STR...S

Birmingham
and West Midlands

First published in 1998 by

Philip's, a division of
Octopus Publishing Group Ltd
2–4 Heron Quays, London E14 4JP

Second colour edition 2002
Second impression with revisions 2003

ISBN 0-540-08124-8

© Philip's 2003

Ordnance Survey

Printed and bound in Spain
by Cayfosa-Quebecor

Contents

III   **Key to map symbols**

IV   **Key to map pages**

VI   **Route planning**

VIII   **Administrative and Postcode boundaries**

1   **Street maps** at 2½ inches to 1 mile

163   **Street maps of centres of Wolverhampton, Birmingham and Coventry** at 5 inches to 1 mile

166   **Index** of towns and villages

167   **Index** of streets, hospitals, industrial estates, railway stations, schools, shopping centres, universities and places of interest

Digital Data

The exceptionally high-quality mapping found in this atlas is available as digital data in TIFF format, which is easily convertible to other bitmapped (raster) image formats.

The index is also available in digital form as a standard database table. It contains all the details found in the printed index together with the National Grid reference for the map square in which each entry is named.

For further information and to discuss your requirements, please contact Philip's on 020 7644 6932 or james.mann@philips-maps.co.uk

(22a)	**Motorway** with junction number		Railway station
	Primary route – dual/single carriageway	Walsall	Private railway station
	A road – dual/single carriageway	South Shields	Metro station
	B road – dual/single carriageway		Tram stop, tram stop under construction
	Minor road – dual/single carriageway		Bus, coach station
	Other minor road – dual/single carriageway		Ambulance station
	Road under construction		Coastguard station
	Pedestrianised area		Fire station
DY7	**Postcode boundaries**		Police station
	County and unitary authority boundaries		Accident and Emergency entrance to hospital
	Railway, railway under construction	H	Hospital
	Tramway, tramway under construction	+	Place of worship
	Miniature railway	i	Information Centre (open all year)
	Rural track, private road or narrow road in urban area	P	Parking
	Gate or obstruction to traffic (restrictions may not apply at all times or to all vehicles)	P&R	Park and Ride
	Path, bridleway, byway open to all traffic, road used as a public path	PO	Post Office
	The representation in this atlas of a road, track or path is no evidence of the existence of a right of way	X	Camping site
58 230 237	**Adjoining page indicators**		Caravan site
			Golf course
	The map area within the pink band is shown at a larger scale on the page indicated by the red block and arrow		Picnic site
		Prim Sch	Important buildings, schools, colleges, universities and hospitals

Acad	**Academy**	Mkt	**Market**
Allot Gdns	**Allotments**	Meml	**Memorial**
Cemy	**Cemetery**	Mon	**Monument**
C Ctr	**Civic Centre**	Mus	**Museum**
CH	**Club House**	Obsy	**Observatory**
Coll	**College**	Pal	**Royal Palace**
Crem	**Crematorium**	PH	**Public House**
Ent	**Enterprise**	Recn Gd	**Recreation Ground**
Ex H	**Exhibition Hall**	Resr	**Reservoir**
Ind Est	**Industrial Estate**	Ret Pk	**Retail Park**
IRB Sta	**Inshore Rescue Boat Station**	Sch	**School**
		Sh Ctr	**Shopping Centre**
Inst	**Institute**	TH	**Town Hall/House**
Ct	**Law Court**	Trad Est	**Trading Estate**
L Ctr	**Leisure Centre**	Univ	**University**
LC	**Level Crossing**	Wks	**Works**
Liby	**Library**	YH	**Youth Hostel**

River Medway	Water name
	River, stream
	Lock, weir
	Water
	Tidal water
	Woods
	Built up area
Church	Non-Roman antiquity
ROMAN FORT	Roman antiquity

The small numbers around the edges of the maps identify the 1 kilometre ational Grid lines ■ The dark grey border on the inside edge of some pages dicates that the mapping does not continue onto the adjacent page

The scale of the maps on the pages numbered in blue is 3.92 cm to 1 km • 2½ inches to 1 mile • 1: 25344

0	¼	½	¾	1 mile
0	250 m	500 m	750 m	1 kilometre

The scale of the maps on pages numbered in red is 7.84 cm to 1 km • 5 inches to 1 mile • 1: 12672

0	220 yards	440 yards	660 yards	½ mile
0	125 m	250 m	375 m	½ kilometre

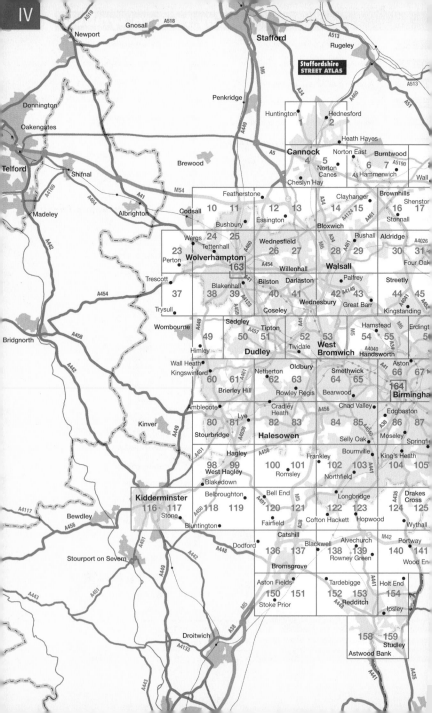

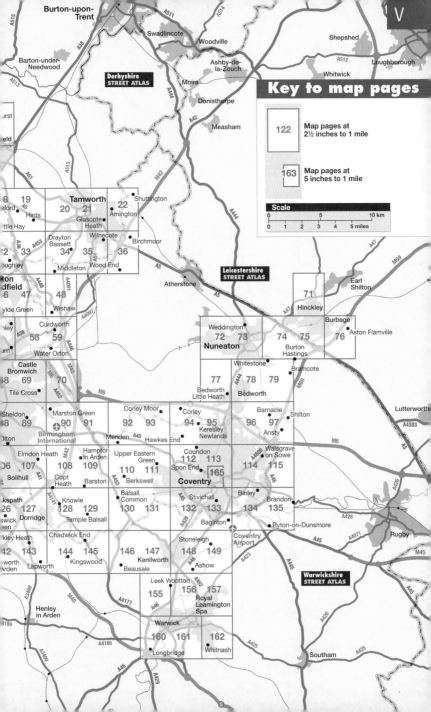

V

Burton-upon-Trent

Swadlincote

Woodville

Shepshed

Whitwick

Loughborough

Barton-under-Needwood

Ashby-de-la-Zouch

Derbyshire STREET ATLAS

Moira

Donisthorpe

Measham

Key to map pages

| 122 | Map pages at 2½ inches to 1 mile |

| 163 | Map pages at 5 inches to 1 mile |

Scale

0 — 5 — 10 km

0 — 1 — 2 — 3 — 4 — 5 miles

Tamworth

Shuttington

20 21 22 Amington

Hints

Glascote Heath

Drayton Bassett Wilncote

34 35 36

Middleton Wood End

Birchmoor

Leicestershire STREET ATLAS

Atherstone

Sutton Coldfield

47 48

Wishaw

Curdworth

58 59

Water Orton

Castle Bromwich

69 70

Tile Cross

Weddington

72 73 74 75

Nuneaton Burton Hastings

Earl Shilton

71

Hinckley

Burbage

76 Aston Flamville

Whitestone

Bramcote

77 78 79

Bedworth Little Heath Bedworth

Sheldon

89 90 91

Birmingham International

Marston Green

Corley Moor

92 93 94 95

Meriden Hawkes End Keresley Newlands

Barnacle

96 97

Shilton

Ansty

Lutterworth

Elmdon Heath

107 108 109

Solihull Copt Heath Barston

Hampton In Arden

Upper Eastern Green

110 111

Berkswell

Coundon

112 113

Spon End

Coventry

114 115

Walsgrave on Sowe

165

Knowle

127 128 129

Dorridge Temple Balsall

130 131

Balsall Common

Stivichall

132 133

Binley

134 135

Brandon

Ryton-on-Dunsmore

Rugby

Baginton

Chadwick End

143 144 145

Lapworth Kingswood

146 147

Beausale

Stoneleigh

148 149

Ashow

Coventry Airport

Warwickshire STREET ATLAS

Henley in Arden

Leek Wootton

155 156 157

Royal Leamington Spa

Warwick

160 161 162

Longbridge Whitnash

Southam

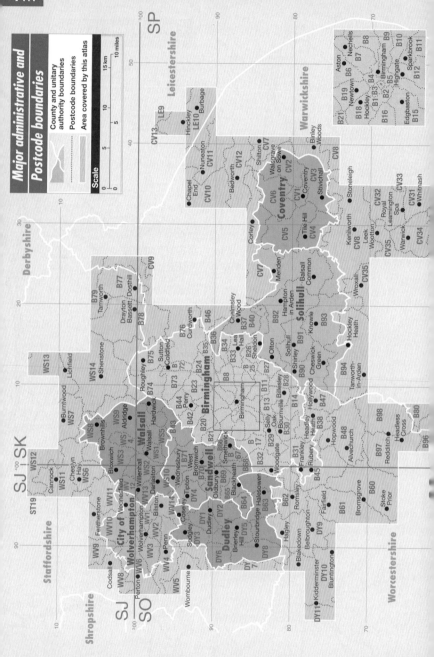

VIII

Major administrative and Postcode boundaries

County and unitary authority boundaries
Postcode boundaries
Area covered by this atlas

Scale
0   5   10   15 km
0   5   10 miles

Shropshire
Staffordshire
Derbyshire
Leicestershire
Warwickshire
Worcestershire

City of Wolverhampton
Walsall
Sandwell
Dudley
Birmingham
Solihull
Coventry

Aston
Nechells
Newtown
Hockley
Birmingham
Highgate
Sparkbrook
Edgbaston

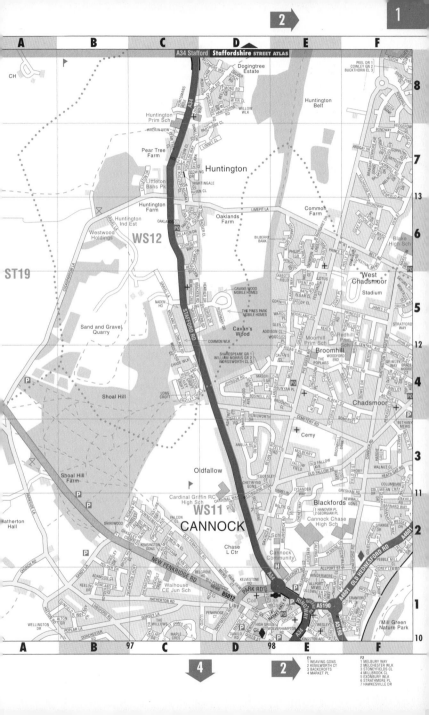

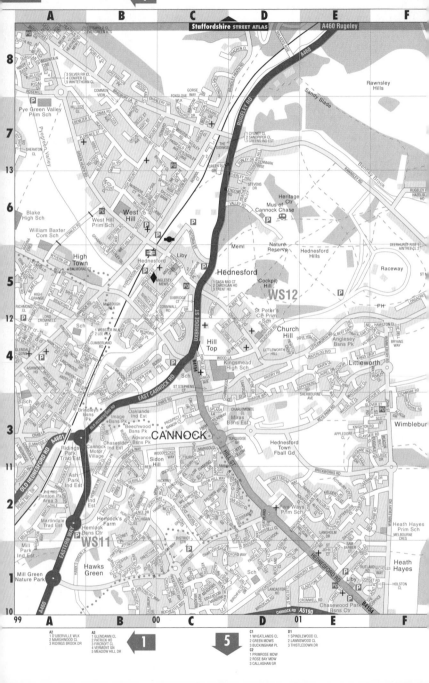

Staffordshire STREET ATLAS

A5127 Burton-upon-Trent (A38)

8

7

13

6

5

12

4

3

11

2

1

10

A B 12 C D 13 E F

Cranberry

Shade House Lock

Middle Lock

Ravenshaw Wood

Black Slough

Woods Farm

Woodend Lock

Trent and Mersey Canal

Fradley Wood

Black Slough Farm

Tomhay Wood

Wood End La

Wood End Farm

Big Lyntus

GORSE LA

New Farm

Full Brook

Fullbrook Farm

Sewage Works

Sprint Course

Little Lyntus

hurst Hall Farm

Curborough Brook

Elmhurst

Corporation Farm

Curborough

Curborough Farm

Curborough Hall Farm

Apsley House

WS13

Curborough House

Brownfield Cottage

Ringway Ind Est

SALISBURY CL

WINCHESTER CL

Nether Stowe

Brownsfields Farm

LICHFIELD

David Willows Prim Sch

Charnwood Prim Sch

THE MILL POND

Streethay Lodge

1 ARMITAGE HO
2 WHITTINGTON HO
3 SHENSTONE HO
4 RIDWARE HO
5 PENNYS CROFT

Chadsmead Prim Sch

Nether Stowe High Sch

Stowe

Scotch Orchard Prim Sch

Lichfield Bsns Ctr

Stowe Pool

TRENT VALLEY COTTS 1
BAILYE CL 2

A5192

A5127 BURTON RD

1 AUGUSTINES WLK
2 PABLS WLK
3 CHRISTOPHER WLK
4 MATTHEWS WLK
5 STEPHENS WLK
6 MARKS WLK
7 PETERS WLK
8 THOMAS GREENWAY
9 JAMES GREENWAY
10 LUKES WLK

8
1 BACKCROFTS
2 HALLCOURT CRES
3 HALLCOURT CL
4 CAXTON CT
5 FAIRMOUNT DR
6 NEW ST

A B C D E F

8

High
House

Dorchester
Rd

Oaks
Dr

Hazelwood
Gr

John Wood
CE Inf Sch

Lyncroft
House
Sch

Cannock

Longford
Prim Sch

Avon Rd

Lyncroft

Rume Hill
Bsns Est

Rumer
Hill

7

A5 Telford

The
Royals

A5

Motel

Wellfield Cl 1
Southgate End 2
Coppice Ct 3
Salcombe Gl 4

A601

Wolverhampton Rd

5 Kingswood Ave 6
6 Langdale Gn

Prospect
Works Bsns Pk

The Cedars
Bsns Ctr

Riding Brook

TA
Ctr

Walsall Rd

Brookfield Dr

Progress
Ind Ctr

Cannock
Chase
Tech Coll

Birch
Bsns
Pk

09

Hotel

WS11

Delta Way
Bsns Ctr

Bridgtown

Delta Way

Bridgtown
Prim Sch

Park
Venture
Est

Green
Lane
Venture
Ctr

6

Wedge's
Mills

Wolverhampton Rd

Watling St

Longford Ind Est

Works

Bsns
Ctr

East St

Leacroft

Wash Brook

CANNOCK

Wyrley Brook
Ret Pk

Phoenix
Ctr

Cannock
Ind Ctr

The Exchange
Ind Est

5

The Winking
Frog
(PH)

Lodge
Hill

Wyrley
Brook
Pk

Walkmill
Bsns Pk

Bennick
Trad Est

Mill La

Walkmill Way

Churchbridge
Pk

Churchbridge

08

Lodge
Farm

Road under construction

Littlewood

Woodman La

4

Middle
Hill

Middle Hill
Farm

South
Staffordshire
Bsns Pk

Coppice La

Wks

Station Rd

Great
Wyrley
High Sch

Moat Hall
Prim Sch

Clay
Pit

P

Cemy

3

WV10

Wheat
Sheaf
(PH)

Laney
Green

Cheslyn Hay
Prim Sch

Cheslyn Hay
High Sch

Cheslyn Hay

Grassmere Cl 1
Old Falls Cl 2
Cheslyn Gr 3

B4156 Low St

Glenthorne
Prim Sch

07

B4156 High St

Liby

2

A462 M6 Junc. 11   A460 Wolverhampton

Wolverhampton Rd

Cemy

WS6

Works

Landywood

Somerford Cl 1
Bluebell La 2
Popular Rd 3
Orion Cl 4
Leander Cl 5
New St 6
Hilton La 7

1

Holly Bush La

Holly
Bush
Farm

B4156

Blacklees
Farm

WV11

Thornley Croft 1
Gilpins Croft 2
Harrison Cl 3
Seymour Cl 4
Charles Cl 5

Works

06

96   A   B   97   C   D   98   E   F

7

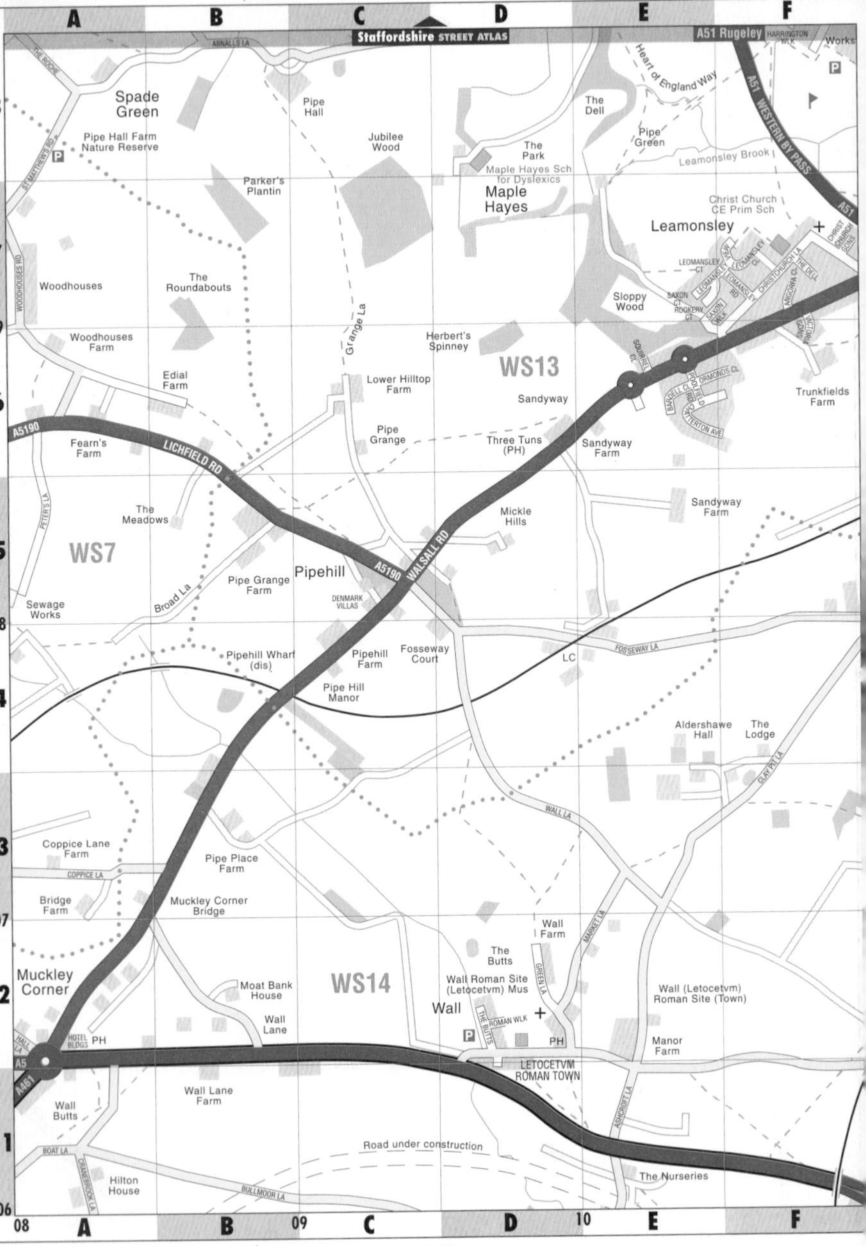

A
B
C
D
E
F
Staffordshire STREET ATLAS
A51 Rugeley
HARRINGTON WLK
Works
ABNALLS LA
THE ROCHE
Spade Green
Pipe Hall
Pipe Hall Farm Nature Reserve
ST MATTHEW'S RD
Jubilee Wood
The Park
Maple Hayes Sch for Dyslexics
Maple Hayes
The Dell
Heart of England Way
Pipe Green
Leamonsley Brook
A51 WESTERN BY PASS
A51
Christ Church CE Prim Sch
Leamonsley
CHRIST CHURCH GDNS
Parker's Plantin
Woodhouses
WOODHOUSES RD
The Roundabouts
Grange La
Sloppy Wood
LEOMANSLEY CT
LEOMANSLEY VIEW
LEOMANSLEY CL
LEOMANSLEY RD
CHRISTCHURCH LA
THE DELL
ANGORFA CL
SAXON CT
ROCKERY CT
SAXON WLK
VICTORIA GDNS
Woodhouses Farm
Herbert's Spinney
WS13
SQUIRREL CL
Edial Farm
Lower Hilltop Farm
POOLFIELD RD
ORMONDS CL
BARDELL CL
CHATTERTON AVE
Sandyway
Trunkfields Farm
A5190
Fearn's Farm
LICHFIELD RD
Pipe Grange
Three Tuns (PH)
Sandyway Farm
PETER'S LA
The Meadows
Mickle Hills
Sandyway Farm
WS7
WALSALL RD
A5190
Pipehill
Pipe Grange Farm
Broad La
DENMARK VILLAS
Sewage Works
FOSSEWAY LA
Pipehill Wharf (dis)
Pipehill Farm
Fosseway Court
LC
Pipe Hill Manor
Aldershawe Hall
The Lodge
CLAY PIT LA
WALL LA
Coppice Lane Farm
COPPICE LA
Pipe Place Farm
Bridge Farm
Muckley Corner Bridge
MARKET LA
Wall Farm
The Butts
Muckley Corner
Moat Bank House
WS14
Wall Roman Site (Letocetvm) Mus
GREEN LA
Wall (Letocetvm) Roman Site (Town)
Wall Lane
Wall
THE BUTTS
ROMAN WLK
HALL LA
HOTEL BLDGS
PH
PH
Manor Farm
A5
A461
LETOCETVM ROMAN TOWN
Wall Butts
Wall Lane Farm
ASHCROFT LA
BOAT LA
Road under construction
CRANEBROOK LA
Hilton House
BULLMOOR LA
The Nurseries
8
7
09
6
5
08
4
3
07
2
1
06
08
09
10

7
17

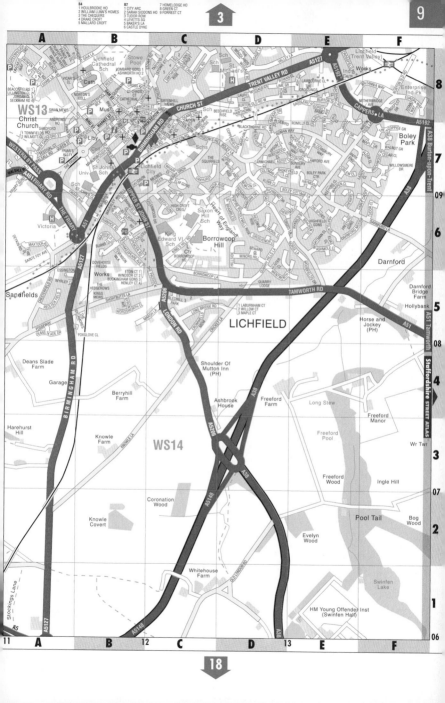

Staffordshire STREET ATLAS

A449 Stafford

8

River Park

Coven Lawn

Cross Green Farm

CH

Three Hammers Farm

HM Prison

7

Shawhall Farm

Brinsford

05

Brinsford Farm

Monarch's Way

6

Coven Heath

Sewage Works

M54

Clewley Coppice

Boundary Ind Est

BROOKHOUSE LA

5

WV9

STAFFORD

Works

04

Cricket Gd

GREENFIELD LA

WV10

MOSELEY RD

4

WOLVERHAMPTON

REDCAR RD 1
AINTREE RD 2
SPRINGFIELD CT 3

STAFFORD RD

1 WEALDEN HATCH
2 WADESMILL LAWNS
3 WILLERBY FOLD
4 WIMSHURST MOW
5 BIBBY'S GN
6 WENDELL CREST

MIRFIELD CL 1
BURNSALL LA 2
GOODMIRE CROFT 3
CROCUS CRES 4
LAVENDER CL 5
CRESSWELL CT 6

Forster Bridge

WOBASTON RD

Works

3

Sports Gd

Marsh Lane Bridge

SLADE RD

St Anthony's RC Prim Sch

Fordhouses

Northcote Farm & Ctry Pk

CARISBROOKE GDNS

DENSTONE GDNS

Crem

Elston Hall Prim Sch

The Northcote Sch
Northcote Recn Ctr
Bushbury

Cemy

03

Usam Trad Est

Beeches Farm

Pendeford High Sch

Liby

Schs

1 HALESWORTH RD
2 ALVERSTOKE CL
3 ASHWELLS GR

2

Rakegate Jun & Inf Schs

THREE TUNS PAR

MARSH LANE PAR

Collingwood Jun & Inf Schs

Liby

Swimming Baths

Bushbury Hall

Bushbury Hill Jun & Inf Schs

Liby

Elston Hall

Moreton Com Sch

HILLCREST AVE

1

BEECH AV

Fordhouse Rd Ind Est

A449

02

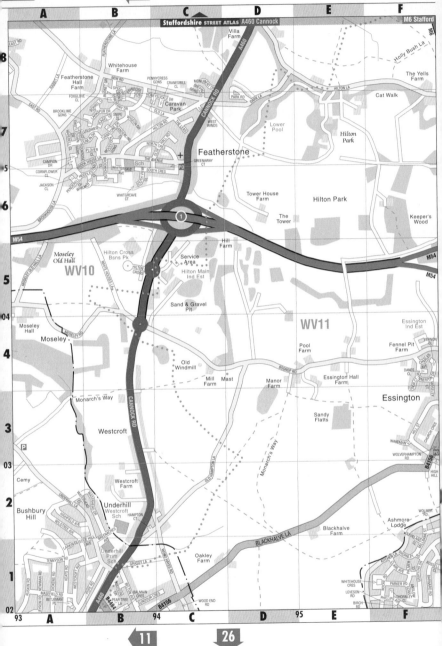

Staffordshire STREET ATLAS A51 Lichfield

Broadfields

Packington Moor

Moor Covert

Common Barn

A51

Tamworth Lane

KNOX'S GRAVE LA

Riding School

A51 HOPWAS HILL

05

Buck's Head Cottages

Sand and Gravel Pit

Packington Farm

Hare Park Wood

PACKINGTON LA

6

WS14

Heart of England Way

Rodbaston Coll

Weeford

Mast

Transmitting Station

The Devil's Dressing Room

5

Buck's Head Farm

B78

Hanging Wood

04

Church Wood

Bourne House

The Lodge

Long Island

Sand and Gravel Pit

Common Plantation

Hints Lane Farm

4

Black Brook

ROCK HILL

WATLING ST

Snake's Hill

Hints Hill

A5

03

3

Rough Leasow

Job's Hill

Hints

Manor Farm

Home Farm

Bangley Lodge

Gorsey Hill

Botley House

2

Sand and Gravel Pit

Crow's Castle

Rookery

Ford

SCHOOL LA

Resr

Bourne Brook

ROOKERY LA

B75

New Plantation

Rookery Farm

White Owl Farm

Roundhill Wood

BROCKHURST LA

1

02

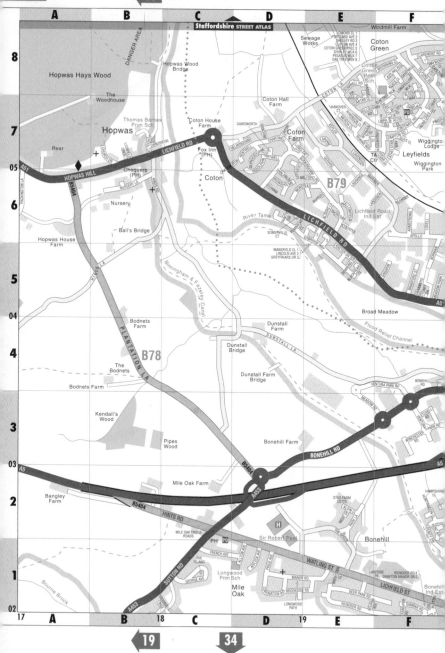

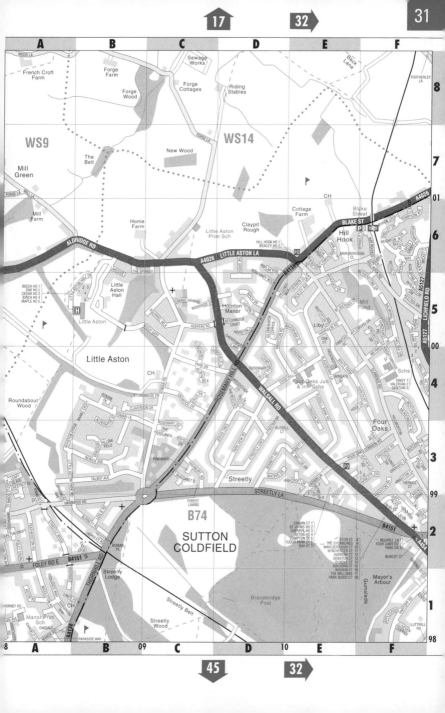

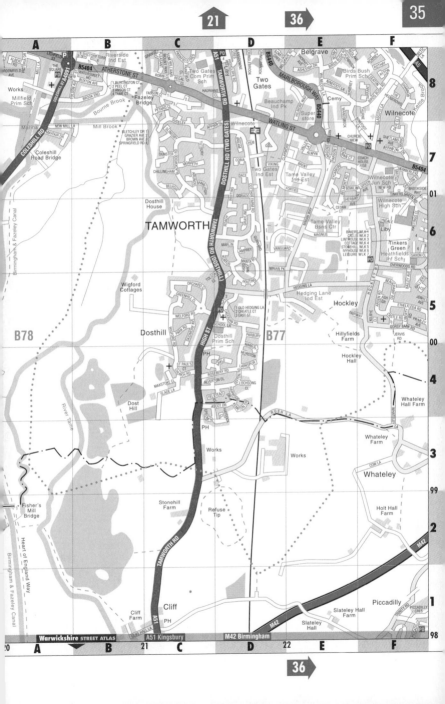

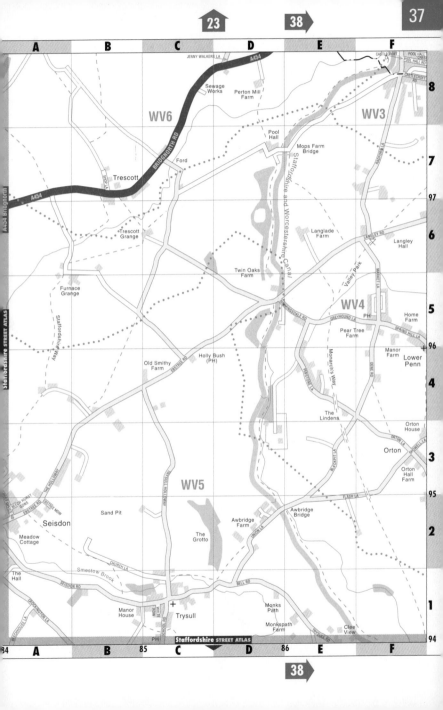

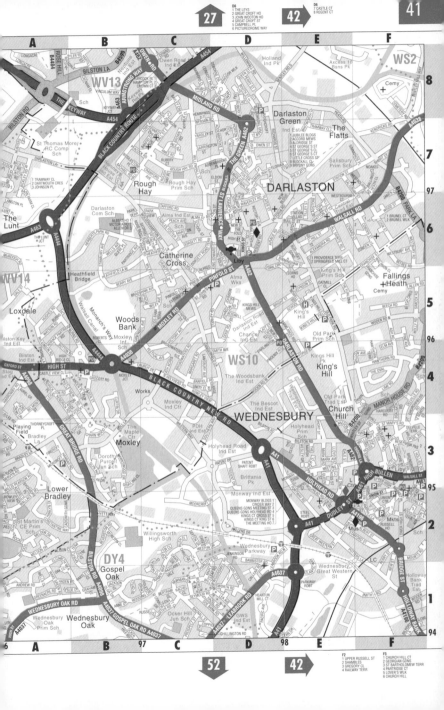

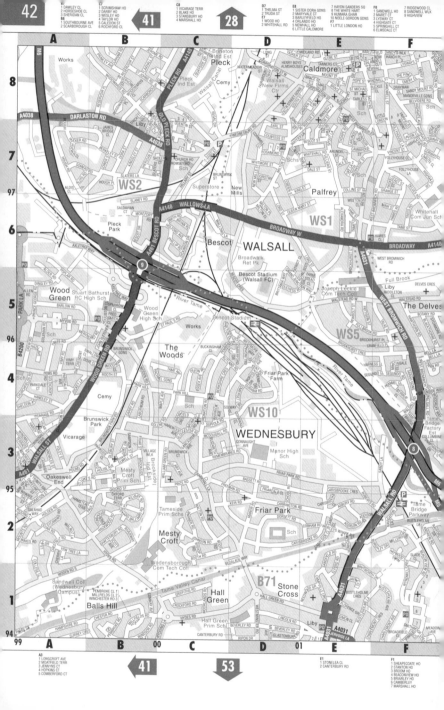

8

7

97

6

5

96

4

B73

SUTTON
COLDFIELD

3

95

2

1

94

A   B   09   C   D   10   E   F

A   B   C   D   E   F

Pool Hollies

Darnel
Hurst

Lady Wood

Upper Nut Hurst

B74

Blackroot
Pool

Meml

Lower Nut Hurst

Keeper's
Pool

Sutton Park

Hill
Hurst

Holly Hurst

Rowton's
Well

Hotel

Westwood
Coppice

Longmoor
Pool

Wyndley
Wood

Banners
Gate

La
Reserve

Powell's Pool

King's
Standing

Banners
Gate
Jun & Inf
Schs

Liby

Longmoor
Sch

New
Oscott

CH

B44

Kingstanding

Superstore

BEGGAR'S
BUSH

Jockey Rd   B4149

Boldmere
Jun & Inf Schs

Liby

Twickenham
Prim Sch

College
Farm

St Mary's
Coll

B23

THORNHILL RD

CHESTER RD

SUTTON OAK RD

KINGSTANDING RD

KINGS RD

COLLEGE RD

CHESTER RD

A453

A453

A4041

B4138

B4138

B4138

A453

A453

B4142

A453

MAXSTOKE
CL

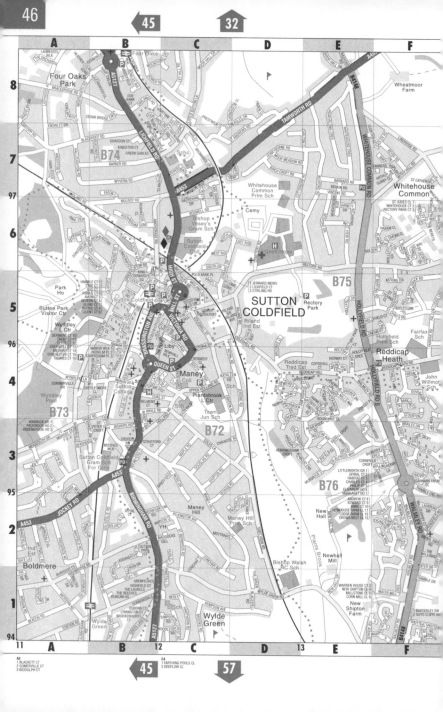

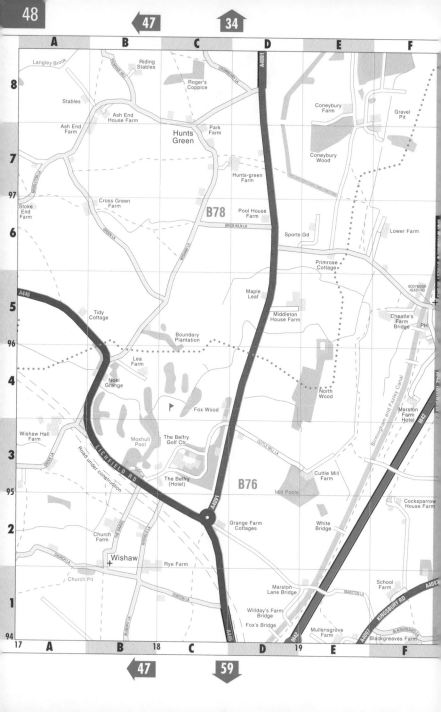

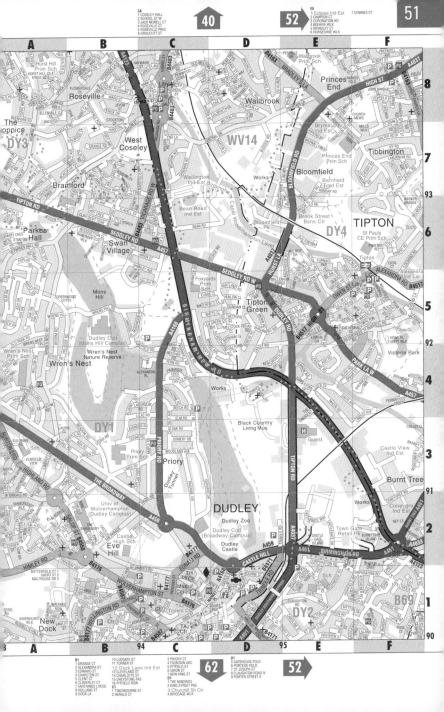

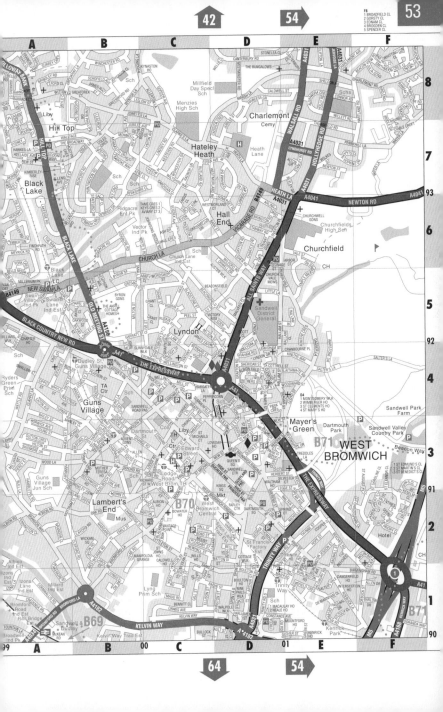

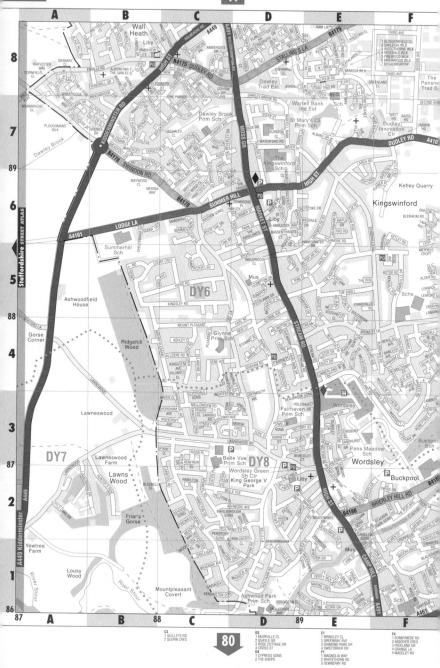

49

80

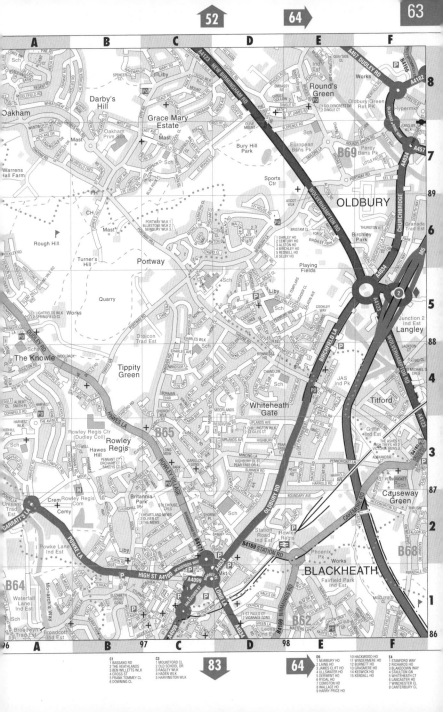

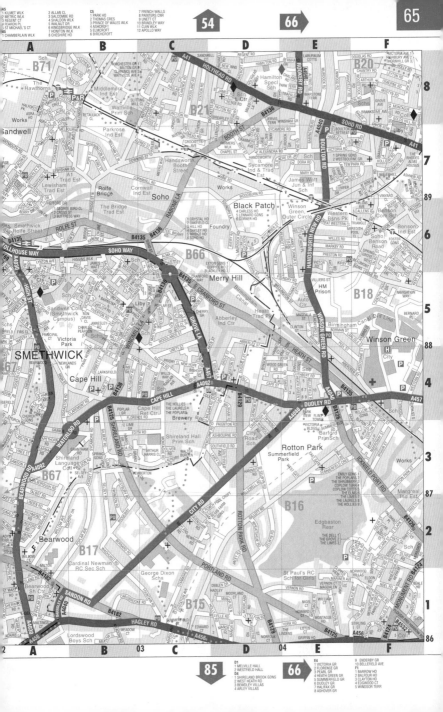

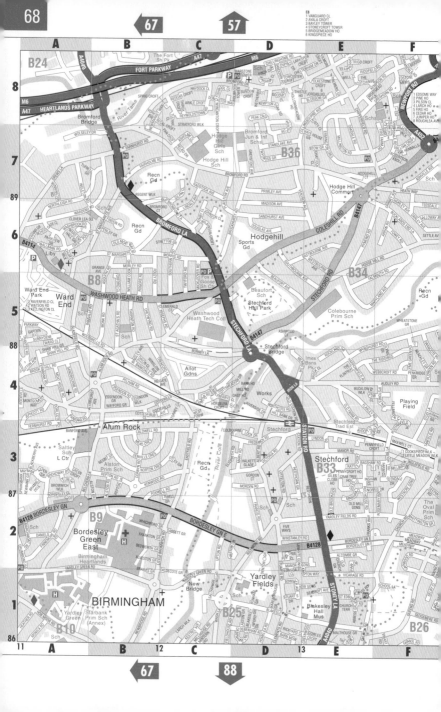

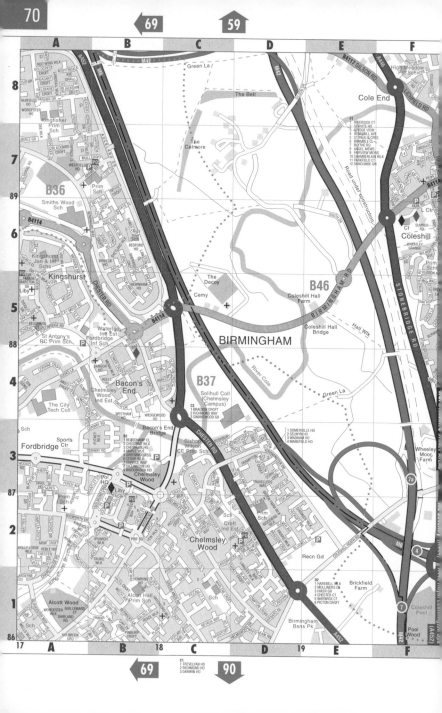

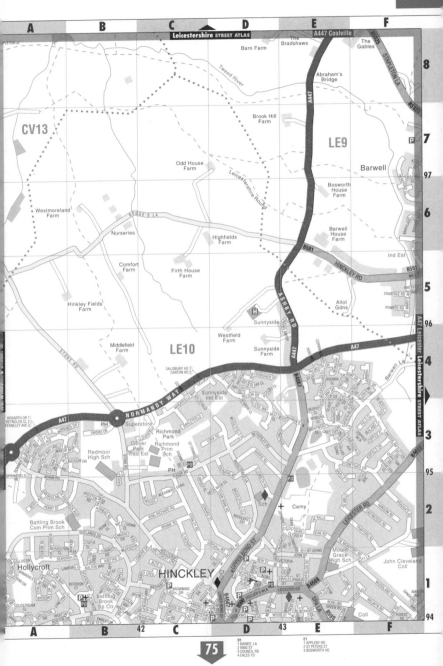

CV13

LE9

Barwell

LE10

HINCKLEY

Hollycroft

D1
1 BAINES' LA
2 KING ST
3 COUNCIL RD
4 EALES YD

E1
1 APPLEBY HO
2 ST PETERS CT
3 BOSWORTH HO

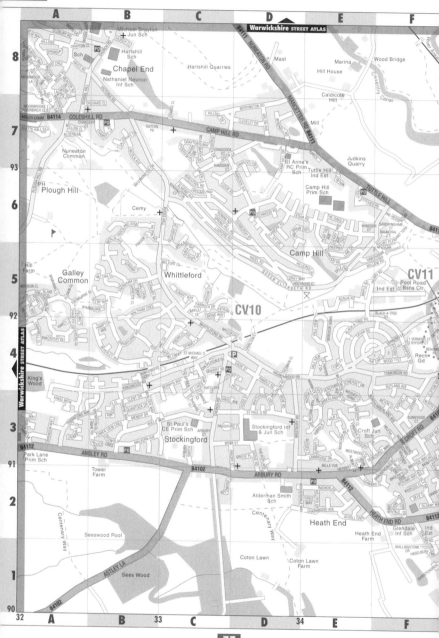

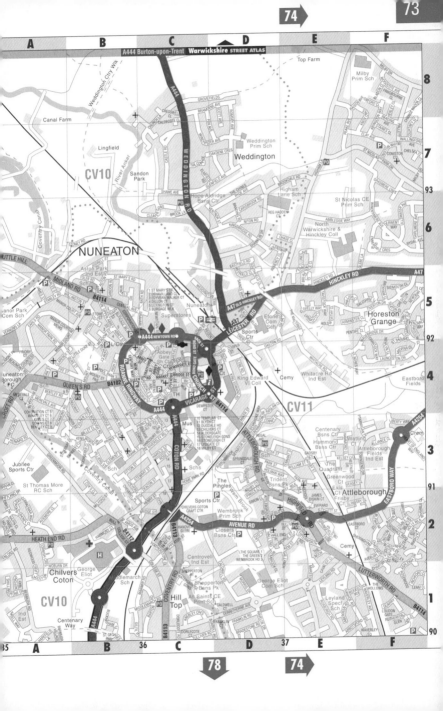

A B C D E F

A5 Tamworth

A47 Hinckley

8

Nuneaton Fields Farm

Meadowcroft Farm

Lodge

WATLING ST

Sterling Pk

Dodwells Bridge Ind Est

A47

DODWELLS RD

Phoenix Bsns Pk

Hinckley Bsns Pk

Knights

Marina

Harrow Brook

7

Callendar Farm

1 CAVERSHAM CL
2 WALLINGFORD AVE

St Nicolas Park

A5

A47

Motel

NEWTON RD

NUFFIELD RD

Harrowbrook Ind Est

TAPADAY RD

STEPHENSON RD

B466

93

ULLSWATER AVE

KESWICK CL

LOWESWATER

RYDAL AVE

Calendar Grove

THE LONG SHOOT

PD

A47

B4666

COVENTRY RD

Hinkley Stadium

6

WINDERMERE AVE

Poplars Farm

Padge Hall Farm

A5

A47 HINCKLEY RD

A4254

Hydes Pastures

5

POST

Ctr

Hydes Pastures

Sketchley Brook

LE10

Moxon's Farm

92

Harrow Brook

HYDES LA

EASTBORO WAY

4

NUNEATON

Eastboro Fields

CV11

A4254

Wheatcroft Farm

Stretton Fields Farm

3

Crem

River Anker

Paul's Ford

91

Hill Farm

2

1 MARCHFONT CL
2 RAINSBROOK DR

WOODLANDS

Fox Covert Cottage

Sinney Fields

1

Gorse Cottage Farm

Attleborough Gorse

Ashby-de-la-Zouch Canal

B4114

90

38 A 39 B C 40 D E F

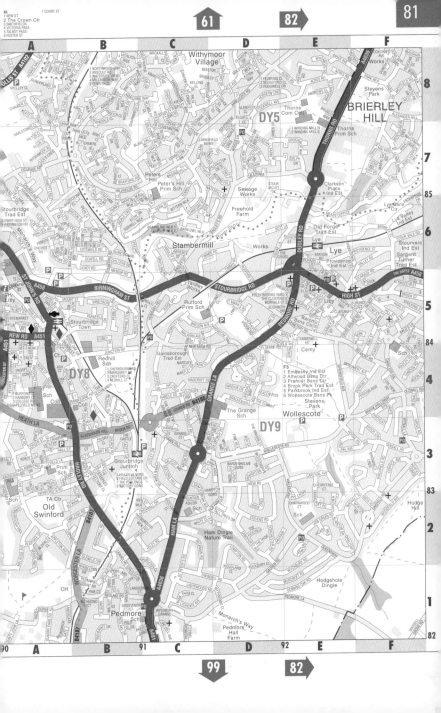

A3
1 HIGHFIELD LA
2 TENBURY HO
3 HONEYBOURNE CL
4 WORCESTER HO
5 BROOME CL
6 PICKERSLEIGH CL
7 MALVERN HO

B3
1 HIGH ST
2 PECKINGHAM ST
3 HAGLEY ST
4 BULL RING
5 GREAT CORNBOW
6 SUMMER HILL
7 POWELL ST
8 PEACHLEY CL

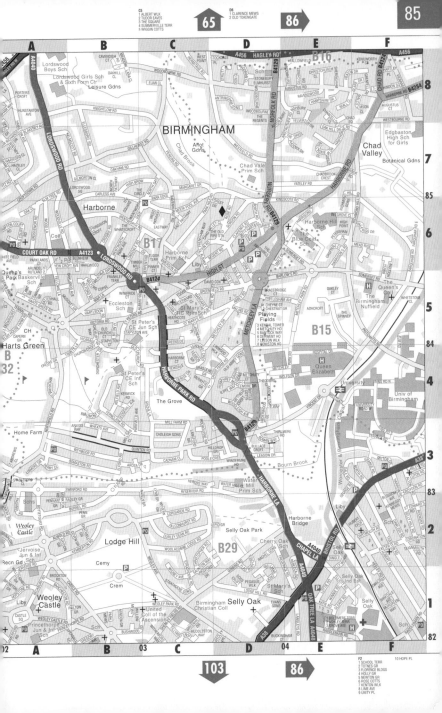

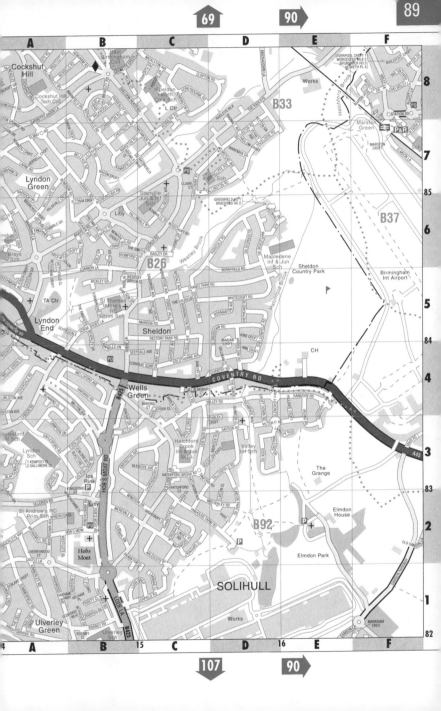

Warwickshire STREET ATLAS

Map grid labels (top): A B C D E F
Map grid labels (bottom): A B C D E F
Vertical grid numbers (right): 8 7 85 6 5 84 4 3 83 2 1 82
Bottom grid numbers: 21 22

146 Lichfield (A38)

B37

The Bogs Farm

Bannerley Rough

Mulliner's Rough

M6

Depot

Todd's Rough

Nursery

B46

STONEBRIDGE RD

Nursery Farm

Ford

Broadwater

Golf & Country Club

Brook Farm

Foxes Den

Refuse Tip

Little Packington

Fish Breeding Farm

The Ash Beds

DENBIGH CNR

A46

Butler's Moors

Packington Park

Park Meadow

Church Farm

River Blythe

Denbigh Spinney

CHESTER HILL

Garden Spinney

Deer Park

Park Farm

Siding Wood

CV7

Packington Hall

84

Hall Pool

Great Pool

Mill Shrubbery

The Wilderness

Beech Lodge

Middle Bickenhill

B92

The Mill Farm

Little Dayhouse Wood

PH

EAST WAY

Dials Pool

P

COVENTRY RD

COVENTRY RD

BIRMINGHAM RD

Stonebridge

A45

The National Motorcycle Mus

Works

Geary's Heath

Pasture Farm

Mills Gorse

Diddington Hill

CH

Diddington Hall

KENILWORTH RD

The Somers

Shadow Brook

A452

Mouldings Green Farm

Molands Bridge

B4102

91

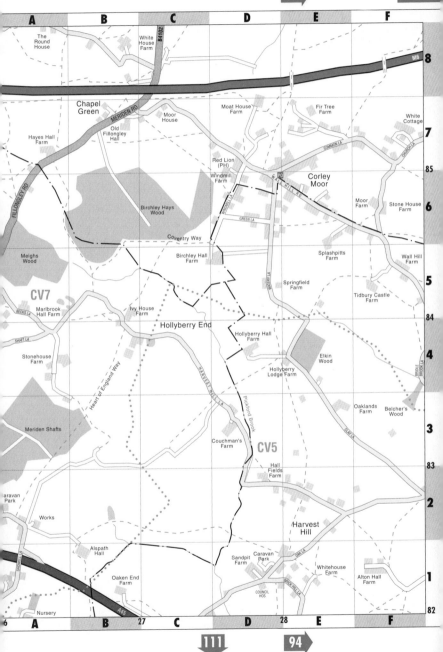

The Round House

White House Farm

B4102

M6

8

Chapel Green

Moor House

Moat House Farm

Fir Tree Farm

White Cottage

7

Hayes Hall Farm

MERIDEN RD

Old Fillongley Hall

Red Lion (PH)

Corley Moor

CHURCH LA

COMMON LA

85

FILLONGLEY RD

Windmill Farm

Moor Farm

Stone House Farm

6

Birchley Hays Wood

TEMPLE LA

GREEN LA

TAN HILL RD

Coventry Way

Birchley Hall Farm

Splashpitts Farm

Wall Hill Farm

5

Meighs Wood

Springfield Farm

PLANT HILL

Tidbury Castle Farm

CV7

Ivy House Farm

Hollyberry End

Hollyberry Hall Farm

84

Marlbrook Hall Farm

BROCK LA

SHAFT LA

Elkin Wood

BRIDE LA

BROOK LA

4

Stonehouse Farm

Heart of England Way

Hollyberry Lodge Farm

Oaklands Farm

Belcher's Wood

HARVEST HILL LA

Meriden Shafts

Pickford Brook

Couchman's Farm

CV5

ELM LA

3

Hall Fields Farm

83

Caravan Park

Works

Harvest Hill

2

SHOWELL LA

Alspath Hall

Sandpit Farm

Caravan Park

Whitehouse Farm

Alton Hall Farm

1

Oaken End Farm

BRICK KILN LA

OAK LA

A45

COUNCIL HOS

Nursery

82

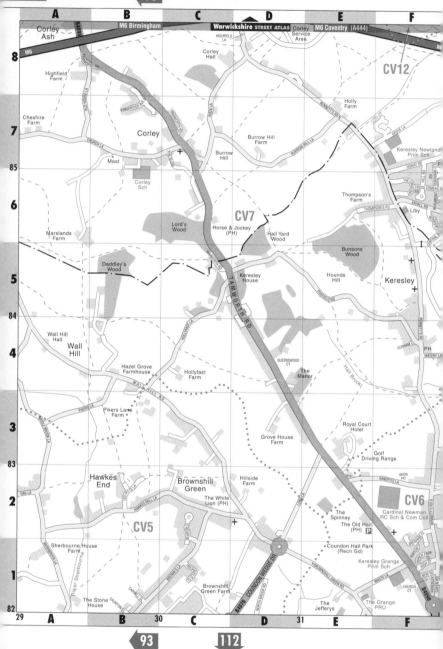

8

7

85

6

5

84

4

3

83

2

1

82

A B C D E F

35 36 37

B1
1 ALICE ARNOLD HO
2 EMILY SMITH HO
3 JOSEPH LATHAM HO
4 DEWIS HO
5 SAMUEL HAYWARD HO

B2
1 CAMELLIA RD
2 WISTARIA CL
3 FUCHSIA CL
4 PEAR TREE CL
5 SPRUCE RD

CV12

Hollyhurst Farm

Hollyhurst

CV7

Sweet Laud's Wood

Weston Hayes Farm

Hawkesbury Hall Farm

Mile Tree Farm

Mile Tree La

Coventry Rd B4113

Coventry Rd

Tolldish Hall Farm

Trossachs Farm

Grove Farm

Hawkesbury Hall

Sowe Fields Farm

CV2

Lenton's Lane Farm

Allot Gdns

Exhall

Coventry Canal

Centenary Way

Hawkesbury

The Greyhound Inn (PH)

Grange Farm

Foxford

Foxford Sch & Com Arts Coll

1 LONGFORD SQ
2 WRENBURY DR
3 KENDRICK CL
4 KEGWORTH CL
5 ELMHURST RD

1 HURN WAY
2 LINSTOCK WAY
3 WORCESTER CT
4 LINGFIELD CT
5 SAPCOTE GR
6 FARMCOTE LODGE

Oxford Canal

Oxford Canal Wlk

CV6

Hall Green

Alderman's Green

Hawkesbury Fields Sch

Alderman's Green Com Prim Sch

Wyken Pool

COVENTRY

Manor House

Sports Gd

Sowe Common

Cemy Potters Green Prim Sch

Woodway Park Sch & Com Coll

Potter's Green

Wood End

St Patrick's RC Prim Sch

Wood End Prim Sch

Cardinal Wiseman RC Sch

Cemy

Little Heath Ind Est

Foleshill CE Prim Sch

OLD CHURCH RD

Longford Park Prim Sch

Liby

Wood End

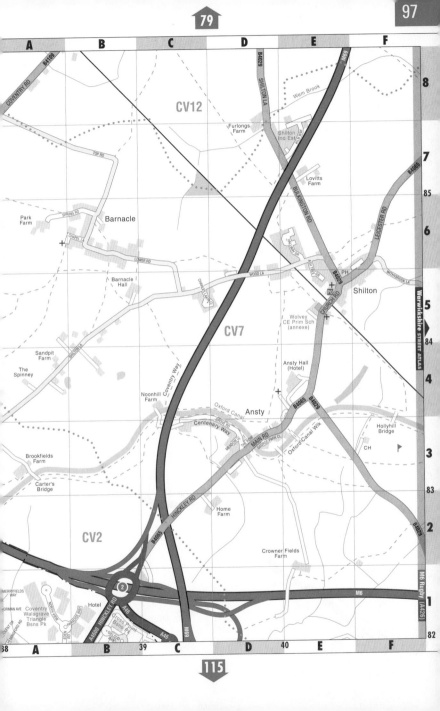

A   B   C   D   E   F

Dovehousefields
Farm

Illeybrook
Farm

Innage
Farm

PH

Illey

8

Hunnington

Blue Bird
Pk

Goodrest
Farm

Illey House
Farm

Potters
Farm

Lower Illey

Breach
Farm

THE CLOSE

RED HILL LA

Frankley
Service
Area

Warstone
Farm

81

7

Hollies
Farm

Twiland
Wood

Kettles
Wood

Raven Hays
Wood

6

Hunnington
Farm

Horsepool
Farm

Long Kettles
Wood

BROADGROVE RD

Yew Tree
Farm

PH

Porch House
Farm

Monarch's Way

FRANKLEY RD

Brookhouse
Farm

Frankley Green La

5

ST KENELM'S RD

B62

B32

80

Romsley

Newbrook
Farm

OLDNALL LA

4

Penny
Fields

St Kenelm's
CE Sch

PH

Ell Wood

Dayhouse
Wood

Long Saw
Croft

Round Saw
Croft

Yew Tree Lane

Yew Tree
Farm

Frankley Hill
Farm

FRANKLEY HILL LA

3

Frankley
Hill

POUND LA

Lower Hill
Barn

79

POPLAR LA

Romsley
Manor Farm

Newtown
Farm

Sandhills
Farm

FABIAN
CL

2

Mast

B45

QUEEN ELIZABETH RD

Holly Hill
Methodist &
CE Inf Sch

Sch

Romsley
Hill

BISHOP CL 1
PRINCE CHARLES CL 2
PRINCESS ANNE DR 3
PRINCE EDWARD DR 4
FISHER CL 5

WITTEN AVE

Mast

Dayhouse
Farm

Gannow Green
Farm

Sch

GANNOW GREEN LA

1

Dayhouse
Bank

P

Visitor
Ctr

Duck Pool
Farm

CROSS FARMS LA

RUBERY LA

North Worcestershire Path

B4551

M5

97

CHERRYHILL LA

98

78

A   B   C   D   E   F

F1
1 BROOKDALE CL
2 CHADDERSLEY CL
3 RUBERY LA S
4 HOLLY HILL
5 CALDY WLK

B7
1 HAMPSHIRE CT
2 DORSET CT
3 DEVON CT
4 BATH CT
5 CHELSEA CT

C7
1 WARWICK CT
2 RUTLAND CT
3 DANBIGH CT
4 RICHMOND CT
5 ESSEX CT
6 NORFOLK CT

7 SUSSEX CT
8 OXFORD CT
9 LINCOLN CT
10 WILTSHIRE CT
11 ASCOT CT
12 ASCOT CT

14 KENDAL CT
15 BRISTOL CT
16 EPSOM CT
17 SANDOWN CT
18 KINGSTON CT

12 GUILDFORD CT
13 ARUNDEL CT

123

104

A1
1 CENTENARY CL
2 TENBY TOWER
3 SANDOWN TOWER
4 WELLINGTON TOWER
A4
1 CUTLERS ROUGH CL
2 SAXON WOOD CL
3 BELL HILL
4 VINEYARD RD

E1
1 BURFORD PARK RD
2 GROVEWOOD DR
3 WHITEBEAM CROFT
F1
1 WARRENS END

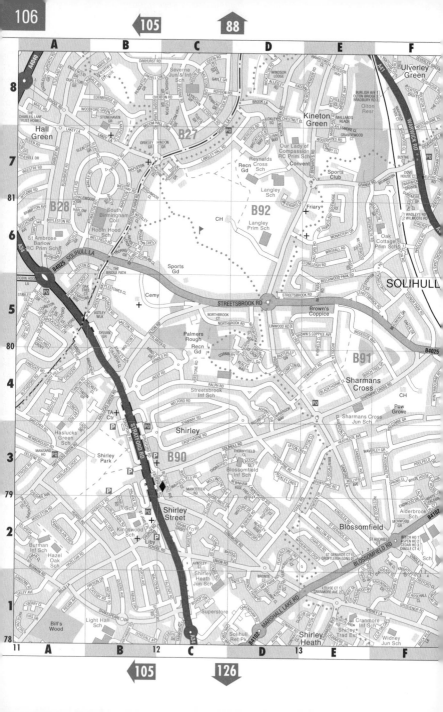

A   B   C   D   E   F

4102

BIRMINGHAM RD
A45

Meriden Bsns Pk
ELM CT

Pinkett's Booth

Pinkett's Wood

Pickford Farm

Pickford

GRACE RD

OLYMPUS CL
PARMASHA DR
LUXOR DR
THEBES
JAMES

8

Millison's Wood

Pickford Green

Pickford Bridge

BIRMINGHAM RD

Windmill Ind Est

Hotel

7

Spring Wood

Pickford Grange Farm

PICKFORD GRANGE LA

Pickford Brook

A45

CH   Hotel

81

6

Brook Farm

CV5

Shirley Woodlands

SHIRLEY LA

Larges Farm

New Home Farm

CHURCH LA

GARDEN FLATS

COVENTRY

5

Oak Farm

Flint's Green

HOCKLEY LA

St Andrew's CE Inf Sch

PH

MELLOWDEW RD

ROSE COTTAGE FLATS

MAGPIE

Sch

DESPARD

Pond Farm Mews

Pond Farm

80

Barnacles Farm

MORGANS CL

ORCHARD

Hockley

KENTHURST

SUTTON AVE

Upper Eastern Green

UPPER EASTERN GREEN LA

FREDERICK NEAL AVE

HOWARD   KIMBERLEY

LOWER EASTERN GREEN LA

LUTHER WAY   UNICORN LA

4

COVENTRY RD

CV7

BROAD LA

CHILTERN HO   MALVERN HO

TILEWOOD AVE

STONEBURY AVE

FAULCONBRIDGE AVE

HANDSWORTH

TREDINGTON RD

Works

The Woodlands Sch

The Meadows Sch

ROSEMARY

HURLMERE

CLYDSON

THOMAS BABB   CROFT
ACTON RD
ASHCOMBE DR

BURY HO
BURNEY
SHEPHERD

Limbrick Wood Sch

3

79

Tilehill Wood (Nature Reserve)

DUNHILL AVE
BLISS
DELIUS ST

CAVENDISH RD

Liby

WICKMANS DR

GLENDALE WAY

Rough Close

PHEASANT
HERONBANK

Conway Farm

DEVEREUX

MAUREEN

TILE HILL LA

Tile Hill Wood Sch & Language Coll

BEECHNUT CL

OAK WAY

BROOKHURST

ENSIGN

CROMES WOOD

HOLYWELL CL

ROOSEVELT DR

BERNERS CRES

NUTBROOK AVE

FRISBY RD

FALSTAFF RD

BOHUN ST

Pig Wood
RC Prim Sch

Limbrick Wood

2

Glebe Farm

BENTON GREEN LA

WINCEBY PL

TANYARD

SAMMONS WAY

CV4

PINNOCK PL

1

B4101   TANNERS LA

Plants Hill Wood

Tile Hill

PLANTS HILL CRES

DRAMSTON CL

GRAVEL

City Coll

Coll

78

26   A   B   27   C   D   28   E   F

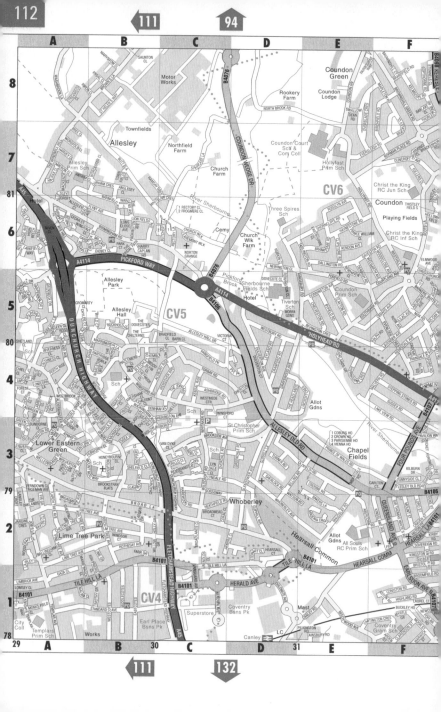

95　　114　　113

F7
1 ADAM RD
2 WARNER ROW
3 ST NICHOLAS CT
4 PARADISE RO

113

A　B　C　D　E　F

A5
1 NETHERMILL RD
2 CHILTERN CT
3 PAKE'S CROFT
4 HUMBERSTONE RD
B3
1 HAWKSWORTH DR

B5
1 WELLINGTON GDNS
2 GARDNER HO
3 GIVENS HO

3 TRAFALGAR HO
4 KERRY'S HO
5 GRINDLEY HO
6 GEORGE POOLE HO
7 DRINKWATER HO

2 COLLETT WLK
3 RIVER CT
4 COMPASS CT
5 MEADOW HO

10 FENNELL HO
11 WINSLOW HO
12 ST THOMAS'S HO
13 ST THOMAS'S CT

8
81
7
6
81
5
80
4
3
79
2
1
78

CV6

COVENTRY

Radford

Great Heath

Paradise

Edgwick

Hillfields

CV2

CV1

CV3

Earlsdon

Spencer Park

Gosford Green

For full street detail of the
highlighted area see page
165.

E4
1 CAWTHORNE CL
2 PENSULA WAY
3 JACQUARD HO
4 LEIGH ST
5 CLARENCE ST
6 THOMAS KING HO
7 NELSON ST
8 WATERLOO ST
9 VERNON ST

E3
1 HILLFIELDS HO
2 JEPHCOTT HO
3 GILBERT CL
4 VAUXHALL CL
5 VERNON CL
6 SPRING CL
7 RAGLAN CT

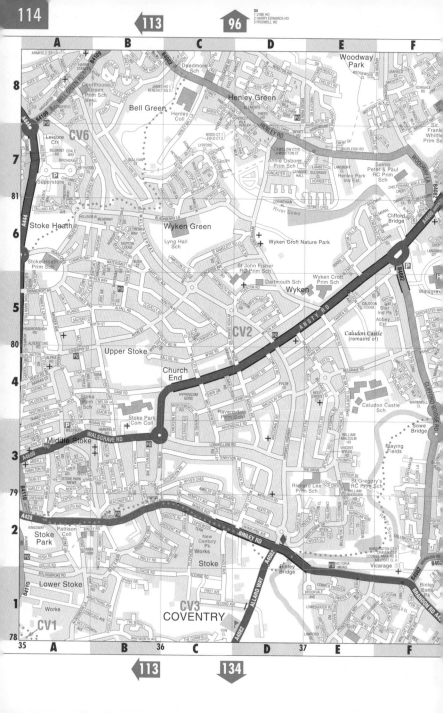

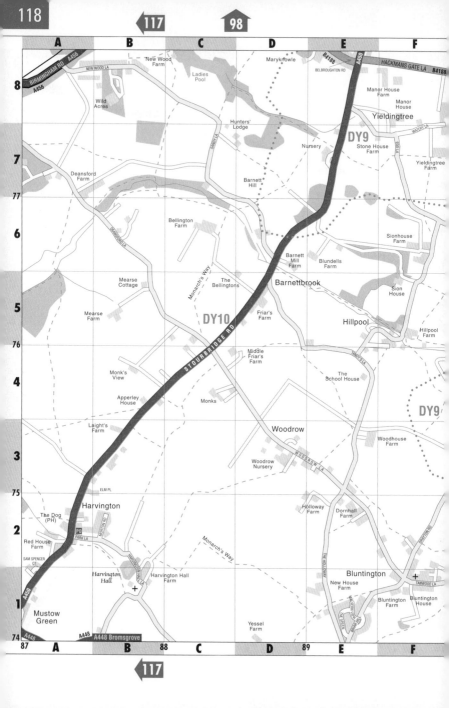

117
98

A   B   C   D   E   F

BIRMINGHAM RD A456
A456
NEW WOOD LA
New Wood Farm

8

Wild Acres

Ladies Pool

Marykfowle

B4188
BELBROUGHTON RD
HACKMANS GATE LA B4188

A450

Manor House Farm
Manor House

Yieldingtree

DY9

Hunters' Lodge

Nursery

Stone House Farm

WATERY LA

7

Deansford Farm

Barnett Hill

Yieldingtree Farm

77

LEASOW LA

Bellington Farm

Sionhouse Farm

6

Barnett Mill Farm

Blundells Farm

Barnettbrook

Monarch's Way

Mearse Cottage

The Bellingtons

Sion House

5

Mearse Farm

Friar's Farm

DY10

Hillpool

Hillpool Farm

76

STOURBRIDGE RD

Middle Friar's Farm

TANHOUSE LA

The School House

DY9

4

Monk's View

Monks

Apperley House

Laight's Farm

Woodrow

WOODROW LA

Woodhouse Farm

3

Woodrow Nursery

ELM PL

75

Harvington

Holloway Farm

Dornhall Farm

The Dog (PH)

PO
PARK LA

Monarch's Way

THE HOLLOWAY

New House Farm

Bluntington

TANWOOD LA

Bluntington House

2

Red House Farm

PARK LA

MILL POOL LANE

Bluntington Farm

SAM SPENCER CT.

Harvington Hall

Harvington Hall Farm

1

A450

Mustow Green

Yessel Farm

A448
A448 A448 Bromsgrove

74

87 A B 88 C D 89 E F

117

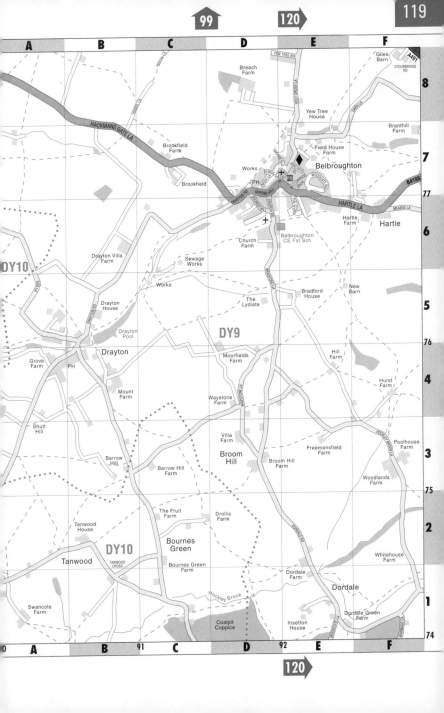

121
102
121
138

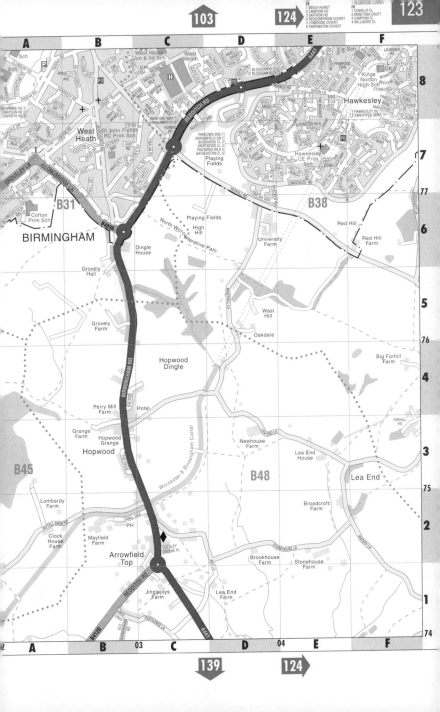

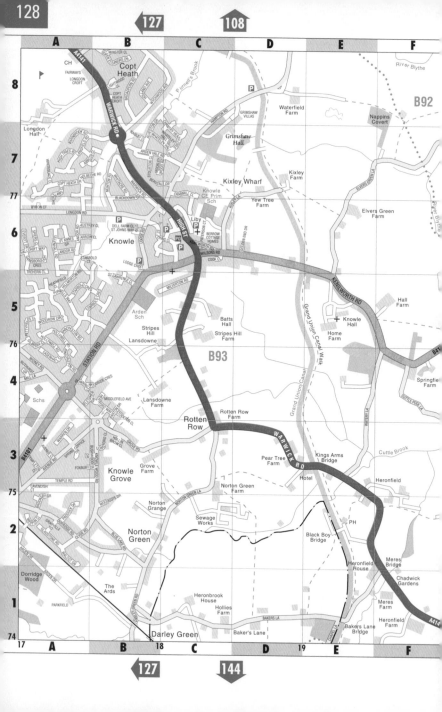

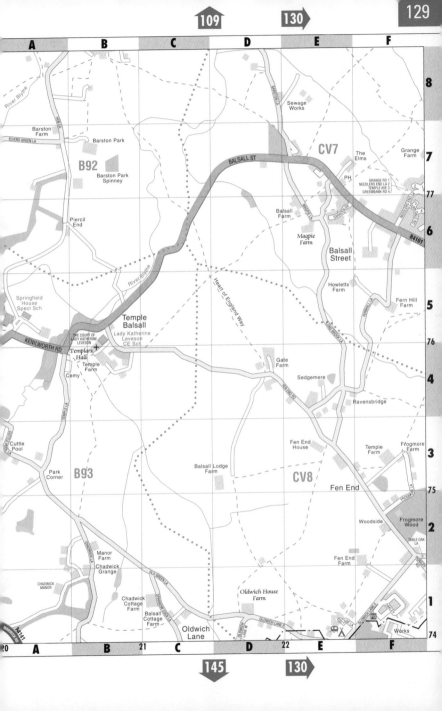

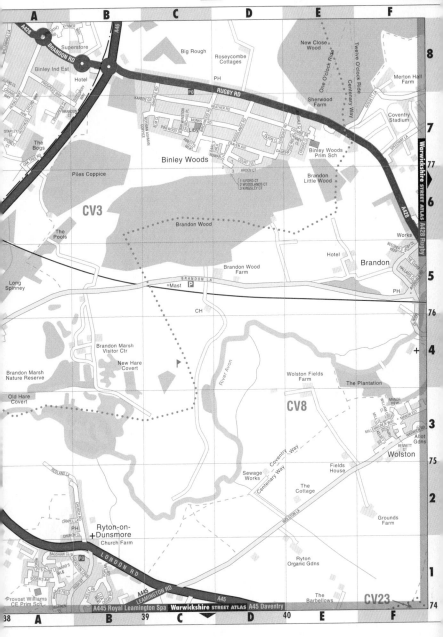

Warwickshire STREET ATLAS A28 Rugby

A   B   C   D   E   F

8

Superstore

Big Rough

New Close Wood

Merton Hall Farm

Binley Ind Est

Roseycombe Cottages

Hotel

PH

RUGBY RD

Coventry Stadium

7

KAREEN GR

WEATHER RD

Sherwood Farm

The Bogs

Libr

77

Binley Woods

Piles Coppice

Binley Woods Prim Sch

Brandon Little Wood

1 ILFORD CT
2 WOODLANDS CT
3 KINGSLEY CT

ARDEN CT

CV3

Brandon Wood

6

The Pools

Works

Brandon

5

Long Spinney

BRANDON LA

Mast

P

Brandon Wood Farm

Hotel

PH

CH

76

Brandon Marsh Visitor Ctr

River Avon

4

New Hare Covert

Wolston Fields Farm

The Plantation

Brandon Marsh Nature Reserve

Old Hare Covert

CV8

MANOR VIEW

3

Wolston

Allot Gdns

75

Coventry Way

Fields House

Sewage Works

Centenary Way

The Cottage

2

Grounds Farm

REDLAND CL

CHURCH LA

Ryton-on-Dunsmore

Church Farm

Ryton Organic Gdns

PH

LONDON RD

1

Provost Williams CE Prim Sch

LEAMINGTON RD

A45

The Barbellows

CV23

74

38   A   B   39   C   D   40   E   F

A B C D E F

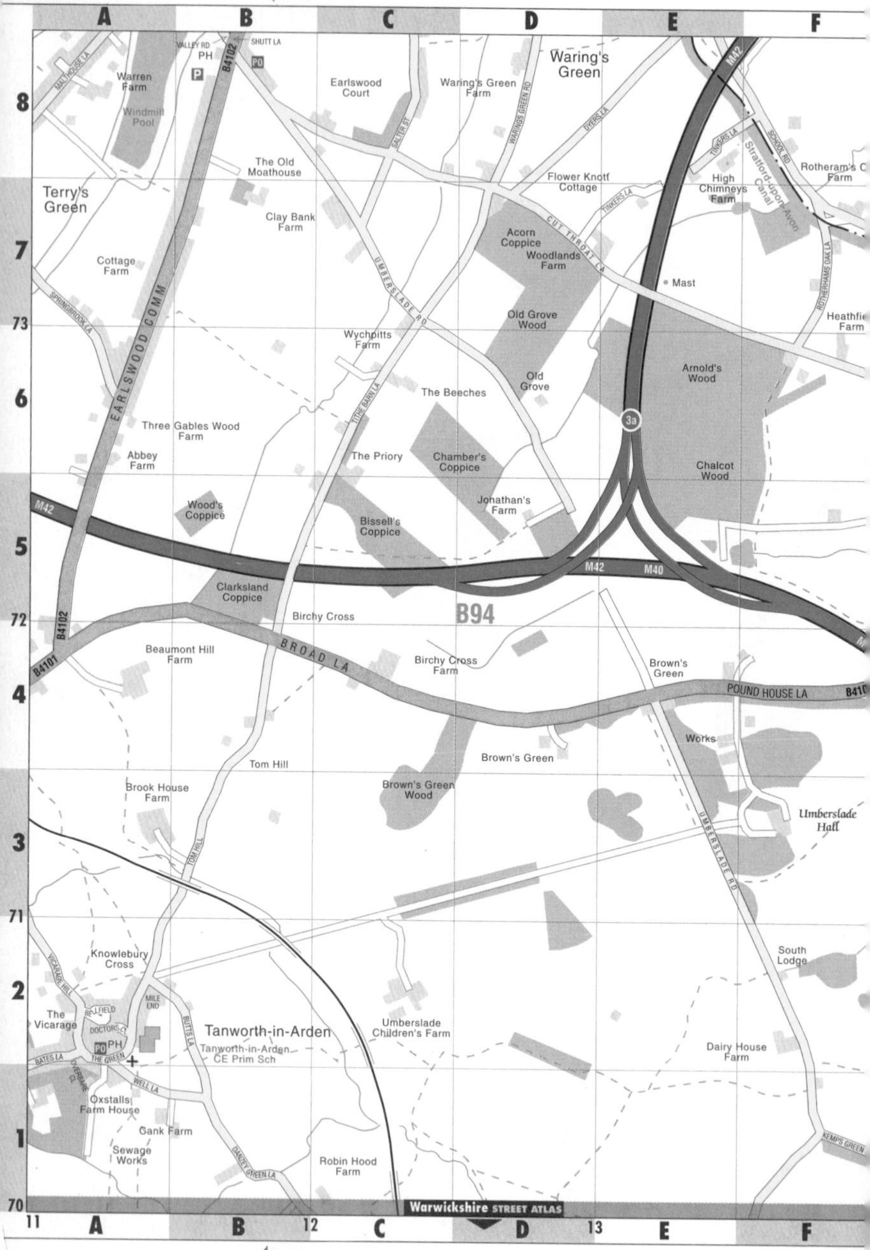

8

Warren Farm

Windmill Pool

VALLEY RD PH

SHUTT LA

P

PO

Earlswood Court

Waring's Green Farm

Waring's Green

M42

The Old Moathouse

Terry's Green

Clay Bank Farm

Flower Knott Cottage

High Chimneys Farm

Rotheram's C Farm

Stratford-upon-Avon Canal

7

Cottage Farm

Acorn Coppice

Woodlands Farm

Mast

Heathfie Farm

73

Wychpitts Farm

Old Grove Wood

Arnold's Wood

6

The Beeches

Three Gables Wood Farm

Old Grove

Abbey Farm

Wood's Coppice

The Priory

Chamber's Coppice

3a

Chalcot Wood

5

Bissell's Coppice

Jonathan's Farm

M42

M40

Clarksland Coppice

72

Birchy Cross

B94

Beaumont Hill Farm

BROAD LA

Birchy Cross Farm

Brown's Green

POUND HOUSE LA

B410

4

Tom Hill

Brown's Green

Works

Brook House Farm

Brown's Green Wood

Umberslade Hall

3

71

Knowlebury Cross

South Lodge

2

The Vicarage

MILE END

Tanworth-in-Arden

Umberslade Children's Farm

Dairy House Farm

PH

PO

Tanworth-in-Arden CE Prim Sch

1

Oxstalls Farm House

Gank Farm

Sewage Works

Robin Hood Farm

70

11 A B 12 C D 13 E F

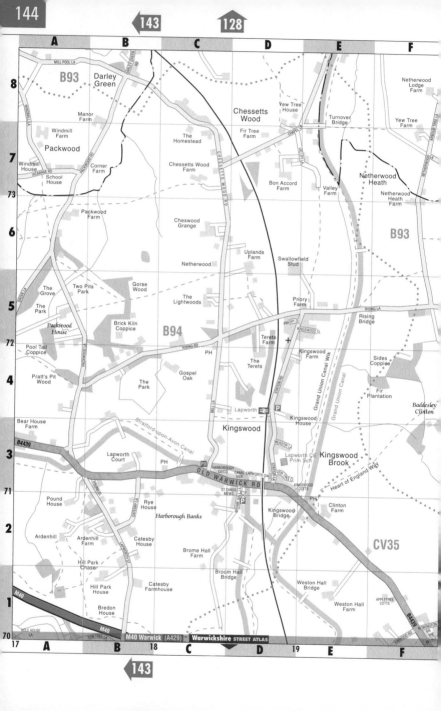

A   B   C   D   E   F

Crackley
Wood

Chase
Farm

Engadine
House

BIRMINGHAM RD

A452

RED LA

MOLLIS LA

8

Camp
Farm

Spring
Farm

The
Spring

7

Little Chase
Farm

South Chase
Farm

BEEHIVE HILL

St Augustine's
RC Prim Sch

UPPER SPRING LA

A429

ORCHARD RD

73

CHASE LA

East Chase
Farm

Priors Field
Prim Sch

GRANGE
AVE

WOODCOTE RD

CORBIE

CLINTON LA

B4103

DE MONTFORT RD

ROSE
COURT

AMHERST RD

QUARRY
RD

BROMLEY
CL

BERKELEY
RD

A429 NEW ST

WATER
TOWER LA

MANOR RD

LAWNSWOOD
GDNS

Sch

WARWICK RD

PRIESTLEY
CT

6

Pleasance
Farm

KENILWORTH

Castle
Green

Castle
Hill

KENILCOURT

AVENUE
RD

CLINTON
AVE

ELIZABETH
RD

CASTLE HILL

HAMMONDS
TERR
PURLIEU LA

HIGH ST

MONTMOUTH
CL

PEARL CL

AVON

BRIDGE ST

PRIORY RD

A452

5

The
Pleasance

High House
Farm

Kenilworth
Castle

Abbey Fields

Finham Brook

ROSEMARY MEWS 3
RICHARDS CL 4
THE ABBEY 5
FIELD HO 6
MONTPELIER HO 7
CONISTON GRANGE 8

KENILWORTH HALL MEWS 1
HOLMES CT 2

72

CV8

CASTLE RD

FORREST RD

BORROWELL LA

B4104

CASTLE
GR

P

LADY
CL

ABBEY HILL

SOUTHBANK
RD

BELMONT
CT

PRIORY
RD

TANNERY

4

Quail
Cottage

Grounds
Farm

Liby

BORROWELL
TERR

P

P

WHATLEY'S

SMALLEY PL

Inchford Brook

Centenary Way

Clinton
Prim Sch

The Mews

Cemy

Oaks
Farm

WALKERS
WAY

OAKS
PREC

PERCY CRES

FARM
RD

BEAUCHAMP RD

ESSEX CL

DUDLEY RD

ROUNDS HILL

P

JOHN O'GAUNT RD

BISHOPS RD

WILLOUGHBY RD

ARCHER RD

COMYN RD

SPRING LA

BRACKEN
RD

SCHOOL LA

SOUTHERN LA

ST JOHN'S

QUEEN'S RD

FIELDING WAY

BRITTAIN LA

MOORLANDS AVE

SERVITE
RD

MOORLANDS
LODGE

ROSELAND RD

LEYCESTER
RD

3

71

Ford

Fernhill
Farm

Bulkington

St John's
Prim Sch

Kenilworth Sch
Castle Hall
Sixth Form

SOVEREIGN

HURT PADDOCKS

2

1

Roundshill
Farm

70

A   B   27   C   D   28   E   F

A B C D E F

8

CV3

Pypes Mill House

Works

Manor Fields

The Rough

Gospel Oak

Chantry Heath Wood

7

73

COVENTRY RD

River Sowe

Stoneleigh Grange

Kings Wood

ACACIA CL
CHAPEL LA
BIRMINGHAM RD
DUDLEY TERR
DALE CL
THE BANK
THE QUEENS
ALMSHOUSES
PRIORY LA
SCHOOL
MEWS

WALKERS CROFT
CARDALL RD

Stoneleigh

Stoneleigh Bridge

Chantry Heath Cottages

6

Motslow Hill

Sowe Mouth

Motslowhill Spinney

River Avon

CH

Cloud Bridge

Coach Bridge

Tantara Lodge

5

72

CV8

Gilbert's Spinney

Centenary Way
Coventry Way

Sewage Works

Stoneleigh Deer Park
Bevis Village

4

National Agricultural Ctr

Stoneleigh Park

Stare Bridge

STONELEIGH RD

Park Farm

Stareton

Waverley Farm

3

71

HOME FARM COTTS

Home Farm

Hares Parlour

Ticknell Spinney

A445 Rugby (A45/A4071)

A445

2

River Avon

Brick Kiln Spinney

Decoy Spinney

Stone House Farm

CV32

LEICESTER LA

COVENTRY RD

Furzen Hill Farm

1

70

Bericote Wood

B4113

Leicester Lane Cotts

A445

2 A B 33 C D 34 E F

Warwickshire STREET ATLAS

F6
1 SUGARBROOK CT
2 Aston Fields Trad Est
3 Silver Birches Bsns Pk

	A	B	C	D	E	F

BROMSGROVE

Sch 7
South Bromsgrove
Com High Sch
(Tech Coll)

Charford

Charford
Fst Sch

Breakback
Hill

East Lodge
Farm

Mast

REGENT
MEWS

YEOMANS
WLK

Spadesbourne Brook

Monarch's Way

ALDERLEY RD 1
WHITFORD CL 2

Foxwalks
Farm

B61

Grafton Manor
House
Fish
Pond

GRAFTON LA

Bowling Green
Farm

BERROW
VIEW

TALBOT

WESLEY WLK

WINTOUR WLK

HEWELL

BROMSGROVE EASTERN BY-PASS

Superstore

West Cr

Sugar Brook

M5 Worcester

WORCESTER RD

HANBURY RD

REDDITCH RD

Stoke
Heath

PLOUGHMANS
WLK

P

Avoncroft Mus
of Historic
Buildings

Ottilie
Hild Sch

Windmill

Tanhouse
Farm

Avoncroft Cattle
Breeding Ctr

E5
1 WAGGONERS CL
2 COUNTINGHOUSE WAY
3 KERRY HILL
4 MARTINGALE CL

Warren
House

Sunningdale

Rectory
Farm

THE
BEECHES

Ewe and
Lamb
(PH)

Fieldview
House

FISH HOUSE LA

Stoke Pound
Farm

Little Intall
Farm

FARFIEL

Brickhouse
Farm

LAKESIDE CL

Little Brick
House Farm

Stoke Prior
Bridge

HANBURY RD

HANEY GARDENS

STOKE POUND LA

BROADMOOR LA

Stoke
Prior

River Salwarpe

Moors
Farm

Nature Reserve

PH

Upton
Warren

Upton Warren
Bridge

Hobden Hall
Farm

Stoke Prior
Fst Sch

P

Ryefields
Farm

B60

Foley
Gardens

Navigation Inn
(PH)

Stoke Wharf

A38 Droitwich

Sailing
Lake

SWAN LA

A38

RYEFIELDS

CLOVENDALE

Worcester and Birmingham Canal

Waste
Pit

Harris
Ind Pk

Sports Gd

Works

Hen Brook

Shaw Lane
Ind Est

WHITFORD CL

Saxon
Bsns Pk

CT

WR9

Sagebury
Farm

Stoke
Works

Weston Hall
Farm

Poolhouse
Farm

ROSEMARY CL

JUBILEE WAY

VERNON CL

SAGEBURY DR

WESTBOURNE RD

B4091

Harbours Hill
Farm

Little
Harbours
Farm

93	A	94	B	C	D	95	E	F

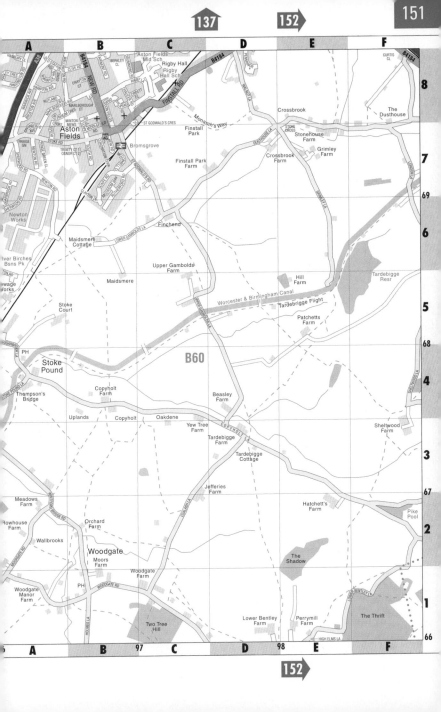

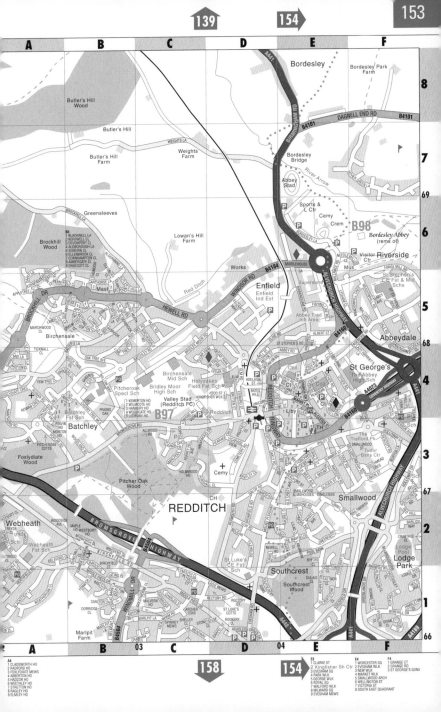

8

Bordesley

Bordesley Park Farm

B4101   DAGNELL END RD   B4101

7

BIRMINGHAM RD

B4101

Bordesley Bridge

River Arrow

69

Abbey Stad

Sports & L Ctr   Cemy   Crem

B98

6

Bordesley Abbey (rems of)

BRIDGELEY LA

Visitor Ctr

Riverside

NEEDLE MILL LA

Mus

Superstore

TORGE MILL LA

St Stephen's CE Fst & Mid Schs

Butler's Hill Wood

Butler's Hill

WEIGHTS LA

Weights Farm

Butler's Hill Farm

Greensleeves

BROCKHILL LA

Lowan's Hill Farm

Brockhill Wood

B9
1 BLACKWELL LA
2 KERSWELL CL
3 DEVONPORT CL
4 ALDBOROUGH LA
5 SISBURN CL
6 ELLENBROOK CL
7 CORNHAMPTON CL
8 AMBERGATE CL
9 DRAYCOTT CL

Works

Red Ditch

Mast

Enfield

WINSFORD RD

Enfield Ind Est

5

HEWELL RD

B4184

MIDDLEHOUSE LA

Abbey Trad Int Area

FISHING ST

B4160

ALBERT ST

Abbeydale

68

ST STEPHEN'S HO

St George's CE Fst & Mid

Birchensale

APPLETREE DR

BROCKHILL DR

PENNYFIELD CL

ST STEPHEN'S HO

ABBEY RD

Coll

St George's The Abbey High Sch

4

Birchensale Mid Sch

Holyoakes Field Fst Sch

ELM LST

ADELAIDE ST

Coll

A4023   COVENTRY HIGHWAY

ALVECHURCH HIGHWAY

Pitcheroak Specl Sch

Bridley Moor High Sch

KINGFISHER WLK

BATES HILL

Coll

B4160

B97

Valley Stad (Reddich FC)

1 KEMERTON HO
2 WILMCOTE HO
3 HANBURY HO
4 WOODGATE HO
5 LEDBURY HO

Reddich

UNICORN HILL

Libry

The Trafford Pk

Batchley Fst Sch

Batchley

PRIORS OAK

BROMSGROVE RD

ALLWOOD

PRIOR HILL

The Trafford Pk

St Tudor Bsns Ctr

Smallwood

3

Foxlydiate Wood

Pitcheroak Cotts

WOODLAND

HOLMWOOD HO

Cemy

PLYMOUTH RD

Smallwood Almshouses

DINGLESIDE

Smallwood

67

Pitcher Oak Wood

CH

REDDITCH

PARSONS RD

HILL

BARLICH WAY

2

Webheath

BROMSGROVE HIGHWAY

BIRCHFIELD RD

Webheath Fst Sch

WINDMILL DR

Birchfield CT

NEWELL HO

The Mayfields

POOL BANK

BYFORD

Lodge Pool Park

CRABTREE CT

Lodge Pool Drive

Lodge Park

Southcrest

SOUTHCREST

1

St Luke's CE Fst Sch

Southcrest Wood

Marlpit Farm

B4504

MALVERN DR

CHARLES

MARLPIT LA

SHELLEY

STONEHOUSE

St Luke's Cotts

RECTORY RD

RECTORY

ROOKERY CL

HEADLESS CROSS

A441

A4189

Dorridge CT

Carlton CT

ASHTON

SPINNEY MEWS

CRABTREE

VICTORIA ST

HIMBLETON

WIREHILL DR

GRIMLEY

66

A4
1 CLADSWORTH HO
2 RADFORD HO
3 FOXLYDIATE MEWS
4 ABBERTON HO
5 HADZOR HO
6 WEETHLEY HO
7 STRETTON HO
8 RAGLEY HO
9 ELMLEY HO

E3
1 CLARKE ST
2 Kingfisher Sh Ctr
3 EVESHAM SQ
4 PARK WLK
5 GEORGE WLK
6 ROYAL SQ
7 WALFORD WLK
8 MILWARD SQ
9 EVESHAM MEWS

E4
1 WORCESTER SQ
2 EVESHAM WLK
3 NEW WLK
4 MARKET WLK
5 SMALLWOOD ARCH
6 WELLINGTON ST
7 VICTORIA ST
8 SOUTH EAST QUADRANT

F4
1 GRANGE CT
2 GRANGE RD
3 ST GEORGE'S GDNS

A   B   C   D   E   F

8

Roundshill Farm

Abattoir

Camp Barn

Woodcote Lodge

Roucil Farm

Little Woodcote

Bannerhill Farm

ROUNCIL LA

Goodrest Cottages

Leek Wootton

CV8

The Lunch

7

DANGER AREA

Mast

Goodrest Farm

Woodcote (County Police HQ)

PH

69

Deer Park Farm

WOODCOTE LA

Terrace Hill Wood

Stone Edge

6

Centenery Way

THE ELMS

Larch Covert

DANGER AREA

Wootton Court

5

DANGER AREA

CH

68

Deer Park

Blacklow Hill

4

Wedgnock Old Park

Prospect Farm

CV35

Gaveston's Cross

Wedgnock Rifle Range

Middle Woodloes

A46

Blackbrake Plantation

3

Loes Farm

67

Woodloes Farm

DWARRIS WLK

Woodloes Park

CV34

1 WEALE GR
2 SHELDON GR

2

WARWICK

Nursery

WARWICK BY-PASS

Ind Est

Wedgnock Ind Est

1

Wedgnock Park Farm

BIRMINGHAM RD
A4177

Grand Union Canal

Woodloes Inf & Jun Schs

COVENTRY RD
A429

Sch

66

A46

A   B   27   C   D   28   E   F

CV8

Chesford Bridge

Bericote Wood

Field Barn Farm

Hotel

Hotel

Blackdown Manor

Cattle Brook

New Farm

Tiger's Island

8

Wootton Spinnies

Works

7

THE MEADOWS

TOMAKIN RD

Tower House

69

Meadow Cottage

Blackdown

Hill Wootton

Leek Wootton

Sewage Works

Hill Wootton Farm

Blackdown Hill Hotel

CV35

6

New House Farm

All Saints CE Prim Sch

Woodland Grange

Cranford

Gaveston Lodge

5

The Warwickshire Nuffield

H

River Avon

68

North Leamington Comm Sch & Art Coll

B4115

4

Sandy Lane Farm

A429

A46

Church Farm

CV32

Old Milverton

ROYAL LEAMINGTON SPA

3

Manor Farm

COVENTRY RD

67

Allot Gdns

THE CLOISTERS
AMBASSADOR CT 2
BELL TOWER MEWS 3

Guy's Well

5 WAYS

2

Guy's Cave

Guy's Cliffe

The Trinity
RC Tech Coll

CV34

Patten's Grove

Milverton

Weir

Sch

1

Cemy

Sch

66

Sch

RUGBY RD

WARWICK PL

WARWICK ST

B4099

A452

A445

Warwickshire STREET ATLAS

8

7

69

6

5

68

4

3

67

2

66

A   B   C   D   E   F

CV32

CV33

Bericote Fields Farm

Cubbington Heath Farm

Oakdene

North Cubbington Wood

Tanner's Barn

West Hill

West Hill Farm

Cubbington

Humber Farm

WILLOW SHEETS MDW

THORN STILE CL.

Cubbington CE Prim Sch

RUGBY RD

WINDMILL CROFT

PH

Our Lady & St Teresa's RC Prim Sch

Schs

CHAMBERLAIN CL.

Hill Farm House

Works

New Manor Farm

Glebe Farm

Tanner's Farm

FORD COTTS

WICKHAM CL

Lillington

Lib

Sch

Mast

Works

Mast

Campion Hills

GRESHAM PL
CHESTNUT SQ
MARSTON CL

St Paul's CE Prim Sch

CH

The Runghills

Ford Farm

White House

River Leam

Redhouse Farm

Offchurch Bury

STONELEIGH RD

B4113

A445

COVENTRY RD

B4453

LEICESTER LA

WESTHILL RD

LILLINGTON RD

CUBBINGTON RD

B4453

A1
1 LOWER VILLIERS ST
2 LANSDOWNE RD
3 KENEDY SQ
4 ST PAUL'S SQ
5 MERCHANTS CT
6 LANSDOWNE CRES
7 WILLES RD
8 HANOVER GDNS
9 WHITTLE CT

A2
1 ACORN CT
2 STOCKTON GR
3 WHITACRE RD
4 SHUCKBURGH GR
5 HELLIDON CL
6 BROWNLOW ST

8

7

65

6

5

64

4

3

63

2

1

62

A B C D E F

Downsell Wood

CH

Morton Stanley Park

The Vaynor Fst Sch

Mid Sch

KEATS RD

Headless Cross

REDDITCH
Superstore

Oakenshaw Wood

Callow Hill

Walkwood Coppice

Walkwood

Windmill La

PH

B97

JUBILEE AVE

EVESHAM RD

Oakenshaw

B98

White House

Lanehouse Farm

Lovelyne Farm

Hunt End

PH

St Augustine's RC High Sch

Stonepits Copse

The Harry David Fst Sch

Crabbs Cross

PH
THE
MAN-TAN

B4504

A448

Slough Farm

The Moors

Thickwaney Brook

Chapel House Farm

Weavers Hill

Upper Huntend Farm

Brookfield

WEAVERS CL

Claverdon CL

New Coppice

A448

Monarch's Way

Foxpits

Wixon Brook

Dagtail La

BROOKHAMPTON CL 1
ALDERMINSTER CL 2

Dagtail End

Eastern Hill

EVESHAM RD

Astwood Hill Farm

Yew Tree House

The Wren's Nest Farm

Manor House La

Astwood Bank Fst Sch

Eastern Hill

ROWSBOROUGH CL

Eastern Hill Farm

CROFTS LA

ASTWOOD LA

B96

Ridgeway Trad Est

B4092

JILL LA

POPLARS LA

Hole Farm

OAK LA

Astwood Court

Sewage Works

Doebank House

Badgers

1 EASTWOOD CT
2 DEWBURY CL
3 POST OFFICE WLK
4 NEW RD

Astwood Bank

B4092 SAMBOURNE LA

Sambourne Lane Farm

A441 Alcester (A422)

02 A B 03 C D 04 E F

A   B   C   D   E   F

8

WILD GOOSE LA   B4497

Arrow Valley Park

The Ilo Ctr

Park Farm

Greenlands

Dingleside Mid Sch

Woodrow

Old Forge Bsns Ctr

The Old Forge

Ipsley Brook

Washford

Washford Ind Est

B98

7

Woodrow Fst Sch

Red Hill

65

B4093

STUDLEY RD

Hill Crest

Kingsley Coll

Washford Farm

PH

BIRMINGHAM RD

A435 Birmingham

6

Wirehill Wood

The Alexandra

Green Lane

Tanhouse Farm

PH

Poplars Trad Est

Washford Bridge

River Arrow

Warwickshire STREET ATLAS

Wirehill

Green Lane Farm

REDDITCH RD

5

Rough Hill Wood

B97

Studley Common

Ind Est

Wapping

B4093

Priory Farm and remains of Priory

PRIORY

64

THE SLOUGH

B4092

Works

B4092

Pear T Dr

St Judes Av

St Chads

Canterbury

Augustine Ave

St Agnes

HIGH ST

LORD DAUGHT 1
OLD VICARAGE 2
GDNS

Lib

P

PO

STUDLEY BRIDGE

Studley Bridge

HARDWICK LA

Thane Cl

4

STATION RD

Badbury Gdns

B80

St Mary's RC Prim Sch

Studley High Sch

Studley

The Park

3

Troy Ind Est

Thomas Town

Studley
St Mary's
CE Jun Sch

Foster Ave

TOME TOWN LA

ALLENDALE

Allendale

ALCESTER RD

63

BRAMSGROVE RD

Littlewood Green

PH

Willow Way

Watty Rd

Holt Lane

Holt Farm

2

B96

Reins Farm

Littlewood Green Farm

Holt Rd

Orchard Way

A435

Spinney Cottage

HILL LA

MIDDLETOWN LA

MUSSON WY

Middletown

Elmdale House

SPERNAL LA

Spernal Ash

B49

1

Sambourne Reins

Perrymill Farm

Sambourne

SAMBOURNE PARK LA

WOOD TERR

SAMBOURNE LA

Warwickshire STREET ATLAS

A435 Alcester

A435

Haydon Way Farm

62

05   A   B   06   C   D   07   E   F

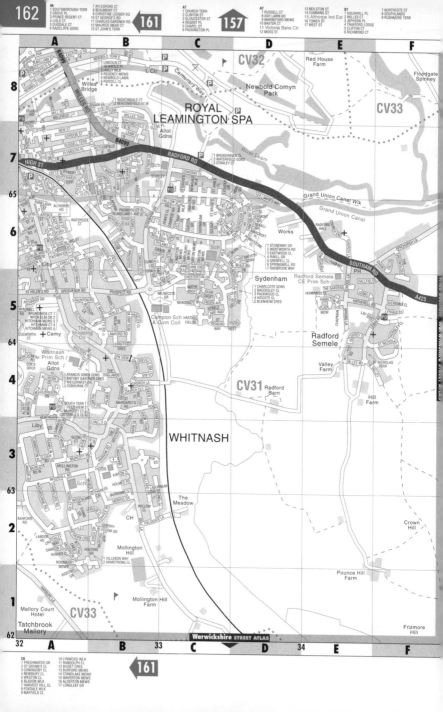

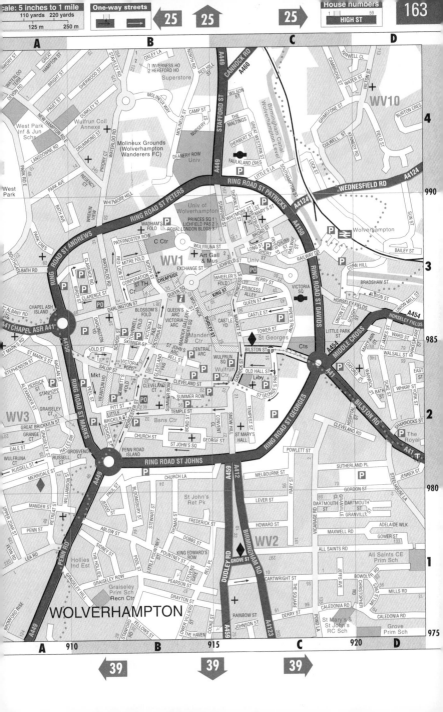

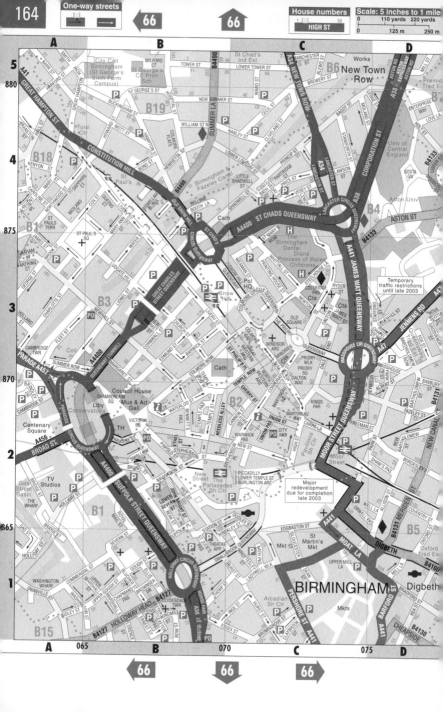

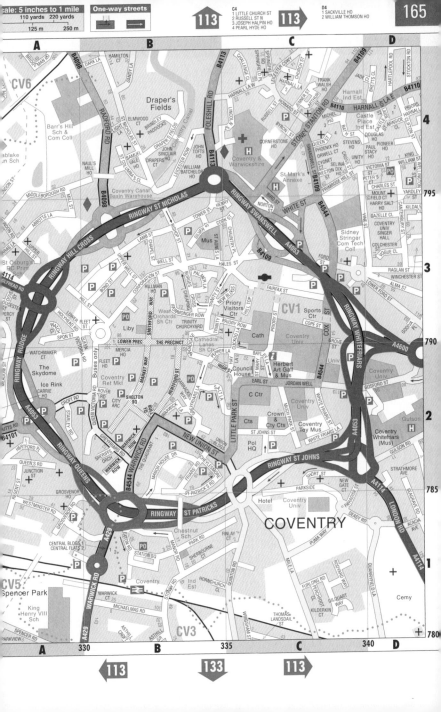

Index

Church Rd **6** Beckenham BR2..........**53** C6

Place name	Location number	Locality, town or village	Postcode district	Page and grid square
May be abbreviated on the map	Present when a number indicates the place's position in a crowded area of mapping	Shown when more than one place has the same name	District for the indexed place	Page number and grid reference for the standard mapping

Public and commercial buildings are highlighted in magenta. Places of interest are highlighted in blue with a star★

Abbreviations used in the index

Acad	Academy	Comm	Common	Gd	Ground	L	Leisure	Prom	Prom
App	Approach	Cott	Cottage	Gdn	Garden	La	Lane	Rd	Road
Arc	Arcade	Cres	Crescent	Gn	Green	Liby	Library	Recn	Recreation
Ave	Avenue	Cswy	Causeway	Gr	Grove	Mdw	Meadow	Ret	Retail
Bglw	Bungalow	Ct	Court	H	Hall	Meml	Memorial	Sh	Shopping
Bldg	Building	Ctr	Centre	Ho	House	Mkt	Market	Sq	Square
Bsns, Bus	Business	Ctry	Country	Hospl	Hospital	Mus	Museum	St	Street
Bvd	Boulevard	Cty	County	HQ	Headquarters	Orch	Orchard	Sta	Station
Cath	Cathedral	Dr	Drive	Hts	Heights	Pal	Palace	Terr	Terrace
Cir	Circus	Dro	Drove	Ind	Industrial	Par	Parade	TH	Town Hall
Cl	Close	Ed	Education	Inst	Institute	Pas	Passage	Univ	University
Cnr	Corner	Emb	Embankment	Int	International	Pk	Park	Wk, Wlk	Walk
Coll	College	Est	Estate	Intc	Interchange	Pl	Place	Wr	Water
Com	Community	Ex	Exhibition	Junc	Junction	Prec	Precinct	Yd	Yard

Index of localities, towns and villages

Aldridge 30 A6	Brownhills 16 B6	Finstall 137 D1	Minworth 58 C5	Tanworth-In-Arden 142 B3
Allesley 112 B7	Bulkington 79 B1	Great Wyrley 5 B3	Moseley 86 F2	Tardebigge 152 B7
Alvechurch 139 B6	Burntwood 7 C5	Hagley 98 E5	Mustow Green 117 F1	Tettenhall Wood 24 C3
Alvecote 22 D6	Burton Green 131 C4	Halesowen 83 D4	Norton Canes 5 F6	Tidbury Green 125 E4
Ansty 97 D4	Burton Hastings 75 A1	Hampton-in-Arden 109 B8	Nuneaton 73 B6	Tipton 51 F6
Ash Green 95 C6	Cannock 1 D2	Handsworth 54 C1	Nurton 23 A3	Trescott 23 B7
Aston Flamville 76 E6	Catherine de Barnes ..108 B6	Harvington 118 B2	Oldbury 63 F6	Trysull 37 C1
Astwood Bank 158 F1	Catshill 137 B8	Hednesford 2 C5	Outwoods 92 C5	Upper Bentley 152 A1
Baginton 133 F2	Chadwick End 145 B7	Himley 49 B3	Perton 23 C4	Upper Marlbrook 121 D2
Balsall Common 130 A7	Chapel End 72 B8	Hinckley 75 B8	Piccadilly 35 F1	Upton Warren 150 A3
Barnacle 97 B6	Chase Terrace 6 E8	Hints 19 D3	Polesworth 36 F8	Wall 8 D2
Barnt Green 138 A7	Cheslyn Hay 4 C3	Hockley Heath 143 D6	Portway 141 A5	Walsall 28 B3
Barston 109 B1	Cheswick Green 126 E4	Hollywood 125 B8	Radford Semele 162 E5	Walsall Wood 15 F4
Barwell 71 F7	Churchill 98 C3	Honiley 146 D5	Redditch 153 C2	Warwick 160 E7
Beausale 146 C2	Clayhanger 15 D6	Hopwas 20 B7	Romsley 101 A4	Water Orton 59 C3
Bedworth 78 B1	Clent 99 F3	Hopwood 123 B3	Rowington Green 145 A1	Wedges Mills 4 B6
Belbroughton 119 E7	Cliff 35 C1	Hunnington 101 B8	Rowney Green 139 E3	Wednesbury 41 D3
Bentley Heath 127 E5	Codsall 10 A3	Huntington 1 D7	Royal Leamington Spa .156 D3	Wednesfield 26 D6
Beoley 154 D7	Coleshill 59 F2	Iverley 98 B7	Ryton-on-Dunsmore ..135 B2	Weeford 19 A4
Berkswell 110 D3	Coleshill 70 F6	Kenilworth 148 D5	Sambourne 159 B1	West Bromwich 53 E3
Bickenhill 90 D1	Corley 94 B7	Keresley 94 F5	Sedgley 50 F7	Whateley 35 F3
Bilston 40 D4	Coven Heath 11 C6	Kidderminster 116 D4	Seisdon 37 A2	White Stitch 92 C3
Binley Woods 135 C7	Coventry 113 C4	Kingswinford 60 F6	Shenstone 18 A5	Whitnash 162 C3
Birchmoor 36 E8	Coventry 165 C1	Knowle 128 B6	Shilton 97 F5	Wildmoor 120 F4
Birmingham 164 C1	Cubbington 157 D6	Lapworth 143 E3	Shuttington 22 F7	Willenhall 27 B4
Birmingham 67 C2	Curdworth 59 B6	Leek Wootton 155 F7	Smethwick 65 A4	Wishaw 48 B2
Blackdown 156 F6	Darlaston 41 E7	Lichfield 9 D5	Solihull 106 F5	Wolston 135 F3
Blackheath 63 E1	Dodford 136 A5	Lickey End 137 C6	Stockingford 72 C3	Wolverhampton 163 B1
Blackwell 138 A5	Dordon 36 F6	Little Aston 31 B4	Stoke Heath 150 D5	Wolverhampton 25 A3
Blakedown 98 C2	Dorridge 127 E3	Little Packington 91 C6	Stoke Pound 151 A4	Wombourne 49 B6
Bluntington 118 E1	Drayton Bassett 34 D5	Lower Clent 99 D4	Stoke Prior 150 C4	Wood End 36 C1
Bournheath 136 D8	Dudley 51 D2	Lower Marlbrook 121 C1	Stone 117 D3	Wroxall 145 E3
Bradnock's Marsh 109 D3	Earlswood 126 B1	Lower Penn 38 A4	Stoneleigh 149 B6	Wylde Green 46 C1
Bramcote 79 E6	Edgbaston 86 A6	Lydiate Ash 121 C3	Stonnall 16 E4	Wythall 124 F2
Brandon 135 F5	Essington 12 F3	Meer End 130 D1	Stourbridge 80 D4	
Brierley Hill 61 E2	Fairfield 120 D3	Meriden 92 D1	Studley 159 F4	
Brinsford 11 D7	Fazeley 34 E8	Middleton 34 A1	Sutton Coldfield 46 D5	
Bromsgrove 136 E2	Featherstone 12 C7	Mile Oak 20 D1	Tamworth 21 B3	

A

A B Row B4 66 F3
A1 Trad Est B66 65 A7
Abberley B77 22 C2
Abberley Cl
Halesowen B63 82 F2
Redditch B98 154 C5
Abberley Ind Ctr B66 65 D5
Abberley Rd Dudley DY3 50 D4
Oldbury B68 84 B8
Abberley St Dudley DY2 62 C8
Smethwick B66 65 D5
Abberton Cl B63 83 C3
Abberton Ct B23 56 C2
Abberton Gr B90 127 B7
Abberton Ho 4 B97 153 A4
Abberton Way CV4 132 E3
Abbess Gr B25 68 E1
Abbey CE Inf Sch CV11 73 B5
Abbey Cl
Bromsgrove B60 137 C2
West Bromwich B71 53 C5
Abbey Cres
Halesowen B63 82 D4
Oldbury B68 64 D1
Abbey Ct CV3 134 B6
Abbey Dr WS3 15 A5
Abbey End CV8 147 F4
Abbey Est CV2 114 F5
Abbey Gate CV11 73 C4
Abbey Gate Sh Ctr CV11 73 C4
Abbey Gdns B67 64 E1
Abbey Gn CV11 73 B5
Abbey High Sch The B98 153 F4
Abbey Hill CV8 147 F5
Abbey Inf Sch B67 64 E2
Abbey Jun Sch B67 64 E1
Abbey Mans 2 B24 57 B6
Abbey Prim Sch WS3 13 E2
Abbey RC Prim Sch B23 57 A5
Abbey Rd
Birmingham, Edgbaston B17 85 D5
Birmingham, Gravelly Hill B23 56 D2
Coventry CV3 134 A6
Dudley, Gornalwood DY3 50 C3
Dudley, Netherton DY2 62 D6
Halesowen B63 82 C4
Kidderminster DY11 116 A6
Redditch B97 153 E4
Smethwick B67 64 E1
Tamworth B77 21 D3
Abbey Sq WS3 13 E2
Abbey St Cannock WS12 2 B7
Dudley DY3 50 C3
Nuneaton CV11 73 B5
Abbey St N B18 66 A5
Abbey The CV8 147 F5
Abbey Trad Ind Area B97 153 E5
Abbey Way CV3 133 F6
Abbeydale Cl CV3 114 F2
Abbeydale Rd B31 103 A2
Abbeyfield Rd
Birmingham B23 56 E8
Wolverhampton WV10 11 E4
Abbeyfields Dr B80 159 E6
Abbot Rd B63 100 C8
Abbots Cl Knowle B93 128 A7
Walsall WS4 29 C6
Abbots Field WS11 1 E5
Abbots Mews DY5 61 D1
Abbots Rd B14 104 E7
Abbots Way
Birmingham B18 66 B6
Warwick CV34 160 D6
Wolverhampton WV3 24 E1
Abbotsbury Cl CV2 115 A4
Abbotsford Ave B43 43 F2
Abbotsford Dr DY1 61 E7
Abbotsford Rd
Birmingham B11 87 C6
Lichfield WS14 9 E7
Nuneaton CV11 73 E1
Abbotsford Sch CV8 147 F6
Abbotts Gn LE10 75 F5
Abbotts La CV1 165 A3
Abbotts Pl WS3 14 D1
Abbotts Rd B24 56 F1
Abbotts St
4 Royal Leamington Spa CV31 161 F7
Walsall WS3 14 D2
Abbotts Wlk CV3 135 C7
Abdon Ave B29 103 C7
Abelia B77 21 F3
Abercorn Rd CV5 112 E2
Aberdeen Cl CV5 112 A5
Aberdeen Rd CV11 73 E1
Aberdeen St B18 65 E4
Aberford Cl WV12 27 D4
Abergavenny Wlk CV3 134 F6
Abigails Cl B26 89 B7
Abingdon Cl WV1 26 B2
Abingdon Rd
Birmingham B23 56 B7
Dudley DY2 62 D3
Walsall WS3 13 F2
Wolverhampton WV1 26 B2
Abingdon Way
Birmingham B35 58 A3
Nuneaton CV11 73 F7
Walsall WS3 13 F2
Ablewell St WS1 28 F1
Ablow St WV2 163 B1
Abnalls La WS13 8 B8
Abney Dr WV14 39 F1
Abney Gr B44 45 B2
Aboyne Cl B5 86 D6
Acacia Ave
Birmingham B37 69 F6
Coventry CV1 113 E1
Walsall WS5 43 A4
Acacia Cl Birmingham B37 69 F6
Dudley DY1 51 A3
Tipton B69 52 B2
Acacia Cres WV8 10 B4
Acacia Ct DY8 80 E6
Acacia Dr WV14 51 B7
Acacia Gr WS12 2 F3
Acacia Rd
Birmingham B30 103 E8
Nuneaton CV10 72 E5
Royal Leamington Spa CV32 156 D1
Acanthus Rd B98 154 F6
Accord Mews WS10 41 D7
Ace Bsns Pk B33 69 D2
Acfold Rd B20 54 E5
Achal Cl CV6 95 F2
Acheson Rd B28,B90 105 F3
Achilees Cl WS6 4 F1
Achilles Cl CV34 161 F2
Achilles Rd CV6 114 A7
Ackleton Gdns WV3 38 F7
Ackleton Gr B29 84 F1
Acocks Green Inf Sch B27 88 B3
Acocks Green Jun Sch B27 88 B3
Acocks Green Sta B27 88 C4
Acorn Cl Bedworth CV12 95 C8
Birmingham, Bournville B30 103 E8
Birmingham, Stockfield B27 88 B5
Cannock WS11 2 C2
Great Wyrley WS6 5 A1
Stoneleigh CV8 149 B7
West Bromwich B70 53 B2
Acorn Ct 1 CV32 157 A2
Acorn Ctr 1 WS1 28 F1
Acorn Gdns B30 104 A7
Acorn Gr Birmingham B1 66 B3
Stourbridge DY8 60 E1
Acorn Rd Catshill B61 137 B8
Halesowen B62 83 C8
Wolverhampton WV11 13 A1
Acorn St Coventry CV3 134 B8
Willenhall WV13 27 C2
Acorn Starter Units WS7 6 D7
Acorn View WS7 7 C6
Acorns The B61 137 A8
Acre Cl CV31 162 A4
Acre La B97 152 E2
Acre Rise WV12 27 B5
Acres Rd DY5 81 E8
Acres The WV3 24 C1
Acton Cl B98 154 D5
Acton Dr DY3 50 B3
Acton Gr Bilston WV14 40 B4
Birmingham B44 45 A2
Acton Ho CV4 111 F3
Ada Rd Birmingham B25 88 B6
Smethwick B66 65 B3
Ada Wrighton Cl WV12 27 C7
Adam Ct WS11 1 D1
Adam Rd 1 CV6 113 F7
Adam St DY11 116 C5
Adam's Hill DY9 99 E4
Adams Brook Dr B32 84 B1
Adams Cl Smethwick B66 64 D7
Tipton DY4 40 F1
Adams Ct DY10 117 A7
Adams Hill B32 84 B1
Adams Ho 3 DY11 116 C6
Adams Rd Brownhills WS8 16 B5
Wolverhampton WV3 38 C8
Adams St Birmingham B7 66 F5
Walsall WS2 28 D2
West Bromwich B70 53 B3
Adamson Cl WS11 1 B1
Adare Dr CV3 133 C8
Adcock Dr CV8 148 B5
Addenbrook Ho
Blackheath B64 82 F8
Sutton Coldfield B73 46 A3
Addenbrook Way DY4 52 D8
Addenbrooke Cres DY11 116 A1
Addenbrooke Dr B73 46 B2
Addenbrooke Pl WS10 41 D7
Addenbrooke Rd
Keresley CV7 95 A6
Smethwick B67 64 F3
Addenbrooke St
Darlaston WS10 41 D7
Walsall WS3 28 C7
Adderley Gdns B8 67 D5
Adderley Park Cl B8 67 E4
Adderley Park Sta B8 67 D3
Adderley Prim Sch B8 67 D4
Adderley Rd B8 67 C4
Adderley Rd S B8 67 C3
Adderley St
Birmingham B9 67 A1
Coventry CV1 113 E4
Adderley Trad Est B8 67 C4
Addingham Cl 2 CV34 155 E1
Addison Cl Cannock WS11 1 E5
Nuneaton CV10 72 A5
Wednesbury WS10 42 E2
Addison Croft DY3 50 A5
Addison Gr WV11 12 B1
Addison Pl Bilston WV14 41 A7
Water Orton B46 59 B3
Addison Rd
Birmingham, King's Heath B14 104 F7
Birmingham, Nechells B7 67 C8
Brierley Hill DY5 61 B2
Coventry CV6 113 A8
Wednesbury WS10 42 E2
Wolverhampton WV3 38 F8
Addison St WS10 41 F2
Addison Terr WS10 41 F2
Adelaide Ave B70 53 A7
Adelaide Ct CV12 78 A2
Adelaide Dr WS12 2 F3
Adelaide Rd CV31,CV32 161 E8
Adelaide St
Birmingham B12 86 F8
Brierley Hill DY5 61 D3
Coventry CV1 165 D4
Redditch B97 153 D4
Adelaide Twr B34 69 C5
Adelaide Wlk WV2 163 D1
Adelphi Ct 3 DY5 61 D2
Adey Rd WV11 26 F8
Adkins La B67 65 A1
Admington Rd B33 89 C8
Admiral Gdns CV8 148 C6
Admiral Parker Dr WS14 17 F5
Admiral Pl B13 86 F4
Admirals Way
Blackheath B65 63 B2
Bramcote CV11 79 E6
Adonis Cl B79 21 C7
Adria Rd B11 87 B4
Adrian Croft B13 87 C1
Adrian Ct 1 B24 57 B6
Adshead Rd DY2 62 C7
Adstone Gr B31 103 A1
Advance Bsns Pk WS11 2 B3
Advent Gdns B70 53 B3
Adwalton Rd WV6 23 F3
Aethelred Ct WV10 25 C6
Affleck Ave B78 20 D1
Agenoria Dr DY8 80 F5
Aggborough Cres DY10 116 E3
Aggborough Stadium (Kidderminster Harriers FC) DY10 116 F4
Agincourt Rd CV3 133 E7
Agmore La B60 138 B3
Agmore Rd B60 138 B4
Aiden Ct WS13 9 C7
Ainsbury Rd CV5 132 E8
Ainsdale Cl Coventry CV6 96 B4
Stourbridge DY8 80 F2
Ainsdale Gdns
Birmingham B24 57 C5
Halesowen B63 82 D2
Ainsworth Rd WV10 11 E4
Aintree Cl Bedworth CV12 78 B4
Cannock WS12 2 F6
Catshill B61 121 A1
Coventry CV6 113 E5
Kidderminster DY11 116 D8
Aintree Dr CV32 157 C3
Aintree Gr B34 69 D6
Aintree Rd WV10 11 D4
Aintree Way DY1 50 F2
Aire Croft B31 103 B1
Airfield Dr WS4,WS9 29 E3
Airport Way B26 90 C3
Aitken Cl B78 21 A2
Aitken Wing B15 86 A6
Ajax Cl WS6 4 F1
Akon Ho CV6 94 F2
Akrill Cl B70 53 B5
Akrill Cottage Homes The B70 53 B5
Al Hira Sch B12 87 A6
Alamein Rd WV13 26 E1
Alan Bray Cl LE10 74 D7
Alan Higgs Way CV4 131 C8
Alandale Ave CV5 111 E4
Alandale Ct CV12 95 C8
Albany Cl DY10 117 B6
Albany Cres WV14 40 C6
Albany Ct CV1 113 A2
Albany Dr WS12 2 E3
Albany Gdns B91 107 E4
Albany Gr
Kingswinford DY6 60 E7
Willenhall WV11 13 C1
Albany Ho B34 69 A7
Albany Rd Birmingham B17 85 C6
Coventry CV5 113 A1
Wolverhampton WV1 163 A3
Albany Terr CV32 156 E1
Albemarle Rd DY8 80 F2
Albermarle Rd DY6 61 A5
Albert Ave 1 B12 87 A6
Albert Bean Cl CV31 162 A4
Albert Bradbeer Inf Sch B31 122 F7
Albert Bradbeer Jun Sch B31 122 F7
Albert Cl B80 159 E4
Albert Clarke Dr WV12 27 C7
Albert Cres CV6 95 B3
Albert Davie Dr WS12 2 E4
Albert Dr B63 82 F2
Albert Ho WS10 41 C6
Albert Pritchard Inf Sch WS10 42 A5
Albert Rd Allesley CV5 111 A8
Birmingham, Aston B6 66 F8
Albert Rd *continued*
Birmingham, Gravelly Hill B23 56 D3
Birmingham, Handsworth B21 54 E1
Birmingham, Harborne B17 85 B5
Birmingham, King's Heath B14 104 F7
Birmingham, Stechford B33 68 D3
Bromsgrove B61 150 E8
Fazeley B78 35 A8
Halesowen B63 82 F3
Hinckley LE10 71 D1
Kidderminster DY10 116 F6
Oldbury B68 84 C8
Tamworth B79 21 B5
Wolverhampton WV6 25 A3
Albert Smith Pl B65 63 A4
Albert St Birmingham B5 164 D3
Brierley Hill DY5 61 D7
Cannock, Broomhill WS11 1 E4
Cannock, Hednesford WS12 2 D5
Coventry CV1 113 E4
Kingswinford DY6 60 B8
Nuneaton CV10 72 E2
Oldbury B69 64 A8
Redditch B97 153 E5
Royal Leamington Spa CV32 156 C1
Stourbridge, Lye DY9 81 E5
Stourbridge, Wollaston DY8 80 F5
Tipton DY4 51 F8
Walsall WS1 28 E2
Warwick CV34 160 D7
Wednesbury WS10 41 F2
West Bromwich B70 53 C1
Albert St E B69 64 B7
Albert Wlk 1 B17 85 C5
Albion Ave WV13 27 C2
Albion Bsns Pk B66 64 E8
Albion Cotts B46 59 B3
Albion Ct Brierley Hill DY5 61 C6
Nuneaton CV11 73 D3
Albion Field Dr B71 53 D4
Albion Ho B70 53 C2
Albion Ind Est
Coventry CV6 113 D7
West Bromwich B70 52 F2
Albion Jun Sch B71 54 A1
Albion Par DY6 60 B8
Albion Pl WS11 1 E4
Albion Rd
Birmingham, Handsworth B21 54 E1
Birmingham, Sparkhill B11 87 D5
Brownhills WS8 15 E8
West Bromwich, Albion B70 53 A2
West Bromwich, Handsworth B71 65 B8
Willenhall WV13 27 B2
Albion Rdbt B70 53 B4
Albion Road Jun Sch WV13 27 C2
Albion St Bilston WV14 40 E6
Birmingham B1 66 C3
Brierley Hill DY5 61 D3
Kenilworth CV8 148 A5
Kingswinford DY6 60 B8
Oldbury B69 52 E1
Tamworth B79 21 C5
Tipton DY4 51 F5
Willenhall WV13 27 C2
Wolverhampton WV1 163 D3
Albion Terr B46 59 B3
Albion Works DY5 61 B3
Alborn Cres B38 123 D8
Albright & Wilson Ho B68 84 E7
Albright Rd B68 64 D4
Albrighton Ho 4 B20 54 F3
Albrighton Rd B63 82 F3
Albrighton Wlk CV11 74 A2
Albury Rd B80 159 E4
Albury Wlk B11 87 A7
Albutts Rd WS11 6 B3
Alcester Dr
Sutton Coldfield B73 45 D3
Willenhall WV13 26 D1
Alcester Gdns B14 104 F7
Alcester Highway B98 158 F8
Alcester Rd
Birmingham B13 86 F3
Finstall B60 137 F1
Hollywood B47 124 F5
Lickey End B60 137 D5
Portway B48 140 F7
Studley B80 159 E3
Tardebigge B60,B97 152 B7
Alcester Rd S
Birmingham, Alcester Lane's End B14 104 E6
Birmingham, Highter's Heath B14 104 F2
Alcester St
Birmingham B12 86 F8
Redditch B98 153 E4
Alcombe Gr B33 68 E2
Alcott Cl B93 127 F2
Alcott Gr B33 69 E3
Alcott Hall Prim Sch B37 70 B1
Alcott La B37 89 F8
Alcove The WS3 14 D2
Aldborough La 4 B97 153 B5
Aldbourne Rd CV1 113 C5
Aldbourne Way B38 123 E7
Aldbury Rd B14 105 A3
Aldbury Rise CV5 112 C4
Aldeburgh Cl WS3 14 A3
Aldeford Dr DY5 81 D8
Alden Hurst WS7 6 F8
Alder Ave DY10 116 E8
Alder Cl Hollywood B47 125 B6
Lichfield WS14 9 F7
Sutton Coldfield B76 57 E7
Alder Coppice DY3 39 C2
Alder Coppice Prim Sch DY3 39 C1
Alder Cres WS5 43 B4
Alder Ct B13 87 A3
Alder Dale WV3 24 E2
Alder Dr B37 70 B1
Alder Gr B62 83 E6
Alder La
Balsall Common CV7 130 C5
Birmingham B30 103 C6
Alder Meadow Cl CV6 95 D4
Alder Park Rd B91 106 F2
Alder Rd Birmingham B12 87 A4
Coventry CV6 96 A2
Kingswinford DY6 60 F5
Wednesbury WS10 42 A5
Alder Way
Bromsgrove B60 137 B2
Sutton Coldfield B74 44 E8
Alderbrook Cl
Redditch B97 153 B5
Sedgley DY3 39 B1
Alderbrook Rd B91 106 F3
Alderbrook Sch B91 106 F2
Alderbrooke Dr CV11 74 A1
Alderdale Ave DY3 39 C3
Alderdale Cres B92 107 E7
Alderflat Pl B7 67 C5
Alderford Cl WV8 24 F8
Aldergate B79 21 B5
Alderham Cl B91 107 D4
Alderhithe Gr B74 31 B3
Alderlea Cl DY8 81 A2
Alderley Cres WS3 28 E5
Alderley Rd B61 150 D8
Alderman Callow Sch & Com Coll CV4 132 A6
Alderman Gee Hall CV12 78 A4
Alderman Harris Prim Sch CV4 131 F7
Alderman Smith Sch CV10 72 D2
Alderman's Green Com Prim Sch CV2 96 C3
Alderman's Green Ind Est CV2 96 D2
Alderman's Green Rd CV2 96 B3
Aldermans La B97 153 B6
Aldermere Rd DY11 116 C8
Alderminster Cl B97 158 E4
Alderminster Rd
Coventry CV5 112 A4
Solihull B91 107 C1
Aldermoor Farm Prim Sch CV3 134 B8
Aldermoor La CV3 114 A1
Aldermore Dr B75 46 F6
Alderney Cl
Bramcote CV11 79 F6
Coventry CV6 95 B2
Alderney Gdns B38 103 D1
Alderpits Rd B34 69 D6
Alders Cl B98 154 A3
Alders Dr B98 154 F4
Alders Gr CV34 160 D4
Alders La Nuneaton CV10 72 A7
Tamworth B79 20 E6
Alders The Bedworth CV12 77 E2
Romsley B62 100 F4
Aldersea Dr B6 66 F7
Aldersgate CV11 73 C3
Aldershaw Rd B26 88 E6
Aldershaws B90 126 A5
Aldersley Ave WV6 24 E7
Aldersley Cl WV6 24 F7
Aldersley High Sch WV8 10 E1
Aldersley Rd WV6 24 F6
Aldersley Stad WV6 24 F6
Aldersmead Rd B31 103 C1
Alderson Rd B8 67 F4
Alderton Cl 3 B91 107 B1
Alderton Dr WV3 38 E8
Alderton Mews 16 CV31 162 C6
Alderwood Pl B91 107 C3
Alderwood Prec DY3 39 C1
Alderwood Rise DY3 50 D5
Aldgate Dr DY5 81 C7
Aldgate Gr B19 66 D5
Aldin Cl B78 20 E2
Aldin Way LE10 71 A3
Aldington Cl B98 153 F1
Aldis Cl Birmingham B28 87 E1
Walsall WS2 42 A7
Aldis Rd WS2 42 A7
Aldrich Ave CV4 111 E2
Aldridge By-Pass WS9 30 A6
Aldridge Cl Birchmoor B78 36 F8
Oldbury B68 64 C4
2 Stourbridge DY8 80 E8
Aldridge Rd Aldridge B74 30 D1
Birmingham B42 55 E4
Hinckley LE10 75 D6
Little Aston B74,WS9 31 B6
Oldbury B68 84 B8
Sutton Coldfield B74 44 E7
Walsall WS4 29 C3
Aldridge Sch WS9 30 A4

Aldridge St WS10 . . . . . . .41 D7
Aldrin Way CV4 . . . . .132 D5
Aldwick Cl CV32 . . . . .157 A4
Aldwych Cl WS9 . . . . .30 B8
Aldwyck Dr WV3 . . . . .38 A8
Aldwyn Ave B13 . . . . .86 F2
Alesworth Dr LE10 . . . . .75 F4
Alex Grierson Cl CV3 . . . .134 E7
Alexander Cl B61 . . . . . . .121 A1
Alexander Ct ◼ CV34 . . . .160 F7
Alexander Gdns
  Birmingham B42 . . . . .55 D3
  Hinckley LE10 . . . . .71 C2
Alexander Hill DY5 . . . . . . .81 FB
Alexander Ind Pk WV14 . . .40 C4
Alexander Rd
  Bedworth CV12 . . . . .78 C3
  Birmingham B27 . . . . .88 C4
  Codsall WV8 . . . . .10 C3
  Smethwick B67 . . . . .64 E2
  Walsall WS2 . . . . .27 F2
Alexander St WV3 . . . . . .163 A2
Alexander Stad B42 . . . . . .55 C6
Alexander Terr B67 . . . . . . .64 F6
Alexandra Ave B21 . . . . . . .65 D7
Alexandra Cres B71 . . . . . .53 E8
Alexandra Ct Dudley DY3 . .50 C3
  Kenilworth CV8 . . . . .148 A4
  Oldbury B68 . . . . .63 F3
Alexandra High Sch DY4 . .52 B6
Alexandra Hospl The
  B98 . . . . .159 C6
Alexandra Ind Est DY4 . . . .51 F5
Alexandra Mews B79 . . . . .21 C5
Alexandra Pl
  Bilston WV14 . . . . .40 D6
  Dudley DY1 . . . . .51 C4
Alexandra Rd
  Birmingham, Handsworth
    B21 . . . . .65 D7
  Birmingham, Highgate B5 . .86 E7
  Birmingham, Stirchley B30 .104 A7
  Coventry CV1 . . . . .113 F4
  Darlaston WS10 . . . . .41 E6
  Rowley Regis B65 . . . . .82 F4
  Royal Leamington Spa
    CV31 . . . . .162 B6
  Tipton DY4 . . . . .52 A6
  Walsall WS1 . . . . .42 E6
  Wolverhampton WV4 . . . . . .39 A5
Alexandra St ◼
  ◼ Dudley DY1 . . . . .51 B1
  Nuneaton CV11 . . . . .73 B4
Alexandra Terr CV6 . . . . . .95 E2
Alexandra Way
  Aldridge WS9 . . . . .30 B5
  Tipton B69 . . . . .52 A2
Alfall Rd CV2 . . . . .114 B5
Alford Cl B45 . . . . .122 C7
Alfred Ct B60 . . . . .150 C2
Alfred Gunn Ho B68 . . . . . .64 B4
Alfred Rd
  Birmingham, Handsworth
    B21 . . . . .65 E8
  Birmingham, Sparkhill B11 . .87 B5
  Coventry CV1 . . . . .113 F4
Alfred Squire Rd WV11 . . . .26 C5
Alfred St
  Birmingham, Aston B6 . . . . .67 B8
  Birmingham, King's Heath
    B14 . . . . .104 F7
  Birmingham, Sparkbrook
    B12 . . . . .87 B5
  Darlaston WS10 . . . . .41 C5
  Smethwick B66 . . . . .65 C7
  Tamworth B79 . . . . .21 A5
  Walsall WS3 . . . . .14 B1
  West Bromwich B70 . . . . . .53 D3
Alfreda Ave B47 . . . . .125 A8
Alfreds Well B61 . . . . .136 C6
Alfreton Cl LE10 . . . . .75 F5
Alfriston Rd CV3 . . . . .133 C4
Alfryth Ct ◼ B15 . . . . .86 C8
Algernon Rd B16 . . . . .65 D4
Alhambra Rd B60 . . . . .137 C1
Alice Arnold Ho ◼ CV2 . . . .96 B1
Alice Cl CV12 . . . . .77 F1
Alice St WV14 . . . . .40 D6
Alice Stevens Sch CV3 . . .134 A6
Alice Wlk WV14 . . . . .40 D6
Alison Cl DY4 . . . . .41 A2
Alison Dr DY8 . . . . .80 E3
Alison Rd B62 . . . . .83 F3
Alison Sq CV6 . . . . .96 B4
All Angels Wlk B68 . . . . . . .64 A4
All Saints CE Inf Sch
  CV12 . . . . .78 C2
All Saints CE Jun Sch
  CV34 . . . . .156 A1
All Saints CE Prim Sch
  Coventry CV1 . . . . .113 E1
  Leek Wootton CV35 . . . . . .156 A5
  Nuneaton CV10 . . . . .72 E7
  West Bromwich B71 . . . . . .53 C6
  Wolverhampton WV2 . . . . .163 D1
All Saints Dr B74 . . . . .32 A2
All Saints Ind Est B18 . . . . .66 A5
All Saints La CV1 . . . . .113 F3
All Saints Rd
  Bedworth CV12 . . . . .77 F1
  Birmingham, King's Heath
    B14 . . . . .104 F7
  Warwick CV34 . . . . .161 B8
  Wolverhampton WV2 . . . . .163 C1
All Saints Sq CV12 . . . . . . .78 B3

All Saints Way B71 . . . . . . .53 D5
All Saints' Rd
  Birmingham, Hockley B18 . .66 B5
  Bromsgrove B61 . . . . .137 A3
  Darlaston WS10 . . . . .41 E6
All Saints' St B18 . . . . .66 A5
All Souls RC Prim Sch
  CV5 . . . . .112 E2
Allan Cl ◼ Smethwick B66 . .65 B5
  ◼ Stourbridge DY8 . . . . . . .80 FB
Allan Rd CV6 . . . . .112 F4
Allard B77 . . . . .21 E2
Allard Ho CV3 . . . . .134 B6
Allard Way CV3 . . . . .134 C6
Allbut St B64 . . . . .62 D1
Allcock St Birmingham B9 . .67 A1
  Tipton DY4 . . . . .52 C8
Allcroft Rd B11 . . . . .87 F2
Allen Cl Birmingham B43 . . .54 E7
  Studley B80 . . . . .159 E3
Allen Dr Darlaston WS10 . . .41 C6
  West Bromwich B70 . . . . . .53 F1
Allen Ho B43 . . . . .54 E7
Allen Rd Tipton DY4 . . . . . . .40 F1
  Wednesbury WS10 . . . . . . .41 F5
  Wolverhampton WV6 . . . . . .25 A3
Allen St Tamworth B77 . . . . .21 C1
  West Bromwich B70 . . . . . .53 B3
Allenby Cl DY6 . . . . .61 A5
Allendale Ave B80 . . . . . . .159 E3
Allendale Cres B80 . . . . . .159 E3
Allendale Ct B80 . . . . .159 E3
Allendale Gr B43 . . . . .54 E8
Allendale Rd
  Birmingham B25 . . . . .88 B7
  Sutton Coldfield B76 . . . . . .57 E8
Allens Ave
  Birmingham B18 . . . . .65 F6
  West Bromwich B71 . . . . . .53 A7
Allens Cl WV12 . . . . .27 B5
Allens Croft Rd B14 . . . . . .104 C6
Allens Farm Rd B31 . . . . . .102 C3
Allens La WS3 . . . . .14 F2
Allens Rd B18 . . . . .65 F6
Allens Rough Prim Sch
  WV12 . . . . .13 C1
Allensmead B77 . . . . .21 C2
Allensmore Cl B98 . . . . . . .154 F2
Allerdale Rd WS8 . . . . .15 E7
Allerton Cl CV2 . . . . .114 C2
Allerton La B71 . . . . .53 C8
Allerton Rd B25 . . . . .88 B7
Allesley Cl B74 . . . . .46 C7
Allesley Croft CV5 . . . . . . .112 A6
Allesley Ct CV5 . . . . .112 A6
Allesley Hall Dr CV5 . . . . .112 C5
Allesley Hall Prim Sch
  CV5 . . . . .112 B4
Allesley Old Rd CV5 . . . . . .112 D3
Allesley Prim Sch CV5 . . . .112 A7
Allesley Rd B92 . . . . .106 D8
Allesley St B6 . . . . .66 E5
Alleston Rd WV10 . . . . .11 D1
Alleston Wlk WV10 . . . . . . .11 D2
Alley The ◼3 . . . . .50 B3
Alleyne Gr B24 . . . . .57 A2
Alleyne Rd B24 . . . . .57 A1
Alliance Cl CV11 . . . . .73 F3
Alliance Way CV2 . . . . .114 A5
Allibone Cl CV31 . . . . .162 A4
Allied Cl CV6 . . . . .95 D2
Allingham Gr B43 . . . . .44 E4
Allington Cl WS5 . . . . .43 D8
Allison St B5 . . . . .164 D2
Allitt Gr CV8 . . . . .148 B5
Allman Rd B24 . . . . .57 C4
Allmyn Dr B74 . . . . .45 A6
Allport Mews WS11 . . . . .1 E1
Allport Rd WS11 . . . . .1 E1
Allport St WS11 . . . . .1 E2
Allsops Cl B65 . . . . .62 F4
Allton Ave B78 . . . . .20 D1
Allton Ct B77 . . . . .21 E3
Allwell Dr B14 . . . . .104 F2
Allwood Gdns B32 . . . . .84 A2
Allwood Ho B97 . . . . .153 C3
Alma Ave DY4 . . . . .52 A7
Alma Cres B7 . . . . .67 B4
Alma Ct CV11 . . . . .79 F6
Alma Ind Est WS10 . . . . . . .41 C6
Alma Pl DY2 . . . . .51 C1
Alma Rd LE10 . . . . .71 D1
Alma St Birmingham B19 . . .66 E6
  Coventry CV1 . . . . .165 D3
  Darlaston WS10 . . . . .41 C6
  Halesowen B63 . . . . .82 C5
  Smethwick B66 . . . . .65 C6
  Walsall WS2 . . . . .28 D4
  Wednesbury WS10 . . . . . . .42 B3
  Willenhall WV13 . . . . .27 B2
  Wolverhampton WV10 . . . . .25 F2
Alma Way B19 . . . . .66 D7
Alma Wks WS10 . . . . .41 D5
Almhouses B24 . . . . .57 A4
Almond Ave
  Kidderminster DY11 . . . . . .116 B8
  Nuneaton CV10 . . . . .72 C6
  Royal Leamington Spa
    CV32 . . . . .156 F3
  Walsall, Bentley WS2 . . . . . .27 E4
  Walsall, Yew Tree WS5 . . . . .43 A4
Almond Cl
  Birmingham B29 . . . . .103 A6
  Cannock WS11 . . . . .2 C2
  Walsall WS3 . . . . .14 F2
Almond Croft B42 . . . . .54 F7
Almond Gr
  Warwick CV34 . . . . .156 A1

Almond Gr continued
  Wolverhampton WV6 . . . . . .25 C4
Almond Rd
  Huntington WS12 . . . . .1 D8
  Kingswinford DY6 . . . . .60 E8
Almond Tree Ave CV2 . . . . .96 E2
Almsbury Ct B26 . . . . .89 C4
Almshouses
  Bedworth CV12 . . . . .78 B3
  Middleton B78 . . . . .34 B1
  Rowington Green CV35 . . .145 A1
  Smethwick B67 . . . . .64 F5
  Stoneleigh CV8 . . . . .149 C6
  ◼ Warwick CV34 . . . . .160 E6
  Wolverhampton WV4 . . . . . .38 F3
Alnwick Cl WS12 . . . . .2 E2
Alnwick Ho B23 . . . . .56 F6
Alnwick Rd WS3 . . . . .14 A4
Alperton Dr DY9 . . . . .81 E2
Alpha Bsns Pk CV2 . . . . . . .96 D1
Alpha Cl B12 . . . . .86 E6
Alpha Ho CV2 . . . . .114 A4
Alpha Way WS6 . . . . .14 A8
Alpine Ct CV8 . . . . .148 A6
Alpine Dr ◼ Cannock WS12 . .2 D4
  Dudley DY2 . . . . .62 B4
Alpine Rise CV3 . . . . .133 A5
Alpine Way WV3 . . . . .24 C2
Alport Croft ◼ B9 . . . . .67 B2
Alspath La CV5 . . . . .111 F4
Alspath Rd CV7 . . . . .92 C1
Alston Cl Cannock WS12 . . . .2 D4
  Solihull B91 . . . . .107 D6
  Sutton Coldfield B74 . . . . . .32 A2
Alston Gr B9 . . . . .68 B3
Alston Ho B69 . . . . .63 D6
Alston Prim Sch B9 . . . . . . .68 B3
Alston Rd Birmingham B9 . . .68 B3
  Oldbury B69 . . . . .63 E7
  Solihull B91 . . . . .107 D6
Alston St B16 . . . . .66 A2
Althorpe Dr B93 . . . . .127 E3
Althorpe Ho CV31 . . . . .162 A6
Althorpe Ind Est ◼5
Alton Cl
  CV31 . . . . .162 A7
Althorpe St CV31 . . . . .162 A7
Alton Ave WV12 . . . . .27 B5
Alton Cl Coventry CV2 . . . . .96 D2
  Redditch B97 . . . . .153 B1
  Wolverhampton WV10 . . . . .11 E3
Alton Gr Cannock WS11 . . . .1 D1
  Dudley DY2 . . . . .51 E1
  West Bromwich B71 . . . . . .53 E7
Alton Rd B29 . . . . .85 F3
Alum Cl CV6 . . . . .113 D8
Alum Dr B9 . . . . .68 B3
Alum Rock Rd B8 . . . . .68 B4
Alum Well Rd WS2 . . . . .28 B1
Alumhurst Ave B8 . . . . .68 B4
Alumwell Cl WS2 . . . . .28 B1
Alumwell Inf & Jun Schs
  WS2 . . . . .28 B2
Alumwell Sch The WS2 . . . .28 A1
Alvaston Cl WS3 . . . . .14 C3
Alvechurch CE First & Mid Sch
  B48 . . . . .139 B6
Alvechurch Highway
  Lydiate Ash B60 . . . . .121 D2
  Redditch B98 . . . . .153 F3
Alvechurch Ho B60 . . . . . . .137 B3
Alvechurch Rd
  Birmingham B31 . . . . .123 B7
  Halesowen B63 . . . . .82 F2
Alvechurch Sta B48 . . . . . .139 A4
Alvecote Cotts B79 . . . . . . .22 D6
Alveley Cl B98 . . . . .154 D4
Alverley Cl DY6 . . . . .60 F4
Alverley Rd CV6 . . . . .113 C6
Alverstoke Cl WV9 . . . . .11 A2
Alverstone Rd CV2 . . . . . . .114 A4
Alveston Cl B77 . . . . .35 C4
Alveston Gr Birmingham B9 . .68 B3
  Knowle B93 . . . . .128 B7
Alveston Pl ◼ CV32 . . . . . .156 F1
Alveston Rd B47 . . . . .125 A7
Alvin Cl Coventry CV3 . . . .114 F1
  Halesowen B62 . . . . .83 F8
Alvington Cl WV12 . . . . .27 D4
Alvis Cl B79 . . . . .20 F7
Alvis Ret Pk CV5 . . . . .113 A3
Alvis Wlk B36 . . . . .59 E1
Alwen St DY8 . . . . .50 F2
Alwin Rd B65 . . . . .63 B2
Alwold Ct B29 . . . . .84 F2
Alwold Rd B29 . . . . .85 A2
Alwynn Wlk B23 . . . . .56 C5
Alwyn Cl WS6 . . . . .4 E3
Alwynn Wlk B23 . . . . .56 C5
Alwyne Freeman Ct
  CV7 . . . . .95 A6
Amal Way B6 . . . . .67 B6
Amanda Ave WV4 . . . . .38 F4
Amanda Dr B26 . . . . .68 F1
Ambassador Cl CV22 . . . . .156 F3
Ambassador Rd B26 . . . . . .90 C4
Ambell Cl B65 . . . . .62 F5
Amber Bsns Village B77 . . .22 B7
Amber Cl B77 . . . . .22 B3
Amber Ct B77 . . . . .22 B3
Amber Dr B69 . . . . .64 A5
Amber Gr B69 . . . . .64 A5
Amber Terr DY10 . . . . .116 F5
Amber Way B62 . . . . .83 C6
Ambergate Cl
  ◼ Redditch B97 . . . . .153 B5
  Walsall WS3 . . . . .14 C3

Ambergate Dr DY6 . . . . .60 C8
Amberley Ave CV12 . . . . . . .79 C2
Amberley Gn B43 . . . . .54 E6
Amberley Gr B6 . . . . .56 A3
Amberley Rd B92 . . . . .88 F4
Amberley Way B74 . . . . .30 E1
Amberwood Cl WS2 . . . . . . .27 D3
Ambion Way LE10 . . . . .71 F1
Amblecote Ave B44 . . . . . . .44 E2
Amblecote Prim Sch DY8 . .80 F7
Amblecote Rd
  Brierley Hill DY5 . . . . .81 D8
  Kidderminster DY10 . . . . . .117 B5
Ambler Gr CV2 . . . . .114 C3
Ambleside
  Birmingham B32 . . . . .84 C1
  Coventry CV2 . . . . .96 E2
Ambleside Cl WV14 . . . . . . .40 E3
Ambleside Dr DY5 . . . . .81 C8
Ambleside Gr WV11 . . . . . . .13 B1
Ambleside Way
  Bromsgrove B60 . . . . .137 B1
  Kingswinford DY6 . . . . .60 D6
  Nuneaton CV11 . . . . .73 E6
Ambrose Cl WV13 . . . . .26 E2
Ambrose Cres DY6 . . . . .60 D8
Ambury Way B43 . . . . .54 D8
Amelas Cl ◼3 DY5 . . . . .61 A1
Amelia Cl CV12 . . . . .79 C3
Amersham Cl
  Birmingham B32 . . . . .84 E5
  Coventry CV5 . . . . .112 B4
Ames Rd WS10 . . . . .41 C7
Amesbury Rd B13 . . . . .86 E3
Amherst Ct ◼2 B92 . . . . . . .88 F1
Amherst Ave B20 . . . . .55 A3
Amherst Rd CV8 . . . . .147 E6
Amhurst Bsns Ctr CV34 . . .160 B7
Amicombe B77 . . . . .22 C1
Amington Croft B75 . . . . . . .32 D3
Amington Heath Com Prim
  Sch B77 . . . . .22 A2
Amington Ind Est B77 . . . . .22 B3
Amington Rd
  Birmingham B25 . . . . .88 B6
  Solihull B90 . . . . .126 A8
  Tamworth B77 . . . . .21 D4
Amiss Gdns B10 . . . . .87 C8
Amity Cl B66 . . . . .65 B5
Amos Ave Nuneaton CV10 . .73 B2
  Wolverhampton WV11 . . . . .26 C7
Amos Jacques Rd CV12 . . .78 A4
Amos La WV11 . . . . .26 C6
Amos Rd DY9 . . . . .81 F2
Amphlett Croft DY4 . . . . . . .52 B4
Amphlett Ct ◼ B60 . . . . . . .137 A2
Amphletts Cl DY2 . . . . .62 E4
Ampton Rd B15 . . . . .86 B7
Amroth Cl B45 . . . . .122 B7
Amroth Mews CV31 . . . . . .162 C6
Amwell Gr B14 . . . . .104 F3
Amy Cl CV6 . . . . .95 F4
Anchor Cl Birmingham B16 . .65 E1
  Tamworth B77 . . . . .21 E4
Anchor Hill DY5 . . . . .61 C1
Anchor La WV14 . . . . .40 B2
Anchor Par WS9 . . . . .30 B6
Anchor Rd Aldridge WS9 . . .30 B6
  Dudley WV14 . . . . .40 C2
Anchorage Rd
  Birmingham B23 . . . . .56 D3
  Sutton Coldfield B74 . . . . . .46 B6
Anchorfields DY10 . . . . . . .116 F6
Anchorway Rd CV3 . . . . . . .133 B4
Anders B79 . . . . .21 A6
Anders Sq WV6 . . . . .23 F3
Andersleigh Dr WV14 . . . . .51 A8
Anderson Cres B43 . . . . . . .43 E2
Anderson Dr CV31 . . . . . . .162 A2
Anderson Gdns DY4 . . . . . .52 A4
Anderson Rd
  Birmingham B23 . . . . .56 E6
  Smethwick B66 . . . . .65 A5
  Tipton DY4 . . . . .52 A4
Anderton Cl B74 . . . . .46 A7
Anderton Park Prim Sch
  B13 . . . . .87 A3
Anderton Rd
  Bedworth CV12 . . . . .77 C1
  Birmingham B11 . . . . .87 C6
  Coventry CV2,CV6 . . . . . . .96 B4
Anderton St B1 . . . . .66 B3
Andover Cres DY6 . . . . .60 F4
Andover Ho B35 . . . . .58 B3
Andover Pl WS11 . . . . .2 A4
Andover St B5 . . . . .66 F2
Andressy Mews B61 . . . . . .137 A5
Andrew Cl WV12 . . . . .27 D6
Andrew Ct B76 . . . . .46 F3
Andrew Dr WV12 . . . . .27 D6
Andrew Gdns B21 . . . . .54 E1
Andrew Rd
  Halesowen B63 . . . . .83 A3
  Tipton DY4 . . . . .41 A1
  West Bromwich B71 . . . . . .42 F2
Andrews Cl DY5 . . . . .81 E8
Andrews Ho WS13 . . . . .9 A7
Andrews Rd WS9 . . . . .16 B1
Anerley Gr B44 . . . . .44 F4
Anerley Rd B44 . . . . .44 F4
Angel Mews ◼ B46 . . . . . . .70 F7
Angel St Dudley DY1 . . . . . .62 B8
  Upper Bentley B97 . . . . . .152 B1
Angela Ave
  Blackheath B65 . . . . .63 D4
  Coventry CV2 . . . . .96 E1

Angela Pl WV14 . . . . .40 D6
Angelica B77 . . . . .21 F4
Angelica Cl ◼7 WS5 . . . . . .43 A3
Angelina St B12 . . . . .86 F7
Angelo Ho B13 . . . . .105 D7
Anglesey Ave B36 . . . . .70 B6
Anglesey Bsns Pk WS12 . . . .2 E4
Anglesey Cl Allesley CV5 . .112 B7
  Burntwood WS7 . . . . .7 E1
Anglesey Cres
  Brownhills WS8 . . . . .2 C5
  Cannock WS12 . . . . .2 C5
Anglesey Mews WS12 . . . . . .2 C5
Anglesey Prim Sch B19 . . . .66 C7
Anglesey Rd
  Brownhills WS8 . . . . .6 F2
  Lichfield WS13 . . . . .3 D2
Anglesey St
  Birmingham B19 . . . . .66 C7
  Cannock WS12 . . . . .2 B5
Angless Way CV8 . . . . .147 F3
Anglia Rd WS11 . . . . .1 D3
Anglian Rd WS9 . . . . .29 D6
Anglo African Ind Pk
  B69 . . . . .52 C6
Angorfa Cl WS13 . . . . .8 F7
Angus Cl Coventry CV5 . . . .112 A4
  Kenilworth CV8 . . . . .148 C6
  West Bromwich B71 . . . . . .53 C6
Anita Ave DY4 . . . . .52 A2
Anita Croft B23 . . . . .56 E2
Ankadine Rd DY8 . . . . .81 B6
Anker Cl WS7 . . . . .7 D6
Anker St CV11 . . . . .73 D3
Anker View B77 . . . . .21 C3
Ankerdine Ct B63 . . . . .83 A3
Ankerdrive B79 . . . . .21 B4
Ankermoor Cl B34 . . . . .69 B6
Ankermoor Ct B77 . . . . .21 E5
Ankermoor Prim Sch
  B77 . . . . .21 E5
Ankerside Sh Ctr B79 . . . . .21 B4
Ann Cres WS11 . . . . .1 E6
Ann Croft B26 . . . . .89 D4
Ann Rd B47 . . . . .125 A3
Ann St WV13 . . . . .27 B3
Annan Ave WV10 . . . . .25 F7
Anne Cl B70 . . . . .52 E3
Anne Cres CV3 . . . . .134 C5
Anne Ct B76 . . . . .46 F3
Anne Gr DY4 . . . . .41 B1
Anne Rd Brierley Hill DY5 . . .62 A1
  Smethwick B66 . . . . .65 D7
  Wolverhampton WV4 . . . . . .39 B6
Annesley Rd B66 . . . . .65 B5
Annie Lennard Inf Sch
  B67 . . . . .64 E3
Annie Osborn Prim Sch
  CV2 . . . . .114 D7
Annscroft B38 . . . . .103 D2
Ansbro Cl B18 . . . . .65 F5
Ansculf Rd DY5 . . . . .61 B1
Ansell Dr CV6 . . . . .96 A5
Ansell Rd
  Birmingham, Gravelly Hill
    B24 . . . . .56 F1
  Birmingham, Sparkbrook
    B11 . . . . .87 C6
  Warwick CV34 . . . . .160 D7
Ansley Cl B98 . . . . .154 F1
Ansley Comm CV10 . . . . . . .72 A7
Ansley Rd CV10 . . . . .72 B3
Ansley Way B92 . . . . .107 D7
Anslow Gdns WV11 . . . . . . .12 E1
Anslow Rd B23 . . . . .56 C5
Anson Ave WS13 . . . . .3 A1
Anson Cl Burntwood WS7 . . . .7 C7
  Great Wyrley WS6 . . . . .4 E4
  Perton WV6 . . . . .23 E5
Anson Ct B78 . . . . .35 B8
Anson Gr B27 . . . . .88 D2
Anson Junc WS2 . . . . .27 E2
Anson Way CV2 . . . . .114 F8
Anstey Croft B37 . . . . .70 A4
Anstey Gr B27 . . . . .88 B1
Anstey Rd B44 . . . . .55 E6
Anstey St B44 . . . . .55 E6
Anston Way WV11 . . . . .26 D7
Anstree Cl WS6 . . . . .4 D1
Anstruther Rd B15 . . . . .85 E8
Ansty Dr WS12 . . . . .2 D1
Ansty Rd CV2 . . . . .114 E5
Antelope Gdns CV34 . . . . .160 C8
Anthony Rd B8 . . . . .67 F4
Anthony Way CV2 . . . . .114 C2
Anton Dr B76 . . . . .58 A6
Antony Gardner Cres
  CV31 . . . . .162 A4
Antony Rd B90 . . . . .106 B1
Antrim Cl CV5 . . . . .112 B7
Antringham Gdns B15 . . . . .85 D8
Antrobus Rd
  Birmingham B21 . . . . .54 E1
  Sutton Coldfield B73 . . . . . .45 F1
Anvil Cres WV14 . . . . .40 C2
Anvil Dr B69 . . . . .63 E6
Anvil Wlk B70 . . . . .52 F4
Apex Bsns Pk WS11 . . . . .5 F4
Apex Rd WS8 . . . . .15 C7
Apley Rd DY8 . . . . .80 E7
Apollo B79 . . . . .20 F6
Apollo Cl WS11 . . . . .2 A5
Apollo Croft B24 . . . . .57 D3
Apollo Rd Oldbury B68 . . . . .64 C6
  Stourbridge DY9 . . . . .82 A5

Apollo Way
Birmingham B20 ... 55 D1
Royal Leamington Spa
CV34 ... 161 D5
[12] Smethwick B66 ... 65 C5
Apperley Way B63 ... 82 B7
Appian Cl
Birmingham B14 ... 104 E5
Tamworth B77 ... 35 D7
Appian Way B90 ... 126 D4
Apple Tree Cl
Birmingham B23 ... 56 B4
Kidderminster DY10 ... 117 B7
Apple Wlk WS11 ... 2 C2
Applebee Rd LE10 ... 75 D6
Appleby Cl B14 ... 104 D5
Appleby Gdns WV11 ... 13 C2
Appleby Gr B90 ... 127 B6
Appleby Ho [1] LE10 ... 71 E1
Applecross B74 ... 31 F1
Applecross Cl CV4 ... 131 F6
Appledore Cl
Cannock WS12 ... 2 E3
Great Wyrley WS6 ... 5 A3
Appledore Ct [3] WS3 ... 28 B8
Appledore Dr CV5 ... 111 F5
Appledore Rd WS5 ... 43 D8
Appledore Terr WS5 ... 43 D8
Appledorne Gdns B34 ... 69 B6
Applesham Cl B11 ... 87 D6
Appleton Ave
Birmingham B43 ... 54 E8
Stourbridge DY8 ... 81 A2
Appleton Cl B30 ... 103 E8
Appleton Cres WV4 ... 39 A5
Appleton Ct [5] B15 ... 86 B7
Appleton Ho B31 ... 102 E5
Appletree Cl
Birmingham B31 ... 102 F1
Catherine de B B91 ... 108 B5
Appletree Cotts CV35 ... 144 F1
Appletree Gr
Aldridge WS9 ... 30 B5
Wolverhampton WV6 ... 25 C5
Appletree La B97 ... 153 B5
Appletrees Cres B61 ... 137 A5
Applewood Gr [5] B64 ... 62 F1
Approach The CV31 ... 161 F6
April Croft B13 ... 87 B3
Apsley Cl B68 ... 84 A7
Apsley Croft B38 ... 104 B2
Apsley Gr Birmingham B24 ... 57 A2
Dorridge B93 ... 127 F2
Apsley Ho B64 ... 62 F2
Apsley Rd B68 ... 84 A7
Aqua Ho CV32 ... 157 A1
Aqueduct La B48 ... 138 F7
Aqueduct Rd B90 ... 105 E1
Aragon Dr
Royal Leamington Spa
CV34 ... 161 D6
Sutton Coldfield B73 ... 46 B6
Aragon Ho CV3 ... 133 C8
Arbor Cl B77 ... 21 D3
Arbor Ct B71 ... 53 E6
Arbor Gate WS9 ... 16 B4
Arbor Way B37 ... 70 C1
Arboretum Rd WS1 ... 29 A3
Arboretum The CV4 ... 132 D3
Arbour Cl CV8 ... 148 B3
Arbour Mews WS11 ... 5 F6
Arbour Tree La B93 ... 144 F7
Arbourtree Ct WV5 ... 49 B7
Arbury Ave
Bedworth CV12 ... 78 A3
Coventry CV6 ... 95 F2
Arbury Cl CV32 ... 157 A4
Arbury Ct CV10 ... 72 C3
Arbury Dr DY8 ... 60 D3
Arbury Garth CV10 ... 72 C3
Arbury Hall Park & Gdns*
CV10 ... 77 D7
Arbury Hall Rd B90 ... 126 D8
Arbury Rd CV10 ... 72 D2
Arbury Wlk B76 ... 58 D5
Arcade WS1 ... 28 E1
Arcade The Coventry CV3 ... 114 B2
Sedgley DY3 ... 50 E5
Arcadian Sh Ctr B5 ... 164 C1
Arcal St DY3 ... 50 E7
Arch Hill St DY2 ... 62 C5
Arch Rd CV2 ... 114 E5
Arch The B5 ... 67 A2
Archbishop Grimshaw Comp
Sch B37 ... 69 F3
Archbishop Ilsley RC Sch
B27 ... 88 C3
Archer Cl Oldbury B68 ... 64 B4
Studley B80 ... 159 D4
Wednesbury WS10 ... 41 E3
Archer Ct DY9 ... 81 E2
Archer Gdns B64 ... 62 C1
Archer Rd
Birmingham B14 ... 105 C4
Kenilworth CV8 ... 147 E3
Redditch B98 ... 153 E4
Walsall WS3 ... 28 E6
Archer Terr B97 ... 153 C1
Archers Cl B23 ... 56 D8
Archery Fields CV34 ... 160 F6
Archery Rd Meriden CV7 ... 92 B1
Royal Leamington Spa
CV31 ... 161 E8
Arches Ind Est The CV5 ... 113 A3
Archibald Rd B19 ... 66 C8
Archway The [2] WS4 ... 28 F3
Arcot Rd B28 ... 87 F2
Ardarth Rd B38 ... 104 A2
Ardav Rd B70 ... 52 F8
Arden Bldgs B93 ... 127 F3
Arden Cl
Balsall Common CV7 ... 130 B7
Meriden CV7 ... 92 C1
Royal Leamington Spa
CV31 ... 162 B5
Stourbridge, Wollaston DY8 ... 80 E7
Stourbridge, Wordsley DY8 ... 60 C3
Tamworth B77 ... 21 E5
Warwick CV34 ... 156 A1
Arden Croft Coleshill B46 ... 59 F1
Solihull B92 ... 89 C4
Arden Ct
Binley Woods CV3 ... 135 D6
Dudley DY3 ... 50 D3
Hampton-in-A B92 ... 109 A7
Sutton Coldfield B72 ... 57 C8
Arden Dr Birmingham B26 ... 88 F7
Dorridge B93 ... 128 A1
Sutton Coldfield, Falcon Lodge
B75 ... 47 B5
Sutton Coldfield, Wylde Green
B73 ... 57 B8
Arden Forest Inf Sch
CV12 ... 79 B3
Arden Gr
Birmingham, Ladywood B16 ... 66 A1
[8] Birmingham, Lozells B19 ... 66 C8
Oldbury B69 ... 64 A5
Arden Ho B60 ... 137 B3
Arden Jun & Inf Sch B11 ... 87 C5
Arden Leys B94 ... 141 D2
Arden Meads B94 ... 143 C6
Arden Oak Rd B26 ... 89 D4
Arden Pl WV14 ... 41 B4
Arden Rd
Birmingham, Acock's Green
B27 ... 88 B4
Birmingham, Aston B6 ... 66 D8
Birmingham, Rubery B45 ... 102 A1
Birmingham, Saltley B8 ... 67 D3
Bulkington CV12 ... 79 C2
Dorridge B93 ... 127 F2
Hollywood B47 ... 125 A6
Kenilworth CV8 ... 148 B3
Nuneaton CV11 ... 74 A1
Smethwick B67 ... 65 A5
Tamworth B77 ... 35 F5
Arden Sch B93 ... 128 B5
Arden St CV5 ... 132 F8
Arden Vale Rd B93 ... 128 B7
Ardencote Rd B13 ... 105 A6
Ardendale [6] B90 ... 126 C8
Arderne Dr B37 ... 70 A1
Ardgay Dr WS12 ... 1 F7
Ardingley Wlk DY5 ... 81 B7
Ardley Cl DY2 ... 62 D8
Ardley Rd B14 ... 105 A5
Aretha Cl DY6 ... 61 A6
Argil Cl WV11 ... 26 D8
Argus Cl B76 ... 46 F3
Argyle Ave B77 ... 21 D4
Argyle Cl Stourbridge DY8 ... 60 E1
Walsall WS4 ... 29 B3
Argyle Rd Walsall WS4 ... 29 B3
Wolverhampton WV2 ... 39 B6
Argyle St Birmingham B7 ... 67 D8
Tamworth B77 ... 21 E4
Argyll Ho [5] WV3 ... 25 C4
Argyll St CV2 ... 114 A3
Ariane B79 ... 20 E7
Arion Cl B77 ... 21 D5
Arkall Cl B79 ... 21 C7
Arkle B77 ... 35 D4
Arkle Croft
Birmingham B36 ... 68 C8
Blackheath B65 ... 62 F6
Arkle Dr CV2 ... 114 F7
Arklet Cl CV10 ... 72 C5
Arkley Gr B28 ... 106 B7
Arkley Rd B28 ... 106 B7
Arkwright Rd
Birmingham B32 ... 84 C5
Walsall WS2 ... 28 B5
Arlen Dr B43 ... 43 D1
Arlescote Cl B75 ... 32 C2
Arlescote Rd B92 ... 89 C2
Arless Way B17 ... 85 B3
Arleston Way B90 ... 126 E8
Arley Cl
Kidderminster DY11 ... 116 A2
Oldbury B69 ... 63 D5
Redditch B98 ... 154 D5
Arley Ct DY2 ... 62 C6
Arley Dr DY8 ... 80 E3
Arley Gr WV4 ... 38 D5
Arley Ho B33 ... 69 A1
Arley Mews CV32 ... 156 E1
Arley Rd Birmingham B29 ... 85 F3
Birmingham, Saltley B8 ... 67 D6
Solihull B91 ... 107 A4
Arley Villas [4] B18 ... 65 D4
Arlidge Cl WV14 ... 40 D4
Arlidge Cres CV8 ... 148 C5
Arlington Ave CV32 ... 156 F2
Arlington Cl DY6 ... 60 D4
Arlington Ct
[2] Royal Leamington Spa
CV32 ... 156 F2
Stourbridge DY8 ... 81 B4
Arlington Gr B14 ... 105 B2
Arlington Ho B15 ... 86 C7
Arlington Mews [5]
CV32 ... 156 F2
Arlington Rd
Birmingham B14 ... 105 B3
West Bromwich B71 ... 53 D6
Arlington Way CV11 ... 73 F2
Arlon Ave CV10 ... 72 D7
Armada Cl B23 ... 56 D1
Armadale Cl LE10 ... 71 A1
Armarna Dr CV5 ... 111 B8
Armfield St CV6 ... 114 A8
Armitage Ho WS13 ... 3 E1
Armorial Rd CV3 ... 133 B7
Armour Cl LE10 ... 75 D5
Armoury Rd B11 ... 87 D6
Armoury Trad Est B11 ... 87 E6
Armscott Rd CV2 ... 114 C6
Armside Cl WS3 ... 15 B4
Armson Rd CV7 ... 78 A1
Armstead Rd WV9 ... 11 A3
Armstrong B79 ... 20 F6
Armstrong Ave CV3 ... 114 B1
Armstrong Cl
Stourbridge DY8 ... 81 B6
Whitnash CV31 ... 162 A2
Armstrong Dr
Birmingham B36 ... 58 F1
Walsall WS2 ... 28 A4
Wolverhampton WV6 ... 25 A5
Armstrong Way WV13 ... 41 B8
Arna Ho CV3 ... 134 B6
Arncliffe Cl CV11 ... 74 A2
Arncliffe Way [4] CV34 ... 155 F1
Arne Rd CV2 ... 115 A6
Arnhem Cl WV11 ... 26 B8
Arnhem Cnr CV3 ... 134 D6
Arnhem Rd WV13 ... 40 E8
Arnhem Way DY4 ... 52 C5
Arnold Ave CV3 ... 133 C5
Arnold Cl Tamworth B79 ... 21 A6
Walsall WS2 ... 27 F3
Arnold Gr
Birmingham B30 ... 103 D4
Solihull B90 ... 106 B4
Arnold Lodge Sch CV32 ... 156 F2
Arnold Rd B90 ... 106 C4
Arnotdale Dr WS12 ... 1 F7
Arnside Cl CV1 ... 165 D4
Arnside Ct B23 ... 56 B4
Arnwood Cl WS2 ... 27 F2
Arosa Dr B17 ... 85 B3
Arran Cl Birmingham B43 ... 43 E3
Cannock WS11 ... 2 A3
Nuneaton CV10 ... 73 A3
Arran Dr B77 ... 35 F7
Arran Rd B34 ... 68 F6
Arran Way
Birmingham B36 ... 70 B7
Hinckley LE10 ... 71 B1
Arras Bvd CV35 ... 160 A7
Arras Rd DY2 ... 51 E2
Arrow Cl B93 ... 128 A6
Arrow Ho [1] B68 ... 84 B8
Arrow Rd WS3 ... 28 E6
Arrow Rd N B98 ... 154 A4
Arrow Rd S B98 ... 154 A4
Arrow Vale Com High Sch
B98 ... 154 E2
Arrow Valley Pk* B98 ... 154 B4
Arrow Wlk B38 ... 104 B1
Arrowcrest Fst Sch B98 ... 154 A2
Arrowdale Rd B98 ... 154 A3
Arrowfield Gn B38 ... 123 D7
Arsenal St B9 ... 67 C1
Arthingworth Cl CV3 ... 114 E1
Arthur Alford Ho CV12 ... 77 D1
Arthur Dr (Road 2)
DY11 ... 116 E1
Arthur Greenwood Ct
WV14 ... 40 C6
Arthur Gunby Cl B75 ... 46 F7
Arthur Harris Cl B66 ... 65 C3
Arthur Pl B1 ... 66 B3
Arthur Rd
Birmingham, Edgbaston B15 ... 86 B7
Birmingham, Erdington B24 ... 57 B4
Birmingham, Handsworth
B21 ... 65 F8
Birmingham, Hay Mills B25 ... 88 B6
Tipton DY4 ... 52 A7
Arthur St Bilston WV14 ... 40 D6
Birmingham B10 ... 67 B1
Cannock, Chadsmoor WS11 ... 1 F4
Cannock, Wimblebury WS12 ... 2 F3
Coventry CV1 ... 165 C4
Kenilworth CV8 ... 148 A5
Redditch B98 ... 154 B3
West Bromwich B70 ... 53 D1
Wolverhampton WV2 ... 39 D7
Arthur Terry Sch B74 ... 32 A3
Artillery Rd CV11 ... 79 F6
Artillery St B9 ... 67 C2
Artingstall Ho B30 ... 104 B8
Artmeis Dr CV34 ... 161 E5
Arton Croft B24 ... 57 A2
Arun Way B76 ... 47 A1
Arundel Birmingham B17 ... 85 A6
Tamworth B77 ... 35 C7
Arundel Ave WS10 ... 41 F3
Arundel Cl [2] CV34 ... 160 F8
Arundel Cres B92 ... 89 A1
Arundel Ct [13] B29 ... 103 C7
Arundel Dr B69 ... 62 F8
Arundel Gr WV6 ... 23 F3
Arundel Ho B23 ... 56 F6
Arundel Pl B11 ... 87 A6
Arundel Rd
Birmingham B14 ... 105 A1
Bromsgrove B60 ... 137 B1
Bulkington CV12 ... 79 C3
Coventry CV3 ... 133 D6
Stourbridge DY8 ... 60 C2
Willenhall WV12 ... 27 C7
Arundel Rd *continued*
Wolverhampton WV10 ... 11 B2
Arundel St WS1 ... 42 E7
Asbury Rd
Balsall Common CV7 ... 130 B5
Wednesbury WS10 ... 42 E2
Ascot Cl Bedworth CV12 ... 78 B4
Birmingham B16 ... 65 F2
Coventry CV3 ... 134 C6
Lichfield WS14 ... 9 D7
Oldbury B69 ... 63 E6
Ascot Ct [11] B29 ... 103 C7
Ascot Dr Cannock WS11 ... 4 C8
Dudley DY1 ... 50 F2
Tamworth B77 ... 35 D4
Wolverhampton WV4 ... 39 A4
Ascot Gdns DY8 ... 60 D2
Ascot Rd B13 ... 86 F2
Ascot Ride CV32 ... 157 C3
Ascot Way B61 ... 121 B1
Ascot Wlk B69 ... 63 E6
Asfare Bsns Pk LE10 ... 75 E1
Ash Ave B12 ... 87 A5
Ash Cl WV8 ... 10 A3
Ash Cres Birmingham B37 ... 69 F6
Kingswinford DY6 ... 60 E6
Ash Ct Oldbury B66 ... 64 C8
Stourbridge DY8 ... 81 A4
Ash Dr Catshill B61 ... 121 B1
Kenilworth CV8 ... 148 A4
Nuneaton CV10 ... 72 A8
West Bromwich B71 ... 53 C6
Ash End House Farm*
B78 ... 48 B8
Ash Gn DY1 ... 51 A5
Ash Gr Ash Green CV7 ... 95 C7
Birmingham, Balsall Heath
B12 ... 87 A5
[11] Birmingham, Bordesley
B9 ... 67 B2
Cannock WS11 ... 1 F4
Dudley DY3 ... 50 C2
Kidderminster DY11 ... 116 B7
Lichfield WS14 ... 9 E8
Stourbridge DY9 ... 81 D3
Tamworth B77 ... 35 F5
Ash Green La CV7 ... 95 D6
Ash Green Sch CV7 ... 95 D6
Ash Hill WV3 ... 24 D2
Ash La Alvechurch B48 ... 123 D2
Great Wyrley WS6 ... 5 A3
Ash Lawn Ho [8] CV31 ... 162 A7
Ash Mews [4] B27 ... 88 C5
Ash Park Ind Est WS11 ... 2 B2
Ash Priors Cl CV4 ... 112 B1
Ash Rd Birmingham B8 ... 67 D4
Dudley DY1 ... 51 B3
Tipton DY4 ... 51 E4
Wednesbury WS10 ... 41 F5
Ash St Bilston WV14 ... 40 E3
Blackheath B64 ... 62 F2
Walsall WS3 ... 14 D1
Wolverhampton WV3 ... 25 A1
Ash Terr B69 ... 52 B1
Ash Tree Ave CV4 ... 112 A2
Ash Tree Ct WS11 ... 1 D4
Ash Tree Dr B26 ... 88 D7
Ash Tree Gr CV7 ... 97 E5
Ash Tree Rd
Birmingham B30 ... 104 A6
Redditch B97 ... 153 B5
Ash View WS12 ... 1 D8
Ash Way B23 ... 56 C7
Ash Wlk B76 ... 46 F2
Ashborough Dr B91 ... 127 C8
Ashbourne Cl WS11 ... 2 A4
Ashbourne Gr [3] B6 ... 66 E8
Ashbourne Rd
Birmingham B16 ... 65 D3
Walsall WS3 ... 14 C3
Wolverhampton, Ettingshall Park
WV4 ... 39 E3
Wolverhampton, Heath Town
WV1 ... 26 A3
Ashbourne Ridge B63 ... 82 D5
Ashbourne Way B90 ... 126 E8
Ashbridge Rd CV5 ... 112 C4
Ashbrook Cres B91 ... 127 C8
Ashbrook Dr B45 ... 122 B8
Ashbrook Gr B30 ... 104 C8
Ashbrook Rd B30 ... 104 C8
Ashburn Gr WV13 ... 27 C2
Ashburton Cl LE10 ... 76 A6
Ashburton Rd
Birmingham B14 ... 104 D5
Coventry CV2 ... 114 E8
Ashbury Covert [3] B30 ... 104 C3
Ashby Cl Birmingham B8 ... 68 C6
Coventry CV3 ... 134 F8
Ashby Ct Nuneaton CV11 ... 73 D3
Solihull B91 ... 107 C1
Ashby Grange LE10 ... 71 E5
Ashby Rd
Hinckley LE9,LE10 ... 71 E5
Tamworth B79 ... 21 C8
Ashcombe Ave B20 ... 54 E3
Ashcombe Dr CV4 ... 111 F3
Ashcombe Gdns B24 ... 57 D3
Ashcott Cl B38 ... 103 D2
Ashcroft Birmingham B15 ... 85 E5
[4] Smethwick B66 ... 65 C5
Tipton DY4 ... 52 A2
[12] Wolverhampton WV4 ... 39 F4
Ashcroft Cl CV2 ... 115 A8
Ashcroft Gr B20 ... 55 D2
Ashcroft Inf Sch B79 ... 21 C7
Ashcroft La Lichfield WS14 ... 8 E1
Shenstone WS14 ... 17 E7
Ashcroft Way CV2 ... 115 B8
Ashdale Cl
Binley Woods CV3 ... 135 E7
Huntington WS12 ... 1 C7
Kingswinford DY6 ... 60 D8
Ashdale Dr B14 ... 105 A1
Ashdale Gr B26 ... 89 A8
Ashdale Rd B77 ... 21 D5
Ashdene Cl
Kidderminster DY10 ... 117 C5
Sutton Coldfield B73 ... 46 A3
Ashdene Gdns
Kenilworth CV8 ... 148 B4
Stourbridge DY8 ... 60 C2
Ashdown Cl
Birmingham, Frankley B45 ... 102 A2
Birmingham, Highgate B13 ... 87 A1
Coventry CV3 ... 134 D8
Ashdown Dr
Nuneaton CV10 ... 72 F2
Stourbridge DY8 ... 60 E3
Ashe Rd CV10 ... 72 B3
Ashen Cl DY3 ... 39 C3
Ashenden Rise WV3 ... 38 A8
Ashenhurst Rd DY1 ... 61 F8
Ashenhurst Wlk DY1 ... 51 A1
Ashes Rd B69 ... 63 F3
Ashes The Oldbury B69 ... 63 F3
Wolverhampton WV11 ... 26 B6
Ashfern Dr B76 ... 57 F7
Ashfield Ave
Birmingham B14 ... 86 F1
Coventry CV4 ... 111 D1
Ashfield Cl WS3 ... 28 F4
Ashfield Cres Dudley DY2 ... 62 C3
Stourbridge DY9 ... 82 A3
Ashfield Ct B38 ... 103 E4
Ashfield Gr
Halesowen B63 ... 82 E2
Wolverhampton WV10 ... 11 C3
Ashfield Ho B28 ... 105 E3
Ashfield Rd Bilston WV14 ... 41 A2
Birmingham B14 ... 86 F1
Kenilworth CV8 ... 148 B4
Wolverhampton, Compton
WV3 ... 24 D2
Wolverhampton, Fordhouses
WV10 ... 11 C3
Ashford Dr Bedworth CV12 ... 78 A3
Sedgley DY3 ... 50 E7
Sutton Coldfield B76 ... 57 F5
Ashford Gdns CV31 ... 161 F3
Ashford Ind Pk WV2 ... 40 A7
Ashford La B94 ... 143 B7
Ashford Rd Hinckley LE10 ... 75 B7
Whitnash CV31 ... 161 F2
Ashford Twr B12 ... 86 F8
Ashfurlong Cl CV7 ... 130 B6
Ashfurlong Cres B75 ... 46 E8
Ashgrove WS7 ... 6 F5
Ashgrove Cl B60 ... 121 D1
Ashgrove Rd B44 ... 44 C2
Ashill Rd B45 ... 122 B7
Ashington Gr CV3 ... 134 A5
Ashington Rd CV12 ... 77 C1
Ashland St
Wolverhampton WV3 ... 25 B1
Wolverhampton WV3 ... 39 B8
Ashlands Cl B79 ... 21 C7
Ashlawn Cres B91 ... 106 D5
Ashlea B78 ... 36 F5
Ashleigh Ct [8] DY2 ... 62 E8
Ashleigh Dr
Birmingham B20 ... 55 B2
Nuneaton CV11 ... 73 F1
Tamworth B77 ... 35 E8
Ashleigh Gr B13 ... 87 B1
Ashleigh Hts B91 ... 107 A5
Ashleigh Mews Cotts
B76 ... 59 C6
Ashleigh Rd Solihull B91 ... 107 B4
Tipton B69 ... 63 C8
Ashley Cl Birmingham B15 ... 86 C7
Kingswinford DY6 ... 60 C4
Stourbridge DY8 ... 80 D2
Ashley Cres CV34 ... 161 B6
Ashley Ct B45 ... 122 A1
Ashley Gdns B8 ... 67 D4
Ashley Ho DY2 ... 62 D4
Ashley Mount WV6 ... 24 D5
Ashley Rd Birmingham B23 ... 56 E3
Walsall WS3 ... 27 F8
Wolverhampton WV4 ... 38 E5
Ashley St WV14 ... 40 E6
Ashley Way CV7 ... 130 B7
Ashmall WS7 ... 7 D4
Ashmead Dr B45 ... 122 C4
Ashmead Gr B24 ... 57 A2
Ashmead Rd WS7 ... 7 A8
Ashmead Rise B45 ... 122 C4
Ashmole Ave WS7 ... 7 E8
Ashmole Cl WS14 ... 9 E6
Ashmole Rd B70 ... 52 F7
Ashmore Ave WV11 ... 13 A1
Ashmore Ind Est WS2 ... 28 E3
Ashmore Lake Rd WV12 ... 27 B4
Ashmore Lake Way
WV12 ... 27 B4
Ashmore Rd
Birmingham B30 ... 103 F5
Coventry CV6 ... 113 B4
Ashmores Cl B97 ... 158 D5
Ashold Farm Rd B24 ... 57 D2
Asholme Cl B36 ... 68 C7

Ashorne Cl
Birmingham B28 . . . . .106 B7
Coventry CV2 . . . . .96 C2
Redditch B98 . . . . .159 D8
Ashover Gr 8 B18 . . . . .65 E4
Ashover Rd B44 . . . . .44 D3
Ashow Cl CV8 . . . . .148 B4
Ashperton Cl B98 . . . . .153 E1
Ashridge Cl CV11 . . . . .78 F8
Ashstead Cl B76 . . . . .58 B6
Ashted Cir B7 . . . . .67 A4
Ashted Lock B7 . . . . .66 F4
Ashted Wlk B7 . . . . .67 B4
Ashton Cl B97 . . . . .153 B1
Ashton Croft
Birmingham B16 . . . . .66 A2
Solihull B91 . . . . .107 A1
Ashton Dr WS4 . . . . .29 C6
Ashton Rd B25 . . . . .88 C7
Ashtree Cl DY5 . . . . .61 B1
Ashtree Gr WV14 . . . . .41 B3
Ashtree Rd Blackheath B64 . . . .62 F2
Oldbury B69 . . . . .63 D8
Tipton B69 . . . . .52 C1
Walsall WS3 . . . . .15 A3
Ashurst Cl CV6 . . . . .96 B5
Ashurst Rd B76 . . . . .57 F7
Ashville Ave B34 . . . . .68 F7
Ashville Dr B63 . . . . .83 A5
Ashwater Dr B14 . . . . .104 D2
Ashway B11 . . . . .87 B5
Ashwell Dr B90 . . . . .106 D4
Ashwells Gr WV9 . . . . .11 A2
Ashwin Rd B21 . . . . .66 A7
Ashwood Ave
Coventry CV6 . . . . .112 F5
Stourbridge DY8 . . . . .60 D2
Ashwood Cl B74 . . . . .44 E8
Ashwood Ct
Birmingham B13 . . . . .87 A3
Birmingham, Stechford B34 . .68 D5
Ashwood Dr B37 . . . . .70 D3
Ashwood Gr WV4 . . . . .39 A5
Ashwood Park Prim Sch
DY5 . . . . .60 D1
Ashwood Rd CV10 . . . . .72 E5
Ashworth Ho
Cannock WS11 . . . . .2 A4
Lichfield WS13 . . . . .9 B8
Ashworth Rd B42 . . . . .44 B1
Askew Bridge Rd DY3 . . . . .50 B3
Askew Cl DY3 . . . . .50 E5
Aspbury Croft B36 . . . . .58 D1
Aspen Cl Birmingham B27 . . . . .88 B2
Coventry CV4 . . . . .111 D1
Sutton Coldfield B76 . . . . .46 F2
Aspen Dr Birmingham B37 . . . .90 C8
Coventry CV6 . . . . .96 C6
Aspen Gdns B20 . . . . .55 B1
Aspen Gr Birmingham B9 . . . . .68 A3
Burntwood WS7 . . . . .6 F8
Hollywood B47 . . . . .125 A5
Willenhall WV12 . . . . .27 E7
Aspen Ho B91 . . . . .106 F2
Aspen Way WV3 . . . . .25 A1
Aspens The WS13 . . . . .3 A1
Asplen Ct CV8 . . . . .148 C4
Aspley Heath B94 . . . . .141 D2
Aspley Heath La B94 . . . . .141 C2
Asquith Dr Cannock WS11 . . . . .2 C2
Tipton B69 . . . . .52 D2
Asquith Rd B8 . . . . .68 B5
Asra Cl B66 . . . . .65 A8
Asra Ho B66 . . . . .65 A8
Astbury Ave B67 . . . . .64 F3
Astbury Cl Walsall WS3 . . . . . . .14 A4
Wolverhampton WV1 . . . . .26 A3
Astbury Ct 4 B68 . . . . .84 B7
Aster Cl Hinckley LE10 . . . . .75 C6
Nuneaton CV11 . . . . .74 A1
Aster Way CV10 . . . . .75 D6
Aster Wlk WV9 . . . . .11 A3
Asthill Croft CV3 . . . . .133 C8
Asthill Gr CV3 . . . . .133 C8
Astley Ave Coventry CV6 . . . . .95 E2
Halesowen B62 . . . . .83 F6
Astley Cl Redditch B98 . . . . . . .159 A7
Royal Leamington Spa
CV32 . . . . .156 D2
Tipton DY4 . . . . .52 A6
Astley Cres B62 . . . . .83 F5
Astley La Bedworth CV12 . . . . .77 C4
Nuneaton CV10 . . . . .72 B1
Astley Rd Birmingham B21 . . . .54 D1
Bromsgrove B60 . . . . .137 C1
Astley Wlk B90 . . . . .106 B5
Aston Bridge B6 . . . . .66 F6
Aston Brook Gr B6 . . . . .66 F5
Aston Brook St E B6 . . . . .66 F5
Aston Bury B15 . . . . .85 D7
Aston Church Rd B7,B8 . . . . . . .67 D6
Aston Cl Bilston WV14 . . . . .41 A4
Shenstone WS14 . . . . .17 F6
Aston Cross Bsns Village
B6 . . . . .67 A6
Aston Ct B23 . . . . .56 C3
Aston Expressway B6 . . . . .66 F6
Aston Expressway (Elevated
Rd) B6 . . . . .67 A8
Aston Fields Mid Sch
B60 . . . . .151 C8
Aston Fields Trad Est
B60 . . . . .150 F6
Aston Flamville Rd LE10 . . .76 C7

Aston Hall* B6 . . . . .66 F8
Aston Hall Rd B6 . . . . .67 B8
Aston La Birmingham B20 . . . . .55 E2
Hinckley LE10 . . . . .76 A4
Aston Manor Cl B20 . . . . .55 E2
Aston Manor Sch B6 . . . . .66 F6
Aston Pk Ind Est CV11 . . . . .73 B5
Aston Rd Birmingham B6 . . . . .66 F5
Bromsgrove B60 . . . . .150 C6
Coventry CV5 . . . . .112 F1
Dudley DY2 . . . . .62 B8
Nuneaton CV11 . . . . .73 B5
Tipton B69 . . . . .52 A1
Willenhall WV13 . . . . .26 E2
Aston Rd N B6 . . . . .66 F6
Aston Science Pk B7 . . . . .66 F4
Aston Seedbed Ctr B7 . . . . .67 A6
Aston St Birmingham B4 . . . . .164 D4
Tipton DY4 . . . . .52 C7
Wolverhampton WV3 . . . . .39 A8
Aston Sta B6 . . . . .67 B8
Aston Tower Com Prim Sch
B6 . . . . .66 F7
Aston Univ B5 . . . . .164 D4
Astons Cl DY5 . . . . .81 D7
Astons Fold DY5 . . . . .81 D7
Astor Dr B13 . . . . .87 C1
Astor Rd Aldridge B74 . . . . .31 A1
Kingswinford DY6 . . . . .60 F5
Astoria Cl W12 . . . . .13 D1
Astoria Gdns WV12 . . . . .13 D1
Astwell Prep Sch B20 . . . . .66 B8
Atcham Cl B98 . . . . .154 F3
Atcheson Cl B80 . . . . .159 E4
Athelney Ct WS3 . . . . .15 A3
Athelstan Gr WV6 . . . . .24 F3
Athelstan Way B27 . . . . .20 F7
Athena Dr CV34 . . . . .161 E5
Athena Gdns CV6 . . . . .96 A1
Atherston Pl CV4 . . . . .132 D6
Atherstone Cl
Redditch B98 . . . . .154 F1
Solihull B90 . . . . .105 E2
Atherstone Rd WV1 . . . . .26 B2
Atherstone St B77,B78 . . . . .35 B8
Athlone Rd WS5 . . . . .43 C8
Athol Cl B32 . . . . .84 F8
Athol Rd CV2 . . . . .115 A6
Athole St B12 . . . . .87 A7
Atholl Cres CV10 . . . . .72 E2
Atkins Way LE10 . . . . .75 E7
Atkinson Dr WV10 . . . . .25 D6
Atlantic Cl 4 WV13 . . . . .27 A1
Atlantic Rd B44 . . . . .44 F1
Atlantic Way WS10 . . . . .41 E1
Atlas Croft WV10 . . . . .25 C6
Atlas Gr B70 . . . . .52 F3
Atlas Trad Est B11 . . . . .87 D5
Attenborough Cl B19 . . . . .66 E5
Attingham Dr
Birmingham B43 . . . . .43 D2
Cannock WS11 . . . . .2 D2
Attleborough Fields Ind Est
CV11 . . . . .73 F3
Attleborough La B46 . . . . .59 A1
Attleborough Rd CV11 . . . . . . .73 D3
Attlee Cl B69 . . . . .52 D2
Attlee Cres WV14 . . . . .40 E2
Attlee Gr WS11 . . . . .2 C2
Attlee Rd WS2 . . . . .27 E3
Attoxhall Rd CV2 . . . . .114 E4
Attwell Pk WV3 . . . . .38 D7
Attwell Rd DY4 . . . . .40 F1
Attwood Bsns Ctr 2 DY9 . . . .81 F5
Attwood Cl B8 . . . . .67 E6
Attwood Cres CV2 . . . . .114 C7
Attwood Gdns WV4 . . . . .39 E5
Attwood Rd WS7 . . . . .6 C7
Attwood St DY9 . . . . .81 F5
Atworth Cl B98 . . . . .159 B5
Aubrey Rd
Birmingham, Beakes Lanes
B32 . . . . .84 E7
Birmingham, Small Heath
B10 . . . . .87 F8
Auchinleck Dr WS13 . . . . .3 C1
Auchinleck Sq 5 B15 . . . . .66 B1
Auckland Dr B36 . . . . .70 B7
Auckland Ho B32 . . . . .84 F4
Auckland Rd
Birmingham B11 . . . . .87 A7
Kingswinford DY6 . . . . .60 E4
Smethwick B67 . . . . .64 E5
Auden Ct WV6 . . . . .23 F4
Audleigh Ho 1 B15 . . . . .86 C8
Audley Dr DY11 . . . . .116 A8
Audley Jun Sch B33 . . . . .68 F4
Audley Rd B33 . . . . .68 F4
Audnam DY8 . . . . .60 F1
Augusta Pl CV32 . . . . .161 F8
Augusta Rd
Birmingham, Acock's Green
B27 . . . . .88 C5
Birmingham, Moseley B13 . . .86 F4
Augusta Rd E B13 . . . . .86 F4
Augusta St B18 . . . . .66 C4
Augustine Ave B80 . . . . .159 D4
Augustine Gr
Birmingham B18 . . . . .65 F6
Sutton Coldfield B74 . . . . .31 F5
Augustines Wlk WS13 . . . . .3 A3
Augustus Cl B46 . . . . .59 F1
Augustus Ct B15 . . . . .85 F8

Augustus Rd
Birmingham B15 . . . . .85 E8
Coventry CV1 . . . . .113 F4
Augustus Rd WS2 . . . . .28 D1
Ault St B70 . . . . .53 D1
Aulton Cres B31 . . . . .103 C1
Aulton Rd B75 . . . . .32 E2
Aulton Way LE10 . . . . .71 B1
Austcliff Cl B97 . . . . .158 D6
Austcliff Dr B91 . . . . .127 C8
Austen Ct CV32 . . . . .157 E5
Austen Pl B15 . . . . .86 B8
Austen Wlk B71 . . . . .53 D6
Austin Cl Birmingham B27 . . . .88 D4
Dudley DY1 . . . . .50 F2
Austin Cote La WS14 . . . . .9 F7
Austin Croft B36 . . . . .58 E1
Austin Dr CV6 . . . . .114 A7
Austin Edwards Dr
CV34 . . . . .161 B8
Austin Ho WS4 . . . . .28 F3
Austin Rise B31 . . . . .122 F7
Austin St WV6 . . . . .25 B4
Austin Way B42 . . . . .55 A5
Austrey Cl B93 . . . . .128 A6
Austrey Gr B29 . . . . .103 A8
Austrey Rd DY6 . . . . .61 A5
Austwick Cl CV34 . . . . .155 E1
Austy Cl B36 . . . . .68 E8
Auto Ctr B18 . . . . .65 E5
Autobase Ind Est B69 . . . . .52 E2
Autumn Berry Gr DY3 . . . . .50 E6
Autumn Cl WS4 . . . . .15 C1
Autumn Dr Dudley DY3 . . . . . . .50 D4
Lichfield WS13 . . . . .3 D2
Walsall WS4 . . . . .15 C2
Autumn Gr B19 . . . . .66 C6
Auxerre Ave B98 . . . . .159 B8
Auxerre Ho B98 . . . . .159 B8
Avalon Cl B24 . . . . .57 B4
Avalon Rd B60 . . . . .137 C2
Ave Maria Cl B64 . . . . .62 E1
Avebury Cl CV11 . . . . .73 F2
Avebury Gr B30 . . . . .104 C7
Avebury Rd B30 . . . . .104 C8
Avenbury Cl B98 . . . . .154 F1
Avenbury Dr B91 . . . . .107 E4
Avenue Cl Birmingham B7 . . . .67 A6
Dorridge B93 . . . . .128 A3
Avenue Rd
Astwood Bank B96 . . . . .158 E1
Birmingham, Aston B7,B6 . . . .67 A6
Birmingham, Erdington B23 . .56 F4
Birmingham, Handsworth
B21 . . . . .54 D2
Birmingham, King's Heath
B14 . . . . .104 D8
Blackheath B65 . . . . .63 D1
Cannock WS12 . . . . .2 E2
Darlaston WS10 . . . . .41 D6
Dorridge B93 . . . . .128 A3
Dudley, Roseville WV14 . . . . . . .51 C8
Dudley, Woodside DY1,DY2 . .61 F6
Kenilworth CV8 . . . . .147 D6
Nuneaton CV11 . . . . .73 D2
Royal Leamington Spa
CV31 . . . . .161 F7
Wolverhampton WV3 . . . . .24 E2
Avenue The
Birmingham, Acock's Green
B27 . . . . .88 D3
Birmingham, Lozells B19 . .66 C8
Blackheath B65 . . . . .63 A3
Blackwell B60 . . . . .138 A6
Blakedown DY10 . . . . .98 B2
Coventry CV3 . . . . .134 A6
Featherstone WV10 . . . . .12 C7
Rowington Green CV35 . . . . .145 A1
Sutton Coldfield B76 . . . . .46 F1
Wolverhampton, Castlecroft
WV3 . . . . .38 B8
Wolverhampton, Penn WV4 . .38 D4
Averill Rd B26 . . . . .69 A1
Avern Cl DY4 . . . . .52 B6
Aversley Rd B38 . . . . .123 D8
Avery Croft B35 . . . . .57 F2
Avery Ct 6 Oldbury B68 . . . . . .84 B7
6 Warwick CV34 . . . . .160 F7
Avery Dell Inst Est B30 . . . . . .104 A6
Avery Dr B27 . . . . .88 D4
Avery Ho B16 . . . . .66 A1
Avery Myers Cl B68 . . . . .64 A5
Avery Rd Smethwick B66 . . . . .65 D6
Sutton Coldfield B73 . . . . .45 C3
Aviary Cl B71 . . . . .53 C6
Aviemore Cl CV10 . . . . .73 A2
Aviemore Cres B43 . . . . .44 B4
Avill B77 . . . . .36 A5
Avill Gr DY11 . . . . .116 C7
Avington Cl DY3 . . . . .50 D7
Avion Cl WS1 . . . . .42 F7
Avion Ctr WV6 . . . . .25 A4
Avocet Cl Birmingham B33 . . . .68 E3
Coventry CV2 . . . . .96 B3
Avocet Dr DY10 . . . . .117 A2
Avon B77 . . . . .36 A5
Avon Bsns Pk WV11 . . . . .4 C7
Avon Cl Brierley Hill DY5 . . . . .61 B7
Bromsgrove B60 . . . . .150 F6
Bulkington CV12 . . . . .79 B6
Perton WV6 . . . . .24 B3
Avon Cres WS3 . . . . .15 A1
Avon Ct Kenilworth CV8 . . . . .147 F5
Sutton Coldfield B73 . . . . .46 B5

Avon Dr
Birmingham, Castle Bromwich
B36 . . . . .69 F7
Birmingham, Moseley B13 . .87 B2
Willenhall WV13 . . . . .27 C2
Wythall B47 . . . . .124 C2
Avon Gr WS5 . . . . .43 A4
Avon Ho Birmingham B15 . . . . .86 D8
Coventry CV4 . . . . .132 C6
Dudley, Dibdale DY3 . . . . .50 E3
5 Dudley, Russell's Hall
DY1 . . . . .61 E8
3 Oldbury B69 . . . . .84 B8
Avon Rd Burntwood WS7 . . . . .6 F5
Cannock WS11 . . . . .4 D8
Halesowen B63 . . . . .82 B5
Kenilworth CV8 . . . . .147 E3
Kidderminster DY11 . . . . .116 B3
Solihull B90 . . . . .106 D1
Stourbridge DY8 . . . . .80 F3
Walsall WS3 . . . . .14 E1
Whitnash CV31 . . . . .162 A3
Avon St Birmingham B11 . . . . . .87 C5
Coventry CV2 . . . . .114 B5
Royal Leamington Spa
CV32 . . . . .157 C4
Wolverhampton WV6 . . . . .24 F3
Avonbank Cl B97 . . . . .158 C6
Avoncroft 8 WV4 . . . . .39 F4
Avoncroft Ho B37 . . . . .70 A2
Avoncroft Mus of Historic
Bldgs* B60 . . . . .150 D6
Avoncroft Rd B60 . . . . .150 D6
Avondale Cl DY6 . . . . .60 E8
Avondale Rd
Birmingham B11 . . . . .87 D4
Brandon CV8 . . . . .135 F5
Coventry CV5 . . . . .133 A8
Royal Leamington Spa
CV32 . . . . .157 C4
Wolverhampton WV6 . . . . .24 F3
Avonlea Rise CV32 . . . . .156 D2
Avonridge Rd DY7 . . . . .78 D1
Awefields Cres B67 . . . . .64 E4
Awlmakers Gr WS3 . . . . .28 D7
Awson St CV6 . . . . .113 F6
Axcess 10 Bsns Pk WS2 . .41 E8
Axholme Rd CV2 . . . . .114 E4
Axletree Way WS10 . . . . .42 B5
Axminster Cl CV11 . . . . .73 F5
Ayala Croft 2 B36 . . . . .68 E8
Aylesbury Cl B94 . . . . .143 C6
Aylesbury Cres B44 . . . . .56 A8
Aylesbury Rd B94 . . . . .143 D7
Aylesdene Ct CV5 . . . . .132 F8
Aylesford Cl DY3 . . . . .39 C2
Aylesford Dr 7 CV31 . . . . .162 A6
Aylesford St
Birmingham B37 . . . . .90 A7
Sutton Coldfield B74 . . . . .31 E5
Aylesford Rd B21 . . . . .54 D1
Aylesford St CV34 . . . . .160 C4
Aylesford St
Coventry CV1 . . . . .113 E4
Royal Leamington Spa
CV31 . . . . .162 A6
Aylesmore Cl
Birmingham B32 . . . . .84 C1
Solihull B92 . . . . .106 E8
Aynho Cl CV5 . . . . .112 A3
Aynsley Cl B90 . . . . .106 C2
Ayre Rd B24 . . . . .57 B4
Ayrshire Cl B36 . . . . .68 D8
Ayrton Cl WV6 . . . . .24 A4
Ayspath Cl CV11 . . . . .74 A2
Azalea Cl Codsall WV8 . . . . .10 B3
Hinckley LE10 . . . . .75 E5
Azalea Gr B9 . . . . .67 E6
Azalea Gr B9 . . . . .67 E2
Azalea Wlk LE10 . . . . .75 E5
Aziz Isaac Cl B68 . . . . .64 C6

B

Babbacombe Rd CV3 . . . . .133 D5
Babington Rd B21 . . . . .65 E7
Bablake Cl CV6 . . . . .112 F8
Bablake Croft B92 . . . . .89 A1
Bablake Jun Sch CV1 . . . . .165 A4
Bablake Sch CV1 . . . . .113 B4
Babors Field WV14 . . . . .40 A3
Babworth Cl WV9 . . . . .11 A2
Baccabox La B47 . . . . .124 C7
Bacchus Rd B18 . . . . .65 E6
Bach Mill Dr B28 . . . . .105 D3
Bache St B70 . . . . .53 D1
Back La Aldridge WS9 . . . . .30 F8
Meriden CV7 . . . . .110 E5
Shenstone WS14 . . . . .17 E1
Solihull B90 . . . . .126 A5
Warwick CV34 . . . . .160 E6
Back Rd Birmingham B38 . . . .103 F2
Kingswinford DY6 . . . . .60 D7
Back St CV11 . . . . .73 C5
Backcester La WS13 . . . . .9 B8
Backcrofts 3 WS11 . . . . .1 E1
Backhouse La WV11 . . . . .26 C4
Badbury Cl B80 . . . . .159 D4
Badbury Gr B80 . . . . .159 D4
Baddesley Cl CV31 . . . . .162 C5
Baddesley Clinton*
B93 . . . . .144 F4
Baddesley Rd B92 . . . . .88 E2
Bader Rd Perton WV6 . . . . .23 E3
Walsall WS2 . . . . .27 F2
Bader Wlk B35 . . . . .57 F2
Badger Brook La B96 . . . . .158 D1

Badger Cl
Cheswick Green B90 . . . . .126 D4
Huntington WS12 . . . . .1 D6
Redditch B98 . . . . .154 D3
Badger Ct WV10 . . . . .25 D4
Badger Dr WV10 . . . . .25 D4
Badger Rd CV3 . . . . .134 D8
Badger Way B90 . . . . .126 D4
Badger Way Stop B90 . . . . .81 E6
Badgers Bank Rd B74 . . . . .31 F5
Badgers Cl WS3 . . . . .15 A5
Badgers Croft B62 . . . . .83 B7
Badgers The B45 . . . . .122 A2
Badgers Way
Birmingham B34 . . . . .69 A5
Cannock WS12 . . . . .1 D1
Badminton Cl DY1 . . . . .50 F3
Badon Covert B14 . . . . .104 D2
Badsey Cl B31 . . . . .103 C4
Badsey Rd B69 . . . . .63 D5
Baggeridge Cl CV3 . . . . .50 A8
Baggeridge Ctry Pk*
DY3 . . . . .49 E6
Baggott St 8 WV2 . . . . .39 C7
Baginton Cl B91 . . . . .107 B5
Baginton Fields Sch
CV3 . . . . .134 B4
Baginton Rd
Birmingham B35 . . . . .58 B4
Coventry CV3 . . . . .133 C5
Bagley Rd DY5 . . . . .81 D6
Bagley St DY9 . . . . .81 C6
Bagnall Cl B25 . . . . .88 D6
Bagnall Rd WV14 . . . . .40 C5
Bagnall St Tipton DY4 . . . . .41 C1
Walsall WS3 . . . . .28 C6
West Bromwich, Golds Hill
B70 . . . . .52 E7
West Bromwich, Mayer's Green
B70 . . . . .53 E2
Bagnall Wlk DY5 . . . . .61 D1
Bagnell Rd B13 . . . . .104 F7
Bagot Way CV34 . . . . .161 E3
Bagridge Cl WV3 . . . . .38 B8
Bagridge Rd WV3 . . . . .38 B8
Bagshaw Cl CV8 . . . . .135 A1
Bagshaw Rd B33 . . . . .68 E3
Bagshawe Croft B23 . . . . .56 D7
Bailey Ave B77 . . . . .35 F5
Bailey Cl Burntwood WS7 . . . . .6 D8
Cannock WS11 . . . . .2 A4
Bailey Rd WV14 . . . . .40 B7
Bailey St
West Bromwich B70 . . . . .53 A4
Wolverhampton WV10 . . . . . .163 D3
Baileys Ct B65 . . . . .63 B3
Baileys Ct WS13 . . . . .3 F1
Baines' La 1 LE10 . . . . .71 D1
Baird Ho B20 . . . . .60 F7
Bakehouse La B93 . . . . .145 B6
Bakeman Ho B26 . . . . .88 D6
Baker Ave
Royal Leamington Spa
CV31 . . . . .161 F6
Wolverhampton WV14 . . . . . . .39 F2
Baker Cl WS7 . . . . .7 F6
Baker House Gr B43 . . . . .54 D7
Baker Rd WV14 . . . . .40 E3
Baker St Bedworth CV6 . . . . . . .96 B6
Birmingham, Handsworth
B21 . . . . .65 F8
Birmingham, Small Heath
B10 . . . . .67 D1
Birmingham, Sparkhill B11 . .87 C5
Burntwood WS7 . . . . .7 A4
Tipton DY4 . . . . .51 E4
West Bromwich B70 . . . . .53 B3
Baker's La Aldridge WS9 . . . . . .30 B6
5 Lichfield WS13 . . . . .9 B7
Knowle B93 . . . . .128 C5
Sutton Coldfield B73,B74 . . . .45 A5
Bakers Mews B93 . . . . .45 B6
Bakers Way WS12 . . . . .2 B5
Bakers Wlk B77 . . . . .35 F6
Bakewell Cl
Coventry CV3 . . . . .134 F8
Walsall WS3 . . . . .14 C3
Balaclava Rd B14 . . . . .104 E8
Balcaskie Cl B15 . . . . .85 E7
Bald's La DY9 . . . . .81 F5
Balden Rd B32 . . . . .84 F7
Baldmoor Lake Rd B23 . . . . . . .56 F6
Baldwin Cl B69 . . . . .52 D2
Baldwin Croft CV6 . . . . .96 B1
Baldwin Gr WS11 . . . . .2 C2
Baldwin Ho B19 . . . . .66 E6
Baldwin Rd
Birmingham B30 . . . . .104 A3
Kidderminster DY10 . . . . .117 B7
Baldwin St Bilston WV14 . . . . . .40 F4
Smethwick B66 . . . . .65 B6
Baldwins La B28 . . . . .105 F4
Balfour B77 . . . . .21 A4
Balfour Cl LE10 . . . . .75 E7
Balfour Cres WV6 . . . . .24 F4
Balfour Ct
Sutton Coldfield B74 . . . . .32 A3
2 Wolverhampton WV6 . . . . .24 F4
Balfour Dr B69 . . . . .52 D2
Balfour Ho B16 . . . . .65 F1
Balfour Rd DY6 . . . . .60 E8
Balfour St B12 . . . . .86 E6
Balham Gr B44 . . . . .45 A1
Balholm B62 . . . . .84 A3
Balking Cl WV14 . . . . .40 B3

Ball Fields DY4 ....52 D5
Ball Ho 5 WS3 ....28 B8
Ball La WV10 ....11 C6
Ballams Wood Dr B31 ....102 B1
Ballantine Rd CV6 ....113 B6
Ballarat Wlk DY8 ....80 F5
Ballard Cres DY2 ....62 D5
Ballard Rd DY2 ....62 D5
Ballard Wlk B37 ....70 A6
Ballingham Cl CV4 ....112 A2
Balliol Bsns Pk WV9 ....10 E3
Balliol Ho B37 ....69 F2
Balliol Rd Coventry CV2 ..114 C4
Hinckley LE10 ....75 F6
Ballot St B66 ....65 B5
Balls Hill WS1 ....28 F2
Balls St WS1 ....28 F2
Balmain Cres WV11 ....12 B1
Balmoral Cl
Coventry CV2 ....114 E6
Halesowen B62 ....83 B7
Lichfield WS14 ....9 D6
Tamworth B79 ....21 B7
Walsall WS4 ....29 D7
Balmoral Ct
Birmingham B1 ....66 C3
Cannock WS11 ....2 A5
Kidderminster DY10 ....117 A5
Nuneaton CV10 ....72 E6
Balmoral Dr Cannock WS12 ..1 F7
Willenhall WV12 ....27 C7
Wombourne WV5 ....38 A1
Balmoral Rd
Birmingham, Erdington B23 ..56 F5
Birmingham, Kingshurst
B36 ....70 A7
Birmingham, Kitwell B32 ..102 B7
Stourbridge DY8 ....60 C2
Sutton Coldfield B74 ....31 F5
Wolverhampton WV4 ....39 A5
Balmoral View DY1 ....50 E2
Balmoral Way
Blackheath B65 ....63 D4
Royal Leamington Spa
CV32 ....157 C6
Walsall WS2 ....28 B4
Balsall Common Prim Sch
CV7 ....130 B5
Balsall Heath Rd B12 ....86 E7
Balsall St WV3 ....129 D7
Balsall St E CV7 ....130 B5
Balthazar Cl CV34 ....161 E4
Baltic Cl WS11 ....1 E2
Baltimore Rd B42 ....55 A5
Balvenie Way DY1 ....50 F4
Bamber Cl WV3 ....38 E8
Bamburgh B77 ....35 C7
Bamburgh Gr CV32 ....156 E3
Bamford Cl WS3 ....14 C3
Bamford Ho WS3 ....14 C3
Bamford Rd Walsall WS3 ..14 C3
Wolverhampton WV3 ....39 A8
Bamford St B77 ....21 D3
Bampfylde Pl B42 ....55 C7
Bampton Ave 4 WS7 ....7 A8
Bamville Rd B8 ....68 A5
Banbrook Cl B92 ....107 D8
Banbury Cl DY3 ....50 E6
Banbury Croft B37 ....69 F2
Banbury Ho B33 ....69 E2
Banbury Rd Cannock WS11 ..4 C8
Warwick CV34 ....161 A3
Banbury St B5 ....66 F2
Bancroft B77 ....21 F3
Bancroft Cl WV14 ....51 B7
Bandywood Cres B44 ....44 F3
Bandywood Rd B44 ....44 F3
Baneberry Dr WV10 ....12 B7
Banfield Ave WS10 ....41 C7
Banfield Rd WS10 ....41 C4
Banford Ave B8 ....68 A4
Banford Rd B8 ....68 A4
Bangham Pit Rd B31 ....102 E6
Bangley La
Drayton Bassett B78 ....33 E6
Tamworth B78 ....34 A8
Bangor Rd B9 ....70 A4
Bangor Rd B9 ....67 D2
Bank Cres WS7 ....6 F5
Bank Croft CV11 ....162 C5
Bank Farm Cl DY9 ....81 C1
Bank Rd
Dudley, Gornalwood DY3 ..50 C2
Dudley, Netherton DY2 .....62 D6
Bank St Bilston WV14 ......40 E3
Birmingham B14 ....86 E1
Blackheath B64 ....62 C1
Brierley Hill DY5 ....61 D3
Cannock WS12 ....2 E1
Dudley WV14 ....51 C8
Stourbridge DY9 ....81 F1
Walsall WS1 ....28 F1
West Bromwich B71 ....53 D6
Wolverhampton WV10 ....25 E5
Bank The CV8 ....149 C6
Bankdale Rd B8 ....68 A4
Bankes Rd B10 ....87 D8
Bankfield Dr CV32 ....156 C1
Bankfield Rd
Bilston WV14 ....40 D5
Tipton DY4 ....52 C8

Bankside, Moseley B13 .....87 D2
Bankside continued
Bankside Cl CV3 ....134 A6
Bankside Cres B74 ....44 F7
Bankside Way WS9 ....16 B2
Bankwell St DY5 ....61 D4
Banky Mdw LE10 ....76 A2
Banner La CV4 ....111 D2
Bannerlea Rd B37 ....69 F5
Bannerley Rd B33 ....69 C1
Banners Ct B73 ....45 B3
Banners Gate Inf Sch
B73 ....45 A4
Banners Gate Jun Sch
B73 ....45 A4
Banners Gate Rd B73 ......45 B3
Banners Gr B23 ....57 A6
Banners La
Halesowen B63 ....82 D6
Redditch B97 ....158 E5
Banners Rd B63 ....82 D6
Banners Wlk B44 ....45 A1
Bannington Ct WV12 ....27 D4
Bannister Rd WS10 ....41 D2
Bannister St B64 ....62 D2
Banquo App
Royal Leamington Spa
CV34 ....161 F2
Royal Leamington Spa
CV34 ....161 F3
Banstead Cl WV2 ....39 E7
Bant Mill Rd B60 ....137 A1
Bantam Gr CV6 ....95 A2
Bantams Cl B33 ....69 C2
Bantock Ave WV3 ....38 F8
Bantock Ct WV3 ....38 E8
Bantock Gdns WV3 ....24 E1
Bantock House Mus
WV3 ....24 F1
Bantock Rd CV4 ....111 E2
Bantock Way B17 ....85 D5
Bantocks The B70 ....53 A6
Banton Cl B23 ....56 D8
Bantry Cl B26 ....89 C4
Baptist End Rd DY2 ....62 C6
Baptist Wlk LE10 ....71 D1
Bar Rd CV3 ....133 E8
Bar Wlk WS9 ....16 E4
Barbara Rd B28 ....105 E4
Barbara St B79 ....21 A5
Barbel Dr WV10 ....26 B4
Barbel Cl WS12 ....2 E2
Barber Inst of Fine Arts The*
B15 ....86 A3
Barberry Ho B38 ....103 F1
Barbers La B91 ....108 C6
Barbican Rise CV2 ....114 E2
Barbourne Cl B91 ....127 B7
Barbridge Cl CV12 ....79 C2
Barbridge Rd CV12 ....79 C3
Barbrook Dr DY5 ....81 B7
Barchester Rd
Birmingham B29 ....85 A1
Knowle B93 ....128 A4
Barclay Ct WV3 ....25 A2
Barclay Rd B67 ....64 E1
Barcliff Ave B77 ....21 E3
Barcroft WV13 ....27 C2
Bard St B11 ....87 C4
Bardenholme Gdns DY9 ..81 D3
Bardfield Cl B31 ....55 A8
Bardley Dr CV6 ....113 C6
Bardon Dr B90 ....106 D2
Bardsey Cl LE10 ....71 B1
Bardwell Cl WV8 ....24 F8
Barford App CV31 ....162 B2
Barford Cl Coventry CV3 ..134 D8
Darlaston WS10 ....41 B3
Redditch B98 ....154 F1
Sutton Coldfield B76 ....46 F4
Barford Cres B 538 ....104 C2
Barford Ho B38 ....86 E8
Barford Prim Sch B16 .....65 F3
Barford Rd
Birmingham B16 ....65 F3
Kenilworth CV8 ....148 B3
Solihull B90 ....106 D2
Barford St B5 ....86 E8
Bargate Dr WV6 ....25 A4
Bargery Rd WV11 ....13 A1
Barham Cl B90 ....127 A5
Bark Piece B32 ....84 C3
Barker Rd B74 ....46 B7
Barker St Birmingham B19 ..66 C6
Oldbury B68 ....64 C6
Barker's Butts La CV6 ..113 A4
Barkers La B47 ....125 A1
Barker's Butts La CV5 ..113 A5
Barlands Croft B34 ....69 C6
Barle Gr B36 ....70 A7
Barleston Dr LE10 ....71 A1
Barley Cl Aldridge WS9 ....30 E2
Cannock WS12 ....2 B5
Dudley DY3 ....50 F7
Wolverhampton WV8 ....10 E1
Barley Croft Perton WV6 ..23 D3
Stoke Heath B60 ....150 E6
Barley Ct CV32 ....156 F2
Barley Lea Ho CV3 ....134 C4
Barley Lea The CV3 ....134 C8
Barley Mow La B61 ....137 B8
Barleyfield LE10 ....71 C3
Barleyfield Ho 3 WS1 .....42 E8
Barleyfield Rise DY6 ....60 A8
Barleyfield Row WS1 ....42 E8
Barlich Way B98 ....154 A2

Barlow Cl
Birmingham B45 ....101 E2
Oldbury B68 ....64 A3
Tamworth B77 ....21 E4
Barlow Dr B70 ....53 F1
Barlow Rd Coventry CV2 ..96 D2
Wednesbury WS10 ....42 A5
Barlow's Rd B15 ....85 E5
Barmouth Cl WV12 ....27 C6
Barn Ave DY3 ....50 C7
Barn Cl Birmingham B30 ..104 B6
Blackheath B64 ....82 E6
Coventry CV5 ....112 C5
Dordon B78 ....36 F6
Halesowen B63 ....82 E2
Lichfield WS13 ....3 H1
Stoke Heath B60 ....150 E6
Stourbridge DY9 ....81 C4
Whitnash CV31 ....162 B3
Barn Croft
Birmingham B32 ....84 E1
Burntwood WS7 ....7 A4
Great Wyrley WS6 ....5 A3
Barns Farm Cl WV14 ....41 A7
Barn Gn WV3 ....38 F7
Barn Mdw B68 ....68 D4
Barn La
Birmingham, Handsworth
B21 ....65 E7
Birmingham, King's Heath
B13 ....105 A7
Solihull B92 ....88 F3
Barn Mdw B25 ....68 D1
Barn Owl Cl DY10 ....117 A2
Barn Owl Dr WS3 ....14 F4
Barn Owl Wlk DY5 ....81 C6
Barn Piece B32 ....84 B3
Barn St B5 ....66 F2
Barnabas Rd B23 ....56 F4
Barnaby Sq WV11 ....11 F4
Barnack Ave CV3 ....133 B5
Barnack Dr CV34 ....155 E1
Barnacle La CV12 ....79 C1
Barnard Cl
Birmingham B37 ....70 D1
Royal Leamington Spa
CV32 ....157 C3
Barnard Pl WV2 ....39 E6
Barnard Rd
Sutton Coldfield B75 ....46 E7
Wolverhampton WV11 ....12 F1
Barnard Way WS11 ....1 C1
Barnbridge B77 ....21 C2
Barnbrook Rd B93 ....128 A7
Barncroft Rd B69 ....63 A8
Barncroft St B70 ....53 A8
Barne Cl CV11 ....79 B7
Barnes Cl B37 ....69 E2
Barnes Hill B29 ....84 F2
Barnes Rd WS14 ....18 A6
Barnesville Cl B10 ....88 A8
Barnet Rd B23 ....56 D5
Barnett Cl Bilston WV14 ...40 D4
Kingswinford DY6 ....60 D4
Barnett Gn DY6 ....60 D4
Barnett La DY6,DY9 ....60 D4
Barnett Rd WV13 ....26 E1
Barnett St
Stourbridge DY9 ....60 D3
Tipton, Tipton Green DY4 ..52 A4
Tipton, Tividale B69 ....52 C2
Barnetts Cl DY10 ....117 B4
Barnetts Gr DY10 ....117 A4
Barnetts La Brownhills WS8 ..6 F1
Kidderminster DY10 ....117 A4
Barnet Cl CV5 ....112 B6
Barnfield Ave CV5 ....112 B6
Barnfield Cl WS14 ....9 B6
Barnfield Dr B92 ....107 F6
Barnfield Gr B20 ....54 E5
Barnfield Rd
Bromsgrove B61 ....136 C1
Halesowen B62 ....83 D7
Tipton DY4 ....52 B6
Wolverhampton WV11 ....26 A2
Barnford Cl B10 ....67 C1
Barnford Cres B68 ....64 B3
Barnfordhill Cl B68 ....64 B4
Barnhurst La WV8 ....10 E2
Barnmoor Rise B91 ....107 C7
Barnpark Covert 9 B14 ..104 C2
Barns Cl WS5 ....15 F4
Barns Croft B74 ....31 B4
Barns La WS4 ....29 D7
Barnsbury Ave B72 ....57 C6
Barnsdale Cres B31 ....102 E4
Barnsley Hall Rd B61 .....137 A6
Barnsley Rd
Birmingham B17 ....65 A1
Bromsgrove B61 ....137 B4
Barnstaple Cl CV5 ....111 F5
Barnstaple Rd B66 ....65 B5
Barnswood Cl
Cannock WS11 ....4 B8
Halesowen B62 ....82 C5
Barnt Green Junc B45 ....138 D8
Barnt Green Rd B45 ....122 C3
Barnwood Cl B98 ....154 D5
Barnwood Rd
Birmingham B32 ....84 F4
Wolverhampton WV8 ....10 E1
Baron Bsns Ctr DY9 ....81 E5
Baron's Croft CV3 ....133 E7
Baron's Field Rd CV3 ...133 E8
Barons Cl B17 ....85 B6
Barons Croft CV10 ....72 C4
Baslow Cl Birmingham B33 ..68 E4

Barpool Rd CV10 ....72 F4
Barr Beacon Sch WS9 ....44 B5
Barr Common Cl WS9 ....30 B3
Barr Common La WS9 ......30 B3
Barr Common Rd WS9 .....30 B3
Barr Lakes La
Aldridge WS9 ....44 A7
Walsall WS9, WS9 ....43 F7
Barr St Birmingham B19 ..66 C5
Dudley DY3 ....50 C3
Barr's Hill Sch & Com Coll
CV1 ....165 A4
Barra Croft B35 ....58 B4
Barrack La B75 ....47 A2
Barrack La B63 ....67 A3
Barrack St Birmingham B7 ..67 A3
Warwick CV34 ....160 E7
West Bromwich B70 ....53 A8
Barracks Cl WS3 ....28 D8
Barracks La
Beausale CV35 ....146 C2
Brownhills WS14 ....16 C8
Walsall WS3 ....28 E8
Barracks Pl WS3 ....28 E8
Barracks Way CV1 ....165 B2
Barrar Cl DY8 ....80 E8
Barras Ct CV2 ....114 A4
Barras Gn CV2 ....114 A4
Barras La CV1 ....113 B3
Barratt Rd B14 ....104 C2
Barratts Croft DY5 ....50 C1
Barratts Rd B14 ....104 D2
Barratts Rd B38 ....104 A1
Barrett Cl DY10 ....117 B6
Barretts La CV7 ....130 C6
Barrett Rd DY8 ....43 C2
Barrie Ave DY10 ....117 C7
Barrie Rd LE10 ....71 D3
Barrington Cl
Walsall WS5 ....43 A3
Wolverhampton WV10 .....11 C1
Barrington Rd
Birmingham B45 ....121 E7
Solihull B92 ....88 F1
Barron Rd B31 ....103 B3
Barrow Cl Coventry CV2 ..115 B6
Redditch B98 ....154 F3
Barrow Hill Rd DY5 ....50 C1
Barrow Ho 1 B16 ....65 F3
Barrow Rd CV8 ....147 F4
Barrow Wlk B5 ....86 E7
Barrowfield Ct CV8 ....147 F4
Barrowfield La CV8 ....147 F4
Barrows La B26 ....89 B6
Barrs Cres B64 ....82 F8
Barrs Rd B64 ....82 E8
Barrs St B68 ....64 A4
Barry Ho 96 D1
Barry Jackson Terr B6 ..66 F7
Barry Rd WS5 ....43 C7
Barsham Cl B5 ....86 C6
Barsham Dr DY5 ....81 C8
Barston Cl CV6 ....96 A2
Barston La
Balsall Common CV7 ......129 D8
Barston B92 ....109 C3
Catherine de B B91 ....108 B2
Hampton-in-A B92 ....108 D3
Solihull B91 ....107 F2
Barston Rd B68 ....84 B7
Bartestree Cl B98 ....154 F1
Bartholomew La B61 ......136 F5
Bartholomew Row B5 .....164 C3
Bartholomew St B5 ....164 C3
Bartic Ave DY6 ....60 F4
Bartleet Rd Redditch B98 ..159 E8
Smethwick B67 ....64 D5
Bartley Cl Coventry CV6 ..95 E2
Tipton DY4 ....41 B1
Warwick CV34 ....160 F7
Bartley Dr B31 ....102 E8
Bartley Green Tech Coll
B32 ....84 C1
Bartley Woods B32 ....84 B2
Barton Cres CV31 ....162 C6
Barton Croft B28 ....105 F6
Barton Dr B93 ....128 B4
Barton Ind Est WV14 ....40 C6
Barton La DY6 ....60 C8
Barton Lodge Rd B28 .....105 E4
Barton Rd Bedworth CV12 ..78 A4
Coventry CV6 ....95 F2
Nuneaton CV10 ....73 C1
Wolverhampton WV4 ....39 F4
Barton St B70 ....53 C2
Barton's Mdw CV2 ....114 B6
Bartons Bank B6 ....66 E7
Barwell Cl Dorridge B93 ..127 E3
Royal Leamington Spa
CV32 ....156 F3
Barwell Ct 8 B9 ....67 B2
Barwell La B37 ....67 B2
Barwell Rd B9 ....67 B2
Barwick St B3 ....164 B3
Basalt Cl WS2 ....28 A3
Basant Cl CV34 ....161 A7
Bascote Cl B97 ....153 B1
Basley Way CV6 ....95 D4
Basford Brook Dr CV6 ......95 F4
Basil Gr B31 ....102 E4
Basil Rd B31 ....102 E4
Basildon Wlk 3 CV2 ......115 A7
Basin La B77 ....35 E7
Baskerville Sch B17 ....85 A5
Baskeyfield Cl WS14 ....9 D7
Baslow Cl Birmingham B33 ..68 E4

Baslow Cl continued
Walsall WS3 ....14 C3
Baslow Rd WS3 ....14 C3
Basons La B68 ....64 D5
Bassano Rd B65 ....63 C1
Bassenthwaite Ct DY6 .....60 D6
Bassett Cl
Sutton Coldfield B76 ....46 E4
Willenhall WV12 ....27 D4
Wolverhampton WV4 ....38 D6
Bassett Croft B10 ....87 B8
Bassett Rd Coventry CV6 ..113 A6
Halesowen B63 ....82 A6
Wednesbury WS10 ....42 D3
Bassett St WS2 ....28 C2
Bassetts Gr B37 ....69 E5
Bassnage Rd B63 ....82 E2
Batchcroft Bilston WV14 ..40 D5
Darlaston WS10 ....41 D8
Batchelor Cl DY8 ....80 F8
Batchley Fst Sch B97 .....153 B4
Batchley Rd B97 ....153 C4
Bate St 3 Walsall WS2 ....28 C3
Wolverhampton WV4 ....40 A3
Bateman Dr B73 ....46 B1
Bateman Rd B46 ....59 F1
Bateman's Acre S 1
CV6 ....113 A4
Batemans La B47 ....124 E5
Bates Cl B76 ....58 B8
Bates Gr WV10 ....26 A4
Bates Hill B97 ....153 C4
Bates La B94 ....144 F1
Bates Rd CV5 ....132 E8
Bath Ave WV1 ....163 A3
Bath Ct 4 B29 ....103 B7
Bath Mdw B63 ....82 E5
Bath Mews DY8 ....80 F5
Bath Pas B5 ....164 C1
Bath Pl 3 CV31 ....162 B7
Bath Rd Brierley Hill DY5 ..62 A2
Cannock WS11 ....1 E5
Nuneaton CV11 ....73 C5
Stourbridge DY8 ....80 F5
Tipton DY4 ....52 A5
Walsall WS1 ....42 E8
Wolverhampton WV1 ......163 A3
Bath St Bilston WV14 .....40 E5
Birmingham B4 ....164 C4
Coventry CV1 ....165 C4
Dudley DY2 ....62 C8
Royal Leamington Spa
CV31 ....161 F7
Sedgley DY3 ....39 E1
Walsall WS1 ....42 E8
Willenhall WV13 ....27 B1
Wolverhampton WV1 ......163 A3
Bath Wlk Wlk Est B12 .....86 E5
Batham Rd DY10 ....117 A8
Batheaston Cl B38 ....123 D7
Bathurst Rd CV6 ....113 A6
Bathway Rd CV3 ....133 A4
Batmans Hill Rd WV14,
DY4 ....40 E1
Batsford Cl B98 ....159 B5
Batsford Rd CV6 ....112 F4
Batson Rise DY5 ....61 A8
Batstone Cl B74 ....95 A1
Battenhall Rd B17 ....85 A5
Battens Cl B98 ....153 F3
Battery Way B11 ....87 C4
Battledown Cl LE10 ......71 B2
Battlefield Hill WV5 ....49 C7
Battlefield La WV5 ....49 B6
Battlefield Terr WV5 ....49 B6
Battling Brook Com Prim Sch
LE10 ....71 B2
Battling Brook Sh Ctr
LE10 ....71 B1
Baughan Ho B24 ....57 D3
Baulk La CV7 ....110 D1
Bavaro Gdns DY5 ....62 A2
Baverstock Rd B14 ....104 E2
Baverstock Sch B14 ....104 E2
Baxter Ave DY10 ....116 F7
Baxter Cl CV4 ....112 A2
Baxter Ct 10 CV31 ....161 F7
Baxter Gdns DY10 ....116 F7
Baxter Rd DY5 ....61 C2
Baxterley Gn
Solihull B91 ....106 D4
Sutton Coldfield B76 ....46 F4
Baxters Gn B90 ....126 B8
Baxters Rd B90 ....126 B8
Bay Tree Cl
Birmingham B38 ....123 D8
Coventry CV2 ....96 D1
Bay Tree 5 WS14 ....17 C8
Bayford Ave
B31 ....122 E6
Birmingham, Sheldon B26 ..89 C4
Bayley Cres WS10 ....41 C8
Bayley Ho WS8 ....16 A6
Bayley La CV1 ....165 C2
Bayley Twr 3 B36 ....68 E8
Bayleys La B24 ....52 C8
Baylie Ct DY8 ....80 F4
Baylie St DY8 ....80 F4
Bayliss Ave Coventry CV6 ..96 A4
Wednesfield WV11 ....26 F8
Wolverhampton WV4 ....40 A3

Bayliss Cl Bilston WV14 .....40 C7
Birmingham B31 .....103 B5
Bayliss Cl WV3 .....24 E2
Baynton Rd WV12 .....27 C8
Bayston Ave WV3 .....38 E8
Bayston Rd B14 .....104 E3
Bayswater Rd
Birmingham B20 .....55 D1
Dudley DY3 .....50 D2
Bayton Rd CV7 .....96 B7
Bayton Road Ind Est CV7 .96 B8
Bayton Way CV7 .....96 C7
Baytree Cl WS3 .....14 A2
Baytree Rd WS3 .....14 A2
Baywell Cl B90 .....127 A7
Bazzard Rd CV11 .....79 F6

Beach Ave
Birmingham B12 .....87 B5
Wolverhampton WV4,WV14 .40 A2
Beach Brook Cl B11 .....87 B5
Beach Cl B31 .....103 C1
Beach Dr B63 .....83 A5
Beach Rd Bilston WV14 .....40 D7
Birmingham B11 .....87 B5
Beach St B63 .....83 A5
Beach Trad Ctr B12 .....87 B5
Beachburn Way B20 .....55 B3
Beachcroft Rd DY6 .....49 C1
Beachwood Ave DY6 .....49 C1
Beacon Cl
Birmingham, Great Barr B43 .43 F1
Birmingham, Rubery B45 .122 A6
Smethwick B66 .....65 A7
Beacon Ct
Birmingham B43 .....43 F1
Sutton Coldfield B74 .....44 F8
Beacon Ctr for the Blind
WV4 .....39 D4
Beacon Dr WS1 .....43 A8
Beacon Hill Aldridge WS9 .30 C1
Birmingham, Aston B6 .....66 E8
Birmingham, Eachway B45 .121 F5
Beacon Hts WS9 .....44 B6
Beacon La
Marlbrook B60,B45 .....121 E4
Sedgley DY3 .....39 E1
Beacon Mews ◼ B43 .....43 F1
Beacon Pas Sedgley DY3 .39 D1
Sedgley DY3 .....50 D8
Beacon Prim Schs WV12 .27 D8
Beacon Rd Aldridge WS9 .30 B1
Birmingham, Kingstanding
B44 .....45 A3
Birmingham, Pheasey WS9,
B43 .....44 C6
Coventry CV6 .....95 D3
Sutton Coldfield B73 .....46 A1
Walsall WS5 .....43 D5
Willenhall WV12 .....27 C8
Beacon Rise Aldridge WS9 .30 B3
Sedgley DY3 .....39 E1
Stourbridge DY9 .....81 D4
Beacon St Lichfield WS13 .....1 A1
Walsall WS1 .....29 A1
Wolverhampton WV14 .....39 F1
Beacon Trad Est WS9 .....30 A6
Beacon View
Birmingham B45 .....122 A6
Walsall WS2 .....27 F3
Beacon View Dr B74 .....44 F5
Beacon View Rd B71 .....42 F2
Beacon Way
Brownhills WS9 .....16 A3
Cannock WS12 .....2 F3
Beaconfields WS3 .....9 A8
Beaconsfield Ave WV4 .....39 D5
Beaconsfield Cres ◼
B12 .....86 E5
Beaconsfield Ct
Nuneaton CV11 .....73 D5
Walsall WS1 .....43 A8
Beaconsfield Dr WV4 .....39 D6
Beaconsfield Rd
Birmingham B12 .....86 E5
Coventry CV2 .....114 A2
Sutton Coldfield B74 .....46 B7
Beaconsfield St
Royal Leamington Spa
CV31 .....162 B7
West Bromwich B71 .....53 C5
Beaconsfield St W CV31 .162 B8
Beaconside Prim Sch
B45 .....121 E6
Beaconview Ho ◼ B71 .....42 F1
Beak St B1 .....164 B2
Beake Ave CV6 .....113 B7
Beakes Rd B67 .....64 F3
Beaks Farm Gdns B16 .....65 D2
Beaks Hill Rd B38 .....103 E2
Beale Cl B35 .....58 A2
Beale Ho B16 .....65 F1
Beale St DY8 .....80 C5
Beales St B6 .....67 B8
Bealeys Ave WV11 .....26 C8
Bealeys Cl WS3 .....14 A3
Bealeys Ct WV11 .....26 C8
Bealeys La WS3 .....14 A2
Beamans Cl B92 .....89 A4
Beaminster Rd B91 .....107 A4
Beamish Cl CV2 .....115 A6
Bean Croft B32 .....84 C2
Bean Rd
Dudley, Dixon's Green DY2 .62 D8
Dudley, Swan Village DY4 .51 C6

Bean Road Ind Est DY4 .....51 C6
Beanfield Ave CV3 .....132 F4
Bear Hill B48 .....139 B5
Beardmore Rd B72 .....57 C8
Bearhill Dr B48 .....139 B6
Bearley Croft B90 .....126 C8
Bearmore Rd B64 .....62 E1
Bearnett Dr WV4 .....38 C2
Bearnett La WV4 .....38 B2
Bearsden Cres LE10 .....71 B2
Bearwood Ho B66 .....65 A4
Bearwood Prim Sch B66 .65 A2
Bearwood Rd B66 .....65 A3
Bearwood Sh Ctr B66 .....65 A1
Beasley Gr B43 .....44 B1
Beaton Cl WV13 .....26 E2
Beaton Rd B74 .....32 A3
Beatrice St WS3 .....28 C6
Beatrice Wlk B69 .....52 A2
Beattie Cl LE10 .....71 D3
Beatty Ho DY4 .....52 B8
Beau Ct WS11 .....1 E4
Beaubrook Gdns DY6 .....60 E3
Beauchamp Ave
Birmingham B20 .....54 F5
Kidderminster DY11 .....116 D3
Royal Leamington Spa
CV32 .....156 F1
Beauchamp Cl
◼ Birmingham B37 .....70 B2
Sutton Coldfield B76 .....58 B7
Beauchamp Ct
Kidderminster DY11 .....116 D3
Royal Leamington Spa
CV32 .....156 F1
Beauchamp Gdns CV34 .161 B6
Beauchamp Hill CV32 .156 E1
Beauchamp Ind Pk B77 .35 D8
Beauchamp Rd
Birmingham B13 .....105 C5
Kenilworth CV8 .....147 F2
Royal Leamington Spa
CV32 .....156 F1
Solihull B91 .....107 B5
Tamworth B77 .....35 F5
Warwick CV34 .....161 B8
Beaudesert Cl B47 .125 A6
Beaudesert Rd
Birmingham B20 .....66 B8
Coventry CV5 .....113 A1
Hollywood B47 .....125 A6
Beaufell Cl CV34 .....155 E1
Beaufort Ave
Birmingham B34 .....68 D5
Kidderminster DY11 .....116 A7
Royal Leamington Spa
CV32 .....157 C5
Beaufort Cl LE10 .....75 E4
Beaufort Dr CV3 .....134 F7
Beaufort Rd
Birmingham, Gravelly Hill
B23 .....56 E2
Birmingham, Ladywood B16 .66 A1
Beaufort Sch B34 .....68 D5
Beaufort Way WS9 .....30 B4
Beaulieu Ave DY6 .....60 F4
Beaulieu Cl DY11 .....116 D8
Beaulieu Pk CV31 .....162 D6
Beaumaris Cl
Coventry CV5 .....111 F5
Dudley DY1 .....50 F4
Beaumaris Ho B31 .....102 D6
Beaumont Ave LE10 .....75 A7
Beaumont Cl
Great Wyrley WS6 .....4 F2
Tipton DY4 .....51 E6
Beaumont Cres CV6 .....113 A4
Beaumont Ct
◼ Coventry CV6 .....113 A4
◼ Royal Leamington Spa
CV31 .....162 A6
Beaumont Dr
Birmingham B17 .....85 B4
Brierley Hill DY5 .....81 B7
Beaumont Gdns B18 .....65 F6
Beaumont Gr B91 .....106 F5
Beaumont Lawns B60 .121 D2
Beaumont Pl CV11 .....73 A4
Beaumont Rd
Birmingham B30 .....103 F6
Great Wyrley WS6 .....4 F2
Halesowen B62 .....83 E8
Keresley CV7 .....95 A6
Nuneaton CV11 .....73 A4
Wednesbury WS10 .....41 F1
Beaumont Way WS11 .....6 A4
Beausale Croft CV5 .....112 A3
Beausale Dr B93 .....128 C7
Beauty Bank B64 .....63 A8
Beauty Bank Cres DY8 .....80 F6
Beauty Bank Prim Sch
DY8 .....80 F6
Beaver Cl WV11 .....26 F5
Beaver Pk B63 .....82 F6
Bebington Cl WV8 .....24 F8
Beccles Dr WV13 .....40 F8
Beck Cl B66 .....65 A4
Beckbury Ave WV4 .....38 C5
Beckbury Rd
Birmingham B29 .....85 A1
Coventry CV2 .....114 F6
Beckenham Ave B44 .....45 B1
Beckensall Cl DY1 .....51 B1
Becket Cl B74 .....31 F6
Beckett St WV14 .....40 F6
Beckfield Cl
Birmingham B14 .....104 E2

Beckfield Cl continued
Walsall WS4 .....29 C8
Beckfoot Dr CV2 .....96 F1
Beckford Croft B93 .....127 F3
Beckford Ct B23 .....56 C2
Beckman Rd DY9 .....81 C2
Beckminster Rd 38 F7
Becks La CV7 .....93 A5
Becks The B48 .....139 A7
Beconsfield Cl B93 .....127 F2
Becton Gr B42 .....55 D7
Bedale Ave LE10 .....71 F2
Bedcote Pl DY8 .....81 B5
Beddoe Cl DY4 .....52 D5
Beddow Ave WV14 .....51 C7
Beddows Rd WS3 .....28 E5
Bede Arc CV12 .....78 B3
Bede Rd Bedworth CV12 .78 A4
Coventry CV6 .....113 B6
Nuneaton CV10 .....72 D3
Bedesfield Wlk B61 .....121 B1
Bedford Cl LE10 .....71 E3
Bedford Dr B75 .....46 E6
Bedford Ho
◼ Birmingham, Erdington
B24 .....56 F4
Birmingham, Kingshurst
B37 .....70 B1
◼ Birmingham WV3 .....25 C4
Bedford Pl Cannock WS12 .....2 B4
◼ Royal Leamington Spa
CV32 .....161 F8
Bedford Rd
Birmingham B12 .....87 A8
Sutton Coldfield B75 .....46 E7
West Bromwich B71 .....53 B7
Bedford St Coventry CV1 .113 A2
Royal Leamington Spa
CV32 .....161 F8
Tipton DY4 .....52 B5
Wolverhampton WV1 .....26 B8
Bedlam Cl F6 .....95 E2
Bedlam Wood Rd B31 .102 C1
Bedworth Cl CV12 .....79 B2
Bedworth Croft DY4 .....52 B4
Bedworth Gr B9 .....68 A3
Bedworth La CV12 .....77 D4
Bedworth Rd
Bedworth CV12 .....78 F2
Bulkington CV12 .....79 A2
Coventry CV6,CV7 .....96 A5
Bedworth Sta CV12 .....78 C2
Bee La WV10 .....11 D3
Beebee Rd WS10 .....41 F5
Beech Ave
Birmingham, Chelmsley Wood
B37 .....70 B1
Birmingham, Quinton B32 .84 D7
◼ Birmingham, Showell Green
B12 .....86 F5
Halesowen B62 .....83 C8
Tamworth B77 .....21 E3
Beech Cl Nuneaton CV10 .72 A8
Rowington Green CV35 .145 A1
Sedgley DY3 .....39 E1
Sutton Coldfield B75 .....32 A4
Tamworth B79 .....21 A8
Wolverhampton WV10 .....25 B8
Beech Cliffe CV34 .....160 F8
Beech Cres Burntwood WS7 .6 F6
Tipton DY4 .....52 C8
Wednesbury WS10 .....41 F5
Beech Ct
Birmingham, Bournville
B30 .....103 E4
Birmingham, Great Barr
B43 .....43 D1
Cannock WS12 .....2 B7
Great Wyrley WS6 .....5 A4
Oldbury B66 .....64 C8
Royal Leamington Spa
CV34 .....161 E2
Beech Dene Gr B23 .....56 E5
Beech Dr CV8 .....148 B5
Beech Farm Croft B31 .103 A3
Beech Gate B74 .....31 C5
Beech Gdns WS14 .....9 C6
Beech Gn DY1 .....51 A5
Beech Gr
Birmingham B14 .....105 A5
Huntington WS12 .....1 D8
Warwick CV34 .....156 B1
Beech Hill Ct B72 .....57 C8
Beech Hill Ho B32 .....102 C8
Beech Hill Rd B72 .....57 C8
Beech Ho Solihull B91 .....106 F2
Sutton Coldfield B74 .....31 B5
Beech Hurst ◼ B38 .123 E8
Beech Hurst Gdns WV5 .37 A2
Beech Mews B64 .....62 E2
Beech Park Dr B45 .....138 C8
Beech Pinc CV12 .....2 A8
Beech Rd
Birmingham, Bournville
B30 .....103 E6
Birmingham, Erdington B23 .56 F8
Bromsgrove B61 .....136 F4
Coventry CV6 .....113 B5
Dudley DY1 .....51 C4
Hollywood B47 .....125 B6
Kingswinford DY6 .....60 E5
Stourbridge DY8 .....80 F3
Tamworth B79 .....21 A8
Tipton B69 .....63 A8
Wednesbury WS10 .....41 F5
Willenhall WV13 .....26 E2
Wolverhampton WV10 .....25 B8

Beech Tree Ave
Coventry CV4 .....112 B2
Wolverhampton WV11 .....26 C8
Beech Tree Cl
Kingswinford DY6 .....60 E8
Redditch B97 .....153 B4
Beech Tree La WV13 .....4 D8
Beech Way B66 .....65 B5
Beech Wlk B38 .....123 E8
Beecham Cl WS9 .....30 A8
Beechcroft Bedworth CV12 .77 F1
Birmingham B15 .....86 A7
Oldbury B68 .....64 C2
Birmingham B45 .....122 C8
Beechcroft Cres B74 .....30 D1
Beechcroft Ct B74 .....32 A1
Beechcroft Dr B61 .....137 B4
Beechcroft Est B63 .....82 C6
Beechcroft Pl WV10 .....25 C6
Beechcroft Rd
Birmingham B36 .....69 B8
Blackheath B64 .....62 F1
Kidderminster DY11 .....116 A8
Beechdale B68 .....84 B7
Beechdale Ave B44 .....44 E2
Beechdale Prim Sch
WS2 .....28 C5
Beechdale Rd WS3 .....27 F8
Beechen Gr WS7 .....6 F8
Beecher Pl B63 .....82 D5
Beecher Rd B63 .....82 D5
Beecher Rd E B63 .....82 D5
Beecher St B63 .....82 D5
Beecher's Keep CV8 .....135 F5
Beeches Ave B27 .....88 C4
Beeches Cl
Birmingham B45 .....121 D8
Kingswinford DY6 .....60 D5
Beeches Ct B45 .....122 B7
Beeches Dr B24 .....57 C5
Beeches Farm Dr B31 .123 A7
Beeches Inf Sch B70 .....53 D3
Beeches Inf Sch The .....
B45 .....102 B2
Beeches Mews DY9 .....98 F4
Beeches Pl WS3 .....28 D6
Beeches Rd
Birmingham B42 .....55 C7
Blackheath B65 .....63 C1
Kidderminster DY11 .....116 C8
Oldbury B68 .....64 C3
Walsall WS3 .....28 D6
West Bromwich B70 .....53 E2
Beeches The
Bedworth CV12 .....77 E2
Birmingham B15 .....86 C8
Sutton Coldfield, Little Aston
B74 .....31 D4
Sutton Coldfield, Wylde Green
B73 .....46 B1
Upton Warren B61 .....150 A4
West Bromwich B70 .....53 E2
Wolverhampton, New Cross
WV11 .....26 B5
Wolverhampton, Newbridge
WV3 .....25 A3
Beeches View Ave B63 .82 C4
Beeches Way B31 .....123 A7
Beeches Wlk B73 .....46 B3
Beechey Cl B43 .....44 D5
Beechfield Ave ◼ B11 .....87 B6
Beechfield Cl B62 .....83 C8
Beechfield Dr DY11 .....116 C8
Beechfield Gr WV14 .....51 B7
Beechfield Rd
Birmingham B11 .....87 B6
Smethwick B67 .....64 F4
Beechfield Rise WS14 .....9 D8
Beechglade B20 .....54 F4
Beechhouse La WV5 .....37 A1
Beechmore Rd B26 .....89 A5
Beechmount Dr B23 .....57 A6
Beechnut Cl
Coventry CV4 .....111 D2
Solihull B91 .....107 D5
Beechnut La B91 .....107 E4
Beechtree Rd WS9 .....15 F3
Beechwood B20 .....54 E3
Beechwood Ave
Coventry CV5 .....132 F8
Hinckley LE10 .....75 D3
Wolverhampton WV11 .....26 C8
Beechwood Bsns Pk WS11 .2 B3
Beechwood Cl
Birmingham B90 .....126 D4
Walsall WS3 .....14 B3
Beechwood Cres B77 .....21 C5
Beechwood Croft
Kenilworth CV8 .....147 F2
Little Aston B74 .....31 C5
Beechwood Ct
◼ Birmingham B30 .....104 C3
Blackheath B64 .....62 E1
Coventry CV5 .....132 F8
Wolverhampton WV6 .....24 C3
Beechwood Dr WV6 .....24 A2
Beechwood Park Rd
B91 .....106 E5
Beechwood Rd
Bedworth CV12 .....78 B4
Birmingham, Great Barr B43 .43 F2
Birmingham, King's Heath
B14 .....104 F5
Dudley DY2 .....51 E1
Nuneaton CV10 .....72 D6
Smethwick B67 .....64 F8
West Bromwich B70 .....53 A3
Beecroft Ave WS13 .....3 B1

Beecroft Ct WS11 .....1 E2
Beecroft Hill Sch WS11 .....1 E2
Beecroft Rd WS11 .....1 E1
Beehive Cl B61 .....121 A1
Beehive Hill CV8 .....147 E7
Beehive La B76 .....59 C6
Beehive Wlk ◼ DY4 .....51 E5
Beeston Cl Birmingham B6 .67 A2
Brierley Hill DY5 .....81 D8
Coventry CV3 .....134 F8
Beet St B65 .....63 C1
Beeton Rd B18 .....65 E6
Beever Rd DY4 .....52 D7
Beggars Bush B73 .....45 D2
Beggars Bush La WV5 .....49 B5
Begonia Cl LE10 .....75 E5
Begonia Dr LE10 .....75 E5
Beighton Cl B74 .....31 F6
Beilby Rd B30 .....104 B5
Belbroughton CE Fst Sch
DY9 .....119 E6
Belbroughton Cl B98 .153 F2
Belbroughton Rd
Blakedown DY10 .....98 D1
Clent DY9 .....99 E2
Halesowen B63 .....82 E3
Stourbridge DY8 .....80 E3
Belchers La B88,B9 .....68 A3
Beldray Rd WV14 .....40 E6
Belfont Trad Est B62 .....83 C4
Belfry Cl Hinckley LE10 .....75 D4
Walsall WS3 .....14 A3
Belfry Dr DY8 .....80 E6
Belfry The WV6 .....23 D4
Belgrade Rd WV10 .....11 B1
Belgrave Ct DY6 .....60 F4
Belgrave High Sch B77 .....21 E1
Belgrave Middleway B5,
B12 .....86 E2
Belgrave Rd
Birmingham B12 .....86 F6
Coventry CV2 .....114 E4
Halesowen B62 .....83 D8
Tamworth B77 .....35 E8
Belgrave Sq CV2 .....114 E4
Belgrave Terr B21 .....66 A7
Belgrave Wlk WS2 .....28 B3
Belgravia Cl B5 .....86 E7
Belgravia Cl B37 .....70 A5
Belgrave Cl B15 .....85 E6
Belgrove Ho WS11 .....1 D1
Belinda Cl WV13 .....26 F3
Bell Barn Rd B15 .....86 C6
Bell Barn Sh Ctr ◼ B15 .86 C8
Bell Cl
Birmingham, Bordesley Green
B9 .....67 E3
Birmingham, Kingshurst
B36 .....70 B6
Darlaston WS10 .....41 D7
Bell Ct CV32 .....156 F2
Bell Dr Birmingham B9 .....67 F3
Cannock WS12 .....2 C7
Coventry CV7 .....95 E7
Walsall WS5 .....43 A5
Bell End B65 .....63 C3
Bell Fold B68 .....64 C6
Bell Green La B38 .....124 B5
Bell Green Rd CV6 .....114 A8
Bell Heath Way B32 .....84 B2
Bell Heather Rd WS8 .....15 C6
Bell Hill B31 .....103 A5
Bell Holloway B31 .....102 F5
Bell La
Birmingham, Kitt's Green
B33 .....69 C1
Birmingham, Northfield
B31 .....103 A4
Studley B80 .....159 E4
Walsall, Wallington Heath
WS3 .....14 B1
Walsall, Yew Tree WS5 .....43 A5
Bell Mdw DY9 .....99 B8
Bell Mead B80 .....159 E4
Bell Meadow Way B14 .104 E1
Bell Pl WV2 .....163 B1
Bell Rd Dudley DY2 .....62 C5
Trysull WV5 .....37 D1
Walsall WS5 .....43 D6
Bell Sh Ctr The B31 .....103 A4
Bell St Bilston WV14 .....40 C6
Bell Tower Mews CV32 .156 F3
Bell Vue Rd B65 .....63 D3
Bellairs Ave CV12 .....77 E1
Bellamy Cl B90 .....106 D1
Bellamy Farm Rd B90 .106 D1
Bellamy La WV11 .....26 C7
Bellbrooke Ct CV6 .....96 B1
Belle Cotts B94 .....143 D5
Belle Isle DY5 .....61 C3
Belle Orch DY11 .....116 B5
Belle Vue B65 .....82 E5
Belle Vue Ave B16 .....65 D4
Belle Vue Dr B62 .....83 E6

Belle Vue Gdns B65 ....63 C3
Belle Vue Prim Sch DY8 ...60 C3
Belle Vue Terr B97 ....62 A1
Belle Wlk B37 ....87 B3
Bellefield Ave **10** B18 ...65 E4
Bellefield Rd B18 ....65 E4
Bellemere Rd B92 ....109 B6
Bellencroft Gdns WV3 ......38 C7
Bellevue Birmingham B5 ....86 D7
  Dudley WV14 ....40 E2
Bellevue Rd Bilston WV14 ..41 A2
  Birmingham B26 ....89 B7
Bellevue St WV14 ....39 F2
Bellfield Birmingham B31 ..102 F4
  Tamworth-In-A B94 ....142 A2
Bellfield Ho B14 ....104 D1
Bellfield Jun & Inf Sch
  B31 ....102 F4
Bellflower Cl WV10 ....12 A7
Bellingham B77 ....22 D1
Bellington Croft **5** B90 ..127 A6
Bellis St B16 ....65 E2
Bellman Cl WS10 ....41 D7
Bells Farm Cl B14 ....104 C2
Bells Farm Inf & Jun Sch
  B14 ....104 C2
Bells La Birmingham B14 ...104 D2
  Stourbridge DY8 ....60 D2
Bells Moor Rd B70 ....53 A6
Bellsize Cl WS11 ....5 F5
Bellview Way CV6 ....96 B1
Bellwood Rd B31 ....102 F4
Belmont Ave WS11 ....1 C2
Belmont Cl Aldridge WS9 ...30 A7
  Great Wyrley WS11 ....5 A4
  Redditch B97 ....153 B1
  Tipton DY4 ....51 F6
Belmont Covert B31 ....103 B6
Belmont Ct
  Royal Leamington Spa
  CV32 ....157 A4
  Sutton Coldfield B27 ......46 B4
Belmont Dr CV32 ....157 A4
Belmont Gdns WV14 ....41 A4
Belmont Mews CV8 ....147 F4
Belmont Pas B4 ....67 A3
Belmont Rd
  Birmingham, Handsworth
  B21 ....65 C8
  Birmingham, Rubery B45 ..122 A6
  Brierley Hill DY5 ....61 D6
  Coventry CV6 ....114 A7
  Smethwick B66 ....65 A2
  Stourbridge DY9 ....81 F4
  Tamworth B77 ....35 E7
  Wolverhampton WV4 ....39 A5
Belmont Rd E B21 ....65 C8
Belmont Row B4 ....67 A3
Belmont St WV14 ....41 A4
Belper B77 ....51 B1
Belper Ind Est B70 ....52 F4
Belper Rd Walsall WS3 .....14 C3
  West Bromwich B70 ....52 F4
Belper Row DY2 ....62 E4
Belsize B77 ....21 E2
Belstone Cl B14 ....104 D6
Belt Rd WS11,WS12 ....2 A5
Belton Ave WV11 ....12 B1
Belton Cl B94 ....143 C5
Belton Gr B45 ....122 C8
Belvedere Ave WV4 ....39 B5
Belvedere Cl
  Burntwood WS7 ....6 F5
  Kidderminster DY10 ....117 A5
  Kingswinford DY6 ....60 F4
  Tamworth B79 ....21 C7
Belvedere Dr B61 ....137 A4
Belvedere Gdns WV6 ....24 E7
Belvedere Rd
  Birmingham B24 ....57 B2
  Coventry CV5 ....133 A8
Belvide Gr B29 ....103 B8
Belvidere Gdns B11 ....87 B5
Belvidere Rd WS1 ....42 F8
Belvoir B77 ....35 C7
Belvoir Cl DY1 ....50 E2
Belvoir Rd B60 ....137 C1
Belwell Dr B74 ....32 A2
Belwell La B74 ....32 A2
Bembridge Cl WV12 ....27 B8
Bembridge Rd B33 ....69 A3
Ben Nevis Way DY8 ....81 A6
Ben Willetts Wlk **3** B65 ..63 C1
Benacre Dr B5 ....66 F2
Benbeck Gr CV4 ....51 C6
Benbow Cl LE10 ....71 D4
Benches Cl WS7 ....6 D6
Bencroft WV8 ....10 B4
Bendall Rd B44 ....45 B2
Benedict Sq CV2 ....114 C8
Benedictine Rd CV3 ....133 C8
Benedon Rd B26 ....89 B7
Bengrove Cl B98 ....159 A7
Benion Rd WS11 ....1 F5
Benmore Ave B5 ....86 D6
Benn Rd CV12 ....79 B2
Bennett Ave DY1 ....51 B6
Bennett Cl CV8 ....135 F3
Bennett Dr CV34 ....161 C7
Bennett Rd B74 ....31 D3
Bennett St
  Birmingham B19 ....66 D8
2 Kidderminster DY11 ..116 C6
Bennett's Fold WV3 ....163 B2
Bennett's Hill
  Birmingham B2 ....164 B2
  Dudley DY2 ....62 E8

Bennett's Rd CV7 ....94 F4
Bennett's Rd S CV6 ....94 F2
Bennetts Rd B8 ....67 D6
Bennetts Well Jun & Inf Sch
  B37 ....69 F3
Bennick Trad Est WS11 .....4 E6
Bennitt Cl B70 ....53 C1
Benson Ave WV4 ....39 D5
Benson Cl Lichfield WS13 ...3 D1
  Perton WV6 ....23 E5
Benson Com Sch B18 ....65 F6
Benson Ind Est B18 ....65 F6
Benson Rd
  Birmingham, Highter's Heath
  B14 ....105 B1
  Birmingham, Hockley B18 ..65 F6
  Coventry CV6 ....95 A1
Benson View B79 ....21 C8
Bent Ave B32 ....84 D6
Bent St DY5 ....61 D4
Benthall Rd CV6 ....95 F2
Bentham Ct B31 ....102 F5
Bentley Br L Pk WV11 ......26 B4
Bentley Cl Redditch B97 ...153 D3
  Royal Leamington Spa
  CV32 ....157 B3
Bentley Ct Coventry CV6 ...95 C4
  Nuneaton CV11 ....73 A4
  Sutton Coldfield B76 ......57 F8
Bentley Dr WV12 ....36 B7
Bentley Drive JMI Sch
  WS2 ....28 B2
Bentley Farm Cl B93 ......127 E4
Bentley Gr B29 ....102 F8
Bentley Heath CE Prim Sch
  B93 ....127 E5
Bentley Heath Cotts
  B93 ....127 F5
Bentley La
  Walsall, Birchills WS2 ....28 B3
  Walsall, Leamore WS2 .....28 A5
  Willenhall WV12 ....27 C5
Bentley Lane Bsns Pk
  WS2 ....28 B3
Bentley Mill Cl WS2 ....27 F1
Bentley Mill La WS2 ....27 F1
Bentley Mill Way WS2 ......28 B3
Bentley New Dr WS2 ....28 B3
Bentley Pl WS2 ....28 B2
Bentley Rd Bedworth CV7 ...78 A1
  Birmingham B36 ....69 C8
  Nuneaton CV11 ....73 A4
  Wolverhampton WV10 ....11 E2
Bentley Rd N WS2 ....27 E1
Bentley Rd S
  Darlaston WS10 ....41 E8
  Walsall WS10 ....27 E1
Bentley Way WV8 ....20 F7
Bentley West Prim Sch
  WS2 ....27 E3
Bentley 1B4 B4
Bentmead Gr B38 ....104 A1
Benton Ave B11 ....87 C6
Benton Cl WV12 ....27 D3
Benton Cres WS3 ....14 D2
Benton Green La CV7 .....110 F2
Benton Rd B11 ....87 C6
Benton's Ct DY11 ....116 C6
Benton's La WS6 ....5 A1
Bentons Mill Croft B7 .....67 C8
Bentree The CV3 ....134 B8
Benyon Ctr The WS2 ....28 A7
Beoley Cl B72 ....46 C1
Beoley Fst Sch B98 ....154 F5
Beoley Gr B45 ....122 A7
Beoley La Beoley B98 .....154 F8
Beoley Rd E B98 ....154 A4
Beoley Rd W B98 ....153 F4
Berberry Cl B30 ....103 D6
Berenska Dr CV32 ....157 A2
Beresford Ave CV6 ....95 E1
Beresford Cres B70 ....53 B3
Beresford Dr B73 ....46 A1
Beresford Rd Oldbury B69 .63 E6
  Walsall WS3 ....28 E8
Berets The B45 ....46 F6
Bericote Croft B27 ....88 D3
Bericote Rd CV32 ....156 E8
Berkeley Cl
  Nuneaton CV11 ....73 B3
  Perton WV6 ....23 F3
  Walsall WS2 ....27 F3
Berkeley Dr DY6 ....60 C7
Berkeley Ho
  Birmingham B23 ....56 F6
  Sutton Coldfield B76 ......57 F8
Berkeley Mews B25 ....88 B7
Berkeley Prec B14 ....104 F2
Berkeley Rd
  Birmingham B25 ....88 B7
  Kenilworth CV8 ....147 E6
  Solihull B90 ....105 F3
Berkeley Rd E B25 ....88 C7
Berkeley Rd N CV5 ....113 A1
Berkeley Rd S CV5 ....133 A8
Berkeley St WS2 ....42 C7
Berkeswell Cl B98 ....154 C7
Berkett Rd CV6 ....95 B2
Berkley Cl B60 ....151 B8
Berkley Cres B13 ....87 C1
Berkley Ct B1 ....66 C1
Berkley St B1 ....66 C1
Bett Rd B20 ....54 F3
Bettany Glade WV10 ....11 E4

Berkshire Cl
  Nuneaton CV10 ....72 E3
  West Bromwich B71 ....53 B7
Berkshire The WS3 ....14 A3
Berkswell CE Prim Sch
  CV7 ....110 C3
Berkswell Dudley DY1 ......50 E3
  Solihull B90 ....107 B8
  Sutton Coldfield B74 .....31 E4
Berkswell Hall CV7 ....110 C3
Berkswell Rd
  Birmingham B24 ....57 B4
  Coventry CV6 ....96 B2
  Meriden CV7 ....110 C7
Berkswell Sta CV7 ....110 D8
Berkswell Windmill*
  ....130 D4
Bermuda Bsns Pk CV10 ....78 A7
Bermuda Cl DY1 ....51 B6
Bermuda Ind Est CV10 .....78 B8
Bermuda Rd CV10 ....73 A1
Bernard Pl B18 ....65 F5
Bernard Rd
  Birmingham B17 ....65 B2
  Oldbury B68 ....64 C2
  Tipton DY4 ....52 B7
Bernard St Walsall WS1 ....29 A1
  West Bromwich B71 ....53 C4
Berners Cl CV4 ....111 E2
Berners St B19 ....66 D7
Bernhard Dr B21 ....65 E8
Bernie Crossland Wlk
  DY10 ....116 F3
Bernwall Cl DY1 ....80 F4
Berrandale Rd B36 ....57 F1
Berrington Dr WV14 ....54 D2
Berrington Gr WV14 ....51 B8
Berrington Wlk B5 ....86 E7
Berrow Cottage Homes
  B93 ....128 C6
Berrow Dr B15 ....85 F7
Berrow View B61 ....150 D7
Berrowside Rd B34 ....69 E6
Berry Ave WS10 ....41 B5
Berry Cl B19 ....66 D6
Berry Cres WS5 ....43 D4
Berry Dr Aldridge WS9 .....29 E5
  Barnt Green B45 ....122 A1
  Smethwick B66 ....65 A6
Berry Hall La B91 ....108 B4
Berry Hill WS12 ....2 C4
Berry Rd Birmingham B8 ....67 D5
  Dudley DY1 ....51 C5
Berry St Birmingham B18 ..65 F6
  Coventry CV1 ....113 E4
  Wolverhampton WV1 ....163 C3
Berryfield Rd B26 ....89 D6
Berryfields Aldridge WS9 ..29 E5
  Stonnall WS9 ....16 E5
Berryfields Rd B76 ....46 F3
Berrymound View B47 ......125 B7
Bertha Rd B11 ....87 D5
Bertie Rd CV8 ....148 A4
Bertie Terr CV32 ....156 E1
Bertram Cl DY4 ....41 C1
Bertram Rd
  1 Birmingham B10 .....67 D1
  Smethwick B67 ....65 A7
Berwick Cl Coventry CV5 ..112 B4
  Warwick CV34 ....155 E2
Berwick Gr
  Birmingham, Frankley B31 .102 D3
  Birmingham, Pheasey B43 ..44 B4
Berwicks La B37 ....70 B1
Berwood Farm Rd B72 ......57 C6
Berwood Gdns B24 ....57 C6
Berwood Gr B92 ....89 B1
Berwood La B24 ....57 E3
Berwood Pk B35 ....58 A2
Berwood Rd B72 ....57 D6
Berwyn Ave CV6 ....95 A1
Berwyn Gr WS6 ....4 F3
Berwyn Way CV10 ....72 C4
Beryl Ave LE10 ....71 A2
Besant Gr B27 ....88 A1
Besbury Cl B93 ....127 E2
Bescot Cres WS1 ....42 D5
Bescot Croft B42 ....55 B6
Bescot Dr WS2 ....42 B6
Bescot Ind Est The WS10 ..41 D4
Bescot Rd WS2 ....42 B6
Bescot St WS1 ....42 E6
Bescot Stadium Sta WS1 ..42 D5
Besford Gr
  Birmingham B31 ....102 D3
  Solihull B90 ....127 B6
Besom Way WS6 ....4 D2
Bessborough Rd B25 ....88 D8
Best Ave CV8 ....148 C7
Best Rd WV14 ....40 D7
Best St B64 ....62 F2
Beswick Gr B33 ....69 A4
Beta Gr B14 ....105 C4
Bethany Mews WS11 ....1 F4
Betjeman Cr DY10 ....117 B5
Betjeman Pl WV10 ....12 A1
Betley Gr B33 ....69 A5
Betony Cl WS5 ....43 A3
Betsham Cl B44 ....44 C5
Bett Rd B20 ....54 F3

Betteridge Dr B76 ....46 E4
Bettina Cl CV10 ....72 E5
Bettman Cl CV3 ....133 E6
Betton Rd B14 ....104 E5
Betty's La WS11 ....6 A4
Bevan Ave WV4 ....39 E4
Bevan Cl Bilston WV14 .....40 F6
  Walsall WS4 ....15 C1
Bevan Lee Rd WS11 ....1 D3
Bevan Rd Brierley Hill DY5 .61 A2
  Tipton DY4 ....52 B4
Bevan Way B66 ....64 F7
Beverley Ave CV10 ....72 B4
Beverley Cl
  Astwood Bank B96 ....158 E2
  Balsall Common CV7 ......130 C7
  Sutton Coldfield B72 ......57 D7
Beverley Court Rd B32 ....84 C6
Beverley Cres WV4 ....39 F4
Beverley Croft B23 ....56 C2
Beverley Ct **1** B62 ......84 A6
Beverley Dr DY6 ....60 C7
Beverley Gr B26 ....89 B5
Beverley Hill WS12 ....2 D6
Beverley Rd
  Birmingham B45 ....122 A7
  Royal Leamington Spa
  CV32 ....156 D1
  West Bromwich B71 ....53 C8
Beverly Dr CV4 ....132 D2
Beverston Rd Perton WV6 .24 A4
  Tipton DY4 ....41 B2
Bevin Rd WS2 ....27 E3
Bevington Cres CV6 ....112 E5
Bevington Rd B6 ....66 F8
Bewdley Ave B12 ....87 A6
Bewdley Dr WV1 ....26 B2
Bewdley Gr B20 ....55 B4
Bewdley Ho B26 ....69 A1
Bewdley Rd
  Birmingham B30 ....104 B8
  Kidderminster DY11 ......116 C6
Bewdley Villas **3** B18 ..65 D4
Bewell Ct B61 ....136 F4
Bewell Head B61 ....136 F4
Bewley Rd WV12 ....27 D4
Bewlys Ave B20 ....54 E4
Bexfield Cl CV5 ....112 A6
Bexhill Gr **3** B15 ......66 C1
Bexley Gr B71 ....53 E7
Bexley Rd B44 ....56 B8
Bexmore Dr WS13 ....3 F1
Beyer Cl B77 ....22 A2
Bhylls Acre Prim Sch
  ....38 B7
Bhylls Cres WV3 ....38 C7
Bhylls La WV3 ....38 C7
Bibbey's Gr WV10 ....11 F4
Bibsworth Ave B13 ....105 D8
Bibury Rd B28 ....105 E7
Bicester Sq B35 ....58 B4
Bickenhill Green Ct B92 ...90 D1
Bickenhill La
  Birmingham B37 ....90 C6
  Birmingham B40 ....90 D4
  Catherine de B B92 ....108 C6
Bickenhill Park Rd B92 ....88 E1
Bickenhill Parkway B37 ....90 D6
Bickenhill Rd B37 ....90 B7
Bickford Rd
  Birmingham B6 ....56 A1
  Wolverhampton WV10 ....25 F5
Bickington Rd B32 ....84 D1
Bickley Ave
  Birmingham B11 ....87 C6
  Sutton Coldfield B74 ......31 E5
Bickley Gr B26 ....89 B5
Bickley Ho B74 ....31 E5
Bickley Rd Bilston WV14 ...41 A7
  Walsall WS4 ....29 C7
Bicknell Croft B14 ....104 E2
Bickton Cl B24 ....57 C5
Biddings La WV14 ....40 B2
Biddles Hill B94 ....141 C6
Biddlestone Gr WS5 ....43 C3
Biddlestone Pl WS10 ......41 B7
Bideford Dr B29 ....85 A2
Bideford Rd
  Coventry CV2 ....114 C7
  Smethwick B66 ....65 B5
Bidford Cl B90 ....106 D2
Bidford Rd B31 ....102 E3
Bierton Rd B25 ....88 C8
Bigbury Cl CV3 ....133 B8
Biggin Cl Birmingham B35 ..58 A3
  Perton WV6 ....23 E5
Biggin Hall Cres B9 ......114 B2
Bigwood Dr
  Birmingham B32 ....84 D1
  Sutton Coldfield B75 ......47 A5
Bilberry Bank WS11 ....1 E6
Bilberry Cres
  Huntington WS12 ....1 C6
  Sutton Coldfield B76 ......46 F3
Bilberry Dr B45 ....122 A6
Bilberry Rd
  Birmingham B14 ....104 C6
  Coventry CV2 ....96 D2
Bilboe Rd WV14 ....41 A3
Bilbrook CE Mid Sch
  ....10 B3
Bilbrook Ct WV8 ....10 B3
Bilbrook Gr
  Birmingham B29 ....84 F2
  Codsall WV8 ....10 B3

Bilbrook Rd WV8 ....10 B4
Bilbrook Sta WV8 ....10 A2
Bilbury Cl B97 ....158 C6
Bilhay La B70 ....53 B5
Bilhay St B70 ....53 B5
Billau Rd WV14 ....40 D2
Billesden Cl CV3 ....134 E8
Billesley La
  Birmingham B13 ....87 A1
  Portway B48 ....140 E6
Billesley Prim Sch B13 ...105 C6
Billing Rd CV5 ....112 D3
Billingham Cl B91 ....127 B8
Billingsley Rd B26 ....89 A8
Billinton Cl CV2 ....114 D2
Bills La B90 ....106 A1
Bills St WS10 ....41 D8
Billsmore Gr B90 ....107 C7
Billy Buns La WV5 ....49 B8
Billy La B45,B60 ....138 A3
Billy Wright Cl WV4 ....38 D6
Bilport La WV13 ....52 F8
Bilston CE Prim Sch
  WV14 ....40 B6
Bilston Central Sta WV14 ..40 E5
Bilston Ind Est WV14 ......41 A4
Bilston Key Ind Est WV14 .41 A4
Bilston La WV13 ....41 A8
Bilston Rd Tipton DY4 .....41 E2
  Wednesbury WS10 ....41 E3
  Willenhall WV13 ....41 A8
  Wolverhampton WV2 ....39 F8
Bilston St Darlaston WV13 .41 D6
  Sedgley DY3 ....50 E8
  Wolverhampton WV1 ....163 C2
  Wednesfield WV13 ....26 F8
Bilton Grange Rd B26 .....88 F8
Bilton Ind Est
  Birmingham B38 ....123 D8
  Coventry CV3 ....113 F1
Binbrook Rd WV12 ....27 D4
Bincomb Ave B26 ....89 B6
Binfield St DY4 ....52 A4
Bingley Ave B8 ....68 B4
Bingley Ent Ctr WV3 ......39 A8
Bingley Prim Sch WV3 .....39 A8
Bingley St WV3 ....39 A8
Binley Cl Birmingham B26 ..88 D6
  Solihull B90 ....126 A8
Binley Gr CV3 ....134 F7
Binley Ind Est CV3 ......135 A8
Binley Rd CV2,CV3 ....114 D1
Binley Woods Prim Sch
  ....135 E7
Binns Cl CV4 ....131 F8
Binstead Rd B44 ....45 A2
Binswood Ave CV32 ....156 F2
Binswood Cl CV2 ....96 D2
Binswood Mans **12**
  CV32 ....156 F2
Binswood Rd B62 ....84 A7
Binswood St CV32 ....156 E1
Binton Cl B98 ....154 F1
Binton Croft B13 ....104 F8
Binton Rd Coventry CV2 ...95 D1
  Solihull B90 ....105 F1
Birbeck Ho B36 ....70 B6
Birbeck Pl DY5 ....61 B6
Birch Ave
  Birmingham B31 ....102 C1
  Brierley Hill DY5 ....62 A2
  Brownhills WS8 ....15 E8
  Burntwood WS7 ....6 F6
  Cannock WS11 ....4 C8
Birch Brook La WS14 ....17 E6
Birch Cl Bedworth CV7 .....78 D4
  Birmingham B30 ....103 E6
  Coventry CV5 ....111 F6
  Sutton Coldfield B76 ......46 F2
Birch Copice DY5 ....62 A1
Birch Cres B69 ....52 B1
Birch Croft Aldridge WS9 ..30 C8
  Birmingham B37 ....70 C1
  Sutton Coldfield B24 ......57 D5
Birch Croft Rd B75 ....46 D2
Birch Ct Birmingham B30 ..103 A4
  Oldbury B66 ....64 D8
  Royal Leamington Spa
  CV34 ....161 E2
Birch Dr Halesowen B62 ....63 E1
  Little Aston B74 ....31 D5
  Stourbridge DY8 ....80 E6
  Sutton Coldfield B75 ......46 F7
Birch End CV34 ....161 B8
Birch Gr
  Balsall Common CV7 ......130 B8
  Birchmoor B78 ....36 D7
  Lichfield WS14 ....9 B8
  Oldbury B68 ....84 D7
Birch Ho B74 ....31 B5
Birch Hollow B15 ....85 F6
Birch La Aldridge WS9 .....16 D1
  Oldbury B68 ....84 D7
  Walsall WS3 ....15 C1
Birch Rd
  Birmingham, Eachway B45 .121 C6
  Birmingham, Witton B6 ....56 A2
  Oldbury B68 ....84 D7
  Sedgley DY3 ....39 F1
  Wednesfield WV11 ....26 F8

Birch Rd E B6 ....56 B2
Birch St Oldbury B68 ....64 C5
Tipton DY4 ....51 F5
Walsall WS2 ....28 D3
Wolverhampton WV1 ...163 B3
Birch Terr DY2 ....62 C4
Birch Tree Gdns WS9 ...30 B5
Birch Tree Gr B91 ....106 F4
Birch Wlk B68 ....84 D8
Birchall St B12 ....66 F1
Birchbrook Ind Pk WS14 .17 E6
Birchcoppice Gdns WV12 .27 E4
Birchcroft ■ B66 ....65 C5
Birchdale WV14 ....40 D7
Birchdale Ave 56 E3
Birchdale Rd B23 ....56 D5
Birchen Coppice Fst Sch
 DY11 ....116 B2
Birchen Coppice Mid Sch
 DY11 ....116 B2
Birchensale Mid Sch
 B97 ....153 C4
Birchensale Rd B97 ....153 C5
Birches Ave WV8 ....10 C1
Birches Barn Ave WV3 ..38 F7
Birches Barn Rd WV3 ...38 F7
Birches Cl B13 ....86 F1
Birches Fst Sch WV8 ...10 B1
Birches Green Inf Sch
 B24 ....57 B2
Birches Green Jun Sch
 B24 ....57 B3
Birches Green Rd B24 ..57 B2
Birches La
 Alvechurch B48 ....138 F6
 Kenilworth CV8 ....148 B3
Birches Park Rd WS8 ...10 A2
Birches Rd WV8 ....10 B2
Birches Rise The CV12 ..79 B4
Birchfield Ave WV6 .....24 B6
Birchfield Cl
 Halesowen B63 ....82 E2
 Wood End CV9 ....36 C1
Birchfield Com Sch B20 .55 D1
Birchfield Cres DY9 .....81 F3
Birchfield Ct B97 ....153 B2
Birchfield Gdns
 ■ Birmingham B6 ....66 D8
 Walsall WS5 ....43 C4
Birchfield La
 Oldbury, Birchley Park B69 .63 F6
 Oldbury, Whiteheath Gate
 B69 ....63 E4
Birchfield Rd
 Birmingham B20 ....55 D2
 Coventry CV6 ....112 F8
 Kidderminster DY11 .....116 B5
 Redditch B97 ....153 B2
 Stourbridge DY9 ....81 F3
Birchfield Twr ■ B20 ...55 D1
Birchfield Way WS5 .....43 C4
Birchfields Dr WV12 .....2 D1
Birchfields Rd WV12 ....27 A5
Birchgate CV6 ....81 F4
Birchglade WV3 ....24 D1
Birchgrave Cl CV6 ......114 A2
Birchills Canal Mus*
 WS2 ....28 C3
Birchills CE Prim Com Sch
 WS2 ....28 D2
Birchills Rd WS2 ....28 D2
Birchley Ho B69 ....63 C6
Birchley Park Ave B69 ..63 E6
Birchley Rise B92 ....88 F4
Birchmoor Cl B28 ....106 B7
Birchmoor Rd B78 ......106 F8
Birchover Rd WS2 ....28 A4
Birchtree Gdns DY5 ....62 A1
Birchtree Hollow WV12 ..27 D5
Birchtree Rd CV10 ....72 C6
Birchtrees B24 ....57 D4
Birchtrees Croft B26 ...88 D5
Birchtrees Dr B33 ....69 D2
Birchway CV32 ....156 C1
Birchwood Ave B78 .....36 F7
Birchwood Cl
 Essington WV11 ....13 A3
 Kidderminster DY11 ....116 A7
Birchwood Cres B12 ....87 B4
Birchwood Cres Sch B78 .36 F7
Birchwood Rd
 Binley Woods CV3 ....135 C7
 Birmingham B12 ....87 A4
 Lichfield WS14 ....9 F7
 Wolverhampton WV4 ....39 A5
Birchwood Wlk DY6 .....60 D8
Birchwoods B32 ....84 B2
Birchy Cl B90 ....125 F6
Birchy Leasowes La
 B90 ....125 E5
Bird Cage Wlk B38 .....103 F2
Bird End B71 ....53 F8
Bird Grove Ct CV1 ....113 D5
Bird Rd CV34 ....161 D4
Bird St Coventry CV1 ...165 C3
 Dudley DY3 ....50 C3
 Lichfield WS13 ....9 B8
Birdbrook Rd B44 ....55 E8
Birdcage Wlk ■ DY2 ...51 D1
Birdie Cl B38 ....103 D1
Birdlip Gr B32 ....84 C6
Birds Bush Prim Sch B77 .35 E8
Birds Bush Rd B77 ......35 F8

Birds Mdw DY5 ....61 B7
Birdwell Croft B13 .....104 F6
Birkdale Ave
 Birmingham B29 ....85 F1
 Blackwell B60 ....138 A5
Birkdale Cl Coventry CV6 ..95 B4
 Nuneaton CV11 ....74 A1
 Stourbridge DY8 ....80 F2
 Wolverhampton WV1 ....26 A2
Birkdale Dr B69 ....63 A7
Birkdale Gr B29 ....104 A8
Birkdale Rd WS3 ....14 A3
Birkenshaw Rd B44 .....55 E8
Birley Gr B63 ....82 C1
Birlingham Ho B60 .....137 B3
Birmingham & Midland Hospl
 For Women The B11 ....87 C3
Birmingham & Midland Mus
 of Transport* B47 .....124 C3
Birmingham Bsns Pk
 B37 ....90 C8
Birmingham Christian Coll
 B29 ....85 C1
Birmingham Coll of Food,
 Tourism & Creative Studies
 B1 ....164 A3
Birmingham Conservatoire
 B3 ....164 A3
Birmingham Dental Hospl
 The B4 ....164 C4
Birmingham Great Pk
 B45 ....122 B8
Birmingham Heartlands
 Hospl B9 ....68 B2
Birmingham Int Airport
 B40 ....90 B4
Birmingham Int Convention
 Ctr* B1 ....66 C2
Birmingham Int Sta B40 .90 D4
Birmingham International
 Convention Ctr* B1 ....66 C2
Birmingham Mus & Art Gal*
 B5 ....66 C3
Birmingham Nature Ctr*
 B5 ....86 C3
Birmingham New Rd
 Dudley DY1,WV14,DY4 ...51 C4
 Wolverhampton WV4 ....39 E4
Birmingham Nuffield Hospl
 The B15 ....85 F5
Birmingham Rd
 Aldridge WS9 ....30 A4
 Allesley CV5 ....111 E7
 Alvechurch B48 ....138 B7
 Birmingham B36 ....69 A8
 Blackheath B65 ....63 C2
 Blakedown DY10 ....98 C2
 Burton Green CV8 ......131 A1
 Coleshill B46 ....59 C5
 Dudley DY1 ....51 E2
 Hagley DY9 ....99 D7
 Halesowen B63 ....83 B4
 Hopwood B31,B48 ......123 B4
 Kenilworth CV8 ....147 C8
 Kidderminster DY10 ...117 D7
 Lichfield WS14 ....9 F4
 Lickey End B60,B61 .....137 B6
 Little Packington CV7 ...91 E3
 Lydiate Ash B45,B61 ...121 D5
 Marlbrook B61 ....121 B1
 Oldbury B69 ....64 A7
 Redditch B97,B98 ....153 E8
 Shenstone WS14 ....18 A4
 Stoneleigh CV8 ....149 B6
 Studley B80,B98 ....159 E7
 Sutton Coldfield B72,B73 .46 B2
 Walsall B43,WS1,WS5 ...43 D5
 Warwick CV34 ....160 B8
 Water Orton B46 ....59 A3
 West Bromwich B71 .....54 A1
 Wolverhampton WV2 ....39 D7
 Wroxall B93,CV35 ....145 D3
Birmingham Sch of Speech &
 Drama B15 ....86 A7
Birmingham St
 Darlaston WS10 ....41 E6
 Dudley DY2 ....51 D1
 Halesowen B63 ....83 B3
 Oldbury B69 ....64 A7
 Stourbridge DY8 ....81 B5
 Walsall WS1 ....28 F1
 Willenhall WV13 ....27 C2
Birmingham Youth Offending
 Services B24 ....56 E2
Birnam B15 ....86 A8
Birnham Ct DY4 ....51 D5
Birstall Wlk B38 ....123 C8
Birvell Ct CV12 ....78 D3
Bisell Way DY5 ....81 C6
Biset Ave DY10 ....117 B5
Bishbury Cl B15 ....85 E5
Bishop Asbury Cres B43 .54 C8
Bishop Challoner RC Sch
 B14 ....104 F8
Bishop Cl
 Birmingham B45 ....101 E1
 Cannock WS11 ....1 D2
Bishop Hall Cres B60 ..150 E7
Bishop Milner RC Sch
 DY1 ....51 A3
Bishop Rd WS10 ....42 F8
Bishop St Birmingham B5 ..86 E8
 Coventry CV1 ....165 B3
Bishop Ullathorne RC Sch
 CV3 ....132 F4
Bishop Vesey's Gram Sch
 B74 ....46 C6

Bishop Walsh RC Sch
 B76 ....46 D1
Bishop Wilson CE Prim Sch
 B37 ....70 C3
Bishop's Ct
 Birmingham, Coleshill Heath
 B37 ....90 E8
 Birmingham, Northfield
 B31 ....103 B3
Bishopgate Bsns Pk
 CV1 ....113 D5
Bishopgate Ind Est CV1 .113 D5
Bishops Cl Dudley DY2 ..62 E8
 Smethwick B66 ....65 C4
Bishops Gate B31 ....103 A2
Bishops Mdw B75 ....32 E3
Bishops Rd B73 ....46 B3
Bishops Way B74 ....31 F6
Bishops Wlk
 Coventry CV5 ....133 B8
 Halesowen B64 ....83 A6
Bishopsgate St B15 .....66 B1
Bishopstone Cl B98 ....154 F2
Bishopton Cl
 Coventry CV5 ....112 B3
 Solihull B90 ....106 C1
Bishopton Rd B67 ....64 F1
Bishton Gr DY2 ....62 D4
Bisley Gr B24 ....57 B2
Bismillah Bldgs B19 ....64 B4
Bissel Dr WS10 ....42 B3
Bissel St WV14 ....40 F5
Bissell Cl B28 ....105 F6
Bissell St
 Birmingham, Highgate B5 ..86 E8
 Birmingham, Quinton B32 ..84 A6
Bisset Cres ■ CV31 ....162 C6
Biton Cl B17 ....85 B5
Bittell Cl Birmingham B31 .122 F7
 Wolverhampton WV10 ..11 E4
Bittell Ct B31 ....122 F7
Bittell Farm Rd B48 ....123 A2
Bittell La B45 ....138 E8
Bittell Rd Alvechurch B48 .139 A8
 Barnt Green B45 ....138 E6
Bittern Wlk DY5 ....81 B8
Bittern Wood Rd DY10 ..117 B3
Bitterne Dr WV6 ....25 A4
Bitterscote La B78 ......21 A2
Black Bank CV7 ....95 F5
Black Country Living Mus*
 DY1 ....51 D3
Black Country New Rd
 Wednesbury WS10 ....41 C4
 West Bromwich B70,DY4 .52 D6
Black Country Route
 Bilston WV14 ....40 E5
 Darlaston WV13,WS10 ..41 A3
 Walsall WS2,WS10 ......27 E1
Black Haynes Rd B29 ...103 A6
Black Horse La ■ DY10 .116 E6
Black Horse Rd CV6 .....96 B6
Black La CV32 ....157 C2
Black Lake B70 ....53 A4
Black Lake La B60,B97 .152 A2
Black Lake Sta B70 .....53 A4
Black Prince Ave CV3 ...133 E6
Black Solls Rd B98 .....154 F5
Black-a-Tree Ct CV10 ...72 F5
Black-a-Tree Rd CV10 ...72 E4
Blackacre Rd DY2 ....62 D8
Blackberry Ave
 Birmingham B9 ....68 A3
 Hockley Heath B94 .....143 C6
Blackberry La 61 E8
 Ash Green CV7 ....95 C5
 Blackheath B65 ....62 F5
 Brownhills WS9 ....16 A4
 Coventry CV6 ....114 C6
 Halesowen B63 ....83 A2
 Sutton Coldfield B74 ...31 E4
Blackberry Way DY2 ....62 A3
Blackbird Croft B36 ....70 A7
Blackbrook Cl DY2 ......62 A3
Blackbrook Rd DY2 .....62 A3
Blackbrook Valley Ind Pk
 DY2 ....62 A5
Blackbrook Way WV10 ..11 E4
Blackburn Ave WV6 .....24 F7
Blackburn Rd CV6 ....95 F3
Blackburne Rd B28 .....105 F6
Blackbushe Cl B17 ......84 F7
Blackcat Cl B37 ....70 A3
Blackdown B77 ....22 C1
Blackdown Rd B45 ......102 A2
Blackfen Rd CV3 ....128 B6
Blackett Ct ■ B73 ....46 A2
Blackfirs La B37,B46 ...90 D7
Blackford Cl
 Halesowen B63 ....82 D2
 Kidderminster DY11 ....116 A1
Blackford Rd
 Birmingham B11 ....87 C4
 Solihull B90 ....126 C8
Blackford St B18 ....65 E5
Blackfriars Ct B79 ....20 E5
Blackgreaves La B76 ...48 F1
Blackhalve La WV11 ....12 D2
Blackham Dr B73 ....57 A7
Blackham Rd WV11 .....26 F8
Blackheath Mkt B65 ....63 C1
Blackheath Trad Est
 B65 ....63 B1
Blackhorse La DY5 ....61 E1
Blackley Ho B60 ....65 C6
Blacklow Rd CV34 ....156 A1
Blackmoor Croft B33 ...69 D2
Blackmore La B60 ......137 A3

Blackpit La WV4 ....37 E3
Blackrock Rd B23 ....56 B6
Blackroot Cl WS7 ....7 D4
Blackroot Ho B73 ....45 C2
Blackroot Rd B74 ....46 B2
Blackshaw Dr CV2 ......114 F6
Blacksmith Way B70 ....53 C2
Blacksmiths La B94 ....143 C6
Blackstitch La B97 ......153 A1
Blackstitch La B97 ......152 F1
Blackthorn Ave WS7 .....6 F4
Blackthorn Cl
 Birmingham B30 ....103 C6
 Coventry CV4 ....132 D5
Blackthorn Cl B98 ......154 E1
Blackthorn Gr CV11 ....73 F2
Blackthorn Rd
 Birmingham, Bournville
 B30 ....103 D6
 Birmingham, Castle Bromwich
 B36 ....69 C8
 Brierley Hill DY8 ....60 F1
 Stourbridge DY8 ....61 A1
Blackthorne Cl
 Dudley DY1 ....50 F4
 Solihull B91 ....106 E4
Blackthorne Rd
 Dudley DY1 ....50 F5
 Kenilworth CV8 ....148 A3
 Lichfield WS14 ....9 D7
 Smethwick B67 ....64 D4
 Walsall WS5 ....42 F5
Blackwatch Rd CV6 .....113 C8
Blackwater Cl DY5 ......61 A6
Blackwell La ■ B97 .....153 B5
Blackwell Rd
 Barnt Green B45,B60 ...138 B5
 Coventry CV6 ....113 E8
 Sutton Coldfield B72 ...46 D1
Blackwell St DY10 ......116 E6
Blackwood Ave WV11 ..26 C8
Blackwood Dr B74 ......44 E8
Blackwood Rd
 Aldridge B74 ....30 E1
 Bromsgrove B60 ....137 B2
 Tamworth B77 ....35 C7
Blackwood Sch B74 ....30 E1
Blades Rd B70 ....52 D4
Bladon Cl CV11 ....73 F8
Bladon Wlk ■ CV31 ....162 C6
Blaenwern Dr B63 ....82 A6
Blagdon Rd B63 ....83 A6
Blair Dr CV12 ....77 D1
Blair Gr B37 ....70 D1
Blake Cl Cannock WS11 ..2 A5
 Hinckley LE10 ....71 C4
 Nuneaton CV10 ....72 A5
Blake Hall Cl DY5 ....81 C7
Blake High Sch WS11 ...1 F6
Blake La B9 ....42 C8
Blake Pl B9 ....67 F2
Blake Rd B61 ....137 B8
Blake St B74 ....31 E6
Blake Street Sta B74 ...31 F6
Blakebrook DY11 ....116 C6
Blakebrook Cl DY11 ....116 C6
Blakebrook Day Special Sch
 DY11 ....116 C6
Blakebrook Gdns DY11 .116 C6
Blakedown CE Prim Sch
 DY10 ....98 C1
Blakedown Rd B63 .....82 F1
Blakedown Sta DY10 ...98 C2
Blakedown Way ■ B69 .63 E4
Blakeland Rd B44 ....55 F8
Blakeland St B9 ....67 F2
Blakelands Ave CV31 ...162 B6
Blakeley Ave WV6 ....24 F7
Blakeley Ct B72 ....57 C8
Blakeley Hall Gdns B69 .64 A7
Blakeley Hall Rd B69 ...64 A7
Blakeley Heath Dr WV5 .49 A5
Blakeley Heath Prim Sch
 WV5 ....49 A5
Blakeley Rise WV6 ......24 F7
Blakeley Wood Rd DY4 .52 D8
Blakemere Ave B25 .....88 E8
Blakemere Cl B98 ......154 F3
Blakemere Ho ■ B16 ...66 A2
Blakemore Cl B32 ....84 D3
Blakemore Dr B75 ......46 F6
Blakemore Rd
 Brownhills WS9 ....16 A3
 West Bromwich B70 .....53 A1
Blakemore ■ WS3 ......28 D8
Blakenall Heath
 Walsall WS3 ....14 D1
 Walsall WS3 ....28 C8
Blakenall Heath Jun Sch
 WS3 ....28 C8
Blakenall La WS3 ....28 C8
Blakenall Row WS3 .....28 C8
Blakeney Ave
 Birmingham B17 ....85 A7
 Stourbridge DY8 ....80 C6
Blakeney Cl DY3 ....50 C6
Blakenhale Jun & Inf Schs
 B33 ....69 B1
Blakenhale Rd B33 ......69 B1
Blakenhall Ind Est WV2 .39 E7
Blakesfield Dr B45 ......121 E2
Blakesley Cl B76 ....57 F5
Blakesley Gr B25 ....88 D8
Blakesley Hall Mus*
 B25 ....68 C1

Blakesley Hall Prim Sch
 B25 ....68 D1
Blakesley Mews B25 ....68 D8
Blakesley Rd B25 ....68 D1
Blakewood Cl B34 ......69 C5
Blandford Ave B36 ......58 E1
Blandford Dr
 Coventry CV3 ....114 F5
 Stourbridge DY8 ....60 E3
Blandford Gdns WS7 ...7 C6
Blandford Rd
 Birmingham B32 ....84 F5
 Royal Leamington Spa
 CV32 ....156 C1
Blandford Way CV35 ...160 A7
Blanefield WV8 ....10 C2
Blanford Mere Prim Sch
 DY6 ....60 E7
Blanning Ct B93 ....127 E3
Blay Ave WS2 ....28 B3
Blaydon Ave B75 ....32 E2
Blaydon Rd WV9,WV10 ..11 A1
Blaythorn Ave B92 ......89 A3
Blaze Hill Rd DY6 ....60 A8
Blaze La B96,B97 ....158 A3
Blaze Pk DY6 ....60 A8
Bleachfield Rd B98 .....154 F8
Bleak Hill Rd B23 ....56 C5
Bleak House Dr WS7 ...6 D8
Bleak St B67 ....64 F4
Bleakhouse Ave B68 ...64 C1
Bleakhouse Jun & Inf Sch
 B68 ....64 C1
Bleakman Ct B30 ....104 A6
Blenheim B31 ....85 B6
Blenheim Ave CV6 ......95 E2
Blenheim Cl Hinckley LE10 .71 F4
 Nuneaton CV11 ....73 F2
 Tamworth B77 ....21 C4
 Walsall WS4 ....29 D7
Blenheim Cres
 Bromsgrove B60 ....151 A8
 Royal Leamington Spa
 CV31 ....162 C5
Blenheim Ct B44 ....55 F8
Blenheim Dr B43 ....54 D8
Blenheim Rd
 Birmingham B13 ....86 F1
 Burntwood WS7 ....7 A8
 Kingswinford DY6 ....61 A6
 Norton Canes WS11 .....6 B4
 Solihull B90 ....106 D2
 Willenhall WV12 ....27 C6
Blenheim Way
 Birmingham, Castle Vale
 B35 ....58 B2
 Birmingham, Old Oscott B44 .55 F8
 Dudley DY1 ....50 E2
Blenheim Wlk CV6 ....95 B4
Bletchley Dr
 Coventry CV5 ....112 B4
 Tamworth B77 ....35 C8
Bletchley Rd B24 ....57 E4
Blewitt Cl B36 ....58 D2
Blewitt St Brierley Hill DY5 .61 C6
 Cannock WS11 ....2 B7
Blews St B6 ....66 E5
Blick Rd CV34 ....161 C4
Blind La Berkswell CV7 ..110 D4
 Kenilworth CV8 ....131 F1
 Tanworth-In-A Arden ...141 D1
Blindpit La B76 ....59 B8
Bliss Ct CV4 ....111 E3
Blithe Cl DY8 ....80 F6
Blithfield Dr DY5 ....81 B7
Blithfield Gr B24 ....57 C5
Blithfield Pl WS11 ....2 B1
Blithfield Rd WS8 ....6 C2
Blockall WS10 ....41 D7
Blockall Cl WS10 ....41 D7
Blockley Cl B97 ....152 E2
Blockley Rd CV12 ....78 C4
Blockley's Yd ■ LE10 ...75 D8
Blondvil St CV3 ....133 D7
Bloomfield Cres WS13 ..3 B2
Bloomfield Ct ■ B42 ...55 A8
Bloomfield Dr WV12 ....13 D1
Bloomfield Dr WV4 ......51 D6
Bloomfield Rd
 Birmingham B13 ....87 B3
 Tipton DY4 ....51 E7
Bloomfield St N B63 ....82 F5
Bloomfield St W B63 ...82 F4
Bloomfield Terr DY4 ....51 C7
Bloomfield Way B79 ....20 F8
Bloomsbury Gr B14 ....104 C7
Bloomsbury St B7 ....67 B5
Bloomsbury Way WS14 ..9 C8
Bloomsbury Wlk ■ B7 ..67 B5
Blossom Ave B29 ....85 F2
Blossom Dr B61 ....137 A5
Blossom Gr
 Birmingham B36 ....68 E8
 Blackheath B64 ....62 F1
 Blossom Hill B24 ....57 C4
Blossom Rd B24 ....57 C4
Blossom's Fold WV1 ...163 B3
Blossomfield Cl
 Birmingham B38 ....123 D8
 Kingswinford DY6 ....60 E8
Blossomfield Ct B38 ...123 D8
Blossomfield Gdns B91 .107 A4
Blossomfield Inf Sch
 B91 ....106 D3
Blossomfield Rd B91 ...106 D3
Blossomville Way ■ B27 .88 C5
Blount Ho DY11 ....116 B8
Blount Terr DY11 ....116 D3
Blounts Rd B23 ....56 D5

Blower's Green Rd DY2 . . .62 B8
Blowers Green Cres DY2 . .62 B7
Blowers Green Rd DY2 . . .62 B7
Blowers Green Prim Sch
DY2 .62 B8
Bloxcidge St B68 . . . . .64 E4
Bloxham Bsns Pk WS2 . . .28 A7
Bloxwich CE Prim Sch
WS3 . . . . .14 B1
Bloxwich Hospl WS3 . . . . .28 B8
Bloxwich L Ctr WS3 . . . . .28 C8
Bloxwich La WS2 . . . . .28 A4
Bloxwich North Sta WS3 . .28 B7
Bloxwich Rd WS2,WS3 . . .28 D5
Bloxwich Rd N WV12 . . . .27 D6
Bloxwich Rd S WV13 . . . . .27 A3
Bloxwich Sta WS3 . . . . . . .14 A1
Blucher St B1 . . . . .164 B1
Blue Ball La B63 . . . . .82 C7
Blue Bell Rd B62 . . . . . . .101 B7
Blue Cedars DY8 . . . . .80 C6
Blue Coat CE Comp Sch
WS1 . . . . .28 F1
Blue Coat CE Inf Sch
WS1 . . . . .28 F1
Blue Coat CE Jun Sch
WS1 . . . . .28 F1
Blue Coat CE Sch CV1 . . .113 F1
Blue Coat Sch The B17 . . .85 E6
Blue La E WS2 . . . . .28 E3
Blue La W WS2 . . . . .28 D2
Blue Lake Rd B93 . . . . . .128 B2
Blue Rock Pl B69 . . . . . . .63 C7
Bluebell Cl Cannock WS12 . .2 B6
Stourbridge DY8 . . . . .60 C2
Bluebell Cres WV11 . . . . .26 D5
Bluebell Croft B31 . . . . .102 F4
Bluebell Dr
Bedworth CV12 . . . . .77 E2
Birmingham B37 . . . . .70 E2
Bluebell La WS6 . . . . .5 A1
Bluebell Rd
Blackheath B64 . . . . .62 E3
Brownhills WS9 . . . . .16 B3
Dudley DY1 . . . . .51 B4
Bluebell Wlk CV4 . . . . . .111 F1
Bluebellwood Cl B76 . . . .47 A3
Bluebird Cl WS14 . . . . .9 D8
Bluebird Trad Est WV10 . .25 C5
Bluestone Wlk B65 . . . . . .63 C6
Blundell Rd B11 . . . . .148 A5
Blundells The CV8 . . . . . . .148 A5
Blyth Ave CV7 . . . . .130 C5
Blyth Cl CV12 . . . . .77 C1
Blyth Ct CV11 . . . . .73 C3
Blythe Cl Burntwood WV7 . . . .
Redditch B97 . . . . .158 D7
Blythe Ct Solihull B91 . . .106 F7
Sutton Coldfield B73 . . . . .46 B5
Blythe Gate B90 . . . . . . .126 F3
Blythe Gr B44 . . . . .44 F4
Blythe Rd B Coleshill B46 . .70 F7
Coventry CV1 . . . . .113 E4
Blythe St B77 . . . . .21 C4
Blythe Valley Pk B90 . . .126 F2
Blythefield Ave B43 . . . . .43 C2
Blytheway B91 . . . . .139 A6
Blythesway B91 . . . . .107 E3
Blythewood Cl B91 . . . . .107 F1
Blythsford Rd B28 . . . . . .106 A4
Blythswood Rd B11 . . . . . .88 A4
Blyton Cl B16 . . . . .65 F3
Boar Croft CV4 . . . . .111 F2
Boar Hound Cl B18 . . . . . .66 A4
Board School Gdns DY3 . .50 E6
Boat La WS14 . . . . .7 F1
Boatman's La WS9 . . . . . . .15 E2
Bobbington Way DY2 . . . .62 E5
Bobs Coppice Wlk DY5 . . .81 F7
Bockenden Rd CV4 . . . . .131 E5
Boddington Cl CV32 . . . .157 E5
Boden Rd B28 . . . . .106 A7
Bodenham Cl B98 . . . . . .154 D3
Bodenham Rd
Birmingham B31 . . . . .102 E1
Oldbury B68 . . . . .84 B8
Bodens La WS4 . . . . .44 B7
Bodiam Ct WV6 . . . . .24 A3
Bodicote Gr B75 . . . . .32 E3
Bodington Cl WS7 . . . . .7 E7
Bodington Rd B75 . . . . . . .32 B3
Bodmin Cl Hinckley LE10 . .71 E4
Walsall WS5 . . . . .43 D7
Bodmin Gr B7 DY5 . . . . . .61 D2
Bodmin Gr B7 B7 . . . . . . .67 B5
Bodmin Rd Coventry CV2 .114 F5
Dudley DY2 . . . . .62 D2
Bodmin Rise WS5 . . . . . . .43 D7
Bodnant Way CV8 . . . . . .148 C6
Bodymoor Heath Rd B76 . .48 F5
Bognop Rd WV11 . . . . .12 D4
Bohun St CV4 . . . . .111 F1
Boldmere Cl B73 . . . . .9 D7
Boldmere Ct B43 . . . . .54 E7
Boldmere Dr B73 . . . . .57 A8
Boldmere Gdns B73 . . . . .57 A8
Boldmere Inst B43 . . . . . . .54 F1
Boldmere Jun Sch B73 . . .45 F1
Boldmere Rd B73 . . . . .57 A8
Boldridge Mews B79 . . . . .21 B5
Bolebridge St B79 . . . . . .21 C4
Boley Cl WS14 . . . . .9 D7
Boley Cottage La WS14 . . .9 E7
Boley La WS14 . . . . .9 D7
Boley Park Ctr WS14 . . . . .9 E7
Boleyn Cl Cheslyn Hay WS6 . .4 D2
Warwick CV34 . . . . .161 C6
Boleyn Rd B45 . . . . .101 E2

Bolingbroke Dr CV34 . . . .161 E3
Bolingbroke Rd CV3 . . . .114 A1
Bolney Rd B32 . . . . .84 E4
Bolton Cl CV3 . . . . .133 C5
Bolton Ct DY4 . . . . .52 C8
Bolton Rd Birmingham B10 .87 C8
Wednesfield WV11 . . . . . . .26 D5
Bolton St B9 . . . . .67 B2
Bolton Way WS3 . . . . .13 F3
Bolyfant Cl CV31 . . . . . . .162 A2
Bomers Field B45 . . . . . .122 C7
Bond Dr B35 . . . . .58 A3
Bond Gate CV11 . . . . .73 C4
Bond Sq B18 . . . . .66 A4
Bond St
Birmingham, Ladywood
B19 . . . . .164 B4
Birmingham, Stirchley B30 .104 A7
Blackheath B65 . . . . .63 E3
Coventry CV1 . . . . .165 B3
Dudley WV14 . . . . .51 A8
Nuneaton CV11 . . . . .73 C5
West Bromwich B70 . . . . . .53 C2
Wolverhampton WV2 . . . .163 B2
Bondfield Rd B30 . . . . . . .105 B6
Bondway WS12 . . . . .1 F8
Bone Mill La WV1 . . . . . . .25 D4
Bonehill Ind Est B78 . . . . .20 F1
Bonehill Rd B78 . . . . .20 E3
Boney Hay Rd WS7 . . . . . . .7 B7
Bonfire Hill DY9 . . . . .120 E6
Bonham Gr B25 . . . . .68 D1
Boningale Way B93 . . . . .127 E3
Bonington Dr CV12 . . . . . .78 A4
Bonner Dr B76 . . . . .57 F5
Bonner Gr WS9 . . . . .29 F5
Bonneville Cl CV5 . . . . . .111 B8
Bonnikson Cl B7 CV31 . . .161 F5
Bonnington Way B43 . . . . .44 D4
Bonsall Rd B23 . . . . .57 A6
Bonville Gdns WV10 . . . . .11 E4
Bont Piece La B97 . . . . . .153 B5
Booth Cl Kingswinford DY6 .61 A6
Lichfield WS13 . . . . .3 A2
Walsall WS3 . . . . .28 D8
Booth St B7 DY5 . . . . .62 D7
Booth Ho WS4 . . . . .28 F3
Booth Rd WS10 . . . . .42 C2
Booth St Birmingham B21 . .65 D7
Cannock WS12 . . . . .2 B6
Darlaston WS10 . . . . .41 D8
Walsall WS3 . . . . .28 C8
Booth's La B42 . . . . .44 B1
Booths Farm Rd B42 . . . . .55 B8
Booths Fields CV6 . . . . . . .95 E2
Bordeaux Cl DY1 . . . . .50 E3
Borden Cl WV8 . . . . .24 F8
Bordesley Abbey* B98 . .153 F6
Bordesley Cir B10 . . . . . . .67 B1
Bordesley Cl B9 . . . . .68 A2
Bordesley Ct CV32 . . . . .157 A3
Bordesley Gn B9 . . . . .67 E2
Bordesley Gn E B9,B33 . . .68 C2
Bordesley Green Girls Sch
B9 .68 A2
Bordesley Green Prim Sch
B9 .68 A2
Bordesley Green Rd B8 . . .67 D2
Bordesley Green Trad Est
B9 .67 D3
Bordesley La B98 . . . . . . .153 E6
Bordesley Middleway
B12 . . . . .87 A8
Bordesley Park Rd B10 . . .67 A1
Bordesley Sta B10 . . . . . . .67 A2
Bordesley St B9 . . . . .67 B2
Bore St WS13 . . . . .9 B7
Borman B79 . . . . .20 F5
Borneo St WS4 . . . . .28 F4
Borough Cres Oldbury B65 .63 F3
Stourbridge DY8 . . . . .80 E5
Borough Cl B63 . . . . .83 B4
Borough Rd B79 . . . . .21 C7
Borough The LE10 . . . . . . .71 D6
Borrington Gdns DY10 . . .117 B4
Borrington Rd DY10 . . . . .117 B5
Borrow St WV13 . . . . .27 A3
Borrowcop Ho WS14 . . . . . .9 C6
Borrowcop La WS14 . . . . . .9 C5
Borrowdale Cl
Brierley Hill DY5 . . . . .81 B8
Coventry CV6 . . . . .113 A8
Borrowdale Dr CV32 . . . .156 D2
Borrowdale Gr B31 . . . . .102 D3
Borrowdale Rd B31 . . . . .102 C3
Borrowell La CV8 . . . . . . .147 E4
Borrowell Terr CV8 . . . . .147 E4
Borwick Ave B70 . . . . .53 A3
Bosbury Terr B30 . . . . . . .104 B7
Boscobel Ave DY4 . . . . . . .51 F4
Boscobel Cl DY1 . . . . .50 F3
Boscobel Cres WS1 . . . . . .25 C4
Boscobel Rd
Birmingham B43 . . . . .43 D2
Cheswick Green B90 . . . . .126 D5
Walsall WS1 . . . . .43 B8
Boscombe Ave B11 . . . . . .87 C6
Boscombe Rd B11 . . . . . . .87 E4
Bosmere Ct B31 . . . . .102 F3
Boss Dr DY2 . . . . .62 C7
Boss Gate Cl WV5 . . . . . . .49 A5
Boston Cl WS12 . . . . .2 E1
Boston Gr B44 . . . . .56 B8
Boston Pl CV6 . . . . .113 D8
Boston Way LE9 . . . . .71 F6
Bosty La WS9 . . . . .29 E5

Boswell Cl
Darlaston WS10 . . . . .41 D5
Tipton WS10 . . . . .41 C1
Boswell Dr CV2 . . . . .115 A7
Boswell Gr CV34 . . . . . . .155 D1
Boswell Rd Bilston WV14 . .40 F7
Birmingham B44 . . . . .55 F6
Cannock WS11 . . . . .1 D4
Sutton Coldfield B74 . . . . .46 C6
Bosworth Cl Dudley DY3 . .51 A6
Hinckley LE10 . . . . .71 A1
Sedgley DY3 . . . . .50 F7
Bosworth Dr B37 . . . . .70 A2
Bosworth Ho B8 LE10 . . . .71 E1
Bosworth Rd B26 . . . . .88 E4
Bosworth Wood Jun & Inf
Sch B36 . . . . .58 F1
Botany Dr DY3 . . . . .50 D6
Botany Rd WS5 . . . . .43 A3
Botany Wlk B7 B16 . . . . . .66 A2
Botha Rd B9 . . . . .67 F2
Botoner Rd CV1 . . . . .113 F2
Bott La Stourbridge DY9 . . .81 E6
Walsall WS1 . . . . .28 F1
Bott Rd CV5 . . . . .132 D8
Botteley Rd B70 . . . . .53 A6
Bottetourt Rd B29 . . . . . . .85 A2
Botteville Rd B27 . . . . .88 C2
Bottle Cotts B17 . . . . .85 D4
Bottrill St CV11 . . . . .73 B5
Boughton Rd B25 . . . . .88 C7
Boulevard The
Brierley Hill DY5 . . . . .61 F2
Sutton Coldfield B73 . . . . .57 B7
Boultbee Rd B72 . . . . .57 C7
Boulters La B B19 . . . . . . .36 D1
Boulton Cir B19 . . . . .66 C6
Boulton Cl WS7 . . . . .7 C8
Boulton Ind Ctr B18 . . . . . .66 B5
Boulton Rd
Birmingham B21 . . . . .65 E7
Smethwick B66 . . . . .65 D6
Solihull B91 . . . . .107 C7
West Bromwich B70 . . . . . .53 E7
Boulton Retreat B21 . . . . .65 E7
Boulton Sq B70 . . . . .53 D1
Boulton Wlk B23 . . . . .56 B4
Boultons La B97 . . . . .158 D6
Boundary Ave B65 . . . . . . .63 E2
Boundary Cl WV13 . . . . . . .26 E1
Boundary Cres DY3 . . . . . .50 C3
Boundary Ct B37 . . . . .69 E2
Boundary Dr B13 . . . . .86 D2
Boundary Hill DY3 . . . . . . .50 C4
Boundary Ho B5 . . . . .86 D5
Boundary Ind Est WV10 . .11 C5
Boundary Pl B21 . . . . .54 B1
Boundary Rd
Brownhills WS9 . . . . .15 F3
Sutton Coldfield B74 . . . . .44 F7
Boundary Way
Wolverhampton, Compton
WV6 . . . . .23 F2
Wolverhampton, Penn WV4 .38 C5
Bourlay Cl B45 . . . . .101 C2
Bourn Mill Dr B6 . . . . .66 F6
Bournbrook Rd B29 . . . . . .86 A2
Bourne Ave Catshill B61 . .120 F1
Fazeley B78 . . . . .20 E1
Halesowen B62 . . . . .83 F4
Tipton DY4 . . . . .52 C7
Bourne Cl
Birmingham B13 . . . . .105 D6
Cannock WS12 . . . . .2 E2
Solihull B91 . . . . .107 E6
Bourne Gn B32 . . . . .84 E6
Bourne Hill Cl DY2 . . . . . . .62 E3
Bourne Rd Birmingham B6 . .67 B7
Coventry CV3 . . . . .114 C1
Bourne St Dudley DY2,DY3 .51 D1
Dudley, Bramford WV14 . . .51 A7
Bourne Vale WS9 . . . . .30 D3
Bourne Way Gdns B29 . . .104 A8
Bourne Wlk B65 . . . . .62 F5
Bournebrook Cl DY2 . . . . . .62 C5
Bournebrook Cres B62 . . . .84 A4
Bournes Cl B63 . . . . .82 F3
Bournes Cres B63 . . . . .82 E4
Bournes Hill B63 . . . . .82 E4
Bournheath Rd B61 . . . . .120 D2
Bournville Coll of F Ed
Birmingham B30 . . . . .103 F7
Birmingham B31 . . . . .103 C7
Bournville Inf Sch B30 . . .103 E7
Bournville Jun Sch B30 . .103 E7
Bournville La B30 . . . . . . .103 E6
Bournville Mews B30 . . . .103 E5
Bournville Sch & Sixth Form
B30 . . . . .103 C6
Bournville Sta B30 . . . . . .104 A7
Bourton Cl B WS5 . . . . . . .43 A3
Bourton Croft B92 . . . . . .106 F8
Bourton Dr CV31 . . . . . . .162 B5
Bourton Rd B92 . . . . .106 F8
Bovey Croft B76 . . . . .58 A7
Bovingdon Rd B35 . . . . . . .58 A3
Bow Ct CV5 . . . . .132 D8
Bow St Bilston WV14 . . . . .40 E6
Birmingham B1 . . . . .164 B1
Willenhall WV13 . . . . .27 A1
Bowater Ave B33 . . . . .68 D1
Bowater Ho
Birmingham B19 . . . . .66 D5
West Bromwich B70 . . . . . .53 C2
Bowater St B70 . . . . .53 C2
Bowbrook Ave B90 . . . . . .127 A5
Bowcroft Gr B24 . . . . .57 C6
Bowden Rd B67 . . . . .64 E6

Bowden Way CV3 . . . . . . .114 F1
Bowdler Rd WV2 . . . . . . .163 D1
Bowen Ave WV4 . . . . .40 A3
Bowen Ct B B13 . . . . .87 B2
Bowen St WV4 . . . . .39 E5
Bowen-cooke Ave WV6 . .23 E6
Bower Ct WS13 . . . . .3 D2
Bower Ho B19 . . . . .66 D6
Bower La DY5 . . . . .82 A8
Bowercourt Cl B91 . . . . .107 B2
Bowers Croft CV32 . . . . .157 A5
Bowes Dr WS11 . . . . .1 F4
Bowes Rd B45 . . . . .121 E7
Bowfell Cl CV5 . . . . .112 B4
Bowker St WV13 . . . . .26 C1
Bowlas Ave B74 . . . . .46 B7
Bowling Green Ave B77 . . .35 F7
Bowling Green Cl
Birmingham B23 . . . . .56 F7
Darlaston WS10 . . . . .41 D7
Bowling Green La
Bedworth CV7,CV12 . . . . . .95 E8
Birmingham B20 . . . . .66 A8
Bowling Green Rd
Dudley DY2 . . . . .62 E2
Hinckley LE10 . . . . .71 E1
Stourbridge DY8 . . . . .80 E5
Bowling Green St CV34 . .160 D6
Bowls Cl CV5 . . . . .112 F3
Bowman Gn LE10 . . . . .75 F6
Bowman Rd B42 . . . . .44 B1
Bowman's Rise WV1 . . . . .26 B3
Bowmans Harbour Island
WV10 . . . . .26 B4
Bowmore Rd B60 . . . . . . .137 B1
Bowness Cl CV6 . . . . .113 A8
Bowness Gr WV11 . . . . . . .13 B1
Bowness Ho B65 . . . . .63 D4
Bowood Cres B31 . . . . . . .103 B2
Bowood Dr WV6 . . . . .24 D6
Bowood End B76 . . . . .46 E3
Bowshot Cl B36 . . . . .58 D1
Bowstoke Rd B43 . . . . .54 C8
Bowyer Rd B8 . . . . .67 E4
Bowyer St B10 . . . . .67 A1
Box Cl CV31 . . . . .162 B3
Box Rd B37 . . . . .90 C8
Box St WS1 . . . . .28 F1
Box Trees Rd B93 . . . . . . .127 C1
Boxhall Cl B6 . . . . .66 F6
Boxhill The CV3 . . . . .114 B1
Boxnott Cl B97 . . . . .153 A2
Boyd Cl CV2 . . . . .115 A8
Boyd Gr B27 . . . . .88 B2
Boyden Cl WS11 . . . . .1 B1
Boydon Cl WV2 . . . . .40 A6
Boyleston Rd B28 . . . . . . .106 A6
Boyne Rd B26 . . . . .89 B7
Boyslade Rd LE10 . . . . . . .75 F6
Boyslade Rd E LE10 . . . . .75 F5
Boyton Gr B44 . . . . .44 F3
Brabazon Gr B35 . . . . .57 F3
Brabham Cres B74 . . . . . . .44 F6
Bracadale Ave B24 . . . . . . .57 A4
Bracadale Cl CV3 . . . . . . .133 D7
Brace St WS1 . . . . .42 E8
Bracebridge Cl CV7 . . . . .130 B6
Bracebridge Ct B17 . . . . . .85 D5
Bracebridge Ho B 45 C2
Bracebridge Rd
Birmingham B24 . . . . .56 F1
Sutton Coldfield B74 . . . . .46 A8
Bracebridge St
Birmingham B6 . . . . .66 E6
Nuneaton CV11 . . . . .73 B3
Braceby Ave B13 . . . . . . .105 C6
Braces La B60 . . . . .121 C1
Brackadale Way B77 . . . . . .9 E6
Bracken Cl Burntwood WS7 . .7 C7
Cannock WS12 . . . . .2 D8
Lichfield WS14 . . . . .9 E6
Wolverhampton WV8 . . . . .10 E1
Bracken Croft B7 B37 . . . .70 C3
Bracken Dr B75 . . . . .47 A5
Bracken Gr B61 . . . . .121 A1
Bracken Park Gdns DY8 . .60 F2
Bracken Rd
Birmingham B24 . . . . .57 C2
Huntington WS12 . . . . .1 C5
Bracken Way
Birmingham B38 . . . . .123 D6
Sutton Coldfield B74 . . . . .44 F6
Bracken Wood WS5 . . . . . .43 D5
Brackenbury Rd B44 . . . . .56 B8
Brackendale Dr
Nuneaton CV10 . . . . .72 F3
Walsall WS5 . . . . .43 B3
Brackendale Sh Ctr
WV12 . . . . .27 D4
Brackendale Way CV5 . . . .81 D4
Brackenfield Rd
Birmingham B44 . . . . .44 D3
Halesowen B63 . . . . .82 E3
Brackenfield View DY1 . . .61 D8
Brackenhill Rd WS7 . . . . . . .7 A8
Brackenhurst Rd CV6 . . .113 A7
Brackenwood Dr WV11 . . .26 F5
Brackleshame Way B77 . . .22 A6
Brackley Ave B20 . . . . .55 C1
Brackley Cl CV6 . . . . .112 F7
Brackleys Way B92 . . . . . .89 A2
Bracknell Wlk B7 CV2 . . .115 A7
Bradburn Rd WV11 . . . . . .26 B8
Bradburne Way B7 . . . . . . .67 A5
Bradbury Cl WS8 . . . . .15 F5
Bradbury La WS12 . . . . .2 B7
Bradbury Rd B92 . . . . . . .107 A8
Braddock Cl CV3 . . . . . . .115 A1

Brade Dr CV2 . . . . .115 B7
Braden Rd WV4 . . . . .38 D4
Brades Cl B63 . . . . .82 B7
Brades Rd B69 . . . . .63 D8
Brades Rise B69 . . . . .63 D8
Bradestone Rd CV11 . . . . .73 D1
Bradewell Rd B36 . . . . .58 D1
Bradfield Cl CV5 . . . . .112 C5
Bradfield Ho B26 . . . . .89 D6
Bradfield Rd B42 . . . . .55 D7
Bradford Cl B43 . . . . .54 F7
Bradford Court Bsns Ctr
B12 . . . . .87 A8
Bradford La
Belbroughton DY9 . . . . . . .119 D5
Walsall WS1 . . . . .28 E1
Bradford Mall WS1 . . . . . .28 E1
Bradford Pl WS1 . . . . .28 E1
Bradford Rd
Birmingham B36 . . . . .69 B7
Brownhills WS8 . . . . .15 E8
Dudley DY2 . . . . .61 F6
Bradford St
Birmingham B12,B5 . . . . . .66 F1
Cannock WS11 . . . . .2 A5
Tamworth B79 . . . . .20 F5
Walsall WS1 . . . . .28 E1
Bradgate Cl WV12 . . . . . . .27 C6
Bradgate Dr B74 . . . . .31 E5
Bradgate Pl B8 B12 . . . . . .87 A6
Bradgate Rd LE10 . . . . . . .71 F2
Brading Rd CV10 . . . . .73 D6
Bradley Croft CV7 . . . . . .130 B6
Bradley La WV14 . . . . .41 A3
Bradley La Sta WV14 . . . . .41 A3
Bradley Rd
Birmingham B34 . . . . .69 D6
Stourbridge DY8 . . . . .80 F6
Wolverhampton WV2 . . . . .39 E7
Bradley St Bilston WV14 . . .40 F4
Brierley Hill DY5 . . . . .61 C7
Tipton DY4 . . . . .51 F2
Bradley Thursfield Ct
DY11 . . . . .116 C7
Bradley's La DY4,WV14 . . .51 E8
Bradlymore Rd DY5 . . . . . .61 D3
Bradleys Cl B64 . . . . .82 E7
Bradmore Cl B7 B91 . . . .107 A1
Bradmore Gr B29 . . . . . . .103 A8
Bradmore Rd WV3 . . . . . . .38 F8
Bradney Gn CV4 . . . . .131 E7
Bradnick Pl CV4 . . . . .111 F1
Bradnock Cl B13 . . . . .105 C7
Bradnock's Marsh La
B92 . . . . .109 E2
Bradshaw Ave
Birmingham B38 . . . . .103 D1
Darlaston WS10 . . . . .41 C5
Bradshaw Cl DY4 . . . . .52 A3
Bradshaw St WV1 . . . . . . .163 D3
Bradshawe Cl B28 . . . . . .105 D3
Bradshaw Rd B30 . . . . . . .104 C4
Bradwell Croft B75 . . . . . .32 E3
Bradwell Ho B31 . . . . .102 D5
Braeburn Cl WS13 . . . . .3 D1
Braemar Ave DY8 . . . . .60 C2
Braemar Cl Coventry CV2 .114 E6
Sedgley DY3 . . . . .39 C1
Willenhall WV12 . . . . .27 B5
Braemar Dr B23 . . . . .56 B5
Braemar Gdns WS12 . . . . . .1 F7
Braemar Rd
Norton Canes WS11 . . . . . . .6 B4
Royal Leamington Spa
CV32 . . . . .157 B4
Solihull B92 . . . . .106 E8
Sutton Coldfield B73 . . . . .46 A2
Braemar Way CV10 . . . . . .73 A2
Braeside Croft B37 . . . . . .70 D2
Braeside Way WS3 . . . . . .14 F3
Bragg Rd B20 . . . . .55 D2
Braggs Farm La B90 . . . . .126 A4
Braham St B79 . . . . .20 D6
Braid Cl B38 . . . . .103 D1
Braidwood Specl Sch
B23 . . . . .56 B6
Brailes Cl B92 . . . . .107 C7
Brailes Dr B76 . . . . .46 F3
Brailes Gr B9 . . . . .68 B1
Brailsford Cl WV11 . . . . . . .26 E8
Brailsford Dr B66 . . . . .65 A5
Brain St B77 . . . . .22 A2
Braithwaite Cl DY6 . . . . . .60 D8
Braithwaite Rd B11 . . . . . .87 B7
Brake La DY8 . . . . .98 E6
Brake The DY8 . . . . .98 F6
Brakesmead CV31 . . . . . .161 F5
Bramah Way DY4 . . . . .52 D3
Bramber B77 . . . . .21 D1
Bramber Dr WV5 . . . . .49 A6
Bramber Way B7 . . . . .80 F2
Bramble Cl
Birmingham, Aston B6 . . . .66 C7
Birmingham, Shenley Fields
B31 . . . . .102 F6
Blackheath B64 . . . . .62 F4
Clayhanger WS8 . . . . .15 E5
Coleshill B46 . . . . .70 F7
Nuneaton CV11 . . . . .73 C2
Willenhall WV12 . . . . .27 C2
Bramble Dell B9 . . . . .68 A3
Bramble Dr
Birmingham B26 . . . . .89 A6
Cannock WS12 . . . . .2 C7
Bramble Gn DY1 . . . . .50 F5

Bramble La WS7 ....7 B8
Bramble St CV1 ....113 E2
Brambles The
  Lichfield WS14 ....9 D6
  Norton Canes WS11 ....6 A5
  Stourbridge DY9 ....81 D3
  Sutton Coldfield B76 ....58 A8
Brambleside DY8 ....60 F1
Bramblewood WV5 ....49 A7
Bramblewood Dr WV3 ....38 E8
Bramblewoods B34 ....69 C5
Brambling B27 ....36 A7
Brambling Rise DY10 ....117 B1
Brambling Wlk
  2 Birmingham B15 ....86 C7
  Brierley Hill DY5 ....81 C6
Bramcote Cl
  Bulkington CV12 ....79 D2
  Hinckley LE10 ....71 F3
Bramcote Dr B91 ....107 C7
Bramcote Hospl CV11 ....79 E7
Bramcote Rd B32 ....84 C5
Bramcote Rise B75 ....46 C7
Bramdean Wlk WV4 ....38 C6
Bramdene Ave CV10 ....73 D8
Bramerton Cl WV11 ....26 A6
Bramford Dr DY1 ....51 B6
Bramford Prim Sch DY1 ....51 B6
Bramley Cl
  Birmingham B43 ....44 D3
  Walsall WS5 ....43 D8
Bramley Croft B90 ....106 C2
Bramley Ct WV11 ....26 C6
Bramley Dr
  Birmingham B20 ....55 B3
  Hollywood B47 ....125 B6
Bramley Mews Ct B27 ....88 C4
Bramley Rd
  Birmingham B27 ....88 C5
  Walsall WS5 ....43 B4
Brampton Ave B28 ....106 A6
Brampton Cres B90 ....106 B6
Brampton Dr WS12 ....2 E2
Brampton Way CV12 ....79 B3
Bramshall Dr B93 ....127 E3
Bramshaw Cl B14 ....104 F2
Bramshill Ct B15 ....86 B8
Bramstead Ave WV6 ....24 B2
Bramston Cres CV4 ....111 F1
Bramwell Dr WS6 ....4 D1
Branwell Gdns CV6 ....95 F5
Brancaster Cl B77 ....22 A5
Branch Rd B38 ....123 E8
Branchal Rd WS9 ....16 C1
Branden Rd B48 ....139 A5
Brandfield Rd CV6 ....112 F8
Brandhall Cl B68 ....64 B1
Brandhall La B68 ....64 A1
Brandhall Prim Sch B68 ....64 B1
Brandhall Rd B68 ....64 A1
Brandon Cl Aldridge WS9 ....30 F3
  Sedgley DY3 ....50 E7
  West Bromwich B70 ....53 A2
Brandon Ct
  Birmingham B31 ....103 B1
  Coventry CV3 ....135 A7
Brandon Gr B31 ....122 F7
Brandon La CV3,CV8 ....135 C5
Brandon Marsh Visitor Ctr★
  CV3 ....135 B4
Brandon Par DY32 ....162 A8
Brandon Pk WV3 ....38 E7
Brandon Pl B34 ....69 D7
Brandon Rd
  Birmingham B28 ....87 E2
  Coventry CV3 ....135 A8
  Halesowen B62 ....63 E1
  Hinckley LE10 ....75 B7
  Solihull B91 ....107 C7
Brandon Thomas Ct B6 ....67 B8
Brandon Way
  Brierley Hill DY5 ....81 E8
  West Bromwich B70 ....53 A2
Brandon Way Ind Est
  B70 ....52 F3
Brandon Wood Farm★
  CV8 ....135 D5
Brandwood Gr B14 ....104 D5
Brandwood Ho B14 ....104 D7
Brandwood Park Rd
  B14 ....104 C4
Brandwood Rd B14 ....104 D5
Branfield Cl WV14 ....51 A8
Branksome Ave B21 ....65 F8
Branksome Rd CV6 ....112 E6
Branscombe Cl B14 ....104 D5
Bransdale Ave CV6 ....95 D3
Bransdale Cl WV6 ....25 B4
Bransdale Rd WS8 ....15 E6
Bransford Ave CV4 ....132 D5
Bransford Rise B91 ....108 B5
Bransford Twr B12 ....86 F8
Branston St B18 ....66 C4
Branstree Dr CV6 ....95 D2
Brantford Rd B25 ....88 C8
Branthill Croft **4** B91 ....107 B1
Brantley Ave WV3 ....24 A1
Brantley Rd B6 ....56 A2
Branton Hill La WS9 ....30 C5
Brantwood Ave WS7 ....7 A5
Brascote Rd LE10 ....71 B1
Brasshouse Inf Sch B66 ....65 A7

Brasshouse La B66 ....65 A7
Brassie Cl B38 ....103 D1
Brassington Ave B72,B73 ....46 B5
Bratch Cl DY2 ....62 C3
Bratch Hollow WS5 ....49 A8
Bratch La WV5 ....49 A8
Brathay Cl CV3 ....133 D6
Bratt St B70 ....53 C4
Braunston Cl B76 ....47 A2
Brawnes Hurst B26 ....69 A1
Bray Ho WV11 ....26 C5
Bray St WV13 ....27 B2
Bray's La CV2 ....114 A3
Brayford
  Brierley Hill DY5 ....81 B7
  Coventry CV3 ....133 C6
Braymoor Rd B33 ....69 E1
Brays Rd B26 ....89 B6
Brays St B26 ....89 A6
Braytoft Cl CV6 ....95 C2
Brazil St CV4 ....111 E2
Breaches La B98 ....159 D8
Breadmarket St WS13 ....9 B8
Breakback Rd B61 ....150 D8
Bream B77 ....35 D7
Bream Cl Birmingham B37 ....70 C2
  Wolverhampton WV10 ....26 A4
Breamore Cres DY1 ....50 F3
Brean Ave B92 ....88 F5
Brearley Cl B19 ....66 E5
Brearley St
  Birmingham, Handsworth
  B21 ....65 D8
  Birmingham, Hockley B19 ....66 D5
Brechin Cl LE10 ....75 A8
Brecknell Rise CV7 ....116 F8
Brecknock Rd B71 ....53 A6
Brecon Ave B61 ....137 A5
Brecon Dr DY8 ....81 B6
Brecon Rd B20 ....66 A8
Brecon Twr ◨ B16 ....66 A2
Bredon Ave Coventry CV3 ....134 F8
  Kidderminster DY11 ....116 A1
  Stourbridge DY9 ....81 C5
Bredon Croft B18 ....66 A6
Bredon Ct Halesowen B63 ....83 A3
  Sutton Coldfield B75 ....32 A4
Bredon Ho B98 ....159 B7
Bredon Rd
  Bromsgrove B61 ....150 D7
  Oldbury B69 ....63 D5
  Stourbridge DY8 ....81 B6
Bredon Terr ◨ B11 ....66 A5
Bredon View B70 ....158 D8
Bree Cl CV5 ....112 A7
Bree's La CV8 ....130 A4
Breech Cl B74 ....44 E7
Breeden Dr B76 ....59 B6
Breedon Rd B30 ....104 A5
Breedon Way WS4 ....15 C1
Breen Rydding Dr WV14 ....51 B8
Breener Ind Est DY5 ....61 B1
Breeze Ave WS11 ....6 B5
Brelades Cl DY1 ....50 E3
Brendon B77 ....22 B1
Brendon Way CV10 ....72 A3
Brenfield Dr LE10 ....75 A8
Brennand Cl B68 ....84 C8
Brennand Rd B68 ....84 B8
Brent B77 ....35 E7
Brent Ho ◨ B31 ....61 E8
Brent Rd B30 ....104 D8
Brentford Rd
  Royal Leamington Spa
  CV31 ....162 A8
  Smethwick B66 ....65 C6
Bridge Ind Est B91 ....107 C7
Bridge Meadow Dr B93 ....127 F6
Bridge Piece B31 ....103 B2
Bridge Rd Birmingham B8 ....67 E3
  Hinckley LE10 ....75 D7
  Tipton DY4 ....52 C7
  Walsall WS4 ....15 B1
Bridge Specl Sch The
  B23 ....56 E4
Bridge St Bilston WV14 ....40 E5
  Birmingham B1 ....164 A2
  Cannock WS11 ....4 E5
  Clayhanger WS8 ....15 E6
  Coventry CV6 ....114 A7
  Dudley WV14 ....51 C8
  Halesowen B62 ....82 C7
  Kenilworth CV8 ....147 F8
  ◨ Kidderminster DY10 ....116 E5
  Nuneaton CV11 ....73 C4
  Nuneaton, Chilvers Coton
  CV11 ....73 D3
  Oldbury B69 ....64 A8
  Redditch B97 ....153 D4
  Stourbridge DY8 ....60 E1
  Tamworth B77 ....21 C5
  Walsall WS1 ....28 F2
  Warwick CV34 ....161 C8
  Wednesbury WS10 ....41 F1
  West Bromwich B70 ....53 B4
  Willenhall WV13 ....26 D1
  Wolverhampton WV10 ....25 E5
Bridge St N B66 ....65 B6
Bridge St S B66 ....65 B6
Bridge St W B19 ....66 D5
Bridge Trad Ctr The B64 ....82 D8
Bridge Trad Est The B66 ....65 B6
Bridge View
  Baginton CV8 ....133 D3
  ◨ Coleshill B46 ....70 F7
Bridge Way WS8 ....15 E6
Bridgeacre Gdns CV3 ....114 F2

Breydon Gr WV13 ....40 F8
Brian Rd B67 ....64 E6
Briansway CV6 ....95 E3
Briar B77 ....22 A3
Briar Ave B24 ....57 A4
Briar Cl Birmingham B24 ....57 A4
  Cannock WS12 ....2 A8
  Hinckley LE10 ....75 F6
  Lickey End B60 ....137 C6
  Royal Leamington Spa
  CV32 ....157 B2
Briar Coppice B90 ....126 D4
Briar Ct
  14 Brierley Hill DY5 ....61 D2
  Dudley DY2 ....62 C6
Briar Hill DY10 ....118 C1
Briar Hill Inf Sch CV31 ....162 B3
Briar Wood Cl WV2 ....40 A7
Briarbeck WS4 ....29 C8
Briardene Ave CV12 ....78 B2
Briarfield Rd B11 ....88 A3
Briarley Ho ◨ B71 ....42 F1
Briarmead LE10 ....75 F4
Briars Cl Brierley Hill DY5 ....61 C4
  Coventry CV2 ....114 C2
  Nuneaton CV11 ....73 E5
Briars The
  Birmingham B23 ....56 D6
  Hagley DY9 ....98 F4
Briarwood DY90 WV90 ....126 D4
Brick Hill La CV5 ....111 E8
Brick Kiln La
  Birmingham B44 ....55 E6
  Dudley DY3 ....50 B3
  Middleton B78 ....48 D6
  Solihull B90,B91 ....126 F8
  Wythall B47 ....124 F4
Brick Kiln St
  Brierley Hill, Hart's Hill
  DY5 ....61 E5
  Brierley Hill, Quarry Bank
  DY5 ....82 A8
  Hinckley LE10 ....75 C8
  Tipton DY4 ....51 F6
Brick St DY3 ....50 D8
Brickfield Rd B25 ....88 B6
Brickheath Rd WV1 ....26 A3
Brickhill Dr B37 ....70 A2
Brickhouse Jun & Inf Sch
  B65 ....63 A3
Brickhouse La
  Stoke Prior B60 ....150 C4
  West Bromwich B70 ....52 E6
Brickhouse La S B64 ....63 A4
Brickhouse Rd B65 ....63 A4
Brickiln Ct ◨ DY5 ....61 D2
Brickiln St WS8 ....15 F7
Brickkiln Prim Sch WV3 ....25 B1
Brickkiln St WV11 ....26 F1
Brickworks Rd WS12 ....2 E2
Brickyard La B80 ....159 C4
Brickyard Rd WS9 ....15 F1
Bridal Path The CV5 ....112 B6
Briddsland Rd B33 ....69 E2
Bridge Ave
  Cheslyn Hay WS6 ....4 E4
  Tipton DY4 ....51 D5

Bridgeburn Rd B31 ....102 E8
Bridgecote CV3 ....134 E6
Bridgefield Wlk B65 ....62 E6
Bridgefoot Wlk WV8 ....10 F1
Bridgeford Rd B34 ....69 B6
Bridgelands Way B20 ....55 D1
Bridgeman Croft B36 ....69 C8
Bridgeman Rd CV6 ....113 B4
Bridgeman St B70 ....28 D1
Bridgemary CV WV10 ....11 E3
Bridgemeadow Ho ◨
  B36 ....68 E8
Bridgend Croft DY5 ....61 B6
Bridgenorth Ho B33 ....69 E3
Bridgeport Rd CV11 ....79 A5
Bridges Rd WS11 ....5 F5
Bridgeside Trad Est B77 ....21 C3
Bridgewater Ave B69 ....64 A4
Bridgewater Cres DY2 ....51 E1
Bridgewater Dr WV14 ....40 C2
Bridgewater St ◨ B77 ....21 D5
Bridgnorth Gr WV12 ....27 A7
Bridgnorth Rd
  Stourbridge DY7,DY8 ....80 C6
  Trescott WV6 ....37 C7
  Wolverhampton WV6 ....24 B2
  Wombourne DY3 ....49 A5
Bridgtown Bsns Ctr WS11 ....4 E6
Bridgtown Prim Sch WS11 ....4 E6
Bridgwater Cl WS9 ....15 F3
Bridle Brook La CV5,CV7 ....94 A3
Bridle Gr B71 ....53 F7
Bridle La B74,WS9 ....44 E7
Bridle Mead B38 ....123 D8
Bridle Path The B90 ....106 B6
Bridle Rd DY8 ....80 D6
Bridle Wood B74 ....44 F7
Bridley Moor High Sch
  B97 ....153 C4
Bridley Moor Rd B97 ....153 C5
Bridport Cl CV2 ....115 A4
Bridport Ho ◨ B31 ....102 E8
Brier Mill Rd B63 ....83 C2
Brier Specl Sch The DY5 ....61 E3
Brierley Hill Prim Sch
  DY5 ....61 D2
Brierley Hill Rd DY8 ....61 A4
Brierley La WV14 ....40 E2
Brierley Rd CV2 ....114 C8
Brierley Trad Est The
  DY5 ....61 C3
Brier Rd B63 ....82 F3
Brigfield Cres B13 ....105 B5
Brigfield Rd B13 ....105 B5
Bright Cres B77 ....21 C2
Bright Rd B68 ....64 B5
Bright St Coventry CV6 ....113 E6
  Darlaston WS10 ....41 D5
  Stourbridge DY8 ....80 D6
  Wolverhampton WV1 ....163 A4
Brightmere Rd CV6 ....113 B4
Brighton Cl WS2 ....28 D3
Brighton Mews ◨ WV3 ....25 A2
Brighton Rd B12 ....87 A5
Brighton St CV2 ....113 F3
Brightstone Cl WV10 ....11 F4
Brightstone Rd B45 ....102 B2
Brightwalton Rd CV3 ....133 D7
Brightwell Cres B93 ....127 E3
Brill Cl CV4 ....132 C5
Brimfield Pl ◨ WV6 ....24 F4
Brimstone La B61 ....136 D7
Brindle Ave CV3 ....114 C2
Brindle Cl B26 ....88 E5
Brindle Ct B23 ....56 B3
Brindlefields Way DY4 ....52 B2
Brindley Ave WV11 ....13 A1
Brindley Cl
  ◨ Stourbridge DY8 ....60 E1
  Walsall WS2 ....27 F5
Brindley Cres WS12 ....2 C8
Brindley Ct
  ◨ Oldbury B68 ....84 B7
  ◨ Tipton DY4 ....51 E5
Brindley Dr B1 ....164 A2
Brindley Heath Rd WS12 ....2 D8
Brindley Paddocks CV1 ....165 B4
Brindley Pl B1 ....66 B2
Brindley Point Apartments
  B16 ....66 B2
Brindley Rd Bedworth CV7 ....96 B8
  Hinckley LE10 ....74 E8
  West Bromwich B71 ....53 A8
Brindley Way ◨ B66 ....65 C5
Brindleys Bsns Pk WS11 ....2 B3
Brineton Gr B29 ....85 A1
Brineton Ind Est ◨ WS2 ....28 C1
Brineton St WS2 ....28 C1
Bringewood Gr B32 ....102 B8
Brinklow Cl B98 ....159 D8
Brinklow Croft B34 ....69 D7
Brinklow Rd
  Birmingham B29 ....84 F2
  Coventry CV3 ....115 A2
Brinklow Twr ◨ B12 ....86 F8
Brinley Way DY6 ....60 C6
Brinsford La WV10 ....11 D7
Brinsford Rd WV10 ....11 D4
Brinsley Cl B91 ....107 B2
Brinsley Rd B26 ....89 B8
Brinton Cl DY11 ....116 C3
Brinton Cres DY11 ....116 C3
Brisbane Cl CV3 ....133 E6
Brisbane Ct CV12 ....78 B2
Brisbane Ho B34 ....69 A6
Brisbane Rd B67 ....64 E5

Brisbane Way WS12 ....2 E1
Briscoe Rd CV6 ....95 D4
Briseley Cl DY5 ....81 D8
Bristam Cl B69 ....63 E6
Bristnall Hall Cres B68 ....64 C3
Bristnall Hall High Sch
  B68 ....64 D3
Bristnall Hall La B68 ....64 D3
Bristnall Hall Rd B68 ....64 C3
Bristnall Ho B11 ....64 D3
Bristol Cl WS11 ....2 B1
Bristol Ct ◨ B29 ....103 C7
Bristol Rd
  Birmingham, Balsall Heath
  B5 ....86 C5
  Birmingham, Gravelly Hill
  B23 ....56 E3
  Coventry CV5 ....112 F2
  Dudley DY2 ....62 D2
Bristol Rd S
  Birmingham B31 ....102 F2
  Birmingham, Longbridge
  B31,B45 ....122 C7
Bristol St Birmingham B15 ....86 D8
  Wolverhampton WV3 ....39 B8
Briston Cl DY5 ....81 C8
Britannia Gdns B65 ....63 C3
Britannia Gn DY3 ....50 B5
Britannia High Sch B65 ....63 D2
Britannia Rd Bilston WV14 ....40 F3
  Blackheath B65 ....63 C2
  Hinckley LE10 ....76 A5
Britannia St
  Coventry CV2 ....113 F3
  Tipton B69 ....52 C2
Britannia Way WS13 ....9 F8
Britford Cl B14 ....104 F3
Briton Rd CV2 ....114 A4
Brittan Cl B34 ....69 E6
Brittania Ph WS10 ....41 D3
Brittania Sh Ctr ◨ LE10 ....75 D8
Brittania Way WS11 ....4 C5
Britten Cl CV11 ....79 A7
Britten St B97 ....153 D4
Britwell Rd B73 ....46 A2
Brixfield Way B90 ....126 B5
Brixham Cl CV11 ....73 F5
Brixham Dr CV2 ....114 C7
Brixham Rd B16 ....65 D4
Broad Acres B31 ....102 E6
Broad Croft DY4 ....52 C6
Broad Ground Rd B98 ....154 B2
Broad Heath Cl B97 ....153 B5
Broad Heath Com Prim Sch
  CV6 ....113 E6
Broad La Birmingham B14 ....104 E4
  Coventry CV5 ....111 D4
  Lichfield WS14 ....9 D6
  Tanworth-In-A B98 ....141 E3
  Walsall, Essington WS3 ....13 A4
  Walsall, Pelsall WS4 ....15 C2
  Wolverhampton, Penn WV3 ....38 E8
Broad La N WV11,WV12 ....27 A7
Broad La S WV11 ....27 A5
Broad Lane Gdns WS3 ....14 A2
Broad Lanes WV14 ....40 C3
Broad Mdw WV9 ....30 B8
Broad Meadow La
  Birmingham B30 ....104 B3
  Great Wyrley WS6 ....5 A5
Broad Oaks B76 ....47 A1
Broad Oaks Rd B91 ....107 A5
Broad Park Rd CV2 ....114 D8
Broad Rd B27 ....88 B3
Broad St Birmingham B14 ....40 D6
  Birmingham B15,B1 ....66 C1
  Brierley Hill DY5 ....61 C6
  Bromsgrove B61 ....136 F4
  Cannock WS11 ....4 E6
  Coventry CV6 ....113 E7
  Dudley WV14 ....51 C8
  Kidderminster DY10 ....116 E7
  Kingswinford DY6 ....60 D5
  Oldbury B69 ....64 A5
  Warwick CV34 ....160 E7
Broad Street Jetty DY4 ....113 E7
Broad Way WS4 ....15 C2
Broadcott Ind Est B64 ....83 A4
Broadfern Rd B93 ....128 B8
Broadfield Cl
  Kingswinford DY6 ....60 D5
  West Bromwich B71 ....42 F1
Broadfield House Glass
  Mus★ DY6 ....60 D5
Broadfield Wlk ◨ B16 ....66 B1
Broadfields B23 ....57 B7
Broadfields Rd B23 ....57 B7
Broadgate CV1 ....165 B3
Broadhaven Cl CV31 ....162 C7
Broadheath Dr WS4 ....29 D8
Broadhidley Dr B32 ....84 B1
Broadlands Cl CV5 ....112 C2
Broadlands Dr DY5 ....61 E5
Broadlands Rise WS13 ....11 D5
Broadlea CV5 ....112 C2
Broadlee B77 ....22 C1
Broadmead Ct CV5 ....112 C2
Broadmeadow Cl B30 ....104 B3
Broadmeadow Ct DY9 ....60 B8
Broadmeadow La WS6 ....5 A3
Broadmeadow Rd WS12 ....40 C7
Broadmeadow Ho B32 ....102 D8

Broadmeadow Inf Sch B30 104 B2
Broadmeadow Jun Sch B30 104 B2
Broadmeadows Cl WV12 27 E8
Broadmeadows Rd WV12 27 E8
Broadmede Ho B67 64 E2
Broadmere Rise CV5 112 A2
Broadmoor Ave B68 64 D2
Broadmoor Cl WV14 40 C4
Broadmoor Rd WV14 40 C3
Broadoaks Cl WS11 5 F6
Broadsmeath B77 21 C1
Broadstone Ave
Halesowen B63 82 B4
Walsall WS3 28 D7
Broadstone Cl WV4 39 D5
Broadstone Rd B26 69 A1
Broadsword Way LE10 75 D4
Broadwalk 5 B1 66 C1
Broadwalk Ret Pk WS1 42 D6
Broadwas Cl B98 154 C5
Broadwater CV5 133 A8
Broadwaters Ave WS10 41 C4
Broadwaters Dr
Hagley DY9 99 B4
Kidderminster DY10 117 A8
Broadwaters Rd WS10 41 C4
Broadway Cannock WS12 1 F6
Coventry CV5 113 A1
Cubbington CV32 157 E5
Oldbury B68 64 C1
Solihull B90 106 B4
Walsall WS5 43 A6
Wolverhampton, Bushbury WV10 11 E2
Wolverhampton, Compton WV3 24 C2
Broadway Ave
Birmingham B9 68 A3
Halesowen B63 83 A2
Broadway Croft
Birmingham B26 89 A6
Oldbury B68 64 C1
Broadway Gdns WV10 11 E2
Broadway Mans CV5 113 A1
Broadway N WS1 29 B2
Broadway Sch B20 55 E2
Broadway Sch The (Aston Campus) B6 66 E8
Broadway The
Birmingham B20 55 E2
Dudley DY1 51 B3
Stourbridge DY8 80 D3
West Bromwich B71 53 B7
Wombourne WV5 49 A5
Broadway W WS1 42 D6
Broadwell Ct CV4 131 F6
Broadwell Ind Pk B69 53 A1
Broadwell Rd Oldbury B69 64 A8
Solihull B92 89 A2
Broadwells Cres CV4 132 A5
Broadyates Gr B25 88 C6
Broadyates Rd B25 88 C6
Brobury Croft B91 106 D4
Brock Rd DY4 52 C4
Brockenhurst Ct B73 46 B1
Brockenhurst Way CV6 96 B6
Brockeridge Cl WV12 13 C1
Brockfield Ho WV10 25 F4
Brockhall Gr B37 69 F5
Brockhill Dr B97 153 A5
Brockhill La
Alvechurch B48 124 B2
Beoley B98 140 F2
Tardebigge B97 152 E8
Brockhurst Ave LE10 75 D4
Brockhurst Cres WS5 42 E4
Brockhurst Dr
Birmingham B28 106 A5
Coventry CV4 111 D2
Wolverhampton WV6 25 A4
Brockhurst Ho 4 WS2 28 D3
Brockhurst La
Solihull B90 126 B5
Weeford B75 33 B7
Brockhurst Pl WS5 42 F5
Brockhurst Rd
Birmingham B36 68 D6
Sutton Coldfield B75 32 D1
Brockhurst St WS1 42 E6
Brockley Cl DY5 61 D3
Brockley Gr B13 86 C1
Brockley Pl B7 67 C7
Brockmoor Cl DY9 81 C2
Brockmoor Prim Sch DY5 61 C3
Brockton Rd B29 85 A1
Brockwell Gr B44 44 E4
Brockwell Rd B44 44 E4
Brockworth Rd B14 104 C2
Brocton Cl WV14 40 A3
Brodick Cl LE10 75 A8
Brodick Rd B35 74 F8
Brodick Way CV10 72 F3
Brogden Cl 4 B71 53 F8
Brome Hall La B94 144 D2
Bromfield Cl B6 66 E7
Bromfield Cres WS10 42 C4
Bromfield Ct WV6 24 B3
Bromfield Rd
Redditch B97 153 D2
Wednesbury WS10 42 C3
Bromford Cl
Birmingham, Erdington B23 56 E5
Birmingham, Handsworth B20 55 A2
Bromford Cres B24 57 A2
Bromford Ct
Birmingham, Turves Green B31 103 B1
Birmingham, Washwood Heath B8 68 B6
Bromford Dale 2 WV6 24 F3
Bromford Dell B31 103 C4
Bromford Dr B36 68 D8
Bromford Hill B20 55 C3
Bromford Ho B73 45 F2
Bromford Jun & Inf Schs B36 68 D7
Bromford La
Birmingham B8,B36 68 C6
West Bromwich B70 53 B2
Bromford Mere 4 B92 88 E1
Bromford Park Ho 3 B13 87 B2
Bromford Rd
Birmingham B36 68 D7
Dudley DY2 62 A6
West Bromwich B69,B70 53 A1
Bromford Rise WV3 163 A1
Bromford Road Ind Est B70 53 A1
Bromford Wlk B43 43 F1
Bromleigh Dr CV2 114 C2
Bromleigh Villas CV8 133 F2
Bromley DY5 61 B5
Bromley Cl Cannock WS12 2 C7
Kenilworth CV8 147 E6
Bromley Gdns WV8 10 A4
Bromley Hills Prim Sch DY6 60 F5
Bromley Ho WV4 39 A5
Bromley La DY6 60 E4
Bromley Lodge WV4 39 A5
Bromley Pl WV4 39 A5
Bromley St Birmingham B9 67 A1
Stourbridge DY9 81 F6
Wolverhampton WV2 39 C7
Bromley-Pensnett Prim Sch The DY5 61 B5
Brompton Dr DY5 81 B7
Brompton Lawns WV6 24 A3
Brompton Pool Rd B28 105 E3
Brompton Rd B44 44 E4
Bromsgrove Eastern By-Pass B60 150 E6
Bromsgrove Highway
Bromsgrove B60 137 D1
Redditch B97 153 B2
Tardebigge B60,B97 152 C6
Bromsgrove Lower Sch B60 136 F1
Bromsgrove Mus* B61 137 A3
Bromsgrove Private Hospl B60 138 B1
Bromsgrove Rd Clent DY9 99 D4
Dodford B61 136 D6
Halesowen B63 83 C4
Kidderminster DY10 117 F2
Redditch B97 153 B3
Romsley B62 101 A5
Studley B80 159 D2
Bromsgrove Sch B61 136 F1
Bromsgrove St
Birmingham B5 164 C1
Halesowen B63 83 C4
Kidderminster DY10 116 E6
Bromsgrove Sta B60 151 B7
Bromwall Rd B13 105 B6
Bromwich Cl CV3 134 F8
Bromwich Dr B75 46 C7
Bromwich La DY9 99 B8
Bromwich Wlk B9 68 A3
Bromwynd Cl WV2 39 B6
Bromyard Ave B76 58 A8
Bromyard Rd B11 87 E3
Bronte Cl B90 106 D1
Bronte Ct Solihull B90 106 D1
Tamworth B79 21 A6
Bronte Dr Cannock WS11 2 C2
Kidderminster DY10 117 C6
Bronte Farm Rd B90 106 D1
Bronte Rd WV2 39 F6
Bronwen Rd WV14 51 C7
Bronze Cl CV11 78 E8
Brook Ave B77 36 A7
Brook Cl Birmingham B33 68 E4
Brownhills WS9 16 A3
Coventry CV1 113 E4
Lichfield WS13 3 A1
Solihull B90 105 F1
Brook Cotts B25 88 A7
Brook Cres Hagley DY9 99 B5
Kingswinford DY6 60 C7
Stourbridge DY9 81 F3
Brook Croft
Birmingham, Lyndon Green B26 89 B7
Birmingham, Marston Green B37 90 B7
Brook Dr B32 84 D1
Brook End Burntwood WS7 7 A4
Fazeley B78 35 B8
Brook Farm Ind Est B94 126 B2
Brook Farm Wlk B37 70 D2
Brook Fields Cl B60 121 C1
Brook Gr WV8 10 B2
Brook Green La B92 109 A1
Brook Hill Rd B8 68 A4
Brook Holloway DY9 81 F4
Brook House La WV10 12 B7
Brook La
Birmingham, Billesley B13 105 B7
Birmingham, Harborne B32 84 F5
Blackheath B64 62 E2
Brook La *continued*
Brownhills WS9 15 F3
Great Wyrley WS6 5 A3
Nuneaton CV10 73 C6
Solihull B92 106 D8
Brook Mdws WV8 10 B4
Brook Meadow Rd
Birmingham B34 69 B6
Walsall WS4 29 D8
Brook Park Trad Est 4 DY9 81 F5
Brook Piece Wlk B35 58 B3
Brook Prim Sch The DY8 60 F1
Brook Rd
Birmingham, Chad Valley B15 85 E7
Birmingham, Eachway B45 121 E7
Bromsgrove B61 136 E1
Cheslyn Hay WS6 4 E4
Fairfield B61 120 C2
Oldbury B68 64 A2
Stourbridge DY8 81 B3
Willenhall WV13 26 E1
Wombourne WV5 49 A6
Brook St Bedworth CV12 78 B5
Bilston WV14 40 E5
Birmingham B3 164 A3
Brierley Hill DY5 82 A8
Dudley, Gornalwood DY3 50 C3
Dudley, Woodsetton DY3 51 A7
Kidderminster DY11 116 C6
Kingswinford DY6 49 B1
Redditch B98 154 A4
Smethwick B66 65 B6
Stourbridge, Amblecote DY8 60 F1
Stourbridge, Lye DY9 81 F5
Stourbridge, Wollaston DY8 80 E5
Tipton DY4 51 E6
Walsall WS2 28 D1
Warwick CV34 160 E6
West Bromwich B70 53 B3
Brook Street Bsns Ctr DY4 51 E6
Brook Terr WV14 40 E5
Brook Vale WS11 4 F8
Brook View Cl B19 66 C6
Brook Wlk B32 84 D2
Brookbank Ave B34 69 D6
Brookbank Gdns DY3 50 B2
Brookbank Rd DY3 50 B2
Brookdale Dudley DY3 50 C3
Hinckley LE10 75 B7
Kidderminster DY10 116 F8
Brookdale Cl B45 102 A1
Brookdale Dr WV4 38 E6
Brookdale Rd CV10 73 E7
Brooke Cl CV34 160 F5
Brooke Rd Cannock WS12 1 F6
Kenilworth CV8 148 B4
Brooke St DY2 62 C8
Brookend Dr B45 121 F7
Brookes Ho 3 WS1 28 F1
Brookfield Cl
Aldridge WS9 16 A1
Redditch B97 158 D4
Brookfield Dr WS11 4 E7
Brookfield Prec B18 66 B4
Brookfield Rd
Aldridge WS9 16 A1
Birmingham B18 66 A5
Codsall WV8 10 B3
Cubbington CV32 157 E5
Hinckley LE10 75 C6
Brookfield Way
Solihull B92 106 D7
Tipton DY4 52 B6
Brookfields Prim Sch B18 66 B4
Brookfields Rd B68 64 C4
Brookford Ave CV6 95 A3
Brookhampton Cl B97 158 E4
Brookhill Cl WV12 13 D1
Brookhill Way WV12 13 D1
Brookhouse Cl WV10 12 B6
Brookhouse La WV10 11 F6
Brookhouse Rd
Blackwell B45 137 F7
Walsall WS5 43 B7
Brookhurst Ct CV32 156 D1
Brookhurst Prim Sch CV32 156 C1
Brookhus Farm Rd B76 58 A8
Brooking Cl B43 44 D4
Brookland Rd
Brownhills WS9 15 F3
Hagley DY9 99 A4
Brooklands
Stourbridge DY8 60 F1
Walsall WS5 43 B3
Brooklands Ave WS6 4 F4
Brooklands Cl B28 87 F1
Brooklands Dr B14 104 E5
Brooklands Gr WS9 15 F3
Brooklands La B98 154 B5
Brooklands Par WV1 26 B2
Brooklands Rd
Birmingham B28 87 F1
Cannock WS11 2 A4
Brooklands Way B37 90 A8
Brooklea CV12 77 F2
Brooklea Gr B38 104 A1
Brooklime Gdns WV10 12 B7
Brooklyn Ave B6 66 F7
Brooklyn Gr Dudley WV14 51 D8
Kingswinford DY6 60 B8
Brooklyn Rd
Burntwood WS7 7 A4
Cannock WS12 2 D1
Brooklyn Rd *continued*
Coventry CV1 113 D6
Brookmans Ave B32 84 D4
Brookmeadow Ct B28 105 D6
Brookpiece Ho B14 104 E2
Brooks Croft B35 58 A2
Brooks Rd B72 57 C8
Brooks Twr B19 66 D7
Brooksbank Dr B64 62 F4
Brooksby Gr B93 128 A2
Brookshaw Way CV2 114 F8
Brookside
Birmingham, Great Barr B43 54 D7
Birmingham, Northfield B31 102 F5
Cheswick Green B90 126 D3
Dudley DY3 50 D2
Hinckley LE10 75 E7
Wednesbury WS10 42 B3
Brookside Ave
Birmingham B13 105 B7
Coventry CV5 112 C3
Kenilworth CV8 147 E4
Brookside Cl
Alvechurch B48 139 B6
Birmingham B23 56 C7
Halesowen B63 82 D3
Brookside Dr B61 136 F8
Brookside Ind Est WS10 42 B3
Brookside Rd B78 20 D1
Brookside Way
Blakedown DY10 98 B2
Kingswinford DY6 60 C7
Tamworth B77 36 A6
Brookstray Flats CV5 112 B3
Brookthorpe Dr WV12 27 C4
Brookvale Ave CV3 114 E1
Brookvale Cl B61 137 B4
Brookvale Gr B92 88 D1
Brookvale Mews B29 86 B2
Brookvale Park Rd B23 56 B4
Brookvale Prim Sch B23 56 B3
Brookvale Rd
Birmingham B23,B6 56 A3
Solihull B92 88 D1
Brookvale Trad Est B6 56 A3
Brookview B67 64 F3
Brookweed B77 22 A3
Brookwillow Rd B63 82 E1
Brookwood Ave B28 105 D5
Brookwood Dr B45 138 C8
Broom Cl B60 137 B2
Broom Covert Rd WS14 18 E8
Broom Cres DY10 117 A6
Broom Dr B14 104 E4
Broom Hall Cres B27 106 B8
Broom Hall Gr B27 106 C8
Broom Ho 3 B71 42 F1
Broom La B90 126 A6
Broom Rd Dudley DY1 51 A5
Walsall WS5 43 B3
Broom St B12 87 A8
Broomcroft Rd B37 69 F5
Broomdene Ave B34 69 A7
Broome Ave B43 54 C7
Broome Cl 5 B63 83 A3
Broome Croft CV6 95 B3
Broome Ct B36 69 C8
Broome Gdns B75 46 C5
Broome La Blakedown DY9 98 F2
Hagley DY9 99 B2
Broome Rd WV10 25 E7
Broomehill Cl DY5 81 C7
Broomfield B67 64 F5
Broomfield Ave B78 35 A8
Broomfield Cl DY11 116 C7
Broomfield Gn DY11 116 C7
Broomfield Pl CV5 113 A2
Broomfield Rd
Birmingham B23 56 D2
Coventry CV5 113 A1
Kidderminster DY11 116 C7
Broomfield Rise CV10 72 F2
Broomfields Ave B91 107 D5
Broomfields Cl B91 107 D5
Broomfields Farm Rd B91 107 D5
Broomhall Ave WV11 26 D6
Broomhill Bank WS11 1 E3
Broomhill Cl
Birmingham B43 54 D8
Cannock WS11 1 E4
Broomhill La B43 54 D8
Broomhill Rd B23 56 B7
Broomhurst B15 85 E8
Broomie Cl B75 46 D4
Broomlea Cl B74 44 E8
Broomy Cl B34 69 A5
Broomybank CV8 148 B6
Brosdale Dr LE10 71 A1
Broseley Ave B31 123 B8
Broseley Brook Cl 1 B9 67 C1
Brosil Ave B20 54 E3
Brotherton Ave B97 152 F2
Brough Cl Birmingham B7 67 B6
Wolverhampton WV4,WV14 39 F3
Brougham St B19 66 B7
Broughton Cres B31 122 D8
Broughton Ct
2 Birmingham, Edgbaston B15 86 B7
1 Birmingham, Pheasey B43 44 D4
Perton WV6 24 A3
Broughton Rd
Birmingham B20 66 A8
Stourbridge DY9 81 D3
Broughton Rd *continued*
Wolverhampton WV3 24 C1
Browett Rd CV6 113 A5
Brown Ave B77 35 C8
Brown Lion St DY4 51 E7
Brown Rd WS10 41 C7
Brown St WV2 39 D7
Brown's Coppice Ave B91 106 E5
Brown's Ct 10 B13 87 B2
Brown's La Allesley CV5 94 C1
Dordon B78 36 F5
Tamworth B79 21 C8
Brownfield Rd B34 69 C7
Brownhills Com Sch WS8 6 F1
Brownhills Rd
Brownhills WS9 16 A4
Norton Canes WS11 6 B4
Brownhills West Prim Sch WS8 6 C2
Brownhills West Sta* WS7 6 C3
Browning Ave CV34 160 C5
Browning Cl
Kidderminster DY10 117 B6
Nuneaton CV10 72 A5
Tamworth B79 20 F8
Willenhall WV12 27 E7
Browning Cres WV10 11 C2
Browning Dr LE10 71 C1
Browning Gr WV6 23 E4
Browning Rd
Burntwood WS7 7 C7
Coventry CV2 114 C3
Dudley DY3 50 A4
Browning St B16 66 B2
Browning Twr B31 103 C3
Brownley Rd B90 126 E7
Brownlow St 6 CV32 157 A2
Brownmead Jun & Inf Sch B34 69 B7
Browns Dr B73 56 F8
Browns Gr B20 54 F3
Browns La B93 127 E6
Brownsea Cl B45 101 F1
Brownsea Dr B1 164 B1
Brownsfield Rd WS13 3 D1
Brownshill Bsns Pk WS8 15 F5
Brownshill Ct CV6 112 F8
Brownshill Green Rd CV6 94 E1
Brownshore La WV11 13 A3
Brownsover Cl B36 58 B1
Brownswall Rd DY3 50 C7
Browsholme B79 20 D6
Broxell Cl CV34 155 C1
Broxwood Pk WV6 24 B3
Bruce Rd Bedworth CV7 95 F7
Coventry CV6 113 B8
Kidderminster DY10 117 B7
Brueton Ave
Bromsgrove B60 151 A8
Solihull B91 107 D3
Brueton Dr
Birmingham B24 57 A3
Redditch B98 154 A3
Brueton Rd WV14 41 A7
Bruford Rd WV3 39 A8
Brunel Cl Birmingham B12 87 A5
Burntwood WS7 7 B8
Coventry CV2 113 F3
Tamworth B79 21 B6
Whitnash CV31 162 B2
Brunel Ct Darlaston WS10 41 F6
Dudley WV14 51 E8
Wombourne WV5 49 A7
Brunel Dr DY4 40 E1
Brunel Gr WV6 23 E5
Brunel Rd Hinckley LE10 75 C8
Oldbury B69 63 D6
Brunel St B1 164 B2
Brunel Way WV2 40 A7
Brunel Wlk WS10 41 F6
Brunslow Cl
Willenhall WV13 27 C1
Wolverhampton WV10 11 C1
Brunswick Arc B1 66 B2
Brunswick Ct
Royal Leamington Spa CV31 162 A5
Wednesbury WS10 42 C3
Brunswick Gate DY8 81 A1
Brunswick Gdns
Birmingham B21 54 F1
Wednesbury WS10 42 B4
Brunswick Ho
Birmingham, Buckland End B34 69 A7
Birmingham, Marston Green B37 89 F8
Brunswick Park Rd WS10 42 B3
Brunswick Rd
Birmingham, Handsworth B21 54 F1
Birmingham, Sparkbrook B12 87 A5
Cannock WS11 1 E2
Coventry CV1 113 B2
Brunswick St
Birmingham B1 66 B2
Royal Leamington Spa CV31 162 A5
Walsall WS2 42 C7
Brunswick Terr WS10 41 F3

Bruntingthorpe Way
CV3 ....138 E8
Brunton Cl CV3 ....115 B1
Brunton Rd B10 ....87 F7
Brushfield Rd B42 .....55 D8
Brutus Dr B46 ....59 E1
Bryan Ave WV4 ....38 D4
Bryan Rd WS2 ....42 C6
Bryans Way WS12 ....2 F4
Bryanston Cl CV2 ....115 A4
Bryanston Ct B91 .....106 F7
Bryanston Rd B91 ....106 F6
Bryant Rd CV7 ....96 A7
Bryant St B18 ....65 E5
Bryce Rd DY5 ....61 B5
Bryher Wlk B45 ....101 E1
Brylan Croft B44 ......55 F6
Brymill Ind Est DY4 ..51 E7
Brympton Rd CV3 ....114 C2
Bryn Arden Rd B26 ....88 E5
Bryn Jones Cl CV3 ...134 F7
Bryn Rd CV6 ....113 F7
Bryndale Ave B14 ....104 C4
Brynmawr Rd WV4,WV14 .40 A3
Brynside Cl B14 ......104 D2
Bryony Cl CV12 ....77 E1
Bryony Croft B23 ......56 B7
Bryony Gdns WS10 .....41 D7
Bryony Rd B29 ....103 B7
Bsns Ctr The B11 ......87 F6
Buchanan Ave WS4 ....29 A3
Buchanan Cl WS4 ......29 A3
Buchanan Rd WS4 .....29 A3
Buckbury Cl DY9 ......81 D2
Buckbury Croft B90 ..127 B6
Buckden B77 ....22 C1
Buckden Cl 2 CV34 ...155 F1
Buckfast Cl
  Bromsgrove B61 .....136 D1
  Coventry CV3 ....133 E5
Buckhold Dr CV5 ......112 B5
Buckingham Cl
  Hinckley LE10 ....71 F4
  Nuneaton CV10 ....73 B1
  Wednesbury WS10 ....42 D4
Buckingham Ct
  Birmingham, Griffin's Hill
  B29 ....132 D6
  Birmingham, Selly Oak B29 .85 D1
Buckingham Dr WV12 ..27 B7
Buckingham Gdns WS14 ..9 B6
Buckingham Gr DY6 ....60 C7
Buckingham Mews B73 .46 A3
Buckingham Pl 3 WS11 ..2 C1
Buckingham Rd
  Birmingham B36 ....69 F7
  Blackheath B65 ....63 D4
  Tamworth B79 ....20 E7
  Wolverhampton WV4 ..39 A5
Buckingham Rise
  Coventry CV5 ....112 B4
  Dudley DY1 ....50 E2
Buckingham St B19 ..164 B4
Buckland Cl WS12 ......2 D1
Buckland End B34 .....69 A6
Buckland Ho 3 B15 ....86 C7
Buckland Rd CV6 .....113 A5
Bucklands End La B34 ..68 F6
Buckle Cl WS1 ....42 E8
Buckler's Yd CV12 .....78 A2
Buckley Ho CV5 ....112 F1
Buckley Rd
  Royal Leamington Spa
  CV32 ....157 C2
  Wolverhampton WV4 ..38 D5
Buckleys Gn B48 .....139 A6
Buckleys The B48 ....139 A6
Bucklow Wlk B33 ......68 E4
Buckminster Dr B93 ..127 E4
Bucknall Cres B32 ...102 A8
Bucknall Ct 14 B13 ...87 B2
Bucknall Ho B14 .....104 E6
Bucknall Rd WV11 .....13 B1
Bucknell Cl B91 ......107 C5
Buckpool Sch DY8 .....60 F3
Buckridge Cl B38 ....123 D7
Buckridge La B90 ....126 A5
Bucks Hill CV10 ....72 C6
Buckton Cl WS14 ....1 F8
Buckton Ct B75 ....32 E2
Budbrook Gr B34 ......69 E6
Budbrooke Cl CV2 .....96 D2
Budbrooke Ind Est
  CV34 ....160 B7
Budbrooke Rd CV34 ..160 B7
Budden Rd WV14 ......51 D7
Bude Rd WS5 ....43 D7
Buffery Rd DY2 ....62 D7
Bufferys Cl B91 ......127 B8
Buildwas Cl WS3 .....13 F2
Bulford Cl B14 ....104 F2
Bulger Rd WV14 ....40 C7
Bulkington La CV11 ...79 A7
Bulkington Rd
  Bedworth CV12 ....78 D2
  Shilton CV7 ....97 E6
Bull La Bilston WV14,WS10 .41 B3
  West Bromwich B70 ...53 A3
  Wombourne WV5 ....49 B7
Bull Ring
  4 Halesowen B63 ......83 B3
  Kidderminster DY10 .116 E6
  Nuneaton CV10 ....73 B2
  Sedgley DY3 ....50 D8
  Willenhall WV13 ....27 A3

Bull Ring Trad Est 2
  B12 ....66 F1
Bull St
  Birmingham, Brookfields
  B4 ....164 C3
  Birmingham, Harborne B17 .85 D5
  Brierley Hill DY5 .....61 B1
  Darlaston WS10 ....41 E6
  Dudley, Gornalwood DY3 .50 C2
  Dudley, Spring Mire DY1 ..62 A8
  Nuneaton CV11 ....73 D2
  West Bromwich B70 ...53 D3
Bull Street Trad Est DY5 .61 B2
Bull Yd CV1 ....165 B2
Bull's Head La CV3 ..114 B2
Bull's La B76 ....47 E1
Bullace Croft B15 .....85 D3
Bulldog La WS13 ....3 B1
Buller St WV4 ....39 E6
Bullfield Ave CV4 ....131 D1
Bullfields Cl B65 ......62 F5
Bullfinch Cl DY1 ......61 E8
Bullfurlong La LE10 ..75 F4
Bullimore Gr CV8 ....148 A2
Bullivents Cl B93 ....127 E3
Bullmeadow La WV5 ..49 A8
Bullmoor La WS14 .....3 B1
Bullock St Birmingham B7 .67 A5
  West Bromwich B70 ...53 D1
Bullock's Row WS1 ....28 F1
Bullows Rd WS8 ....15 C6
Bulwell Cl B6 ....67 A7
Bulwer Rd CV6 ....113 A6
Bulwick Cl CV3 ......115 B1
Bumble Hole La B61 ..136 C7
Bunbury Gdns B30 ...103 D4
Bunbury Rd B30,B31 ..103 C4
Bundle Hill B63 ....83 A4
Bungalows The
  West Bromwich, Charlemont
  B71 ....53 E8
  West Bromwich, Stow Village
  B70 ....52 F6
Bunker's Hill La WV14 .40 E7
Bunn's La DY1,DY2 ....51 F1
Bunny Stile La WV11 ..26 B6
Buntsford Dr B60 ....150 F6
Buntsford Hill B60 ..150 C5
Buntsford Park Rd B60 .150 F6
Bunyan Pl WV11 ....1 E4
Burbage CE Inf Sch LE10 .76 A5
Burbage CE Jun Sch
  LE10 ....75 F6
Burbage Cl WV10 ......25 E6
Burbage Rd LE10 ......76 A7
Burbages La CV6 ......95 D4
Burbery St 3 DY4 .....52 A8
Burberry Gr CV7 .....130 A6
Burbidge Rd B9 ....67 E3
Burbury Cl Bedworth CV12 .78 C4
  Royal Leamington Spa
  CV32 ....157 C2
Burbury St CV34 .....161 B8
Burbury St
  Birmingham, Lozells B19 .66 C6
  Birmingham, Newtown B19 .66 C6
Burcher Gn DY10 .....117 B5
Burcombe Twr B23 ....57 B6
Burcot Ave
  Bromsgrove B60 .....137 B4
  Wolverhampton WV1 ..26 A2
Burcot Cl B74 ....31 F2
Burcot Ho B60 ....137 B3
Burcot La
  Bromsgrove, Burcot B60 .137 B3
  Bromsgrove, Stoney Hill
  B60 ....137 C4
Burcote Rd B24 ....57 D3
Burcott Ct 3 CV34 ...155 F1
Burdock Cl Cannock WS11 ..2 B3
  Walsall WS5 ....43 A3
Burdock Ho B38 ......103 F1
Burdock Rd B29 ......103 A6
Burdons Cl B34 ....69 A5
Bure Gr WV13 ....27 D1
Burfield Rd B63 ....82 C6
Burford Cl Solihull B92 .89 A3
  Walsall WS5 ....43 A4
Burford Ct
  10 Birmingham B13 ...87 B2
  Stourbridge DY8 ......81 A4
Burford Mews 15 CV31 .162 C6
Burford Park Rd B38 .123 E8
Burford Rd
  Birmingham B44 ....55 F7
  Hollywood B47 ....125 A6
Burgage Pl CV11 ......73 C4
Burgage Wlk CV11 ....73 B5
Burges CV1 ....165 B3
Burges Gr CV34 ......155 F1
Burgess Croft B92 ...107 F7
Burgh Way WS2 ....28 A4
Burghley Cl CV11 .....73 F2
Burghley Dr
  Kidderminster DY11 ..116 C5
  West Bromwich B71 ...42 F2
Burghley Wlk DY5 .....81 B8
Burgoyne St WS11 .....2 A5
Burhill Way B37 ....70 B5
Burke Ave B13 ....87 D2
Burkitt Dr DY4 ....52 C8
Burland Ave WV6 .....24 E6
Burleigh Cl
  Balsall Common CV7 .130 B7
  Willenhall WV12 ......27 B6
Burleigh Croft WS7 ...7 A4
Burleigh Rd Hinckley LE10 .71 C2
  Wolverhampton WV3 ..39 A8

Burleigh St WS1 ....29 A1
Burleton Rd B33 ......69 E2
Burley Cl B90 ....105 F2
Burley Wlk B38 ......123 C8
Burlington Arc B2 ...164 B2
Burlington Ave B70 ...53 E1
Burlington Cl DY10 ..117 B4
Burlington Ct B78 .....35 B8
Burlington Rd
  Birmingham B10 ....67 F1
  Coventry CV2 ....113 F4
  Nuneaton CV10 ....78 B7
  West Bromwich B70 ...53 E1
Burlington St B6 ......66 E6
Burlish Ave 3 B92 ....88 F1
Burman Cl B90 ....106 A2
Burman Dr B46 ....70 F5
Burman Inf Sch B90 .106 A2
Burman Rd B90 ....106 A1
Burmarsh Wlk WV8 ..24 F8
Burmese Way B65 .....62 F5
Burn Cl B66 ....65 A4
Burnaby Cl CV10 ......72 B5
Burnaby Rd CV6 ....95 B1
Burnaston Cres B90 .127 C6
Burnaston Rd B28 ....87 E1
Burnbank Gr B24 ......57 B4
Burncross Way WV10 .25 F6
Burnel Rd B29 ....85 B2
Burnell Gdns WV3 ....38 C8
Burnet Gr WV10 ....12 B8
Burnett Ho 2 B69 .....63 D5
Burnett Rd B74 ....31 B2
Burney La B8 ....68 C4
Burnfields Cl WS9 .....30 A7
Burnham Ave
  Birmingham B25 ....88 C6
  Wolverhampton WV10 .25 C8
Burnham Cl DY6 ....60 F4
Burnham Ct
  Birmingham B23 ....56 C2
  18 Brierley Hill DY5 ..61 D2
Burnham Gn WS11 .....4 B8
Burnham Mdw B28 ..106 A6
Burnham Rd
  Birmingham B44 ....55 E7
  Coventry CV3 ....134 A6
Burnham Rise CV11 ...74 A6
Burnhill Gr B29 ......103 A8
Burnlea Gr B31 ......103 C1
Burns Ave Tipton DY4 ..52 A7
  Warwick CV34 ....160 C5
Burns Cl
  Kidderminster DY10 .117 B6
  Lichfield WS14 ....9 B6
  Redditch B97 ....158 C8
  Stourbridge DY8 ......81 A8
Burns Dr B79 ....7 C7
Burns Pl WS10 ....41 A5
Burns Rd Coventry CV2 .114 B3
  Royal Leamington Spa
  CV32 ....157 B4
  Tamworth B79 ....21 A6
  Wednesbury WS10 ....41 B5
Burns Wlk CV12 ....78 C1
Burnsall Cl
  Birmingham B37 ....69 F2
  Wolverhampton WV9 ..11 A3
Burnsall Gr CV5 .....132 D8
Burnsall Rd CV5 .....132 D8
Burnside CV3 ....115 A2
Burnside Ct B73 ....46 A1
Burnside Gdns WS5 ..43 D6
Burnside Way B31 ...122 F7
Bursnips Rd WV11 ....13 C4
Burton Ave WS4 ....29 B8
Burton Cl Allesley CV5 .94 C2
  Stone DY10 ....117 D1
Burton Cres CV10 ...163 D4
Burton Farm Rd WS4 ..29 B3
Burton Green CE Prim Sch
  CV8 ....131 B3
Burton Ind Est B64 ...82 E8
Burton La Bramcote CV11 .79 F7
  Redditch B98 ....153 F3
Burton Old Rd
  Lichfield WS13 ....3 F1
  Lichfield WS14 ....9 F8
Burton Old Rd E WS14 ..9 D8

Burton Old Rd W WS14 ...9 D8
Burton Rd Dudley DY1 ...50 F4
  Lichfield WS13 ....3 F1
  Wolverhampton WV10 .25 E3
Burton Wood Dr B20 ..55 D2
Bury Hill Rd B69 ......63 D8
Bury Ho CV4 ....111 F3
Bury Mound Ct B90 .105 C2
Bury Rd CV31 ....161 F7
Buryfield Rd B91 ....107 B6
Busby Cl CV3 ....134 F7
Bush Ave B66 ....65 C5
Bush Cl CV4 ....111 F3
Bush Ct CV2 ....114 B6
Bush Gr Birmingham B21 .54 C1
  Walsall WS3 ....15 A2
Bush Rd Dudley DY2 ..62 C2
  Tipton DY4 ....51 E4
Bush St WS10 ....41 D7
Bushbury Ave CV4 ...111 F2
Bushbury Croft B37 ..70 C3
Bushbury Hill Jun & Inf Scts
  WV10 ....11 F1
Bushbury La
  Wolverhampton, Bushbury
  WV10 ....11 E2
  Wolverhampton, Elston Hall
  WV10 ....25 D7
Bushbury Rd
  Birmingham B33 ....69 A5
  Wolverhampton WV10 .26 A5
Bushell Dr B91 ......107 D4
Bushey Cl B74 ....30 F2
Bushey Fields Hospl DY5 .61 E7
Bushey Fields Rd DY1 ..61 E7
Bushfield Ct WV14 ....40 C5
Bushley Cl B98 ......159 A7
Bushley Croft B91 ...127 B8
Bushman Way B34 ....69 E5
Bushmore Rd B28 ...106 A7
Bushway Cl DY5 ....61 A2
Bushwood Ct B15 ....86 C8
Bushwood Dr B93 ...128 B3
Bushwood Rd B29 ....85 B1
Bushy End CV34 .....161 E4
Busill Jones Prim Sch
  WS3 ....27 F8
Bustleholme Ave B71 .42 F1
Bustleholme Cres B71 .42 E1
Bustleholme La B71 ..42 E2
Butcher's La CV5 ....112 C6
Butchers La B63 ......82 C7
Butchers Rd B92 ....109 A6
Butcroft Gdns WS10 .41 E6
Bute Cl Birmingham B45 .101 E1
  Hinckley LE10 ....71 C1
  Willenhall WV12 ......27 B6
Butler Cl CV8 ....148 C7
Butler Rd B92 ....88 F3
Butler St
  Astwood Bank B96 ...158 E1
  West Bromwich B70 ...53 A4
Butler's Hill La B97 .153 B5
Butler's Rd B20 ....55 A3
Butlers Cl
  Birmingham, Handsworth
  B20 ....55 A3
  Birmingham, Perry Common
  B73 ....45 D1
Butlers Cres CV7 .....78 A1
Butlers End CV35 ...146 C2
Butlers La B74 ....32 A3
Butlers Lane Sta B74 .32 A3
Butlers Prec 2 WS1 ..28 E2
Butlin Rd CV6 ....95 C4
Butlin St B7 ....67 C7
Butt La Allesley CV5 .112 A8
  Hinckley LE10 ....71 F1
Butt Lane Cl LE10 .....71 E1
Butter Wlk B38 ......123 C8
Buttercup Cl 6 WS5 ..43 A3
Buttercup Dr B60 ...137 C6
Butterfield Cl WV6 ..23 D3
Butterfield Ct DY1 ....51 A2
Butterfield Rd DY5 ...61 B7
Butterfly Way 4 B64 .62 F1
Buttermere B77 ....36 B7
Buttermere Ave CV11 .74 A6
Buttermere Cl
  Brierley Hill DY5 ......81 B7
  Cannock WS11 ....2 A3
  Coventry CV3 ....134 F7
  Wolverhampton WV6 ..24 D8
Buttermere Ct WV6 ..23 F4
Buttermere Dr
  Birmingham B32 ....84 F3
  Essington WV11 ....13 A2
Buttermere Gr WV11 ..13 B1
Butterworth Cl WV14 .40 A1
Butterworth Dr CV4 .132 A6
Buttery Rd B67 ....64 E6
Buttons Farm Rd WV4 .38 D3
Buttress Way B66 .....65 A6
Butts CV1 ....165 A2
Butts Cl WS11 ....5 E4
Butts La Norton Canes WS11 .5 E4
  Stone DY10 ....117 D1
Butts Rd Coventry CV1 .113 B2
  Walsall WS4 ....28 F3
  Wolverhampton WV4 ..38 E4
Butts St WS4 ....28 F3
Butts The Lichfield WS14 ..8 D2
  Walsall WS4 ....28 F3
Butts Way WS11 ....5 E4
Buxton Ave B78 ....35 B8

Buxton Cl WS3 ....14 C3
Buxton Rd
  Birmingham B23 ....56 B7
  Dudley DY2 ....62 A6
  Sutton Coldfield B73 ..57 A8
  Walsall WS3 ....14 C3
By Pass Rd B77 ....22 A5
By Byfield Cl B33 ....69 E5
Byfield Pl CV7 ....130 D5
Byfield Rd CV6 ......112 E5
Byfleet Cl WV14 ......40 A3
Byford Cl B98 ....153 E2
Byford Ct CV10 ....72 F4
Byford St CV10 ....72 F4
Byford Way B37 ......90 B8
Byland B77 ....21 D3
Byland Way WS3 .....13 F2
Bylands Cl B61 ......136 E1
Byng Kenrick Central Sch
  B33 ....69 D3
Bypass Link B91 ....107 F3
Byrchen Moor Gdns DY5 .61 B7
Byrne Rd WV2 ....39 D7
Byron Ave Bedworth CV12 .78 D2
  Birmingham B23 ....56 B3
  Lichfield WS14 ....9 B5
  Warwick CV34 ....160 C4
Byron Cl Birmingham B10 .87 D7
  Kidderminster DY10 .117 B5
Byron Cres DY1 ....51 B6
Byron Croft Sedgley DY3 .50 A5
  Sutton Coldfield B74 ..31 F6
Byron Ct Knowle B93 .128 A6
  Sutton Coldfield B74 ..32 A5
Byron Gdns B71 ....53 B5
Byron Pl WS11 ....1 F5
Byron Rd Birmingham B10 .87 D7
  Redditch B97 ....158 D8
  Tamworth B79 ....21 A7
  Willenhall WV12 ......27 E7
Byron St Brierley Hill DY5 .61 D7
  Coventry CV1 ....165 C4
  West Bromwich B71 ...53 B5
Byron Way B61 ......137 A8
Bywater Cl CV3 ......133 B5
Bywater Ho 4 WS1 ...28 F1
Byways WS3 ....14 C3

C

Caban Cl B31 ....102 E5
Cable & Wireless Coll
  CV4 ....131 E6
Cable Dr WS2 ....28 C5
Cable Gr WV6 ....23 E4
Cabot Gr WV6 ....23 E4
Cadbury Coll B38 ...103 F1
Cadbury Dr B35 ....58 A2
Cadbury Ho B19 ......66 D5
Cadbury Rd B13 ......87 B4
Cadbury Way B17 .....85 B5
Cadbury World* B30 .103 F7
Cadden Dr CV4 ......112 B2
Caddick Cres B71 ....53 D7
Caddick Rd B42 ....44 C3
Caddick St WV14 .....51 A8
Cadeby Cl LE10 ....71 B3
Cadet Dr B90 ....106 A3
Cadgwith Gdns WV14 .41 A2
Cadine Gdns B13 .....86 A5
Cadle Rd WV10 ....25 E7
Cadleigh Gdns B17 ...85 C3
Cadman Cl CV12 ......78 C3
Cadman Cres WV10 ..26 A7
Cadman's La WS6,WS3 .14 D6
Cadnam Cl
  Birmingham B17 ......85 C3
  Willenhall WV13 ......41 B8
Cadogan Rd B77 ......35 D5
Caen Cl CV35 ....160 A7
Caernarfon Dr CV11 ..73 D3
Caernarvon Cl WV12 .27 C7
Caernarvon Way DY1 .50 E2
Caesar Rd CV8 ......147 E3
Caesar Way B46 ......59 E1
Cairn Dr WS2 ....27 F2
Cairndhu Dr DY10 ..117 B7
Cairns St WS2 ....28 C3
Caister B77 ....22 A6
Caister Dr WV13 ......40 F8
Caistor Cl B78 ....34 B8
Caithness Cl CV5 ...112 A4
Cakemore Rd B65 ....63 E2
Cala Dr B15 ....86 B7
Calcot Dr WV6 ....24 E8
Calcott Ho CV3 ......134 B5
Caldecote Cl CV11 ...73 C3
Caldecote Gr B9 ......68 C1
Caldecote Rd CV6 ..113 C5
Caldeford Ave B90 ..127 A7
Calder B77 ....36 A8
Calder Ave WS1 ......29 A2
Calder Cl Bulkington CV12 .79 B2
  Coventry CV3 ....133 E7
Calder Dr B76 ....58 A7
Calder Gr B20 ....54 E2
Calder Rise DY3 ......50 F6
Calder Twr 2 B20 ....55 D1
Calderfields Cl WS4 ..29 A3
Caldmore Com Prim Sch
  WS1 ....42 E8
Caldmore Gn WS1 ....42 E8
Caldmore Rd WS1 ....42 E8
Caldon Cl LE10 ....75 B8

Caldwell Cres DY11 ....116 D5
Caldwell Ct
  Nuneaton CV11 ....73 D1
  Solihull B91 ....107 C5
Caldwell Gr B91 ....107 C5
Caldwell Ho B70 ....53 C2
Caldwell Rd
  Birmingham B9 ....68 B3
  Nuneaton CV11 ....73 D1
Caldwell St B71 ....53 D8
Caldy Wlk 5 B45 ....101 F1
Cale Cl B77 ....21 C2
Caledon St 5 WS2 ......42 C7
Caledonia DY5 ....81 D7
Caledonia Rd WV2 ......163 D1
Caledonia St WS11 ......40 E6
Caledonian B77 ....21 F2
Caledonian Cl WS5 ......43 C3
Calewood Rd DY5 ....A2
Caliban Mews CV34 ....161 E3
California Rd B32 ....84 E2
California B69 ....83 B8
California Way B32 ......84 F3
Californian Gr WS7 ......6 F8
Callaghan Gr 5 WS11 ....2 C2
Callcott Dr DY5 ....81 D7
Callear Rd WS10 ....41 D1
Callendar Cl CV11 ....74 A7
Calley Cl DY4 ....52 A3
Callis Wlk B77 ....35 F6
Callow Hill La B97 .....158 B6
Callow Rd B48 ....139 A6
Callowbridge Rd B45 ...121 F7
Callowbrook La B45 ....121 F7
Callows La 5 DY10 ....116 E6
Calmere Cl CV2 ....114 F8
Calpurnia Ave CV34 ...161 E2
Calshot Prim Sch B42 ...55 B8
Calshot Rd B42 ....55 A8
Calstock Rd WS12 ....43 E6
Calthorpe Mans 4 B15 ..66 B1
Calthorpe Rd
  Birmingham, Edgbaston B15 .86 B8
  Birmingham, Handsworth Wood
  B20 ....55 C2
  Walsall WS5 ....43 D6
Calthorpe Sch B12 ..87 A8
Caludon Castle Sch
  CV2 ....114 E4
Caludon Lodge CV2 ...114 E5
Caludon Park Ave CV2 .114 E5
Caludon Rd CV2 ....114 A4
Calver Gr B44 ....44 D3
Calverley Rd B38 .....123 D8
Calvert Cl CV3 ....133 D6
Calverton Gr B43 ....54 E8
Calves Croft WV13 ......27 A3
Calvin Cl WV10 ....11 D3
Calving Hill WV11 ....1 E2
Cam Gdns DY5 ....61 B6
Cam Ho BY71 ....61 E8
Camberley 6 B71 ....42 F1
Camberley Cres WV4 ....39 E2
Camberley Gr WV4 ......39 A4
Camberley Rd B23 ......56 E6
Camberley Rd DY6 ......61 A4
Camberwell Terr CV31 .162 A7
Camborne Cl B6 ....66 E7
Camborne Cl WV11 .....73 F5
Camborne Rd WS5 ......43 D7
Camborne Ct 4 WS5 ...43 D7
Cambourne Rd
  Blackheath B65 ....63 C3
  Hinckley LE10 ....75 F6
Cambria Dr B28 ....105 F8
Cambria Cl B90 ....125 E2
Cambria St WS11 ....1 D4
Cambrian B77 ....22 A2
Cambridge Ave
  Birmingham B1 ....106 C3
  Sutton Coldfield B73 ...57 B8
Cambridge Cl WS9 ......30 B8
Cambridge Cres B15 ....86 D7
Cambridge Dr
  Birmingham B37 ....69 F1
  Nuneaton CV10 ....72 E3
Cambridge Gdns CV32 .157 A1
Cambridge Rd
  Birmingham B13 ....86 F1
  Dudley DY2 ....62 A7
  Smethwick B66 ....65 A7
Cambridge St
  Birmingham B1 ....164 A2
  Coventry CV1 ....113 E5
  Walsall WS1 ....42 E7
  West Bromwich B70 ....53 B2
  Wolverhampton WV10 .163 C4
Cambridge Twr B1 .....164 A2
Cambridge Way B27 .....88 D4
Camden Cl
  Birmingham B36 ....69 A8
  Walsall WS5 ....43 A4
Camden Dr
  Birmingham B1 ....66 C3
  Tamworth B77 ....21 E3
Camden St
  Birmingham B18,B1 ....66 B4
  Brownhills WS9 ....15 F4
  Coventry CV2 ....114 A4
  Walsall WS1 ....42 E8
Camden Way DY6 ....49 D1
Camellia Gdns
  Brierley Hill DY8 ......60 E2
  Wolverhampton WV9 ...10 F3
Camellia Rd 1 CV2 .....96 B2
Camelot Cl WS11 ....1 F4

Camelot Gr CV8 ....148 C5
Camelot Way B10 ....87 C8
Cameo Dr DY9 ....81 F5
Cameron Cl Allesley CV5 .112 A7
  Royal Leamington Spa
  CV32 ....157 A4
Cameron Rd WS4 ....29 B3
Camford Gr B14 ....104 F3
Camhouses B77 ....22 B1
Camino Rd B32 ....84 F3
Camomile Cl 5 WS5 ....43 A3
Camp Hill Birmingham B12 .87 A8
  Stourbridge DY8 ....60 E1
Camp Hill Cir B12 ......87 A8
Camp Hill Dr CV10 ......72 D7
Camp Hill Ind Est B12 ..87 A7
Camp Hill Middleway
  B12 ....87 A7
Camp Hill Prim Sch CV10 .72 E6
Camp Hill Rd CV10 .....72 C7
Camp La
  Birmingham, Handsworth
  B21 ....54 C2
  Birmingham, King's Norton
  B38 ....103 F3
Camp Rd B75 ....32 D6
Camp St Birmingham B9 ..67 C1
  Wednesbury WS10 .....41 F2
  Wolverhampton WV1 ..163 B4
Camp Wood Cl B30 ....103 F8
Campbell Cl
  Nuneaton CV11 ....72 A4
  Tamworth B79 ....20 F8
  Walsall WS4 ....29 B3
Campbell Pl 8 WS10 ....41 D6
Campbell St DY5 ....61 C4
Campbells Gn B26 ......89 B4
Campden Cl B97 ....158 D6
Campden Gn B92 ....89 A3
Campion Cl
  Birmingham B38 ......123 F8
  Coventry CV3 ....133 D6
  Walsall WS5 ....43 A3
Campion Cl 2 DY4 .....51 E5
Campion Dr
  Featherstone WV10 .....12 A7
  Tamworth B77 ....21 C3
Campion Gr CV32 ......157 A2
Campion Gn B63 ....82 D3
Campion Ho
  2 Birmingham B38 ....123 E8
  Wolverhampton WV10 .25 F4
Campion Sch & Com Coll
  CV31 ....162 C5
Campion Terr CV32 ....157 A1
Campion Way B90 .....126 A5
Camplea Croft B37 .....70 A2
Camplin Cres B20 ......54 E5
Campling Cl CV12 ......79 B2
Campriano Dr CV34 ...161 A8
Campton Cl LE10 ....75 E7
Campville Cres B71 .....42 E1
Campville Gr B37 ....69 F5
Camrose Croft
  Birmingham, Balsall Heath
  B12 ....86 F5
  Birmingham, Castle Bromwich
  B34 ....68 F6
Camrose Gdns WV9 ....11 A3
Camrose Twr B7 ....67 B6
Camsey La WS7 ....7 E8
Camville CV3 ....115 A2
Canal La B24 ....57 A3
Canal Rd CV6 ....113 F8
Canal Side Dudley DY2 ..62 E4
  Hopwood B48 ....123 B2
Canal Side Ind Est DY5 ..61 C1
Canal St Brierley Hill DY5 ..61 C1
  Dudley, Roseville WV14 .51 C8
  Dudley, Tipton Green DY1 .51 D4
  Oldbury B69 ....64 A7
Canal View Ind Est DY5 ..61 B1
Canal Way CV110 ....74 F7
Canalside Brs 144 D3
Canalside CI Walsall WS3 .14 F1
  Wednesbury WS10 .....42 E2
Canary Gr B19 ....66 C6
Canberra 2 EB CV12 ....77 F2
Canberra Ho B34 ....69 E6
Canberra Rd Coventry CV6 .96 C4
  Walsall WS5 ....43 C6
Canberra Way
  4 Birmingham B12 .....86 F8
  Hinckley LE10 ....75 E4
Canford Cl
  Birmingham B12 ....86 F7
  Coventry CV3 ....133 D6
Canford Cres CV3 .....132 E7
Canley Ford CV4,CV5 ..132 E7
Canley Rd CV5 ....132 D8
Canley Sta CV5 ....112 D1
Cannel Rd WS7 ....6 D6
Cannes Ct CV4 ....132 D6
Canning Cl WS5 ....43 B6
Canning Gdns B18 .....65 E4
Canning Rd Tamworth B77 ..21 F4
  Walsall WS5 ....43 B6
Canning St LE10 ....71 C1
Cannock Chase High Sch
  WS11 ....1 E2
Cannock Chase Tech Coll
  Cannock, Blackfords WS11 ..1 D1
  Cannock, Bridgton WS11 ..1 E7
Cannock Com Hospl WS11 ..1 E2
Cannock Ind Ctr WS11 ...4 D5

Cannock Motor Village
  WS11 ....2 B3
Cannock Rd
  Burntwood WS7 ....7 B7
  Cannock WS11,WS12 ...2 A5
  Cannock, Heath Hayes WS12 .5 C8
  Featherstone WV10 .....12 C7
  Norton Canes WS7 ......8 A1
  Willenhall WV12 ....27 C7
Cannock Sta WS11 ......1 E1
Cannock Sta WS11 ......1 A1
Cannocks La CV4 ......132 D6
Cannon Cl CV4 ....132 F6
Cannon Dr WV14 ....40 D2
Cannon Hill Gr 2 B12 ..86 E5
Cannon Hill Pl 1 B12 ...86 E5
Cannon Hill Rd
  Birmingham B12 ....86 E5
  Coventry CV4 ....132 D5
Cannon Park District Ctr
  CV4 ....132 C6
Cannon Park Prim Sch
  CV4 ....132 D5
Cannon Park Rd CV4 ..132 E5
Cannon Rd WV5 ....49 A6
Cannon St
  Birmingham B2 ....164 C2
  Walsall WS2 ....28 E4
  Willenhall WV13 ....27 B2
Cannon St N WS2 ......28 E4
Canon Dr CV7 ....95 D6
Canon Hudson Cl CV3 .134 C6
Canon Maggs CE Jun Sch
  CV12 ....78 B2
Canon Young Rd CV31 .162 B3
Canterbury Ave WV13 ..27 D2
Canterbury Cl
  Kenilworth CV8 ....148 C3
  Lichfield WS13 ....3 C3
  8 Oldbury B65 ....63 E4
  Studley B80 ....159 C4
  Tamworth B79 ....20 B3
  Walsall WS13 ....15 A4
  West Bromwich B71 ....53 E8
Canterbury Cross Prim Sch
  B20 ....55 D1
Canterbury Dr
  Birmingham B37 ....90 A7
  Burntwood WS7 ....7 E7
  Perton WV6 ....23 E4
Canterbury Rd
  Birmingham B20 ....55 D1
  Kidderminster DY11 ..116 A6
  West Bromwich B71 ....53 D8
  Wolverhampton WV4 ...38 E5
Canterbury St CV1 ....165 D3
Canterbury Twr 1 B1 ...66 B3
Canterbury Way
  Cannock WS12 ....2 B1
  Nuneaton CV11 ....74 A8
Cantlow Cl CV5 ....112 A3
Cantlow Ho 2 B12 .....86 F7
Cantlow Rd B13 ....105 A6
Cantlow Ho B10 ....71 C4
Canute Cl WS1 ....42 F7
Canvey Cl B45 ....101 E1
Canwell Ave B37 ....69 F5
Canwell Dr B75 ....33 B5
Canwell Gate B75 ......32 E4
Canwell Gdns WV14 ....40 C4
Capcroft Rd B13 ......105 B6
Cape Cl WS8 ....16 A6
Cape Hill B66 ....65 C4
Cape Rd Ntr B66 ....65 C4
Cape Ind Est CV34 ....160 E7
Cape Prim Sch B66 ....65 C4
Cape Rd CV34 ....160 D8
Cape St Birmingham B18 .65 D4
  West Bromwich B70 ....52 E4
Capener Rd B43 ....44 A2
Capern Gr B32 ....84 F5
Capethorn Rd B66 .....65 A3
Capilano Rd B23 ....56 C7
Capmartin Rd CV6 .....95 A2
Cappers La WS13,WS14 .9 F8
Capponfield Cl WV14 ...40 B3
Capstone Ave
  Birmingham B18 ....66 A4
  Wolverhampton WV10 .25 C8
Captain's Cl WV3 ....24 D2
Captains Pool Rd DY10 .117 A1
Capulet Cl CV3 ....134 C6
Capulet Dr CV34 ......161 E3
Caradoc B77 ....22 A2
Caradoc Cl CV2 ....114 D7
Caradoc Hall CV2 .....114 D7
Carcroft Rd B25 ....88 D8
Cardale Croft 1 CV3 ..134 F8
Cardale St B65 ....52 F4
Carder Cres WV14 .....40 D4
Carder Dr DY5 ....61 C2
Cardiff Cl CV3 ....134 D5
Cardiff St WV3 ....39 B8
Cardigan Cl B71 ....53 C7
Cardigan Dr WV12 .....27 B6
Cardigan Ho WV12 .....2 C5
Cardigan Pl WS12 ......2 C5
Cardigan Rd CV12 ......77 C1
Cardigan St B4 ....66 F3
Cardinal Cres B61 ....136 D1
Cardinal Dr DY10 .....117 B3
Cardinal Griffin RC High Sch
  WS11 ....1 D2
Cardinal Newman RC Sch &
  Com Coll CV6 ....94 F2

Cardinal Newman RC Sec Sch
  B17 ....65 A2
Cardinal Way WS11 ....1 D2
Cardinal Wiseman RC Sch
  Birmingham B44 ....44 F2
  Coventry CV2 ....96 E1
Carding Ct CV5 ....111 F4
Cardington Ave B42 ....44 B1
Cardington Cl B98 ....154 F3
Cardoness Pl DY1 ......50 F2
Cardy Cl B97 ....153 B4
Careless Gn DY9 ....81 F4
Carew B77 ....36 A5
Carey St CV6 ....114 B8
Carfax WS11 ....4 E8
Cargill Cl CV6 ....95 F5
Carhampton Rd B75 ....47 A5
Carillon Gdns B65 ......63 C3
Carisbrook Rd CV10 ....73 D6
Carisbrooke B77 ....22 A2
Carisbrooke Ave B37 ...90 C8
Carisbrooke Cl WS10 ...42 E3
Carisbrooke Cres WS10 .42 E3
Carisbrooke Dr B62 ....83 D3
Carisbrooke Gdns WV10 .11 E3
Carisbrooke Rd
  Birmingham B17 ....65 B1
  Perton WV6 ....24 A3
  Wednesbury WS10 .....42 E2
  Wolverhampton WV10 .11 E3
Carl Eynon Ct 2 WS3 ...28 B8
Carl St WS2 ....28 C7
Carlcroft B77 ....22 B2
Carless Ave B17 ....85 B7
Carless Ho B66 ....65 C6
Carless St WS1 ....42 E8
Carlisle Rd WS11 ....4 B7
Carlisle St B18 ....65 A5
Carlton Ave Aldridge B74 .31 A2
  Bilston WV14 ....40 F7
  Birmingham B21 ....54 E1
  Stourbridge DY8 ....81 E3
  Wolverhampton WV11 ..26 A8
  Cannock B Bulkington CV12 .79 B3
  Cannock WS12 ....2 D1
  Dudley DY1 ....51 C6
Carlton Bank B98 .....154 F3
Carlton Cl Birmingham B75 .46 F7
Carlton Cres
  Burntwood WS7 ....7 A8
  Tamworth B79 ....20 F8
Carlton Croft B74 ......31 A2
Carlton Ct Coventry CV5 .112 F2
Carlton Gdns CV5 .....133 A8
Carlton Ho
  5 Royal Leamington Spa
  CV32 ....161 F8
  Sutton Coldfield B75 ...32 B2
Carlton Mews Flats B36 .69 D7
Carlton Rd Birmingham B9 .67 D1
  Coventry CV6 ....95 F1
  Smethwick B66 ....65 A8
  Wolverhampton WV3 ...39 A7
Carlyle Ave DY10 .....117 B6
Carlyle Bsns Pk B70 ...52 F5
Carlyle Gr WV10 ....26 A8
Carlyle Rd
  Birmingham, Edgbaston B16 .65 E1
  Birmingham, Lozells B19 ..66 C8
  Blackheath B65 ....63 C2
  Bromsgrove B60 ......151 B8
  Wolverhampton WV10 .26 A8
Carmel Cl WS12 ....2 C5
Carmel Gr B32 ....84 B1
Carmelite Rd CV1 .....113 E2
Carmichael Cl WS14 ....9 D7
Carmodale Ave B42 ....55 B5
Carnbroe Ave CV3 ....134 F7
Carnegie Ave DY4 .....52 B4
Carnegie Cl CV3 ......134 B5
Carnegie Dr WS10 .....42 A3
Carnegie Rd B65 ....63 B2
Carnford Rd B26 ....89 B7
Carnforth Cl DY6 ......60 B7
Carnforth Rd B60 .....137 B1
Carnoustie B77 ....22 C5
Carnoustie Cl
  Bromsgrove B61 ......150 D8
  Nuneaton CV11 ....79 C8
  Sutton Coldfield B75 ...46 C8
  Walsall WS3 ....14 A3
Carnwath Rd B73 ......45 E2
Carol Ave B61 ....136 D3
Carol Cres Halesowen B63 .82 F5
  Wednesfield WV11 .....26 E6
Carol Gdns DY8 ....81 F8
Caroline Cl CV11 ....78 F7
Caroline Rd B13 ....86 F4
Caroline St
  Birmingham B3 ....164 A4
  Dudley DY2 ....51 E1
  West Bromwich B70 ....53 B2
Carpathian Ct 4 B18 ..66 C4
Carpathian The 5 B18 ..66 C4
Carpenter Glade B63 ..82 D5
Carpenter Pl 7 B12 ....87 A6
Carpenter Rd B15 ......86 B7
Carpenter's Rd B19 ....66 C7
Carpenters Cl LE10 ....75 F5
Carpenters Ct 8 B12 ...86 F6
Carpet Trades Way
  DY11 ....116 D7
Carrick Cl WS3 ....15 A5
Carrie Ho CV1 ....165 A2
Carriers Cl WS2 ....27 F1
Carriers Fold WV5 ......49 B7

Carrington Rd WS10 ....42 D2
Carroll Wlk DY10 .....117 C5
Carroway Head Hill B78 .33 D4
Carrs La B4 ....164 C2
Carrway Ct CV7 ....95 D5
Carshalton Gr WV2 .....39 E7
Carshalton Rd B44 .....45 A2
Cartbridge Cres WS3 ...28 F6
Cartbridge La WS4 .....29 A6
Cartbridge La S WS4 ...29 A5
Cartbridge Wlk WS3 ...29 A6
Carter Ave Codsall WV8 .10 B3
  Kidderminster DY11 ..116 C4
Carter Ct DY11 ....116 C4
Carter Rd Birmingham B43 .43 F2
  Coventry CV3 ....134 A8
  Wolverhampton WV6 ...25 B5
Carter's Gn B70 ....53 B4
Carter's La
  Birmingham B62 ....84 A3
  Halesowen B62 ....83 F4
Carters Cl
  Bromsgrove B61 ......150 D7
  Sutton Coldfield B76 ...46 E3
Carters Hurst B33 ......69 B1
Cartersfield La WS9 ....16 E6
Carthorse La B97 .....153 B5
Carthusian Rd CV3 ....133 C7
Cartland Rd
  Birmingham, Sparkbrook
  B11 ....87 C6
  Birmingham, Stirchley B14,
  B30 ....104 C7
Cartmel Cl CV3 ....133 B1
Cartmel Ct B23 ....56 B4
Cartway The WV6 ......23 D4
Cartwright Gdns B69 ..52 C2
Cartwright Ho WS3 ....14 B1
Cartwright Rd
  Stoke Prior B60 ......150 D2
  Sutton Coldfield B75 ...32 C3
Cartwright St WV2 ....163 C1
Carvell Cl CV5 ....94 A6
Carver Cl CV2 ....114 E2
Carver Gr B24 ....57 C6
Carver Gdns DY8 ....80 E2
Carver St B1 ....66 B4
Casa Mio Ct WS12 ......2 C5
Cascade Cl CV3 ....133 E6
Case La CV35 ....145 E1
Casern View B75 ....47 A6
Casewell Rd DY6 ....60 C8
Casey Ave B23 ....56 D8
Cash Joynson Ave WS10 .41 C8
Cash's Bsns Ctr CV1 ..113 D5
Cash's La CV1 ....113 D6
Cashmore Ave CV31 ...161 F1
Cashmore Rd
  Bedworth CV12 ....77 E1
  Kenilworth CV8 ....148 C4
Casia Gr CV8 ....148 C4
Caslon Cres DY8 ....80 D4
Caslon Flats B63 ....82 C4
Caslon Prim Sch B63 ..82 C4
Caslon Rd B63 ....82 C6
Caspian Way CV2 .....115 A8
Cassandra Cl
  Brierley Hill DY5 ......50 C1
  Coventry CV4 ....132 D3
Cassandra Gr CV34 ...161 D4
Cassowary Rd 2 B20 ...54 F3
Castello Dr B36 ....58 D8
Castle Bromwich Bsns Pk
  B35 ....58 A1
Castle Bromwich Hall Gdns*
  B36 ....69 E8
Castle Bromwich Jun Sch
  B36 ....69 E7
Castle Cl Blackheath B64 .63 B1
  Brownhills WS8 ....6 F2
  Coventry CV3 ....133 D6
  Solihull B92 ....89 B1
  Tamworth B77 ....21 E4
  Warwick CV34 ....160 E6
Castle Cres B36 ....69 C8
Castle Croft B68 ....84 D8
Castle Ct
  7 Brownhills WS10 ....41 D6
  Hinckley LE10 ....75 D6
  Kenilworth CV8 ....148 A6
Castle Dr Coleshill B46 ..70 F5
  Willenhall WV12 ....27 B5
Castle Dyke WS13 ......9 B7
Castle Gate Island DY2 ..51 E2
Castle Gr CV8 ....147 D5
Castle Hill Kenilworth CV8 .147 E4
  Stourbridge DY8 ....81 B3
Castle High Sch DY1 ...51 B2
Castle Hill Dudley DY1 ...51 D2
  Kenilworth CV8 ....147 E4
  Warwick CV34 ....160 E6
Castle Ho B33 ....69 B2
Castle Hts B64 ....83 B8
Castle La Solihull B92 ..89 A2
  Warwick CV34 ....160 E6
Castle Mews 5 CV34 ..160 E6
Castle Mill Rd DY1 .....51 C4
Castle Place Ind Est
  CV1 ....165 D4
Castle Rd
  Birmingham, Kings Norton
  B30 ....103 F4

Castle Rd continued
Birmingham, Weoley Castle
B29 .... 85 B1
Brownhills WS9 .... 16 A3
Kenilworth CV8 .... 147 E5
Wolverhampton DY11 .... 116 E5
Nuneaton CV10 .... 73 C7
Studley B80 .... 159 F4
Tamworth B77 .... 35 F5
Tipton DY4 .... 51 D4
Castle Rd E B68 .... 84 D8
Castle Rd W B68 .... 84 C8
Castle Specl Sch WS3 .... 28 E7
Castle Sq B29 .... 85 A1
Castle St
Astwood Bank B96 .... 158 E2
Brownhills WS8 .... 6 F2
Coventry CV1 .... 165 D4
Darlaston WS10 .... 41 D8
Dudley DY1 .... 51 D1
Dudley, Roseville WV14 ... 51 C8
Hinckley LE10 .... 75 D8
Sedgley DY3 .... 50 D8
Tipton DY4 .... 51 E5
Warwick CV34 .... 160 E6
West Bromwich B70 .... 53 A8
Wolverhampton WV1 ..... 163 C3
Castle Tine DY8 .... 81 B3
Castle Vale Ent Pk B76 ... 58 C4
Castle Vale Ind Est B76 .. 58 A5
Castle Vale Sch B35 ...... 58 B3
Castle View Dudley DY1 .. 51 B2
Tamworth B77 .... 21 C3
Castle View CI WS10 .... 41 A4
Castle View Ind Est DY4 . 51 E5
Castle View Rd WV14,
WS10 .... 41 B4
Castle VI WV1 .... 163 C3
Castlebridge Gdns WV11 . 26 F7
Castlebridge Rd WV11 .... 27 A6
Castlecroft WS11 .... 5 E5
Castlecroft Ave WV3 ...... 38 A8
Castlecroft Gdns WV3 .... 38 C8
Castlecroft La WV6 .... 23 F1
Castlecroft Prim Sch
WV3 .... 38 B8
Castlecroft Rd
Bilston WV14 .... 40 F7
Wolverhampton WV3 .... 38 B8
Castleditch La B98 ...... 158 E7
Castleford CI B11 .... 87 C4
Castleford Rd B11 .... 87 C4
Castleford Jun Mix Inf Sch
WS9 .... 16 A3
Castlefort Rd WS9 .... 16 A3
Castlegate Dr DY1 .... 51 E2
Castlegate Mews 4
CV34 .... (not clear)
Castlegate Way DY1 ...... 51 E2
Castlehall B77 .... 22 A2
Castlehill Rd WS9 .... 16 C3
Castlehills Dr B36 .... 69 A8
Castlemaine Dr LE10 ..... 71 E3
Castlereagh CV10 .... 25 C6
Castleton CI B15 .... 86 B7
Castleton Rd
Birmingham B42 .... 55 D7
Walsall WS3 .... 14 C3
Castleton St DY2 .... 62 C4
Caswell Rd
Royal Leamington Spa
CV31 .... 162 B6
Sedgley DY3 .... 50 C8
Cat & Kittens La WV10 ... 11 E6
Cat La B34 .... 69 B7
Cater Dr B76 .... 46 F2
Caterham Dr DY6 .... 60 F3
Catesby Dr DY6 .... 60 D8
Catesby Ho B37 .... 69 F4
Catesby La B94 .... 144 B2
Catesby Rd Coventry CV6 113 B8
Solihull B90 .... 106 B1
Cateswell Rd B11,B28 .... 87 F2
Cathcart Rd DY8 .... 80 E5
Cathedral Ave DY11 ..... 116 A6
Cathedral CI DY4 .... 51 E5
Cathedral Ct WS13 .... 9 B8
Cathedral Lanes Sh Ctr
CV1 .... 165 B3
Cathedral Rise WS13 ...... 9 A8
Cathel Dr B42 .... 55 A7
Catherine CI B60 .... 150 F8
Catherine Ct B24 .... 57 C4
Catherine de Barnes La
Bickenhill B92 .... 90 D1
Catherine de B B92 .... 108 C7
Catherine Dr B73 .... 46 A6
Catherine Rd WV14 .... 40 A1
Catherine St
Birmingham B6 .... 67 A7
Coventry CV2 .... 113 F3
Catherine Ward Hall
CV12 .... 78 B5
Catherines CI B91 .... 108 B4
Catherton CI CV4 .... 41 C1
Catholic La DY3 .... 50 D7
Catisfield Cres WV8 ...... 10 F1
Cato St B7 .... 67 B5
Cato St N B7 .... 67 C5
Caton Gr B28 .... 106 A7
Catshill Fst Sch B61 .... 137 A8
Catshill Mid Sch B61 .... 136 F8
Catshill Rd WS8 .... 16 A7
Cattell Dr B75 .... 47 B5
Cattell Rd Birmingham B9 . 67 C1

Cattell Rd continued
Warwick CV34 .... 160 E7
Cattells Gr B7 .... 67 C6
Cattermole Gr B43 .... 44 C3
Cattock Hurst Dr B72 .... 57 D7
Causeway B65 .... 63 C2
Causeway Green Prim Sch
B68 .... 64 A4
Causeway Green Rd B68 .. 64 A4
Causeway Rd WV14 .... 51 D8
Causeway The B25 .... 88 D7
Causey Farm Rd B63 .... 100 C8
Cavalier Cir WV10 .... 11 E4
Cavalier CI CV11 .... 73 E2
Cavan's CI WS11 .... 1 E4
Cavandale Ave B44 .... 44 E1
Cavans CI CV3 .... 135 A8
Cavans Way CV3 .... 135 A8
Cavans Wood Mobile Homes
WS12 .... 1 D5
Cavell CI WS2 .... 28 D2
Cavell Rd Burntwood WS7 . 7 E8
Dudley DY2 .... 51 F1
Cavendish B79 .... 20 E7
Cavendish CI
Birmingham B38 .... 104 B1
Kingswinford DY6 .... 60 D4
Marlbrook B60 .... 121 C1
Cavendish Ct
Birmingham B17 .... 85 B8
Dorridge B93 .... 128 A3
Cavendish Dr Hagley DY9 . 98 F4
Kidderminster DY10 ...... 117 B7
Cavendish Gdns
Walsall WS2 .... 28 A4
Wolverhampton WV1 ...... 26 C1
Cavendish Rd
Birmingham B16 .... 65 D4
Coventry CV4 .... 111 E2
Halesowen B62 .... 83 F4
Walsall WS2 .... 28 A4
Cavendish Way WS9 ...... 30 B5
Caversham CI CV11 .... 74 A7
Caversham PI B73 .... 46 B4
Caversham Rd B44 .... 45 A2
Cawdon Gr B93 .... 127 F3
Cawdor Cres B16 .... 65 F1
Cawnpore Rd CV6 .... 95 B2
Cawthorne CI 1 CV1 ... 113 E4
Caxton Ct 8 WS3 .... 14 B8
Caxton Gr B44 .... 45 C1
Caxton St WS11 .... 4 E8
Caynham CI B98 .... 154 D4
Caynham Rd B32 .... 102 B8
Cayton Gr B23 .... 56 F6
Ce Prim Sch ofSt Edmund &
St John DY2 .... 51 E1
Cearl Ct B27 .... 88 C2
Cecil Ct CV31 .... 162 A8
Cecil Dr B69 .... 52 D2
Cecil Leonard Knox Cres
CV11 .... 79 F6
Cecil Rd
Birmingham, Gravelly Hill
B24 .... 56 F3
Birmingham, Selly Park B13 . 86 C1
Cecil St Birmingham B19 . 164 C4
Cannock WS11 .... 1 F4
Stourbridge DY8 .... 80 F5
Walsall WS4 .... 28 F3
Cecily Rd CV3 .... 133 E7
Cedar Ave
Birmingham B36 .... 69 C8
Brownhills WS8 .... 16 A8
Dudley WV14 .... 51 B7
Ryton-on-D CV8 .... 135 B1
Cedar Bridge Croft B74 ... 46 B8
Cedar CI Birmingham B30 103 E6
Burntwood WS7 .... 7 A6
Cannock WS12 .... 2 A8
Lichfield WS14 .... 9 F7
Oldbury B68 .... 84 C8
Royal Leamington Spa
CV32 .... 157 A4
Stourbridge DY8 .... 80 D2
Walsall WS5 .... 43 B4
Cedar Cres DY11 .... 116 C6
Cedar Ct Allesley CV5 ... 112 A6
Birmingham B43 .... 54 B8
Hinckley LE10 .... 76 A6
Tamworth B77 .... 35 E6
Cedar Dr Aldridge B74 .... 30 E1
Birmingham, Pype Hayes
B24 .... 57 C5
Birmingham, West Heath
B31 .... 123 B7
Bromsgrove B60 .... 137 A1
Kidderminster DY11 ...... 116 C7
Tamworth B79 .... 21 A8
Cedar Gr Bilston WV14 .... 40 F7
Codsall WV8 .... 10 B3
Great Wyrley WS6 .... 5 A4
Hagley DY9 .... 99 A6
Warwick CV34 .... 156 A1
Wolverhampton WV3 .... 38 F7
Cedar Ho Birmingham B36 . 68 F8
Little Aston B74 .... 31 B5
Solihull B91 .... 106 F1
Cedar Park Rd
Redditch B97 .... 153 D4
Willenhall WV12 .... 13 C1
Cedar Rd
Birmingham B30 .... 103 E6
Burntwood WS7 .... 7 A7
Dudley DY1 .... 51 B3
Nuneaton CV10 .... 72 D6
Redditch B97 .... 153 D4

Cedar Rd continued
Tipton DY4 .... 51 D5
Wednesbury WS10 .... 42 A2
Willenhall WV13 .... 26 E2
Cedar Terr B60 .... 137 A1
Cedar View B97 .... 153 C4
Cedar Way
Birmingham B31 .... 102 F1
Wolverhampton WV11 ...... 26 C7
Cedar Wlk 8 B37 .... 70 D2
Cedar Wood Dr CV7 ..... 130 B6
Cedar Wood Rd DY3 ...... 50 D5
Cedarhill Dr WS11 .... 1 F3
Cedarhurst
Birmingham B32 .... 85 A5
Solihull B91 .... 107 C3
Cedars Ave
Birmingham B27 .... 88 C4
Coventry CV6 .... 112 F5
Kingswinford DY6 .... 60 D4
Wombourne WV5 .... 49 A5
Cedars Bsns Ctr The
WS11 .... 4 D7
Cedars Hort Unit The
WV14 .... 24 D2
Cedars Mews The 3
CV32 .... 161 D8
Cedars Rd CV7 .... 78 B1
Cedars The
Birmingham B25 .... 68 E1
8 Wolverhampton, Newbridge
WV6 .... 24 F3
Wolverhampton, Tettenhall
WV6 .... 24 D5
Cedarwood B74 .... 46 B8
Cedarwood Croft B42 .... 54 F8
Cedric CI CV3 .... 134 C5
Celandine B77 .... 21 C3
Celandine CI DY6 .... 60 C4
Celandine Rd
Coventry CV2 .... 96 D2
Dudley DY1 .... 51 A4
Celandine Way CV12 ...... 77 E2
Celbury Way B43 .... 54 D8
Celtic Rd WS11 .... 1 E3
Celts CI B65 .... 63 C4
Cemetery La B18 .... 66 B5
Cemetery Rd
Cannock WS11 .... 1 E4
Darlaston WS10 .... 41 F8
Oldbury B68 .... 64 C6
Redditch B97 .... 153 D3
Smethwick B67 .... 64 F4
Stourbridge DY9 .... 81 E5
Sutton Coldfield B75 ...... 46 D6
Willenhall WV13 .... 27 A2
Cemetery St Bilston WV14 . 40 C6
Cheslyn Hay WS6 .... 4 C3
Cemetery Way WS3 .... 14 B1
Centaur Rd CV5 .... 112 F1
Centenary Bsns Ctr CV11 . 73 E3
Centenary CI 1 B31 .... 103 A1
Centenary Dr B21 .... 54 E1
Centenary Rd CV4 .... 132 D7
Centenary Sq B1 .... 164 A2
Central Arc WV1 .... 163 B2
Central Ave Bilston WV14 . 40 E7
Birmingham B31 .... 122 F8
Blackheath, Cradley Heath
B64 .... 82 D7
Blackheath, Rowley Regis
B65 .... 63 C2
Cannock WS11 .... 2 A5
Coventry CV2 .... 114 A2
Nuneaton CV11 .... 73 B5
Royal Leamington Spa
CV31 .... 161 F6
Stourbridge DY9 .... 81 E3
Tipton DY4 .... 51 F7
18 Wolverhampton WV4 .... 39 F4
Central Bldgs CV3 ...... 165 B1
Central Bsns Pk B33 ...... 69 D1
Central Dr Dy6,CV7 .... 95 A5
Central City Ind Est CV6 113 F5
Central CI WS3 .... 14 A1
Central Dr
Dudley, Groveland DY3 ... 50 D2
Dudley, West Cosley WV14 . 50 D7
Walsall WS3 .... 14 A1
Central Flats WS3 .... 165 B1
Central Gr B27 .... 88 C2
Central Park Dr B18 ...... 65 F5
Central Park Ind Est DY2 . 62 E3
Central Rd B60 .... 137 A2
Central Sq B23 .... 57 A4
Central Trad Est
Darlaston WS10 .... 41 E6
Wolverhampton WV2 .... 39 F8
Central Way DY5 .... 61 E1
Centre Ct B63 .... 83 B3
Centre La B63 .... 83 B3
Centre Link Ind Est B7 ... 67 B6
Centreway The B14 ...... 105 D4
Centrovell Ind Est CV11 .. 73 C2
Centurion CI B46 .... 59 F1
Centurion Pk B77 .... 36 B6
Centurion Way B77 .... 36 B6
Century Ho B69 .... 63 D6
Century Ind Est B44 ...... 44 E3
Century Pk
Birmingham, Bordesley Green
B9 .... 67 C2
Birmingham, Marston Green
B26 .... 64 A8
Century Rd B69 .... 64 A8
Century Twr B5 .... 86 C5
Ceolmund Cres B37 ...... 70 B2
Chace Ave CV3 .... 134 C6

Chace Prim Sch CV3 ..... 134 C6
Chaceley CI CV2 .... 115 A8
Chaceley Gr B23 .... 56 F7
Chaceley Gr B23 .... 56 F7
Chad Rd Birmingham B15 . 85 F8
Dudley DY1,WV14 .... 51 B7
Chad Sq B15 .... 85 E8
Chad Vale Prim Sch B15 . 85 D7
Chad Valley CI B17 ...... 85 D6
Chadbrook Crest B15 .... 85 E7
Chadbury Croft 8 B91 . 127 B8
Chadbury Rd B63 .... 83 C3
Chadcote Way B61 ...... 120 F1
Chadderley CI 2 B45 .. 101 F1
Chaddesley CI
Oldbury B69 .... 63 D5
Redditch B98 .... 153 F1
Chaddesley Dr DY9 ...... 81 B1
Chaddesley Gdns 2
DY10 .... 117 A5
Chaddesley Rd
Birmingham B31 .... 103 D2
Halesowen B63 .... 82 F2
Kidderminster DY10 ...... 117 A5
Chadley CI B91 .... 107 A6
Chadsgrove Specl Sch
B61 .... 136 F8
Chadshunt CI B36 .... 58 D2
Chadsmead Prim Sch
WS13 .... 3 A1
Chadsmoor CE Jun Sch
WS11 .... 2 A3
Chadsmoor Ind Est WS11 .. 2 A4
Chadstone Terr B7 .... 67 B6
Chadstone CI B90 .... 127 B6
Chadswell Hts WS13 ...... 3 D2
Chadwell Dr B90 .... 106 B6
Chadwell La DY9 .... 120 F7
Chadwick Ave B45 ...... 122 B6
Chadwick CI
Coventry CV5 .... 112 B3
Wolverhampton WV4 .... 38 C6
Chadwick La
Chadwick End B93 .... 145 B8
Knowle B93 .... 129 A2
Chadwick Manor B93 ... 129 A1
Chadwick Mews
Chadwick End B93 .... 145 B6
Redditch B98 .... 159 A7
Chadwick Rd B75 .... 46 F5
Chadworth Ave B93 ..... 127 E3
Chaffcombe Rd B26 ...... 89 C7
Chaffinch CI Cannock WS12 . 2 B4
Sedgley DY3 .... 39 C3
Chaffinch Dr
Birmingham B36 .... 70 B7
Kidderminster DY10 ...... 116 F2
Chaffinch Rd DY9 .... 81 D3
Chain Wlk B19 .... 66 D7
Chainmakers CI WV14 .... 40 E3
Chainshop Mus DY2 .... 62 B1
Chalcot Dr WS12 .... 2 A7
Chalcot Gr B20 .... 54 F5
Chaldon CI WV9 .... 11 A1
Chale Gr B14 .... 105 A3
Chalfield B79 .... 20 D6
Chalfont Ave WS11 .... 4 C7
Chalfont CI
Bedworth CV12 .... 78 A4
Coventry CV5 .... 112 B4
Chalfont PI DY9 .... 81 E2
Chalfont Rd B20 .... 55 C1
Chalford Rd B23 .... 56 C8
Chalford Way B90 .... 106 C1
Chalgrove Ave B38 ...... 103 E1
Chalgrove Cres B91 ..... 107 B1
Challenge Bsns Pk CV1 . 113 D5
Challenge CI CV1 .... 165 C4
Challenge Way WV10 ..... 25 D1
Challenor Ave WV13 ...... 26 D1
Chalybeate CI B45 ...... 101 F1
Chamberlain CI
Cubbington CV32 .... 157 E5
Tipton B69 .... 52 D2
Chamberlain Cres B90 .. 106 A2
Chamberlain Ct
3 Birmingham, Hockley
B18 .... 66 C4
Birmingham, King's Heath
B14 .... 86 E1
Chamberlain Ho B16 ..... 66 A1
Chamberlain Rd B13 .... 105 A6
Chamberlain Sq B3 ..... 164 B2
Chamberlain Wlk
8 Coleshill B46 .... 70 F7
8 Smethwick B66 .... 65 B5
Chamberlain's La WV4 ... 38 E3
Chamberlaine St CV12 ... 78 B3
Champ ny DY10 .... 116 F2
Chance Croft B68 .... 84 B8
Chance Fields CV31 .... 162 F6
Chancel Ind Est
Darlaston WS10 .... 41 D5
Kidderminster DY10 ...... 117 B6
Willenhall WV13 .... 27 B2
Chancel Ind Est The
WV1 .... 26 A1
Chancel Way
Birmingham B6 .... 55 F5
Halesowen B62 .... 83 C6
Chancellor's CI B15 ...... 85 E8
Chancellors CI CV4 ..... 132 D4
Chancery Ct CV10 .... 72 A7
Chancery Dr WS12 .... 2 C7
Chancery La CV10 .... 72 B7
Chancery Way DY5 .... 61 F2
Chanders Rd CV34 ...... 155 D1
Chandler Dr WV4 .... 38 D3

Chandler Ho B65 .... 63 D4
Chandlers CI WV9 .... 11 A1
Chandlers CI CV31 ...... 161 D7
Chandlers CI
Redditch B97 .... 158 D7
Wolverhampton WV9 ...... 11 A1
Chandlers Dr B77 .... 22 B5
Chandlers Keep WS8 ..... 16 A6
Chandlers Rd CV31 ...... 162 A2
Chandos Ave B13 .... 86 F3
Chandos Ct 18 CV32 ... 156 F1
Chandos Prim Sch B12 .. 86 E8
Chandos St Coventry CV2 113 A3
Nuneaton CV11 .... 73 B3
Royal Leamington Spa
CV32 .... 156 F1
Change Brook CI CV11 ... 73 F8
Channon Dr DY5 .... 81 D8
Chanston Ave B14 ...... 104 E4
Chanterelle Gdns WV4 ... 39 B4
Chantrey Cres
Bilston WV14 .... 40 F7
Birmingham B43 .... 44 D4
Chantries The CV1 ...... 113 E5
Chantry Ave WS3 .... 28 C8
Chantry CI B47 .... 125 A7
Chantry Ct B13 .... 86 F3
Chantry Ho B62 .... 84 A6
Chantry Heath Cres
B93 .... 128 C7
Chantry Rd
Birmingham, Handsworth
B21 .... 65 F8
Birmingham, Moseley B13 . 86 F3
Stourbridge DY7 .... 80 C7
Chantry The CV34 ...... 156 A1
Chapel Ash WV3 .... 25 B2
Chapel Ash Island WV1 . 163 A3
Chapel Ave WS8 .... 6 E2
Chapel CI B64 .... 83 B8
Chapel Ct
Astwood Bank B96 .... 158 E1
Brierley Hill, Barrow Hill
DY5 .... 61 C7
4 Brierley Hill, Silver End
DY5 .... 61 D2
Chapel Dr
Balsall Common CV7 ...... 130 B8
Brownhills WS8 .... 6 E2
Wythall B47 .... 124 F3
Chapel Farm CI CV3 .... 134 C6
Chapel Fields Jun Sch
B92 .... 88 F3
Chapel Fields Rd B92 .... 88 F3
Chapel Gn WV13 .... 27 B2
Chapel House La B63 .... 82 C6
Chapel House St B12 .... 66 F1
Chapel La Barnacle CV7 .. 97 B6
Belbroughton DY9 .... 120 D7
Beoley B98 .... 154 F8
Birmingham, Great Barr
B43,WS9 .... 44 A5
Birmingham, Selly Oak B29 . 85 E2
Lapworth B94 .... 144 D7
Lichfield WS14 .... 9 C7
Romsley B62 .... 100 C6
Rowney Green B48 .... 139 F4
Ryton-on-D CV8 .... 135 B2
Walsall B43 .... 43 F4
Wythall B47 .... 124 E2
Chapel PI DY11 .... 116 D6
Chapel Rd B96 .... 158 E1
Chapel Row CV34 .... 160 E7
Chapel Sq WS6 .... 4 D3
Chapel St
Astwood Bank B96 .... 158 E1
Bedworth CV12 .... 78 C3
Bilston WV14 .... 40 F4
Birmingham B5 .... 164 D3
Birmingham, Handsworth
B21 .... 65 D7
Brierley Hill, Barrow Hill
DY5 .... 61 C7
Brierley Hill, Quarry Bank
DY5 .... 61 F1
Brierley Hill, Silver End DY5 . 61 D2
Bromsgrove B60 .... 137 A2
Brownhills WS8 .... 6 E2
Cannock WS12 .... 2 A7
Coventry CV1 .... 165 B3
Dudley DY2 .... 62 D4
Hagley DY9 .... 99 A5
Halesowen B63 .... 83 A3
Kidderminster DY11 ...... 116 D6
Kingswinford DY6 .... 60 B8
Norton Canes WS11 .... 5 F5
Nuneaton CV11 .... 73 C4
Oldbury B69 .... 63 E7
Redditch B97 .... 153 D1
8 Royal Leamington Spa
CV31 .... 162 A7
Stourbridge, Lye DY9 ...... 81 E5
Stourbridge, Wollaston DY8 . 81 A4
Stourbridge, Wordsley DY8 . 60 D3
Tipton DY4 .... 51 E5
Walsall, Blakenall Heath
WS3 .... 28 D8
Walsall, Pelsall WS3 .... 15 A3
Warwick CV34 .... 160 E7
West Bromwich B70 .... 53 B3
Wolverhampton WV2 .... 39 D7
Chapel View B67 .... 64 F4
Chapel Wlk
Birmingham B30 .... 104 A2
Bromsgrove B60 .... 137 A2
Dudley DY3 .... 50 C2
Chapelfield Mews DY8 ... 81 A4

Chapelfield Rd B45 .....122 A7
Chapelhouse Rd B37 .....69 F1
Chapelon B77 ....22 A2
Chapelwood Gr B42 .....55 D5
Chaplain Rd WS12 ....2 E2
Chapman CI CV34 ......162 E5
Chapman Ctr CV34 .....161 C8
Chapman Ctr The
(Birmingham Sch of Speech
& Drama) B1 ....164 B2
Chapman Rd B10 ....87 C8
Chapman St B70 ....53 B3
Chapmans Hill B62 ....101 B1
Chapmans Pas B1 ......164 B1
Chapter Ho B10 ....53 A5
Chard Rd CV3 ....134 D8
Charfield CI B30 ......103 D7
Charford Fst Sch B60 ..150 F7
Charford Rd B60 ......150 F8
Charingworth Rd B92 ...89 C3
Charity Rd CV7 ....95 A7
Charlbury Ave B37 .....69 F2
Charlbury Cres B26 .....88 F8
Charlbury Mews CV31 ..162 C6
Charlbury Twr 8 B5 ....86 E8
Charlecote CI B98 .....154 D2
Charlecote Croft B90 ..126 C8
Charlecote Dr
Birmingham B23 ....56 E7
Dudley DY1 ....50 E2
Charlecote Gdns
Royal Leamington Spa
CV31 ....162 D5
Sutton Coldfield B73 ....57 A8
Charlecote Rd CV6 .....95 A2
Charlecote Rise 1 WV13 .40 F8
Charlecote Twr 4 B15 ..66 C1
Charlecote Wlk CV11 ....78 F8
Charlecott CI B13 .....105 D7
Charlemont Ave B71 ....53 E8
Charlemont CI WS5 .....43 E2
Charlemont Cres B71 ...42 E1
Charlemont Gdns WS5 ..43 C6
Charlemont Jun & Inf Sch
B71 ....53 E8
Charlemont Rd
Walsall WS5 ....43 C6
West Bromwich B71 .....53 F8
Charlemont CI WS12 ....2 D3
Charles Ave
Blackheath B65 ....63 C4
Essington WV11 ....12 F4
Wolverhampton WV4 ....39 B5
Charles Burns Sch B13 .86 E1
Charles Ct Birmingham B8 .67 D4
Cheslyn Hay WS6 ....4 D1
Charles Cres WS3 ......15 A5
Charles Ct
8 Birmingham B13 .....87 B2
Sutton Coldfield B76 ...46 F3
Warwick CV34 ....160 C7
1 Warwick, Emscote
CV34 ....160 C7
Charles Dr B77 ....67 B6
Charles Eaton Rd CV12 ..77 F3
Charles Edward Rd B26 .88 D6
Charles Foster St WS10 .41 C6
Charles Gardner Rd 6
CV31 ....161 F6
Charles Hayward Bglws
WV4 ....39 D3
Charles Henry St B12 ..86 F8
Charles Holland St WV13 .27 B2
Charles Lakin CI CV7 ...97 C5
Charles Lane Trust Homes
The B28 ....106 A8
Charles Pearson Ct B65 .63 B5
Charles Rd
Birmingham, Aston B6 ..56 A1
Birmingham, Bordesley Green
B9,B10 ....67 E1
Birmingham, Handsworth
B20 ....55 C1
Brierley Hill DY5 ....62 B1
Halesowen B63 ....82 F4
Solihull B91 ....106 E2
Stourbridge DY8 ....80 E4
Tipton DY4 ....52 A7
Charles St Coventry CV1 .165 D4
Hinckley LE10 ....71 E1
Kidderminster DY10 ...116 F6
Nuneaton CV11 ....73 A5
Redditch B97 ....153 C1
Smethwick B66 ....65 C7
Walsall WS2 ....28 D2
Warwick CV34 ....161 A8
West Bromwich B70 ....52 E5
Willenhall WV13,WV1 ...27 C3
Charles Wesley Ct WV3 .39 A7
Charles Wlk B65 ....63 C5
Charlesdale Dr W59 ....30 B4
Charlesworth Ave B90 .127 B6
Charleville Rd B19 .....66 B7
Charlewood Rd CV6 .....95 B2
Charlock Gr WS11 ......2 C3
Charlotte Ct B69 ....52 A2
Charlotte Rd
Birmingham, Edgbaston B15 .86 C7
Birmingham, Stirchley B30 .104 A6
Tipton DY4 ....41 C2
Charlotte St
Birmingham B3 ....164 A3
1 Dudley DY1 ....51 B1
Royal Leamington Spa
CV31 ....161 F6
Walsall WS1 ....29 A2
Charlton Dr B64 ....82 D7
Charlton PI B8 ....67 D5

Charlton Rd B44 ....56 A8
Charlton St
Brierley Hill DY5 ....61 A3
4 Dudley DY1 ....51 A4
Charminster Ave B25 ...88 D8
Charminster Dr CV3 ...133 D4
Charnley Dr B75 ....32 E2
Charnwood Ave
Nuneaton CV10 ....72 E2
Sedgley DY3 ....39 D2
Charnwood Bsns Pk
WV14 ....40 C5
Charnwood CI
Bilston WV14 ....41 B3
Birmingham B45 ....102 B3
Brierley Hill DY5 ....81 B8
Cannock WS12 ....2 C3
Hinckley LE10 ....71 E2
Lichfield WS13 ....3 E1
Charnwood Ct DY9 .....81 E2
Charnwood Ho WS13 ...3 B2
Charnwood Prim Sch
WS13 ....3 B1
Charnwood Rd
Birmingham B42 ....54 F7
Hinckley LE10 ....71 D2
Walsall WS5 ....43 A4
Charnwood Way CV32 ..157 C3
Charter App CV34 ......160 D5
Charter Ave CV4 ....132 B7
Charter CI WS11 ....5 E4
Charter Cres B64 ......83 B8
Charter Ho CV4 ....132 A7
Charter Gr CV7 ....41 C1
Charter St DY5 ....61 E5
Charterfield Dr
Cannock WS12 ....2 C1
Kingswinford DY6 ....60 D7
Charterfield Sh Ctr DY6 .60 D8
Charterhouse Dr B91 ..107 C1
Charterhouse Rd CV1 ..113 E2
Charters Ave WV8 ......10 B1
Charters The WS13 ......3 B1
Chartist Rd B8 ....67 D6
Chartley CI Dorridge B93 .127 E3
Perton WV6 ....23 F4
Chartley Rd
Birmingham B23 ....56 D1
West Bromwich B71 ....53 D6
Chartway The WS3 .....15 B4
Chartwell B79 ....20 D7
Chartwell CI Dudley DY1 .51 B6
Chartwell Ct CV11 .....73 F1
Chartwell Dr
Cheswick Green B90 ...126 D5
Sutton Coldfield B74 ...31 D4
Wolverhampton WV10 ..11 D1
Chartwell Grange B64 ..83 A7
Chase Ave WS6 ....4 E3
Chase CI CV11 ....73 E6
Chase Gr B24 ....57 D6
Chase L Ctr WS11 ....1 D2
Chase La CV8 ....147 B7
Chase Park Ind Est WS7 ..6 D7
Chase Rd
Brierley Hill DY3,DY5 ...50 C1
Brownhills WS8 ....7 A1
Burntwood WS7 ....7 B6
Walsall WS3 ....14 F1
Chase Terrace High Sch
WS7 ....7 A8
Chase Terrace Prim Sch
WS7 ....6 F7
Chase The
Sutton Coldfield B74 ...57 D7
Wolverhampton WV6 ...25 B6
Chase Vale WS7 ....6 E6
Chase View WV4 ....39 E2
Chase Wlk WS12 ....1 C4
Chaselands WS7 ....6 D2
Chaseley Ave WS11 ....1 C2
Chaseley Croft WS11 ...1 C2
Chaseley Gdns WS11 ...7 C7
Chaseside Dr WS11 .....2 B3
Chaseside Ind Est WS11 .2 B3
Chasetown Com Sch WS7 .6 E5
Chasetown High Sch WS7 .6 E4
Chasetown Ind Est WS7 ..6 E7
Chasetown Sta* WS7 ....6 D5
Chasewater Country Pk*
WS7 ....6 A6
Chasewater Heath Bsns Pk
WS7 ....6 D5
Chasewater Heaths Sta*
WS7 ....6 D6
Chasewater Light Rly*
WS11 ....6 A6
Chasewater Raceway WS8 .6 C3
Chasewater Water Sports
Venue* WS8 ....6 C3
Chasewater Way WS11 ..1 C2
Chasewood Park Bsns Ctr
WS12 ....2 E1
Chater Dr B76 ....47 A1
Chaters CI DY3 ....51 A5
Chatham CI CV31 ......134 C8
Chatham Rd B31 ......103 A3
Chatillon CI CV34 .....161 E3
Chatsworth B79 ....20 C7
Chatsworth Ave B43 ...43 C1
Chatsworth CI
Cheswick Green B90 ...126 E5
Hinckley LE10 ....75 F6
Sutton Coldfield B72 ...57 D7
Willenhall WV12 ....27 B5
Chatsworth Cres WS4 ..29 D7

Chatsworth Dr
Cannock WS11 ....2 A4
Nuneaton CV11 ....73 F2
Chatsworth Gdns
Royal Leamington Spa
CV31 ....162 D6
Wolverhampton WV6 ...24 A7
Chatsworth Gr CV8 ....148 C5
Chatsworth Rd B62 ....83 A7
Chatsworth Rise CV3 ..133 E6
Chatsworth Twr 7 B15 ..86 C8
Chattaway Dr CV7 .....130 B6
Chattaway St B7 ....67 C7
Chatterton Ave WS13 ...3 A4
Chatterton Wlk 4 DY10 .117 B6
Chattle Hill B46 ....59 E2
Chattock Ave B91 .....107 E3
Chattock CI B36 ....68 E7
Chatwell Gr B29 ....85 B2
Chatwin PI WV14 ....40 E3
Chatwin St B66 ....64 D7
Chatwins Wharf DY4 ...51 F5
Chaucer Ave Dudley DY3 .50 A5
Tipton DY4 ....52 B8
Willenhall WV12 ....27 E8
Chaucer CI
Birmingham B23 ....56 B3
Dudley WV14 ....51 D8
Lichfield WS14 ....9 B6
Stourbridge DY8 ....81 A8
Tamworth B79 ....21 A6
Chaucer Cres DY10 ...117 C5
Chaucer Dr CV10 ....72 A4
Chaucer Gr B27 ....88 B2
Chaucer Ho B63 ....82 B5
Chaucer Rd
Bromsgrove B60 ....151 B8
Walsall WS3 ....28 E8
Chauntry PI CV1 ......165 C3
Chauson Gr B91 ....127 A8
Chavasse Rd B72 ......46 D3
Chawn Hill DY9 ....81 C3
Chawn Park Dr DY9 ....81 C3
Chawnhill CI DY9 ......81 C3
Cheadle Dr B23 ....56 D8
Cheam CI CV6 ....96 A1
Cheam Gdns WV6 ......24 E8
Cheapside
Birmingham B5,B12 ...164 D1
3 Willenhall WV13 ......27 A1
Cheapside Ind Est 1 B12 .66 F1
Cheatham St B7 ....67 C6
Cheatle Ct B77 ....35 D5
Checketts St WS2 .....28 C2
Checkley CI B90 ....106 A4
Checkley Croft B76 ....57 F8
Cheddar Rd B12 ....86 E6
Chedworth CI
Birmingham B29 ......103 B6
Redditch B98 ....154 C5
Cheedon CI B93 ....127 E2
Chelford Cres DY6 .....61 A3
Chells Gr B13 ....105 B5
Chelmar CI B36 ....69 F8
Chelmar Dr DY5 ....61 A6
Chelmarsh CV6 ....113 C6
Chelmarsh Ave WV3 ...38 B8
Chelmarsh CI B98 .....154 C7
Chelmorton Rd B42 ....55 D7
Chelmscote Rd B92 ....88 F1
Chelmsley Ave B46 ....70 F6
Chelmsley Circ B37 ...70 B3
Chelmsley Gr B33 .....69 E3
Chelmsley La B37 ......90 A8
Chelmsley Rd B37 .....70 C2
Chelmsley Wood Ind Est
B37 ....70 B4
Chelney Wlk CV3 .....115 A1
Chelsea B37 ....70 A8
Chelsea CI
Birmingham B32 ....84 F4
Nuneaton CV11 ....73 F7
Chelsea Ct 8 B29 .....103 B7
Chelsea Dr B74 ....31 E4
Chelsea Trad Est B7 ...67 A6
Chelsey Rd CV6 ....60 C6
Chelsey Rd DY2 ....54 E4
Chelston Dr WV6 ......24 E4
Chelston Rd B31 ......102 E2
Cheltenham Ave B61 ..121 B1
Cheltenham CI
Bedworth CV12 ....78 B4
Wolverhampton WV6 ...25 B5
Cheltenham Croft CV2 .114 F7
Cheltenham Dr
Birmingham B36 ....68 D8
Kingswinford DY6 ......60 B6
Cheltondale Rd B90 ...126 C8
Cheltondale Rd B91 ...106 F6
Chelveston Cres B91 ..107 B1
Chelveston Rd CV6 ....112 E5
Chelwood Gdns WV14 ..40 B5
Chelwood Gr CV2 ......96 C4
Chelworth Rd B38 .....104 B2
Chem Rd WV14 ....40 C5
Chenet Way WS11 ......1 E2
Chenies CI CV5 ....112 B3
Cheniston Rd WV12 ....27 C7
Chepstow CI
Coventry CV3 ....134 C5
Perton WV6 ....23 F4
Chepstow Dr B61 .....121 B1
Chepstow Gr B45 .....122 B6
Chepstow Rd Walsall WS3 .13 F1

Chepstow Rd continued
Wolverhampton WV10 ..11 D5
Chepstow Villas 5 B12 ..87 B5
Chepstow Way WS3 ....13 F1
Chequer St
Bulkington CV12 ....79 C2
Wolverhampton WV3 ...39 A6
Chequerfield Dr WV4 ..39 A6
Chequers Ave DY9 .....81 E1
Chequers Ct WS11 .....6 A5
Chequers The 3 WS13 ..9 B8
Cherhill Covert 1 B14 ..104 C2
Cherington CI B98 ....154 F1
Cherington Rd B29 ....104 A8
Cheriton CI CV5 ....112 D4
Cheriton Gr WV6 ....23 E3
Cheriton Wlk B23 ......56 B3
Cherrington CI B31 ...102 F7
Cherrington Dr WS6 ....4 C1
Cherrington Gdns
Stourbridge DY9 ....99 C7
Wolverhampton WV6 ...24 B2
Cherrington Way B91 .107 B1
Cherry Bank WS12 .....2 A2
Cherry Blossom Gr
CV31 ....162 B2
Cherry CI Burntwood WS7 ..6 F6
Coventry CV6 ....95 D2
Cherry Cres
Birmingham B24 ....56 F3
Bromsgrove B61 ......136 E2
Cherry Dr Birmingham B9 ..67 B1
1 Blackheath B64 ......82 E8
Cherry Gr DY1 ....50 F4
Cherry Gr Smethwick B66 .65 C5
Stourbridge DY8 ....80 E4
Wolverhampton WV11 ..26 C7
Cherry Hill Ave B45 ...138 C8
Cherry Hill Dr B45 ....138 C8
Cherry Hill Rd B45 ....138 C8
Cherry Hill Wlk DY1 ...62 A8
Cherry La Himley DY3 ..49 C3
Sutton Coldfield B73 ...57 A7
Wednesbury WS10 .....42 A2
Cherry Lea B34 ....69 B6
Cherry Oak Sch B29 ...85 D2
Cherry Orch
Blackheath B64 ....62 F1
Kenilworth CV8 ....148 A5
Lichfield WS10,WV14 ..116 F6
Lichfield WS14 ....9 C7
Cherry Orchard Ave B63 .82 F5
Cherry Orchard Cres B63 .82 F6
Cherry Orchard Dr B61 .136 E3
Cherry Orchard Rd B20 .55 A4
Cherry Pit La B98 .....141 A1
Cherry Rd DY4 ....51 F7
Cherry St Birmingham B2 .164 C2
Halesowen B63 ....82 F5
Stourbridge DY8 ....80 E4
Tamworth B79 ....21 B5
Wolverhampton WV3 ...25 B1
Cherry Tree Ave
Nuneaton CV10 ....72 E6
Walsall WS5 ....43 A3
Cherry Tree Croft B27 .88 C5
Cherry Tree Gdns WV8 ..10 B3
Cherry Tree La
Codsall WV8 ....10 B3
Halesowen B63 ....82 D1
Cherry Tree Rd
Huntington WS12 ....1 D8
Kingswinford DY6 ......60 D8
Norton Canes WS11 ....6 B5
Cherry Tree Wlk
Redditch B97 ....153 B4
Tamworth B79 ....21 A8
Cherry Way CV8 ....148 A5
Cherry Wlk B47 ....125 B5
Cherrybrook Way CV2 ..96 C1
Cherryl Ho B31 ....31 E3
Cherrytree Ct DY9 .....81 E3
Cherrywood Ct WV14 ..40 C1
Cherrywood Cres 3
B91 ....127 C8
Cherrywood Ct B92 ....89 A2
Cherrywood Gn WV14 ..40 D8
Cherrywood Gr CV5 ...111 F5
Cherrywood Ind Est B9 ..67 D3
Cherrywood Rd
Aldridge B74 ....30 D1
Birmingham B9 ....67 E2
Sutton Coldfield B74 ...44 D8
Chervil CI B42 ....55 C7
Chervil Rise WV10 .....25 F3
Cherwell B77 ....21 D1
Cherwell CI LE10 ....75 A8
Cherwell Ct B73 ....46 B5
Cherwell Dr
Birmingham B36 ....69 F8
Brownhills WS8 ....6 D1
Cherwell Gdns 7 B6 ...66 D8
Chesford Cres
Coventry CV6 ....96 B2
Warwick CV34 ....156 B1
Chesham St B12 ......162 B7
Cheshire Ave B90 ....106 A2
Cheshire CI DY8 ....60 D8
Cheshire Gr
Kidderminster DY11 ...116 A7
Perton WV6 ....23 E4
Cheshire Ho 8 B66 ....65 B5
Cheshire Rd
Birmingham B6 ....56 A2

Cheshire Rd continued
Smethwick B67 ....65 A4
Walsall WS2 ....27 F2
Chesholme Rd CV6 ....95 B2
Cheshunt Ho 8 B37 ....70 B2
Chesils The CV3 ......133 D6
Cheslyn Dr WS6 ....4 D2
Cheslyn Gr B14 ....105 A3
Cheslyn Hay High Sch
WS6 ....4 C3
Cheslyn Hay Prim Sch
WS6 ....4 C3
Chessetts Gr B13 .....105 A6
Chessetts Wood Rd
B94 ....144 C7
Chesshier St LE10 .....71 C1
Chester Ave WV6 ......24 F7
Chester CI
Birmingham B37 ....70 A4
Cannock WS11 ....2 B1
Lichfield WS13 ....3 C3
Willenhall WV13 ....27 D2
Chester Ct 4 B37 ......70 D2
Chester Gdns B73 .....45 E1
Chester Hayes Ct B24 ..57 C5
Chester PI WS2 ....28 B1
Chester Rd Aldridge B74 ..30 A8
Birmingham, Castle Bromwich
B36 ....69 E7
Birmingham, Chelmsley Wood
B37 ....90 F8
Blackheath B64 ....82 E8
Dudley DY2 ....62 A8
Hampton-in-A B46,B92,CV7 .91 B5
Stonnall WS9 ....16 D3
Sutton Coldfield B23,B24,
B35,B73 ....57 C4
West Bromwich B71 ....42 B1
Chester Rd N
Birmingham B73 ....45 B4
Brownhills WS8 ....6 D1
Kidderminster DY10 ...117 A7
Chester Rd S DY10 ....116 F4
Chester Rise B68 ......84 B8
Chester Road Sta B73 ..57 A7
Chester St Birmingham B6 .67 A6
Coventry CV1 ....113 B3
Wolverhampton WV6 ...25 B3
Chesterfield CI B31 ...103 B2
Chesterfield Ct
Birmingham B38 ......103 E4
Brownhills WS9 ....1 C6
Chesterfield Rd WS14 ..9 A5
Chestergate Croft B24 ..57 D4
Chesterton Ave B12 ...87 B5
Chesterton CI
Redditch B97 ....158 D4
Solihull B91 ....106 C5
Chesterton Ct B13 .....86 F1
Chesterton Dr
Nuneaton CV10 ....72 A5
Royal Leamington Spa
CV31 ....162 C5
Chesterton Rd
Birmingham B12 ....87 B5
Coventry CV6 ....113 A4
Wolverhampton WV10 ..26 A8
Chesterton Way B79 ...21 A7
Chesterwood
Aldridge WS9 ....30 F2
Hollywood B47 ....125 A6
Chesterwood Gdns B20 .55 D2
Chesterwood Rd B13 .104 F6
Chestnut Ave Dudley DY1 .51 B3
Kenilworth CV8 ....147 F3
Tamworth B79 ....21 B7
Tipton DY4 ....51 F7
Chestnut CI Aldridge B24 ..31 A3
Birmingham B27 ....88 B4
Cannock WS11 ....2 C2
Solihull B92 ....106 D8
Stourbridge DY8 ....80 D3
Chestnut Cres CV10 ...72 E5
Chestnut Ct
Birmingham B36 ....69 E7
Coventry CV3 ....134 B8
Royal Leamington Spa
CV34 ....161 E2
Chestnut Dr
Birmingham, Buckland End
B36 ....69 B7
Birmingham, Erdington B24 .57 C4
Birmingham, Rednal B45 ..122 D4
Cheslyn Hay WS6 ....4 F3
Great Wyrley WS6 ......4 F3
Nuneaton CV11 ....73 E3
Shenstone WS14 ....17 F5
Walsall WS4 ....29 B8
Wolverhampton WV11 ..49 A5
Chestnut Gr
Birmingham B17 ....85 D5
Coventry CV4 ....112 A2
Kidderminster DY10 ...116 B8
Kingswinford DY6 ......60 D7
Tamworth B77 ....21 C3
Wolverhampton WV11 ..26 C7
Chestnut PI
Birmingham B14 ......104 E8
Walsall WS3 ....28 D6
Chestnut Rd
Astwood Bank B96 ....158 E1
Bedworth CV12 ....78 D4
Birmingham B13 ....87 A4
Bromsgrove B61 ......136 F4
Oldbury B68 ....84 C7

Chestnut Rd continued
Walsall WS3 ....28 E6
Wednesbury WS10 ....42 A2
Chestnut Sch CV1 ....165 B1
Chestnut Sq CV32 ....157 B2
Chestnut Tree Ave CV4 ....112 A2
Chestnut Way WV3 ....38 D8
Chestnut Wlk ◨ B37 ....70 B2
Chestnuts Ave 89 B7
Chestnuts The
Bedworth CV12 ....77 E2
Wolverhampton WV11 ....26 B6
Chestom Rd WV14 ....40 B5
Cheston Ind Est B7 ....67 B7
Cheston Rd B7 ....67 B6
Cheswell Cl WV6 ....24 B2
Cheswick Cl
Coventry CV6 ....114 A7
Willenhall WV13 ....40 F8
Cheswick Green Prim Sch
B90 ....126 E4
Cheswick Way B90 ....126 D4
Cheswood Dr B76 ....58 B6
Chesworth Rd B60 ....137 B1
Chettle Croft B92 ....107 F7
Chettle Rd WV14 ....40 F3
Chetton Ave CV6 ....113 C6
Chetton Gn WV10 ....11 B3
Chetwode Cl CV5 ....112 B4
Chetwood Cl WV6 ....25 A5
Chetwynd Cl WS2 ....27 D3
Chetwynd Dr CV11 ....79 B7
Chetwynd Gdns WS11 ....1 D3
Chetwynd Jun Sch CV11 ....79 A7
Chetwynd Rd
Birmingham B8 ....68 B5
Wolverhampton WV2 ....39 B6
Cheveley Ave B45 ....122 B7
Chevening Cl DY3 ....50 E7
Cheveral Ave CV6 ....113 B6
Cheveral Rd CV12 ....78 A3
Cheverel Pl CV11 ....73 B2
Cheverel St CV11 ....73 B3
Cheveridge Cl B91 ....107 A2
Cheverton Rd B31 ....102 E4
Cheviot B77 ....22 C1
Cheviot Cl CV10 ....72 B3
Cheviot Ct B75 ....32 A4
Cheviot Rd
Stourbridge DY8 ....81 A6
Wolverhampton WV2 ....39 F7
Cheviot Rise Cannock WS12 ....2 C5
Royal Leamington Spa
CV32 ....157 C3
Cheviot The CV4 ....132 D6
Cheviot Way B63 ....82 D2
Cheylesmore CV1 ....165 B2
Cheylesmore Cl B73 ....46 B4
Cheyne Cl B17 ....85 D5
Cheyne Gdns B28 ....105 E3
Cheyne Wlk DY5 ....81 C7
Cheyney Cl WV6 ....25 A5
Chichester Ave DY2 ....62 D5
Chichester Cl CV11 ....74 A7
Chichester Ct B73 ....46 B5
Chichester Dr
Birmingham B32 ....84 A5
Cannock WS12 ....2 C1
Chichester Gr B37 ....70 B1
Chickock Hill CV3 ....133 B6
Chiel Cl CV5 ....111 F4
Chigwell Cl B35 ....58 A3
Chilcote Cl B28 ....105 F4
Chilcote Prim Sch B28 ....105 F4
Childs Ave WV14 ....40 A2
Childs Oak Cl CV7 ....130 A6
Chilgrove Gdns WV6 ....24 C5
Chilham Dr B37 ....70 C2
Chillaton Rd CV6 ....95 B2
Chillenden Ct WV13 ....27 C2
Chillingham B77 ....35 C7
Chillinghome Rd B36 ....68 D8
Chillinghome Twr B36 ....57 F1
Chillington Cl WS6 ....4 F1
Chillington Dr
Codsall WV8 ....10 A4
Dudley DY1 ....50 F3
Chillington Fields WV1 ....26 A1
Chillington Ho WV4 ....24 E5
Chillington Pl WV14 ....40 C5
Chillington Rd DY4 ....41 C1
Chillington St WV1 ....25 F1
Chillington Wlk B65 ....63 D3
Chillington Works Ind Est
WV1 ....25 F1
Chiltern Cl
Cheslyn Hay WS6 ....4 D1
Dudley DY3 ....50 D3
Halesowen B63 ....82 D1
Chiltern Ct
◨ Coventry CV6 ....113 A5
Sutton Coldfield B75 ....32 A4
Chiltern Dr WV13 ....26 D1
Chiltern Ho
Coventry CV5 ....111 D4
Redditch B98 ....154 E1
Chiltern Leys ◨ CV6 ....113 A4
Chiltern Rd
Stourbridge DY8 ....81 B6
Tamworth B77 ....22 C1
Chilterns The
Coventry CV5 ....112 B4
Oldbury B69 ....63 E5
Chilton Ct B23 ....56 C2
Chilton Rd B14 ....105 D4

Chilvers Coton Com Inf Sch
CV11 ....73 B3
Chilvers Coton Craft Ctr
CV11 ....73 C2
Chilvers Ct CV11 ....73 C4
Chilvers Gr B37 ....69 F5
Chilwell Cl B91 ....107 B1
Chilwell Croft B19 ....66 E6
Chilworth Ave WV11 ....26 F7
Chilworth Cl
◨ Birmingham B6 ....66 F6
Nuneaton CV11 ....78 E8
Chimes Cl B33 ....69 E1
Chimney Rd DY4 ....52 D6
Chimes The CV10 ....73 D7
Chingford Cl DY8 ....60 C4
Chingford Rd
Birmingham B44 ....56 A8
Coventry CV6 ....96 A4
Chinley Gr B44 ....45 C1
Chinn Brook Rd B13 ....105 C5
Chip Cl B38 ....103 D2
Chipperfield Rd B36 ....68 E8
Chipstead Rd B23 ....56 E7
Chipstone Cl B91 ....107 C1
Chirbury Gr B31 ....103 B1
Chirk Cl DY10 ....116 E2
Chirton Gr B14 ....104 D6
Chiseldon Croft B14 ....105 A3
Chisholm Gr B27 ....106 C8
Chiswell Rd B18 ....65 E4
Chiswick Ct ◨ B23 ....56 E2
Chiswick Ho B15 ....86 C8
Chiswick Wlk B37 ....70 E2
Chivenor Ho B35 ....58 A2
Chivenor Jun & Inf Sch
B35 ....58 A2
Chivington Cl B90 ....127 B6
Chorley Ave B34 ....68 F6
Chorley Gdns WV14 ....40 B5
Chorley Way CV6 ....113 C6
Christ Church CE Inf Sch
Wolverhampton, Dunstall Hill
WV6 ....25 B4
Wolverhampton, Tettenhall Wood
WV6 ....24 B3
Christ Church CE Jun Sch
WV6 ....24 C4
Christ Church CE Prim Sch
Dudley WV14 ....40 D1
Lichfield WS13 ....8 F7
Oldbury B69 ....64 A8
Walsall WS3 ....28 D8
Christ Church Gdns WS13 ....8 F7
Christ Church Gr WS1 ....43 A7
Christ Church Prim Sch
B61 ....87 B7
Christ the King RC Inf Sch
CV6 ....112 F6
Christ the King RC Jun Sch
CV6 ....112 F7
Christ the King RC Prim Sch
B44 ....56 A8
Christchurch Cl
Birmingham B15 ....85 E8
Nuneaton CV10 ....72 F1
Christchurch La WS13 ....8 F7
Christchurch Rd CV6 ....113 A5
Christine Cl DY4 ....41 C2
Christine Ledger Sq ◨
CV31 ....162 A6
Christopher Hooke Ho
CV6 ....113 E8
Christopher Rd
Birmingham B29 ....85 C2
Halesowen B62 ....83 E3
Wolverhampton WV2 ....163 B2
Christopher Wlk WS13 ....3 A3
Chub B77 ....35 D7
Chubb St WV1 ....163 C3
Chuckery Prim Sch WS1 ....29 A1
Chuckery Rd WS1 ....29 A1
Chudleigh Gr B43 ....54 D8
Chudleigh Rd
Birmingham B23 ....56 E4
Coventry CV2 ....114 E7
Church Ave
Birmingham, Handsworth
B20 ....55 C1
Birmingham, Moseley B13 ....86 F3
Clent DY9 ....99 F3
Stourbridge DY8 ....81 A7
Water Orton B46 ....59 B3
Church Cl Birmingham B37 ....70 A6
Drayton Bassett B78 ....34 E5
Hinckley LE10 ....76 A5
Nuneaton CV10 ....72 B8
Ryton-on-D CV8 ....96 C8
Shenstone WS14 ....18 A5
Whitnash CV31 ....162 B4
Wood End CV9 ....36 C1
Wythall B47 ....124 F3
Church Cres WV11 ....12 F3
Church Croft
Birmingham B17 ....85 B4
Halesowen B63 ....83 A4
Church Cross View DY1 ....61 D8
Church Ct
Astwood Bank B96 ....158 E2
◨ Blackheath B64 ....62 E1
Coventry CV4 ....94 F1
Stourbridge DY8 ....81 A5
Walsall WS1 ....28 E1
Church Down Ct B97 ....158 D6
Church Dr
Birmingham B30 ....104 B7
Hopwas B78 ....20 B7
Kenilworth CV8 ....147 F5

Church End CV31 ....162 E6
Church Farm Barn & Cotts
DY10 ....98 B3
Church Gdns
Smethwick B67 ....65 A4
Wolverhampton WV10 ....26 A4
Church Gn Bilston WV14 ....40 D8
Birmingham B20 ....55 A2
Church Gn E B98 ....153 E4
Church Gn W B97 ....153 E4
Church Gr B13 ....105 C5
Church Hill
Belbroughton DY9 ....119 D6
Beoley B98 ....154 D8
Birmingham, Frankley Green
B32 ....102 B6
Birmingham, Northfield
B31 ....103 B3
Brierley Hill DY5 ....61 D2
Cannock WS12 ....2 D5
Cubbington CV32 ....157 E5
Royal Leamington Spa
CV32 ....161 E8
◨ Walsall WS1 ....28 F1
◨ Wednesbury WS10 ....41 F3
Wolverhampton WV4 ....38 E4
Church Hill Cl B91 ....107 C2
Church Hill Ct ◨ WS10 ....41 F3
Church Hill Dr WV6 ....24 E5
Church Hill Mid Sch
B98 ....154 D6
Church Hill Rd
Birmingham B20 ....55 C1
Solihull B91 ....107 C3
Wolverhampton WV6 ....24 D5
Church Hill St B67 ....64 F6
Church Hill Way B98 ....154 D6
Church Ho
Brierley Hill DY5 ....61 C2
Walsall WS2 ....42 C7
Church La Ash Green CV7 ....95 E7
Aston Flamville LE10 ....76 F1
Berkswell CV7 ....110 C3
Bickenhill B92 ....90 E2
Birmingham, Aston B6 ....67 A8
Birmingham, Handsworth
B20 ....55 A2
Birmingham, Kitt's Green
B33 ....69 A3
Bromsgrove B61 ....136 F2
Brownhurst WS7 ....7 D3
Corley CV7 ....94 B7
Coventry, Middle Stoke
CV2 ....114 B3
Coventry, Upper Eastern Green
CV5 ....111 C5
Cubbington CV32 ....157 E5
Curdworth B76 ....59 B6
Halesowen B63 ....83 B4
Lapworth B94 ....143 E3
Leek Wootton CV35 ....155 F6
Meriden CV7 ....110 E8
Middleton B78 ....34 C1
Nuneaton CV10 ....73 C7
Radford Semele CV31 ....162 E6
Royal Leamington Spa
CV32 ....157 A3
Seisdon WV5 ....37 B2
Shuttington B79 ....22 E7
Stoneleigh CV8 ....149 C6
Stonnall WS9 ....16 E4
Tamworth B79 ....21 B5
West Bromwich B71 ....53 C6
Whitnash CV31 ....162 B4
Wishaw B76 ....48 A2
Wolverhampton WV2 ....163 B2
Church Lane Ind Est B71 ....53 C6
Church Mews Tipton DY4 ....51 E8
Walsall WS3 ....28 B8
Church Moat Way ◨
WS3 ....28 B8
Sutton Coldfield B75 ....32 C3
Church Rd
Astwood B96 ....158 E2
Baginton CV8 ....133 F2
Belbroughton DY9 ....119 D6
Birmingham, Aston B6 ....67 B7
Birmingham, Edgbaston B15 ....86 A7
Birmingham, Erdington B24 ....57 A4
Birmingham, Moseley B13 ....87 A3
Birmingham, Northfield
B31 ....103 A4
Birmingham, Perry Barr
B42 ....55 D5
Birmingham, Sheldon B26 ....89 C6
Birmingham, South Yardley
B25 ....88 B8
Birmingham, Stechford B33 ....68 F2
Blackheath B65 ....63 C4
Bromsgrove B61 ....136 F2
Brownhills WS8 ....15 F7
Burntwood WS7 ....7 D7
Catshill B61 ....136 F8
Dodford B61 ....136 A2
Dudley, Daisy Bank WV14 ....40 D1
Dudley, Netherton DY2 ....62 C4
Halesowen B63 ....82 C7
Huntington WS11 ....1 A2
Kingswinford DY6 ....60 E2
Norton Canes WS11 ....5 E4
Nuneaton, Chapel End CV10 ....72 B8
Nuneaton, Stockingford
CV10 ....72 C3
Perton WV6 ....23 E4

Church Rd continued
Redditch, St George's
B97 ....153 E4
Redditch, Webheath B97 ....152 F2
Ryton-on-D CV8 ....135 B2
Shenstone WS14 ....17 F5
Shilton CV7 ....97 E5
Smethwick B67 ....65 A4
Solihull B90 ....106 B2
Stonnall WS9 ....16 E3
Stourbridge, Lye DY9 ....81 E5
Stourbridge, Old Swinford
DY8 ....81 B3
Sutton Coldfield, Erdington
B73 ....56 F8
Sutton Coldfield, Maney B72,
B73 ....46 B3
Tamworth B77 ....35 C4
Walsall WS3 ....15 A3
Wednesfield WV11 ....27 D6
Wolverhampton, Bradmore
WV3 ....38 F7
Wolverhampton, Oxley
WV10 ....11 C1
Wolverhampton, Tettenhall
WV6 ....24 E5
Wolverhampton, Tettenhall Wood
WV6 ....24 B3
Wombourne WV5 ....49 B7
Church Row B34 ....68 E6
Church Sq ◨ B69 ....64 A7
Church St ◨ Bilston WV14 ....40 D5
Birmingham B3 ....164 B3
Birmingham, Lozells B19 ....66 C7
Blackheath B64 ....62 E1
Brierley Hill, Barrow Hill
DY5 ....61 D7
Brierley Hill, Quarry Bank
DY5 ....61 F1
Brierley Hill, Silver End DY5 ....62 C2
Bromsgrove B61 ....136 F2
Bulkington CV12 ....79 C2
Burntwood WS7 ....6 E5
Cannock WS11 ....1 E1
Cannock, Bridgtown WS11 ....4 D6
Cannock, Chadsmoor WS11 ....2 A4
Claybanger WS8 ....15 E6
Coventry CV1 ....165 C4
Darlaston WS10 ....41 D6
Darlaston, Moxley WS10 ....41 C4
Dudley, Gornalwood DY3 ....50 D3
Dudley, Kate's Hill DY2 ....62 C8
Hagley DY9 ....99 A5
Halesowen B62 ....63 D1
Hinckley LE10 ....76 A5
Kidderminster DY10 ....116 D6
Lichfield WS13,WS14 ....9 C8
Nuneaton CV11 ....73 D4
Oldbury B69 ....64 A8
Royal Leamington Spa
CV31 ....162 A7
Stourbridge DY8 ....81 A5
Studley B80 ....159 E3
Tamworth B79 ....21 B5
Tipton DY4 ....52 A2
Walsall WS1 ....28 F1
West Bromwich, Hateley Heath
B71 ....53 C6
West Bromwich, Lyng B70 ....53 C4
Willenhall WV13 ....27 B2
Wolverhampton WV2 ....163 B2
Wolverhampton, Heath Town
WV10 ....26 A4
Wolverhampton, New Cross
WV11 ....26 C5
Church Terr
Cubbington CV32 ....157 E5
◨ Royal Leamington Spa
CV31 ....162 A7
Sutton Coldfield B75 ....32 C3
Church View
Aldridge WS9 ....30 B6
Birmingham B11 ....87 C6
Brownhills WS9 ....15 F3
Dudley DY3 ....50 D3
Tamworth B77 ....35 F7
Church View Cl WS3 ....28 D8
Church View Dr B64 ....62 F1
Church Way
Bedworth CV12 ....78 B2
Walsall WS4 ....15 C2
Church Wlk Allesley CV5 ....112 C6
Birmingham B8 ....68 A6
Blackheath B65 ....63 C4
Hinckley LE10 ....75 D8
Kidderminster DY11 ....116 C6
◨ Royal Leamington Spa
CV31 ....161 F7
Nuneaton, Weddington
WV10 ....38 F7
Wolverhampton WV6 ....24 E5

Churchfields
◨ Birmingham B43 ....44 D4
Bromsgrove B61 ....136 F3
Kidderminster DY10 ....116 E7
Churchfields Ave DY4 ....51 D4
Churchfields Gdns B61 ....136 F3
Churchfields High Sch
B71 ....53 E6
Churchfields Rd
Bromsgrove B61 ....136 F3
Wednesbury WS10 ....42 A4
Churchill Ave
Coventry CV6 ....113 E8
Kenilworth CV8 ....148 A6
Churchill Cl B69 ....52 C2
Churchill Dr
Blackheath B65 ....63 B2
Stourbridge DY8 ....81 A7
Churchill Gdns DY3 ....50 C7
Churchill Ho ◨ CV32 ....161 F8
Churchill La B20 ....98 B3
Churchill Par B77 ....47 A5
Churchill Pl B33 ....69 B1
Churchill Rd
Bromsgrove B61 ....136 F3
Catshill B61 ....121 A1
Halesowen B63 ....82 F2
Shenstone WS14 ....18 A5
Sutton Coldfield, Falcon Lodge
B75 ....47 A5
Sutton Coldfield, New Oscott
B73 ....45 C3
Walsall WS2 ....27 E3
Churchill Sh Ctr ◨ DY5 ....51 D1
Churchill Wlk ◨ DY4 ....52 A8
Churchover Cl B76 ....57 D6
Churchside Way WS9 ....16 B2
Churchstone Cl B61 ....136 F8
Churchward Cl DY8 ....81 B6
Churchward Gr WV5 ....49 A8
Churchwell Ct
Halesowen B63 ....83 B2
Wombourne WV5 ....49 A6
Churchwell Gdns B71 ....53 E6
Churchyard Rd DY4 ....52 B5
Churn Hill Rd WS9 ....30 B4
Churns Hill La DY3 ....49 B3
Churston Cl WS3 ....14 A3
Chylds Ct CV5 ....112 A5
Cicero App CV34 ....161 E2
Cider Ave DY5 ....81 E8
Cinder Bank DY2 ....62 C6
Cinder Bank Island DY2 ....62 B7
Cinder Bk DY2 ....62 C6
Cinder Rd Burntwood WS7 ....6 E7
Dudley DY3 ....50 B2
Cinder Way WS10 ....41 E3
Cinquefoil Leasow DY4 ....52 C6
Circle The
Birmingham B17 ....85 C6
Nuneaton CV10 ....72 E4
Circuit Cl WV13 ....27 B3
Circular Rd B27 ....88 C2
Circus Ave B37 ....70 C2
Cirencester Cl B60 ....137 B2
City Arc Birmingham B2 ....164 C2
Coventry CV1 ....165 B2
◨ Lichfield WS13 ....9 B7
City Coll
Birmingham, Sparkbrook
B11 ....87 A7
Birmingham, Sparkhill B11 ....87 D5
City Coll Birmingham (St
George's Sixth Form
Campus) B19 ....164 B5
City Coll Coventry CV1 ....113 A2
City Coll Coventry (Butts Ctr)
CV1 ....113 B1
City College Coventry (Tile
Hill Ctr) CV4 ....111 F1
City Est B64 ....82 D8
City Hospl B18 ....65 F4
City of Wolverhampton Coll
(Bilston Campus) WV14 ....40 B7
City Rd Birmingham B16 ....65 C2
Tipton B69 ....63 C8
City View Birmingham B8 ....67 E5
City Road Prim Sch B16 ....65 D3
City Tech Coll The B37 ....70 A4
City Trad Est B16 ....66 A3
City View B8 ....67 D4
Civic Cl B1 ....66 C2
Cladsworth Ho ◨ B97 ....153 A4
Claerwen Gr B31 ....102 E5
Claines Cres DY10 ....117 B5
Claines Rd
Birmingham B31 ....103 C4
Halesowen B63 ....82 D5
Clandon Cl B14 ....104 C2
Clanfield Ave WV11 ....26 F7
Clapgate Gdns WV14 ....40 A3
Clapgate La B32 ....84 C2
Clapham Sq CV31 ....162 B7
Clapham St CV31 ....162 B6
Clapham Terr CV31 ....162 B7
Clapham Terrace Com Prim
Sch CV31 ....162 B7
Clarborough Dr B74 ....31 F5
Clare Ave WV11 ....12 F1
Clare Ct CV12 ....78 A2
Clare Cres WV14 ....39 F2
Clare Dr B15 ....85 F8
Clare Rd Walsall WS3 ....29 A6
Wolverhampton WV10 ....25 E7

Clare Witnell Cl DY11 . . . . . . 116 B8
Clare's Ct DY11 . . . . 116 C6
Clarel Ave B8 . . . . 24 F7
Claregate Prim Sch WV6 . . . . 24 F7
Claremont Cl CV12 . . . . 79 B4
Claremont Cotts DY3 . . . . 50 E8
Claremont Ct B64 . . . . 62 E1
Claremont Mews WV3 . . . . . . 39 A7
Claremont Pl ■ B18 . . . . 66 A5
Claremont Rd
  Birmingham, Hockley B18 . . .66 B6
  Birmingham, Sparkbrook
  B11 .87 B7
  Royal Leamington Spa
  CV31 . . . . .161 F6
  Sedgley DY3 . . . . .50 E8
  Smethwick B66 . . . . .65 B4
  Tamworth B79 . . . . .21 A8
  Wolverhampton WV3 . . . . . . .39 B7
Claremont St
  Bilston WV14 . . . . .40 C6
  Blackheath B64 . . . . .62 E1
Claremont Way B63 . . . . 83 A3
Claremont Wlk CV5 . . . . 112 C6
Clarence Ave B21 . . . . 65 C8
Clarence Ct
  ■ Hinckley LE10 . . . . 75 E8
  Oldbury B68 . . . . .64 C2
Clarence Gdns B74 . . . . 31 F2
Clarence Mews ■ B17 . . . . . . 85 D6
Clarence Rd Bilston WV14 . . . . 40 F7
  Birmingham, Gravelly Hill
  B23 .56 D3
  Birmingham, Handsworth
  B21 .65 C8
  Birmingham, Harborne B17 . . .85 D6
  Birmingham, King's Heath
  B13 .87 A1
  Birmingham, Sparkhill B11 . . .87 B7
  Dudley DY2 . . . . .62 D6
  Hinckley LE10 . . . . .75 E8
  Sutton Coldfield B74 . . . . . . .31 F4
  Wolverhampton WV1 . . . . . . 163 B3
Clarence St
  ■ Coventry CV1 . . . . 113 E4
  Dudley DY3 . . . . .50 E5
  Kidderminster DY10 . . . . . . .116 F6
  Nuneaton CV11 . . . . .73 A4
  Royal Leamington Spa
  CV31 . . . . .162 A6
  Wolverhampton WV1 . . . . . . 163 B3
Clarence Terr ■ CV32 . . . . . . 156 F1
Clarendon Pl ■ B17 . . . . 85 C5
Clarendon Ave CV32 . . . . 156 F1
Clarendon Cres CV32 . . . . . . 156 E1
Clarendon Dr DY4 . . . . 52 D8
Clarendon Ho LE10 . . . . 75 B7
Clarendon Pl
  Halesowen B62 . . . . .84 A6
  Royal Leamington Spa
  CV32 . . . . .156 E1
  Walsall WS3 . . . . .14 F3
Clarendon Rd
  Birmingham B16 . . . . .65 E1
  Hinckley LE10 . . . . .75 C7
  Kenilworth CV8 . . . . 148 A3
  Smethwick B67 . . . . .64 F4
  Sutton Coldfield B75 . . . . . . .32 C3
  Walsall WS4 . . . . .15 C2
  Wolverhampton WV3 . . . . . . .25 A2
Clarendon St
  Coventry CV5 . . . . .112 F1
  Royal Leamington Spa
  CV32 . . . . .157 A1
  Walsall WS3 . . . . .14 F3
  Wolverhampton WV3 . . . . . . .25 A2
Clarewell Ave B91 . . . . 127 B8
Clarion Way WS11 . . . . 1 E5
Clark Rd WV3 . . . . 24 F2
Clark St Birmingham B16 . . . . . 65 E2
  Coventry CV6 . . . . .96 A1
  Stourbridge DY8 . . . . .80 E4
Clarke Ho WS3 . . . . 14 B1
Clarke St ■ B97 . . . . 153 E3
Clarke's Ave CV8 . . . . 148 A3
Clarke's La B71 . . . . 53 C7
Clarkes Gr DY4 . . . . 52 D6
Clarkes La WV12,WV13 . . . . . . 27 C3
Clarkson Dr CV31 . . . . 162 A4
Clarkson Place Ind Est
  DY5 .81 E7
Clarkson Rd WS10 . . . . 42 A3
Clarry Dr B74 . . . . 45 F8
Clary Gr WS5 . . . . 43 A3
Clatterbach La DY9 . . . . 100 A4
Claughton Cl DY11 . . . . 116 C5
Claughton Rd DY2 . . . . 51 D1
Claughton Road N ■
  DY2 .51 D1
Claughton St DY11 . . . . 116 C5
Clausen Cl B43 . . . . 44 E4
Clavedon Cl B31 . . . . 102 E7
Claverdon Cl
  Brownhills WS8 . . . . .16 A8
  Redditch B97 . . . . .158 D4
  Solihull B91 . . . . 106 E3
Claverdon Dr
  Birmingham B43 . . . . .54 D7
  Little Aston B74 . . . . .31 C4
Claverdon Gdns B27 . . . . 88 B5
Claverdon Ho B13 . . . . 105 A7
Claverdon Rd CV5 . . . . 112 B3
Claverley Ct ■ DY1 . . . . 51 B1
Claverley Dr WV4 . . . . 38 D5
Clay Ave CV11 . . . . 73 F7
Clay Dr B32 . . . . 84 A5
Clay La Allesley CV5 . . . . 93 E3

Clay La continued
  Birmingham B26 . . . . .88 E5
  Coventry CV2 . . . . .114 A4
  Oldbury B69 . . . . .64 A3
Clay Pit La Lichfield WS14 . . . . . .8 F3
  Solihull B90 . . . . 126 A5
Claybrook Dr B98 . . . . 159 F7
Claybrook Fst Sch B98 . . . . . . 159 F7
Claybrook St B5 . . . . 164 C1
Claycroft Pl DY9 . . . . 81 E5
Claycroft Terr DY1 . . . . 51 B6
Claydon Gr ■ B14 . . . . 105 A3
Claydon Rd DY6 . . . . 49 C1
Claygate Rd WS12 . . . . 2 E3
Clayhanger La WS8 . . . . 15 D6
Clayhanger Rd WS8 . . . . 15 F6
Claymore B77 . . . . 35 E7
Claypit Cl B70 . . . . 53 A3
Claypit La
  Bournheath B61 . . . . .120 E1
  West Bromwich B70 . . . . .53 A4
Clayton Cl WV2 . . . . 39 C7
Clayton Dr
  Birmingham B36 . . . . .69 C7
  Bromsgrove B60 . . . . .151 B7
Clayton Gdns B45 . . . . 122 A2
Clayton Ho ■ B16 . . . . 65 F1
Clayton Rd Birmingham B8 . . . . 67 D5
  Coventry CV6 . . . . .112 E5
  Dudley WV14 . . . . .51 B7
Clayton Wlk B35 . . . . 58 A2
Clear View DY6 . . . . 60 B6
Clearwell Gdns DY1 . . . . 50 F3
Clearwell Rd B98 . . . . 154 C3
Cleasby B77 . . . . 22 C1
Cleaver Gdns CV10 . . . . 73 C6
Clee Ave DY11 . . . . 116 C2
Clee Hill Dr WV3 . . . . 24 A1
Clee Hill Rd DY3 . . . . 50 C4
Clee Rd Birmingham B31 . . . . . 123 A8
  Dudley DY2 . . . . .62 A7
  Oldbury B68 . . . . .64 C4
  Stourbridge DY8 . . . . .81 A6
Clee View Mdw ■ DY3 . . . . . . 39 D2
Cleeton St WS12 . . . . 2 C6
Cleeve B77 . . . . 21 D3
Cleeve Cl B98 . . . . 154 D5
Cleeve Dr B74 . . . . 31 F6
Cleeve Ho B24 . . . . 57 A2
Cleeve Rd
  Birmingham B14 . . . . .105 C4
  Walsall WS3 . . . . .13 F3
Cleeve Way WS3 . . . . 13 F3
Cleeves Ave CV34 . . . . 161 D6
Clem Atlee Ct WV13 . . . . 40 D8
Clematis B77 . . . . 21 F3
Clematis Dr WV9 . . . . 10 F3
Clemens St CV31 . . . . 162 A7
Clement Pl WV14 . . . . 40 D7
Clement Rd Bilston WV14 . . . . 40 D7
  Halesowen B62 . . . . .63 D1
Clement St Birmingham B1 . . . . 66 B3
  Nuneaton CV11 . . . . .73 B3
  Walsall WS2 . . . . .28 D5
Clements Cl B69 . . . . 63 F4
Clements Rd B25 . . . . 88 D8
Clements St CV2 . . . . 114 A3
Clemson St WV13 . . . . 27 A2
Clennon Rise CV2 . . . . 114 D8
Clensmore St DY10 . . . . 116 D7
Clent Ave
  Kidderminster DY11 . . . . . . .116 B1
  Redditch B97 . . . . .158 D7
Clent Ct B5 . . . . 51 D1
Clent Dr Hagley DY9 . . . . 99 D6
  Nuneaton CV10 . . . . .72 B3
Clent Fst Sch DY9 . . . . 99 E2
Clent Hill Dr B65 . . . . 63 A5
Clent Ho Bromsgrove B60 . . . 137 B3
  Halesowen B63 . . . . .83 A2
Clent Rd
  Birmingham, Handsworth
  B21 .54 D1
  Birmingham, Rubery B45 . . .121 E8
  Oldbury B68 . . . . .64 B1
  Stourbridge DY8 . . . . .81 A6
Clent View B66 . . . . 65 B3
Clent View Rd
  Birmingham B32 . . . . .84 A1
  Halesowen B63 . . . . .82 C2
Clent Villas B12 . . . . 87 B4
Clent Way B32 . . . . 102 A8
Cleobury Cl B97 . . . . 153 B5
Cleobury La B94 . . . . 126 A3
Cleopatra Gr CV34 . . . . 161 E4
Cleton St DY4 . . . . 52 B3
Cleton Street Bsns Pk
  DY4 .52 B3
Clevedon Ave B36 . . . . 69 E8
Clevedon Rd B12 . . . . 86 E6
Cleveland Cl
  Willenhall WV13 . . . . .26 D1
  Wolverhampton WV11 . . . . . .12 F1
Cleveland Ct
  ■ Birmingham B13 . . . . .87 B2
  ■ Royal Leamington Spa
  CV32 . . . . .156 F2
  Wolverhampton WV3 . . . . . . 163 B2
Cleveland Dr
  Barnt Green B45 . . . . .122 A2
  Cannock WS11 . . . . .2 B4
Cleveland Pas ■ WV1 . . . . . . 163 B2
Cleveland Rd
  Bulkington CV12 . . . . .79 B3
  Coventry CV2 . . . . .114 A4
  Hinckley LE10 . . . . .75 C8

Cleveland Rd continued
  Wolverhampton WV2 . . . . . . 163 C2
Cleveland St
  ■ Dudley, New Dock DY1 . . . .51 B1
  ■ Dudley, Old Dock DY1 . . . .62 B8
  Stourbridge DY8 . . . . .80 E4
  Wolverhampton WV1 . . . . . . 163 B2
Cleves Cres CV3 . . . . 134 D7
Cleves Cres WS6 . . . . 4 F1
Cleves Dr B45 . . . . 121 E7
Cleves Rd B45 . . . . 121 E8
Clewley Dr WV9 . . . . 11 B3
Clewley Gr B32 . . . . 84 B5
Clews Cl WS1 . . . . 42 E7
Clews Rd B98 . . . . 158 F7
Cleweshaw La B38 . . . . 124 C4
Cley Cl B5 . . . . 86 D6
Cliffden Gr CV8 . . . . 148 C6
Cliff Hall La B78 . . . . 35 C1
Cliff Rock Rd B45 . . . . 122 B7
Cliffe Ct CV32 . . . . 156 D1
Cliffe Dr B33 . . . . 69 C3
Cliffe Rd CV32 . . . . 156 D1
Cliffe Way CV34 . . . . 161 A8
Clifford Bridge Prim Sch
  CV3 .115 A3
Clifford Bridge Rd CV3 . . . . . 114 F4
Clifford Cl B77 . . . . 21 F3
Clifford Rd
  Bentley Heath B93 . . . . .127 F4
  Smethwick B67 . . . . .64 F1
  West Bromwich B70 . . . . .53 B2
Clifford St
  Birmingham B19 . . . . .66 D7
  ■ Dudley DY1 . . . . .62 B8
  Tamworth B77 . . . . .21 E3
  Wolverhampton WV6 . . . . . . .25 A3
Clifford Wlk B19 . . . . 66 D7
Clift Gr WV12 . . . . 27 D6
Clifton Ave Aldridge WS9 . . . . . 16 C1
  Cannock WS11 . . . . .4 F7
  Clayhanger WS8 . . . . .15 D7
  Tamworth B79 . . . . .21 A7
Clifton Cl Birmingham B6 . . . . . 66 F7
  Oldbury B69 . . . . .64 A4
  Redditch B98 . . . . .159 E8
Clifton Cres B91 . . . . 106 F1
Clifton Ct Hinckley LE10 . . . . . 71 F1
  ■ Royal Leamington Spa
  CV31 . . . . .162 B7
Clifton Dr B73 . . . . 46 B6
Clifton Gdns WV8 . . . . 10 C3
Clifton Gn B28 . . . . 106 A5
Clifton Jun Sch B12 . . . . 87 A5
Clifton La B71 . . . . 53 E8
Clifton Rd
  Birmingham, Aston B6 . . . . . . .66 F7
  Birmingham, Balsall Heath
  B12 .87 A5
  Birmingham, Castle Bromwich
  B36 .69 E8
  Halesowen B62 . . . . .83 E8
  Kidderminster DY11 . . . . . . .116 A1
  Nuneaton CV10 . . . . .72 F4
  Smethwick B67 . . . . .64 F3
  Sutton Coldfield B73 . . . . . . .46 B5
  Wolverhampton WV6 . . . . . . .24 D5
Clifton Road Ind Est B12 . . . . 86 F5
Clifton St Blackheath B64 . . . . . 62 F1
  Coventry CV1 . . . . .165 D4
  Dudley WV14 . . . . .51 A8
  Sedgley WV14 . . . . .39 F1
  Stourbridge DY8 . . . . .80 F4
  Wolverhampton WV3 . . . . . . .25 B2
Clifton Terr B23 . . . . 56 F4
Clifton Way LE10 . . . . 71 A1
Clinic Dr Nuneaton CV11 . . . . . 73 C3
  Stourbridge DY9 . . . . .81 E5
Clinton Ave
  Kenilworth CV8 . . . . 147 D6
  Warwick CV35 . . . . 160 A7
Clinton Cres WS7 . . . . 7 B8
Clinton Gr B90 . . . . 106 E1
Clinton La CV8 . . . . 147 C3
Clinton Prim Sch CV14 . . . . . . 41 A7
  Coleshill B46 . . . . .70 F7
  Coventry CV6 . . . . .95 F2
  Solihull B90 . . . . 106 E1
Clinton St Birmingham B18 . . . 65 E3
  ■ Royal Leamington Spa
  CV31 . . . . .162 A7
Clipper View B16 . . . . 65 E1
Clipston Rd B8 . . . . 67 F4
Clipstone Rd CV6 . . . . 112 E6
Clissold Cl B12 . . . . 86 E7
Clissold Pas B18 . . . . 66 A4
Clissold St B18 . . . . 66 A4
Clive Cl B75 . . . . 32 D2
Clive Rd
  Balsall Common CV7 . . . . . . .130 C5
  Birmingham B32 . . . . .84 D7
  Bromsgrove B60 . . . . .151 B8
  Burntwood WS7 . . . . .7 A7
  Redditch B97 . . . . .153 D5
Clive St B71 . . . . 53 C5
Cliveden Ave
  Aldridge WS9 . . . . .16 B1
  Birmingham B42 . . . . .55 D4
Cliveden Coppice B74 . . . . 31 F1
Cliveden Wlk CV11 . . . . 78 E8
Clivedon Way B62 . . . . 83 B7
Cliveland St B19 . . . . 164 C4
Clivesway LE10 . . . . 71 C2
Clock La B92 . . . . 90 D2
Clockfields Dr DY5 . . . . 61 A1
Clockmill Ave WS3 . . . . 14 F3
Clockmill Pl WS3 . . . . 14 F3

Clockmill Rd WS3 . . . . 14 E3
Clodeshall Rd B8 . . . . 67 E4
Cloister Croft CV2 . . . . 114 F6
Cloister Crofts CV32 . . . . 156 F3
Cloister Dr B62 . . . . 83 D3
Cloister Way CV32 . . . . 156 F3
Cloisters The
  Royal Leamington Spa
  CV32 . . . . .156 F3
  Studley B80 . . . . 159 D4
  Walsall WS4 . . . . .28 F3
Clonmel Rd B30 . . . . 104 A6
Clopton Cres B37 . . . . 70 C4
Clopton Rd B33 . . . . 89 C8
Close The
  Birmingham, Beech Lanes
  B17 .84 F7
  Birmingham, Griffin's Hill
  B29 . . . . .103 D8
  Brandon CV8 . . . . .135 F5
  Dudley DY3 . . . . .50 C4
  Halesowen B63 . . . . .82 D6
  Hollywood B47 . . . . .125 A5
  Hunnington B62 . . . . .101 A7
  Kenilworth CV8 . . . . 148 A6
  Lichfield WS13 . . . . .9 B8
  Royal Leamington Spa
  CV31 . . . . .162 A5
  Solihull B92 . . . . 106 F8
  Wednesbury WS10 . . . . .41 E3
  Tipton DY4 . . . . .52 C6
Closers Bsns Ctr CV11 . . . . . . 73 D2
Clothier Gdns WV13 . . . . 27 A3
Clothier St WV13 . . . . 27 A3
Clothier Street Prim Sch
  WV13 . . . . .27 A3
Cloud Gn CV4 . . . . 132 D5
Cloudbridge Dr B92 . . . . 107 F7
Cloudsley Gr B92 . . . . 88 F3
Clovelly Gdns CV2 . . . . 114 C5
Clovelly Ho B32 . . . . 102 A8
Clovelly Rd CV2 . . . . 114 B5
Clovelly Way CV11 . . . . 73 E5
Clover Ave B37 . . . . 70 D2
Clover Ct B38 . . . . 103 D2
Clover Dr B32 . . . . 84 D2
Clover Hill WS5 . . . . 43 E8
Clover La DY6 . . . . 60 B7
Clover Lea Sq B8 . . . . 68 A6
Clover Ley WV10 . . . . 25 F3
Clover Mdws WS12 . . . . 2 C1
Clover Piece DY4 . . . . 52 C6
Clover Pk Trad Est LE10 . . . . . 71 B3
Clover Rd B29 . . . . 103 A7
Clover Ridge WS6 . . . . 4 D4
Cloverdale Perton WV6 . . . . . . 23 D4
  Stoke Prior B60 . . . . .150 C3
Cloverdale CV10 . . . . 95 B4
Cloverfield CL10 . . . . 71 C3
Cloweswood La B94 . . . . 141 F8
Club Cotts WV10 . . . . 11 C6
Club La WV10 . . . . 11 C6
Club Row DY3 . . . . 50 E5
Club View B38 . . . . 103 D2
Clun Cl B69 . . . . 52 A1
Clun Rd B31 . . . . 102 F6
Clunbury Croft B34 . . . . 69 B5
Clunbury Rd B31 . . . . 123 A8
Clunes Ave CV11 . . . . 73 E6
Clusters The DY9 . . . . 81 E5
Clyde Ave B62 . . . . 83 E8
Clyde Ct B73 . . . . 46 B5
Clyde Mews DY5 . . . . 61 B6
Clyde Rd Bulkington CV12 . . . . 79 A2
  Dorridge B93 . . . . .128 A2
Clyde St Birmingham B12 . . . . . 67 A1
  Blackheath B64 . . . . .62 E1
Clyde Twr ■ B19 . . . . 66 D7
Clydesdale B26 . . . . 89 B5
Clydesdale Rd
  Birmingham B32 . . . . .84 B6
  Clayhanger WS8 . . . . .15 C6
Clydesdale Twr B1 . . . . 164 B1
Co-Operative St CV2 . . . . 96 B3
Coal Hauage Rd WS11 . . . . .35 D7
Coal Pool La WS3 . . . . 28 F5
Coalash La B60 . . . . 151 C2
Coalbourn La B77 . . . . 80 F7
Coalbourn Way B65 . . . . 61 A3
Coalbourne Gdns B63 . . . . 82 C6
Coalburnhill Glassworks*
  B94 .80 F7
Coalheath La WS4 . . . . 29 C8
Coalmeadow Cl WS3 . . . . 13 F3
Coalpit Fields Rd CV12 . . . . . . 78 C1
Coalpool Pl WS3 . . . . 28 F6
Coalport Rd WV1 . . . . 26 A1
Coalway Ave
  Birmingham B26 . . . . .89 C4
  Wolverhampton WV3 . . . . . . .38 A6
Coalway Gdns WV3 . . . . 38 D7
Coalway Rd Walsall WS3 . . . . . 28 E5
  Wolverhampton WV3 . . . . . . .38 A6
Coat of Arms Bridge Rd
  CV3 .133 A6
Coates Rd DY10 . . . . 117 B7
Coatsgate Wlk WV8 . . . . 10 F2
Cob La B30 . . . . 103 C6
Cobbett Rd WS7 . . . . 6 D7
Cobble Wlk B18 . . . . 66 A5
Cobbles The B72 . . . . 57 D7
Cobbs Rd CV8 . . . . 147 D6
Cobbs Wlk B65 . . . . 63 A5
Cobden Ave CV31 . . . . 162 C5
Cobden Cl Cannock WS12 . . . . . 2 C7
  Darlaston WS10 . . . . .41 F6
  Tipton DY4 . . . . .51 F8
Cobden Gdns B12 . . . . 86 E6

Cobden Ho WV2 . . . . 39 D7
Cobden St Coventry CV6 . . . . 113 E5
  Darlaston WS10 . . . . .41 F6
  Kidderminster DY11 . . . . . . .116 D5
  Stourbridge DY9 . . . . .80 E5
  Walsall WS1 . . . . .42 D7
Cobham Bsns Ctr B9 . . . . 67 D2
Cobham Cl
  Birmingham B35 . . . . .57 F3
  Bromsgrove B60 . . . . .150 F7
Cobham Court Mews
  DY9 .99 D6
Cobham Rd
  Birmingham B9 . . . . .67 D2
  Halesowen B63 . . . . .83 B4
  Kidderminster DY10 . . . . . . .116 E4
  Stourbridge DY8 . . . . .81 B2
  Wednesbury WS10 . . . . .42 E2
Cobley Hill B48 . . . . 138 E4
Cobnall Rd B61 . . . . 121 A2
Cobs Field B30 . . . . 103 C6
Coburg Croft DY4 . . . . 52 C6
Coburg Ho CV5 . . . . 112 E3
Cochran Cl DY5 . . . . 32 D2
Cochrane Cl
  Stourbridge DY9 . . . . .99 C8
  Tipton DY4 . . . . .52 C6
Cochrane Rd DY2 . . . . 61 F5
Cock Hill La B45 . . . . 121 F8
Cockermouth Cl CV32 . . . . . . 156 D2
Cocksheds La B62 . . . . 83 C8
Cockshut Hill B26 . . . . 89 A8
Cockshut Hill Tech Coll
  B26 .89 A8
Cockshutt La B61 . . . . 136 D7
Cockshutts La WV12 . . . . 39 D7
Cocksmead Croft B14 . . . . 104 D5
Cocksmoor Ho B14 . . . . 104 D7
Cocksparrow La WS12,
  WS10 . . . . 1 B5
Cocksparrow St CV34 . . . . . . 160 D7
Cockspur St B78 . . . . 36 E7
Cockthorpe Cl B17 . . . . 84 F7
Cocton Cl WV6 . . . . 23 E5
Codsall Com High Sch
  WV8 .10 A4
Codsall La WS14 . . . . 10 A4
Codsall Mid Sch WV8 . . . . 10 A3
Codsall Rd Blackheath B64 . . . 82 E8
  Codsall WV8 . . . . .10 C1
  Wolverhampton WV6 . . . . . . .24 D7
Cofield Rd B73 . . . . 45 D3
Cofton Church La B45 . . . . . . 122 D3
Cofton Cl B97 . . . . 153 B5
Cofton Ct B45 . . . . 122 D7
Cofton Gr B31 . . . . 122 E6
Cofton Lake Rd B45 . . . . 122 C3
Cofton Prim Sch B31 . . . . 123 A6
Cofton Rd B31 . . . . 123 B7
Cokeland Pl B64 . . . . 82 D8
Colaton Cl WV10 . . . . 25 E4
Colbourne Ct B33 . . . . 68 D3
Colbourne Gr CV32 . . . . 156 D2
Colbourne Rd
  Tamworth B78 . . . . .21 A2
  Tipton DY4 . . . . .52 A4
Colbrand Gr B15 . . . . 86 D8
Colbrook B77 . . . . 21 D1
Coldbath Rd B13 . . . . 105 B8
Coldfield Dr B98 . . . . 158 E7
Coldridge Cl WV8 . . . . 10 D1
Coldstream Cl LE10 . . . . 71 A1
Coldstream Dr DY8 . . . . 60 E3
Coldstream Rd B76 . . . . 57 E8
Coldstream Way B42,86 . . . . . 55 F1
Cole Bank Rd B28 . . . . 105 E8
Cole Ct B37 . . . . 70 B2
Cole Gn B90 . . . . 105 F2
Cole Hall La B34 . . . . 69 A5
Cole St DY2 . . . . 62 E4
Cole Valley Rd B28 . . . . 105 D6
Colebourne Prim Sch
  B33 .68 E5
Colebourne Rd B13 . . . . 105 D6
Colebridge Cres B46 . . . . 70 F8
Colebrook Cl CV3 . . . . 114 F2
Colebrook Croft B90 . . . . 105 F2
Colebrook Rd
  Birmingham B11 . . . . .87 D5
  Solihull B90 . . . . 105 F2
Coleby Cl CV4 . . . . 131 D7
Coleford Cl Redditch B97 . . . . 153 A2
  Stourbridge DY8 . . . . .60 C2
Coleford Dr B37 . . . . 70 A2
Colehill B79 . . . . 21 B5
Colehurst Croft B90 . . . . 126 F6
Coleman Rd WS10 . . . . 42 A5
Coleman St Coventry CV4 . . . . 111 F3
  Wolverhampton WV6 . . . . . . .24 F4
Colemeadow Rd
  Birmingham B13 . . . . .105 B6
  Coleshill B46 . . . . .70 F7
  Redditch B98 . . . . .154 F6
Colenso Rd B16 . . . . 65 D4
Coleraine Rd B42 . . . . 55 A6
Coleridge Cl
  Redditch B97 . . . . .158 C8
  Tamworth B79 . . . . .21 A6
  Walsall WS3 . . . . .15 A3
  Willenhall WV12 . . . . .27 E7
Coleridge Dr WV6 . . . . 23 E4
Coleridge Pas B4 . . . . 164 C3
Coleridge Rd
  Birmingham B43 . . . . .54 E7

Coleridge Rd
Coventry CV2 ....114 C3
Coleridge Rise DY3 ....50 A4
Coles Cres B71 ....53 B7
Coles La
Sutton Coldfield B72 ......46 C3
West Bromwich B71 ....53 B7
Colesbourne Ave B14 ...104 C2
Colesbourne Rd B92 ......89 B3
Colesden Wlk WV4 ....38 C6
Coleshill CE Prim Sch
B46 ....70 F6
Coleshill Dr B97 ....158 C5
Coleshill Heath Rd
Birmingham B37 ....90 C7
Coleshill B37,B46 ....92 F6
Coleshill Heath Sch B37 ..70 C1
Coleshill Ind Est B46 ....59 F2
Coleshill Rd
Birmingham, Hodgehill B34,
B36 ....68 E6
Birmingham, Marston Green
B37 ....90 B8
Curdworth B76 ....59 C5
Fazeley B78 ....35 A7
Nuneaton CV10 ....72 A7
Water Orton B46 ....59 B2
Coleshill St
Birmingham B5 ....164 D3
Fazeley B78 ....35 A8
Sutton Coldfield B72 ....46 C5
Coleside Ave B13 ....105 D7
Coleview Cres B33 ....69 E3
Coleville Rd B76 ....58 B6
Coley Cl LE10 ....75 D7
Coley La B31 ....103 A2
Colgreave Ave B13 ....87 D2
Colina Cl CV3 ....134 C5
Colindale Rd B44 ....45 A3
Colinwood Cl WS6 ....4 F1
Colldene Rd CV6 ....95 D1
Colleen Ave B30 ....104 B3
College Cl WS10 ....42 A1
College Ct WV6 ....24 D4
College Dr
Birmingham B20 ....54 F2
Royal Leamington Spa
CV32 ....156 F2
College Farm Dr B73 ......45 D1
College High Sch The
B44 ....56 B6
Coleshill Rd B73 ....46 B4
College La
Balsall Common CV8 ....129 E1
Hinckley LE10 ....71 E1
Tamworth B79 ....21 B5
College Rd
Birmingham, Alum Rock B8 .67 E4
Birmingham, Handsworth
B20 ....54 E2
Birmingham, Moseley B13 .87 C2
Birmingham, Perry Common
B44 ....56 B7
Birmingham, Quinton B32 ..84 A6
Bromsgrove B60 ....137 A2
Kidderminster DY10 ....116 E4
Stourbridge DY8 ....81 A4
Wolverhampton WV6 ....24 D4
College St
Birmingham B18 ....66 A4
Nuneaton CV10 ....73 C1
College View WV6 ....24 D3
College Wlk B60 ....137 A2
Collet Rd WV6 ....23 E5
Collets Brook B75 ....33 A2
Collett B77 ....22 A1
Collett Cl DY8 ....81 A6
Collett Wlk 2 CV1 ....113 B3
Colletts Gr B37 ....69 F4
Colley Ave WV10 ....25 F7
Colley Gate B63 ....82 C6
Colley La B63 ....82 C6
Colley Lane Prim Sch
B63 ....82 C6
Colley Orch B63 ....82 C6
Colley St B70 ....53 D3
Collier Cl Cheslyn Hay WS6 ..4 D2
Walsall WS8 ....15 C7
Colliers Cl WV12 ....27 B6
Colliers Fold DY5 ....61 B5
Colliery Dr WS3 ....13 F3
Colliery La CV7 ....78 B1
Colliery La N CV7 ....78 B1
Colliery Rd Smethwick B71 ..65 A8
West Bromwich B71 ....54 A1
Wolverhampton WV1 ....25 F2
Collindale Ct DY6 ....49 D1
Colling Wlk B37 ....70 C3
Collingbourne Ave B36 ...68 E8
Collingdon Ave B26 ....89 C6
Collings Ho B16 ....66 A1
Collingwood Dr B43 ....44 D3
Collingwood Ho B43 ....44 D3
Collingwood Jun & Inf Schs
WV10 ....11 E1
Collingwood Rd
Coventry CV5 ....113 A2
Wolverhampton WV10 ......11 E2
Collins Cl B32 ....84 A5
Collins Gr CV4 ....132 D5
Collins Hill WS13 ....3 A2
Collins Rd Brownhills WS8 ..16 A5
Royal Leamington Spa
CV34 ....161 D5

Collins Rd continued
Wednesbury WS10 ....42 C3
Collins St Walsall WS1 ....42 E7
West Bromwich B70 ....52 F3
Collinson Cl B98 ....154 A1
Collis Cl B60 ....150 E7
Collis St DY8 ....80 F8
Collister Cl B90 ....106 B4
Columbine Cl WS5 ....42 F3
Colly Croft B37 ....69 F5
Collycroft Pl B27 ....88 B5
Colman Ave WV11 ....26 F6
Colman Cres B68 ....64 C2
Colman Hill B63 ....82 D5
Colman Hill Ave B63 ......82 C6
Colmers Farm Inf Sch
B45 ....122 B8
Colmers Farm Jun Sch
B45 ....122 B8
Colmers Farm Sch B45 ..122 B8
Colmers Wlk B31 ....102 D1
Colmore Ave B14 ....104 D7
Colmore Circus Queensway
B4 ....164 C3
Colmore Cres B13 ....87 B1
Colmore Dr B75 ....47 A5
Colmore Flats B19 ....164 B4
Colmore Gate B2 ....164 C3
Colmore Inf Sch B14 ....104 D7
Colmore Rd B14 ....104 D7
Colmore Row B3 ....164 B3
Coln Cl B31 ....102 D6
Colonial Ind Pk B64 ....82 D7
Colonial Rd B9 ....67 F2
Colshaw Rd DY8 ....80 C4
Colston Rd B24 ....57 B2
Colt Cl B74 ....44 E7
Coltham Rd WV12 ....27 D7
Coltishall Croft B35 ....57 A2
Coltman Cl WS14 ....9 D7
Colton Hills Com Sch
WV4 ....39 B4
Colts Cl LE10 ....75 D4
Colts La B98 ....154 D3
Coltsfoot Cl WV11 ....26 C5
Coltsfoot View WS6 ....4 E2
Columbia Cl B5 ....86 D7
Columbia Gdns CV12 ......78 C2
Columbian Cres WS7 ....6 F8
Columbian Dr WS11 ....1 F3
Columbine Way CV17 ....7 C1
Colville Cl B12 ....87 B5
Colville Rd B12 ....87 B5
Colville Wlk B12 ....87 B5
Colwall Rd DY3 ....50 D4
Colwall Wlk B27 ....88 D4
Colworth Rd B31 ....102 F4
Colyere Cl CV7 ....95 A6
Colyns Gr B33 ....68 F5
Combe Fields Rd CV3 .....115 F4
Comber Croft B13 ....105 D8
Comber Dr DY5 ....61 B6
Comberford Ct 5 WS10 ..42 A3
Comberford Dr WS10 ......42 D4
Comberford Rd B79 ....21 A7
Comberton Ave DY10 ....117 B5
Comberton Ct 5 DY10 ..117 A5
Comberton Fst Sch
DY10 ....117 B4
Comberton Gdns DY10 ..117 B4
Comberton Hill DY10 .....116 F5
Comberton Mans 4
DY10 ....117 A5
Comberton Mid Sch
DY10 ....117 B4
Comberton Park Rd
DY10 ....117 B4
Comberton Pl DY10 ......116 F5
Comberton Rd
Birmingham B26 ....89 B8
Kidderminster DY10 ....117 B4
Comberton Terr DY10 ....116 F5
Combine Cl B75 ....32 D4
Comet Rd B26 ....90 C4
Commainge Cl CV34 .....160 D7
Commercial Rd
Walsall WS2 ....28 A7
Wolverhampton WV1 ....25 E1
Commercial St B1 ....164 A1
Commissary Rd B26 ....90 A3
Common La
Birmingham, Sheldon B26 ..89 B6
Birmingham, Washwood Heath
B8 ....67 F6
Cannock WS11 ....2 A3
Corley CV7 ....93 E7
Kenilworth CV8 ....148 B7
Tamworth B79 ....21 B4
Common Rd WV5 ....49 A6
Common Side WS8 ....16 A6
Common View WS12 ....2 B7
Common Way CV2 ....114 A6
Common Wlk WS12 ....1 C5
Commonfield Croft B8 ....67 D5
Commonside
Brierley Hill WV5 ....61 C6
Walsall WS3 ....15 A2
Communication Row
B15 ....66 C1
Compass Cl 4 CV1 ....113 B3
Compton Cl
Redditch B98 ....153 E2
Royal Leamington Spa
CV32 ....157 C2
Solihull B91 ....106 D4
Compton Croft B37 ....70 D1

Compton Ct Dudley DY2 ...62 C6
Sutton Coldfield B74 ....31 F3
7 Wolverhampton WV3 ....25 A2
Compton Dr Dudley DY2 ...62 F8
Kingswinford DY6 ....60 D5
Sutton Coldfield B74 ....44 E7
Compton Gr
Halesowen B63 ....82 C4
Kingswinford DY6 ....60 D5
Compton Grange B64 ......82 C8
Compton Hill Dr WV3 ......24 D2
Compton Ho B33 ....69 B2
Compton Park Recn Ctr
WV6 ....24 E3
Compton Rd
Birmingham B24 ....56 E1
Blackheath B64 ....62 C1
Coventry CV6 ....95 D2
Halesowen B62 ....83 F5
Stourbridge DY9 ....81 D2
Tamworth B79 ....20 F7
Wolverhampton WV3 ....24 F2
Compton Rd W WV3 ....24 C2
Comrie Cl CV2 ....114 F6
Comsey Rd B43 ....44 B3
Comwall Cl WS3 ....28 C7
Comyn St CV32 ....157 B1
Conchar Cl B72 ....46 C2
Conchar Rd B72 ....46 C2
Concorde Rd B26 ....90 C4
Concorde Twr B35 ....57 F2
Condor Gr WS12 ....2 C1
Condover Cl WS2 ....27 D3
Condover Rd B31 ....123 B8
Conduit Rd WS11 ....6 A4
Conduit St WS13 ....9 B8
Coney Gn DY8 ....81 B5
Coney Green Dr B31 ......122 F8
Coneybury Wlk B76 ....58 D5
Coneyford Rd B34 ....69 C6
Coneygre Ind Est DY4 .....51 F2
Coneygre Rd DY4 ....52 A3
Congleton Cl
Coventry CV6 ....95 C2
Redditch B97 ....153 B5
Congrave Wlk CV12 ....78 A2
Congreve Cl CV34 ....155 F2
Conifer Cl Bedworth CV12 ..78 C4
Brierley Hill DY5 ....81 C8
Cannock WS11 ....2 A8
Conifer Ct B13 ....86 E2
Conifer Dr
Birmingham, Handsworth
B21 ....65 E7
Birmingham, Northfield
B31 ....103 B3
Conifer Gr
Bromsgrove B61 ....136 F3
3 Royal Leamington Spa
CV31 ....161 F5
Conifer Paddock
Coventry CV3 ....114 E1
Halesowen B62 ....83 E8
Conifer Rd B74 ....44 E8
Conifers The CV8 ....148 B3
Coningsby Cl 3 CV31 ....162 C6
Coningsby Dr DY11 ....116 A8
Conington Gr B17 ....85 A5
Coniston Ave B92 ....88 F4
Coniston Cl
Birmingham B28 ....105 F7
Bromsgrove B60 ....137 B1
Bulkington CV12 ....79 C3
Coniston Cres B43 ....54 F7
Coniston Rd
Birmingham B23 ....56 D4
Coventry CV5 ....112 F1
Royal Leamington Spa
CV32 ....156 D1
Wolverhampton WV6 ....24 D8

Constables The B68 ....64 B2
Constance Ave B70 ....53 D1
Constance Cl CV12 ....95 F8
Constance Rd B5 ....86 D5
Constantine La B46 ....59 F1
Constantine Way WV14 ...41 A2
Constitution Hill
Birmingham B19 ....164 B4
1 Dudley DY2 ....62 D8
Constitution Hill E DY2 ...62 D8
Convent Cl Cannock WS11 ..4 D8
Kenilworth CV8 ....148 A7
Wolverhampton WV1 ....163 C2
Conway Ave
Birmingham B32 ....84 B6
Coventry CV4 ....131 D8
Oldbury B68 ....64 B2
West Bromwich B71 ....42 B1
Conway Cl Dudley DY1 .....51 C6
Kingswinford DY6 ....60 F4
Solihull B90 ....106 D1
Conway Cres WV12 ....27 C7
Conway Gr B43 ....54 D7
Conway Ho
Birmingham B31 ....102 D6
Walsall WS3 ....28 C6
Conway Prim Sch B11 .....87 C6
Conway Rd
Birmingham, Fordbridge
B37 ....70 B3
Birmingham, Sparkbrook
B11 ....87 C6
Bromsgrove B60 ....136 F1
Cannock WS11 ....23 F3
Royal Leamington Spa
CV32 ....161 D8
Solihull B90 ....106 D1
Conwy Cl Nuneaton CV11 ..73 D3
Walsall WS2 ....28 A4
Conybere St B12 ....86 F7
Conyworth Cl B27 ....88 D4
Cook Ave DY2 ....62 D7
Cook Cl Knowle B93 ....128 C6
Perton WV6 ....23 E4
Cook Rd WS3 ....14 D2
Cook St Birmingham B7 ...67 C7
Coventry CV1 ....165 B3
Darlaston WS10 ....41 F6
Cooke Cl Coventry CV6 ....96 A4
Warwick CV34 ....155 F2
Cookes Croft B31 ....103 B2
Cookesley Cl B43 ....44 D4
Cookley Cl B63 ....82 F2
Cookley Way B69 ....63 E5
Cookley Wharf Ind Est
DY5 ....61 B4
Cooknell Dr DY8 ....60 E2
Cooks La B37 ....70 A4
Cooksey La B44 ....44 F4
Cooksey Rd B10 ....87 C8
Cookspiece Wlk B33 ....68 F3
Coombe Abbey Ctry Pk*
CV3 ....115 E4
Coombe Abbey Visitor Ctr*
CV3 ....115 E4
Coombe Ave CV3 ....134 C7
Coombe Croft WV9 ....11 A3
Coombe Ct CV3 ....115 A2
Coombe Dr CV3 ....135 E7
Coombe Hill B64 ....83 B8
Coombe Park Rd CV3 ....114 F2
Coombe Rd
Birmingham B20 ....55 E1
Solihull B90 ....106 C2
Coombes La B31 ....114 B2
Coombes Rd B62 ....83 B7
Coombeswood Way B65 ..63 B3
Cooper & Jordan CE Prim
Sch WS9 ....30 C6
Cooper Ave DY5 ....61 A2
Cooper Cl
Bromsgrove B60 ....150 E6
West Bromwich B70 ....53 E2
Cooperage Rd CV3 ....134 F7
West Bromwich B70 ....53 D3
Wolverhampton WV2 ....39 F8
Cooper's Bank Rd DY5 ....50 C1
Cooper's La B67 ....65 A5
Coopers Hill B48 ....138 E6
Coopers Rd B20 ....55 A4
Cope Arnolds Cl CV6 ....95 F4
Cope St Birmingham B18 ..66 A2
Coventry CV1 ....165 C3
Darlaston WS10 ....41 C6
Walsall WS3 ....28 C6
Cope's Dr B79 ....21 B7
Copeley Hill B23 ....56 D1
Copes Cres WV10 ....26 A7
Cophall St DY4 ....52 D5
Cophams Cl B92 ....89 C2
Copland Pl CV4 ....111 E1
Coplow Cl CV7 ....130 A6
Coplow Cotts B16 ....65 F3
Coplow St B16 ....65 F3
Coplow Terr B16 ....65 F3
Copnor Gr B26 ....88 E6
Coppenhall Gr B33 ....69 A3
Copper Beech Cl CV6 ......95 E1
Copper Beech Dr
Kingswinford DY6 ....49 D1
Wombourne WV5 ....49 B6
Copper Beech Gdns B20 ..55 A2
Copperas St CV2 ....96 B2

Copperbeach Dr 2 B12 ...87 A5
Copperbeech Cl B32 ....84 F5
Copperfield Rd CV2 ....114 B3
Copperfields WS14 ....9 D7
Copperkins Rd WS12 ....2 E4
Coppermill Cl WS12 ....1 F7
Coppice Ash Croft B19 ....66 D8
Coppice Ave DY9 ....81 F3
Coppice Cl
Birmingham, Eachway B45 ..121 F7
3 Birmingham, Erdington
B24 ....56 F3
Brierley Hill DY5 ....61 F1
Burntwood WS7 ....6 F8
Cheslyn Hay WS6 ....4 D4
Cheswick Green B90 ....126 C4
Hinckley LE10 ....71 F2
Redditch B97 ....153 C3
Sedgley DY3 ....50 C7
Solihull B92 ....107 A7
Wolverhampton WV11 ....13 A1
Coppice Cres WS8 ....15 D7
Coppice Ct WS11 ....4 B7
Coppice Dr
Birmingham B27 ....88 B2
Dordon B78 ....36 F7
Coppice Farm Way
Walsall WV11 ....13 B1
Willenhall WV12 ....27 B8
Coppice Gr WS14 ....9 F7
Coppice Ho
Birmingham, Acock's Green
B27 ....88 A2
Birmingham, Handsworth
B66 ....65 D6
Willenhall WV12 ....27 C7
Coppice Hollow B32 ....84 B1
Coppice Hts DY11 ....116 B1
Coppice Jun Sch B92 ....107 C7
Coppice La Aldridge WS9 ..15 F1
Brierley Hill DY5 ....62 A1
Brownhills WS8 ....15 D8
Burntwood WS7,WS14 ....8 A3
Cheslyn Hay WS6 ....4 D4
Middleton B78 ....33 D2
Willenhall WV12 ....27 C6
Wolverhampton WV6 ....24 B6
Coppice Oaks B13 ....87 A3
Coppice Prim Sch The
B47 ....125 A6
Coppice Rd
Birmingham B13 ....87 A3
Blackheath B64 ....82 E7
Brownhills WS8,WS9 ....15 F4
Dudley WV14 ....51 A8
Solihull B92 ....107 C7
Whitnash CV31 ....162 B2
Wolverhampton WV3 ....38 D8
Coppice Rise DY5 ....62 A2
Coppice Sch B75 ....32 B1
Coppice Side WS8 ....15 D7
Coppice Side Ind Est
WS8 ....15 C8
Coppice St Dudley DY1 ....51 D4
Tipton DY4 ....51 E5
West Bromwich B70 ....53 A4
Coppice The
Birmingham, Frankley B31 ..102 C2
Birmingham, Handsworth Wood
B20 ....55 A2
Cannock WS12 ....2 E1
Coventry CV3 ....134 B8
Hagley DY8 ....98 F5
Hinckley LE10 ....75 F8
Nuneaton CV10 ....73 C7
Tipton DY4 ....52 C6
Willenhall WV12 ....27 C6
Coppice View Rd B73 ......45 A4
Coppice Way 7 B37 ....70 B2
Coppice Wlk
Cheswick Green B90 ....126 D4
Hinckley LE10 ....71 F3
Copplestone Cl B34 ....69 B6
Copps Rd CV32 ....161 D8
Copsey Hall Gr WV9 ....16 B1
Copsy Nook La WS7 ....7 C5
Copse Cl B31 ....103 A2
Copse Cres WS3 ....15 A4
Copse Dr CV5 ....111 B8
Copse Rd DY2 ....62 B3
Copse The Bedworth CV7 ..96 A8
Sutton Coldfield B74 ....31 F1
Copsehill Ct B75 ....46 E4
Copsewood Ave CV11 ......79 B7
Copsewood Terr CV3 .....114 C2
Copston Gr B29 ....103 B8
Copstone Dr B93 ....127 F3
Copt Heath Croft B93 ....128 B8
Copt Heath Dr B93 ....128 A7
Copt Oak Cl CV4 ....131 C6
Copthall Rd B21 ....54 C2
Copthorne Ave WS7 ....6 F4
Copthorne Rd
Birmingham B44 ....44 E3
Coventry CV6 ....112 F8
Wolverhampton WV3 ....39 A7
Copyholt La
Stoke Prior B60 ....151 D3
Upper Bentley B60,B97 ...152 A3
Coral Cl Coventry CV5 ....112 C2
Hinckley LE10 ....75 F4
Corbett Cl B31 ....70 C2
Corbett Cl B60 ....150 C1
Corbett Cres DY8 ....81 A7
Corbett Dr B60 ....150 C1
Corbett Ho 8 DY8 ....80 F8

Corbett Hospl DY8 .80 F7
Corbett Ind Est DY2 .62 C6
Corbett Inf Sch B66 .65 B5
Corbett Rd
Brierley Hill DY5 .61 E1
Hollywood B47 .125 A7
Kidderminster DY11 .116 A8
Corbett St B66 .65 B4
Corbetts Cl B92 .109 B7
Corbin Rd B78 .36 F6
Corbison Cl CV34 .155 D1
Corbizum Ave B80 .159 D4
Corbridge Ave B44 .44 F1
Corbridge Rd B73 .45 F2
Corbyn Rd Birmingham B9 .68 B3
Dudley DY1 .61 F8
Corbyns Cl DY5 .61 B7
Corbyns Hall La DY5 .61 B7
Corbyns Hall Rd DY5 .61 B7
Cordelia Gn CV34 .161 D4
Cordley St B70 .53 B4
Corfe Cl Birmingham B32 .84 F5
Coventry CV2 .114 F5
Perton WV6 .23 F3
Corfe Dr B69 .63 A8
Corfe Rd WV14 .51 A8
Corfton Dr WV6 .24 C3
Coriander Cl
Birmingham B45 .102 B2
Stoke Prior B60 .150 C1
Corinne Cl B45 .122 A6
Corinne Croft B37 .70 A4
Corinthian Pl CV2 .114 D6
Coriolanus Sq CV34 .161 F3
Corisande Rd B29 .85 C2
Corley Ave B31 .103 B3
Corley Cl B90 .105 E1
Corley Sch CV7 .94 B6
Corley View CV7 .95 C6
Cormorant Gr DY10 .117 B3
Corn Hill Walsall WS5 .43 E8
Wolverhampton WV10 .163 D3
Corn Mdws CV12 .78 C2
Corn Mill Cl
Birmingham B32 .84 E1
Sutton Coldfield B76 .46 F1
Cornbow Ctr B63 .83 B3
Cornbrook Rd B29 .102 F7
Cornbury Gr B91 .106 D4
Corncrake Cl B72 .46 D2
Corncrake Dr B36 .70 A7
Corncrake Rd DY1,DY3 .50 E3
Corndon Cl DY11 .116 B2
Cornel B77 .21 F4
Cornel Cl B37 .90 C8
Cornelius St CV3 .133 D8
Corner Ho B66 .65 D6
Corner La B97 .152 E2
Corner Stone Country Club
B31 .103 B5
Cornerstone B13 .86 F3
Cornerstone Ho CV1 .165 C4
Cornerway B38 .123 F7
Cornet's End La CV7 .110 B6
Cornets End La CV7 .109 E7
Cornfield Hinckley LE10 .71 C4
Wolverhampton WV8 .10 F2
Cornfield Ave B60 .150 D6
Cornfield Cl DY6 .60 A8
Cornfield Croft
Birmingham B37 .70 D3
Sutton Coldfield B76 .46 F3
Cornfield Dr WS14 .9 E7
Cornfield Pl B65 .62 F4
Cornfield Rd
Birmingham B31 .103 B4
Blackheath B65 .62 F4
Cornfield The CV3 .114 C1
Cornflower Cl WV10 .12 A7
Cornflower Cres DY2 .62 F8
Cornflower Rd WS8 .15 D6
Corngreaves Jun & Inf Sch
B64 .62 D1
Corngreaves Rd B64 .82 E7
Corngreaves The B34 .69 B6
Corngreaves Trad Est
B64 .82 D7
Corngreaves Wlk B64 .82 E7
Cornhampton Cl 7 B97 .153 B5
Cornhill WS11 .1 E5
Cornhill Gr
Birmingham B30 .104 C7
Kenilworth CV8 .148 C5
Cornish Cres CV10 .73 A2
Cornmill Cl WS1 .42 D7
Cornmill Gr WV6 .23 D3
Cornovian Cl WV6 .23 E5
Corns Ho WS10 .41 E6
Cornwall Ave Oldbury B68 .84 B8
Tamworth B78 .21 A1
Cornwall Cl Aldridge WS9 .16 A1
Kingswinford DY6 .60 D8
3 Warwick CV34 .160 F8
Wednesbury WS10 .42 D3
Cornwall Gate WV12 .27 B5
Cornwall Ind Est
Birmingham B8 .67 C4
Smethwick B66 .65 C7
Cornwall Pl
Royal Leamington Spa
CV32 .156 D1
Walsall WS2 .27 E3
Cornwall Rd
Birmingham, Handsworth
B20 .54 F2
Birmingham, Rubery B45 .101 E1
Cannock WS12 .2 B5
Coventry CV1 .113 E1
Cornwall Rd *continued*
Smethwick B66 .65 C7
Stourbridge DY8 .80 D8
Walsall WS5 .43 B7
Wolverhampton WV6 .24 C4
Cornwall St B3 .164 B3
Cornwall Twr B18 .66 B5
Cornwall Way LE10 .71 E4
Cornwallis Rd B70 .53 A1
Cornwell Cl Redditch B98 .159 B5
Tipton DY4 .52 A5
Cornyx La B91 .107 D6
Coronation Ave
Mile Oak B78 .20 D1
Willenhall WV13 .27 D2
Coronation Cres B79 .22 F7
Coronation Ct CV11 .73 B4
Coronation Ho 3 DY4 .51 E5
Coronation Rd
Bilston WV14 .40 C6
Birmingham, Great Barr
B43 .43 E4
Birmingham, Selly Oak B29 .85 F2
Birmingham, Washwood Heath
B8 .67 F6
Brownhills WS9 .16 A3
Coventry CV1 .113 F4
Tipton DY4 .52 B8
Walsall WS4 .15 B2
Wednesbury WS10 .42 C4
Wolverhampton WV10 .26 A5
Coronation St B79 .21 A5
Coronation Terr B60 .151 B7
Coronation Way DY10 .117 B5
Coronel Ave CV6 .95 E4
Corporation Rd DY2 .51 F1
Corporation St
Birmingham B2 .164 C3
Birmingham, New Town Row
B4 .164 C4
Coventry CV1 .165 B3
Kidderminster DY10 .116 E5
Nuneaton CV11 .73 B5
Tamworth B79 .21 B5
Walsall WS1 .42 E8
Wednesbury WS10 .42 A2
Wolverhampton WV1 .163 B3
Corporation St W WS1 .42 D8
Corpus Christi RC Prim Sch
Birmingham B33 .68 D2
Wednesfield WV11 .27 A8
Corpus Christi RC Sch
CV3 .134 D7
Correen B77 .22 C1
Corrie Croft
Birmingham, Bartley Green
B32 .102 B7
Birmingham, Lyndon Green
B26 .89 B7
Corrin Gr DY6 .60 C8
Corron Hill B63 .83 B4
Corser St Dudley DY1 .51 A2
Stourbridge DY8 .81 A3
Wolverhampton WV1 .25 F1
Corsican Cl Burntwood WS7 .7 A8
Willenhall WV12 .27 E7
Corsican Dr WS12 .2 A8
Corston Mews CV31 .162 C6
Cort Dr WS7 .7 B8
Corunna Rd CV34 .160 C7
Corve Gdns WV6 .24 E5
Corve View DY3 .39 C1
Corvedale Ho WV1 .26 B1
Corvedale Rd B29 .103 A6
Corville Gdns B26 .89 C4
Corville Rd B62 .83 F6
Corwen Croft B31 .102 E6
Cory Croft DY4 .52 A5
Coseley Hall 1 WV14 .51 C8
Coseley Rd WV14 .40 C4
Coseley Road Island
WV14 .40 C4
Coseley Sch The WV14 .40 B1
Coseley Sta WV14 .40 C1
Cosford Cl Redditch B98 .154 F1
Royal Leamington Spa
CV32 .157 B3
Cosford Cres B35 .58 A3
Cosford Ct WV6 .23 E5
Cosford Dr DY2 .62 E5
Cosgrove Wlk WV8 .10 F1
Cossington Rd B23 .56 E7
Costers La B98 .154 F2
Costock Cl B37 .90 B8
Cot La DY6,DY8 .60 C5
Coten End CV34 .160 F7
Coten End Prim Sch
CV34 .160 F7
Cotes Rd LE10 .75 F5
Cotford Rd B14 .105 A2
Cotheridge Cl B90 .127 C6
Cotleigh Gr B43 .44 D3
Cotman Cl Bedworth CV12 .78 A4
Birmingham B43 .44 C3
Cotman Dr LE10 .71 A3
Coton Gr B90 .105 E2
Coton Green Prec B79 .20 F7
Coton Green Prim Sch
B79 .20 F8
Coton La Birmingham B23 .56 F4
Tamworth B79 .20 E8
Coton Rd Nuneaton CV11 .73 C3
Wolverhampton WV4 .39 B5
Cotsdale Rd WV4 .38 E3
Cotsford B91 .107 A3
Cotswold Ave WS6 .4 F3
Cotswold Cl Aldridge WS9 .16 C1
Birmingham B45 .102 B2
Cotswold Cl *continued*
Cannock WS12 .2 A8
Kidderminster DY11 .116 C2
Oldbury B69 .63 E5
Cotswold Cres CV10 .72 B3
Cotswold Croft B63 .82 C1
Cotswold Ct
Sutton Coldfield B75 .32 A4
Wolverhampton WV3 .39 A6
Cotswold Dr CV3 .133 C3
Cotswold Gr WV12 .13 B1
Cotswold Ho 6 B14 .105 A3
Cotswold Rd Cannock WS12 .2 A8
Stourbridge DY8 .81 B6
Wolverhampton WV2 .39 F7
Cotswold Way B61 .137 A5
Cottage Cl Burntwood WS7 .6 F5
Cannock WS12 .2 D5
Royal Leamington Spa
CV31 .162 C6
Wolverhampton WV11 .26 C6
Cottage Ct WS7 .6 F5
Cottage Dr B60 .121 D1
Cottage Farm La B60 .121 C1
Cottage Farm Lodge CV6 .95 A1
Cottage Farm Rd
Coventry CV6 .95 A2
Tamworth B77 .35 D7
Cottage Gdns B45 .121 F6
Cottage La Burntwood WS7 .6 F5
Marlbrook B60 .121 C1
Minworth B76 .58 D6
Wolverhampton WV10 .11 D3
Cottage Mews WS9 .30 E4
Cottage St
Brierley Hill DY5 .61 D3
Kingswinford DY6 .60 D7
Cottage View WV8 .10 B4
Cottage Wlk B77 .35 F6
Cottages The
Birmingham B24 .67 F8
Halesowen B63 .82 E6
Cotterell Ct 3 WS4 .28 F3
Cotteridge Inf & Jun Sch
B30 .104 A5
Cotteridge Rd B30 .104 A4
Cotterill's Cl CV31 .162 B3
Cotterills Ave B8 .68 C4
Cotterills La B8 .68 C4
Cotterills Rd DY4 .52 B7
Cottesbrook Cl CV3 .114 E1
Cottesbrook Inf Sch B27 .88 D4
Cottesbrook Jun Sch
B27 .88 C4
Cottesbrook Rd B27 .88 D4
Cottesfield Cl B8 .68 B4
Cottesmore Cl B71 .53 F8
Cottesmore Ho 7 B20 .54 F3
Cottle Cl WS2 .27 F3
Cotton Dr CV8 .148 C6
Cotton La B13 .87 A2
Cotton Mill Spinney
CV32 .157 E6
Cotton Pool Rd B61 .136 E2
Cottrell St B71 .53 D4
Cottrells Cl B14 .105 C4
Cottrells Mews B46 .59 B2
Cottsmeadow Dr B8 .68 C4
Cotwall End Ho DY3 .50 C7
Cotwall End Nature Ctr*
DY3 .50 C6
Cotwall End Prim Sch
DY3 .50 D7
Cotwall End Rd DY3 .50 C5
Cotysmore Rd B75 .46 D7
Couchman Rd B8 .67 E4
Coughton Dr CV31 .162 D5
Coulter Gr WV6 .23 D4
Coulter La WS7 .7 E8
Council Cres WV12 .27 C4
Council Ho* B3 .164 B2
Council Hos CV5 .93 D1
Council Rd 3 LE10 .71 D1
Coundon Court Sch & Com
Coll CV6 .112 E7
Coundon Gn CV6 .112 E8
Coundon Prim Sch CV6 .112 E5
Coundon Rd CV1 .113 B3
Coundon St CV1 .165 A4
Coundon Wedge Dr
CV5 .112 D7
Counterfield Dr B65 .62 F5
Countess Dr WS4 .29 D7
Countess Rd CV11 .73 A4
Countess St WS1 .42 D7
Countess's Croft The
CV3 .133 D7
Countinghouse Way 2
B60 .150 E6
County Bridge Prim Sch
WS2 .27 E1
County Cl
Birmingham, Stirchley B30 .104 C6
Birmingham, Woodgate B32 .84 D3
County Dr B78 .21 A2
County La DY7 .98 D8
County Park Ave B62 .83 D3
Court Cres DY6 .60 C5
Court Dr WS14 .17 F4
Court Farm Prim Sch
B23 .56 E6
Court Farm Rd B23 .56 E6
Court Farm Way B29 .102 F7
Court La B23 .56 E7
Court Leet CV3 .135 D7
Court Leet Rd CV3 .133 E7
Court Oak Gr B32 .84 F6
Court Oak Rd B17 .85 A6
Court of Lady Katherine
Leveson The B93 .129 B5
Court Par WS9 .30 B6
Court Pas DY1 .51 C1
Court Rd
Birmingham, Balsall Heath
B12 .86 E6
Birmingham, Sparkhill B11 .87 C4
Wolverhampton, Lanesfield
WV4 .40 A3
Wolverhampton, Newbridge
WV6 .24 F4
Court St 2 Blackheath B64 .62 F1
Royal Leamington Spa
CV31 .162 A7
7 Stourbridge DY8 .81 A5
Court Way WS2 .28 E2
Courtaulds Way CV6 .113 D6
Courtenay Gdns B43 .43 E2
Courtenay Rd B44 .55 E8
Courthouse Croft CV8 .148 C4
Courthouse Green Prim Sch
CV6 .114 A8
Courtland Ave CV6 .112 F5
Courtland Rd DY6 .60 E8
Courtlands Cl B5 .86 C6
Courtlands The WV6 .24 E4
Courtney DY10 .116 E2
Courtney Cl CV11 .73 F7
Courtway Ave B14 .105 B1
Courtyard The
Coleshill B46 .59 F2
Solihull B91 .107 C4
Stoke Prior B60 .150 D2
Warwick CV34 .160 F5
Cousins St WV2 .39 D7
Cove Pl CV2 .114 C7
Coveley Gr B18 .66 A5
Coven Cl WS3 .15 A5
Coven Gr B29 .85 B2
Coven St WV10 .25 D4
Coventry & Warwickshire
Hospl CV1 .165 C4
Coventry Airport CV8 .134 B2
Coventry Bsns Pk CV5 .112 D1
Coventry Canal Basin
Warehouse CV1 .165 B4
Coventry Cath Church of St
Michael* CV1 .165 C3
Coventry City FC CV1 .113 F3
Coventry Council Ho
CV1 .165 C2
Coventry Gram Sch CV5 .112 F1
Coventry Highway B98 .154 C4
Coventry Muslim Sch
CV6 .113 E8
Coventry Prep Sch CV3 .133 B8
Coventry Railway Ctr
CV8 .134 A3
Coventry Rd
Aston Flamville LE10 .76 F1
Baginton CV8 .133 F2
Barnacle CV7,CV12 .97 A8
Bedworth, Hawkesbury CV2,
CV7 .96 E6
Bedworth, Springfield CV12 .78 B2
Berkswell CV7 .110 E3
Birmingham B10,B25,B26 .88 C6
Bulkington CV12 .79 B1
Coventry CV3 .115 F3
Cubbington CV32 .157 E7
Hampton-in-A B92 .91 B3
Hinckley LE10 .75 B7
Hinckley, Sketchley LE10 .75 F5
Kenilworth CV8 .148 A7
Nuneaton CV10 .78 C7
Solihull B26,B92 .90 C2
Stoneleigh CV8,CV3 .149 C7
Warwick CV34 .160 F8
Coventry Ret Mkt CV1 .165 B2
Coventry Road Exhall
CV7 .96 A8
Coventry St
Birmingham B5 .164 D2
Coventry CV2 .114 A4
Kidderminster DY10 .116 F6
Nuneaton CV11 .73 C4
Stourbridge DY8 .81 A5
Wolverhampton WV1 .26 A2
Coventry Sta CV1 .165 B1
Coventry Toy Mus*
CV1 .165 C2
Coventry Univ
Coventry CV1 .165 C1
Coventry CV1 .165 C2
Coventry CV1 .165 C3
Coventry CV1 .165 D2
Coventry Univ Singer Hall
CV1 .165 C3
Coventry Walsgrave Triangle
Bsns Pk CV2 .97 A1
Cover Croft B76 .47 A1
Coverdale Rd B92 .89 A4
Covers The B80 .159 E6
Covert La DY8 .80 D2
Covert The WV8 .10 E1
Covey Cl WS13 .3 D1
Cow La B78 .35 F3
Cowdray Cl CV31 .162 C7
Cowles Croft B25 .68 E1
Cowley B77 .21 E2
Cowley Cl B36 .58 F1
Cowley Dr
Birmingham B27 .88 D4
Dudley DY1 .50 F2
Cowley Gn WS12 .1 F8
Cowley Gr B11 .87 E5
Cowley Rd
Birmingham B11 .87 E5
Coventry CV2 .114 D4
Cowper Cl Warwick CV34 .155 E1
Willenhall WV12 .27 E7
Cowper Rd LE10 .75 D6
Cowper Wlk DY10 .117 C6
Cowslip Cl
1 Birmingham, Hawkesley
B38 .123 F8
Birmingham, Selly Oak
B29 .103 A7
Cowslip Wlk DY5 .81 C6
Cox Rd WV14 .40 E1
Cox St Birmingham B3 .164 B4
Coventry CV1 .165 C3
Cox's Cl CV10 .73 B3
Cox's La B64 .62 F2
Cox's Orch CV31 .162 A4
Coxcroft Ave DY5 .81 F8
Coxmoor Cl WS3 .13 F3
Coxwell Ave WV10 .25 C5
Coxwell Gdns B16 .65 F2
Coyne Cl DY4 .51 D5
Coyne Rd B70 .53 B2
Cozens Cl CV12 .78 A4
Crab La Cannock WS11 .2 A3
Willenhall WV12 .13 D1
Crab Mill Cl B38 .123 E7
Crab Tree Ho B33 .68 E3
Crabbe St DY9 .81 F5
Crabbs Cross La B97 .158 E5
Crabmill Cl B93 .128 C7
Crabmill La
Birmingham B38 .124 D8
Coventry CV6 .113 F7
Crabourne Rd DY2 .62 B2
Crabtree Cl
Birmingham B31 .103 C2
Hagley DY9 .99 B6
Redditch B98 .154 A2
West Bromwich B71 .53 F8
Crabtree Dr
Birmingham B37 .69 F2
Bromsgrove B61 .136 F3
Crabtree Gr CV31 .162 C6
Crabtree La B61 .136 E3
Crabtree Rd Barwell LE9 .71 F5
Birmingham B18 .66 A5
Walsall WS1 .29 A2
Crackley Cotts CV8 .148 B8
Crackley Cres CV8 .148 B8
Crackley La Coventry CV4 .131 F3
Kenilworth CV8 .148 A7
Crackley Way DY2 .62 A6
Craddock Ct CV10 .72 C7
Craddock Dr CV10 .72 C7
Craddock Rd B67 .64 E6
Craddock St WV6 .25 B4
Cradley CE Prim Sch
B63 .82 C7
Cradley Cl B98 .154 F2
Cradley Croft B21 .54 C3
Cradley Fields B63 .82 D5
Cradley Forge DY5 .82 A8
Cradley Heath Factory Ctr
B64 .82 B8
Cradley Heath Sta B64 .82 B8
Cradley High Sch B63 .82 B6
Cradley Park Rd DY2 .62 D2
Cradley Rd Blackheath B64 .82 C8
Dudley DY2 .62 D3
Cradock Rd B8 .67 E5
Craig Cl CV31 .162 B6
Craig Croft B37 .70 D2
Craigends Ave CV3 .134 E6
Crail Gr B43 .44 B4
Crakston Cl CV2 .114 E2
Cramlington Rd B42 .55 A8
Crammond Cl LE10 .75 B8
Cramnore Cl DY4 .52 A8
Cramp Hill WS10 .41 D6
Cramper's Field CV6 .113 A5
Cranborne Chase CV2 .115 A5
Cranbourne Ave WV4 .39 E3
Cranbourne Cl B45 .102 B2
Cranbourne Gr B44 .56 A8
Cranbourne Pl B71 .53 D4
Cranbourne Rd
Birmingham B44 .45 A1
Stourbridge DY8 .81 B4
Cranbrook Ct WV13 .27 C2
Cranbrook Gr WV6 .23 F3
Cranbrook Rd B21 .54 C2
Cranby St B8 .67 C5
Crane Cl CV34 .155 D1
Crane Ct WS1 .29 A3
Crane Dr WS7 .7 A4
Crane Field WS13 .3 B1
Crane Rd WV14 .40 F3
Crane St DY11 .116 C6
Crane Terr WV6 .24 E5
Craneberry Rd B37 .69 E3
Cranebrook Hill B78 .33 E5
Cranebrook La
Stonnall WS14 .16 F7
Wall WS14 .17 A8
Cranehouse Rd B44 .45 A2
Cranemoor Cl B7 .67 C6
Craner's Rd CV1 .113 F4
Cranes Park Rd B26 .89 C5
Cranesbill Cl WV10 .12 C7
Cranesbill Rd B29 .103 A6
Cranfield Gr B26 .88 F8
Cranfield Pl WS5 .42 F5

Cranfield Rd WS7 ....7 A7
Cranford Gr **6** B91 ......107 B1
Cranford Pl WS11 ....1 F1
Cranford Rd
  Coventry CV5 ....112 C4
  Wolverhampton WV3 ....38 D8
Cranford St B66 ....65 C5
Cranford Way B66 ....65 C5
Cranham Cl B97 ....153 B1
Cranham Dr DY6 ....60 E5
Cranhill Cl B92 ....89 B1
Crankhall La WS10 ....42 C3
Cranleigh Cl Aldridge WS9 .30 B5
  Willenhall WV12 ....13 C1
Cranleigh Ho B23 ....56 F6
Cranleigh Pl B44 ....55 B5
Cranleigh Way WS14 ....9 E7
Cranmer Ave WV12 ....27 D2
Cranmer Cl WS6 ....4 D1
Cranmer Gr
  Royal Leamington Spa
    CV34 ....161 D3
  Sutton Coldfield B74 ......31 F6
Cranmere Ave B44 ....24 A6
Cranmere Ct WV6 ....24 A6
Cranmoor Cres B43 ....83 A5
Cranmore Ave
  Birmingham B21 ....65 D7
  Solihull B90 ....126 E8
Cranmore Bvd B90 ....126 D8
Cranmore Dr B90 ....106 E1
Cranmore Inf Sch B91 ....106 E1
Cranmore Rd
  Birmingham B36 ....58 E1
  Solihull B90 ....126 D8
  Wolverhampton WV3 ....24 F3
Cransley Gr B91 ....107 A1
Crantock Cl WV11 ....13 C1
Crantock Rd B42 ....55 C4
Crantock Way CV11 ....73 F4
Cranwell La WV5 ....49 A5
Cranwell Gr B24 ....57 D3
Cranwell Rise B78 ....20 C1
Cranwell Way B35 ....58 A3
Crathie Cl CV2 ....114 F6
Crathorne Ave WV10 ....11 C1
Craufurd Ct DY8 ....81 A3
Craufurd St DY8 ....81 A3
Craven B77 ....22 B1
Craven Ave CV3 ....135 D7
Craven Ct CV3 ....114 F2
Craven St Coventry CV5 ..112 F2
  Wolverhampton WV2 ....39 F6
Crawford Ave
  Darlaston WS10 ....41 C7
  Smethwick B67 ....64 F4
  Wolverhampton WV4 ....39 F3
Crawford Ct CV32 ....157 B5
Crawford Rd
  Sutton Coldfield B76 ......57 F8
  Wolverhampton WV3 ....25 A2
Crawford St B8 ....67 D5
Crawley Wlk **1** B64 .....62 D1
Crawshaws Rd B36 ....58 C1
Crayford Rd B44 ....45 A1
Craythorne Ave B20 ....54 E4
Crecy Cl B76 ....46 E4
Crecy Rd CV3 ....133 E7
Credenda Rd B70 ....53 A1
Crediton Cl CV11 ....73 F5
Cregoe St B15 ....86 C8
Cremore Ave B8 ....67 E5
Cremore Rd B75 ....32 B2
Cremorne Wlk B75 ....32 B2
Crendon Cl B80 ....159 E5
Crendon Rd B65 ....63 A6
Crescent Arc B91 ....107 C3
Crescent Ave
  Birmingham B18 ....66 B6
  Brierley Hill DY5 ....61 C1
  Coventry CV3 ....114 C2
Crescent Grange Rd The
  DY9 ....81 C4
  Cradley Heath B64 DY2 ....62 B7
Crescent Rd
  Darlaston WS10 ....41 D6
  Dudley DY2 ....62 B5
  Kidderminster DY11 ......116 C5
  Willenhall WS13 ....27 C2
  Crescent Sta The WV14 ....40 D6
Crescent The
  Bilston WV14 ....40 D6
  Birmingham, Coleshill Heath
    B37 ....90 E8
  Birmingham, Great Barr
    B43 ....44 A1
  Birmingham, Hockley B18 ..66 B6
  Birmingham, Sparkbrook
    B12 ....87 B5
  Blackheath, Cradley Heath
    B64 ....83 A7
  Blackheath, Rowley Regis
    B65 ....63 C2
  Bromsgrove B60 ....136 F1
  Dudley DY1 ....51 E4
  Great Wyrley WS6 ....5 A2
  Hagley DY9 ....98 F5
  Hampton-in-A B92 ....109 B7
  Keresley CV7 ....94 F6
  Solihull, Lode Heath B91 ..107 B4
  Solihull, Shirley B90 ....106 A4
  Walsall WS1 ....43 A8
  Wednesbury WS10 ....42 A4
  Willenhall WS10,WV13 .....27 C1
  Wolverhampton WV6 ....24 B3

Crescent Twr B1 ....66 C2
Cressage Ave B31 ....103 A1
Cressage Rd CV2 ....115 A6
Cressett Ave DY5 ....61 C4
Cressett La DY5 ....61 C4
Cressida Cl CV34 ....144 D5
Cressington Dr B74 ....32 A1
Cresswell Cl CV10 ....73 C8
Cresswell Cres WS3 ....13 F2
Cresswell Ct WV10 ....11 A3
Cresswell Gr B24 ....57 D4
Cresswell Ho CV6 ....113 B7
Crest The
  Birmingham B31 ....123 C7
  Royal Leamington Spa
    CV32 ....157 D3
Crest View
  Birmingham B14 ....105 B4
  Sutton Coldfield B74 .....44 F8
Crestwood B77 ....22 A5
Crestwood Ave DY11 .....116 A5
Crestwood Dr B44 ....55 E7
Crestwood Glen WV6 ......24 E7
  Crestwood Park Prim Sch
    DY6 ....61 A5
Crestwood Sch The DY6 ...60 F5
Creswell Rd B28 ....106 B7
Creswick Gr B45 ....122 C7
Crew La CV8 ....148 C6
Crew Rd WS10 ....42 A4
Creynolds Cl B90 ....126 D3
Creynolds La B90 ....126 E4
Crick La B20 ....66 A8
Cricket Cl Coventry CV5 .112 C2
  Walsall WS5 ....43 B7
Cricket La WS14 ....9 C5
Cricket Mdw Dudley DY3 ..50 E5
  Wolverhampton WV10 ......11 E4
Cricketers Mdw B64 ......82 F7
Cricklewood Dr B62 ......83 D3
Crigdon B77 ....22 C1
Crimmond Rise B63 ....82 E5
Crimscote Cl B90 ....126 F6
Cringlebrook B77 ....21 D1
Cripps Rd WS2 ....27 E3
Crockett St DY1 ....51 A2
Crockett's La B66 ....65 A6
Crocketts Ave B21 ....65 D7
  Crocketts Lane Inf Sch
    B66 ....65 B5
Crocketts Rd B21 ....65 D8
Crockford Dr B75 ....32 B3
Crockford Rd B71 ....42 C1
Crockington La WV5 ......37 A1
Crocus Cres WV9 ....11 A2
Croft Apartments **2**
  WV13 ....27 A2
Croft Cl Birmingham B25 ..88 E6
  Redditch B98 ....154 D3
  Warwick CV34 ....161 C7
Croft Cres WS8 ....15 D7
Croft Ct B36 ....69 B8
Croft Down Rd B92 ....89 D4
Croft Fields CV12 ....78 B2
Croft Gdns WS7 ....7 A8
Croft Ho **2** WS1 ....28 E1
Croft Ind Est B37 ....70 D2
Croft Jun Sch CV10 ....72 F3
Croft La WV10 ....26 A7
Croft Par WS9 ....30 B6
Croft Pool CV12 ....77 F2
Croft Rd Bedworth CV12 ..77 F2
  Birmingham B26 ....88 E8
  Coventry CV1 ....165 A2
  Leek Wootton CV35 ....156 A7
  Nuneaton CV10 ....72 F3
Croft St Tamworth B79 ....21 B6
  Walsall WS2 ....28 D3
  Willenhall WV13 ....27 A2
  Croft Street JMI Sch
    WS2 ....28 D3
Crofte The
  Birmingham B31 ....103 B2
  Blakedown DY10 ....98 C2
  Bulkington CV12 ....79 B2
  Cheslyn Hay WS6 ....4 E2
  Coventry CV6 ....95 F4
  Dudley DY2 ....61 F6
  Kidderminster DY11 ......116 A4
  Meriden CV7 ....92 C1
  Sedgley DY3 ....39 E1
  Walsall WS5 ....43 A8
Croftdown Rd B17 ....85 A7
Crofters Cl DY8 ....81 B4
Crofters Ct B15 ....85 E6
Crofters Wlk **1** WS8 ...10 E1
Croftfield Gdns B91 .....106 E2
Crofts La B96 ....158 B2
Crofts The B68 ....58 A8
Croftway The B20 ....54 E6
Croftwood Rd DY9 ....81 D4
Cromane Sq B43 ....54 E7
Cromarty Cl CV5 ....112 A5
Cromdale B77 ....22 C1
Cromdale Cl CV10 ....72 A3
Cromdale Dr B63 ....82 D3
Crome Rd B43 ....44 D3
Cromer Gdns WV6 ....24 F5
Cromer Rd
  Birmingham B12 ....87 A5
  Lichfield WS13 ....3 B1
  Royal Leamington Spa
    CV32 ....157 B2
Cromes Wood CV4 ....111 D1
Crompton Ave B20 ....55 C1
Crompton Cl WS2 ....28 A5
Crompton Ct Codsall WV8 .10 B4
  Warwick CV34 ....160 D6

Crompton Rd
  Birmingham, Handsworth
    B20 ....55 C1
  Birmingham, Nechells B7 ..67 C8
  Birmingham, Rubery B45 ..101 D1
  Tipton DY4 ....52 A4
Crompton St CV34 ....160 D6
Cromwell Cl
  Blackheath B65 ....63 A5
  Walsall WS2 ....27 E4
Cromwell Ct WS6 ....5 A1
Cromwell Dr DY2 ....62 F8
  Cromwell Inf & Jun Sch
    B7 ....67 B6
Cromwell La
  Birmingham B31 ....102 E8
  Coventry CV4,CV8 ....131 C6
Cromwell Rd
  Cannock WS12 ....2 C7
  Tamworth B79 ....20 E8
  Wolverhampton WV10 ......11 E4
Cromwell St
  Birmingham B7 ....67 B6
  Coventry CV6 ....113 F6
  Dudley DY2 ....62 E8
  West Bromwich B71 ......53 D4
Cromwells Mdw WS14 ....9 C5
Crondal Pl B15 ....86 B7
Crondal Rd CV7 ....96 B7
  Cronehills Jun & Inf Sch
    B70 ....53 D3
Cronehills Linkway B70 ...53 D3
Cronehills St B70 ....53 D3
Crook La Aldridge WS9 ....30 B1
Crooked La WS9 ....44 A7
Crookham Cl B17 ....84 F7
Crookhay La B71 ....53 B8
Crooks La B80 ....159 D3
Croome Cl
  Birmingham B17 ....87 B3
  Coventry CV6 ....112 F4
  Redditch B98 ....154 F1
Cropredy Rd B31 ....123 B8
Cropthorne Cl B98 ......159 B7
Cropthorne Dr B47 ......125 B7
Cropthorne Ho B60 ......137 B3
Cropthorne Rd B90 ......106 C3
Crosbie Rd
  Birmingham B17 ....85 B6
  Coventry CV5 ....112 E3
Crosby Cl Birmingham B1 ..66 B3
  Wolverhampton WV6 ....24 F5
Cross Cheaping CV1 ......165 B3
Cross Cl B64 ....62 F2
Cross Farm Rd B17 ....85 D4
Cross Farms La B45 .....101 F1
Cross Fields Rd **4** CV34 160 F8
Cross Ho WV2 ....39 C7
Cross Keys WS13 ....9 B8
Cross La Birmingham B43 ..43 E1
  Cubbington CV32 ....157 E4
  Lichfield WS14 ....9 B6
  Sedgley DY3 ....39 E1
Cross Pl DY3 ....39 E1
  Cross Point Bsns Pk
    CV2 ....114 D8
Cross Rd Coventry CV6 ..113 F8
  Keresley CV7 ....94 F6
  4 Royal Leamington Spa
    CV32 ....156 D1
Cross Road Ind Est CV6 ..113 F7
Cross St Bilston WV14 ....40 F2
  Birmingham B21 ....65 C8
  4 Blackheath B65 .....63 C1
  Burntwood WS7 ....6 E8
  Cannock, Bridgtown WS11 ..4 E1
  Cannock, Heath Hayes WS12 ..2 E1
  Cheslyn Hay WS6 ....4 D2
  Coventry CV1 ....165 C4
  Dudley DY1 ....51 C1
  Halesowen B63 ....83 A3
  1 Kingswinford DY6 ....60 D3
  Kingswinford, Wall Heath
    DY6 ....60 B8
  Kingswinford, Wordsley
    DY6 ....60 D6
  Nuneaton CV10 ....72 D3
  Oldbury B68 ....64 A4
  Royal Leamington Spa
    CV32 ....157 A1
  Smethwick B66 ....65 A6
  Stourbridge DY8 ....80 E5
  Tamworth B79 ....21 B5
  Tamworth, Kettlebrook B77 ..21 C3
  Walsall WS3 ....15 A1
  9 Warwick CV34 ......160 F7
  Wednesbury WS10 ....41 E3
  1 Willenhall WV13 ....27 A1
  Wolverhampton WV1 ....25 F1
Cross St N WV1 ....25 D4
Cross St S WV2 ....39 C7
Cross The
  Kingswinford DY6 ....60 D6
  Stourbridge DY9 ....81 E6
Cross Walks Rd DY9 ......81 E5
Cross Wlk B69 ....63 C8
Crossfell B77 ....22 B1
Crossfield Rd
  Birmingham B33 ....69 A3
  Lichfield WS13 ....3 B2
Crossgate Rd Dudley DY2 ..61 F6
  Redditch B98 ....159 C7
  Crossings Ind Est The **4**
    WS3 ....28 B8
Crossings The WS14 ....9 E8
Crosskey Cl B33 ....69 E2
Crossland Cres WV6 ......24 F7
Crossland Row LE10 ....76 A6

Crossley Ct CV6 ....113 F7
Crossley Ret Pk DY11 ...116 D6
Crossley St DY2 ....62 D4
Crossley Wlk B60 ....150 E7
Crossway La B44 ....56 E7
Crossway Rd CV3 ....133 B4
Crossways LE10 ....75 F5
Crossways Ct B44 ....56 B7
Crossways Gn B44 ....56 B7
Crossways Sh Ctr WV10 ...26 A3
Crosswells Rd B68 ....64 B5
Crowberry Cl WS8 ....15 D6
Crowberry La B78 ....48 C8
Crowden Rd B77 ....22 A1
Crowesbridge Mews
  WV14 ....51 B8
Crowhill Rd CV11 ....74 A1
Crowhurst Rd B31 ......122 E7
Crowland Ave WV6 ....23 E4
Crowle Dr DY9 ....81 C5
Crowmere Rd CV2 ....114 F7
Crown Cl Blackheath B65 ..63 D4
  Bromsgrove B61 ....136 F2
  Sedgley DY3 ....39 D1
Crown Ct Darlaston WS10 ..41 C8
  Sutton Coldfield B74 .....13 C3
  Crown Ctr The **2** DY8 ..81 A5
Crown Gn CV6 ....95 E2
Crown Ho CV5 ....112 E3
Crown La Iverley CV10 ....98 F2
  Kidderminster DY10 .....116 E6
  Stourbridge DY8 ....80 F5
  Sutton Coldfield B74 .....31 E3
Crown Mdw B48 ....139 A7
Crown Rd
  Birmingham, Bordesley Green
    B9 ....67 D2
  Birmingham, King's Heath
    B30 ....104 A4
Crown St WV1 ....25 D4
Crown Terr CV31 ....161 F7
Crown Way CV32 ....157 B3
Crown Wharf Sh Pk WS2 ..28 D2
Crown Wlk DY4 ....52 A2
Crownhill Rd LE10 ....75 B4
Crownmeadow Dr WV4 .....52 D7
Crows Nest Cl B76 ....46 F3
Crowther Gdns B63 ......82 C7
Crowther Gr WV6 ....24 F4
Crowther Rd
  Birmingham B23 ....56 D5
  Wolverhampton WV6 ....24 F5
Crowther St
  Kidderminster DY11 .....116 C6
  Wolverhampton WV10 ......25 E4
Croxall Way B66 ....65 B5
Croxdene Ave WS3 ....14 A1
Croxhall St CV12 ....78 C3
Croxley Dr WS12 ....2 C3
Croxley Gdns WV13 ....40 F8
Croxstalls Ave WS3 ......28 A8
Croxstalls Cl WS3 ....14 A1
Croxstalls Pl WS3 ....28 A8
Croxstalls Rd WS3 ....28 A8
Croxton Gr B33 ....69 A4
Croy Dr B35 ....58 B4
Croyde Ave B42 ....55 A8
Croydon Cl CV3 ....133 E6
Croydon Rd
  Birmingham, Bournbrook
    B29 ....86 B7
  Birmingham, Erdington B24 ..57 A2
Crucible The WV4 ....40 D2
Crummock Cl CV6 ....95 D3
Crump Ho WS1 ....28 F1
Crumpfields La B97 .....152 F1
Crusader Cl B69 ....63 E5
Crutchley Ave B78 ....21 A2
Crutchley Way CV31 .....162 A2
Crychan Cl B45 ....102 B2
Cryersoak Cl B90 ....127 B7
Cryfield Grange Rd CV4,
  CV8 ....132 C2
Cryfield Hts CV4 ....132 D2
Crystal Ave DY8 ....61 F1
Crystal Dr B66 ....64 C8
Crystal Ho B66 ....64 C8
Crystal L Ctr DY8 ....81 A5
  Cubbington CE Prim Sch
    CV32 ....157 F5
Cubbington Rd
  Coventry CV6 ....96 A2
  Royal Leamington Spa
    CV32 ....157 B3
Cubley Rd B28 ....87 E1
Cuckoo Cl WS11 ....2 C2
Cuckoo La CV1 ....165 C3
Cuckoo Rd B7 ....67 D8
Cuin Rd B66 ....65 C5
Cuin Wlk **11** B66 .....65 C5
Culey Gr B33 ....69 D2
Culey Wlk B37 ....70 D2
Culford Dr B32 ....102 D8
Culham Cl B27 ....88 D2
Cullwick St WV1 ....40 A8
Culmington Rd B31 .....123 F8
Culmore Cl WV12 ....27 D4
Culmore Rd B62 ....83 E1
Culpepper Cl CV10 ....72 E4
Culverhouse Dr DY5 ......61 A1
Culverley Cres B93 .....127 F6
Culvert Way B66 ....64 D7
Culwell St WV10 ....163 C4
Culwell Trad Est WV10 ...25 F4
Culworth Cl CV31 ....161 F5
Culworth Ct
  Coventry CV6 ....113 E7

Culwarth Ct continued
  Royal Leamington Spa
    CV31 ....162 A5
Culworth Row CV6 ....113 E8
Cumberford Ave B33 ......69 E1
Cumberland Ave **3** B5 ..86 E2
Cumberland Cl DY6 ....60 E4
Cumberland Cres
  Burntwood WS7 ....7 A8
  Royal Leamington Spa
    CV32 ....157 C3
Cumberland Dr
  Nuneaton CV10 ....72 E3
  Tamworth B78 ....21 A1
Cumberland Ho **7** WV3 ..25 C4
Cumberland Rd
  Bilston WV14 ....40 D1
  Cannock WS11 ....2 A4
  Oldbury B68 ....64 B1
  West Bromwich B71 ......53 D7
  Willenhall WV13 ....27 D2
Cumberland St B1 ....66 B2
Cumberland Wlk B75 .....47 B5
Cumbernauld Wlk **7**
  CV2 ....115 A7
Cumbrae Dr LE10 ....71 B2
Cumbria Cl CV1 ....113 A3
Cumbria Way B8 ....67 D6
Cumbrian Croft B63 .....82 D2
  West Bromwich B71 ......53 D7
Cumbrian La **14** CV11 ..73 C4
Cundall Cl CV31 ....162 B6
Cunnery The CV8 ....149 A3
Cunningham Rd
  Perton WV6 ....23 E4
  Walsall WS2 ....27 E2
Cupfields Ave DY4 ....52 C8
Cupfields Cres DY4 ......52 C7
Cur La B97 ....152 D3
Curbar Rd B42 ....55 C6
Curborough Rd WS13 ......3 B2
Curdale Rd B32 ....102 B8
Curdworth La B76 ....59 A8
Curdworth Prim Sch B76 ..59 C6
Curlew B77 ....36 A7
Curlew Cl
  Kidderminster DY10 .....117 B2
  Lichfield WS14 ....9 E7
Curlew Hill WS11 ....2 A4
Curlews Cl B23 ....56 C8
Curlieu Cl CV35 ....160 A7
Curral Rd B65 ....63 C3
Curran Cl CV31 ....162 B4
Curriers Cl CV4 ....131 D7
Curslow La DY10 ....117 F1
Curtin Dr WS10 ....41 B4
Curtis Cl Finstall B60 ..151 F8
  Smethwick B66 ....65 C4
Curtis Rd CV2 ....114 D6
Curzon Ave CV6 ....113 E8
Curzon Cl LE10 ....75 F7
Curzon Cr CV31 ....162 C6
Curzon St Birmingham B4 ..67 A3
  Wolverhampton WV2 ....39 D7
Cut Throat La B94 ......142 D7
Cuthbert Rd B18 ....65 E4
Cutler St B66 ....65 B6
Cutlers Rough Cl B31 ...102 F5
Cutsdean Cl B31 ....102 F6
Cutshill Cl B36 ....69 C8
Cutting The WS4 ....28 F4
Cuttle Mill La B76 ......48 D3
Cuttle Pool La B93 .....128 F4
Cutworth Cl B76 ....47 B3
Cwerne Ct DY3 ....50 C3
Cygnet Cl Alvechurch B48 .139 A7
  Cannock WS12 ....2 C7
  Wolverhampton WV6 ....24 C2
Cygnet Ct CV11 ....165 C4
Cygnet Dr B79 ....20 F5
Cygnet Gr B23 ....56 B6
Cygnet La DY5 ....61 C7
Cygnet Rd B70 ....53 A3
Cygnus B70 ....52 F5
Cymbeline Way CV34 ....161 E4
Cypress Ave DY3 ....50 D5
Cypress Croft CV3 .....134 F8
Cypress Ct DY10 ....117 A4
Cypress Gdns
  1 Kingswinford DY6 ...60 D4
  Walsall WS5 ....43 C4
Cypress Gr B31 ....102 E1
Cypress La CV31 ....162 B3
Cypress Rd Dudley DY2 ...51 F1
  Walsall WS5 ....43 C4
Cypress Sq **2** B27 .....88 C5
Cypress Way B31 ....122 F8
Cyprus Ave B96 ....158 D2
Cyprus Cl B29 ....103 A7
Cyprus St Oldbury B69 ...64 A8
  Wolverhampton WV2 ....39 C6
Cyril Gr B10 ....87 C8
Cyril Rd B10 ....87 D8

D

D'aubeny Rd CV4 ....132 C8
D'Eyncourt Jun & Inf Sch
  WV11 ....26 B7
D'Eyncourt Rd WV10 ......26 A8
D'Urberville Cl WV2 ......39 F6
D'Urberville Rd WV2 ......39 F6
D'Urberville Wlk **1** WS11 ..2 A2
Dace B77 ....35 D7
Dace Rd WV10 ....26 B4
Dacer Cl B30 ....104 B5
Dad's La B13 ....86 C1
Dadford View DY5 ....61 B2

Daffern Rd CV7 .... 78 A1
Daffodil Cl DY3 .... 50 E7
Daffodil Pl WS5 .... 43 C8
Daffodil Rd WS13 .... 43 D8
Daffodil Way B31 .... 122 E8
Dagger La B71 .... 53 E4
Dagnall Rd B27 .... 88 D3
Dagnell End Rd B98 .... 154 B7
Dagtail La B97 .... 158 D3
Dahlia Cl Hinckley LE10 .... 75 E6
  Wolverhampton WV1 .... 26 C1
Daimler Cl B36 .... 58 F1
Daimler Rd
  Birmingham B14 .... 105 D3
  Coventry CV6 .... 113 C5
Dainton Gr B32 .... 84 C1
Daintree Croft CV3 .... 133 C7
Daintry Dr B78 .... 20 B7
Dairy Cl B68 .... 52 B5
Dairy Ct B68 .... 84 D7
Daisy Bank WS12 .... 1 F8
Daisy Bank WS13 .... 15 B2
Daisy Bank Cres WS5 .... 43 D8
Daisy Dr B23 .... 56 A5
Daisy Farm Rd B14 .... 105 B3
Daisy Mdw DY4 .... 52 C6
Daisy Rd B16 .... 65 F2
Daisy St Dudley WV14 .... 40 D2
  Wolverhampton WV6 .... 25 A4
Daisy Wlk WV9 .... 11 A3
Dalbeg Cl WV8 .... 24 E8
Dalbury Rd B28 .... 105 E5
Dalby Cl CV3 .... 134 E8
Dalby Rd WS3 .... 28 F6
Dale Cl Birmingham B43 .... 43 D1
  Catshill B61 .... 136 F7
  Smethwick B66 .... 65 A3
  Tipton DY4 .... 52 C6
  Warwick CV34 .... 161 A8
Dale Ct WV1 .... 25 A3
Dale Dr WS7 .... 7 B7
Dale End Birmingham B4 .... 164 C3
  Darlaston WS10 .... 41 C6
  Nuneaton CV10 .... 72 E5
Dale End Cl LE10 .... 75 A7
Dale Hill B60 .... 137 F6
Dale Meadow Cl CV7 .... 130 B6
Dale Rd Birmingham B29 .... 85 E3
  Halesowen B62 .... 83 E8
  Redditch B98 .... 153 F5
  Stourbridge DY8 .... 80 F2
Dale St Bilston WV14 .... 41 A5
  Royal Leamington Spa
  CV32 .... 161 E8
  Smethwick B66 .... 65 A3
  Walsall WS1 .... 42 E7
  Wednesbury WS10 .... 41 E3
  Wolverhampton WV3 .... 163 A2
Dale Terr B69 .... 63 C8
Dale Wlk B25 .... 88 B7
Dalecote Ave B92 .... 107 E8
Dalehouse Flats CV8 .... 148 B6
Dalehouse La CV8 .... 148 D7
Dales Cl WV6 .... 25 B6
Dales Inf Sch The B77 .... 36 B8
Dales Jun Sch B77 .... 36 B8
Dalesman Cl DY6 .... 60 B7
Daleview Rd B14 .... 105 C4
Daleway Rd CV3 .... 133 B4
Dalewood Croft B26 .... 88 F6
Dalewood Rd B37 .... 69 F5
Daley Cl B1 .... 66 B3
Daley Rd WV14 .... 40 F2
Dalkeith Rd B73 .... 45 F3
Dalkeith St WS2 .... 28 C3
Dallas Rd B23 .... 56 D5
Dallimore Cl B92 .... 89 A3
Dallington Rd CV6 .... 112 E6
Dalloway Cl B5 .... 86 D6
Dalmahoy Cl CV11 .... 79 C8
Dalmeny Rd CV4 .... 131 D7
Dalston Cl DY2 .... 62 D6
Dalston Rd B27 .... 88 C4
Dalton Ct B23 .... 56 B3
Dalton Gdns CV2 .... 114 F4
Dalton Rd Bedworth CV12 .... 78 A2
  Coventry CV5 .... 113 B1
  Walsall WS2 .... 28 A3
Dalton St Birmingham B4 .... 164 C3
  Wolverhampton WV3 .... 39 B8
Dalton Way B4 .... 164 C3
Dalvine Rd DY2 .... 62 B2
Dalwood Cl WV14 .... 51 B7
Dalwood Way CV6 .... 96 B4
Dam St WS13 .... 9 B8
Dama Rd B78 .... 34 F8
Damar Creft B14 .... 104 D4
Dame Agnes Gr CV6 .... 114 B8
Dame Elizabeth Cadbury Sch
  & Sixth Form B30 .... 103 D7
Dame Ellen Pinsent Speci
  Sch B13 .... 105 A7
Damien Cl B67 .... 64 F5
Damson Cl Redditch B97 .... 158 C6
  Wednesfield WV12 .... 27 A6
Damson La B92 .... 107 E7
Damson La B91 .... 107 B7
Damson Parkway B91,
  B92 .... 107 F2
Damson Wood Inf Sch
  B92 .... 107 D7
Danbigh Cft ● B29 .... 103 C7
Danbury Cl B76 .... 47 A2
Danbury Rd B90 .... 106 B2
Danby Gr B24 .... 57 B2
Dando Rd DY2 .... 62 D8
Dandy Bank Rd DY6 .... 61 A8

Dandy's Wlk WS1 .... 42 F8
Dane Gr B13 .... 104 D8
Dane Rd CV2 .... 114 B4
Dane Terr B65 .... 63 C5
Danehill Wlk WV8 .... 24 F8
Danehurst Ctr WV1 .... 26 A3
Danelagh Cl CV2 .... 20 F7
Danes Cl WV11 .... 12 F4
Danesbury Cres
  Birmingham B44 .... 56 A8
  Royal Leamington Spa
  CV31 .... 162 D6
Danescourt Rd WV6 .... 24 D6
Danesmoor Rd B26 .... 88 E7
Danesmore Park Jun & Inf
  Sch WV11 .... 13 A1
Daneswood Dr WS9 .... 15 F3
Daneswood Rd CV3 .... 135 E7
Daneways Cl B74 .... 45 A8
Danford Cl DY8 .... 81 A4
Danford Gdns B10 .... 87 C8
Danford La B91 .... 106 E3
Danford Rd B47 .... 124 F6
Danford Way B43 .... 54 D8
Dangerfield Ho B70 .... 53 E1
Dangerfield La WS10 .... 41 C4
Daniel Ave CV10 .... 72 C3
Daniels La WS9 .... 30 C5
Daniels Rd B9 .... 68 A2
Danilo Rd WS11 .... 1 D1
Danks St B12 .... 52 A2
Danzey Cl B98 .... 159 B5
Danzey Gr B14 .... 104 C3
Danzey Green La B94 .... 142 B1
Danzey Green Rd B36 .... 58 B1
Daphne Cl CV2 .... 96 C3
Darby Cl WV14 .... 40 A2
Darby End Rd DY2 .... 62 E4
Darby Ho ② WS2 .... 62 E4
Darby Rd Oldbury B68 .... 64 C5
  Wednesbury WS10 .... 42 B4
Darby St B65 .... 63 C1
Darbys Hill Rd B69 .... 63 B7
Dare Rd B23 .... 56 E4
Dare's Wlk LE10 .... 71 D1
Darell Croft B76 .... 46 E3
Daren Cl B36 .... 69 F8
Darfield Wlk ② B12 .... 86 F8
Darges La ▲ 4 F4
Dark La
  Astwood Bank B96 .... 158 D1
  Bedworth CV12 .... 77 D1
  Belbroughton DY9 .... 119 F8
  Birchmoor B78 .... 36 D6
  Brinsford WV10 .... 11 D8
  Coventry CV1 .... 165 B4
  Featherstone WV10,WV11 .... 12 D7
  Great Wyrley WS6 .... 5 C1
  Hollywood B38,B47 .... 124 E7
  Romsley B62 .... 100 F4
  Stoke Heath B60 .... 150 D6
Darkhouse La WV14 .... 40 C2
Darlaston Com Sch
  WS10 .... 41 B6
Darlaston Ct CV7 .... 92 D1
Darlaston La WV14 .... 41 A7
Darlaston Rd Walsall WS2 .... 42 A8
  Wednesbury WS10 .... 41 E4
Darlaston Road Ind Est
  WS10 .... 41 D5
Darley Ave B34 .... 68 F6
Darley Dr WV6 .... 25 B5
Darley Green Rd B93 .... 128 B1
Darley Ho B69 .... 63 D6
Darley Mead Ct B91 .... 107 E4
Darley Rd LE10 .... 75 E6
Darley Way B74 .... 45 A7
Darleydale Ave B44 .... 44 E1
Darlington St
  Darlaston WS10 .... 41 D5
  Wolverhampton WV1 .... 163 B3
  Darlington WV1 .... 163 B3
Darlston Row CV7 .... 92 B1
Darnbrook B77 .... 22 C1
Darnel Croft ⑤ B10 .... 67 B1
Darnel Hurst Rd B75 .... 32 D3
Darnick Rd B73 .... 45 D2
Darnley Rd ⑤ B16 .... 66 A2
Darris Rd B29 .... 104 A8
Dart B77 .... 36 A5
Dart Cl LE10 .... 75 A8
Dart St B9 .... 67 B1
Dartford Rd WS3 .... 13 F1
Dartington Way CV11 .... 78 F8
Dartmoor Cl B45 .... 102 A2
Dartmouth Ave
  Cannock WS11 .... 4 C8
  Stourbridge DY8 .... 80 E1
  Walsall WS3 .... 28 E6
  Willenhall WV13 .... 27 A2
Dartmouth Cir B6 .... 66 F5
Dartmouth Cl WS3 .... 28 E5
Dartmouth Cres WV14 .... 41 A7
Dartmouth Dr WV12 .... 30 A5
Dartmouth Ho ② WS3 .... 28 F6
Dartmouth Middleway
  B7 .... 66 F4
Dartmouth Pl WS3 .... 28 F6

Dartmouth Rd
  Birmingham B29 .... 85 F2
  Coventry CV2 .... 114 C5
  Smethwick B66 .... 64 F8
Dartmouth Sch CV2 .... 114 D5
Dartmouth Sq B70 .... 53 D2
Dartmouth St
  West Bromwich B70 .... 53 B3
  Wolverhampton WV2 .... 163 C1
  Wolverhampton WV2 .... 163 D1
Dartmouth Street Sta
  B70 .... 53 B3
Darvel Rd WV12 .... 27 D4
Darwall St WS1 .... 42 E8
Darwall Pk B77 .... 22 B2
Darwin Cl Burntwood WS7 .... 7 A3
  Cannock WS12 .... 2 E2
  Coventry CV2 .... 115 A6
  Hinckley LE10 .... 71 E3
  Lichfield WS13 .... 9 A8
Darwin Ct Bedworth CV12 .... 78 A2
  Perton WV6 .... 23 E4
Darwin Ho
  ⑧ Birmingham B37 .... 70 D1
  Kingswinford DY6 .... 60 F7
Darwin Pl WS2 .... 28 B6
Darwin Rd WS2 .... 28 B6
Darwin St B12 .... 86 F8
Dassett Gr B9 .... 68 C2
Dassett Rd B93 .... 127 F4
Datchet Cl CV5 .... 112 C4
Datteln Rd WS11 .... 2 A1
Dauntsey Covert B14 .... 104 D2
Davena Dr B29 .... 84 E2
Davena Gr WV14 .... 40 D3
Davenham Rd B60 .... 137 C1
Davenport Dr
  Birmingham B35 .... 58 C3
  Bromsgrove B60 .... 137 B1
Davenport Lodge Sch
  CV5 .... 133 B8
Davenport Rd
  Coventry CV5 .... 133 B8
  Wednesfield WV11 .... 26 E6
  Wolverhampton WV6 .... 24 B5
Davenport Terr LE10 .... 75 E8
Daventry Gr B32 .... 84 D6
Daventry Rd CV3 .... 133 D7
Davey Cl WV7 .... 6 F4
Davey Rd Birmingham B20 .... 55 E1
  West Bromwich B70 .... 53 A5
David Cox Ct B17 .... 85 A5
David Garrick Gdns WS13 .... 3 B2
David Peacock Cl CV3 .... 52 A5
David Rd Bedworth CV7 .... 95 F8
  Birmingham B20 .... 55 B2
  Coventry CV1 .... 113 F2
  Tipton DY4 .... 52 A5
Davids The B31 .... 103 C5
Davidson Ave CV31 .... 162 A7
Davidson Rd WS14 .... 9 B7
Davies Ave ⑦ Oldbury B69 .... 64 A4
  Walsall WS3 .... 14 B1
Davies Rd CV7 .... 95 F7
Davis Ave DY4 .... 51 E4
Davis Cl CV32 .... 156 D2
Davis Gr B25 .... 88 D6
Davis Rd Tamworth B77 .... 21 F4
  Willenhall WV12 .... 27 D8
Davison Rd B67 .... 64 F3
Davy Rd WS2 .... 28 A5
Daw End WS4,WS9 .... 29 C6
Daw End La WS4 .... 29 C6
Daw End Specl Sch WS4 .... 29 C6
Dawberry Cl B14 .... 104 D5
Dawberry Fields Rd
  B14 .... 104 D5
Dawberry Rd B14 .... 104 C5
Dawes Ave B70 .... 53 C1
Dawes Cl CV2 .... 114 A3
Dawes La WS8 .... 7 A1
Dawley Brook Prim Sch
  DY6 .... 60 C7
Dawley Cl ❶ WS2 .... 42 B7
Dawley Cres B37 .... 70 B1
Dawley Rd DY6 .... 60 C8
Dawley Trad Est DY6 .... 60 D8
Dawlish Wlk ② CV2 .... 115 A7
Dawlish Cl CV11 .... 73 E5
Dawlish Dr CV3 .... 133 D5
Dawlish Rd
  Birmingham B29 .... 85 F2
  Dudley DY1 .... 51 C5
  Smethwick B66 .... 65 B5
Dawn Dr DY4 .... 41 C2
Dawn Rd B31 .... 102 E6
Dawney Dr B75 .... 32 A4
Dawson Ave WV14 .... 39 F2
Dawson Cl CV31 .... 162 A2
Dawson Rd
  Birmingham B21 .... 65 F8
  Bromsgrove B61 .... 136 E2
Dawson Sq WV14 .... 40 C5
Dawson St Smethwick B66 .... 65 A3
  Walsall WS3 .... 28 D8
Day Ave WV11 .... 26 E7
Day Cl CV32 .... 156 E1
Day St WS2 .... 28 E3
Day's La CV2 .... 113 F3
Daybrook Cl B97 .... 153 B5
Dayhouse Bank B62 .... 101 B1
Daylesford Inf Sch B92 .... 89 A3
Daylesford Rd B92 .... 89 A3
Days Cl CV1 .... 113 E3

Daytona Dr CV5 .... 111 B8
De Havilland Dr B35 .... 58 A2
De Marnham Cl B70 .... 53 E1
De Montfort Ho B37 .... 69 F5
De Montfort Rd
  Hinckley LE10 .... 71 E1
  Kenilworth CV8 .... 147 E6
De Montfort Way CV4 .... 132 D5
De Moram Gr B92 .... 107 F7
De Somerley Ho ❶ B69 .... 64 A7
De-Compton Cl CV7 .... 95 A7
De-La-Bere Cres LE10 .... 76 A6
Deacon St CV11 .... 73 C3
Deakin Ave WS8 .... 6 F1
Deakin Rd
  Birmingham B24 .... 57 A3
  Sutton Coldfield B75 .... 46 E7
Deakins Rd B25 .... 88 B7
Deal Ave WS7 .... 7 A8
Deal Dr B69 .... 52 A1
Dean Cl Birmingham B44 .... 56 B8
  Hinckley LE10 .... 71 E2
  Stourbridge DY8 .... 81 B6
  Sutton Coldfield B72 .... 57 B7
Dean Ct
  ⑤ Brierley Hill DY5 .... 61 D2
  Perton WV6 .... 23 E6
Dean Rd Birmingham B23 .... 56 F5
  Hinckley LE10 .... 71 E2
  Walsall WS4 .... 29 C7
Dean Rd W LE10 .... 71 E2
Dean St Birmingham B5 .... 164 C1
  Coventry CV2 .... 114 A3
  Sedgley DY3 .... 50 D8
Dean's Rd WV1 .... 26 B2
Deanbrook Cl B90 .... 127 A6
Deanery CE Prim Sch
  B76 .... 57 F8
Deanery Row WV1 .... 163 B4
Deans Cl B98 .... 154 D5
Deans Croft 9 C8
Deans Pl WS3 .... 28 F6
Deans Slade Dr WS14 .... 9 A5
Deans Way CV7 .... 95 D6
Deanscroft Dr B60 .... 137 C6
Deansfield High Sch
  WV1 .... 26 C2
Deansfield Rd WV1 .... 26 A2
Deansford La DY10 .... 118 B6
Deanston Croft CV2 .... 96 F1
Deansway
  Bromsgrove B61 .... 136 E2
  Warwick CV34 .... 155 E1
Deansway Ho DY10 .... 117 A7
Deansway The DY10 .... 117 A7
Dearman Rd B11 .... 87 B7
Dearmont Rd B31 .... 122 E7
Dearne Ct DY3 .... 51 A6
Deasy Ho CV3 .... 134 B5
Deasy Rd CV1 .... 165 C1
Deavall Way WS11 .... 2 B2
Debden Cl B93 .... 127 E2
Debenham Cres B25 .... 88 A8
Debenham Rd B25 .... 68 D1
Deblen Dr B16 .... 65 E1
Deborah Cl WV4 .... 39 C6
Dee Gr Birmingham B38 .... 123 E8
Dee Ho ② CV1 .... 61 E8
Dee Rd WS3 .... 14 E1
Dee Wlk B36 .... 70 A7
Deedmore Rd CV2 .... 96 D1
Deedmore Sch CV2 .... 114 C8
Deegan Cl CV2 .... 114 A5
Deelands Rd B45 .... 121 F8
Deeley ② B77 .... 22 A1
Deeley Cl Birmingham B15 .... 86 C7
  Blackheath B64 .... 82 C7
Deeley Dr DY4 .... 52 C6
Deeley Pl WS3 .... 28 B8
Deeley St Brierley Hill DY5 .... 61 E1
  Walsall WS3 .... 28 B8
Deepdale B77 .... 22 D2
Deepdale Ave B26 .... 89 B4
Deepdale La DY3 .... 50 E3
Deeplow Cl ② B72 .... 46 C4
Deepmoor Rd B33 .... 68 F3
Deepmore Ave WS2 .... 28 B8
Deepwood Cl WS4 .... 29 B6
Deepwood Gr B32 .... 102 B8
Deer Barn Hill B98 .... 154 A1
Deer Cl Huntington WS12 .... 1 C6
  Norton Canes WS11 .... 6 B7
Deer Leap The CV8 .... 148 B6
Deer Park Rd B78 .... 20 E1
Deer Park Way B91 .... 107 C1
Deer Wlk WV8 .... 10 F2
Deerdale Way CV3 .... 134 F8
Deerfold Cres WS7 .... 7 B7
Deerham Cl B23 .... 56 D7
Deerhill B77 .... 22 C1
Deerhurst B98 .... 154 C7
Deerhurst Cl B98 .... 154 C7
Deerhurst Rd
  Birmingham B20 .... 54 F5
  Coventry CV6 .... 95 B2
Deerhurst Rise WS12 .... 2 F6
Deerpark Dr CV34 .... 160 E8
Defford Ave WS4 .... 15 C1
Defford Cl B97 .... 152 E1
Defford Dr B68 .... 64 B4
Dehavilland Cl CV31 .... 73 B5
Deighton Rd WS5 .... 43 C2
Delage Cl CV6 .... 96 B4
Delamere Cl B36 .... 58 D1
Delamere Dr WS5 .... 43 C3

Delamere Rd
  Bedworth CV12 .... 77 F2
  Birmingham B28 .... 105 F7
  Willenhall WV12 .... 27 C7
Delamere Way CV32 .... 157 C4
Delancey Keep B75 .... 47 A5
Delaware Rd CV3 .... 133 C5
Delf Ho CV2 .... 96 D1
Delhi Ave CV6 .... 95 D1
Delhurst Ave WV4 .... 39 E3
Delhurst Rd B44 .... 44 D1
Delius Ho ❷ B16 .... 66 B4
Delius St CV4 .... 111 E3
Dell Cl CV3 .... 134 B3
Dell Farm Cl B93 .... 128 B6
Dell Rd Birmingham B30 .... 104 A5
  Brierley Hill DY5 .... 61 B5
Dell The
  Birmingham, Edgbaston B16 .... 65 F2
  Birmingham, Shenley Fields
  B31 .... 102 D6
  Cannock WS12 .... 2 F4
  Lichfield WS13 .... 8 F7
  Solihull B92 .... 89 A1
  Stourbridge DY8 .... 80 E6
  Tamworth B79 .... 21 B6
Della Dr B32 .... 102 D8
Dellow Gr B48 .... 139 A5
Dellows Cl B38 .... 123 D7
Dellway Ct DY8 .... 80 E6
Delmore Way B76 .... 58 B6
Delph La DY5 .... 81 E7
Delph La DY5 .... 81 D8
Delph Dr DY5 .... 81 D1
Delph Road Ind Est DY5 .... 61 C1
Delphinium Cl B9 .... 67 C3
Delphi Cl CV34 .... 161 E4
Delrene Rd B28,B90 .... 105 F3
Delta Way WS11 .... 4 D7
Delta Way Bsns Ctr WS11 .... 4 D6
Deltic B77 .... 22 A1
Delves Cres Walsall WS5 .... 43 A5
  Wood End CV9 .... 36 C1
Delves Green Rd WS5 .... 43 A5
Delves Jun Sch WS5 .... 43 A5
Delves Rd WS1 .... 42 F7
Delville Rd WS10 .... 41 F4
Delville Terr WS10 .... 41 F4
Dempster Ct CV11 .... 73 C4
Dempster Rd CV12 .... 78 A4
Demuth Way B69 .... 63 F6
Denaby Gr B14 .... 105 D4
Denbigh Cl DY1 .... 50 F2
Denbigh Cnr B46 .... 91 A6
Denbigh Cres B71 .... 53 B6
Denbigh Dr
  Wednesbury WS10 .... 42 D4
  West Bromwich B71 .... 53 B6
Denbigh Rd
  Coventry CV6 .... 112 E5
  Tipton DY4 .... 52 C4
Denbury Cl WS12 .... 2 D1
Denby Bldgs ⑮ CV32 .... 161 F8
Denby Cl Birmingham B7 .... 67 B5
  Royal Leamington Spa
  CV32 .... 157 C3
Denby Croft B90 .... 127 B6
Dencer Cl B45 .... 122 A8
Dencer Dr CV8 .... 148 C4
Dencil Cl B63 .... 82 D5
Dene Ave DY6 .... 60 C4
Dene Court Rd B92 .... 88 F1
Dene Hollow B13 .... 105 C7
Dene Rd Stourbridge DY8 .... 80 F3
  Wombourne WV4 .... 37 F4
Denegate Cl B76 .... 58 B6
Denehurst Cl B45 .... 122 A1
Denehurst Way CV10 .... 72 F3
Denemoor Ct CV8 .... 148 B5
Denewood Ave B20 .... 55 B2
Denewood Way CV8 .... 148 C6
Denford Gr B14 .... 104 D5
Dengate Cl CV7 .... 130 B7
Denham Ave CV5 .... 112 C4
Denham Ct B23 .... 56 C2
Denham Gdns WV3 .... 38 B8
Denham Rd B27 .... 88 C5
Denholm Rd B73 .... 45 D2
Denholme Gr B14 .... 105 A3
Denis Rd LE10 .... 75 D5
Denise Dr Birmingham B17 .... 85 C4
  Birmingham, Kingshurst B37 .... 69 F4
  Dudley WV14 .... 51 B8
Denleigh Rd DY6 .... 60 E4
Denmark Cl WV6 .... 25 A4
Denmark Rise WS12 .... 2 D7
Denmark Villas WS13 .... 8 C5
Denmead Dr WV11 .... 26 F8
Denmore Gdns WV1 .... 26 C2
Dennett Cl CV34 .... 155 F2
Dennfield Dr WS6 .... 4 C2
Dennis B77 .... 21 E2
Dennis Hall Rd DY8 .... 81 A8
Dennis Rd Birmingham B12 .... 87 B4
  Coventry CV2 .... 114 B6
Dennis St DY8 .... 81 A8
Denshaw Croft CV2 .... 115 A8
Denshaw Rd B14 .... 104 D6
Denston Ct B74 .... 31 F2
Denstone Gdns WV10 .... 11 F3
Dent St B79 .... 21 C5
Denton Cl CV8 .... 147 D6
Denton Croft B93 .... 127 D3

Denton Gr
Birmingham, Great Barr
B43 ....54 D7
Birmingham, Stechford B33 ..68 D2
Denton Rd DY9 ....82 A4
Denver Rd B14 ....105 A2
Denville Cl WV14 ......40 E7
Denville Cres B9 ....68 B3
Denville Rd CV32 ......157 A3
Derby Ave WV6 ....24 F7
Derby Dr B37 ....70 B2
Derby Rd LE10 ....71 D1
Derby St Birmingham B9 ..67 A2
Walsall WS2 ....28 E4
Dereham Cl B8 ....67 C4
Dereham Ct CV32 ......157 A2
Dereham Wlk WV14 .....40 E2
Dereton Cl DY1 ....61 E8
Derick Burcher's Mall 5
DY10 ....116 E6
Dering Cl CV2 ....114 D8
Deronda Cl CV12 ....78 A3
Derron Ave B26 ....88 E5
Derry Cl B17 ....85 A3
Derry St Brierley Hill DY5 ..61 D2
Wolverhampton WV2 ....163 C1
Derrydown Cl B23 ......56 E3
Derrydown Rd B42 ......55 B5
Dersingham Dr CV6 .....96 B2
Derwent B77 ....21 D1
Derwent Cl Aldridge WS9 ..30 F3
Brierley Hill DY5 ....61 B6
Coventry CV5 ....111 E4
Royal Leamington Spa
CV32 ....156 D1
Willenhall WV13 ....27 C2
Derwent Ct B73 ....46 B5
Derwent Gr
Birmingham B13 ....86 C1
Burntwood WS7 ....7 D6
Cannock WS11 ....4 D8
Derwent Ho
Birmingham B17 ....85 D5
Kidderminster DY10 ....116 F7
5 Oldbury B69 ....63 D5
Derwent Rd
Bedworth CV12 ....78 A2
Birmingham B30 ....104 C8
Coventry CV6 ....95 A2
Wolverhampton WV6 ....24 E8
Derwent Way
Bromsgrove B60 ....137 B1
Nuneaton CV11 ....73 F6
Desborough Ho 8 B14 ..105 A3
Desdemona Ave CV34 ..161 E4
Desford Ave B42 ....55 C7
Despard Rd CV5 ....111 D4
Dettonford Rd B32 ....102 B8
Devereux Cl
Birmingham B36 ....69 C8
Coventry CV4 ....111 C1
Devereux Ho B79 ....21 A4
Devereux Rd
Sutton Coldfield B75 .....22 C1
West Bromwich B70 ....53 E1
Deveron Ct LE10 ....71 B1
Deveron Way LE10 ......71 B1
Devey Dr DY4 ....52 D6
Devine Croft DY4 ......52 A5
Devitts Cl B90 ....126 F7
Devon Cl Birmingham B20 ..54 F2
Nuneaton CV10 ....72 F3
Devon Cres Aldridge WS9 ..16 A1
Dudley DY2 ....61 F7
West Bromwich B71 ....53 C6
Devon Ct
3 Birmingham B29 ....103 B7
Cannock WS11 ....4 C8
Devon Gn WS11 ....4 B8
Devon Gr CV2 ....114 B6
Devon Ho 4 B31 ....30 F8
Devon Rd
Birmingham B45 ....101 F1
Cannock WS11 ....4 F8
Smethwick B67 ....84 E7
Stourbridge DY8 ....80 E7
Wednesbury WS10 ....43 C1
Willenhall WV13 ....27 D1
Wolverhampton WV1 ......163 A4
Devon St B7 ....67 C5
Devonport Cl 3 B97 ..153 B5
Devonshire Ave B18 ....65 F6
Devonshire Ct B74 .....32 A2
Devonshire Dr
Tamworth B79 ....21 A1
West Bromwich B71 ....53 E3
Devonshire Inf Sch B67 ..64 E5
Devonshire Jun Sch B67 ..64 E5
Devonshire Rd
Birmingham B20 ....54 F2
Smethwick B67 ....64 E6
Devonshire St B18 .....66 A6
Devonshire Villas B10 ..87 D8
Devoran Cl Bedworth CV7 ..96 B8
Wolverhampton WV6 ....25 B4
Dewberry Dr WS5 ....43 A3
Dewberry Rd 3 DY8 .....60 F1
Dewbury Cl B96 ....158 E1
Dewhurst Croft B33 ....69 B3
Dewis Ho 8 CV2 ....96 B1
Dewsbury Ave CV3 .....133 B5
Dewsbury Cl DY8 ....60 E3
Dewsbury Dr
Burntwood WS7 ....7 C6
Wolverhampton WV4 ....39 A4

Dewsbury Gr B42 ....55 C5
Dexter Ho B67 ....64 F6
Dexter Way B78 ....36 F8
Deykin Ave B6 ....56 B2
Deykin Avenue Jun & Inf Sch
B6 ....56 B2
Deykin Rd WS13 ....9 A6
Dial Cl B14 ....104 E2
Dial House La CV5 ......95 B1
Dial La Stourbridge DY8 ..80 E8
West Bromwich B70 ....52 F6
Diamond Ct 3 B64 .....62 D1
Diamond Gr WS11 ....2 C2
Diamond Park Dr 3 DY8 ..60 E1
Diana Cl WV5 ....16 B3
Diana Dr CV2 ....96 E1
Diana Princess of Wales
Childrens Hospl B4 ...164 C3
Diane Cl DY4 ....41 B2
Dibble Cl WV12 ....27 D5
Dibble Rd B67 ....64 F6
Dibdale Cl DY3 ....50 D3
Dibdale Rd DY1 ....50 F3
Dibdale Rd W DY1 ......50 E3
Dibdale St Dudley DY1 ..51 A2
Sedgley DY1 ....50 F2
Dice Pleck B31 ....103 C2
Dick Sheppard Ave DY4 ..52 B8
Dickens Cl Dudley DY3 ..50 B5
Nuneaton CV10 ....72 A4
Dickens Gr 8 B14 .....105 A3
Dickens Heath Rd
Solihull B90 ....126 A5
Solihull B90 ....126 A6
Dickens Rd Coventry CV6 ..113 A8
Dudley WV14 ....40 D2
Wolverhampton WV10 ......12 A1
Dickins Rd CV34 ......156 B1
Dickinson Ave WV10 ....25 F8
Dickinson Dr
Sutton Coldfield B76 ....46 E4
Walsall WS2 ....42 C6
Dickinson Rd WV5 ......49 A5
Didcot Cl B97 ....158 C5
Diddington Ave B28 ...106 A5
Diddington La B92,CV7 ..91 C1
Didgley Gr B37 ....70 A5
Didsbury Rd CV7 ....78 A1
Digbeth Birmingham B5 ..164 D1
Walsall WS1 ....28 E1
Digbey Cl CV5 ....112 B6
Digby Cres B46 ....59 B3
Digby Ct 3 B27 ....88 C3
Digby Dr B37 ....90 B6
Digby Ho B37 ....69 F4
Digby Pl CV7 ....92 C1
Digby Rd Coleshill B46 ..70 F6
Kingswinford DY6 ....60 D8
Sutton Coldfield B73 .....46 B4
Dilcock Way CV4 ......131 F7
Dilke Rd WS9 ....29 F5
Dillam Cl CV6 ....96 A4
Dilliars Wlk B70 ......53 A5
Dillington Ho 6 B37 ..70 B2
Dillon Ct CV11 ....73 B5
Dillotford Ave CV3 ...133 D6
Dilloways La WV13 .....40 F8
Dilwyn Cl B98 ....154 F1
Dimbles Hill B23 ......3 B1
Dimbles La WS13 ....3 A2
Dimmingsdale Bank B32 ..84 C4
Dimmingsdale Rd WV4 ..37 E5
Dimminsdale WV13 ......27 A1
Dimmock St WV4 ....39 E5
Dimmocks Ave WV14 ....51 D8
Dimsdale Gr B31 ......102 E3
Dimsdale Rd B31 ......102 D3
Dinedor Cl B98 ....154 D3
Dingle Ave B64 ....82 E8
Dingle Cl
Birmingham B30 ....103 D7
Coventry CV6 ....113 A4
Dudley DY2 ....62 E7
Dingle Com Prim Sch
........................61 A4
Dingle Ct B91 ....106 F1
Dingle Hollow B69 .....63 D8
Dingle La Solihull B91 ..106 F2
Willenhall WV13 ....27 A4
Dingle Mead B14 ......104 C4
Dingle Rd Clayhanger WS8 ..15 E6
Dudley DY2 ....62 E7
Kingswinford DY6 ....60 A4
Stourbridge DY9 ....81 C2
Dingle St B69 ....63 E8
Dingle The
Birmingham B29 ....85 E2
Cheswick Green B90 ......126 D5
Nuneaton CV10 ....72 E6
Oldbury B69 ....63 D8
Wolverhampton WV3 ....24 D1
Dingle View DY3 ....50 C7
Dingleside B98 ....153 E2
Dingleside Mid Sch B98 ..159 B8
Dingley Rd
Bulkington CV12 ....79 B2
Wednesbury WS10 ....42 A5
Dinham Gdns DY1 ....50 E3
Dinmore Ave B31 ......103 B4
Dinmore Cl B98 ....154 D3
Dinsdale Wlk WV6 ......25 A5
Dippons Dr WV6 ....24 A3
Dippons Ho WV6 ....24 A3
Dippons Mill Cl WV6 ...24 A3
Dirtyfoot La WV4 ......38 A5
Discovery Cl DY4 ......52 C5
Discovery Way CV3 ....135 B7
District Ctr WV11 .....2 C1

Ditch The WS1 ....28 F1
Ditchford Cl B97 .....158 D4
Ditton Gr B31 ....122 F6
Dixon Cl Birmingham B35 ..58 A2
Tipton DY4 ....52 C6
Dixon Ct DY10 ....117 C8
Dixon Ho B16 ....66 A1
Dixon Rd B10 ....87 B8
Dixon St
Kidderminster DY10 ......116 E5
Wolverhampton WV2 ....39 E7
Dixon's Green Rd DY2 ..62 E8
Dixons Green Ct 7 DY2 ..62 E8
Dobbins Oak Rd DY9 ....81 E1
Dobbs Mill Cl B29 .....86 B2
Dobbs St WV2 ....163 B1
Dobson La CV31 ....162 A4
Dock La 9 DY1 ....51 B1
Dock Lane Ind Est 12
DY1 ....51 B1
Dock Meadow Dr WV4 ...40 A4
Dock Rd DY8 ....60 F2
Dock The Catshill B61 ..137 A8
Stourbridge B61 ....81 F5
Dockar Rd B31 ....102 E2
Dockers Cl CV7 ....130 C7
Doctor's Piece CV3 ....27 B2
Doctors Cl B94 ....142 A2
Doctors Hill
Bournheath B61 ....136 D8
Stourbridge DY9 ....81 C3
Doctors La
Kingswinford DY6 ....60 A4
Shenstone WS14 ....18 A6
Dodd Ave CV34 ....161 C7
Doddington Gr B32 ....102 B8
Dodford Cl B45 ....121 F7
Dodford Fst Sch B61 ..136 A5
Dodford Ho B60 ....137 B3
Dodford Rd B61 ....120 D1
Dodgson Cl DY10 ....96 A4
Dodwells Bridge Ind Est
LE10 ....74 E8
Dodwells Rd LE10 ......74 F8
Doe Bank Ct B74 ....44 D5
Doe Bank La
Birmingham B43,WS9 .....44 D5
Coventry CV1 ....113 A3
Doe Bank Rd DY4 ....41 C1
Dog Kennel La
Solihull B90 ....126 D7
8 Walsall WS1 ....28 F1
Dog La Tamworth B77 ...22 B6
Weeford WS14 ....19 A4
Dogberry Cl CV3 ......134 C6
Dogberry Way CV34 ....161 F2
Doggs Lane Croft B27 ..88 B2
Dogkennel La
Halesowen B63 ....83 B3
Oldbury B68 ....64 A5
Doglands The CV31 ....162 B4
Dolben La B98 ....154 D3
Dollery Dr B5 ....86 A5
Dollis Gr B44 ....44 F3
Dolman St B7 ....67 B4
Dolman Rd B6 ....66 C8
Dolobran Rd B11 ....87 B7
Dolomite Ave CV4 .....112 D1
Dolphin Cl WS3 ....14 F1
Dolphin Ho WS3 ....15 A1
Dolphin La WV12 ....27 D8
Dolphin La B27 ....88 C1
Dolphin Rd
Birmingham B11 ....87 D5
Redditch B98 ....154 A5
Dolton Way DY4 ....51 E6
Doman Rd DY11 ....116 B7
Dolphin Cl WS3 ....4 D7
Dom Gr WS11 ....4 D7
Donaldbain Cl CV4 ....132 A4
Doncaster Cl CV2 .....114 F2
Doncaster Way B36 .....68 C8
Donegal Cl CV4 ....132 A7
Donegal Rd B74 ....44 F5
Dongan Rd CV34 ....161 D7
Donibristle Croft B35 ..58 A4
Donnington Ave CV6 ...112 E5
Donnington Cl B98 ....154 C5
Donnington Ho B33 .....69 B2
Donnithorne Ave CV10,
CV11 ....73 D1
Donovan Dr B73 ....46 B6
Dooley Cl WV13 ....26 E2
Doone Cl CV2 ....114 E6
Dora Herbert Ct B12 ...86 E5
Dora Rd Birmingham, B10 ..87 E8
Birmingham, Handsworth
B21 ....65 D1
West Bromwich B70 ....53 C1
Dora St WS2 ....42 B7
Dorado B77 ....35 D7
Doran Cl B63 ....82 D1
Doranda Way B71 ....53 F1
Dorcas Cl CV11 ....79 C8
Dorchester Cl WV12 ...27 C8
Dorchester Ct B91 ....107 A4
Dorchester Dr B17 .....85 B4
Dorchester Rd
Cannock WS11 ....1 A1
Hinckley LE10 ....76 B7
Solihull B91 ....107 A4
Stourbridge DY9 ....81 D2
Willenhall WV12 ....13 C1
Dorchester Way
Coventry CV2 ....115 A4
Nuneaton CV11 ....74 A7

Dordale Rd DY9 ....119 E2
Dordon Cl B90 ....105 E1
Dordon Rd B78 ....36 F8
Doreen Gr B24 ....57 B2
Doris Rd Birmingham, B11 ..87 B4
Birmingham, Bordesley Green
B9 ....67 D2
Coleshill B46 ....70 A7
Dorking Gr B15 ....66 C1
Dorlcote Rd B8 ....68 A4
Dorlecote Cl CV10 .....73 C1
Dorlecote Pl CV10 .....78 C8
Dorlecote Rd CV10 .....78 C8
Dormer Ave B77 ....21 D5
Dormer Harris Ave CV4 ..111 B1
Dormer Ho 3 CV32 ....156 F2
Dormer Pl CV32 ....161 F8
Dormie Cl B38 ....103 D1
Dormington Rd B44 ....44 F3
Dormston Cl
Redditch B98 ....153 F1
Solihull B91 ....127 C8
Dormston Dr
Birmingham B29 ....84 F2
Sedgley DY3 ....50 E8
Dormston Sch The DY3 ..50 E8
Dormston Trad Est DY1 ..50 F4
Dornie Dr B38 ....123 A7
Dorncliffe Ave B33 ....89 D7
Dorney Cl CV5 ....132 E8
Dornie Dr B38 ....103 F1
Dornton Rd B30 ....104 C8
Dorothy Gdns B20 ......55 A2
Dorothy Goodman Specl Sch
LE10 ....71 D2
Dorothy Pattison Hospl
WS2 ....28 C3
Dorothy Powell Way CV2 ..96 F1
Dorothy Purcell Jun Sch
WV14 ....41 B3
Dorothy Rd
Birmingham B11 ....88 B5
Smethwick B67 ....65 A4
Dorothy St WS1 ....42 D7
Dorridge Cl B97 ......152 E8
Dorridge Croft B93 ...127 F2
Dorridge Jun & Inf Schs
B93 ....128 A2
Dorridge Rd B93 ......128 A2
Dorridge Sta B93 .....127 F2
Dorrington Gn B42 .....55 A5
Dorrington Prim Sch
B42 ....55 A5
Dorrington Rd B42 .....55 A5
Dorset Cl
Birmingham B45 ....101 F2
Nuneaton CV10 ....72 F3
Tamworth B78 ....21 A1
Dorset Cotts B30 .....104 A6
Dorset Ct 3 B29 ......103 B7
Dorset Dr WS9 ....16 B1
Dorset Pl WS3 ....28 C7
Dorset Rd Birmingham B8 ..67 C6
Cannock WS12 ....2 E1
Coventry CV1 ....113 C5
Smethwick B17 ....65 B3
Stourbridge DY8 ....80 D8
Dorset Twr B18 ....66 B4
Dorsett Rd
Darlaston WS10 ....41 C6
Wednesbury WS10 ....42 D2
Dorsett Road Terr WS10 ..41 C6
Dorsheath Gdns B23 ....56 F4
Dorsington Rd B27 .....88 D1
Dorstone Covert B14 ..104 C2
Dorville Cl B38 ....123 D8
Dosthill Prim Sch B77 ..35 D5
Dosthill Rd (Two Gates)
B77 ....35 D7
Dotterel Pl DY10 .....117 A1
Douay Rd B24 ....57 B6
Double Row DY2 ....62 E4
Doughty St DY4 ....52 C5
Douglas Ave
Birmingham B36 ....68 D6
Oldbury B68 ....64 D5
Douglas Davies Cl WV12 ..27 C4
Douglas Ho CV1 ....165 D4
Douglas Pl WV10 ......25 C6
Douglas Rd
Birmingham B27 ....88 C4
Birmingham, Handsworth
B21 ....65 F8
Dudley WV14 ....51 D8
Halesowen B62 ....63 E1
Hollywood B47 ....125 A7
Oldbury B68 ....64 D4
Sutton Coldfield B72 ....46 C3
Douglass Rd DY2 ....62 E8
Doulton Cl
Birmingham B32 ....84 F3
Coventry CV2 ....96 E1
Doulton Dr B66 ....65 A6
Doulton Rd
Blackheath B65 ....63 A4
Oldbury B64,B65 ....62 F4
Doulton Trad Est B65 ....62 F4
Dove Cl Bedworth CV12 ..77 E3
Birmingham B25 ....88 E8
Huntington WS12 ....1 C4
Hinckley LE10 ....75 A8
Kidderminster DY10 .....117 B2
Walsall WS1 ....29 A1
Wednesbury WS10 ....41 A8
Dove Dr DY8 ....81 A8
Dove Gdns B38 ....104 B2
Dove Hollow Cannock WS12 ..2 E4
Great Wyrley WS6 ....4 F1

Dove House Ct B91 ....106 F7
Dove House La B91 ....107 A8
Dove Ridge DY8 ....81 A7
Dove Way B36 ....69 FB
Dovebridge Cl B76 .....46 F4
Dovecote Cl
Coventry CV6 ....112 D5
Solihull B91 ....107 B8
Tipton DY4 ....52 C5
Wolverhampton WV6 ......24 C4
Dovecote Rd B61 ......136 C1
Dovecotes Prim Sch
WV8 ....10 E1
Dovecotes The
Coventry CV5 ....112 B5
Sutton Coldfield B75 ....32 B3
Dovedale WS11 ....2 A3
Dovedale Ave
Coventry CV6 ....95 F2
Solihull B90 ....106 B1
Walsall WS3 ....15 B5
Willenhall WV12 ....27 B4
Dovedale Ct WV4 ....39 F2
Dovedale Dr B28 ......105 F5
Dovedale Rd
Birmingham B23 ....56 C7
Kidderminster DY11 .....116 A8
Wolverhampton WV4 ....39 E3
Dovehouse Fields WS14 ..9 B6
Dovehouse La B91 .....106 F7
Dovehouse Pool Rd 1
B6 ....66 B8
Dover Cl B32 ....102 A7
Dover Farm Cl B77 .....36 B8
Dover Ho WS3 ....28 C7
Dover St Bilston WV14 ..40 D6
Birmingham B18 ....66 A6
Coventry CV1 ....165 A3
Dovercourt Ho 1 B15 ..86 D8
Dovercourt Rd B26 .....89 C5
Doverdale Ave DY10 ...117 B5
Doverdale Cl
Halesowen B63 ....82 E5
Redditch B98 ....159 B7
Doveridge Cl B91 .....106 E6
Doveridge Rd B28 .....105 E5
Doversley Rd B14 .....104 C5
Dovestone B77 ....22 D1
Dovey Dr B76 ....58 A7
Dovey Rd Birmingham B13 ..87 D2
Tipton B69 ....63 D8
Dowar Rd B45 ....122 C7
Dowells Cl B13 ....86 F2
Dowells Gdns DY8 ......60 D3
Dower Rd B75 ....32 B1
Doweries The B45 .....121 F8
Dowler's Hill Cres B98 ..159 A8
Dowley Croft B23 ......57 B8
Dowles Rd DY11 ....116 B2
Downcroft Ave B38 ....103 E2
Downderry Way CV6 ...114 A6
Downend Cl WV10 ......11 F4
Downey Cl B11 ....87 B7
Downfield Cl WS3 ......14 A4
Downfield Dr DY3 ......50 E6
Downham Cl WS5 ....29 E1
Downham Pl WV3 ....38 F8
Downham Wood WS5 .....43 E8
Downie Rd WV8 ....10 C3
Downing Cl
18 Blackheath B65 ....63 C1
Knowle B93 ....128 A4
Wednesfield WV11 ....27 A7
Downing Cres 6 B68 ...84 B7
Downing Dr B79 ....20 E5
Downing St
Halesowen B63 ....83 A5
Smethwick B66 ....65 C7
Downland Cl B38 .....103 F1
Downs Rd WV13 ....41 C8
Downs The Aldridge WS9 ..30 D2
Wolverhampton WV10 .....25 C6
Downsell Rd B97 ......153 A2
Downsfield Rd B26 .....89 B7
Downside Rd B24 ....56 F8
Downton Cl CV2 ....115 A8
Downton Cres B33 ......69 E3
Dowty Ave CV12 ....77 D1
Dowty Way WV9 ....11 A3
Doyle Dr CV6 ....95 F3
Dr Phillips Sh Ctr The
CV2 ....114 D8
Dragoon Fields B60 ...151 B8
Drake Cl WS3 ....14 B1
Drake Cres DY11 ......116 A7
Drake Croft 4 WS13 ....9 C8
Drake Ct WS3 ....14 B1
Drake Ho WS2 ....52 A7
Drake Rd Birmingham B23 ..56 C3
Smethwick B66 ....64 F7
Walsall WS3 ....14 C1
Drake St Coventry CV6 ..113 D7
West Bromwich B71 ....53 C5
Drake Way LE10 ....71 D4
Drake's Gn WV14 ....41 A3
Drakes Cl B97 ....158 C6
Drakes Cross Par B47 ..125 A5
Drakes Hill Cl DY8 ....80 C4
Drancy Ave WV12 ....27 D6
Draper Cl CV8 ....148 C2
Draper's Fields CV1 ...165 B4
Drapers Ct CV11 ......165 B4
Drawbridge Rd B90 ....125 E8

Draycote Cl B92 ....107 D6
Draycott Ave B23 ....56 D5
Draycott Cl
■ Redditch B97 ....153 B5
Wolverhampton WV4 ....38 C5
Draycott Cres B77 ....21 D1
Draycott Dr B31 ....102 E7
Draycott Rd
Coventry CV2 ....114 C7
Smethwick B66 ....64 E7
Drayman Cl WS1 ....42 F8
Draycott Cl Nuneaton CV10 ..72 A8
Redditch B98 ....159 D8
Sutton Coldfield B75 ....32 B3
Drayton Cres CV5 ....111 D5
Drayton Cl
Bromsgrove B60 ....151 B8
Warwick CV34 ....155 E2
Drayton La E 34 C5
Drayton Manor Dr
Drayton Bassett B78 ....34 F7
Fazeley B78 ....34 F8
Drayton Manor Pk B78 ....34 E7
Drayton Rd
Bedworth CV12 ....78 D2
Belbroughton DY9 ....119 B5
Birmingham B14 ....104 F8
Smethwick B66 ....65 A1
Solihull B90 ....126 A8
Drayton St Walsall WS2 ......28 C2
Wolverhampton WV2 ....163 B1
Drayton St E WS2 ....28 C2
Drayton Way CV10 ....72 C7
Dreadnought Rd DY5 ....61 B8
Dreamwell Ind Est B11 ....88 A6
Dreel The B15 ....85 E7
Dreghorn Rd B36 ....68 A6
Drem Ct B35 ....58 A2
Dresden Cl WV1 ....40 A4
Drew Cres
Kenilworth CV8 ....148 A4
Stourbridge DY9 ....81 D2
Drew Rd DY9 ....81 D3
Drews Ho B14 ....104 D1
Drews Holloway B63 ....82 D5
Drews Holloway S B63 ....82 D5
Drews La B8 ....68 A7
Drews Meadow Cl ■
B14 ....104 C2
Driffield Cf B98 ....154 D2
Driffold B73 ....46 B3
Driftwood Cl B38 ....123 D7
Drinkwater Ho ■ CV1 ....113 B2
Drive Fields WV4 ....38 B6
Drive The
Birmingham, Gravelly Hill
B23 ....56 E2
Birmingham, Handsworth
B20 ....55 B2
Brierley Hill DY5 ....61 C5
Coventry CV2 ....114 E3
Halesowen B63 ....83 A3
Hopwood B48 ....123 B3
Redditch B97 ....152 C7
Shenstone WS14 ....18 E8
Walsall, High Heath WS4 ....15 C1
Walsall, Pelsall WS11 ....14 E2
Wolverhampton WV6 ....24 C5
Droicon Trad Est B65 ....63 C5
Dronfield Rd CV2 ....114 B3
Drovers Way B60 ....150 E6
Droveway The WV9 ....10 F2
Droxford Wlk WV8 ....10 E1
Droylsdon Park Rd CV3 .....134 B6
Druid Park Rd WV12 ....13 C1
Druid Rd CV2 ....133 D8
Druid St LE10 ....71 D1
Druids Ave Aldridge WS9 ....30 C8
Blackheath B65 ....63 D4
Druids La B14 ....104 D1
Druids Wlk WS9 ....16 A3
Drummond Cl
Coventry CV6 ....112 F7
Wolverhampton WV11 ....13 A2
Drummond Gr B43 ....44 C3
Drummond Rd
Birmingham B9 ....68 A2
Bromsgrove B60 ....151 B8
Stourbridge DY9 ....81 F4
Drummond St WV1 ....163 B4
Drummond Way B37 ....70 C2
Drury La Solihull B91 ....107 C3
Drybrook Cl B38 ....123 E8
Drybrooks Cl CV7 ....130 B6
Dryden Cl Kenilworth CV8 ...147 F3
Tipton DY4 ....52 A7
Willenhall WV12 ....27 E8
Dryden Gr B27 ....88 B2
Dryden Pl WS3 ....28 C7
Dryden Rd Tamworth B79 ....21 A6
Walsall WS3 ....28 C7
Wolverhampton WV10 ....11 F1
Drylea Gr B36 ....68 F8
Dual Way WV4 ....1 D8
Dubarry Ave DY6 ....60 C7
Duchess Rd
Birmingham B16 ....66 A1
Walsall WS1 ....42 D5
Duck La WV8 ....10 E3
Duckhouse Rd WV11 ....26 D7
Duddeston Dr B8 ....67 D4
Duddeston Manor Rd B7 ....67 A4
Duddeston Mill Rd B7,B8 ....67 C4
Duddeston Mill Trad Est
B8 ....67 C4
Duddeston Sta B7 ....67 B4
Dudding Rd WV4 ....39 D5

Dudhill Rd B65 ....63 A3
Dudhill Wlk B65 ....63 A3
Dudley Castle* DY1 ....51 D2
Dudley Central Trad Est
DY2 ....62 C8
Dudley Cl B65 ....63 A5
Dudley Coll (International
Glass Ctr) DY5 ....61 D3
Dudley Coll (Wolverhampton
Street Coll) DY1 ....51 C2
Dudley Coll Mons Hill
DY1 ....51 B5
Dudley Gdns WV11 ....26 E6
Dudley Gr B32 ....157 B2
Dudley Gr B23 ....65 E4
Dudley Innovation Ctr
DY6 ....60 F7
Dudley L Ctr DY1 ....51 B1
Dudley Park Rd B27 ....88 C3
Dudley Port DY4 ....52 A3
Dudley Port Sta DY4 ....52 B4
Dudley Rd Birmingham B18 ..65 E4
Blackheath B65 ....63 A5
Brierley Hill DY5,DY6 ....60 E6
Dudley DY1 ....50 C6
Halesowen B63 ....83 A5
Himley DY3 ....49 D3
Kenilworth CV8 ....147 F2
Kingswinford, Barrow Hill
DY6 ....60 F7
Kingswinford, Wall Heath
DY6 ....60 D8
Oldbury B69 ....63 F8
Stourbridge DY9 ....81 E5
Tipton DY4 ....51 E5
Wolverhampton WV2 ....39 D7
Dudley Rd E B69 ....52 D1
Dudley Rd W B69 ....52 B2
Dudley Rise LE10 ....75 D6
Dudley Row DY1 ....51 D1
Dudley Southern Bypass
DY2 ....62 C7
Dudley Terr CV8 ....149 B6
Dudley Wlk WV4 ....39 C5
Dudley Wood Ave DY2 ......62 C2
Dudley Wood Prim Sch
DY2 ....62 C2
Dudley Wood Rd DY2 ....62 C2
Dudley Zoo* DY1 ....51 D2
Duggins La CV4,CV7 ....131 B8
Duke Barn Field CV2 ....114 A5
Duke St Blackheath B65 .....63 B2
Coventry CV5 ....112 F2
Dudley DY3 ....50 D5
Nuneaton CV11 ....73 B4
Royal Leamington Spa
CV32 ....157 A1
Stourbridge DY8 ....81 A6
Sutton Coldfield B72 ....46 B4
Wednesfield WS10 ....26 D5
West Bromwich B70 ....53 C1
Wolverhampton, Penn Fields
WV3 ....39 A7
Wolverhampton, Springfield
WV1 ....163 D2
Dukes Rd
Birmingham B30 ....104 A3
Dordon B78 ....36 F6
Dulais Cl B98 ....153 E1
Dulvern Gr B14 ....104 D5
Dulverton Ave CV5 ....112 D4
Dulverton Ct CV5 ....112 D4
Dulverton Rd B6 ....56 B1
Dulwich Gr B44 ....56 B8
Dulwich Rd B44 ....56 A8
Dumble Pit La B48 ....140 F7
Dumblederry Ct WS9 ....30 C7
Dumblederry La
Aldridge WS9 ....29 F6
Walsall WS9 ....29 E7
Dumolo's La B77 ....21 F3
Dumphouse La B48 ....140 C3
Dunard Rd B90 ....105 F3
Dunbar Cl Birmingham B32 ..84 D1
Kidderminster DY10 ....117 C6
Dunbar Gr B43 ....44 B4
Dunblane Dr CV32 ....157 B1
Dunblane Way LE10 ....71 A2
Duncalfe Dr B75 ....32 B3
Duncan Edwards Cl DY1 ....62 A8
Duncan Ho B71 ....46 B1
Duncan St WV2 ....39 C7

Dunchurch Cl
Balsall Common CV7 ....130 B7
Redditch B98 ....154 F1
Dunchurch Cres B73 ....45 C3
Dunchurch Dr B31 ....102 E7
Dunchurch Highway
CV5 ....112 A4
Dunchurch Ho ■ B15 ....86 E8
Dunclent Cres DY10 ....117 E3
Dunclent La DY10 ....117 E3
Duncombe Gr ■ B17 ....85 A7
Duncombe St DY8 ....80 D5
Duncroft Ave CV6 ....112 F7
Duncroft Rd B26 ....89 A8
Duncroft Wlk DY1 ....51 B6
Duncumb Rd B75 ....47 A5
Dundale La WS6 ....4 D2
Dundas Ave DY2 ....62 F8
Dunedin B77 ....22 A1
Dunedin Dr B45 ....122 B1
Dunedin Ho B32 ....84 F4
Dunedin Rd B44 ....44 F3
Dunham Croft B93 ....127 D3
Dunhill Ave CV4 ....111 E3
Dunkirk Ave B70 ....53 E3
Dunkirk Pl CV3 ....134 F7
Dunkley St WV1 ....163 B4
Dunley Croft B90 ....126 F6
Dunley Ct B23 ....56 C2
Dunlin Cl
Featherstone WV10 ....12 B7
Kidderminster DY10 ....116 F2
Dunlop Rd B97 ....158 D5
Dunlop Way B35 ....57 F2
Dunnerdale Rd WS8 ....15 D7
Dunnigan Rd B32 ....84 F3
Dunnose Cl CV6 ....113 E8
Dunns Bank DY5 ....81 F7
Dunrose Cl CV2 ....114 E2
Dunsfold Cl WV14 ....40 A3
Dunsfold Croft ■ B6 ....66 F6
Dunsford Cl DY5 ....81 B7
Dunsford Rd B66 ....65 A2
Dunsink Rd B6 ....55 F1
Dunslade Cres DY5 ....81 F8
Dunslade Rd B23 ....56 F7
Dunsley Dr DY8 ....60 E3
Dunsley Gr WV4 ....39 A4
Dunsmore Ave CV3 ....134 C6
Dunsmore Dr DY5 ....81 F8
Dunsmore Gr B91 ....106 F7
Dunsmore Rd B28 ....87 E2
Dunstall Ave WV6 ....25 C4
Dunstall Cl B97 ....153 B2
Dunstall Gr B29 ....102 F8
Dunstall Hill WV6 ....25 C5
Dunstall Hill Jun & Inf Sch
WV6 ....25 C4
Dunstall Hill Trad Est
WV6 ....25 C5
Dunstall La Hopwas B78 ....20 D4
Wolverhampton WV6 ....25 B5
Dunstall Park Race Course
WV6 ....25 A6
Dunstan Croft B90 ....126 C8
Dunstan St ■ B15 ....85 B4
Dunster B77 ....35 C7
Dunster Cl B30 ....104 C4
Dunster Gr WV6 ....23 F3
Dunster Pl CV6 ....95 D3
Dunster Rd B37 ....70 D2
Dunston Cl
Great Wyrley WS6 ....13 E8
Kingswinford DY6 ....60 D7
Dunston Dr WV7 ....7 A8
Dunsville Dr CV2 ....114 F8
Dunton Cl B75 ....32 A4
Dunton Hall Rd B90 ....126 A8
Dunton La B78 ....48 C1
Dunton Rd B37 ....69 F5
Dunton Trad Est B7 ....67 D7
Dunvegan Cl
Coventry CV3 ....115 A2
Kenilworth CV8 ....148 C4
Dunvegan Rd B24 ....57 A4
Duport Rd LE10 ....75 F7
Durant Cl B45 ....101 D1
Durban Rd B66 ....65 C4
Durbar Ave CV6 ....113 D8
Durham Ave WV13 ....27 C1
Durham Cl
Bromsgrove B61 ....136 C4
Keresley CV7 ....94 F4
Tamworth B78 ....21 A2
Durham Cres CV5 ....112 B7
Durham Croft B37 ....70 B2
Durham Dr B71 ....53 D7
Durham Ho ■ WV3 ....25 C4
Durham Pl WS2 ....28 B1
Durham Rd
Birmingham B11 ....87 B4
Blackheath B65 ....63 E4
Dudley DY2 ....62 D2
Stourbridge DY8 ....80 F8
Walsall WS2 ....42 B8
Wednesbury WS10 ....42 D4
Durham Twr ■ B1 ....66 B3
Durley Dean Rd B29 ....85 C2
Durley Dr B73 ....45 C3
Durley Rd B25 ....88 C6
Durlston Cl B77 ....21 F5

Durslade Gr B28 ....106 A8
Durnford Croft B14 ....104 E1
Dursley Cl Solihull B92 ......107 B8
Dursley La Redditch B98 .....154 F8
Willenhall WV12 ....27 D4
Dursley Rd WS11 ....1 B2
Dursley Way WS7 ....7 A7
Dusthouse La B60 ....151 D7
Dutton Rd CV2 ....96 D3
Dutton's La B75 ....32 E4
Duxford Cl B97 ....158 B8
Duxford Rd B42 ....55 B7
Dwarris Wlk CV34 ....155 E2
Dwellings La B32 ....84 B5
Dyas Ave B42 ....55 A7
Dyas Rd Birmingham B44 ....44 E1
Hollywood B47 ....125 A7
Dyce Cl B35 ....58 A4
Dyce La B94 ....142 D8
Dyers Cl CV11 ....79 F6
Dymoke St B12 ....86 F8
Dymond Rd CV6 ....95 D3
Dynes Wlk B67 ....65 A5
Dyott Rd B13 ....87 A1
Dysart Cl CV1 ....113 E4
Dyson Cl WS2 ....27 F3
Dyson St CV4 ....111 E3
Dysons Gdns B8 ....67 E5

E

Eachelhurst Rd B24,B76 ....57 F5
Eachus Rd WV14 ....51 D8
Eachway B45 ....121 F6
Eachway Farm Cl B45 ......122 A6
Eachway La B45 ....122 A6
Eacott Cl CV6 ....95 A3
Eadgar Ct B43 ....54 D7
Eadie Mews B97 ....153 D1
Eagle Cl CV10 ....72 D4
Eagle Cl Blackheath B65 .....63 A4
Cheslyn Hay WS6 ....4 D2
Dudley DY1 ....50 F1
Nuneaton CV11 ....79 B8
Eagle Croft B14 ....104 E2
Eagle Ct WV3 ....39 A7
Eagle Dr B77 ....22 A4
Eagle Gdns B24 ....57 B3
Eagle Gr Birmingham B36 ...70 A8
Cannock WS12 ....2 C1
Eagle Ho CV1 ....113 D5
Eagle Ind Est DY4 ....52 E7
Eagle La Kenilworth CV8 ....147 F3
Tipton DY4 ....52 D6
Eagle Rd B98 ....154 E5
Eagle St Coventry CV1 ......113 D5
Royal Leamington Spa
CV31 ....162 A6
Tipton DY4 ....52 C6
Wolverhampton, Monmore Green
WV2 ....39 E8
Wolverhampton, Penn Fields
WV3 ....39 A7
Eagle St E CV1 ....113 D5
Eagle Trad Est B63 ....83 A4
Eales Yd ■ LE10 ....71 D1
Ealing Gr B44 ....45 A1
Ealingham B77 ....22 B1
Eardisley Cl B98 ....154 F1
Earl Place Bsns Pk CV4 .....112 B1
Earl St Bedworth CV12 ......78 C2
Bilston WV14 ....40 D5
Coventry CV1 ....165 C2
Kingswinford DY6 ....60 D4
Royal Leamington Spa
CV32 ....157 A1
Earl's Court Rd B17 ....85 A6
Earl's Wlk CV3 ....133 D7
Earls Cl B97 ....152 F2
Earls Court Rd B17 ....85 A6
Earls Ferry Gdns B32 ....102 A7
Earls High Sch The B63 .....83 B4
Earls Rd Nuneaton CV11 ....73 A5
Earls Rivers Ave CV34 ......161 D3
Earls Way B63 ....83 B4
Earlsbury Gdns B20 ....55 D1
Earlsdon Ave N CV5 ....112 F1
Earlsdon Ave S CV5 ....133 A8
Earlsdon St CV5 ....132 F8
Earlsmead Rd B21 ....65 C7
Earlsmere B94 ....126 B1
Earlston Way B43 ....54 D8
Earlswood Comm B94 ......142 A6
Earlswood Cres CV9 ....11 A3
Earlswood Ct B20 ....55 A2
Earlswood Dr B74 ....46 C7
Earlswood Ho ■ B5 ....86 E7
Earlswood Rd
Dorridge B93 ....127 D2
Kingswinford DY6 ....60 E8
Earlswood Sta B94 ....141 C6
Early Bury Birmingham B8 ...67 D3
Walsall WS3 ....13 F2
Easedale Cl
Coventry CV3 ....133 B6
Nuneaton CV11 ....74 A6
Easemore Rd B98 ....153 E3
Easenhall Cl B93 ....128 A4
Easenhall La B98 ....154 E1

Easmore Cl B14 ....104 D2
East Ave Bedworth CV12 ....78 D2
Coventry CV2 ....114 A2
Tipton B69 ....63 C7
Wolverhampton WV11 ....26 C6
East Birmingham Coll
B33 ....89 B8
East Birmingham Coll
Bordesley Green Campus
B9 ....68 A2
East Car Park Rd B40 ....90 F4
East Cl LE10 ....75 D7
East Croft Rd WV4 ....38 C5
East Dene CV32 ....157 B2
East Dr B35 ....86 C4
East Farm Croft B10 ....87 D8
East Gate B16 ....65 E3
East Gn WV4 ....38 C6
East Gr CV31 ....162 A6
East Holme B9 ....67 C2
East Meadway B33 ....69 E3
East Mews B44 ....44 D2
East Park Jun Sch WV1 .....40 A8
East Park Trad Est WV1 .....40 A8
East Park Way WV1 ....26 A1
East Pathway B17 ....85 C6
East Rd Bromsgrove B60 ....137 A1
Featherstone WV10 ....12 B8
Tipton DY4 ....52 B8
Wolverhampton WV4 ....39 F4
East Rise B75 ....46 D6
East St Brierley Hill DY5 ....82 A8
Cannock WS11 ....4 E6
Coventry CV1 ....113 E3
Dudley, Gornalwood DY3 ....50 D3
Dudley, Kate's Hill DY2 .....62 E8
Kidderminster DY10 ....116 F6
Tamworth B77 ....35 D5
Walsall WS2 ....42 F3
Wolverhampton WV1 ....163 D2
East View B77 ....21 E3
East View Rd B72 ....46 D2
East Way B92 ....91 B3
Eastacre WV13 ....41 A2
Eastboro Ct CV11 ....73 E2
Eastbourne Fields CV11 .....74 A4
Eastboro Way CV11 ....73 F2
Eastbourne Ave B34 ....68 E6
Eastbourne Cl CV6 ....112 E6
Eastbourne House Sch
B27 ....88 C4
Eastbourne St WS4 ....28 F3
Eastbrook Cl B76 ....46 D4
Eastbury Dr B92 ....89 A3
Eastcote Cl B90 ....106 D3
Eastcote Cres WS7 ....7 A5
Eastcote La B92 ....108 C4
Eastcote Rd
Birmingham B27 ....88 A1
Wolverhampton WV10 ....25 F5
Eastcotes CV4 ....112 B1
Eastdean Cl B23 ....56 D6
Eastern Ave
Brierley Hill DY5 ....61 B2
Lichfield WS13 ....3 C2
Eastern Green Jun Sch
CV5 ....111 D5
Eastern Green Rd CV5 ......111 F4
Eastern Hill B96 ....158 F2
Eastern Rd
Birmingham B29 ....86 B3
Sutton Coldfield B73 ....46 B1
Eastern Way B92 ....2 A1
Easterton Croft B14 ....104 E2
Eastfield Cl WS9 ....30 B4
Eastfield Dr B92 ....107 E8
Eastfield Gr WV1 ....25 F2
Eastfield Jun & Inf Sch
WV1 ....25 F2
Eastfield Rd
Birmingham B9 ....68 C3
Nuneaton CV10 ....73 D6
Royal Leamington Spa
CV32 ....162 A8
Tipton DY4 ....52 A7
Wolverhampton WV1 ....25 F2
Eastgate WS7 ....7 A4
Eastgate Ho ■ CV34 ....160 E6
Eastgate Mews ■ CV34 .....160 E6
Eastgate St WS7 ....6 E8
Eastham Rd B13 ....105 C6
Eastholme Ave B23 ....69 A4
Eastlake Cl B43 ....44 D3
Eastlands Gr CV5 ....112 E4
Eastlands Rd B13 ....87 A1
Eastleigh DY3 ....50 C8
Eastleigh Ave CV5 ....132 F7
Eastleigh Croft B76 ....58 A7
Eastleigh Dr B62 ....101 A4
Eastleigh Gr B25 ....88 D8
Eastley Cres CV34 ....160 B8
Eastmoor Cl B74 ....31 B2
Eastney Cres WV8 ....24 F8
Eastnor Cl
Kidderminster DY10 ....116 E2
Redditch B98 ....153 E1
Eastnor Gr CV31 ....162 B7
Eastnor Gdns WV11 ....26 F5
Easton Gr Birmingham B27 ..88 C1
Hollywood B47 ....125 B7
Eastridge Croft WS14 ....18 A5
Eastville B31 ....103 B3
Eastward Glen WV8 ....10 C1

Edge Hill Dr Perton WV6 . . . . . .23 E3
Sedgley DY3 . . . . .39 C2
Edge Hill Rd B74 . . . . .31 E4
Edge St WV14 . . . . .51 D8
Edgefield Rd CV2 . . . . .115 A8
Edgehill Pl CV4 . . . . .111 C1
Edgehill Rd B31 . . . . .103 B1
Edgemond Ave B24 . . . . .57 F4
Edgemoor Mdw WS12 . . . . . . .2 C1
Edgewick Com Prim Sch
CV6 . . . . .113 E8
Edgewood Cl B64 . . . . .82 F8
Edgewood Dr B45 . . . . .122 B1
Edgewood Rd
Birmingham, King's Norton
B38 . . . . .123 F7
Birmingham, Rednall B45 . . . .122 B6
Edgeworth Cl
Redditch B98 . . . . .154 C5
Willenhall WV12 . . . . .27 C4
Edgeworth Ho WS13 . . . . .3 A2
Edgmond Cl B98 . . . . .154 D4
Edgware Rd B23 . . . . .56 D5
Edgwick Park Ind Est
CV6 . . . . .113 F8
Edgwick Rd CV6 . . . . .113 F7
Edgwood Ct 4 B16 . . . . .65 F1
Edinburgh Ave WS2 . . . . .27 F3
Edinburgh Cl DY10 . . . . .116 E8
Edinburgh Cres
Royal Leamington Spa
CV31 .161 F6
Stourbridge DY8 . . . . .60 C1
Edinburgh Ct B24 . . . . .57 D7
Edinburgh Dr
Walsall WS4 . . . . .29 D7
Willenhall WV12 . . . . .27 B6
Edinburgh La WS2 . . . . .28 B4
Edinburgh Rd
Bilston WV14 . . . . .40 F3
Dudley DY2 . . . . .62 D6
Nuneaton CV10 . . . . .72 D6
Oldbury B68 . . . . .64 B6
Walsall WS5 . . . . .43 B8
Edinburgh Villas CV8 . . . . . . .133 F2
Edingale Rd CV2 . . . . .114 F8
Edison Cl WS12 . . . . .2 C1
Edison Gr B32 . . . . .84 C6
Edison Rd
Curdworth B46,B76 . . . . .59 F4
Walsall WS2 . . . . .28 B5
Edison Wlk WS2 . . . . .28 B5
Edith Rd B66 . . . . .65 C3
Edmondes Cl CV34 . . . . .155 F1
Edmonds Cl B33 . . . . .69 B2
Edmonds Ct
Birmingham, Gilbertstone
B10 . . . . .87 D7
Birmingham, Small Heath
B10 . . . . .87 D7
Edmonds Rd B68 . . . . .64 C2
Edmondscote Rd CV32 . . . . .161 D8
Edmonton Ave B44 . . . . .45 B1
Edmonton Cl WS11 . . . . .2 B2
Edmonton Ho B5 . . . . .86 D7
Edmund Cl WV12 . . . . .27 C6
Edmund Rd
Birmingham B8 . . . . .67 D4
Coventry CV1 . . . . .113 D5
Dudley DY2 . . . . .50 E6
Edmund St B3 . . . . .164 B3
Ednall La B60 . . . . .136 F1
Ednam Cl 3 B71 . . . . .53 F8
Ednam Gr WV5 . . . . .38 A1
Ednam Rd Dudley DY1 . . . . . . .51 C2
Wolverhampton WV4 . . . . .39 C5
Edsome Way B36 . . . . .68 F8
Edstone Cl B93 . . . . .127 F4
Edstone Mews B36 . . . . .68 F8
Edward Ave WS9 . . . . .30 B7
Edward Bailey Cl CV3 . . . . . .134 E7
Edward Cl WV14 . . . . .40 E3
Edward Ct
Birmingham B16 . . . . .65 C1
Sutton Coldfield B76 . . . . .46 F3
Tamworth B77 . . . . .21 F4
Walsall WS1 . . . . .43 A8
Edward Fisher Dr DY4 . . . . . .52 A5
Edward Rd Bedworth CV12 . . .78 C2
Birmingham, Balsall Heath
B12 . . . . .86 E5
Birmingham, Highter's Heath
B14 . . . . .105 A1
Coventry CV6 . . . . .95 A3
Halesowen B63 . . . . .82 F4
Oldbury B68 . . . . .64 A4
Perton WV6 . . . . .23 E5
Smethwick B67 . . . . .65 A4
Tipton DY4 . . . . .52 A7
Water Orton B46 . . . . .59 C3
Edward St Birmingham B1 . . .66 C3
Cannock WS11 . . . . .1 E4
Coventry CV6 . . . . .113 E5
Darlaston WS10 . . . . .41 E6
3 Dudley DY1 . . . . .51 B1
Hinckley LE10 . . . . .71 C2
Nuneaton CV11 . . . . .73 C3
Oldbury B69 . . . . .64 A4
Redditch B97 . . . . .153 D4
Royal Leamington Spa
CV32 .156 C1
Tamworth B79 . . . . .21 A5
Walsall WS2 . . . . .28 C3
Warwick CV34 . . . . .160 D7
West Bromwich B70 . . . . .53 C3
Wolverhampton WV4 . . . . .39 F5

Edward Street Hospl
B70 . . . . .53 C3
Edward Tyler Rd CV7 . . . . . . .78 A1
Edwards Ctr 7 LE10 . . . . . . .75 D8
Edwards Rd CV8 . . . . .148 C5
Edwards Rd
Birmingham B24 . . . . .57 A4
Burntwood WS7 . . . . .6 F5
Dudley DY2 . . . . .62 C4
Sutton Coldfield B75 . . . . .32 D3
Edwin Ave (Road 4)
DY10 .116 F1
Edwin Cres B60 . . . . .150 F8
Edwin Ct Bromsgrove B60 . . .150 F8
Bromsgrove B60 . . . . .150 F7
Edwin Phillips Dr B71 . . . . . .53 B8
Edwin Rd B30 . . . . .104 B7
Edyth Rd CV2 . . . . .114 E4
Edyvean Walker Ct CV11 . . .73 B5
Eel St B69 . . . . .63 F7
Effingham Rd B13 . . . . .105 C7
Egbert Cl B6 . . . . .67 B7
Egelwin Cl WV6 . . . . .23 E5
Egerton Ct 4 B85 . . . . .81 A7
Egerton Rd Aldridge B74 . . . .30 F1
Birmingham B24 . . . . .57 B2
Wolverhampton WV10 . . . . .11 E3
Egg La DY9,DY10 . . . . .119 A5
Egghill La B31,B45 . . . . .102 B3
Eggington Rd DY8 . . . . .60 B6
Eginton Rd B28 . . . . .105 E5
Eglamour Way CV34 . . . . . . .161 F3
Egmont Gdns WV11 . . . . .26 F5
Egret Ct DY10 . . . . .117 A1
Egret Wlk CV2 . . . . .96 B3
Eider Cl DY10 . . . . .117 B1
Eights Croft WS7 . . . . .6 D8
Eileen Gdns B37 . . . . .69 E4
Eileen Rd B11 . . . . .87 C3
Elan Cl Dudley DY3 . . . . .50 D3
Royal Leamington Spa
CV32 .157 C3
Elan Rd Birmingham B31 . . . .102 C2
Sedgley DY3 . . . . .50 D3
Elbow St B64 . . . . .62 F2
Elbury Croft B93 . . . . .127 F5
Elcock Dr B42 . . . . .55 D5
Eld Rd CV6 . . . . .113 E7
Eldalade Way WS10 . . . . .42 D2
Elder Cl WS11 . . . . .2 C2
Elder La WS7 . . . . .7 C7
Elder Way B23 . . . . .56 D2
Elderberry Cl DY8 . . . . .80 F8
Elderberry Way CV2 . . . . . . .114 B6
Elderfield Rd B30 . . . . .104 B3
Elderfield Cl B98 . . . . .154 E7
Elderfield Gr B91 . . . . .127 B7
Elderside Cl WS8 . . . . .15 F8
Eldon Ct WS1 . . . . .28 E8
Eldon Dr B76 . . . . .57 F7
Eldon Rd
Birmingham, Edgbaston B16 . .65 F2
Birmingham, Woodgate B32 . . .84 A3
Halesowen B62 . . . . .83 F5
Eldon St Darlaston WS10 . . . .41 D7
Walsall WS1 . . . . .28 F1
Eldorado Cl B80 . . . . .159 D4
Eldridge Cl WV9 . . . . .10 F2
Eleanor Rd WV14 . . . . .40 D6
Electra Park Ind Pk B6 . . . . .56 B1
Electric Ave B6 . . . . .56 B1
Elford Cl B14 . . . . .104 E5
Elford Gr Bilston WV14 . . . . . .40 C4
Birmingham B37 . . . . .70 C3
Elford Rd
Birmingham B17,B29 . . . . .85 B3
West Bromwich B71 . . . . .42 E2
Elgar Cl Cannock WS11 . . . . . .1 E5
Lichfield WS13 . . . . .3 A2
Nuneaton CV11 . . . . .79 A7
Elgar Cres DY5 . . . . .61 D7
Elgar Mews 2 B60 . . . . .136 F2
Elgar Rd CV6 . . . . .114 B8
Elgin Cl Sedgley DY3 . . . . .39 E1
Stourbridge DY8 . . . . .81 A7
Elgin Ct WV6 . . . . .23 E4
Elgin Gr B25 . . . . .88 C7
Elgin Rd WS3 . . . . .14 A4
Elias Cl WS14 . . . . .9 E6
Eliot Cl Tamworth B79 . . . . . . .21 A7
Warwick CV34 . . . . .155 E2
Eliot Croft WV14 . . . . .40 D2
Eliot St B7 . . . . .67 C8
Eliot Wlk DY10 . . . . .117 C6
Elizabeth Ave
Bilston WV14 . . . . .40 F3
Wednesbury WS10 . . . . .42 C3
Wolverhampton WV4 . . . . .39 B5
Elizabeth Cres B68 . . . . .64 D2
Elizabeth Ct
2 Birmingham B27 . . . . .88 C2
8 Coventry CV6 . . . . .113 A4
Warwick CV34 . . . . .161 B6
Redditch Dr B79 . . . . .21 A6
Elizabeth Gr Dudley DY2 . . . .62 F7
Solihull B90 . . . . .106 C2
Elizabeth Ho
Stourbridge DY9 . . . . .81 E5
Sutton Coldfield B76 . . . . .46 F4
14 Walsall WS5 . . . . .43 B4
Elizabeth Mews B69 . . . . .52 A2
Elizabeth Prout Gdns
B65 . . . . .63 B1
Elizabeth Rd
Birmingham, Moseley B13 . . . .86 C2
Birmingham, New Oscott
B73 . . . . .45 D1
Birmingham, Stechford B33 . . .68 D3

Elizabeth Rd continued
Cannock WS11 . . . . .1 E6
Halesowen B63 . . . . .82 F3
Hinckley LE10 . . . . .71 D2
Royal Leamington Spa
CV31 .161 F6
Walsall WS5 . . . . .43 C7
West Bromwich B70 . . . . .52 D4
Elizabeth Way
Halesowen B63 . . . . .83 A3
Redditch B97 . . . . .153 D5
Elizabeth Wlk DY4 . . . . .41 A2
Elkington Croft B90 . . . . .127 A6
Elkington St
Birmingham B6 . . . . .66 E5
Coventry CV6 . . . . .113 F8
Elkstone Cl B92 . . . . .89 E3
Elkstone Covert B14 . . . . . . .104 C2
Ellacombe Rd CV2 . . . . .114 D8
Elland Gr B27 . . . . .88 D2
Ellards Dr WV11 . . . . .26 F5
Ellen St B18 . . . . .66 B4
Ellenbrook Cl 8 B97 . . . . . . .153 B5
Ellenvale Cl WV14 . . . . .51 A8
Ellerbeck B77 . . . . .22 B1
Ellerby Gr B24 . . . . .57 E4
Ellerdene Cl B98 . . . . .158 D6
Ellerman Gdns CV6 . . . . .95 F3
Ellerside Gr B31 . . . . .102 F2
Ellerslie Cl DY5 . . . . .81 D8
Ellerslie Rd B13 . . . . .105 C7
Ellerton Rd B44 . . . . .45 B1
Ellerton Wlk WV10 . . . . .25 F5
Ellesboro' Rd B17 . . . . .85 B7
Ellesmere Rd
Bedworth CV12 . . . . .78 A2
Birmingham B8 . . . . .67 D4
Ellice Dr B36 . . . . .70 B7
Elliot Cl 1 WV4 . . . . .39 F4
Elliot Gdns B45 . . . . .122 B5
Elliott Cl WS11 . . . . .1 F5
Elliott Rd B29 . . . . .85 E1
Elliott Way B6 . . . . .55 E3
Elliott's Rd DY4 . . . . .51 E5
Elliotts La WV8 . . . . .10 A3
Ellis Ave DY5 . . . . .61 A2
Ellis Park Dr CV3 . . . . .115 B1
Ellis St B1 . . . . .164 B1
Ellis Wlk WS11 . . . . .4 F8
Ellison St B70 . . . . .53 C1
Elliston Ave B44 . . . . .55 F8
Elliston Gr CV31 . . . . .162 C6
Ellowes Hall Sch The
DY3 . . . . .50 C5
Ellowes Rd DY3 . . . . .50 C4
Ellys Rd CV1 . . . . .113 C5
Elm Ave Bilston WV14 . . . . . . .40 D6
Birmingham B12 . . . . .87 A5
Wednesbury WS10 . . . . .41 F4
Wolverhampton WV11 . . . . .26 B5
Elm Bank B13 . . . . .87 A3
Elm Bank Cl CV32 . . . . .157 A4
Elm Cl Binley Woods CV3 . . .135 C7
Dudley DY3 . . . . .50 B2
Stourbridge DY8 . . . . .80 D2
Elm Cres DY4 . . . . .52 A6
Elm Croft B68 . . . . .84 C7
Elm Ct Allesley CV5 . . . . .111 B8
Birmingham B13 . . . . .86 F4
Oldbury B66 . . . . .64 C8
Redditch B97 . . . . .153 D4
Walsall WS5 . . . . .43 A4
Elm Dale Rd WV4 . . . . .39 A5
Elm Dr Birmingham B43 . . . . . .43 D1
Blakedown DY10 . . . . .98 B2
Halesowen B62 . . . . .63 E1
Elm Farm Ave B37 . . . . .89 F7
Elm Farm Rd WV2 . . . . .39 D7
Elm Gdns WS14 . . . . .9 C7
Elm Gn DY1 . . . . .51 A5
Elm Gr
Balsall Common CV7 . . . . .130 C6
Birmingham B37 . . . . .69 F6
Bromsgrove B61 . . . . .137 A4
Codsall WV8 . . . . .10 A3
Huntington WS12 . . . . .1 D8
Elm Lodge B92 . . . . .109 A7
Elm Pl DY10 . . . . .118 B3
Elm Rd
Birmingham, Bournville
B30 . . . . .103 F8
Birmingham, Edgbaston B15 . .85 F3
Dudley DY1 . . . . .51 C4
Kidderminster DY10 . . . . .117 A6
Kingswinford DY6 . . . . .60 E6
Norton Canes WS11 . . . . .6 B5
Redditch B97 . . . . .153 D4
Royal Leamington Spa
CV32 .157 B3
Sutton Coldfield B76 . . . . .46 F2
Walsall WS3 . . . . .28 D6
Elm St Willenhall WV13 . . . . . .27 C2
Wolverhampton WV3 . . . . .25 A1
Elm Street Inf Sch WV13 . . . .27 C2
Elm Terr B69 . . . . .52 B1
Elm Tree Ave CV4 . . . . .112 B2
Elm Tree Cl LE10 . . . . .75 F8
Elm Tree Gr B63 . . . . .82 D6
Elm Tree Rd
Birmingham, Harborne B17 . . .85 A7
Birmingham, Stirchley B30 . . .104 A6
Bulkington CV12 . . . . .79 D2
Elm Tree Rise B92 . . . . .109 B6
Elm Tree Way B64 . . . . .62 F1
Elm Tree Wlk B79 . . . . .20 B7
Elm Way CV10 . . . . .72 A8
Elmay Rd B26 . . . . .89 A7
Elmbank Gr B20 . . . . .54 E5

Elmbank Rd
Kenilworth CV8 . . . . .147 E6
Walsall WS5 . . . . .43 C4
Elmbridge Cl B63 . . . . .82 D5
Elmbridge Dr B90 . . . . .127 B6
Elmbridge Rd B44 . . . . .55 E6
Elmbridge Way DY3 . . . . .50 E6
Elmcroft 5 B66 . . . . .65 C5
Elmcroft Ave B32 . . . . .84 A1
Elmcroft Gdns WV10 . . . . .11 E3
Elmcroft Rd B26 . . . . .88 F7
Elmdale B62 . . . . .84 A7
Elmdale Cres B31 . . . . .102 E4
Elmdale Dr Aldridge WS9 . . . .30 D8
Kidderminster DY10 . . . . .117 C5
Elmdale Gr B31 . . . . .102 E4
Elmdale Rd WV14 . . . . .51 A7
Elmdene Cl CV8 . . . . .148 B4
Elmdon Cl Solihull B92 . . . . . .89 D2
Wolverhampton WV10 . . . . .11 A1
Elmdon Coppice B92 . . . . . . .107 F7
Elmdon Ct B37 . . . . .90 A7
Elmdon La
Birmingham B37 . . . . .90 A6
Solihull B26 . . . . .90 A3
Elmdon Park Rd B92 . . . . .89 D2
Elmdon Rd
Birmingham, Acock's Green
B27 . . . . .88 C8
Birmingham, Marston Green
B37 . . . . .90 A7
Birmingham, Selly Park B29 . . .86 A3
Wolverhampton WV10 . . . . .11 A1
Elmdon Trad Est B37 . . . . .90 C5
Elmfield Ave B24 . . . . .57 F4
Elmfield Cres B13 . . . . .86 F2
Elmfield Rd
Birmingham B36 . . . . .69 F7
Nuneaton CV10 . . . . .73 C7
Elmfield Rudolf Steiner Sch
Ltd DY8 . . . . .81 A3
Elmfield View DY1 . . . . .51 A3
Elmhurst B15 . . . . .85 D8
Elmhurst Ave B65 . . . . .63 C3
Elmhurst Cl B97 . . . . .158 D4
Elmhurst Dr
Burntwood WS7 . . . . .7 A4
Kingswinford DY6 . . . . .60 F4
Elmhurst Rd
Birmingham B21 . . . . .54 E1
Coventry CV6 . . . . .96 A4
Elmley Cl Dudley WV14 . . . . . .51 B7
Kidderminster DY11 . . . . .116 B3
Elmley Ct B23 . . . . .56 C2
Elmley Gr
Birmingham B30 . . . . .104 B2
Perton WV6 . . . . .23 F3
Elmore Cl Birmingham B37 . . .70 A4
Coventry CV3 . . . . .134 D8
Elmore Green Cl WS3 . . . . . . .28 B8
Elmore Green Prim Sch
WS3 . . . . .14 B1
Elmore Green Rd WS3 . . . . . .14 B1
Elmore Rd B33 . . . . .69 A3
Elmore Row WS3 . . . . .14 B1
Elms Cl Birmingham B38 . . . .123 C8
Solihull B91 . . . . .107 D5
Elms Dr WS11 . . . . .1 C1
Elms Farm Prim Sch B33 . . . .89 C7
Elms Rd B27 . . . . .46 C3
Elms The Bedworth CV12 . . . .77 E2
Birmingham B17 . . . . .65 E6
Leek Wootton CV35 . . . . .155 F6
Wolverhampton WV11 . . . . .26 B5
Elmsdale WV6 . . . . .24 A2
Elmsdale Ave CV6 . . . . .95 F2
Elmsdale Ct 8 WS1 . . . . .42 F8
Elmstead Ave B33 . . . . .89 D7
Elmstead Cl WS5 . . . . .29 E1
Elmstead Twr 2 B5 . . . . .86 E7
Elmstead Wood WS5 . . . . .29 E1
Elmstone Cl B97 . . . . .158 C5
Elmtree Rd Aldridge B74 . . . . .30 D1
Sutton Coldfield B74 . . . . .44 D8
Elmwood Ave
Coventry CV6 . . . . .112 F5
Essington WV11 . . . . .13 A3
Elmwood Cl
Balsall Common CV7 . . . . .130 C7
Cannock WS11 . . . . .2 A3
Elmwood Ct
Birmingham B5 . . . . .86 D6
Coventry CV1 . . . . .165 B4
Sutton Coldfield B74 . . . . .45 A1
Elmwood Gdns B20 . . . . .55 A2
Elmwood Gr B47 . . . . .125 A6
Elmwood Rd
Birmingham B24 . . . . .57 C2
Stourbridge DY8 . . . . .60 C2
Sutton Coldfield B74 . . . . .45 A5
Elmwood Rise DY3 . . . . .39 B1
Elmwoods B32 . . . . .84 B2
Elphin Cl CV6 . . . . .95 A4
Elphinstone End B24 . . . . .57 C6
Elsma Rd B68 . . . . .84 C8
Elston Hall La WV10 . . . . .11 D1
Elston Hall Prim Sch
WV10 . . . . .11 D2
Elstree Rd B23 . . . . .56 E5
Elswick Gr B44 . . . . .56 B8
Elswick Pl B44 . . . . .45 B1
Elsworth Gr B25 . . . . .88 C6
Elsworth Ho B31 . . . . .103 C2
Eltham Gr B44 . . . . .45 B1
Eltham Rd CV3 . . . . .133 C7
Elton Cl
Royal Leamington Spa
CV32 .157 C2

Elton Cl *continued*
Wolverhampton WV10 .....11 E4
Elton Croft B93 ....127 F4
Elton Gr B27 ....88 A2
Eltonia Croft B26 ....89 B6
Elunda Gr WS7 ....6 E5
Elva Croft B36 ....58 F1
Elvers Green La B92,B93 .128 E7
Elvetham Rd B15 ....86 C8
Elviron Dr WV6 ....24 B5
Elwell Cres DY1 ....50 F5
Elwell St
Wednesbury WS10 ....42 B3
West Bromwich B70 ....52 E5
Elwells Cl WV14 ....40 A3
Elwy Circ CV7 ....95 C6
Elwyn Rd B73 ....46 A3
Ely Cl Birmingham B37 .....70 B2
Blackheath B65 ....63 E4
Cannock WS11 ....2 B1
Coventry CV2 ....115 A6
Kidderminster DY11 ......116 A6
Ely Cres B71 ....53 B7
Ely Gr B32 ....84 F4
Ely Pl WS2 ....28 B1
Ely Rd WS2 ....28 B1
Emay Cl B70 ....52 F8
Embankment The DY5 ....61 E3
Embassy Dr
Birmingham B15 ....86 B8
Oldbury B69 ....63 E8
Embassy Ind Est 1 DY9 ..81 F5
Embassy Rd B69 ....63 E8
Embassy Wlk CV2 ....114 D8
Emberton Way B77 ....21 F5
Embleton Cl LE10 ....71 B1
Embleton Gr B34 ....69 A6
Emerald Ct Birmingham B8 .68 C5
5 Solihull B92 ....88 F1
Emerald Way CV31 ....161 F5
Emerson Cl DY3 ....50 A4
Emerson Gr WV10 ....25 F8
Emerson Rd
Birmingham B17 ....85 C6
Coventry CV2 ....114 C3
Wolverhampton WV10 ......25 F8
Emery Cl Birmingham B23 ..56 D1
Coventry CV2 ....114 E7
Walsall WS1 ....42 F8
Emery Ct DY10 ....116 E7
Emery St WS1 ....42 F8
Emily Gdns B16 ....65 F3
Emily Rd B26 ....88 D6
Emily Smith Ho 2 CV2 ...96 B1
Emily St Birmingham B12 ...86 F7
West Bromwich B70 ....53 B2
Emmanuel Rd
Burntwood WS7 ....7 B7
Sutton Coldfield B73 ......57 B8
Emmeline St B9 ....67 B1
Emmott Dr CV31 ....162 B5
Empire Cl WS9 ....29 F8
Empire Ind Est WS9 ....15 F1
Empire Ind Pk WS9 ....29 F8
Empire Rd CV4 ....111 E2
Empress Way WS10 ....41 D8
Emscote Dr B73 ....57 B7
Emscote Gn B91 ....106 E2
Emscote Inf Sch CV34 ...161 B8
Emscote Lawn Prep Sch
CV34 ....161 A8
Emscote Rd
Birmingham B6 ....55 F1
Coventry CV3 ....114 C2
Warwick CV34 ....161 B8
Emsworth Cres WV9 ....11 A2
Emsworth Gr B14 ....104 D6
Ena Rd CV1 ....113 D5
End Hall Rd WV6 ....24 A3
Endemere Rd CV6 ....113 D7
Enderby Cl B93 ....127 F4
Enderby Dr WV4 ....39 A5
Enderby Gr 9 B18 ....65 E4
Enderby Rd B23 ....56 C7
Enderley Cl WS3 ....14 B3
Enderley Dr WS3 ....14 B3
Endhill Rd B44 ....45 A3
Endicott Rd B6 ....55 F1
Endmoor Gr B23 ....56 D6
Endsleigh Gdns CV31 ....162 B6
Endsleigh Gr B28 ....106 A8
Endwood Court Rd B20 ...55 A2
Endwood Ct
Birmingham B11 ....87 D4
Birmingham, Handsworth Wood
B20 ....55 A2
Endwood Dr
Little Aston B74 ....31 C4
Solihull B91 ....106 F2
Enfield Cl B23 ....56 F6
Enfield Ind Est B97 ......153 D5
Enfield Rd
Birmingham B15 ....86 B8
Blackheath B65 ....63 D3
Coventry CV2 ....114 B3
Redditch B97 ....158 D5
Enford Cl B34 ....69 D6
Engadine Rd B60 ....137 C1
Engine La Bilston WS10 ....41 A4
Brierley Hill DY5 ....61 F4
Stourbridge DY9 ....81 D6
Tamworth B77 ....22 A2
Walsall WS8 ....15 C8
Engine St Oldbury B69 .....64 B6
Smethwick B66 ....65 B6
England Cres CV31 ......161 E7
England Ho 9 CV32 .....156 F2
Englestede Cl B20 ....54 F3
Engleton Rd CV6 ....113 A6
Englewood Dr B28 ....106 A8
English Martyrs Prim Sch
B11 ....87 C4
Ennerdale Cl
Brownhills WS8 ....15 E7
Royal Leamington Spa
CV32 ....156 D2
Ennerdale Cres CV11 .....73 F6
Ennerdale Dr
Halesowen B63 ....82 D2
Perton WV6 ....23 F4
Ennerdale La CV2 ....114 F4
Ennerdale Rd
Birmingham B43 ....54 F6
Wolverhampton WV6 ......24 D8
Ennersdale Bglws B46 .....59 F1
Ennersdale Cl B46 ....59 F1
Ennersdale Rd B46 ....59 F1
Enright Cl CV32 ....156 E2
Ensall Dr DY8 ....60 E1
Ensbury Cl WV12 ....27 D4
Ensdale Row WV13 ....27 A1
Ensdon Gr B44 ....45 B1
Ensford Cl B74 ....31 E5
Ensign Bsns Ctr CV4 ....131 F6
Ensign Cl CV4 ....111 D1
Ensor Cl CV11 ....74 A6
Ensor Dr B78 ....22 F1
Enstone Rd
Birmingham B23 ....57 A7
Dudley DY1 ....61 F8
Enterprise Dr
Stourbridge DY9 ....81 F6
Sutton Coldfield B74 ......44 E7
Enterprise Gr WS3 ....15 B5
Enterprise Ho B92 ....109 A6
Enterprise Ind Pk WS13 ....9 F8
Enterprise Trad Est DY5 ..61 F3
Enterprise Way B7 ....164 D4
Enterprise Workshops
DY6 ....61 A7
Enville Cl Birmingham B37 ..70 B1
Walsall WS3 ....14 A3
Enville Gr B11 ....87 D5
Enville Pl DY8 ....80 E5
Enville Rd Dudley DY3 .....50 D4
Kingswinford DY6 ....60 B8
Wolverhampton WV4 ......38 C4
Enville St DY8 ....80 F5
Epperston Ct CV31 ......161 F7
Epping Cl
Birmingham B45 ....102 B2
Walsall WS3 ....28 F6
Epping Gr B44 ....56 A7
Epping Way CV32 ....157 C4
Epsom Cl Bedworth CV12 ..78 B4
Lichfield WS14 ....9 D7
Perton WV6 ....23 F4
Redditch B97 ....158 C8
Tamworth B77 ....35 C4
Epsom Ct 16 B29 ....103 C7
Epsom Dr CV3 ....134 C6
Epsom Gr B44 ....56 B8
Epsom Rd Catshill B61 ...121 A1
Royal Leamington Spa
CV32 ....157 C4
Epwell Gr B44 ....55 F6
Epwell Rd B44 ....55 F6
Epworth Ct DY5 ....61 B5
Erasmus Rd B11 ....87 A7
Erasmus Way WS13 ....9 A8
Ercall Cl B23 ....56 A6
Erdington Coll B24 ....57 A4
Erdington Hall Prim Sch
B24 ....56 F1
Erdington Hall Rd B24 ....56 F2
Erdington Ind Pk B24 .....57 F4
Erdington Rd WS9 ....30 C3
Erdington Sta B23 ....56 F5
Eric Grey Cl CV2 ....114 A5
Erica Ave CV12 ....77 F2
Erica Cl B29 ....103 A8
Erica Dr CV31 ....162 B2
Erica Rd WS5 ....43 B3
Eringden B77 ....22 B1
Erithway Rd CV3 ....133 B4
Ermington Cres B36 ......68 E7
Ermington Rd WV4 ....39 D4
Ernesford Grange Prim Sch
CV3 ....114 E1
Ernesford Grange Sch & Com
Coll CV3 ....134 D8
Ernest Clarke Cl WV12 ...27 C4
Ernest Ct B38 ....104 A1
Ernest Rd Birmingham B12 .87 B4
Dudley DY2 ....51 F1
Smethwick B67 ....64 E6
Ernest Richards Rd CV12 .78 B4
Ernest St B1 ....164 B1
Ernsford Ave CV3 ....114 B1
Ernsford Cl B93 ....127 F2
Erskine Cl LE10 ....71 A2
Erskine St B7 ....67 B3
Erwood Cl B97 ....153 B2
Esher Dr CV3 ....133 E7
Esher Rd Birmingham B44 ..44 F4
West Bromwich B71 ....53 D6
Esk Ho 1 DY1 ....61 E8
Eskdale Cl WV1 ....26 A2
Eskdale Rd LE10 ....75 A7
Eskdale Wlk
Brierley Hill DY5 ....81 B8
Coventry CV3 ....134 D7
Eskrett St WS12 ....2 C5
Esme Rd B11 ....87 B4
Esmond Cl B30 ....103 D5
Essendon Gr B8 ....68 B4
Essendon Rd B8 ....68 B4
Essendon Wlk B8 ....68 B4
Essex Ave
Kingswinford DY6 ....60 B5
Wednesbury WS10 ....42 C4
West Bromwich B71 ....53 D7
Essex Cl Coventry CV5 ....112 B3
Kenilworth CV8 ....147 E2
Essex Ct
5 Birmingham B29 ......103 C7
Warwick CV34 ....160 E8
Essex Dr WS12 ....2 B4
Essex Gdns DY8 ....80 D7
Essex Ho 2 WV3 ....25 C4
Essex Rd Dudley DY2 ......62 A6
Sutton Coldfield B75 ......32 D2
Essex St Birmingham B5 ..164 C1
Walsall WS2 ....28 E5
Essington Cl Lichfield WS14 ..9 A5
Shenstone WS14 ....18 A7
Stourbridge DY8 ....60 E1
Essington Ind Est WV11 ..12 F4
Essington Rd WV12 ....13 B1
Essington St B16 ....66 B1
Essington Way WV1 ......26 B1
Este Rd B26 ....69 A1
Esterton Cl CV6 ....95 C2
Estone Wlk B6 ....66 F7
Estria Rd B15 ....86 B7
Estridge La WS6 ....5 A2
Etchell Rd B78 ....20 F3
Ethel Rd B17 ....85 D5
Ethel St Birmingham B2 ..164 B2
Oldbury B68 ....64 A4
Smethwick B67 ....64 F2
Ethelfield Rd CV2 ....114 B3
Ethelfleda Rd B77 ....35 F5
Ethelfleda Terr WS10 .....41 F3
Ethelred Cl B74 ....32 A3
Etheridge Rd WV14 ....40 D7
Eton Cl DY3 ....50 F6
Eton Ct Lichfield WS14 ......9 B6
Sutton Coldfield B74 ......31 F2
Eton Dr DY8 ....81 A3
Eton Rd B12 ....87 B4
Eton Wlk DY9 ....99 A6
Etone Com Sch CV11 .....73 D5
Etone Ct CV11 ....73 B5
Etruria Way WV14 ....40 E7
Etta Gr B44 ....44 F4
Ettingley Cl B98 ....159 B5
Ettingshall Park Farm La
WV4 ....39 E4
Ettingshall Prim Sch
WV14 ....40 B6
Ettingshall Rd WV2 ......40 A7
Ettington Cl B93 ....127 D2
Ettington Rd
Birmingham B6 ....66 E8
Coventry CV5 ....112 A3
Ettymore Cl DY3 ....50 D8
Ettymore Rd DY3 ....50 D8
Ettymore Rd W DY3 ....50 C8
Etwall Rd B28 ....105 E6
Euan Cl B17 ....85 C8
Eunal Ct B97 ....158 E5
Euro Bsns Pk B69 ....52 D1
Euro Ct B13 ....87 B2
Europa Ave B70 ....53 F2
Europa Way Lichfield WS13 ..9 F8
Royal Leamington Spa
CV34 ....161 D5
European Bsns Pk B69 ...63 E7
Eustace Rd CV12 ....79 D1
Euston Cres CV3 ....134 C6
Euston Pl CV32 ....161 F8
Euston Sq 1 CV32 ......161 F8
Eva Rd Birmingham B18 ...65 D6
Oldbury B68 ....64 D3
Evans Cl Bedworth CV12 ...78 C3
Dudley DY4 ....51 C5
Evans Croft B78 ....21 A1
Evans Gdns B29 ....85 D1
Evans Gr CV31 ....162 A2
Evans Pl WV14 ....40 E7
Evans St Willenhall WV13 ..26 D1
Wolverhampton, Cinder Hill
WV4,WV14 ....39 F1
Wolverhampton, Dunstall Hill
WV6 ....25 B4
Evason Ct B6 ....55 E1
Eve La DY1 ....50 F5
Evelyn Ave CV6 ....95 F2
Evelyn Croft B73 ....57 A8
Evelyn Rd B11 ....87 D4
Evenlode Cl Redditch B98 .153 F1
Solihull B92 ....89 B3
Evenlode Cres CV6 ......112 F5
Evenlode Gr WV13 ....27 D1
Evenlode Rd B92 ....89 B3
Everard Ct CV11 ....73 E2
Everdon Rd CV6 ....95 B2
Everene Ho 1 B27 ....88 C3
Everest Cl B66 ....64 F8
Everest Rd
Birmingham B20 ....55 A3
Walsall WS2 ....27 F3
Everglade Rd CV9 ....36 C1
Evergreen Cl WV14 ....51 B8
Evergreen Hts WS12 ....2 A8
Everitt Dr B93 ....128 A6
Evers St DY5 ....82 A8
Eversfield Prep Sch
B91 ....107 B4
Eversleigh Rd CV6 ......112 E7
Eversley Dale B24 ....57 A2
Eversley Gr Sedgley DY3 ..39 C2
Wolverhampton WV11 .....26 C6
Eversley Rd 2 B9 ....67 D1
Everton Rd B8 ....68 C4
Eves Croft B32 ....84 C1
Evesham Cres WS3 ....13 F3
Evesham Ct DY11 ....116 D5
Evesham Ho B60 ....137 B3
Evesham Mews 9 B97 ...153 E3
Evesham Rd B96,B97 ....158 E3
Evesham Rise DY2 ....62 D3
Evesham Sq 3 B97 ......153 E3
Evesham St B97 ....153 E3
Evesham Wlk
Coventry CV4 ....132 D5
2 Redditch B97 ....153 E4
Eveson Rd DY8 ....80 E2
Ewart Rd WS2 ....27 E3
Ewell Rd B24 ....57 B4
Ewhurst Ave B29 ....85 F1
Ewhurst Cl WV13 ....40 F8
Ewloe Cl DY10 ....116 E1
Exbury Cl WV9 ....10 F2
Exbury Way CV11 ....78 E8
Excelsior Gr WS3 ....15 B5
Exchange Ind Est The
WS11 ....4 E5
Exchange St
Brierley Hill DY5 ....61 D4
Kidderminster DY10 .....116 E6
Wolverhampton WV1 .....163 B3
Exchange The WS3 ....14 B1
Exe Croft B31 ....123 B8
Exeter Cl Coventry CV3 ...134 D8
Kidderminster DY11 .....116 A6
Exeter Dr Birmingham B37 ..89 F8
Tamworth B79 ....20 E5
Exeter Ho 8 B24 ....56 F4
Exeter Pas B1 ....164 B1
Exeter Pl WS2 ....28 B1
Exeter Rd Birmingham B29 ..85 F2
Cannock WS11 ....4 B8
Dudley DY2 ....62 D2
Smethwick B66 ....65 B5
Exeter St B1 ....164 B1
Exford Cl DY5 ....81 B7
Exhall Cedars Inf Sch
CV7 ....96 A8
Exhall Cl Redditch B98 ...154 D5
Solihull B91 ....106 E2
Exhall Ct B23 ....56 C2
Exhall Gn CV7 ....95 F7
Exhall Grange Sch CV7 ...95 C5
Exhall Rd CV7 ....95 A6
Exham Cl CV34 ....155 E1
Exhibition Way B40 ....90 D4
Exis Ct CV11 ....73 E2
Exley B77 ....21 D1
Exminster Rd CV3 ....133 E5
Exmoor Ct B61 ....137 A4
Exmoor Dr
Bromsgrove B61 ....137 A4
Royal Leamington Spa
CV32 ....157 C4
Exmoor Gn WV11 ....26 C7
Exmouth Cl CV2 ....114 C7
Exon Ct DY4 ....51 F6
Exonbury Wlk 5 WS11 .....1 F2
Expressway The B70 .....53 C4
Exton Cl Ash Green CV7 ....95 C6
Wednesfield WV11 ....26 F8
Exton Gdns B66 ....65 D6
Exton Way B8 ....67 D5
Eyffler Cl CV34 ....160 D7
Eyland Gr WS1 ....28 F2
Eymore Cl B29 ....103 B6
Eynsham Ct WV6 ....24 E5
Eyre St B18 ....66 A3
Eyston Ave DY4 ....52 D8
Eyton Cl B98 ....154 D3
Eyton Croft B12 ....86 F7
Ezekiel La WV12 ....27 C6

F

Fabian Cl
Birmingham B45 ....102 A2
Coventry CV3 ....134 D7
Fabian Cres B90 ....106 B1
Fabius Cl LE10 ....75 C7
Facet Rd B38 ....104 A2
Factory La B61 ....136 F1
Factory Rd
Birmingham B18 ....66 A6
Hinckley LE10 ....71 D1
Tipton DY4 ....51 E6
Factory St WS10 ....41 C6
Fair Isle Dr CV10 ....72 F2
Fair Lady Dr WS7 ....6 D8
Fair Oaks Dr WS6 ....14 A8
Fairbanks Cl CV2 ....115 A7
Fairbourne Ave
Birmingham B44 ....44 E2
Blackheath B65 ....63 E4
Fairbourne Gdns B97 ....158 C7
Fairbourne Twr B23 ......57 A6
Fairbourne Way CV6 .....112 E8
Fairburn Cres WS3 ....15 B5
Faircroft CV8 ....147 F3
Faircroft Ave B76 ....57 F6
Faircroft Rd B36 ....58 D1
Fairdene Way 3 B43 .....54 D8
Fairfax Ct 6 CV34 ....160 F7
Fairfax Rd
Birmingham B31 ....123 A8
Sutton Coldfield B75 ......46 F5
Wolverhampton WV10 .....11 E3
Fairfax Sch B75 ....46 F5
Fairfax St CV1 ....165 C3
Fairfield Cl WS12 ....2 D1
Fairfield Ct CV3 ....134 A7
Fairfield Dr
Halesowen B62 ....63 E1
Walsall WS3 ....15 B4
Fairfield Fst Sch B61 ...120 D3
Fairfield Gr B62 ....63 E1
Fairfield Ho B60 ....137 B3
Fairfield Mount WS1 .....42 F8
Fairfield Park Ind Est
B62 ....63 E1
Fairfield Rd
Birmingham B14 ....104 E8
Bournheath B61 ....120 D1
Dudley DY2 ....62 D7
Halesowen B63 ....83 A2
Halesowen, Hurst Green
B62 ....63 E1
Stourbridge DY8 ....60 F2
Fairfield Rise
Meriden CV7 ....92 C1
Stourbridge DY8 ....80 D5
Fairfields Hill B78 ....36 F8
Fairford Cl Redditch B98 ..154 E7
Solihull B91 ....106 D5
Fairford Gdns
Burntwood WS7 ....7 C6
Stourbridge DY8 ....60 E3
Fairford Rd B44 ....55 F6
Fairgreen Gdns DY5 ....61 C5
Fairgreen Way
Aldridge B74 ....31 A1
Birmingham B29 ....85 F1
Fairground Way WS1 .....42 D8
Fairhaven Croft B62 ......63 E1
Fairhaven Prim Sch DY8 ..60 D3
Fairhill Way B11 ....87 C7
Fairhills DY3 ....50 D8
Fairholme Rd B36 ....68 B7
Fairhurst Dr CV32 ....156 E3
Fairlands Pk CV4 ....132 F6
Fairlawn B15 ....86 A7
Fairlawn Cl
Royal Leamington Spa
CV32 ....156 D1
Willenhall WV12 ....13 C1
Fairlawn Dr DY6 ....60 D4
Fairlawn Way WV12 ....13 C1
Fairlawns Birmingham B26 ..69 A1
Sutton Coldfield B76 ......58 A8
Fairlie Cres B38 ....103 D1
Fairlight Dr B45 ....122 A1
Fairmead Rise B38 ......103 E1
Fairmile Cl CV3 ....134 C8
Fairmile Rd B63 ....83 A6
Fairmont Rd B60 ....151 B8
Fairmount Dr 5 WS11 .....4 E8
Fairoak Dr
Bromsgrove B60 ....150 F6
Wolverhampton WV6 ......24 B3
Fairview Ave B42 ....55 B6
Fairview Cl
Cheslyn Hay WS6 ....4 D2
Tamworth B77 ....21 F5
Wolverhampton WV11 .....26 B7
Fairview Cres
Kingswinford DY6 ....60 F6
Wolverhampton WV11 .....26 B7
Fairview Ct WS2 ....27 D2
Fairview Gr WV11 ....26 B7
Fairview Mews 9 B46 .....70 F7
Fairview Rd Dudley DY1 ...51 A3
Wolverhampton, Penn WV4 .38 C4
Wolverhampton, Scotlands
WV11 ....26 B7
Fairview Wlk CV6 ....95 E2
Fairway Birmingham B31 ..102 E3
Cannock WS11 ....4 D6
Nuneaton CV11 ....79 B8
Tamworth B77 ....35 F5
Walsall WS4 ....15 D1
Fairway Ave B69 ....63 A8
Fairway Ct B77 ....22 B3
Fairway Dr B45 ....121 F6
Fairway Gn WV14 ....40 D8
Fairway Prim Sch B38 ...103 D1
Fairway Rd B68 ....63 F2
Fairway Rise CV8 ....148 C6
Fairway The
Birmingham B38 ....103 D2
Hinckley LE10 ....75 F7
Fairways B93 ....128 A8
Fairways Ave DY8 ....80 E2
Fairways Cl
Coventry CV5 ....112 A6
Stourbridge DY8 ....80 E2
Fairways Dr B60 ....138 B5
Fairways The CV32 .....156 D2
Fairyfield Ave B43 ....43 D1
Fairyfield Ct B43 ....43 D1
Fakenham Croft B17 ......84 F7
Falcon B77 ....36 A6
Falcon Ave CV3 ....134 F8
Falcon Cl Cannock WS11 ....1 C2
Cheslyn Hay WS6 ....4 C2
Kidderminster DY10 .....116 E2
Nuneaton CV11 ....79 B8
Falcon Cres WV14 ....39 F2
Falcon Lodge Cres B75 ...47 A6
Falcon Pl B69 ....63 C7
Falcon Rd B68 ....63 F2
Falcon Rise DY8 ....80 C6
Falcon View B30 ....104 A4
Falcon Way DY1 ....50 F1
Falcondale Rd WV12 ......13 C1

Falconers Gn LE10 ....75 F6
Falconhurst Rd B29 ....85 C2
Falconry Ctr* DY9 ....98 F3
Falcons The B75 ....47 B5
Falfield Cl B65 ....63 D6
Falfield Gr B31 ....122 E7
Falkener Ho CV6 ....113 E7
Falkland Cl CV4 ....131 D7
Falkland Croft B30 ....104 B6
Falkland Way B36 ....70 B5
Falkwood Gr B93 ....127 F6
Falindale Rd B26 ....89 B6
Fallings Heath Cl WS10 ....30 C5
Fallings Park Ind Est
  ....25 F5
Fallow Field Cannock WS11 ..1 E3
  Lichfield WS13 ....3 C3
  Little Aston B74 ....31 B3
Fallow Hill CV31 ....162 C6
Fallow Rd B78 ....20 F1
Fallow Wlk B32 ....84 A2
Fallowfield
  Birmingham B15 ....85 E8
  Perton WV6 ....23 D4
  Wolverhampton WV8 ....10 E2
Fallowfield Ave B28 ....105 F5
Fallowfield Rd
  Blackheath B65 ....63 A3
  Halesowen B63 ....82 D3
  Solihull B92 ....89 D3
  Walsall WS5 ....43 E8
Fallowfields CV6 ....95 C4
Fallowfields Cl B61 ....136 E3
Fallows Ho B19 ....66 E5
Fallows Rd B11 ....87 C6
Falmouth Cl CV11 ....74 A5
Falmouth Dr
  Hinckley LE10 ....71 E4
  Tamworth B77 ....21 F5
Falmouth Rd
  Birmingham B34 ....68 F6
  Walsall WS5 ....43 D7
Falna Cres DY9 ....20 F7
Falstaff Ave B47 ....125 A6
Falstaff Cl Nuneaton CV11 ..74 A1
  Sutton Coldfield B76 ....58 B7
Falstaff Ct B75 ....47 C5
Falstaff Gr CV34 ....161 E3
Falstaff Ho B13 ....105 D7
Falstaff Rd Coventry CV4 ..111 E1
  Solihull B90 ....106 C1
Falstone Rd B33 ....45 D2
Fanad Ho B23 ....56 E3
Fancott Dr CV8 ....147 F6
Fancott Rd B31 ....103 A5
Fancourt Ave WV4 ....38 D4
Fane Rd WV11 ....13 B2
Fanshawe Rd B27 ....88 C1
Far Gosford St CV1 ....113 E2
Far Highfield B76 ....46 E4
Far Hill Cl B71 ....53 F8
Far Lash LE10 ....75 F7
Far Moor La B98 ....154 F5
Far View WS9 ....16 B2
Far Wood Rd B31 ....102 E8
Faraday Ave
  Birmingham B32 ....84 D5
  Curdworth B46,B76 ....59 F5
Faraday Ct B32 ....84 D5
Faraday Ho 5 B15 ....86 C8
Faraday Rd Hinckley LE10 ..74 E7
  Walsall WS2 ....28 B6
Farber Rd CV2 ....115 A6
Farbrook Way WV12 ....27 B6
Farclose Ho B15 ....86 C7
Farcroft Ave
  Birmingham B21 ....65 D8
  Coventry CV5 ....111 D4
Farcroft Gr B21 ....54 D1
Farcroft Rd B21 ....54 D1
Fardon Way B23 ....56 D8
Fareham Cres WV4 ....38 C6
Farewell La WS7 ....7 E6
Farfield
  Kidderminster DY10 ....116 F5
  Stoke Prior B60 ....150 F4
Farfield Cl B31 ....103 B2
Farfield Studios DY10 ......116 F5
Faringdon B77 ....21 F1
Farlands Dr DY8 ....81 A3
Farlands Gr B43 ....54 F7
Farlands Rd DY8 ....81 A3
Farleigh Dr WV3 ....38 A8
Farleigh Rd WV6 ....24 A3
Farley Ctr The B70 ....53 D2
Farley La B62 ....100 F1
Farley Rd B23 ....56 B4
Farley St
  Royal Leamington Spa
  CV31 ....162 B7
  Tipton DY4 ....52 D5
Farlow Cl Coventry CV6 ...114 A6
  Redditch B98 ....154 C4
Farlow Croft B37 ....89 F8
Farlow Rd B31 ....103 C3
Farm Ave B68 ....64 A3
Farm Cl Birmingham B33 ....68 F3
  Cannock WS12 ....2 C3
  Codsall WV8 ....10 B2
  Coventry CV6 ....95 B3
  Kidderminster DY11 ....116 B2
  Sedgley DY3 ....50 B7
  Solihull B92 ....89 C2
  Tamworth B79 ....21 C7
Farm Croft B19 ....66 C6
Farm House Way B43 ....43 E4
Farm Rd Birmingham B11 ....87 B7
  Blackheath B65 ....63 A4
  Brierley Hill DY5 ....61 E1
  Dudley DY2 ....62 A4
  Hinckley LE10 ....75 E6
  Kenilworth CV8 ....147 E2
  Oldbury B68 ....64 A3
  Redditch B98 ....154 A3
  Royal Leamington Spa
  CV32 ....157 B3
  Smethwick B67 ....64 E3
  Tipton DY4 ....52 B7
  Wolverhampton WV3 ....38 C8
Farm St Birmingham B19 ....66 C6
  Walsall WS2 ....28 E4
  West Bromwich B70 ....53 C1
Farman B9 ....67 B2
Farman Rd CV5 ....113 A2
Farmbridge Cl WS2 ....27 D3
Farmbridge Rd WS2 ....27 D3
Farmbridge Way WS2 ....27 D3
Farmbrook Ave WV10 ....11 D3
Farmcote Ct B97 ....158 D4
Farmcote Lodge CV2 ....96 B4
Farmcote Rd
  Birmingham B33 ....69 A4
  Coventry CV2 ....96 B4
Farmcroft Rd DY9 ....81 E5
Farmdale Gr B45 ....122 A6
Farmer Rd B10 ....88 A8
Farmer Ward Rd CV8 ....148 A3
Farmer Way DY4 ....41 C1
Farmers Cl B76 ....46 E4
Farmers Ct B63 ....82 F4
Farmers Rd B60 ....150 E7
Farmers Wlk B21 ....65 D7
Farmhouse Rd WV12 ....27 D5
Farmhouse Way
  Solihull B90 ....127 B7
  Willenhall WV12 ....27 D5
Farmoor Gr B34 ....69 E6
Farmoor Way WV10 ....11 E4
Farmside CV3 ....134 D5
Farmside Cl DY9 ....82 A3
Farmside Gr WV4 ....10 F2
Farmstead Cl WS1 ....42 E5
Farmstead Rd B92 ....89 C2
Farmstead The CV8 ....134 B8
Farnborough Cl B98 ....154 F1
Farnborough Ct B75 ....32 C2
Farnborough Dr B90 ....126 F6
Farnborough Rd B35 ....58 B3
Farnbury Croft B38 ....104 B2
Farncote Dr B74 ....31 F3
Farndale Ave
  Coventry CV6 ....95 D3
  Wolverhampton WV6 ....24 F5
Farndale Cl DY5 ....81 B6
Farndale Jun Sch WV6 ....25 A4
Farndon Ave B37 ....90 C3
Farndon Cl CV12 ....79 B3
Farndon Rd B8 ....67 F4
Farneway LE10 ....71 B1
Farnham Cl B43 ....54 F8
Farnham Rd B21 ....54 E2
Farnhurst Rd B36 ....68 B7
Farnol Rd B26 ....68 F1
Farnworth Gr B36 ....58 E1
Farquhar Rd
  Birmingham, Edgbaston B15 ..85 F6
  Birmingham, Moseley B13 ..86 F3
Farquhar Rd E B15 ....85 F6
Farr Dr CV4 ....112 B2
Farran Way B43 ....54 E7
Farren Rd
  Birmingham B31 ....102 D1
  Coventry CV2 ....114 E5
Farrier Cl
  Bromsgrove B60 ....150 E6
  Sutton Coldfield B76 ....57 F8
Farrier Rd B43 ....44 D3
Farrier Way DY6 ....60 A7
Farriers Mill WS3 ....14 E4
Farriers The B26 ....89 B5
Farriers Way
  Hinckley LE10 ....75 F6
  Nuneaton CV11 ....73 F2
Farrington Ho 5 WS2 ....28 D3
Farrington St WS2 ....28 D3
Farrington Rd
  Birmingham B23 ....56 B5
  Wolverhampton WV4 ....39 E3
Farrow Rd B44 ....44 E3
Farthing La CV34 ....164 A3
Farthing La
  Curdworth B76 ....59 C6
  Redditch B97 ....153 B5
  Sutton Coldfield B72 ....46 B4
Farthing Pools Cl 1 B72 ....46 C4
Farthings La DY2 ....62 A7
Farthings Lodge 7 DY1 .....51 F8
Farthings The B17 ....85 D6
Farvale Rd B76 ....58 C6
Faseman Ave CV4 ....111 F3
Fashoda Rd B29 ....86 B1
Fasson Cl B77 ....35 C8
Fast Pits Rd B25 ....88 C7
Fastlea Rd B32 ....84 D1
Fastmoor Oval B33 ....69 E1
Fatherless Barn Cres
  ....82 D5
Faulconbridge Ave CV5 ....111 E4
Faulconbridge Way
  CV34 ....161 E3
Faulkland Cres WV1 ....163 C4
Faulkner Cl DY8 ....80 F4
Faulkner Rd B92 ....89 B1

Faulkners Farm Dr B23 .....56 B6
Faulkner Dr DY5 ....61 B7
Faultlands Cl CV11 ....78 F8
Faversham Cl
  Willenhall WS2 ....27 D3
  Wolverhampton WV8 ....24 E8
Fawdry Cl B73 ....46 B5
Fawdry St Birmingham B9 ...67 A2
  Smethwick B66 ....65 C5
  Wolverhampton WV1 ....163 A4
Fawley Cl Coventry CV3 ...134 C6
  Willenhall WV13 ....26 F1
Fawley Gr B14 ....104 B5
Fawn Cl WS12 ....1 C6
Faygate CV3 ....114 F3
Fazeley Rd Tamworth, B78 ..21 A4
  Tamworth, Fazeley B78 .....21 B2
Fazeley St B5 ....66 F2
Fearnings Cotts B97 ....158 D5
Fearon Pl 3 B66 ....65 A5
Featherbed La
  Coventry CV4 ....132 A5
  Redditch B97 ....158 C5
Featherston Dr LE10 ....75 E6
Featherston Rd B74 ....31 A2
Featherstone Cl
  Nuneaton CV10 ....73 C2
  Solihull B90 ....106 D2
Featherstone Cres B90 ...106 D2
Featherstone La B62 ....83 E7
Featherstone Prim Sch
  ....56 E4
Featherstone Rd B14 ....104 E6
Feckenham Ho B60 ....137 B3
Feckenham Rd
  Astwood Bank B96 ....158 E2
  Redditch, Headless Cross
  B97 ....158 C8
  Redditch, Hunt End B97 ...158 C4
Fecknam Way WS13 ....3 C1
Feilding Cl CV2 ....115 A6
Feilding Way CV10 ....72 A5
Felbrigg Cl DY5 ....81 D8
Feldings The B24 ....57 C4
Feldon La B62 ....83 E7
Felgate Cl B90 ....127 A6
Fell Gr Birmingham B21 .....54 C2
  Royal Leamington Spa
  CV32 ....157 C3
Fellbrook Cl B33 ....68 F3
Fellmeadow Rd B33 ....69 A3
Fellmeadow Way DY3 ....50 E7
Fellmore Gr CV31 ....162 D7
Fellows Ave DY6 ....60 C8
Fellows La B17 ....84 F4
Fellows Rd WV14 ....40 D7
Fellows St WV2 ....163 B1
Felspar Rd B77 ....22 B3
Felstead Cl B77 ....35 C4
Felsted Way B7 ....67 A4
Felstone Rd B44 ....44 E1
Feltham Cl B33 ....69 E1
Felton Cl Coventry CV2 ......96 E1
  Redditch B98 ....154 E1
Felton Croft B33 ....69 A3
Felton Gr B91 ....107 C1
Fen Cl DY10 ....116 E8
Fen End Rd CV8 ....129 E4
Fenbourne Cl WS4 ....29 C8
Fenchurch Cl WS2 ....28 D4
Fencote Ave B37 ....70 A4
Fenmere Cl WV4 ....39 D3
Fenn Rise Stourbridge DY8 ..60 D3
  Willenhall WV12 ....27 B5
Fenn St B77 ....21 E1
Fennel Cl WS6 ....4 E3
Fennel Croft B34 ....69 B7
Fennel Rd DY5 ....81 C7
Fennell Ho 10 CV1 ....113 B2
Fennis Cl B93 ....127 F3
Fens Cres DY5 ....61 C5
Fens Pool Ave DY5 ....61 C6
Fenside Ave CV3 ....133 D4
Fensway The B34 ....69 A5
Fenter Cl B13 ....86 F5
Fentham Cl B92 ....109 B6
Fentham Ct B92 ....106 F8
Fentham Gn B92 ....109 A7
Fentham Rd
  Birmingham, Aston B6 ....66 E8
  Birmingham, Gravelly Hill
  B23 ....56 E3
  Hampton-in-Arden B92 .....109 A6
Fenton Rd
  Birmingham B27 ....88 B5
  Hollywood B47 ....125 A7
Fenton St Brierley Hill DY5 ..61 D3
  Smethwick B66 ....64 E7
Fenton Way B27 ....88 B5
Fenwick Cl B97 ....153 B1
Fereday Rd WS9 ....16 B3
Fereday St DY4 ....51 F8
Fereday's Croft DY3 ....50 D7
Ferguson Dr DY11 ....116 A1
Ferguson Rd B68 ....64 D5
Ferguson St WV11 ....13 A1
Fern Ave DY4 ....51 F7
Fern Cl Coventry CV2 ....96 D2
  Dudley WV14 ....51 B8
  Walsall WS4 ....15 D1
Fern Dale Rd CV7 ....129 F6
Fern Dell Cl WS11 ....1 C2
Fern Dr WS6 ....5 A4
Fern Gr Coventry CV7 ....77 E2
Fern Leys WV3 ....24 D1
Fern Rd Birmingham B24 ....57 A4
  Dudley DY1 ....51 C4
  Huntington WS12 ....1 D5

Fern Rd continued
  Wolverhampton WV3 ....163 A1
Fernbank Cl B63 ....82 E2
Fernbank Cres WS5 ....43 C4
Fernbank Rd B8 ....68 A4
Ferncliffe Rd B17 ....85 B4
Ferndale Ave B43 ....54 F7
Ferndale Cl Burntwood WS7 ..7 B6
  Catshill B61 ....121 A1
  Hagley DY9 ....99 A5
  Nuneaton CV11 ....73 E5
Ferndale Cres
  Birmingham B12 ....87 A8
  Kidderminster DY11 ....116 B8
Ferndale Ct B46 ....70 F6
Ferndale Dr CV8 ....148 A3
Ferndale Pk DY9 ....99 C8
Ferndale Prim Sch B28 ......54 E8
Ferndale Rd
  Binley Woods CV3 ....135 D7
  Birmingham B28 ....105 F8
  Essington WV11 ....13 B3
  Oldbury B68 ....64 A2
  Sutton Coldfield B74 ....44 F8
Ferndene Rd B11 ....88 A3
Ferndown Ave B26 ....69 A1
Ferndown Cl
  Birmingham B26 ....69 A1
  Coventry CV4 ....112 A3
  Walsall WS3 ....14 B4
Ferndown Gdns WV11 ....26 F5
Ferndown Rd B91 ....107 C5
Ferneley Ave LE10 ....71 A3
Ferness Cl LE10 ....71 B2
Ferness Rd LE10 ....71 B2
Ferney Hill Ave B97 ....153 C3
Fernhill Ct CV8 ....147 E6
Fernhill Ct B23 ....56 C2
Fernhill Dr CV32 ....157 B1
Fernhill Gr B44 ....44 F3
Fernhill La CV7,CV8 ....129 F5
Fernhill Lodge B93 ....127 C4
Fernhurst Dr DY5 ....61 B7
Fernhurst Rd B8 ....68 A3
Fernleigh B60 ....137 A1
Fernleigh Ave WS7 ....7 A8
Fernleigh Ct B91 ....107 C5
Fernleigh Gdns DY8 ....60 C3
Fernleigh Rd WS4 ....29 B3
Fernley Ave B29 ....86 B2
Fernley Rd B11 ....87 C4
Fernside Gdns B13 ....87 B3
Fernside Rd WV13 ....26 D3
Fernwood Cl
  Redditch B98 ....159 B5
  Sutton Coldfield B73 ....45 E1
Fernwood Croft
  Birmingham B14 ....104 E6
  Tipton DY4 ....51 F4
Fernwood Rd B73 ....56 E8
Fernwoods B32 ....84 B2
Ferrers Cl Coventry CV4 ...111 F2
  Sutton Coldfield B75 ....32 D2
Ferrers Rd B77 ....21 D4
Ferrie Gr WS8 ....15 E8
Ferris Gr B27 ....88 A1
Festival Ave WS10 ....41 C4
Festival Cl Cannock WS11 ..1 E5
  Lichfield WS13 ....9 A7
Festival Mews WS12 ....1 F6
Festival Way WV6 ....25 B5
Fetherston Cres CV8 ....135 B1
Fetherston Ct 4 WS11 ......1 C5
Ffernfall Ct B23 ....56 E5
Fibbersley WV13 ....26 F4
Fibbersley Bank WV13 ....26 F4
Fiddlers Gn B92 ....109 A7
Field Ave B31 ....102 F5
Field Barn Rd CV35 ....160 A7
Field Cl Birmingham B26 ....89 A6
  Bromsgrove B60 ....150 E6
  Hinckley LE10 ....71 F3
  Kenilworth CV8 ....148 B5
  Stourbridge DY9 ....61 A2
  Walsall, Blakenall Heath
  WS3 ....28 C8
  Walsall, Pelsall WS4 ....15 B2
Field Cottage Dr DY8 ....81 B3
Field Cottage Ct CV2 ....114 D7
Field Farm La B98 ....154 D2
Field Farm Rd B77 ....21 D1
Field Head La CV34 ....160 B6
Field Head PI WV6 ....24 B4
Field Ho WS8 ....147 F5
Field La Birmingham B32 ...102 B8
  Clent DY9 ....99 D4
  Great Wyrley WS6 ....4 E3
  Solihull B91 ....108 A5
  Stourbridge DY8 ....81 A3
  Walsall WS4 ....15 B2
Field March CV3 ....134 C5
Field Maple Rd DY8 ....60 E4
Field Mews DY2 ....62 E2
Field Rd Dudley DY2 ....51 E2
  Lichfield WS13 ....3 B3
  Tipton DY4 ....52 A8
  Walsall WS3 ....14 C1
Field Rd Ind Est WS3 ....28 C8
Field St Bilston WV14 ....40 D3
  Cannock WS11 ....1 F3
  Willenhall WV13 ....27 A2
  Wolverhampton WV10 ....163 D4
Field View CV4 ....131 F8
Field View Cl CV7 ....96 A8
Field View Dr B65 ....63 F3
Field Way B94 ....143 C6
Field Wlk WS9 ....30 B7
Fieldfare WS7 ....7 D5

Fieldfare Cl B64 ....62 F4
Fieldfare Croft B36 ....70 A8
Fieldfare Ct DY10 ....117 A1
Fieldfare Rd DY9 ....81 D6
Fieldgate La
  Kenilworth CV8 ....147 F6
  Whitnash CV31 ....162 B2
Fieldgate Lawn CV8 ....147 F6
Fieldgate Trad Est WS1 ......28 F1
Fieldhead Rd B11 ....88 A3
Fieldhouse La B62 ....100 E4
Fieldhouse Rd
  Birmingham B25 ....88 C8
  Burntwood WS7 ....7 A7
  Wolverhampton WV4 ....39 E4
Fieldon Cl B90 ....106 C2
Fields The CV8 ....160 F8
Fields Ct CV34 ....160 F8
Fields The WV8 ....10 B4
Fieldside La CV3 ....114 F3
Fieldside Wlk WV14 ....40 D8
Fieldview Cl WV14 ....40 E2
Fieldways Ct B47 ....125 A7
Fiery Hill Dr B45 ....138 C8
Fiery Hill Rd B45 ....138 C8
Fife Rd CV5 ....113 A1
Fife St CV11 ....73 A4
Fifield Cl CV11 ....73 D2
Fifield Gr B33 ....68 F3
Fifth Ave Birmingham B9 ....67 F2
  Wolverhampton WV10 ....25 C7
Filey B77 ....21 F3
Filey Cl WS11 ....4 C8
Filey Rd WV10 ....11 B2
Fillingham Cl B37 ....70 D1
Fillongley Rd CV7 ....92 E3
Filton Ave WS7 ....7 A8
Filton Croft B35 ....58 A4
Fimbrell Cl DY5 ....81 A8
Finbury Cl B92 ....88 F1
Finch Cl Blackheath B65 ....62 E4
  Coventry CV6 ....95 D2
Finch Croft CV7 ....130 B7
Finch Dr B74 ....45 A6
Finch Rd B19 ....66 C8
Finchall Croft B92 ....107 E7
Fincham Cl WV9 ....11 A3
Finchdene Gr WV3 ....24 D1
Finches End B34 ....69 C5
Finchfield Cl DY8 ....80 C4
Finchfield Gdns WV3 ....24 E1
Finchfield Hill WV3 ....24 C1
Finchfield La WV3 ....38 C8
Finchfield Rd WV3 ....24 E1
Finchfield Rd W WV3 ....24 D1
Finchley Ave 1 B19 ....66 C8
Finchley Cl DY3 ....50 C7
Finchley Rd B44 ....45 B1
Finchmead Rd B33 ....69 E2
Finchpath Rd B70 ....53 A6
Findlay Rd B14 ....86 E1
Findon Cl Bulkington CV12 ..79 C3
  Redditch B97 ....153 A5
Findon Rd B8 ....68 B6
Findon St DY10 ....116 F6
Finford Croft CV7 ....130 B6
Fingal Cl CV3 ....34 A2
Finger Post Dr WS3 ....15 A5
Fingest Cl CV5 ....112 B4
Finham Cres CV8 ....148 B6
Finham Flats CV8 ....148 B6
Finham Green Rd CV3 .....133 B3
Finham Park Sch CV3 ......133 A4
Finham Prim Sch CV3 .....133 B3
Finham Rd CV8 ....148 B6
Finings Ct 7 CV32 ....156 F2
Finlarigg Dr B15 ....85 E6
Finlay Ct CV1 ....165 C1
Finmere Rd B28 ....105 F8
Finnemore Cl CV3 ....133 B5
Finnemore Rd B9 ....68 A2
Finney Well Cl WV14 ....40 B3
Finsbury Dr DY5 ....81 C7
Finsbury Gr B23 ....56 D6
Finstall Cl Birmingham B7 ..67 A4
  Sutton Coldfield B72 ....46 C1
Finstall Rd Blakedown B60 ..137 B1
Finstall Rd
  Bromsgrove B60 ....151 C8
Finstall B60 ....137 D1
Finwood Cl B92 ....107 E8
Finwood Rd CV35 ....144 F3
Fir Ave B12 ....87 A5
Fir Cl WS12 ....1 D8
Fir Croft DY5 ....81 C8
Fir Gr Birmingham B14 .....104 F5
  Coventry CV4 ....112 A2
  Stourbridge DY9 ....81 A6
  Wolverhampton WV3 ....25 A1
Fir St DY3 ....49 F7
Fir Tree Ave CV4 ....112 B2
Fir Tree Cl
  Birmingham B44 ....55 F7
  Redditch B97 ....153 D4
  Tamworth B79 ....20 E7
Fir Tree Dr Dudley DY3 ......50 F7
  Walsall WS5 ....43 B4
Fir Tree Gr
  Nuneaton CV11 ....78 D8
  Sutton Coldfield B73 ....45 F1
Fir Tree Prim Sch WS5 ......43 A4
Fir Tree Rd WV3 ....38 D8
Firbank Cl B30 ....04 A3
Firbank Way WS3 ....14 F2
Firbarn Cl B76 ....46 D3
Firbeck Gr B44 ....45 A1
Firbeck Rd B44 ....45 A1

Fircroft Bilston WV14 ....41 A3
Birmingham B31 ....102 F8
Solihull B91 ....106 F6
■9 Wolverhampton WV4 ....39 F4
Fircroft Cl
■3 Cannock WS11 ....2 A3
Stoke Heath B60 ....150 D6
Fircroft Coll B29 ....103 D8
Fircroft Ho B37 ....70 A2
Fire Station Rd B26 ....90 C5
Firecrest Cl
Birmingham B23 ....56 B7
Cannock WS11 ....2 C2
Firecrest Way DY10 ....117 B1
Firethorn Cres CV31 ....162 A2
Firhill Croft B14 ....104 D2
Firleigh Dr CV12 ....79 D2
Firmstone Ct DY8 ....80 E7
Firmstone St DY8 ....80 E7
Firs Cl Marlbrook B60 ....121 D1
Smethwick B67 ....65 A5
Firs Cl The DY10 ....117 A5
Firs Dr B90 ....106 A1
Firs Farm Dr B36 ....68 F7
Firs Ho B36 ....68 F8
Firs La B67 ....65 A5
Firs Prim Sch B36 ....68 F8
Firs Rd DY6 ....60 E6
Firs St DY2 ....51 D1
Firs The Bedworth CV12 ....77 E2
Birmingham B11 ....87 C6
Cannock WS11 ....2 A2
Coventry CV5 ....133 B8
Kidderminster DY10 ....117 A5
Meriden CV7 ....92 B1
Wolverhampton WV11 ....26 B5
Firsbrook Cl WV6 ....25 A5
Firsbrook Ho WV6 ....25 A5
Firsby Rd B32 ....84 E5
Firsholm Cl B73 ....57 A7
First Ave
Birmingham, Bordesley Green B9 ....67 E1
Birmingham, Selly Oak B29 ....86 B3
Birmingham, Tyburn B35 ....58 A5
Birmingham, Witton B6 ....55 F2
Brownhills WS8 ....16 A8
Coventry CV3 ....114 C1
Kingswinford DY6 ....61 A8
Sedgley DY6 ....50 A1
Wolverhampton WV10 ....25 E6
First Exhibition Ave B40 ....90 D4
First Meadow Piece B32 ....84 E4
Firsvale Rd WV11 ....26 F5
Firsway WV6 ....24 A2
Firswood Rd B33 ....69 C1
Firth Dr Birmingham B14 ....105 B5
Halesowen B62 ....83 E8
Firth Park Cres B62 ....83 E8
Firtree Rd B24 ....57 B2
Fish Hill B97 ....153 E4
Fish House La B60 ....150 E4
Fisher Cl B45 ....101 E2
Fisher Rd Coventry CV6 ....113 E8
Oldbury B69 ....64 C7
Walsall WS3 ....13 F2
Fisher St Brierley Hill DY5 ....61 B2
Cannock WS12 ....1 F8
Dudley DY2 ....51 D1
Tipton, Burnt Tree DY4 ....52 A3
Tipton, Great Bridge DY4 ....52 D5
Willenhall WV13 ....27 C2
Wolverhampton WV3 ....39 B8
Fisher's Ct CV34 ....160 D4
Fishers Dr B90 ....125 F5
Fishing Line Rd B97 ....153 E5
Fishley Cl WS3 ....14 C4
Fishley La WS3 ....14 D5
Fishponds Rd CV8 ....147 E3
Fishpool Cl B36 ....68 C8
Fishpool La CV7 ....91 B5
Fistral Gdns WV3 ....38 F7
Fitchet's Bank WS7 ....7 F6
Fithern Cl DY3 ....50 E5
Fitters Mill Cl B5 ....86 E6
Fitton Ave DY6 ....61 A5
Fitton St CV11 ....73 B3
Fitz Roy Ave B17 ....84 F7
Fitzgerald Pl DY5 ....81 B6
Fitzguy Cl B70 ....53 E1
Fitzmaurice Rd WV11 ....27 A7
Fitzroy Cl CV2 ....115 B6
Fitzroy Rd B31 ....102 D3
Fitzwarren Specl Sch DY4 ....52 A6
Five Fields Rd WV12 ....27 A5
Five Oaks Rd WV13 ....40 E8
Five Ways Birmingham B33 ....68 D2
Birmingham, Bordesley Green B9 ....67 D2
Birmingham, Ladywood B16 ....66 B1
Blackheath B64 ....82 C8
Churchill DY10 ....98 A5
Dudley DY3 ....50 D3
Wolverhampton, Dunstall Hill WV3 ....25 C4
Wolverhampton, Merry Hill WV3 ....38 C7
Wroxall CV35 ....145 F1
Five Ways Prim Sch WS12 ....2 D2
Five Ways Rd CV35 ....145 F1
Five Ways Sta B15 ....86 B8
Fivefield Rd CV7 ....94 E5
Fives Gr WS7 ....6 C8
Flackwell Rd B23 ....56 E7
Fladbury Cl Dudley DY2 ....62 D3
Redditch B98 ....159 B8
Fladbury Cres B29 ....85 D1
Fladbury Gdns B20 ....66 C8
Fladbury Pl ■3 B19 ....66 C7
Flamboro' Cl CV3 ....134 F8
Flamborough Cl B34 ....69 A7
Flamborough Way WV14 ....51 B7
Flamville Rd LE10 ....76 B5
Flanders Cl B98 ....154 D5
Flanders Dr DY6 ....60 D8
Flash La WV4 ....37 E2
Flash Rd B69 ....64 A7
Flatlea B31 ....102 F4
Flats La WS14 ....19 A6
Flats The B61 ....136 F3
Flatts The WS10 ....41 E7
Flaunden Cl CV5 ....112 B4
Flavel Cres CV31 ....161 F7
Flavel Rd B60 ....150 E7
Flavell Ave WV14 ....40 D1
Flavell Cl B32 ....84 B1
Flavell St DY1 ....51 B6
Flavells La
Birmingham B25 ....88 C8
Dudley DY3 ....50 B2
Flax Cl B47 ....125 A5
Flax Gdns B38 ....123 F8
Flax Hill Jun Sch B79 ....21 B7
Flaxhall St WS2 ....42 B8
Flaxley Cl B33 ....68 F3
Flaxley Rd B33 ....68 E4
Flaxton Gr B33 ....69 A4
Flaxton Wlk WV6 ....25 A5
Flecknoe Cl B36 ....58 C1
Flecknose St CV3 ....134 C6
Fledburgh Dr B76 ....46 D4
Fleet Ho CV1 ....165 B2
Fleet St Birmingham B3 ....164 A3
Coventry CV1 ....165 B3
Fleetwood Gr B26 ....69 A1
Fleetwood Ho ■3 B13 ....86 F4
Fleming Pl WS2 ....28 A6
Fleming Rd
Birmingham B32 ....84 D5
Hinckley LE10 ....74 F7
Walsall WS2 ....28 A6
Fletchamstead Highway CV5 ....132 D7
Fletcher Gr B93 ....128 B4
Fletcher Rd Hinckley LE10 ....75 E7
Walsall WV12 ....13 D1
Willenhall WV12 ....27 D8
Fletcher St DY9 ....81 F5
Fletcher's La WV13 ....27 C2
Fletchworth Gate CV5 ....132 D8
Fletton Gr B14 ....105 A3
Fleur de-lys Ct CV34 ....161 B8
Flinkford Cl WS5 ....43 D6
Flinn Cl WS14 ....9 D7
Flint Cl DY10 ....116 E2
Flint Green Rd B27 ....88 B3
Flint Ho ■3 WV3 ....25 C4
Flint Twr B18 ....65 E4
Flintham Cl B92 ....88 E3
Flintway The B33 ....68 E4
Flood St DY2 ....51 D1
Flood Street Island DY2 ....62 D8
Floodgate St B5 ....66 F1
Flora Cl B79 ....21 C7
Flora Rd B25 ....88 B7
Florence Ave
Birmingham B11 ....87 C5
■5 Sutton Coldfield B73 ....57 B7
Wolverhampton WV4 ....40 A4
Florence Bldgs ■3 B29 ....85 F2
Florence Cl CV12 ....95 F8
Florence Dr ■4 B73 ....57 B7
Florence Gr
■2 Birmingham B18 ....65 E4
West Bromwich B71 ....42 E1
Florence Pl ■10 B12 ....87 A6
Florence Rd
Birmingham, Acock's Green B27 ....88 D4
Birmingham, Handsworth B21 ....65 D8
Birmingham, King's Heath B14 ....104 F8
Codsall WV8 ....10 C3
Oldbury B69 ....63 E7
Smethwick B66 ....65 B4
Sutton Coldfield B73 ....57 B7
Tipton DY4 ....52 A7
West Bromwich B70 ....53 E1
Florence St
Birmingham B1 ....164 B1
Cannock WS12 ....2 B7
Walsall WS1 ....29 A1
Florence Villas B11 ....87 C7
Florendine Com Prim Sch B77 ....21 F5
Florendine St B77 ....21 F5
Florian Gr WS10 ....41 E7
Florian Way LE10 ....71 A1
Florida Way DY6 ....61 A6
Flowerdale Cl WV14 ....51 B8
Flowerdale Dr CV2 ....114 B6
Floyd Gr CV7 ....130 C7
Floyds La WS4 ....29 C6
Floyer Rd B10 ....67 F1
Flude Rd CV7 ....95 C6
Flyford Cl B98 ....153 F1
Flyford Croft B29 ....84 F2
Flynt Ave CV5 ....112 B6
Fockbury Mill La B61 ....136 E5
Fockbury Rd B61 ....136 B5
Foden Cl WS14 ....17 F6
Foden Rd B42 ....55 A7
Foinavon Cl B65 ....62 F6
Fold St WV1 ....163 B2
Fold The Birmingham B38 ....104 A1
Darlaston WS10 ....41 D6
Wolverhampton WV4 ....38 F4
Foldyard Cl B76 ....58 A8
Foleshill CE Prim Sch CV6 ....96 A2
Foleshill Rd CV1,CV6 ....113 D6
Foley Ave WV6 ....24 C3
Foley Church Cl B74 ....31 A2
Foley Ct B74 ....30 F1
Foley Dr WV6 ....24 C3
Foley Gdns B60 ....150 E3
Foley Ind Est DY11 ....116 D3
Foley Park Fst Sch DY11 ....116 D3
Foley Rd Birmingham B8 ....68 B5
Stourbridge DY9 ....81 C2
Foley Rd E B74 ....31 A2
Foley Rd W B74 ....30 E1
Foley St WS10 ....42 A3
Foley Wood Cl B74 ....30 E1
Foliot Fields B25 ....88 D8
Folkes Rd DY9 ....82 A6
Folkestone Croft B36 ....68 E8
Folkland Gn CV6 ....113 A7
Folliott Rd B33 ....69 B3
Folly The B97 ....158 D8
Follyhouse Cl WS1 ....42 F7
Follyhouse La WS1 ....42 F7
Fontenaye Rd B79 ....20 F7
Fontley Cl B26 ....69 A2
Fontmell Cl CV2 ....115 A4
Fontwell Rd WV10 ....11 D4
Footherley La WS14 ....17 E3
Footherley Rd WS14 ....17 F5
Ford Brook La WS3 ....15 B2
Ford Cotts CV33 ....157 F2
Ford Rd B61 ....136 E1
Ford St Birmingham B18 ....66 B5
Coventry CV1 ....165 C3
Nuneaton CV10 ....72 E4
Smethwick B67 ....64 F6
Walsall WS2 ....42 C7
Fordbridge Cl B97 ....153 C1
Fordbridge Inf Sch B37 ....70 A5
Fordbridge Rd B37 ....70 A5
Forde Way Gdns B38 ....123 D7
Forder Gr B14 ....105 A2
Fordfield Rd B33 ....69 C4
Fordham Gr WV9 ....11 A3
Fordhouse La B30 ....104 B6
Fordhouse Rd
Bromsgrove B60 ....137 B1
Wolverhampton WV10 ....11 D1
Fordhouse Road Ind Est WV10 ....25 D8
Fordraught La B62 ....101 B1
Fordrift The B37 ....90 A6
Fordrough B25 ....87 F7
Fordrough Ave B9 ....67 E3
Fordrough La B9 ....67 E2
Fordrough The
Birmingham B31 ....103 C1
Hollywood B90 ....125 C7
Sutton Coldfield B74 ....32 A1
Fords Rd B90 ....125 E7
Fordwater Rd B74 ....44 F6
Fordwell Cl CV5 ....112 F3
Fore St B2 ....164 C2
Foredraft Cl B32 ....84 C2
Foredraft St B63 ....82 D5
Foredraught B80 ....159 E4
Foredrift Cl B98 ....153 E2
Foredrove La B92 ....107 E7
Foregate St B96 ....158 E1
Foreland Way CV6 ....95 A3
Forelands Gr B61 ....150 D8
Forest Ave WS3 ....28 D7
Forest Cl Lickey End B60 ....137 B6
Smethwick B66 ....64 E7
Sutton Coldfield B74 ....44 E7
Forest Ct Birmingham B13 ....87 A3
Coventry CV5 ....112 A4
Dorridge B93 ....127 F3
Willenhall WV12 ....27 C8
Forest Dale B45 ....122 B6
Forest Dr Birmingham B17 ....85 D6
Blackheath B64 ....62 F3
Forest Gate WV12 ....27 D8
Forest Glade WS6 ....4 F2
Forest Hill Rd B26 ....89 C5
Forest La WS2 ....28 D5
Forest Lawns B74 ....31 C3
Forest Oak Specl Sch B36 ....58 E1
Forest Pk B76 ....46 E4
Forest Pl WS3 ....28 E6
Forest Rd
Birmingham, Moseley B13 ....87 A3
Birmingham, South Yardley B25 ....88 C6
Dorridge B93 ....127 F3
Dudley DY1 ....51 C4
Hinckley LE10 ....75 F8
Oldbury B68 ....84 C7
Forest View B97 ....158 E6
Forest Way
Great Wyrley WS6 ....5 A1
Hollywood B47 ....125 B6
Nuneaton CV10 ....72 E2
Forester Way DY10 ....116 E3
Forester's Rd CV3 ....133 E6
Forfar Wlk B38 ....103 D2
Forfield Pl CV31 ....162 A7
Forfield Rd CV6 ....112 E5
Forge Cl Burntwood WS7 ....7 D5
Wolverhampton WV8 ....10 E1
Forge Croft B76 ....58 B6
Forge Dr B61 ....136 F3
Forge La
Aldridge, Leighswood WS9 ....30 A5
Aldridge, Mill Green WS9 ....30 F7
Belbroughton DY9 ....119 D7
Blackheath B64 ....82 B8
Blakedown DY10 ....98 B1
Burntwood WS7 ....7 F6
Halesowen B62 ....83 C5
Kingswinford DY6 ....60 A8
Lichfield WS13 ....3 A1
Shenstone B74,WS14 ....31 C7
Sutton Coldfield B76 ....58 B5
West Bromwich B71 ....54 A6
Forge Mill Farm* B71 ....54 B6
Forge Mill Needle Mus* B98 ....153 F6
Forge Mill Rd B98 ....153 F6
Forge Rd Darlaston WS10 ....41 C6
Kenilworth CV8 ....148 A6
Stourbridge DY8 ....80 F6
Walsall WS3 ....14 F5
Willenhall WV12 ....27 C4
Forge St Cannock WS12 ....2 C4
Wednesbury WS10 ....41 E4
Forge The B63 ....82 B8
Forge Trad Est B62 ....83 C5
Forge Way Coventry CV6 ....95 C3
Oldbury B69 ....63 E6
Forhill Ho B38 ....123 F3
Forknell Ave CV2 ....114 C5
Formans Rd B11 ....87 E3
Formans Trad Est B11 ....87 D3
Formby Ave WV6 ....23 D4
Formby Way WS3 ....14 A3
Forrell Gr B31 ....123 B7
Forrest Ave Cannock WS11 ....4 E8
Essington WV11 ....13 A4
Forrest Ct ■9 WS13 ....9 B7
Forrest Rd CV8 ....147 E4
Forrester St WS2 ....28 C2
Forrester Street Prec ■3 WS2 ....28 C2
Forresters Cl LE10 ....75 F6
Forresters Rd LE10 ....75 F6
Forryan Rd LE10 ....75 F7
Forshaw Heath La B94 ....141 A7
Forshaw Heath Rd B94 ....125 C1
Forster St Birmingham B7 ....67 A3
Smethwick B67 ....64 E7
Forsythia Cl B31 ....102 F8
Forsythia Gr WV8 ....10 A3
Fort Cres WS9 ....16 A3
Fort Ind Pk The B35 ....57 F1
Fort Parkway B24,B35, B36 ....57 D1
Fort Sh Pk The B24 ....57 C1
Forth Dr B37 ....70 B4
Forth Gr B38 ....123 E8
Forth Way B62 ....83 E8
Forties B77 ....35 E7
Fortnum Cl B33 ....69 D2
Forton Cl WV6 ....24 B2
Forum Rd B40 ....90 E3
Forward Cotts B48 ....138 F6
Forward Rd B26 ....90 A3
Fosberry Cl CV34 ....161 B8
Fosbrooke Rd B10 ....88 A8
Fossdale Rd B77 ....36 A8
Fosseway WS14 ....9 A5
Fosseway Dr B23 ....56 E8
Fosseway La WS13,WS14 ....8 E4
Fosseway Rd CV3 ....133 B4
Fossil Dr B45 ....122 A7
Foster Ave Cannock WS12 ....1 F6
Studley B80 ....159 E3
Wolverhampton WV14 ....40 B1
Foster Gdns B18 ....65 F6
Foster Gn WV6 ....23 E3
Foster Pl DY8 ....80 E6
Foster Rd Coventry CV6 ....113 B7
Wolverhampton WV10 ....25 E7
Foster St Darlaston WS10 ....41 D7
■6 Stourbridge DY8 ....81 A5
Walsall WS3 ....28 D8
Foster St E DY8 ....81 A5
Foster Way B5 ....86 C5
Fotherley Brook Rd WS9 ....30 F5
Founder Cl CV4 ....132 A8
Foundry La
Smethwick B66 ....65 D6
Walsall WS3 ....14 E3
Foundry Prim Sch B18 ....65 E6
Foundry Rd
Birmingham B18 ....65 E5
Kingswinford DY6 ....60 C8
Foundry St Dudley WV14 ....40 C1
Kingswinford DY6 ....60 C8
Tipton DY4 ....51 E8
Fountain Arc ■4 DY1 ....51 C1
Fountain Cl B31 ....122 E6
Fountain La
Dudley DY4,WV14 ....51 E8
West Bromwich B69 ....53 A1
Fountain Rd B17 ....65 C1
Fountains Rd WS3 ....13 E2
Fountains Way WS3 ....13 E2
Four Acres B32 ....84 C4
Four Ashes Rd B93 ....127 E4
Four Crosses Rd WS4 ....15 C1
Four Dwellings High Sch B32 ....84 B5
Four Dwellings Inf Sch B32 ....84 C5
Four Dwellings Jun Sch B32 ....84 B5
Four Oaks Cl B98 ....158 D8
Four Oaks Common Rd B74 ....31 F3
Four Oaks Ct B74 ....32 B1
Four Oaks Inf Sch B74 ....31 E4
Four Oaks Jun Sch B74 ....31 E4
Four Oaks Rd B74 ....32 A1
Four Oaks Sta B74 ....46 B8
Four Pounds Ave CV5 ....112 F3
Four Stones Cl B91 ....107 A1
Four Stones Gr B5 ....86 D6
Four Winds Rd DY2 ....62 E6
Fourlands Ave B72 ....57 D7
Fourlands Rd B31 ....102 E6
Fourth Ave
Birmingham, Bordesley Green B9 ....67 F2
Birmingham, Selly Oak B29 ....86 C3
Brownhills WS8 ....7 A1
Wolverhampton WV10 ....25 E6
Fow Oak CV4 ....111 C2
Fowey Cl B76 ....58 A7
Fowey Rd B34 ....68 F6
Fowgay Dr B91 ....106 F1
Fowler Cl Perton WV6 ....23 E6
Smethwick B66 ....65 A8
Fowler Rd Coventry CV6 ....113 B4
Sutton Coldfield B75 ....47 B5
Fowler St Birmingham B7 ....67 B6
Wolverhampton WV2 ....39 C6
Fowlmere Rd B42 ....55 B8
Fownhope Cl B98 ....154 E3
Fox & Goose Sh Ctr B8 ....68 C5
Fox Ave Nuneaton CV10 ....73 D7
Willenhall WV13 ....27 A2
Fox Covert DY8 ....80 E5
Fox Cres B11 ....87 D4
Fox Foot Dr DY5 ....61 C4
Fox Glove Way ■3 B23 ....56 B7
Fox Gr B27 ....88 A2
Fox Green Cres B27 ....88 A2
Fox Hill B29 ....103 C8
Fox Hill Cl B29 ....103 C8
Fox Hill Rd B75 ....32 F2
Fox Hollies L Ctr B27 ....88 B1
Fox Hollies Rd
Birmingham B27,B28 ....88 A1
Sutton Coldfield B76 ....47 B2
Fox Hollies Sch B27 ....88 A1
Fox Hollow WV6 ....24 C2
Fox La Bromsgrove B61 ....150 E8
Lichfield WS13 ....3 A5
Fox Mill Est B11 ....87 D3
Fox St Birmingham B5 ....164 D3
Dudley DY1 ....51 C6
Fox Wlk WS9 ....16 B3
Fox's La WV6 ....25 C4
Foxbury Dr B93 ....128 B3
Foxcote Ave B21 ....65 E7
Foxcote Cl Redditch B98 ....154 F4
Solihull B90 ....126 D8
Foxcote Dr B90 ....126 D8
Foxcote La B63,DY9 ....82 B4
Foxcroft Cl WS7 ....7 B5
Foxdale Dr DY5 ....61 B3
Foxdale Gr B33 ....69 C3
Foxdale Wlk ■8 CV31 ....162 C6
Foxes Cl B60 ....138 B5
Foxes Mdw
Birmingham B30 ....103 F4
Sutton Coldfield B76 ....58 A8
Foxes Rake WS11 ....1 E3
Foxes Ridge B64 ....82 E8
Foxes Way
Balsall Common CV7 ....130 B6
Warwick CV34 ....160 D4
Foxfield B31 ....102 F4
Foxfield Dr DY8 ....81 A3
Foxfields Way WS12 ....1 C7
Foxford Cl
Birmingham B36 ....58 D1
Sutton Coldfield B72 ....57 D7
Foxford Cres CV2 ....96 B4
Foxford Sch & Com Arts Coll CV6 ....96 A5
Foxglove B77 ....22 A4
Foxglove Cl
Bedworth CV12 ....77 E1
Birmingham B27 ....88 B1
Coventry CV6 ....95 C2
Featherstone WV10 ....12 B7
Lichfield WS14 ....9 A5
Walsall WS3 ....15 A5
Wednesfield WV11 ....26 E5
Foxglove Cres B37 ....69 E3
Foxglove Rd DY1 ....51 A4
Foxglove Way
Birmingham B21 ....65 D7
Lickey End B60 ....137 C6
Foxglove Wlk WS12 ....2 C7
Foxhill Barns B48 ....138 E5
Foxhill Cl WS12 ....2 D2
Foxhill La B48 ....138 E5
Foxhill's Cl WS7 ....7 A5
Foxhills Cl CV11 ....74 C1
Foxhills Pk DY2 ....62 C4
Foxhills Rd
Stourbridge DY8 ....60 D1
Wolverhampton WV4 ....38 C4
Foxholes La B97 ....158 A6
Foxholes The DY10 ....116 F8
Foxhollies Dr B63 ....82 E4
Foxhollow B61 ....150 D8
Foxhope Cl B38 ....104 B2
Foxhunt Rd B63 ....82 E2

Foxland Ave
Birmingham B45 ....122 C7
Great Wyrley WS6 ....5 A3
Foxland Cl
Birmingham B37 ....70 D2
Cheswick Green B90 ....126 D4
Foxlands Ave WV4 ....38 D3
Foxlands Cres WV4 ....38 C3
Foxlands Dr Dudley DY3 ...50 D5
Sutton Coldfield B72 ....57 D7
Wombourne WV4 ....38 D3
Foxlea Rd B63 ....82 D1
Foxley Dr B91 ....108 B5
Foxlydiate Cres B97 .....153 A4
Foxlydiate La B97 ....152 F3
Foxlydiate Mews 8
B97 ....153 A4
Foxmeadow Cl DY3 ....50 E7
Foxoak Ent Ctr B64 ....62 D1
Foxoak St B64 ....62 D1
Foxtail Way WS12 ....2 E4
Foxton Rd Birmingham B8 ..67 F4
Coventry CV3 ....114 C1
Foxwalks Ave B61 ....150 D8
Foxwell Gr B9 ....68 C3
Foxwell Rd B9 ....68 C3
Foxwood Ave B43 ....44 B2
Foxwood Gr B37 ....69 F5
Foxwood Rd B78 ....36 F8
Foxyards Cl DY4 ....51 D5
Foxyards Rd Dudley DY4 ...51 C5
Foxyards Rd DY4 ....51 D5
Foyle Rd B38 ....103 F1
Fozdar Cres WV14 ....40 B1
Fradley Cl B30 ....103 D4
Framefield Dr B91 ....107 F6
Framlingham Gr
Kenilworth CV8 ....148 C6
Perton WV6 ....24 A3
Frampton Cl
Birmingham, Bournville
B30 ....103 D7
Birmingham, Chelmsley Wood
B37 ....70 D3
Frampton Way B43 ....44 D5
Frampton Wlk CV2 ....114 F4
Frances Ave CV34 ....161 A7
Frances Cres CV12 ....78 A3
Frances Dr WS3 ....14 B2
Frances Havergal Cl 2
CV31 ....161 F6
Frances Rd Baginton CV8 ..133 F5
Birmingham, Balsall Heath
B30 ....104 A5
Birmingham, Lozells B19 ....66 C8
Birmingham, Stockland Green
B23 ....56 D3
Franche Fst Sch DY11 ....116 B8
Franche Mid Sch DY11 ...116 B8
Franche Rd DY11 ....116 C8
Franchise Gdns WS10 .....41 F6
Franchise St
Birmingham B42 ....55 E2
Darlaston WS10 ....41 F6
Kidderminster DY11 ......116 C6
Francis Cl
1 Kingswinford DY6 ....60 D8
Sutton Coldfield B74 ....44 F8
Francis Gibbs Gdns
CV31 ....162 A4
Francis Rd
Birmingham, Acock's Green
B27 ....88 C3
Birmingham, Edgbaston B16 ..66 A1
Birmingham, South Yardley
B25 ....88 A6
Birmingham, Stechford B33 ..68 D2
Bromsgrove B60 ....150 F7
Lichfield WS13 ....3 A2
Smethwick B67 ....64 D4
Stourbridge DY8 ....80 C5
Francis St Birmingham B7 ..67 A4
Coventry CV6 ....113 E7
Wednesbury WS10 ....53 D1
Wolverhampton WV1 ....25 F2
Francis Ward Cl B71 ....53 A8
Francis Wlk B31 ....123 A7
Franciscan Rd CV3 ....133 D8
Frank F Harrison Comp Sch
WS2 ....27 F2
Frank Rd B67 ....64 E6
Frank St Birmingham B12 ..86 F7
Nuneaton CV11 ....73 B3
Frank Tommey Cl 8 B65 ..63 C1
Frank Walsh Ho CV1 ......165 C4
Frankburn Rd B74 ....44 F8
Frankfort St B19 ....66 D6
Frankholmes Dr B90 ......127 A6
Frankland Rd CV6 ....96 A1
Frankley Ave B62 ....83 F5
Frankley Beeches Rd
B31 ....102 D3
Frankley Com High Sch
B45 ....101 F1
Frankley Gn B32 ....101 E5
Frankley Green La B32 ...101 E5
Frankley Hill La B32 ......102 A4
Frankley Ind Pk B45 ......102 B1
Frankley La B31,B32 ......102 D6
Frankley Lodge Rd B32 ..102 D4
Frankley Rd B68 ....84 B8
Frankley Terr B17 ....85 B5
Franklin Cl CV11 ....73 D1
Franklin Gr WS7 ....7 B7
Franklin Gr CV4 ....111 E1

Franklin Rd
Birmingham B30 ....103 F5
Nuneaton CV11 ....73 D1
Whitnash CV31 ....162 A3
Franklin St B18 ....65 E5
Franklin Way B30 ....103 F6
Franklyn Cl WV6 ....23 E5
Frankpledge Rd CV3 ....133 E7
Franks Way B33 ....68 E2
Frankton Ave CV3 ....133 C5
Frankton Cl Redditch B98 ..159 E8
Solihull B92 ....89 B2
Frankton Gr B9 ....68 B2
Frankwell Dr CV2 ....96 E1
Fraser Cl CV10 ....72 B6
Fraser Rd Birmingham B11 ..87 D5
Coventry CV6 ....95 A1
Fraser St WV14 ....40 E6
Frayne Ave DY6 ....60 C7
Freasley Cl B90 ....106 D3
Freasley Rd B34 ....69 D6
Fred Lee Gr CV3 ....133 D4
Fred Smith Cl WS10 ....42 E5
Freda Eddy Ct 8 DY10 ...116 E6
Freda Rd B70 ....53 D1
Freda Rise B69 ....63 D8
Fredas Gr B17 ....85 A4
Frederick Ave LE10 ....71 A3
Frederick Bird Prim Sch
CV2 ....113 F5
Frederick Ct B77 ....21 E3
Frederick Early Ho B98 ...159 B7
Frederick Neal Ave CV5 ..111 D6
Frederick Rd
Birmingham, Aston B6 ....66 F8
Birmingham, Edgbaston B15 ..86 B8
Birmingham, Erdavelly Hill
B23 ....56 E2
Birmingham, Selly Oak B29 ..85 D2
Birmingham, Sparkhill B11 ..87 C4
Birmingham, Stechford B33 ..68 D3
Oldbury B68 ....84 D7
Sutton Coldfield B73 ....46 A2
Wolverhampton WV11 ....26 C5
Frederick Rd (Road 1)
DY10 ....116 F1
Frederick St
Birmingham B1 ....66 C4
Walsall WS2 ....28 D1
West Bromwich B70 ....53 D1
Wolverhampton WV2 ....163 B1
Frederick William St
WV13 ....27 B2
Fredericks Cl DY8 ....80 E4
Freeburn Cswy CV4 ....132 C7
Freeford Gdns WS14 ....9 E6
Freehold St CV1 ....113 F4
Freeland Gr 8 DY6 ....60 F4
Freeman Cl CV10 ....72 D4
Freeman Ct DY11 ....116 B3
Freeman Dr B76 ....46 F4
Freeman Pl WV14 ....40 E8
Freeman Rd
Birmingham B7 ....67 B6
Wednesbury WS10 ....42 D3
Freeman St
Birmingham B5 ....164 C2
Coventry CV6 ....113 F6
Wolverhampton WV10 ....25 F2
Freeman's La LE10 ....76 A5
Freemans Cl CV32 ....156 E2
Freemantle Ct B37 ....69 F5
Freemantle Dr WS12 ....2 E4
Freemantle Ho B24 ....57 D3
Freemount Sq B43 ....54 E7
Freer Dr WS7 ....7 E7
Freer Rd B6 ....66 E8
Freer St Nuneaton CV11 ......73 E2
Walsall WS1 ....28 F2
Freesland Rise CV10 ....72 B6
Freeth Rd WS8 ....7 A1
Freeth St Birmingham B16 ..65 F2
Oldbury B69 ....63 E8
Freezeland St WV14 ....40 B6
Fremantle Ho B34 ....69 E6
Fremont Dr DY1 ....50 E3
French Ave B78 ....20 C1
French Rd DY2 ....51 F1
French Walls 7 B66 ....65 C5
Frensham Cl
Birmingham B37 ....70 C2
Cheslyn Hay WS6 ....4 E4
Frensham Dr CV10 ....72 B6
Frensham Way B17 ....85 C6
Frenshaw Gr B44 ....55 F7
Freshfield Cl CV5 ....94 C1
Freshwater Dr DY5 ....81 B8
Freshwater Gr 1 LE10 ....162 C6
Freton Cl CV6 ....113 F7
Frevill Rd CV6 ....114 B8
Freville Cl B79 ....21 A5
Friar Park Rd WS10 ....42 D3
Friar St WS10 ....42 E3
Friar's Alley WS13 ....9 B7
Friardale Cl WS10 ....42 D3
Friars Cl
Binley Woods CV3 ....135 E7
Dudley DY9 ....60 D3
Friars Gorse DY7 ....80 C8
Friars St CV34 ....160 D6
Friars Wlk
Birmingham B37 ....70 D2
Tamworth B77 ....21 C3
Friars' Rd CV1 ....165 B2
Friary Ave Lichfield WS13 ....9 A6
Solihull B90 ....127 A6
Friary Cl Birmingham B20 ..54 F3

Friary Cres WS4 ....29 C6
Friary Dr B74 ....31 F3
Friary Gdns
Birmingham B21 ....54 D2
Lichfield WS13 ....9 A7
Friary Rd Birmingham B20 ..54 E3
Lichfield WS13 ....9 A7
Friary The WS13 ....9 A7
Friary St CV11 ....73 E3
Friary The WS13 ....9 A7
Friday Bridge 8 B1 ....66 C1
Friday La B92 ....108 D4
Friesland Dr WV1 ....26 B3
Friezeland Rd B62 ....28 B2
Friezland La WS8 ....16 A5
Friezland Way WS8 ....16 A5
Frilsham Way CV5 ....112 B4
Fringe Gn B60 ....151 A7
Fringe Green Cl B60 ....151 A7
Fringe Meadow Rd B98 ...154 F6
Frinton Gr B21 ....65 C7
Frisby Ct CV11 ....73 E2
Frisby Rd CV4 ....111 E2
Friston Ave B16 ....66 B1
Friswell Dr CV6 ....113 F8
Friswell Ho 8 CV2 ....114 D8
Frith Way LE10 ....71 A3
Frobisher Cl
Great Wyrley WS6 ....4 F1
Hinckley LE10 ....71 D4
Frobisher Rd CV3 ....133 C5
Frobisher Way B66 ....64 D7
Frodesley Rd B26 ....89 B8
Frog La
Balsall Common CV7 ....130 A5
Lichfield WS13 ....9 B7
Froggatt Rd WV14 ....40 D7
Froggatts Ride B76 ....46 F3
Frogmere Cl CV5 ....112 C6
Frogmill Com Jun Sch
B45 ....102 B2
Frogmill Rd B45 ....102 B2
Frogmoor Ho B26 ....88 E7
Frogmore La CV8 ....129 F2
Frome Cl DY3 ....50 D2
Frome Dr WV11 ....26 C5
Frome Rd 4 DY1 ....61 E8
Frome Way B14 ....104 D6
Front Cotts B48 ....138 F6
Frost St WV2 ....40 A6
Froxmere Cl B91 ....127 D8
Froyle Cl WV6 ....24 C5
Froysell St WV13 ....27 B2
Fryer Ave CV32 ....156 E3
Fryer Rd B31 ....123 B7
Fryer St WV1 ....163 C3
Fryers Cl WS3 ....28 A7
Fryers Rd WS2,WS3 ....28 A7
Frythe Cl CV8 ....148 C6
Fuchsia Cl 8 CV2 ....96 B2
Fuchsia Dr WV9 ....10 F3
Fugelmere Cl B17 ....84 F7
Fulbroke Cl B98 ....154 C5
Fulbrook Gr B29 ....102 F8
Fulbrook Rd Coventry CV2 ..96 D2
Dudley DY1 ....51 A1
Fulfen Prim Sch WS7 ....7 D7
Fulford Dr B76 ....58 B5
Fulford Gr B26 ....89 C6
Fulford Hall Rd B90,B94 ..125 D2
Fulham Rd B11 ....87 B5
Fullbrook Cl B90 ....127 A5
Fullbrook Rd WS5 ....42 E5
Fullelove Rd WS8 ....16 A7
Fullers Cl CV6 ....112 F7
Fullerton Cl WV8 ....10 E1
Fullwood Cl CV2 ....96 E2
Fullwood Cres DY1,DY2 ....61 H6
Fullwoods End WV14 ....40 C1
Fulmar Cres DY10 ....117 B2
Fulmer Wlk B18 ....66 A3
Fulton Cl B60 ....137 B1
Fulwell Gr B44 ....56 B8
Fulwell Mews B37 ....90 B8
Fulwood Ave B62 ....83 F8
Furber Pl DY6 ....60 F6
Furlong La B63 ....82 D6
Furlong Mdw B31 ....103 C2
Furlong Rd CV1 ....165 C1
Furlong The WS10 ....41 E5
Furlong Wlk DY3 ....50 D4
Furlongs Rd DY3 ....50 D6
Furlongs The
Stourbridge DY8 ....81 B3
Wolverhampton WV11 ....26 B5
Furnace Cl CV12 ....78 D3
Furnace Hill B63 ....83 B5
Furnace La B63 ....83 B5
Furnace Par DY4 ....51 E6
Furnace Rd
Bedworth CV12 ....78 D4
Dudley DY2 ....62 C8
Furness B77 ....21 D3
Furness Cl WS3 ....13 F1
Furnivall Cres WS13 ....3 D1
Furrows The B60 ....150 D6
Furst St WS8 ....16 A8
Furze Way WS5 ....43 E8
Furzebank Way WV12 ....27 E4
Fylde Ho CV2 ....114 D4
Fynford Rd CV6 ....113 B5

Gables The *continued*
Sutton Coldfield B24 ....57 D4
Gaddesby Rd B14 ....104 F8
Gadds Dr B65 ....63 D4
Gads Gn DY2 ....62 D5
Gads Green Cres DY2 ....62 E6
Gads La Dudley DY1 ....51 C1
West Bromwich B70 ....53 A3
Gadsby Ave WV11 ....27 A7
Gadsby Cl CV11 ....73 E3
Gadsby St CV11 ....73 E3
Gadshill CV34 ....161 E4
Gadwall Croft B23 ....56 B3
Gaelic Rd WS11 ....1 D4
Gagarin B79 ....20 F5
Gaia La WS13 ....9 B8
Gaia Stowe WS13 ....3 B1
Gaiafields Rd WS13 ....3 B1
Gaialands Cres WS13 ....3 B1
Gail Cl WS9 ....16 B4
Gail Pk WV3 ....38 D7
Gailey Croft B44 ....44 E3
Gainford Cl WV8 ....10 F1
Gainford Rd B44 ....45 C1
Gainford Rise CV3 ....115 A3
Gains La WS3,WS11 ....5 D2
Gainsborough Ave LE10 ...71 A3
Gainsborough Cres
Birmingham B43 ....44 D4
Knowle B93 ....128 A6
Gainsborough Dr
Bedworth CV12 ....78 A4
Mile Oak B78 ....34 B8
Perton WV6 ....24 A4
Royal Leamington Spa
CV31 ....162 D6
Gainsborough Hill DY8 ....81 A3
Gainsborough Mews
DY11 ....116 B5
Gainsborough Pl DY1 ....50 D2
Gainsborough Rd B42 ....55 B6
Gainsborough Trad Est
DY9 ....81 C4
Gainsbrook Cres WS11 ......5 F5
Gainsford Dr B62 ....83 B6
Gairloch Rd WV11 ....13 B1
Gaitskell Terr B69 ....52 D2
Gaitskell Way B66 ....64 F7
Galahad Way WS10 ....42 A2
Galbraith Cl WV14 ....51 D8
Gale Wlk B65 ....62 F5
Galena Cl B77 ....22 B2
Galena Way B6 ....66 C6
Galey's Rd CV3 ....133 D8
Gallagher Bsns Pk CV6 ....95 E5
Gallagher Cl 15 B13 ....87 B2
Gallagher Rd CV12 ....78 A2
Gallagher Ret Pk CV6 .....113 F8
Gallery Sq 4 WS1 ....28 E2
Galliards The CV4 ....132 D4
Galliers Cl B77 ....35 F5
Galloway Ave B34 ....68 F6
Galloway Cl CV3 ....57 F7
Gallows Hill CV34 ....161 B4
Gallus Dr LE10 ....71 A1
Galmington Dr CV3 ....133 B6
Galton Cl
Sutton Coldfield B24 ....57 F4
Tipton DY4 ....52 C6
Galton Dr DY2 ....62 B6
Galton Ho B67 ....64 F2
Galton Rd B67 ....64 F1
Galton Twr B1 ....164 A2
Galtons La DY9 ....120 A7
Galway Rd WS7 ....7 C7
Gamesfield Gn WV3 ....24 F1
Gammage St DY2 ....62 B8
Gamson Cl DY10 ....116 E4
Ganborough Cl B98 ....154 E1
Gandy Rd WV12 ....27 A7
Gannahs Farm Cl B76 ......46 F3
Gannow Green La B45 ....101 D1
Gannow Manor Cres
B45 ....101 E2
Gannow Manor Gdns
B45 ....101 F1
Gannow Rd B45 ....121 E7
Gannow Wlk B45 ....121 E7
Ganton Rd WS3 ....14 A3
Ganton Wlk WV8 ....24 F8
Garage Cl B77 ....21 D5
Garden Cl
Birmingham, Frankley B45 ..102 A2
Birmingham, Ward End B8 ..68 A5
Hinckley LE10 ....75 D6
Knowle B93 ....127 F6
Garden Cres WS3 ....14 F3
Garden Croft WS9 ....30 B7
Garden Ct
Warwick, Emscote CV34 ....161 C8
Warwick, Packmores CV34 ..160 F7
Garden Flats CV5 ....111 D5
Garden Gr Bedworth CV12 ..95 F8
Birmingham B20 ....54 E6
Garden Rd LE10 ....71 D1
Garden St WS2 ....28 E3
Garden Wlk Bilston WV14 ..40 F6
Dudley DY3 ....50 C2
Gardeners Cl DY11 ....116 C8
Gardenia Dr CV5 ....112 B6
Gardens The
Birmingham B23 ....56 E3
Kenilworth CV8 ....148 A3
Radford Semele CV31 ......162 E5
Gardner Ho B7 ....162 B6
Gardner Way CV8 ....148 A2
Garfield Rd B26 ....89 B8
Garganey Ct DY10 ....116 F1

Garibaldi Terr B60 ....137 A1
Garland Cres B62 ....83 E8
Garland St B9 ....67 C3
Garland Way B31 ....103 C4
Garlands Croft CV7 ....95 A6
Garlands The WV11 ....26 C7
Garlick Dr CV8 ....148 C6
Garman Cl B43 ....43 E2
Garner Cl WV14 ....40 D3
Garner Rd B44 ....44 B3
Garner Cl WV9 ....16 E4
Garnet Cl 4 B92 ....88 F1
Garnett Dr B75 ....46 E6
Garnette Cl CV10 ....72 B5
Garrard Gdns B73 ....46 B5
Garratt St DY5 ....61 D8
Garratt Cl B68 ....64 C4
Garratt St B71 ....53 E5
Garratt's La B65 ....63 A2
Garratts Wlk B14 ....104 E2
Garret Cl DY6 ....60 D8
Garrett St CV11 ....73 E2
Garretts Green La B26,
B33 ....89 A8
Garrick Cl Coventry CV5 ...111 C4
Dudley DY1 ....50 F3
Garrick Rise WS7 ....7 B7
Garrick St WV1 ....163 C2
Garrigill B77 ....22 B1
Garrington St WS10 ....41 C7
Garrison Cl 6 B9 ....67 B2
Garrison La B9 ....67 C2
Garrison St B9 ....67 B3
Garston Way 4 B43 ....54 D8
Garth Cres CV3 ....134 D8
Garth Ho CV3 ....134 D8
Garth The
Birmingham B14 ....105 D4
Lichfield WS13 ....3 B2
Garway Cl Redditch B98 ...154 E1
Royal Leamington Spa
CV32 ....156 F4
Garway Gr B25 ....88 C6
Garwood Rd B26 ....68 F2
Gas Sq B61 ....136 F1
Gas St Birmingham B1 ......66 C2
Royal Leamington Spa
CV31 ....161 F7
**Gas Street Basin * B1 .....164 A2
Gatacre St CV3 ....50 D3
Gatcombe Cl WV10 ....11 F4
Gatcombe Rd DY1 ....50 E2
Gate La Dorridge B93 ....127 C3
Sutton Coldfield B73 ....45 F2
Gate St Birmingham B8 ......67 D5
Sedgley DY3 ....50 E7
Tipton DY4 ....52 B2
Gatehouse CV31 ....161 D7
Gatehouse Fold 6 DY2 .....51 D1
Gatehouse La CV12 ....78 A2
Gatehouse Trad Est WS8 ....7 A1
Gateley Rd B68 ....84 D7
Gateside Rd CV6 ....95 E2
Gatis St WV6 ....25 A5
Gatwick Rd B35 ....58 B4
Gauden Rd DY9 ....81 D2
Gaulby Wlk CV3 ....115 A1
Gaunt Cl WS6 ....5 A1
Gaunts The B48 ....139 B6
Gaveston Cl 2 CV34 ....160 F8
Gaveston Rd
Coventry CV6 ....112 F6
Royal Leamington Spa
CV32 ....156 E1
Gavin Way B6 ....55 F4
Gawne La B64 ....62 F3
Gawsworth B79 ....20 D7
Gay Hill La B38 ....124 B8
Gaydon Cl Coventry CV6 ...114 A8
Perton WV6 ....24 B3
Redditch B98 ....153 F1
Gaydon Gr B29 ....85 A2
Gaydon Pl B73 ....46 B4
Gaydon Rd Aldridge WS9 ...30 A4
Solihull B92 ....89 D3
Gayer St CV6 ....96 A1
Gayfield Ave DY5 ....61 E1
Gayhurst Cl CV3 ....134 E8
Gayhurst Dr B25 ....88 E8
Gayle B77 ....22 A1
Gayle Gr B27 ....106 C8
Gayton Rd B71 ....53 D6
Gaywood Croft B15 ....86 C8
Gaza Cl CV4 ....112 A1
Gazelle Cl CV1 ....165 D3
Geach St B19 ....66 D6
Geach Twr B19 ....66 D5
Gedney Cl B90 ....105 C3
Gee St B19 ....66 D6
Geeson Cl B35 ....58 B4
Gemini Dr WS11 ....4 F6
Geneva Rd DY4 ....51 D5
Genge Ave WV4 ....39 E4
Genners App B31 ....102 D8
Genners La B31 ....102 D7
Genthorn Cl WV4 ....39 F4
Gentian B74 ....31 F4
Gentian Cl B31 ....102 F6
Geoffery Cl CV2 ....114 B5
Geoffery Cl B76 ....58 B7
Geoffrey Pl B11 ....87 C3
Geoffrey Rd
Birmingham B11 ....87 C3
Solihull B90 ....105 F3
George Arthur Rd B8 ....67 D5
George Ave
Blackheath B65 ....63 D2
Mile Oak B78 ....20 C1

George Betts Prim Sch B66 64 C7
George Bird Cl B66 65 A6
George Cl DY2 62 E8
George Dance Cl 2 DY10 117 B6
George Dixon Jun & Inf Sch B17 65 C2
George Dixon Sch B17 65 C2
George Eliot Ave CV12 78 D2
George Eliot Com Sch CV11 73 D1
George Eliot Hospl CV10 73 B2
George Eliot Rd CV1 113 D5
George Eliot Sch CV11 78 D8
George Eliot St CV11 73 C2
George Fentham Prim Sch B92 109 B6
George Frederick Rd B73 45 A4
George Henry Rd DY4 52 E6
George Hodgkinson Cl CV4 111 F3
George La WS13 9 C8
George Marston Rd CV3 114 E1
George Park Cl Ansty CV7 97 D3
Coventry CV2 96 C1
George Poole Ho 6 CV1 113 B2
George Rd
Alvechurch B48 139 A5
Birmingham, Edgbaston B15 86 B8
Birmingham, Great Barr B43 43 F2
Birmingham, Perry Common B73 45 D1
Birmingham, Selly Oak B29 85 E3
Birmingham, South Yardley B25 88 A6
Birmingham, Stockland Green B23 56 C3
Dudley, Daisy Bank WV14 40 D1
Dudley, Tipton Green DY4 51 D6
Halesowen B63 82 F4
Oldbury B68 64 C2
Solihull B91 107 D3
Warwick CV34 161 A8
Water Orton B46 59 C3
George Robertson Cl CV3 134 E7
George Rose Gdns WS10 41 C6
George Salter High Sch B70 53 A4
George St
Birmingham, Balsall Heath B12 86 F5
Birmingham, Brookfields B3 164 A3
Birmingham, Handsworth B21 65 C8
Birmingham, Lozells B19 66 B7
1 Bromsgrove B61 136 F2
Cannock WS12 2 D4
Coventry CV1 113 E5
Dudley DY1 51 B6
Hinckley LE10 75 D8
Kidderminster DY10 116 F6
Nuneaton CV11 73 E2
Royal Leamington Spa CV31 162 A7
Stourbridge DY8 60 F1
Tamworth B79 21 B4
Walsall WS1 28 E1
West Bromwich B70 53 D2
Willenhall WV13 27 A4
Wolverhampton WV2 163 C2
Wolverhampton, Ettingshall WV2 40 A7
George St W B18 66 A4
George Street Ringway CV12 78 B3
George Wlk 5 B97 153 E3
Georgian Gdns 2 WS10 41 F3
Georgian Pl WS11 1 E2
Georgina Ave WV14 40 D3
Gerald Rd DY8 80 E7
Geraldine Rd B25 88 B7
Geranium Gr B9 67 F3
Geranium Rd DY2 62 F8
Gerard B79 20 E7
Gerard Ave CV4 132 B8
Gerardsfield Rd B33 69 E2
Germander Dr WS5 43 A3
Gerrard Cl B19 66 D7
Gerrard Rd WV13 26 E1
Gerrard St
Birmingham B19 66 C7
1 Warwick CV34 160 E6
Gervase Dr DY1 51 C3
Geston Rd DY1 61 F8
Gettings Cl WS7 7 F7
Gheluvelt Ave DY10 116 F7
Gibb La B61 137 A8
Gibb St B9 66 F1
Gibbet Hill Rd CV4 132 B3
Gibbet La DY7 80 B4
Gibbins Rd B29 85 D2
Gibbons Cl CV4 111 F2
Gibbons Gr WV6 24 F4
Gibbons Hill Rd DY3 39 D2
Gibbons Ind Pk DY6 61 A7
Gibbons La DY5 61 A7
Gibbons Rd
Sutton Coldfield B75 32 B3
Wolverhampton WV6 24 F4
Gibbs Cl CV2 115 B6
Gibbs Hill Rd B31 123 C7
Gibbs Rd Redditch B98 154 A5
Gibbs Rd *continued*
Stourbridge DY9 82 A5
Gibbs St WV6 25 A4
Gibson Cres CV12 78 A1
Gibson Dr Birmingham B20 66 B8
Smethwick B66 65 A6
Gibson Rd Birmingham B20 66 B8
Perton WV6 23 E3
Gideon Cl B25 88 D6
Gideons Cl DY3 50 D5
Gielgud Way CV2 115 B8
Giffard RC Prim Sch WV6 24 F5
Giffard Rd Bilston WV1 40 B7
Wolverhampton WV10 11 F3
Giffard Way CV34 155 E1
Gifford Ct 13 DY5 61 D2
Giffords Croft WS13 3 A1
Gig Mill Prim Sch DY8 80 E3
Gigg La B76 48 B3
Gigmill Way DY8 80 E4
Gilbanks Rd DY8 80 D7
Gilberry Cl B93 128 A4
Gilbert Ave B69 63 B7
Gilbert Cl
3 Coventry CV1 113 E3
Wednesfield WV11 27 A7
Gilbert Ent Pk WV12 27 B4
Gilbert La WV5 49 B7
Gilbert Rd
Bromsgrove B60 150 E7
Lichfield WS13 3 C2
Smethwick B66 65 B3
Gilbert Scott Way DY10 116 F7
Gilbert St DY4 52 A2
Gilbert Wlk WS13 3 C2
Gilberts Ct WS4 29 A4
Gilbertstone Ave B26 88 E5
Gilbertstone Cl B98 153 E1
Gilbertstone Prim Sch B26 88 E5
Gilbeys Cl DY8 60 E1
Gilby Rd B16 66 A1
Gilchrist Dr B15 85 E8
Gildas Ave B38 104 A1
Giles Cl Birmingham B33 68 E3
Coventry CV6 95 C2
Solihull B92 107 F7
Giles Close Ho B33 68 E3
Giles Rd Lichfield WS13 3 A3
Oldbury B68 64 B5
Gilfil Rd CV10 73 B1
Gill St Dudley DY2 62 E4
West Bromwich B70 53 C1
Gilldown Pl B15 86 B7
Gillespie Croft B6 66 F7
Gillet Cl CV11 73 B3
Gillhurst Rd B17 85 C7
Gillians Wlk CV2 115 A8
Gilling Gr B34 69 A6
Gillingham Cl WS10 42 D4
Gillity Ave WS5 43 C8
Gillity Cl WS5 43 C8
Gillity Ct 3 WS5 43 D7
Gilliver Rd B90 106 B2
Gillman Cl B26 89 D4
Gillott Cl B91 107 E3
Gillott Rd B16 65 D2
Gillows Croft B90 127 A7
Gillscroft Rd B33 69 A3
Gillway B79 21 B8
Gilmorton Cl
Birmingham B17 85 B7
Solihull B91 107 C1
Gilpin Cl B8 68 C7
Gilpin Cres WS3 15 A4
Gilpins Croft WS6 4 D1
Gilquart Way CV1 165 C1
Gilson Dr B46 70 D8
Gilson Rd B46 70 E8
Gilson St DY4 52 C8
Gilson Way B37 70 A5
Gilwell Rd B34 69 E6
Gingko Wlk 2 CV31 161 F5
Gipsy Cl CV7 130 B5
Gipsy La
Balsall Common CV7 130 C5
Birmingham B23 56 B5
Nuneaton CV10,CV11 78 D7
Willenhall WV13 27 B1
Girdlers Cl CV3 133 B5
Girtin Cl CV12 78 A4
Girton Ho B36 69 F8
Girton Rd WS11 4 F8
Girvan Gr CV32 157 C5
Gisborn Cl B10 87 B8
Gisburn Cl CV34 155 F1
Givens Ho 9 CV1 113 B2
GK Davies Trad Est DY9 82 A6
Glade Ave WS7 7 A8
Glade The Aldridge B74 30 E1
Birmingham B26 89 D4
Cannock WS11 1 C2
Coventry CV5 111 F3
Stourbridge DY9 81 E5
Wolverhampton WV8 10 E1
Glades The WS9 30 B7
Gladeside Cl WS4 29 D8
Gladman Bsns Quarter WV9 10 F3
Gladstone Cl LE10 71 E4
Gladstone Dr
Stourbridge DY8 80 D6
Tipton B69 52 D3
Gladstone Gr 3 DY6 60 D8
Gladstone Rd
Birmingham, Gravelly Hill B23 56 D3
Gladstone Rd *continued*
Birmingham, South Yardley B26 88 D6
Birmingham, Sparkbrook B11 87 B6
Cannock WS12 2 E1
Dorridge B93 128 A2
Stourbridge DY8 80 D6
Gladstone St
Birmingham B6 67 B8
Darlaston WS10 41 E6
Walsall WS2 28 D4
West Bromwich B71 53 C5
Gladstone Terr LE10 75 E8
Gladys Rd Birmingham B25 88 B7
Smethwick B67 64 F2
Gladys Terr B67 65 A2
Glaisdale Ave CV6 95 E3
Glaisdale Gdns WV6 25 A5
Glaisdale Rd B28 106 B8
Glaisedale Gr WV13 27 C2
Glaisher Dr WV10 25 C6
Glamis Rd WV12 27 B7
Glamorgan Cl CV3 134 D5
Glanville Dr B75 32 A4
Glasbury Croft B38 123 E7
Glascote Cl B90 106 A4
Glascote Ct B77 21 E4
Glascote Gr B34 69 C6
Glascote Heath Prim Sch B77 22 A2
Glascote La B77 35 F8
Glascote Rd
Tamworth B77 22 B2
Tamworth, Glascote Heath B77 21 E3
Glasscroft Cotts WS7 7 F7
Glasshouse Hill DY8 81 B3
Glasshouse La
Kenilworth CV8 148 D4
Tanworth-in-A B94 143 F6
Glaston Dr B91 107 A1
Glastonbury Cl DY11 116 A6
Glastonbury Cres WS3 13 E2
Glastonbury Rd
Birmingham B14 105 C5
West Bromwich B71 42 D1
Glastonbury Way WS3 13 E1
Gleads Croft B62 84 A3
Gleaston Wlk WV1 26 C1
Gleave Rd Birmingham B29 85 E1
Whitnash CV31 162 A3
Glebe Ave CV12 77 E1
Glebe Cl Coventry CV4 132 A7
Redditch B98 154 D2
Glebe Cres CV8 148 A3
Glebe Ct CV31 162 A3
Glebe Dr B73 56 F8
Glebe Farm Rd B33 69 A5
Glebe Fields B76 59 B6
Glebe La Nuneaton CV11 73 F6
Stourbridge DY8 80 E4
Glebe Pl Darlaston WS10 41 B6
Royal Leamington Spa CV31 162 B7
Glebe Rd Alvechurch B48 139 A7
Hinckley LE10 71 F1
Nuneaton CV11 73 D4
Solihull B91 107 D5
Willenhall WV13 40 F8
Glebe St WS1 42 E8
Glebe The
Belbroughton DY9 119 E6
Beoley B98 154 F7
Corley CV7 94 C7
Glebe Way CV7 130 A7
Glebefarm Gr CV3 114 F3
Glebefields Prim Sch DY4 52 A8
Glebefields Rd DY4 52 A7
Glebeland Cl B16 66 B1
Gledhill Pk WS14 9 C5
Gleeson Dr CV34 155 E1
Glen Bank LE10 71 E1
Glen Cl Cannock WS11 1 E5
Walsall WS4 29 A3
Glen Ct Codsall WV8 10 A4
Wolverhampton WV6 24 E2
Glen Devon Cl B45 102 A2
Glen Ho DY1 61 D8
Glen Park Rd DY3 50 D2
Glen Rd Dudley DY3 50 E6
Stourbridge DY8 80 F3
Glen Rise B13 105 C6
Glen Side B32 84 D2
Glen The B60 138 A5
Glenavon Rd B14 105 A3
Glenbarr Cl LE10 75 A8
Glenbarr Dr LE10 75 A8
Glencoe Dr WS11 2 A4
Glencoe Rd
Birmingham B16 65 C4
Coventry CV3 114 B1
Glencroft Rd B92 89 D4
Glendale Ave CV8 148 A6
Glendale Cl
Halesowen B63 83 B4
Wolverhampton WV3 38 C8
Glendale Ct B77 36 B6
Glendale Dr
Birmingham B33 68 F3
Wombourne WV5 49 A6
Glendale Gdns WS11 2 A4
Glendale Inf Sch CV10 72 F2
Glendale Twr 5 B23 57 B6
Glendale Way CV4 111 C2
Glendawn Cl 1 WS11 2 A3
Glendene Cres B38 123 C7
Glendene Dr 2 B43 54 D8
Glendene Rd WS12 2 D6
Glendon Gdns CV12 79 C3
Glendon Rd B23 56 D6
Glendon Way B93 127 E3
Glendower App CV34 161 E3
Glendower Ave CV5 112 D3
Glendower Rd
Aldridge WS9 16 B1
Birmingham B42 55 D4
Gleneagles B77 22 B5
Gleneagles Cl
Hinckley LE10 75 D4
Nuneaton CV11 74 C1
Gleneagles Dr
Birmingham B43 43 E3
Blackwell B60 138 A5
Sutton Coldfield B75 46 D8
Tipton B69 63 A7
Gleneagles Rd
Birmingham B26 89 A8
Coventry CV2 114 E6
Perton WV6 23 D5
Walsall WS3 13 F3
Glenelg Dr DY8 81 B2
Glenelg Mews WS5 43 D5
Glenfern Gdns CV8 134 E2
Glenfern Rd WV14 51 A8
Glenfield Tamworth B77 21 C1
Wolverhampton WV8 10 E2
Glenfield Ave CV10 73 D7
Glenfield Cl
Redditch B97 158 D6
2 Solihull B91 127 C8
Sutton Coldfield B76 46 E3
Glenfield Gr B29 86 A1
Glengarry Cl B32 102 B7
Glengarry Gdns WV3 24 F1
Glenhill Dr B38 124 A8
Glenhurst Cl WS2 27 D3
Glenmead Prim Sch B44 55 D8
Glenmead Rd B44 55 D8
Glenmore Ave WS7 7 A6
Glenmore Cl WV3 38 E7
Glenmore Dr
Birmingham B38 103 D2
Coventry CV6 95 F5
Glenmount Ave CV6 95 F5
Glenn St CV6 95 D3
Glenpark Rd B8 67 F5
Glenridding Cl CV6 95 F5
Glenrosa Wlk CV4 132 A7
Glenroy Cl CV2 114 E6
Glenroyde B38 123 E7
Glenside Ave B92 89 C3
Glenthorne Dr WS6 4 E3
Glenthorne Ho WS6 4 D2
Glenthorne Prim Sch WS6 4 E3
Glenthorne Rd B24 57 A2
Glenthorne Way B24 57 A2
Glentworth B76 47 A2
Glentworth Ave CV6 95 A2
Glentworth Gdns WV6 25 B5
Glenville Ave CV9 36 C1
Glenville Dr B23 56 E5
Glenwood Cl DY5 81 D8
Glenwood Dr B90 126 D4
Glenwood Gdns CV12 78 A5
Glenwood Rd B38 123 D8
Glenwood Rise WS9 16 D3
Globe St WS10 41 F1
Gloster Dr CV8 147 F6
Gloucester Cl
Lichfield WS13 3 B3
Nuneaton CV11 74 A7
Gloucester Ho
4 Birmingham B24 56 F4
4 Wolverhampton WV3 25 C4
Gloucester Pl WV13 27 D2
Gloucester Rd Dudley DY2 62 D2
Walsall WS5 43 C8
Wednesbury WS10 42 C3
Gloucester St
Birmingham B5 164 C1
Coventry CV1 113 B3
3 Royal Leamington Spa CV31 162 A7
Wolverhampton WV6 25 B4
Gloucester Way
Birmingham B37 70 A1
Cannock WS11 2 B1
Glover Cl
Birmingham B28 105 F6
Warwick CV34 160 B4
Glover Rd B75 47 A5
Glover St Birmingham B9 67 A2
Cannock WS12 2 F3
Coventry CV3 133 D8
Redditch B98 153 E3
West Bromwich B70 53 D1
Glover's Trust Homes B73 56 F7
Glovers Cl CV7 92 C1
Glovers Croft B37 69 F3
Glovers Field Dr B7 67 C7
Glovers Rd B10 87 D8
Glyde Ct B27 88 B2
Glyme Dr WV6 24 E5
Glyn Ave WV14 41 B3
Glyn Dr WV14 41 B3
Glyn Farm Rd B32 84 C6
Glyn Rd B32 84 D6
Glyndebourne B79 20 D7
Glyne Ct B73 46 B5
Glynn Cres B63 82 B7
Glynne Ave DY6 60 D5
Glynne Prim Sch DY6 60 C4
Glynside Ave B32 84 D6
Godfrey Cl CV31 162 E5
Godiva Pl CV1 165 D3
Godiva Trad Est CV6 113 F8
Godolphin B79 20 D7
Godrich Ho B13 87 B3
Godson Cres DY11 116 C3
Godson Pl DY11 116 C3
Goffs Cl B32 84 F3
Gofton B77 36 A8
Gold Cl CV11 78 E8
Goldacre Cl CV31 161 F4
Goldcrest B77 36 A6
Goldcrest Cl DY2 62 D2
Goldcrest Croft B36 70 A8
Goldcrest Dr DY10 117 B2
Golden Acres La CV3 134 F7
Golden Croft B20 54 F1
Golden Cross La B61 121 B1
Golden End Dr B93 128 D6
Golden Hillock Rd
Birmingham B11 87 D6
Dudley DY2 62 C3
Golden Hillock Sch & Specialist Sports Coll B11 87 D5
Goldencrest Dr B69 63 E8
Goldfinch Cl B30 103 D8
Goldfinch Rd DY9 81 C3
Goldicroft Rd WS10 42 A4
Goldieslie Cl B73 46 B2
Goldieslie Rd B73 46 B2
Golds Hill Gdns B21 65 F7
Golds Hill Rd B21 65 F8
Golds Hill Way DY4 52 D7
Goldsborough B77 22 A1
Goldsmith Ave CV34 160 C5
Goldsmith Pl B79 21 A7
Goldsmith Rd
Birmingham B14 104 F8
Walsall WS3 28 E7
Goldsmith Wlk DY10 117 C5
Goldstar Way B33 69 C2
Goldtel Ind Est WV4 40 A5
Goldthorn Ave WV4 39 B6
Goldthorn Cl CV5 111 D4
Goldthorn Cres WV4 39 A6
Goldthorn Hill WV2,WV4 39 C6
Goldthorn Park Jun & Inf Sch WV4 39 D5
Goldthorn Pl DY11 116 C2
Goldthorn Rd
Kidderminster DY11 116 C2
Wolverhampton WV2,WV3 39 B6
Goldthorne Ave
Birmingham B26 89 C4
Cannock WS11 1 F2
Goldthorne Cl B97 153 C1
Goldthorne Wlk DY5 81 D8
Golf Dr CV11 74 B1
Golf La Bilston WV14 40 D7
Whitnash CV31 162 B2
Golson Cl B75 46 F6
Gomeldon Ave B14 104 F3
Gomer St WV13 27 A2
Gomer St W WV13 27 A2
Gonville Ho B36 69 F8
Gooch Cl DY8 81 B6
Gooch St B5 86 E8
Gooch St N B5 86 E8
Good Hope Hospl B75 46 D6
Good Shepherd RC Sch CV6 95 F1
Goodall Gr B43 44 E5
Goodall St WS1 28 F1
Goodby Rd B13 86 D3
Goode Ave B18 66 A5
Goode Cl Oldbury B68 64 C4
Warwick CV34 160 C7
Goode Croft CV4 111 F2
Goodeve Wlk B75 47 B5
Goodfellow St CV32 156 C1
Goodison Gdns B24 57 B5
Goodleigh Ave B45 122 E6
Goodman Cl B28 105 F6
Goodman St B1 66 B3
Goodman Way CV4 111 C1
Goodrest Ave B62 84 A5
Goodrest Croft B14 105 C4
Goodrest La B38 123 F6
Goodrich Ave WV6 24 A3
Goodrich Cl B98 154 F2
Goodrich Covert 10 B14 104 C2
Goodway Ct 7 CV34 160 F7
Goodway Ho 5 CV32 161 D8
Goodway Rd
Birmingham B44 55 F8
Solihull B92 89 E4
Goodwin Cl DY11 116 C7
Goodwood Cl
Birmingham B36 68 D8
Coventry CV3 134 C6
Lichfield WS14 9 D7
Goodwood Dr B74 44 F7
Goodwood Rd B61 121 B1
Goodwyn Ave B68 84 C7
Goodyear Ave WV10 25 E7
Goodyear Rd B67 64 E2
Goodyers End La CV12 95 D8
Goodyers End Prim Sch CV12 95 E8
Goosehill Cl B98 154 E1
Goosehills Rd LE10 75 E5
Goosemoor La B23 56 F7
Goostry Cl B77 21 D5
Goostry Rd B77 21 D5

Gopsal St B4 .....67 A3
Gopsall Rd LE10 .....71 D2
Gorcott La B90 .....126 A5
Gordon Ave
Birmingham B19 .....66 D7
West Bromwich B71 .....53 C8
Wolverhampton WV4 .....39 F3
Gordon Cl Bedworth CV12 ..78 C4
Tipton B69 .....52 D2
Gordon Cres DY5 .....61 E5
Gordon Ct B33 .....68 D3
Gordon Dr DY4 .....52 C6
Gordon Pl WV14 .....40 C5
Gordon Rd
Birmingham, Harborne B17 .85 D6
Birmingham, Lozells B19 .....66 C8
Gordon St
5 Birmingham B9 .....67 B2
Coventry CV1 .....113 B2
Darlaston WS10 .....41 E6
Royal Leamington Spa CV31 .....162 A7
Wolverhampton WV2 .....163 C2
Gorey Cl WV12 .....27 B8
Gorge Rd WV14,DY3 .....39 F1
Goring Rd CV2 .....114 A4
Gorleston Gr B14 .....105 B2
Gorleston Rd B14 .....105 B2
Gorse Cl
Birmingham, Fordbridge B37 .....69 F2
Birmingham, Selly Oak B29 .....103 A8
Gorse Dr WS12 .....1 D5
Gorse Farm Rd
Birmingham B43 .....54 E8
Nuneaton CV11 .....79 B8
Gorse Green La DY9 .....120 C8
Gorse La Lichfield WS13 .....3 F6
Lichfield WS14 .....9 E6
Gorse Meadow Dr B45 ..138 B8
Gorse Rd Dudley DY1 .....51 A4
Sedgley DY3 .....50 E8
Wednesfield WV11 .....27 A8
Gorse Way WS12 .....2 C8
Gorsebrook Rd WV6 .....25 B5
Gorsefield Rd B34 .....69 C5
Gorsemoor Prim Sch WS12 .....2 D1
Gorsemoor Rd WS12 .....2 D1
Gorsemoor Way WV11 .....13 B3
Gorseway Burntwood WS7 .....7 B5
Coventry CV5 .....112 C3
Gorsey La Cannock WS11 .....1 C1
Coleshill B46 .....59 F2
Great Wyrley WS6 .....4 F1
Norton Canes WS3 .....5 E1
Wythall B47 .....125 A3
Gorsey Way Aldridge WS9 ..29 E5
Coleshill B46 .....59 E2
Gorsly Piece B32 .....84 C4
Gorstey Lea WS7 .....7 C7
Gorstie Croft B43 .....54 E8
Gorsty Ave DY5 .....61 C3
Gorsty Bank WS14 .....9 E8
Gorsty Cl 2 B71 .....53 F8
Gorsty Hill Rd B65 .....83 B8
Gorsy Bank Rd B77 .....35 F5
Gorsy Rd B32 .....84 D5
Gorsy Way CV10 .....72 D5
Gorsymead Gr B31 .....102 C2
Gorton Croft CV7 .....130 B7
Gorway Cl WS1 .....42 F7
Gorway Gdns WS1 .....43 A7
Gorway Rd WS1 .....43 A7
Goscote Cl Redditch B97 .153 A5
Walsall WS3 .....28 F7
Goscote Hospl WS3 .....28 F8
Goscote Ind Est WS3 .....14 E1
Goscote La WS3 .....28 F8
Goscote Lodge Cres WS3 .....29 A7
Goscote Pl WS3 .....29 A7
Goscote Rd WS3 .....15 A1
Gosford Dr LE10 .....71 A1
Gosford Ind Est CV1 .....113 F2
Gosford Park Prim Sch CV1 .....113 F2
Gosford St
Birmingham B12 .....86 F6
Coventry CV1 .....165 D2
Gosford Wlk B92 .....89 B1
Gosmoor Ho B26 .....88 E7
Gospel End Rd DY3 .....50 B8
Gospel End St DY3 .....50 D8
Gospel Farm Rd B27 .....106 B8
Gospel La B27 .....106 C8
Gospel Oak Rd
Coventry CV6 .....95 B4
Tipton DY4 .....41 B1
Gosport Cl WV1 .....40 B7
Gosport Rd CV6 .....113 E8
Goss Croft B29 .....85 D1
Goss The DY5 .....61 D1
Gossett La CV8 .....135 F7
Gossey La B33 .....69 C2
Gossey Lane Jun & Inf Sch B33 .....69 C2
Gosta Gn B4 .....164 D4
Gotham Rd B26 .....88 E6
Goths Cl B65 .....63 C4
Gough Ave WV11 .....26 B8
Gough Rd
Birmingham, Edgbaston B15 .86 C7
Birmingham, Sparkhill B11 ..87 D5
Gough Rd *continued*
Dudley WV14 .....40 C1
Gough St Birmingham B1 .164 B1
Willenhall WV13 .....27 C2
Wolverhampton WV1 .....163 C3
Gould Ave E DY11 .....116 A2
Gould Ave W DY11 .....116 A1
Gould Firm La WS9 .....30 E6
Gould Rd CV35 .....160 A7
Governor's Ct CV34 .....160 D8
Gowan Rd B8 .....67 E4
Gower Ave DY6 .....60 F4
Gower Ho B62 .....83 F6
Gower Rd Halesowen B62 ..83 F6
Sedgley DY3 .....50 B8
Gower St Birmingham B19 ..66 D7
Walsall WS2 .....42 B7
Willenhall WV13 .....27 A2
Wolverhampton WV2 .....163 D1
Gowland Dr WS11 .....1 B1
Gowrie Cl LE10 .....71 B2
Goya Cl WS11 .....2 C2
Gozzard St WV14 .....40 E5
Grace Mary Prim Sch B69 .....63 C7
Grace Moore Ct WS11 .....1 F4
Grace Rd Allesley CV5 .....111 A8
Birmingham B11 .....87 C7
Tipton, Summer Hill DY4 ....52 A7
Tipton, Tividale B69 .....63 C8
Gracechurch Sh Ctr B72 ..46 B5
Gracemere Cres B28 .....105 E3
Gracewell Homes B13 ..105 D8
Gracewell Rd B13 .....87 D1
Grafton Cl B98 .....159 B7
Grafton Cres B60 .....150 E8
Grafton Ct
Birmingham B23 .....56 C2
Coventry CV4 .....132 B7
4 Wolverhampton WV6 .....24 F4
Grafton Dr WV13 .....26 D1
Grafton Gdns DY3 .....50 B3
Grafton Gr 1 B19 .....66 C7
Grafton Ho
Bromsgrove B60 .....137 B3
Wolverhampton WV4 .....39 E5
Grafton La B61 .....150 C7
Grafton Pl WV14 .....40 E7
Grafton Rd
Birmingham, Handsworth B21 .....54 D1
Birmingham, Sparkbrook B11 .....87 B7
Oldbury B68 .....63 F2
Solihull B90 .....105 C2
West Bromwich B71 .....53 D4
Grafton St CV1 .....113 F2
Graham Cl Coventry CV6 ...96 B1
Tipton DY4 .....41 B1
Graham Cres B45 .....122 A7
Graham Ho B74 .....30 F2
Graham Rd
Birmingham, Saltley B9 .....67 F3
Birmingham, South Yardley B25 .....88 C6
Halesowen B62 .....83 C8
Stourbridge DY6 .....60 D4
West Bromwich B71 .....53 D4
Graham St
Birmingham, Hockley B1 ....66 C3
Birmingham, Lozells B19 ....66 C7
Nuneaton CV11 .....73 C5
Grainger Cl DY4 .....52 D6
Grainger Ct WS11 .....1 D2
Grainger St DY2 .....62 D7
Grainger's La B64 .....82 D8
Graiseley Ct WV3 .....163 B2
Graiseley Hill WV2 .....163 B1
Graiseley La WV11 .....26 C5
Graiseley Prim Sch WV2 .....163 B1
Graiseley Row WV2 .....163 B1
Graiseley St WV3 .....163 A2
Graith Cl B28 .....105 E3
Grammar School La B63 .83 A4
Grampian Rd DY8 .....81 A6
Granada Trad Est B69 .....63 F6
Granary Cl Cannock WS12 ...2 B5
Kingswinford DY6 .....60 A8
Granary La B76 .....46 F3
Granary Rd
Stoke Heath B60 .....150 E6
Wolverhampton WV8 .....10 E1
Granary The WS9 .....30 B6
Granborough Cl CV3 .....134 F8
Granborough Ct CV32 ...157 A3
Granbourne Rd WS2 .....27 D4
Granby Ave B33 .....69 C1
Granby Bsns Pk B33 .....69 D1
Granby Cl Hinckley LE10 ....75 C7
Redditch B98 .....154 F4
Solihull B92 .....106 E7
Granby Rd Hinckley LE10 ....75 C7
Nuneaton CV10 .....72 F3
Grand Cl B66 .....65 B3
Grand Depot Rd CV11 .....79 F6
Grand Junction Way WS1 .....42 D5
Grandborough Dr B91 ..107 A1
Grandys Croft B37 .....69 F2
Granefield Ct 4 B9 .....67 D1
Grange Ave Aldridge WS9 ..16 A1
Birmingham B8 .....68 B6
Burntwood WS7 .....7 B7
Coventry, Binley CV3 .....134 F7
Coventry, Finham CV3 .....133 C3
Kenilworth CV8 .....147 E7
Sutton Coldfield B75 .....32 C3
Grange Cl Nuneaton CV10 ..72 C7
Tamworth B77 .....35 C8
Warwick CV34 .....161 C8
Grange Cres
Birmingham B45 .....121 F8
Halesowen B63 .....83 B3
Walsall WS4 .....29 B8
Grange Ct 1 Dudley DY1 ..51 B1
1 Redditch B98 .....153 F4
Stourbridge DY9 .....81 C3
Willenhall WS2 .....27 D2
Wolverhampton WV3 .....163 A2
Grange Dr Cannock WS11 ....1 F2
Hinckley LE10 .....75 E5
Grange Farm Dr B38 ....123 D8
Grange Farm Prim Sch CV3 .....133 B5
Grange Hill B62 .....83 C2
Grange Hill Rd B38 .....103 E1
Grange La
Alvechurch B48 .....139 B3
4 Kingswinford DY6 .....60 F4
Stourbridge DY9 .....81 D4
Sutton Coldfield B75 .....32 C3
Grange Mews The 1 CV32 .....156 D1
Grange PRU The CV6 .....94 E1
Grange Rd
Balsall Common CV7 .....129 F7
Birmingham, Aston B6 .....66 E8
Birmingham, Bordesley Green B10 .....67 D1
Birmingham, Erdington B24 .57 C5
Birmingham, King's Heath B14 .....104 E8
Birmingham, Selly Oak B29 ..85 F3
Blackheath B64 .....83 B8
Burntwood WS7 .....7 A5
Coventry CV6 .....96 B5
Dorridge B93 .....127 E2
Dudley, New Dock DY1 .....51 B1
Dudley, Roseville WV14 .....51 B7
Halesowen B63 .....83 C3
Kidderminster DY11 .....116 B7
Norton Canes WS11 .....6 B6
2 Redditch B98 .....153 F4
Royal Leamington Spa CV32 .....157 B3
Smethwick B66 .....65 A3
Solihull B91 .....106 E7
Stourbridge DY9 .....81 C4
Tanworth-in-A B94 .....143 E8
West Bromwich B70 .....53 B3
Wolverhampton, Blakenhall WV2 .....39 B6
Wolverhampton, Tettenhall WV6 .....24 C4
Grange Rise B38 .....123 F7
Grange Sch The DY9 .....81 D4
Grange St Dudley DY1 .....51 B1
Walsall WS1 .....42 F7
Grange The
Cubbington CV32 .....157 F5
Halesowen B62 .....83 F6
Royal Leamington Spa CV32 .....157 B1
Royal Leamington Spa, Myton CV34 .....161 C7
Wombourne WV5 .....49 A7
Grange Wlk CV6 .....96 B5
Grangefield Cl WV8 .....10 F1
Grangehurst Prim Sch CV6 .....96 B4
Grangemouth Rd CV6 ...113 B7
Grangers La B98 .....158 F5
Grangewood Ct
Solihull B92 .....106 E7
Sutton Coldfield B73 .....57 A7
Granhill Cl B98 .....159 A8
Granleigh Ct CV32 .....157 E5
Granoe Cl CV3 .....134 E8
Granshaw Cl B38 .....103 F1
Grant Cl Kingswinford DY6 .60 D8
West Bromwich B71 .....53 C5
Grant Ct B30 .....104 A5
Grant Rd Bedworth CV7 ....78 A1
Coventry CV3 .....114 B2
Grant St Birmingham B15 ..86 D8
Walsall WS3 .....28 B8
Grantham Rd
Birmingham B11 .....87 B6
Smethwick B66 .....65 B3
Grantham St CV2 .....113 F3
Grantley Cres DY6 .....60 C7
Grantley Dr B37 .....70 B3
Granton Cl B14 .....104 D5
Granton Rd B14 .....104 D5
Grantown Gr WS3 .....14 A4
Granville B77 .....21 F1
Granville Cl
Bromsgrove B60 .....137 B1
Wolverhampton WV2 .....163 C1
Granville Crest DY10 ....117 B6
Granville Dr DY6 .....60 F5
Granville Gdns LE10 .....75 C8
Granville Rd
Blackheath B64 .....83 B8
Dorridge B93 .....128 A2
Hinckley LE10 .....75 C8
Granville Sq B1 .....66 C1
Granville St
Birmingham B1 .....164 A1
Royal Leamington Spa CV32 .....157 A2
Willenhall WV13 .....27 A3
Wolverhampton WV2 .....163 C1
Grapes Cl CV6 .....113 B5
Grasdene Gr B17 .....85 C4
Grasmere Ave
Aldridge B74 .....31 A2
Coventry CV3 .....132 F6
Perton WV6 .....23 F4
Grasmere Cl
Birmingham B43 .....54 F7
Kidderminster DY10 .....116 E7
Kingswinford DY6 .....60 B7
Wolverhampton, Tettenhall WV6 .....24 E8
Wolverhampton, Wood End WV11 .....26 C7
Grasmere Cres CV11 .....73 F7
Grasmere Ho 13 B69 .....63 D5
Grasmere Pl WS11 .....1 E5
Grasmere Rd
Bedworth CV12 .....78 B2
Birmingham B21 .....65 F7
Grasscroft Dr CV3 .....133 E6
Grassholme B77 .....36 A8
Grassington Ave CV34 ...155 F1
Grassington Dr
Birmingham B37 .....69 F1
Nuneaton CV11 .....74 A2
Grassmere Ct WS6 .....4 D3
Grassmere Dr DY8 .....80 F3
Grassmoor Rd B38 .....103 E2
Grassy La WV11 .....12 B1
Graston Cl B16 .....66 A2
Gratham Cl DY5 .....81 B7
Gratley Croft WS12 .....1 C4
Grattidge Rd B27 .....88 D2
Gratton Ct CV3 .....132 F6
Gravel Bank B32 .....84 D2
Gravel Hill Coventry CV4 ..111 F1
Wombourne WV5 .....49 B6
Gravel La WS12 .....1 C5
Gravel Pit La B48 .....139 E3
Gravel The B76 .....48 B2
Gravelly Ct 4 B23 .....56 E2
Gravelly Hill B23 .....56 E2
Gravelly Hill N B23 .....56 E3
Gravelly Hill Sta B23 .....56 E2
Gravelly Ind Pk B24 .....67 F8
Gravelly La
Birmingham B23 .....56 F5
Stonnall WS9 .....16 F3
Gray Cl DY10 .....117 B6
Gray Rd WS12 .....1 F6
Gray St B9 .....67 B2
Graydon Ct B74 .....46 B7
Grayfield Ave B13 .....87 A3
Grayland Cl B27 .....88 B2
Graylands The CV3 .....133 C4
Grayling B77 .....35 D6
Grayling Cl WS10 .....41 B3
Grayling Rd DY9 .....81 C6
Grayling Wlk
Birmingham B37 .....70 C3
Wolverhampton WV10 .....26 B4
Grays Rd B17 .....85 D6
Grayshott Cl
Birmingham B23 .....56 E5
Bromsgrove B61 .....136 E3
Grayston Ave B77 .....21 E4
Grayswood Ave CV5 .....112 D4
Grayswood Park Rd B32 ..84 C6
Grayswood Rd B31 .....122 F7
Grazebrook Croft B32 ..102 D8
Grazebrook Ind Pk DY2 ...62 B6
Grazebrook Rd DY2 .....62 C7
Grazewood Cl WV12 .....27 B7
Grazier Ave B77 .....35 C8
Grazing La B97 .....152 F2
Greadier St WV12 .....27 C5
Great Arthur St B66 .....64 F7
Great Barn La B97 .....153 B1
Great Barr Prim Sch B44 .44 D1
Great Barr Sch B44 .....44 D1
Great Barr St B9 .....67 A2
Great Brickkiln St WV3 ....25 B1
Great Bridge DY4 .....52 D5
Great Bridge Ind Est DY4 .52 C7
Great Bridge Prim Sch DY4 .....52 C6
Great Bridge Rd WV14 .....41 B3
Great Bridge St B70 .....52 E5
Great Brook St B7 .....67 A4
Great Charles St WS8 .....15 F8
Great Charles Street Queensway B3 .....164 B3
Great Colmore St B15 ....86 D8
Great Cornbow 5 B63 .....83 B3
Great Croft Ho 2 WS10 ..41 D6
Great Croft St 4 WS10 ..41 D6
Great Francis St B7 .....67 B4
Great Hampton Row B19 .....164 A4
Great Hampton St
Birmingham B18 .....164 A4
Wolverhampton WV1 .....25 B4
Great Hockings La B97 ..152 E2
Great King St B19 .....66 C5
Great King St N B19 .....66 C6
Great Lister St B7 .....67 A4
Great Moor Rd WV6 .....23 A3
Great Stone Rd B31 .....103 A3
Great Tindal St B16 .....66 A2
Great Western Arc B2 ...164 C3
Great Western Cl B18 .....65 E6
Great Western Dr B64 .....63 A1
Great Western St
Wednesbury WS10 .....41 E2
Wolverhampton WV1 .....163 C4
Great Western Way DY4 ..52 D6
Great Wood Rd B10 .....67 C1
Great Wyrley High Sch WS6 .....4 F3
Greatfield Rd DY11 .....116 B4
Greatheed Rd CV32 .....156 E2
Greatmead B77 .....21 C1
Greatorex Ct B71 .....53 B8
Greaves Ave WS5 .....43 C8
Greaves Cl Walsall WS5 ...43 C8
Warwick CV34 .....161 C7
Greaves Cres WV12 .....27 C8
Greaves Rd DY2 .....62 D5
Greaves Sq B38 .....104 B1
Greaves The B76 .....58 F6
Grebe Cl B23 .....56 B3
Green Acres B27 .....88 B2
Green Acres Rd B38 .....123 D8
Green Ave B28 .....87 E1
Green Bank Ave B28 .....87 E1
Green Barns La WS14 .....32 C8
Green Bower Dr B61 .....137 A5
Green Cl Studley B80 .....159 E3
Whitnash CV31 .....162 B4
Wythall B47 .....125 A3
Green Croft B9 .....68 A3
Green Ct
Birmingham, Gravelly Hill B23 .....56 E2
Birmingham, Hall Green B28 .....105 F8
8 Lichfield WS13 .....9 B7
Green Dr Birmingham B32 ..84 C1
Wolverhampton WV10 .....25 C7
Green Field The CV3 .....134 B8
Green Gables
Hollywood B47 .....125 A7
Sutton Coldfield B74 .....46 B7
Green Heath Rd WS12 .....2 A7
Green Hill Cl B60 .....137 D6
Green Hill Way B90 .....106 B5
Green La Aldridge WS9 .....30 E5
Balsall Common CV7 .....130 B7
Birmingham, Bordesley Green B9 .....67 E1
Birmingham, Castle Bromwich B36 .....69 E8
Birmingham, Great Barr B43 .....43 D1
Birmingham, Handsworth B21 .....65 C8
Birmingham, Hawkesley B38 .....123 E8
Birmingham, Newton B43 ...54 D8
Birmingham, Quinton B32 ..84 C6
Brownhills WS8 .....7 B2
Cannock WS11 .....4 E6
Catshill B61 .....121 A1
Coleshill B46 .....70 F5
Corley CV7 .....93 D6
Coventry CV3 .....133 B4
Dudley DY3 .....50 F5
Halesowen B62 .....63 D1
Kingswinford DY6 .....60 D7
Lichfield WS14 .....8 D2
Middleton B78 .....48 B6
Nuneaton CV10 .....72 C7
Redditch B97 .....158 A7
Solihull B90 .....105 E1
Stourbridge DY9 .....81 E5
Studley B80 .....159 B5
Tamworth B77,B78 .....36 D7
Walsall, Birchills WS2,WS3 ..28 C5
Walsall, High Heath WS9 ....15 D3
Walsall, Pelsall WS4,WS9 ...15 A4
Warwick CV34 .....160 F8
Wolverhampton WV6 .....24 F7
Green Lane Ind Est B9 ....67 E1
Green Lane Venture Ctr WS11 .....4 E6
Green Lanes Bilston WV14 .40 C7
Sutton Coldfield B73 .....57 B8
Green Lanes Prim Sch B36 .....69 F8
Green Leigh B23 .....56 F8
Green Mdw
Stourbridge DY9 .....99 B7
Wednesfield WV11 .....26 E5
Green Mdws 2 WS11 .....2 C1
Green Meadow Prim Sch B29 .....102 F7
Green Meadow Rd
Birmingham B29 .....103 A7
Willenhall WV12 .....27 B7
Green Oak Rd WV8 .....10 B2
Green Park Ave WV14 .....40 C8
Green Park Dr WV14 .....40 C8
Green Park Rd
Birmingham B31 .....102 E2
Bromsgrove B60 .....137 B2
Dudley DY2 .....62 F8
Green Park Sch WV14 .....40 B8
Green Rd Birmingham B28 ..87 E1
Dudley DY2 .....62 D7
Green Rock La WS3 .....14 D1
Green Rock Prim Sch WS3 .....14 E1
Green Slade Cres B60 ...121 C1
Green Slade Gr WS12 .....2 C7
Green St Birmingham B12 ..66 F1
Dudley WV14 .....51 C8
Kidderminster DY10 .....116 E5
Oldbury B69 .....64 A7
Smethwick B67 .....64 F5
Stourbridge DY8 .....80 F5
Walsall WS2 .....28 C3
West Bromwich B70 .....64 E8
Green Street Ind Est DY10 .....116 E4
Green Sward La B98 ....154 D1
Green The Aldridge WS9 ....30 C6
Birmingham B31 .....102 C2

Green The *continued*
Birmingham, Castle Bromwich
B36 ....69 B7
Birmingham, Erdington B23 .57 A4
Birmingham, King's Norton
B38 ....103 F2
4 Birmingham, Quinton
B32 ....84 A6
Bluntington DY10 ....118 E1
Darlaston WS10 ....41 D7
Fazeley B78 ....20 E2
Hagley DY9 ....98 F4
Nuneaton CV11 ....73 E2
Oldbury B68 ....64 B1
Solihull B91 ....107 D5
Stoneleigh CV8 ....149 C6
Stourbridge DY8 ....60 D2
Sutton Coldfield B72 ....46 D1
Tamworth B77 ....22 B8
Walsall WS3 ....14 B1
Wood End B78 ....36 C4
Green Way WS9 ....16 B2
Green Wickets B13 ....104 E6
Green Wlk WR17 ....84 F7
Greenacre Cl B77 ....22 B8
Greenacre Dr WV8 ....10 B2
Greenacre Rd DV4 ....41 A1
Greenacres Sedgley DY3 ....39 B1
Sutton Coldfield B76 ....58 A8
Wolverhampton WV6 ....24 B5
Greenacres Ave WV10 ....12 B2
Greenacres Cl WS9 ....30 D2
Greenacres Prim Sch
Bilston WV14 ....40 F6
Tamworth B77 ....22 B5
Greenacres Rd B61 ....136 E3
Greenaleigh Rd B14 ....105 D3
Greenaway Cl B43 ....44 C3
Greenaway Ct WV10 ....12 C7
Greenbank B45 ....138 D8
Greenbank Gdns DY8 ....60 E2
Greenbank Rd CV7 ....129 F6
Greenbush Dr B63 ....83 A5
Greencroft Bilston WV14 ......40 D6
Kingswinford DY6 ....60 D4
Lichfield WS13 ....3 A2
Greendale Cl B61 ....138 A8
Greendale Rd CV5 ....112 D3
Greenend Rd B13 ....86 F2
Greenfels Rise DY2 ....62 F8
Greenfield Ave
Balsall Common CV7 ....130 A7
Blackheath B64 ....62 B1
Marlbrook B60 ....121 D1
Stourbridge DY8 ....80 F5
Greenfield Cl WV5 ....49 A7
Greenfield Cotts B48 ....139 A5
Greenfield Cres B15 ....86 A8
Greenfield Croft WV14 ....40 D2
Greenfield Ho B26 ....89 D6
Greenfield La WV10 ....11 E5
Greenfield Prim Sch
Stourbridge DY8 ....80 F5
Walsall WS4 ....29 C8
Greenfield Rd
Birmingham, Harborne B17 ......85 D5
Birmingham, Newton B43 ....54 D7
Smethwick B67 ....64 E4
Greenfield View DY3 ....59 B7
Greenfields Aldridge WS9 .....30 B7
Cannock WS11 ....1 E2
Redditch B98 ....153 E2
Greenfields Rd
Kingswinford DY6 ....60 E6
Walsall WS3 ....15 D2
Wombourne WV5 ....49 A5
Greenfinch Cl
Birmingham B36 ....70 A7
Kidderminster DY10 ....117 A3
Greenfinch Rd
Birmingham B36 ....70 A7
Stourbridge DY9 ....119 A7
Greenford Cl B97 ....153 B5
Greenford Ho B23 ....56 B6
Greenford Rd B14 ....105 C3
Greenheart B77 ....22 A4
Greenhill Blackwell B60 .....137 F4
Lichfield WS13 ....9 C8
Wombourne WV5 ....49 B6
Greenhill Ave DY10 ....116 F7
Greenhill Cl
Tamworth B77 ....35 C5
Willenhall WV12 ....27 B5
Greenhill Ct
Halesowen B62 ....83 E7
Sutton Coldfield B72 ....57 C8
Wombourne WV5 ....49 B5
Greenhill Dr B29 ....85 C1
Greenhill Gdns
Birmingham B43 ....43 E2
Halesowen B62 ....83 D6
Wombourne WV5 ....49 B5
Greenhill Inst Est DY10 ....117 A7
Greenhill News WS13 ....9 C8
Greenhill Oak DY10 ....116 F7
Greenhill Rd
Birmingham, Handsworth
B21 ....54 D2
Birmingham, Moseley B13 ......87 A1
Dudley DY3 ....50 E5
Halesowen B62 ....83 D6
Sutton Coldfield B72 ....57 C8
Whitnash CV31 ....162 B4
Greenhill Way WS9 ....16 B1
Greenholm Prim Sch
B44 ....55 E7
Greenholm Rd B44 ....55 E7

Greenhough Rd WS13 ....9 A8
Greenhurst B45 ....122 A1
Greening Dr B15 ....86 B7
Greenland Ave CV5 ....111 F5
Greenland Cl DY6 ....60 E8
Greenland Ct
Birmingham B8 ....67 C6
Coventry CV5 ....111 F5
Greenland Rd B29 ....86 B1
Greenlands Bsns Ctr
B98 ....154 B2
Greenlands Dr B98 ....158 F8
Greenlands Rd B37 ....70 C1
Greenlawns DY4 ....52 B8
Greenlea B77 ....36 A8
Greenleaf Cl CV5 ....112 A3
Greenleas Gdns B63 ....83 C3
Greenleighs DY3 ....39 D3
Greenly Rd WV4 ....39 D5
Greenmoor Rd
Hinckley LE10 ....75 D5
Nuneaton CV10 ....73 A3
Greenoak Cres
Birmingham B30 ....104 C8
Dudley WV14 ....51 A7
Greenodd Dr CV6 ....95 F5
Greenridge Rd B20 ....54 F3
Greenroyde DY9 ....81 B1
Greens Ind Est WS12 ....2 C7
Greens Rd CV6 ....95 A1
Greens The WV6 ....23 E3
Greens Yd CV12 ....78 B3
Greensand Dr WV14 ....40 D2
Greenside
Birmingham B17 ....85 C5
Cheswick Green B90 ....126 D4
Stoke Prior B60 ....150 C2
Greenside Cl CV11 ....74 C1
Greenside Rd B24 ....57 C5
Greenside Way WS5 ....43 A4
Greensill Ave DY4 ....51 F8
Greenslade Croft B31 ....103 A2
Greenslade Rd
Sedgley DY3 ....39 B2
Solihull B90 ....105 C2
Walsall WS5 ....43 C7
Greensleeves B74 ....31 F1
Greensleeves Cl CV6 ....95 B2
Greenstead Rd B13 ....87 D1
Greensward Cl CV8 ....148 B6
Greensward The CV3 ....115 A2
Greenswar WV11 ....26 B8
Greenvale B31 ....102 F5
Greenvale Ave B26 ....89 D6
Greenway Birmingham B20 ......54 F6
Nuneaton CV11 ....79 B8
Sedgley DY3 ....39 A2
Warwick CV34 ....155 E1
Greenway Ave 2 DY8 ....60 E1
Greenway Dr B73 ....45 C3
Greenway Gdns
Birmingham B38 ....123 E7
Sedgley DY3 ....39 E1
Greenway Rd WV14 ....40 E4
Greenway St B9 ....67 C1
Greenway The
Birmingham, Marston Green
B37 ....90 A6
Birmingham, New Oscott
B73 ....45 B3
Hagley DY9 ....98 F5
Greenway Wlk B33 ....69 E1
Greenways
Birmingham B31 ....102 F8
Halesowen B63 ....82 C6
Stourbridge DY8 ....88 D8
Greenways The CV32 ....157 B3
Greenwood B25 ....88 D8
Greenwood Ave
Birmingham B27 ....88 B1
Blackheath B65 ....63 D3
Oldbury B68 ....64 C5
Greenwood Cl B14 ....104 E5
Greenwood Cotts DY1 ....51 A5
Greenwood Cl
Nuneaton CV11 ....73 E3
Royal Leamington Spa
CV32 ....157 B1
Greenwood Dr WV14 ....9 B6
Greenwood Pk
Aldridge WS9 ....16 C2
Cannock WS11 ....2 B8
Greenwood Pl B44 ....45 B1
Greenwood Rd
Aldridge WS9 ....16 B2
West Bromwich B71 ....53 B8
Wolverhampton WV10 ....11 D1
Greenwood Sq 5 B37 ....70 B2
Greenwood Terr B82 ....70 B2
Greenwoods The DY8 ....80 E5
Greet Prim Sch B11 ....87 D4
Greethurst Dr B13 ....87 C2
Greets Green Ind Est B70 ....52 F3
Greets Green Rd B70 ....52 F3
Greetville Cl B34 ....69 A5
Gregg Ct WS11 ....2 C2

Grendon Cl Coventry CV4 .....111 C1
Redditch B98 ....154 D1
Grendon Dr B73 ....45 D3
Grendon Gdns WV3 ....38 D6
Grendon Rd
Birmingham B14 ....106 A3
Solihull B92 ....106 A3
Grendon Sch B14 ....105 A3
Grenfell Cl CV31 ....162 D6
Grenfell Dr B73 ....46 B1
Grenfell Dr B15 ....85 F8
Grenfell Rd WS3 ....14 D3
Grenville Ave CV2 ....114 B3
Grenville Cl WS2 ....27 D3
Grenville Dr
Birmingham B23 ....56 B3
Smethwick B66 ....64 C5
Grenville Pl B70 ....52 E3
Grenville Rd Dudley DY1 ......50 E1
Solihull B90 ....106 B2
Gresham Ave CV32 ....157 B2
Gresham Pl CV32 ....157 B2
Gresham Rd
Birmingham B28 ....105 F6
Cannock WS11 ....1 F3
Nuneaton CV10 ....78 B8
Oldbury B68 ....64 C6
Gresham St CV2 ....114 A2
Gresham Twr B12 ....86 F8
Gresley B77 ....21 F1
Gresley Cl B74 ....32 A4
Gresley Gr B23 ....56 C2
Gresley Rd CV2 ....114 D7
Gresley Row WS13 ....9 C8
Gressel La B33 ....69 D3
Grestone Ave B20 ....54 E4
Grestone Prim Sch B20 ....54 E4
Greswold Cl CV4 ....111 F1
Greswold Gdns B34 ....69 A5
Greswold Prim Sch B91 ....107 C6
Greswold St B71 ....53 B5
Greswolde Dr B24 ....57 B4
Greswolde Park Rd B27 ....88 B4
Greswolde Rd
Birmingham B11 ....87 D3
Birmingham B33 ....106 E6
Royal Leamington Spa
CV31 ....162 A5
Solihull B91 ....106 F1
Greswold e The CV3 ....162 F6
Gretton Cres WS9 ....29 F5
Gretton Rd Aldridge WS9 ......29 F5
Birmingham B23 ....56 D7
Greville Dr B15 ....86 C6
Greville Rd
Kenilworth CV8 ....147 F4
Warwick CV34 ....156 B1
Greville Smith Ave
CV31 ....162 B4
Grevis Cl B13 ....86 F4
Grevis Rd B25 ....68 E1
Grey Mill Cl B90 ....126 F6
Grey Tree Cres B93 ....127 E3
Grey's Rd B80 ....159 E3
Greycoat Rd CV6 ....95 A2
Greyfort Cres B92 ....88 E1
Greyfriars Cl Dudley DY1 ......50 E3
Solihull B92 ....88 E1
Greyfriars Ct CV6 ....113 A7
Greyfriars Dr
Bromsgrove B61 ....136 D2
Tamworth B79 ....20 E6
Greyfriars La CV1 ....165 B2
Greyfriars Rd CV1 ....165 B2
Greyhound La
Stourbridge DY8 ....80 D2
Wolverhampton WV4 ....37 E5
Greyhurst Croft 5 B91 ....127 B8
Greysbrooke WS14 ....18 A5
Greysbrooke Prim Sch
WS14 ....18 A6
Greystoke Ave B36 ....68 D7
Greystoke Dr DY6 ....60 D6
Greystone Cl B98 ....154 C5
Greystone Pas 15 DY1 ....51 B1
Grice St B70 ....69 F8
Griff La Nuneaton CV10 ....78 A6
Nuneaton, Griff CV10 ....78 B6
Griff Specl Sch The CV10 ....78 B8
Griffin Cl
Birmingham B31 ....103 B6
Kidderminster DY10 ....117 B6
Griffin Cl B5 ....86 C5
Griffin Gdns B17 ....85 D4
Griffin Ho B16 ....65 E1
Griffin Ind Est B65 ....63 F3
Griffin Rd Birmingham B23 ....56 C5
Kidderminster DY10 ....116 E6
Warwick CV34 ....161 C7
Griffin St Dudley DY2 ....62 E4
West Bromwich B70 ....53 D3
Wolverhampton WV1 ....25 F1
Griffins Brook Cl B30 ....103 D7
Griffins Brook La B30 ....103 D6
Griffiths Dr
Wolverhampton WV11 ....13 A1
Wombourne WV5 ....49 A5
Griffiths Rd Dudley DY1 ....51 A6
West Bromwich B71 ....42 C1
Willenhall WV12 ....27 D8
Griffiths St DY4 ....51 E6
Grigg Gr B31 ....102 E1
Grimley Cl B98 ....153 F1
Grimley La B60 ....151 E6
Grimley Rd 2 B31 ....103 D2
Grimley Way WS11 ....1 E4
Grimpits La B38 ....124 A7
Grimshaw Rd B27 ....88 A1
Grimshaw Villas B93 ....128 D8

Grimston Cl CV3 ....115 A2
Grimstone St WV10 ....163 C4
Grindle Rd CV6 ....95 F4
Grindleford Rd B42 ....55 D7
Grindley Ho 5 CV1 ....113 B2
Grindsbrook B77 ....36 A8
Gristhorpe Rd B29 ....104 A8
Grizebeck Dr CV5 ....112 A5
Grizedale Cl B45 ....102 B2
Grocott Rd WS10 ....41 A4
Grosmont Ave 8 B12 ....87 A6
Grosvenor Ave
Aldridge B74 ....30 F1
Birmingham B20 ....55 C2
Kidderminster DY10 ....117 A6
Grosvenor Cl
Lichfield WS14 ....9 D6
Sutton Coldfield B75 ....32 C1
Wolverhampton WV10 ....11 D2
Grosvenor Cres
Hinckley LE10 ....76 A6
Wolverhampton WV10 ....11 D2
Grosvenor Ct
Birmingham, Erdington B23 ....57 A5
Birmingham, Handsworth
B20 ....55 C2
Dudley DY3 ....50 D2
4 Royal Leamington Spa
CV32 ....156 F1
Shenstone WS14 ....17 F6
Stourbridge DY9 ....81 B1
Wednesfield WV11 ....26 E5
Wolverhampton, Tettenhall
WV6 ....24 A3
Grosvenor Gdns B61 ....137 B5
Grosvenor Ho CV1 ....165 A2
Grosvenor Pk WV9 ....10 E3
Grosvenor Rd
Birmingham, Aston B6 ....67 B8
Birmingham, Handsworth
B20 ....55 C2
Birmingham, Harborne B17 ......85 A6
Coventry CV1 ....165 A1
Dudley DY3 ....50 D2
Oldbury B68 ....64 A3
Royal Leamington Spa
CV31 ....162 A5
Solihull B91 ....106 F1
Wolverhampton, Bushbury
WV10 ....11 D2
Wolverhampton, Ettingshall Park
WV4 ....39 E3
Grosvenor Road S DY3 ....50 D2
Grosvenor Sh Ctr B31 ....103 A4
Grosvenor Sq B28 ....105 F6
Grosvenor St
Birmingham B5 ....164 D3
Wolverhampton WV10 ....25 F3
Grosvenor St W B16 ....66 B1
Grosvenor Way DY5 ....81 E7
Grotto La WV6 ....24 E5
Groucutt St WV14 ....51 C8
Grounds Dr B74 ....31 F3
Grounds Rd B74 ....31 F3
Grout St B70 ....52 E4
Grove Ave
Birmingham, Handsworth
B21 ....55 C1
Birmingham, Moseley B13 ......87 A2
Halesowen B63 ....82 F3
Solihull B91 ....107 C5
Grove Cl WS11 ....1 C7
Grove Cottage Rd B9 ....67 D2
Grove Cres
Brierley Hill DY5 ....61 C5
Walsall WS3 ....14 F3
Grove Ct Birmingham B43 ......54 F6
Coventry CV5 ....112 B7
Grove Farm Dr B75 ....46 F5
Grove Fields CV10 ....73 D8
Grove Gdns
Birmingham B20 ....54 F2
Bromsgrove B61 ....137 A6
Grove Hill WS5 ....29 E1
Grove Hill Rd B21 ....54 F1
Grove La
Birmingham, Handsworth
B20 ....55 C1
Birmingham, Harborne B17 .....85 C4
Keresley CV7 ....94 F1
Lapworth B94 ....143 F4
Norton Canes WS3 ....5 C1
Smethwick B66 ....64 D5
Wishaw B76 ....47 F2
Wolverhampton WV6 ....24 B2
Grove Mews B31 ....123 B8
Grove Pk Hinckley LE10 ....76 A6
Kingswinford DY6 ....60 C8
Grove Pl Nuneaton CV10 ....72 D3
13 Royal Leamington Spa
CV31 ....162 A6
Grove Prim Sch
Birmingham B21 ....65 F8
Wolverhampton WV10 ....163 D1
Grove Rd Ansty CV7 ....97 D3
Birmingham, King's Heath
B14 ....104 D6
Birmingham, Sparkhill B11 ......87 C2
Dorridge B93 ....128 B3
Hinckley LE10 ....76 A6
Nuneaton CV10 ....72 D3
Oldbury B68 ....64 A1
Solihull B91 ....107 C5
Wolverhampton WV3 ....81 F3
Grove Sch Coventry CV5 ......165 C3
Dudley DY2 ....62 E8
Redditch B98 ....153 E4

Grove St *continued*
Royal Leamington Spa
CV32 ....161 E8
Smethwick B66 ....65 D4
Wolverhampton WV2 ....163 C1
Wolverhampton, Springfield
WV10 ....25 F3
Grove Terr WS1 ....28 F1
Grove The Bedworth CV12 ......78 C3
Birmingham, Edgbaston B16 ...65 F2
Birmingham, Great Barr
B43 ....43 E1
Birmingham, Lozells B19 ....66 B7
Birmingham, Redhall B45 ....22 A7
Birmingham, Saltley B8 ....67 C4
Birmingham, West Heath
B31 ....123 B8
Blackheath B65 ....63 C2
Brierley Hill DY5 ....103 C1
Burntwood WS7 ....6 D8
Coleshill B46 ....70 F4
Hampton-in-A B92 ....91 A1
Hinckley LE10 ....75 C8
Little Aston B74 ....31 D6
Studley B80 ....159 D3
Walsall WS5 ....43 E3
Wolverhampton, Lanesfield
WV4 ....39 E5
Wolverhampton, New Cross
WV11 ....26 B6
Grove Vale Ave B43 ....43 C1
Grove Vale Prim Sch
B43 ....43 D1
Grove Villas B64 ....82 D7
Grove Way B74 ....44 F7
Grovefield Cres CV7 ....130 C8
Grovehurst Pk CV8 ....149 B2
Groveland Rd DY4 ....52 A5
Grovelands Cres WV10 ....11 D3
Grovelands Ind Est CV7 ....96 A6
Grovelley La B31,B45 ....122 E5
Groveside Way WS3 ....15 A5
Grovewood Dr 2 B38 ....103 E1
Guardhouse Rd CV6 ....113 A8
Guardian Angels RC Prim Sch
B34 ....69 E6
Guardian Ct
Birmingham, Frankley B31 .....102 D3
Birmingham, Gilbertstone
B26 ....88 F7
8 Bromsgrove B60 ....137 A2
Solihull B91 ....107 D3
Guardian Ho B68 ....84 C7
Guardians Way B31 ....102 E8
Guernsey Dr B36 ....70 A6
Guest Ave WV11 ....26 C8
Guest Gr B19 ....66 C3
Guest Hospl DY1 ....51 E3
Guild Ave WS3 ....28 D8
Guild Cl B16 ....66 A2
Guild Cotts The 12 CV34 ....160 E6
Guild Croft B19 ....66 C6
Guild Ct 4 B60 ....136 E2
Guild Rd Bromsgrove B60 ....136 F1
Coventry CV6 ....113 D7
Guildford Cl CV11 ....116 A6
Guildford Croft B37 ....89 F8
Guildford Ct
12 Birmingham B29 ....103 C7
Coventry CV6 ....113 D7
Guildford Dr B19 ....66 D7
Guildford St **4** B19 ....66 D7
Guildhall Mews The 7
WS1 ....28 E2
Guildmarsh Cl B37 ....70 B1
Guisborough Rd CV3 ....134 E8
Guinness Cl B98 ....158 D8
Guiting Cl B97 ....153 B1
Guiting Rd B29 ....103 A7
Gulistan Cl CV32 ....156 E1
Gulistan Rd CV32 ....156 E1
Gullane Cl B38 ....103 D1
Gullet The B78 ....22 F1
Gullick Way CV5 ....6 D8
Gulliman's Way CV31 ....162 D7
Gullswood Cl B14 ....104 D2
Gulson Hospl CV1 ....165 D2
Gulson Rd CV1 ....113 A1
Gumbleberrys Cl B8 ....68 C4
Gun La CV2 ....114 A5
Gunbarrel Ind Ctr B63 ....82 F6
Gundry Cl CV31 ....162 A7
Gungate B79 ....21 B5
Gunmakers Wlk B19 ....66 D7
Gunner Gr B75 ....47 A6
Gunner La B45 ....121 D7
Gunners Cl B48 ....159 E4
Gunnery Terr 3 CV32 ....56 E3
Gunns Way B92 ....106 D7
Guns La B70 ....53 B4
Guns Village Ind Sch B70 ......53 B4
Guns Village Jun Sch
B70 ....53 A3
Gunstock Cl B74 ....44 E7
Gunter Rd B24 ....57 E3
Gunton Ave CV3 ....134 C6
Guphill Ave CV5 ....112 D2
Guphill La CV5 ....112 D3
Gupta Trad Est B69 ....52 F1
Gurnard B77 ....35 D6
Gurnard Cl WV12 ....13 A1
Gurney Cl CV4 ....111 B3
Gurney Pl WS2 ....28 A5
Gurney Rd WS2 ....28 A5

Guthrie Cl B19 .66 D6
Guthrum Cl
Birmingham B23 .56 E8
Perton WV6 .23 F5
Gutter The DY9 .120 E7
Gutteridge Ave CV6 .95 A2
Guy Ave WV10 .25 E6
Guy Pl E 11 CV32 .156 F1
Guy Pl W 10 CV32 .156 F1
Guy Rd CV8 .147 F2
Guy St
Royal Leamington Spa CV32 .156 F1
Warwick CV34 .160 F7
Guy's Almshouses B79 .21 B5
Guy's Cl CV34 .161 A8
Guy's Cliffe Ave CV32 .156 D2
Guy's Cliffe Rd CV32 .161 E8
Guy's Cliffe Terr CV34 .160 F7
Guy's Cross Park Rd CV34 .160 F8
Guy's La DY3 .50 B2
Guy's Wlk B61 .137 A5
Guys Cl B79 .20 F7
Guys Cliffe Ave B76 .46 F1
Guys Motors Ind Pk WV10 .25 F5
Gwalia Gr B23 .56 F4
Gwendoline Ave LE10 .71 A2
Gwendoline Way WS9 .16 B4
GWS Ind Est WS10 .41 D1
Gypsy La Kenilworth CV8 .147 F2
Redditch B97 .152 C5
Water Orton B46 .59 D2

H

Habberley La DY11 .116 A8
Habberley Rd
Blackheath B65 .63 D2
Kidderminster DY11 .116 B7
Habberley St 1 DY11 .116 C6
Habberly Croft 1 B91 .107 B1
Habitat Ct B76 .46 F3
Hack St B9 .67 A1
Hackett Cl WV14 .39 F1
Hackett Ct 2 B69 .64 A7
Hackett Dr B66 .64 D7
Hackett Rd B65 .63 E3
Hackett St DY4 .52 C7
Hackford Rd WV4 .39 F4
Hackmans Gate La DY9 .119 B7
Hackwood Ho 10 B69 .63 D5
Hackwood Rd WS10 .42 B2
Hadcroft Grange DY9 .81 D4
Hadcroft Rd DY9 .81 C4
Haddock Rd WV14 .40 C7
Haddon Cres WV12 .27 C7
Haddon Croft B63 .82 C1
Haddon End CV3 .133 E6
Haddon Rd
Birmingham B42 .55 D6
Royal Leamington Spa CV32 .157 B2
Haddon St CV6 .114 A8
Haddon Twr 4 B15 .86 D8
Haden Cl Blackheath B64 .83 A7
Stourbridge DY8 .60 D2
Haden Cres WV11 .26 F6
Haden Cross Dr B64 .83 A7
Haden Ct 5 WV3 .25 A2
Haden Hill WV3 .25 A2
Haden Hill Rd B63 .83 B6
Haden Park Rd B64 .82 F7
Haden Rd Blackheath B64 .62 E2
Tipton DY4 .41 A1
Haden St B12 .86 F6
Haden Way B12 .86 F6
Haden Wlk 2 B65 .63 C3
Hadendale B64 .83 A7
Hadfield Cl B24 .57 E3
Hadfield Croft B19 .66 C5
Hadfield Way B37 .70 A4
Hadland Rd B33 .69 B1
Hadleigh Croft B76 .58 A6
Hadleigh Rd CV3 .133 C4
Hadley Cl Dudley DY2 .62 E4
Hollywood B47 .125 A5
Hadley Croft B66 .65 A7
Hadley Ct B16 .65 D1
Hadley Pl WV14 .40 C7
Hadley Rd Bilston WV14 .40 C7
Walsall WS2 .27 F6
Hadley St B68 .64 A4
Hadley Way WS2 .28 A6
Hadlow Croft B33 .89 D7
Hadrian Cl CV32 .157 B4
Hadrian Dr B46 .59 F1
Hadrians Cl B77 .35 D8
Hadyn Gr B26 .89 B6
Hadzor Ho 5 B97 .153 A4
Hadzor Rd B68 .84 D8
Hafren Cl B45 .102 B2
Hafton Gr B9 .67 D1
Haggar St WV2 .39 C6
Hagley Cl DY9 .99 C6
Hagley Cswy DY9 .100 B8
Hagley Ct DY3 .50 D3
Hagley Hill DY9 .99 E7
Hagley Ho B60 .137 B3
Hagley Mews DY9 .99 D6
Hagley Park Dr B45 .122 A6
Hagley Prim Sch DY9 .99 B5
Hagley RC High Sch DY8 .98 F6
Hagley Rd Birmingham B16 .65 C1
Halesowen B63 .82 E2
Stourbridge DY8 .81 B3
Hagley Rd W B32,B68 .84 D7
Hagley St 3 B63 .83 B3
Hagley Sta DY9 .99 A6
Hagley View Rd DY2 .62 C8
Hagley Villas B12 .87 B4
Hagley Wood La DY9, B62 .100 B7
Haig Cl Cannock WS11 .2 A5
Sutton Coldfield B75 .46 C7
Haig Pl B13 .105 A7
Haig Rd DY2 .51 F1
Haig St B71 .53 C5
Hailes Park Cl WV2 .39 E6
Hailsham Rd B23 .56 F5
Hailstone Cl B65 .63 A5
Haines Cl DY4 .52 B4
Haines St B70 .53 D2
Hainfield Dr B91 .107 E5
Hainge Rd B69 .52 C1
Hainult Cl DY8 .60 D4
Halas Ind Est B62 .83 C5
Halberd Cl LE10 .75 D5
Halberton St B66 .65 D4
Haldane Ct B33 .69 B2
Haldon Gr B31 .122 E7
Hale Gr B24 .57 D4
Halecroft Ave WV11 .26 D5
Hales Cres B67 .64 E4
Hales Gdns B23 .56 C8
Hales La B67 .64 E4
Hales Park Ind Est CV6 .95 E4
Hales Rd Halesowen B63 .83 A4
Wednesbury WS10 .42 A5
Hales St CV1 .165 C3
Hales Way B69 .63 F7
Halesbury Ct B63 .82 F2
Halesbury Sch B62 .83 E7
Halescroft Sq B31 .102 E6
Halesmere Way B63 .83 C3
Halesowen CE Prim Sch B63 .83 B4
Halesowen Coll (e-commerce Ctr) B62 .83 C8
Halesowen Coll (Walton Campus) B63 .83 A3
Halesowen Coll (Whittingham main campus) B63 .83 B5
Halesowen Ind Pk B62 .83 B6
Halesowen Rd
Dudley BY2,B64 .62 D4
Halesowen B62 .83 F6
Lydiate Ash B61 .121 C3
Halesowen St
Blackheath B65 .63 C1
Oldbury B69 .63 F7
Halesworth Rd WV9 .10 F2
Halewood Gr B28 .106 A7
Haley St WV12 .27 C5
Halfcot Ave DY9 .81 C3
Halford Cres WS3 .28 F5
Halford Gr B24 .57 E4
Halford La CV6 .95 A2
Halford Lodge CV6 .95 A2
Halford Rd B91 .106 E6
Halford St B79 .21 A5
Halford's La B66 .65 A8
Halfords Pk B66 .65 A8
Halfpenny Field Wlk B35 .58 A3
Halfshire La DY10 .98 B1
Halfway Cl B44 .55 E6
Halifax Cl CV5 .112 A7
Halifax Gr 7 B18 .65 E4
Halifax Ho B5 .86 D7
Halifax Rd B90 .106 B2
Haliscombe Gr 4 B6 .66 E8
Halkett Glade B33 .68 D3
Hall Brook Rd CV6 .95 A4
Hall Cl CV8 .149 B6
Hall Cres B71 .53 C6
Hall Dale Cl B28 .105 F5
Hall Dr Baginton CV8 .133 E3
Birmingham B37 .90 A7
Hagley DY9 .99 D6
Hall End Nuneaton CV11 .73 D2
Wednesbury WS10 .41 F3
Hall End Pl CV11 .73 D2
Hall Gr WV14 .51 C8
Hall Green Inf Sch B28 .105 F7
Hall Green Jun Sch B28 .105 F7
Hall Green Prim Sch B71 .42 D1
Hall Green Rd
Coventry CV2,CV6 .96 B2
West Bromwich B71 .42 D1
Hall Green Sch B28 .105 E8
Hall Green Sta B28 .87 F1
Hall Hays Rd B34 .69 E7
Hall La Brownhills WS9 .15 E3
Burntwood, Hammerwich WS7 .7 E4
Burntwood, Muckley Corner WS7,WS14 .7 F2
Coventry CV2 .114 F6
Dudley DY2 .62 C6
Great Wyrley WS6 .5 A3
Hagley DY9 .99 D6
Tipton DY4 .52 B8
Walsall WS3 .14 F3
Wolverhampton WV14 .39 F1
Hall Mdw Hagley DY9 .99 D7
Wedges Mills WS11 .4 B6
Hall Park St WV14 .40 B7
Hall Rd
Birmingham, Castle Bromwich B36 .69 A8
Hall Rd *continued*
Birmingham, Handsworth B20 .66 A8
Birmingham, Saltley B8 .67 D4
Hinckley LE10 .75 D5
Royal Leamington Spa CV32 .156 F1
Smethwick B67 .64 E4
Hall St Bilston WV14 .40 E5
Birmingham B18 .164 A4
Blackheath B64 .62 F2
Darlaston WS10 .41 B7
Dudley DY2 .51 D1
Oldbury B68 .64 B5
Sedgley DY3 .50 D8
Stourbridge DY8 .81 A3
Tipton DY4 .51 E5
Walsall WS2 .28 D3
West Bromwich B70 .53 C2
Willenhall WV13 .27 B1
Wolverhampton WV11 .26 C5
Hall St E WS10 .41 C7
Hall St S B70 .64 D8
Hall Wlk B46 .70 F4
Hall's Cl CV31 .162 B3
Halladale B38 .103 F1
Hallam Cl B71 .53 E5
Hallam Cres WV10 .25 E6
Hallam Dr B71 .53 E5
Hallam Rd CV6 .95 B2
Hallam St Birmingham B12 .86 E5
West Bromwich B71 .53 D5
Hallams Cl CV8 .135 F5
Hallbridge Cl WS3 .14 F2
Hallbridge Way B69 .52 B2
Hallchurch Rd DY2 .61 F6
Hallcourt Cl 3 WS11 .4 E8
Hallcourt Cres 2 WS11 .4 E8
Hallcourt La WS11 .4 E8
Hallcroft Cl B72 .57 C7
Hallcroft Way
Aldridge WS9 .30 C5
Knowle B93 .128 A6
Hallens Dr WS10 .41 D2
Hallet Dr WV3 .163 A2
Hallewell Rd B16 .65 D3
Hallfield Sch B15 .86 A7
Hallfields CV31 .162 E5
Hallgreen St WV14 .40 E2
Hallmoor Rd B33 .69 B3
Hallmoor Sch B33 .69 B3
Hallot Cl B23 .56 D8
Halloughton Rd B74 .46 A7
Hallowfields Cl B98 .153 E1
Hallstead Rd B13 .105 B5
Hallway Dr CV7 .97 E6
Halsbury Gr B44 .56 B8
Halstead Gr B91 .127 A8
Halston Rd WS7 .7 B8
Halswelle Gr B43 .44 E4
Halton Rd B73 .45 E2
Halton St DY2 .62 C5
Haltonlea B77 .36 A8
Ham Dingle Prim Sch DY9 .81 C2
Ham La Kingswinford DY6 .49 E1
Stourbridge DY9 .81 C2
Hamar Way B37 .70 B1
Hamberley Ct B18 .65 D5
Hamble B77 .21 D2
Hamble Cl DY5 .61 A6
Hamble Ct B73 .46 B5
Hamble Gr WV6 .23 E4
Hamble Rd
Birmingham B42 .43 F1
Wolverhampton WV4 .38 C6
Hambledon Cl WV9 .11 A2
Hambleton Rd B63 .82 D2
Hambletts Rd B70 .53 A3
Hambrook Cl WV6 .25 A5
Hambury Dr B14 .104 D7
Hamelin St WS11 .1 E3
Hamilton Ave
Birmingham B17 .85 A7
Halesowen B62 .83 C3
Stourbridge DY8 .80 D6
Hamilton Cl
Bedworth CV12 .77 C1
Cannock WS12 .2 F4
Hinckley LE10 .71 A2
Lickey End B60 .137 C6
Sedgley DY3 .50 C8
Stourbridge DY8 .60 C2
Hamilton Ct
1 Birmingham B13 .86 F4
Coventry CV1 .165 B4
Nuneaton CV10 .72 D4
Hamilton Dr
Birmingham B29 .103 D8
Stourbridge DY8 .60 C2
Studley B80 .159 D3
Tipton B69 .52 C2
Hamilton Gdns WV10 .11 F3
Hamilton Ho
3 Birmingham B5 .86 D7
Walsall WS3 .14 C1
Hamilton Lea WS11 .6 A6
Hamilton Rd
Birmingham B21 .65 D8
Coventry CV2 .114 A3
Kidderminster DY11 .116 B3
Radford Semele CV31 .162 E5
Redditch B97 .158 C8
Smethwick B67 .64 E2
Tipton DY4 .52 C6
Hamilton Specl Sch B21 .65 D8
Hamilton St WS3 .14 D1
Hamilton Terr CV32 .161 F8
Hamlet Cl CV11 .74 B1
Hamlet Gdns B28 .105 F8
Hamlet Rd B28 .105 F8
Hamlet The
Leek Wootton CV35 .156 A7
Norton Canes WS11 .5 E5
Hammer Bank DY5 .82 A8
Hammersley Cl B63 .82 C7
Hammersley St CV12 .77 E1
Hammerwich Hospl WS7 .7 B5
Hammerwich La WS7 .7 F3
Hammerwich Rd WS7 .7 D5
Hammond Ave WV10 .25 E8
Hammond Bsns Ctr CV11 .73 E3
Hammond Cl CV11 .73 E3
Hammond Dr B23 .56 F5
Hammond Rd CV2 .113 F4
Hammond Way DY8 .81 A7
Hammonds Terr CV8 .147 D5
Hampden Cl DY5 .82 A8
Hampden Retreat B12 .86 E6
Hamps Cl WS7 .7 D7
Hampshire Cl
Coventry CV3 .134 F8
Tamworth B78 .20 F2
Hampshire Ct 1 B29 .103 B7
Hampshire Dr B15 .85 E8
Hampshire Rd B71 .42 A1
Hampson Cl B11 .87 B6
Hampstead Cl WV11 .26 D6
Hampstead Glade B63 .83 C2
Hampton Ave
Bromsgrove B60 .151 A8
Nuneaton CV10 .72 B4
Hampton Cl
Coventry CV6 .113 F6
Redditch B98 .159 A7
Sutton Coldfield B73 .45 C2
Tamworth B79 .21 C7
Hampton Court Rd B17 .85 A6
Hampton Ct
Essington WV10 .12 B2
Hampton-in-A B92 .109 B6
Solihull B91 .107 D4
Hampton Dr B74 .46 B8
Hampton Gdns DY9 .81 D3
Hampton Gn WS11 .4 E7
Hampton Gr
Royal Leamington Spa CV32 .157 B1
Walsall WS3 .15 A4
Hampton Grange CV7 .92 B1
Hampton La
Meriden CV7 .109 E8
Solihull B91 .108 B5
Hampton Pl WS10 .41 C8
Hampton Rd
Birmingham, Aston B6 .66 D8
Birmingham, Stockland Green B23 .56 D4
Coventry CV6 .113 F6
Knowle B93 .128 C8
Warwick CV34 .160 B5
Wolverhampton WV10 .11 B1
Hampton St
Birmingham B19 .164 B4
Cannock WS11 .4 D7
Dudley, Netherton DY2 .62 C5
Dudley, Roseville WV14 .51 B8
Warwick CV34 .160 D6
Hampton View WV10 .25 F3
Hampton- in -Arden Sta B92 .109 B7
Hams La B76 .59 F6
Hams Rd B8 .67 D4
Hamstead Hall Ave B20 .54 E5
Hamstead Hall Rd B20 .54 F4
Hamstead Hall Sec Sch B20 .54 E6
Hamstead Hill B20 .54 F4
Hamstead Ho B43 .54 F7
Hamstead Jun & Inf Sch B43 .54 D7
Hamstead Rd
Birmingham, Hanmtead B43 .54 D7
Birmingham, Lozells B19, B20 .66 B7
Hamstead Sta B42 .54 F6
Hamstead Terr WS10 .42 A2
Hanam Cl B75 .46 F6
Hanbury Cl
Bromsgrove B60 .151 A8
Halesowen B63 .82 F1
Hanbury Cres WV4 .38 E6
Hanbury Croft B27 .88 E3
Hanbury Ct DY8 .81 A4
Hanbury Hill DY8 .81 A4
Hanbury Ho B97 .153 B4
Hanbury Rd
Bedworth CV12 .78 C4
Brownhills WS8 .6 F2
Dorridge B93 .127 F4
Norton Canes WS11 .5 F5
Stoke Heath B60 .150 D4
Tamworth B77 .21 F4
West Bromwich B70 .53 A3
Hanbury's Farm Prim Sch B77 .21 D1
Hanch Pl WS1 .42 F8
Hancock Gn CV4 .131 F8
Hancock Rd B8 .67 F4
Hancox St B68 .64 B2
Handcross Gr CV3 .133 A5
Handel Ct WS11 .2 C2
Handel Wlk WS13 .3 C2
Handley Gr
Birmingham B31 .102 C2
Warwick CV34 .155 D1
Handley St WS10 .42 A4
Handley's Cl CV8 .135 A1
Handsworth Cl B21 .65 D7
Handsworth Coll B6 .66 E8
Handsworth Coll (City Coll Birmingham) B21 .65 F8
Handsworth Cres CV5 .111 E4
Handsworth Dr B43 .44 A3
Handsworth Gram Sch B21 .65 F8
Handsworth New Rd B18 .65 E6
Handsworth Wood Boys' Sch B20 .54 F2
Handsworth Wood Girls' Sch B20 .54 F2
Handsworth Wood Rd B20 .55 A2
Handsworth, Booth Street Sta B21 .65 C7
Hanford Cl CV6 .113 E6
Hanger Rd B26 .90 A3
Hanging La B31 .102 E2
Hangleton Dr B11 .87 D6
Hangman's La LE10 .71 E3
Hanley Cl B63 .82 E4
Hanley Ct B23 .56 C2
Hanley St B19 .164 C4
Hanley Villas 1 B12 .87 B5
Hanlith B77 .36 A8
Hannaford Way WS11 .1 F2
Hannafore Rd B16 .65 D3
Hannah Rd WV14 .41 A3
Hanney Hay Rd WS7,WS8 .7 B3
Hannon Rd B14 .104 E5
Hanover Cl B6 .66 E7
Hanover Ct Hinckley LE10 .75 E6
Redditch B97 .158 D8
Tamworth B79 .20 E7
Walsall WS2 .27 E1
Wolverhampton WV6 .24 C4
Hanover Dr B24 .67 F8
Hanover Gdns 8 CV32 .157 A1
Hanover Glebe CV11 .73 C2
Hanover Ho 6 DY8 .80 F8
Hanover Pl
Bromsgrove B60 .136 F1
Cannock WS11 .1 E2
Hanover Rd B65 .63 C4
Hanover St B61 .136 F1
Hans Cl CV2 .113 F4
Hansell Dr B93 .127 E2
Hansom Rd
Birmingham B32 .84 C5
Hinckley LE10 .71 F2
Hanson Ct 2 LE10 .75 D8
Hanson Gr B92 .88 F5
Hanson Way CV6 .96 A4
Hanson's Bridge Rd B24 .57 F5
Hanwell Cl B76 .58 B7
Hanwood Cl
Birmingham B12 .86 F8
Coventry CV5 .111 D4
Hanwood Ho 1 B12 .86 F8
Hanworth Cl CV32 .157 C2
Hanworth Rd CV34 .160 D8
Harald Cl WV6 .23 E5
Harbeck Ave B44 .55 F8
Harberrow Cl DY9 .99 A6
Harbet Dr B40 .90 E4
Harbinger Rd B38 .104 B2
Harborne Ct B17 .85 C4
Harborne Hill Sch B15 .85 E6
Harborne La B17 .85 D3
Harborne Park Rd B17 .85 C4
Harborne Prim Sch B17 .85 C6
Harborne Rd
Birmingham B15 .85 E7
Oldbury B68 .84 E8
Harborough Cotts B94 .144 D3
Harborough Ct B74 .32 A2
Harborough Dr
Aldridge WS9 .30 B5
Birmingham B36 .58 D1
Harborough Rd CV6 .95 B2
Harborough Wlk DY9 .81 B2
Harbours Cl B61 .150 D7
Harbours Hill DY9 .120 E6
Harbury Cl Redditch B98 .154 D1
Sutton Coldfield B76 .58 B6
Harbury La CV33,CV34 .161 E2
Harbury Rd B12 .86 D5
Harby Cl B37 .90 B8
Harcourt CV3 .134 E5
Harcourt Dr Dudley DY3 .50 D2
Sutton Coldfield B74 .31 F4
Harcourt Gdns CV11 .73 C3
Harcourt Ho B79 .21 A4
Harcourt Rd
Birmingham B23 .56 E7
Blackheath B64 .82 F8
Wednesbury WS10 .41 F4
Harden Cl WS3 .28 E7
Harden Ct B31 .102 E1
Harden Gr WS3 .28 E7
Harden Keep B66 .65 A4
Harden Manor Ct B63 .83 C3
Harden Prim Sch WS3 .28 E7
Harden Rd WS3 .28 E7
Harden Vale B63 .82 E5
Hardie Ct 2 WV4 .39 F4
Hardie Gn WS11 .1 F3
Harding St WV14 .40 D2
Hardon Rd WV4 .39 F5
Hardware St B70 .53 D4
Hardwick Cl CV5 .112 A4
Hardwick Ct Aldridge B74 .30 F2
Tamworth B79 .21 C5
Hardwick Dr B62 .83 A7

Hardwick La B80 ....159 F4
Hardwick Rd Aldridge B74 .31 A2
Solihull B92 ....88 E4
Hardwicke Way DY9 ......81 D5
Hardwike Wlk B14 ......104 D2
Hardwyn Cl CV3 ....115 A1
Hardy Ave DY10 ....117 A6
Hardy Cl Hinckley LE10 ....71 D4
Nuneaton CV10 ....72 A4
Hardy Rd Coventry CV6 ...113 A8
Walsall WS3 ....28 E8
Wednesbury WS10 ....42 A3
Hardy Sq WV2 ....39 F6
Hare & Hounds La CV10 ..73 A2
Hare Gr B31 ....102 D3
Hare St WV14 ....40 F5
Harebell B77 ....22 A4
Harebell Cl Cannock WS12 ..2 D2
Featherstone WV10 ....12 A7
Walsall WS5 ....43 A3
Harebell Cres DY1 ....51 A4
Harebell Gdns B38 ......123 F8
Harebell Wlk 1 B37 .....70 D2
Harefield Ho CV2 ....114 B3
Harefield La CV12 ....77 F8
Harefield Rd
Coventry CV2 ....114 B3
Nuneaton CV11 ....73 C4
Haresfield B90 ....126 A5
Haresfield Cl B97 ....153 D3
Harewell Dr B75 ....32 C1
Harewood B17 ....85 B6
Harewood Ave
Birmingham B43 ....43 C2
Wednesbury WS10 ....42 C3
Harewood Cl B28 ....105 E5
Harewood Rd CV5 ....112 C2
Harford St B18,B19 ......164 A5
Hargate La B71 ....53 D4
Hargate Prim Sch B71 ...53 C4
Harger Ct CV8 ....147 F4
Harger Mews CV8 ....147 F4
Hargrave Cl
Coventry CV3 ....115 A1
Water Orton B46 ....59 B3
Hargrave Rd B90 ....105 D1
Hargreave Cl B76 ....57 F8
Hargreaves Ct DY11 .....116 C3
Hargreaves St WV1 ....40 A7
Harington Rd CV6 ....113 A5
Harland Cl B61 ....136 D3
Harland Rd B74 ....32 A3
Harlech Cl
Birmingham B32 ....102 A7
Kenilworth CV8 ....148 C5
Tipton B69 ....52 A1
Harlech Ho 2 WS3 ......28 C6
Harlech Rd WV12 ....27 C6
Harlech Twr B23 ....57 A6
Harlech Way Dudley DY1 ...50 F2
Kidderminster DY10 ......116 E2
Harleston Rd B44 ....55 F8
Harlestones Ho DY8 ......80 F7
Harley Cl WS8 ....16 A6
Harley Dr WV14 ....40 B4
Harley Grange 6 DY2 ....62 E8
Harley St CV2 ....114 A3
Harlow Gr B28 ....106 A6
Harlow Wlk 8 CV2 .....115 A7
Harlstones Cl DY8 ....81 A8
Harlyn Cl WV14 ....41 A2
Harman Rd B72 ....57 B6
Harmar Cl CV34 ....155 D1
Harmer Cl CV2 ....115 A7
Harmer St B18 ....66 A5
Harmon Rd DY8 ....80 C5
Harmony Ct CV10 ....73 B2
Harnall Cl B90 ....126 E7
Harnall Ind Est CV1 .....165 C4
Harnall La CV1 ....165 C4
Harnall La E CV1 ....113 E4
Harnall La W CV1 ....165 C4
Harnall Row
Coventry CV1 ....113 E2
Coventry CV1 ....113 E3
Harness Cl WS5 ....42 F4
Harold Evers Way DY10 .116 F7
Harold Rd Birmingham B16 .65 F1
Coventry CV2 ....114 D2
Smethwick B67 ....64 E3
Harold St CV11 ....73 C3
Harpenden Dr CV5 ....112 A5
Harper Ave WV11 ....26 C7
Harper Bell Sch The B12 .87 A8
Harper Rd Bilston WV14 ...40 D6
Coventry CV1 ....113 E2
Harper St WV13 ....27 A2
Harpers Rd
Birmingham, Highter's Heath
B14 ....105 A1
Birmingham, Northfield
B31 ....103 A2
Harport Rd B98 ....154 A1
Harpur Cl WS4 ....29 A4
Harpur Rd WS4 ....29 A4
Harrier Rd B27 ....88 D2
Harriers Gn DY10 ....117 B8
Harriers Ind Est DY10 ...116 F5
Harriet Cl DY5 ....61 B5
Harringay Dr DY8 ....80 E3
Harringay Rd B44 ....45 A2
Harrington Ct CV3 ....114 F2
Harrington Way CV10 ....78 A7
Harrington Wlk WS13 ......3 F8
Harringworth Ct WS4 .....29 C8
Harriott Dr CV34 ....161 D4
Harris Ct B18 ....66 A6
Harris Dr
2 Birmingham B42 ......55 A8
Smethwick B66 ....65 B3
Harris Ind Pk B60 ....150 E2
Harris Rd Coventry CV3 ...114 B2
Warwick CV34 ....160 C8
Harrison Cl
Cheslyn Hay WS6 ....4 D1
Walsall WS3 ....14 C1
Harrison Cres CV12 ....78 A2
Harrison Ct DY8 ....61 A1
Harrison Ho B14 ....104 F3
Harrison Rd
Birmingham B24 ....56 F4
Cannock WS11 ....4 E7
Redditch B97 ....158 C8
Stourbridge DY8 ....61 A1
Sutton Coldfield B74 ....31 E5
Walsall WS4 ....15 C2
Harrison St WS3 ....14 C1
Harrison Way CV31 ......161 F5
Harrison's Fold DY2 ......62 C5
Harrison's Rd B15 ....85 E6
Harrisons Gn B15 ....85 E6
Harrisons Pleck B13 ......86 F3
Harrold Ave B65 ....63 E3
Harrold Rd B65 ....63 E3
Harrold St DY4 ....52 C7
Harrold Terr B19 ....66 C8
Harrop Way DY8 ....80 E8
Harrow Cl Coventry CV6 ...96 A4
Hagley DY9 ....99 A6
Stoke Heath B60 ....150 E6
Harrow Ct B74 ....31 F2
Harrow Rd
Birmingham B29 ....85 F3
Kingswinford DY6 ....49 D1
Whitnash CV31 ....162 B3
Harrow St WV1 ....25 B4
Harrowbrook Ind Est
LE10 ....74 E7
Harrowbrook Rd LE10 .....74 E7
Harrowby Dr DY4 ....52 A4
Harrowby Pl WV13 ....27 D1
Harrowby Rd
Bilston WV14 ....41 A4
Wolverhampton WV10 .....11 C2
Harrowfield Rd B33 ....68 E4
Harry Caplan Ho CV5 ....112 B6
Harry Cheshire Com High
Sch DY11 ....116 B6
Harry Edwards Ho 2
CV2 ....114 D8
Harry Perks St WV13 .....27 A3
Harry Price Ho 9 B69 ....63 D5
Harry Rose Rd CV2 ......114 E3
Harry Salt Ho CV1 ....165 D3
Harry Stanley Ho CV6 ...114 A8
Harry Taylor Fst Sch The
B97 ....158 E6
Harry Taylor Ho B98 .....154 A4
Harry Truslove Cl CV6 ...113 A7
Harry Weston Rd CV3 ...115 A1
Hart Dr B73 ....57 A8
Hart Rd Birmingham B24 ...57 A5
Willenhall WV11 ....26 D4
Hart St WS1 ....42 E8
Hartfield Cres B27 ....88 B2
Hartfields Way B65 ....62 F5
Hartford Cl B17 ....85 A7
Hartford Rd B60 ....137 B1
Hartill Rd WV4 ....38 D3
Hartill St WV13 ....41 B8
Hartington Cl B93 ....127 E3
Hartington Cres CV5 ....112 F1
Hartington Gn LE10 ....75 E6
Hartington Rd B19 ....66 D7
Hartland Ave
Coventry CV2 ....114 B5
Dudley WV14 ....51 A8
Hartland Rd
Birmingham B31 ....122 E6
Dudley DY4 ....51 D5
West Bromwich B71 ....53 F8
Hartland St DY5 ....61 D7
Hartle La DY9 ....119 F6
Hartlebury Cl
Cannock WS11 ....2 C2
Dorridge B93 ....127 F3
Redditch B98 ....154 E7
Hartlebury Rd
Halesowen B63 ....82 F2
Oldbury B69 ....63 D5
Hartledon Rd B17 ....85 B5
Hartlepool Rd CV1 ......165 D4
Hartley Dr WS9 ....30 B4
Hartley Gr B44 ....45 B3
Hartley Pl B15 ....85 F8
Hartley Rd B44 ....45 B3
Hartley St WV3 ....25 A2
Hartleyburn B77 ....36 A8
Harton Way B14 ....104 C5
Hartopp Rd
Birmingham B8 ....67 E4
Sutton Coldfield B74 ......45 F8
Hartridge Wlk CV5 ......112 B4
Harts Cl B17 ....85 D6
Harts Green Rd B17 ....85 A5
Harts Rd B8 ....67 E5
Hartsbourne Dr B62 ....83 D4
Hartshill Ho B27 ....88 E2
Hartshill Rd
Birmingham B34 ....69 A6
Solihull B27 ....88 D2
Hartshill Sch CV10 ....72 B8
Hartshorn St WV14 ....40 D5
Hartside Cl B63 ....82 D2
Hartslade WS14 ....9 E6
Hartswell Dr B13 ....104 F6
Hartwell Cl B91 ....107 B1
Hartwell La WS6 ....5 A3
Hartwell Rd B24 ....57 B2
Harvard Cl DY1 ....50 F4
Harvard Rd B92 ....89 B4
Harvest Cl
Birmingham B30 ....104 B6
Dudley DY3 ....50 E5
Stoke Heath B60 ....150 E6
Harvest Ct B65 ....63 A4
Harvest Fields Way B75 ..32 E3
Harvest Gdns B68 ....64 A4
Harvest Hill Cl 7 CV31 ..162 C6
Harvest Hill La CV5,CV7 ...93 C4
Harvest Rd Blackheath B65 .63 A3
Smethwick B67 ....64 D3
Harvest Wlk B65 ....63 A3
Harvester Way DY6 ....60 A8
Harvesters Cl
Aldridge WS9 ....30 E2
Coventry CV3 ....115 A2
Harvesters Rd WV12 ......27 D5
Harvesters Way WV12 ....27 D5
Harvesters Wlk WV8 ......10 E1
Harvey Cl CV5 ....112 A7
Harvey Ct B33 ....69 D3
Harvey Dr B75 ....32 C2
Harvey Mews B30 ......103 D7
Harvey Rd
Birmingham B26 ....88 D7
Walsall WS2 ....28 B5
Harvey Works Ind Est
B63 ....82 F6
Harveys Terr DY2 ....62 D4
Harvills Hawthorn B70 ...52 F7
Harvills Hawthorn Prim Sch
B70 ....52 F7
Harvine Wlk DY8 ....80 E3
Harvington Cl
Kidderminster DY11 .....116 A8
Redditch B97 ....153 B5
Harvington Dr B90 ......127 B6
Harvington Hall* DY10 ..118 B1
Harvington Hall La
DY10 ....118 B1
Harvington Ho DY8 ....81 A6
Harvington Rd
Birmingham B29 ....103 A8
Bromsgrove B60 ....151 A8
Dudley WV14 ....40 B1
Halesowen B63 ....82 F1
Oldbury B68 ....84 A8
Harvington Way B76 ......58 A8
Harvington Wlk 3 B65 ...63 C3
Harwell Cl B79 ....21 C7
Harwin Cl WV6 ....24 F7
Harwood Dr Hinckley LE10 .71 F4
Tamworth B77 ....35 D4
Harwood Gr 1 B90 .....126 C8
Harwood Rd WS13 ....3 B3
Harwood St B70 ....53 B3
Hasbury CE Prim Sch
B63 ....82 F2
Hasbury Cl B63 ....82 E2
Hasbury Rd B32 ....102 B8
Haselbech Rd CV3 ......114 F1
Haselbury Cnr CV10 ......72 F1
Haseley Cl Redditch B98 ..154 E1
Royal Leamington Spa
CV31 ....162 B5
Haseley Rd
Birmingham B21 ....65 E7
Coventry CV2 ....96 C1
Solihull B91 ....106 E6
Haselor Rd B73 ....45 E1
Haselour Rd B37 ....69 F5
Hasilwood Sq CV3 ......114 B2
Haskell St WS1 ....42 F7
Haslucks Croft B90 .....106 A3
Haslucks Green Rd
Solihull, Major's Green
B90 ....125 E7
Solihull, Shirley B90 ....106 B4
Haslucks Green Sch
B90 ....106 A3
Hassop Rd B42 ....55 D7
Hastang Fields CV31 ....162 C5
Hastings Cl B77 ....35 F6
Hastings Ct DY1 ....50 E2
Hastings High Sch LE10 ..75 F7
Hastings Rd
Birmingham B23 ....56 B7
Bromsgrove B60 ....150 E7
Coventry CV2 ....114 A4
Haswell Rd B63 ....82 D4
Hatch Heath Cl WV5 .....49 A7
Hatcham Rd B44 ....45 C2
Hatchett St B19 ....66 E5
Hatchford Ave B92 ....89 C3
Hatchford Brook Inf Sch
B92 ....89 C3
Hatchford Brook Jun Sch
B92 ....89 C3
Hatchford Brook Rd B92 .89 C3
Hatchford Ct B92 ....89 C3
Hatchford Prim Sch B37 ..69 F2
Hatchford Wlk B37 ....70 B1
Hateley Dr WV4 ....39 E4
Hateley Heath Prim Schs
B71 ....53 B7
Hatfield Cl
Birmingham B23 ....56 D8
Redditch B98 ....154 E1
Hatfield Rd
Birmingham B19 ....66 D8
Stourbridge DY9 ....81 C4
Hathaway Cl
Balsall Common CV7 ....130 B7
Willenhall WV13 ....40 F8
Hathaway Dr
Nuneaton CV11 ....74 A1
Warwick CV34 ....155 E2
Hathaway Rd
Coventry CV4 ....111 D1
Solihull B90 ....106 B1
Sutton Coldfield B74 ......32 A4
Hatherden Dr B76 ....47 A2
Hatherell Rd CV31 ......162 E5
Hathersage Rd B42 ....55 D7
Hatherton Croft WS11 ......1 C1
Hatherton Gdns WV10 ....11 E2
Hatherton Gr B29 ....84 F1
Hatherton Lane Prim Sch
WS2 ....28 A6
Hatherton Pl WS9 ....30 A7
Hatherton Rd
Bilston WV14 ....40 F6
Cannock WS11 ....1 C1
Walsall WS1 ....28 E2
Hatherton St
Cheslyn Hay WS6 ....4 C2
Walsall WS1,WS4 ....28 E3
Hattersley Gr B11 ....88 A3
Hatton Cres WV10 ....26 A7
Hatton Gdns B42 ....55 B7
Hatton Rd Cannock WS11 ...1 A1
Wolverhampton WV6 ......24 F3
Hatton St WV14 ....40 E4
Hattons Gr WV8 ....10 B2
Haughton Rd B20 ....55 D1
Haunch La B13 ....105 A5
Haunchwood Dr B76 ......57 F7
Haunchwood Rd CV10 ....72 D4
Havacre La WV14 ....40 C1
Havefield Ave WS14 ....9 E7
Havelock Cl WV3 ....38 F8
Havelock Rd
Birmingham, Handsworth
B20 ....55 C1
Birmingham, Saltley B8 ....67 D5
Birmingham, Sparkhill B11 ..87 E4
Haven Croft B43 ....54 D8
Haven Dr B27 ....88 B3
Haven The
Birmingham B14 ....105 D4
Stourbridge DY8 ....60 D2
Wolverhampton WV2 ....163 B1
Havendale Cl CV6 ....113 B5
Haverford Dr B45 ....122 B6
Havergal Wlk B63 ....82 B4
Haverhill Cl WS3 ....14 A3
Hawbridge Cl B90 ....127 B6
Hawbush Gdns DY5 ....61 A1
Hawbush Prim Sch DY5 ..61 B2
Hawbush Rd
Brierley Hill DY5 ....61 A2
Walsall WS3 ....28 E6
Hawcroft Gr B34 ....69 C6
Hawes Cl WS1 ....42 F6
Hawes La B65 ....63 B3
Hawes Rd WS1 ....42 F6
Haweswater Dr DY6 ......60 D6
Hawfield Cl B69 ....63 C7
Hawfield Gr B72 ....57 C7
Hawfield Rd B69 ....63 C7
Hawfinch B77 ....36 A5
Hawfinch Rise DY10 ....117 A2
Hawford Ave DY10 ......117 B6
Hawk Cl CV11 ....79 B8
Hawker Dr B35 ....57 F2
Hawkes Cl B30 ....104 A7
Hawkes Dr CV34 ....161 D4
Hawkes La B70 ....53 A7
Hawkes Mill La CV5 ......94 B2
Hawkes St B10 ....87 D8
Hawkesbury Cl B98 .....154 D5
Hawkesbury Fields Sch
CV2 ....96 C3
Hawkesbury La CV2 ......96 D5
Hawkesbury Rd B90 .....105 F1
Hawkesford Cl
Birmingham B36 ....69 A8
Sutton Coldfield B74 ......32 B1
Hawkesford Rd B33 ......69 D3
Hawkesley CE Prim Sch
B38 ....123 E7
Hawkesley Cres B31 ....103 A1
Hawkesley Dr B31 ......122 F8
Hawkesley End B38 .....123 E7
Hawkesley Mill La B31 ..102 F2
Hawkesley Rd DY1 ....61 F8
Hawkesley Sq B38 ....123 E7
Hawkesmoor Dr WS14 .....9 D8
Hawkestone Cres B70 ....53 A6
Hawkestone Rd B29 .....103 A7
Hawkesville Dr 7 WS11 ...1 F2
Hawkeswell Cl B92 ......106 E8
Hawkeswell Dr DY6 ....49 D1
Hawkesworth Dr CV8 ....148 A6
Hawkesyard Rd B24 ......56 E1
Hawkhurst Rd B14 ....104 F2
Hawkin's Pl WV14 ....40 F3
Hawkinge Dr B35 ....58 A4
Hawkins Cl Birmingham B5 .86 E6
Hinckley LE10 ....71 D4
Lichfield WS13 ....3 B2
Hawkins Croft DY4 ....52 A3
Hawkins Dr WS11 ....4 C4
Hawkins Rd CV5 ....113 A2
Hawkins St B70 ....53 A8
Hawkley Cl WV1 ....26 B2
Hawkley Rd WV1 ....26 B2
Hawkmoor Gdns B38 ....124 A8
Hawks Cl WS6 ....4 D2
Hawks Green La WS11 .....2 A2
Hawksford Cres WV10 ....25 E7
Hawkshead Dr B93 ......127 F6
Hawkside B77 ....36 B8
Hawksmill Ind Est B9 ....67 C1
Hawksmoor Dr WV6 ....23 D3
Hawkstone Cl DY11 .....116 D8
Hawkstone Ct WV6 ....23 D5
Hawkswell Ave WV5 ......49 A5
Hawkswell Dr
Kingswinford DY6 ....60 D8
Willenhall WV13 ....40 F8
Hawkswood Dr
Balsall Common CV7 ....130 B7
Wednesbury WS10 ....41 B3
Hawkswood Gr B14 ......105 B3
Hawksworth B77 ....21 F2
Hawksworth Dr 1 CV1 ..113 B3
Hawkyard Ct WS11 ....2 A4
Hawley Cl WS4 ....28 F4
Hawley Ct B43 ....43 E1
Hawley Rd LE10 ....75 D7
Hawnby Gr B76 ....47 A2
Hawne Cl B63 ....82 E6
Hawne La B63 ....82 F6
Hawnelands The B63 ......82 F5
Hawskford Cres WV10 ....25 D7
Hawthorn Ave WS6 ....5 A1
Hawthorn Brook Way
B23 ....56 E8
Hawthorn Cl
Birmingham, Erdington B23 .56 F7
Birmingham, Spring Vale B9 .67 B1
Lichfield WS14 ....9 D8
Hawthorn Coppice DY9 ...99 A6
Hawthorn Cres LE10 ......75 E4
Hawthorn Croft B68 ....84 D7
Hawthorn Ct CV4 ....111 E1
Hawthorn Gr
9 Birmingham B19 ....66 C8
Kidderminster DY11 .....116 A6
Hawthorn La CV4 ....111 E1
Hawthorn Park Dr 1
B20 ....54 F3
Hawthorn Pk B20 ....54 E3
Hawthorn Pl WS2 ....27 E3
Hawthorn Prim Sch B44 ..56 A7
Hawthorn Rd Aldridge B74 .31 A1
Bilston WV1 ....40 B8
Birmingham B44 ....56 A7
Brierley Hill DY5 ....81 E8
Bromsgrove B61 ....137 B4
Redditch B97 ....153 A4
Royal Leamington Spa
CV31 ....161 F6
Tipton DY4 ....52 B8
Walsall WS4 ....15 B1
Walsall, Bescot WS5 ......42 F5
Walsall, Shelfield WS4 ....29 B8
Wednesbury WS10 ....41 F4
Wylde Green B72 ....46 C1
Hawthorn Terr WS10 .....41 F4
Hawthorn Way CV10 .....72 A8
Hawthornden Ct B76 .....57 D7
Hawthorne Ave B79 ....21 B8
Hawthorne Cres WS7 ......7 A6
Hawthorne Dr B47 ......125 B6
Hawthorne Gr DY3 ....50 D2
Hawthorne Ho WV10 .....25 F3
Hawthorne Rd
Birmingham, Castle Bromwich
B36 ....69 F7
Birmingham, Edgbaston B15 .85 E7
Birmingham, King's Norton
B30 ....103 D5
Cannock WS12 ....2 F3
Cheslyn Hay WS6 ....4 E4
Dudley DY1 ....51 C4
Essington WV11 ....13 A3
Halesowen B63 ....82 E2
Huntington WS12 ....1 D8
Wednesfield WV11 ....27 A5
Willenhall WV12 ....27 D7
Wolverhampton WV2 ......39 D6
Hawthorne Terr CV10 ....72 F5
Hawthorns Sta The B71 ..65 A8
Hawthorns The
Birmingham B13 ....86 F3
Hagley DY9 ....98 F4
1 Kidderminster DY10 ..117 A5
Oldbury B68 ....84 D7
Wolverhampton WV11 ......26 B6
Hawthorns The (West
Bromwich Albion FC)
B21 ....54 B1
Haxby Ave B34 ....69 A6
Hay Cl DY11 ....116 C7
Hay Gn DY9 ....81 D5
Hay Gr WS8 ....15 F8
Hay Green Cl B30 ....103 D6
Hay Green La B30 ......103 D6
Hay Hall Rd B11 ....87 F5
Hay Hill WS5 ....43 E8
Hay La Coventry CV1 ....165 C2
Solihull B90 ....127 A6
Hay Pk B5 ....86 D6
Hay Rd B25 ....88 A7
Hay Wood La B93,CV35 .145 A3
Haybarn The B76 ....58 A8
Haybridge Ave DY8 ....98 F5
Haybridge High Sch DY8 .98 F6
Haybrook Dr B11 ....87 F4
Haycock Pl WS10 ....41 C8
Haycroft Ave B8 ....67 E5
Haycroft Dr B74 ....32 A4

Haydn Sanders Sq **7**
WS1 ....42 E8
Haydock Cl
Birmingham B36 ....68 C8
Coventry CV6 ....96 B4
Tamworth B77 ....35 D4
Wolverhampton WV6 .....25 B5
Haydock Rd B61 ....121 B1
Haydon Cl B93 ....122 F2
Haydon Croft B33 ....69 A3
Haydon Way B49 ....159 F1
Haye House Gr B36 ....68 E7
Hayes Cres B68 ....64 D5
Hayes Croft B38 ....123 F7
Hayes Gr B24 ....57 D6
Hayes Green Rd CV12 ...95 F8
Hayes La Bedworth CV7 ..96 A8
Stourbridge DY9 ....82 A6
Hayes Mdw B72 ....57 D7
Hayes Rd Nuneaton CV10 ..72 A8
Oldbury B68 ....64 D5
Hayes St B70 ....53 A4
Hayes The
Birmingham B31 ....123 C7
Stourbridge DY9 ....82 A5
Willenhall WV12 ....27 B6
Hayes Trad Est DY9 ....82 A6
Hayes View Dr WS6 ....4 E4
Hayes Way WS11,WS12 ....2 C1
Hayfield Ct B13 ....87 B2
Hayfield Gdns B13 ....87 C2
Hayfield Rd B13 ....87 B2
Hayford Cl B98 ....154 A5
Hayland Rd B23 ....56 E6
Hayle B77 ....21 D2
Hayle Ave CV34 ....159 A4
Hayle Cl Birmingham B38 ..104 B2
Nuneaton CV11 ....74 A5
Hayley Ct
Kingswinford DY6 ....60 D6
Sutton Coldfield B74 ....57 F5
Hayley Green Rd B32 ...102 B8
Hayley Park Rd B63 ....100 C8
Hayling Cl B45 ....101 F1
Hayling Gr WV2 ....39 B6
Hayloft Cl B60 ....150 E6
Haylofts The B63 ....82 C1
Haymarket The WS6 ....10 E1
Haymoor WS14 ....9 E7
Haynes Cl B61 ....137 B8
Haynes La WS5 ....43 B4
Haynestone Rd CV6 ......112 E6
Haypits Cl B71 ....53 E7
Hayrick Dr DY6 ....60 B7
Hays Kent's Moat The
B26 ....69 A1
Hays La CV11 ....75 B7
Hayseech B64 ....83 A7
Hayseech Rd B63 ....82 F6
Hayton Gn Cv4 ....131 F8
Haytor Ave B14 ....104 D5
Haytor Rise CV2 ....114 C7
Haywain Cl WV9 ....10 F2
Hayward Rd B75 ....46 C7
Hayward's La CV7 ....51 B8
Hayward's Gn CV6 ....113 A7
Haywards Cl
Birmingham B23 ....56 E5
Walsall WS3 ....14 F3
Haywharf Rd DY5 ....61 B5
Haywood Dr
Halesowen B62 ....83 C8
Wolverhampton WV6 ......24 D4
Haywood Rd B33 ....69 E2
Haywood's Farm B71 ....42 F2
Haywood St B71 ....20 F8
Hayworth Rd WS13 ....3 C2
Hazel Ave Birmingham B73 ..45 C1
Wednesbury WS10 ....42 A4
Hazel Cl Nuneaton CV10 ...72 A8
Royal Leamington Spa
CV32 ....157 A2
Hazel Croft
Birmingham, Chelmsley Wood
B37 ....70 B1
Birmingham, Northfield
B31 ....103 A3
Hazel Dr B47 ....125 B5
Hazel Gdns
Birmingham B27 ....88 C5
Codsall WV8 ....10 A4
Hazel Gr Bedworth CV12 ..78 D3
Bilston WV14 ....40 E7
Hockley Heath B94 ....143 C6
Lichfield WS14 ....9 C7
Stourbridge DY8 ....80 C3
West Bromwich B70 ....53 C1
Wolverhampton WV11 ......26 C7
Wombourne WV5 ....49 A7
Hazel La WS6 ....5 B2
Hazel Oak Sch B90 ....106 A2
Hazel Rd Birmingham B45 ..121 F6
Coventry CV6 ....96 B4
Dudley DY1 ....51 C2
Kingswinford DY6 ....60 E5
Nuneaton CV10 ....72 D5
Redditch B97 ....153 C5
Tipton DY4 ....41 D1
Wolverhampton WV3 ....38 E7
Hazelbank B38 ....103 E2
Hazelbeach Rd B8 ....67 F5
Hazelbeech Rd B70 ....53 A3
Hazeldene Gr **5** B36 ....66 E8
Hazeldene Rd
Birmingham B33 ....89 D7

Hazeldene Rd continued
Halesowen B63 ....82 E2
Hazeley Cl B17 ....85 A7
Hazelgarth B77 ....36 B8
Hazelhead St Georges (Ind
Est) CV1 ....113 F2
Hazelhurst Rd
Birmingham, Castle Bromwich
B36 ....69 E7
Birmingham, King's Heath
B14 ....104 E7
Hazell Way CV10 ....73 A1
Hazelmead Ct B73 ....57 A7
Hazelmere Dr
Burntwood WS7 ....6 F4
Wolverhampton WV3 ....24 A1
Hazelmere Rd B28 ....105 F8
Hazeloak Rd B90 ....106 A6
Hazels The DY9 ....98 F5
Hazelslade Ho WS12 ....2 F6
Hazelton Cl Catshill B61 ..137 A8
2 Solihull B91 ....107 B1
Hazelton Rd B61 ....121 C1
Hazeltree Croft B27 ....88 B2
Hazeltree Gr B93 ....127 E3
Hazelville Gr B28 ....106 A6
Hazelville Rd B28 ....106 A7
Hazelwell Cres B30 ....104 B6
Hazelwell Fordrough
B30 ....104 B6
Hazelwell La B30 ....104 B7
Hazelwell Rd B30 ....104 A6
Hazelwell St B30 ....104 A7
Hazelwood Cl
Cheslyn Hay WS6 ....4 D2
Kidderminster DY11 ....116 B4
Hazelwood Dr WV11 ....26 A5
Hazelwood Gr
Cannock WS11 ....2 B2
Willenhall WV12 ....27 D5
Hazelwood Rd
Aldridge B74 ....30 D1
Birmingham B27 ....88 B2
Hazlemere Cl CV5 ....112 B4
Hazlemere Dr B74 ....32 B1
Hazlemere Gr WS11 ....48 B8
Hazlewood Rd DY1 ....50 F5
Hazlitt Gr B30 ....103 D4
Headborough Rd CV2 ....114 A5
Headborough Wlk WS9 ...16 B1
Headingley Rd B21 ....54 C1
Headington Ave CV4 ....95 A2
Headland Dr B8 ....67 D5
Headland Rd WV3 ....24 A1
Headlands The
Coventry CV5 ....112 D4
Little Aston B74 ....31 C3
Headless Cross Dr B97 ..153 D1
Headley Croft B38 ....123 D8
Headley Dr B97 ....158 D8
Headley Heath La B38 ...124 B6
Headway Rd WV10 ....11 C3
Heale Cl B63 ....82 A7
Healey B77 ....21 E2
Healey Ct CV34 ....160 F7
Health Centre Rd CV4 ...132 C4
Heanor Croft B6 ....67 B8
Heantun Croft WV10 ....26 A5
Heantun Ct WV3 ....23 B1
Heantun Ho WV3 ....163 B2
Heantun Lodge WV14 ......40 C6
Heantun Mill Ct WS10 .....41 D1
Heantun Rise WV3 ....25 C4
Heanton Rowen WV3 ....29 C3
Hearsall Com Prim Sch
CV5 ....112 F2
Hearsall Comm CV5 ....112 F2
Hearsall Ct CV4 ....112 D2
Hearsall Golf Course
CV5 ....132 E2
Hearsall La CV5 ....112 F2
Heart of England Sch
CV7 ....130 C6
Heart of England Way
CV11 ....73 B4
Heart Of The Country Ctr*
WS14 ....18 E8
Heartland Mews B65 ....63 B2
Heartlands High Sch B7 ...67 B4
Heartlands Parkway B7 ...67 D2
Heartlands Pl B8 ....67 E4
Heath Acres WS10 ....41 C4
Heath Ave CV12 ....77 C1
Heath Bridge Cl WS4 ....29 A8
Heath Cl Birmingham B30 ..103 D5
Bromsgrove B60 ....150 E6
Stonnall WS14 ....16 C5
Tipton DY4 ....52 B5
Heath Cres CV2 ....114 A6
Heath Croft B31 ....123 A7
Heath Croft Rd B75 ....32 D1
Heath Ct **2** B12 ....86 F5
Heath End Rd
Bedworth CV12 ....120 D7
Nuneaton CV10 ....72 F2
Heath Farm Rd
Codsall WV8 ....10 B2
Stourbridge DY8 ....80 E3
Heath Gap Rd WS11 ....1 F3
Heath Gdns B91 ....107 D6
Heath Gn DY1 ....50 F5
Heath Gr WV8 ....10 B3
Heath Green **4** B18 .....65 E4
Heath Green Rd B18 ....65 E4
Heath Green Way CV4 ....131 C6
Heath Hayes Prim Sch
WS12 ....2 F2

Heath Hill Rd WV6 ....23 E1
Heath Ho B14 ....104 F2
Heath House La WV8 ....23 E8
Heath La
Kidderminster DY10 ....117 C1
Stourbridge DY8 ....81 A4
West Bromwich B71 ....53 D7
Heath Lane Hospl B71 .....53 D7
Heath Mill La B9 ....67 A1
Heath Park High Sch
WV11 ....26 A5
Heath Rd Bedworth CV12 ..77 F1
Birmingham B30 ....103 D5
Coventry CV2 ....114 A4
Darlaston WS10 ....41 E8
Dudley DY2 ....62 C2
Hollywood B47 ....125 A7
Solihull B91 ....107 D6
Willenhall WV12 ....13 D1
Heath Rd S B31 ....103 B4
Heath Rise B14 ....105 A1
Heath St Birmingham B18 ..65 E4
Blackheath B65 ....63 C1
Smethwick B66 ....65 B5
Stourbridge DY8 ....80 F4
Tamworth B79 ....21 C5
Heath St S B18 ....65 F4
Heath Terr
Beausale CV35 ....146 C2
Royal Leamington Spa
CV32 ....156 E1
Heath Trad Pk B66 ....65 D5
Heath View Cannock WS12 ..5 E8
Walsall WS2 ....27 F3
Heath Way
Birmingham B34 ....69 B6
Cannock WS11 ....2 B2
Heath-Mount Jun & Inf Sch
B12 ....86 F6
Heathbank Dr WS12 ....1 C6
Heathbrook Ave DY6 ....60 E8
Heathcliff Rd
Birmingham B11 ....87 F4
Dudley DY2 ....62 E8
Heathcote Ave B91 ....106 E3
Heathcote Ct CV6 ....36 E7
Heathcote Ct CV6 ....113 A7
Heathcote Ho B17 ....85 C5
Heathcote La CV34 ....161 D4
Heathcote La
Royal Leamington Spa
CV34 ....161 D4
Warwick CV34 ....161 A5
Heathcote Rd
Birmingham B30 ....104 A5
Whitnash CV31 ....162 A4
Heathcote St CV6 ....113 A7
Heathcote Way CV34 .....161 D4
Heather Ave WS5 ....43 B4
Heather Cl
Birmingham B36 ....70 A8
Nuneaton CV10 ....72 F3
Walsall WS3 ....28 A8
Wednesfield WV11 ....26 E5
Heather Court Gdns B74 ..46 A8
Heather Croft B44 ....44 F3
Heather Ct B13 ....86 D3
Heather Dale B13 ....86 D2
Heather Dr Bedworth CV12 ..77 E2
Birmingham B45 ....121 F6
Huntington WS12 ....7 B5
Heather Gr Solihull B91 ..107 E6
Willenhall WV12 ....27 E4
Heather Ho B38 ....103 F1
Heather Mews WS12 ....2 A8
Heather Rd
Binley Woods CV3 ....135 D7
Birmingham, Great Barr
B43 ....54 D8
Birmingham, Small Heath
B10 ....87 E8
Cannock WS12 ....2 A8
Coventry CV2 ....96 C2
Dudley DY1 ....51 C4
Smethwick B67 ....64 E6
Walsall WS3 ....28 A8
Heather Valley WS12 ....2 D6
Heatherleigh Rd B36 ......69 F8
Heathfield Ave B20 ....66 B8
Heathfield Cl
Blackheath B64 ....62 F7
Knowle B93 ....128 A5
Heathfield Cres DY11 ....116 B4
Heathfield Ct **1** B19 .....66 B7
Heathfield Rd B30 ....14 B2
Heathfield Foundation Sch
The B64 ....62 F2
Heathfield Gdns DY8 ....80 F4
Heathfield La WS10 ....41 C6
Heathfield La W WS10 ......41 B6
Heathfield Prim Sch B19 ..66 C8
Heathfield Rd
Birmingham, King's Heath
B14 ....104 F8
Birmingham, Lozells B19 ..66 C8
Coventry CV5 ....112 C2
Halesowen B63 ....82 F3
Redditch B97 ....153 A1
Sutton Coldfield B74 ....31 F3
Heathfield Way B64 ....62 F1
Heathfields Inf Sch B77 ...35 F6
Heathgreen Cl B37 ....70 D3
Heathland Ave B34 ....69 A7
Heathland Cl WS12 ....2 D2
Heathlands CV36 ....60 E8
Heathlands Cres B73 ......45 F1
Heathlands Gr B31 ....103 A1

Heathlands Prim Sch
B34 ....68 F7
Heathlands Rd B73 ....45 F1
Heathlands The
2 Blackheath B65 ....63 C1
Stourbridge DY8 ....81 B4
Heathleigh Rd B38 ....123 C8
Heathley La B78 ....34 E5
Heathmere Ave B25 ....88 D8
Heathmere Dr B37 ....70 B2
Heathside Dr
Birmingham B38 ....104 B2
Walsall WS3 ....15 A4
Heathy Farm Cl B32 ....84 B2
Heathy Rise B32 ....84 A2
Heaton Cl WV10 ....11 E5
Heaton Dr Birmingham B15 ..85 E8
Sutton Coldfield B73 ....45 F8
Heaton Rd B91 ....107 A7
Heaton St B18 ....66 A5
Hebden B77 ....36 B8
Hebden Ave CV34 ....155 F1
Hebden Gr
Birmingham B28 ....105 E3
Willenhall WV11 ....13 B1
Hebden Way CV11 ....74 A2
Heckley Rd CV7 ....96 A7
Heddle Gr CV6 ....114 B8
Heddon Pl B7 ....67 A3
Hedera Cl WS5 ....43 B3
Hedera Rd B98 ....154 F6
Hedgefield Gr B63 ....82 C4
Hedgefield Way CV4 ......131 F8
Hedgerow Cl WS12 ....1 F7
Hedgerow Dr DY6 ....49 D1
Hedgerow Wlk
Coventry CV6 ....95 B4
Wolverhampton WV8 ....10 E1
Hedgerows The
Lichfield WS14 ....9 B5
Nuneaton CV10 ....72 F6
Romsley B62 ....100 F4
Tamworth B77 ....35 F8
Hedges Way B60 ....137 B1
Hedgetree Croft B37 ....70 C2
Hedging La B77 ....35 E5
Hedging Lane Ind Est
B77 ....35 E5
Hedgings The B34 ....69 B6
Hedgley Gr B33 ....69 A4
Hedingham Gr B37 ....70 D2
Hedley Croft B35 ....58 B4
Hednesford Rd
Brownhills WS8 ....6 C2
Cannock, Blackfords WS11 ..1 F2
Cannock, Heath Hayes WS12 ..2 E1
Norton Canes WS11 ....6 F5
Hednesford St WS11 ....28 B5
Hednesford Sta WS12 ....2 B5
Heeley Rd B29 ....85 F1
Heemstede La CV32 ....157 A2
Heera Cl CV6 ....113 B8
Hefford Dr B66 ....65 A6
Hele Rd CV3 ....133 D6
Helen St CV6 ....113 F6
Helena Cl CV10 ....72 E3
Helena St B1 ....66 C3
Helenny Cl WV11 ....26 A5
Helford Cl DY4 ....51 D4
Helga St WV10 ....25 C4
Heligan Pl WS12 ....2 E2
Hellaby Cl B72 ....46 A4
Hellaby Ct B73 ....57 A7
Hellidon Cl **5** CV32 ....157 A2
Hellier Ave DY4 ....52 B4
Hellier Rd WV10 ....11 E2
Hellier St DY2 ....62 C8
Helming Dr WV1 ....26 B3
Helmingham Rd B29 ....20 D7
Helmsdale Rd CV32 ....157 B5
Helmsdale Way DY3 ....51 A7
Helmsley Cl DY5 ....81 C8
Helmsley Rd WV11 ....26 C8
Helmswood Dr B37 ....90 C8
Helston Cl Nuneaton CV10 ..74 A5
Stourbridge DY8 ....60 C2
Tamworth B79 ....21 C8
Walsall WS5 ....43 D7
Helston Rd WS5 ....43 D7
Helstone Gr B11 ....88 A3
Hembs Cres B43 ....54 C8
Hemdale CV11 ....74 A4
Heming Rd B98 ....159 E8
Hemingford Rd CV2 ....115 A8
Hemlingford Croft B37 ....90 A7
Hemlingford Rd
Birmingham B37 ....69 F6
Sutton Coldfield B76 ....58 A6
Hemlock Bsns Ctr WS11 ...2 B3
Hemlock Pk WS11 ....2 B2
Hemlock Way WS11 ....2 B3
Hemming St DY11 ....116 C4
Hemmings Cl
Radford Semele CV31 .....162 E5
Stourbridge DY8 ....80 F5
Wolverhampton WV10 .....25 E3
Hemmings St WS10 ....41 C8
Hemplands Rd DY8 ....80 F5
Hempole La DY4 ....52 D6
Hemsby Cl CV4 ....132 A7
Hemsworth Dr CV12 ....79 B2
Hemyock Rd B29 ....103 B8
Hen La CV6 ....95 D3
Henbury Rd B27 ....88 D4
Henderson Cl CV5 ....112 A6
Henderson Way B65 ....63 C1
Henderson Wlk DY4 ....52 B8
Hendon Cl Dudley DY3 ....50 D2

Hendon Cl continued
Wolverhampton WV10 .....25 E7
Hendon Rd B11 ....87 B5
Hendre Cl CV5 ....112 D2
Heneage Pl **8** B7 ....67 A4
Heneage St B7 ....67 A4
Heneage St W B7 ....66 F4
Henfield Cl WV11 ....26 D7
Hengham Rd B26 ....69 A1
Henley Cl Burntwood WS7 ..7 B5
Nuneaton CV11 ....73 F8
Sutton Coldfield B73 ....57 B8
Tamworth B79 ....21 C6
Tipton DY4 ....52 D5
Walsall WS3 ....14 E1
Henley Coll CV2 ....114 C8
Henley Cres B91 ....107 B7
Henley Ct Coventry CV2 ..114 D7
Lichfield WS14 ....9 E5
Henley Dr B74 ....32 A3
Henley Mill La CV2 ....114 C7
Henley Park Ind Est
CV2 ....114 E7
Henley Rd Coventry CV2 ..114 D7
Royal Leamington Spa
CV31 ....162 B5
Wolverhampton WV10 .....11 B1
Henley St B11 ....87 B7
Henley Wlk CV2 ....114 D8
Henleydale **8** B90 ....126 C8
Henlow Rd B14 ....105 A2
Henn Dr DY4 ....40 E1
Henn St B74 ....52 A8
Hennalls The B36 ....68 F7
Hennals Ave B97 ....152 F2
Henne Dr WV14 ....40 C1
Henrietta St
Birmingham B19 ....164 B4
Coventry CV6 ....113 E5
Henry Boteler Rd CV4 ....132 B7
Henry Boys' Almshouses
WS1 ....42 D8
Henry Rd B25 ....88 C7
Henry St Coventry CV1 ...165 B3
Hinckley LE10 ....71 A2
Kenilworth CV8 ....148 A5
Nuneaton CV11 ....73 C2
Walsall WS2 ....28 D1
Henry Tanday Ct **4**
CV32 ....156 E1
Henry Wlk B60 ....150 E7
Hensborough B90 ....126 A5
Hensel Dr WV3 ....38 C8
Henshaw Gr B25 ....88 C7
Henshaw Rd B10 ....87 D8
Henson Rd CV12 ....79 C1
Henstead St B5 ....86 D8
Hentland Cl B98 ....154 D4
Henwood Cl WV6 ....24 C3
Henwood La B91 ....108 B4
Henwood Rd WV6 ....24 C3
Hepburn Cl WS9 ....30 A4
Hepburn Edge B24 ....57 B4
Hepworth Cl WV6 ....23 F4
Hepworth Rd CV3 ....115 B1
Herald Ave CV5 ....112 D1
Herald Bsns Pk CV3 ....134 F7
Herald Ct **2** B21 ....51 C1
Herald Rd B26 ....90 C4
Herald Way
Coventry CV3 ....135 A7
Hinckley LE10 ....75 D4
Heralds Ct **6** CV34 ......161 B8
Herbert Art Gall & Mus*
CV1 ....165 C2
Herbert Rd Aldridge WS9 ..16 A1
Birmingham, Handsworth
B21 ....54 F1
Birmingham, Small Heath
B10 ....87 C8
Smethwick B67 ....65 A1
Solihull B91 ....107 B4
Herbert St Bilston WV14 ...40 B6
Nuneaton CV10 ....72 E3
Redditch B98 ....153 E4
West Bromwich B70 ....53 D3
Herbert's La CV8 ....148 A5
Herberts Park Rd WS10 ...41 B6
Herbhill Cl WV4 ....39 D4
Hereford Ave B12 ....87 A6
Hereford Cl Aldridge WS9 ..30 A8
Barwell LE9 ....71 F6
Birmingham B45 ....102 A2
Kidderminster DY11 ....116 A5
Nuneaton CV10 ....72 E4
Hereford Ho WV1 ....163 B4
Hereford Pl B71 ....53 B7
Hereford Rd
Bramcote CV11 ....79 F6
Cannock WS12 ....2 D2
Dudley DY2 ....62 E3
Oldbury B68 ....84 B7
Hereford Sq B8 ....67 C5
Hereford St WS2 ....28 E4
Hereford Walk B37 ....21 A2
Hereford Wlk B37 ....70 C2
Hereward Coll CV4 ....111 F1
Hereward Rise B62 ....83 C5
Herford Way LE10 ....75 F6
Heritage Cl B68 ....64 C4
Heritage Ct
Coventry CV1 ....132 D3
Lichfield WS14 ....9 D6
Heritage The **6** WS1 ....28 E1

Heritage Way
Birmingham B33 ....**69** D3
Tipton DY4 ....**52** B5
Hermes Ct CV34 ....**161** E5
Hermes Cres CV2 .....**114** E6
Hermes Ct B74 ....**31** F3
Hermes Rd
Birmingham B26 ....**90** C4
Lichfield WS13 ....**3** D1
Hermit St DY3 ....**50** D5
Hermit's Croft CV3 ...**133** D8
Hermitage Dr B76 ......**47** A4
Hermitage La B78 ....**22** E1
Hermitage Rd
Birmingham, Edgbaston B15 .**85** C8
Birmingham, Gravelly Hill
B23 ....**56** E3
Coventry CV2 ....**114** D4
Solihull B91 ....**107** C6
Hermitage The B91 ...**148** A3
Hern Rd DY5 ....**81** C6
Hernall Croft B26 ......**89** A7
Herne Ct B18 ....**66** A4
Hernefield Rd B34 .....**69** B6
Hernehurst B32 ....**84** C6
Heron Cl Alvechurch B48 .**139** A7
  Cheswick Green B90 ....**126** D4
Heron Cl B73 ....**57** B7
Heron Ho CV3 ....**114** B2
Heron Mill WS3 ....**14** E3
Heron Rd B68 ....**64** A2
Heron Way B45 ....**121** F7
Herondale WS12 ....**2** B4
Herondale Cres DY8 ...**80** C4
Herondale Rd
Birmingham B26 ....**88** F6
Stourbridge DY8 ....**80** C4
Heronfield Cl B98 .....**154** C5
Heronfield Dr B31 ....**122** F6
Heronfield Way B91 ..**107** E5
Heronry The WV6 ....**23** F2
Herons Way B29 ....**85** C3
Heronsville Ho DY4 ....**52** B3
Heronswood Dr DY5 ....**61** D1
Heronswood Rd
Birmingham B45 ....**122** B6
Kidderminster DY10 ......**117** A2
Heronville Dr B70 ....**53** A7
Heronville Rd B70 ....**53** A6
Herrick Rd Birmingham B8 .**67** E5
  Coventry CV2 ....**114** D3
Herrick St WV3 ....**163** A2
Herringshaw Croft B76 .**46** E3
Herbert Austin Dr B60 .**121** C1
Hertford Pl CV1 ....**165** A2
Hertford St
Birmingham B12 ....**87** A5
Coventry CV1 ....**165** B2
Hertford Way B93 ......**128** B4
Hervey Gr B24 ....**57** D6
Hesket Ave B68 ....**64** C1
Hesketh Cres B23 ....**56** C5
Hesketh Pl B37 ....**89** F8
Hesleden B77 ....**36** B8
Heslop Cl CV3 ....**134** F8
Hessian Cl WV14 ....**40** B2
Hestia Dr B29 ....**103** E8
Heston Ave B42 ....**55** B8
Hetton Cl CV34 ....**155** E1
Hever Ave B44 ....**45** A1
Hever Cl DY1 ....**50** E3
Hewell Ave B60 ....**150** F7
Hewell Cl
Birmingham B31 ....**122** F7
Kingswinford DY6 ....**49** D1
Redditch B97 ....**152** C6
Hewell La
Barnt Green B45 ....**138** D8
Redditch B60,B97 ....**152** D6
Hewell Rd
Barnt Green B45 ....**138** D8
Redditch B97 ....**153** D4
Hewitson Gdns B67 .....**64** F2
Hewitt Ave CV6 ....**113** B4
Hewitt Cl WS13 ....**3** A2
Hewitt St WS10 ....**41** C5
Hewston Croft WS12 ....**2** D4
Hexby Cl CV2 ....**115** A6
Hexham Way DY1 ....**50** D7
Hexton Cl B90 ....**105** D2
Hexworthy Ave CV3 ...**133** B5
Heybarnes Cir B10 ....**87** F7
Heybarnes Rd B10 ....**88** A8
Heybrook Cl CV2 ....**114** C7
Heycott Gr B38 ....**104** C2
Heycroft CV4 ....**132** D4
Heydon Rd
Brierley Hill DY5 ....**61** B6
Finstall B60 ....**137** D1
Heyford Cl CV7 ....**96** D3
Heyford Gr B91 ....**127** C8
Heyford Way B35 ....**58** B5
Heygate Way WS9 ....**16** B1
Heyland Cnr B10 ....**67** F1
Heyley Croft WS12 ....**2** C4
Heynesfield Rd B33 .....**69** C3
Heythrop Gr B13 ....**105** D8
Heyville Croft CV8 .....**148** C3
Heywood Cl CV4 ....**114** A7
Hibberd Ct CV8 ....**147** F4
Hibbert Rd WV1,WV2 ...**40** A8
Hickman Gdns B16 ......**65** C1
Hickman Rd Bilston WV14 .**40** C5
  Birmingham B11 ....**87** B6
  Brierley Hill DY5 ....**61** C4
  Tipton DY4 ....**51** F8
Hickman St DY9 ....**81** C6

Hickman's Ave B64 ......**62** E2
Hickmans Cl B62 ....**84** A6
Hickmerelands La DY3 .**39** C1
Hickory Ct WS11 ....**2** C2
Hickory Dr B17 ....**65** A2
Hicks Cl CV34 ....**155** E2
Hidcote Ave B76 ....**58** A8
Hidcote Cl Nuneaton CV11 .**78** F8
  Royal Leamington Spa
  CV31 ....**162** C5
Hidcote Gr
Birmingham, Garret's Green
B33 ....**89** C8
Birmingham, Marston Green
B37 ....**90** A7
Hidcote Rd CV8 ....**148** C6
Hidson Rd B23 ....**56** C5
Higgins Ave WV14 ....**40** D2
Higgins La B32 ....**84** C5
Higgins Wlk B66 ....**65** B6
Higgs Field Cres B64 ...**63** B1
Higgs Rd WV11 ....**13** A1
High Arcal Dr DY3 ....**50** F7
High Arcal Rd DY3 ....**49** F4
High Arcal Sch The DY3 .**50** F6
High Ash Cl CV7 ....**95** F7
High Ave B64 ....**82** F8
High Bank WS11 ....**4** B8
High Beech CV5 ....**112** A6
High Beeches B43 ....**43** D1
High Brink Rd B46 ....**70** F7
High Broome Ct B78 .....**21** A3
High Brow B17 ....**85** B7
High Bullen WS10 ....**41** F3
High Clere B64 ....**83** A7
High Croft Aldridge WS9 .**16** B2
  Birmingham B43 ....**43** C1
High Croft Cres WS14 ...**9** C7
High Elms La B60 ....**151** E1
High Ercal Ave DY5 ....**61** C2
High Farm Rd
Halesowen, Hasbury B63 .**82** F3
Halesowen, Hurst Green
B62 ....**83** F8
High Gn WS11 ....**1** D1
High Grange WS11 ....**2** A5
High Green Ct WS11 ....**1** D1
High Haden Cres B64 ...**83** A8
High Haden Rd B64 ......**83** A8
High Hill WV11 ....**13** A2
High Holborn DY3 ....**50** D7
High House Dr B45 .....**121** F3
High House La B60 ......**152** A6
High Leasowes B63 ......**83** A4
High Mdws
Stoke Heath B60 ....**150** D7
Wolverhampton WV6 ....**24** C3
Wombourne WV5 ....**49** B6
High Meadow Fst Sch
B46 ....**70** F8
High Meadow Rd B38 ..**104** A2
High Mount St WS12 .....**2** B6
High Oak DY5 ....**61** C7
High Park Cl
Coventry CV5 ....**111** F3
Sedgley DY3 ....**50** D8
Smethwick B66 ....**65** B5
High Park Cnr B7 ....**67** B6
High Park Cres DY3 ....**39** D1
High Park Rd B63 ....**82** C5
High Park St B7 ....**67** B6
High Point B15 ....**85** E6
High Rd WV12 ....**27** C5
High Ridge WS9 ....**29** F5
High Ridge Cl
Aldridge WS9 ....**29** E5
Bilston WS10 ....**41** A4
High St Aldridge WS9 ....**30** B6
  Astwood Bank B96 ....**158** E1
  Bedworth CV12 ....**78** B2
  Belbroughton DY9 ....**119** E7
  Bilston WV14 ....**40** D5
  Bilston, Moxley WS10 .....**41** A4
  Birmingham B4 ....**164** C2
  Birmingham, Aston B6,B19 .**66** E7
  Birmingham, Erdington B23 .**56** F4
  Birmingham, Harborne B17 .**85** D6
  Birmingham, King's Heath
  B14 ....**104** E8
  Birmingham, Quinton B32 .**84** A6
  Birmingham, Saltley B8 ...**67** D5
  Blackheath, Cradley Heath
  B64 ....**82** C8
  Blackheath, Rowley Regis
  B65 ....**63** C1
  Brierley Hill, Barrow Hill
  DY5 ....**61** C7
  Brierley Hill, Brockmoor
  DY5 ....**61** C4
  Brierley Hill, Quarry Bank
  DY5 ....**82** A8
  Bromsgrove B61 ....**137** A2
  Brownhills, Catshill WS8 ..**15** F8
  Brownhills, Walsall Wood
  WS9 ....**15** F3
  Burntwood, Chase Terrace
  WS7 ....**6** E8
  Burntwood, Chasetown WS7 .**6** F6
  Cheslyn Hay WS6 ....**4** D2
  Clayhanger WS8 ....**15** D6
  Coleshill B46 ....**70** F7
  Coventry CV1 ....**165** C2
  Coventry, Keresley CV6 ....**94** F1
  Cubbington CV32 ....**157** E5
  Darlaston WS10 ....**41** D6
  Dudley DY1 ....**51** C1

High St continued
  7 Dudley, Old Dock DY1 ..**62** B8
  1 Halesowen B63 ....**83** B3
  Hampton-in-A B92 ....**109** A7
  Kenilworth CV8 ....**147** E5
  Kidderminster DY10 ......**116** E6
  Kingswinford DY6 ....**60** E6
  Kingswinford, Wall Heath
  DY6 ....**60** C8
  Knowle B93 ....**128** C6
  Norton Canes WS11 ....**6** B5
  Nuneaton CV11 ....**73** B4
  Royal Leamington Spa
  CV31 ....**162** A7
  Ryton-on-D CV8 ....**135** B1
  Sedgley DY3 ....**50** D8
  Smethwick B66 ....**65** A5
  Solihull B91 ....**107** C3
  Solihull, Shirley B90 .....**105** D2
  Stourbridge DY8 ....**81** A5
  Stourbridge, Amblecote DY8 .**80** F7
  Stourbridge, Lye DY9 .....**81** E5
  Stourbridge, Wollaston DY8 .**80** E7
  Stourbridge, Wordsley DY8 .**60** E2
  Studley B80 ....**159** E4
  Sutton Coldfield B72 ....**46** C5
  Tamworth B77 ....**35** C5
  Tipton, Princes End DY4 ..**51** F8
  Tipton, Tipton Green DY4 .**51** E5
  Walsall WS1 ....**28** E1
  Walsall, Pelsall WS3 ....**15** A4
  Walsall, Wallington Heath
  WS3 ....**14** B1
  Warwick CV34 ....**160** E6
  Wednesfield WV11 ....**26** D5
  West Bromwich B70 ....**53** C3
  Wolverhampton WV6 ......**24** D4
  Wombourne WV5 ....**49** B7
High St Duchess Par
B70 ....**53** D3
High St Princess Par
B70 ....**53** D3
High Street Bordesley
B12 ....**67** A1
High Street Deritend
B12 ....**66** F1
High Timbers B45 ....**101** F1
High Trees B20 ....**54** F3
High Trees Cl B98 ....**158** F7
High Trees Ho B69 ....**63** F3
High Trees Rd B93 ......**128** A7
High View WV14 ....**39** F1
High View Dr CV7 ....**95** C7
High View Rd CV32 .....**157** C5
High Wood Cl DY6 ....**60** C6
Higham La CV11 ....**73** E7
Higham Lane Sch CV10 .**73** D6
Higham Way
Hinckley LE10 ....**75** E7
Wolverhampton WV10 ......**25** E6
Higham Way Ho LE10 ...**75** E7
Highams Cl B65 ....**63** B3
Highbridge Rd
Dudley DY2 ....**62** B3
Sutton Coldfield B73 ....**46** A1
Highbrook Cl WV9 ....**11** A2
Highbury Ave
Birmingham B21 ....**65** F8
Blackheath B65 ....**63** D3
Highbury Cl B65 ....**63** D3
Highbury Ct B13 ....**104** E7
Highbury Gn CV10 ....**72** C7
Highbury Rd
Birmingham B14 ....**104** D8
Oldbury B68 ....**64** A5
Smethwick B66 ....**64** D7
Sutton Coldfield B74 ....**31** C3
Highclare Sch B13 ....**89** A3
Highclare Sch (The Abbey)
B23 ....**57** A5
Highclare Sch-St Paul's
B23 ....**46** C7
Highcliffe Rd B77 ....**35** D8
Highcrest Cl B31 ....**123** A7
Highcroft WS3 ....**15** B6
Highcroft Ave DY8 ....**60** F2
Highcroft Cl B92 ....**89** C2
Highcroft Cres CV32 ...**156** C1
Highcroft Dr B74 ....**31** E3
Highcroft Hospl B23 .....**56** F4
Highcroft Rd B23 ....**56** E3
Highdown Cres B90 .....**127** A6
Highdown Rd CV31 .....**162** B6
Highfield CV7 ....**92** C1
Highfield Ave
Bilston WV14 ....**40** E4
Burntwood WS7 ....**7** B7
Redditch B97 ....**158** D8
Tamworth B77 ....**22** A5
Walsall WS4 ....**29** C8
Wolverhampton WV10 ......**12** A2
Highfield Cl
Birmingham B28 ....**105** D5
Burntwood WS7 ....**7** B7
Kenilworth CV8 ....**147** E4
Highfield Cres
Blackheath B65 ....**63** B1
Halesowen B63 ....**82** D6
Wolverhampton WV11 ......**26** B6
Highfield Ct Cannock WS11 .**2** B5
  Sutton Coldfield B73 ....**46** B1
Highfield Gdns WS13 .....**9** E6
Highfield Inf & Jun Sch
B8 ....**67** E5
Highfield La
Birmingham B32 ....**84** B4
Clent DY9 ....**100** A3

Highfield La continued
  Corley CV7 ....**94** D8
  1 Halesowen B63 ....**83** A3
Highfield Mews B63 .....**82** D6
Highfield Pl B14 ....**105** D5
Highfield Rd
Birmingham, Edgbaston B15 .**86** A8
Birmingham, Moseley B13 .**87** B3
Birmingham, Newton B43 .**54** C7
Birmingham, Saltley B8 ...**67** E5
Birmingham, Yardley Wood
B14,B28 ....**105** D5
Blackheath B65 ....**63** B1
Bromsgrove B61 ....**150** E8
Burntwood WS7 ....**7** C7
Cannock WS12 ....**2** E1
Coventry CV2 ....**114** A2
Dudley DY2 ....**51** E1
Halesowen B63 ....**82** D5
Kidderminster DY10 ......**117** A8
Nuneaton CV11 ....**73** C2
Redditch B97 ....**158** D8
Smethwick B67 ....**65** A5
Stourbridge DY8 ....**61** A2
Studley B80 ....**159** D4
Tipton DY4 ....**52** B8
Walsall WS3 ....**15** A4
Highfield Rd N WS3 ......**14** F5
Highfield Terr CV32 ....**156** D1
Highfield Way WS9 ....**16** B2
Highfields
Bromsgrove B61 ....**136** E1
Burntwood WS7 ....**7** B7
Highfields Ct WV4 ....**38** D6
Highfields Dr
Dudley WV14 ....**40** D3
Wombourne WV5 ....**49** A5
Highfields Grange WS6 ..**4** D1
Highfields Pk WS6 ....**4** F1
Highfields Prim Sch
Blackheath B65 ....**83** C8
Burntwood WS7 ....**7** C7
Dudley WV14 ....**40** C2
Highfields Rd
Burntwood WS7 ....**6** F4
Dudley WV14 ....**40** F4
Hinckley LE10 ....**71** E1
Sch WV4 ....**38** D5
Highfields The WV6 ......**24** A3
Highgate Aldridge B74 ...**31** A1
  Dudley DY3 ....**50** E5
Highgate Ave Walsall WS1 .**42** F8
  Wolverhampton WV4 ....**38** D6
Highgate Bsns Ctr B12 .**87** B6
Highgate Cl
Birmingham B12 ....**86** F7
Kidderminster DY11 ....**116** A4
Walsall WS1 ....**42** F8
Highgate Ct WS1 ....**42** F8
Highgate Dr WS1 ....**42** F7
Highgate Ho B5 ....**86** E8
Highgate Middleway B12 .**86** F7
Highgate Pl B12 ....**87** A7
Highgate Prim Sch DY2 .**61** F6
Highgate Rd
Birmingham B12 ....**87** A6
Dudley DY1,DY2 ....**61** F6
Walsall WS1 ....**42** F7
Highgate Sq B12 ....**86** F7
Highgate St
Birmingham B12 ....**86** F7
Blackheath B64 ....**62** F2
Highgrove Coventry CV4 .**131** F5
  Wolverhampton WV6 ....**24** C3
Highgrove Cl
Tamworth B79 ....**21** B7
Willenhall WV12 ....**27** B7
Highgrove Pl DY1 ....**50** F2
Highland Ho B62 ....**83** C8
Highland Mews WV14 ....**40** D1
Highland Rd
Birmingham, Great Barr
B43 ....**43** E3
Blackheath B64 ....**62** E2
Cannock WS12 ....**1** C4
Coventry CV5 ....**112** F1
Dudley DY1 ....**51** A3
Kenilworth CV8 ....**148** C7
Royal Leamington Spa
CV32 ....**157** B4
Highland Ridge B62 ......**83** E5
Highlands Cl CV34 ......**161** A8
Highlands Ct B90 ....**126** E8
Highlands Rd
Birmingham B90 ....**126** F8
Wolverhampton WV3 ....**38** D8
Highley Cl
Kidderminster DY11 ....**116** B2
Redditch B98 ....**154** E4
Highmoor Cl
Bilston WV14 ....**40** D3
Willenhall WV12 ....**27** B7
Highmoor Rd B65 ....**63** B3
Highmore Dr B32 ....**102** C8
Highover Dr B75 ....**32** A4
Highpark Ave DY8 ....**80** D5
Highter's Heath La B14 .**105** A2
Highter's Heath Sch
B14 ....**105** B3
Highters Cl B13 ....**105** A3
Highters Rd B14 ....**105** A3
Hightown B63 ....**82** C6

Hightree Cl B32 ....**84** B1
Highview **9** WS1 ....**42** F8
Highview Dr DY6 ....**60** F4
Highview St DY2 ....**51** E1
Highwaymans Croft
CV4 ....**132** D5
Highwood Ave B92 ....**89** A1
Highwood Croft B38 ...**103** D1
Hiker Gr B37 ....**70** D2
Hilary Cres DY1 ....**51** B6
Hilary Dr Aldridge WS9 ..**30** A5
  Sutton Coldfield B76 ....**47** A3
  Wolverhampton WV3 ....**38** D7
Hilary Gr B31 ....**102** F4
Hilary Rd Coventry CV4 .**132** E6
  Nuneaton CV10 ....**72** F5
Hilden Rd B7 ....**67** B4
Hilderic Cres DY1 ....**61** F7
Hilderstone Rd B25 ......**88** C6
Hildicks Cres WS3 ....**28** F7
Hildicks Pl WS3 ....**29** A7
Hill Ave WV4 ....**39** F3
Hill Avenue Jun & Inf Sch
WV4 ....**39** F3
Hill Bank DY9 ....**81** F5
Hill Bank Dr B33 ....**68** D4
Hill Bank Rd
Birmingham B38 ....**104** A2
Halesowen B63 ....**82** D6
Hill Cl Birmingham B31 .**103** C1
  Royal Leamington Spa
  CV32 ....**157** A3
  Sedgley DY3 ....**39** E1
Hill Crest
Birmingham B13 ....**86** E2
Dudley DY2 ....**51** E1
Hill Croft Rd B14 ....**104** C6
Hill Farm Ave CV11 ....**74** B1
Hill Farm Prim Sch CV6 .**113** B7
Hill Fray Dr CV3 ....**134** A5
Hill Gr B20 ....**55** C2
Hill Grove Cres DY10 ...**117** A4
Hill Ho B66 ....**65** C6
Hill Hook Rd B74 ....**31** E5
Hill Hook Rd B74 ....**31** F5
Hill House La B33 ....**68** F3
Hill La
Alvechurch B47,B48 ....**124** D1
Birmingham B43 ....**43** E2
Bromsgrove B60 ....**136** F1
Clent DY9 ....**99** E4
Middleton B75 ....**33** B2
Hill Pas B64 ....**62** E2
Hill Pk WS9 ....**16** B4
Hill Pl WV11 ....**13** A1
Hill Rd Keresley CV7 ....**94** F6
  Stourbridge DY8 ....**81** E5
  Tipton B69 ....**52** A2
  Willenhall WV13 ....**26** E2
Hill Rise View B60 ......**137** C6
Hill Side Coventry CV2 ..**114** A6
  Dudley DY3 ....**50** C4
Hill St Bedworth CV12 ....**78** B5
  Bilston WV14 ....**40** E3
  Birmingham B2,B19 ....**66** E3
  Brierley Hill DY5 ....**61** D8
  Brierley Hill B64 ....**164** B2
  Brierley Hill, Silver End DY5 .**61** D2
  Burntwood WS7 ....**6** E5
  Cannock WS12 ....**2** C3
  Coventry CV1 ....**165** A3
  Darlaston WS10 ....**41** E6
  Dudley, Netherton DY2 ....**62** D5
  Dudley, Upper Gornal DY3 .**50** D5
  Essington WV11 ....**12** F3
  Halesowen B63 ....**83** A3
  Hinckley LE10 ....**75** E8
  Kidderminster DY11 ....**116** D6
  Norton Canes WS11 ....**5** F6
  Nuneaton CV10 ....**72** D4
  Royal Leamington Spa
  CV32 ....**157** A1
  Smethwick B66 ....**65** A6
  Stourbridge DY8 ....**80** F4
  Stourbridge, Lye DY9 .....**81** F5
  Tipton DY4 ....**51** F4
  Walsall WS1 ....**28** F1
  Warwick CV34 ....**160** E6
Hill The B32 ....**84** E2
Hill Top Coventry CV1 ...**165** C3
  Redditch B97 ....**152** F1
  West Bromwich B70 ....**53** A7
Hill Top Ave
Tamworth B79 ....**21** B8
Hill Top Cl B44 ....**55** E6
Hill Top Ind Est B70 .....**52** F8
Hill Top Rd
Birmingham B31 ....**102** F3
Dudley B68 ....**64** C2
Hill Top Wlk WS9 ....**16** C1
Hill View WS9 ....**16** B2
Hill Village Rd B75 ....**32** A4
Hill West Inf Sch B74 ...**31** F4
Hill West Jun Sch B74 ..**31** F4
Hill Wood WS3 ....**14** F2

Hill Wood Rd B75 ....32 C5
Hill Wootton Rd CV32,
  CV35 ....156 C6
Hillaire CI B38 ....104 C2
Hillaries Rd B23 ....56 D2
Hillary Ave WS10 ....42 C3
Hillary Crest DY3 ....50 E5
Hillary Prim Sch WS2 ....42 C7
Hillary St WS2 ....42 C7
Hillbank B69 ....63 D8
Hillbank Rd B27 ....88 D2
Hillbrook Gr B33 ....68 F3
Hillbrow Cres B62 ....83 F8
Hillbury Dr WV12 ....27 B8
Hillcrest Ave
  Birmingham B43 ....43 E2
  Halesowen B63 ....82 B7
  Wolverhampton WV10 ....11 E1
Hillcrest Bsns Pk DY2 ....62 C4
Hillcrest CI Dudley DY2 ....62 C5
  Tamworth B79 ....21 B6
Hillcrest Gdns WV12 ....27 D5
Hillcrest Ind Est B64 ....82 D8
Hillcrest Pk B47 ....140 F8
Hillcrest Rd
  Birmingham B43 ....43 E2
  Dordon B78 ....36 F7
  Nuneaton CV10 ....72 E5
  Romsley B62 ....101 A4
  Sutton Coldfield B72 ....46 C1
Hillcrest Rise WS7 ....7 B4
Hillcrest Sch & Com Coll The
  DY2 ....62 C5
Hillcrest Sch & Sixth Form
  Ctr B32 ....84 E3
Hillcroft Ho B14 ....104 F2
Hillcroft Rd DY5 ....60 E7
Hillcross Wlk B36 ....68 F8
Hilldene Rd DY6 ....60 C4
Hilldrop Gr B17 ....85 D3
Hilleys Croft B37 ....69 F2
Hillfield Mews ■ B91 ....127 B8
Hillfield Rd
  Birmingham B11 ....87 D3
  Solihull B91 ....107 A1
  Solihull, Hillfield B91 ....107 B1
Hillfield Wlk B65 ....62 F5
Hillfields B67 ....64 D3
Hillfields Ho ■ CV1 ....113 E3
Hillfields Rd DY5 ....61 B7
Hillgrove Gdns DY10 ....117 A4
Hillhurst Gr B36 ....58 D1
Hilliard CI CV12 ....78 B4
Hilliards Croft B42 ....55 A8
Hillingford Ave B43 ....44 D3
Hillman B77 ....21 E2
Hillman Dr DY2 ....62 E7
Hillman Gr B36 ....58 F1
Hillman Ho WV1 ....165 B3
Hillmeads Dr DY2 ....62 F7
Hillmeads Rd B38 ....104 A1
Hillmorton B74 ....31 F3
Hillmorton CI B98 ....154 E6
Hillmorton Rd
  Coventry CV2 ....96 C1
  Knowle B93 ....128 A5
  Sutton Coldfield B74 ....31 F4
Hillmount CI B28 ....87 E2
Hillrise .... LE10 ....75 F8
Hillsborough Ho B27 ....88 E2
Hillside Brownhills WS8 ......16 A6
  Lichfield WS14 ....9 D6
  Nuneaton CV10 ....72 A8
  Redditch B98 ....153 D2
Hillside Ave
  Blackheath B65 ....83 B8
  Brierley Hill DY5 ....82 A8
  Halesowen B63 ....82 D6
Hillside CI
  Birmingham B32 ....102 A8
  Brownhills WS8 ....16 A6
  Burntwood WS7 ....6 E5
  Cannock WS12 ....2 A7
Hillside Cres WS3 ....14 F3
Hillside Croft B92 ....89 E4
Hillside Ct B43 ....43 E2
Hillside Dr
  Birmingham, Great Barr
    B42 ....43 D2
  Birmingham, Kingshurst B37 ..69 F4
  Kidderminster DY11 ....116 A7
  Lickey End B61 ....137 B6
  Nuneaton CV10 ....72 C7
  Sutton Coldfield B74 ....44 F7
Hillside Gdns
  Birmingham B37 ....69 F4
  Wolverhampton WV1 ....26 A3
Hillside Ho
  Birmingham, Gravelly Hill
    B23 ....56 C6
  Birmingham, Great Barr
    B43 ....43 D2
  Dudley DY1 ....51 A5
  Hinckley LE10 ....75 D6
  Sutton Coldfield B74 ....32 A4
Hillstone Gdns WV10 ....25 F8
Hillstone Jun & Inf Sch
  B34 ....69 D5
Hillstone Rd B34 ....69 D5
Hilltop DY9 ....81 F3
Hilltop CI CV8 ....145 E8
Hilltop Ct DY3 ....50 E3
Hilltop Dr B36 ....68 D7

Hilltop Rd DY2 ....62 E8
Hillview CI Halesowen B63 ....82 E6
  Lickey End B60 ....137 C6
Hillview Rd
  Birmingham B45 ....121 E8
  Lickey End B60 ....137 C6
Hillville Gdns DY8 ....81 B3
Hillwood Ave B90 ....127 A6
Hillwood CI DY6 ....60 C4
Hillwood Common Rd
  B75 ....32 B6
Hillwood Rd
  Birmingham B31 ....102 E7
  Halesowen B62 ....83 C7
Hilly Rd WV14 ....40 E2
Hillyfields Rd B23 ....56 C4
Hilmore Way B77 ....35 E8
Hilsea CI WV8 ....10 F1
Hilston Ave
  Halesowen B63 ....82 F4
  Wolverhampton WV4 ....38 C4
Hilton Ave
  Birmingham B28 ....105 F4
  Nuneaton CV10 ....72 B6
Hilton CI Stourbridge DY8 ....81 A7
  Walsall WS3 ....14 A2
Hilton Cross WV10 ....12 B5
Hilton Cross Bsns Pk
  WV10 ....12 A8
Hilton Ct Coventry CV5 ....112 F2
  Sutton Coldfield B72 ....57 C8
Hilton Dr B72 ....57 C8
Hilton La
  Essington WV10,WV11 ....12 E8
  Great Wyrley WS6 ....5 F2
  Great Wyrley, Warstone
    WV11 ....13 B7
Hilton Main Ind Est
  WV11 ....12 C5
Hilton Park Service Area ....
Hilton PI WV14 ....40 F5
Hilton Rd Burntwood WS7 ......6 C8
  Featherstone WV10 ....12 C7
  Tipton B69 ....63 C8
  Willenhall WV12 ....13 C1
  Wolverhampton WV4 ....39 F4
Hilton St
  West Bromwich B70 ....53 A3
  Wolverhampton WV10 ....163 D4
Hilton Trad Est WV4 ....39 F4
Himbleton CI B98 ....153 F1
Himbleton Croft ■ B90 ......127 A6
Himley Ave DY1 ....50 F2
Himley CI Birmingham B43 ....43 C2
  Willenhall WV12 ....27 B5
Himley Cres WV4 ....39 E3
Himley Gdns DY3 ....49 F4
Himley Gr B45 ....122 B6
Himley Hall* DY3 ....49 A2
Himley La Bedworth CV12 .....77 D2
  Dudley DY1,DY3 ....49 A2
Himley Rise B90 ....126 E4
Himley St DY1 ....51 A1
Hinbrook Rd DY1 ....50 E1
Hinchliffe Ave WV14 ....40 B2
Hinckes Rd WV6 ....24 B5
Hinckley & District Hospl
  LE10 ....75 D8
Hinckley & District Mus*
  LE10 ....71 D1
Hinckley Bsns Pk LE10 ....74 F8
Hinckley Coll LE10 ....71 F1
Hinckley Ct ■ B68 ....84 B7
Hinckley Rd
  Ansty CV7,CV7 ....97 C2
  Aston Flamville LE10 ....76 D7
  Aston Flamville LE10 ....76 D8
  Barwell LE9 ....71 E5
  Burton Hastings CV11 ....75 A1
  Burton Hastings CV11 ....75 D1
  Burton Hastings LE10 ....75 E1
  Coventry CV2 ....115 A8
  Hinckley LE10 ....76 A6
  Nuneaton CV11 ....73 E5
Hinckley Sta LE10 ....75 D7
Hincks St WV2 ....40 A7
Hind CI CV34 ....155 F2
Hindhead Rd B14 ....105 C4
Hindip CI B63 ....82 F2
Hindlow CI B7 ....67 A2
Hindon Gr B27 ....106 C7
Hindon Sq B15 ....85 F8
Hindon Wlk B32 ....84 C2
Hingeston St B18 ....66 B4
Hingley Croft WS9 ....30 F3
Hingley Ind Pk B64 ....62 C1
Hingley Rd DY9 ....82 A6
Hingley St B64 ....62 D1
Hinksford CI DY6 ....60 D8
Hinstock CI WV4 ....39 A4
Hinstock Rd B20 ....54 F1
Hintlesham Ave B15 ....85 D5
Hinton Ave B48 ....139 A6
Hinton Fields B61 ....136 E7
Hinton Gr WV11 ....26 F5
Hintons Coppice B93 ....127 E6
Hints Ct B78 ....19 D2
Hints La Hopwas B78 ....20 B5
  Weeford B78 ....19 F4
Hints Rd Hopwas B78 ....20 A6
  Mile Oak B78 ....20 C2
Hipkins St DY4 ....51 E7
Hiplands Rd B62 ....83 F4
Hipsley CI B36 ....58 C1

Hipsmoor CI B37 ....69 F3
Hipswell Highway CV2 ....114 D3
Hirdemonsway B90 ....126 A5
Hiron Croft CV3 ....133 C8
Hiron The CV3 ....133 C8
Hiron Way CV34 ....160 B7
Histons Hill WV8 ....10 A3
Hitchcock CI B67 ....64 D5
Hitches La B15 ....86 B7
Hitchman CI CV31 ....162 A5
Hitchman Mews CV31 ....162 A5
Hitchman Rd CV31 ....162 A5
Hither Green La B98 ....153 F7
Hitherside B90 ....126 B5
Hive Ind Ctr The B18 ....66 A6
HM Young Offender Inst
  (Swinfen Hall) WS14 ....9 E1
Hoarestone Ave CV11 ....79 A7
Hoarstone B98 ....98 F5
Hob Green Prim Sch DY9 ......81 E2
Hob Green Rd DY9 ....81 E2
Hob La
  Balsall Common CV7 ....130 E4
  Burton Green CV8 ....131 A3
  Coventry CV8 ....129 A8
Hob Moor Rd B10,B25 ....88 C8
Hob's Mdw B92 ....89 B2
Hob's Moat Rd B92 ....89 B3
Hob's Rd WS13 ....3 E1
Hobacre CI B45 ....122 A8
Hobart Croft ■ B7 ....67 A4
Hobart Ct B74 ....32 A3
Hobart Dr WS5 ....43 C6
Hobart Rd Cannock WS12 ......2 E1
  Tipton DY4 ....40 E1
Hobbis Ho B38 ....123 C7
Hobble End La WS6 ....14 B7
Hobgate CI WV10 ....25 F4
Hobgate Rd WV10 ....25 F4
Hobhouse CI B42 ....54 D8
Hobley St WV13 ....27 C2
Hobmoor Croft B25 ....88 D7
Hobmoor Prim Sch B25 ....88 D8
Hobnock Rd WV11 ....13 B5
Hobs Hole La WS9 ....30 D7
Hobs Rd WS10 ....42 A4
Hobson CI B18 ....66 A5
Hobson Rd B29 ....86 B1
Hockett St CV3 ....133 D8
Hocking Rd CV2 ....114 A1
Hockley Brook CI B18 ....66 A5
Hockley Brook La DY9 ....119 F3
Hockley Centre Trad Est ....
  B18 ....66 A6
Hockley Cir B18 ....66 B6
Hockley CI B19 ....66 D6
Hockley Cir B19 ....66 B6
Hockley Ctr ■ B18 ....66 C4
Hockley Heath Prim Sch
  B94 ....143 C6
Hockley Hill B18 ....66 B5
Hockley La Coventry CV5 .....111 C5
  Dudley DY2 ....62 C6
Hockley Pool CI B18 ....66 B5
Hockley Rd
  Birmingham B23 ....56 D4
  Dudley WV14 ....51 A7
  Tamworth B77 ....35 F5
Hockley St B19 ....66 C5
Hodge Hill Ave DY9 ....81 F3
Hodge Hill Cotts DY10 ....117 C7
Hodge Hill Com Sch B36 ......68 C7
Hodge Hill Gr B34 ....68 E6
Hodge Hill Sch B36 ....68 C7
Hodge La B77 ....22 B6
Hodgehill Ct B36 ....68 E7
Hodgett's La
  Berkswell CV7 ....130 F7
  Coventry CV7,CV8 ....131 A6
Hodgetts CI B67 ....64 D3
Hodgetts Dr B63 ....100 C8
Hodgkins CI WS8 ....16 A6
Hodgson Twr B19 ....66 D6
Hodnell CI B36 ....58 C1
Hodnet CI Bilston WV14 ......40 B5
  Kenilworth CV8 ....148 B5
Hodnet Dr DY5 ....61 C6
Hodnet Gr B15 ....86 E8
Hodnet PI WS11 ....2 B2
Hodson Ave WV13 ....27 C1
Hodson CI WV11 ....26 F8
Hodson Way WS11 ....2 B2
Hoff Beck Ct ■ B9 ....67 B2
Hogarth CI Bedworth CV12 ....78 A4
  Birmingham B43 ....44 D5
  Hinckley LE10 ....71 A3
Hogarth Ho ■ B15 ....86 C8
Hoggs La B31 ....102 E4
Holbeach Rd B33 ....69 B2
Holbeache La DY6 ....49 D1
Holbeache Rd DY6 ....60 C8
Holbeche Rd
  Knowle B93 ....128 A7
  Sutton Coldfield B75 ....47 B5
Holbein CI CV12 ....78 A4
Holberg Gr WV11 ....26 F5
Holborn Ave CV6 ....95 C2
Holborn Hill B6,B7 ....67 B7
Holborn St Ch Ctr DY3 ....50 D7
Holborow Rd B37 ....70 A1
Holbrook La CV6 ....95 D2
Holbrook Park Est CV6 ......113 D8
Holbrook Prim Sch CV6 ....95 E1
Holbrook Twr B36 ....68 D8
Holbrook Way CV6 ....95 D1
Holbury CI WV9 ....11 A2

Holcombe Rd B11 ....88 A3
Holcroft Rd
  Halesowen B63 ....82 C5
  Kingswinford DY6 ....49 C1
  Stourbridge DY9 ....81 C4
Holcroft St Tipton DY4 ....52 A2
  Wolverhampton WV2 ....39 F7
Holden CI B23 ....56 E2
Holden Cres WS3 ....28 F5
Holden Croft DY4 ....52 A3
Holden PI WS3 ....28 E5
Holden Rd
  Wednesbury WS10 ....42 A2
  Wolverhampton WV4 ....38 D3
Holdens The B28 ....105 E6
Holder Rd Birmingham WS11 ..1 B2
Holder Rd
  Birmingham, South Yardley
    B25 ....88 C7
  Birmingham, Sparkbrook
    B11 ....87 A6
Holders Gdns B13 ....86 C2
Holders La B13 ....86 C2
Holdford Rd B6 ....55 F2
Holdgate Rd B29 ....103 C7
Hole Farm Rd B31 ....103 D7
Hole Farm Way B38 ....123 F7
Hole House La B94 ....143 F1
Hole La B31 ....103 C5
Holford Ave WS2 ....42 C6
Holford Dr B42,B6 ....55 F4
Holford Way B6 ....55 F3
Holifast Rd B72 ....57 C7
Holioak Dr CV34 ....161 B6
Holland Ave Knowle B93 .....128 B8
  Oldbury B68 ....64 D4
Holland Ho B19 ....66 D5
Holland Ind Pk WS10 ....41 D8
Holland Rd Bilston WV14 .....40 E7
  Birmingham B43 ....54 D7
  Coventry CV6 ....113 A6
  Sutton Coldfield B72 ....46 C4
Holland St
  Birmingham B3 ....164 A3
  ■ Dudley DY1 ....62 B8
  Sutton Coldfield B72 ....46 C4
  Tipton DY4 ....52 A2
Holland's Way WS3 ....14 D3
Hollands PI WS3 ....14 D1
Hollands Rd WS3 ....14 D1
Hollaway Ct B63 ....82 D5
Hollemeadow Ave WS3 ....28 D7
Holliars Gr B37 ....69 F5
Hollicombe Terr CV2 ....114 D8
Holliday Rd
  Birmingham, Erdington B24 ..57 A4
  Birmingham, Handsworth
    B21 ....65 F7
Holliday St
  Birmingham B1 ....164 A2
  Birmingham B1 ....66 C1
Hollie Lucas Rd B13 ....104 F7
Hollier's Wlk LE10 ....71 D1
Holliers Walk Prim Sch
  LE10 ....71 D1
Hollies Ave WS11 ....1 F1
Hollies Croft B5 ....86 C5
Hollies Ct WS11 ....1 F1
Hollies Dr Halesowen B62 ....83 E6
  Wednesbury WS10 ....41 F6
Hollies Ind Est WV2 ....163 B1
Hollies La WV6 ....23 A4
Hollies Park Rd WS11 ....1 F1
Hollies Rise B64 ....62 E8
Hollies St ■ DY5 ....61 D7
Hollies The
  Birmingham B45 ....122 A1
  Birmingham, Aston B6 ....67 B8
  Birmingham, Winson Green
    B16 ....66 A8
  Smethwick B66 ....65 C4
  Wolverhampton WV1 ....163 B1
Hollin Brow CI B93 ....128 B3
Hollingberry La B76 ....46 F3
Hollings Gr B91 ....127 B8
Hollington Cres B33 ....69 A4
Hollington Rd WV1 ....26 B1
Hollington Way B90 ....127 C7
Hollinwell CI
  Nuneaton CV11 ....79 C8
  Walsall WS3 ....14 A3
Hollis La CV8 ....147 E8
Hollis Rd CV3 ....114 A2
Hollister Dr B32 ....84 F3
Hollow Cres CV6 ....113 A5
Hollow Croft B31 ....103 B3
Hollow Croft Rd WV12 ....27 B7
Hollow The B13 ....86 F3
Holloway
  Birmingham B31 ....102 E5
  Tamworth B79 ....21 B4
Holloway Bank
  Wednesbury WS10 ....41 F1
  West Bromwich B70 ....53 A8
Holloway Bank Trad Est
  WS10 ....41 F1
Holloway Circus Queensway ..
  B1 ....164 B1
Holloway Dr B98 ....154 B3
Holloway Field CV6 ....113 A6
Holloway Head B1 ....164 B1
Holloway La B98 ....153 F3

Holloway Pk B98 ....154 A3
Holloway St Dudley DY3 ....50 D4
  Wolverhampton WV1 ....40 A7
Holloway St W DY3 ....50 D4
Holloway The
  Alvechurch B48 ....139 D3
  Bluntington DY10 ....118 E2
  Seisdon WV5 ....37 A3
  Stourbridge DY8 ....80 F7
  Warwick CV34 ....146 C6
  Wolverhampton WV6 ....24 C2
Hollowmeadow Ho B36 ....68 D8
Hollows The CV11 ....73 F1
Hollowtree La B60 ....138 A3
Holly Ave
  Birmingham, Balsall Heath
    B12 ....87 A5
  Birmingham, Selly Oak B29 ..86 B1
Holly Bank CV5 ....133 A8
Holly Bush Gr B32 ....84 D7
Holly CI Hinckley LE10 ....75 E5
  Sutton Coldfield B76 ....46 F2
  Tamworth B79 ....21 B7
  Willenhall WV12 ....27 C6
Holly Ct Birmingham B23 .....57 A5
  Walsall WS5 ....43 A4
Holly Dell B38 ....104 B2
Holly Dr Birmingham B27 .....88 B2
  Hollywood B47 ....125 B7
  Ryton-on-D CV8 ....135 B1
Holly Farm Bsns Pk
  CV8 ....146 B7
Holly Gr
  Birmingham, Bournville
    B30 ....103 F8
  Birmingham, Lozells B19 ....66 B8
  ■ Birmingham, Selly Oak
    B29 ....85 F2
  Bromsgrove B61 ....136 F3
  Coventry CV4 ....112 B2
  Stourbridge DY8 ....80 F5
  Wolverhampton WV3 ....38 F7
Holly Grange Rd B64 ....64 D7
Holly Hall Rd DY2 ....62 A7
Holly Hall Sch DY1 ....61 F8
Holly Hill
  ■ Birmingham B45 ....101 F1
  Great Wyrley WS6 ....13 E8
Holly Hill Meth & CE Inf Sch
  B45 ....101 F2
Holly Hill Rd
  Birmingham B45 ....102 A2
  Shenstone WS14 ....11 D5
Holly La Aldridge WS9 ....30 F8
  Balsall Common CV7 ....130 A8
  Birmingham, Erdington B24 ..57 C4
  Birmingham, Marston Green
    B37 ....90 B3
  Brownhills WS9 ....16 A4
  Great Wyrley WS6 ....13 F8
  Huntington WS12 ....1 C7
  Portway B48 ....140 F5
  Smethwick B66 ....64 C6
  Sutton Coldfield B74 ....32 A3
  Wishaw B76 ....47 D4
Holly Lodge High Sch
  B67 ....64 D6
Holly Lodge Wlk B37 ....69 F2
Holly Park Dr B24 ....57 C4
Holly Park Ind Est B24 ......57 C2
Holly PI B29 ....86 B2
Holly Rd
  Birmingham, Edgbaston
    B16 ....65 D1
  Birmingham, Handsworth
    B20 ....66 A8
  Birmingham, King's Norton
    B30 ....104 A4
  Blackheath B65 ....63 B1
  Bromsgrove B61 ....136 F4
  Dudley DY1 ....51 A3
  Oldbury B68 ....84 C8
  Wednesbury WS10 ....41 F5
  West Bromwich B71 ....53 E8
Holly St Cannock WS12 ....1 F6
  Dudley DY1 ....61 E6
  Royal Leamington Spa
    CV32 ....157 B1
  Smethwick B67 ....64 F5
Holly Stitches Rd CV10 .....72 E6
Holly View WV11 ....13 A3
Holly Wlk Baginton CV8 .....133 E2
  Nuneaton CV11 ....73 F2
  Royal Leamington Spa
    CV32 ....157 A1
Holly Wood B44 ....44 A1
Hollybank Ave WV11 ....13 A3
Hollybank CI WS3 ....14 A2
Hollybank Gr B63 ....82 D1
Hollybank Rd B13 ....105 A6
Hollyberry Ave B91 ....127 A8
Hollyberry Croft B34 ....69 C6
Hollybrow B29 ....103 B7
Hollybush La
  Coventry CV6 ....96 A4
  Stourbridge DY8 ....80 F7
  Wolverhampton WV4 ....38 B4
Hollybush Wlk ■ B64 ....62 D1
Hollycot Gdns B12 ....86 F6
Hollycroft LE10 ....71 C1
Hollycroft Cres LE10 ....71 C1
Hollycroft Gdns WV6 ....24 D6
Hollycroft Rd B21 ....54 D1
Hollydale Rd
  Birmingham B24 ....57 C3
  Blackheath B65 ....63 D2
Hollyfast La CV7 ....94 C4
Hollyfast Prim Sch CV6 .....112 V7

Hollyfast Rd CV6 ....112 E6
Hollyfaste Rd B33 ....69 B1
Hollyfield Ave B91 ......106 E3
Hollyfield Cres B75 ......46 E4
Hollyfield Ct B75 ....46 E5
Hollyfield Dr
 Barnt Green B45 ....122 A1
 Sutton Coldfield B75 .....46 E5
Hollyfield Prim Sch B75 ..46 F5
Hollyfield Rd B75 ....46 E5
Hollyfield Rd S B76 ......46 F4
Hollyhedge Cl
 Birmingham B31 ....102 D6
 Walsall WS2 ....28 C2
Hollyhedge La WS2 ....28 C2
Hollyhedge Prim Sch
 B71 ....53 E8
Hollyhedge Rd B71 ....53 E7
Hollyhill La WS14 ....17 E5
Hollyhock Rd
 Birmingham B27 ....88 A2
 Dudley DY2 ....51 F1
Hollyhurst Bedworth CV12 .77 F1
 Water Orton B46 ....59 C2
Hollyhurst Dr B90 ....60 E3
Hollyhurst Gr
 Birmingham B26 ....88 E6
 Solihull B90 ....126 B8
Hollyhurst Rd B73 ....45 B3
Hollymoor Way
 Birmingham B31 ....102 B1
 Birmingham B31 ....102 D1
Hollymount B62 ....84 A7
Hollyoak Croft B31 ......123 B8
Hollyoak Gr B91 ....107 A1
Hollyoak Rd B74 ....44 F6
Hollyoak St B71 ....53 D4
Hollyoak Way WS11 ....1 F1
Hollyoake CI B68 ....64 A2
Hollypiece Ho B27 ....88 A2
Hollywell Rd
 Birmingham B26 ....89 B6
 Knowle B93 ....128 A5
Hollywell St WV14 ....40 A1
Hollywood By-Pass
 Birmingham B47 ....104 F1
Hollywood B38,B47 ......124 E6
Hollywood Croft B42 ......54 F8
Hollywood Gdns B47 .....125 A8
Hollywood La B47 ....125 B7
Hollywood Prim Sch
 B14 ....105 A1
Holm View Cl WS14 ....17 F6
Holman Cl WV13 ....26 E2
Holman Rd WV13 ....26 E2
Holman St DY11 ....116 C5
Holman Way CV11 ....73 D3
Holmbridge Gr WS4 ......15 D2
Holmcroft Coventry CV2 ..114 F8
 ☑ Wolverhampton WV4 ....39 F4
Holmcroft Rd DY10 ......117 A5
Holme Mill WV10 ....11 D4
Holme Way WS4 ....29 B7
Holmes Cl B43 ....54 E7
Holmes Ct WS8 ....147 F5
Holmes Dr
 Birmingham B45 ....121 F6
 Coventry CV5 ....111 D5
Holmes La B60 ....151 B1
Holmes Rd
 Whitnash CV31 ....162 B3
 Willenhall WV12 ....27 D6
Holmes The WV10 ....11 D3
Holmesfield Rd B42 ......55 C7
Holmewood Cl CV8 ......148 B5
Holmewood Ct CV8 ......148 B5
Holmfield Rd CV2 ....114 B3
Holmsdale Rd CV6 ....113 E7
Holmwood Ave DY11 .....116 A6
Holmwood Dr B97 ......153 C3
Holmwood Rd B97 ......153 C3
Holmwood Rd B10 ....67 D1
Holroyd Ho CV4 ....111 F2
Holston Cl WS12 ....2 F1
Holsworth Cl B77 ....21 D1
Holsworthy Cl CV11 ......73 E5
Holt Cres WS11 ....2 B2
Holt Ct B7 ....38 B4
Holt Farm Prim Sch B62 ..63 E1
Holt Gdns B80 ....159 E2
Holt Hill B98 ....154 F8
Holt Ho B61 ....137 A3
Holt La B62 ....100 D4
Holt Rd Halesowen B62 ....63 E1
 Hinckley LE10 ....75 E6
 Studley B80 ....159 E2
Holt St B7 ....64 D4
Holt The CV32 ....157 B3
Holte Dr B75 ....32 D2
Holte Rd
 Birmingham, Aston B6 ....56 A1
 Birmingham, Sparkhill B11 .87 D5
Holte Sch B19 ....56 A6
Holtes Wlk B6 ....67 B8
Holton Ct WV13 ....27 C2
Holtshill La WS1 ....28 E2
Holtwick B77 ....36 B8
Holy Cross Ct CV2 ......114 E4
Holy Cross Gn DY9 ....99 E2
Holy Cross La DY9 ......119 E8
Holy Cross RC Prim Sch
 B76 ....47 A3
Holy Family RC Prim Sch
 Birmingham B10 ....87 F7
 Coventry CV5 ....95 B3
Holy Name RC Prim Sch
 B43 ....43 E1
Holy Oaks Cl B98 ....154 E2

Holy Rosary RC Prim Sch
 WV1 ....26 A1
Holy Souls RC Prim Sch
 B27 ....88 C3
Holy Trinity CE Prim Sch
 Birmingham B20 ....55 C2
 Brownhills WS8 ....15 E6
 West Bromwich B70 ....53 D1
Holy Trinity RC Prim Sch
 WV14 ....40 E6
Holy Trinity RC Sch B10 ..87 C8
Holy Well Cl B16 ....66 A2
Holyhead C Ltr B21 ......65 D8
Holyhead Prim Sch
 WS10 ....41 E3
Holyhead Rd
 Birmingham B21 ....65 D8
 Codsall WV8 ....23 E7
 Coventry CV5 ....112 E5
 Darlaston WS10 ....41 C4
 Wednesbury WS10 ....41 E3
Holyhead Road Ind Est
 WS10 ....41 D3
Holyhead Sch B21 ....65 D8
Holyhead Way B21 ....65 D8
Holyoak Cl Bedworth CV12 .77 F1
 ☑ Birmingham B6 ....55 F1
Holyoakes Field First Sch
 B97 ....153 D4
Holyoakes La B97 ....152 C5
Holyoke Gr CV31 ....162 B2
Holyrood Ct CV10 ....72 D5
Holyrood Gr B6 ....66 E8
Holywell Cl CV4 ....111 D1
Holywell La B45 ....121 D6
Holywell Prim Sch B45 ...121 D6
Holywell Rise WS14 ......9 C6
Home Farm CV35 ....155 F6
Home Farm Cotts CV8 ...149 A3
Home Farm Cres CV31 ...162 B4
Home Meadow Ct B13 ....86 F3
Home Meadow Ho B27 ....88 A2
Home Meadow La B98 ...154 E6
Home Park Rd CV11 ......73 C3
Homecroft Rd B26 ....88 E8
Homedene Rd B31 ....102 E7
Homefield Rd WV8 ....10 C3
Homelands B42 ....55 B7
Homelea Rd B25 ....88 D8
Homeledge Ho B44 WS13 ..9 B7
Homemead Gr B45 ......121 F7
Homer CI CV34 ....161 E5
Homer Hill Rd B63 ....82 C7
Homer Rd Solihull B91 ..107 B3
 Sutton Coldfield B75 .....32 D2
Homer St B12 ....86 F5
Homers Fold WV14 ....40 D5
Homerton Rd B44 ....45 B1
Homestead Cl DY3 ....50 E5
Homestead Dr B75 ....32 C3
Homestead Rd B33 ....69 B1
Homeward Way CV3 .....115 A1
Homewood Cl B76 ....46 E3
Honesty Cl WS8 ....15 E6
Honeswode Cl B20 ....66 A8
Honeyborne Rd B75 ......46 D7
Honeybourne B77 ....21 D2
Honeybourne Cl
 Coventry CV5 ....112 B3
 ☑ Halesowen B63 ....83 A3
Honeybourne Rd
 Birmingham B33 ....89 C8
 Halesowen B63 ....83 C3
Honeybourne Sch B28 ...105 F8
Honeybourne Way WV13 ..27 C2
Honeycomb Way B31 .....102 E3
Honeyfield Rd CV1 ......113 D5
Honeysuckle Ave DY6 ....60 E7
Honeysuckle Cl B32 ......84 B5
Honeysuckle Dr
 Coventry CV2 ....96 B2
 Featherstone WV10 ....12 C7
 Walsall WS5 ....43 A3
Honeysuckle Gr ☑ B27 ...88 C5
Honeysuckle Way WS6 ....5 B8
Honeytree Cl CV6 ....60 F3
Honiley Ct CV2 ....96 D1
Honiley Dr B73 ....45 C2
Honiley Rd
 Birmingham B33 ....69 A2
 Honiley CV8 ....146 B6
 Meer End CV8 ....130 A1
Honiley Way CV2 ....96 D1
Honister Cl DY5 ....61 F1
Honiton Cl B31 ....102 E4
Honiton Cres B31 ....102 E4
Honiton Rd CV2 ....114 C5
Honiton Way WS9 ....29 F5
Honiton Wlk ☑ B66 ......65 B5
Honnington Ct ☑ B29 ....84 F1
Honor Ave WV4 ....39 E5
Hoo Farm Ind Est DY10 ..116 F1
Hoo Rd DY10 ....116 E4
Hoobrook Ent Ctr DY10 ..116 E2
Hoobrook Ind Est DY10 ..116 E2
Hood Gr B30 ....103 D4
Hood St CV1 ....113 E3
Hook Dr B74 ....31 F4
Hook La WS14 ....17 C3
Hooper St B18 ....65 F4
Hoopers La B96 ....158 E1
Hoosen Cl B62 ....84 A7
Hope Aldridge Bsns Ctr
 CV10 ....73 C6
Hope Cl CV7 ....95 A7
Hope Pl ☑ B29 ....85 F2
Hope Rd DY4 ....52 A6
Hope St Birmingham B5 ..86 E8

Hope St continued
 Coventry CV1 ....113 B2
 Dudley DY2 ....62 C8
 Halesowen B62 ....83 D8
 Stourbridge DY8 ....60 D3
 Walsall WS1 ....42 E8
 West Bromwich B70 ....53 E2
Hope Terr DY2 ....62 C5
Hopedale Cl CV2 ....114 E3
Hopedale Rd B32 ....84 C5
Hopgardens Ave B60 ....137 B2
Hopkins Ct ☑ WS10 .....42 A3
Hopkins Dr B71 ....53 E7
Hopkins Rd CV6 ....113 A4
Hopkins St ☑ 52 A2
Hopleys Cl B77 ....21 E4
Hopstone Gdns WV4 .....38 F4
Hopstone Rd B29 ....85 A1
Hopton Cl Coventry CV5 ..112 A4
 Perton WV6 ....23 F3
Hopton Cres WV11 ......26 D6
Hopton Crofts CV32 ....156 C2
Hopton Dr DY10 ....116 E1
Hopton Gdns DY1 ....51 A3
Hopton Gr B13 ....105 C5
Hopton Mdw WS12 ....2 C1
Hopwas Gr B37 ....69 F5
Hopwas Hill B79 ....20 A6
Hopwood Cl B63 ....83 A2
Hopwood Gr B31 ....122 E6
Hopyard Cl DY3 ....50 B3
Hopyard Gdns WV14 .....40 B3
Hopyard La Dudley DY3 ...50 B3
 Redditch B98 ....154 D4
Hopyard Rd WS2 ....27 E2
Horace Partridge Rd
 WS10 ....41 A5
Horace St WV14 ....51 A8
Horatio Dr B13 ....86 F4
Hordern Cl WV6 ....24 F5
Hordern Cres DY5 ....81 D8
Hordern Gr WV6 ....24 F5
Hordern Rd WV6 ....24 F5
Hornbeam B77 ....22 A4
Hornbeam Dr CV2 ....103 B7
Hornbeam Dr CV4 ....111 D1
Hornbeam Gr CV31 .....162 C6
Hornbeam Wlk WV3 ......25 A1
Hornbrook Gr B92 ......106 C7
Hornby Gr B14 ....105 C4
Hornby Rd WV4 ....39 C5
Hornchurch Cl CV1 .....165 B1
Horndean Cl CV6 ....113 E8
Horne Way B34 ....69 E5
Horner Way B62 ....63 C1
Horning Dr WV14 ....40 C3
Horninghold Cl CV3 ....134 E8
Hornsey Cl CV2 ....114 E8
Hornsey Gr B44 ....45 A2
Hornsey Rd B44 ....45 A2
Hornton Cl B74 ....31 D5
Horrell Rd
 Birmingham B26 ....89 B7
 Solihull B90 ....105 F2
Horse Fair
 Birmingham B1 ....164 B1
 Kidderminster DY10 .....116 E7
Horse Shoe Rd CV6 ......96 A4
Horse Shoes La B26 .....89 B5
Horsecroft Dr B71 ....54 A8
Horsefair The ☑ LE10 ...75 D8
Horsehills Dr WV3 ....24 E2
Horsela Croft B8 ....68 C8
Horseley Fields WV1 ....163 D3
Horseley Heath DY4 .....52 C5
Horseley Rd DY4 ....52 C5
Horsepool LE10 ....76 A5
Horseshoe Cl ☑ WS2 ....42 B7
Horseshoe The B68 .....64 C2
Horseshoe Wlk ☑ DY4 ...51 E5
Horsfall Rd B75 ....47 A5
Horsford Rd CV3 ....133 E6
Horsham Ave DY8 ....60 C3
Horsley Rd Birmingham B43 ..44 D4
 Little Aston B74 ....31 B2
Horton Cl Darlaston WS10 ..41 D7
 Sedgley DY3 ....50 C8
Horton Pl WS10 ....41 D7
Horton Sq Birmingham B12 ..86 E7
Horton St Darlaston WS10 ..41 D7
 West Bromwich B70 ......53 C2
Hosiery St CV12 ....78 C2
Hospital Dr B15 ....85 E4
Hospital La
 Bedworth CV12 ....77 B1
 Cheslyn Hay WS6 ....4 B2
 Dudley WV14 ....51 B7
Hospital Rd WS7 ....7 B5
Hospital St
 Birmingham B19 ....164 B4
 Birmingham, Newtown B19 .66 D6
 Tamworth B79 ....21 B5
 Walsall WS2 ....28 D4
 Wolverhampton WV2 .....163 C2
Hossil La
 Belbroughton DY9 ......119 C8
 Clent DY9 ....99 D1
Hotchkiss Way CV3 .....135 A7
Hotel Bldgs WS14 ....8 A2
Hothersall Dr B73 ....45 D2
Hothorpe Cl CV3 ....114 F1
Hotspur Rd B44 ....44 F1
Hough Pl WS2 ....42 B7

Hough Rd
 Birmingham B14 ....104 D6
 Walsall WS2 ....42 A7
Houghton Ct B28 ....105 D4
Houghton St Oldbury B69 ..63 F6
 West Bromwich B70 ......53 C2
Houlbrooke Ho ☑ WS14 ...9 C8
Houldey Rd B31 ....103 B1
Houldsworth Cres CV6 ...95 C4
Houliston Cl WS10 ....42 B5
Houndsfield Cl B47 .....125 B5
Houndsfield Farm B47 ...125 B5
Houndsfield Gr B47 .....125 A5
Houndsfield La B47 .....125 C6
Housman Cl B60 ....150 E8
Housman Ct B60 ....137 A3
Housman Pk B60 ....137 A2
Housman Wlk DY10 .....117 C6
Houting DY7 ....35 D5
Houx The DY8 ....80 E8
Hove Ave CV5 ....111 E4
Hove Rd B27 ....88 C3
Hovelands Cl CV2 ......114 C8
Hoveton Cl B98 ....154 B2
Howard Ave B61 ....136 E3
Howard Cl CV5 ....111 E4
Howard Cres CV3 ....134 E7
Howard Ct B16 ....65 E1
Howard Rd Bilston WV14 ..40 F3
 Birmingham, Handsworth
 B20 ....55 B2
 Birmingham, King's Heath
 B14 ....104 E7
 Birmingham, Newton B43 .54 C8
 Birmingham, South Yardley
 B25 ....88 C7
 Nuneaton CV10 ....73 A3
 Redditch B98 ....144 D4
 Solihull B92 ....88 E3
 Wednesfield WV11 ....26 F8
Howard Rd E B13 ....104 F7
Howard St
 Birmingham B19 ....164 B4
 Coventry CV1 ....165 C4
 Tipton DY4 ....52 B5
 West Bromwich B70 ......52 F7
Howard Wlk CV31 ......162 D6
Howat Rd CV7 ....94 F7
Howcotte Gn CV4 ......131 E8
Howden Pl B33 ....69 A5
Howdle's La WS8 ....6 E2
Howe Cres WV12 ....27 C6
Howe St ☑ B4 ....66 F3
Howell Rd WV2 ....39 E7
Howells Cl CV12 ....77 D1
Howes Com Prim Sch
 CV3 ....133 E5
Howes Croft B35 ....58 A2
Howes La CV3 ....133 D3
Howford Gr B7 ....67 B4
Howl Pl DY4 ....51 E5
Howland Cl WV9 ....10 F2
Howlette Rd CV4 ....111 E2
Howley Ave B44 ....44 F1
Howley Grange Prim Sch
 B62 ....83 F5
Howley Grange Rd B62 ...84 A4
Hoylake B77 ....22 B4
Hoylake Cl Nuneaton CV11 .74 B1
 Walsall WS3 ....14 B4
Hoylake Dr B69 ....63 A7
Hoyland Way B30 ......103 E8
HRS Bsns Pk B33 ....69 C1
Huband Ct B98 ....154 A5
Hubert Croft B29 ....85 F2
Hubert Rd B29 ....85 F2
Hubert St B6 ....66 F5
Hucker Cl WS2 ....42 A7
Hucker Rd WS2 ....42 A7
Huddesford Dr CV7 .....130 C8
Huddisdon Cl ☑ CV34 ..155 F1
Huddleston Way B29 ....85 C1
Huddlestone Cl WV10 ...12 B6
Huddocks View WS3 .....14 F5
Hudson Ave B46 ....70 F6
Hudson Cl WS11 ....2 B1
Hudson Dr WS7 ....7 C6
Hudson Gr WV6 ....23 E5
Hudson Rd
 Birmingham B20 ....55 A4
 Tipton DY4 ....52 A4
Hudson's Dr B30 ....104 A4
Hudswell Dr DY5 ....81 D8
Huggins Cl CV7 ....130 C7
Hugh Gaitskill Ct WV14 ...40 C8
Hugh Porter Way WV6 ...24 F6
Hugh Rd Birmingham B10 ..67 D1
 Coventry CV3 ....114 A2
 Smethwick B67 ....64 E5
Hugh Villas B10 ....67 E1
Hughes Ave WV3 ....38 E7
Hughes Cl Warwick CV34 .155 D2
 Whitnash CV31 ....162 A2
Hughes Pl WV14 ....40 D7
Hughes Rd Bilston WV10 ..41 A5
 Wednesbury WS10 ....41 A5
Hughes The CV34 ......160 F6
Huins Cl B69 ....154 A4
Hulbert Dr DY2 ....62 B6
Hulbert Ind Est DY2 .....62 B6
Hulland Pl DY5 ....61 C3
Hullbrook Rd B13 ......105 C6
Hulme Cl CV3 ....115 B1
Humara Ghar ☑ WS1 ....42 E8

Humber Ave
 Coventry CV1 ....113 F1
 Coventry CV3 ....113 F2
 Sutton Coldfield B76 .....58 A7
Humber Gdns B63 ....82 C5
Humber Gr B36 ....58 F1
Humber Ho DY1 ....61 D8
Humber Rd Coventry CV3 .134 A8
 Wolverhampton WV3 ......25 A1
Humber Twr ☑ B7 ....67 A4
Humberstone Rd
 ☑ Coventry CV6 ....113 A5
 Sutton Coldfield B24 .....57 E4
Hume St
 Kidderminster DY11 ....116 C5
 Smethwick B66 ....65 B4
Humpage Rd B9 ....67 E2
Humphrey Ave B60 .....150 F7
Humphrey Burton's Rd
 CV3 ....133 C8
Humphrey Middlemore Dr
 B17 ....85 D4
Humphrey St DY3 ....50 D3
Humphrey-Davy Rd
 CV12 ....95 D8
Humphries Cres WV14 ...40 F2
Humphries Dr DY10 ....116 F2
Humphries Ho WS8 ......15 F7
Humphries Rd WV10 ....25 D6
Humphris St CV34 ......161 B8
Hundred Acre Rd B74 ....44 F7
Hungary Cl DY9 ....81 C5
Hungary Hill DY9 ....81 C5
Hungerfield Rd B36 .....58 C1
Hungerford Rd DY8 .....80 E2
Hungry La WS14 ....18 F5
Hunningham Gr ☑ B91 .127 B8
Hunnington Cl B32 ......84 A1
Hunnington Cres B63 ...83 B2
Hunscote Cl B90 ....105 F1
Hunscote Ho B90 ......105 F1
Hunslet Cl B32 ....84 F4
Hunslet Rd
 Birmingham B32 ....84 F4
 Burntwood WS7 ....7 B8
Hunstanton Ave B17 .....84 F8
Hunstanton Cl DY5 ......81 C7
Hunt End La CV7 ....158 C5
Hunt Terr CV4 ....132 B7
Hunt's La WV12 ....27 D6
Hunter Ave WS7 ....7 B7
Hunter Cl WS14 ....9 D6
Hunter Cres WS3 ....28 E7
Hunter Ct B5 ....86 D5
Hunter Rd WS11 ....4 E8
Hunter St WV6 ....25 A4
Hunter Terr CV5 ....132 D8
Hunters' Ride DY7 ......60 B2
Hunters Cl Bilston WV14 ..41 A7
 Coventry CV3 ....115 A2
Hunters Hill Sch B60 ...137 F6
Hunters Rd B19 ....66 B7
Hunters Rise B63 ....82 D1
Hunters Vale B19 ....66 C6
Hunters Wlk B23 ....56 C8
Huntingdon Cl
 Redditch B98 ....154 F2
 Tamworth B78 ....20 F2
Huntingdon Gdns B63 ...82 C7
Huntingdon Rd
 Coventry CV5 ....133 A8
 West Bromwich B71 .....53 B7
Huntingdon Way CV10 ...72 E3
Huntington Ho B23 ......56 B6
Huntington Ind Est WS12 .3 B8
Huntington Prim Sch
 WS12 ....1 C8
Huntington Rd WV12 ....27 D8
Huntington Terrace Rd
 WS11 ....1 F4
Huntingtree Prim Sch
 B63 ....82 E3
Huntingtree Rd B63 .....82 E3
Huntlands Rd B63 ....82 F2
Huntley Dr B91 ....107 B4
Huntly Rd B16 ....66 A1
Hunton Ct ☑ B23 ....56 E2
Hunton Hill B23 ....56 E3
Hunton Rd B23 ....56 E3
Hunts Mill Dr DY5 ......50 D2
Hunts Rd B30 ....104 B7
Huntsmans Gate WS7 ....7 B8
Huntsmans Rise WS12 ...1 C8
Hurcott Ct DY10 ....117 A8
Hurcott La DY10 ....117 A8
Hurcott Rd DY10 ....117 B8
Hurdis Rd B90 ....106 A2
Hurdlow Ave B18 ....66 B5
Hurlbutt Rd CV34 ......161 C4
Hurley Cl
 Royal Leamington Spa
 CV32 ....157 A2
 Sutton Coldfield B72 .....46 C2
 Walsall WS5 ....43 D6
Hurley Gr B37 ....69 D3
Hurleys Fold DY2 ....62 C5
Hurlingham Rd B44 ......45 A1
Hurn Way CV6 ....96 B4
Huron Cl WS11 ....2 B2
Hurricane Way B35 ......58 A2
Hurst Bsns Pk DY5 ......62 A4
Hurst Cl B36 ....69 E7
Hurst Ct DY9 ....81 F5

Hurst Green Prim Sch B62 .....83 E8
Hurst Green Rd
Bentley Heath B93 .....127 F4
Halesowen B62 .....83 F8
Minworth B76 .....58 D6
Hurst Hill Ct WV14 .....51 A8
Hurst Hill Prim Sch WV14 .....51 A8
Hurst La Birmingham B34 .....69 E6
Brierley Hill DY5 .....61 F3
Tipton DY4 .....52 C5
Hurst La N B36 .....69 F7
Hurst Rd Bedworth CV12 .....78 B3
Coventry CV6 .....96 A4
Dudley WV14 .....40 A1
Sedgley WV14 .....75 D8
Smethwick B67 .....64 D2
Hurst St B5 .....164 C1
Hurst The
Birmingham B13 .....105 D7
Hollywood B47 .....125 A6
Hurst Wlk CV6 .....96 A4
Hurstbourne Cres WV1 .....26 B1
Hurstcroft Rd B33 .....69 B3
Hurstway The B23 .....56 C8
Hurstwood Rd B23 .....56 C8
Huskisson Ct WV10 .....25 C6
Hussey Rd Brownhills WS8 .....15 E8
Norton Canes WS11 .....5 F5
Husum Way DY10 .....117 C7
Hut Hill La WS6 .....5 A4
Hutton Ave B8 .....67 D5
Hutton Rd
Birmingham, Handsworth B20 .....55 C1
Birmingham, Saltley B8 .....67 D5
Huxbey Dr B92 .....107 F8
Huxley Cl WV9 .....11 A3
Hyacinth Way LE10 .....75 D5
Hyatt Sq DY5 .....81 C7
Hyatts Wlk B65 .....62 F5
Hyde Cl B60 .....137 B2
Hyde Pl CV32 .....161 E8
Hyde Rd Coventry CV2 .....114 E4
Kenilworth CV8 .....148 A5
Wednesfield WV11 .....26 C6
Hyde The DY9 .....81 D2
Hydes La LE10 .....74 E4
Hydes Rd
Wednesbury WS10 .....42 B2
West Bromwich B71 .....42 C1
Hydesville Tower Sch WS1 .....29 A2
Hyett Way WV14 .....41 B2
Hylda Rd B20 .....55 B1
Hylstone Cres WV11 .....26 D6
Hylton St B18 .....66 C5
Hypericum Gdns CV2 .....114 C4
Hyperion Dr WV4 .....39 A3
Hyperion Rd
Stourbridge DY7 .....80 C7
Sutton Coldfield B36 .....57 F1
Hyron Hall Rd B27 .....88 C2
Hyssop Cl Birmingham B7 .....67 A5
Cannock WS11 .....2 B3
Hytall Rd B90 .....105 C2
Hythe Gr B25 .....88 D8

I-Max Bsns Pk B11 .....88 A6
Ibberton Rd B14 .....105 B3
Ibex Cl CV3 .....114 F1
Ibis Cl DY10 .....117 B3
Ibis Gdns DY6 .....61 A6
Ibstock Cl B98 .....154 E4
Ibstock Dr DY8 .....81 A4
Ibstock Ho B98 .....154 E4
Ibstock Rd CV6 .....96 A5
Icknield Cl B74 .....31 A1
Icknield Fst Sch B98 .....154 D1
Icknield Port Rd B16 .....65 F3
Icknield Sq B16 .....66 A3
Icknield St
Alvechurch B38 .....124 B2
Beoley B98 .....140 C2
Birmingham B18 .....66 A3
Redditch, Church Hill B98 .....154 C7
Redditch, Ipsley B98 .....154 D2
Rowney Green B48 .....140 B6
Icknield Street Dr B98 .....159 D7
Ida Rd Walsall WS2 .....28 C2
West Bromwich B70 .....53 D1
Idbury Rd B44 .....56 A7
Ideal Bldgs **7** DY11 .....116 D6
Ideal Wks DY9 .....82 A6
Iden Rd CV1 .....113 E4
Idmiston Croft B14 .....104 F2
Idonia Rd WV6 .....23 F5
Ilam Pk CV8 .....148 C5
Ilex Ct CV34 .....161 A7
Ilford Cl CV12 .....78 A3
Ilford Ct CV3 .....135 D7
Ilford Dr CV3 .....133 B5
Ilford Rd B23 .....56 D6
Ilfracombe Gr CV3 .....133 A5
Iliffe Ho LE10 .....75 B7
Iliffe Way B17 .....85 D4
Ilkley Gr B37 .....69 F2
Illey Cl B31 .....102 C1
Illey La Birmingham B32 .....102 A7
Halesowen B62 .....101 E8

Illeybrook Sq B32 .....84 D2
Illshaw WV9 .....11 A3
Illshaw Heath Rd B90, B94 .....126 D2
Ilmington Cl
Coventry CV3 .....133 B5
Redditch B98 .....154 D1
Ilmington Dr B73 .....45 C3
Ilmington Rd B29 .....84 F1
Ilminster Cl LE10 .....76 B7
Ilsham Gr B31 .....122 E6
Ilsley Rd B23 .....56 E4
Image Bsns Pk WS12 .....2 B3
Imber Rd DY10 .....117 A1
Imex Auto Ctr DY4 .....52 A3
Imex Bsns Pk
Birmingham, Bordesley Green B9 .....67 D2
Birmingham, Stechford B33 .....68 C4
Tipton DY4 .....52 A3
Wolverhampton WV2 .....39 C7
Imex Ho WV2 .....39 B7
Imogen Gdns CV34 .....161 E3
Imperial Ave DY10 .....116 F8
Imperial Gr DY10 .....116 F8
Imperial Rd B9 .....67 E1
Imperial Rise B46 .....59 E2
Impney Cl B98 .....154 E6
Impsley Cl B36 .....69 B8
Inca Cl CV3 .....134 F8
Ince Rd WS10 .....41 C7
Incestre Dr B43 .....43 D1
Inchbrook Rd CV8 .....148 C7
Inchcape Ave B20 .....55 A3
Inchford Ave CV34 .....155 E2
Inchford Cl CV11 .....73 F1
Inchford Rd B92 .....107 E7
Inchlaggan Rd WV10 .....25 F6
Infantry Pl B75 .....47 A6
Ingatestone Dr DY8 .....60 C5
Inge St B5 .....164 C1
Ingestre Cl Cannock WS11 .....2 B1
Walsall WS3 .....13 F3
Ingestre Dr B43 .....43 C1
Ingestre Ho WV6 .....24 E5
Ingestre Rd
Birmingham B28 .....106 A7
Wolverhampton WV10 .....11 C1
Ingeva Dr B45 .....122 A1
Ingham Way B17 .....85 A8
Ingle Ct CV31 .....161 E7
Ingleby Gdns WV6 .....25 A5
Ingledew Cl WS2 .....27 D3
Inglefield Rd B33 .....68 F3
Inglemere Gr B29 .....102 F7
Inglenook Dr B20 .....55 A2
Ingleside Villas **8** B11 .....87 C5
Ingleton Cl CV11 .....74 A2
Ingleton Ho **2** B15 .....86 D8
Ingleton Rd B8 .....68 A7
Inglewood Ave WV3 .....38 F8
Inglewood Cl
Kingswinford DY6 .....60 D5
Royal Leamington Spa CV32 .....157 A3
Inglewood Gr B74 .....30 E2
Inglewood Rd B11 .....87 C5
Ingoldsby Rd B31 .....103 C3
Ingot Cl WS2 .....28 B6
Ingram Gr B27 .....88 A2
Ingram Pit La B77 .....22 A5
Ingram Pl WS3 .....14 D1
Ingram Rd Coventry CV5 .....132 D8
Walsall WS3 .....14 D1
Inhedge St DY3 .....50 E5
Inhedge The DY1 .....51 C1
Inkberrow Rd B63 .....82 F7
Inkerman Gr WV10 .....25 F2
Inkerman Ho B19 .....66 E6
Inkerman St
Birmingham B7 .....67 B4
Wolverhampton WV10 .....25 F3
Inland Rd B24 .....57 B2
Innage Cl CV31 .....162 B8
Innage Rd B31 .....103 B4
Innage The B47 .....125 A5
Innis Rd CV5 .....132 E8
Innisfree House Sch B47 .....125 C4
Innsworth Dr B35 .....58 A4
Insetton Cl B98 .....154 D4
Inshaw Cl B33 .....68 E3
Institute Rd B14 .....104 F8
Instone Rd Coventry CV6 .....95 A1
Halesowen B63 .....83 A3
Instow Cl WV12 .....27 B8
Insull Ave B14 .....105 B1
Intended St B63 .....82 F7
International Ho B43 .....54 F6
Intersection Ho B70 .....53 E1
Intown WS1 .....28 F2
Intown Row WS1 .....28 F2
Inverary Cl CV8 .....148 C4
Inverclyde Rd B20 .....55 A3
Inverness Cl CV5 .....112 A4
Inverness Ho WV1 .....163 B4
Inverness Rd B31 .....102 F3
Invicta Rd CV3 .....134 D6
Inworth WV9 .....11 B3
Io Ctr The B98 .....159 C8
Ipsley Alders Marsh Nature Reserve* B98 .....155 E3
Ipsley Church La B98 .....154 C1
Ipsley Fst Sch B98 .....158 F8
Ipsley Gr B23 .....56 A5
Ipsley La B98 .....154 D2
Ipsley St B98 .....155 C2
Ipstones Ave B33 .....68 F4

Ipswich Cres B42 .....55 B7
Ipswich Wlk B37 .....70 B2
Ireland Green Rd B70 .....53 B2
Ireton Cl CV4 .....111 C1
Ireton Rd Birmingham B20 .....55 A4
Wolverhampton WV10 .....11 E3
Iris Cl Birmingham B29 .....103 B8
Dudley DY2 .....51 F1
Hinckley LE10 .....75 E5
Tamworth B79 .....21 C6
Iris Dr B14 .....104 D3
Irnham Rd B74 .....32 B1
Iron Bridge Wlk DY9 .....99 B8
Iron La B33 .....68 D4
Ironmonger Row CV1 .....165 B3
Ironstone Rd WS7 .....6 E8
Irvan Ave B70 .....52 F5
Irvine Cl WS3 .....28 B7
Irvine Rd WS3 .....28 B7
Irving Cl DY3 .....50 A4
Irving Rd Coventry CV1 .....113 E2
Solihull B92 .....89 E3
Tipton DY4 .....41 A1
Irving St B1 .....66 D1
Irwell J77 .....21 E2
Irwin Ave B45 .....122 C7
Isaac Walton Pl B70 .....52 E7
Isambard Dr CV6 .....95 F5
Isbourne Way **1** B9 .....67 B2
Isis Cl B73 .....46 B5
Isis Gr Birmingham B36 .....69 F8
Willenhall WV13 .....27 C2
Isis Ho DY1 .....61 D8
Island Cl LE10 .....71 E2
Island Dr DY10 .....116 E4
Island Rd B21 .....54 C1
Island The B78 .....20 C1
Islington B63 .....83 A4
Islington Cres CV9 .....36 C1
Islington Row Middleway B15 .....86 C8
Ismere Rd B24 .....57 B2
Itchen Gr WV6 .....23 E4
Ithon Gr B38 .....123 E8
Ivanhoe Ave CV11 .....73 E1
Ivanhoe Rd
Birmingham B43 .....44 C3
Lichfield WS14 .....9 B6
Wolverhampton WV2 .....40 A6
Ivanhoe St DY2 .....62 A8
Ivatt B77 .....21 F2
Ivatt Cl WS4 .....29 B7
Iverley Dr DY10 .....98 C5
Iverley Rd B63 .....83 C4
Iverley Wlk DY9 .....81 C2
Ivor Rd Birmingham B11 .....87 B4
Coventry CV6 .....95 F2
Redditch B97 .....153 D2
Ivy Ave Birmingham B12 .....87 A5
Birmingham B12 .....87 B5
Ivy Cl WS11 .....4 D8
Ivy Croft WV9 .....10 F3
Ivy Farm La CV4 .....132 D6
Ivy Gdns WS11 .....6 A5
Ivy Gr Brownhills WS8 .....16 A4
Nuneaton CV10 .....72 A6
Ivy House Rd B69 .....63 D6
Ivy La Birmingham B9 .....67 A2
Romsley B62 .....100 D5
Ivy Lodge Cl B37 .....90 A7
Ivy Rd
Birmingham, Handsworth B21 .....66 A7
Birmingham, Stirchley B30 .....104 A6
Dudley DY1 .....51 D5
Sutton Coldfield B73 .....45 F1
Tipton DY4 .....51 F7
Ivy Way B90 .....126 A6
Ivybridge Gr B42 .....55 C3
Ivybridge Rd CV3 .....133 D6
Ivydale Ave B26 .....89 C5
Ivyfield Rd B23 .....56 B5
Ivyhouse La WV14 .....51 B8
Ivyhouse Rd B38 .....123 C8
Ivyhouse Wlk B77 .....35 F6
Izod St B97 .....153 D4
Izons La B70 .....53 A1
Izons La Ind Est B70 .....53 A1
Izons Rd B70 .....53 C3

J

Jacey Rd Birmingham B16 .....65 D2
Solihull B90 .....106 B4
Jack Cade Way CV34 .....161 E4
Jack David Ho CV4 .....52 D5
Jack Holden Ave WV14 .....40 A2
Jack Newell Ct **3** WV14 .....51 C8
Jack O'Watton Bsns Pk B46 .....59 D2
Jackdaw Cl DY3 .....39 C2
Jackdaw Dr B36 .....70 A8
Jacker's Rd CV7 .....96 B4
Jacklin Dr CV3 .....133 C4
Jackmell Rd LE10 .....74 D8
Jackson Ave B8 .....67 E4
Jackson Cl
Birmingham B11 .....87 B7
Featherstone WV10 .....12 A6
Keresley CV7 .....95 A7
Norton Canes WS11 .....5 E4
Oldbury B68 .....64 A5
Tipton DY4 .....41 B1

Jackson Ct continued
Oldbury B69 .....63 F4
Jackson Dr B67 .....64 D5
Jackson Gr CV8 .....148 C4
Jackson Ho **9** B69 .....64 A7
Jackson Rd
Birmingham B8 .....67 F4
Coventry CV6 .....95 D1
Lichfield WS13 .....3 B3
Jackson St Oldbury B68 .....64 B4
Stourbridge DY9 .....81 E6
Wolverhampton WV6 .....25 B4
Jackson Way B32 .....84 A5
Jackson Wlk B35 .....58 A2
Jackwood Gn CV12 .....95 C8
Jacmar Cres B67 .....64 E6
Jacob Dr CV4 .....132 D6
Jacob's Hall La WS6 .....5 B1
Jacobean La B93 .....108 B1
Jacoby Pl B5 .....86 C5
Jacox Cres CV8 .....148 C5
Jacquard Cl CV3 .....133 D4
Jacquard Ho **3** CV1 .....113 E4
Jade Cl CV1 .....165 D4
Jade Gr WS11 .....2 C2
Jaffray Cres B24 .....56 F3
Jaffray Ct B23 .....56 E3
Jaffray Rd B24 .....56 F3
Jaguar B77 .....21 E2
Jakeman Cl B98 .....154 E4
Jakeman Rd B12 .....86 E5
James Beattie Ho WV6 .....24 C4
James Bridge Cl WS2 .....42 B7
James Brindley Sch (Parkway Ctr) B15 .....86 C8
James Brindley Sch (Willow Ctr) B13 .....86 E1
James Cl Darlaston WS10 .....41 F7
Smethwick B67 .....65 A5
James Clift Ho **3** B69 .....63 D5
James Ct
Birmingham, King's Norton B38 .....103 F2
5 Birmingham, Moseley B13 .....87 B2
Warwick CV34 .....160 F7
James Dawson Dr CV5 .....111 B8
James Dee Cl DY5 .....62 A1
James Diskin Ct CV11 .....73 E2
James Eaton Cl B71 .....53 A5
James Galloway Cl CV3 .....134 E7
James Green Rd CV4 .....111 F2
James Greenway WS13 .....3 A2
James Ho Birmingham B19 .....66 C6
Coventry CV2 .....114 C8
James Hutchens Ct WS7 .....6 F5
James Memi Homes The **4** B7 .....67 C7
James Rd
Birmingham, Great Barr B43 .....54 D8
Birmingham, Tyseley B11 .....87 F6
Coleshill B46 .....70 F8
Kidderminster DY10 .....117 A8
James Scott Rd B63 .....82 A6
James St Bilston WV14 .....40 D6
Birmingham B3 .....164 A3
Cannock WS11 .....1 F5
Nuneaton CV11 .....73 A5
Willenhall WV13 .....27 A3
James Turner St B18 .....65 C8
James Watt Dr B19 .....66 C8
James Watt Ho B66 .....65 B5
James Watt Jun & Inf Sch B21 .....65 E7
James Watt Queensway B4 .....164 C3
James Watt St
Birmingham B4 .....164 C3
West Bromwich B71 .....53 B8
Jamescroft CV3 .....134 E6
Jameson Rd B6 .....67 C8
Jameson St WV6 .....25 B4
Jane Lane Cl WS2 .....27 F4
Jane Lane Specl Sch WS2 .....27 F3
Janice Gr B14 .....105 B4
Janine Ave WV11 .....26 E7
Jaques Cl B46 .....59 B2
Jardine Cres CV4 .....111 F2
Jardine Rd B6 .....55 F1
Jarvis Cl LE10 .....71 C4
Jarvis Cres B69 .....64 A4
Jarvis Rd B23 .....56 F6
Jarvis Way B24 .....67 A8
JAS Ind Pk B65 .....63 E4
Jasmin Croft B14 .....104 E3
Jasmine Cl WV9 .....11 A3
Jasmine Gr
Bromsgrove B61 .....136 F4
Codsall WV8 .....10 B3
Coventry CV3 .....134 C8
Royal Leamington Spa CV32 .....157 A2
Jasmine Rd Dudley DY2 .....51 F1
Tamworth B77 .....22 A4
Jasmine Way WS10 .....41 D7
Jason Cl B77 .....21 D5
Jason Rd DY9 .....81 F4
Jay Park Cres DY10 .....117 B2
Jay Rd DY6 .....60 D8
Jayne Cl
Wednesfield WV11 .....26 D7
West Bromwich B71 .....42 E1
Jays Ave DY4 .....52 B4
Jays Cres B48 .....123 B1
Jayshaw Ave B43 .....54 E8
Jeal Cl B47 .....124 E2

Jean Dr DY4 .....52 D6
Jeavons Pl WV14 .....40 C5
Jedburgh Ave WV6 .....23 E4
Jedburgh Gr CV3 .....133 A4
Jeddo St WV2 .....163 B1
Jeffcock Rd WV3 .....39 A7
Jefferies Cl LE10 .....71 E2
Jefferson Cl B71 .....53 B8
Jeffrey Ave WV4 .....39 F5
Jeffrey Cl CV12 .....95 C8
Jeffrey Rd B65 .....63 E3
Jeffrey Woods Cross CV1 .....113 F4
Jeffries Ho **1** B69 .....64 A7
Jeffs Ave WV2 .....163 C1
Jeliff St CV4 .....111 F2
Jelleyman Cl DY11 .....116 C6
Jellicoe Ho **9** CV4 .....52 A8
Jellicoe Way LE10 .....71 D3
Jenkins Ave CV5 .....111 F4
Jenkins Cl WV14 .....40 C5
Jenkins St B10 .....87 C8
Jenkinson Rd WS10 .....41 D1
Jenks Ave WV10 .....25 E8
Jennens Rd B4 .....66 F3
Jenner Cl WS2 .....28 A6
Jenner Ho WS2 .....27 F6
Jenner Rd WS2 .....28 A6
Jenner St Coventry CV1 .....165 C4
Wolverhampton WV2 .....163 D2
Jennifer Wlk B25 .....88 E8
Jennings St B64 .....62 F2
Jenny Cl WV14 .....40 E1
Jenny Walkers La WV5 .....23 D1
Jennyns Ct **8** WS10 .....42 A3
Jensen B77 .....21 E2
Jenton Rd CV31 .....162 B6
Jephcott Ho **2** CV1 .....113 E3
Jephcott Rd B8 .....68 A4
Jephson Ct CV2 .....96 A5
Jephson Dr B26 .....88 F7
Jephson Pl **3** CV31 .....162 B7
Jeremy Gr B92 .....89 B3
Jeremy Rd WV4 .....39 C5
Jerome Ct B74 .....30 F1
Jerome Dr WS11 .....4 A6
Jerome Prim Sch WS11 .....5 F5
Jerome Rd
Norton Canes WS11 .....6 A5
Sutton Coldfield B72 .....46 D4
Walsall WS2 .....28 B1
Jerome Way WS7 .....7 C7
Jerrard Dr B75 .....46 C6
Jerrard Mews B75 .....46 C5
Jerry's La Birmingham B23 .....56 E6
Weeford WS14 .....19 B8
Jersey Cl B98 .....154 D7
Jersey Croft B36 .....70 B6
Jersey Rd B8 .....67 D4
Jerusalem Wlk DY10 .....116 E7
Jervis Cl DY5 .....61 D4
Jervis Cres B74 .....31 D3
Jervis Ct **2** WS1 .....28 F2
Jervis Pk B74 .....31 C4
Jervis Rd B77 .....35 F5
Jervis Terr B21 .....65 D8
Jervoise Dr B31 .....103 B5
Jervoise Jun & Inf Sch B29 .....85 A1
Jervoise La B71 .....42 E1
Jervoise Rd B29 .....85 A2
Jervoise St B70 .....53 A4
Jesmond Gr B24 .....57 E4
Jesmond Rd CV1 .....113 F4
Jessel Rd WS2 .....28 C2
Jessie Rd WS9 .....16 B3
Jesson Cl WS1 .....43 A7
Jesson Ct WS1 .....43 A8
Jesson Rd Dudley DY3 .....51 A6
Sutton Coldfield B75 .....47 A5
Walsall WS1 .....43 A8
Jesson St B70 .....53 E3
Jesson's C E Prim Sch DY1 .....51 B1
Jessop Dr B77 .....21 E5
Jevon St WV14 .....51 B8
Jevons Rd B73 .....45 A3
Jew's La DY3 .....50 E4
Jewellery Quarter Sta B18 .....66 B4
Jiggins La B32 .....84 B4
Jill Ave B43 .....43 C1
Jill La B96 .....159 B2
Jillcot Rd B92 .....89 B3
Jim Forrest Cl **4** CV3 .....134 F8
Jinnah Cl B12 .....86 F8
Joan of Arc Ho CV3 .....133 E6
Joan St WV2 .....39 E6
Joan Ward St CV3 .....133 D8
Joan's Cl CV31 .....162 C6
Joanna Dr CV3 .....133 C3
Job's La CV4 .....112 A2
Jockey Field DY3 .....50 E6
Jockey La WS10 .....42 A4
Jockey Rd B73 .....46 A2
Jodrell St CV11 .....73 B6
Joe O'Brien Cl CV3 .....134 C6
Joe Williams Cl **7** CV3 .....134 F8
Joeys La WV8 .....10 C3
John Bosco Cl B71 .....53 B5
John Bright Cl DY4 .....51 F8
John Bright St B1 .....164 B2
John Cleveland Coll LE10 .....71 F1
John F Kennedy Wlk **4** DY4 .....52 B8
John Fletcher Cl WS10 .....42 B4
John Grace St CV3 .....133 D8

John Gulson Prim Sch
CV1 ....113 D5
John Harper St WV13 ....27 B2
John Ho CV1 ....8 B1
John Howell Dr CV4 ....52 A5
John Kempe Way B12 ....87 A2
John Knight Rd CV12 ....78 B5
John McGuire Cres CV3 ....134 E7
John Nash Sq CV8 ....147 F3
John Nichols St LE10 ....75 B7
John O'Gaunt Rd CV8 ....147 E3
John of Gaunt Ho CV3 ....133 E6
John Rd B62 ....83 F3
John Riley Dr WV12 ....27 C8
John Rous Ave CV4 ....132 B7
John Shelton Com Prim Sch
CV6 ....95 D4
John Shelton Dr CV6 ....95 D4
John Sinclair Ho CV1 ....165 B4
John Smith Ho ⑪ B1 ....66 C3
John St Bedworth CV12 ....78 A2
Birmingham B19 ....66 B7
Blackheath B65 ....63 C1
Brierley Hill DY5 ....61 A4
Cannock, Wimblebury WS12 ....2 F3
Hinckley LE10 ....71 E1
Nuneaton, Coton CV11 ....73 C2
Nuneaton, Stockingford
CV10 ....72 E3
Oldbury B69 ....64 A7
Royal Leamington Spa
CV32 ....161 F8
Stourbridge DY8 ....60 F1
Tamworth B77 ....21 E4
Walsall WS2 ....28 E3
West Bromwich, Guns Village
B70 ....53 B4
West Bromwich, Swan Village
B70 ....52 F5
Willenhall WV13 ....27 A1
Wolverhampton WV2 ....40 A6
John St N B71 ....53 B5
John Tofts Ho CV1 ....165 B4
John Willmott Sch B76 ....46 F4
John Wood CE Inf Sch
WS11 ....4 D8
John Wooton Ho ❸
WS10 ....41 D6
John's La
Tipton, Dudley Port DY4 ....52 C3
Tipton, Tividale B69 ....52 C3
Johndory B77 ....35 D6
Johns Cl B80 ....159 C4
Johns Gr B43 ....54 C8
Johns La WS6 ....5 A3
Johnson Ave WV11 ....26 C5
Johnson Cl
Birmingham, Sparkhill B11 ....87 C5
Birmingham, Ward End B8 ....68 C6
Darlaston WS10 ....41 D5
Lichfield WS13 ....3 C1
Redditch B98 ....154 A5
Johnson Dr B35 ....57 F3
Johnson Pl WV14 ....41 A7
Johnson Rd
Bedworth CV12 ....78 C3
Birmingham B23 ....57 A6
Burntwood WS7 ....6 F8
Cannock WS11 ....1 D4
Coventry CV6 ....114 A8
Darlaston WS10 ....41 D5
Wednesbury WS10 ....42 C2
Willenhall WV13 ....27 D7
Johnson St
Birmingham B7 ....67 C6
Wolverhampton WV2 ....40 B7
Wolverhampton, Cinder Hill
WV14 ....39 F1
Wood End CV9 ....36 C1
Johnsons Bridge Rd B71 ....53 C6
Johnsons Gr B68 ....84 D8
Johnston St B70 ....53 D1
Johnstone St B19 ....66 D8
Joiners Croft B92 ....107 E8
Joinings Bank B68 ....64 B4
Jon Baker Ct LE10 ....75 E8
Jonathan Rd CV2 ....114 F8
Jones Ho WS2 ....28 D3
Jones La Burntwood WS7 ....7 F7
Great Wyrley WS6 ....5 B1
Jones Rd Bedworth CV7 ....78 A1
Walsall WV12 ....13 D1
Willenhall WV12 ....27 D8
Wolverhampton WV10 ....25 C6
Jones Wood Cl B76 ....58 A7
Jonesfield Cres WS11 ....26 B2
Jonkel Ave B77 ....36 A5
Jonquil Cl B23 ....56 C7
Jordan Cl Kenilworth CV8 ....148 B2
Lichfield WS13 ....9 A8
Smethwick B66 ....65 B5
Sutton Coldfield B75 ....32 B1
Jordan Ho B36 ....68 E8
Jordan Leys CV4 ....52 B5
Jordan Pl WV14 ....40 F5
Jordan Rd B75 ....32 C2
Jordan Way WS9 ....16 B1
Jordan Well CV1 ....165 C2
Jordans Cl B97 ....158 D6
Jordans The CV5 ....112 C4
Joseph Cash Prim Sch
CV6 ....113 C7
Joseph Chamberlain VI Form
Coll B12 ....86 F6
Joseph Creighton Cl
CV3 ....134 E7
Joseph Dewsbury Cl WS7 ....6 F8
Joseph Edward Cox Inf Sch
WS10 ....42 D2
Joseph Halpin Ho ❸
CV11 ....165 C4
Joseph Latham Ho ❸
CV2 ....96 B1
Joseph Leckie Com Tech Coll
WS5 ....42 E5
Joseph Luckman Rd
CV12 ....78 B4
Joseph St B69 ....63 F6
Joseph Turner Prim Sch
WS10 ....41 E6
Josiah Mason Coll B23 ....56 C4
Josiah Rd B31 ....102 D2
Jourdain Pk CV34 ....161 E3
Jovian Dr CV1 ....71 A1
Jowett B77 ....21 E2
Jowett's La B71 ....53 B8
Joyberry Dr DY8 ....81 A3
Joyce Pool CV34 ....160 E7
Joynson St WS10 ....41 E5
Jubilee Ave
Redditch B97 ....158 D7
West Bromwich B71 ....53 B7
Jubilee Bldgs WS10 ....41 D7
Jubilee Cl
Great Wyrley WS6 ....4 F2
Walsall WS3 ....28 E6
Jubilee Cres CV6 ....113 B7
Jubilee Dr N DY11 ....116 B2
Jubilee Dr S DY11 ....116 B2
Jubilee Dr S WV11 ....26 D2
Jubilee Park Jun & Inf Sch
DY4 ....52 B8
Jubilee Rd Bilston WV14 ....41 A4
Birmingham B45 ....101 C2
Tipton DY4 ....52 B8
Jubilee St B71 ....53 D8
Jubilee Terr
Bedworth CV12 ....78 B4
Stoke Prior B60 ....150 C1
Jubilee Trad Ctr B5 ....66 E1
Judd Cl CV6 ....95 C4
Judds La CV6 ....95 E4
Judge Cl B69 ....64 A7
Judge Rd DY5 ....81 F7
Juggins La B94 ....141 B7
Julia Ave B24 ....57 F4
Julia Gdns B71 ....53 D8
Julian Cl Catshill B61 ....137 A8
Coventry CV2 ....114 F8
Great Wyrley WS6 ....5 A3
Wolverhampton WV1 ....26 B2
Julian Rd WV1 ....26 B2
Julie Croft WV14 ....40 E1
Juliet Cl CV11 ....74 A1
Juliet Dr CV34 ....161 F3
Juliet Rd B62 ....83 F3
Julius Dr B46 ....59 F1
Junction 2 Ind Est B69 ....63 F5
Junction 6 Ind Pk B6 ....56 B2
Junction Rd
Birmingham B21 ....65 C8
Bromsgrove B61 ....136 F1
Stourbridge DY8 ....81 B4
Stourbridge, Amblecote DY8 ....60 E1
Wolverhampton WV2 ....40 B7
Junction St
Coventry CV1 ....165 A2
Dudley DY2 ....62 B8
Oldbury, Brades Village B69 .....64 C7
Walsall WS1 ....42 D7
Junction St S B69 ....64 A5
Junction The ❶ DY4 ....80 E8
June Cres B37 ....70 C2
June Croft B26 ....89 D5
Juniper Cl B76 ....46 F3
Juniper B77 ....22 A4
Juniper Cl Bedworth CV12 ....77 E2
Birmingham B27 ....88 C1
Juniper Dr CV10 ....117 A4
Juniper Dr Coventry CV5 ....111 F5
Sutton Coldfield B76 ....58 A7
Walsall WS5 ....43 B4
Juniper Ho B36 ....68 F7
Juniper Rise B63 ....82 C5
Juno Dr CV31 ....161 F5
Jury Rd DY5 ....81 F7
Jury St CV34 ....160 E6
Justice Cl CV31 ....162 A4
Jutland Rd B13 ....105 B8

K

Kanzan Rd CV2 ....96 B4
Kareen Gr CV3 ....135 C7
Karen Cl CV10 ....72 E7
Karen Way DY5 ....81 D8
Karlingford Cl CV5 ....132 D8
Kate's Hill Comm Prim Sch
DY2 ....62 E8
Katherine Rd B67 ....64 F2
Kathleen Ave CV12 ....77 E1
Kathleen Rd
Birmingham B25 ....88 C7
Sutton Coldfield B72 ....46 C4
Katie Rd B29 ....85 E1
Katmandu Rd B60 ....137 C1
Katrine Cl CV10 ....72 C5
Kayne Cl DY6 ....60 C7
Keanscott Dr B68 ....64 C4
Keasdon Gr WV14 ....40 F6
Keating Gdns B75 ....32 A4
Keatley Ave B33 ....69 E2
Keats Ave Birmingham B10 ......87 D7
Cannock WS11 ....1 E5
Keats Cl Dudley DY3 ....50 A5
Nuneaton CV10 ....72 A4
Stourbridge DY8 ....60 F8
Sutton Coldfield B74 ....31 F6
Tamworth B79 ....20 F8
Keats Dr WV14 ....40 D2
Keats Gr Birmingham B27 ....88 B1
Wolverhampton WV10 ....26 A8
Keats Ho ❸ Oldbury B68 ....64 C4
Reddith B97 ....158 C8
Keats Pl DY10 ....117 B6
Keats Rd Coventry CV2 ....114 D2
Walsall WS3 ....28 F8
Willenhall WV12 ....27 E7
Wolverhampton WV10 ....12 A1
Keble Cl Burntwood WS7 ....7 C7
Cannock WS11 ....4 E8
Keble Gr Birmingham B26 ....89 B6
Walsall WS5 ....43 A7
Keble Ho B37 ....70 A2
Keble Wlk B79 ....21 A6
Kebull Gr CV4 ....131 E8
Kedleston Cl WS3 ....14 A3
Kedleston Ct B28 ....105 F4
Kedleston Rd B28 ....105 F5
Keegan Wlk WS2 ....27 F4
Keel Dr B13 ....87 D1
Keele Cl B98 ....154 E6
Keeley Ho B37 ....70 A4
Keeley St B9 ....67 B2
Keeling Dr WS11 ....1 B1
Keeling Rd CV8 ....148 B5
Keelinge St DY4 ....52 B5
Keen St B66 ....65 F5
Keenan Dr CV12 ....77 D1
Keeper's Cl WS7 ....7 A6
Keepers Cl Brownhills WS9 .....15 F3
Kingswinford DY6 ....60 B8
Lichfield WS14 ....9 E7
Keepers Gate Cl B74 ....46 C7
Keepers Ho B73 ....45 C2
Keepers La Codsall WV8 ....10 A1
Wolverhampton WV6,WV8 ....24 A7
Keepers Rd B74 ....31 C5
Keepers Wlk CV12 ....77 D1
Keer Ct B9 ....67 B2
Kegworth Cl CV6 ....96 A4
Kegworth Rd B23 ....56 C2
Keir Cl CV32 ....157 A2
Keir Hardy Wlk B69 ....63 D7
Keir Pl DY8 ....80 E8
Keir Rd WS10 ....42 D2
Keith Rd CV32 ....157 B4
Keith Winter Cl B61 ....136 E6
Kelby Cl B31 ....102 E4
Kelby Rd B31 ....102 F4
Keldy Cl WV6 ....24 F5
Kele Rd CV4 ....132 A7
Kelfield Ave B17 ....85 B4
Kelham Pl B92 ....89 B1
Kelia Dr B67 ....64 F6
Kellett Rd B7 ....67 A4
Kelling Cl DY5 ....81 C8
Kellington Cl B8 ....67 F4
Kelmarsh Dr B91 ....107 C8
Kelmscote Rd CV6 ....112 F8
Kelmscott Rd B17 ....85 B7
Kelsall Cl WV1 ....26 B2
Kelsall Croft B1 ....66 B3
Kelsey Cl Birmingham B7 ....67 A4
Nuneaton CV11 ....73 E3
Kelsey La CV7 ....130 D5
Kelsey's Cl CV8 ....135 F3
Kelso Gdns WV6 ....23 D4
Kelsull Croft B37 ....70 A2
Kelston Ct B15 ....86 A6
Kelvedon Gr B91 ....107 C4
Kelverdale Gr B14 ....104 C4
Kelverley Gr B71 ....43 A1
Kelvestone Ho WS11 ....1 D1
Kelvin Ave CV2 ....114 D5
Kelvin Cl DY11 ....116 A8
Kelvin Dr WS11 ....2 A3
Kelvin Pl WS2 ....28 B6
Kelvin Rd
Birmingham B31 ....103 B1
Royal Leamington Spa
CV32 ....157 C5
Walsall WS2 ....28 B6
Kelvin Way Trad Est WV14 ......53 C1
Kelway CV3 ....115 A2
Kelway Ave B43 ....44 B3
Kelwood Dr B63 ....83 A5
Kelynmead Rd B33 ....69 A2
Kem St CV11 ....73 E2
Kemberton Cl WV3 ....24 C1
Kemberton Rd
Birmingham B29 ....85 B2
Wolverhampton WV3 ....24 C1
Kemble Cl WV12 ....27 D5
Kemble Croft B5 ....86 E7
Kemble St B35 ....58 A3
Kemelstowe Cres B63 ....100 C8
Kemerton Ho B97 ....153 B4
Kemerton Way B90 ....126 F6
Kempe Rd B33 ....69 A4
Kempley Ave CV2 ....114 C2
Kemps Green Rd
Balsall Common CV7 ....130 B6
Tanworth-in-A B94 ....143 A1
Kempsey Cl
Halesowen B63 ....82 E4
Oldbury B69 ....63 E4
Redditch B98 ....159 B7
Solihull B92 ....89 A3
Kempsey Covert B38 ....123 E7
Kempsey Ho B32 ....102 A8
Kempsford Cl B98 ....158 F6
Kempson Ave
Sutton Coldfield B72 ....46 C1
West Bromwich B71 ....53 B5
Kempson Rd B36 ....68 F8
Kempsons Gr WV14 ....40 B3
Kempthorne Ave WV10 ....25 E8
Kempthorne Gdns WS3 ....14 A2
Kempthorne Rd WV14 ....40 F6
Kempton Cres CV32 ....157 C4
Kempton Ct B61 ....121 A1
Kempton Dr
Great Wyrley WS6 ....4 F2
Tamworth B77 ....35 D4
Kempton Park Rd B36 ....68 D8
Kempton Way DY8 ....80 E3
Kemsey Dr WV14 ....40 F6
Kemshead Ave B31 ....122 E8
Kemsley Rd B14 ....104 F2
Kenchester Cl B98 ....154 F2
Kenchester Ho ❷ B16 ....66 A2
Kendal Ave
Birmingham B45 ....122 B7
Coleshill B46 ....70 F7
Royal Leamington Spa
CV32 ....156 C2
Kendal Cl
Bromsgrove B60 ....137 B1
Nuneaton CV11 ....74 A6
Wolverhampton WV6 ....24 F6
Kendal Ct
⑭ Birmingham, Selly Oak
B29 ....103 C7
Birmingham, Stockland Green
B23 ....56 B3
Brownhills WS9 ....15 F4
Cannock WS11 ....4 F8
Kendal Dr B45 ....122 D1
Kendal Gr B92 ....107 F8
Kendal Rd B11 ....87 B7
Kendal Rise
Coventry CV5 ....112 C4
Oldbury B68 ....64 B3
Wolverhampton WV6 ....24 F6
Kendal Rise Rd B45 ....122 B7
Kendal Tower B17 ....85 D5
Kendal Ho ⑪ B69 ....63 D5
Kendall Rise DY6 ....60 D6
Kenderine Montessori Sch
CV5 ....133 A8
Kendon Ave CV6 ....112 E6
Kendrick Ave B34 ....69 E5
Kendrick Cl Coventry CV6 ....96 A4
Solihull B92 ....107 F6
Kendrick Pl WV14 ....41 A4
Kendrick Rd Bilston WV14 ....41 A4
Sutton Coldfield B76 ....57 F5
Wolverhampton WV10 ....25 F6
Kendrick St WS10 ....42 A3
Kendricks Rd WS10 ....41 F7
Kenelm Ct Coventry CV3 ....134 C5
Kenelm Rd
Birmingham B10 ....87 E8
Dudley WV14 ....40 C1
Oldbury B68 ....64 A3
Sutton Coldfield B73 ....46 B4
Kenelm's Ct B62 ....101 A4
Kenilcourt CV8 ....147 D6
Kenilworth Castle*
CV8 ....147 D5
Kenilworth Cl
Birmingham B97 ....158 D6
Stourbridge DY8 ....60 D2
Sutton Coldfield B74 ....46 A8
Tipton DY4 ....51 D4
Kenilworth Cres
Walsall WS2 ....28 A4
Wolverhampton WV4 ....39 E4
Kenilworth Ct
Birmingham, Edgbaston B15 ...85 F8
Birmingham, Gravelly Hill
B24 ....56 E2
❷ Cannock WS11 ....1 E1
Coventry CV3 ....133 C8
Dudley DY1 ....61 F8
Kenilworth Dr
Cannock WS11 ....1 D4
Kidderminster DY10 ....116 E2
Nuneaton CV11 ....73 B3
Kenilworth Hall Mews
CV8 ....147 F5
Kenilworth Ho
Birmingham B13 ....105 A6
❸ Walsall WS3 ....28 C6
Kenilworth Rd
Balsall Common CV7,CV8 ....130 D4
Birmingham B20 ....55 E2
Coventry CV4 ....132 B2
Cubbington CV32 ....157 C6
Hampton-in-A B92 ....109 E5
Kenilworth CV8 ....148 C8
Knowle B93 ....128 E5
Lichfield WS14 ....9 B6
Meriden CV7 ....91 D1
Oldbury B68 ....64 A3
Perton WV6 ....23 F4
Royal Leamington Spa
CV32 ....156 E5
Tamworth B77 ....21 E4
Kenilworth Sch CV8 ....148 C5
Kenilworth Sch Castle Hall
Sixth Form CV8 ....147 F2
Kenilworth St ⑱ CV32 ....156 F1
Kenley Gr B30 ....104 B3
Kenley Way ❷ B91 ....106 D4
Kenmare Way WV11 ....26 C4
Kenmore Ave WS12 ....1 F7
Kenmore Dr LE10 ....71 B2
Kenmore Rd B33 ....89 C8
Kennan Ave CV31 ....161 F6
Kennedy Cl
Kidderminster DY10 ....116 F3
Sutton Coldfield B72 ....46 C4
Tamworth B77 ....21 C1
Kennedy Cres
Darlaston WS10 ....41 C7
Dudley DY3 ....50 D4
Kennedy Croft B26 ....89 A7
Kennedy Ct WV8 ....80 F5
Kennedy Gr B30 ....104 B6
Kennedy Rd WV10 ....163 D4
Kennedy Sq ❸ CV32 ....157 A1
Kenneggy Mews B29 ....85 F2
Kennerley Rd B25 ....88 D6
Kennet B77 ....22 A3
Kennet Cl Brownhills WS8 ....6 C2
Coventry CV2 ....114 C8
Kennet Gr B36 ....69 F8
Kennet Ho ❺ DY1 ....61 E8
Kenneth Gr B23 ....56 B5
Kennford Cl B65 ....63 C6
Kennington Rd WV10 ....25 F5
Kenpas Highway CV3 ....133 A5
Kenrick Croft B35 ....57 F2
Kenrick Ho B16 ....66 A1
Kenrick Way B70 ....64 E8
Kensington Ave B12 ....87 A4
Kensington Ct
Coventry CV5 ....113 A1
Nuneaton CV10 ....72 C6
Kensington Dr
Sutton Coldfield B74 ....31 F5
Tamworth B79 ....21 B7
Kensington Gdns
WS11 ....1 C2
Stourbridge DY8 ....60 C1
Kensington Ho ❸ B37 ....5 C8
Kensington Rd
Birmingham B29 ....86 B2
Coventry CV5 ....113 A1
Willenhall WV12 ....27 B7
Kensington St B19 ....66 D6
Kenswick Dr B63 ....83 A2
Kent Ave Fazeley B78 ....20 F2
Walsall WS2 ....28 B3
Kent Cl Aldridge WS9 ....16 B1
Coventry CV3 ....133 E6
Kidderminster DY10 ....116 E3
Walsall WS2 ....28 E5
West Bromwich B71 ....53 C7
Kent Close Jun & Inf Sch
B71 ....53 B7
Kent Dr LE10 ....71 F4
Kent Pl Cannock WS12 ....2 F1
Dudley DY2 ....62 A6
Kent Rd Birmingham B45 ......101 F1
Halesowen B62 ....83 F5
Stourbridge DY8 ....80 D7
Wednesbury WS10 ....42 D4
Wolverhampton WV2 ....39 E7
Kent St Birmingham B5 ....66 E1
Dudley DY3 ....50 E5
Walsall WS2 ....28 E5
Kent St N B18 ....65 F5
Kent's Cl B92 ....88 F3
Kenthurst Cl CV5 ....111 A4
Kentish Rd B21 ....65 C8
Kentmere Cl CV2 ....96 E2
Kentmere Twr ❹ B23 ....57 B6
Kenton Ave WV6 ....24 F4
Kenton Wlk ❽ B29 ....85 F2
Kents Ho B33 ....69 B2
Kentwell B77 ....20 D7
Kenward Croft B17 ....84 F7
Kenway B47 ....125 A7
Kenwick Rd B17 ....85 B4
Kenwood Rd B9 ....68 B3
Kenwyn Gn CV7 ....96 B8
Kenyon Cl
Bromsgrove B60 ....137 A1
Stourbridge DY8 ....81 A2
Kenyon St B18 ....164 A4
Kepler B79 ....20 E7
Keppel St CV1 ....113 E5
Kerby Rd B23 ....56 D4
Keresley Brook Rd CV6 ....95 A2
Keresley Cl Coventry CV6 ....95 A2
Solihull B91 ....107 C5
Keresley Gr B29 ....84 F2
Keresley Green Rd CV6 ....94 F1
Keresley Grange Prim Sch
CV6 ....94 F1
Keresley Green Rd CV6 ....94 F1
Keresley Newland Prim Sch
CV7 ....94 F7
Keresley Rd CV6 ....113 A8
Kernthorpe Rd B14 ....104 D4
Kerr Dr DY4 ....51 E8
Kerria Ctr B77 ....22 A4
Kerria Rd B77 ....22 B4
Kerridge Cl WV9 ....11 A2
Kerrls Way CV3 ....115 A1
Kerry Cl Barwell LE9 ....71 F7
Birmingham B31 ....102 F6
Brierley Hill DY5 ....61 C4
Kerry Ct WS1 ....43 A8
Kerry Hill ❸ B60 ....150 E6
Kerry's Ho CV1 ....113 B2
Kersley Gdns WV11 ....26 F5
Kerswell Cl ❷ B97 ....153 B5

Kerswell Dr B90 . . . . .127 A5
Kesterton Rd B74 . . . . .31 E5
Kesteven Cl B15 . . . . .86 B6
Kesteven Rd B71 . . . . .53 C7
Keston Rd B44 . . . . .44 F4
Kestrel B77 . . . . .36 A6
Kestrel Ave B25 . . . . .88 C8
Kestrel Cl Birmingham B23 . .56 D6
   Hinckley LE10 . . . . .75 F6
   Kidderminster DY10 . . . . . .116 E3
Kestrel Croft 2 CV3 . . . . . .134 F8
Kestrel Dr B74 . . . . .31 F5
Kestrel Gr
   Birmingham B30 . . . . .103 D8
   Cannock WS12 . . . . .2 E1
   Willenhall WV12 . . . . .27 C8
Kestrel Rd Dudley DY1 . . . .51 A1
   Halesowen B63 . . . . .82 B7
   Oldbury B68 . . . . .63 F2
Kestrel Rise B24 . . . . .24 F7
Kestrel View B60 . . . . .137 C7
Kestrel Way WS6 . . . . .4 C2
Keswick Cl CV11 . . . . .74 A6
Keswick Dr CV6 . . . . .60 D6
Keswick Gn CV32 . . . . .156 D1
Keswick Gr B74 . . . . .30 F2
Keswick Ho B69 . . . . .63 D5
Keswick Rd B92 . . . . .89 A4
Keswick Wlk CV2 . . . . .114 F4
Ketley Croft B12 . . . . .86 F7
Ketley Fields DY6 . . . . .61 A5
Ketley Hill Rd DY1 . . . . .61 F8
Ketley Rd DY6 . . . . .60 F7
Kettlebrook Rd
   Solihull B90 . . . . .127 C6
   Tamworth B77 . . . . .21 C3
Kettlehouse Rd B44 . . . . . . .44 F3
Kettles Wood Dr B32 . . . . . .84 C2
Kettlesbank Rd DY3 . . . . . . .50 B2
Kettlewell Cl CV34 . . . . . . .155 E1
Kettlewell Way B37 . . . . . . .69 F1
Ketton Gr B33 . . . . .89 D7
Kevilliok St CV3 . . . . .133 D6
Kew Cl Birmingham B37 . . . .69 F3
   Kenilworth CV8 . . . . .148 C5
Kew Dr DY1 . . . . .51 A2
Kew Gdns B33 . . . . .68 E1
Kew Ho CV4 . . . . .111 F3
Kewstoke Cl WV12 . . . . .13 B1
Kewstoke Croft B31 . . . . . .102 E6
Kewstoke Rd WV12 . . . . .13 C1
Key Bsns Pk B24 . . . . .57 D3
Key Cl WS12 . . . . .2 C4
Key Hill B18 . . . . .66 B5
Key Hill Dr B18 . . . . .66 B5
Key Ind Pk WV13 . . . . .26 D3
Keyes Dr DY6 . . . . .49 D1
Keynell Covert B30 . . . . . .104 C2
Keynes Dr WV14 . . . . .40 E6
Keys Cres B71 . . . . .53 C6
Keyse Rd B75 . . . . .46 F7
Keyspark Rd WS12 . . . . .2 E3
Keyte Cl DY4 . . . . .52 A5
Keyway Jct WV13 . . . . .41 B8
Keyway Ret Pk WV13 . . . . . .41 B8
Keyway The WV13 . . . . .41 A8
Keyworth Cl DY4 . . . . .52 B5
Khybar Cl WS10 . . . . .41 C8
Kidd Croft DY4 . . . . .41 C2
Kidderminster Coll
   DY10 . . . . .116 E4
Kidderminster General Hospl
   DY11 . . . . .116 C5
Kidderminster Rd
   Bromsgrove B61 . . . . .136 C3
   Hagley DY9 . . . . .99 B5
   Iverley DY7,DY10 . . . . .98 C7
   Kingswinford DY6 . . . . .60 B7
Kidderminster Rd S DY9 . .98 F3
Kidderminster Sta DY10 . .116 F5
Kidderminster Town Sta*
   DY10 . . . . .116 F5
Kidson Eventide Homes
   WV6 . . . . .24 F5
Kielder Cl Cannock WS12 . . . .2 E2
   Walsall WS5 . . . . .43 C3
Kielder Dr CV10 . . . . .72 E2
Kielder Gdns DY9 . . . . .81 B1
Kier's Bridge Cl DY4 . . . . . .52 B3
Kilburn Dr Coventry CV5 . .112 E1
   Kingswinford DY6 . . . . .49 E1
Kilburn Gr B44 . . . . .44 F3
Kilburn Pl DY2 . . . . .62 D6
Kilburn Rd B44 . . . . .44 F3
Kilby Ave B16 . . . . .66 A2
Kilby Gn LE10 . . . . .75 F6
Kilby Rd CV31 . . . . .162 C5
Kilbye Cl B77 . . . . .35 F5
Kilcote Rd B90 . . . . .105 C2
Kildale Cl CV1 . . . . .165 D3
Kilderkin Ct CV1 . . . . .165 B1
Kildwick Way 5 CV34 . . . .155 E1
Kilmarie Cl LE10 . . . . .71 A1
Kilmet Wlk 1 B67 . . . . .65 A5
Kilmore Croft B36 . . . . .68 E8
Kilmorie Rd
   Birmingham B27 . . . . .88 C5
   Cannock WS11 . . . . .1 C2
Kiln Cl Nuneaton CV10 . . . . .72 E3
   Royal Leamington Spa
   CV32 . . . . .157 A1
   Studley B80 . . . . .159 C4
Kiln Croft B65 . . . . .63 A3
Kiln La Birmingham B11 . . . .88 B6

Kiln La continued
   Solihull B90 . . . . .126 A5
Kiln Way Polesworth B78 . . .22 F1
   Shilton CV7 . . . . .97 A7
Kilnsey Gr CV34 . . . . .155 E1
Kilpeck Cl B98 . . . . .154 F2
Kilsall Ct 12 WV3 . . . . .25 C4
Kilsby Gr B91 . . . . .127 C8
Kilvert Rd WS10 . . . . .42 B2
Kilworth Ho 6 CV32 . . . . .156 F1
Kimberley B77 . . . . .35 F7
Kimberley Ave B8 . . . . .67 E5
Kimberley Cl Aldridge B74 . .31 A2
   Coventry CV5 . . . . .111 F4
   Redditch B98 . . . . .154 B7
Kimberley Pl WV14 . . . . .51 B7
Kimberley Rd
   Baginton CV8 . . . . .133 F2
   Bedworth CV12 . . . . .78 C4
   Smethwick B66 . . . . .65 A7
   Solihull B92 . . . . .89 A1
Kimberley Rise B71 . . . . . . .53 A7
Kimberley St WV3 . . . . .25 A1
Kimberley Wlk B76 . . . . .58 D6
Kimble Cl CV5 . . . . .112 A4
Kimble Gr B24 . . . . .57 D3
Kimbolton Dr B60 . . . . .138 A5
Kimpton Cl B14 . . . . .104 E2
Kinman Croft B74 . . . . .45 A7
Kinchford Cl B91 . . . . .127 B8
Kineton Cl B98 . . . . .154 D1
Kineton Croft B32 . . . . .102 D8
Kineton Green Inf Sch
   B92 . . . . .88 D1
Kineton Green Rd B92 . . . .106 D8
Kineton Ho B13 . . . . .105 A6
Kineton La B94 . . . . .127 A1
Kineton Rd
   Birmingham B45 . . . . .121 E7
   Coventry CV2 . . . . .114 C6
   Kenilworth CV8 . . . . .148 C4
   Sutton Coldfield B73 . . . . . .45 E1
Kineton Rise DY3 . . . . .39 C2
Kinfare Dr WV6 . . . . .24 B4
Kinfare Rise DY3 . . . . .50 E4
King Charles Ave WS2 . . . .27 E2
King Charles Cl DY11 . . . . .116 C6
King Charles Ct B44 . . . . . . .45 B2
King Charles I High Sch
   DY10 . . . . .117 A5
King Charles Prim Sch
   WS2 . . . . .27 F2
King Charles Rd B62 . . . . . .83 F4
King Charles Sq 4
   DY10 . . . . .116 E6
King David Jun & Inf Sch
   B13 . . . . .86 F2
King Edmund St DY1 . . . . . .51 B2
King Edward Ave B61 . . . .136 F5
King Edward IV Handsworth
   Sch B21 . . . . .66 A7
King Edward Rd
   Birmingham B13 . . . . .86 F3
   Bromsgrove B61 . . . . .136 F5
   Coventry CV1 . . . . .113 F4
   Nuneaton CV11 . . . . .73 D4
King Edward St WS10 . . . . .41 D6
King Edward VI Aston Sch
   B6 .66 F8
King Edward VI Camp Hill
   Schs B14 . . . . .104 D7
King Edward VI Coll
   Nuneaton CV11 . . . . .73 D4
   Stourbridge DY8 . . . . .81 A6
King Edward VI Five Ways
   Sch B32 . . . . .102 C8
King Edward VI High Sch for
   Girls B15 . . . . .86 A6
King Edward VI Sch WS14 . .9 C6
King Edward's Row
   WV2 . . . . .163 B1
King Edward's Sch B15 . . . .86 A4
King Edward's Sq B73 . . . . .46 B5
King Edwards Gdns B20 . . .66 B8
King Edwards Rd B1 . . . . . . .66 B2
King Edwards Wharf B16 . .66 B2
King George Ave B61 . . . . .136 F4
King George Cl B61 . . . . . .136 F4
King George Cres WS4 . . . .29 B6
King George Pl WS4 . . . . . . .29 B6
King George VI Ave WS5 . .29 C1
King George's Ave
   Bedworth CV12 . . . . .78 B5
   Coventry CV6 . . . . .95 F2
King George's Way LE10 . .75 B7
King Henry VIII Sch
   CV3 . . . . .133 A1
King Richard Rd LE10 . . . . .71 C2
King Richard St CV2 . . . . . .113 F3
King St Bedworth CV12 . . . .78 D2
   Bilston WV14 . . . . .40 E3
   Birmingham B11 . . . . .87 A7
   Blackheath B64 . . . . .62 F1
   Brierley Hill DY5 . . . . .82 A8
   Brownhills WS9 . . . . .16 A6
   Burntwood WS7 . . . . .6 F5
   Dudley DY2 . . . . .51 C1
   Dudley, Roseville WV14 . . .51 A8
   Halesowen B63 . . . . .83 A4
   8 Hinckley LE10 . . . . .71 D1
   Royal Leamington Spa
   CV32 . . . . .157 A1
   Smethwick B66 . . . . .65 B7
   Stourbridge, Lye DY9 . . . . .81 E5
   Stourbridge, Wollaston DY8 .80 E6

King St continued
   Tamworth B79 . . . . .21 B5
   Walsall WS1 . . . . .42 D7
   Wednesbury WS10 . . . . . . .41 E3
   Willenhall WV13 . . . . .27 B2
   Wolverhampton WV1 . . . .163 C3
King Street Pas
   Brierley Hill DY5 . . . . .82 A8
   2 Dudley DY2 . . . . .51 D1
King William St
   Coventry CV1 . . . . .113 E4
   Stourbridge DY8 . . . . .80 F8
King's Ave B69 . . . . .52 B2
King's CE Sch The WV6 . . . .24 B5
King's Cl B11 . . . . .87 B3
King's Heath Boys Sch
   B13 . . . . .105 A6
King's High Sch for Girls The
   CV34 . . . . .160 E7
King's Hill Day Hospl
   WS10 . . . . .41 E5
King's Hill Field WS10 . . . .41 E5
King's Hill La CV8 . . . . .133 B2
King's Hill Prim Sch
   WS10 . . . . .41 E5
King's Hill Rd B4 WS14 . . . . .9 C6
King's Norton Boys Sch
   B30 . . . . .103 E4
King's Norton Girls Sch
   B30 . . . . .103 F5
King's Norton Sta B30 . . . .103 F4
King's Rd Birmingham B44 . .44 E3
   Kidderminster DY11 . . . . .116 C6
King's Rise Com Prim Sch
   B44 . . . . .45 A2
Kingfield Rd
   Coventry CV1,CV6 . . . . . . .113 D7
   Solihull B90 . . . . .105 C2
Kingfisher B77 . . . . .36 A6
Kingfisher Ave CV10 . . . . . .72 C5
Kingfisher Cl
   Birmingham B26 . . . . .89 A6
   Sedgley DY3 . . . . .39 C2
Kingfisher Ct B48 . . . . .139 A7
Kingfisher Dr
   Birmingham B36 . . . . .70 A8
   Cannock WS12 . . . . .2 C5
   Stourbridge DY8 . . . . .60 A6
Kingfisher Ent Pk B98 . . . .154 A3
Kingfisher Gr
   Kidderminster DY10 . . . . .117 B3
   Willenhall WV12 . . . . .27 C8
Kingfisher Ind Est B70 . . . .52 E6
Kingfisher Prim Sch B36 . .70 A8
Kingfisher Sh Ctr 2
   B97 . . . . .153 E3
Kingfisher Veiw B34 . . . . . .69 A5
Kingfisher Way B30 . . . . . .103 D8
Kingfisher Wlk B97 . . . . . . .153 E3
Kingham Cl Dudley DY3 . . . .50 C2
   Redditch B98 . . . . .154 A3
Kingham Covert B14 . . . . .104 D2
Kingland Dr CV32 . . . . .156 C1
Kings Ave WS12 . . . . .2 C4
Kings Bsns Pk B44 . . . . .44 E3
Kings Cl B14 . . . . .104 C6
Kings Croft
   Birmingham, Castle Bromwich
   B36 . . . . .69 F7
   Birmingham, Sheldon B26 . .89 A5
   Cannock WS12 . . . . .2 C4
Kings Ct Stourbridge DY8 . .80 F5
   Sutton Coldfield B75 . . . . . .32 B3
   Tipton DY4 . . . . .52 A4
Kings Ct Cross St WS10 . . .41 E3
Kings Ct King St WS10 . . . . .41 E3
Kings Gdn B20 . . . . .103 E4
Kings Gdns CV12 . . . . .78 C2
Kings Gr CV2 . . . . .114 B3
Kings Green Ave B38 . . . . .103 F2
Kings Heath Jun Sch
   B14 . . . . .86 F1
Kings Hill Cl WS10 . . . . .41 E5
Kings Hill Pk WS10 . . . . . . .41 E5
Kings Ho B24 . . . . .57 A4
Kings Mdw CV10 . . . . .72 C3
Kings Mews WS14 . . . . .9 B5
Kings Norton Bsns Ctr
   B30 . . . . .123 F8
Kings Norton L Ctr B38 . . .123 F8
Kings Norton Prim Sch
   B30 . . . . .104 A2
Kings Par B4 . . . . .164 C2
Kings Park Dr CV3 . . . . . . .115 B1
Kings Rd
   Birmingham, Kingstanding
   B44,B73 . . . . .45 B2
   Birmingham, Stirchley B14 .104 C6
   Birmingham, Stockland Green
   B23 . . . . .56 D4
   Birmingham, Tyseley B11 . . .88 A6
   Sedgley DY3 . . . . .50 B8
   Walsall WS4 . . . . .29 C7
Kings Road Ind Est B25 . . .88 A6
Kings Sq Dudley WV14 . . . . .51 A8
   West Bromwich B70 . . . . . .53 D3
Kings Terr B14 . . . . .104 D6
Kingsbridge Ho B31 . . . . . .56 B6
Kingsbridge Rd
   Birmingham B32 . . . . .84 D1
   Nuneaton CV10 . . . . .73 D6

Kingsbridge Wlk 6 B66 . . .65 B5
Kingsbrook Dr B91 . . . . . . .127 B8
Kingsbury Ave B24 . . . . .57 D3
Kingsbury Bsns Pk B76 . . .58 E6
Kingsbury Cl
   Minworth B76 . . . . .58 D5
   Walsall WS4 . . . . .29 B4
Kingsbury Rd
   Birmingham, Birches Green
   B24 . . . . .57 B3
   Birmingham, Tyburn B24,
   B35 . . . . .57 E3
   Coventry CV6 . . . . .112 E5
   Curdworth B76 . . . . .59 B7
   Minworth B76,B35,B37 . . .58 A5
   Sutton Coldfield B35,B76 . .58 B5
   2 Tipton DY4 . . . . .52 A8
Kingsbury Sch B24 . . . . .57 A2
Kingsclere Wlk CV4 . . . . . . .38 C6
Kingscliff Rd B10 . . . . .88 A8
Kingscote Cl B98 . . . . .154 D7
Kingscote Gr CV3 . . . . .133 A4
Kingscote Rd
   Birmingham B15 . . . . .85 E6
   Dorridge B93 . . . . .127 E2
Kingscroft Cl B74 . . . . .45 A8
Kingscroft Rd B74 . . . . .45 B7
Kingsdene Ave DY6 . . . . . . .60 C4
Kingsdown Ave B42 . . . . . . .55 A6
Kingsdown Rd B31 . . . . .84 F1
Kingsfield Ind Est CV1 . . . .113 C6
Kingsfield Rd B14 . . . . .104 E8
Kingsford Cl B36 . . . . .58 D1
Kingsford Ct B92 . . . . .89 B3
Kingsford Nouveau DY6 . . .61 A5
Kingsgate Ho B37 . . . . .70 A2
Kingshayes Rd WS9 . . . . . . .16 B1
Kingshill Dr B38 . . . . .103 F2
Kingsholm Cl CV3 . . . . .115 B1
Kingshurst CV31 . . . . .162 E6
Kingshurst Ho B37 . . . . .69 F5
Kingshurst Inf Sch B37 . . . .70 A6
Kingshurst Jun Sch B37 . . .70 A6
Kingshurst Rd
   Birmingham B31 . . . . .103 A3
   Solihull B90 . . . . .105 F1
Kingshurst Way B37 . . . . . .69 F5
Kingsland Ave CV5 . . . . . . .112 F2
Kingsland Dr B93 . . . . .127 E4
Kingsland Jun & Inf Sch
   B44 . . . . .44 F4
Kingsland Rd
   Birmingham B44 . . . . .44 F4
   Wolverhampton WV1 . . . . .25 B3
Kingslea Rd B91 . . . . .106 E2
Kingsleigh Croft B75 . . . . .32 B2
Kingsleigh Dr B36 . . . . .69 A8
Kingsleigh Rd B20 . . . . .55 B2
Kingsley Ave
   Cannock WS12 . . . . .2 C7
   Redditch B98 . . . . .154 A3
   Wolverhampton WV6 . . . . .24 B4
Kingsley Cl B79 . . . . .21 A6
Kingsley Coll B98 . . . . .159 C6
Kingsley Cres CV12 . . . . . . .79 B3
Kingsley Ct
   Binley Woods CV3 . . . . . . .135 D6
   Birmingham B25 . . . . .88 B8
Kingsley Gr DY3 . . . . .50 A5
Kingsley Prep Sch B93 . . . .128 A4
Kingsley Rd
   Birmingham, Balsall Heath
   B12 . . . . .87 A6
   Birmingham, King's Norton
   B30 . . . . .103 D4
   Kingswinford DY6 . . . . .60 C5
Kingsley St Dudley DY2 . . .62 C5
   Walsall WS2 . . . . .42 B7
Kingsley Terr CV2 . . . . .114 E8
Kingsley Wlk CV2 . . . . .114 F7
Kingslow Ave WV4 . . . . .38 D6
Kingsmead High Sch
   WS12 . . . . .2 C4
Kingsmead Mews CV3 . . . .134 C6
Kingsmere Cl B24 . . . . .56 F2
Kingsoak Gdns DY2 . . . . . . .62 E2
Kingspiece Ho 6 B36 . . . . .68 E8
Kingstanding Ctr B44 . . . . .44 F3
Kingstanding Rd B44 . . . . . .55 F7
Kingstanding Specl Sch
   B44 . . . . .45 A1
Kingsthorne Prim Sch
   B14 . . . . .104 D2
Kingsthorpe Rd B14 . . . . . .105 A3
Kingston Arc WS11 . . . . .1 E1
Kingston Cl B79 . . . . .21 C7
Kingston Ct
   1 Birmingham, Selly Oak
   B29 . . . . .103 C7
   Sutton Coldfield B74 . . . . . .46 B7
Kingston Dr LE10 . . . . .71 E4
Kingston Ind Est B9 . . . . . . .67 B1
Kingston Mews CV31 . . . . .162 C6
Kingston Rd
   Birmingham B9 . . . . .67 B1
   Coventry CV5 . . . . .112 F2
Kingston Row B1 . . . . .66 C2
Kingsville Rd DY6 . . . . .61 A5
Kingsway Cannock WS12 . . . .2 A4
   Coventry CV2 . . . . .114 A3
   Essington WV11 . . . . .13 A4
   Nuneaton CV11 . . . . .73 B4
   Oldbury B68 . . . . .84 B7
   Royal Leamington Spa
   CV31 . . . . .161 F6
   Stourbridge DY8 . . . . .80 E8
   Wolverhampton WV10 . . . .26 A6

Kingsway Ave 8 DY4 . . . . .52 A8
Kingsway Com Prim Sch
   CV31 . . . . .161 F6
Kingsway Dr B38 . . . . .103 F2
Kingsway Ho CV12 . . . . .78 C2
Kingsway Rd WV10 . . . . .26 A6
Kingswear Ave WV6 . . . . . . .23 F3
Kingswinford Rd DY1 . . . . .61 F7
Kingswinford Sch The
   DY6 . . . . .60 D7
Kingswood Ave
   Cannock WS11 . . . . .4 C7
   Corley CV7 . . . . .94 B8
Kingswood Cl
   Coventry CV6 . . . . .95 D1
   Lapworth B94 . . . . .144 E5
   Solihull B90 . . . . .106 D1
Kingswood Cotts B94 . . . .144 D3
Kingswood Croft B7 . . . . . . .67 C7
Kingswood Dr
   Birmingham B30 . . . . .104 C3
   Great Wyrley WS6 . . . . .5 A3
   Norton Canes WS11 . . . . . . .5 F5
   Sutton Coldfield B74 . . . . . .44 F5
Kingswood Gdns
   Nuneaton CV10 . . . . .72 B4
   Wolverhampton WV4 . . . . .38 F6
Kingswood Ho B14 . . . . . . .104 E2
Kingswood Rd
   Birmingham, Coft Common
   B31 . . . . .122 F7
   Birmingham, Moseley B13 . .87 A4
   Kingswinford DY6 . . . . .60 C4
   Nuneaton CV10 . . . . .72 B4
Kington Cl WV12 . . . . .27 B8
Kington Gdns B37 . . . . .69 F2
Kington Way B33 . . . . .68 E1
Kiniths Cres B71 . . . . .53 E5
Kiniths Way
   Halesowen B62 . . . . .83 E4
   West Bromwich B71 . . . . . .53 E4
Kinlet Cl Redditch B98 . . . .154 E3
   Wolverhampton WV3 . . . . .38 A8
Kinlet Gr B31 . . . . .103 C2
Kinloch Dr DY1 . . . . .50 F3
Kinnerley St WS1 . . . . .29 A1
Kinnersley Cl B98 . . . . .154 E3
Kinnersley Cres B69 . . . . . .63 D5
Kinnerton Cres B29 . . . . . . .84 F2
Kinross Ave WS12 . . . . .1 F7
Kinross Cl CV10 . . . . .72 C2
Kinross Cres B43 . . . . .44 B4
Kinross Rd CV32 . . . . .157 B4
Kinross Way LE10 . . . . .71 A1
Kinsall Gn B77 . . . . .36 C6
Kinsey Gr B14 . . . . .104 F4
Kinsham Dr B91 . . . . .127 B8
Kintore Croft B32 . . . . .102 B7
Kintyre Cl
   Birmingham B45 . . . . .101 C1
   Hinckley LE10 . . . . .71 B1
Kintyre The CV2 . . . . .115 B7
Kinver Ave
   Kidderminster DY11 . . . . .116 A1
   Willenhall WV12 . . . . .27 B5
Kinver Cl CV2 . . . . .96 E1
Kinver Cres WS9 . . . . .16 C1
Kinver Croft
   Birmingham B12 . . . . .86 E7
   Sutton Coldfield B76 . . . . . .58 A8
Kinver Ct B11 . . . . .87 D4
Kinver Dr Hagley DY9 . . . . . .99 C5
   Wolverhampton WV4 . . . . .38 C5
Kinver Rd B31 . . . . .103 D2
Kinver St DY8 . . . . .60 E1
Kinwalsey La CV7 . . . . .92 F6
Kinwarton Cl B26 . . . . .88 D6
Kipling Ave Dudley WV14 . .40 B1
   Warwick CV34 . . . . .160 C4
Kipling Cl Nuneaton CV10 . .72 A5
   Tipton DY4 . . . . .52 A8
Kipling Rd
   Birmingham B30 . . . . .103 C4
   Coventry CV6 . . . . .113 A8
   Dudley DY3 . . . . .50 A5
   Willenhall WV12 . . . . .27 E8
   Wolverhampton WV10 . . . .11 D2
Kipling Rise B79 . . . . .20 F8
Kipling Wlk 3 DY10 . . . . . .117 B6
Kirby Ave CV34 . . . . .155 F1
Kirby Cl Bilston WV14 . . . . . .40 E3
   Brandon CV8 . . . . .135 F5
   Coventry CV1 . . . . .113 D6
Kirby Cnr CV4 . . . . .132 B5
Kirby Corner Rd CV4 . . . . .132 B6
Kirby Dr DY1 . . . . .50 E3
Kirby Rd Birmingham B18 . .65 E6
   Coventry CV5 . . . . .112 F2
Kirfield Dr LE10 . . . . .75 F7
Kirkby Gn B73 . . . . .46 B3
Kirkdale Ave CV6 . . . . .95 D3
Kirkham Gdns DY6 . . . . .61 C6
Kirkham Gr B33 . . . . .68 F4
Kirkham Way DY4 . . . . .52 A5
Kirkland Way B78 . . . . .34 B8
Kirkside Gr WS8 . . . . .15 F7
Kirkstall Cl WS3 . . . . .13 F2
Kirkstall Cres WS3 . . . . .13 F2
Kirkstone
   Birmingham B43 . . . . .54 F6
   Wombourne WV5 . . . . .49 A6
Kirkstone Ct DY5 . . . . .81 B8
Kirkstone Cres B43 . . . . . . .54 F6
Kirkstone Rd CV12 . . . . .78 A2
Kirkstone Way DY5 . . . . .81 B8
Kirkstone Wlk CV11 . . . . . . .74 A6
Kirkwall Rd B32 . . . . .100 A8
Kirkwood Ave B23 . . . . .56 F7

Kirmond Wlk WV6 . . . . .25 C5
Kirstead Gdns WV6 . . . . .24 B3
Kirtley B77 . . . . .21 E2
Kirton Cl Coventry CV6 . . . . . .94 F1
  Whitnash CV31 . . . . .162 B3
Kirton Gr Birmingham B33 . .69 A4
  Solihull B91 . . . . .107 A1
  Wolverhampton WV6 . . . . . . .24 C4
Kitchen La
  Wednesfield WV11 . . . . .26 F8
  Wolverhampton WV11 . . . .12 F1
Kitchener Rd
  Birmingham B29 . . . . .86 B1
  Coventry CV6 . . . . .113 E8
  Dudley DY2 . . . . .51 F1
Kitchener St B66 . . . . .65 D6
Kite La B97 . . . . .153 A5
Kitebrook Cl
  Redditch B98 . . . . .154 E4
  Solihull B90 . . . . .127 A7
Kites Cl CV34 . . . . .155 E2
Kites Nest La CV35 . . . . . . .146 C1
Kitsland Rd B34 . . . . .69 E6
Kitswell Gdns B32 . . . . .102 A8
Kitt's Green Rd B33 . . . . . . .69 B3
Kittermaster Rd CV7 . . . . . . .92 C1
Kittiwake Dr
  Brierley Hill DY5 . . . . .81 D7
  Kidderminster DY10 . . . . . .117 B3
Kittoe Rd B74 . . . . .32 A3
Kitwell Jun & Inf Sch
  B32 .102 A7
Kitwell La B32 . . . . .102 A8
Kitwood Ave B78 . . . . .36 F6
Kitwood Dr B92 . . . . .107 D7
Kixley La B93 . . . . .128 C6
Klaxon Ind Est B11 . . . . . . .87 F4
Klevedon Cl CV11 . . . . .74 A1
Knapton Cl LE10 . . . . .71 A3
Knaresdale Cl DY5 . . . . .81 C8
Knaves Castle Ave WS8 . . . .6 F2
Knebley Cres CV10 . . . . .73 C1
Knebworth Cl B44 . . . . .55 E8
Knibbs Sh Ctr The CV34 .160 E7
Knight Ave CV1 . . . . .113 E1
Knight Ct B75 . . . . .47 C5
Knight Ho B13 . . . . .105 D7
Knightcote Dr
  Royal Leamington Spa
  CV32 . . . . .161 E8
  Solihull B91 . . . . .127 B8
Knightley Cl CV32 . . . . .157 E5
Knightley Rd B91 . . . . .106 F2
Knightlow Ave CV3 . . . . . . .134 C6
Knightlow Cl CV8 . . . . .148 C3
Knightlow Rd B17 . . . . .85 B8
Knighton Cl B74 . . . . .31 F3
Knighton Ct B23 . . . . .56 E2
Knighton Dr B74 . . . . .31 F3
Knighton Rd
  Birmingham B11 . . . . .103 C4
  Cannock WS12 . . . . .2 E3
  Dudley DY2 . . . . .62 D4
  Sutton Coldfield B74 . . . . . . .31 D5
Knights Ave WV6 . . . . .24 E6
Knights Cl
  Birmingham B23 . . . . .56 E2
  Hinckley LE10 . . . . .75 D4
Knights Cres WV6 . . . . .24 E7
Knights Ct Hinckley LE10 . . .74 E8
  Norton Canes WS11 . . . . .6 C5
Knights Hill WS9 . . . . .30 B3
Knights Rd B11 . . . . .88 A4
Knights Templar Way
  CV4 .112 A1
Knights Wood Cl B75 . . . . . .46 D7
Knightsbridge Ave CV12 . . .78 C4
Knightsbridge Cl B74 . . . . . .31 F4
Knightsbridge Ct B37 . . . . . .69 F5
Knightsbridge Rd B92 . . . . .89 B1
Knightsfield Cl B73 . . . . .45 C3
Knightsford Cl B97 . . . . . . .152 F2
Knightstone Ave B18 . . . . . .66 A4
Knightwick Cres B23 . . . . . .56 C5
Knipersley Rd B73 . . . . .57 A7
Knoll Cl WS7 . . . . .7 A5
Knoll Croft Aldridge WS9 . . .16 C1
  Cheswick Green B90 . . . . . .126 D4
  Coventry CV3 . . . . .133 C6
Knoll Dr Coventry CV3 . . . .133 C6
  Warwick CV34 . . . . .155 E1
Knoll Sch The CV11 . . . . . .116 A2
Knoll The Birmingham B32 . .84 C1
  Kingswinford DY6 . . . . .60 C6
Knollcroft B16 . . . . .66 A2
Knott Cl B93 . . . . .61 D2
Knottesford Cl B80 . . . . . . .159 C3
Knotts Farm Rd DY6 . . . . . .61 A4
Knottsall La B68 . . . . .64 B3
Knowesley Cl B60 . . . . .137 B2
Knowlands Rd B90 . . . . .127 A8
Knowle CE Prim Sch
  B93 .128 C6
Knowle Cl
  Birmingham B45 . . . . .122 D7
  Redditch B98 . . . . .154 C6
Knowle Hill CV8 . . . . .148 C4
Knowle Hill Rd DY2 . . . . . . .62 B4
Knowle La WS14 . . . . .9 F3
Knowle Rd
  Birmingham B11 . . . . .87 D3
  Blackheath B65 . . . . .63 A4
  Hampton-in-A B92 . . . . .108 E2
Knowle Wood Rd B93 . . . . .128 B3
Knowles Ave CV10 . . . . .72 C4
Knowles Dr B74 . . . . .46 A7
Knowles Rd WV1 . . . . .25 F1

Knowles St WS10 . . . . .42 A3
Knox Cres CV11 . . . . .73 F8
Knox Rd WV2 . . . . .37 F5
Knox's Grave La WS14,
  B78 . . . . .19 D7
Knutswood Cl B13 . . . . .105 D7
Kohima Dr DY8 . . . . .80 D6
Kossuth Rd WV14 . . . . .40 A1
Kurtus B77 . . . . .35 D6
Kwikform Bldg CV6 . . . . . . .95 E4
Kyle Cl WV10 . . . . .11 B1
Kyles Way B32 . . . . .102 B7
Kynaston Cres WV8 . . . . . . .10 B2
Kynaston Ho B71 . . . . .53 C8
Kyngsford Rd B33 . . . . .69 D3
Kynner Way CV3 . . . . .135 B8
Kynoch Wks B6 . . . . .55 F3
Kyotts Lake Rd B11 . . . . . . .87 B7
Kyotts Lake Unit Factory
  B11 . . . . .87 B7
Kyrwicks La B11 . . . . .87 A7
Kyter La B36 . . . . .69 B8

L

Laburnham Ct WS14 . . . . .9 C5
Laburnham Rd DY6 . . . . .60 C6
Laburnum Ave
  Birmingham B37 . . . . .69 F6
  Cannock WS11 . . . . .4 E7
  Coventry CV6 . . . . .112 F5
  Kenilworth CV8 . . . . .148 A4
  Smethwick B67 . . . . .64 F4
  Tamworth B79 . . . . .21 B8
Laburnum Cl
  Bedworth CV12 . . . . .77 E2
  Birmingham B37 . . . . .69 F6
  Cannock WS11 . . . . .4 E7
  Hollywood B47 . . . . .125 A5
  Redditch B98 . . . . .153 E2
  Stourbridge DY8 . . . . .80 E7
Laburnum Dr
  Sutton Coldfield B76 . . . . . . .47 A3
  Whitnash CV31 . . . . .162 B3
Laburnum Gr
  Birmingham B13 . . . . .86 F3
  Bromsgrove B61 . . . . .136 F4
  Burntwood WS7 . . . . .6 F6
  Kidderminster DY11 . . . . . .116 B8
  Nuneaton CV10 . . . . .72 D6
  Walsall WS2 . . . . .27 F3
  Warwick CV34 . . . . .156 B1
Laburnum Ho WS4 . . . . .15 D1
Laburnum Rd Bilston WV1 . .40 B8
  Birmingham B30 . . . . .16 A3
  Brownhills WS9 . . . . .16 A3
  Dudley DY1 . . . . .51 C4
  Tipton DY4 . . . . .51 F7
  Walsall WS5 . . . . .43 C4
  Wednesbury WS10 . . . . .42 B4
  Wolverhampton WV4 . . . . . .39 F3
Laburnum St
  Stourbridge DY8 . . . . .80 E7
  Wolverhampton WV3 . . . . . .163 B4
Laburnum Trees B47 . . . . .124 F7
Laburnum Villas B11 . . . . . .87 C5
Laburnum Way B31 . . . . . .103 A1
Laceby Gr B13 . . . . .87 D1
Lacell Cl CV34 . . . . .155 E1
Ladbroke Dr B76 . . . . .46 F2
Ladbroke Gr B90 . . . . .106 C8
Ladbroke Pk CV34 . . . . .155 E1
Ladbrook Cl B98 . . . . .158 E7
Ladbrook Gr DY3 . . . . .50 B3
Ladbrook Rd
  Coventry CV5 . . . . .112 A4
  Solihull B91 . . . . .107 C2
Ladbury Gr WS5 . . . . .43 A4
Ladbury Rd WS5 . . . . .43 A3
Ladeler Gr B33 . . . . .69 E2
Ladies Wlk DY3 . . . . .50 D8
Lady Bank B32 . . . . .102 B7
Lady Bracknell Mews
  B31 .103 D4
Lady Brades Ho B69 . . . . . .64 A7
Lady Byron La B93 . . . . . . .127 F8
Lady Grey Ave CV34 . . . . . .162 A3
Lady Grey's Wlk DY8 . . . . . .80 D5
Lady Harriet's La B98 . . . . .153 F4
Lady Katherine Leveson CE
  Sch B93 . . . . .129 B5
Lady La Coventry CV6 . . . . . .95 F4
  Earlswood B90,B94 . . . . . .126 B3
  Kenilworth CV8 . . . . .147 B4
Lady Warwick Ave CV12 . . .78 D2
Ladycroft Birmingham B16 . .66 B2
  Cubbington CV32 . . . . .157 E5
Ladyfields Way CV6 . . . . . . .95 C2
Ladygrove Cl B98 . . . . .159 A8
Ladymead Dr CV6 . . . . .95 B2
Ladymoor Rd WV14 . . . . . . .40 C5
Ladypool Ave B11 . . . . .87 B6
Ladypool Cl
  Halesowen B62 . . . . .83 C4
  Walsall WS4 . . . . .29 A5
Ladypool Prim Sch B11 . . . .87 B6
Ladypool Rd B11,B12 . . . . . .87 A5
Ladysmith Rd B63 . . . . .82 C6
Ladywell Cl WV5 . . . . .49 A8
Ladywell Wlk B5 . . . . .164 C1
Ladywood Cl DY5 . . . . .61 F2
Ladywood Middleway
  B16 . . . . .66 A2

Ladywood Rd
  Birmingham B16 . . . . .66 A1
  Sutton Coldfield B74 . . . . . . .46 A8
Laertes Gr CV34 . . . . .161 F2
Laggan Cl CV10 . . . . .72 C5
Lagonda B77 . . . . .21 E3
Lagrange B79 . . . . .20 E6
Laing Ho B69 . . . . .63 D5
Lair The B78 . . . . .36 F8
Lake Ave WS5 . . . . .43 C7
Lake Cl WS5 . . . . .43 C7
Lake St DY3 . . . . .50 D3
Lake View Rd CV5 . . . . .112 F4
Lakedown Cl B14 . . . . .104 E1
Lakefield Cl B28 . . . . .106 A8
Lakefield Cl B28 . . . . .106 B7
Lakefield Rd WV11 . . . . .26 E5
Lakehouse Ct B23 . . . . .56 E8
Lakehouse Gr B38 . . . . .103 D3
Lakehouse Rd B73 . . . . .56 F8
Lakeland Dr B77 . . . . .36 A7
Lakeland Ho CV34 . . . . . . .161 A7
Lakenheath B79 . . . . .21 C7
Laker Cl DY8 . . . . .81 A7
Lakes Cl CV11 . . . . .116 C7
Lakes Halt The B94 . . . . . . .141 F8
Lakes Rd B23 . . . . .56 A6
Lakeside Bedworth CV12 . . .78 A2
  Little Aston B74 . . . . .31 B5
  Redditch B97 . . . . .152 D7
Lakeside Cl WS13 . . . . .26 E3
Lakeside Ct
  Norton Canes WS11 . . . . .6 B6
  Brierley Hill DY5 . . . . .81 B8
  Upton Warren B61 . . . . .150 B4
Lakeside Dr
  Birmingham B20 . . . . .55 A4
  Brierley Hill DY5 . . . . .81 B8
Lakeside Ind Est B98 . . . . .154 B3
Lakeside Pk B65 . . . . .20 F1
Lakeside Prim Sch
  Tamworth B77 . . . . .21 E2
  Willenhall WV13 . . . . .26 E3
Lakeside Rd B70 . . . . .53 A6
Lakeside Wlk B23 . . . . .56 C3
Lakeview CI B43 . . . . .44 B2
Lakewood Dr B45 . . . . .102 B1
Lakey La B28 . . . . .106 B8
Lakey Lane Jun & Inf Sch
  B28 .106 B7
Lakin Cl CV34 . . . . .160 F8
Lakin Ho CV34 . . . . .160 F8
Lakin Rd CV34 . . . . .160 F8
Lamb Cl B34 . . . . .69 F5
Lamb Cres WV5 . . . . .49 A6
Lamb St CV1 . . . . .165 B3
Lambah Cl WV14 . . . . .40 F7
Lambert Cl B23 . . . . .56 D6
Lambert Ct
  Kingswinford DY6 . . . . .60 D8
  Warwick CV34 . . . . .160 D6
Lambert Dr WS7 . . . . .7 A8
Lambert End B70 . . . . .53 B3
Lambert Fold DY2 . . . . .62 E8
Lambert Rd WV10 . . . . .25 C6
Lambert St B70 . . . . .53 B3
Lambeth Cl
  Birmingham B37 . . . . .70 B4
  Coventry CV2 . . . . .114 D7
Lambeth Rd Bilston WV14 . .40 B7
  Birmingham B44 . . . . .44 E3
Lambourn Cl WS3 . . . . .14 C2
Lambourn Cres CV31 . . . . .162 C6
Lambourn Rd
  Birmingham B23 . . . . .56 D4
  Willenhall WV13 . . . . .27 D1
Lambourne Cl
  Coventry CV5 . . . . .112 A4
  Great Wyrley WS6 . . . . .4 F3
  Lichfield WS14 . . . . .9 E8
Lambourne Gr B37 . . . . .69 E2
Lambourne Way
  Brierley Hill DY5 . . . . .81 B8
  Norton Canes WS11 . . . . .6 A5
Lamerton Cl CV2 . . . . .114 C6
Lamford Cl LE10 . . . . .71 B1
Lamintone Dr CV32 . . . . . .156 D2
Lammas Cl B92 . . . . .89 C1
Lammas Croft CV31 . . . . . .162 A3
Lammas La CV34 . . . . .160 D6
Lammas Ho CV6 . . . . .113 A4
Lammas Rd Coventry CV6 .112 F4
  Stourbridge DY8 . . . . .60 C3
Lammas Wlk CV34 . . . . . . .160 D7
Lammermoor Ave B43 . . . . .43 F2
Lamont Ave B32 . . . . .84 F4
Lamorna Cl
  Nuneaton CV11 . . . . .73 F4
  Wolverhampton WV3 . . . . . .38 B8
Lamport Ho B14 . . . . .105 A3
Lamprey B77 . . . . .35 D6
Lanark Cl DY6 . . . . .61 A7
Lanark Croft B35 . . . . .57 F3

Lancaster Pl
  Kenilworth CV8 . . . . .147 E2
  Walsall WS3 . . . . .14 C2
Lancaster Rd
  Brierley Hill DY5 . . . . .61 C2
  Hinckley LE10 . . . . .75 D8
Lancaster St B4 . . . . .164 C4
Lance Cl LE10 . . . . .75 C6
Lancelot Cl B8 . . . . .67 E3
Lancelot Ho DY10 . . . . .117 C8
Lancelot Pl B70 . . . . .52 E4
Lanchester Cl B79 . . . . .20 E7
Lanchester Rd
  Birmingham B38 . . . . .104 A1
  Coventry CV6 . . . . .113 B6
Lanchester Way B36 . . . . . . .58 F1
Lancia Cl CV6 . . . . .96 B4
Lancing Rd CV12 . . . . .79 C2
Land La B37 . . . . .90 A7
Land Oak Dr DY10 . . . . . . .117 B7
Lander Cl B45 . . . . .122 A6
Landgate Rd B21 . . . . .54 C2
Landor Ho CV31 . . . . .162 A2
Landor Rd Knowle B93 . . . .128 A6
  Redditch B98 . . . . .154 A1
  Warwick CV34 . . . . .160 D8
  Whitnash CV31 . . . . .162 A3
Landrail Wlk B36 . . . . .70 A8
Landrake Rd DY6 . . . . .61 A5
Landsberg B77 . . . . .20 F6
Landsdown Pl B18 . . . . .66 A5
Landseer Dr LE10 . . . . .71 B3
Landseer Gr B43 . . . . .44 D4
Landsgate DY8 . . . . .81 A1
Landswood Cl B44 . . . . .45 A1
Landswood Rd B68 . . . . .64 C4
Landswood Ent Pk WS6 . . .13 F8
Landywood Gn WS6 . . . . . . .4 E2
Landywood La WS6 . . . . .4 C2
Landywood Prim Sch
  WS6 . . . . .13 F8
Landywood Sta WS6 . . . . . . .4 F2
Lane Ave WS2 . . . . .28 B3
Lane Cl WS2 . . . . .28 B3
Lane Croft B76 . . . . .58 A8
Lane Cl B3 WV3 . . . . .25 C4
Lane Green Ave WV8 . . . . . .10 B3
Lane Green Ct WV8 . . . . . . .10 B3
Lane Green Fst Sch WV8 . .10 B4
Lane Green Rd WV8 . . . . . . .10 C2
Lane Green Rd Masionettes
  WV8 .10 C3
Lane Green Sh Par WV8 . . .10 B3
Lane Rd WV4 . . . . .40 A3
Lane St WV14 . . . . .40 D3
Lanes Sh Ctr The B73 . . . . .57 B7
Lanesfield Dr WV4 . . . . .40 A4
Lanesfield Drive Ind Est
  WV4 . . . . .40 A4
Lanesfield Jun & Inf Sch
  WV4 . . . . .40 A4
Laneside CV3 . . . . .134 E6
Laneside Ave B74 . . . . .44 F7
Laneside Dr LE10 . . . . .71 F3
Laneside Gdns WS2 . . . . . . .28 B2
Lanfear Ct LE10 . . . . .75 C8
Langbank Ave CV3 . . . . . . .134 D7
Langbay Ct CV2 . . . . .114 F6
Langcliffe Ave CV34 . . . . . .155 F1
Langcomb Rd B90 . . . . .126 A8
Langdale Ave CV6 . . . . .95 D3
Langdale Cl
  Clayhanger WS8 . . . . .15 E6
  Royal Leamington Spa
  CV32 . . . . .157 D3
Langdale Croft B21 . . . . . . .65 E7
Langdale Dr B77 . . . . .22 A6
Langdale Dr Bilston WV14 . .40 D7
  Cannock WS11 . . . . .4 C7
  Nuneaton CV11 . . . . .74 A6
Langdale Gn WS11 . . . . .4 C7
Langdale Rd
  Birmingham B43 . . . . .54 F7
  Hinckley LE10 . . . . .75 A8
Langdale Way DY9 . . . . .81 D4
Langdon St B27 . . . . .67 B2
Langdon Wlk B27 . . . . .88 C4
Langfield Rd B93 . . . . .128 A7
Langford Ave B43 . . . . .54 E8
Langford Cl WS1 . . . . .29 A1
Langford Croft B91 . . . . . . .107 C2
Langford Gr B17 . . . . .85 C3
Langham Cl B26 . . . . .89 A7
Langham Gr B74 . . . . .30 F1
Langholm Dr
  Birmingham B44 . . . . .45 D1
  Cannock WS12 . . . . .2 E2
Langland Dr DY3 . . . . .50 C8
Langley Ave WV14 . . . . .51 C8
Langley Cl B98 . . . . .154 D1
Langley Cres B68 . . . . .64 B4
Langley Croft CV4 . . . . .112 A2
Langley Dr B35 . . . . .58 A2
Langley Gdns Oldbury B68 . .64 B4
  Wolverhampton WV3 . . . . . .38 D7
Langley Gr B10 . . . . .87 D8
Langley Green Rd B69 . . . . .64 A4
Langley Green Sta B68 . . . .64 B5
Langley Hall Dr B75 . . . . . . .47 B5
Langley Hall Rd
  Solihull B92 . . . . .106 C7
  Sutton Coldfield B75 . . . . . . .47 B5
Langley Heath Dr B76 . . . . .47 A3
Langley High Sch B68 . . . . .64 A4
Langley High St B69 . . . . . . .64 A4
Langley Mede B68 . . . . .64 B5

Langley Prim Sch
  Oldbury B69 . . . . .64 A5
  Solihull B92 . . . . .106 D6
Langley Rd
  Birmingham B10 . . . . .87 D8
  Oldbury B68 . . . . .64 B4
  Whitnash CV31 . . . . .162 A4
  Wolverhampton WV3,WV4 . .38 B7
Langley Rise B92 . . . . .89 D3
Langley Sch B92 . . . . .106 D7
Langley Specl Sch B75 . . . .47 A6
Langley Wlk B37 . . . . .70 D2
Langleys Rd B29 . . . . .85 E1
Langlodge Rd CV6 . . . . .95 B2
Langmead Cl WS2 . . . . .27 D3
Langnor Rd CV2 . . . . .114 C6
Langsett Rd WV10 . . . . .25 E4
Langstone Rd
  Birmingham B14 . . . . .105 D3
  Dudley DY1 . . . . .50 F1
Langton Cl
  Birmingham B36 . . . . .70 B6
  Coventry CV3 . . . . .134 E8
Langton Ct WS13 . . . . .3 A1
Langton Pl WV14 . . . . .41 A6
Langton Rd B8 . . . . .67 E4
Langtree Ave B91 . . . . .107 B1
Langtree Cl WS12 . . . . .2 D1
Langwood Cl CV4 . . . . .132 B8
Langwood Ct B36 . . . . .69 B8
Langworth Ave B27 . . . . . . .88 C5
Lannacombe Rd B31 . . . . . .122 E6
Lansbury Ave WS10 . . . . . . .41 C4
Lansbury Cl CV2 . . . . .114 E7
Lansbury Dr WS11 . . . . .1 C4
Lansbury Gn B64 . . . . .83 B8
Lansbury Rd B64 . . . . .83 B8
Lansbury Wlk 6 DY4 . . . . . .52 A8
Lansdale Ave B91 . . . . .107 F8
Lansdown Cl Coventry CV6 .116 C5
  Halesowen B63 . . . . .82 E6
Lansdowne Cir CV32 . . . . .157 A1
Lansdowne Cl
  Bedworth CV12 . . . . .78 A3
  Dudley, Tansley Hill DY2 . . . .62 F8
  Dudley, West Coseley
  WV14 . . . . .51 A7
Lansdowne Cres
  6 Royal Leamington Spa
  CV32 . . . . .157 A1
  Studley B80 . . . . .159 D3
  Tamworth B77 . . . . .35 D8
Lansdowne Ct DY9 . . . . .81 C1
Lansdowne Rd
  Bilston WV14 . . . . .40 E7
  Birmingham, Erdington B24 .56 F3
  Birmingham, Handsworth
  B21 . . . . .66 A8
  Halesowen, Hasbury B63 . . .82 D2
  Halesowen, Hurst Green
  B62 . . . . .63 E1
  8 Royal Leamington Spa
  CV32 . . . . .157 A1
  Studley B80 . . . . .159 D3
  Wolverhampton WV1 . . . . .163 A4
Lansdowne St
  Birmingham B18 . . . . .65 F4
  Coventry CV2 . . . . .113 F3
Lant Cl CV7 . . . . .131 B7
Lantern Rd DY2 . . . . .62 C2
Lapal La B62 . . . . .84 A2
Lapal La N B62 . . . . .83 E3
Lapal La S B32,B62 . . . . . . .83 F2
Lapal Prim Sch B62 . . . . . . .83 F4
Lapley Cl WV1 . . . . .26 B2
Lapath Ho B32 . . . . .102 D8
Lapper Ave WV4 . . . . .39 F2
Lapwing B77 . . . . .36 A6
Lapwing Cl
  Cheswick Green B90 . . . . .4 C1
  Kidderminster DY10 . . . . . .117 B1
Lapwing Croft B23 . . . . .56 C7
Lapwing Dr B92 . . . . .109 B7
Lapwood Ave DY6 . . . . .61 A5
Lapworth CE Prim Sch
  B94 .144 D3
Lapworth Cl B98 . . . . .158 F7
Lapworth Dr B73 . . . . .45 C3
Lapworth Gr B12 . . . . .86 F6
Lapworth Oaks B94 . . . . . .144 D3
Lapworth Rd Coventry CV2 .96 D1
  Wythall B94 . . . . .126 B1
Lapworth Rd CV2 . . . . .96 D1
Lapworth St B94 . . . . .144 D4
Lapworth Sta B94 . . . . .144 D4
Lara Cl B17 . . . . .85 B8
Lara Gr DY4 . . . . .52 A2
Larch Ave B21 . . . . .54 D2
Larch Cl WS14 . . . . .9 E7
Larch Croft
  Birmingham B37 . . . . .70 B2
  Tipton B69 . . . . .52 B2
Larch Gr Sedgley DY3 . . . . . .50 E7
  Warwick CV34 . . . . .156 A1
Larch Ho Birmingham B36 . .68 F8
  Stourbridge DY8 . . . . .80 C6
Larch Rd DY6 . . . . .60 E7
Larch Tree Ave CV4 . . . . . .112 A2
Larch Wlk B25 . . . . .88 C7
Larches Cottage Gdns
  DY11 . . . . .116 C3
Larches La WV3 . . . . .25 A2
Larches Pas B12 . . . . .86 F6
Larches Rd DY11 . . . . .116 D4
Larches St B11 . . . . .87 B6

Larches The
Bedworth CV7 ....96 B8
Wolverhampton WV11 ....26 B5
Larchfield Cl B20 ....55 B3
Larchmere Dr
Birmingham B28 ....105 F8
Bromsgrove B61 ....136 E3
Essington WV11 ....13 B3
Larchwood Cres B74 ....44 E8
Larchwood Gn WS11 ....2 A4
Larchwood Gn WS5 .....43 B4
Larchwood Rd
Bedworth CV7 ....78 B1
Walsall WS5 ....43 A4
Larcombe Dr WV4 ....39 C5
Large Ave WS10 ....41 C4
Lark Cl B14 ....105 A2
Lark Hall Inf Sch B79 ...21 A8
Lark Meadow Dr B37 ...69 F3
Larkfield Ave B36 ....69 B8
Larkfield Rd B98 ....154 A1
Larkfield Way CV5 .....112 A6
Larkhill DY10 ....116 E7
Larkhill Rd B14 ....104 D1
Larkin Cl Bulkington CV12 .79 B3
Wolverhampton WV10 ....12 A1
Larkin Gr CV2 ....114 F6
Larks Mill WS3 ....14 E4
Larksfield B66 ....65 B4
Larksfield Mews DY5 ...81 C7
Larkspur B77 ....35 D4
Larkspur Ave WS7 ......7 A5
Larkspur Croft B36 ....68 D8
Larkspur Ct
Bedworth CV12 ....95 C8
Halesowen B62 ....83 F7
Larkspur Dr WV10 ......12 B7
Larkspur Rd DY2 ....62 F8
Larkspur Way WS8 .....15 D6
Larkswood Dr
Sedgley DY3 ....50 D7
Wolverhampton WV4 .....38 C3
Larne Rd B26 ....89 A7
Lashbrooke Ho B45 ....121 F7
Lassington Cl B98 ......154 E4
Latches Cl WS10 ....41 E6
Latchford Cl B98 ....154 E6
Latelow Rd B33 ....69 A2
Lath La B66 ....64 D8
Latham Ave B43 ....54 E7
Latham Cres DY4 ....52 A3
Latham Rd CV5 ....113 A2
Latham Gr B33 ....68 F5
Latimer Cl CV8 ....147 F2
Latimer Gdns B15 ......86 D7
Latimer Pl B18 ....65 E6
Latimer Rd B48 ....139 A5
Latimer St WV13 ....27 B3
Latymer Cl B76 ....58 A7
Lauder Cl Sedgley DY3 ...39 C1
Willenhall WV13 ....26 D1
Lauderdale Ave CV6 ....95 D3
Lauderdale Cl WS8 .....15 E6
Lauderdale Gdns WV10 ..11 E3
Laughton Cl B31 ....123 B7
Launce Gr CV34 ....161 F2
Launceston Cl
Tamworth B77 ....21 D2
Walsall WS5 ....43 D7
Launceston Dr CV11 ...73 F4
Launceston Rd WS5 ....43 D7
Launde The B28 ....105 E3
Laundry Cotts CV35 ...145 E4
Laundry Rd B66 ....65 C3
Laureates Wlk B74 .....46 A8
Laurel Ave B12 ....87 A5
Laurel Bank B79 ....21 B6
Laurel Bank Mews B60 .137 F4
Laurel Cl Coventry CV2 ..96 E2
Dudley DY1 ....51 A3
Lichfield WS14 ....9 D8
Redditch B98 ....153 E2
Laurel Ct Birmingham B13 .87 A2
Coventry CV5 ....112 F1
Laurel Dr Burntwood WS7 ..7 C7
Cannock WS12 ....2 E4
Nuneaton CV10 ....72 A7
Smethwick B66 ....65 A8
Sutton Coldfield B74 ....44 E8
Laurel Gdns
Birmingham B21 ....54 E1
3 Birmingham, Stockfield
B27 ....88 C5
Laurel Gr Bilston WV14 ..41 A4
Birmingham B30 ....103 E6
Bromsgrove B61 ....136 F4
Wolverhampton WV4 ....38 E6
Laurel La B63 ....83 B3
Laurel Rd
Birmingham, Handsworth
B21 ....54 F1
Birmingham, King's Norton
B30 ....104 A4
Dudley DY1 ....51 A3
Tipton DY4 ....51 F7
Walsall WS5 ....43 B4
Laurels Cres CV7 ......130 C6
Laurels The
Bedworth CV12 ....77 E2
Birmingham, Ladywood B16 .65 F3
Birmingham, Sheldon B26 .89 C5
Oldbury B68 ....84 B6
Smethwick B66 ....65 C4
Sutton Coldfield B73 ....46 B1

Laurence Ct B31 ....103 B5
Laurence Gr WV6 ....24 E7
Lauriston Cl DY1 ....50 E3
Lavender Ave CV6 ......112 F5
Lavender Cl WV9 ....10 F3
Lavender Gdns **1** B23 ..56 B7
Lavender Gr WV14 ......40 F6
Lavender Hall La CV7 ...110 C2
Lavender Ho B38 ....123 F8
Lavender La DY8 ....80 D3
Lavender Rd Dudley DY1 .51 B3
Tamworth B77 ....21 F4
Lavendon Rd B42 ....55 B5
Lavenham Cl CV11 ....79 C8
Lavinia Rd B62 ....83 E3
Law Cl B69 ....52 D2
Law Cliff Rd B42 ....55 B6
Law St B71 ....53 C5
Lawden Rd B10 ....87 B8
Lawford Ave WS14 ....9 F2
Lawford Cl Birmingham B7 .67 A3
Coventry CV3 ....114 E1
Lawford Gr Birmingham B5 .86 E8
Solihull B90 ....105 D2
Lawford Rd CV31 ....162 B5
Lawfred Ave WV11 ......26 D5
Lawley Cl Coventry CV4 .112 A2
Walsall WS4 ....15 B1
Lawley Middleway B4 ...67 A3
Lawley Rd WV14 ....40 B6
Lawley St Dudley DY1 ...51 A1
West Bromwich B70 ......52 F3
Lawley The B63 ....82 D1
Lawn Ave DY8 ....80 A4
Lawn Gr WV9 ....11 A7
Lawn Rd WV2 ....39 F6
Lawn St DY8 ....80 E4
Lawnoaks Cl WS8 ....6 D2
Lawns The Bedworth CV12 .77 C2
Hinckley LE10 ....75 E8
Lawnsdale Cl B46 ....70 F7
Lawnsdown Rd DY5 .....81 F6
Lawnsfield Gr B23 ......56 D7
Lawnside Gn WV14 ......40 D8
Lawnswood Hinckley LE10 .75 A8
Stourbridge DY7 ....60 A2
Sutton Coldfield B76 ....58 A8
Lawnswood Ave
Burntwood WS7 ....6 F5
Solihull B90 ....106 D3
Stourbridge DY8 ....60 C3
Wolverhampton, Parkfield
WV4 ....39 E4
Wolverhampton, Tettenhall
WV6 ....24 E8
Lawnswood Cl **2** WS11 ..2 D1
Lawnswood Dr
Brownhills WS9 ....16 A3
Stourbridge WS9 ....60 A2
Sutton Coldfield B21 ....54 C1
Lawnswood Rd
Dudley DY3 ....50 D5
Stourbridge DY8 ....60 D3
Lawnswood Rise WV6 ...24 F8
Lawnwood Rd DY2 ......62 C2
Lawrence Ave
Wednesfield WV11 ....26 F6
Wolverhampton WV10 ....26 A4
Lawrence Cl
6 Oldbury B68 ....84 B8
Tamworth B79 ....21 A6
Lawrence Dr B76 ....58 D6
Lawrence Gdns CV8 ....148 A6
Lawrence La B64 ....62 E1
Lawrence Rd CV7 ....96 A8
Lawrence Saunders Rd
CV6 ....113 B5
Lawrence St
Stourbridge DY9 ....81 C6
Willenhall WV13 ....27 A3
Lawrence Wlk B43 ......44 D4
Lawson Cl WS9 ....30 B4
Lawson St B4 ....164 C4
Lawton Ave B29 ....86 B2
Lawton Cl Blackheath B65 .63 D6
Hinckley LE10 ....74 F8
Lawton Ct WV3 ....25 B1
Laxey Rd B16 ....65 D3
Laxford Cl B12 ....86 E6
Laxton Cl DY6 ....61 A5
Laxton Gr B25 ....68 D1
Lay Gdns CV31 ....162 E5
Lazy Hill Birmingham B38 .104 B2
Stonnall WS9 ....16 D2
Lazy Hill Rd WS9 ....16 C1
Le Hanche Cl CV7 ......116 D6
Le More B74 ....32 A2
Lea Ave WS10 ....41 D1
Lea Bank Ave DY11 ....116 B5
Lea Bank Rd DY2 ....62 C3
Lea Croft Rd B97 ......158 D5
Lea Cswy The DY11 ....116 B6
Lea Dr B26 ....89 A6
Lea End La B48 ....123 D3
Lea Ford Rd B33 ....69 C4
Lea Green Ave DY4 .....51 D5
Lea Green La B47 ......125 C5
Lea Hall Rd B33 ....69 A2
Lea Hall Sta B33 ....69 B2
Lea Hill Rd B20 ....55 C2
Lea Ho Birmingham B15 ..86 D7
Lea House Rd B30 .....104 A7
Lea La WS6 ....5 A3
Lea Manor Dr WV4 .....38 E4
Lea Park Rise B61 .....136 F5
Lea Rd Birmingham B11 ..87 D4
Wolverhampton WV3 .....39 B8

Lea St DY10 ....116 F6
Lea Street Fst Sch DY10 .116 F6
Lea The Birmingham B33 ..69 A2
Kidderminster DY11 ....116 A5
Lea Vale Rd B67 ....80 F3
Lea Village B33 ....69 C2
Lea Wlk Birmingham B45 .121 F8
Ryton-on-D CV8 ....135 B1
Lea Wood Gr DY11 ....116 A5
Lea Yield Cl B30 ....104 A7
Leabon Gr B17 ....85 C4
Leabrook B26 ....88 B8
Leabrook Rd DY4,WS14 ..41 D1
Leabrook Rd N WS10 ....41 D2
Leach Green La B45 ....122 B6
Leach Heath La B45 ....122 A7
Leacliffe Way WS9 ......16 D3
Leacote Dr WV6 ....24 C4
Leacrest Rd CV6 ....95 A2
Leacroft WV12 ....27 C7
Leacroft Ave WV10 ......25 E8
Leacroft Cl WS9 ....16 C1
Leacroft Gr B71 ....53 B7
Leacroft La WS11 ....4 F5
Leacroft Rd DY6 ....60 E8
Leadbeater Ho **6** WS3 ..28 B8
Leadbetter Dr B61 ....136 D2
Leaf Cl CV3 ....133 D4
Leaf La CV3 ....133 E5
Leafdown Cl WS12 ....2 D3
Leafenden Ave WS7 ......7 A6
Leafield Cl CV2 ....114 F8
Leafield Cres B33 ....69 A5
Leafield Gdns B62 ......83 D8
Leafield Rd B92 ....89 C1
Leaford Way DY6 ....60 F5
Leafy Glade B74 ....31 A1
Leafy Rise DY3 ....50 D4
Leagh Cl CV8 ....148 B7
Leahill Croft B37 ....69 F2
Leaholme Gdns DY9 ....81 B2
Leahouse Gdns B68 ....64 A3
Leahouse Rd B68 ....64 A3
Leahurst Cres B17 ......85 C4
Leaholme Ct CV5 ......132 F8
Leam Cl CV11 ....73 F1
Leam Cres B92 ....89 B1
Leam Dr WS7 ....7 D7
Leam Gn CV4 ....132 D5
Leam Rd CV31 ....161 D7
Leam St CV31 ....162 B7
Leam Terr CV31 ....162 B8
Leamington Rd
Birmingham B12 ....87 B5
Coventry CV3 ....133 C6
Kenilworth CV8 ....148 B2
Ryton-on-D CV8 ....135 B1
**Leamington Spa Art Gallery
& Mus*** CV32 ....161 E7
Leamington Spa Sta
CV31 ....161 F7
Leamore Cl WS11 ....5 F5
Leamore Ind Est WS2 ..28 C6
Leamore La WS2 ....28 B6
Leamore Prim Sch WS2 .28 C7
Leamount Dr B44 ....45 C2
Leander Cl WS6 ....4 F1
Leander Gdns B14 .....104 F5
Leander Rd DY9 ....81 F4
Leandor Dr B74 ....45 A7
Lear Gr CV34 ....161 E4
Lear Rd WV5 ....49 B8
Leas Cl CV12 ....78 A3
Leas The WV10 ....12 C7
Leason La WV10 ....26 A7
Leasow Dr B15 ....85 D3
Leasow The WS9 ....29 E5
Leasowe
Birmingham B45 ....121 F8
Tipton DY4 ....51 E4
Leasowe Rd
Birmingham B45 ....121 F8
Tipton DY4 ....51 E4
Leasowes Ave CV3 .....132 F4
Leasowes Ct B63 ....82 F3
Leasowes Dr WV4 ......38 D6
Leasowes La B62 ....83 A4
Leasowes Prim Sch B62 ..83 A4
Leasowes Rd B14 ....87 A1
Leather St B19 ....66 E6
Leatherhead Cl B6 ......66 F6
Leaveston Dr B26 ....89 A5
Leaward Cl CV10 ....72 E2
Lebanon Gr WS7 ....6 F8
Lechlade Cl B98 ....154 B7
Lechlade Rd B43 ....54 E8
Leckie Rd WS2 ....28 E4
Ledbrook Rd CV32 .....157 E5
Ledbury Cl Aldridge WS9 .16 C1
Birmingham B16 ....66 A2
Redditch B98 ....154 F2
Ledbury Dr WV1 ....26 A1
Ledbury Ho
Birmingham B33 ....69 E2
Redditch B97 ....153 B4
Ledbury Rd CV31 ......162 D6
Ledbury Way B76 ....58 A8
Ledsam Gr B32 ....84 F6
Ledsam St B16 ....66 A2
Ledwell B90 ....126 A5
Lee Bank Ho
B15 ....164 A1
Lee Bank Middleway
B15 ....86 C8
Lee Cl CV34 ....155 E2
Lee Cres B15 ....86 C8
Lee Ct WS9 ....15 F3

Lee Gdns B67 ....64 E5
Lee Mount B15 ....86 C8
Lee Rd Blackheath B64 ..82 F8
Hollywood B47 ....125 A7
Royal Leamington Spa
CV31 ....161 E6
Lee St B70 ....53 A8
Lee The CV5 ....112 C4
Lee Wlk WS11 ....2 B4
Leebank Rd B63 ....82 E2
Leech St DY4 ....52 C5
Leeder Cl CV6 ....95 C2
Leedham Ave B77 ....21 D5
Leeming Cl CV4 ....132 C5
Lees Rd WV14 ....40 F3
Lees St B18 ....65 F6
Lees Terr WV14 ....40 F3
Leeson Wlk B17 ....85 D5
Legge La Birmingham B1 ..66 C3
Bilston WV14 ....40 D1
Legge St Birmingham B4 .164 D4
West Bromwich B70 ......53 E3
Wolverhampton WV2 .....39 E6
Legion Cl WS11 ....6 A6
Legion Rd B45 ....121 E7
Legs La WV10 ....11 F3
Leicester Cl B67 ....64 E1
Leicester Cswy CV1 ...113 D5
Leicester Ct CV12 ......79 C2
Leicester La
Cubbington CV32 ....149 E1
Royal Leamington Spa
CV32 ....157 C6
Leicester Pl B71 ....53 C7
Leicester Rd
Bedworth CV12 ....78 B4
Hinckley LE10 ....71 F2
Nuneaton CV11 ....73 D5
Shilton CV7 ....97 F6
Leicester Row CV1 ....165 B4
Leicester St
Bedworth CV12 ....78 B3
Bulkington CV12 ....79 C2
Royal Leamington Spa
CV32 ....157 A1
Walsall WS1 ....28 E2
Wolverhampton WV6 .....25 A4
Leigh Ave Burntwood WS7 ..7 B7
Coventry CV3 ....133 C3
Leigh CE Prim Sch CV4 .131 D8
Leigh Cl WS4 ....29 A4
Leigh Ct Birmingham B23 .56 C2
Walsall WS4 ....29 A3
Leigh Inf & Jun Sch B8 .67 E6
Leigh Rd Birmingham B8 ..67 E6
Sutton Coldfield B75 ....47 B5
Walsall WS4 ....29 A4
Leigh St **4** CV1 ....113 E4
Leigham Dr B17 ....85 A7
Leighs Cl WS4 ....15 C1
Leighs Rd WS4 ....15 C1
Leighswood Ave WS9 ...30 B7
Leighswood Cl WS11 ....5 F5
Leighswood Ct WS9 .....30 B6
Leighswood Gr WS9 ....30 A7
Leighswood Ind Est WS9 .30 A6
Leighswood Rd WS9 .....30 A6
Leighton Cl
Birmingham B43 ....44 C3
Coventry CV4 ....132 D2
Dudley DY1 ....50 E2
Royal Leamington Spa
CV32 ....157 C4
Leighton Rd Bilston WV14 .41 A4
Birmingham B13 ....87 A2
Wolverhampton WV6 .....38 F6
Leisure Wlk B77 ....35 F6
Leith Gr B38 ....123 E8
Lelant Gr B17 ....85 A5
Lellow St B71 ....53 C8
Lemar Ind Est B30 .....86 B1
Lemon Rd B70 ....53 A8
Len Davies Rd WV12 ....27 B7
Lench Cl Halesowen B62 ..63 C1
Redditch B97 ....153 A5
Lench St B4 ....164 C4
Lench's Cl B13 ....87 A3
**Lench's Trust Almshouses
3** Birmingham, Edgbaston
B12 ....87 A8
3 Birmingham, Highgate
B12 ....86 F7
3 Birmingham, Ladywood
B16 ....66 B1
Lenchs Gn B5 ....86 E7
Lenchs Trust B32 ......84 E4
Lennard Gdns B66 ......65 D6
Lennox Cl CV3 ....134 C6
Lennox Gdns WV3 ....39 A8
Lennox Gr B73 ....57 A7
Lennox St B19 ....66 D5
Lenton Croft B26 ....88 E4
Lenton's La CV2 ....96 E4
Lenwade Rd B68 ....84 D8
Leofric Cl **3** B15 ......86 C8
Leofric St CV6 ....113 A5
Leomansley Cl WS13 .....8 E7
Leomansley Rd WS13 ....8 E7
Leomansley View WS13 ..8 E7
Leominster Ho B33 .....69 E2
Leominster Rd B11 ......87 E3
Leomansley View WS13 ..8 E7
Leona Ind Est B62 ......63 D1
Leonard Ave **5** B19 ....66 D7
Leonard Gr B19 ....66 D7

Leonard Parkins Ho
CV12 ....79 D2
Leonard Rd
Birmingham B19 ....66 D8
Stourbridge DY8 ....80 C5
Leontes Mdws CV34 ....161 E3
Leopold Ave B20 ....54 F5
Leopold Rd CV1 ....113 F4
Leopold St B12 ....86 F8
Lepid Gr B29 ....85 D2
Lerryn Cl DY6 ....60 F5
Lerwick Cl DY6 ....60 F5
Lesingham Dr CV4 .....111 E1
Lesley Bentley Ho **6** B11 .66 C3
Lesley Dr DY6 ....60 E4
Lesley Rd DY4 ....41 B1
Leslie Rd
Birmingham, Edgbaston B16 .65 F2
Birmingham, Handsworth
B20 ....55 D2
Little Aston B74 ....31 B2
Wolverhampton WV10 ....25 F4
Leslie Rise B69 ....63 C8
Lesscroft Cl WV9 ....11 A2
Lester Gr WS9 ....30 E2
Lester St WV14 ....40 F5
Leswell Gr DY10 ......116 F6
Leswell La DY10 ......116 F6
Leswell St DY10 ......116 F6
Letchlade Cl CV2 ......114 C8
Letheren's La B43 ......68 D2
Leve La WV13 ....27 B1
Level St DY5 ....61 E3
Leven Cl LE10 ....75 B8
Leven Croft B76 ....58 A7
Leven Dr WV12 ....13 B1
Leven Way CV2 ....115 A8
Levenwick Way DY6 .....61 A5
Lever St WV2 ....163 C1
Leveretts The B21 ......54 C3
Leverton Rise WV10 ....25 C6
Leveson Ave WS6 ....4 E2
Leveson Cl DY2 ....62 E8
Leveson Cres CV7 .....130 B6
Leveson Ct
1 Willenhall WV13 ....27 A2
2 Wolverhampton WV6 ...25 A4
Leveson Dr DY4 ....51 E6
Leveson Rd WV11 ....26 F8
Leveson St WV13 ....27 A2
Leveson Wlk **1** DY2 ....62 E8
Levett Rd B77 ....22 B5
Levetts Fields WS14 .....9 C7
Levetts Hollow WS11 .....1 D3
Levetts Sq **4** WS13 .....9 B7
Levington Rd WV6 ....23 F5
Lewis Ave WV1 ....26 B2
Lewis Cl Lichfield WS14 ..9 E7
Willenhall WV12 ....27 D5
Lewis Gr WV11 ....26 D7
Lewis Rd
Birmingham B30 ....104 C7
Coventry CV1 ....113 D5
Oldbury B68 ....84 B7
Radford Semele CV31 ...162 F5
Stourbridge DY9 ....81 D5
Lewis St Bilston WV14 ...40 E6
Tipton DY4 ....52 D5
Walsall WS2 ....28 D3
Lewisham Rd
Smethwick B66 ....65 A7
Wolverhampton WV10 ....11 B2
Lewisham St B71 ....53 D4
Lewisham Trad Est B66 ..65 A7
Lewkner Almshouses The
B48 ....139 A5
Lewthorn Rise WV4 .....39 D4
Lexington Ct CV11 ......73 B5
Lexington Gn DY5 ....81 C7
Ley Hill Farm Rd B31 ..102 E5
Ley Hill Prim Sch B31 .102 E5
Ley Hill Rd B75 ....46 C8
Ley Rise DY3 ....39 C1
Leybourne Cres WV9 ....10 F2
Leybourne Gr B25 ......88 C6
Leybrook Rd B45 ....122 B8
Leyburn Cl Coventry CV6 ..95 E2
Nuneaton CV11 ....74 A2
Walsall WS2 ....27 D3
Leyburn Rd B16 ....66 A1
Leycester Cl B31 ......123 A7
Leycester Cl **2** CV34 ..160 E6
Leycester Pl **10** CV34 ..160 E6
Leycester Rd CV8 .....148 A2
Leycroft Ave B33 ....69 D3
Leydon Croft B38 ......104 B2
Leyes La CV8 ....148 C5
Leyfields WS13 ....3 B2
Leyfields Cres CV34 ...160 D4
Leyland Ave WV3 ....24 F1
Leyland Croft WS3 .....14 F1
Leyland Rd
Bulkington CV12 ....79 A2
Coventry CV5 ....112 D4
Nuneaton CV11 ....73 E1
Tamworth B77 ....21 E3
Leyland Spec! Sch CV11 .73 E1
Leyman Cl B14 ....105 C4
Leymere Cl CV7 ....92 C1
Leys Cl DY9 ....81 C2
Leys Cres DY5 ....61 B3
Leys Ind Est DY5 ....61 A3
Leys La CV7 ....92 C1
Leys Rd DY5 ....61 B3
Leys The Birmingham B31 .103 B5
1 Darlaston DY4 ....41 D6

Leys Wood Croft B26 ....89 B6
Leysdown Gr B27 ....106 C8
Leysdown Rd B27 ....106 C8
Leyside CV1 ....134 E5
Leysters CI B98 ....154 E3
Leyton CI DY5 ....81 D8
Leyton Gr B44 ....45 A1
Leyton Rd B21 ....65 F4
Libards Gate ◀ B91 ....127 C8
Libbards Way B91 ....127 B8
Liberty Rd B77 ....35 F5
Liberty Way CV11 ....73 F3
Libra CI B70 ....22 F7
Library CI LE10 ....76 A5
Library Rd CV4 ....132 B5
Library Way B45 ....121 F7
Lich Ave WV11 ....26 E7
Lichen CI WV12 ....1 C6
Lichen Gn CV4 ....132 D5
Lichfield (Trent Valley) Sta
  WS13 ....9 F8
Lichfield Bsns Ctr WS13 ....3 D1
Lichfield Cath* WS13 ....9 B8
Lichfield Cathedral Sch
  WS13 ....9 B8
Lichfield City Sta WS14 ....9 B7
Lichfield CI CV11 ....74 A7
Lichfield Coll WS13 ....9 B7
Lichfield Cres B78 ....20 E7
Lichfield CE Solihull B90 ....105 D2
  Sutton Coldfield B75 ....46 C5
  Walsall WS4 ....29 A4
Lichfield Pas WV1 ....163 C3
Lichfield Rd
  Birmingham B6 ....67 B8
  Brownhills WS8 ....16 A8
  Brownhills, New Town WS8,
  WS14 ....7 C1
  Brownhills, Shire Oak WS8,
  WS9 ....16 B5
  Burntwood WS7 ....7 D6
  Cannock WS11 ....5 B8
  Coventry CV3 ....133 D8
  Sutton Coldfield B74 ....32 A3
  Tamworth B78,B79 ....20 C6
  Walsall WS4 ....29 B4
  Walsall, Highbridge WS3 ....15 B5
  Walsall, New Invention 13 E1
  Walsall, Rushall WS4 ....29 B6
  Walsall, Wallington Heath
  WS3 ....14 C2
  Water Orton B46,B76 ....59 D4
  Wednesfield WV11 ....26 E6
  Wishaw B76,B78 ....48 B3
Lichfield Road Ind Est
  B79 ....20 E6
Lichfield St Bilston WV14 ....40 E5
  Fazeley B78 ....20 F1
  Tamworth B79 ....21 A5
  Tipton DY4 ....51 F8
  Walsall WS1 ....28 F2
  Wolverhampton WV1 ....163 C3
Lichwood Rd WV11 ....26 F7
Lickey Coppice B45 ....122 C4
Lickey End Fst Sch B60 ....137 C6
Lickey Gr DY11 ....116 B2
Lickey Grange Dr B60 ....121 E1
Lickey Hills Country Pk*
  B45 ....122 B3
Lickey Hills Jun & Inf Sch
  B45 ....121 F3
Lickey Rd
  Birmingham B45 ....122 C6
  Stourbridge DY8 ....81 B6
Lickey Rock B60 ....121 D1
Lickey Sq B45 ....122 A2
Liddiard Ct DY8 ....80 E6
Liddon Gr B27 ....106 C8
Liddon Rd B27 ....106 C8
Lidford CI B14 ....104 C4
Lifford La B30 ....104 B4
Lifford Way CV3 ....135 A7
Lifton Croft DY6 ....60 F5
Light Hall Sch B90 ....126 B8
Light La CV1 ....165 B4
Lightfields Wlk B65 ....63 B2
Lighthorne Ave B16 ....66 B2
Lighthorne Rd B91 ....107 C6
Lightning Way B31 ....123 B7
Lightoak CI B97 ....158 C6
Lightwood CI B93 ....128 B8
Lightwood Rd DY1 ....51 A3
Lightwoods Hill B67 ....84 E8
Lightwoods Jun & Inf Sch
  B68 ....84 D8
Lightwoods Rd
  Smethwick B67 ....65 A1
  Stourbridge DY9 ....81 F1
Lilac Ave
  ◀ Birmingham, Balsall Heath
  B12 ....87 A5
  Birmingham, Perry B44 ....55 F2
  Cannock WS11 ....1 D6
  Coventry CV6 ....112 F5
  Sutton Coldfield B74 ....44 E8
  Tipton DY4 ....51 E7
  Walsall WS5 ....43 A4
Lilac Cl Hinckley LE10 ....75 E6
  Redditch B98 ....153 E2
Lilac Cr Burntwood WS7 ....6 F7
  Walsall WS2 ....27 E3
  Warwick CV34 ....156 A1
  Wednesbury WS10 ....42 A2
Lilac Ho WS4 ....15 D1
Lilac La WS6 ....14 A8
Lilac Rd Bedworth CV12 ....78 D5

Lilac Rd continued
  Bilston WV1 ....40 B8
  Dudley DY1 ....51 C4
  Tamworth B79 ....21 A8
  Willenhall WV12 ....27 E7
Lilac Way B62 ....83 F8
Lilacvale Way CV4 ....132 D5
Lilian Gr WV14 ....40 E1
Lileshall CI B98 ....154 E3
Lileshall Cres WV2 ....39 D7
Lileshall Rd B26 ....89 B7
Lilley CI CV6 ....95 C2
Lilley Green Rd B48 ....140 D5
Lilley La B31 ....123 B8
Lillington Ave CV32 ....156 F2
Lillington CI Lichfield WS13 ....9 A8
  Royal Leamington Spa
  CV32 ....157 A3
  Sutton Coldfield B75 ....47 A4
Lillington Gr B34 ....69 D5
Lillington Prim Sch
  CV32 ....157 B3
Lillington Rd
  Coventry CV2 ....96 D1
  Royal Leamington Spa
  CV32 ....157 A3
  Solihull B90 ....126 B8
Lily Green La B97 ....153 A4
Lily Rd B26 ....88 D7
Lily St B77 ....53 C5
Lilycroft La B38 ....124 A7
Limberlost CI B20 ....55 A3
Limbrick Ave CV4 ....132 A1
Limbrick CI B90 ....105 F2
Limbrick Wood Prim Sch
  CV4 ....111 F3
Limbury Gr B92 ....107 F8
Lime Ave
  ◀ Birmingham B29 ....85 F2
  Royal Leamington Spa
  CV32 ....157 A4
  Walsall WS2 ....27 E3
Lime CI Great Wyrley WS6 ....4 F4
  Hollywood B47 ....125 A5
  Tipton DY4 ....51 E5
  Walsall WS2 ....27 E3
  West Bromwich B70 ....53 A4
Lime Ct Birmingham B11 ....87 C4
  Kidderminster DY10 ....117 A4
Lime Gr Bilston WV14 ....40 C7
  Birmingham B25,B26 ....88 D6
  Birmingham, Balsall Heath
  B12 ....86 F6
  Birmingham, Chelmsley Wood
  B37 ....70 B1
  Birmingham, Lozells B19 ....66 C8
  Birmingham, Small Heath
  B10 ....87 D8
  Bromsgrove B61 ....136 F4
  Burntwood WS7 ....7 C6
  Coventry CV4 ....112 B2
  Kenilworth CV8 ....148 A4
  Lichfield WS14 ....9 D8
  Nuneaton CV10 ....72 D3
  Smethwick B66 ....65 B3
  Smethwick B66 ....65 B3
  Sutton Coldfield B73 ....57 B7
  Walsall WS4 ....29 C6
Lime Kiln CI B38 ....123 D7
Lime La Norton Canes WS3 ....6 A1
  Walsall WS3 ....15 A8
Lime Rd Huntington WS12 ....1 D8
  Sedgley DY3 ....39 F1
  Wednesbury WS10 ....41 F4
Lime St Dudley WV14 ....51 A3
  Walsall WS1 ....29 A1
  Wolverhampton WV3 ....39 B8
Lime Tree Ave
  Coventry CV4 ....112 A2
  Wolverhampton WV6 ....24 A3
Lime Tree Cres B97 ....153 B4
Lime Tree Croft B31 ....103 C2
Lime Tree Gdns WV8 ....10 B3
Lime Tree Rd
  Birmingham, Acock's Green
  B27 ....88 C5
  Birmingham, Saltley B8 ....67 F6
  Codsall WV8 ....10 B4
  Walsall WS5 ....43 A4
Limehurst Ave WV3 ....24 C1
Limehurst Rd WS4 ....29 C6
Limekiln La
  Birmingham B14 ....105 A4
  Earlswood B94 ....126 D1
Limepit La Dudley DY1 ....51 A3
  Huntington WS11,WS12 ....1 D6
Limes Ave Blackheath B65 ....63 C2
  Brierley Hill DY5 ....61 C5
Limes Rd Dudley DY1 ....51 B3
  Wolverhampton WV6 ....24 A8
Limes The Bedworth CV12 ....77 C2
  Birmingham, Gravelly Hill
  B24 ....56 F2
  Birmingham, Ladywood B16 ....66 A2
  Birmingham, Moor Park
  B16 ....65 F3
  Birmingham, Sparkbrook
  B11 ....87 C6
  Walsall WS1 ....29 A2
  Wolverhampton WV1 ....26 B5
Limes View DY3 ....50 E7
Limescroft CI WS4 ....29 B7
Limetree Rd B74 ....30 D1
Linacre Ho B37 ....69 F2
Linaker Rd CV3 ....134 C5
Linchmere Rd B21 ....54 C2
Lincoln Ave
  Nuneaton CV10 ....72 B7

Lincoln Ave continued
  Tamworth B79 ....20 E6
  Willenhall WV13 ....27 D2
Lincoln CI Birmingham B27 ....88 E3
  Lichfield WS13 ....3 C3
  Warwick CV34 ....155 E1
Lincoln Croft WS14 ....17 F6
Lincoln Ct
  ◉ Birmingham B29 ....103 C7
  Royal Leamington Spa
  CV32 ....162 A8
Lincoln Dr WS11 ....4 F8
Lincoln Gn WV10 ....11 D2
Lincoln Gr B37 ....70 A1
Lincoln Ho WV10 ....25 E3
Lincoln Rd
  Birmingham B27 ....88 D2
  Bromsgrove B61 ....136 E4
  Dudley DY2 ....62 D2
  Smethwick B67 ....64 E2
  Walsall WS1 ....42 D1
  West Bromwich B71 ....42 E3
Lincoln Rd N B27 ....88 E3
Lincoln St Birmingham B12 ....86 E6
  Coventry CV1 ....165 C4
  Wolverhampton WV10 ....25 E3
Lincoln Twr B16 ....66 A1
Lincroft Cres CV5 ....112 E4
Lindale Ave B36 ....68 C6
Lindale Cres DY5 ....81 B6
Linden Ave
  Birmingham B43 ....54 D8
  Burntwood WS7 ....7 A8
  Halesowen B62 ....83 E7
  Kidderminster DY10 ....117 A7
  Tipton B69 ....63 D8
Linden CI Tamworth B77 ....21 A1
  Warwick CV34 ....155 E2
  Willenhall WS2 ....27 D2
Linden Ct B91 ....107 E4
Linden Dr DY8 ....81 A3
Linden Gdns WV1 ....163 A4
Linden Glade B63 ....83 A4
Linden Gr DY10 ....117 A7
Linden La WV12 ....27 E6
Linden Lea Bedworth CV12 ....78 B3
  Wolverhampton WV3 ....24 D1
Linden Rd
  Birmingham B30 ....103 E7
  Dudley DY1 ....51 B3
  Hinckley LE10 ....71 C1
  Smethwick B66 ....65 A4
Linden View WS12 ....2 B4
Lindens Dr B74 ....44 F6
Lindens Prim Sch B74 ....44 F6
Lindens The
  Birmingham, Beech Lanes
  B32 ....84 E7
  Birmingham, Edgbaston
  B15 ....65 D1
  Wolverhampton WV6 ....24 E3
Lindenwood B73 ....46 B6
Lindford Way B38 ....104 B2
Lindhurst Dr B94 ....143 C6
Lindisfarne B77 ....21 D3
Lindisfarne Dr CV8 ....148 C6
Lindley Ave DY4 ....51 D4
Lindley Rd Bedworth CV12 ....77 D2
  Coventry CV3 ....114 B2
Lindon CI WS8 ....16 A6
Lindon Dr WS8 ....15 F7
Lindon Rd WS8 ....15 F5
Lindon Wood WS8 ....16 A6
Lindrick CI WS3 ....13 F3
Lindridge Dr B76 ....58 D6
Lindridge Rd
  Birmingham B23 ....56 C5
  Solihull B90 ....105 F1
  Sutton Coldfield B75,B76 ....47 B6
Lindrosa Rd B74 ....30 F3
Lindsay Rd B42 ....44 B1
Lindsey Ave B31 ....103 C2
Lindsey Cres CV8 ....148 A1
Lindsey Pl DY5 ....61 C3
Lindsey Rd B71 ....53 C7
Lindsworth App B30 ....104 C3
Lindsworth Ct ◉ B30 ....104 C3
Lindsworth Rd B30 ....104 C3
Lindsworth Specl Sch
  B30 ....104 C3
Lineholt CI B98 ....159 A6
Linehouse La
  Catshill B60 ....137 D8
  Marlbrook B60 ....121 D1
Linen St CV34 ....160 D6
Linfield Gdns CV8 ....39 C1
Linford Gr B25 ....68 D8
Linford Wlk CV2 ....96 F1
Linforth Dr B74 ....45 A7
Ling Ho WV10 ....25 F3
Ling Rd WS12 ....2 B6
Lingard CI B7 ....67 B5
Lingard Ho B76 ....57 F8
Lingard Rd B75 ....47 A5
Lingen CI B98 ....154 E3
Lingfield Ave
  Birmingham B44 ....44 F1
  Wolverhampton WV10 ....11 C5
Lingfield CI WS6 ....4 E3
Lingfield Ct
  ◉ Birmingham B43 ....54 D7
  Coventry CV6 ....96 B4
Lingfield Dr WS6 ....4 E3
Lingfield Gdns B34 ....69 B6
Lingfield Gr WV6 ....23 F4
Lingfield Rd WS11 ....6 A5

Lingfield Way DY6 ....61 A5
Lingfield Wlk B61 ....121 B1
Lingham Cl B91 ....107 D7
Lingwood Dr CV10 ....72 F3
Linhope Dr DY6 ....61 A5
Link One Ind Pk CV4 ....52 E6
Link Rd Birmingham B16 ....65 E3
  Brownhills WS9 ....16 B3
  Wombourne WV5 ....49 A7
Link The B27 ....88 A1
Links Ave WV6 ....24 D7
Links Cres B68 ....84 B8
Links Dr Birmingham B45 ....122 A5
  Solihull B91 ....107 B6
  Stourbridge DY8 ....80 F6
Links Rd Birmingham B14 ....105 A1
  Coventry CV6 ....113 B8
  Oldbury B68 ....84 B8
  Wolverhampton WV4 ....39 A3
Links Side Way WS9 ....30 C8
Links The DY10 ....117 A4
Links View Aldridge B74 ....31 B1
  Halesowen B62 ....83 D4
Linkswood CI B13 ....87 B3
Linkway B11 ....161 E6
Linkway Ret Pk WS11 ....4 B6
Linkwood Ind Est B98 ....80 F6
Linley CI WS9 ....29 E5
Linley Dr WV10 ....11 E1
Linley Gr
  Birmingham B14 ....104 C6
  Dudley DY3 ....50 B2
Linley Lodge Ind Est
  WS9 ....29 E6
Linley Rd WS4 ....29 D7
Linley Wood Rd WS9 ....29 E5
Linnet CI Birmingham B30 ....103 E8
  Coventry CV3 ....134 D5
  Halesowen B62 ....83 B6
  Huntington WS12 ....1 D7
Linnet Gr Birmingham B23 ....56 B6
  Willenhall WV12 ....27 C8
Linnet Rise DY10 ....116 F1
Linpole Wlk B14 ....104 D2
Linsey Rd B92 ....89 C2
Linslade CI WV4 ....39 D6
Linstock Way CV6 ....96 B4
Linthouse La WV11 ....26 E8
Linthouse Wlk B77 ....35 F6
Linthurst Fst Sch B60 ....138 A6
Linthurst Newtown B60 ....138 A7
Linthurst Rd B45,B60 ....138 A7
Linthy B77 ....22 B1
Linton Ave B91 ....107 A1
Linton CI Halesowen B63 ....82 D5
  Redditch B98 ....154 F2
Linton Croft WV14 ....40 D5
Linton Mews B98 ....154 F2
Linton Rd
  Birmingham, Acock's Green
  B11 ....88 A4
  Birmingham, Great Barr
  B43 ....44 C3
  Blackheath B64 ....62 F3
  Wolverhampton WV4 ....38 E5
Linton Wlk B23 ....56 C3
Linwood Dr Cannock WS12 ....1 E7
  Coventry CV2 ....96 F1
Linwood Rd
  Birmingham B21 ....65 E8
  Dudley DY1 ....106 D5
  Solihull B91 ....106 E5
Linwood Wlk B97 ....85 D4
Lion Fields Ave CV5 ....112 B6
Lion Ind Est WS9 ....30 A8
Lion Pas DY8 ....80 F5
Lion Sq DY10 ....116 E6
Lion St
  Kidderminster DY10 ....116 E6
  Stourbridge DY8 ....80 F5
Lion's Den WS7,WS14 ....7 E2
Lionel St B3 ....164 B3
Liskeard CI CV11 ....74 A5
Liskeard Rd WS5 ....43 D7
Lisko CI DY5 ....81 A8
Lisle Ave DY11 ....116 D3
Lisle Ct ◉ CV31 ....162 A5
Lismore CI B45 ....101 E1
Lismore Croft CV2 ....115 B7
Lismore Dr
  Birmingham B17 ....85 A3
  Hinckley LE10 ....71 C1
Lisson Gr B44 ....44 F4
Listelow CI B36 ....69 B8
Lister CI Tipton DY4 ....52 A4
  Walsall WS2 ....28 B5
Lister Rd Dudley DY2 ....62 D7
  Kidderminster DY11 ....116 B4
  Walsall WS2 ....28 B5
Lister St Birmingham B7 ....66 F4
  Nuneaton CV11 ....73 D3
  Willenhall WV13 ....40 D4
Listowel Rd B14 ....104 D6
Lisures Dr B76 ....46 D4
Little Acre B97 ....158 D6
Little Albert St WS2 ....28 E2
Little Ann St B5 ....66 F2
Little Aston Hall Dr B74 ....31 B5
Little Aston Hospl B74 ....31 B5
Little Aston La B74 ....31 C6
Little Aston Park Rd B74 ....31 A3
Little Aston Prim Sch
  B74 ....31 D4
Little Aston Rd WS9 ....30 D6
Little Barr St B9 ....67 A2
Little Barrow Wlk WS13 ....3 A1
Little Birches WV3 ....38 F8

Little Bloxwich CE Prim Sch
  WS3 ....14 D3
Little Bricklin St WV3 ....163 B2
Little Bromwich Rd B9 ....68 C2
Little Broom St B12 ....87 A8
Little Caldmore ◀ WS1 ....42 E8
Little Church La B79 ....21 B5
Little Church St ◀ CV1 ....165 C4
Little Clothier St WV13 ....27 A3
Little Clover CI ◀ B7 ....67 C7
Little Comm WS3 ....15 A4
Little Cornbow B63 ....83 B3
Little Cottage St ◀ DY5 ....61 D2
Little Cote B43 ....43 C1
Little Cross St WS10 ....41 D7
Little Cryfield CV4 ....132 C1
Little Duke St CV11 ....73 B4
Little Edward St B9 ....67 A2
Little Farm CV3 ....134 D5
Little Field CV2 ....114 A5
Little Fields Way B69 ....63 F7
Little Forge Rd B98 ....159 C8
Little Francis Gr ◀ B7 ....67 B5
Little Gorway WS1 ....42 F7
Little Grebe Rd DY10 ....117 B3
Little Green La ◀ B9 ....67 C1
Little Green Lanes B73 ....57 B7
Little Hall Rd B7 ....67 B5
Little Hardwick Rd WS9 ....30 D2
Little Hay La WS14 ....18 C3
Little Heath Croft B34 ....69 E7
Little Heath Ind Est CV6 ....96 A2
Little Heath La B60 ....137 D6
Little Heath Prim Sch
  CV6 ....95 F1
Little Hill WS10 ....41 F3
Little Hill Gr B38 ....104 A1
Little Hill Way B32 ....84 D2
Little John St DY5 ....61 D4
Little Johnson's La
  Aldridge WS9 ....30 B1
  Walsall WS9 ....44 B8
Little La
  West Bromwich B71 ....53 D5
  Willenhall WV12 ....27 D7
Little Lawns CI WS9 ....16 A4
Little London WS1 ....42 F8
Little London Ho WS1 ◀ 42 F7
Little London Jun Mix Inf Sch
  WV13 ....27 A2
Little Meadow Croft
  B31 ....102 F4
Little Meadow Wlk B33 ....68 F3
Little Moor Hill B67 ....64 F5
Little Newport St ◀ WS1 ....28 E1
Little Oaks Dr DY7 ....60 A2
Little Oaks Rd B6 ....66 E8
Little Park St
  Coventry CV1 ....165 C2
  Wolverhampton WV1 ....163 C3
Little Pitts CI B24 ....57 D5
Little Pk B32 ....84 B4
Little Potter St ◀ DY5 ....61 D2
Little Pountney St WV2 ....163 B1
Little Shadwell St B4 ....164 C4
Little South St CV1 ....113 E3
Little St DY2 ....51 D1
Little Station St ◀ WS2 ....28 E2
Little Sutton B75 ....46 C8
Little Sutton Prim Sch
  B75 ....32 D3
Little Sutton Rd B75 ....32 D2
Little Wood Wood WV13 ....27 A2
Little Woods B97 ....158 E6
Little's La ◀ WV1 ....163 C4
Littlecote DY7 ....20 D7
Littlecote Croft ◀ B14 ....105 A3
Littlecote Dr B23 ....56 F7
Littlemead Ave B31 ....103 C1
Littlemead Rd B90 ....125 E8
Littleover Ave B28 ....105 F6
Littleshaw Croft B47 ....125 C4
Littleshaw La B47 ....125 C4
Littlethorpe CV3 ....134 D6
Littleton Bsns Pk WS12 ....1 C7
Littleton CI
  Kenilworth CV8 ....148 A7
  Sutton Coldfield B76 ....47 A2
Littleton Croft ◉ B91 ....127 C8
Littleton Dr WS12 ....1 C7
Littleton Rd WV12 ....27 D7
Littleton St E WS1 ....28 F3
Littleton St W WS1 ....28 E3
Littlewood CI ◉ B91 ....127 B8
Littlewood La WS6 ....4 E4
Littlewood Rd WS6 ....4 E4
Littleworth Ave DY1 ....51 B6
Littleworth Gr B76 ....46 F4
Littleworth Hill WS12 ....2 C4
Littleworth Rd CV11 ....73 B4
Litton B77 ....22 C1
Liveridge CI B93 ....127 F6
Liverpool Croft B37 ....89 F8
Liverpool St B9 ....67 A2
Livery St Birmingham B3 ....164 B3
  Birmingham B3 ....164 B4
  Royal Leamington Spa
  CV32 ....161 F8
Livingstone Ave WV6 ....23 D5
Livingstone Rd
  Bilston WV14 ....40 B5
  Birmingham, Handsworth
  B20 ....55 D1

Livingstone Rd continued
Birmingham, King's Heath
B14 ....104 E6
Coventry CV6 ....113 E7
Walsall WS3 ....14 E2
West Bromwich B70 ....53 B1
Lizafield Ct 🅱 B66 ....64 E7
Llewellyn Rd CV31 ......162 A6
Lloyd Cl CV11 ....73 D2
Lloyd Cres CV2 ....114 E3
Lloyd Dr WV4 ....38 C2
Lloyd George Gr WS11 ..2 C2
Lloyd Hill WV4 ....38 C3
Lloyd Ho B19 ....66 C6
Lloyd Rd Birmingham B20 .55 A4
Wolverhampton WV6 ....24 D5
Lloyd Roberts Bldgs WV4 .38 F1
Lloyd St Birmingham B10 ..87 D8
Cannock WS11 ....1 D1
Dudley DY2 ....62 D8
Wednesbury WS10 ....41 E3
West Bromwich B71 ....53 E4
Wolverhampton WV6 ....24 D4
Lloyds Rd B62 ....83 C8
Loach Dr CV2 ....96 B4
Lobelia Cl LE10 ....75 E1
Locarno Prim Sch DY4 ..52 A6
Locarno Rd DY4 ....52 A6
Lochalsh Gr WV11 ....13 B1
Lochmore Cl LE10 ....75 A8
Lochmore Dr LE10 ....75 A8
Lochmore Way LE10 ......75 A8
Lochranza Croft B43 ....43 E2
Lochsong Ct B77 ....35 D4
Lock Cl B97 ....153 A4
Lock Dr B33 ....68 D3
Lock Keepers Cl WS11 ....5 F4
Lock Keepers Reach
B48 ....138 F6
Lock La CV34 ....160 D8
Lock St WV1 ....163 C4
Locke Cl CV6 ....95 A1
Locket Cl WS2 ....27 F4
Lockfield Cl DY8 ....60 F2
Lockhart Cl CV8 ....148 A4
Lockhart Dr B75 ....32 C1
Lockheed Cl 🅱 CV31 ...161 F5
Lockhurst La CV6 ....113 D7
Locking Croft B35 ....58 B3
Lockington Croft B62 ....83 F6
Lockley Cl WV10 ....25 F4
Locks The CV31 ....161 D7
Locks View DY8 ....60 E1
Lockside WS9 ....29 F7
Locksmith Cl WV13 ....27 B2
Lockton Rd B30 ....104 C8
Lockwood Rd B31 ....102 F4
Lode Heath Sch B91 ....107 C6
Lode La B91 ....107 C6
Loder Cl CV4 ....111 F3
Lodge Cl Halesowen B62 ..83 E3
Hinckley LE10 ....76 A5
Walsall WS5 ....43 D6
Lodge Cres Dudley DY2 ..62 A4
Hagley DY9 ....99 B5
Warwick CV34 ....160 D4
Lodge Croft
Birmingham B31 ....102 E6
Knowle B93 ....128 B6
Lodge Farm B88 ....88 F8
Lodge Farm Cl B76 ......46 F3
Lodge Farm Jun Mix Inf Sch
WV12 ....27 E4
Lodge Farm Mid Sch
B98 ....154 A2
Lodge Forge Trad Est
B64 ....82 C7
Lodge Gr WS9 ....30 A5
Lodge Green La CV7 ......92 F2
Lodge Green La N CV7 ...92 F2
Lodge Hill Rd B29 ....85 D1
Lodge La Cheslyn Hay WS11 .4 C5
Kingswinford DY6 ....60 B6
Lodge Pool Dr B98 ......153 F1
Lodge Pool Prim Sch B33 .69 B3
Lodge Rd Bilston WV14 ...40 F4
Birmingham B18 ....65 F5
Birmingham B18 ....66 B5
Coventry CV3 ....114 B1
Darlaston WS10 ....41 D5
Knowle B93 ....128 B6
Redditch B98 ....153 E3
Smethwick B67 ....64 E7
Walsall, Pelsall WS4 ....15 B1
Walsall, The Chuckery WS5 .43 B1
West Bromwich B70 ....53 C3
Wolverhampton WV10 ......25 E4
Lodge Rd/ West Bromwich
TH Sta B70 ....53 C3
Lodge St Oldbury B69 ....64 A7
Willenhall WV13 ....27 C5
Lodge View WS6 ....4 C2
Lodgefield Rd B62 ....83 B7
Lodgepool Cl B44 ....55 E6
Loeless Rd B33 ....69 A3
Lofthouse Cres B31 ....102 F3
Lofthouse Gr B31 ....102 F3
Lofthouse Rd B20 ....54 F3
Loftus Cl B29 ....102 F8
Loftus Ct WS7 ....7 A5
Logan Cl WV10 ....25 C6
Logan Rd CV2 ....114 C7
Loie Cl CV6 ....96 A4
Lollard Croft CV3 ....133 D8
Lomaine Dr B30 ....103 E4

Lomas Dr B31 ....102 E3
Lomas St WV1 ....25 C4
Lomax Cl WS13 ....3 A1
Lomax Rd WS12 ....2 E7
Lombard Ave DY2 ....62 D3
Lombard Gdns WS13 ....9 B8
Lombard St
Birmingham B12 ....86 F8
Lichfield WS13 ....9 B8
West Bromwich B70 ....53 C3
Lombard St W B70 ....53 C3
Lombardy Croft 🅱 B62 ...84 A4
Lombardy Gdns WV12 .....27 E7
Lombardy Gr WS7 ....6 F8
Lomita Cres B77 ....35 D8
Lomond Cl
Birmingham B34 ....69 E6
Hinckley LE10 ....75 B8
Tamworth B79 ....20 F8
Lomond Rd DY3 ....39 C1
Lomond Way CV10 ....72 C5
Lomsey Cl CV4 ....112 A1
London Hts DY1 ....51 A2
London La
Bromsgrove B60 ....151 F7
Tardebigge B60 ....152 A6
London Rd
Birmingham B20 ....55 C2
Coventry, Cheylesmore
CV3 ....133 E7
Coventry, Willenhall CV3 ..134 B5
Hinckley LE10 ....75 F8
Lichfield WS14 ....9 C5
Middleton B75,B78 ....47 D7
Ryton-on-D CV8 ....135 B1
Shenstone B75,WS14 ....32 F7
Sutton Coldfield B75 ....33 A4
Walsall WS4 ....18 F3
London St B66 ....65 C5
Londonderry Gr B67 ......64 F5
Londonderry La B67 ......64 E4
Londonderry Rd B68 .....64 D4
Lones Rd B71 ....65 B8
Long Acre Birmingham B7 .67 C7
Kidderminster DY10 ......116 F7
Long Acre St WS2 ....28 D3
Long Acre Trad Est B7 ...67 B7
Long Bridge Rd WS14 .....9 C5
Long Brook La CV7,CV8 .129 F5
Long Cl DY9 ....99 A4
Long Close Ave CV5 .....112 B6
Long Close Wlk B35 ......58 A3
Long Compton Dr DY9 ....99 A6
Long Croft WS12 ....1 C4
Long Furrow WV8 ....10 E1
Long Hyde Rd B67 ....64 F1
Long Innage B63 ....82 B6
Long Knowle La WV11 ....26 B8
Long Knowle Prim Sch
WV11 ....26 C8
Long La Allesley CV5,CV4,CV7 .94 D2
Great Wyrley WS6 ....13 E6
Halesowen B62 ....83 E8
Long La Trad Est B62 ....83 D8
Long Leasow B29 ....103 B7
Long Ley WV10 ....25 F3
Long Ley Prim Sch WV10 .25 F3
Long Leys Croft B46 ......59 B2
Long Leys Ct B46 ....59 B2
Long Mdw B65 ....59 B2
Long Meadow Dr DY3 .....33 B2
Long Meadow Rd B60 ...137 C6
Long Mill Ave WV11 ....26 B7
Long Mill N WV11 ....26 B7
Long Mill S WV11 ....26 B7
Long Mynd B63 ....82 D1
Long Mynd Cl WV11 ....13 B1
Long Mynd Rd B31 ......102 F6
Long Nuke Rd B31 ....102 E7
Long Saw Dr B31 ....102 E5
Long Shoot The CV11 .....74 C6
Long St Birmingham B11 ..87 A6
Bulkington CV12 ....79 D2
Walsall WS2 ....28 D1
Wolverhampton WV1 ....163 C3
Long Wood B30 ....103 E5
Longacre WS10 ....41 A8
Longacre Ind Est B7 ......67 C7
Longacres Cannock WS12 ..2 F5
Little Aston B74 ....31 C4
Longbank Rd B69 ....63 C8
Longboat La DY8 ....60 E1
Longborough Cl B97 ....158 B6
Longbow Rd B29 ....102 F7
Longbridge La B31 ......122 E8
Longbridge Sta B31 .....122 E8
Longcroft Ave WS10 ......42 A3
Longcroft Cl B35 ....58 A3
Longcroft The
Halesowen B63 ....82 E4
Walsall WS4 ....29 C7
Longdales Rd B38 ....123 E7
Longdon Ave WV4 ....39 D5
Longdon Cl B98 ....159 B7
Longdon Croft B93 ......128 A8
Longdon Dr B74 ....31 E3
Longdon Rd B93 ....128 A6
Longfellow Ave CV34 ....160 C4
Longfellow Cl B97 ....158 C7
Longfellow Gn DY10 .....117 C6
Longfellow Pl WS11 ....1 E4
Longfellow Rd
Birmingham B30 ....103 D4
Coventry CV2 ....114 C3
Dudley DY3 ....50 B5
Longfellow Wlk B79 ......20 F8

Longfield Cl
Birmingham B28 ....105 F6
Longfield Ho B77 ....21 E4
Longfield Dr B74 ....31 D4
Longfield Ho
Coventry CV6 ....114 A8
Wolverhampton WV10 ......25 F3
Longfield Rd
Birmingham B31 ....102 E8
Royal Leamington Spa
CV31 ....162 B6
Stourbridge DY9 ....81 D5
Longford Cl
Birmingham B32 ....102 A7
Dorridge B93 ....128 B3
Longford Ct WS11 ....4 A8
Longford Gn WS11 ....4 C7
Longford Gr B44 ....45 A3
Longford Ind Est WS11 ....4 B8
Longford Park Prim Sch
CV6 ....96 A3
Longford Prim Sch WS11 ..4 C8
Longford Rd
Bedworth CV7 ....96 A6
Birmingham B44 ....45 A2
Cannock WS11 ....4 C7
Coventry CV6 ....96 A4
Wolverhampton WV10 ......26 A4
Longford Sq CV6 ....96 A4
Longham Croft B32 ....84 E4
Longhurst Croft B31 ....123 B7
Longlake Ave WV6 ....24 B3
Longlands Cl B38 ....123 C8
Longlands Dr B77 ....21 F4
Longlands Ho B31 ....87 B5
Longlands Rd B62 ....83 E3
Longlands The
Barnt Green B45 ....138 D7
Wombourne WV5 ....49 A6
Longleat Birmingham B43 ..43 C2
Tamworth B79 ....20 D7
Longleat Dr
Cheswick Green B90 ....126 E5
Dudley DY1 ....50 E2
Longleat Gr 🅱 CV31 ...162 C6
Longleat Rd WS9 ....16 A1
Longleat Twr 🅱 B15 .....66 C1
Longley Ave B76 ....58 D5
Longley Cres B26 ....88 E4
Longleys Croft CV34 .....160 D4
Longmeadow Cres B34 ...69 E6
Longmeadow Dr B74 .....31 A3
Longmeadow Gr B31 ....123 A6
Longmeadow Rd WS5 ....43 E8
Longmoor Cl
Redditch B97 ....153 B5
Wednesfield WV11 ....26 F5
Longmoor Rd
Birmingham B73 ....45 B3
Halesowen B63 ....82 E3
Longmoor Specl Sch
B73 ....45 B3
Longmore Ave WS2 ....27 F1
Longmore Cl B73 ....45 A5
Longmore Ho B73 ....45 C3
Longmore Rd B90 ....106 D2
Longmore St
Birmingham B12 ....86 E7
Wednesbury WS10 ....41 F3
Longshaw Gr B34 ....69 D6
Longstone Cl B90 ....127 B6
Longstone Rd B42 ....55 D7
Longville Ct CV3 ....134 A6
Longwill Prim Sch For Deaf
Children B31 ....103 A5
Longwood Cl CV4 ....131 F6
Longwood Path B78 ......20 D1
Longwood Prim Sch B78 .20 D1
Longwood Rd
Aldridge WS9 ....30 B2
Birmingham B45 ....122 A7
Lonicera Cl WS5 ....43 B3
Lonscale Dr CV3 ....133 B5
Lonsdale Cl
Birmingham B33 ....68 D2
Willenhall WV12 ....27 B5
Lonsdale Rd Bilston WV14 .40 F6
Birmingham B17 ....85 B6
Royal Leamington Spa
CV31 ....157 B4
Smethwick B66 ....64 D7
Walsall WS5 ....43 C6
Wolverhampton WV3 ....39 B7
Lord Austin Dr B60 ......121 E1
Lord Cromwell Ct WS11 ...2 A5
Lord Lytton Ave CV2 ....114 D2
Lord St Bilston WV14 .....40 E3
Birmingham B7 ....66 F5
Coventry CV5 ....112 F2
Walsall WS1 ....42 E6
Wolverhampton WV3 ....39 A8
Lord St W WV14 ....40 E3
Lord's Dr WS2 ....28 E3
Lords La B80 ....159 E2
Lordsmere Cl WV14 ....40 D1
Lordswood Boys Sch
B17 ....65 A1
Lordswood Cl B97 ....152 F2
Lordswood Girls Sch & Sixth
Form Ctr B17 ....85 A8
Lordswood Rd B17 ....65 A1
Lordswood Sq B17 ....85 B7
Lorenzo Cl CV3 ....134 D6
Lorimer Way B43 ....44 D4
Lorne Gr DY10 ....117 A6
Lorne St Burntwood WS7 ..7 A7
Kidderminster DY10 ......117 A5

Lorne St continued
Tipton DY4 ....51 F8
Lorrainer Ave DY5 ....81 A8
Lorton B79 ....20 D7
Lothersdale B77 ....36 C8
Lothians Rd Walsall WS3 ..15 A5
Wolverhampton WV6 ....24 E6
Lottie Rd B29 ....85 E1
Lotus B77 ....21 E1
Lotus Croft B67 ....64 F4
Lotus Ct B16 ....65 C1
Lotus Dr Blackheath B64 ..62 F2
Cannock WS11 ....1 E1
Lotus Way B65 ....62 F5
Loudon Ave CV6 ....113 A5
Loudon Gate CV11 ....73 F1
Loughshaw B77 ....22 C1
Loughton Gr B63 ....82 F4
Louis Ct B67 ....64 F5
Louisa Pl 🅱 B18 ....66 A5
Louisa St 🅱 B1 ....66 C3
Louise Croft B14 ....104 E2
Louise Ct
🅱 Birmingham B27 ....88 C3
Solihull B91 ....106 E5
Louise Ho DY5 ....61 D6
Louise Lorne Rd B13 .....86 F4
Louise Rd B21 ....65 F7
Louise St DY3 ....50 C3
Lovage Rd B98 ....154 F6
Lovatt Cl DY4 ....41 C1
Lovatt Pl WS11 ....1 C3
Lovatt St WV1 ....163 A3
Love La Birmingham B47 ..66 F4
Great Wyrley WS6 ....5 B3
Hinckley LE10 ....75 D8
Hollywood B47 ....124 F7
Stourbridge, Lye DY9 ....81 F5
Stourbridge, Old Swinford
DY8 ....81 A1
Wall WS13 ....42 E7
Wolverhampton WV6 ....24 D6
Love Lyne B97 ....158 B5
Loveday Dr CV32 ....156 E2
Loveday Ho B70 ....53 D3
Loveday St B4 ....164 C4
Lovelace Ave B91 ....127 D8
Lovell B79 ....20 F6
Lovell Cl CV12 ....96 B4
Lovell Rd CV12 ....78 A3
Lover's Wlk 🅱 WS10 .....41 F3
Lovett Ave B69 ....63 D5
Lovetts Cl LE10 ....74 F8
Low Ave B43 ....43 F2
Low Hill Cres WV10 ....25 E8
Low Hill La WV10 ....25 C8
Low St WS6 ....4 D3
Low Thatch B38 ....123 E7
Low Town B69 ....64 A7
Low Wood Rd B23 ....56 E5
Lowans Hill View B97 ...153 C4
Lowbridge Cl WV12 ....27 C5
Lowbrook La B90 ....125 D4
Lowcroft Gdns WV10 .....25 E8
Lowden Croft B26 ....88 E4
Lowdham B77 ....22 C1
Lowe Ave WS10 ....41 C7
Lowe Dr Kingswinford DY6 .60 E4
Sutton Coldfield B73 ....45 C3
Lowe Rd CV6 ....95 A2
Lowe St 🅱 Birmingham B12 .87 A8
Wolverhampton WV6 ....25 B4
Lower Ave CV31 ....161 F7
Lower Beeches Rd B31 ..102 C2
Lower Bentley La B60 ...151 F1
Lower Bond St LE10 ....71 D1
Lower Chapel St B69 ......52 C2
Lower Church La DY4 ......52 B5
Lower City Rd B69 ....52 E3
Lower Common La B97 ..153 B2
Lower Dartmouth St B9 ..67 B2
Lower Darwin St B12 ......86 F8
Lower Derry St DY5 ....61 D2
Lower Eastern Green La
CV5 ....111 F4
Lower Essex St B5 ....66 E1
Lower Farm WV9 ....16 E4
Lower Farm Prim Sch
WS3 ....14 C3
Lower Ford St CV1 ....165 D3
Lower Forster St WS1 ....28 F2
Lower Gambolds La
B60 ....151 B6
Lower Gn DY4 ....51 E5
Lower Grinsty La B97 ....158 A8
Lower Ground Cl 🅱 B6 ..55 F1
Lower Hall La WS1 ....28 F2
Lower Hall St WV13 ....27 B1
Lower High St
Blackheath B64 ....82 C8
Stourbridge DY8 ....80 F6
Wednesbury WS10 ....41 F2
Lower Higley Cl B32 ......84 E4
Lower Holyhead Rd
CV1 ....165 A3
Lower Horseley Fields
WV1 ....26 A7
Lower House La CV9 ......36 F2
Lower Ladyes Hills CV8 ..148 A6
Lower Leam St CV31 .....162 B7
Lower Lichfield St WV13 ..27 B2
Lower Loveday St B19 ...164 C4
Lower Mill St DY11 ....116 D6
Lower Moor B18 ....103 E8
Lower North St WS4 ....28 E3
Lower Par The B72 ....46 C5
Lower Parklands DY11 ...116 C5

Lower Prec CV1 ....165 B3
Lower Prestwood Rd
WV11 ....26 C7
Lower Queen St B72 ....46 C4
Lower Rd Barnacle CV7 ....97 C6
Cannock WS12 ....2 D3
Lower Reddicroft B73 .....46 C5
Lower Rushall St WS1 .....28 F2
Lower Sandford St WS13 ..9 A7
Lower Severn St B1 ......164 B2
Lower Shepley La B60 ...137 E6
Lower St WV6 ....24 E5
Lower Temple St B2 ......164 B2
Lower Tower St B19 .....164 C5
Lower Trinity St B9 ....67 A1
Lower Valley Rd DY5 ......61 A2
Lower Vauxhall WV1 ......25 A3
Lower Villiers St
🅱 Royal Leamington Spa
CV32 ....157 A1
Wolverhampton WV2 ....39 C7
Lower Walsall St WV1 .....25 F1
Lower White Rd B32 ......84 D5
Lowercroft Way B74 ....31 E6
Lowerpark B77 ....21 C1
Lowerstack Croft B37 .....69 F3
Lowes Ave CV34 ....155 E1
Lowesmoor Rd B26 ....89 C7
Loweswater Cl CV11 ......74 A6
Loweswater Dr DY3 ....50 D3
Loweswater Ho B38 ......104 B1
Loweswater Rd CV3 ......114 E1
Lowfield Cl B62 ....84 A3
Lowfield La B97 ....153 B5
Lowforce B77 ....22 C1
Lowhill La B45 ....122 D6
Lowland Ct B64 ....62 F1
Lowland Rd WS12 ....1 C5
Lowlands Ave
Sutton Coldfield B74 ....44 E8
Wolverhampton WV6 ....24 E6
Lowlands Ct WV6 ....24 E6
Lowlands La B98 ....154 D3
Lowndes Rd DY8 ....80 E6
Lowrey Ct B68 ....64 A3
Lowry Cl Bedworth CV12 ..78 A4
Perton WV6 ....23 D1
Smethwick B67 ....64 F6
Willenhall WV13 ....26 E2
Lowther Ct 🔟 DY5 ....61 D2
Lowther St CV2 ....113 F4
Loxdale Park Ind Est
WV14 ....40 E4
Loxdale Prim Sch WV14 ..40 E4
Loxdale Sidings WV14 ....40 F4
Loxdale St Bilston WV14 ..40 F4
Wednesbury WS10 ....41 E2
Loxdale Sta WV14 ....40 F4
Loxley Ave
Birmingham B14 ....105 C3
Solihull B90 ....105 F1
Loxley Cl
Birmingham B31 ....102 E8
Coventry CV2 ....96 D2
Redditch B98 ....154 D6
Loxley Ct CV2 ....96 D2
Loxley Rd Smethwick B67 ..64 F1
Sutton Coldfield B75 ....32 D3
Loxley Sq B92 ....106 D8
Loxley Way CV32 ....157 A2
Loxton Cl B74 ....31 D5
Loynells Rd B45 ....122 B7
Loyns Cl B37 ....69 E3
Lozells Inf & Jun Sch
B19 ....66 C7
Lozells Rd B19 ....66 C7
Lozells St B19 ....66 C7
Lozells Wood Cl 🅱 B19 ..66 C7
Lucas Ct CV32 ....161 D8
Lucas Ho CV32 ....156 F2
Lucas Rd LE10 ....75 D6
Lucas St B35 ....58 B4
Luce Cl B35 ....58 B4
Luce Rd WV10 ....25 C6
Lucerne Ct CV2 ....96 C3
Lucerne St B23 ....56 C6
Lucian Cl CV2 ....115 B7
Lucknow Rd WV12 ....27 B5
Lucy Edwards Ct CV11 ..116 C5
Lud La B79 ....21 A5
Luddington Rd B92 ....107 E8
Ludford Cl B75 ....46 E7
Ludford Rd
Birmingham B32 ....84 A1
Nuneaton CV10 ....72 C6
Ludgate B79 ....21 A5
Ludgate Ave DY11 ....116 A4
Ludgate Cl B46 ....59 B3
Ludgate Ct WS5 ....43 D7
Ludgate Hill B3 ....164 B3
Ludgate St DY1 ....51 B1
Ludlow Cl Birmingham B37 .70 C2
Cannock WS11 ....2 C2
Willenhall WV12 ....27 B6
Ludlow Ho
🅱 Birmingham B13 ....105 A6
Willenhall WV12 ....28 C6
Ludlow La WS2 ....28 A4
Ludlow Rd Birmingham B8 .67 E4
Coventry CV5 ....113 A2
Kidderminster DY10 ......116 E3
Redditch B97 ....153 E3
Ludlow Way B74 ....31 F5
Ludmer Way B20 ....55 C1
Ludstone Ave WV4 ....38 D5
Ludstone Rd B29 ....84 F1
Ludworth Ave B37 ....90 B8
Luff Cl CV3 ....134 B8

Lugtrout La
Catherine de B B91 ....108 A6
Solihull B91 ....107 F6
Lukes Wlk WS13 ....3 A2
Lulworth Cl B63 ....82 C6
Lulworth Pk CV8 ....148 C6
Lulworth Rd
  Birmingham B28 ....88 A1
  Burntwood WS7 ....7 A7
Lulworth Wlk WV4 ....38 C6
Lumley Gr B37 ....70 D2
Lumley Rd WS1 ....29 A1
Lumsden Cl CV2 ....114 F8
Lunar Cl CV4 ....132 C5
Lundy Cl LE10 ....71 B1
Lundy View B36 ....70 B6
Lunn Ave CV8 ....147 E3
Lunn Poly Ho ⬛ CV12 ...156 F1
Lunns Croft WS13 ....9 C8
Lunt Jct The WV14 ....41 A6
Lunt Pl WV14 ....41 A6
Lunt Rd Bilston WV14 .....40 F6
  Birmingham B32 ....84 D5
Lunt The * CV8 ....133 E3
Lupin Cl LE10 ....75 D5
Lupin Gr Birmingham B9 ...67 F3
  Walsall WS5 ....43 B4
Lupin Rd DY2 ....51 F1
Lupton Ave CV3 ....133 C7
Lupton Cl B60 ....137 A1
Lusbridge Cl B63 ....82 B4
Luscombe Rd CV2 ....114 E8
Luther Way CV5 ....111 F4
Lutley Ave B63 ....82 E4
Lutley Cl WV3 ....38 E7
Lutley Dr DY9 ....81 C3
Lutley Gr B32 ....84 B3
Lutley La B63 ....82 C2
Lutley Mill Rd B63 ....82 E4
Lutley Prim Sch B63 ......82 D1
Luton Rd B29 ....85 F3
Lutterworth Rd
  Coventry CV2 ....114 C5
  Hinckley LE10 ....76 C3
  Nuneaton CV11 ....79 C8
Luttrell Rd B74 ....32 A1
Luxor La CV5 ....111 B8
Lyall Gdns B45 ....101 E1
Lyall Gr B27 ....88 A2
Lychgate Ave DY9 ....81 C1
Lychgate Cl LE10 ....76 A4
Lychgate La LE10 ....76 C5
Lyd Cl WV11 ....26 B8
Lydate Rd B62 ....83 F4
Lydbrook Covert ⬛ B38 .123 E8
Lydbury Gr B33 ....69 A4
Lydd Croft B35 ....58 B4
Lyddington Dr B62 ....83 B7
Lyde Gn B63 ....82 B7
Lydford Cl CV2 ....114 C7
Lydford Gr B24 ....57 A1
Lydford Rd WS3 ....14 B3
Lydgate Ct Bedworth CV12 78 A4
  Nuneaton CV11 ....13 C3
Lydgate Rd Coventry CV6 113 B5
  Kingswinford DY6 ....60 F6
Lydget Gr B23 ....56 D7
Lydham Cl Bilston WV14 ...40 B4
  Birmingham B44 ....44 B8
  Redditch B98 ....153 E5
Lydia Croft B74 ....31 E6
Lydian Cl WV6 ....25 B4
Lydiate Ash Rd B60 ......121 C3
Lydiate Ave B31 ....102 D1
Lydiates Cl DY3 ....50 B7
Lydney Cl Redditch B98 ..154 D7
  Willenhall WV12 ....27 C4
Lydney Gr B31 ....102 F3
Lydstep Gr CV31 ....162 C7
Lye Ave B32 ....84 A2
Lye Bsns Ctr DY9 ....81 F6
Lye Close La B32 ....84 A2
Lye Cross Rd B69 ....63 B7
Lye Sta DY9 ....81 F6
Lye Valley Ind Est DY9 ...81 F6
Lyecroft Ave B37 ....70 D2
Lygon Cl B98 ....154 A5
Lygon Gr B32 ....84 E4
Lyme Green Rd B33 ....68 F4
Lymedene Rd B42 ....55 B5
Lymer Rd WV10 ....11 C1
Lymesy St CV3 ....133 D7
Lymington Cl CV6 ....113 D8
Lymington Ct B73 ....46 B1
Lymington Dr CV6 ....96 B6
Lymington Rd WV13 ......27 D2
Lymore Croft CV2 ....115 A8
Lymsey Croft DY8 ....60 C3
Lynbrook Cl Dudley DY2 ..62 D5
  Hollywood B47 ....125 A7
Lynbrook Rd CV5 ....132 D8
Lynch The Nuneaton CV11 .73 D2
  Polesworth B78 ....22 F1
Lynchgate Ct CV4 ....132 C6
Lynchgate Ho CV4 ....132 C6
Lynchgate Rd CV4 ....132 C6
Lyncourt Gr B32 ....84 B6
Lyncroft House Sch WS11 .4 E8
Lyncroft L Ctr WS11 ....4 E8
Lyncroft Rd B11 ....87 F2
Lyndale B77 ....35 F6
Lyndale Cl CV5 ....112 C3
Lyndale Dr WV11 ....26 E6
Lyndale Rd Coventry CV5 112 C3
  Dudley DY2 ....62 E6
  Sedgley DY3 ....39 B2
Lyndale Rd B61 ....136 E3
Lyndenwood B97 ....153 A2

Lyndholm Rd DY10 ....117 A6
Lyndhurst Cl Coventry CV6 .96 B6
  Hinckley LE10 ....76 A7
Lyndhurst Croft CV5 .....111 C4
Lyndhurst Dr
  Kidderminster DY10 .....116 E8
  Stourbridge DY8 ....60 F1
Lyndhurst Rd
  Birmingham B24 ....56 F2
  Cannock WS12 ....2 E1
  West Bromwich B71 ....53 D4
  Wolverhampton WV3 ......39 A7
Lyndon B71 ....53 D5
Lyndon Cl
  Birmingham, Castle Bromwich
  B36 ....69 C8
  Birmingham, Handsworth
  B20 ....55 C2
  Halesowen B63 ....82 F4
  Sedgley DY3 ....39 E1
Lyndon Croft B37 ....90 B7
Lyndon Cl CV32 ....161 E8
Lyndon Gr
  Kingswinford DY6 ....60 B8
  West Bromwich B71 ....53 D4
Lyndon Green Inf Sch
  B26 ....89 A6
Lyndon Green Jun Sch
  B26 ....89 A6
Lyndon Ho B31 ....103 B3
Lyndon Rd
  Birmingham B33 ....68 E3
  Birmingham, Eachway B45 121 E7
  Solihull B92 ....88 F2
  Sutton Coldfield B73 .....46 B5
Lyndon Sch B92 ....89 A3
Lyndworth Rd B30 ....104 D8
Lyne Ho ⬛ CV2 ....114 D8
Lyneham Cl Hinckley LE10 .71 A1
  Tamworth B79 ....21 C8
Lyneham Gdns B76 ....58 B6
Lyneham Way B35 ....57 F3
Lynfield Ct B38 ....123 F7
Lyng Cl CV5 ....112 A4
Lyng Hall Sch CV2 ......114 C6
Lyng La B70 ....53 C2
Lyng Prim Sch B70 ....53 C1
Lynmouth Cl
  Aldridge WS9 ....30 A5
  Nuneaton CV11 ....73 E5
Lynmouth Rd CV2 ....114 E8
Lynn Gr B29 ....85 C2
Lynn La WS14 ....17 D6
Lynton Ave Smethwick B66 .65 A6
  West Bromwich B71 ....53 C7
  Wolverhampton WV6 ......24 F6
Lynton Cl CV34 ....155 E1
Lynton Ho B23 ....56 B6
Lynton Rd Birmingham B6 .67 B7
  Coventry CV6 ....95 F1
Lynval Rd DY5 ....81 F7
Lynwood Ave DY6 ....60 A6
Lynwood Cl WV12 ....27 E8
Lynwood Dr DY10 ....98 C2
Lynwood Wlk ⬛ CV31 ...162 C6
Lyon Ct B72 ....46 C5
Lyons Gr B11 ....87 C3
Lysander Rd B45 ....102 A2
Lysander Way WV11 ......1 E3
Lyster Cl CV34 ....160 B8
Lysway Cl ⬛ WS1 ....42 F8
Lysways St WS1 ....42 F8
Lythall Cl CV31 ....165 E2
Lythalls La CV6 ....95 E2
Lythalls Lane Ind Est CV6 .95 E1
Lytham B77 ....22 A2
Lytham Cl Stourbridge DY8 .80 F2
  Sutton Coldfield B76 .....58 B6
Lytham Croft B15 ....66 C1
Lytham Gr WS3 ....14 A4
Lytham Rd WV6 ....23 D4
Lythwood Dr DY5 ....81 C8
Lyttelton Rd
  Birmingham, Edgbaston
  B16 ....65 D1
  Birmingham, Stechford B33 .68 D3
  Stourbridge DY8 ....80 D5
  Warwick CV34 ....160 E8
Lyttleton Cl
  Coventry CV2 ....115 A1
  Dudley DY2 ....62 C4
Lyttleton Ho B63 ....82 D4
Lyttleton Pl DY9 ....99 C6
Lyttleton St B70 ....53 C2
Lytton Ave WV4 ....38 E4
Lytton Gr B27 ....88 B1
Lytton La B32 ....84 F3

M

Maas Rd B31 ....103 A4
Mabey Ave B98 ....153 F5
Macadam Cl WS7 ....7 B8
Macarthur Rd B64 ....82 C8
Macaulay Ho B32 ....64 C4
Macaulay Rd CV2 ....114 D4
Macbeth App CV34 ......161 D4
Macdonald Cl B69 ....52 D2
Macdonald Rd CV2 .....114 D3
Macdonald St B5 ....86 D4
Mace St B64 ....62 E1
Macefield Cl CV2 ....96 D2
Macgregor Cres B77 .....21 F3
Macgregor Tithe B79 ....21 B5

Machin Rd B23 ....56 F4
Mackadown La B33 ....69 D2
Mackay Rd WS3 ....14 D2
Mackenzie Ct CV5 ....111 A8
Mackenzie Rd B11 ....87 C2
Macmillan Rd B65 ....63 C2
Macmillan Cl B60 ....52 C2
Macrome Rd WV6 ....24 E8
Madam's Hill Rd B90 ...126 D7
Maddocks Hill B72 ....46 C2
Maddocks Hill B72 ....56 E6
Madeira Ave WV8 ....10 A2
Madeira Croft CV5 ......112 E2
Madeira Ct DY8 ....60 D6
Madeley Rd
  Belbroughton DY9 ......120 D6
  Birmingham B11 ....87 C5
  Kingswinford DY6 ....61 A4
  Redditch B98 ....154 F5
Madin Rd DY4 ....51 E4
Madinatul Uloom Al-Islamiya
  Sch DY10 ....117 D1
Madison Ave
  Birmingham B36 ....69 C8
  Walsall WS2 ....28 B8
Madley Cl B45 ....121 E8
Madox Cl B79 ....20 E8
Madresfield Dr B63 ......83 B2
Madrona B77 ....22 B4
Maer Cl B65 ....63 A3
Mafeking Rd B66 ....65 A7
Mafeking Villas B62 .....83 B7
Magdala St B18 ....65 E5
Magdalen Cl DY1 ....51 A2
Magdalen Ct B16 ....65 E1
Magdalene Rd WS1 ....43 A7
Magee Cl LE10 ....71 C2
Magee Dr WS6 ....4 E3
Magness Cres WV12 .....27 C5
Magnet Wlk B23 ....56 C3
Magnet Wlk B77 ....22 A4
Magnolia Cl
  Birmingham B29 ....103 A7
  Coventry CV3 ....133 B5
Magnolia Gr WV8 ....10 B3
Magnolia Way ⬛ DY8 ....60 F1
Magnum Cl B74 ....44 F7
Magpie B77 ....35 E6
Magpie Cl DY2 ....62 E3
Magpie Ho CV5 ....111 D5
Magpie La CV7 ....108 A6
Magpie Way DY10 ....117 B2
Maguire Ind Est CV4 ....131 F8
Magyar Cres CV11 ....79 A8
Maidavale Cres CV3 ....133 C4
Maidendale Rd DY6 ......60 B7
Maidensbridge Dr DY6 ...60 C8
Maidensbridge Gdns
  DY6 ....49 B1
Maidensbridge Prim Sch
  DY6 ....49 B1
Maidensbridge Rd DY6 ...49 B1
Maidstone Dr
  Burntwood WS7 ....7 D6
  Stourbridge DY8 ....60 E3
Maidstone Rd B20 ....55 E1
Maidwell Dr B90 ....126 E8
Main Rd Ansty CV7 ....97 D3
  Birmingham B26 ....89 F3
  Meriden CV7 ....110 D8
  Tamworth B79 ....21 B8
Main St Birmingham B11 ..87 A7
  Brandon CV8 ....135 F4
  Shenstone WS14 ....17 F6
  Stonall WS9 ....16 D4
Main Terr B11 ....87 A7
Mainstone Cl B98 ....154 E3
Mainstream Forty Seven Ind
  Pk B7 ....67 C5
Mainstream Way B7 ......67 C5
Mainwaring Dr B75 ....32 E2
Maisemore Cl B98 ......154 D6
Maitland B77 ....21 F2
Maitland Ho B34 ....69 E6
Maitland Rd
  Birmingham B8 ....67 F4
  Dudley DY1 ....50 E1
Majestic Way B65 ....63 D4
Major Ct ⬛ B13 ....87 B2
Major St WV2 ....39 E7
Majuba Rd B16 ....65 C4
Makepeace Ave CV34 ...155 F1
Malam Cl CV4 ....112 A1
Malcolm Ave
  Birmingham B24 ....57 C5
  Bromsgrove B61 ....136 E3
Malcolm Ct WV11 ....25 A3
Malcolm Gr B45 ....122 A7
Malcolm Rd B90 ....106 B1
Malcolmson Cl B15 ....85 F8
Maldale B77 ....22 C1
Malfield Ave B97 ....152 F3
Malham Rd Tamworth B77 .36 C8
  Warwick CV34 ....155 F1
Malin Ct B23 ....56 C8
Malins Rd Birmingham B17 .85 D5
  Wolverhampton WV4 ......39 F5
Malins The CV34 ....161 B6
Malkit Cl WS2 ....27 F4
Mallaby Cl B90 ....126 A8
Mallard Ave
  Kidderminster DY10 .....117 B3
  Nuneaton CV10 ....72 C6
Mallard Cl
  Birmingham B27 ....88 C3

Mallard Cl continued
  Brierley Hill DY5 ....81 C7
  Redditch B98 ....153 F5
  Walsall WS3 ....15 A5
Mallard Court ⬛ WS13 ....9 C8
Mallard Dr
  Birmingham B23 ....56 B3
  Hinckley LE10 ....75 A7
  Oldbury B69 ....63 E2
Mallard Rd B80 ....159 F4
Mallards Reach B92 .....106 E8
Mallender Dr B93 ....127 F6
Mallerin Croft CV10 ......72 B5
Mallicot Cl WS13 ....3 D1
Mallin Gdns DY1 ....61 E8
Mallin St B66 ....64 C8
Mallory Cres WS3 ....14 D2
Mallory Dr
  Kidderminster DY11 .....116 D8
  Warwick CV34 ....160 D7
Mallory Rd WV6 ....23 E3
Mallory Rise B13 ....87 C1
Mallow Cl WV5 ....95 E4
Mallow Cl WS5 ....43 A6
Mallow Cl WV6 ....25 B5
Mallow Rise ⬛ B23 ......56 B7
Mallows Cl WS10 ....41 D6
Malmesbury Rd
  Birmingham B10 ....87 E7
  Coventry CV6 ....95 A3
Malpas Dr B32 ....102 C8
Malpas Wlk WV10 ....26 A4
Malpass Rd DY5 ....81 F7
Malt Cl B17 ....85 D6
Malt Mill La B62 ....83 D8
Malt Mill Lane Trad Est
  B62 ....83 D8
Malthouse B64 ....64 E7
Malthouse Croft B6 ......66 E8
Malthouse Dr DY1 ....51 A2
Malthouse Gdns B19 ....66 D7
Malthouse La
  Birmingham B8 ....67 B6
  Birmingham, Great Barr
  B42 ....55 D8
  Earlswood B94 ....141 E7
  Kenilworth CV8 ....147 E6
  Wolverhampton WV6 ......24 C6
Malthouse Rd DY5 ....51 E5
Malthouse Row B37 ......90 A8
Maltings Ct B17 ....65 A1
Maltings The
  Aldridge WS9 ....30 C6
  Nuneaton CV11 ....73 E5
  Royal Leamington Spa
  CV32 ....156 F2
  Studley B80 ....159 D4
  Wolverhampton WV1 .....163 C4
Malton Ave B65 ....63 D6
Malton Gr B13 ....105 B7
Malvern Ave
  Nuneaton CV11 ....72 B3
  Stourbridge DY9 ....81 C5
Malvern Ct
  West Bromwich B71 ....53 D5
  Willenhall WV12 ....27 B4
Malvern Cres DY2 ....61 F6
Malvern Ct
  Birmingham B27 ....88 C4
  Sutton Coldfield B74 .....31 F2
  Wolverhampton WV10 ....25 D8
Malvern Dr Aldridge WS9 ..30 C8
  Kidderminster DY10 .....116 E3
  Sutton Coldfield B76 .....58 A8
  Wolverhampton WV11 ....26 B1
Malvern Hill Rd B7 ......67 C7
Malvern Ho
  Coventry CV5 ....111 D4
  ⬛ Halesowen B63 ....83 A3
  Redditch B97 ....153 C1
Malvern Park Ave B91 ..107 D3
Malvern Rd
  Balsall Common CV7 ....130 C6
  Barnt Green B45 ....122 A2
  Birmingham, Acock's Green
  B27 ....88 D4
  Birmingham, Handsworth
  B21 ....54 C1
  Bromsgrove B61 ....150 D7
  Coventry CV5 ....112 F4
  Oldbury B68 ....64 B8
  Redditch B97 ....153 D8
Malvern St B12 ....87 A5
Malvern View
  Bluntington DY10 ....118 E1
  Kidderminster DY11 .....116 B3
  Malvern View Rd DY3 ...50 D4
Mamble Rd DY8 ....80 E5
Mammoth Dr WV10 ....25 D6
Manby Cl WV6 ....25 A4
Manby Rd B35 ....58 A4
Manby St DY4 ....51 F8
Mancetter Rd
  Nuneaton CV10 ....72 D7
  Solihull B90 ....106 C3
Manchester St
  Birmingham B6 ....164 C5
  Oldbury B69 ....64 B7
Mancroft Cl DY6 ....60 B7
Mancroft Gdns WV6 ......24 C5
Mancroft Rd WV6 ....24 C5
Mandale Rd WV10 ....25 D6
Mandarin Ave DY10 .....117 B3
Mandarin Cl LE10 ....75 A6
Mander Ctr WV1 ....163 B3
Mander Gallery B1 ......163 B3
Mander Gr CV34 ....160 C4

Mander Sq WV1 ....163 B3
Mander St WV3 ....163 A1
Manderley Cl
  Coventry CV5 ....111 C5
  Sedgley DY3 ....39 C2
Mandeville Gdns CV6 ....60 C6
Mandeville Gdns WS1 ....42 F8
Mandeville Way B61 ....136 F5
Maney Cnr B72 ....46 B4
Maney Hill Prim Sch B72 .46 D2
Maney Hill Rd B72 ....46 C2
Manfield Ave CV2 ....115 A7
Manfield Rd WV13 ....26 C3
Manifold Cl WS7 ....7 D6
Manilla Grange B70 .....53 B2
Manilla Rd B29 ....86 B1
Manitoba Croft ⬛ B38 .123 F8
Manley Cl B70 ....53 A3
Manley Rd WS13 ....3 C1
Manloves ⬛ WV3 ....39 A8
Manning Ct B14 ....104 F3
Manningford Rd B14 ....104 E3
Manor Abbey Rd B62 ....83 E4
Manor Ave Cannock WS11 ..1 D1
  Great Wyrley WS6 ....5 A4
  Kidderminster DY11 .....116 A7
Manor Cl Birmingham B16 .65 D1
  Codsall WV8 ....10 B4
  Hinckley LE10 ....71 C4
  Kidderminster DY11 .....116 A6
  Willenhall WV13 ....26 F3
  Wolverhampton WV4 ......38 F4
Manor Court Ave CV11 ...73 B5
Manor Court Mews CV11 .73 A5
Manor Court Rd
  Bromsgrove B60 ....150 F8
  Nuneaton CV11 ....73 A5
Manor Ct Dorridge B93 ..127 F2
  Dudley DY2 ....62 C5
  Kenilworth CV8 ....148 A6
  Royal Leamington Spa
  CV31 ....161 F7
  Walsall WS2 ....28 C1
Manor Dr Dudley DY3 ....50 B3
  Sutton Coldfield B73 .....46 B4
  Swindon DY3 ....49 F4
Manor Farm Com Sch
  WS4 ....29 B6
Manor Farm Craft Ctr*
  B79 ....125 F2
Manor Farm Dr WV12 ....27 D5
Manor Farm Rd B11 ......87 E4
Manor Gdns
  Birmingham B33 ....68 D2
  Wednesbury WS10 ....41 F4
  Wombourne WV5 ....49 B7
Manor Hall Mews CV3 ..134 D6
Manor High Sch WS10 ...42 D3
Manor Hill B73 ....46 B4
Manor Ho B36 ....69 F5
Manor Hospl WS2 ....28 C1
Manor House Ct
  Aston Flamville LE10 .....76 E6
  Birmingham B29 ....84 F1
Manor House Dr CV1 ...165 B2
Manor House La
  Aldworth Bank B46 ......158 E3
  Birmingham B26 ....88 F7
  Water Orton B46 ....59 B3
Manor House Pk WV8 ....10 B4
Manor House Rd WS10 ...41 F4
Manor Ind Est WS2 ......28 C1
Manor Jun & Inf Sch
  WV14 ....40 B2
Manor La Halesowen B62 .83 E4
  Honiley CV8,CV35 ......144 B1
  Lydiate Ash B61 ....121 C4
  Stourbridge DY8 ....80 D3
  Wroxall CV35 ....145 F4
Manor Mews B80 ....159 E4
Manor Park Com Sch
  CV11 ....73 A5
Manor Park Rd B31 .....102 C1
Manor Park Prim Sch
  Birmingham B6 ....67 A8
  Coventry CV3 ....133 D7
Manor Park Rd
  Birmingham B36 ....69 D8
  Nuneaton CV11 ....73 A5
Manor Pk DY6 ....60 D6
Manor Pl LE10 ....71 D1
Manor Prim Sch
  Aldridge B74 ....31 A1
  Drayton Bassett B78 .....34 E5
  Manor Rd Aldridge B74 ...31 A1
  Birmingham, Birchfield B6 .55 F1
  Birmingham, Edgbaston
  B16 ....65 D1
  Birmingham, Stechford B33 .68 E3
  Coventry CV1 ....165 B1
  Dorridge B93 ....127 F3
  Kenilworth CV8 ....147 F6
  Oak Side B78 ....20 D1
  Royal Leamington Spa
  CV32 ....157 B3
  Smethwick B67 ....107 C5
  Solihull B91 ....107 C6
  Studley B80 ....159 E4
  Sutton Coldfield, Maney B73 .46 B4
  Sutton Coldfield, Streetly
  B74 ....45 A8
  Tamworth B79 ....21 D4

Manor Rd *continued*
Tipton DY4 ....51 F4
Upper Bentley B97 ....152 B1
Walsall WS2 ....28 C2
Wednesbury WS10 ....42 D2
Wolverhampton, Ettingshall
WV4 ....40 A5
Wolverhampton, Oxley
WV10 ....25 C7
Wolverhampton, Penn WV4 .38 F4
Wythall B47 ....125 A3
Manor Rd B116 ....65 D1
Manor Rise Burntwood WS7 .7 A5
Lichfield WS14 ....9 C7
Manor Road Prec 2
WS2 ....28 C2
Manor Side Ind Est B98 .154 E6
Manor Sq B91 ....107 C3
Manor St Hinckley LE10 ......71 C1
Wolverhampton WV6 ....24 D5
Manor Terr CV8 ....148 A6
Manor View CV8 ....135 F3
Manor Way
Halesowen B62,B63 ....83 D3
Hinckley LE10 ....75 D5
Manor Way Prim Sch
B63 ....83 C2
Manor Wlk Solihull B91 ...107 C3
Sutton Coldfield B73 ....46 B4
Manorford Ave B71 ....43 A1
Manorial Rd B75 ....32 E3
Mansard Cl
Wolverhampton, Bradmore
WV3 ....38 F8
Wolverhampton, Scotlands
WV10 ....26 B8
Mansard Ho B90 ....106 A3
Manse Cl CV7 ....78 A1
Manse Gdns B80 ....159 E3
Mansel Rd B10 ....87 E8
Mansel St CV6 ....113 E8
Mansell Cl B63 ....82 B7
Mansell Rd Redditch B97 .158 D7
Tipton DY4 ....52 A8
Mansfield Cl B79 ....20 E6
Mansfield Green Com Sch
B6 ....66 E8
Mansfield Ho B37 ....70 D3
Mansfield Rd
Birmingham, Aston B6 ....66 E8
Birmingham, South Yardley
B25 ....88 C5
Mansion Cl DY1 ....51 A3
Mansion Cres B67 ....64 E4
Mansion Ct B62 ....83 E7
Mansion Dr Burntwood WS7 .7 D4
Tipton DY4 ....52 C5
Manston St 1 LE10 ....75 D8
Manston Cl WV4 ....38 D5
Manston Dr WV6 ....23 E5
Manston Rd B26 ....89 B7
Manston View B79 ....21 C8
Manta Rd B77 ....35 D6
Mantilla Dr CV3 ....133 B5
Manton Croft B93 ....127 E3
Manton Ho B19 ....66 E7
Manway Cl B20 ....54 F4
Manwoods Cl B20 ....55 B2
Maple Ave Bedworth CV7 .78 B1
Wednesbury WS10 ....42 C4
Maple Bank B15 ....86 A7
Maple Bsns Pk B7 ....67 B6
Maple Cl Birmingham B21 ..54 E1
Burntwood WS7 ....6 F7
Dudley WV14 ....51 A7
Hinckley LE10 ....75 E5
Kidderminster DY11 ....116 B8
Stourbridge DY8 ....80 D2
Maple Cres WS11 ....1 C1
Maple Croft B13 ....104 F5
Maple Ct Bilston WV14 ....40 F2
2 Birmingham B24 ....56 F3
Lichfield WS14 ....9 C7
Oldbury B66 ....64 D8
Maple Dr Birmingham B44 .56 C8
Dudley DY3 ....50 B2
Huntington WS12 ....1 C8
Walsall, Shelfield WS4 ....29 B8
Walsall, Yew Tree WS5 ....43 B4
Maple Gn DY1 ....51 A5
Maple Gr Bilston WV14 ....40 F4
Birmingham, Aston B19 ....66 D8
Birmingham, Kingshurst B37 .69 F6
Kingswinford DY6 ....60 E6
Lichfield WS14 ....9 F7
Warwick CV34 ....156 A1
Wolverhampton WV3 ....24 C2
Maple Hayes Sch for
Dyslexics WS13 ....8 C8
Maple Ho Little Aston B74 ..31 B5
Redditch B97 ....153 B2
Walsall WS4 ....15 D1
Maple Leaf B37 ....90 B8
Maple Leaf Ind Est WS2 .....28 A3
Maple Leaf Rd WS10 ....41 C1
Maple Rd
Birmingham, Eachway B45 .121 F6
Birmingham, Selly Oak
B30 ....103 C8
Dudley DY1 ....51 C3
Halesowen B62 ....83 D8
Nuneaton CV10 ....72 E5
Royal Leamington Spa
CV31 ....161 F6

Maple Rd *continued*
Sutton Coldfield B72 ....46 C3
Walsall WS3 ....14 F2
Wolverhampton WV3 ....38 E8
Maple Rise Oldbury B68 .....64 C2
Tamworth B77 ....22 A4
Maple Row 4 DY5 ....61 D2
Maple St WS3 ....14 D2
Maple Tree La B63 ....82 C6
Maple Way B31 ....102 F1
Maple Wlk 4 B37 ....70 B2
Maplebeck Ct B91 ....107 C5
Maplebeck Cl WS5 ....113 A3
Mapledene B13 ....87 B2
Mapledene Inf Sch B26 ......89 D6
Mapledene Jun Sch B26 ......89 D6
Maples The
Bedworth CV12 ....77 E2
Wolverhampton WV11 ....26 B8
Mapleton Rd
Birmingham B28 ....106 B7
Coventry CV6 ....112 F8
Maplewood B76 ....58 A8
Mapperley Cl CV2 ....115 A8
Mapperley Gdns B13 ....86 C3
Mappleborough Rd B90 ....105 E1
Marans Croft B38 ....123 D7
Marble Alley B80 ....159 E4
Marbury Cl B38 ....103 D2
Marbury Mews DY5 ....61 D1
March Cl WS6 ....4 D1
March End Rd WV11 ....26 D5
March Way Aldridge WS9 ...16 C1
Coventry CV3 ....134 D7
Marchant Rd
Bilston WV14 ....40 D7
Hinckley LE10 ....75 C8
Wolverhampton WV6 ....24 F2
Marchfont Cl CV11 ....74 A1
Marchmont Rd B10 ....68 A2
Marchmount Rd B72 ....57 C8
Marchwood Cl B97 ....153 A5
Marcliff Cres B90 ....105 C2
Marconi Pl WS12 ....2 C7
Marcos Dr B36 ....58 F1
Marcot Rd B92 ....88 F5
Marcroft Pl CV13 ....162 D6
Marden Cl WV13 ....26 F1
Marden Gr B31 ....123 A7
Marden Wlk B23 ....56 C3
Mardol Cl CV2 ....114 D7
Mardon Rd B26 ....89 C5
Maree Gr WV11 ....13 B1
Maret Ct 2 WS1 ....42 F8
Marfield Cl B76 ....58 A6
Margam Cres WS3 ....13 F2
Margam Terr WS3 ....13 F2
Margam Way WS3 ....13 F2
Margaret Ave
Bedworth CV12 ....78 B3
Halesowen B63 ....82 F4
Margaret Cl DY5 ....81 E8
Margaret Dr Cannock WS11 .1 E6
Stourbridge DY8 ....81 B4
Margaret Gdns B67 ....64 E5
Margaret Rd B17 ....85 C7
Margaret Ho B76 ....46 F3
Margaret Rd
Birmingham B73 ....45 D1
Birmingham, Harborne B17 ..85 C5
Darlaston WS10 ....41 C4
Walsall WS2 ....27 E3
Margaret St
Birmingham B3 ....164 B3
West Bromwich B70 ....53 B2
Margaret Vine Ct B62 ....63 F1
Margeson Cl CV2 ....114 E2
Margesson Dr B45 ....122 D1
Margetts Cl CV8 ....147 F4
Margreal Ind Est B16 ....65 F3
Marholm Cl WV9 ....10 F2
Maria St B70 ....64 E8
Marian Croft B26 ....89 D5
Marie Brock Cl CV4 ....112 B1
Marie Dr B27 ....106 B8
Marigold Cl WS11 ....2 C3
Marigold Cres DY1 ....51 A4
Marigold Dr LE10 ....75 E5
Marina Cl CV4 ....131 E7
Marina Cres WS12 ....2 A5
Marine Cres DY8 ....60 E1
Marine Dr B44 ....55 E6
Marine Gdns DY8 ....60 E1
Mariner B79 ....20 E6
Mariner Ave B16 ....65 E1
Marion Cl DY5 ....61 C2
Marion Rd Coventry CV6 .113 D7
Smethwick B67 ....64 E5
Marion Way B28 ....105 E7
Marita Cl DY2 ....62 E3
Marjoram Cl B38 ....123 F8
Marjorie Ave B30 ....104 B3
Mark Antony Dr CV34 ......161 D4
Mark Ave WS10 ....41 E3
Mark Cl B98 ....153 E2
Mark Ho B13 ....29 A3
Mark Rd WS10 ....41 E3
Markby Rd B18 ....65 E6
Market Cnr Bagington CV8 .133 F2
7 Royal Leamington Spa
CV31 ....161 F6
Market End Cl CV12 ....77 C2
Market Hall St WS11 ....1 E1
Market La Lichfield WS14 ......8 E2

Market La *continued*
Wombourne WV4 ....37 F5
Market Pl Blackheath B65 ...63 C1
Bromsgrove B61 ....136 F2
4 Cannock WS11 ....1 E1
Dudley DY1 ....51 D1
Hinckley LE10 ....75 D8
Nuneaton CV11 ....73 C4
Redditch B98 ....153 E4
Tamworth B79 ....21 B4
Tipton DY4 ....52 D5
Walsall WS3 ....14 B1
Warwick CV34 ....160 E6
Wednesbury WS10 ....41 F2
Willenhall WV13 ....27 A1
Market Sq B64 ....82 C8
Market St
Bromsgrove B61 ....136 F2
Cannock WS12 ....2 C5
Kidderminster DY10 ....116 E5
Kingswinford DY6 ....60 D6
Lichfield WS13 ....9 B8
Oldbury B69 ....64 A8
Stourbridge DY8 ....81 A5
Tamworth B79 ....21 B4
Warwick CV34 ....160 D6
Wolverhampton WV1 ....163 C2
Market Way Bilston WV14 ..40 D5
Coventry CV1 ....165 B2
Hagley DY9 ....99 C6
Market Wlk 4 B97 ....153 E4
Markfield Rd B26 ....89 B8
Markford Wlk B19 ....66 D6
Markham Cres B92 ....89 F1
Markham Croft WV9 ....11 A2
Markham Dr
Kingswinford DY6 ....60 E4
Whitnash CV31 ....162 B3
Markham Rd B73 ....45 C3
Marklew Cl WS8 ....16 A5
Marks Cl WS11 ....1 D1
Marks Mews 7 CV34 ....160 E6
Marks Wlk WS12 ....3 A2
Marksbury Cl WV6 ....25 A5
Marl Rd DY2 ....62 B4
Marl Top B38 ....103 F2
Marlbank Rd DY8 ....61 A1
Marlborough Ave B60 ....151 A8
Marlborough Cl
Hinckley LE10 ....76 B7
Sutton Coldfield B74 ....31 E6
Marlborough Ct
Bromsgrove B60 ....151 B8
Lichfield WS13 ....9 B8
Sutton Coldfield, Falcon Lodge
B75 ....47 A6
Sutton Coldfield, Four Oaks
B74 ....31 F2
Marlborough Dr
Royal Leamington Spa
CV31 ....162 D5
Stourbridge DY8 ....81 A3
Marlborough Gdns
Stourbridge DY8 ....60 D2
Wolverhampton WV6 ....24 E4
Marlborough Gr B25 ....68 D1
Marlborough Ind Est
WV2 ....39 D7
Marlborough Inf Sch
B10 ....67 E1
Marlborough Jun Sch
B10 ....67 E1
Marlborough Rd
Birmingham, Castle Bromwich
B36 ....69 D8
Birmingham, Small Heath
B10 ....67 E1
Coventry CV2 ....114 A3
Dudley DY3 ....50 F6
Nuneaton CV11 ....73 B3
Smethwick B66 ....65 A3
Marlborough St
2 Birmingham B19 ....116 E5
Walsall WS3 ....14 B1
Marlborough Way B77 ....21 F2
Marlbrook Cl B92 ....89 C4
Marlbrook Dr WV4 ....39 B6
Marlbrook La B60 ....121 D2
Marlcliff Gr B13 ....105 A6
Marlcroft CV3 ....134 E5
Marldon Rd B14 ....104 E6
Marlene Croft B37 ....70 C1
Marler Rd CV4 ....131 F7
Marley Hts B27 ....88 D4
Marley Rd DY6 ....61 A4
Marlfield Farm Fst Sch
B98 ....154 C6
Marlfield La
Redditch B98 ....154 B4
Redditch B98 ....154 B5
Marlin B77 ....35 D6
Marling Croft B92 ....107 F7
Marlissa Dr CV6 ....95 E2
Marloes Wlk CV31 ....162 C6
Marlow Cl Coventry CV5 ..112 B4
Dudley DY2 ....62 E3
Marlow Rd
Birmingham B23 ....56 D5
Tamworth B77 ....21 C5
Marlow St Blackheath B65 .63 B1
Walsall WS2 ....28 E3
Marlowe Cl DY10 ....117 B6
Marlowe Dr WV12 ....27 A7
Marlpit La Redditch B97 ....153 C1
Sutton Coldfield B75 ....32 D3
Marlpit Rise B75 ....32 E3
Marlpool Ct DY11 ....116 C8

Marlpool Dr
Redditch B97 ....153 C3
Walsall WS3 ....15 A1
Marlpool Fst Sch DY11 .116 C8
Marlpool La DY11 ....116 C8
Marlpool Pl DY11 ....116 C8
Marlston Wlk CV5 ....112 B4
Marlwood Cl CV6 ....95 F4
Marmion Dr B43 ....43 F2
Marmion Gr DY1 ....62 A8
Marmion Ho B70 ....52 F6
Marmion St B79 ....21 B5
Marmion Way B70 ....52 F6
Marne Cl CV34 ....161 A8
Marnel Dr WV3 ....38 E7
Marner Cres CV6 ....113 B5
Marner Rd Bedworth CV12 .78 A3
Nuneaton CV10 ....73 B1
Marnhull Cl CV2 ....114 F4
Marquis Dr B62 ....83 A7
Marrick B77 ....22 C1
Mariners La CV5 ....112 B5
Marriott Rd
Bedworth CV12 ....77 D2
Coventry CV6 ....113 A4
Dudley DY2 ....62 C4
Smethwick B66 ....64 D7
Marroway St B16 ....65 F3
Marrowfat La B21 ....65 F7
Mars Cl WV14 ....40 A1
Marsdale Dr CV10 ....72 E3
Marsden Cl B92 ....88 E1
Marsden Rd B98 ....153 E3
Marsett B77 ....36 C8
Marsh Cres DY8 ....60 D3
Marsh End B38 ....124 A8
Marsh Gr DY10 ....116 E8
Marsh Hill B23 ....56 C4
Marsh Hill Jun & Inf Sch
B23 ....56 C4
Marsh Ho CV2 ....115 A7
Marsh La Birmingham B23 .56 E5
Bradnock's Marsh B92 ....109 D5
Curdworth B76 ....59 D5
Hampton-in-A B92 ....109 B6
Lichfield WS14 ....9 B6
Solihull B91 ....107 E3
Walsall WS2 ....28 E2
Water Orton B46 ....59 C3
West Bromwich B71 ....53 D8
Wolverhampton WV10 ....11 B2
Marsh Lane Par WV10 ....11 C2
Marsh St WS2 ....28 E2
Marsh The WS10 ....41 E3
Marsh Way B61 ....120 F1
Marshall Cl WS9 ....30 B4
Marshall Gr B44 ....55 F7
Marshall Ho
4 Walsall WS2 ....42 C8
8 West Bromwich B71 ....42 F1
Marshall Lake Rd B90 ......106 D1
Marshall Rd Bedworth CV7 .95 F8
Oldbury B68 ....64 C1
Willenhall WV13 ....26 D1
Marshall St
Birmingham B1 ....164 B1
Smethwick B67 ....64 D7
Tamworth B77 ....21 E5
Marshalls Ind Est CV2 ....39 C7
Marsham Cl CV34 ....161 B8
Marsham Court Rd B91 .106 F7
Marsham Rd B14 ....104 F3
Marshbrook Cl
Coventry CV2 ....96 E3
Sutton Coldfield B24 ....57 E4
Marshbrook Rd B24 ....57 D4
Marshdale Ave CV6 ....95 E3
Marshfield B90 ....126 B5
Marshfield Cl B98 ....154 B7
Marshfield Dr CV4 ....132 D2
Marshfield Gdns B24 ....56 F2
Marshland Way WS2 ....27 E1
Marshmont Way B23 ....56 D8
Marshwood Cl 2 WS11 ....2 A2
Marshwood Croft B62 ....84 A3
Marsland Cl B17 ....85 B5
Marsland Rd B92 ....106 E8
Marston Ave WS10 ....41 C6
Marston Cl
Royal Leamington Spa
CV32 ....157 B2
Stourbridge DY8 ....80 D4
Marston Croft B37 ....89 F7
Marston Dr B37 ....70 A5
Marston Gr B43 ....54 C8
Marston Green Jun & Inf
Schs B37 ....90 A7
Marston Green Sta B37 ......89 F7
Marston Ind Est WV2 ....39 C7
Marston La
Bedworth CV12 ....78 D5
Nuneaton CV11 ....78 E8
Wishaw B76 ....48 E1
Marston Rd
Birmingham B29 ....102 F8
Cannock WS12 ....1 C6
Dudley DY1 ....61 E8
Sutton Coldfield B73 ....57 A7
Wolverhampton WV2 ....39 C7
Walsall WS13 ....3 C2
Tamworth B79 ....27 C2
Market Cl DY35 ....68 D6
Martham Dr WV6 ....24 B2
Martin Cl Birmingham B26 .88 D6
Bromsgrove B61 ....136 E1
Coventry CV5 ....111 E4
Dudley WV14 ....51 D7
Martin Croft WS13 ....3 A1
Martin Dr WV12 ....27 C5

Martin Hill St DY2 ....62 C8
Martin Rd Bilston WV14 ....40 F3
Tipton DY4 ....52 A4
Walsall WS5 ....43 C8
Martin Rise B37 ....89 F8
Martin St WV4 ....39 F5
Martindale 1 ....2 A2
Martindale Rd CV7 ....96 C8
Martindale Trad Est WS11 ..2 A2
Martindale Wlk DY5 ....81 B6
Martineau Sq B2 ....164 C2
Martineau Twr B19 ....66 D5
Martineau Way B2 ....164 C2
Martingale Cl
4 Bromsgrove B60 ....150 E6
Walsall WS5 ....42 F4
Martinique Sq CV34 ....160 D6
Martins Rd CV12 ....77 E1
Martlesham Sq B35 ....58 A4
Martley Cl B98 ....159 B7
Martley Croft
Birmingham B32 ....84 E4
Solihull B91 ....127 B8
Martley Ct DY9 ....81 C4
Martley Dr DY9 ....81 C4
Martley Rd Oldbury B69 ......63 D5
Walsall WS4 ....15 C2
Marton Ave WS7 ....7 A8
Marton Cl B7 ....67 B6
Martyrs' Cl The CV3 ....133 D8
Marwood Cl CV11 ....78 F2
Marwood Croft B74 ....31 A2
Mary Ann St
Birmingham B3 ....164 B4
Wolverhampton WV1 ....163 D2
Mary Elliot Specl Sch
WS2 ....28 E4
Mary Herbert St CV3 ....133 D7
Mary Macarthur Dr B64 .62 C1
Mary Rd
Birmingham, Handsworth
B21 ....65 E7
Birmingham, Stechford B33 .68 D3
Tipton B69 ....63 C8
West Bromwich B70 ....53 D1
Mary Slessor St CV3 ....134 D7
Mary St
Birmingham, Balsall Heath
B12 ....86 E5
Birmingham, Brookfields
B3 ....164 A4
Cannock WS12 ....2 B7
Walsall WS2 ....28 D3
Mary Vale Rd B30 ....103 F6
Maryland Ave B34 ....68 F5
Maryland Cl LE9 ....71 F6
Maryland Dr B31 ....103 B5
Maryland Rd DY5 ....81 F7
Marylebone Cl DY8 ....81 A7
Marystow Cl CV5 ....112 B8
Maryvale Ct Lichfield WS14 .9 D7
2 Walsall WS1 ....42 E8
Maryvale RC Prim Sch
B44 ....44 E1
Marywell Cl B32 ....102 B7
Masefield Ave Dudley DY1 .51 C7
Warwick CV34 ....160 C4
Masefield Cl Bilston WV14 ..40 F2
Lichfield WS14 ....9 B6
Masefield Dr B79 ....21 A7
Masefield Gdns 1 DY10 .117 B6
Masefield Gr WS11 ....1 E4
Masefield Rd Dudley DY3 ...50 A4
Walsall WS3 ....28 E1
Wolverhampton WV10 ....12 A1
Masefield Rise B62 ....83 D3
Masefield Sq B31 ....103 C4
Masham Cl B33 ....68 E3
Mashie Gdns B38 ....103 D1
Maslen Pl B63 ....83 B3
Maslin Dr WV14 ....40 A1
Mason Ave CV32 ....157 C3
Mason Cl B97 ....158 D7
Mason Cotts B24 ....57 B5
Mason Cres WV4 ....38 E5
Mason Ct LE10 ....75 B8
Mason La B94 ....125 F1
Mason Rd Birmingham B24 .57 A4
Coventry CV6 ....95 F1
Kidderminster DY11 ....116 C6
Redditch B97 ....158 D8
Walsall WS2 ....28 B5
Mason St Dudley WV14 ....51 B7
West Bromwich B70 ....53 B4
Wolverhampton WV2 ....39 C7
Mason's Way B92 ....88 E2
Masonleys Rd B31 ....102 D3
Masons Cl B63 ....82 C6
Masons Way B92 ....88 E2
Massbrook Gr WV10 ....25 F6
Massbrook Rd WV10 ....25 F6
Masser Rd CV6 ....95 D4
Masshouse Circus
Queensway B4 ....164 C3
Masshouse La
Birmingham, Digbeth B5 ......164 D3
Birmingham, King's Norton
B38 ....103 D1
Masters La B62 ....63 E1
Masters Rd CV31 ....162 A4
Matchborough Ctr B98 .....154 E1
Matchborough Way
B98 ....154 E1
Matchlock Cl B74 ....44 E7
Matfen Ave B73 ....45 F2
Math Mdw B32 ....84 F5
Mathe Croft CV31 ....162 C5
Matlock Cl Dudley DY2 ....62 D3

Matlock CI continued
Walsall WS3 . . . . .14 C3
Matlock Dr WV14 . . . . .2 A4
Matlock Rd
Birmingham B11 . . . . .87 F3
Coventry CV1 . . . . .113 D6
Walsall WS3 . . . . .14 C3
Matlock Villas 2 B12 . . . . . . .87 B5
Matterson Rd CV6 . . . . .113 A5
Matthew Boulton Coll
B15 .86 D8
Matthew Boulton Com Prim
Sch B21 . . . . .65 E7
Matthew La (Road 3)
DY10 . . . . .116 F1
Matthews CI B65 . . . . .63 B1
Matthews Wlk WS13 . . . . .3 A2
Mattox Rd WV11 . . . . .26 D6
Matty Rd B68 . . . . .64 C4
Maud Rd Water Orton B46 .59 D3
West Bromwich B70 . . . . . . .53 C1
Maudslay Rd CV5 . . . . .112 E2
Maughan St
Brierley Hill DY5 . . . . .82 A8
Dudley DY1 . . . . .51 B1
Maund CI B60 . . . . .150 E7
Maureen CI CV4 . . . . .111 C1
Maurice Gr WV10 . . . . .26 A6
Maurice Mead Ct 12
CV31 . . . . .162 A6
Maurice Rd
Birmingham B14 . . . . .104 C5
Smethwick B67 . . . . .64 E2
Mavis Gdns B68 . . . . .84 B8
Mavis Rd
Birmingham B31 . . . . .102 E1
Cannock WS12 . . . . .2 B7
Mavor Dr CV12 . . . . .77 D1
Maw St WS1 . . . . .42 F6
Mawgan Dr WV14 . . . . .9 D6
Mawnan CI CV7 . . . . .96 B8
Max Rd Birmingham B32 . . . .84 D5
Coventry CV6 . . . . .112 F5
Maxholm Rd B74 . . . . .44 E8
Maxstoke CI
Birmingham B32 . . . . .102 A7
Meriden CV7 . . . . .92 B1
Redditch B98 . . . . .154 D1
Sutton Coldfield B73 . . . . . .45 E2
Tamworth B77 . . . . .35 C4
Walsall WS3 . . . . .14 A3
Maxstoke Croft B90 . . . . . .126 C8
Maxstoke Gdns CV31 . . . . .161 F6
Maxstoke La CV7 . . . . .92 B2
Maxstoke Rd B73 . . . . .45 E1
Maxstoke St B9 . . . . .67 B2
Maxted Rd B23 . . . . .56 C7
Maxtock Ave WS13 . . . . .9 A6
Maxwell Ave B20 . . . . .55 B1
Maxwell CI WS14 . . . . .9 C7
Maxwell Ct B33 . . . . .68 F3
Maxwell Rd WV2 . . . . .163 C1
May Ave B12 . . . . .87 A5
May Farm CI B47 . . . . .125 A6
May La Birmingham B14 . . . .104 F5
Hollywood B47 . . . . .125 A7
May St Coventry CV6 . . . . . .113 E8
Walsall WS3 . . . . .28 D6
May Tree Gr B20 . . . . .54 F3
May Trees B47 . . . . .124 F6
Mayall Dr B75 . . . . .32 D4
Mayama Rd B78 . . . . .34 F8
Maybank B9 . . . . .67 F3
Maybank CI WS14 . . . . .9 D8
Maybank PI B44 . . . . .55 E6
Maybank Rd DY2 . . . . .62 C3
Mayberry CI B14 . . . . .105 B2
Maybridge Dr B91 . . . . .127 B8
Maybrook Ind Est WS8 . . . .15 E5
Maybrook Rd
Brownhills WS8 . . . . .15 F5
Sutton Coldfield B76 . . . . . .58 A5
Maybush Gdns WV10 . . . . . .11 C1
Maycock Rd CV6 . . . . .113 D7
Maycroft CI WS12 . . . . .1 C7
Maydene Croft B12 . . . . . . .86 F6
Mayfair Birmingham B37 . . .69 F5
Stourbridge DY9 . . . . .81 D2
Mayfair CI Birmingham B44 .56 B7
Dudley DY1 . . . . .51 A2
Mayfair Dr
Drayton Bassett B78 . . . . . . .35 A7
Kingswinford DY6 . . . . .60 C7
Mayfair Gdns Tipton DY4 .52 A4
Wolverhampton WV3 . . . . . .24 D2
Mayfield B77 . . . . .36 C8
Mayfield Ave B29 . . . . .86 B2
Mayfield CI
Bedworth CV12 . . . . .78 B3
Catshill B61 . . . . .120 F1
Kidderminster DY11 . . . . . . .116 A8
8 Royal Leamington Spa
CV31 . . . . .162 C6
Solihull B91 . . . . .107 C1
Mayfield Cres B65 . . . . .63 A3
Mayfield Ct B13 . . . . .87 A2
Mayfield Dr CV8 . . . . .148 C4
Mayfield Prep Sch WS1 .43 A8
Mayfield Rd
Birmingham, Acock's Green
B11 .88 A3
Birmingham, Lozells B19 . . . .66 C8
Birmingham, Moseley B13 . . .87 A3
Birmingham, Stirchley B30 .104 A6
Coventry CV5 . . . . .113 A1
Dudley DY1 . . . . .63 F1
Halesowen B62 . . . . .83 E3
Halesowen, Hasbury B63 . . .82 E2

Mayfield Rd continued
Nuneaton CV11 . . . . .73 E2
Sutton Coldfield, Boldmere
B73 .46 A2
Sutton Coldfield, Streetly
WV4 .44 F8
Wolverhampton WV4 . . . . . . .26 B1
Mayfield Sch B19 . . . . .66 C6
Mayfield Specl Sch B19 .66 C8
Mayfield The WV1 . . . . .26 B1
Mayfields The B98 . . . . .153 E2
Mayflower CI B19 . . . . .66 D6
Mayflower Dr
Brierley Hill DY5 . . . . .61 A7
Coventry CV2 . . . . .114 A8
Mayford Gr B13 . . . . .105 B6
Maygrove Rd DY6 . . . . .60 C7
Mayhurst CI
Hollywood B47 . . . . .125 C6
Tipton DY4 . . . . .52 A8
Mayhurst Rd B47 . . . . .125 B6
Mayland Dr B74 . . . . .45 A5
Mayland Rd B16 . . . . .65 C2
Maynard Ave
Bedworth CV12 . . . . .95 D8
Stourbridge DY8 . . . . .80 D3
Warwick CV34 . . . . .161 A7
Mayo Dr CV8 . . . . .148 A4
Mayor's Croft CV4 . . . . . . .132 B7
Mayou Ct WS3 . . . . .15 A4
Maypole CI B64 . . . . .82 B8
Maypole Ct WV5 . . . . .49 A6
Maypole Dr DY8 . . . . .80 E5
Maypole Fields B63 . . . . . . .82 A7
Maypole Gr B14 . . . . .105 B2
Maypole Hill B63 . . . . .82 A7
Maypole La B14 . . . . .105 A2
Maypole Rd B68 . . . . .64 B1
Maypole St WV5 . . . . .49 B7
Mayswood Dr WV6 . . . . .23 F1
Mayswood Gr B32 . . . . .84 D4
Mayswood Rd B92 . . . . .89 C2
Maythorn Ave B76 . . . . .58 A6
Maythorn Gdns
Codsall WV8 . . . . .10 A4
Wolverhampton WV6 . . . . . . .24 C3
Maythorn Gr 3 B91 . . . . . . .127 B8
Maytree CI B37 . . . . .70 A2
Maywell Dr B92 . . . . .107 F8
Maywood CI DY6 . . . . .60 B6
McBean Rd WV6 . . . . .24 F4
McCalla Ho WV3 . . . . .25 B1
McConnell CI B60 . . . . .151 B7
McDonnell Dr CV6 . . . . .95 F6
McDougall Rd WS10 . . . . . . .42 C3
McGeough Wlk WS11 . . . . . .2 B5
McGhie St WS12 . . . . .2 A5
McGregor CI 13 B6 . . . . .55 F1
McKean Rd Oldbury B69 . . . .64 A8
West Bromwich B70 . . . . . . .53 C1
Mcken Ct B70 . . . . .53 C1
Mclean Rd WV10 . . . . .11 E3
McMahon Rd CV12 . . . . .95 E8
Meaburn CI B29 . . . . .103 A7
Mead CI WS9 . . . . .30 B6
Mead Cres B9 . . . . .68 B3
Mead Rise B15 . . . . .85 F6
Mead The DY3 . . . . .50 B8
Meadfoot Ave B14 . . . . .104 F3
Meadfoot Dr DY6 . . . . .60 B7
Meadfoot Rd CV3 . . . . .134 E6
Meadow Ave B71 . . . . .53 F8
Meadow Brook Rd B31 . . .102 F5
Meadow CI Aldridge B74 . . .30 F2
Ansty CV7 . . . . .97 D3
Birmingham B17 . . . . .85 B1
Hockley Heath B94 . . . . . . .143 C6
Royal Leamington Spa
CV32 . . . . .157 C4
Walsall WS4 . . . . .29 C8
Meadow Croft
Cannock WS12 . . . . .1 C4
Hagley DY9 . . . . .98 F4
Perton WV6 . . . . .23 D3
Wythall B47 . . . . .125 A3
Meadow Ct
Birmingham B17 . . . . .85 A6
Nuneaton CV11 . . . . .73 B4
Meadow Dr
Hampton-in-A B92 . . . . .109 B7
Hinckley LE10 . . . . .76 A7
Meadow Gr
Great Wyrley WS6 . . . . .5 A2
Solihull B92 . . . . .88 D1
Meadow Grange Dr
WV12 . . . . .27 B7
Meadow Green Prim Sch
B47 .125 A3
Meadow Hill CI DY11 . . . . .116 A5
Meadow Hill Dr 5 B61 . . . . .1 A8
Meadow Hill Rd B38 . . . . . .103 E2
Meadow Ho 5 CV1 . . . . . . .113 B3
Meadow La
Alvechurch B48 . . . . .139 B6
Coven Heath WV10 . . . . .11 C6
Lapworth B94 . . . . .144 D3
Wednesfield WV12 . . . . .27 A5
Wolverhampton WV14 . . . . . .40 B2
Wombourne WV5 . . . . .49 B8
Meadow Lark CI WS12 . . . . .2 B4
Meadow Mills Ind Est
DY10 . . . . .116 E5
Meadow Pk B79 . . . . .20 F5
Meadow Pleck La B90 . . . .126 A8
Meadow Rd Aldridge WS9 . . .30 B7
Birmingham, Harborne B17 . .65 B1
Birmingham, Quinton B32 . . .84 A6

Meadow Rd continued
Catshill B61 . . . . .136 F8
Coventry CV6 . . . . .95 B4
Dudley DY1 . . . . .51 B3
Halesowen B62 . . . . .83 C8
Nuneaton CV10 . . . . .72 A8
Oldbury B68 . . . . .64 B3
Smethwick B67 . . . . .65 A4
Tamworth B78 . . . . .20 E3
Warwick CV34 . . . . .161 A7
Wolverhampton WV3 . . . . . . .38 D8
Wythall B47 . . . . .125 A3
Meadow Rise
Balsall Common CV7 . . . . . .130 C7
Birmingham B30 . . . . .103 D7
Meadow St Blackheath B64 .82 F8
Coventry CV1 . . . . .165 A2
Nuneaton CV11 . . . . .73 B5
Tamworth B77 . . . . .21 C3
1 Wolverhampton WV1 . . .25 B2
Meadow Vale WV8 . . . . .10 B2
Meadow View
Birmingham B13 . . . . .105 C8
Burntwood WS7 . . . . .7 D6
Sedgley DY3 . . . . .39 C1
Meadow View JMI Sch
B43 .44 D5
Meadow View Terr WV6 . .24 E4
Meadow Way
Cannock WS12 . . . . .2 C1
Stourbridge DY8 . . . . .60 C2
Meadow Wlk
Birmingham B14 . . . . .104 E1
Blackheath B64 . . . . .82 D8
Meadowbank Grange WS6 .4 E4
Meadowbrook Gdns WV8 .10 B4
Meadowbrook Rd
Halesowen B63 . . . . .82 E3
Lichfield WS13 . . . . .3 B3
Meadowcroft CI CV4 . . . . .131 F8
Meadowfield Rd B45 . . . . . .122 A6
Meadowfields CI DY8 . . . . . .61 C3
Meadowhill Cres B98 . . . . .153 F5
Meadowhill Dr DY8 . . . . .60 E2
Meadowhill Rd B98 . . . . . . .153 F5
Meadowlands Dr WS4 . . . . .15 D1
Meadowpark Rd DY8 . . . . . .80 D8
Meadows Fst Sch B61 . . . .137 A3
Meadows Gr WV8 . . . . .10 A4
Meadows Prim Sch The
B31 .102 E1
Meadows Sch The CV4 . . .111 E3
Meadows The
Aldridge WS9 . . . . .29 E5
Hinckley LE10 . . . . .76 A7
Leek Wootton CV35 . . . . . . .156 A7
Stourbridge DY9 . . . . .99 B7
Studley B80 . . . . .159 E4
Wolverhampton WV8 . . . . . . .10 B2
Meadowside CI B43 . . . . .43 E1
Meadowside Rd B74 . . . . . . .31 F3
Meadowsweet Ave B38 . .123 F8
Meadowsweet Way
Cannock WS12 . . . . .2 E4
Kingswinford DY6 . . . . .61 A6
Meadowvale Rd B60 . . . . . .137 C6
Meadthorpe Rd B44 . . . . . . .55 D8
Meadvale Rd B45 . . . . .122 B6
Meadway Birmingham B33 . .68 F1
Coventry CV2 . . . . .114 B6
Meadway CI WS12 . . . . .2 C3
Meadway N CV2 . . . . .114 B6
Meadway St WS7 . . . . .7 A5
Meadway The
Hinckley LE10 . . . . .75 F7
Redditch B97 . . . . .153 C1
Wolverhampton WV6 . . . . . . .24 A5
Meadwood Ind Est WV4 .40 E5
Mears CI B23 . . . . .56 D8
Mears Coppice DY5 . . . . . . .81 E6
Mears Dr B33 . . . . .68 D4
Mearse CI B18 . . . . .66 A5
Mearse La
Barnt Green B45 . . . . .122 A1
Belbroughton DY9 . . . . .120 B6
Mease Ave WS7 . . . . .7 D6
Mease Croft 2 B9 . . . . .67 B2
Measham Gr B26 . . . . .88 E5
Measham Way WV11 . . . . . .26 F7
Meaton Gr B32 . . . . .102 B8
Medcroft Ave B20 . . . . .54 E4
Medici Rd B60 . . . . .137 C2
Medina B77 . . . . .21 E1
Medina CI WV10 . . . . .11 F4
Medina Rd
Birmingham B11 . . . . .87 E4
Coventry CV6 . . . . .95 E1
Medina Way DY6 . . . . .60 C6
Medland Ave CV3 . . . . .132 F5
Medley Gdns DY4 . . . . .52 E4
Medley Gr CV31 . . . . .161 F3
Medley Rd B11 . . . . .87 D5
Medlicott Rd B11 . . . . .87 C6
Medway B77 . . . . .21 E1
Medway CI DY5 . . . . .81 A6
Medway Croft B36 . . . . .69 F7
Medway Ct B73 . . . . .46 B5
Medway Gr B38 . . . . .123 E8
Medway Rd WS8 . . . . .6 C2
Medway Twr B7 . . . . .67 B5
Medway Wlk WS8 . . . . .6 C2
Medwin Gr B23 . . . . .56 D7
Meer End B38 . . . . .123 D7
Meer End Rd CV8 . . . . .130 D1
Meerash La WS7 . . . . .7 A2
Meerhill Ave B90 . . . . .127 A6
Meeting Ho The WS10 . . . .41 E3
Meeting House La
Balsall Common CV7 . . . . . .130 C6

Meeting House La continued
Birmingham B31 . . . . .103 A4
Meeting La DY5 . . . . .61 B1
Meeting Lane Ind Est
DY5 .61 B1
Meeting St Dudley DY2 . . . . .62 C5
Tipton DY4 . . . . .52 D5
Wednesbury WS10 . . . . .41 E3
Meg La WS7 . . . . .7 C8
Meir Rd B98 . . . . .159 C8
Melbourne Ave
Birmingham, Newtown B19 .66 C6
Birmingham, Selly Oak B66 .65 B7
Bromsgrove B61 . . . . .136 E4
Melbourne CI
Bromsgrove B61 . . . . .136 E3
Kingswinford DY6 . . . . .60 E4
Nuneaton CV11 . . . . .78 E8
West Bromwich B70 . . . . . . .53 A7
Melbourne Cres WS12 . . . . . .2 F2
Melbourne Ct 13 CV12 . . . .77 F2
Melbourne Gdns WS5 . . . . .43 B6
Melbourne Ho B34 . . . . .69 E6
Melbourne Rd
Bromsgrove B61 . . . . .136 E3
Cannock WS12 . . . . .2 F2
Coventry CV5 . . . . .113 A2
Halesowen B63 . . . . .83 B5
Smethwick B66 . . . . .65 B7
Melbourne St WV2 . . . . .163 C2
Melbury CI WV3 . . . . .25 A1
Melbury Gr B14 . . . . .105 A3
Melbury Gr B14 . . . . .104 E5
Melbury Way 1 WS11 . . . . .1 F2
Melchester Wlk 2 WS11 . .1 F2
Melchett Rd B30 . . . . .104 A4
Melcote Gr B44 . . . . .55 F6
Meldon Dr WV14 . . . . .41 A2
Meldrum Rd CV10 . . . . .72 D4
Melen St B97 . . . . .153 D4
Melford B79 . . . . .20 E6
Melford CI DY3 . . . . .39 C2
Melford Hall Rd B91 . . . . . .106 F7
Melford CI Coventry CV3 . .114 F2
Nuneaton CV10 . . . . .72 C5
Melfort Gr B14 . . . . .105 A3
Melfort Gr B14 . . . . .105 A3
Melhsam CI B14 . . . . .105 A3
Mell Sq B91 . . . . .107 C4
Mellis Gr B23 . . . . .56 A5
Mellish Ct WS4 . . . . .29 A3
Mellish Dr WS4 . . . . .29 B3
Mellish Rd WS4 . . . . .29 B3
Mellor Dr B74 . . . . .31 E3
Mellors CI B17 . . . . .85 A4
Mellowdew Rd
Coventry CV2 . . . . .114 C4
Stourbridge DY8 . . . . .80 F8
Mellowship Rd CV5 . . . . . . .111 D5
Mellwaters B77 . . . . .36 C8
Melmerby B77 . . . . .36 C8
Melplash Ave B91 . . . . .107 A4
Melrose Ave
Bedworth CV12 . . . . .95 D8
Birmingham, Sparkbrook
B12 .87 A6
Birmingham, Sparkhill B11 . .87 C6
Stourbridge DY8 . . . . .81 A2
Sutton Coldfield B73 . . . . . .45 E2
West Bromwich B71 . . . . . . .42 D1
Melrose CI
Birmingham B38 . . . . .103 F1
Hinckley LE10 . . . . .75 B8
Melrose Dr WS4 . . . . .29 A3
Melrose Dr Cannock WS12 . . .1 F7
Perton WV6 . . . . .23 E4
Melrose Gr B19 . . . . .66 B7
Melrose PI B66 . . . . .64 D8
Melrose Rd B20 . . . . .55 D1
Melstock CI DY4 . . . . .51 D5
Melstock Rd B14 . . . . .104 D7
Melton Ave B92 . . . . .89 B4
Melton Dr B15 . . . . .86 B7
Melton Rd
Birmingham B14 . . . . .104 F8
Royal Leamington Spa
CV32 . . . . .157 B4
Melverley Gr B44 . . . . .55 F7
Melverton Ave WV10 . . . . . .25 E8
Melville CI CV7 . . . . .96 A8
Melville Hall 1 B16 . . . . . . .65 D1
Melville Rd
Birmingham B16 . . . . .65 D1
Coventry CV1 . . . . .113 A3
Redditch B80 . . . . .87 B6
Memorial CI WV13 . . . . .27 A2
Memory La
Darlaston WS10 . . . . .41 D8
Wolverhampton WV11 . . . . . .26 B5
Menai CI WV12 . . . . .27 C6
Menai Wlk B37 . . . . .70 B4
Mendip Ave B8 . . . . .67 E5
Mendip CI
Bromsgrove B61 . . . . .137 A5
Dudley DY3 . . . . .50 D3
Wolverhampton WV2 . . . . . . .39 F7
Mendip Dr CV10 . . . . .72 B3
Mendip Ho B98 . . . . .154 D6
Mendip Rd Birmingham B8 .67 E5
Halesowen B63 . . . . .82 C6
Stourbridge DY8 . . . . .81 B6
Mendip Way B77 . . . . .22 C4
Menin Cres B13 . . . . .105 B7
Menin Rd
Birmingham B13 . . . . .105 B8
Tipton DY4 . . . . .51 D5
Mentone Ct B20 . . . . .54 F3
Menzies High Sch B71 . . . .53 C8
Meon Gr Birmingham B33 . . .89 B8

Meon Gr continued
Perton WV6 . . . . .23 F4
Meon Rise DY9 . . . . .81 C3
Meon Way WV11 . . . . .26 F7
Meranti CI WV12 . . . . .27 C8
Mercer Ave
Coventry CV2 . . . . .114 A5
Water Orton B46 . . . . .59 A3
Mercer Gr WV11 . . . . .26 D7
Mercers Mdw CV7 . . . . .95 A6
Merchants Ct 5 CV32 . . . .157 A1
Merchants Way WS9 . . . . . . .30 A7
Mercia Ave CV8 . . . . .147 F4
Mercia Bsns Village
CV4 .131 F6
Mercia CI
Bromsgrove B60 . . . . .150 F7
Tamworth B79 . . . . .20 E7
Mercia Dr WV6 . . . . .23 E5
Mercia Ho CV1 . . . . .165 B3
Mercia Way CV34 . . . . .161 B7
Mercian CI 8 WS14 . . . . .9 C7
Mercian PI B77 . . . . .22 A3
Mercian Way B77 . . . . .22 B3
Mercot CI B98 . . . . .159 A6
Mercury Ct B77 . . . . .22 B3
Mercury Rd WS11 . . . . .2 A5
Mere Ave B35 . . . . .58 B3
Mere CI WV12 . . . . .27 A5
Mere Croft WS11 . . . . .5 F4
Mere Dr B75 . . . . .32 B2
Mere Green CI B75 . . . . .32 C2
Mere Green Comb Sch
B75 .32 B2
Mere Green Rd B75 . . . . . . .32 C2
Mere Oak Rd WV6 . . . . .23 E5
Mere Pool Rd B75 . . . . .32 E2
Mere Rd Birmingham B23 . . .56 D3
Stourbridge DY8 . . . . .80 E3
Mere View WS4 . . . . .29 C8
Merecote Rd B92 . . . . .106 D7
Meredith Gn DY11 . . . . .116 A1
Meredith Pool CI B18 . . . . . .65 F6
Meredith Rd
Coventry CV2 . . . . .114 D2
Dudley DY3 . . . . .50 A5
Wolverhampton WV11 . . . . . .26 C8
Meredith St B64 . . . . .62 D1
Meres Rd B63 . . . . .82 C5
Mereside Way B92 . . . . . . .106 E8
Merevale Ave
Hinckley LE10 . . . . .75 C7
Nuneaton CV11 . . . . .73 A4
Merevale CI Hinckley LE10 .75 C7
Redditch B98 . . . . .159 D8
Merevale Ct CV11 . . . . .73 A4
Merevale Rd B92 . . . . .89 B2
Merganser B77 . . . . .36 A6
Merganser Way WV10 . . . .117 B3
Meriden Ave DY8 . . . . .80 D6
Meriden Bsns Pk CV5 . . . .111 B8
Meriden CE Prim Sch
CV7 .92 C1
Meriden CI
Birmingham B25 . . . . .88 B7
Cannock WS11 . . . . .4 B8
Stourbridge DY8 . . . . .80 D6
Meriden Cr 3 WV4 . . . . .39 F4
Meriden Dr B37 . . . . .70 A6
Meriden Hill CV7 . . . . .110 E8
Meriden Rd
Berkswell CV7 . . . . .110 C4
Corley CV7 . . . . .93 B7
Hampton-in-A B92 . . . . .109 C7
Wolverhampton WV10 . . . . . .25 A8
Meriden Rise B92 . . . . .89 D3
Meriden St
Birmingham B5 . . . . .164 D2
Meridian PI B60 . . . . .137 A1
Merino Ave B31 . . . . .123 A8
Merlin CI Birmingham B35 . .58 A3
Cannock WS11 . . . . .1 C2
Dudley DY1 . . . . .61 F8
Tamworth B77 . . . . .36 A6
Merlin Dr DY10 . . . . .117 B3
Merlin Gr B26 . . . . .89 B5
Merrick CI B63 . . . . .82 D2
Merrick Ct LE10 . . . . .75 F5
Merrick Rd WV11 . . . . .27 A6
Merridale Ave WV3 . . . . .24 F2
Merridale Cres WV3 . . . . . . .25 A2
Merridale Ct WV3 . . . . .24 F1
Merridale Gdns WV3 . . . . . .25 A2
Merridale Gr WV3 . . . . .24 E1
Merridale Jun & Inf Sch
WV3 .25 A1
Merridale La WV3 . . . . .25 A2
Merridale Rd WV3 . . . . .25 A2
Merridale St WV3 . . . . .163 A2
Merridale St W WV3 . . . . . .39 A8
Merriemont Dr B45 . . . . . . .122 A1
Merrifield Gdns LE10 . . . . . .75 E5
Merrill CI WS6 . . . . .4 C2
Merrill Gdns B60 . . . . .121 D2
Merrills Hall Island
WV11 . . . . .26 D4
Merrington CI 5 B91 . . . . .127 C8
Merrion's CI B43 . . . . .43 F4
Merrishaw Rd B31 . . . . .123 A8
Merritt's Brook La B31 . . .102 E5
Merritts Brook CI B29 . . . .103 A5
Merritts Hill B31 . . . . .102 E6

Merrivale Rd
Coventry CV5 ....112 E3
Halesowen B62 ....83 F8
Smethwick B66 ....63 A2
Merry Hill DY5 ....61 F2
Merry Hill Ctr DY5 ....61 F3
Merryfield CI B92 ......107 D7
Merryfield Gr B17 ......85 C4
Merryfield Rd DY1 ......50 E1
Merryfields Way CV2 .....96 F1
Merryhill Dr B18 ....65 F6
Merryhills Ent Pk WV10 ..25 F5
Merse Rd B98 ....154 E6
Mersey Gr B38 ....123 E8
Mersey Rd
Bulkington CV12 ....79 A3
Walsall WS3 ....14 E1
Merstal Dr B92 ....107 F7
Merstone CI WV14 ......40 C6
Merstone Sch B37 ......70 A1
Merstowe CI B27 ....88 B3
Merton CI
Kidderminster DY10 ......117 B7
Oldbury B68 ....64 B2
Merton Ct WS7 ....6 F5
Merton Ho B37 ....69 F2
Merton Rd B13 ....87 B3
Mervyn Pl WV14 ....41 A3
Mervyn Rd Bilston WV14 ..41 A3
Birmingham B21 ....54 E1
Meryhurst Rd WS10 .....42 B5
Merynton Ave CV4 .....132 E5
Meschines St CV3 ......133 D6
Mesnes Gn WS14 ....9 C7
Messenger La B70 ......53 D3
Messenger Rd B66 ......65 B6
Mesty Croft Prim Sch
WS10 ....41 F3
Metalloys Ind Est B76 ...58 B5
Metcalf CI WS7 ....7 C8
Metcalfe CI WS12 ....2 C6
Metchley Croft B90 ....126 F6
Metchley Ct B17 ....85 D4
Metchley Dr B17 ....85 D5
Metchley La B17 ....85 D5
Metchley Park Rd B15 ...85 E4
Metfield CI B79 ....21 C8
Metfield Croft
Birmingham B17 ....85 D4
Kingswinford DY6 ....60 F6
Metlin Gr B33 ....69 E3
Metric WIk B67 ....65 A5
Metro Way B66 ....65 C7
Mews Rd CV32 ....156 E1
Mews The Bedworth CV12 ..78 B2
Birmingham B27 ....88 B3
Blackheath B65 ....63 B2
Cannock WS11 ....1 D1
Kenilworth CV8 ....147 E3
Meynell Ho B20 ....54 F3
Meyrick Rd B70 ....53 A6
Meyrick WIk B16 ....65 F1
Miall Park Rd B91 .....106 E5
Miall Rd B28 ....106 A4
Mica CI B77 ....22 B2
Michael Blanning Gdns
B93 ....127 E3
Michael Ct B5 ....86 D6
Michael Dr B15 ....86 C6
Michael Drayton Jun Sch
CV10 ....72 A8
Michael Rd
Darlaston WS10 ....41 B7
Smethwick B67 ....64 E6
Michaelmas Rd CV3 ....165 B1
Michaelwood CI B97 ....152 F2
Michel Ho CV1 ....165 C4
Michell CI CV3 ....134 B8
Michelle CI B13 ....105 A5
Michigan CI WS11 ....2 B2
Mickle Mdw B46 ....59 B3
Micklehill Dr B90 .....126 B8
Mickleover Rd B8 ....68 C5
Mickleton B77 ....36 C8
Mickleton Ave B33 ......89 C8
Mickleton CI B98 ......158 E7
Mickleton Rd
Coventry CV5 ....133 A8
Solihull B92 ....106 D8
Mickley Ave WV10 ....25 E5
Midacre WV13 ....27 A1
Middelburg CI CV11 ......74 A1
Middle Acre Rd B32 .....84 E2
Middle Ave WV13 ....40 A8
Middle Bickenhill La B92 ..91 A4
Middle Cres WS3 ....29 A7
Middle Cross WV1 ......163 D3
Middle Dr B45 ....122 D4
Middle Entry B79 ....21 B4
Middle Field Rd B31 ....103 D2
Middle Gdns WV13 ....27 B2
Middle House Dr B60 ...121 D1
Middle La
Wolverhampton WV9 ....11 A5
Wythall B38 ....124 D5
Middle Leaford B34 ......69 A5
Middle Leasowe B12 .....84 D4
Middle Meadow Ave B32 ..84 C5
Middle Park CI B29 ....103 B8
Middle Park Rd B29 ....103 C8
Middle Piece Dr B97 ...153 B1
Middle Rd
Upper Bentley B60 ......152 A2
Wildmoor B61 ....120 F4

Middle Ride CV3 ....134 E5
Middle Vauxhall 4 WV1 ..25 A2
Middleborough Rd CV1 ..165 A4
Middlecotes CV4 ....112 B1
Middlefield WV8 ....10 E2
Middlefield Ave
Halesowen B62 ....63 F1
Knowle B93 ....128 B4
Middlefield CI
Halesowen B62 ....63 F1
Hinckley LE10 ....71 D2
Middlefield Ct LE10 .....71 D2
Middlefield Dr CV3 .....115 B1
Middlefield Gdns B62 ....83 E8
Middlefield Ho B14 ....104 F3
Middlefield La Hagley DY9 ..99 B6
Hinckley LE10 ....71 D3
Middlefield PI LE10 .....71 D3
Middlefield Rd
Bromsgrove B60 ....151 B7
Tipton B69 ....63 A8
Middlefield Dr CV3 .....115 A1
Middlefield Rd B31 .....115 A1
Middlehouse La B97 ....153 E6
Middlemarch Bsns Pk
CV3 ....134 C2
Middlemarch Rd
Coventry CV6 ....113 C7
Nuneaton CV10 ....73 C1
Middlemarch Sch CV10 ..73 B1
Middlemist Gr B43 ......54 F6
Middlemore Bsns Pk
WS9 ....29 C6
Middlemore CI B80 ....159 D3
Middlemore Ind Est B66 ..65 B8
Middlemore La WS9 ......30 A6
Middlemore La W WS9 ...29 C6
Middlemore Rd
Birmingham B31 ....103 B3
Smethwick B66 ....65 B8
Middlepark Rd DY1 ......61 F8
Middlesmoor B77 ....36 C8
Middleton CI
Redditch B98 ....154 F2
Walsall WS5 ....42 F5
Middleton Gdns B30 ....103 D4
Middleton Grange B31 ..103 C4
Middleton Hall ....
* Middleton B78 ....34 E1
Middleton Hall Rd B30 ..103 C4
Middleton La B78 ....47 F6
Middleton Rd
Aldridge B74 ....31 A1
Birmingham B14 ....104 F7
Bromsgrove B61 ....136 F4
Brownhills WS8 ....7 A1
Solihull B90 ....106 A2
Middleton Trad Est
WV13 ....26 E1
Middletown B80 ....159 D1
Middleton La B96,B80 ..159 D1
Middletree Rd B63 ......82 C7
Midfield Dr B75 ....60 C3
Midgley Dr B74 ....32 A2
Midhill Dr B65 ....63 C6
Midhurst Dr WS12 ....2 C7
Midhurst Gr WV6 ....24 C5
Midhurst Rd B30 ....104 B3
Midland Air Mus* CV8 ..134 B3
Midland Dr B72 ....46 C5
Midland Ct B3 ....164 A4
Midland Dr B72 ....
Midland Oak Trad Est
CV6 ....95 E2
Midland Rd
Birmingham B30 ....103 F5
Coventry CV6 ....113 E5
Darlaston WS10 ....41 C8
Huntington WS12 ....1 C5
Nuneaton CV11 ....73 A5
Walsall WS1 ....28 E1
Midland St B9 ....67 C5
Midpoint Park Ind Est
B76 ....58 C5
Midvale Dr B14 ....104 D2
Mikado Rd B60 ....137 D2
Milburn B77 ....36 C8
Milburn Hill Rd CV4 ...132 B6
Milburn Rd B44 ....45 A3
Milby CI CV11 ....73 C3
Milby Dr CV11 ....74 A7
Milby Prim Sch CV11 ....73 F8
Milcote CI B98 ....159 A7
Milcote Dr
Sutton Coldfield B73 .....45 C3
Willenhall WV13 ....26 D1
Milcote Rd
Birmingham B29 ....103 A8
Smethwick B67 ....64 F1
Solihull B91 ....107 A4
Milcote Way DY6 ....60 B7
Mildenhall B79 ....21 C8
Mildenhall Rd B42 ......44 A1
Mildred Rd B64 ....62 E2
Mildred Way B65 ....63 C6
Mile End B94 ....142 A2
Mile Flat DY6 ....60 A1
Mile La CV1 ....165 C11
Mile Oak Cross Rds B78 ..20 C2
Mile Tree La CV2 ....96 F7
Milebrook Gr B32 ......102 B8
Milebush Ave B36 ....58 D1
Miles Gr DY2 ....62 F7

Miles Mdw CV6 ....96 B1
Miles Meadow CI WV12 ..27 C8
Milestone Dr WV6 ......24 A3
Milestone Dr DY9 ....98 F4
Milestone Ho 2 B14 ...113 B2
Milestone La B21 ....65 D8
Milestone Way WV12 .....27 C8
Milfoil CI LE10 ....74 F7
Milford Ave
3 Birmingham B12 ....87 A6
Willenhall WV12 ....27 C5
Milford CI Allesley CV5 ..112 B6
Birmingham B28 ....106 A6
Redditch B97 ....158 C6
Stourbridge DY8 ....60 E3
Milford Copse B17 ......85 B5
Milford Croft B65 ....62 F6
Milford Ct
Birmingham B19 ....164 B5
Royal Leamington Spa
CV31 ....162 A8
Milford Gr B90 ....127 C7
Milford Pl B14 ....104 E8
Milford Rd
Birmingham B17 ....85 B5
Wolverhampton WV2 ....39 C7
Milholme Gr B92 ....107 D8
Milk St B5 ....66 F1
Milking Bank DY1 ....50 E2
Milking Bank Prim Sch
DY1 ....50 E2
Mill Bank DY3 ....50 D4
Mill Bank Mews CV8 ...148 B6
Mill Burn Way 3 B9 .....67 B2
Mill CI Blakedown DY10 ..98 B2
Bromsgrove B60 ....150 F6
Coventry CV2 ....96 B3
Dudley DY3 ....50 D6
Hollywood B47 ....125 A7
Nuneaton CV11 ....73 F1
Wolston CV8 ....135 F3
Mill Cres WS11 ....2 B2
Mill Croft WV14 ....40 C6
Mill Dr B66 ....65 B5
Mill End CV8 ....148 A6
Mill Farm Rd B17 ....85 C3
Mill Gdns
Birmingham B14 ....105 D5
Smethwick B67 ....64 F3
Mill Gn WV10 ....11 D4
Mill Gr WV8 ....10 B3
Mill Green Nature Pk
WS11 ....1 F1
Mill Hill Baginton CV8 ..133 D3
Smethwick B67 ....64 F3
Mill Hill Rd LE10 ....71 C1
Mill Ho B8 ....68 D4
Mill House CI CV32 ....161 D8
Mill House Dr CV32 ....161 C8
Mill House Terr CV32 ..161 C8
Mill La Aldridge WS9 .....30 F7
Bentley Heath B93 ......127 F4
Birmingham, Digbeth B5 ..164 D1
Birmingham, Northfield
B31 ....103 A2
Birmingham, Woodgate Valley
B32 ....84 E2
Blakedown DY10 ....98 B2
Bramcote CV11 ....79 F8
Bromsgrove B61 ....136 F2
Bulkington CV12 ....79 A3
Burntwood WS7 ....7 D3
Chesyln Hay WS11 ....4 D5
Coventry CV3 ....114 F2
Cubbington CV32 ....157 F5
Earlswood B94 ....141 B8
Fazeley B78 ....35 A8
Hanbury B60 ....151 E1
Kidderminster, Blakebrook
DY11 ....116 D6
Kidderminster, Hoobrook
DY10 ....116 F2
Lapworth B94 ....144 C4
Little Aston WS9 ....31 A7
Oldbury B69 ....64 B5
Shenstone WS14 ....18 A6
Solihull B91 ....107 C4
Stonnall WS9,WS14 ......17 A4
Tamworth B79 ....21 C5
Tettenhall Wood WV6 .....24 B1
Walsall WS3,WS4 ....28 F4
Wildmoor B61 ....120 F3
Willenhall WV12 ....27 C5
Wolverhampton WV11 ......26 E1
Wombourne WV5 ....49 B6
Wythall B47,B94 ....125 B1
Mill La Arc B91 ....107 C3
Mill Park Ind Est WS11 ..2 A1
Mill Pk WS11 ....2 A1
Mill Pl WS3 ....28 E4
Mill Pleck B80 ....159 E3
Mill Pool CI DY9 ....99 A5
Mill Pool Ho WV4 ......144 A8
Mill Pool Rd WS12 ....2 B6
Mill Race La Coventry CV6 ..96 B3
Stourbridge DY8 ....81 A6
Mill Rd Blackheath B64 ...82 E7
Brownhills WS8 ....16 A7
Royal Leamington Spa
CV31 ....162 A8
Walsall WS3 ....15 C1
Mill St Barwell LE9 .....71 F5
Bedworth CV12 ....78 B3

Mill St continued
Bilston WV14 ....40 C5
Brierley Hill DY5 ....61 C8
Cannock WS11 ....1 E1
Coventry CV1 ....165 A3
Darlaston WS10 ....41 C6
Halesowen B63 ....82 C7
Kidderminster DY11 .....116 D6
Nuneaton CV11 ....73 C4
Redditch B97 ....153 D4
Royal Leamington Spa
CV31 ....162 A7
Stourbridge DY8 ....60 E7
Sutton Coldfield B72 .....46 C5
Tipton DY4 ....52 D5
Walsall WS2 ....28 E3
Warwick CV34 ....160 F6
West Bromwich B70 ....53 C4
Willenhall WV13 ....27 A3
Mill Stream CI WV8 .....10 B4
Mill Terr CV12 ....78 B5
Mill View Birmingham B33 ..69 C4
Hinckley LE10 ....71 D2
Mill WIk CV11 ....73 C4
Mill WIk The B31 ......102 F1
Millais CI CV12 ....78 A4
Millais Rd LE10 ....71 A3
Millard Ind Est B70 .....53 B1
Millard Rd WV14 ....40 B1
Millbank Malvern View
B17 ....85 D4
Millbank St WV11 ....12 F1
Millbrook CI 4 WS11 ....1 F2
Millbrook Ct B62 ....83 A7
Millbrook Dr
Birmingham B31 ....122 E8
Shenstone WS14 ....17 F6
Millbrook Rd B14 ......104 C6
Millbrook Way DY5 ......81 B8
Millcroft CI B32 ....84 E2
Millcroft Rd B74 ....45 A8
Milldale CI DY10 ....116 E8
Milldale Cres WV10 .....11 D3
Milldale Rd WV10 ....11 D4
Millenium Forge DY1 ....51 D5
Millenium Pk B70 ....53 A5
Millennium CI WS3 ......15 A3
Millennium Gdns B64 ....62 F2
Millennium Way
Codsall WV8 ....10 B4
Wolston CV8 ....135 F3
Miller CI B60 ....150 E6
Miller Cres WV14 ....40 A1
Miller St B6 ....66 E5
Millers CI WS12 ....27 F1
Millers Ct
1 Kidderminster DY11 ..116 D6
Solihull B90 ....105 F2
Millers Gn LE10 ....75 F6
Millers Green Dr DY6 ....60 A8
Millers Rd CV34 ....160 E8
Millers Vale WS12 ....2 D1
Millersdale CI WS3 ......14 E3
Millersdale Dr B71 ......42 F2
Millfield Birmingham B31 ..103 A4
Royal Leamington Spa
CV31 ....162 A8
Millfield Ave
Walsall, High Heath WS4 ..15 B1
Walsall, Little Bloxwich
WS3 ....14 D3
Millfield Day Specl Sch
B71 ....53 A3
Millfield Gdns 2 DY11 ..116 D6
Millfield Prim Sch
Brownhills WS8 ....16 A7
Fazeley B78 ....35 A8
Millfield Rd
Birmingham B20 ....54 F5
Brownhills WS8 ....136 E1
Brownhills WS8 ....116 A7
Millfield View B63 ......82 E4
Millfields B33 ....69 E3
Millfields CI B71 ....42 B1
Millfields Fst Sch B61 ..136 E1
Millfields Rd
Bilston WV4,WV4 ....40 B5
West Bromwich B71 ....42 B1
Millhaven Ave B30 .....104 B6
Millhouse Ct CV6 ......113 F7
Millhouse Rd B25 ....88 C8
Millicent CI WS12 ....2 B6
Millicent PI 11 B12 .....87 A6
Millichip Rd WV14 ......26 E1
Millington Rd
Birmingham B36 ....68 E7
Tipton DY4 ....40 F1
Wolverhampton WV10 .....25 E6
Millison Gr B90 ....127 A7
Millmead Rd B32 ....84 E1
Millpool Gdns B14 .....104 F3
Millpool Hill B14 ......104 F4
Millpool Way B66 ....65 A4
Millrace Rd B98 ....153 E5
Mills Ave B76 ....46 F4
Mills CI WV11 ....26 B8
Mills Cres WV2 ....163 D1
Mills Rd WV2 ....163 D1
Mills WIk DY4 ....51 F7

Millsborough Rd
B98 ....153 F3
Millside B28 ....105 E3
Millstone CI B76 ....46 F1
Millsum Ho 6 WS1 ....28 F1
Millthorpe CI B8 ....68 B5
Millwalk Dr WV9 ....11 A3

Millward St
Birmingham B9 ....67 C1
West Bromwich B70 ....53 A3
Millwright CI DY4 ....52 B5
Milner CI CV12 ....79 D2
Milner Cres CV2 ....96 E1
Milner Rd B29 ....86 A1
Milner Way B13 ....105 D8
Milnes Walker Ct B44 ....44 E1
Milo Cres B78 ....21 A2
Milrose Way CV4 ....131 F8
Milsom Gr B34 ....69 D6
Milstead Rd B26 ....69 A1
Milston CI B14 ....104 E1
Milton Ave
2 Birmingham B12 ....87 A6
Tamworth B79 ....21 A7
Warwick CV34 ....160 C5
Milton CI Bedworth CV12 ..78 D1
Bentley Heath B93 ......127 F4
Hinckley LE10 ....71 C1
Kidderminster DY11 .....116 A6
Redditch B97 ....158 C8
Walsall WS1 ....42 D6
Willenhall WV12 ....27 E7
Milton Cres
Birmingham B25 ....88 D7
Dudley DY3 ....50 A5
Milton Ct Perton WV6 ....23 C4
Smethwick B66 ....65 A1
Milton Dr DY9 ....99 D7
Milton Gr Birmingham B21 ..65 C8
Birmingham B29 ....85 F3
Milton Ho B63 ....82 B5
Milton PI WS1 ....42 D6
Milton Rd
Bentley Heath B93 ......127 F4
Cannock WS11 ....1 E4
Catshill B61 ....137 A8
Dudley WV14 ....51 D8
Smethwick B67 ....64 E5
Wolverhampton WV10 ......26 A5
Milton St Birmingham B19 ..66 E6
Brierley Hill DY5 ....61 D7
Coventry CV2 ....114 A4
Walsall WS1 ....42 D7
West Bromwich B71 ....53 B5
Milverton CI
Halesowen B63 ....83 A6
Sutton Coldfield B76 .....57 F7
Milverton Cres 1 CV32 ..156 E1
Milverton Cres W 3
CV32 ....156 E1
Milverton Ct
CV32 ....161 E8
Milverton Hill CV32 ....161 E8
Milverton House Prep Sch
CV11 ....73 D3
Milverton Lodge 2
CV32 ....156 E1
Milverton Prim Sch
CV32 ....156 E1
Milverton Rd
Birmingham B23 ....56 A4
Coventry CV2 ....96 D2
Knowle B93 ....128 C5
Milverton Terr CV32 ...161 E8
Milward Sq 8 B97 ......153 E3
Mimosa CI B29 ....103 B7
Mimosa WIk DY6 ....60 E8
Mincing La B65 ....63 D3
Mindelsohn Way B15 ....85 C6
Minden Gr B29 ....85 B1
Minehead Rd Dudley DY1 ..61 D8
Wolverhampton WV10 ......11 B2
Miner St WS2 ....28 C3
Miners WIk B78 ....22 C3
Minerva CI Tamworth B77 ..21 D5
Willenhall WV12 ....27 E4
Minerva La WV1 ....25 E1
Minewood CI WS3 ....13 F3
Minith Rd WV14 ....51 D8
Miniva Dr B76 ....47 A2
Minivet Dr B12 ....86 E6
Minley Ave B17 ....84 F7
Minories B4 ....164 C3
Minories The 1 CV1 .....51 D1
Minors Hill WS14 ....9 D6
Minstead Rd B24 ....56 D6
Minster CI Blackheath B65 ..63 E3
Knowle B93 ....128 B8
Minster Ct B10 ....87 D7
Minster Rd CV1 ....113 B3
Minster The WV3 ....39 A7
Minster WIk B61 ....136 F8
Minsterley CI WV3 ......38 E8
Minsterpool Wlk WS13 ....9 B8
Minton CI WV1 ....26 A1
Minton Rd B32 ....86 F5
Minton Mews B60 ......151 B8
Mintor Rd
Birmingham B32 ....84 F4
Coventry CV2 ....96 E1
Minworth CI B97 ....153 B2
Minworth Ind Pk B76 ....58 B5
Minworth Jun & Inf Sch
..........................58 D5
Minworth Rd B46 ....59 A3
Miranda CI
Birmingham B45 ....102 A2
Coventry CV3 ....134 D7
Miranda Dr CV34 ....161 E2
Mira Bsns Pk Est WS12 ...2 D3
Mirfield CI WV9 ....11 A3
Mirfield Rd
Birmingham B33 ....69 B2
Solihull B91 ....107 A6

Mission Cl B64 .....63 A1
Mission Dr DY4 .....52 A3
Mistletoe Dr WS5 .....43 B3
Mistral Cl LE10 .....75 F8
Mitcham Cl WS12 .....1 F7
Mitcham Gr B44 .....45 B1
Mitchel Rd DY6 .....60 F4
Mitcheldean Covert
B14 .....104 D2
Mitchell Ave
 Coventry CV4 .....132 A7
 Dudley WV14 .....40 B1
Mitchell Ho
 Coventry CV4 .....132 A7
 Warwick CV34 .....160 E7
Mitchell Rd CV12 .....78 C2
Mitchell's Ct B79 .....21 B5
Mitford Dr B92 .....107 D7
Mitre Cl Essington WV11 .....13 A3
 Willenhall WV12 .....27 D7
Mitre Ct B61 .....137 A3
Mitre Fold WV1 .....163 B3
Mitre Rd Cheslyn Hay WS6 .....4 D2
 Stourbridge DY9 .....81 E5
Mitten Ave B45 .....102 A1
Mitton Rd B20 .....54 E2
Moat Ave CV3 .....132 F5
Moat Coppice B62 .....84 A1
Moat Croft
 Birmingham B37 .....70 A2
 Sutton Coldfield B76 .....58 B7
Moat Dr
 Drayton Bassett B78 .....34 E5
 Halesowen B62 .....63 F1
Moat Farm Dr
 Bedworth CV12 .....95 C8
 Birmingham B32 .....84 C2
Moat Farm Inf Sch B68 .....64 C3
Moat Farm Jun Sch B68 .....64 C3
Moat Farm Way WS3 .....15 A5
Moat Gn CV35 .....160 A1
Moat Green Ave WV11 .....26 E7
Moat Hall Prim Sch WS6 .....4 F3
Moat House La B80 .....159 F8
Moat House La CV4 .....132 C7
Moat House La E WV11 .....26 E7
Moat House Prim Sch
WV11 .....26 E7
Moat House Rd B8 .....68 A4
Moat La
 Birmingham, Digbeth B5 .....164 C1
 Birmingham, South Yardley
B26 .....88 E7
 Great Wyrley WS6 .....5 A2
 Solihull B91 .....107 C6
Moat Mdws B32 .....84 E4
Moat Rd Oldbury B68 .....64 B3
 Tipton DY4 .....52 A7
 Walsall WS2 .....28 C2
Moat St WV13 .....27 A2
Moat Way LE9 .....71 F6
Moatfield Mid Sch B98 .....154 E1
Moatfield Terr 2 WS10 .....42 A3
Moathouse La W WV11 .....26 D7
Moatmead Wlk B36 .....68 E8
Moatside Cl WS3 .....15 A5
Moatway The B38 .....123 E7
Mob La WS4 .....15 C3
Mobberley Rd WV14 .....40 A1
Mockley Wood Rd B93 .....128 B7
Modbury Ave B32 .....84 D1
Modbury Cl CV3 .....133 D5
Moden Cl DY3 .....50 D6
Moden Hill DY3 .....50 D6
Moat Jul B63 .....82 A2
Moillett St B18 .....65 D4
Moilliett Ct B66 .....65 C6
Moira Cres B14 .....105 C4
Moises Hall Rd WV5 .....49 B7
Moland St B4 .....164 C4
Mole St B11 .....87 B6
Molesworth Ave CV3 .....114 A1
Molhay Gdns 4 B42 .....55 A8
Molineux Grounds
 (Wolverhampton Wanderers
 FC) WV1 .....163 B4
Molineux St WV1 .....163 B4
Molineux Way WV1 .....163 B4
Mollington Cres B90 .....106 C3
Mollington Rd CV31 .....162 D2
Molyneux Rd DY2 .....62 E2
Momus Bvd CV2 .....114 C2
Mona Rd B23 .....56 F5
Monarch Dr DY4 .....52 C6
Monarch Ho B68 .....64 B2
Monarch Inf Sch B11 .....88 A5
Monarch Way DY2 .....62 C4
Monastery Dr B91 .....106 E6
Monckton Rd B68 .....84 A7
Moncrieff Dr CV31 .....162 C5
Moncrieffe Cl DY2 .....62 E8
Moncrieffe St WS1 .....29 A1
Money La B61 .....121 A7
Monica Rd B10 .....87 F8
Monins Ave DY4 .....52 A2
Monk Cl DY4 .....52 A2
Monk Rd B8 .....68 B5
Monk's Croft The CV3 .....133 C7
Monks Dr B80 .....159 D4
Monks Field Cl CV4 .....112 A1
Monks Kirby Rd B76 .....46 F3
Monks Path B97 .....152 F4
Monks Rd
 Binley Woods CV3 .....135 C7
 Coventry CV1 .....113 F2
Monks Way Tamworth B77 .....21 F5
 Warwick CV34 .....160 D6

Monkseaton Rd B72 .....46 B2
Monksfield Ave B43 .....43 D1
Monkshood Mews B22 .....56 B7
Monkshood Retreat
B38 .....123 F8
Monkspath Solihull B90 .....127 A6
 Sutton Coldfield B76 .....46 F1
Monkspath Bsns Pk
B90 .....126 F8
Monkspath Cl B90 .....126 D7
Monkspath Hall Rd B90 .....127 B7
Monkspath Jun & Inf Sch
B90 .....127 B6
Monksway B38 .....104 B1
Monkswell Cl
 Birmingham B10 .....87 D7
 Brierley Hill DY5 .....61 D1
Monkswood Cres CV2 .....114 D8
Monkswood Rd B31 .....103 C2
Monkton Rd B29 .....85 A2
Monmer Cl WV13 .....27 B3
Monmer Cl WV13 .....27 B5
Monmer La WV12,WV13 .....27 B4
Monmore Bsns Pk WV2 .....39 F7
Monmore Park Ind Est
WV2 .....40 A6
Monmore Rd WV1 .....40 A7
Monmouth Cl
 Coventry CV5 .....112 B3
 Kenilworth CV8 .....147 F6
Monmouth Dr
 Sutton Coldfield B73 .....45 D3
 West Bromwich B71 .....53 B7
Monmouth Gdns CV10 .....72 E3
Monmouth Ho B33 .....69 E2
Monmouth Rd
 Birmingham B32 .....102 D8
 Smethwick B67 .....84 E8
 Walsall WS2 .....27 E3
Monnington Ho CV8 .....148 B7
Mons Rd DY2 .....51 F1
Monsal Ave WV10 .....25 E4
Monsal Rd B42 .....55 C7
Monsaldale Cl WV6 .....23 F1
Monsieurs Hall La B61 .....136 B3
Montague Ho B16 .....65 E1
Montague Rd
 Birmingham, Birches Green
B24 .....57 A1
 Birmingham, Edgbaston B16 .....65 E1
 Birmingham, Handsworth
B21 .....65 B8
 Smethwick B66 .....65 B5
 Warwick CV34 .....161 A8
Montague St
 Birmingham, Aston B6 .....67 B8
 Birmingham, Bordesley B9 .....67 A2
Montalt Rd CV3 .....133 E7
Montana Ave B42 .....55 A5
Montana Wlk CV10 .....72 E3
Monteagle Dr DY6 .....49 D1
Montford Gr DY3 .....50 D7
Montfort Rd Coleshill B46 .....70 F5
 Walsall WS2 .....42 B6
Montfort Wlk B32 .....84 A2
Montgomery Bsns Ctr
B11 .....87 C7
Montgomery Cl
 Catshill B61 .....121 A1
 Coventry CV3 .....134 C4
Montgomery Cres DY5 .....81 F7
Montgomery Croft B11 .....87 C7
Montgomery Prim Sch
B11 .....87 C7
Montgomery Rd
 Royal Leamington Spa
CV31 .....161 F4
 Walsall WS2 .....27 E2
Montgomery St B11 .....87 C7
Montgomery Way B8 .....68 A4
Montgomery Wlk 1 B71 .....53 D4
Montjoy Cl CV3 .....134 D7
Montley B77 .....36 C8
Montpelier Ho CV8 .....147 F5
Montpelier Rd B24 .....57 A1
Montpellier Cl CV3 .....133 C6
Montpellier Gdns DY1 .....50 E2
Montpellier St B12 .....87 A6
Montreal Ho B5 .....86 D7
Montrose Ave CV32 .....157 B5
Montrose Cl LE10 .....71 F5
Montrose Dr
 Birmingham B35 .....58 A4
 Dudley DY1 .....62 A8
 Nuneaton CV10 .....72 F3
Montsford Cl B93 .....127 E3
Monument Ave DY9 .....81 E4
Monument La
 Barnt Green B45 .....121 F4
 Sedgley DY3 .....50 E3
 Sedgley DY3 .....39 E1
Monument Rd B16 .....65 F2
Monway Bldgs WS10 .....41 E3
Monway Ind Est WS10 .....41 E3
Monway Terr WS10 .....41 E3
Monwode Lea La B46 .....91 C6
Monyhull Hall Rd B30 .....104 D3
Monyhull Hospl B14 .....104 D3
Moodyscroft Rd B33 .....69 C3
Moon's La WS6 .....4 D1
Moons Moat Dr B98 .....154 E5
Moons Moat First Sch
B98 .....154 D5
Moons Pk B98 .....154 E6
Moor Cl WS7 .....7 B7
Moor Ct B24 .....56 F3
Moor Ctr The DY5 .....61 D3

Moor End Ct B24 .....57 B4
Moor End La B24 .....57 B4
Moor Green Jun Sch
B13 .....86 C1
Moor Green La B13 .....86 D2
Moor Hall Dr Clent DY9 .....100 A1
 Sutton Coldfield B75 .....32 D1
Moor Hall Prim Sch B75 .....32 C2
Moor Ho B14 .....104 C2
Moor La Birmingham B6 .....56 A4
 Blackheath B65 .....63 B3
 Shenstone WS14 .....17 E2
 Tamworth, Amington B79 .....22 A6
 Tamworth, Bolehill B77 .....21 D5
Moor Leasow B31 .....103 C2
Moor Meadow Rd B75 .....46 D7
Moor Pk Perton WV6 .....23 D5
 Walsall WS3 .....14 B3
Moor Pool Ave B17 .....85 C6
Moor Rd CV10 .....72 A8
Moor St Brierley Hill DY5 .....61 C3
 Coventry CV5 .....112 F1
 Tamworth B79 .....21 A4
 Wednesbury WS10 .....42 B2
 West Bromwich B70 .....53 C2
Moor St S WV2 .....39 C7
Moor Street Ind Est DY5 .....61 C3
Moor Street Queensway
B5 .....164 C2
Moor Strest B5 .....164 C2
Moor The B76 .....58 A8
Moorbrooke CV10 .....72 A7
Moorcroft Cl
 Nuneaton CV11 .....74 B1
 Redditch B97 .....158 B6
Moorcroft Dr WS10 .....41 C2
Moorcroft Gdns B97 .....158 B6
Moorcroft Pl 5 B7 .....67 A4
Moorcroft Rd B13 .....86 E3
Moordown Ave B92 .....89 A2
Moore Cl Coventry CV6 .....96 A5
 Perton WV6 .....23 F4
 Sutton Coldfield B74 .....31 F6
 Warwick CV34 .....155 E2
Moore Cres B68 .....64 C3
Moore Rd WV12 .....27 D8
Moore St Cannock WS12 .....2 C7
 Wolverhampton WV1 .....25 F1
Moore Wlk CV34 .....161 C7
Moore's Row B5 .....66 F1
Moorend Ave B37 .....70 B2
Moorfield Ave B93 .....127 F6
Moorfield Dr
 Bromsgrove B61 .....136 F3
 Halesowen B63 .....83 A5
 Sutton Coldfield B73 .....57 A8
Moorfield Rd
 Birmingham B34 .....69 B6
 Wolverhampton WV2 .....39 C7
Moorfield The B34 .....69 B6
Moorfoot Ave B63 .....82 C1
Moorgate B79 .....21 A5
Moorgate Cl B98 .....154 E6
Moorgate Prim Sch B79 .....21 A5
Moorgate Rd B60 .....151 A2
Moorhill Prim Sch WS11 .....1 E4
Moorhill Rd CV31 .....162 A3
Moorhills Croft B90 .....126 B8
Moorings The
 Brierley Hill DY5 .....62 A4
 Oldbury B69 .....63 E8
 Royal Leamington Spa
CV31 .....161 D7
Moorland Ave WV10 .....25 C6
Moorland Cl B16 .....65 D1
Moorland Rd
 Birmingham B16 .....65 D1
 Cannock WS11 .....1 E5
 Walsall WS3 .....28 A8
Moorlands Ave B47 .....147 F3
Moorlands Ct B65 .....63 D4
Moorlands Dr B90 .....106 C2
Moorlands Lodge 147 F3
Moorlands Prim Sch B71 .....53 B8
Moorlands Rd B71 .....42 C1
Moorlands The B74 .....45 F8
Moorpark Cl CV11 .....79 C8
Moorpark Rd B31 .....103 A1
Moors Croft B32 .....84 B1
Moors La B31 .....102 E7
Moors Mill La DY4 .....52 D7
Moors The B36 .....68 F8
Moorside Gdns WS2 .....28 B3
Moorside Rd B14 .....105 D3
Moorsom St B6 .....66 E5
Moorville Wlk B11 .....87 A7
Moorwood Cres CV10 .....72 A8
Moorwood La CV10 .....72 A7
Morar Cl B35 .....58 C4
Moray Cl Halesowen B62 .....83 E8
 Hinckley LE10 .....75 A8
Morcom Rd B11 .....87 E5
Morcroft WV14 .....41 A3
Mordaunt Dr B75 .....32 E2
Morden Rd B33 .....68 D3
Mordiford Cl B98 .....154 E4
Moreall Mdws CV4 .....132 D3
Moreland Croft B76 .....58 B6
Morelands The B31 .....103 B1
Morestead Ave B26 .....89 C5
Moreton Ave
 Birmingham B43 .....44 C3
 Wolverhampton WV4 .....39 E4
Moreton Cl
 Birmingham B32 .....84 F5
 Tipton DY4 .....41 B2

Moreton Com Sch WV10 .....11 F1
Moreton Rd Solihull B90 .....106 C2
 Wolverhampton WV10 .....11 D1
Moreton St Birmingham B1 .....66 B4
 Cannock WS11 .....1 F4
Morfa Gdns CV6 .....112 D5
Morford Rd WS9 .....30 A7
Morgan Cl Studley B80 .....159 F2
 Willenhall WV12 .....27 B4
Morgan Ct B24 .....57 C6
Morgan Gr B36 .....58 F1
Morgan Rd B78 .....21 A2
Morgans Rd CV5 .....111 C4
Morgrove Ave B93 .....127 F6
Morillon Cl DY10 .....117 A1
Morjon Dr B43 .....43 F2
Morland Cl CV12 .....79 D2
Morland Dr LE10 .....71 B3
Morland Rd
 Birmingham B43 .....44 C4
 Coventry CV6 .....95 C2
Morley Gr WV6 .....25 C4
Morley Rd Birmingham B8 .....68 B6
 Burntwood WS7 .....7 B7
Morley Road Sh Ctr WS7 .....7 B7
Morlich Rise DY5 .....81 B8
Morlings Dr WS7 .....7 B8
Morning Pines DY8 .....80 E4
Morningside
 Coventry CV5 .....133 B8
 Sutton Coldfield B73 .....46 B6
Mornington Rd B66 .....65 B7
Morpeth B77 .....35 C7
Morrell St CV32 .....156 F1
Morris Ave Coventry CV2 .....114 D4
 Walsall WS2 .....27 E2
Morris Cl B27 .....88 D4
Morris Croft B36 .....58 F1
Morris Ct 3 WV4 .....39 F4
Morris Dr Nuneaton CV11 .....73 D1
 Whitnash CV31 .....162 B2
Morris Field Croft B28 .....105 E4
Morris Hill B78 .....36 F7
Morris Rd B8 .....68 C6
Morris St B70 .....53 C1
Morris Wlk B60 .....150 E8
Morrison Ave WV10 .....25 D8
Morrison Rd DY4 .....52 C4
Morse Rd CV31 .....162 B3
Morsefield La B98 .....154 D1
Morston B77 .....35 D4
Mortimer Rd CV8 .....147 F2
Mortimers Cl B14 .....105 B1
Mortlake Cl CV6 .....95 A1
Morton Ho B97 .....153 A3
Morton La B97 .....158 B7
Morton Rd
 Brierley Hill DY5 .....81 D7
 Harvington DY10 .....118 B2
Morvale Ct DY9 .....81 E5
Morvale Gdns DY9 .....81 E5
Morvale St DY9 .....81 E5
Morven Rd B73 .....46 A3
Morville Cl B93 .....127 D3
Morville Croft WV14 .....40 B5
Morville Rd DY2 .....62 E4
Morville St B16 .....66 B2
Mosborough Cres B19 .....66 C5
Mosedale Dr WV11 .....26 F5
Moseley Ave CV6 .....113 A4
Moseley CE Prim Sch
B13 .....86 F2
Moseley Ct
 Essington WV11 .....12 F3
 Willenhall WV13 .....26 D1
Moseley Dr B37 .....89 F8
Moseley Gate B13 .....86 F3
Moseley Hall Hospl B13 .....86 E3
Moseley Old Hall* WV10 .....12 A5
Moseley Old Hall La
WV10 .....12 A5
Moseley Park Sch WV14 .....40 E8
Moseley Rd Bilston WV14 .....40 E8
 Birmingham B12 .....86 F6
 Kenilworth CV8 .....148 B3
 Willenhall WV14,WV13 .....26 D1
 Wolverhampton WV10 .....12 A4
Moseley St Birmingham B12 .....86 F8
 Tipton DY4 .....52 C7
 Wolverhampton WV6 .....25 C4
Moss Cl Aldridge WS9 .....30 A5
 Huntington WS12 .....1 C5
 Walsall WS4 .....29 A3
Moss Dr B72 .....46 C3
Moss Gdns WV14 .....40 B3
Moss Gr Birmingham B14 .....104 D6
 Kenilworth CV8 .....148 B7
 Kingswinford DY6 .....60 D7
Moss House Cl B15 .....66 B1
Moss La B98 .....154 F8
Moss Lane Cl B98 .....154 F8
Moss Rd WS11 .....2 A3
Moss St Royal Leamington Spa
CV31 .....162 A7
 Walsall WS1 .....28 F2
Mossbank Ave WS7 .....7 A6
Mossdale B77 .....36 C8
Mossdale Cl CV6 .....113 B6
Mossdale Cres CV10 .....72 F2
Mossdale Way DY3 .....50 D3
Mossfield Rd B14 .....104 F7
Mossley Cl WS3 .....13 F1

Mossley La WS3 .....13 F2
Mossley Prim Sch WS3 .....13 F2
Mosspaul Cl CV32 .....156 D2
Mossvale Cl B64 .....62 F1
Mossvale Gr B8 .....68 F5
Mosswood Rd WS11 .....4 D7
Mostyn Cres B71 .....53 A1
Mostyn Ho
 Birmingham, Edgbaston B16 .....65 F2
 Birmingham, Handsworth
B21 .....65 F8
Mostyn Rd
 Birmingham B16 .....65 F2
 Birmingham, Handsworth B21 .....65 F8
Mostyn St WV1 .....25 B4
Mother Teresa Ho B70 .....53 B3
Mott Cl DY4 .....52 B3
Mott St B19 .....164 B4
Mottistone Cl CV3 .....133 D6
Mottram Cl B70 .....53 B3
Mottrams Cl B72 .....46 C2
Moule Cl DY11 .....116 C6
Mounds The B38 .....123 E8
Moundsley Gr B14 .....105 A3
Moundsley Ho B14 .....104 F2
Mount Ave
 Brierley Hill DY5 .....61 C3
 Cannock WS12 .....2 B7
Mount Carmel RC Fst Sch
B97 .....153 A2
Mount Cl Birmingham B13 .....86 F4
 Cheslyn Hay WS6 .....4 E2
 Dudley DY3 .....50 C2
 Wombourne WV5 .....49 A7
Mount Ct WV6 .....24 B2
Mount Dr Bedworth CV12 .....78 A3
 Wombourne WV5 .....49 A7
Mount Field Ct CV1 .....165 D4
Mount Gdns CV5 .....133 B8
Mount Grace High Sch
LE10 .....71 E4
Mount La Clent DY9 .....99 E4
 Dudley DY3 .....50 C2
Mount Nod Prim Sch
CV5 .....112 A3
Mount Nod Way CV5 .....112 B3
Mount Pleasant
 Bilston WV14 .....40 E6
 Birmingham, King's Heath
B14 .....86 F1
 Birmingham, Small Heath
B10 .....67 B1
 Brierley Hill DY5 .....81 E1
 Cheslyn Hay WS6 .....4 E2
 Kingswinford DY6 .....60 C4
 Redditch B97 .....153 D2
 Tamworth B77 .....35 C8
Mount Pleasant Ave B21 .....54 E1
Mount Pleasant Cotts
CV2 .....115 A7
Mount Pleasant Ct 1
B10 .....67 B1
Mount Pleasant Prim Sch
DY5 .....61 E1
Mount Pleasant Rd CV12 .....78 A3
Mount Pleasant Terr
 Dudley WV14 .....51 B8
 West Bromwich B70 .....53 C2
Mount Rd
 Birmingham B21 .....65 D7
 Blackheath B65 .....63 E3
 Burntwood WS7 .....7 B6
 Fairfield B61 .....120 E2
 Hinckley LE10 .....75 D8
 Stourbridge, Stamberhill
DY8 .....81 B5
 Stourbridge, Wordsley DY8 .....60 E2
 Tipton B69 .....52 B3
 Walsall WS3 .....15 A4
 Willenhall WV13 .....40 E8
 Wolverhampton, Lanesfield
WV4 .....39 F2
 Wolverhampton, Penn WV4 .....39 A4
 Wolverhampton, Tettenhall Wood
WV6 .....24 A3
 Wombourne WV5 .....49 A7
Mount Road Ind Est WS7 .....7 B6
Mount Side St WS12 .....2 C7
Mount St Birmingham B7 .....67 C7
 Cannock WS12 .....2 B7
 Coventry CV5 .....112 F2
 Halesowen B63 .....83 A3
 Nuneaton CV11 .....73 E3
 Redditch B98 .....153 E3
 Stourbridge DY8 .....81 B5
 Tipton DY4 .....52 C6
 Walsall WS1 .....42 E8
Mount Street Bsns Ctr
B7 .....67 C6
Mount Street Ind Est B7 .....67 D7
Mount Street Pas WS1 .....73 B4
Mount The
 Birmingham B23 .....56 D1
 Blackheath B64 .....83 A3
 Coventry CV3 .....133 E8
 Curdworth B76 .....59 C6
Mount Vernon Dr B61 .....137 A5
Mount View B75 .....46 E4
Mountain Ash Dr DY9 .....81 C2
Mountain Ash Rd WS8 .....15 E5
Mountain Pine Cl WS12 .....2 A8
Mountbatten Ave CV8 .....148 C3
Mountbatten Cl B70 .....53 F2
Mountbatten Rd WS2 .....42 A7
Mountfield Cl B14 .....105 A2
Mountford Cl B65 .....63 C3
Mountford Cres WS9 .....30 C8

216 Mou – New

Mountford Dr B75 46 B8
Mountford La WV14 40 D6
Mountford Rd B90 105 D1
Mountford St B11 87 D5
Mountjoy Cres B92 89 C3
Mountrath St WS1 28 E1
Mounts Rd WS10 41 F2
Mounts Way B7 67 C7
Mountserrat Rd B60 137 B1
Mountwood Covert WV6 24 B3
Mouse Hill WS3 14 F3
Mouse La DY11 116 B8
Mousehall Farm Rd DY5 81 D7
Mousesweet Cl DY2 62 E4
Mousesweet La DY2 62 E3
Mousesweet Wlk B64 82 B8
Mowbray Cl B45 102 A2
Mowbray St
Birmingham B5 86 E8
Coventry CV2 113 F3
Mowe Croft B37 90 B7
Mows Hill Rd B94 143 A1
Moxhull Cl WV12 13 C1
Moxhull Dr B76 57 E7
Moxhull Gdns WV12 13 C1
Moxhull Rd B37 70 A5
Moxley Ind Ctr WS10 41 C4
Moxley Inf Sch WS10 41 B4
Moxley Jct WS10 41 B4
Moxley Rd WS10 41 C5
Moyle Cres CV5 111 D4
Moyle Dr B63 82 B7
Moyses Croft B66 65 A8
Mozart Ct WS11 2 C2
Much Park St CV1 165 C2
Muchall Rd WV4 39 A5
Mucklow Hill B62 83 D5
Mucklow Hill Trad Est
B62 83 C5
Muirfield B77 22 C5
Muirfield Cl
Nuneaton CV11 79 C8
Walsall WS3 14 A3
Muirfield Cres B69 63 B7
Muirfield Gdns B38 103 D1
Muirville Cl 1 DY8 60 D3
Mulberry Cl CV32 157 A2
Mulberry Dr
Birmingham B13 87 B1
5 Warwick CV34 160 F8
Mulberry Gn DY1 50 F5
Mulberry Pl WS3 13 F1
Mulberry Rd
Birmingham B30 103 C5
Cannock WS11 1 E3
Coventry CV6 114 A7
Walsall WS3 14 A1
Mulberry Way CV10 72 A8
Mulberry Wlk B74 44 E8
Muldoon Cl WS11 2 B4
Mull Cl B45 101 E1
Mull Croft B36 70 B7
Mullard Dr CV31 162 B3
Mullensgrove Rd B37 70 A5
Mullett Rd WV11 26 B7
Mullett St DY5 61 B5
Mulliner St CV6 113 F5
Mulliners Cl 2 B37 70 D2
Mullion Croft B38 103 E1
Mulroy Rd B74 46 B6
Mulwych Rd B33 69 E3
Munnings Dr LE10 71 A3
Munro Cl DY10 117 C6
Munsley Cl B98 154 F2
Munslow Gr B31 122 F8
Muntz Cres B94 143 C6
Muntz Ho B16 66 A1
Muntz St B10 87 D8
Murcott Ct CV31 162 A3
Murcott Rd E CV31 162 A3
Murcott Rd W CV31 162 A3
Murcroft Rd DY9 81 E1
Murdoch Rd WV14 41 A6
Murdock Ct WV12 27 D7
Murdock Gr B21 65 E7
Murdock Rd
Birmingham B21 65 E8
Smethwick B66 65 D6
Murdock Way 1 WS2 28 A5
Murray Ct Birmingham B20 55 A2
Sutton Coldfield B73 46 A3
Murray Ho WV14 40 D5
Murray Rd CV6 113 A7
Murrayfield Way CV3 115 B1
Murrell Cl B5 86 D7
Murton B77 36 C8
Mus of British Road
Transport* CV1 165 B3
Mus of Cannock Chase*
WS12 2 D6
Mus of the Jewellery
Quarter* B19 66 C5
Musborough Cl B36 58 C1
Muscott Gr B17 85 B5
Muscovy Rd B23 56 C3
Musgrave Cl B76 46 E3
Musgrave Rd B18 65 F6
Mushroom Hall Rd B68 64 B5
Musk La DY3 50 B3
Musk La W DY3 50 B3
Muswell Cl B91 107 D5
Muxloe Cl WS3 14 A3
Myatt Ave Aldridge WS9 29 F5
Burntwood WS7 7 A7
Wolverhampton WV2 39 E6
Myatt Cl WV2 39 E6
Myatt Way WS9 29 F5
Myddleton St B18 66 A4
Myles Ct DY5 61 D4
Mylgrove CV3 133 D3
Mynors Cres B47 125 A6
Myring Dr B75 46 F5
Myrtle Ave
4 Birmingham, Balsall Heath
B12 87 A5
Birmingham, Highter's Heath
B14 104 F2
Redditch B98 153 E2
Myrtle Cl WV12 27 E7
Myrtle Gr
10 Birmingham B19 66 C8
Coventry CV5 112 F1
Wolverhampton WV3 38 E6
Myrtle Pl B29 86 B2
Myrtle Rd DY1 51 B3
Myrtle St WV2 39 F6
Myrtle Terr DY4 41 B2
Myton Cres CV34 161 C6
Myton Crofts CV31 161 D7
Myton Dr B90 105 D1
Myton Gdns CV34 161 A6
Myton La CV34 161 C6
Myton Rd CV31,CV34 161 B6
Myton Sch CV34 161 B6
Mytton Cl DY2 51 E1
Mytton Gr DY4 51 E5
Mytton Rd
Birmingham B30 103 C5
Water Orton B46 58 F3
Myvod Rd WS10 42 A5

N

Naden Ho WS12 1 C5
Naden Rd B19 66 B6
Nadin Rd B73 57 A8
Naesby Rd WV6 23 F3
Nafford Gr B14 104 F2
Nagersfield Rd DY5 61 A2
Nailcote Ave CV4 131 C8
Nailcote La CV7 131 A7
Nailers Cl Birmingham B32 83 F2
Stoke Heath B60 150 E6
Nailers Cl 3 B60 136 F2
Nailers Dr WS7 7 D6
Nailors Fold WV14 40 D2
Nailstone Cres B27 106 C8
Nailsworth Rd
Dorridge B93 127 D2
Redditch B98 153 F2
Nairn Cl Birmingham B28 105 F5
Nuneaton CV10 73 A2
Redditch B98 154 E4
Nairn Rd WS3 14 A4
Nally Dr WV14 40 A2
Nanaimo Way DY6 61 A4
Nansen Prim Sch B8 67 F5
Nansen Rd Birmingham B8 67 F5
Birmingham, Sparkhill B11 87 C3
Nantmel Gr B32 102 C8
Naomi Way WS9 16 B4
Napier B77 21 E3
Napier Dr DY4 52 C6
Napier Rd Walsall WS2 28 A5
Wolverhampton WV2 39 D7
Napier St CV1 113 E3
Napton Cl B98 154 D1
Napton Dr CV32 157 A2
Napton Gn CV5 112 A3
Napton Gr B29 84 F2
Narberth Way CV2 114 F8
Narraway Gr DY4 52 D8
Narrow La Brownhills WS8 15 F8
Halesowen B62 83 E8
Walsall WS2 42 B7
Narrowboat Way DY5,
DY2 62 A5
Narrows The 1 LE10 75 E8
Naseby Cl Coventry CV3 134 F8
Redditch B98 154 D6
Naseby Dr B63 82 D2
Naseby Ho 4 B14 105 A3
Naseby Rd Birmingham B8 67 F5
Solihull B91 107 B6
Nash Ave WV6 23 E3
Nash Cl B65 63 C1
Nash Croft B37 90 B8
Nash Ho B15 86 D8
Nash La
Belbroughton DY9 119 D7
Lichfield WS13 3 A5
Nash Rd B98 154 B1
Nash Sq B42 55 D4
Nashe Cl DY10 117 C5
Nately Gr B29 85 C3
Nathan Cl B75 46 C8
Nathaniel Newton Inf Sch
CV10 72 B8
National Ag Ctr* CV8 149 A4
National Ex Ctr B40 90 E4
National Indoor Arena*
B1 66 B2
National Lock Mus*
WV13 27 A1
National Motorcycle Mus
The* B92 91 A2
National Sea Life Ctr*
B1 66 B2
Naul's Mill Ho CV1 165 B4
Naunton Cl B29 103 A7
Naunton Rd WS2 28 A3
Navenby Cl B90 105 C3
Navigation Dr DY5 62 A4
Navigation La B71 42 F2
Navigation Rdbt DY4 52 E6
Navigation St
Birmingham B2 164 B2
Walsall WS2 28 D1
Wolverhampton WV1 25 E1
Navigation Way
Birmingham B18 65 F5
Cannock WS11 2 A2
Coventry CV6 114 A8
West Bromwich B70 52 F2
Nayland Croft B28 106 A5
Naylor Cl DY11 116 B3
Naylors Gr DY3 50 E4
Neachells Ct WV13 26 E1
Neachells La
Wednesfield WV11 26 D5
Willenhall WV13 26 D3
Neachells Lane Ind Est
WV11 26 D4
Neachells Lane Island
WV11 26 D4
Neachless Ave WV5 49 A5
Neachley Gr B33 68 F4
Neal Ct CV2 115 A8
Neale Ave CV5 112 A6
Neale Cl CV12 79 C1
Neale Ho
West Bromwich B70 53 D1
Wolverhampton WV2 39 C7
Neale St WS2 28 C2
Neander B79 20 F6
Near Lands Cl B32 84 B4
Near Oak Ho B32 102 D8
Nearhill Rd B38 123 C8
Nearmoor Rd B34 69 D6
Neasden Gr B44 56 B8
Neath Rd WS3 13 F2
Neath Way Dudley DY3 51 A6
Walsall WS3 13 F2
Nebsworth Cl B90 106 D5
Nechells Inf & Jun Sch
B7 67 C8
Nechells Park Rd B7 67 C7
Nechells Parkway B7 67 A5
Nechells Pl B7 67 C5
Needham St B7 67 C7
Needhill Cl B93 127 F6
Needle Cl B80 159 E4
Needle Mill La B98 153 E6
Needlers End La CV7 130 A7
Needless Alley B2 164 B2
Needwood Cl WV2 39 B6
Needwood Dr WV4 39 F4
Needwood Gr B71 42 E1
Needwood Hill WS13 3 A2
Needwood Ho B27 88 D3
Neighbrook Cl B97 152 F2
Neilston St 13 CV31 162 A7
Nelson Ave Bilston WV14 40 C7
Warwick CV34 161 A8
Nelson Dr Cannock WS12 2 F4
Hinckley LE10 71 D4
Nelson Ho DY4 52 A7
Nelson La CV34 161 A8
Nelson Mandela Sch B12 87 B5
Nelson Prim Sch B1 66 B3
Nelson Rd Birmingham B6 55 F1
Dudley DY1 51 B1
Nelson St Birmingham B1 66 B3
7 Coventry CV1 113 E4
Oldbury B69 64 B6
West Bromwich B71 53 C5
Willenhall WV13 27 B3
Nemesia B77 22 B4
Nene Cl Coventry CV3 134 D7
Stourbridge DY8 81 A5
Nene Way B36 69 F8
Neptune Ind Est WV13 41 B8
Neptune St DY4 51 E5
Nesbit Gr B9 68 B3
Nesfield Cl B38 103 C1
Nesfield Gr B92 109 B7
Nesscliffe Gr B23 56 D7
Nest Comm WS3 14 F5
Neston Gr B33 68 C2
Nestor Ho B13 105 D7
Nether Beacon WS13 3 A1
Nether La WS7 7 D8
Nether Stowe High Sch
WS13 3 B1
Netheravon Cl B14 104 D1
Netherbridge Ave WS14 9 E7
Netherbrook Prim Sch
DY2 62 D2
Netherby Rd DY3 50 C8
Nethercote Gdns B90 105 E3
Netherdale Cl B72 57 C7
Netherdale Rd B14 105 A1
Netherend Cl B63 82 A7
Netherend La B63 82 B7
Netherend Sq B63 82 A7
Netherfield B98 159 A8
Netherfield Gdns B27 88 B3
Nethergate DY3 50 F5
Netherley Rd LE10 71 D3
Nethermill Rd 1 CV6 113 A5
Netherstone Gr B74 31 F5
Netherstowe WS13 3 C2
Netherstowe La WS13 3 D2
Netherton Bsns Pk DY2 62 E3
Netherton CE Prim Sch
DY2 62 B4
Netherton Gr B33 69 C3
Netherwood Cl B91 106 E6
Netherwood La B93 145 A7
Nethy Dr WV6 24 B5
Netley Gr B11 87 F3
Netley Ho B32 84 F5
Netley Rd WS3 13 E2
Netley Way WS3 13 E2
Network Pk B7 67 C4
Nevada Way B37 70 C1
Neve Ave WV10 25 F8
Nevill Cl CV31 161 F6
Nevill St B79 21 A5
Neville Ave
Kidderminster DY11 116 D3
Wolverhampton WV4 39 D5
Neville Cl B98 154 A5
Neville Ct
Birmingham B13 104 F6
Kidderminster DY11 116 D3
5 Warwick CV34 160 E6
Neville Gr CV34 155 F1
Neville Rd
Birmingham, Castle Bromwich
B36 58 E1
Birmingham, Stockland Green
B23 56 C3
Solihull B90 105 F1
Neville St B77 21 E3
Neville Wlk B35 58 A2
Nevin Gr B42 55 C5
Nevis Ct WV6 24 E2
Nevis Gr WV12 13 B1
Nevison Gr B43 44 B4
New Art Gall The* WS2 28 E2
New Ash Dr CV5 111 F5
New Barns La WS14 17 B3
New Bartholomew St
B5 164 D2
New Birmingham Rd B69,
DY2 52 B1
New Bldgs Coventry CV1 165 C3
Darlaston WS10 41 E6
Halesowen B63 82 A7
Hinckley LE10 71 D1
New Bond St
Birmingham B9 67 B1
2 Dudley DY2 62 D8
New Brook St 3 CV32 161 E8
New Canal St B5 164 D2
New Century Pk CV3 114 C2
New Century Way CV11 73 B4
New Church Rd B73 57 A8
New Cole Hall La B33,
B34 69 B5
New College Cl WS1 43 A7
New Coventry Rd B26 89 A5
New Croft B19 66 E7
New Cross Ave WV10 26 B4
New Cross Hospl WV11 26 B5
New Cross Ind Est WV1 26 A3
New Cross Junc WV10 26 B4
New Cross St
Darlaston WS10 41 D5
Tipton DY4 51 E5
New Ct 7 DY5 61 D2
New Dudley Rd DY6 60 C8
New England B62 83 E7
New England Cl B69 52 E1
New Ent Workshops B18 66 A5
New Farm Rd DY9 81 C4
New Forest Rd WS3 28 F6
New Gas St B70 53 A5
New Gate Ct CV1 165 C2
New Hall Dr
Sutton Coldfield, Maney
B75 46 D4
Sutton Coldfield, Wylde Green
B76 46 E2
New Hall Inf Sch B75 47 B5
New Hall Jun Sch B75 47 B5
New Hall Pl WS10 42 A3
New Hall St WV13 27 B2
New Hampton Rd E
WV1 163 A4
New Hampton Rd W
WV6 24 F4
New Heath Cl WV11 26 B5
New Henry St B68 64 B4
New Hope Rd B66 65 C4
New Horse Rd WS6 4 E3
New Inn Rd 2 B19 66 D8
New Inns Cl B21 65 D8
New Inns La B45 101 E1
New Invention Inf & Jun Schs
WV12 27 C7
New John St
Birmingham B6 66 E5
Halesowen B62 83 C8
New John St W B19 66 D5
New King St 7 DY1 51 C1
New Landywood La WS6 13 E7
New Leasow B76 58 A7
New Market St B3 164 B3
New Meadow Cl B31 103 B2
New Meadow Rd B98 154 B3
New Meeting St B69 64 A8
New Mill La B78 35 A7
New Mill St DY2 51 C1
New Mills St WS1 42 D7
New Moseley Rd 4 B12 87 A8
New Oscott Inf Sch B73 45 C3
New Oscott Jun Sch B73 45 C3
New Penkridge Rd WS11 1 C1
New Pool Rd B64 82 B8
New Railway St WV13 27 B2
New Rd Aldridge WS9 30 A5
Ash Green CV7 95 B6
Astwood Bank B96 158 E1
Birmingham B45 121 F7
Bromsgrove B60 137 A1
New Rd *continued*
Bromsgrove, Sidemoor
B61 136 E3
Brownhills WS8 15 F7
Burntwood WS7 7 B6
Coventry CV6 94 F1
Dudley DY2 62 C7
Fairfield B61 120 E2
Featherstone WV10 12 B8
Halesowen B63 83 B4
Hinckley LE10 76 A6
Hollywood B47 125 A8
Kidderminster DY10 116 E5
Shenstone WS14 17 F6
Shuttington B79 22 E8
Solihull B91 107 D3
Stourbridge DY8 81 A5
Studley B80 159 E3
Tamworth B77 35 F7
Tipton DY4 52 D6
Water Orton B46 59 B3
Willenhall WV13 27 A1
Wolverhampton, Newbridge
WV6 24 E4
Wolverhampton, Scotlands
WV10 26 B8
New Row B78 34 E5
New Rowley Rd DY2 62 E7
New Shipton Cl B76 46 F1
New Spring St B18 66 A4
New Spring St N B18 66 A4
New St Bedworth CV12 78 C2
Birchmoor B78 36 E7
Birmingham, Castle Bromwich
B36 69 B8
Birmingham, Digbeth B2 164 C2
Birmingham, Erdington B23 56 F5
Birmingham, Frankley B45 102 A1
Brierley Hill DY5 82 A8
Bulkington CV12 79 D2
Burntwood, Chase Terrace
WS7 6 E8
Burntwood, Chasetown WS7 6 E5
Cannock, Bridgtown WS11 4 D6
Cannock, Hednesford WS12 2 C4
6 Cannock, Mill Green
WS11 4 E8
Cubbington CV32 157 E5
Darlaston WS10 41 D6
Dudley, Eve Hill DY1 51 D1
Dudley, Gornalwood DY3 50 C3
Essington WV11 13 A3
Fazeley B78 35 B8
Great Wyrley WS6 5 A1
Hinckley LE10 71 D1
Kenilworth CV8 147 F6
Kingswinford, Wall Heath
DY6 60 C8
Kingswinford, Wordsley
DY6 60 D4
Royal Leamington Spa
CV31 162 A7
Smethwick B66 65 B6
Stourbridge, Wollaston DY8 80 F5
Stourbridge, Wordsley DY8 60 D2
Tamworth, Bolehill B77 21 E4
Tamworth, Mount Pleasant
B77 21 C1
Tipton DY4 51 F5
Walsall, High Heath WS4 15 D1
Walsall, Rushall WS4 29 B7
Walsall, The Chuckery WS1 28 F1
Walsall, Wallington Heath
WS3 14 B1
Warwick CV34 160 E6
Wednesbury WS10 41 F1
West Bromwich B71 53 D3
West Bromwich, Hill Top
B70 53 A7
West Bromwich, Mayer's Green
B70 53 D3
Willenhall WV13 26 E1
Wolverhampton, Ettingshall
WV2 40 A6
Wolverhampton, Merry Hill
WV3 38 D7
Wolverhampton, Parkfield
WV4 39 E6
New St N B71 53 D3
New Street Sta B2 164 B2
New Summer St B19 164 B4
New Swan La B70 53 A5
New Town
Brierley Hill DY5 61 C4
Dudley DY2 62 D1
New Town La B64 62 D1
New Town Row B6 66 E5
New Union St CV1 165 B2
New Village DY2 62 C2
New Wharf Cotts B60 152 B7
New Wlk 3 B97 153 E4
New Wood Cl DY7 80 C8
New Wood Dr B31 102 D1
New Wood Gr WS9 16 A3
New Wood La DY10 118 B8
Newark Croft B26 89 B6
Newark Rd Dudley DY2 62 D2
Willenhall WV12 27 C7
Newbank Gr B9 68 A3
Newbold Cl
Bentley Heath B93 127 F5
Coventry CV3 114 F1
Newbold Comyn Pk*
CV32 162 D8
Newbold Croft B7 67 B5
Newbold Ct B63 83 B3
Newbold Lawn CV32 162 A8
Newbold Pl CV32 162 A8

Newbold St CV32 .....162 A8
Newbold Terr CV32 ...162 A8
Newbold Terr W CV32 .162 B8
Newbolds Rd WV10 ....26 A6
Newbolt Rd WV14 .....40 E6
Newbolt St WS5 ......42 E5
Newborough Dr B28, B90 ....105 F3
Newborough Rd
Birmingham B28 .....105 F4
Solihull B90 ....106 A3
Newbourne Hill B48 ..139 E4
Newbridge Ave WV6 ...24 E3
Newbridge Cres WV6 ..24 E4
Newbridge Dr WV6 ....24 E3
Newbridge Gdns WV6 ..24 E4
Newbridge Mews **3** WV6 ....24 E4
Newbridge Prep Sch WV6 ....24 E4
Newbridge Rd
Birmingham B9 ....68 B1
Kingswinford DY6 ....60 C8
Newbridge St WV6 ....24 F4
Newburgh Cres CV34 .160 E8
Newburn Prim Sch CV34 ....160 C4
Newburn Croft B32 ...84 B5
Newbury Cl Catshill B61 ..121 B1
Great Wyrley WS6 .....4 F2
Halesowen B62 ....83 D3
4 Royal Leamington Spa CV31 ....162 C6
Newbury Ho **8** B69 ..63 D6
Newbury La B69 ......63 D6
Newbury Rd
Birmingham B19 ......66 E7
Norton Canes WS11 ...6 A5
Stourbridge DY8 .....60 D1
Wolverhampton WV10 ..11 C2
Newbury Wlk B65 ....63 C6
Newby Cl CV3 ....133 E6
Newby Gr B37 ....70 B5
Newcastle Croft B35 ..58 C3
Newchurch Gdns **8** B24 ..56 E2
Newcombe Rd
Birmingham B21 ......54 D2
Coventry CV5 ....113 A1
Newcomen Cl
Bedworth CV12 ....95 D8
Burntwood WS7 ....7 C8
Newcomen Ct WS4 ....29 B7
Newcomen Dr CV4 ....51 F3
Newcomen Rd CV12 ...77 D1
Newcott Cl CV9 ......88 F7
Newcroft Gr B26 .....88 E7
Newdegate Pl CV11 ...73 C4
Newdegate St CV11 ...73 C4
Newdigate CV31 ......162 C5
Newdigate Cl CV12 ...78 A4
Newdigate Prim Sch CV12 ....77 C1

Newhouse Farm Cl B76 .46 F3
Newick Ave B74 ......31 B3
Newick Gr B14 ....104 C4
Newick St DY2 ....62 C4
Newington Cl CV6 ....112 D6
Newington Rd B37 ....90 B8
Newland Cl Redditch B98 .159 B7
Walsall WS4 ....15 C2
Newland Ct B23 ......56 C3
Newland Gdns B64 ...82 E7
Newland Gr DY2 .....61 F7
Newland La CV7 ......95 B7
Newland Rd
Birmingham B9 ....67 F1
Coventry CV1 ....113 D5
Royal Leamington Spa CV32 ....157 C3
Newlands Cl
Kidderminster DY11 ..116 C7
Willenhall WV13 .....27 A1
Newlands Ct Cannock WS12 .5 E8
Coventry CV3 ....113 F2
Newlands Dr B62 .....83 E7
Newlands Gn B66 ....65 A4
Newlands La
Birmingham B37 .....90 A6
Norton Canes WS12 ...5 D8
Newlands Rd
Bentley Heath B93 ...127 F4
Birmingham B30 .....104 C7
Newlands The
Birmingham B34 .....69 C7
Studley B80 ....159 D3
Newlyn Cl Lichfield WS14 ..9 D7
Nuneaton CV11 ....73 F4
Newlyn Rd
Birmingham B31 .....102 F3
Blackheath B64 .....82 D8
Newman Ave WV4 ....39 F4
Newman Cl CV12 .....78 B4
Newman Coll of Higher Ed B32 ....102 C8
Newman College Cl B32 ....102 C8
Newman Pl WV14 ....40 F7
Newman Rd
Birmingham B24 .....56 F4
Tipton DY4 ....41 C1
Wolverhampton WV10 ..12 A1
Newman Way B45 ...122 A6
Newmans Cl B66 .....65 C4
Newmarket Cl
Coventry CV6 ....96 B4
Wolverhampton WV6 ..25 A5
Newmarket Rd WS11 ..5 E4
Newmarket Way B36 ..68 B7
Newmarsh Rd B76 ....58 A6
Newmore Gdns WS5 ..43 C5
Newnham Gr B23 .....56 E6
Newnham Ho B36 ....70 B5
Newnham Rd
Birmingham B16 .....65 C2
Coventry CV1 ....113 F5
Royal Leamington Spa CV32 ....157 B3
Newnham Rise B90 ..106 D3
Newport B 21 F5
Newport Cl B897 ....158 B6
Newport Rd
Birmingham, Balsall Heath B12 ....87 A4
Birmingham, Buckland End B36 ....68 F8
Coventry CV6 ....95 D1
Newport St
3 Walsall WS1 ......28 E1
Wolverhampton WV10 ..25 E4
Newquay Cl Hinckley LE10 .71 E4
Nuneaton CV11 ....73 F5
Walsall WS5 ....43 E7
Newquay Rd WS5 ....43 D7
Newshire Ind Est B11 .87 D6
Newsholme Cl **1** CV34 ..155 E1
Newstead B79 ....20 D6
Newstead Ave LE10 ..75 F4
Newstead Cl CV11 ...73 F2
Newstead Rd B44 ....45 B3
Newstead Way CV3 ..115 B1
Newton Cl
Birmingham B43 .....43 C1
Coventry CV2 ....114 F7
Redditch B98 ....159 A6
Newton Gdns B43 ...54 B8
Newton Gr **8** B29 ..85 F2
Newton Ind Est B19 ..67 D2
Newton Manor Cl B43 .54 D8
Newton Pl
Birmingham B18 .....66 A7
Walsall WS2 ....28 B6
Newton Rd
Birmingham, Balsall Heath B11 ....87 B5
Birmingham, Newton B43 ..54 B8
Bromsgrove B60 .....151 A2
Hinckley LE10 ....74 E7
Knowle B93 ....128 B2
Walsall WS2 ....28 B5
West Bromwich B71 ..53 F6
Newton Sq B43 ......43 E1
Newton St
Birmingham B4 ......164 C3
West Bromwich B71 ..53 E7
Newton Works B60 ..151 A6
Newton's Coll WS13 ..9 B8
Newtown Bldgs CV12 .78 B3
Newtown Dr B19 .....66 C6
Newtown La
Romsley B62 ....101 D2

Newtown La continued
Wildmoor B62 ....120 D8
Newtown Middleway B6 ..66 E5
Newtown Prim Sch B70 .52 D3
Newtown Rd
Bedworth CV12 ....78 A2
Nuneaton CV11 ....73 D3
Newtown Sh Ctr B19 ..66 E6
Newtown St B64 .....62 D2
Ney Cl DY4 ....51 F2
Niall Cl B15 ....85 E8
Niblett Hill B61 .....136 B7
Nicholas Chamberlaine Comp Sch CV12 ....78 D3
Nicholas Cl CV12 ....78 C3
Nicholas Rd B74 .....44 E8
Nicholls Cl WV14 ....40 B1
Nicholls Fold WV11 ..26 D5
Nicholls Rd DY4 .....40 E1
Nicholls St Coventry CV2 ..113 F4
West Bromwich B70 ..53 E2
Nicholls Way WS12 ...2 F1
Nichols Cl B92 ......107 F7
Nicholson Cl CV34 ..155 F1
Nickson Rd CV4 .....111 E1
Nigel Ave B31 ....103 A5
Nigel Ct B16 ....65 C2
Nigel Rd Birmingham B8 ..67 E6
Dudley DY1 ....51 A2
Nightingale B77 .....36 A6
Nightingale Ave B36 ..70 A8
Nightingale Cl
Brierley Hill DY5 .....81 D7
Willenhall WV12 .....27 C8
Nightingale Ct
Royal Leamington Spa CV31 ....162 B8
Solihull B91 ....107 C4
Nightingale Dr
Kidderminster DY10 ..117 B2
Tipton DY4 ....52 C5
Nightingale La CV5 ..132 E7
Nightingale Pl WV14 .40 D7
Nightingale Wlk
1 Birmingham B15 ..86 C7
Burntwood WS7 ....7 E7
Nightwood Gr B23 ..56 C6
Nijon Cl B21 ....54 D1
Nimbus B77 ....35 D4
Nimmings Cl B62 ...122 F6
Nimmings Rd B62 ...63 D1
Nine Days La B98 ...159 B6
Nine Elms La WV10 ..25 E4
Nine Leasowes B66 ..64 E7
Nine Locks Ridge DY5 ..61 D2
Nine Pails Wlk B70 ..53 D1
Nineacres Dr B37 ....70 A3
Ninefoot La
Tamworth, Belgrave B77 ..35 E8
Tamworth, Wilnecote B77 ..35 E7
Ninestiles Tech Coll B27 ..88 B1
Nineveh Ave B21 ....65 F7
Nineveh Rd B21 .....65 F7
Ninfield Rd B27 .....88 A4
Ninian Pk B77 ....35 D4
Ninian Way B77 .....35 E6
Nirvana Cl WS11 .....1 C2
Nith Pl DY1 ....51 B3
Niton Rd CV10 ....73 A4
Niven Cl CV5 ....112 A6
No Name Rd WS7 .....6 E7
Noakes Ct WV10 .....41 F7
Noble Cl CV34 ......160 D5
Nock St DY4 ....52 C7
Nocke Rd WV11 .....12 E3
Nod Rise CV5 ....112 B3
Noddy Park Rd WS9 ..30 B6
Noddy Pk WS9 ....30 B7
Node Hill B80 ......159 D3
Node Hill Cl B80 ...159 D3
Noel Ave B12 ....87 A6
Noel Ct B97 ....158 C8
Noel Rd B16 ....65 F1
Noele Gordon Gdns **10** WS1 ....42 E8
Nolan Cl CV6 ....95 D4
Nonant Gr B37 ......54 D8
Nonsuch Prim Sch B32 ..84 D2
Nook The Brierley Hill DY5 ..61 B5
Cheslyn Hay WS6 .....4 C1
Nuneaton CV11 ....73 F7
Nooklands Croft B33 ..69 A2
Noose Cres WV13 ...26 E2
Noose La WV13 ......26 E3
Nora Rd B11 ....87 C3
Norbiton Rd B44 ....56 A8
Norbreck Cl B43 .....43 D1
Norbury Ave WS3 ...15 A3
Norbury Cl B98 .....154 B7
Norbury Cres WV4 ..40 A4
Norbury Dr DY5 .....61 D1
Norbury Gr B92 .....89 A3
Norbury Rd Bilston WV14 ..40 F6
Birmingham B44 .....44 F3
West Bromwich B70 ..53 A7
Wolverhampton WV10 ..25 F6
Norcombe Gr B90 ..127 A7
Nordic Drift CV2 ...115 A6
Nordley Rd WV11 ....26 C5
Norfolk Ave B71 .....53 D7
Norfolk Cl
Birmingham B30 .....104 B6
Hinckley LE10 ....75 D4

Norfolk Cres
Aldridge WS9 ....30 B8
Nuneaton CV10 ....72 E4
Norfolk Ct
Birmingham B16 .....65 D1
6 Birmingham, Selly Oak B29 ....103 C7
Norfolk Dr Tamworth B78 ..21 A1
Wednesbury WS10 ...42 D4
Norfolk Gdns B75 ...46 B7
Norfolk Gr WS6 ......4 F1
Norfolk Ho B30 .....104 A3
Norfolk House Sch B15 ..85 D8
Norfolk New Rd WS2 ..28 A4
Norfolk Pl WS2 .....28 D5
Norfolk Rd
Birmingham B45 ....101 F2
Birmingham, Edgbaston B15 ....85 D8
Birmingham, Erdington B23 ..56 F5
Dudley DY2 ....62 A7
Oldbury B68 ....80 D8
Stourbridge DY8 ....80 B7
Sutton Coldfield B75 ..46 C7
Wolverhampton WV3 ..39 A8
Norfolk St Coventry CV1 ..113 B3
Royal Leamington Spa CV32 ....157 A1
Norfolk Terr CV4 ...132 B7
Norgrave Rd B92 ...89 C2
Norlan Dr B14 ......104 F3
Norland Rd B27 .....88 C1
Norley Gr B13 ......105 C7
Norman Ashman Coppice CV3 ....135 C7
Norman Ave
Birmingham B32 .....84 E7
Coventry CV2 ....96 F1
Nuneaton CV11 ....73 B4
Norman Cl B79 ......20 E7
Norman Place Rd CV6 ..112 F7
Norman Rd
Birmingham B31 .....103 B3
Smethwick B67 .....64 E2
Walsall WS5 ....43 D7
Norman St
Birmingham B18 .....65 E5
Dudley DY2 ....62 E7
Norman Terr B65 ....63 C4
Normanby Mdws CV31 ..162 A2
Normandy Cl CV35 ..160 A7
Normandy Rd B20 ..55 E1
Normandy Way LE10 ..71 C3
Normansell Terr B6 ..67 B8
Normanton Ave B26 ..89 D5
Normanton Twr B23 ..57 A6
Norrington Gr B31 ..102 C3
Norrington Rd B31 ..102 D3
Norris Dr B33 ....68 E3
Norris Rd B6 ....55 F1
Norris Way B75 .....46 D5
North Ave Bedworth CV12 ..78 D2
Birmingham B40 .....90 F5
Coventry CV2 ....114 A3
Wolverhampton WV11 ..26 C6
North Birmingham Coll B44 ....55 E7
North Bromsgrove High Sch B60 ....137 B3
North Brook Rd CV6 ..112 D8
North Cl Cubbington CV32 ..157 E5
Hinckley LE10 ....75 E6
North Cres WV10 ....12 C7
North Dr
Birmingham, Balsall Heath B5 ....86 C5
Birmingham, Lozells B20 ..66 B8
Sutton Coldfield B75 ..46 C6
North East Worcestershire Coll (Bromsgrove Campus) [137] B3
North East Worcestershire Coll (Redditch Campus) B98 ....153 E4
North Gate B17 .....85 C7
North Gn WV4 ......38 D6
North Holme B9 ....67 C2
North Leamington Com Sch & Arts Coll CV32 ...156 F4
North Leamington Com Sch & Arts Coll (Sixth Form) CV32 ....156 F2
North Oval DY3 .....50 E5
North Park Rd B23 ..56 B3
North Pathway B17 ..85 B7
North Rd
Birmingham, Handsworth B20 ....55 E2
Birmingham, Harborne B17 ..85 D6
Birmingham, Selly Oak B29 ..85 F3
Bromsgrove B60 ....137 A2
Tipton DY4 ....52 B8
Wolverhampton WV1 ..25 C4
Wolverhampton, Parkfield WV4 ....39 F5
North Roundhay B33 ..69 A4
North Springfield DY3 ..39 E1
North St Brierley Hill DY5 ..61 C2
Cannock WS11 ....1 C6
Coventry CV2 ....114 B5
Dudley DY2 ....51 D1
Nuneaton CV10 ......72 F3
Smethwick B67 .....64 F5
Walsall WS2,WS4 ...28 D1
Wolverhampton WV1 ..163 B3
North Street Ind Est DY5 ..61 C2

North View CV2 ......97 A1
North View Dr DY5 ...61 E5
North Villiers St CV32 ..157 A1
North Walsall Prim Sch WS2 ....28 E4
North Warwick St **1** B9 ..67 D1
North Warwickshire & Hinckley Coll LE10 ..71 E1
North Warwickshire & Hinckley Coll
Hinckley LE10 ....75 F8
Nuneaton CV11 ....73 E6
North Western Arc B2 ..164 C3
North Western Rd B66 ..65 A6
North Western Terr B18 ..65 F7
North Wlk B31 ......103 C1
Northam Wlk WV6 ...25 B4
Northampton St B18 ..66 B4
Northanger Rd B27 ..88 B2
Northbourne Dr DY11 ..78 F7
Northbrook Ct B90 ..106 D5
Northbrook Rd B90 ..106 C5
Northbrook St B16 ..65 F4
Northcliffe Hts DY11 ..116 C7
Northcote Rd B33 ...68 D4
Northcote St
6 Royal Leamington Spa CV31 ....162 B7
Walsall WS2 ....28 D4
Northcott Rd
Bilston WV14 ....40 F4
Dudley DY2 ....62 D4
Northdale WV6 ......24 A4
Northdown Rd B91 ..106 F1
Northey Rd CV6 .....113 D8
Northfield Children's Farm* B31 ....102 C3
Northfield Gr WV3 ..38 C7
Northfield Manor Jun & Inf Sch B29 ....103 B7
Northfield Rd
Birmingham, Harborne B17, B32 ....85 A3
Birmingham, King's Norton B30 ....103 E4
Coventry CV1 ....113 F2
Dudley DY2 ....62 D4
Hinckley LE10 ....75 C7
Northfield Road Prim Sch DY2 ....62 D5
Northfield Sta B31 ..103 B2
Northfields Way WS8 ..15 D7
Northfleet Twr B31 ..102 C2
Northgate Aldridge WS9 ..30 A7
Blackheath B64 .....82 D8
Brownhills WS9 ......16 A1
Warwick CV34 ......160 E7
Northgate Cl DY11 ..116 A4
Northgate St DY4 ...160 E7
Northgate Way WV9 ..30 A8
Northicote Recn Ctr WV10 ....11 E3
Northland Rd B91 ..106 E1
Northlands Rd B13 ..87 A1
Northleach Ave B14 ..104 D2
Northleach Cl B98 ..154 B5
Northleigh Rd B8 ....68 A6
Northleigh Rd B13 ..69 A2
Northolt Dr B35 .....58 A4
Northolt Gr B42 .....43 F1
Northover Cl WV9 ...11 A2
Northside Cl B98 ...158 E7
Northside Dr B74 ...44 F8
Northumberland Ave
Kidderminster DY11 ..116 D3
Nuneaton CV10 ......72 F3
Northumberland Cl B78 ..21 A1
Northumberland
Coventry CV1 ....113 A3
Royal Leamington Spa CV32 ....156 E2
Northumberland St B7 ..67 A4
Northvale Cl CV8 ...148 B6
Northway Birmingham B40 ..90 F5
Royal Leamington Spa CV31 ....162 A5
Sedgley DY3 ....39 C2
Northwick Cres B91 ..107 B1
Northwood Ct **1** DY5 ..61 D2
Northwood Park Cl WV10 ....11 E3
Northwood Park Rd WV10 ....11 E3
Northwood St B3 ...164 A4
Northwood Way DY5 ..61 D1
Northycote Farm & Ctry Pk* WV10 ....11 F3
Northycote La WV10 ..11 F4
Norton Canes High Sch WS11 ....6 A7
Norton Canes Prim Sch WS11 ....6 A6
Norton Cl
Birmingham B31 .....103 A3
Redditch B98 ....154 F2
Smethwick B66 .....65 C5
Tamworth B79 ......21 C7
Wolverhampton WV4 ..38 C3
Norton Cres Bilston WV14 ..41 F3
Birmingham B9 ......68 B3
Dudley DY2 ....62 E3
Norton Dr CV34 ....155 E2

Norton Rd WS11 .....6 B6
Norton Gate B38 .....103 F1
Norton Grange
  Allesley CV5 .....112 C6
  Walsall WS3 .....5 F4
Norton Grange Cres WS11 .5 F4
Norton Green La
  Knowle B93 .....128 C2
  Norton Canes WS11 .....5 F4
Norton Hall La WS11 .....5 F4
Norton Hill Dr CV2 .....114 E6
Norton La Burntwood WS7 ...7 C6
  Great Wyrley WS6 .....5 A4
  Norton Canes WS11 .....5 B7
  Tidbury Green B47,B90,
  B94 .....125 E3
Norton Lakeside Sta*
  WS7 .....6 C6
Norton Mews B61 .....137 A4
Norton Rd Coleshill B46 .....70 FB
  Kidderminster DY10 .....117 B6
  Norton Canes WS11,WS12 .5 FB
  Stourbridge DY8 .....80 E2
  Walsall WS3 .....15 A5
Norton Springs WS11 .....5 F5
Norton St Birmingham B18 .66 A6
  Coventry CV1 .....165 C3
Norton Terr
  Birmingham B30 .....104 B6
  Norton Canes WS11 .....5 F6
Norton Twr B1 .....66 C2
Norton Vw B14 .....104 D7
Norton Wlk B23 .....56 C3
Nortune Cl B38 .....103 D2
Norwich Cl Lichfield WS13 .3 C3
  Coventry CV1 .....74 A8
Norwich Croft B37 .....69 F1
Norwich Dr
  Birmingham B17 .....84 F8
  Coventry CV3 .....133 B5
Norwich Rd Dudley DY2 .62 D2
  Walsall WS2 .....28 B1
Norwood Ave B64 .....82 E7
Norwood Cl LE10 .....71 E3
Norwood Gr
  Birmingham B19 .....66 B7
  Coventry CV2 .....96 E2
Norwood Ho 11 CV32 .156 F2
Norwood Rd
  Birmingham B9 .....67 E2
  Brierley Hill DY5 .....61 C3
Norwood Villas B16 .....65 F1
Nottingham Dr WV12 .....27 C7
Nottingham New Rd
  WS2 .....28 A5
Nottingham Way WS5 .....61 F2
Nova Croft CV5 .....111 C4
Nova Ct B43 .....44 B1
Nova Scotia St B4 .....164 D3
Nowell St WS10 .....41 E5
Nuffield Ho B36 .....70 A8
Nuffield Hospl WV6 .....24 C4
Nuffield Rd Coventry CV6 .114 A7
  Hinckley LE10 .....74 E7
Nugent Cl B6 .....66 F7
Nugent Gr B90 .....126 D3
Nuneaton Borough Football
  Club CV11 .....73 A4
Nuneaton Mus & Art Gal*
  CV11 .....73 C3
Nuneaton Rd
  Bedworth CV12 .....78 B4
  Bulkington CV12 .....79 B4
  Nuneaton CV10 .....72 D8
Nuneaton Sta CV11 .....73 C5
Nunts La CV6 .....95 B3
Nunts Park Ave CV6 .....95 B4
Nursery Ave Aldridge WS9 .30 B5
  Birmingham B12 .....86 F5
Nursery Cl
  Birmingham B30 .....103 F5
  Hagley DY9 .....99 A4
  Kidderminster DY11 .....116 B8
Nursery Dr B30 .....103 F5
Nursery Gdns
  Solihull B90 .....125 E8
  Stourbridge DY8 .....60 F1
Nursery La Hopwas B78 .....20 B6
  Royal Leamington Spa
  CV31 .....162 A5
  Sutton Coldfield B74 .....31 A2
Nursery Rd
  Birmingham, Harborne B15 .85 D7
  Birmingham, Lozells B19 ....66 C6
  Walsall WS3 .....28 B7
Nursery St WV1 .....163 B4
Nursery View Cl WS9 .....30 E2
Nursery Wlk WV6 .....24 C4
Nurton Bank WV6 .....23 A3
Nutbrook Ave CV4 .....111 E2
Nutbush Dr B31 .....102 D6
Nutfield Wlk B32 .....84 F5
Nutgrove Cl B14 .....104 F7
Nuthatch Dr DY5 .....81 C8
Nuthurst B75 .....47 B4
Nuthurst Dr WS11 .....4 F4
Nuthurst Gr
  Bentley Heath B93 .....128 A4
  Birmingham B14 .....104 F2
Nuthurst Grange Rd
  B94 .....143 C4
Nuthurst Rd
  Birmingham B31 .....122 F6
  Lapworth B94 .....143 A2

Nutley Dr DY4 .....52 D8
Nutmeg Gr WS1 .....29 A2
Nutt's La LE10 .....75 A7
Nuttall Gr B21 .....65 C7
Nymet B77 .....35 E8

O
O'Connor Dr DY4 .....41 C1
O'Hare Ho WS4 .....28 F3
O'keeffe Cl B11 .....87 B6
Oak Apple Rd B61 .....137 B8
Oak Ave Birmingham B12 .87 A7
  Great Wyrley WS6 .....5 A1
  Huntington WS12 .....1 D8
  Walsall WS2 .....27 E3
  West Bromwich B70 .....53 B3
Oak Bank B18 .....66 A6
Oak Barn Rd B62 .....83 E8
Oak Cl Baginton CV8 .....133 F2
  Bedworth CV12 .....78 C4
  Birmingham B17 .....85 A6
  Hinckley LE10 .....75 E5
  Tipton DY4 .....41 A1
Oak Cottage Prim Sch
  B91 .....106 F6
Oak Cotts B14 .....105 C2
Oak Cres Tipton B69 .....52 B1
  Walsall WS3 .....28 D6
Oak Croft B37 .....69 E3
Oak Ct Coventry CV3 .....133 F7
  Halesowen B63 .....82 F2
  Oldbury B66 .....64 C8
  Royal Leamington Spa
  CV34 .....161 E2
  Stourbridge DY8 .....81 A4
  Sutton Coldfield B74 .....31 E5
  Walsall WS5 .....43 A4
Oak Dr Birmingham B23 .56 C7
  Chapel End CV10 .....72 A8
Oak Farm Cl B76 .....58 A7
Oak Farm Craft Ctr*
  B78 .....34 B5
Oak Farm Rd B30 .....103 E5
Oak Gn Dudley DY1 .....51 A5
  Wolverhampton WV6 .....24 B3
Oak Gr Birmingham B31 .102 E1
  Kidderminster DY10 .....117 A5
  Wolverhampton WV11 .....26 B7
Oak Hill WV3 .....24 C1
Oak Hill Dr B15 .....85 E7
Oak Ho Great Wyrley WS6 ..5 A1
  Little Aston B74 .....31 B5
Oak House (Mus)* B70 ...53 B2
Oak Ind Pk The DY6 .....49 B4
Oak La Allesley CV5 .....93 E1
  Barston B92 .....109 B1
  Kingswinford DY6 .....49 F1
  West Bromwich B70 .....53 B3
Oak Leaf Dr B13 .....87 A3
Oak Leasow B32 .....84 B4
Oak Leys WV3 .....24 C1
Oak Meadow Jun & Inf Sch
  WV11 .....27 A1
Oak Park Rd DY8 .....60 F1
Oak Rd Brownhills WS9 .16 A3
  Catshill B61 .....137 B8
  Dudley DY1 .....51 C3
  Oldbury B68 .....84 C7
  Tipton DY4 .....51 E6
  Walsall, High Heath WS4 ..15 C1
  Walsall, Pelsall Wood WS3 .14 F5
  West Bromwich B70 .....53 B2
  Wolverhampton WV3 .....25 A1
Oak St Blackheath B64 .....62 D1
  Brierley Hill DY5 .....61 F1
  Dudley, Darby End DY2 ....62 E4
  Dudley, West Coseley DY1,
  WV14 .....51 B7
  Kingswinford DY6 .....60 D6
  Wolverhampton WV3 .....25 A1
Oak Street Trad Est DY5 ..61 F1
Oak Tree Ave
  Coventry CV3 .....133 A6
  Redditch B97 .....153 B4
Oak Tree Cl
  Bentley Heath B93 .....127 E4
  Royal Leamington Spa
  CV32 .....157 A2
Oak Tree Cres B62 .....83 F6
Oak Tree Ct
  Birmingham B28 .....106 A5
  Royal Leamington Spa
  CV32 .....157 A2
Oak Tree Gdns 2 DY8 ....61 A1
Oak Tree La
  Birmingham B29 .....85 E1
  Hollywood B47 .....125 B6
  Sambourne B96 .....159 B2
Oak Tree Pk B98 .....154 F6
Oak Tree Rd
  Birmingham B8 .....67 D6
  Coventry CV3 .....135 A7
Oak Tree Wlk B79 .....20 F7
Oak Trees B47 .....125 A7
Oak View WS2 .....27 E3
Oak Way Coventry CV4 .....111 D2
  Sutton Coldfield B76 .....46 F2
Oak Wlk The B31 .....103 A1
Oakalls Ave B60 .....137 B2
Oakcroft Rd B13 .....105 C7
Oakdale B74 .....31 A1
Oakdale Cl
  Brierley Hill DY5 .....61 A7
  Oldbury B68 .....64 A2

Oakdale Rd
  Binley Woods CV3 .....135 C7
  Birmingham B36 .....68 E7
  Oldbury B68 .....64 A2
Oakdale Trad Est CV6 .....49 E1
Oakden Pl WV11 .....116 C7
Oakdene Cl WS6 .....4 D2
Oakdene Cres CV10 .....73 D7
Oakdene Dr B45 .....138 C8
Oakdene Rd WS7 .....7 A6
Oaken Dr Solihull B91 .106 F5
  Willenhall WV12 .....27 E7
Oaken Gdns WS7 .....7 A8
Oaken Grange WS6 .....4 F1
Oaken Pk WV8 .....10 A2
Oakenfield WS13 .....3 A2
Oakenhayes Cres
  Brownhills WS8 .....6 F1
  Sutton Coldfield B76 .....58 C5
Oakenhayes Dr WS8 .....6 F1
Oakenshaw Rd
  Redditch B98 .....154 A1
  Solihull B90 .....106 D1
Oakeswell St WS10 .....42 A3
Oakey Cl CV6 .....95 F4
Oakfield Ave
  Birmingham, Balsall Heath
  B12 .....87 A6
  Birmingham, Sparkbrook
  B11 .....87 C6
  Dudley DY1 .....51 B6
  Kingswinford DY6 .....60 E5
Oakfield Cl Smethwick B66 .65 C6
  Stourbridge DY8 .....60 F1
Oakfield Ct DY5 .....61 D2
Oakfield Dr
  Birmingham B45 .....122 D4
  Walsall WS3 .....15 B5
Oakfield Ho CV3 .....115 A1
Oakfield Rd
  Birmingham, Balsall Heath
  B12 .....86 E5
  Birmingham, Erdington B24 .56 F3
  Birmingham, Selly Oak B29 ..86 B3
  Codsall WV8 .....10 C2
  Coventry CV6 .....113 F6
  Kidderminster DY11 .....116 B5
  Smethwick B66 .....65 C6
  Stourbridge B66 .....61 A1
  Stourbridge, Wollascote
  B99 .....81 F2
Oakfields Way B91 .....108 B5
Oakford Dr CV5 .....111 F6
Oakhall Dr B93 .....127 F4
Oakham Ave DY2 .....62 E7
Oakham Cl B98 .....159 A5
Oakham Cres
  Bulkington CV12 .....79 D2
  Dudley DY2 .....62 E7
Oakham Ct 9 DY2 .....62 E8
Oakham Dr DY2 .....62 F8
Oakham Ho 7 B14 .....105 A3
Oakham Prim Sch B69 ....63 B7
Oakham Rd
  Birmingham B17 .....85 B7
  Dudley DY2 .....62 F7
  Tipton B69 .....63 A7
Oakham Way B92 .....89 A1
Oakhill Ave DY10 .....116 E4
Oakhill Cl B17 .....85 B8
Oakhill Cres B27 .....106 B8
Oakhill Dr DY5 .....81 B7
Oakhill Prim Sch B27 .....21 F2
Oakhill Rd WS11 .....1 F2
Oakhurst WS14 .....9 C7
Oakhurst Ct B72 .....57 C8
Oakhurst Dr B60 .....137 A3
Oakhurst Rd
  Birmingham B27 .....106 B8
  Sutton Coldfield B72 .....57 C8
Oakington Ho B35 .....58 A3
Oakland Cl B91 .....107 E4
Oakland Dr DY3 .....50 A2
Oakland Gr B61 .....137 B4
Oakland Ho B74 .....32 A4
Oakland Rd
  Birmingham, Handsworth
  B21 .....65 E8
  Birmingham, Moseley B13 .87 A3
  Walsall WS3 .....28 E7
Oaklands
  Birmingham, Moseley B13 .87 A3
  Birmingham, Northfield
  B31 .....102 F4
  Curdworth B76 .....59 B5
  Halesowen B62 .....84 A4
  Wolverhampton WV5 .....39 B8
Oaklands Ave B17 .....85 B5
Oaklands Cl WS12 .....1 C6
Oaklands Croft B76 .....58 B7
Oaklands Ct B64 .....148 A2
Oaklands Dr B20 .....54 F2
Oaklands Grn B20 .....40 D8
Oaklands Ind Est WS12 ....2 B3
Oaklands Prim Sch B27 ...88 C2
Oaklands Rd
  Sutton Coldfield B74 .....46 B8
  Wolverhampton WV3 .....39 B8
Oaklands The
  Birmingham B37 .....90 A7
  Coventry CV4 .....112 A2
  Halesowen B62 .....83 F6
  Wolverhampton WV10 ....117 A7
Oaklands Way
  Birmingham B31 .....102 C1
  Walsall WS3 .....15 B3
Oaklea Dr B64 .....62 F2
Oakleaf Cl B32 .....84 C2

Oakleigh B31 .....103 C2
Oakleigh Ct 8 WV3 .....25 B2
Oakleigh Dr Codsall WV8 ..10 A3
  Sedgley DY3 .....50 C7
Oakleigh Rd DY8 .....81 B2
Oakleigh Trad Est WV14 ...40 B2
Oakleigh Wlk DY6 .....60 E8
Oakleighs DY8 .....60 C1
Oakley CV8 .....129 F1
Oakley Ave Aldridge WS9 ..30 B5
  Tipton DY4 .....52 A6
Oakley Cl WS13 .....3 B2
Oakley Ct Bedworth CV12 ..77 D1
  Birmingham B15 .....85 E5
Oakley Gr WV4 .....38 D5
Oakley Ho
  Bromsgrove B60 .....137 A1
  Smethwick B66 .....65 C4
Oakley Rd
  Birmingham, Sparkbrook
  B10 .....87 C7
  Birmingham, Stirchley B30 .104 B5
  Wolverhampton WV4 .....38 D5
Oakley Wood Dr B91 .....107 E4
Oakley Wood Rd CV33 ..161 F1
Oakly Rd B97 .....153 D3
Oakmeadow Cl
  Birmingham, Acock's Green
  B26,B27 .....88 D4
  Birmingham, Tile Cross B33 ..69 D3
Oakmeadow Way B24 .....57 D3
Oakmoor Rd CV6 .....96 A4
Oakmount Cl WS3 .....14 F3
Oakmount Rd B74 .....45 A7
Oakridge Cl
  Redditch B98 .....154 C7
  Willenhall WV12 .....27 C4
Oakridge Dr WV12 .....27 C4
Oakridge Rd CV32 .....157 C4
Oakroyd Cres CV10 .....72 D7
Oaks Cres WV3 .....25 A1
Oaks Dr Cannock WS11 ....1 C1
  Featherstone WV10 .....11 F8
  Wolverhampton WV3 .....25 B2
  Wombourne WV5 .....49 A5
Oaks Pl CV6 .....96 A3
Oaks Prec CV8 .....147 E3
Oaks Rd CV8 .....147 E2
Oaks The Bedworth CV12 ..77 F2
  Birmingham B34 .....69 B7
  Birmingham, Hawkesley
  B38 .....123 F7
  Royal Leamington Spa
  CV32 .....161 D8
  Smethwick B67 .....64 F6
  Sutton Coldfield B76 .....47 A3
  Wolverhampton, Merridale
  WV3 .....25 A5
  Wolverhampton, New Cross
  WV11 .....26 B5
Oakslade Dr B92 .....107 E8
Oakstreet Ent Ctr B64 ....62 D1
Oakthorpe Dr B37 .....69 F5
Oakthorpe Gdns B69 .....52 A2
Oaktree Cl B48 .....139 A7
Oaktree Farm Mobile Homes
  Pk B94 .....141 B7
Oakwood Cl
  Brownhills WS9 .....15 E4
  Essington WV11 .....13 B3
  Shenstone WS14 .....18 A6
Oakwood Cres DY2 .....61 F6
Oakwood Croft B91 .....107 C1
Oakwood Ct B63 .....83 A4
Oakwood Dr
  Birmingham B14 .....104 D4
  Sutton Coldfield B74 .....44 E8
Oakwood Gr CV34 .....156 A1
Oakwood Rd
  Birmingham B11 .....87 C3
  Hollywood B47 .....125 A6
  Smethwick B67 .....64 F4
  Sutton Coldfield B73 .....45 E1
  Walsall WS3 .....28 E7
Oakwood Sch WS9 .....16 A3
Oakwood St B70 .....53 B5
Oakwoods WS11 .....4 D8
Oakworth Cl CV2 .....114 F8
Oasis The DY9 .....98 F5
Oast Ho B8 .....68 D4
Oasthouse Cl
  Kingswinford DY6 .....60 A7
  Stoke Heath B60 .....150 D6
Oaston Rd
  Birmingham B36 .....69 D8
  Nuneaton CV11 .....73 D4
Oatfield Cl WS7 .....7 A4
Oatlands Cl CV6 .....95 C4
Oatlands Way WV6 .....23 D3
Oatlands Wlk 3 B14 ....104 C2
Oatmill Cl WS10 .....41 E5
Oban Dr CV10 .....73 A2
Oban Rd Coventry CV6 .....95 F5
  Hinckley LE10 .....75 A7
  Solihull B92 .....88 F1
Oberon Cl
  Birmingham B45 .....102 A2
  Nuneaton CV11 .....74 A1
  Royal Leamington Spa
  CV34 .....161 E4
Oberon Dr B90 .....106 B1
Occupation Rd
  Brownhills WS9 .....16 A4
  Coventry CV4 .....114 C3
Occupation St DY1 .....51 A2
Ocean Dr WS10 .....41 E1

Ockam Croft B31 .....103 C2
Ocker Hill Inf Sch DY4 ...52 C8
Ocker Hill Jun Sch DY4 ..41 C1
Ocker Hill Rd DY4 .....52 C8
Oddicombe Croft CV3 ...133 D5
Oddingley Ct B23 .....56 C3
Oddingley Rd B31 .....103 C2
Odell Cres WS3 .....28 C7
Odell Pl B5 .....86 C5
Odell Rd WS3 .....28 B7
Odell Way WS3 .....28 B7
Odensil Grn B92 .....89 B2
Odiham Cl B79 .....21 C7
Odin Cl WS11 .....2 A5
Odnall La DY9 .....99 F3
Odstone Dr LE10 .....74 F8
Offa Dr CV8 .....148 A4
Offa Rd CV31 .....162 B5
Offa St B79 .....21 B5
Offa's Dr WV6 .....23 E5
Offadrive B79 .....21 B5
Offchurch La CV31 .....162 F6
Offchurch Rd CV32 .....157 C4
Offenham Cl B98 .....154 B6
Offenham Covert B38 ...123 E8
Offini Cl B70 .....53 F2
Offmoor Rd B32 .....102 B8
Offmore Ct DY10 .....117 C6
Offmore Farm Cl DY10 .117 C6
Offmore Fst Sch DY10 ..117 B6
Offmore La DY10 .....117 A6
Offmore Rd DY10 .....116 A6
Offwell Rd B98 .....154 D1
Ogbury Cl B14 .....104 C2
Ogley Cres WS8 .....16 A7
Ogley Dr B75 .....47 A5
Ogley Hay Ind Sch WS8 ..15 F7
Ogley Hay Rd
  Burntwood, Chase Terrace
  WS7 .....7 A8
  Burntwood, New Town St,
  WS8 .....7 B8
Ogley Rd WS8 .....16 A7
Ogley Vale WS7 .....7 B8
Okeford Way CV10 .....73 A1
Okehampton Dr B71 .....53 C6
Okehampton Rd CV3 ...133 E5
Okement Dr WV11 .....26 D5
Oken Ct CV34 .....160 D7
Oken Rd CV34 .....160 D8
Olaf Pl CV2 .....115 A7
Old Abbey Gdns B17 .....85 D4
Old Acre Dr B21 .....65 E7
Old Bakery Ct DY9 .....99 A6
Old Bank Pl B72 .....46 C5
Old Bank Rd B31 .....103 B2
Old Barn Rd
  Birmingham B30 .....103 D6
  Stourbridge DY8 .....61 A1
Old Beeches B23 .....56 C8
Old Bell Rd B23 .....57 B6
Old Birchills WS2 .....28 C3
Old Birmingham Rd
  Alvechurch B48 .....139 B8
  Catshill B60 .....137 C8
  Marlbrook B60,B45 .....121 C1
Old Bridge St B19 .....66 C6
Old Bridge Wlk B65 .....62 F5
Old Bromford La B8 .....68 C6
Old Brookside B33 .....68 E2
Old Bush St DY5 .....61 E3
Old Bush Trad Est DY5 ..61 E3
Old Camp Hill B12 .....87 A8
Old Canal Wlk DY4 .....52 B5
Old Castle Gr WS8 .....6 F2
Old Chapel Rd B67 .....64 F3
Old Chapel Wlk B68 .....64 A4
Old Chester Rd S DY10 .116 E2
Old Church CE Prim Sch
  WS10 .....41 C6
Old Church Cl B17 .....85 B5
Old Church Gn B33 .....68 E2
Old Church Rd
  Birmingham B31 .....85 B4
  Coventry CV6 .....96 A1
  Water Orton B46 .....59 B3
Old Crescent Ct 1 B68 ..64 B8
Old Crest Ave B98 .....153 E2
Old Croft La B34 .....69 C7
Old Cross St DY4 .....51 E5
Old Crown Ct B32 .....84 B1
Old Crown Mews CV2 ....96 D5
Old Damson La B92 .....90 A2
Old Dickens Heath Rd
  B90 .....126 A5
Old Dominion Wks WV1 ..40 A7
Old End La WV14 .....51 C7
Old Fallings Cres WV10 ..25 F6
Old Fallings Jun Sch
  WV10 .....26 A8
Old Fallings La WV10 .....25 F8
Old Fallow Ave WS11 .....1 E3
Old Fallow Rd WS11 .....1 E3
Old Falls Cl WS6 .....4 D3
Old Farm Dr WV8 .....10 A4
Old Farm Gr B14 .....105 D5
Old Farm Mdw WV3 .....38 C8
Old Farm Rd B33 .....68 E3
Old Fire Sta The B17 .....85 D6
Old Fordrove B76 .....46 D3
Old Forest Way B34 .....69 B6
Old Forge Bsns Ctr B98 ..159 C8
Old Forge Dr B98 .....159 C8
Old Forge Trad Est DY9 ..81 E6
Old Grange Rd B11 .....87 C4
Old Green La CV8 .....129 C1

Old Grove Gdns DY9 ....81 D3
Old Hall Cl DY8 ....81 A8
Old Hall Ct WS9 ....44 A5
Old Hall Ind Est WS3 ...28 C8
Old Hall La
 Norton Canes WS11,WS12 ..5 B7
 Walsall WS9 ....44 B5
Old Hall Specl Sch WS7 ..27 E5
Old Hall St WV1 ....163 C2
Old Ham La DY9 ....81 D2
Old Hampton La WV11 ...12 C2
Old Hawne La B63 ....83 A5
Old Heath Cres WV1 .....26 A1
Old Heath Rd WV1 ....26 A2
Old Hedging La B77 .....35 D5
Old Hednesford Rd WS11,
 WS12 ....2 A3
Old Hill WV6 ....24 D5
Old Hill Prim Sch B64 ..62 F1
Old Hill Sta B64 ....83 A8
Old Hinckley Rd CV10 ...73 D5
Old Hobicus La B68 .....64 B5
Old Horns Cres B43,B44 ..44 C2
Old House La Corley CV7 ..94 A7
 Romsley B62 ....101 B1
Old Kingsbury Rd B76 ...58 C5
Old La Featherstone WV10 .12 C7
 Rowney Green B48 ....140 D4
 Walsall WS3 ....28 C8
Old Langley Hall WV6 ..23 F2
Old Landywood La WS6 ..13 D2
Old Langley Hall B75 ...47 C4
Old Level Way DY2 ......62 D4
Old Lime Gdns B38 .....123 E8
Old Lindens Cl B74 .....44 E7
Old Lode La B92 ....89 C3
Old London Rd WS14 .....9 D1
Old Manor Cl B78 ....34 E5
Old Manor Flats WV6 ...24 D5
Old Masters Cl WS1 .....29 A1
Old Meadow Rd B31 .....123 C7
Old Meeting Rd WV14 ...51 C8
Old Meeting Yd CV12 ....78 B3
Old Mill Ave CV4 ....132 D5
Old Mill Cl B90 ....105 D2
Old Mill Gdns
 Birmingham B33 ....68 E2
 Walsall WS4 ....15 C2
Old Mill Gr B20 ....55 C2
Old Mill Rd B46 ....70 F7
Old Milverton CV32 ....156 C3
Old Milverton La CV32 ..156 E5
Old Milverton Rd CV32 ..156 C2
Old Moat Dr B31 ....103 B3
Old Moat Way B8 ....68 B6
Old Oak Cl WS9 ....30 D8
Old Oak Rd B38 ....104 A2
Old Oscott Hill B44 ....44 F2
Old Oscott La B44 ......55 E8
Old Park Cl B6 ....66 E7
Old Park La B6 ....64 A5
Old Park Prim Sch WS10 ..41 E5
Old Park Rd Dudley DY1 ..51 A5
 Wednesbury WS10 ....41 E5
Old Park Special Sch
 DY1 ....61 F8
Old Park Rd East WS10 ..41 E4
Old Park Wlk B6 ....66 E7
Old Penkridge Mews
 WS11 ....1 D1
Old Penkridge Rd WS11 ...1 C2
Old Penn's Yd CV12 ....78 A2
Old Pk B29 ....103 A5
Old Pl WS3 ....28 C8
Old Pleck Rd WS2 ....42 C7
Old Port Cl DY4 ....52 B2
Old Portway B38 ....123 E7
Old Postway B19 ....66 D7
Old Quarry Cl B45 .....121 F8
Old Quarry Dr DY3 .....50 D5
Old Rd CV7 ....92 E1
Old Rectory Gdns WS9 ..30 C6
Old Rectory La B48 ....139 B7
Old School Cl WV13 ....27 A2
Old School Dr B65 ......63 C3
Old School Mews CV32 ..157 B3
Old School Yd The B77 ..22 A5
Old Scott Cl B33 ....69 C2
Old Smithy Pl B18 ......66 A5
Old Snow Hill B3 ....164 B4
Old Stone Cl B45 ......164 C3
 Warwick CV34 ....160 E6
Old Sq The **1** WS1 .....28 E1
Old Stables Wlk **2** B7 ..67 C7
Old Stafford Rd WV11 ...11 C8
Old Station Rd
 Birmingham B33 ....68 D4
 Bromsgrove B60 ....137 A1
 Hampton-in-A B92 ......109 A8
Old Stone Cl B45 ......101 F1
Old Stone Yd CV32 .....156 E5
Old Stowheath La WV1 ..26 C1
Old Stratford Rd B60 ...137 C2
Old Swinford Hospital Sch
 DY8 ....81 A4
Old Tokengate **2** B17 ..85 D6
Old Town Cl B38 ......103 F2
Old Town La WS3 ....14 F3
Old Union Mill B16 ....66 B2
Old Vicarage Cl
 Walsall WS3 ....15 A2
 Wombourne WV5 ....49 B6
Old Vicarage Gdns B80 .159 E4
Old Walsall Rd B42 ....54 F7
Old Warstone La WV11 ..13 B8
Old Warwick Ct **1** B92 ..88 C1

Old Warwick Rd
 Lapworth B94,CV35 ....144 D3
 Royal Leamington Spa
  CV31 ....161 E7
 Solihull B92 ....88 C1
Old Waste La CV7 ......130 E6
Old Well Cl WS4 ....29 B7
Old Wharf Rd DY8 ......80 A2
Old Winnings Rd CV7 ...94 F6
Old Woodyard The DY9 ..99 D6
Oldacre Cl B76 ....57 D6
Oldacre Rd B68 ....84 A7
Oldany Way CV10 ....73 D7
Olderberrow Cl **1** B90 ..127 A6
Oldbury Cl B98 ....154 B6
Oldbury Ct B79 ....21 B5
Oldbury Green Ret Pk
 B69 ....63 F8
Oldbury Ho B68 ....64 C2
Oldbury Rd
 Blackheath B65 ....63 D2
 Nuneaton CV10 ....72 A8
 Smethwick B66 ....64 D7
 West Bromwich B70 .....52 F2
Oldbury Ring Way B69 ..64 D7
Oldbury Road Ind Est
 West Bromwich B70 .....52 F2
Oldbury St WS10 ....42 B3
Olde Hall La WS6 ....4 F3
Olde Hall Rd WV10 .....12 C7
Oldfield Dr DY8 ....81 A3
Oldfield Rd
 Birmingham B12 ....87 A6
 Coventry CV5 ....112 E3
 Dudley WV14 ....51 A8
Oldfield Trad Est B64 ..82 D8
Oldfields Blackheath B64 ..82 D8
 Hagley DY9 ....99 A6
 Lane CV2 ....114 E4
Oldhouse Farm Cl B28 .105 F6
Oldington Gr **1** B91 ..127 B8
Oldington Trad Est
 DY11 ....116 B1
Oldknow Jun Sch B10 ..87 E7
Oldknow Rd B10 ....87 E7
Oldnall Cl DY9 ....81 F4
Oldnall Rd
 Kidderminster DY10 ...117 A4
 Stourbridge B63,DY9 ...82 A4
Oldsvinford CE Prim Sch
 DY8 ....81 A3
Oldway Dr B91 ....107 E2
Oldwich La E
 Honiley CV8 ....145 E8
 Knowle CV8 ....129 D1
Oldwich La W B93 ......145 C8
Olga Dr DY4 ....41 B1
Olinthus Ave WV11 .....26 E7
Olive Ave Coventry CV2 .114 D5
 Wolverhampton WV4 ....39 E5
Olive Dr B62 ....83 C8
Olive Hill Prim Sch B62 ..83 D7
Olive Hill Rd B62 ......83 D8
Olive La B62 ....83 C8
Olive Mount B69 ....63 D8
Olive Pl B14 ....104 E7
Oliver Cl **1** DY2 ....62 E8
Oliver Cres WV14 ....40 F2
Oliver Ct B65 ....63 B2
Oliver Rd
 Birmingham, Erdington B23 ..56 F6
 Birmingham, Ladywood B16 ..65 F2
 Smethwick B66 ....65 C3
Oliver St Birmingham B7 ..67 B5
 Coventry CV6 ....113 F6
Oliver Way CV2 ....115 B8
Ollerton Rd B26 ....88 F7
Ollison Dr B74 ....30 F2
Olliver Cl B62 ....83 C4
Oloreshaw Rd B26 ......89 D5
Olton Ave CV5 ....111 E4
Olton Bridge B92 .....106 F8
Olton Bvd E B27 ....88 C2
Olton Bvd W B11 ....87 F3
Olton Mere B92 ....88 E1
Olton Pl CV11 ....72 F4
Olton Rd B90 ....106 B5
Olton Sta B92 ....88 E1
Olton Wharf B92 ....88 E1
Olympus Ave CV34 ....161 D5
Olympus Cl CV5 ....111 B8
Olympus Dr DY4 ....52 D6
Omar Rd CV2 ....114 D2
Ombersley Cl Oldbury B69 ..63 D5
 Redditch B98 ....159 C7

Orchard Ave continued
 Solihull B91 ....107 D5
Orchard Cl
 Birmingham B21 ....54 F1
 Blackheath B65 ....63 A3
 Cheslyn Hay WS6 ....4 E3
 Coleshill B46 ....70 F6
 Curdworth B76 ....59 B7
 Hagley DY9 ....99 B4
 Halesowen B63 ....82 C6
 Hinckley LE10 ....76 A5
 Nuneaton CV10 ....72 B8
 Sutton Coldfield B73 ...57 A8
 Tamworth B77 ....35 C5
 Walsall WS4 ....29 C5
 Willenhall WV13 ....27 B1
Orchard Cres
 Coventry CV3 ....133 C8
 Stoke Prior B60 ....150 C3
 Wolverhampton WV3 ....38 B7
Orchard Croft B45 ....138 D8
Orchard Ct
 Birmingham, Erdington B23 ..57 A5
 Birmingham, Stockland Green
  B23 ....56 B4
 Blackheath B65 ....63 B3
 Coventry CV3 ....115 A1
 Kingswinford DY6 ......60 D6
 Wolverhampton WV3 ....38 B7
Orchard Dr
 Birmingham B31 ....122 F7
 Coventry CV5 ....111 C4
Orchard Gdns WS12 ....1 F6
Orchard Gr Aldridge WS9 .30 B4
 Dudley DY3 ....50 B3
 Sutton Coldfield B74 ...31 F3
 Wolverhampton WV4 ....39 A4
Orchard Ho CV6 ....96 A4
Orchard La Codsall WV8 ..10 B3
 Kenilworth CV8 ....148 C3
 Stourbridge DY9 ....81 E6
Orchard Meadow Wlk
 B35 ....58 B3
Orchard Pl B80 ....159 F8
Orchard Rd
 Birmingham B24 ....57 B5
 Bromsgrove B61 ....136 F4
 Dudley DY2 ....62 C2
 Hockley Heath B94 ....143 C6
 Walsall WS5 ....43 B3
 Willenhall WV13 ....27 B1
 Wolverhampton WV11 ...26 C7
Orchard Ret Pk CV3 ...134 D4
Orchard Rise B26 ......88 F7
Orchard Sch The
 Smethwick B66 ....64 E7
 Smethwick B67 ....65 A5
Orchard St Bedworth CV12 ..78 B4
 Brierley Hill DY5 ....61 D3
 Hinckley LE10 ....75 E8
 Kidderminster DY10 ...116 E6
 Nuneaton CV11 ....73 D4
 Redditch B98 ....153 E3
 Tamworth, Kettlebrook B77 ..21 C3
 Tamworth, The Leys B79 ..21 B5
 Tipton DY4 ....51 F2
Orchard The Bilston WV14 ..40 E5
 Birmingham B37 ....89 F8
 Bromsgrove B61 ....136 F4
 Burntwood WS7 ....7 B7
 Oldbury B68 ....64 C4
 Walsall WS3 ....14 D2
 Wolverhampton WV6 ....24 E6
Orchard Villas
 Fairfield B61 ....120 D2
 Wythall B47 ....124 F1
Orchard Way
 Birmingham, Acock's Green
  B27 ....88 D2
 Birmingham, Perry Common
  B23 ....56 C6
Ostler Cl DY6 ....60 B7
Oswald Rd CV32 ......161 D8
Oswald St B98 ....153 E3
Oswestry Cl B97 ......158 C7
Oswestry Ct B11 ....87 B6
Oswin Gr CV2 ....114 C4
Oswin Pl WS3 ....28 F5
Oswin Rd WS3 ....28 F5
Othello Ave CV34 .....161 F3
Other Rd B98 ....153 E3
Otley Gr B9 ....68 C3
Ottawa Twr **2** B5 ......86 D7
Otter Croft B34 ....69 D5
Otterburn Cl WS12 ......2 E2
Otters Rest CV31 ....162 C5
Otterstone Cl DY3 ......39 C2
Ottery B77 ....36 B5
Ottilie Hild Sch B60 ..150 E5
Oughton Rd B12 ....87 A7
Oulsham Ct **11** B13 ....87 B2
Oundle Cl DY11 ....116 D8
Oundle Ct B74 ....31 F2
Oundle Rd B44 ....55 F7
Ounsdale Cres WV5 ....49 A7
Ounsdale Dr DY2 ....62 C4
Ounsdale Rd WV5 ......49 A7
Ounty John La DY9 .....99 A2
Our Lady & Kenelm RC Sch
 B63 ....83 A4
Our Lady & St Chad's RC Sch
 WV10 ....25 D3
Our Lady & St Rose of Lima
 RC Prim Sch B29 ......85 B1
Our Lady & St Teresa's RC
 Prim Sch CV32 ....157 D5
Our Lady of Compassion RC
 Prim Sch B92 ....106 D7
Our Lady of Fatima RC Prim
 Sch B17 ....84 F7

Ormond Pl WV14 ....40 F6
Ormond Rd B45 ....101 F1
Ormonds Cl WS13 ....8 E6
Ormsby Gr B27 ....106 B7
Ormscliffe Rd B45 ....122 B6
Orphanage Rd B24 .....57 B6
Orpington Dr CV6 ......95 D4
Orpington Rd B44 ......44 E3
Orpwood Rd B33 ....69 B2
Orsino Cl CV34 ....161 E2
Orslow Wlk WV10 ....26 A5
Orton Ave B76 ....58 A6
Orton Cl B46 ....59 A3
Orton Gr WV4 ....38 D4
Orton La WV4,WV5 ......38 A2
Orton Rd CV6 ....95 D4
Orton Way B35 ....58 A1
Orwell Cl Nuneaton CV10 ..72 A5
 Stourbridge DY8 ....80 D4
 Wednesfield WV11 ......26 F5
Orwell Ct CV1 ....165 C4
Orwell Dr
 Birmingham B38 ....123 C8
 West Bromwich B71 ....53 D6
Orwell Pas B5 ....164 C2
Orwell Rd Coventry CV1 .113 F1
 Walsall WS1 ....43 B8
Osbaston Cl
 Coventry CV5 ....111 E4
 Hinckley LE10 ....71 F3
Osberton Dr DY1 ....50 F2
Osborn Ct B73 ....46 B3
Osborn Rd B11 ....87 C6
Osborne Cl Birmingham B6 ..67 A7
 Brierley Hill DY5 ....81 F8
 Kidderminster DY10 ...117 B6
Osborne Ct CV31 ......162 A4
Osborne Dr WS10 ......41 D8
Osborne Gr B19 ....66 C7
Osborne Jun & Inf Sch
 B23 ....57 A5
Osborne Rd
 Birmingham, Erdington B23 ..56 F5
 Birmingham, Handsworth
  B21 ....65 E8
 Coventry CV5 ....133 A8
 West Bromwich B70 ....53 C3
 Wolverhampton WV4 ...38 F5
Osborne Rd S **1** B23 ...56 F4
Osborne Twr B6 ....67 A8
Osbourne Croft B90 ...126 D5
Oscott Ct B6 ....55 F3
Oscott Ct B23 ....56 E8
Oscott Gdns B42 ....55 F3
Oscott Rd B6,B42 ......55 E3
Oscott School La B44 ...44 E2
Osier Gr B23 ....56 B6
Osier Pl WV1 ....25 F2
Osier St WV1 ....25 F2
Oslo Gdns CV2 ....115 A7
Osmaston Rd
 Birmingham B17 ....85 B3
 Stourbridge DY8 ....80 F2
Osmington Gr B63 ......82 D6
Osnor Ct B60 ....151 B7
Osprey B77 ....36 A5
Osprey Cl Coventry CV2 .115 B6
 Nuneaton CV11 ....79 B8
Osprey Dr DY1 ....50 F1
Osprey Ho B80 ....159 D4
Osprey Park Dr DY10 ..117 B3
Osprey Rd
 Birmingham, Acock's Green
  B27 ....88 D2
Our Lady of Lourdes RC Prim
 Sch B13 ....105 D5
Our Lady of the Angels RC Inf
 Sch CV11 ....73 C3
Our Lady of the Assumption
 RC Prim Sch CV4 .....111 E1
Our Lady Of the Wayside RC
 Prim Sch B90 ....126 C8
Our Lady's RC Prim Sch
 B33 ....69 D2
Out Wood Dr B31 ......102 D1
Outermarch Rd CV6 ...113 C7
Outfields B13 ....104 E6
Outlands Dr LE10 ......71 B2
Outmore Rd B33 ....69 C2
Outwood Cl B98 ....158 E7
Oval Prim Sch The B33 ..68 F2
Oval Rd Birmingham B24 ..56 F1
 Tipton DY4 ....51 F6
Oval The
 Dudley DY1 ....61 E8
 Smethwick B67 ....64 D2
 Wednesbury WS10 ....41 F4
Over Brunton Cl B31 ..103 B2
Over Green Dr B37 .....69 F5
Over Mill Dr B29 ....86 B2
Over Pool Rd B8 ....68 A6
Over St CV6 ....114 A8
Overbare Cl B94 ......142 A1
Overberry Cl CV2 ......96 D2
Overbrook Cl DY3 .....50 C2
Overbury Cl
 Birmingham B31 ....103 C3
 Halesowen B63 ....83 A3
Overbury Rd B31 ......103 C3
Overdale Ave B76 ......58 E1
Overdale Cl WV12 .....27 C5
Overdale Ct B13 ....86 F4
Overdale Dr WS2,WV13 ..27 D3
Overdale Rd
 Birmingham B32 ....84 E5
 Coventry CV5 ....112 C3
Overell Gr CV32 ......156 D2
Overend Rd B63,B64 ...82 D7
Overend St B70 ....53 D2
Overfield Dr WV14 .....40 A3
Overfield Rd
 Birmingham B32 ....84 F1
 Dudley DY1 ....61 E8
Overhill Rd WS7 ....7 B5
Overlea Ave B27 ....88 B3
Overmoor Cl B19 ......66 C7
Overseal Rd WV11 .....26 E8
Overslade Cres CV6 ...112 E8
Overslade Rd B91 .....106 F2
Oversley Rd B76 ....58 A6
Overstrand WV9 ....10 F3
Overton Cl B28 ....106 A6
Overton Dr B46 ....59 C3
Overton Gr B27 ....106 C8
Overton La WS7 ....7 C4
Overton Pl Birmingham B7 ..67 A3
 West Bromwich B71 ....53 D6
Overton Rd B27 ....106 C8
Overton Wlk WV4 ....38 C6
Overtons Cl CV31 .....162 F5
Overwood Croft B8 .....67 E3
Overwoods Rd B77 .....36 A4
Owen Pl WV14 ....40 D6
Owen Rd Darlaston WS10 ..41 C8
 Willenhall WV13 ....41 C8
 Wolverhampton WV3 ...39 A8
Owen Road Ind Est
 WV13 ....27 C1
Owen St Darlaston WS10 ..41 D7
 Dudley DY2 ....62 E8
 Tipton DY4 ....51 E5
Owenford Rd CV6 .....113 C7
Owens Croft B38 ......104 A1
Owens Way B64 ....63 A1
Oxnall Rd B24 ....69 C6
Ox Cl CV2 ....114 A6
Ox Leasow B32 ....84 C2
Ox Leys Rd B75,B76 ...47 D3
Ox St DY3 ....50 D4
Oxbarn Ave WV3 ....38 E7
Oxbow Way DY10 ......116 E8
Oxbridge Way B79 .....20 E6
Oxendon Way CV3 .....134 E8
Oxenton Croft B63 .....82 D2
Oxford Cl Birmingham B8 ..68 B5
 Great Wyrley WS6 ....4 F3
 Nuneaton CV11 ....73 F8
Oxford Ct **3** B29 ......103 C2
Oxford Dr Birmingham B27 ..88 D4
 Stourbridge DY8 ....80 F4
Oxford Gr WS11 ....1 C8
Oxford Pl **1** CV32 ....156 F1
Oxford Rd
 Birmingham, Acock's Green
  B27 ....88 C3
 Birmingham, Erdington B23 ..56 F4
 Birmingham, Moseley B13 ..87 A2
 Cannock WS11 ....4 F8
 Ryton-on-D CV8 ....134 F1
 Smethwick B66 ....53 B3
 West Bromwich B70 ....53 B3
Oxford Row **14** CV34 ..156 F1
Oxford St Bilston WV14 ..40 F5
 Birmingham, Digbeth B5 .164 D2
 Birmingham, Stirchley B30 ..104 A7
 Coventry CV1 ....113 E3
 Dudley DY1 ....51 B1
 Kidderminster DY10 ...116 E5

Oxford St *continued*
Royal Leamington Spa
CV32 ....156 F1
Walsall WS2 ....42 C7
Wednesbury WS10 ....42 B3
Wolverhampton WV1 ....163 D2
Oxford Street Ind Pk
WV14 ....40 F5
Oxford Street Island
WV14 ....40 E5
Oxford Terr WS10 ....42 B2
Oxford Trad Est B5 ....164 D1
Oxhayes Cl CV7 ....130 C6
Oxhill Cl B98 ....154 E1
Oxhill Rd Birmingham B21 ....54 E2
Solihull B90 ....105 C2
Oxleasow Rd B98 ....154 E4
Oxley Ave WV10 ....25 C6
Oxley Cl Dudley DY2 ....62 B2
Great Wyrley WS6 ....4 F1
Oxley Dr CV3 ....133 C3
Oxley Gr B29 ....103 A8
Oxley Jun & Inf Sch
WV10 ....25 C7
Oxley La WV1 ....163 B4
Oxley Links Rd WV10 ....25 B8
Oxley Moor Rd
Wolverhampton WV10 ....25 A8
Wolverhampton, Blakeley Green
WV9 ....24 F8
Wolverhampton, Oxley WV9,
WV10 ....11 B1
Oxley St WV1 ....25 C4
Oxlip Cl WS5 ....43 A3
Oxpiece Dr B36 ....68 D8
Oxstall Cl B76 ....58 D5
Oxted Cl WV11 ....26 F5
Oxted Croft B23 ....56 E3
Oxwood La B32 ....101 D4

P

Pace Cres WV14 ....41 A2
Pacific Ave WS10 ....41 D1
Packenham Dr B76 ....57 F8
Packhorse La B38,B47 ....124 E6
Packington Ave
Allesley CV5 ....112 B6
Birmingham B34 ....69 D5
Packington Ct B74 ....31 E4
Packington La
Little Packington CV7 ....91 C6
Outwoods B46,CV7 ....92 B8
Weeford B78 ....19 F5
White Stitch CV7 ....92 A3
Packington Pl 6 CV31 ....162 A7
Packmore St CV34 ....160 F8
Packmores B90 ....126 A5
Packwood Cl
Bentley Heath B93 ....127 E4
Birmingham B20 ....55 A2
Nuneaton CV11 ....78 F8
Redditch B97 ....152 F1
Royal Leamington Spa
CV31 ....162 C5
Willenhall WV13 ....40 F8
Packwood Cotts B93 ....127 F1
Packwood Ct
1 Birmingham B29 ....84 F1
Solihull B91 ....107 C5
Packwood Dr B43 ....43 D1
Packwood Gn CV5 ....112 A3
Packwood Ho
Birmingham B15 ....86 C8
* Lapworth B94 ....144 A5
Sutton Coldfield B73 ....46 A3
Packwood La B94 ....144 A4
Packwood Mews 5
CV34 ....161 B8
Packwood Rd
Birmingham B26 ....89 B8
Lapworth B94 ....144 A7
Tipton B69 ....52 A1
Padarn Cl DY3 ....39 C1
Padbury WV9 ....11 B3
Padbury Ho B31 ....102 D5
Paddiford Pl CV10 ....72 C3
Paddington Rd B21 ....54 C1
Paddington Wlk WS2 ....27 F4
Paddock Dr
Birmingham B26 ....89 A7
Dorridge B93 ....128 A2
Paddock La Aldridge WS9 ....30 A5
Great Wyrley WS6 ....5 A3
Redditch B98 ....158 E7
Walsall WS1 ....28 F1
Paddock The
Bilston WV14 ....40 D1
Birmingham B31 ....103 C4
Dudley DY3 ....50 E5
Lichfield WS14 ....9 C5
Perton WV6 ....23 D4
Stoke Heath B60 ....150 D6
Stourbridge DY9 ....99 C8
Paddock View WV6 ....25 B5
Paddocks Cl B78 ....22 F1
Paddocks Gn B18 ....66 A5
Paddocks Rd B47 ....124 F6
Paddocks The
Bulkington CV12 ....79 B3
Kenilworth CV8 ....148 B5
Warwick CV34 ....160 F7
Paddys Wide Water Est
DY5 ....61 C5

Padgate Cl B35 ....58 B3
Padgets La B98 ....154 D4
Padmore Ct CV31 ....162 B6
Padstow B77 ....21 F5
Padstow Cl CV11 ....73 F5
Padstow Rd
Birmingham B24 ....57 D4
Coventry CV4 ....131 E8
Padua Rd B60 ....137 C1
Paganal Dr B70 ....53 E1
Paganel Dr DY1 ....51 C3
Paganel Inf Sch B29 ....85 A2
Paganel Jun Sch B29 ....85 A2
Paganel Rd B29 ....85 A2
Pagat Mews B76 ....47 A2
Page Rd CV4 ....131 E7
Pageant Ct B12 ....86 E5
Pages Cl B75 ....46 C5
Pages Ct B43 ....43 E1
Pages La B43 ....43 E1
Paget Cl Bromsgrove B61 ....136 E2
Dudley WV14 ....51 B8
Paget Ct CV2 ....96 B3
Paget Ho DY4 ....52 B3
Paget Prim Sch B24 ....57 C4
Paget Rd Birmingham B24 ....57 D4
Wolverhampton WV3,WV6 ....24 F3
Paget St WV1 ....163 A4
Pagham Cl WV9 ....10 F2
Pagnell Gr B13 ....105 C6
Paignton Rd B16 ....65 D3
Pailton Cl CV2 ....96 C2
Pailton Gr B29 ....85 B1
Pailton Rd B90 ....106 B5
Painswick Cl
Redditch B98 ....158 E6
Walsall WS5 ....43 B3
Painswick Rd B28 ....105 F7
Paint Cup Row DY2 ....62 C2
Painters Cnr 8 B66 ....65 C5
Painters Croft WV14 ....40 E1
Pake's Croft 3 CV6 ....113 A5
Pakefield Rd B30 ....104 C3
Pakenham Cl B76 ....57 F8
Pakenham Ho B76 ....57 F8
Pakenham Rd B15 ....86 C7
Pakenham Village B15 ....86 C7
Pakfield Wlk B6 ....66 F8
Palace Cl B65 ....63 D4
Palace Dr B66 ....64 D8
Palace Rd B9 ....67 E1
Pale La B17 ....84 F8
Pale St DY3 ....50 E5
Palefield Rd B90 ....126 F6
Palermo Ave CV3 ....133 E6
Palethorpe Rd DY4 ....52 A8
Palfrey Jun & Inf Schs
WS1 ....42 D7
Palfrey Rd DY8 ....80 D5
Pallasades Sh Ctr The
B2 ....164 B2
Pallett Dr CV11 ....73 F7
Palm Croft DY5 ....81 C8
Palm Tree Ave CV2 ....96 C2
Palmcourt Ave B28 ....105 E7
Palmer Cl WV11 ....12 F1
Palmer La CV1 ....165 B3
Palmer Rd Hinckley LE10 ....71 B2
Whitnash CV31 ....162 B4
Palmer St B9 ....67 A2
Palmers Cl Codsall WV8 ....10 C1
Solihull B90 ....106 B5
Palmers Cross Prim Sch
WV6 ....24 D8
Palmers Gr B36 ....68 E8
Palmers Rd B98 ....154 F5
Palmers Way WV8 ....10 C1
Palmerston Dr B69 ....52 D2
Palmerston Rd
Birmingham B11 ....87 B6
Coventry CV5 ....132 F8
Palmvale Croft B26 ....89 A6
Palmyra Rd B60 ....137 C2
Palomino Pl B16 ....65 F2
Pamela Rd B31 ....103 A3
Pan Croft B36 ....68 C7
Pancras Cl CV2 ....96 E1
Pandora Rd CV2 ....114 E7
Pangbourne Cl CV11 ....73 F8
Pangbourne Rd CV2 ....114 C8
Pangfield Pk CV5 ....112 C4
Panjab Gdns B67 ....64 F6
Pannel Croft B19 ....66 D6
Panther Croft B34 ....69 D5
Papenham Gn CV4 ....132 A8
Paper Mill Dr B98 ....154 B5
Paper Mill End B44 ....55 D6
Papworth Dr B61 ....136 F5
Papyrus Way B36 ....57 F1
Par Gn B38 ....103 D1
Parade Birmingham B1 ....164 A3
Royal Leamington Spa
CV32 ....161 F8
Parade The
Birmingham B37 ....70 A5
Blackheath B64 ....82 E8
Brownhills WS8 ....6 E1
Dudley DY1 ....51 B2
6 Hinckley LE10 ....75 D8
Kingswinford DY6 ....60 B7
Nuneaton CV11 ....73 C3
Sutton Coldfield B72 ....46 C5
Parade View WS8 ....15 E8
Paradise DY2 ....62 D8
Paradise Circus Queensway
B1,B3 ....164 A2
Paradise Ct B28 ....105 D6
Paradise Gr WS3 ....14 F3

Paradise Ho 4 CV6 ....113 F7
Paradise La
Birmingham B28 ....105 E6
Walsall WS3 ....14 F3
Wolverhampton WV10 ....11 E8
Paradise Row B60 ....136 F2
Paradise St
Birmingham B3 ....164 B2
Coventry CV1 ....165 C1
Warwick CV34 ....160 F8
Paradise Way CV2 ....97 B1
Paradise Works CV6 ....113 F7
Paragon Way CV7 ....96 B8
Parbrook Cl CV4 ....131 E8
Parbury B77 ....35 D5
Parchments The WS13 ....3 B1
Pardington Cl B92 ....107 E8
Pargeter Ct 1 WS2 ....28 C2
Pargeter Rd B67 ....64 F2
Pargeter St
Stourbridge DY8 ....80 F4
Walsall WS2 ....28 C3
Parish Gdns DY9 ....81 C1
Parish Hill B61 ....120 D1
Parisienne Ho CV5 ....112 E2
Park App B23 ....56 C2
Park Ave
1 Birmingham, Balsall Heath
B12 ....86 F5
Birmingham, Hockley B18 ....66 A6
Birmingham, King's Norton
B30 ....104 A5
Blackheath B65 ....63 C3
Burntwood WS7 ....7 B5
Coleshill B46 ....70 F6
Coventry CV6 ....95 C3
Norton Canes WS11 ....6 A5
Nuneaton CV11 ....73 E3
Oldbury B68 ....64 B3
Smethwick B67 ....64 F4
Solihull B91 ....107 D3
Studley B80 ....159 E3
Tipton DY4 ....51 E5
Willenhall WV13 ....26 F2
Wolverhampton WV1 ....163 A4
Wolverhampton, Goldthorn Park
WV4 ....39 C5
Wombourne WV5 ....49 A5
Park Bldgs DY3 ....50 C4
Park Butts Ringway
DY11 ....116 D6
Park Cir B6 ....66 F7
Park Cl Brownhills WS8 ....15 F8
Cheslyn Hay WS6 ....4 E3
Dudley DY1 ....51 B7
Kenilworth CV8 ....148 B5
Solihull B92 ....89 D2
Sutton Coldfield B24 ....57 D5
Tipton B69 ....63 C7
Park Cres
West Bromwich B71 ....53 D4
Wolverhampton WV1 ....163 A3
Park Croft
Chase Terrace WS7 ....6 C8
Hollywood B47 ....125 A5
Park Ct Allesley CV5 ....112 B6
Blackheath B65 ....63 C3
Kidderminster DY11 ....116 D5
Redditch B98 ....154 A3
Sutton Coldfield B73 ....45 F1
Park Dale Ct WV1 ....25 A3
Park Dale E WV1 ....25 A3
Park Dale W WV1 ....25 A3
Park Dr Little Aston B74 ....31 C4
Royal Leamington Spa
CV31 ....161 E7
Sutton Coldfield B74 ....31 F2
Wolverhampton WV4 ....39 C5
Park Edge B17 ....85 C7
Park End WS14 ....9 E7
Park End Dr B32 ....84 D1
Park Farm Ind Est B98 ....159 C7
Park Farm Rd
Birmingham B43 ....44 B3
Tamworth B77 ....21 C1
Park Gr Birmingham B10 ....87 D8
Water Orton B46 ....59 C2
Park Hall Cl WS5 ....43 C6
Park Hall Cres B36 ....69 C8
Park Hall Inf Sch WS5 ....43 C7
Park Hall Jun Sch WS5 ....43 C7
Park Hall Rd Walsall WS5 ....43 D6
Wolverhampton WV4 ....39 D5
Park Hall Sch B36 ....58 E1
Park Head Cres DY2 ....62 B8
Park Head Rd DY2 ....62 B8
Park Hill Birmingham B13 ....86 E4
Blackheath B65 ....63 B1
Kenilworth CV8 ....148 B5
Wednesbury WS10 ....42 C4
Park Hill Dr B20 ....54 F4
Park Hill Jun Sch CV8 ....148 C5
Park Hill La Allesley CV5 ....112 A6
Coventry CV5 ....112 A5
Park Hill Prim Sch
Birmingham B13 ....86 F4
Coventry CV5 ....112 A4
Wednesbury WS10 ....42 C4
Park Hill Rd
Birmingham B17 ....85 C6
Smethwick B67 ....65 A5
Park Hill St DY2 ....62 E8
Park Ho 1 B66 ....65 C5
Park Inn DY4 ....52 A4
Park La Berkswell CV7 ....110 B2
Birmingham, Aston B6 ....66 F7
Birmingham, Castle Vale
B35 ....58 C4

Park La *continued*
Birmingham, Handsworth
B21 ....54 B3
Fazeley B78 ....20 E2
Great Wyrley WS6 ....5 A3
Halesowen B63 ....82 B6
Harvington DY10 ....118 A2
Kidderminster DY11 ....116 D6
Kingswinford DY6 ....60 E7
Nuneaton CV10 ....72 A3
Oldbury B69 ....64 A6
Shenstone WS14 ....18 B4
Wednesbury WS10 ....42 A5
Wolverhampton WV10 ....25 E6
Park La E DY4 ....52 B4
Park La W DY4 ....51 F4
Park Lane Ind Est
West Bromwich B21 ....54 B1
Wolverhampton WV10 ....25 E5
Park Lane Trad Est B69 ....64 A6
Park Lime Dr WS4 ....29 B4
Park Lime Pits Ctry Pk
WS4 ....29 C4
Park Mall WS1 ....28 E2
Park Meadow Ave WV14 ....40 C8
Park Mews B29 ....85 B1
Park Paling The CV3 ....133 E7
Park Pl B7 ....67 C7
Park Rd Bedworth CV12 ....78 B2
Bilston WV14 ....40 C5
Birmingham, Aston B6 ....67 A7
Birmingham, Hockley B18 ....66 A6
Birmingham, Moseley B13 ....86 F4
Birmingham, Sparkhill B11 ....87 C3
Birmingham, Stockland Green
B23 ....56 C2
Brierley Hill DY5 ....81 F8
Burntwood, Chase Terrace
WS7 ....6 F8
Burntwood, Chasetown WS7 ....7 B5
Cannock WS11 ....1 D1
Coleshill B46 ....70 F6
Coventry CV1 ....165 B1
Darlaston WS10 ....41 C6
Dudley, Lower Gornal DY3 ....50 C4
Dudley, Netherton DY2 ....62 C6
Dudley, West Coseley DY1 ....51 B7
Featherstone WV10 ....12 D8
Hagley DY9 ....99 B6
Halesowen B63 ....82 B5
Hinckley LE10 ....75 E8
Kenilworth CV8 ....148 A6
Norton Canes WS11 ....6 A5
Royal Leamington Spa
CV32 ....157 A4
Smethwick B67 ....64 F1
Solihull B91 ....107 D3
Stourbridge DY8 ....80 D5
Sutton Coldfield B73 ....46 B5
Tamworth B77 ....35 C5
Tipton B69 ....63 C8
Walsall, Daw End WS4 ....29 C5
Walsall, The Chuckery WS5 ....43 D5
Walsall, Wallington Heath
WS3 ....14 B1
Willenhall WV13 ....26 F3
Park Rd E WV1 ....163 A4
Park Rd N B6 ....67 A7
Park Rd S B18 ....66 B5
Park Rd W
Stourbridge DY8 ....80 D5
Wolverhampton WV1 ....25 A3
Park Retreat B66 ....65 B5
Park Ridge B74 ....46 A7
Park Ridge Dr B63 ....82 B6
Park Rise
Kidderminster DY11 ....116 D5
Wolverhampton WV3 ....24 E2
Park Sch B79 ....21 A7
Park Sq B37 ....90 D8
Park St
Birmingham, Aston B6 ....67 A7
Birmingham, Digbeth B5 ....164 D2
Blackheath, Cradley Heath
B64 ....62 E2
Blackheath, Rowley Regis
B65 ....63 D1
Cannock WS11 ....4 E6
Cheslyn Hay WS6 ....4 E3
Coventry CV6 ....113 E7
Darlaston WS10 ....41 C5
Kidderminster DY11 ....116 D5
Kingswinford DY6 ....60 D6
Nuneaton CV11 ....73 D3
Oldbury B69 ....63 F6
Royal Leamington Spa
CV32 ....156 F1
Stourbridge, Amblecote DY8 ....80 F8
Stourbridge, Lye DY9 ....81 F5
Stourbridge, Stambermill
DY8 ....81 A5
Tamworth B79 ....21 A5
Tipton DY4 ....52 A5
Walsall WS1 ....28 E2
Wednesbury WS10 ....41 F3
West Bromwich B70 ....53 D3
Park St Arc 3 WS1 ....28 E2
Park St S WV2 ....39 C6
Park Street Gdns DY11 ....116 D6
Park Terr Birmingham B21 ....65 E8
Darlaston WS10 ....41 B6
Park The B97 ....152 C7
Park Trad Est B18 ....66 A6
Park Tree Wlk B24 ....57 D4
Park Venture Ctr WS11 ....4 E6
Park View
Birmingham, Rotton Park
B18 ....65 E4

Park View *continued*
Birmingham, Small Heath
B10 ....87 D7
Coventry CV3 ....114 A2
Darlaston WS10 ....41 C6
Hockley Heath B94 ....143 C6
Sutton Coldfield B73 ....46 A6
Park View Cl CV7 ....96 A8
Park View Ct WS11 ....1 D1
Park View Rd
Birmingham B31 ....102 F3
Stourbridge DY9 ....81 F4
Sutton Coldfield B74 ....31 D3
Park View Sch B8 ....67 F5
Park Villas 10 B9 ....67 B2
Park Way
Birmingham B45 ....122 B8
Redditch B98 ....154 A5
Wolverhampton WV11 ....13 A1
Park Wlk Brierley Hill DY5 ....81 F8
4 Redditch B97 ....153 E3
Park Wood Ct B74 ....31 F2
Park Wood La CV4 ....131 D7
Parkbrook Ind Est 5
DY9 ....81 F5
Parkdale DY3 ....50 D8
Parkdale Ave WS10 ....42 A4
Parkdale Cl B24 ....56 F2
Parkdale Ct WS10 ....42 A4
Parkdale Dr B31 ....123 A7
Parkdale Rd B26 ....89 D6
Parker Ho B14 ....104 F3
Parker Paul Ind Est WV2 ....39 C7
Parker Rd WV11 ....12 F1
Parker St Birmingham B16 ....65 F1
Walsall WS3 ....14 A1
Parkes Ave WV8 ....10 B2
Parkes Fold DY4 ....51 F8
Parkes Hall Rd DY1 ....51 A6
Parkes Ho 8 B69 ....64 A7
Parkes La Dudley DY3 ....51 A7
Tipton DY4 ....51 F8
Parkes St Brierley Hill DY5 ....61 D3
Smethwick B67 ....64 F4
Warwick CV34 ....160 D7
Willenhall WV13 ....27 B1
Parkeston Cres B44 ....45 C1
Parkfield Birmingham B32 ....84 A2
Dorridge B93 ....128 A1
Parkfield Ave B77 ....21 C1
Parkfield Cl
Birmingham B15 ....86 C7
Halesowen B62 ....84 A5
Redditch B98 ....154 B6
Tamworth B77 ....35 C8
Parkfield Colliery WV4 ....39 F5
Parkfield Cres
Tamworth B77 ....35 C8
Wolverhampton WV2 ....39 E6
Parkfield Ct 11 B46 ....70 F7
Parkfield Dr
Birmingham B36 ....58 C1
Kenilworth CV8 ....148 B5
Parkfield Gr WV2 ....39 E6
Parkfield High Sch WV4 ....39 E5
Parkfield Inf & Jun Sch
B8 ....67 E3
Parkfield Jun & Inf Sch
WV4 ....39 E5
Parkfield Rd
Birmingham B8 ....67 E4
Coleshill B46 ....70 F6
Dudley DY2 ....62 E6
Keresley CV7 ....95 A6
Oldbury B68 ....64 A3
Stourbridge DY8 ....81 B5
Wolverhampton WV2,WV4 ....39 E6
Parkgate Prim Sch CV6 ....95 B3
Parkgate Rd CV6 ....95 C3
Parkhall Croft B34 ....69 C7
Parkhill Dr CV5 ....112 A5
Parkhill Rd Burntwood WS7 ....7 A8
Sutton Coldfield B76 ....57 F6
Parkhouse Ave WV11 ....26 B6
Parkhouse Dr B23 ....56 B5
Parkhouse Gdns DY3 ....50 C4
Parkland Ave DY11 ....116 B5
Parkland Cl CV6 ....95 C3
Parklands B91 ....107 A3
Parklands Ave CV32 ....157 C4
Parklands Ct B17 ....85 A6
Parklands Dr B74 ....45 F8
Parklands Gdns WS1 ....43 A8
Parklands Rd
Darlaston WS10 ....41 E5
Wolverhampton WV1 ....26 A1
Parklands The
Birmingham B23 ....56 D5
Kingswinford DY6 ....60 D6
Stourbridge DY9 ....81 D3
Wolverhampton WV3 ....24 D1
Parkrose Ind Est B66 ....65 B7
Parks Cres WV11 ....13 A3
Parkside Birmingham B32 ....84 C2
Coventry CV1 ....165 C2
Tamworth B77 ....21 E1
Parkside Ave WV13 ....26 E2
Parkside Cl WS10 ....42 B3
Parkside Ct LE10 ....75 E8
Parkside Ind Est WV1 ....25 F1
Parkside Jun Sch B66 ....65 B5
Parkside La WS11 ....1 A2
Parkside Mid Sch B61 ....137 A3
Parkside Rd
Birmingham B20 ....54 E6
Halesowen B63 ....82 D5
Parkside Way
Aldridge B74 ....31 A1

Parkside Way continued
Birmingham B31 ....102 C1
Parkway Ave B61 ....150 D8
Parkstone Cl WS4 ....13 C1
Parkstone Rd CV6 ....95 F2
Parkview CV5 ....165 A1
Parkview Cres WS2 ....28 A4
Parkview Ct DY6 ....60 B8
Parkview Dr
Birmingham B8 ....68 A6
Brownhills WS8 ....6 F2
Parkview Rd WV14 ....40 C8
Parkview Trad Est B38 ....103 F3
Parkville Ave B17 ....95 B3
Parkville Cl WV6 ....95 C3
Parkville Highway CV6 ......95 B3
Parkway Birmingham B8 ....68 A5
Coventry CV2 ....115 B8
Parkway Ind Ctr B7 ....67 A4
Parkway Rd DY1 ....51 A2
Parkway Rdbt WV10 ....41 E1
Parkway The Perton WV6 ..23 F4
Walsall WS4 ....29 C8
Parkwood Cl WS8 ....16 A5
Parkwood Croft B43 ....44 B1
Parkwood Ct CV8 ....148 B5
Parkwood Dr B73 ....45 C2
Parkwood Rd B61 ....136 E3
Parkyn St WV2 ....39 E8
Parliament St
Birmingham, Aston B6 ......66 F6
Birmingham, Small Heath
B10 ....87 C8
West Bromwich B70 ....53 D1
Parlows End B38 ....123 D7
Parmington Cl B97 ....158 B6
Parmiter Ho CV32 ....156 F2
Parolles Cl CV34 ....161 E3
Parr Ct CV34 ....161 D6
Parrotts Gr CV2 ....96 D5
Parry Rd Coventry CV2 ....114 C7
Kidderminster DY11 ......116 B3
Wednesfield WV11 ....27 A8
Parson St B77 ....35 F3
Parson's Hill B30 ....104 B2
Parson's La LE10 ....75 F8
Parson's Nook CV2 ....114 A5
Parsonage Dr
Birmingham B45 ....122 D4
Halesowen B63 ....82 A7
Parsonage St Oldbury B69 ..64 B7
West Bromwich B71 ....53 D6
Parsons Hill B68 ....64 B2
Parsons Hollow B77 ....35 E7
Parsons Rd B98 ....153 E2
Parsons St DY1 ....51 C1
Parsons Way CV7 ....27 F6
Partons Rd B14 ....104 D6
Partridge Ave WS10 ....41 B6
Partridge Cl
Birmingham B37 ....70 D3
Huntington WS12 ....1 D7
Partridge Croft
Coventry CV6 ....96 A1
Lichfield WS13 ....9 C8
Partridge Ct
Birmingham B4 ....164 C4
◆ Wednesbury WS10 ......41 F3
Partridge Gr DY10 ....117 A2
Partridge La B97 ....158 A7
Partridge Mill WS3 ....14 E3
Partridge Rd
Birmingham B26 ....69 A1
Stourbridge DY8 ....80 C4
Passey Rd B13 ....87 D2
Passfield Ave WS12 ....22 C7
Passfield Rd B33 ....69 A3
Pasture Gate WS11 ....1 C2
Pasture View 14 F2
Pastures The WV6 ....23 D4
Pastures Wlk B38 ....123 D7
Pat Davis Ct DY10 ....116 E7
Patch La B98 ....158 F6
Patent Dr WS10 ....41 D3
Patent Shaft Rdbt WS10 ..41 D3
Paternoster Row
Birmingham B5 ....66 F2
◆ Kidderminster DY11 ..116 D6
Wolverhampton WV1 ....163 B3
Paterson Ct B93 ....128 C6
Paterson Pl WS8 ....16 B5
Pathlow Cres B90 ....106 A1
Patience Gr CV34 ....161 F3
Patios The DY11 ....116 C7
Paton Gr B13 ....86 F2
Patricia Ave
Birmingham B14 ....105 C4
Wolverhampton WV4 ....39 D5
Patricia Cl CV4 ....111 C1
Patricia Cres DY1 ....51 B7
Patricia Dr DY1 ....52 A2
Patrick Gregory Rd
WV11 ....26 F6
Patrick Ho ◆ WV11 ....2 A3
Patrick Rd B26 ....88 E7
Patriot Cl WS1 ....42 D5
Patshull Ave WV10 ....11 B3
Patshull Cl B43 ....43 D1
Patshull Gr WV10 ....11 B3
Patshull Ho WV6 ....24 E5
Patshull Pl ◆ B19 ....66 C7
Pattens Rd B14 ....105 C4
Patterdale Rd
Birmingham B23 ....56 D4
Cannock WS11 ....2 A4
Patterdale Way DY5 ....81 B8
Patterton Dr B76 ....58 A7
Pattingham Rd WV6 ....23 C2

Pattison Coll CV3 ....114 A2
Pattison Gdns B23 ....56 D2
Pattison St WS5 ....42 E5
Paul Byrne Ct B20 ....55 B1
Paul Pursehouse Rd
WV14 ....40 D3
Paul St Dudley WV14 ....40 A1
Wednesbury WS10 ....42 B2
Wolverhampton WV2 ....163 B2
Paul Stacy Ho CV1 ....165 D4
Paul Vale DY4 ....52 B5
Pauline Ave CV6 ....96 B2
Pauls Coppice WS8 ....16 A5
Pauls Wlk WS13 ....3 A3
Pavenham Dr B5 ....86 C4
Pavilion Ave B67 ....64 D3
Pavilion Gdns
Bromsgrove B61 ....136 F5
Dudley DY2 ....62 C2
Pavilion Rd B6 ....55 F3
Pavilion The B77 ....22 B3
Pavilion Way CV5 ....112 F3
Pavilions Sh Ctr B4 ......164 C2
Pavilion Cl WS9 ....30 C7
Pavior's Rd WS7 ....6 E4
Paxford Cl B98 ....154 B6
Paxford Way B31 ....102 F6
Paxmead Cl CV6 ....95 B1
Paxton Ave WV6 ....23 E3
Paxton Cl B60 ....137 B1
Paxton Rd
Birmingham B18 ....66 A5
Coventry CV6 ....113 A4
Stourbridge DY9 ....82 A4
Payne Cl CV32 ....157 A2
Payne St B65 ....63 C1
Payne's La CV1 ....113 F3
Paynell Cl CV6 ....95 B1
Paynton Wlk ◆ B15 ....86 D8
Payton Cl B69 ....52 E1
Payton Rd B21 ....65 D8
PDH Ind Est
Wednesbury WS10 ....41 C3
Willenhall WV13 ....26 D3
Peace Cl WS6 ....4 E3
Peace Wlk B37 ....70 B1
Peach Ave WS10 ....41 C6
Peach Ley Rd B29 ....102 F7
Peach La WV4 ....39 A2
Peachley Cl ◆ B63 ....83 B3
Peacock Ave Coventry CV2 ..96 F1
Wednesfield WV11 ....27 A7
Peacock Cl DY4 ....52 B4
Peacock Mews DY10 ......116 E8
Peacock Rd
Birmingham B13 ....104 F6
Darlaston WS10 ....41 B7
Peacocks Est B64 ....62 C1
Peacocks The CV34 ......160 B2
Peak Croft B36 ....68 D8
Peak Dr DY3 ....50 E3
Peak House Rd B43 ....43 E4
Peak Rd DY8 ....81 B6
Peake Ave CV11 ....73 E7
Peake Cres WS8 ....15 F5
Peake Dr DY4 ....52 B4
Peake Rd WS8 ....16 A5
Peakman Cl B45 ....122 A6
Peakman St B98 ....153 E4
Peaks L Ctr B79 ....21 B3
Peal St WS1 ....42 F1
Pear Tree Ave
Nuneaton CV10 ....72 E6
Tipton DY4 ....51 F5
Pear Tree Cl
Birmingham, Grove Vale
B43 ....43 B1
Birmingham, Stechford B33 ..68 D2
◆ Coventry CV2 ....1 C7
Huntington WS12 ....1 C7
Kidderminster DY10 ......117 B7
Shuttington B79 ....22 E7
Solihull B90 ....105 D2
Pear Tree Cres B90 ......105 C2
Pear Tree Ct
Birmingham B43 ....54 C8
Blackheath B65 ....63 D3
Pear Tree Dr
Birmingham B43 ....43 C1
Blackheath B65 ....63 D3
Pear Tree Gr B90 ....105 D2
Pear Tree La
Brownhills WS8 ....6 C2
Dudley WV14 ....51 D8
Wolverhampton WV11 ......26 B8
Pear Tree Rd
Birmingham B34 ....69 C6
Birmingham, Grove Vale
B43 ....43 B1
Smethwick B67 ....64 F4
Pears Cl DY1 ....61 E8
Pearl Gr
Birmingham, Acock's Green
B27 ....88 B3
◆ Birmingham, Rotton Park
B18 ....65 E3
Pearl Hyde Ho ◆ CV1 ..165 C4
Pearl Hyde Prim Sch
CV2 ....115 A5
Pearman Rd
Birmingham B45 ....101 D1
Smethwick B66 ....65 A3
Pearmans Croft B47 ......125 A6
Pears Cl CV3 ....147 F5
Pearsall Dr B69 ....63 E8
Pearson Ave CV6 ....96 B2
Pearson Ct WV12 ....27 D4
Pearson St Blackheath B64 ..62 E1

Pearson St continued
Brierley Hill DY5 ....61 D3
Stourbridge DY9 ....81 F4
West Bromwich B70 ....53 B4
Wolverhampton WV2 ....163 B1
Peart Dr B80 ....159 C4
Peartree Ave WV13 ....27 B3
Peartree Dr DY8 ....81 A2
Peartree Ind Est DY2 ......62 A6
Peartree La
Blackheath B64 ....62 E1
Dudley DY2 ....62 A6
Peascroft La WV14 ....40 E6
Peasefield Cl B21 ....65 C8
Pebble Cl Stourbridge DY8 ..81 B5
Tamworth B77 ....22 B3
Pebble Island Way
CV31 ....162 C5
Pebble Mill Cl WS11 ....1 F2
Pebble Mill Dr WS11 ....2 A2
Pebble Mill Rd B5 ....86 C4
Pebblebrook Way DY4 ......78 C1
Pebworth Ave B90 ....127 B6
Pebworth Cl
Birmingham B29 ....86 B2
Coventry CV5 ....112 B3
Redditch B98 ....154 C7
Pebworth Gr
Birmingham B33 ....89 C8
Dudley DY1 ....51 B3
Peckham Rd B44 ....45 A2
Peckingham St ◆ B63 ......83 B3
Peckover Cl B65 ....63 C1
Peddimore La B76 ....58 C7
Pedmore CE Prim Sch
DY9 ....81 C1
Pedmore Cl B98 ....159 B7
Pedmore Court Rd DY8 ..81 B1
Pedmore Gr B44 ....44 F2
Pedmore Hall La DY9 ......99 C8
Pedmore La Hagley DY9 ..99 F8
Stourbridge DY9 ....81 E1
Pedmore Rd
Brierley Hill DY5, DY2 ......61 F4
Stourbridge DY9 ....81 E5
Pedmore Road Ind Est
DY5 ....61 F4
Pedmore Wlk B69 ....63 D5
Peel Cl Coventry CV6 ......113 E6
Darlaston WS10 ....41 D8
Drayton Bassett B78 ......34 E5
Hampton-in-A B92 ....109 B6
Willenhall WV13 ....27 A2
Peel Ct Cannock WS11 ......1 E1
Fazeley B78 ....35 B8
Peel Dr WS12 ....1 F8
Peel Ho B79 ....21 A4
Peel La CV6 ....113 F5
Peel Rd CV34 ....160 D6
Peel St Birmingham B18 ..65 E5
Coventry CV6 ....113 E6
Dudley DY2 ....62 E8
Kidderminster DY11 ......116 D5
Tipton DY4 ....52 A4
West Bromwich B71 ....53 C5
Willenhall WV13 ....27 A1
Wolverhampton WV3 ....163 B2
Peel Way B69 ....52 D2
Peel Wlk B17 ....84 F7
Peelers Way B77 ....21 C1
Pegasus Ct B62 ....83 F5
Pegasus Prim Sch B35 ....58 B3
Pegasus Wlk
Birmingham B29 ....85 D1
Tamworth B79 ....20 F7
Pegleg Wlg ◆ B14 ....104 C2
Pegmill Cl CV3 ....133 F8
Pelham Dr DY1 ....51 A2
Pelham Lodge DY10 ......117 A5
Pelham Rd B8 ....68 A5
Pelham St WV3 ....25 B1
Pelsall La Walsall WS4 ....15 A1
Walsall, Little Bloxwich
WS3 ....14 D3
Walsall, Shelfield WS4 ....29 B8
Pelsall Rd WS8 ....15 D7
Pelsall Village Sch WS4 ..14 F4
Pemberly Rd B27 ....88 A2
Pemberton Cl B66 ....65 B3
Pemberton Cres WS10 ....42 D5
Pemberton Rd
Dudley WV14 ....40 D1
West Bromwich B70 ....53 A6
Pemberton St B18 ....66 B4
Pembridge Cl
Birmingham B32 ....102 A7
Brierley Hill DY5 ....61 F1
Redditch B98 ....154 D2
Pembridge Rd B93 ....127 E3
Pembroke Ave WV2 ....40 A7
Pembroke Cl
Bedworth CV12 ....77 C1
Tamworth B79 ....20 D6
◆ Warwick CV34 ....160 F8
West Bromwich B71 ....42 B1
Willenhall WV12 ....27 B6
Pembroke Croft B28 ......106 A5
Pembroke Ct ◆ CV32 ....156 F2
Pembroke Gdns DY8 ......60 C2
Pembroke Ho ◆ WS3 ......28 D6
Pembroke Rd
Birmingham B12 ....87 A4
Smethwick B71 ....42 B1
Pembroke Way
Birmingham, Vauxhall B8 ..67 C5
Birmingham, Yardley Wood
B28 ....106 A5
Nuneaton CV11 ....73 D3

Pembroke Way continued
West Bromwich B71 ....53 B7
Pembrook Rd CV6 ....95 C2
Pembury Ave CV6 ....96 A3
Pembury Croft B44 ....45 A1
Penarth Gr CV3 ....134 E7
Penbury Cl B14 ....104 F5
Penbury Ct B74 ....44 F6
Pencombe Dr WV4 ....39 C7
Pencraig Cl CV8 ....148 C5
Pencroft Rd B34 ....69 C7
Penda Cl B20 ....66 A8
Penda Gr WV6 ....23 F5
Pendeen Rd B14 ....105 C4
Pendeford Ave WV6 ....24 E8
Pendeford Bsns Pk WV9 ..10 F3
Pendeford Hall La WV9 ..10 D5
Pendeford High Sch
WV10 ....11 B2
Pendeford La WV9 ....11 A3
Pendeford Mill La WV8 ..10 C3
Pendeford Mill Nature
Reserve* WV8 ....10 E4
Pendene Ct WV4 ....39 A5
Pendenis Cl CV6 ....114 A8
Pendennis Cl B30 ....103 D5
Pendennis Dr B69 ....63 A8
Penderel Ct CV6 ....95 C3
Penderel St WS3 ....14 C1
Penderell Cl WV10 ....12 A6
Penderell Cl
Birmingham B37 ....70 A3
Codsall WV8 ....10 A3
Pendigo Way
Birmingham B40 ....90 E3
Birmingham B40 ....90 F4
Pendinas Dr WV8 ....10 B3
Pendine Ct ◆ CV32 ......161 D8
Pendle Hill WS12 ....2 C4
Pendleton Gr B27 ....106 B8
Pendock Ct B23 ....56 C3
Pendragon Rd B42 ....55 C4
Pendrel Cl WS6 ....13 F8
Pendrell Cl
Birmingham B37 ....70 A3
Codsall WV8 ....10 A3
Pendrill Rd WV10 ....11 E3
Penfields Rd DY8 ....81 B6
Penge Gr B44 ....44 E3
Penhallow Dr WV4 ....39 E5
Penhurst Ave B20 ....55 D1
Penk Dr WS7 ....7 D6
Penk Rise WV6 ....24 B4
Penkridge Cl WS2 ....28 D3
Penkridge Ct WS11 ....1 D1
Penkridge Gr B33 ....68 F4
Penkridge St WS2 ....28 D3
Penley Gr B8 ....68 B6
Penmanor B60 ....151 D8
Penn Cl WS3 ....14 C1
Penn Common Rd WV4 ....54 C1
Penn Croft La WV4 ....39 A1
Penn Fields Sch WV3 ......38 F7
Penn Gr B29 ....85 B2
Penn Hall Sch WV4 ....38 E3
Penn Ho CV4 ....111 C1
Penn Hospl WV4 ....38 E4
Penn Ind Est B64 ....62 D1
Penn La B94 ....141 C4
Penn Rd Blackheath B65 ..63 E3
Sedgley DY3 ....49 F8
Wolverhampton WV2,WV3,
WV4 ....39 A6
Penn Road Island WV2 ..163 B2
Penn St Birmingham B4 ..67 A3
Blackheath B64 ....62 E1
Wolverhampton WV3 ....163 A1
Pennant Ct B65 ....63 B3
Pennant Gr B29 ....85 A2
Pennant Rd
Blackheath, Cradley Heath
B64 ....62 D1
Blackheath, Rowley Regis
B65 ....63 B3
Hinckley LE10 ....75 D5
Pennard Gr B32 ....84 F4
Penncricket Ct B68 ....63 E3
Penncricket La B65,B68 ..63 E3
Penncroft WV4 ....38 E4
Penndale Cl B24 ....57 C6
Pennhouse Ave WV4 ......38 F5
Pennine Dr Cannock WS11 ..1 D3
Sedgley DY3 ....50 D3
Pennine Rd B61 ....137 A5
Pennine Way
Birmingham B8 ....67 D6
Nuneaton CV10 ....72 B3
Stourbridge DY8 ....60 E2
Tamworth B77 ....36 C8
Willenhall WV12 ....27 D4
Pennington Cl B70 ....53 A2
Pennington Way CV6 ....113 E8
Penns Cl CV32 ....157 E5
Penns Ct B76 ....57 E2
Penns La Coleshill B46 ....70 F7
Sutton Coldfield B72,B76 ..57 D7
Penns Lake Rd B76 ....57 E2
Penns Prim Sch B72 ......57 D6
Penns Wood Cl DY3 ....39 C2
Penns Wood Dr B76 ....57 F7
Pennwood La WV4 ....38 D6
Pennwood Ct WV4 ....38 F3
Penny Cress Gn WS11 ......1 C4
Penny Ct WS6 ....13 D8
Penny Farthing Arc DY3 ..50 D8
Penny Park La CV6 ....95 A3
Penny Royal Cl DY3 ....50 D2
Pennyacre Rd B14 ....104 C2
Pennycress Gdns WV10 ..12 C7
Pennycroft Ho B33 ....68 E3
Pennyfield Croft B33 ......68 E3

Pennyfold Cl B97 ....153 A5
Pennyhill La B71 ....54 C1
Pennyroyal Cl WS5 ....43 B3
Pennyroyal Cl WS5 ....43 B3
Pennystone Cl CV31 ......162 D6
Penrice Dr B69 ....52 A1
Penrith Cl Brierley Hill DY5 ..81 B8
Royal Leamington Spa
CV32 ....156 C2
Penrith Croft B32 ....102 D8
Penrith Gr B37 ....70 C2
Penrose Cl CV4 ....132 A7
Penryhn Cl CV8 ....148 C5
Penryn Cl Nuneaton CV11 ..74 A4
Walsall WS5 ....43 D7
Penryn Rd WS5 ....43 D7
Pens Meadow Sch DY8 ..60 E3
Pensby Cl B13 ....105 D8
Pensett Trad Est The
DY6 ....50 A1
Pensford Rd B31 ....103 C3
Pensham Croft B90 ....127 A6
Penshaw Cl WV9 ....11 A2
Penshaw Gr B13 ....87 D1
Penshurst Rd B60 ....137 C1
Penshurst Way CV11 ......78 F8
Pensilva Way ◆ CV1 ......113 E4
Pensnett Rd
Brierley Hill DY5 ....61 C4
Dudley DY1 ....61 F7
Pensnett Sch of Tech
DY5 ....61 B6
Pensnett Trad Est The
DY6 ....60 F8
Penstock Ct DY10 ....117 C8
Penstock Dr B69 ....64 A4
Penstone La WV4 ....73 F5
Pentire Cl CV11 ....73 F5
Pentire Rd WS14 ....9 C6
Pentland Cl LE10 ....71 B1
Pentland Croft B12 ....86 F7
Pentland Gdns WV6 ....22 E2
Pentos Dr B11 ....87 D3
Pentridge Cl B76 ....57 F5
Penwood Gdns WV14 ......51 C8
Penzance Cl LE10 ....71 C4
Penzance Way CV11 ......74 A3
Penzer Dr B45 ....138 D8
Penzer St DY6 ....60 D7
Peolsford Rd WS3 ....15 A4
Peony Wlk B23 ....56 B3
Peplins Way B30 ....104 B3
Peplow Rd B33 ....69 A4
Pepper Hill DY8 ....81 A4
Pepper La CV1 ....165 B2
Pepper Wood Dr B31 ....102 C1
Pepperbox Dr DY4 ....52 A5
Peppercorn Cl B61 ....120 C3
Pepys Cnr CV4 ....111 E3
Pepys Ct B43 ....54 E7
Perch Ave B37 ....70 A3
Perch Cl WV10 ....26 B4
Perch Rd WS2 ....28 A4
Perchfoot Cl CV1 ....165 C1
Percival Rd B16 ....65 C1
Percy Bsns Pk B69 ....63 F7
Percy Cres CV8 ....147 E2
Percy Rd Birmingham B11 ..87 D4
Kenilworth CV8 ....147 E2
Warwick CV34 ....160 E8
Percy Shurmer Prim Sch
B12 ....86 E7
Percy St CV1 ....165 A3
Percy Terr ◆ CV32 ....156 D1
Peregrine Cl DY1 ....50 F1
Peregrine Dr CV5 ....112 A5
Peregrine Gr DY10 ....117 A2
Pereira Rd B17 ....85 C7
Perimeter Rd
Birmingham B40 ....90 D4
Birmingham B40 ....90 D4
Perivale Gr WV14 ....51 D8
Perivale Way DY8 ....81 A8
Periwinkle Cl WS8 ....15 D6
Perkins Cl DY1 ....51 C6
Perks Rd WV11 ....13 A1
Perott Dr B75 ....32 D2
Perrett Wlk ◆ DY11 ......116 D6
Perrin Ave DY11 ....116 B4
Perrins Gr B8 ....68 A6
Perrins La DY9 ....81 F4
Perrins Rise DY9 ....81 F4
Perrott Gdns DY5 ....61 B3
Perry Ave Birmingham B42 ..55 C6
Wolverhampton WV10 ......25 F8
Perry Barr Sta B20 ....55 D2
Perry Barr Stad (Greyhound)
B42 ....55 D3
Perry Beeches Inf Sch
B42 ....55 C8
Perry Beeches Jun Sch
B42 ....55 C8
Perry Cl DY2 ....62 D8
Perry Common Jun & Inf Sch
B23 ....56 B7
Perry Common Rd B23 ....56 C6
Perry Green B45 ....101 D1
Perry Hall Dr WV12 ....27 B5
Perry Hall Jun and Inf Sch
WV11 ....26 F6

Perry Hall Rd WV11 ....26 F6
Perry Hill Cres B68 ....84 B7
Perry Hill Ho B68 ....84 C8
Perry Hill Rd B68 ....84 B7
Perry Hill Rd B68 ....84 B7
Perry La B61 ....136 F2
Perry Park Cres B42 ....55 C6
Perry Park Rd B44 ....63 B1
Perry St Bilston WV14 ....40 E3
Darlaston WS10 ....41 D8
Smethwick B66 ....65 A7
Tipton DY4 ....52 A4
Wednesbury WS10 ....41 F2
Perry Trad Est WV14 ....40 E3
Perry Villa Dr B42 ....55 D5
Perry Wlk B23 ....56 B6
Perry Wood Rd B42 ....55 A8
Perrycrofts Cres B79 ....21 C7
Perryfields Cl B98 ....158 F6
Perryfields Cres B61 ....136 F5
Perryfields High Sch B68 ....84 A8
Perryfields Prim Sch B68 ....84 A7
Perryfields Rd B61 ....136 D4
Perryford Dr B91 ....127 C8
Perrymill La B96 ....159 B1
Perrywell Rd Birmingham A4 ....56 A4
Birmingham B6 ....55 F4
Persehouse St WS1 ....28 F2
Pershore Ave B29 ....86 B2
Pershore Cl WS3 ....13 F2
Pershore Ct DY11 ....116 D5
Pershore Pl CV4 ....132 E6
Pershore Rd Birmingham, Balsall Heath B5 ....86 C4
Birmingham, Breedon Cross B30 ....104 A5
Birmingham, Ten Acres B30 ....104 A8
Halesowen B63 ....83 A2
Kidderminster DY11 ....116 A6
Walsall WS3 ....13 F2
Pershore Rd S B30 ....103 F3
Pershore St B5 ....164 C1
Pershore Way WS3 ....13 F2
Perth Rd WV12 ....27 B6
Perth Rise CV5 ....112 A4
Perton Brook Vale W6 ....23 F2
Perton Fst Sch WV6 ....23 E5
Perton Gr Birmingham B29 ....103 A8
Wolverhampton WV6 ....23 F2
Perton Mid Sch WV6 ....24 A5
Perton Rd WV6 ....23 F2
Perton Sandown Fst Sch WV6 ....23 F4
Pestilence La Alvechurch B48 ....139 C8
Alvechurch B48 ....139 D8
Petard Cl B77 ....35 C8
Petchells Cl DY5 ....61 B5
Peter Ave WV14 ....40 F2
Peter Hall La CV7 ....115 F6
Peter's Finger B60 ....136 F1
Peter's Hill Prim Sch DY5 ....81 C7
Peter's Hill Rd DY5 ....81 C6
Peter's La B47 ....8 A5
Peterborough Dr WS12 ....2 C1
Peterbrook Cl B98 ....158 F7
Peterbrook Prim Sch B90 ....105 D2
Peterbrook Rd B90 ....105 D1
Peterbrook Rise B90 ....105 D1
Peterdale Dr WV4 ....38 F3
Peterhead B77 ....21 F5
Peterlee Wlk 6 CV2 ....115 A7
Peters Ave B31 ....102 F2
Peters St B70 ....53 A7
Peters Wlk Coventry CV6 ....96 A4
Lichfield WS13 ....3 A2
Petersbourne Ct B28 ....105 F8
Petersfield WS11 ....1 F4
Petersfield Ct B28 ....105 F8
Petersfield Dr B65 ....63 E3
Petersfield Rd B28 ....105 E7
Petersham Pl B15 ....85 E6
Petersham Rd B44 ....45 C1
Petford St B64 ....62 E1
Petitor Cres CV2 ....96 C1
Petland Trad Ctr B98 ....154 D4
Peto Gr CV34 ....161 F2
Petitt Cl B14 ....104 E2
Petton Cl B98 ....154 F3
Pettyfield Cl B26 ....89 A6
Pettyfields Cl B93 ....128 A5
Petworth Cl 3 WV13 ....40 F8
Petworth Gr B26 ....88 E6
Pevensey Cl B69 ....62 F6
Pevensey Rd B60 ....137 C1
Peverell Dr B28 ....105 F7
Peveril Dr CV3 ....133 B5
Peveril Gr B76 ....46 E4
Peveril Rd Perton WV6 ....23 F4
Wolverhampton WV6 ....39 E3
Pevril Way B43 ....43 F2
Peyto Cl CV6 ....95 C2
Pheasant Cl Bedworth CV12 ....77 D1
Kidderminster DY10 ....117 A2
Pheasant Croft B36 ....70 A8

Pheasant La B98 ....158 F7
Pheasant Oak CV4 ....111 C2
Pheasant Rd B67 ....64 D1
Pheasant St DY5 ....61 C3
Pheasey Park Farm Prim Sch B43 ....44 C4
Philip Ct 1 Royal Leamington Spa CV31 ....161 F6
Sutton Coldfield B76 ....46 F3
Philip Gr WS11 ....1 E6
Philip Rd Halesowen B63 ....82 F3
Tipton DY4 ....52 D5
Philip Sidney Rd B11 ....87 E3
Philip St WS11 ....40 D1
Philip Victor Rd B20 ....54 F1
Phillimore Rd B8 ....67 D5
Phillip Docker Ct CV12 ....79 B2
Phillip Rd WS2 ....42 C6
Phillippes Rd 6 CV34 ....155 F1
Phillips Ave WV11 ....12 F1
Phillips St B6 ....66 E6
Phillips Street Ind Est B6 ....66 F6
Phillips Terr B98 ....153 F4
Phipson Rd B11 ....87 B3
Phoenix Bsns Pk Birmingham B7 ....67 A6
Hinckley LE10 ....74 E8
Phoenix Ct B5 ....86 C5
Phoenix Ctr WS11 ....4 E6
Phoenix Gn B15 ....85 E7
Phoenix Ho CV1 ....165 C4
Phoenix Ind Est Bilston WV14 ....40 F4
Tipton B70 ....52 E5
Willenhall WV11 ....26 D3
Phoenix Pk B62 ....63 E2
Phoenix Pk Ind Est CV7 ....96 B7
Phoenix Rd Cannock WS11 ....2 A2
Tipton DY4 ....51 F6
Willenhall WV11 ....26 D3
Phoenix Rise Birmingham B23 ....56 B7
Wednesbury WS10 ....41 E4
Wolverhampton WV2 ....39 C6
Phoenix St West Bromwich B70 ....52 F4
Wolverhampton WV2 ....39 D6
Phoenix Way CV6 ....95 E3
Picasso Cl WS11 ....2 C2
Piccadilly Birmingham B2 ....164 B2
Piccadilly B78 ....35 F1
Piccadilly Cl B37 ....70 C1
Piccadilly Cres B78 ....35 F1
Pickard St CV34 ....161 A7
Pickenham Rd B14 ....105 A1
Pickering Croft B32 ....84 D1
Pickering Rd WV11 ....26 D5
Pickersleigh Cl 6 B63 ....83 A3
Pickford Cl CV11 ....74 A1
Pickford Grange La CV5 ....111 C7
Pickford Green La CV5 ....111 C7
Pickford St B5 ....66 F2
Pickford Way CV5 ....112 B6
Pickrell Rd WV14 ....40 B1
Pickwick Cl B13 ....87 B2
Pickwick Gr B13 ....87 C2
Pickwick Pl WV14 ....40 E4
Picton Croft 8 B37 ....70 D2
Picton Gr B13 ....105 B6
Picturedrome Way 8 WS10 ....41 D6
Piddock Rd B66 ....65 A5
Pier St WS8 ....15 F7
Pierce Ave B92 ....88 E3
Piercy St B70 ....53 A3
Piers Cl CV34 ....160 F8
Piers Rd B21 ....66 A7
Piggots Croft B37 ....69 F3
Pike Cl Birmingham B20 ....54 F1
Hinckley LE10 ....75 D5
Pike Dr B37 ....70 C3
Pike Hill B60 ....138 A7
Pike Rd WS2 ....28 A4
Pikehelve St B70 ....52 F3
Pikehorne Croft B36 ....58 D2
Pikers La CV7 ....94 A3
Pikes Pool La B60 ....137 E2
Pikes The B45 ....121 F8
Pikewater Rd B9 ....67 D1
Pilgrims Gate LE10 ....76 A6
Pilkington Ave B72 ....46 C2
Pilkington Rd CV5 ....132 D8
Pillaton Dr WS12 ....1 C6
Pilling Cl CV2 ....114 F8
Pilson Cl B36 ....68 F8
Pimbury Rd WV12 ....27 D7
Pimlico Ct B97 ....50 D3
Pimpernel Dr WS5 ....43 A3
Pinbury Croft B37 ....70 B1
Pinchers Cl DY9 ....81 B6
Pine Ave Smethwick B66 ....64 E7
Wednesbury WS10 ....41 F4
Pine Cl Great Wyrley WS6 ....4 F4
Kingswinford DY6 ....60 D5
Solihull B91 ....106 F2
Tamworth B79 ....21 B8
Wolverhampton WV3 ....25 A1
Pine Ct Coventry CV5 ....111 C4
Royal Leamington Spa CV32 ....157 B3
Stourbridge DY9 ....81 B1
Wolverhampton WV11 ....26 C6
Pine Gn DY1 ....51 A5
Pine Gr Barnt Green B45 ....121 F2
Birmingham B14 ....105 A5
Burntwood WS7 ....6 F5

Pine Ho B36 ....68 F8
Pine Leigh B74 ....32 B1
Pine Rd Dudley DY1 ....51 C4
Tipton B69 ....52 B3
Pine Sq B37 ....70 B2
Pine St WS3 ....14 D2
Pine Tree Ave CV4 ....112 A2
Pine Tree Cl B97 ....152 F3
Pine Tree Ct CV12 ....78 C4
Pine Tree Rd CV12 ....78 D4
Pine Wlk Birmingham B31 ....103 B3
Stourbridge DY9 ....81 D3
Pine Woods B32 ....84 A2
Pineapple Gr B30 ....104 C8
Pineapple Inf & Jun Sch B14 ....104 C5
Pineapple Rd B30 ....104 C7
Pinehurst CV32 ....157 E6
Pinehurst Dr B38 ....103 F3
Pineneedle Croft WV12 ....27 E4
Pineridge Dr DY11 ....116 B5
Pines Park Mobile Homes The WS12 ....1 D7
Pines Specl Sch The B36 ....68 F8
Pines The Bedworth CV12 ....77 A1
Birmingham B45 ....102 A1
Cheswick Green B90 ....126 D5
Coventry CV4 ....131 D7
Lichfield WS14 ....9 F7
Walsall WS1 ....42 E8
Wolverhampton WV3 ....24 D1
Pinetree Dr B74 ....30 D1
Pineview B31 ....102 F2
Pinewall Ave B38 ....104 A1
Pineways Stourbridge DY8 ....60 C2
Sutton Coldfield B74 ....31 C3
Pineways Dr WV6 ....24 E4
Pineways The B69 ....63 C5
Pinewood Ave Binley Woods CV3 ....135 C7
Birmingham B32 ....84 A1
Pinewood Cl Birmingham, Eachway B45 ....121 D8
Birmingham, Great Barr B44 ....55 E7
Brownhills WS8 ....6 E1
Walsall WS5 ....43 B4
Willenhall WV12 ....27 E7
Wolverhampton WV3 ....38 A8
Wombourne WV5 ....49 A6
Pinewood Dr Birmingham B31 ....102 F8
Halesowen B62 ....84 A7
Pinewood Gr CV5 ....133 B8
Pinewood Wlk DY6 ....60 E8
Pinewoods Birmingham B31 ....102 F8
Halesowen B62 ....84 A7
Pinewoods Ave DY9 ....98 F4
Pinewoods Cl DY9 ....98 F4
Pinewoods Ct DY9 ....98 F4
Pinfield Dr B45 ....122 B1
Pinfold WS3 ....28 C8
Pinfold Cres WV4 ....38 D6
Pinfold Ct WS10 ....41 C5
Pinfold Gdns WV11 ....26 D5
Pinfold Gr WV4 ....38 D6
Pinfold Hill WS14 ....17 F6
Pinfold La Chelsyn Hay WS6 ....4 C2
Norton Canes WS11 ....5 E4
Walsall WS9 ....44 B6
Wolverhampton WV4 ....38 E5
Pinfold Rd B91 ....107 E5
Pinfold St Bilston WV14 ....40 D5
Birmingham B2 ....164 B2
Darlaston WS10 ....41 D5
Oldbury B69 ....64 A8
Pinfold Street Extension WS10 ....41 C5
Pinfold Street JMI Sch WS10 ....41 C5
Pingle Cl B71 ....42 F1
Pingle Ct CV11 ....73 D2
Pingle La WS7 ....7 D5
Pinkney Pl B68 ....64 C3
Pinley Fields CV3 ....134 B8
Pinley Gr B43 ....44 A3
Pinley Way 2 B91 ....107 A1
Pinner Ct B17 ....85 C6
Pinner Gr B32 ....84 E4
Pinner's Croft CV2 ....114 A5
Pinnock Pl CV4 ....111 F1
Pinson Gdns WV13 ....26 F1
Pinson Rd WV13 ....26 F2
Pintail Dr B23 ....56 C2
Pintail Gr DY10 ....117 B3
Pinto Cl B16 ....65 F2
Pinvin Ho B97 ....153 A3
Pinza Croft B36 ....68 D8
Pioli Pl WS2 ....28 D5
Pioneer Cl B97 ....153 D4
Pioneer Ho CV1 ....165 D4
Pipe Hall Farm Nature Reserve* WS13 ....8 A8
Piper Cl WV6 ....23 F4
Piper Pl DY8 ....80 F8
Piper Rd WV3 ....38 A8
Piper's La CV8 ....148 A5
Piper's Row WV1 ....163 C3
Pipers Cl B61 ....150 D7
Pipers Cft WS13 ....3 A2
Pipers Gn B28 ....105 F5
Pipers Rd B98 ....159 D7
Pipes Mdw WV14 ....40 E5
Pipit Ct DY10 ....117 A2
Pippin Ave B63 ....82 B7
Pirbright Cl WV14 ....40 E3
Pirrey Cl WV14 ....40 E1

Pit Leasow Cl B30 ....104 B8
Pitcairn Cl B30 ....104 B6
Pitcairn Dr B62 ....83 B5
Pitcairn Ho B67 ....64 E2
Pitcairn Rd B67 ....64 E1
Pitcheroak Cotts B97 ....153 A3
Pitcheroak Specl Sch B97 ....153 B4
Pitclose Rd B31 ....103 B1
Pitfield Rd B33 ....69 D1
Pitfield Row 10 DY1 ....51 B1
Pitfield St 9 DY1 ....51 C1
Pitfields Cl B68 ....84 A8
Pitfields Rd B68 ....84 A8
Pithall Rd B34 ....69 D5
Pitman Rd B32 ....84 C5
Pitmaston Ct B13 ....86 D3
Pitmaston Rd B28 ....106 B6
Pitmeadow Ho B14 ....104 E2
Pitsford St B18 ....66 B4
Pitt La B92 ....89 C8
Pitt St Birmingham B4 ....67 A3
Wolverhampton WV3 ....163 B2
Pitts Farm Rd B24 ....57 C6
Pitts La B10 ....116 C6
Pixall Dr B15 ....86 A8
Pixhall Wlk B35 ....58 B3
Plainview Cl WS9 ....30 E2
Plaistow Ave B36 ....68 C7
Plane Gr B37 ....70 B1
Plane Tree Cl DY10 ....116 F7
Plane Tree Rd WS5 ....43 C4
Planet Rd DY5 ....61 D4
Planetary Ind Est WV13 ....26 C4
Planetary Rd WV13 ....26 C3
Planetree Cl B60 ....137 B2
Plantree Rd B74 ....44 D8
Plank La B46 ....59 A2
Planks La WV5 ....49 A7
Plant Cl DY8 ....60 F1
Plant St Blackheath B64 ....62 D1
Stourbridge DY8 ....60 E2
Plant Way WS3 ....14 F4
Plantagenet Pk CV34 ....161 E3
Plantation La Himley DY3 ....49 B3
Hopwas B78 ....20 B4
Plantation Rd WS5 ....43 A4
Plantation The DY5 ....61 B7
Plants Brook Rd B76 ....57 F6
Plants Cl Great Wyrley WS6 ....14 A8
Sutton Coldfield B73 ....45 D1
Plants Gr B24 ....57 D5
Plants Hill Cres CV4 ....111 E1
Plants Hollow DY5 ....61 D1
Plantsbrook L Ctr B72 ....46 C4
Plantsbrook Sch B72 ....46 C4
Plascom Rd WV1 ....26 A1
Plato Cl CV34 ....161 E5
Platt St Cannock WS11 ....2 A5
Darlaston WS10 ....41 D5
Platts Cres DY8 ....80 E8
Platts Dr DY8 ....80 F8
Platts Rd DY8 ....80 E8
Playdon Gr B14 ....105 A3
Pleasant Cl DY6 ....60 C4
Pleasant Mead WS9 ....29 E5
Pleasant St Kidderminster DY10 ....116 E7
West Bromwich, Hill Top B70 ....53 A8
West Bromwich, Lambert's End B70 ....53 C2
Pleasant View CV3 ....50 D2
Pleasant Way CV32 ....157 A2
Pleck Bsns Pk WS2 ....28 C1
Pleck Ho B14 ....104 C1
Pleck Ind Est WS2 ....42 C8
Pleck Rd WS2 ....28 C1
Pleck Wlk B38 ....104 A1
Plestowes Cl B90 ....106 B6
Pleydell Cl CV3 ....134 C5
Plimsoll Gr B32 ....84 C5
Plimsoll St DY11 ....116 D5
Plough & Harrow Rd B16 ....65 F1
Plough Ave B32 ....84 C2
Plough Hill Rd CV10 ....72 A6
Ploughmans Pl B75 ....32 D4
Ploughmans Wlk Kingswinford DY6 ....60 A7
Lichfield WS13 ....3 C3
Stoke Heath B60 ....150 D6
Wolverhampton WV8 ....10 F1
Plover Cl WV10 ....12 B7
Plover Gr DY10 ....117 B1
Ploverdale Cres DY6 ....61 A6
Plowden Rd B33 ....68 F4
Plume St B6 ....67 C8
Plumstead Rd B44 ....56 B8
Plym Cl WV11 ....26 C5
Plymouth Cl Birmingham B31 ....123 A7
Coventry CV2 ....114 C7
Redditch B97 ....153 C1
Plymouth Ct B97 ....153 C1
Plymouth Dr B45 ....138 A8
Plymouth Pl CV31 ....162 A7
Plymouth Rd Barnt Green B45 ....138 A8
Birmingham B30 ....104 B7
Redditch B97 ....153 D2
Pochard Cl DY10 ....116 F1
Poets Cnr B10 ....87 D7
Poins Cl CV34 ....161 F3
Pointon Cl WV14 ....40 A2
Poitiers Rd CV3 ....133 D6
Polden Cl B63 ....82 C1

Polesworth Cl B98 ....154 D1
Polesworth Gr B34 ....69 B6
Polesworth High Sch B78 ....36 F7
Pollard Rd B27 ....88 C1
Pollards The B23 ....56 E8
Polly Brooks Yd DY9 ....81 E5
Polo Fields DY9 ....81 B1
Polperro Dr CV5 ....112 A5
Pomeroy Cl CV4 ....131 D7
Pomeroy Rd Birmingham, Pheasey B43 ....44 C4
Birmingham, Woodgate B32 ....84 C1
Pommel Cl B45 ....42 F4
Pond Cres WV2 ....39 C7
Pond Farm Mews CV5 ....111 C5
Pond Gr WV2 ....39 E7
Pond La WV2 ....39 D7
Pondthorpe CV3 ....134 E6
Ponesfield Rd WS13 ....3 B2
Ponesgreen WS13 ....3 B2
Pontypool Ave CV3 ....134 F6
Pool Ave WS11 ....6 B5
Pool Bank B98 ....153 E2
Pool Bank St CV11 ....73 B4
Pool End Cl B93 ....127 F6
Pool Farm Rd B27 ....88 C1
Pool Field Ave B31 ....102 E7
Pool Furlong DY9 ....99 E1
Pool Gn WS9 ....30 A5
Pool Green Terr WS9 ....30 A5
Pool Hall Cres WV3 ....38 A8
Pool Hall Rd WV3 ....38 A8
Pool Hayes Com Sch WV12 ....27 B5
Pool Hayes La WV11, WV12 ....27 B5
Pool Hayes Prim Sch WV12 ....27 B5
Pool La B69 ....63 F3
Pool Mdw Cheslyn Hay WS6 ....4 D1
Sutton Coldfield B76 ....58 A8
Pool Meadow Cl Birmingham B13 ....87 C1
Solihull B91 ....107 F2
Pool Rd Burntwood, Brownhills West WS7 ....6 E3
Burntwood, Highfields WS7 ....6 F4
Halesowen B63 ....83 B3
Nuneaton CV10 ....72 F5
Smethwick B66 ....65 B5
Studley B80 ....159 E4
Wednesfield WV11 ....27 A6
Pool Road Bsns Ctr CV10 ....72 F5
Pool St Birmingham B6 ....66 F6
Dudley DY1 ....51 A6
Walsall WS1 ....28 F1
Wolverhampton WV2 ....163 B1
Pool View Great Wyrley WS6 ....5 A4
Walsall WS4 ....29 D7
Pool Way B33 ....69 A2
Poole Cres Birmingham B17 ....85 C3
Brownhills WS8 ....6 D2
Dudley WV14 ....40 D2
Poole Rd CV6 ....113 A5
Poole St Stourbridge DY8 ....80 E4
Wolverhampton WV10 ....25 E4
Poole's Way CV7 ....7 C7
Poolehouse Rd B43 ....43 E3
Pooles Ct DY10 ....116 D5
Pooles La WV12 ....27 D8
Pooley La B79 ....22 F2
Poolfield Dr B91 ....106 F3
Poolfield Rd WS13 ....8 B6
Poolhead La Earlswood B94 ....141 C7
Tanworth-In-A B94 ....141 E5
Poolside Gdns CV3 ....133 A5
Pooltail Wlk B31 ....102 D1
Pope Gr WS12 ....1 F6
Pope Rd WV10 ....12 A1
Pope St Birmingham B1 ....66 B3
Smethwick B66 ....65 B7
Pope's La B69 ....64 B7
Popes La Birmingham B30,B31,B38 ....103 D3
Wolverhampton WV6 ....24 A6
Poplar Ave Bedworth CV12 ....78 D2
Birmingham, Balsall Heath B12 ....87 A5
Birmingham, Coleshill Heath B37 ....90 C8
Birmingham, Edgbaston B17 ....65 B2
2 Birmingham, Erdington B23 ....56 F4
Birmingham, King's Heath B14 ....104 F8
6 Birmingham, Lozells B19 ....66 C8
Brownhills WS8 ....16 A8
Burntwood WS7 ....6 A5
Cannock WS11 ....1 F4
Oldbury B69 ....64 A4
Sutton Coldfield B75 ....46 F7
Tipton, Tipton Green DY4 ....51 D5
Tipton, Tividale B69 ....63 C8
Walsall, Bentley WS2 ....27 C4
Walsall, New Tree WS5 ....43 A4
West Bromwich B70 ....53 E2
Wolverhampton WV11 ....26 B7
Poplar Cl Catshill B61 ....136 F6
Tipton B69 ....52 C1
Walsall WS2 ....27 E4
Wombourne WV5 ....49 B6
Poplar Cres Dudley DY1 ....51 B3

Poplar Cres continued
Stourbridge DY8 ....80 D3
Poplar Dr
Barnt Green B45 ....138 D8
Birmingham, Washwood Heath
B8 ....67 D6
Birmingham, Witton WS5 ..55 F5
Poplar Gr
7 Birmingham B19 ....66 C8
Ryton-on-D CV8 ......135 B1
Smethwick B66 ....65 B3
West Bromwich B70 .....53 E1
Poplar Ho CV12 ....78 C2
Poplar La Cannock WS11 ...1 B1
Romsley B62 ....101 A4
Poplar Rd Bilston WV14 ...40 F7
Birmingham, Moseley B14 ..86 E1
Birmingham, Sparkhill B11 .87 C5
Brownhills WS8 ....16 A8
Coventry CV5 ....112 F1
Dorridge B93 ....127 F3
Great Wyrley WS6 ....5 A1
Kidderminster DY11 ...116 C4
Kingswinford DY6 ....60 E5
Oldbury B69 ....64 A8
Redditch B97 ....153 A3
Smethwick B66 ....65 B3
Solihull B91 ....107 C4
Stourbridge DY8 ....80 E3
Wednesbury WS10 ....42 A5
Wolverhampton WV3 .....39 A6
Poplar Rise
Sutton Coldfield B74 .....31 D6
Tipton B69 ....63 C8
Poplar Row DY11 .....116 C4
Poplar St
Norton Canes WS11 ......5 F5
Smethwick B66 ....65 C5
Wolverhampton WV2 .....39 D6
Poplar Trad Est B6 ....55 F5
Poplar Trees B47 .....125 A6
Poplars Dr B36 ....69 B8
Poplars La B96 ....158 A1
The Poplars
Birmingham, Rotton Park
B16 ....65 F3
Birmingham, Sparkhill B11 .87 C6
Brierley Hill DY5 ....61 A7
Nuneaton CV10 ....72 D3
Smethwick B66 ....65 C4
Stourbridge DY8 ....80 E8
Poplars Trad Est B80 ..159 D6
Poplarwoods B32 ......84 B2
Poppy Dr **3** WS5 .....43 A3
Poppy Gr B8 ....67 F4
Poppy La B24 ....57 C5
Poppyfield Ct CV4 .....132 D3
Poppymead B23 ....56 B8
Porchester Cl
Brownhills WS9 ....16 A2
Coventry CV3 ....115 A2
Porchester Dr B19 ......66 D6
Porchester St B19 ......66 D6
Porlock Cl CV3 ....133 E5
Porlock Cres B31 ......102 D3
Porlock Rd DY8 ....81 A6
Port Hope Rd B11 ......87 A7
Port La WV8,WV9 ......10 B8
Portal Rd WS2 ....27 F2
Portchester Dr WV11 ...26 D5
Porter Cl Coventry CV4 ..131 E8
Sutton Coldfield B72 .....57 B7
Porter St **5** DY2 .....51 D1
Porter Street S **3** DY2 .51 D1
Porters Croft B17 ......85 A8
Porters Field **6** DY2 ..51 D1
Porters Way B9 ....67 E2
Portersfield Ind Est B64 .82 D8
Portersfield Rd B64 ....82 C8
Portershill Dr B90 .....106 C1
Portfield Dr CV4 ......132 A3
Portfield Gr B23 ....57 A6
Porthkerry Gr DY3 .....50 B7
Porthouse Gr WV14 ....40 A3
Portia Ave B90 ....106 B1
Portia Cl CV11 ....74 A1
Portia Way CV34 ......161 E3
Portland Ave
Aldridge WS9 ....30 B5
Tamworth B79 ....20 F8
Portland Cres DY9 ......81 B1
Portland Ct Aldridge WS9 .30 B6
9 Royal Leamington Spa
CV32 ....161 F8
Portland Dr Hinckley LE10 .71 E4
Nuneaton CV10 ....72 C4
Stourbridge DY9 ....81 B1
Portland Pl Cannock WS11 .4 C7
Dudley WV14 ....51 B7
Portland Pl E CV32 ....161 F8
Portland Pl W **5** CV32 .161 E8
Portland Rd Aldridge WS9 .30 B6
Birmingham B16 ....65 F1
Portland St
Birmingham B6 ....67 A7
Royal Leamington Spa
CV32 ....161 F8
Walsall WS2 ....28 E1
Portland Terr **6** B18 ...66 A5
Portleys La B78 ....34 D4
Portman Rd B13 ....104 F7
Portmanteau Mews
B94 ....143 C6
Portobello Cl WV13 .....26 D1
Portobello Rd B70 ......53 A8
Portree Ave CV3 ....114 F2

Portrush Ave B38 .....103 D1
Portrush Rd WV6 ......23 D4
Portsdown Cl WV11 ....25 F7
Portsdown Rd B63 .....82 D2
Portsea Cl CV3 ....133 D6
Portsea St WS3 ....28 C6
Portswood Dr WV9 .....10 F1
Portway Cl Coventry CV4 .131 E8
Kingswinford DY6 ....60 E5
Royal Leamington Spa
CV31 ....162 D6
Solihull B91 ....106 E1
Portway Hill B65 ....63 A5
Portway Rd Bilston WV14 .40 E7
Blackheath B65 ....63 B5
Oldbury B69 ....63 F7
Wednesbury WS10 ......60 E5
Portway The DY6 ......60 E5
Portway Wlk B65 ....63 C6
Portwrinkle Ave CV6 ...114 A6
Poseidon Way CV34 ...161 F4
Posey Cl B21 ....54 C3
Post Office Rd WV5 .....37 A2
Post Office Wlk B96 ...158 E1
Postbridge Rd CV3 .....133 D5
Poston Croft B14 ......104 D3
Potter Cl B23 ....56 D8
Potter Ct **2** DY5 ......61 D2
Potters Green Prim Sch
CV2 ....96 E2
Potters Green Rd CV2 ...96 E1
Potters La Birmingham B6 .66 E7
Wednesbury WS10 ......41 F2
Potters Rd CV12 ....77 E1
Potterton Way B66 .....64 F8
Pottery Rd Oldbury B68 ..64 F1
Smethwick B66 ....65 A7
Potton Cl CV3 ....134 C6
Potts Cl CV8 ....148 C4
Pouk Hill Cl WS2 ....28 A3
Pouk La WS14 ....16 F7
Poultney Rd CV6 ......113 A6
Poultney St B70 ....52 F7
Poulton Cl B13 ....87 A2
Pound Cl Berkswell CV7 ..110 D3
Lapworth B94 ....144 B3
Oldbury B68 ....63 F3
Pound Gn B8 ....67 F6
Pound House La
Tanworth-in-A B94 .....142 F4
Tanworth-in-A, Nuthurst
B94 ....143 A4
Pound La
Birmingham B32 ....101 F3
Royal Leamington Spa
CV32 ....157 A3
Pound Rd
Birmingham B14 ......104 E2
Oldbury B68 ....63 F3
Wednesbury WS10 ......42 A3
Poundley Cl B36 ....69 C8
Pountney St WV2 ......163 B1
Pourbaix Ho WS13 ......9 B6
Powell Ave B32 ....84 B5
Powell Pl Bilston WV14 ...40 E3
Tipton DY4 ....52 C5
Powell Rd CV2 ....114 A4
Powell St Birmingham B1 ..66 B3
7 Halesowen B63 .....83 B3
Wolverhampton WV10 ...25 F4
Powell Way CV11 ......73 C4
Powells Ho B73 ....45 C2
Power Cres B16 ....66 A2
Power Way DY4 ....52 D8
Powers Cl CV2 ....156 F1
Powers Rd LE9 ....71 F5
Powick Rd B23 ....56 D1
Powis Ave DY4 ....52 B7
Powis Gr CV8 ....148 C5
Powke La B64 ....63 A2
Powke Lane Ind Est B65 .63 A2
Powlers Cl DY9 ....81 E2
Powlett St WV2 ....163 C2
Poxon Rd WS9 ....16 A3
Poynings The WV6 .....24 E6
Poyser Rd CV10 ....78 C8
Pratts La B80 ....159 F7
Precinct The
Coventry CV1 ....165 B3
Tamworth B79 ....21 B5
Willenhall WV12 ....27 C7
Premier Bsns Ctr **5** DY9 .81 F5
Premier Bsns Pk WS2 ...28 D1
Premier Ct B30 ....104 C3
Premier Partnership Ind Est
DY3 ....51 B7
Premier St B7 ....67 D8
Premier Trad Est B7 ....66 F5
Prescelly Cl CV10 ....72 B3
Prescelly Ct CV8 ......147 F5
Prescot Rd DY9 ....81 C3
President Kennedy Sch &
Com Coll CV6 ....95 B4
Prestbury Rd B6 ....66 E8
Presthope Rd B29 .....103 B7
Preston Ave B76 ....46 E3
Preston Cl Coventry CV4 .131 F7
Redditch B98 ....154 B6
Preston Ho **4** WS1 .....28 F1
Preston Rd
Birmingham, Hockley B18 .65 E6
Birmingham, South Yardley
B26 ....88 D7
Hinckley LE10 ....71 B2
Prestons Row WV14 ....40 A3
Prestwick Cl B75 ....46 C7
Prestwick Rd
Birmingham B35 ....58 B4

Prestwick Rd continued
Kingswinford DY6 ....60 C6
Prestwood Ave WV11 ...26 D7
Prestwood Dr DY7 ......80 A7
Prestwood Rd
Birmingham B29 ....103 B8
Wolverhampton WV11 ...26 A5
Prestwood Rd W WV11 ..26 B7
Pretoria Rd B9 ....67 E3
Priam Cir CV34 ....161 F3
Priam Gr WS3 ....15 B5
Price Ave B78 ....20 C4
Price Cres WV14 ....40 D7
Price Rd Cubbington CV32 .157 E5
Stourbridge DY9 ....82 A6
Wednesbury WS10 ......42 C3
Price St Bilston WV14 ...40 F5
Birmingham B4 ....164 C4
2 Dudley DY2 ....62 E8
Smethwick B66 ....65 B5
West Bromwich B70 .....53 C3
Prices Rd DY3 ....50 C3
Pridmore Rd CV6 ......113 D7
Priest Meadow Cl B96 ..158 D1
Priest St B64 ....62 F1
Priestfield Cl B44 ......44 D8
Priestfield Rd B97 .....158 E5
Priestfield St WV14 .....40 B6
Priestfield Sta WV2 .....40 A7
Priesthills Rd LE10 ......75 D8
Priestland Rd B34 ......69 B7
Priestley Cl
Birmingham B20 ....55 A2
Halesowen B63 ....82 B6
Priestley Rd
Birmingham B11 ....87 A4
Walsall WS2 ....28 A1
Priestley Smith Specl Sch
B23 ....56 B6
Primley Ave
Birmingham B36 ....68 D7
Tamworth B77 ....35 F5
Walsall WS2 ....28 B2
Primley Cl WS2 ....28 B2
Primrose Ave
Birmingham B11 ....87 C5
Tipton DY4 ....52 C8
Wolverhampton WV10 ...11 E3
Primrose Bank B68 .....64 B4
Primrose Cl
Blackheath B64 ....82 B8
Lickey End B60 ....137 C6
Walsall WS3 ....14 E3
Primrose Cres DY1 .....51 C4
Primrose Croft B28 ....105 F5
Primrose Dr
Bedworth CV12 ....77 E1
Hinckley LE10 ....75 E5
Primrose Gdns
Birmingham B38 ....123 F8
Codsall WV8 ....10 A3
Featherstone WV10 ....12 B7
Primrose Hill
Birmingham B38 ....124 A8
Smethwick B67 ....64 D4
Stourbridge DY8 ....60 E1
Warwick CV34 ....155 E2
Primrose Hill Prim Sch
B38 ....123 F8
Primrose Hill St CV1 ...165 C4
Primrose Hill Trad Est
DY2 ....62 D4
Primrose La
Birmingham B28 ....105 F5
Solihull B90 ....126 A5
Wolverhampton WV10 ...26 A8
Primrose Mdw **1** WS11 ..2 C2
Primrose Pk DY5 ....61 D6
Primrose Rd DY2 ....62 C4
Primrose Terr B38 .....123 E8
Primrose Woods B32 ...84 B2
Primroses The WS5 .....43 B4
Primsland Cl B90 ......127 C7
Prince Albert Inf & Jun Sch
B6 ....66 E8
Prince Albert St B9 ......67 D1
Prince Andrew Cres
B45 ....101 E2
Prince Charles Cl B45 ..101 E2
Prince Charles Rd WV14 .40 F3
Prince Edward Dr B45 ..101 E1
Prince George Rd WS10 .42 A5
Prince Of Wales La B14 .105 C3
Prince Of Wales Rd
CV5 ....112 E3
Prince of Wales **3**
B66 ....65 C4
Prince Philip Cl B45 ...101 E2
Prince Rd B30 ....104 A3
Prince Regent Ct **3**
CV31 ....161 F6
Prince Rupert Mews
WS13 ....9 A8
Prince Rupert's Way
WS13 ....9 A8
Prince St Blackheath B64 ..82 D8
Brownhills WS9 ....16 A7
Cannock WS12 ....1 E6
Walsall WS2 ....42 C8
Prince William Cl
Birmingham B23 ....56 D2
Coventry CV6 ....112 E6
Prince's Ave
Nuneaton CV11 ....73 B3
Walsall WS1 ....29 B1
Prince's Dr CV31 ......161 D7

Prince's Rd B69 ....52 B2
Prince's St Nuneaton CV11 .73 C3
Royal Leamington Spa
CV32 ....157 B1
Prince's Way B91 ....107 B3
Princep Cl B43 ....44 D4
Princes Ave WS1 ....43 A8
Princes Cl CV3 ....134 B8
Princes Dr Codsall WV8 ..10 A2
Coventry CV6 ....96 B1
Kenilworth CV8 ....148 B7
Princes End Ind Pk DY4 ..40 E1
Princes End Prim Sch
DY4 ....51 E7
Princes Gate B91 ......107 B4
Princes Gdns WV8 .....10 A2
Princes Rd DY8 ....80 D3
Princes Sq WV1 ....163 C3
Princess Alice Dr B73 ...45 D2
Princess Alley WV1 ....163 C3
Princess Anne Dr B45 ..101 E2
Princess Anne Rd
Bilston WV14 ....40 F3
Walsall WS2 ....27 F3
Princess Cl WS7 ....6 E7
Princess Cres B63 ......82 E6
Princess Ct WV10 ......26 A5
Princess Gr B71 ....53 D8
Princess of Wales Com Hospl
The B61 ....137 A4
Princess Rd
Birmingham B5 ....86 E7
Hinckley LE10 ....75 E8
Oldbury B68 ....64 D2
Princess Sq WV14 ......40 F3
Princess St Burntwood WS7 .6 E8
Cannock WS11 ....1 C5
Coventry CV6 ....113 F7
Wolverhampton WV1 ...163 C3
Princess Way WS10 .....41 C8
Princethorpe Cl
Birmingham B34 ....69 D7
Solihull B90 ....106 A2
Princethorpe Inf Sch
B29 ....85 A1
Princethorpe Jun Sch
B29 ....85 A1
Princethorpe Rd B29 ....85 A1
Princethorpe Twr B12 ...86 E7
Princethorpe Way CV3 .134 E8
Princeton Gdns WV9 ...10 F2
Principal Ct B67 ....65 A5
Pringle Ho B76 ....46 F4
Prior Ave B60 ....150 C3
Prior Cl DY10 ....117 C5
Prior Deram Wlk CV4 ...132 C7
Priors Cl CV7 ....130 B6
Priors Field Prim Sch
CV8 ....147 D7
Priors Harnall CV1 ....165 D4
Priors Mill DY3 ....50 E5
Priors Oak B97 ....153 B4
Priors The CV12 ....78 C2
Priors Way B23 ....56 C8
Priorsfield Rd
4 Coventry CV6 ....113 A4
Kenilworth CV8 ....147 F4
Priorsfield Rd N **3** CV6 .113 A4
Priorsfield Rd S CV6 ...113 A4
Priory Ave B29 ....86 B2
Priory Cl Dudley DY1 ....51 B2
Lapworth B94 ....144 D5
Smethwick B66 ....65 C4
Stourbridge DY8 ....81 B3
Tamworth B79 ....20 F7
West Bromwich B70 .....53 F2
Priory Croft CV8 ....148 A4
Priory Ct Brownhills WS9 .16 B4
Coventry CV5 ....113 A1
3 Dudley DY1 ....51 C1
Nuneaton CV11 ....73 A4
Solihull B91 ....127 B7
Studley B80 ....159 E5
Priory Cts The B2 .....164 C3
Priory Dr B68 ....64 B5
Priory Field Cl WV14 ....39 F1
Priory Green Prim Sch
WV9 ....11 A1
Priory Ho Halesowen B63 .82 F5
Kenilworth CV8 ....147 F4
Priory Hospl The B5 ....86 C5
Priory JMI Sch WS3 .....28 B7
Priory La DY3 ....50 D7
Priory Mews CV34 ....160 E7
Priory New Way Ind Est
B6 ....66 F5
Birmingham Prim Sch DY1 .51 C1
Priory Queensway The
B4 ....164 C3
Priory Rd
Birmingham, Aston B6 ...67 B8
Birmingham, Edgbaston B5,
B15 ....86 C6
Birmingham, Strichley B14 .104 C7
Birmingham, Warstock
B28 ....105 D3
Cannock WS12 ....2 D4
Dudley DY1 ....51 C3
Halesowen B62 ....83 F4
Kenilworth CV8 ....148 A4
Stourbridge DY8 ....81 B3
Warwick CV34 ....160 E7
Priory Row CV1 ....165 C3
Priory St B15 ....86 B6

Priory Sq Birmingham B4 .164 C3
Studley B80 ....159 E5
Priory St Coventry CV1 ..165 C3
Dudley DY1 ....51 C1
Nuneaton CV10 ....72 D3
Royal Leamington Spa
CV31 ....161 F6
Priory Terr CV31 ......162 A7
Priory The DY3 ....50 D8
Priory Visitors Ctr*
CV1 ....165 C3
Priory Wlk
Birmingham B4 ....164 C3
Hinckley LE10 ....71 E1
Sutton Coldfield B72 .....57 C7
8 Warwick CV34 ....160 F7
Prioryate Way B9 ......67 E3
Pritchard Ave WV11 ....26 E6
Pritchard Cl B66 ....65 B5
Pritchard St
Brierley Hill DY5 ....61 B3
Wednesbury WS10 ......42 A3
Pritchatts Rd B15 ....85 F5
Pritchett Ave WV4 .....39 F3
Pritchett Rd B31 ......123 B7
Pritchett St B6 ....66 E5
Pritchett Twr **4** B10 ...67 B1
Private Way B45 ....122 C4
Privet Cl B44 ....44 E3
Privet Rd CV2 ....96 B2
Probert Rd WV10 ....11 B1
Proctor St B7 ....67 A5
Proctors Barn La B98 ..154 B4
Proffitt Ave CV6 ....96 A1
Proffitt Cl Brownhills WS8 .16 A5
Walsall WS2 ....28 E4
Proffitt St WS2 ....28 E4
Progress Cl CV3 ....135 A7
Progress Dr WS11 ....4 F6
Progress Ind Ctr WS11 ...4 F7
Progress Way CV3 ....135 A8
Prole St WV10 ....25 E4
Promenade The DY5 ....61 D2
Prophets Cl B97 ....153 D3
Prospect Dr WS13 ......9 F8
Prospect Gdns DY8 .....81 A4
Prospect Hill
Kidderminster DY10 ...116 E6
Redditch B97 ....153 E4
Stourbridge DY8 ....81 A4
Prospect La
Kidderminster DY10 ...116 E6
Solihull B91 ....106 D4
Prospect Manor Ct **2** CV3 .2 C3
Prospect Pk WS11 ....4 D7
Prospect Pl B12 ....86 F5
Prospect Rd
Birmingham B13 ....86 F1
Burntwood WS7 ....7 B6
Dudley DY3 ....50 C2
Halesowen B62 ....83 C5
Royal Leamington Spa
CV31 ....162 B5
Prospect Rd N B98 ....154 A4
Prospect Rd S B98 ....154 A4
Prospect Row Dudley DY2 .62 D8
Stourbridge DY8 ....81 A3
Prospect St Bilston WV14 .40 E6
Tamworth B79 ....21 A5
Tipton DY4 ....41 C1
Prospect Trad Est **2** B1 .66 C3
Prosper Mdw DY6 ......60 F7
Prospero Cl B45 ....102 A2
Prospero Dr CV34 .....161 E3
Prosser St Bilston WV14 ..40 D5
Wolverhampton WV10 ...25 E5
Prossers Wlk B46 ....70 F7
Proud Cross Ringway
DY11 ....116 C6
Proud's La WV14 ....40 D7
Provence Cl WV10 ......25 F4
Providence Cl WS3 .....28 C7
Providence Dr DY9 .....81 E6
Providence Ind Est DY9 .81 E6
Providence La WS3 .....28 C6
Providence Rd B61 ....136 F3
Providence Row WV14 ..51 B8
Providence St
Blackheath B64 ....62 D1
Coventry CV5 ....132 F8
Stourbridge DY9 ....81 C5
Tipton DY4 ....52 C5
Providence Terr WS10 ...41 C6
Provost Williams CE Prim
Sch CV8 ....135 A1
Pruden Ave WV4 ......39 F3
Pryor Rd B68 ....64 C4
Ptarmigan Pl CV11 ......73 F3
Puckering's La **11** CV34 .160 E6
Pudsey Dr B75 ....32 C3
Pugh Cres WS2 ....27 E2
Pugh Rd Bilston WV14 ...40 E8
Birmingham B6 ....67 A7
Wolverhampton WV4,WV14 .39 F2
Pughe's Cl LE10 ....76 A6
Pugin Cl WV6 ....23 D3
Pugin Gdns B23 ....56 D8
Pullman Cl B77 ....22 A2
Puma Way CV1 ....165 C1
Pump St
Kidderminster DY10 ...116 E4
Oldbury B69 ....64 A7
Pumphouse La
Blackwell B45,B60 .....137 F7
Redditch B97 ....152 D1

Puppy Gn DY4 ....52 B5
Purbeck Cl B63 ....82 D1
Purbeck Croft B32 ....84 F4
Purbrook B77 ....35 E8
Purcell Rd WV1 ....40 A8
Purcell Ave Lichfield WS13 .3 C2
 Nuneaton CV11 ....79 A7
Purcell Cl CV32 ....4 A8
Purcell Rd Coventry CV6 ..114 B8
 Wolverhampton WV10 ....25 D8
Purdy Rd WV14 ....40 E2
Purefoy Rd
 Birmingham B13 ....105 C5
 Coventry CV3 ....133 D8
Purley Gr B23 ....56 A5
Purlieu La CV8 ....147 D5
Purnells Way B93 ....128 A5
Purser Dr CV34 ....160 B4
Purshall Cl B97 ....153 C3
Purslet Rd WV1 ....26 A2
Purslow Gr B31 ....103 A1
Purton Mews CV32 ....162 C6
Putney Ave B20 ....55 C1
Putney La B62 ....101 B1
Putney Rd B20 ....55 C1
Putney Wlk B37 ....70 B3
Puxton Dr DY11 ....116 D8
Puxton La DY11 ....116 C7
Pye Green Rd WS11 ....1 E4
Pye Green Valley Prim Sch
 WS12 ....2 A7
Pyeharps Rd LE10 ....75 E5
Pype Hayes Cl B24 ....57 D4
Pype Hayes Rd B24 ....57 D4
Pyt Pk CV5 ....112 D4
Pytchley Ho ▣ B20 ....54 F3
Pytman Dr B76 ....58 A7

Q
Quadrangle The B90 ....126 E8
Quadrant The
 Coventry CV1 ....165 B2
 Nuneaton CV11 ....73 E3
 Sedgley DY3 ....39 D1
Quadrille Lawns WV9 ......10 F2
Quail Gn WV6 ....23 F2
Quail Park Dr DY10 ....117 A2
Qualcast Rd WV1,WV10 ....25 F2
Quantock Cl
 Birmingham B45 ....102 B2
 Brownhills WS8 ....16 A4
 Halesowen B63 ....82 D2
Quantock Dr
 Kidderminster DY10 .....117 A6
 Nuneaton CV10 ....72 B3
Quantock Rd DY8 ....81 B6
Quantry La DY9 ....120 F8
Quarrington Gr B14 ......105 A3
Quarry Bank Prim Sch
 DY5 ....62 A1
Quarry Cl Cheslyn Hay WS6 .4 E3
 Leek Wootton CV35 ....155 F7
Quarry Fields CV35 ....155 F7
Quarry Hill B63 ....82 F2
Quarry Hills La WS14 ....9 D6
Quarry House Cl B45 .....101 F1
Quarry La
 Birmingham B31 ....103 A2
 Bromsgrove B61 ....150 D8
 Halesowen B63 ....83 A2
 Nuneaton CV11 ....73 F1
 Rowington Green CV35 ..145 C1
Quarry Lodge WS14 ....9 D5
Quarry Park Rd DY8 ....99 A8
Quarry Rd
 Birmingham B29 ....103 A8
 Dudley DY2 ....62 B1
 Kenilworth CV8 ....147 E6
Quarry Rise B69 ....63 B8
Quarry St CV32 ....161 C8
Quarry The DY10 ....116 F8
Quarry Wlk B45 ....122 A7
Quarry Yd CV10 ....72 C4
Quarryfield La CV1 ....165 C1
Quarrywood Gr CV2 ....114 A4
Quasar Ctr ▣ WS1 ....28 E2
Quatford Gdns WV10 ......25 E5
Quayle Gr ▣ DY8 ....60 D3
Quayside B69 ....63 E8
Quayside Dr WS2 ....42 C8
Quebec Ho ▣ B37 ....86 D7
Queen Alexandra Coll
 B17 ....85 A6
Queen Eleanors Dr B93 ..128 B8
Queen Elizabeth Ave
 WS2 ....27 F2
Queen Elizabeth Ct B19 ..66 B6
Queen Elizabeth Hospl
 B15 ....85 E4
Queen Elizabeth Rd
 Birmingham B45 ....101 E2
 Kidderminster DY10 .....117 B5
 Nuneaton CV10 ....72 D5
Queen Elizabeth's Mercian
 Sch B79 ....21 C6
Queen Isabel's Ave CV3 ..133 D8
Queen Margaret's Rd
 CV4 ....132 C8
Queen Mary St WS1 ....42 D6
Queen Mary's Gram Sch
 WS1 ....43 A8
Queen Mary's High Sch
 WS4 ....28 F3
Queen Mary's Rd
 Bedworth CV12 ....78 C5
 Coventry CV6 ....113 E8
Queen Philippa St CV3 ..133 D6
Queen Sq WV1 ....163 B3
Queen St
 Astwood Bank B96 ....158 E1
 Bedworth CV12 ....78 C2
 Bilston, Bunker's Hill WV14 .40 E5
 Bilston, Moxley WS10 ....41 B4
 Birmingham B12 ....87 B5
 Blackheath B64 ....62 D1
 Brierley Hill, Pesnett DY5 ..61 C6
 Brierley Hill, Quarry Bank
  DY5 ....82 A8
 Brownhills WS9 ....15 F7
 Burntwood WS7 ....6 F5
 Cannock, Blackfords WS11 .1 D1
 Cannock, High Town WS11 .2 A5
 Cheslyn Hay WS6 ....4 D3
 Coventry CV1 ....165 C4
 Cubbington CV32 ....157 E5
 Darlaston WS10 ....41 D6
 Halesowen B63 ....83 A4
 Kidderminster DY10 .....116 E7
 Kingswinford DY6 ....60 D7
 Lichfield WS13 ....9 A7
 Oldbury B69 ....64 A8
 Redditch B98 ....153 E4
 Royal Leamington Spa
  CV32 ....157 A1
 Stourbridge, Wollaston DY8 .80 F6
 Stourbridge, Wordsley DY8 ..60 E3
 Sutton Coldfield B72 ......46 C4
 Tipton DY4 ....51 F8
 Walsall WS2 ....28 D1
 Wednesbury WS10 ....41 E3
 West Bromwich B70 ....53 D3
 Wolverhampton WV1 .....163 A3
Queen Street Pas DY5 .....82 A8
Queen Victoria Prim Sch
 DY3 ....50 E8
Queen Victoria Rd
 Coventry CV1 ....165 B2
 Coventry CV1 ....165 B3
Queen's Arc WV1 ....163 B3
Queen's Ave B69 ....52 A1
Queen's Cl CV8 ....147 F3
Queen's Coll The B15 .....85 F5
Queen's Cotts B97 ....153 B4
Queen's Cres B69 ....81 A7
Queen's Croft Com Sch
 ....9 B7
Queen's Cross CV1 ....62 B8
Queen's Ct WV10 ....26 A6
Queen's Dr CV35 ....145 A1
Queen's Lea WV12 ....27 C5
Queen's Park Ct LE10 .....75 E8
Queen's Park Flats ▣
 LE10 ....75 E8
Queen's Park Rd B32 ....84 F6
Queen's Park Terr ▣
 LE10 ....75 E8
Queen's Rd
 Birmingham B23 ....56 C3
 Coventry CV1 ....165 A2
 Hinckley LE10 ....75 E8
 Kenilworth CV8 ....147 F3
 Nuneaton CV11 ....73 B4
 Oldbury B68 ....64 D4
 Smethwick B67 ....64 D4
 Stourbridge DY8 ....80 F6
 Tipton DY4 ....51 F5
 Walsall WS5 ....43 B6
Queen's Ride B12 ....86 D4
Queen's Sq
 Warwick CV34 ....160 D5
 West Bromwich B70 ......53 D3
Queens Arc CV11 ....73 C4
Queens Ave
 Birmingham B14 ....104 E8
 Solihull B90 ....106 B1
Queens Cl CE Jun Sch CV11 .73 A4
Queens Cl Birmingham B24 .56 F2
 Smethwick B67 ....65 A5
Queens Court Trad Est
 B70 ....52 F3
Queens Cres WV14 ....40 A1
Queens Ct
 Birmingham B3 ....164 B4
 Brierley Hill DY5 ....61 C6
 Nuneaton CV11 ....73 A4
Queens Dr
 Birmingham B30 ....104 A4
 Blackheath B65 ....63 D4
 Burntwood WS7 ....6 F5
Queens Dr The B62 ....83 C5
Queens Gdns
 Bilston WV14 ....40 D7
 Dudley DY2 ....62 C4
Queens Gdns Holyhead Rd
 WS10 ....41 E3
Queens Gdns Meeting St
 WS10 ....41 E3
Queens Head Rd B21 ......65 E7
Queens Hill DY9 ....119 D7
Queens Hospital Cl B15 ..66 C1
Queens Ovah Hassar Mus
 The* CV34 ....160 E6
Queens Par WS3 ....14 B1
Queens Rd
 Birmingham, Aston B6 ....67 A8
 Birmingham, Yardley B26 ..68 F1
 Sedgley DY3 ....50 E8
 Walsall WS11 ....29 C7
Queens Sq WS11 ....1 E1

Queens Way B78 ....36 F6
Queensbridge Rd B13 .....86 E2
Queensbridge Sch B13 ....86 E2
Queensbury Specl Sch
 B24 ....56 F2
Queensland Ave CV5 .....112 F2
Queenspark CV31 ....161 E6
Queensway Birmingham B6 .55 F2
 Halesowen B63 ....83 B3
 Nuneaton CV10 ....73 E6
 Oldbury B68 ....64 B1
 Royal Leamington Spa
  CV31 ....161 E6
 Stourbridge DY9 ....81 E2
 Sutton Coldfield B74 ......45 A8
 Tamworth B79 ....21 A8
Queensway (Tunnel)
 B3 ....164 B3
Queensway Cl B68 ....64 B1
Queensway Trad Est
 Birmingham B5 ....164 D3
 Royal Leamington Spa
  CV31 ....161 E6
Queenswood Ct CV7 ....94 D4
Queenswood Rd
 Birmingham B13 ....87 A4
 Sutton Coldfield B75 ......32 B1
Quenby Dr DY1 ....51 A3
Quentin Dr DY1 ....61 F8
Queslade Cl B43 ....44 A1
Queslett Rd B43 ....44 C2
Queslett Rd E B74,B43 ....44 F5
Quibery Cl B98 ....154 F3
Quicksand La WS9 ....29 F4
Quigley Ave B9 ....67 B2
Quillets Rd ▣ DY8 ....60 C5
Quilletts Cl CV6 ....96 A1
Quilter Cl Dudley WV14 ...51 A8
 Walsall WS2 ....27 F3
Quilter Rd B24 ....57 B2
Quince B77 ....22 A3
Quince Tree Sch B77 ......22 A3
Quincey Dr B24 ....57 C3
Quincy Rise DY5 ....81 C7
Quinn Cl CV3 ....134 B7
Quinneys La B98 ....159 B6
Quinton Ave WS6 ....4 F2
Quinton Church Prim Sch
 B32 ....84 A6
Quinton Cl Redditch B98 .154 D1
 Solihull B92 ....89 D3
Quinton Expressway B32 ..84 B4
Quinton Flats CV3 ....133 D7
Quinton La B32 ....84 D6
Quinton Par CV3 ....133 D7
Quinton Pk CV3 ....133 D7
Quinton Rd
 Birmingham B17 ....85 C3
 Coventry CV1 ....165 C1
Quinton Rd W B32 ....84 D4
Quintondale ▣ B90 ....106 C8
Quonians La WS13 ....9 B8
Quorn Cres ▣ DY8 ....60 C3
Quorn Rd B24 ....57 B2
Quorn Ho ▣ B20 ....54 F3
Quorn Way CV3 ....134 E7

R
Rabbit La WV10 ....12 A8
Rabone La B66 ....65 C6
Raby Cl B69 ....62 F8
Raby St WV2 ....163 C2
Race Leys Inf Sch CV12 ...78 B3
Race Leys Jun Sch CV12 ..78 B4
Racecourse La DY8 ....80 F1
Racecourse Rd WV6 ....25 A5
Rachael Gdns WS10 ....42 C4
Rachel Cl DY4 ....41 C1
Rachel Gdns B29 ....85 D2
Radbourne Dr B74 ....46 C6
Radbourne Dr B63 ....82 A7
Radbourne Rd B90 ....106 D3
Radbrook Way CV31 ......162 D6
Radcliffe Dr B62 ....83 E6
Radcliffe Gdns CV31 .....162 A6
Radcliffe Rd CV5 ....132 E8
Radcliffe Twr ▣ B12 ....86 F8
Raddens Rd B62 ....83 F3
Raddington Dr B92 ....106 E8
Raddlebarn Farm Dr
 B29 ....103 F8
Raddlebarn Prim Sch
 B29 ....85 F1
Raddlebarn Rd B29 ....103 F8
Radford Cl WS5 ....43 D7
Radford Cir ▣ CV6 ....113 A4
Radford Dr WS4 ....15 C2
Radford Hall CV31 ....162 E6
Radford Ho Coventry CV6 ..113 A7
 ▣ Redditch B97 ....153 A4
Radford La WV3,WV4 ....37 F7
Radford Prim Sch CV6 ..113 B5
Radford Rd
 Alvechurch B48 ....139 D7
 Birmingham B29 ....103 A6
 Coventry CV1,CV6 ....113 A6
 Royal Leamington Spa
  CV31 ....162 C7
Radford Rise B91 ....107 E5
Radford Semele CE Prim Sch
 CV31 ....162 E5
Radley Dr CV10 ....73 A1
Radley Gr B29 ....85 A2
Radley Rd Stourbridge DY9 .81 F4

Radley Rd continued
 Walsall WS4 ....29 C7
Radleys JMI Sch WS4 ......29 D7
Radleys The B33 ....89 D8
Radleys Wlk B33 ....89 D8
Radlow Cres B37 ....90 B8
Radmore Cl WS7 ....6 D8
Radmore Rd LE10 ....71 D3
Radnor Cl B45 ....102 B2
Radnor Croft WS5 ....43 C3
Radnor Ct WS9 ....15 F4
Radnor Dr CV10 ....72 E2
Radnor Gn B71 ....53 C7
Radnor Ho B31 ....102 D6
Radnor Rd
 Birmingham B20 ....66 B8
 Oldbury B68 ....84 B7
 Sedgley DY3 ....50 C8
Radnor Rise WS12 ....2 B4
Radnor St B18 ....66 A6
Radnor Wlk CV2 ....114 F8
Radstock Ave B36 ....69 A8
Radstock Rd WV12 ....13 C1
Radway Cl B98 ....154 B6
Radway Ind Est B90 ......126 E7
Radway Rd B90 ....126 E8
Raeburn Rd B43 ....44 C4
Raeside Dr B45 ....102 B1
RAF Cotts B35 ....57 F2
Raford Rd B23 ....56 D6
Ragian Ave Perton WV6 ...23 F3
Ragian Ave B66 ....65 C4
Raglan Cl Aldridge WS9 ...30 F3
 Nuneaton CV11 ....73 D4
 Sedgley DY3 ....50 B7
Raglan Ct
 Bromsgrove B60 ....137 A1
 ▣ Coventry CV1 ....113 E3
Raglan Gr CV8 ....148 B5
Raglan Ho B33 ....69 A2
Raglan Rd
 Birmingham, Balsall Heath
  B5 ....86 D5
 Birmingham, Handsworth
  B21 ....65 C8
 Smethwick B66 ....65 C4
Raglan St Brierley Hill DY5 .61 C4
 Coventry CV1 ....165 D3
 Wolverhampton WV3 ....163 A2
Raglan Way B37 ....70 D1
Ragley Cl Knowle B93 ....128 A7
 Walsall WS3 ....14 A1
Ragley Cres B60 ....151 A8
Ragley Dr
 Birmingham, Grove Vale
  B43 ....43 D2
 ▣ Willenhall WV13 ....40 F8
Ragley Ho ▣ B97 ....153 A4
Ragley Way CV11 ....73 F2
Ragley Wlk ▣ B65 ....63 C3
Raglis Cl B97 ....153 A1
Ragnall Ave B33 ....89 D7
Raikes La WS14 ....17 C7
Rail Bridge Est B70 ....53 A1
Railswood Dr WS3 ....15 A3
Railway Cl B80 ....159 D4
Railway Dr Bilston WV14 ..40 E5
 Wolverhampton WV1 ....163 C3
Railway La WV13 ....27 A1
Railway Rd
 Birmingham B20 ....55 F2
 Sutton Coldfield B73 ......46 B5
Railway St Bilston WV14 ...40 E5
 Cannock WS11 ....4 E8
 Norton Canes WS11 ....6 A8
 Tipton DY4 ....52 C5
 West Bromwich B70 ....53 B4
 Wolverhampton WV1 ....163 C3
Railway Terr
 Bedworth CV12 ....78 C2
 Birmingham, Aston B7 ....67 A4
 Birmingham, Hamstead B42 .54 F6
 ▣ Wednesbury WS10 ......41 F2
Railway View B10 ....87 C7
Railwayside Cl B66 ....64 E7
Railwharf Sidings DY2 ....62 D4
Rainbow St Dudley WV14 ..40 D2
 Wolverhampton WV2 ....163 C1
Rainford Way B38 ....123 C8
Rainham Cl DY4 ....51 D5
Rainsbrook Dr
 Nuneaton CV11 ....74 A1
 Solihull B90 ....126 F6
Rainscar B77 ....36 B7
Raison Ave CV11 ....73 F8
Rake Hill WS7 ....7 B8
Rakegate Jun & Inf Sch
 WV10 ....11 B1
Raleigh Cl Birmingham B21 .54 B1
 Hinckley LE10 ....71 D4
Raleigh Croft B43 ....43 E3
Raleigh Ind Est B21 ....54 B1
Raleigh Rd Bilston WV14 ...41 A3
 Birmingham B9 ....67 D2
 Coventry CV2 ....114 B2
Raleigh St Walsall WS2 ....28 D2
 West Bromwich B71 ......53 C4
Ralph Barlow Gdns B44 ..56 B8
Ralph Rd Birmingham B8 ..67 D4
 Coventry CV6 ....112 F5
 Solihull B90 ....106 C4
Ralphs Mdw B32 ....84 D2
Ralston Cl WS3 ....14 A4
Ramillies Cres WS6 ....4 F1
Ramp Rd B26 ....90 C5

Ramsay Cl B71 ....53 F8
Ramsay Cres CV5 ....112 B7
Ramsay Rd Oldbury B68 ...64 C1
 Tipton DY4 ....51 E7
Ramsay St WS3 ....28 A5
Ramsden Ave CV10 ....72 D6
Ramsden Cl B29 ....103 B7
Ramsden Ct CV10 ....72 C7
Ramsey Cl
 Birmingham B45 ....101 F1
 Hinckley LE10 ....71 B1
Ramsey Rd
 ▣ Birmingham B7 ....67 C7
 Royal Leamington Spa
  CV31 ....162 B7
Ran-tan The B97 ....158 E5
Ranby Rd CV2 ....113 F4
Randall Ave B48 ....139 A6
Randall Cl DY6 ....60 F4
Randall Rd CV8 ....147 F3
Randle Dr B75 ....32 C3
Randle Rd Nuneaton CV10 .72 D4
 Stourbridge DY9 ....81 C4
Randle St CV6 ....113 B5
Randolph Cl ▣ CV31 .....162 C6
Randwick Gr B44 ....44 E1
Ranelagh Ho WV2 ....87 D7
Ranelagh Rd WV2 ....87 D7
Ranelagh St CV31 ....162 A6
Ranelagh Terr CV31 ....161 F6
Range Meadow Cl CV32 .156 C3
Rangemoor CV3 ....134 D6
Rangeways Rd
 Kidderminster DY11 .....116 A8
 Kingswinford DY6 ....60 F4
Rangeworthy Cl B97 ......158 C7
Rangifer Rd B78 ....20 F1
Rangoon Rd B92 ....89 E4
Ranleigh Ave DY6 ....60 F2
Rann Cl B16 ....66 A1
Rannoch Cl
 Brierley Hill DY5 ....81 B8
 Hinckley LE10 ....75 B8
Rannoch Cl CV2 ....72 C5
Rannock Cl CV3 ....114 F2
Ranscombe Dr DY3 ....50 D2
Ransom Rd
 Birmingham B23 ....56 C4
 Coventry CV6 ....113 E8
Ranton Park Area 3 WS11 ..2 A2
Ranulf Croft CV3 ....133 C7
Ranulf St CV3 ....133 C7
Ranworth Rise WV4 ....39 D4
Raphael Cl CV5 ....112 C3
Rashwood Cl B94 ....143 B6
Ratcliff Way B47 ....52 D6
Ratcliff Wlk ▣ B69 ....64 A7
Ratcliffe Cl DY3 ....50 F6
Ratcliffe Ct CV10 ....72 C4
Ratcliffe Rd Hinckley LE10 .75 F6
 Solihull B91 ....107 C7
 Wednesfield WV11 ....27 A6
Rathbone Cl Bilston WV14 .40 D5
 Birmingham B5 ....86 E7
 Keresley CV7 ....95 A6
Rathbone Rd B67 ....64 F2
Rathlin Cl WV9 ....10 F3
Rathlin Croft B36 ....70 B6
Rathmore Cl DY8 ....80 E2
Rathvilly St B31 ....103 B3
Rathwell Cl WV9 ....11 A1
Rattle Croft B33 ....89 A3
Raveloe Dr CV11 ....73 D1
Raven Cl Cannock WS12 ....2 E4
 Cheslyn Hay WS6 ....4 D2
 Huntington WS12 ....1 C7
Raven Cragg Rd CV5 .....132 E8
Raven Cres WV11 ....26 F8
Raven Ct ▣ DY5 ....61 D2
Raven Hays Rd B31 ....102 C2
Raven Rd WS5 ....43 B6
Raven Way CV11 ....73 F2
Raven Wlk ▣ B15 ....86 C7
Ravenall Cl B34 ....69 B7
Ravenfield Cl ▣ B8 ....68 A5
Ravenhayes La B32 ....102 A6
Ravenhill Dr WV8 ....10 A4
Ravenhurst Dr B43 ....43 E3
Ravenhurst Mews B23 ....56 E3
Ravenhurst Rd B17 ....85 C6
Ravenhurst St B12 ....87 A8
Ravens Bank Dr B98 ......154 E2
Ravens Bank Fst Sch
 B98 ....154 D6
Ravens Ct WS8 ....15 F7
Ravensbourne Gr WV13 ...27 C2
Ravenscroft B80 ....80 C6
Ravenscroft Rd
 Solihull B92 ....107 A8
 Willenhall WV12 ....27 B5
Ravensdale Ave CV32 ....156 C2
Ravensdale Cl WS5 ....43 B7
Ravensdale Gdns WS5 ....43 B7
Ravensdale Prim Sch
 CV2 ....114 D4
Ravensdale Rd
 Birmingham B10 ....87 F7
 Coventry CV2 ....114 D4
Ravenshaw La B91 ....108 A4
Ravenshaw Rd B16 ....65 C2
Ravenshaw Way B91 .....108 A3
Ravenshill Rd B14 ....105 D4
Ravensholme WV6 ....23 F7
Ravensitch Wlk DY5 ....61 E1
Ravensmere Rd B98 ......154 E1
Ravensthorpe Cl CV3 ....134 E8

Ravenstone B77 .....36 B8
Ravenswood B15 .....85 E8
Ravenswood Cl B74 .....46 B8
Ravenswood Dr B91 .....106 F1
Ravenswood Dr S B91 .....106 E1
Ravenswood Hill B46 .....70 F7
Rawdon Gr B44 .....56 B8
Rawlett High Sch B79 .....21 A8
Rawlings Rd B67 .....65 A2
Rawlins Croft B35 .....58 C3
Rawlins St B16 .....66 A1
Rawlinson Rd CV32 .....157 B2
Rawnsley Dr CV8 .....148 C6
Rawnsley Rd WS12 .....2 E7
Ray Ct B74 .....31 F3
Ray Hall La
  Birmingham B43 .....54 B8
  West Bromwich B43,B71 .....43 A1
Raybolds Bridge St WS2 .....28 C4
Raybon Croft B45 .....122 A6
Raybould's Fold DY2 .....62 C5
Rayford Dr B71 .....43 A2
Raygill B77 .....36 B8
Rayleigh Rd B27 .....88 D3
Rayleigh Rd WV3 .....39 A8
Raymond Ave B42 .....55 B6
Raymond Cl Coventry CV6 .....95 F5
  Walsall WS2 .....28 D5
Raymond Gdns WV11 .....26 B6
Raymond Rd B8 .....67 E4
Raymont Gr B43 .....44 B4
Raynor Cres CV12 .....77 D1
Raynor Rd WV10 .....25 F6
Raynsford Wlk CV34 .....155 D1
Raywoods The CV10 .....72 F3
Rea Ave B45 .....121 E8
Rea Bsns Pk B7 .....67 C4
Rea Cl B31 .....123 A7
Rea Fordway B45 .....101 F1
Rea St B5 .....164 D1
Rea St S B5 .....164 D1
Rea Terr B5 .....66 F2
Rea Twr B19 .....66 C5
Rea Valley Dr B31 .....103 B2
Reabrook Rd B31 .....122 F8
Read St CV1 .....113 E3
Readers Wlk B43 .....43 F1
Reading Ave CV11 .....73 F7
Reading Cl CV2 .....96 B3
Reansway Sq WV6 .....25 A4
Reapers Cl WV12 .....27 D5
Reapers Wlk WV8 .....10 F1
Rear Cotts B48 .....138 F6
Reardon Ct CV34 .....155 E1
Reaside Cres B14 .....104 B5
Reaside Croft B12 .....86 E6
Reaside Sch B45 .....101 E1
Reaview Dr B29 .....86 B2
Reay Nadin Dr B73 .....45 B4
Reaymer Cl WS2 .....28 B6
Rebecca Dr B29 .....85 E2
Rebecca Gdns WV4 .....38 F4
Recreation Rd
  Bromsgrove B61 .....136 F3
  Coventry CV6 .....96 A3
Recreation St DY2 .....62 D5
Rectory Ave WS10 .....41 D6
Rectory Cl Allesley CV5 .....112 C6
  Bedworth CV7 .....78 A1
  Drayton Bassett B78 .....34 E5
  Stourbridge DY8 .....81 B3
  Whitnash CV31 .....162 B4
Rectory Ct B97 .....153 D1
Rectory Dr CV7 .....78 A1
Rectory Fields CV8 .....60 E2
Rectory Gdns
  Birmingham B36 .....69 A8
  Oldbury B68 .....64 C5
  Solihull B91 .....107 D3
  Stourbridge DY8 .....81 B3
Rectory Gr B18 .....65 E6
Rectory La Allesley CV5 .....112 C6
  Birmingham B36 .....69 A8
  Upton Warren B61 .....150 A4
Rectory Park Ave B75 .....46 E4
Rectory Park Cl B75 .....46 E4
Rectory Park Ct B75 .....46 E4
Rectory Park Rd B26 .....89 C5
Rectory Rd
  Birmingham B31 .....103 B3
  Redditch B97 .....153 D1
  Solihull B91 .....107 C3
  Stourbridge DY8 .....81 B3
  Sutton Coldfield B75 .....46 E6
Rectory St DY8 .....60 E3
Red Brick Cl B64 .....82 D7
Red Brook Rd WS2 .....28 A5
Red Deeps CV11 .....78 D8
Red Hall Jun Sch DY3 .....50 C3
Red Hill Redditch B98 .....153 F2
  Stourbridge DY8 .....81 B4
Red Hill Cl B80 .....159 E6
Red Hill Gr B38 .....123 F7
Red Hill Rd B62 .....101 A7
Red Hill St WV1 .....163 B4
Red House Ave WS10 .....42 B3
Red House Ind Est WS9 .....30 A6
Red House La WS9 .....29 F5
Red House Park Rd B43 .....43 E2
Red House Rd B33 .....68 E2
Red La Burton Green CV8 .....131 C2
  Coventry CV6 .....113 F5
  Kenilworth CV8 .....147 D8
  Sedgley DY3 .....50 B8
Red Leasowes Rd B63 .....83 A3
Red Lion Ave WS11 .....6 A4
Red Lion Cl B69 .....52 A1

Red Lion Cres WS11 .....6 A4
Red Lion La WS11 .....6 B4
Red Lion St
  Alvechurch B48 .....139 B6
  Redditch B98 .....153 E4
  Wolverhampton WV1 .....163 B3
Red River Rd WS2 .....28 A5
Red Sands Rd DY10 .....116 E8
Red Wing Wlk B36 .....70 A8
Redacre Rd B73 .....45 F2
Redacres WV6 .....24 E6
Redbank Ave B23 .....56 C3
Redbourn Rd WS3 .....14 A4
Redbrook Cl WS12 .....2 D2
Redbrook Covert 7
  B38 .....123 E8
Redbrooks Cl B91 .....107 A1
Redburn Dr B14 .....104 D2
Redcap Croft CV6 .....95 D4
Redcar Cl Catshill B61 .....121 B1
  Royal Leamington Spa
  CV32 .....157 C4
Redcar Croft B36 .....68 C8
Redcar Rd Coventry CV1 .....113 E5
  Wolverhampton WV10 .....11 D4
Redcliff B77 .....21 F5
Redcliffe Dr WV5 .....49 B6
Redcotts Cl WV10 .....26 A8
Redcroft Dr B24 .....57 C5
Redcroft Rd DY2 .....62 E6
Reddal Hill Prim Sch
  B64 .....62 E1
Reddal Hill Rd B64 .....62 E2
Reddicap Heath Rd B75 .....46 F4
Reddicap Hill B75 .....46 E4
Reddicap Trad Est B76 .....46 D4
Reddicroft B72,B73 .....46 C5
Reddings La B11,B28 .....87 E3
Reddings Rd B13 .....86 E2
Reddings The B47 .....125 A5
Redditch Ho B33 .....69 E2
Redditch Rd
  Alvechurch, Arrowfield Top
  B48 .....139 B8
  Alvechurch, Rowney Green
  B48 .....139 C3
  Birmingham B31,B38 .....123 C8
  Hopwood B48 .....123 B1
  Stoke Heath B60 .....150 D5
  Studley B80 .....159 D5
Redditch Ringway B97 .....153 D4
Redditch Sta B97 .....153 D4
Redditch Wlk 4 CV2 .....115 A7
Redesdale Ave CV6 .....112 F5
Redfern Ave CV8 .....148 A6
Redfern Cl B92 .....89 B1
Redfern Dr WS7 .....7 B5
Redfern Park Way B11 .....88 A5
Redfern Rd B11 .....88 A5
Redfly La DY5 .....61 C6
Redford Cl B13 .....87 B2
Redgate Cl B38 .....103 D2
Redgrave Cl CV2 .....115 B8
Redhall Rd
  Birmingham B32 .....84 E7
  Dudley DY3 .....50 C2
Redhill Ave WV5 .....49 A6
Redhill Cl Stourbridge DY8 .....81 B4
  Tamworth B79 .....21 C7
Redhill Ct DY9 .....81 B4
Redhill Jun & Inf Sch
  B25 .....88 A6
Redhill La B45,B61 .....121 C5
Redhill Prim Sch WS11 .....1 F4
Redhill Rd
  Birmingham, King's Norton
  B38 .....123 D7
  Birmingham, Tyseley B25 .....88 A6
  Cannock WS11 .....1 F4
  Redhill Sch DY8 .....81 B4
Redhouse Cl B93 .....127 E4
Redhouse Cone & Mus*
  DY8 .....60 E1
Redhouse Ind Est WS9 .....29 F6
Redhouse JMI Sch WV9 .....29 E5
Redhouse Rd WV6 .....24 B5
Redhouse St WS1 .....42 E7
Redhurst Dr WV10 .....11 B3
Redlake B77 .....35 E8
Redlake Dr DY9 .....99 B8
Redlake Rd DY9 .....81 B1
Redland Cl Coventry CV2 .....96 E2
  Marlbrook B60 .....121 C1
Redland La CV8 .....135 A2
Redland Rd CV31 .....162 B5
Redlands Cl B91 .....107 D5
Redlands Rd B91 .....107 D5
Redlands Way B31 .....31 A1
Rediff Ave B36 .....58 D1
Redlock Field WS14 .....9 A5
Redmead Cl B30 .....103 C4
Redmoor Gdns WV4 .....39 A5
Redmoor High Sch LE10 .....71 B3
Redmoor Way B76 .....58 D6
Rednal Hill Jun & Inf Schs
  B45 .....122 C7
Rednal Hill La B45 .....122 A6
Rednal Mill Dr B45 .....122 C7
Rednal Rd B38 .....103 E1
Rednal Dr B7 .....332 C3
Rednell Ho B69 .....63 D6
Redoak Ho WV10 .....25 F3
Redpine Crest WV12 .....27 D5
Redruth Cl Coventry CV6 .....114 A8
  Kingswinford DY6 .....60 D8
  Nuneaton CV11 .....74 A4
  Walsall WS5 .....43 D7
Redruth Rd WS5 .....43 D7

Reds Dr B97 .....153 C4
Redstart Ave DY10 .....117 B2
Redstone Cl B98 .....154 C6
Redstone Dr WV11 .....26 F5
Redstone Farm Rd B28 .....106 B6
Redthorn Gr B33 .....68 D3
Redthorne Gr CV8 .....148 B8
Redvers Rd B9 .....67 E1
Redway St B75 .....46 E4
Redwell Cl B77 .....21 D5
Redwing B77 .....36 A6
Redwing Cl WS7 .....7 D5
Redwing Ct DY10 .....117 A1
Redwing Dr WS12 .....1 C7
Redwing Gr B23 .....56 B7
Redwood Ave DY1 .....50 F5
Redwood Bsns Pk B66 .....64 C7
Redwood Cl Aldridge B74 .....30 F2
  Birmingham B30 .....103 E4
Redwood Croft
  Birmingham B14 .....104 E7
  Nuneaton CV10 .....73 A1
Redwood Dr
  Burntwood WS7 .....6 F8
  Cannock WS11 .....2 A3
  Tipton B69 .....52 B2
Redwood Gdns B27 .....88 B5
Redwood Ho B37 .....69 F5
Redwood Rd
  Birmingham B30 .....103 E4
  Dudley WV14 .....40 D2
  Walsall WS5 .....43 B4
Redwood Way WV12 .....27 B8
Reed Sq B35 .....58 B4
Reedham Gdns WV4 .....38 D5
Reedly Rd WV12 .....13 C1
Reedmace B77 .....21 C2
Reedmace Cl B38 .....123 F8
Reedswood Cl WS2 .....28 C3
Reedswood Gdns WS2 .....28 C3
Reedswood La WS2 .....28 C3
Reedswood Way WS2 .....28 B4
Rees Dr Coventry CV3 .....133 D4
  Wombourne WV5 .....49 B7
Reeve Ct DY10 .....117 A1
Reeve Dr CV8 .....148 A4
Reeve La WS13 .....9 B8
Reeves Gdns WV8 .....10 A4
Reeves Rd
  Birmingham B14 .....104 C6
  Hinckley LE10 .....75 F6
Reeves St WS3 .....28 B8
Reflex Ind Pk WV13 .....27 A3
Reform St B70 .....53 D3
Reg Hadden Ct CV10 .....73 D6
Regal Cl B77 .....35 C8
Regal Croft B36 .....68 B8
Regal Dr WS2 .....42 C8
Regan Ave B90 .....106 A1
Regan Cres B23 .....56 E6
Regan Ct B75 .....47 C5
Regan Ho B13 .....105 D7
Regatta Dr CV32 .....161 F8
Regency Cl
  7 Birmingham B9 .....67 D1
  Nuneaton CV10 .....73 D6
Regency Ct Coventry CV5 .....132 F8
  Walsall WS1 .....43 A7
  Wolverhampton WV1 .....163 B4
Regency Dr
  Birmingham B38 .....103 F2
  Coventry CV3 .....132 F5
  Kenilworth CV8 .....147 F3
Regency Gdns B14 .....105 C3
Regency Ho
  Birmingham B16 .....66 A1
  Royal Leamington Spa
  CV32 .....162 A8
Regency Mews CV12 .....162 A8
Regency Wlk B74 .....31 D5
Regent Ave B69 .....52 A1
Regent Cl Birmingham B5 .....86 D6
  Halesowen B63 .....83 A4
  Kingswinford DY6 .....60 C6
  Tipton B69 .....63 A8
Regent Ct
  8 Darlaston WS10 .....41 D6
  5 Hinckley LE10 .....75 D8
  8 Smethwick B66 .....65 A5
Regent Dr B69 .....52 A1
Regent Gr CV32 .....161 F8
Regent Ho Oldbury B68 .....64 B2
  6 Walsall WS2 .....28 D3
Regent Mews B60 .....150 E8
Regent Par B1 .....66 B3
Regent Park Rd B10 .....67 C1
Regent Pl Birmingham B1 .....66 C4
  4 Royal Leamington Spa
  CV31 .....162 A7
  Tipton B69 .....52 B2
Regent Rd
  Birmingham, Handsworth
  B21 .....65 D8
  Birmingham, Harborne B17 .....85 D6
  Tipton B69 .....52 A1
  Wolverhampton WV4 .....38 F5
Regent Specl Sch B69 .....52 A1
Regent St Bedworth CV12 .....78 C4
  Bilston WV14 .....40 D6
  Birmingham, Hockley B1 .....66 C4
  Birmingham, Stirchley B30 .....104 A7
  Blackheath B64 .....62 F2
  Coventry CV1 .....165 A2
  Dudley DY1 .....51 C6
  Hinckley LE10 .....75 D8
  Nuneaton CV11 .....73 D5
  Royal Leamington Spa
  CV32 .....161 F8

Regent St continued
  Smethwick B66 .....65 A6
  Tipton DY4 .....51 E8
  Willenhall WV13 .....27 A3
Regent Wlk B8 .....68 B7
Regents Park Com Prim Sch
  B10 .....87 B8
Regents Park Rd B60 .....137 C2
Regents The B15 .....85 D8
Regiment Ct CV6 .....95 A1
Regina Ave B44 .....55 E8
Regina Cl B45 .....101 E2
Regina Cres
  Coventry CV2 .....115 A7
  Wolverhampton WV6 .....24 B4
Regina Dr Birmingham B42 .....55 D3
  Walsall WS4 .....29 B4
Reginald Rd
  Birmingham B8 .....67 D4
  Smethwick B67 .....64 F2
Regis Beeches WV6 .....24 C5
Regis Gdns B65 .....63 C2
Regis Heath Rd B65 .....63 E2
Regis Ho B68 .....64 C2
Regis Rd Blackheath B65 .....63 C2
  Wolverhampton WV6 .....24 C5
Regis Wlk CV2 .....114 F7
Reid Ave WV12 .....27 D6
Reid Cl WS7 .....7 F7
Reid Rd B68 .....64 D1
Reigate Ave B8 .....68 B4
Reignier Pl CV34 .....161 F2
Reindeer Rd B78 .....20 E1
Relay Dr B77 .....36 C7
Reliance Trad Est WV4 .....40 B5
Relko Dr B36 .....68 C7
Relton Mews CV6 .....113 F6
Rembrandt Cl
  Cannock WS11 .....2 D2
  Coventry CV3 .....112 C3
Remburn Gdns CV34 .....160 F8
Remembrance Rd
  Coventry CV3 .....134 D6
  Wednesbury WS10 .....42 C3
Remington Dr WS11 .....4 F8
Remington Pl WS2 .....28 C5
Remington Rd WS2 .....28 C5
Rene Rd B77 .....21 E5
Renfrew Cl DY8 .....60 C3
Renfrew Gdns DY11 .....116 C5
Renfrew Sq B35 .....58 B4
Renfrew Wlk CV4 .....132 A8
Renison Rd CV12 .....77 E1
Rennie Gr B32 .....84 D5
Rennison Dr WV5 .....49 A6
Renolds Cl CV4 .....112 C2
Renown Ave CV4 .....132 C3
Renown Cl DY5 .....61 B7
Renton Gr WV10 .....11 A1
Renton Rd WV10 .....11 A1
Repington Rd N B77 .....22 A5
Repington Rd S B77 .....22 A5
Repington Way B75 .....47 B5
Repton Ave WV6 .....23 E3
Repton Cl WS11 .....4 B8
Repton Dr CV6 .....96 B2
Repton Gr B9 .....68 B3
Repton Ho B23 .....56 F8
Repton Rd B9 .....68 B3
Reservoir Cl WS2 .....42 B8
Reservoir Pas WS10 .....41 F3
Reservoir Pl WS2 .....42 B8
Reservoir Rd
  Birmingham, Edgbaston B16 .....65 F2
  Birmingham, Rednall B45 .....122 C3
  Birmingham, Selly Oak B29 .....85 C3
  Birmingham, Stockland Green
  B23 .....56 C4
  Blackheath B65 .....63 D3
  Cannock WS12 .....2 D4
  Kidderminster DY11 .....116 C3
  Oldbury B68 .....64 C4
  Solihull B92 .....106 F8
  Reservoir Retreat B16 .....65 F2
Reservoir St WS2 .....42 B8
Reswood Cl 3 B24 .....156 F3
Retallack Cl B66 .....65 B8
Retford Dr B76 .....46 E4
Retford Gr B25 .....88 C6
Retreat Gdns DY3 .....50 E7
Retreat St
  Astwood Bank B96 .....158 E1
  Wolverhampton WV3 .....163 A1
Retreat The B64 .....62 E1
Revesby Wlk 4 B7 .....67 A4
Revival St WS3 .....28 C8
Rex Cl CV4 .....131 D8
Reyde Cl B97 .....153 A2
Reynalds Cross Sch
  B92 .....106 D7
Reynard Cl B97 .....152 F3
Reynards Cl DY3 .....51 A7
Reynolds Cl Hinckley LE10 .....71 A3
  Lichfield WS13 .....3 B2
Reynolds Ct B68 .....84 B8
Reynolds Gr WV6 .....23 F5
Reynolds Ho B19 .....66 E7
Reynolds Rd
  Bedworth CV12 .....78 A4
  Birmingham B21 .....65 E7
Reynolds Wlk WV11 .....27 A7
Reynoldstown Rd B36 .....68 C8
Rhayader Rd B31 .....102 E5
Rhodes Alms Houses The
  B25 .....65 F7
Rhodes Cl DY3 .....50 D8
Rhone Cl B11 .....87 C3
Rhoose Croft B35 .....58 B3

Rhuddlan Way DY10 .....116 E1
Rhyl Rd CV11 .....79 F6
Rhys Thomas Cl WV12 .....27 D4
Ribbesford Ave WV10 .....25 B8
Ribbesford Cl B63 .....82 E6
Ribbesford Cres WV14 .....40 D1
Ribble Cl CV12 .....79 B2
Ribble Ct B73 .....46 B5
Ribble Rd CV3 .....113 F2
Ribble Wlk B36 .....69 F8
Ribblesdale B77 .....36 B7
Ribblesdale Ave LE10 .....71 E3
Ribblesdale Rd B29,B30 .....104 A8
Ribbonbrook CV11 .....73 D3
Ribbonfields CV11 .....73 D3
Rich Cl CV34 .....161 E7
Richard Cooper Rd WS14 .....17 F5
Richard Joy Cl CV6 .....95 C2
Richard Lee Prim Sch
  CV2 .....114 E3
Richard Lighton Ho 6
  B1 .....66 C3
Richard Pl WV5 .....43 C8
Richard Rd WS5 .....43 C8
Richard St Birmingham B7 .....66 F5
  West Bromwich B70 .....53 B3
Richard St S B70 .....53 C2
Richard St W B70 .....53 B2
Richard Williams Rd
  WS10 .....42 B2
Richards Cl
  Birmingham B31 .....122 F6
  Blackheath B65 .....63 E4
  Kenilworth CV8 .....147 F5
Richards Ct WS11 .....5 F6
Richards Gr CV31 .....162 A5
Richards Ho
  2 Birmingham B69 .....63 E4
  8 Walsall WS2 .....28 D3
Richards Rd DY4 .....40 F1
Richards St WS10 .....41 D7
Richardson Cl CV34 .....155 F1
Richardson Dr DY8 .....80 E8
Richardson Ho B14 .....52 C8
Richardson Way CV2 .....115 B8
Richbarn Rd B33 .....50 F4
Riches St WV6 .....24 F3
Richford Gr B33 .....69 D2
Richmere Ct WV6 .....24 B3
Richmond Aston Dr DY4 .....52 A5
Richmond Ave
  Birmingham B12 .....86 F5
  Wolverhampton WV3 .....24 F1
Richmond Cl
  Birmingham B20 .....55 A3
  Cannock WS11 .....2 A5
  Tamworth B79 .....21 A5
Richmond Croft B42 .....54 F6
Richmond Ct
  8 Birmingham B29 .....103 C2
  Halesowen B63 .....82 E3
  Oldbury B68 .....64 C5
  6 Royal Leamington Spa
  CV31 .....162 B7
  Stourbridge DY9 .....81 B1
  2 Sutton Coldfield B72 .....57 B7
Richmond Dr
  Lichfield WS14 .....9 D7
  Perton WV6 .....23 F3
  Wolverhampton WV3 .....24 E1
Richmond Gdns
  Stourbridge DY8 .....80 F7
  Wombourne WV5 .....49 A5
Richmond Gr DY8 .....80 E8
Richmond Hill B68 .....64 C5
Richmond Hill Gdns B15 .....85 E7
Richmond Hill Rd B15 .....85 F6
Richmond Ho 2 B37 .....70 C1
Richmond Mews WV3 .....25 A1
Richmond Pk DY6 .....60 C8
Richmond Pl B14 .....104 F8
Richmond Prim Sch
  LE10 .....71 C3
Richmond Rd
  Birmingham, Eachway B45 .....121 F7
  Birmingham, Hockley B18 .....66 B6
  Birmingham, Yardley B33 .....68 D2
  Dudley DY2 .....62 C8
  Hinckley LE10 .....71 C3
  Hollywood B47 .....125 C7
  Nuneaton CV11 .....73 A2
  Sedgley DY3 .....50 E7
  Smethwick B66 .....65 A2
  Solihull B92 .....88 F2
  Sutton Coldfield B73 .....46 B6
  Wolverhampton WV3 .....24 E1
Richmond St
  Coventry CV2 .....114 A3
  Halesowen B63 .....83 A4
  Walsall WS1 .....28 F3
  West Bromwich, Great Bridge
  B70 .....52 F6
Richmond St S B70 .....52 F6
Richmond Way 2 B37 .....70 C3
Rickard Cl B93 .....127 E6
Rickman Dr B15 .....86 D8
Rickyard Cl
  Birmingham, Northfield
  B29 .....103 A6
  Birmingham, Yardley B25 .....68 D1
Rickyard La B98 .....154 D5
Rickyard Piece B32 .....84 E4
Riddfield Rd B36 .....68 E8
Ridding La WS10 .....41 F2
Riddings Cres WS3 .....14 F4

Riddings Hill CV7 ....130 C8
Riddings The
  Birmingham B33 ....68 F4
  Coventry CV5 ....132 E7
  Stourbridge DY9 ....81 D2
  Sutton Coldfield B76 ....58 B8
  Tamworth B77 ....21 E5
  Wolverhampton WV10 ...26 A7
Riddon Dr LE10 ....75 B8
Ridewell Gr CV31 ....162 A1
Ridgacre Ent Pk B71 ....53 B6
Ridgacre La B32 ....84 C6
Ridgacre Rd
  Birmingham B32 ....84 C6
  West Bromwich B71 .....53 B6
Ridgacre Rd W B32 .....84 A6
Ridge Cl Birmingham B13 .105 C6
  Willenhall WS2 ....27 D3
Ridge Cl CV5 ....112 A6
Ridge Gr DY9 ....81 C5
Ridge La WV11 ....26 D7
Ridge Prim Sch The DY8 .80 C5
Ridge Rd DY6 ....60 C5
Ridge St DY8 ....80 C6
Ridge Way WS9 ....30 B4
Ridgefield Rd B62 ....83 C7
Ridgeley Cl CV34 ....155 E2
Ridgemount Dr B38 .....123 D8
Ridgethorpe CV3 ....134 E6
Ridgewater Cl B45 .....122 B6
Ridgeway Birmingham B17 .65 B2
  Dudley DY3 ....50 D7
Ridgeway Ave
  Coventry CV5 ....133 C6
  Halesowen B62 ....84 A6
Ridgeway Ct B80 ....159 E2
Ridgeway Ct WS2 ....27 F2
Ridgeway Dr WV4 ......38 F3
Ridgeway Prim Sch WS7 .7 A5
Ridgeway Rd
  Stourbridge DY8 ....60 F2
  ■ Tipton DY4 ....52 A8
Ridgeway Sch CV34 ....156 A1
Ridgeway The
  Birmingham B23 ....56 A5
  Burntwood WS7 ....7 A4
  Hinckley LE10 ....75 D6
  Warwick CV34 ....156 A1
Ridgeway Trad Est B96 .158 E1
Ridgewood B34 ....69 B6
Ridgewood Ave DY8 ....80 C7
Ridgewood Cl
  Royal Leamington Spa
  CV32 ....156 C1
  ■ Walsall WS1 ....42 F8
Ridgewood Dr B75 .....32 B1
Ridgewood Gdns B44 ...55 F7
Ridgewood High Sch
  DY8 ....80 C5
Ridgewood Rise B77 ....22 A5
Ridgley Rd CV4 ....131 E8
Ridgmont Croft B32 ....84 E5
Riding Cl B71 ....53 F7
Riding Way WV12 ....27 D6
Ridings Brook Dr ■ WS11 .2 A2
Ridings La B98 ....154 B6
Ridings Park Trad Est
  WS11 ....2 A3
Ridley St B1 ....164 A1
Ridpool Prim Sch B33 ...69 B3
Ridpool Rd B33 ....69 B3
Ridware Ho WS13 ....3 E1
Rifle Range Rd DY11 ...116 B3
Rifle St WV14 ....51 A8
Rigby Cl CV34 ....161 D4
Rigby Dr WS11 ....1 F4
Rigby Hall Sch B60 ....151 C8
Rigby La B60 ....151 C8
Rigby St WS10 ....42 A1
Rigdale Cl CV2 ....114 E2
Righton Ho B77 ....21 D1
Riland Ave B75 ....46 D5
Riland Ct B72 ....57 C7
Riland Gr B75 ....46 C5
Riland Ind Est B75 .....46 D5
Riland Rd B75 ....46 D5
Riley B77 ....21 E3
Riley Cl CV8 ....148 D4
Riley Cres WV4 ....39 A6
Riley Dr B36 ....59 A1
Riley Rd B14 ....105 D3
Riley Sq CV2 ....96 B1
Riley St WV13 ....27 B2
Rills The LE10 ....71 E2
Rilstone Rd B32 ....84 F5
Rindleford Ave WV4 ....38 C6
Ring Rd N B15 ....6 E7
Ring Rd N B15 ....85 F4
Ring Rd S B15 ....85 F3
Ring Road St Andrews
  WV1 ....163 A3
Ring Road St Davids
  WV1 ....163 C3
Ring Road St Georges
  WV2 ....163 C2
Ring Road St Johns
  WV2 ....163 B2
Ring Road St Marks
  WV1 ....163 B2
Ring Road St Patricks
  WV1 ....163 C4
Ring Road St Peters
  WV1 ....163 B3
Ring The B25 ....88 C8
Ringhills Rd WV8 ....10 B2

Ringinglow Rd B44 .....44 D2
Ringmere Ave B36 .....69 B7
Ringswood Rd B92 .....88 E4
Ringway WS11 ....1 E1
Ringway Hill Cross CV1 .165 A3
Ringway Ind Est WS13 ..3 C3
Ringway Queens CV1 ...165 A2
Ringway Rugge CV1 ....165 A2
Ringway St Johns CV1 ..165 C2
Ringway St Nicholas
  CV1 ....165 B3
Ringway St Patricks
  CV1 ....165 B1
Ringway Swanswell
  CV1 ....165 C3
Ringway Whitefriars
  CV1 ....165 C3
Ringwood Ave WS9 ....30 B5
Ringwood Dr B45 ......102 A1
Ringwood Highway CV2 .96 E2
Ringwood Rd WV10 ....11 D1
Rinhill Gr CV31 ....162 D6
Ripley Cl B69 ....62 F8
Ripley Gr B23 ....56 B5
Riplingham ■ CV32 ....156 F2
Ripon Cl CV5 ....112 B8
Ripon Dr B71 ....42 D1
Ripon Rd
  Birmingham B14 ....105 C4
  Walsall WS2 ....28 B2
  Wolverhampton WV10 ..25 C7
Rippingille Rd B43 .....44 C4
Ripple Rd B30 ....104 B7
Risborough Cl CV5 .....112 C3
Rischale Way WS4 .....29 D8
Risdale Cl CV32 ....156 D2
Rise Ave B45 ....122 A7
Rise The
  Birmingham, Great Barr
  B42 ....55 A8
  Birmingham, Marston Green
  B37 ....90 A7
  Hopwood B48 ....123 B4
  Kingswinford DY6 ......60 E5
Riseley Cres B5 ....86 D7
Rising Brook WV6 .....24 B4
Rising La
  Chadwick End B93 ....145 B5
  Lapworth B94,B93 ....144 F5
Rising Rd B94 ....144 C5
Rissington Ave B29 ...104 A8
Ritchie Cl B13 ....87 A1
Rivendell Ct B93 ......142 C2
Rivendell Gdns WV6 ...24 B5
River Brook Dr B30 ...104 B8
River Cl Bedworth CV12 ..77 F1
  Royal Leamington Spa
  CV32 ....161 D8
River St ■ CV1 ....113 B3
River Lee Rd B11 ......87 E5
River St B5 ....67 A2
River Wlk CV2 ....96 C2
Riverbank Rd WV13 ...27 D2
Riverdrive B78,B79 ....21 B3
Riverfield Gr B77 ......21 D5
Riverford Croft CV4 ...132 D4
Rivermead CV11 ....73 A4
Rivermead Pk B34 .....69 A6
Riverside ■ CV32 .....161 A8
Riverside Rd B14 .....105 D3
Riverside Cl
  Coventry CV3 ....134 A7
  Lickey End B60 ....137 C6
Riverside Cres B28 ...105 D4
Riverside Ct
  Birmingham B38 ......103 D3
  ■ Coleshill B46 ......70 F7
Riverside Dr
  Birmingham, Cannon Hill
  B29 ....86 C3
  Birmingham, Stechford B33 .68 D4
  Solihull B91 ....107 E2
Riverside Gdns WV8 ...10 B5
Riverside Ind Est
  Fazeley B78 ....35 B8
  Tamworth B78 ....21 B1
Riversleigh Dr DY8 ....80 E8
Riversleigh Rd CV32 ..156 C1
Riversley Rd CV11 .....73 C3
Riverway WS10 ....42 B2
Rivington Cl DY8 ......80 E4
Rivington Cres B44 ....45 C1
Ro-Oak Rd CV6 ....112 B5
Roach B77 ....35 D6
Roach Cl Birmingham B37 .70 C3
  Brierley Hill DY5 .....61 D5
Roach Cres WV11 ......26 F8
Roach Pool Croft B16 ..65 C2
Road No 1 DY10 ....116 F2
Road No 2 DY10 ....116 E2
Road No 3 DY10 ....116 E2
Roanne Ringway CV11 ..73 B4
Robert Ave B23 ....56 E6
Robert Cl Coventry CV3 .134 C4
  Tamworth B79 ....20 F7
Robert Cramb Ave CV4 .131 F8
Robert Ct
  ■ Birmingham, Pheasey
  B43 ....44 D4
  Birmingham, Wake Green
  B13 ....87 B2
Robert Rd Bedworth CV7 .95 FB
  Birmingham B20 ....55 B1
  Tipton DY4 ....51 F6
Robert St DY3 ....50 D4
Robert Wynd WV14 ....40 A1

Roberts Cl Bilston WS10 .41 B4
  Brownhills WS9 ....15 F2
Roberts Ct B24 ....55 D7
Roberts Green Rd DY3 ..50 E4
Roberts La WS9 ....99 B8
Roberts Prim Sch DY3 ..50 D4
Roberts Rd
  Birmingham B27 ....88 D3
  Walsall WS3 ....28 F5
  Wednesbury WS10 .....42 E2
Robertson Knoll B36 ...68 F7
Robertsons Gdns ■ B7 .67 C7
Robeson Cl DY4 ....51 D5
Robey's La B78 ....22 D3
Robin Cl Birmingham B36 .70 A8
  Huntington WS12 ....1 C7
  Kingswinford DY6 ......61 A6
  Tamworth B77 ....35 C8
  Hinckley LE10 ....71 D4
  Solihull B92 ....89 B1
Robin Gr WV11 ....26 C7
Robin Hood Cres B28 ..105 E7
Robin Hood La B28 ....105 E7
Robin Hood Rd
  Brierley Hill DY5 ......61 F2
  Coventry CV3 ....134 C6
Robin Hood Sch B28 ..106 B6
Robin Rd B23 ....56 B5
Robin Wlk WS2 ....27 F3
Robin's Cl DY8 ....81 A3
Robina Cl CV32 ....157 B2
Robinia B77 ....22 A4
Robins Bsns Pk B70 ...52 E7
Robins Cl WS6 ....4 D1
Robins Gr CV34 ....160 C4
Robins Hill Dr B48 ....139 A5
Robins Rd WS7 ....6 E7
Robins Way CV10 .....72 A3
Robinsfield Dr B31 ...123 A7
Robinson Cl D B79 ....20 D7
Robinson Rd
  Bedworth CV12 ....95 D8
  Burntwood WS7 ....6 F8
Robinson's Way LE10 ..75 F4
Robinson's Way R76 ...58 D5
Robottom Cl WS2 .....28 B6
Robson Cl WS8 ....15 F5
Rocester Ave WV11 ....26 E7
Rochdale Wlk B10 .....87 C7
Roche Rd WS3 ....13 F1
Roche The WS13 ....8 A8
Roche Way WS3 ....13 F1
Rochester Ave WS7 ...7 A7
Rochester Cl
  Nuneaton CV11 ....73 B3
  Redditch B97 ....158 C8
Rochester Croft WS2 ..28 A4
Rochester Rd
  Birmingham B31 ......103 A4
  Coventry CV5 ....132 E8
Rochester Way WS11 ..2 C1
Rochester Wlk DY10 ..117 C5
Rochford Cl
  Birmingham B45 ......121 E7
  Halesowen B63 ....82 F2
  Sutton Coldfield B76 ..58 A8
  ■ Walsall WS2 ....42 C7
Rochford Ct
  Royal Leamington Spa
  CV31 ....161 E7
  Solihull B90 ....127 A6
Rochford Gr WV4 .....38 D5
Rock Ave B45 ....122 C7
Rock Cl CV6 ....96 B1
Rock Cotts B DY11 ...116 D6
Rock Gr B92 ....88 E3
Rock Hill
  Bromsgrove B61 ......150 D7
  Weeford B78,WS14 ....19 C4
Rock La CV7 ....94 C2
Rock Mill La CV32 ....161 C8
Rock Rd Sedgley WV14 .50 F8
  Solihull B92 ....88 E3
Rock St DY3 ....50 E5
Rock The WV6 ....24 D5
Rocken End CV6 ......113 D8
Rocket Pool Dr WV14 ..41 A2
Rockford Cl B98 ....158 F5
Rockford Rd B42 ....55 A7
Rockingham Cl
  Dorridge B93 ....127 D2
  Dudley DY3 ....50 B3
  Walsall WS3 ....14 B1
Rockingham Dr
  Nuneaton CV11 ....78 F7
  Perton WV6 ....23 F3
Rockingham Gdns B74 ..46 B6
Rockingham Hall Gdns
  DY9 ....99 D7
Rockingham Rd B25 ...88 D8
Rockland Dr B33 ......68 C4
Rockland Gdns WV13 ..40 F8
Rocklands Cres WS13 ..3 D1
Rocklands Dr B75 .....46 B8
Rocklands Sch WS13 ...9 C8
Rockley Gr B45 ....122 B7
Rockley Rd B65 ....63 A6
Rockmead Ave B44 ....44 F2
Rockmoor Cl B37 ......69 E3
Rockrose Gdns WV10 ..12 A7
Rockville Rd B8 ....68 A4
Rockwell La B48 ......139 E4
Rockwood Rd B27 .....88 B4
Rocky La
  Birmingham, Aston B6 .67 A6
  Birmingham, Great Barr
  B42 ....55 B5

Rocky La continued
  Birmingham, Nechells Green
  B7 ....67 B6
  Catshill B61 ....136 E7
  Kenilworth CV8 ....148 D2
Rodbaston Coll WS14 ..19 A5
Rodborough Rd
  Birmingham B9 ....88 B7
  Dorridge B93 ....127 E3
Rodbourne Rd B17 ....85 C3
Roddis Cl B23 ....56 D8
Roden Ave DY10 ......117 A7
Roderick Dr WV11 ....26 D7
Roderick Rd B11 ......87 C5
Rodhouse Cl CV4 .....111 D1
Rodlington Ave B44 ...44 F1
Rodman Cl B15 ....85 D8
Rodney Cl Birmingham B16 .66 A2
  Hinckley LE10 ....71 D4
  Solihull B92 ....89 B1
Rodney Rd B92 ....89 B1
Rodway Cl
  Birmingham B19 ......66 E7
  Brierley Hill DY5 ......81 D7
  Wolverhampton WV4 ..39 D3
Rodway Dr CV5 ....111 D4
Rodwell Gr B44 ....56 A8
Rodyard Way CV1 .....165 C1
Roe Cl CV34 ....160 F8
Roebuck Cl B34 ....69 E5
Roebuck Glade WV12 ..27 E4
Roebuck La
  Smethwick B66 ....64 F8
  West Bromwich B70 ...53 E1
Roebuck Pl WS3 ....28 E6
Roebuck Rd WS3 .....28 E6
Roebuck St B70 ....53 F1
Roedean Cl B44 ....56 B7
Roford Cl DY3 ....50 E5
Rogerfield Rd B23 ....57 A6
Rogers Cl WV11 ......13 A2
Rogers Rd B8 ....68 B5
Rogers Way CV34 ....160 B4
Rokeby Cl B76 ....58 C8
Rokeby Cl LE(A)LE10 ..71 C6
Rokeby Cl B76 ....46 E4
Rokeby Rd B43 ....43 F2
Rokeby Wlk B34 ......69 A6
Rokewood Cl DY6 .....49 D1
Rokholt Cres WS11 ....1 C1
Rolan Dr B90 ....125 E8
Roland Ave CV6 ....95 C3
Roland Gdns ■ B19 ...66 C8
Roland Gr ■ B19 ......66 C8
Roland Mount CV6 ....95 C3
Roland Rd B19 ....66 C8
Roland Terr ■ B19 ....66 C8
Rolfe St B66 ....65 A6
Rollason Cl CV6 ......113 C8
Rollason Rd
  Birmingham B24 ......57 A3
  Coventry CV6 ....113 B8
  ■ Dudley DY2 ....62 D8
Rollason's Yd CV6 ....96 A3
Rollesby Dr WV13 ....40 F8
Rolling Mill Cl B5 .....86 F7
Rollingmill St WS2 ....28 C1
Rollswood Dr B91 ....107 A4
Rollswood Dr WV13 ...27 C2
Roma Rd B11 ....87 E5
Roman Cl WS8 ....6 E2
Roman Ct
  Birmingham B38 ......124 B8
  Cannock WS11 ....4 E5
  Tamworth B77 ....35 E7
Roman La B74 ....31 B4
Roman Pk Coleshill B46 .59 F1
  Little Aston B74 ....31 B4
Roman Pl B74 ....31 B2
Roman Rd Coventry CV2 .114 B3
  Little Aston B74 ......31 C4
Roman Rd (Sandy La)
  DY8 ....80 C3
Roman View WS11 ....4 F5
Roman Way
  Birmingham B15 ......85 D8
  Blackheath B65 ....63 C3
  Bromsgrove B61 ......137 B4
  Coleshill B46 ....59 F2
  Coventry CV3 ....133 D3
  Lichfield WS14 ....9 D7
  Wolverhampton B79 ...20 E7
Roman Way Fst Sch
  B98 ....154 E3
Roman Wlk WS14 .....8 D2
Romans Grange B74 ..31 C5
Romany Rd B45 ......101 D1
Romany Way DY8 .....80 C3
Romeo Arbour CV34 ..161 E3
Romford Cl B26 ....89 B6
Romford Rd CV6 ....95 B2
Romilly Ave B20 ....55 B3
Romilly Cl Lichfield WS14 ..9 E7
  Stourbridge DY8 ......80 E6
  Sutton Coldfield B76 ..47 A4
Romney B77 ....35 F8
Romney Cl
  Birmingham B28 ......105 F7
  Hinckley LE10 ....71 A3
Romney House Ind Est
  WS10 ....41 B7
Romney Way B43 .....44 D4
Romsey Ave CV10 ....73 D8
Romsey Gr WV10 .....11 C3
Romsey Ho WS2 ......42 C7
Romsey Rd WV10 .....11 C3
Romsey Way WS3 ....13 F3
Romsley Cl
  Birmingham B45 ......121 E8

Romsley Cl continued
  Halesowen B63 ....83 B2
  Redditch B98 ....154 F3
  Walsall WS4 ....15 C2
Romsley Hill Grange
  B62 ....100 F1
Romsley Rd
  Birmingham B32 ......102 B8
  Coventry CV6 ....113 C6
  Oldbury B68 ....64 B2
  Stourbridge DY9 ......81 C5
Romulus Cl B20 ....55 B3
Ron Davis Cl B66 ......65 B5
Ronald Gr B36 ....58 D1
Ronald Rd B9 ....67 E2
Ronald Rd B9 ....67 D2
Rood End Prim Sch B68 .64 C6
Rood End Rd B69 .....64 C7
Rooker Ave WV2 ......39 F6
Rooker Cres WV2 .....39 F6
Rookery Ave
  Brierley Hill DY5 ......61 A2
  Wolverhampton WV4 ..40 A3
Rookery Cl B97 ......153 D1
Rookery Ct WS13 .....8 E7
Rookery La Aldridge WS9 .30 B6
  Coventry CV5 ....95 B4
  Weeford B75,B78 ....19 C2
  Wolverhampton WV4 ..39 F6
Rookery Parr WV9 ....30 B6
Rookery Pk DY5 ......61 B5
Rookery Rd
  Birmingham, Handsworth
  B21 ....54 E1
  Birmingham, Selly Oak B29 .85 F2
  Wolverhampton WV14,WV4 .40 A3
  Wombourne WV5 .....49 B6
Rookery Rise WV5 ....49 B6
Rookery Road Jun & Inf Schs
  B21 ....54 E1
Rookery St WV11 .....26 C5
Rookery The B62 .....84 A2
Rooks Mdw DY9 ......99 B6
Rookwood Dr WV6 ...23 F2
Roosevelt Dr CV4 ....111 E2
Rooth St WS10 ....42 B4
Roper Way DY3 ......50 F6
Roper Wlk DY3 ....50 F6
Rosafield Ave B62 ....83 F6
Rosalind Ave DY1 ....51 B6
Rosalind Gr WV11 ....27 A5
Rosamond St WS1 ...42 D7
Rosamund's Rise Suth B8 .67 E3
Rosary Rd B23 ....56 D3
Rosary Villas ■ B11 ..87 C5
Rosaville Cres CV5 ...112 A6
Rose Ave Alvechurch B48 .139 A5
  Coventry CV6 ....112 F5
  Kingswinford DY6 ....60 F5
  Oldbury B68 ....64 C3
Rose Bay Mdw ■ WS11 ..2 C2
Rose Cl B66 ....65 C5
Rose Cottage Dr ■ DY8 .60 D3
Rose Cottage Flats CV5 .111 D5
Rose Cotts
  ■ Birmingham, Selly Oak
  B29 ....85 F2
  Birmingham, Stirchley B30 .104 A6
Rose Croft CV8 ....147 E6
Rose Ct
  Balsall Common CV7 ..130 B8
  Dudley DY2 ....51 F1
  ■ Solihull B91 ....15 E5
Rose Hill
  Barnt Green B45 ......122 B4
  Brierley Hill DY5 ......62 A1
  Willenhall WV13 ....41 A8
Rose Hill Cl B36 ......69 B8
Rose Hill Gdns WV13 ..27 B1
Rose Hill Rd B21 ......66 A7
Rose La Burntwood WS7 ..7 C7
  Dodford B61 ....136 A6
  Nuneaton CV11 ....73 C3
  Tipton B69 ....52 C2
Rose Rd Birmingham B17 ..85 D6
  Coleshill B46 ....70 F8
Rose St WV14 ....40 F2
Rose Terr B45 ....138 D8
Rosebank Dr WS3 ....28 E4
Rosebay Ave B38 ....123 F8
Roseberry Ave CV2 ...96 C1
Rosebery Rd
  Smethwick B66 ....65 C4
  Tamworth B77 ....35 D4
Rosebery St
  Birmingham B18 ....66 A4
  Wolverhampton WV3 ..25 B1
Roseberiars B90 .....125 E7
Rosecroft Rd B26 ....89 C6
Rosedale Ave
  Birmingham B23 ......56 E5
  Smethwick B66 ....65 C3
Rosedale CE Inf Sch
  WV12 ....27 D5
Rosedale Gr B25 .....88 C8
Rosedale Pl WV13 ....41 A8
Rosedale Rd B25 .....88 C8
Rosedale Wlk DY6 ....60 E8
Rosedene Dr B20 .....54 F2
Rosefield Croft B6 ....66 F4
Rosefield Ct B68 ......65 A4
Rosefield Pl ■ CV32 ..161 F8
Rosefield Rd B67 ......65 A4
Rosefield St CV32 ....162 A8
Rosefield Wlk ■ CV32 .161 F8
Rosegreen Cl CV3 ....133 E6
Rosehall Cl Redditch B98 .158 E6
  Solihull B91 ....106 F1

Rosehill WS12 .... 1 F8
Rosehip Cl WS5 .... 43 A3
Rosehip Dr CV2 .... 114 B6
Roseland Ave DY2 .... 51 F1
Roseland Rd CV8 .... 147 F3
Roseland Way 7 B15 .... 66 B1
Roselands Ave CV2 .... 114 D8
Roseleigh Rd B45 .... 122 B6
Rosemary Ave
  Bilston WV14 .... 40 F6
  Cheslyn Hay WS6 .... 4 D3
  Wolverhampton WV4 .... 39 C6
Rosemary Cl
  Clayhanger WS8 .... 15 D6
  Coventry CV4 .... 111 E3
Rosemary Cres
  Dudley DY1 .... 51 A6
  Sedgley DY1 .... 50 F6
  Wolverhampton WV4 .... 39 C6
Rosemary Cres W WV4 .... 39 B5
Rosemary Ct B74 .... 31 D4
Rosemary Dr
  Huntington WS12 .... 1 D5
  Little Aston B74 .... 31 C3
  Stoke Prior B60 .... 150 C1
Rosemary Hill CV8 .... 147 F5
Rosemary Hill Rd B74 ..... 31 B4
Rosemary La DY8 .... 80 D3
Rosemary Mews CV8 .... 147 F5
Rosemary Nook B74 .... 31 D5
Rosemary Rd
  Birmingham B33 .... 68 F2
  Cheslyn Hay WS6 .... 4 D3
  Halesowen B63 .... 82 E2
  Kidderminster DY10 ...... 117 B7
  Tamworth B77 .... 21 F4
  Tipton DY4 .... 52 A6
Rosemary Way LE10 .... 75 B7
Rosemoor Dr DY5 .... 81 B7
Rosemount
  Birmingham B32 .... 84 E5
  Wolverhampton WV6 .... 24 D5
Rosemount Cl CV2 .... 114 E7
Rosemullion Cl CV7 .... 96 B8
Rosetti Cl DY10 .... 117 C6
Roseville Cl 4 WV14 ...... 51 C8
Roseville Gdns WV8 .... 10 A4
Roseville Prec 5 WV14 .... 51 C8
Rosewood CV11 .... 73 F1
Rosewood Cl
  Hinckley LE10 .... 75 F6
  Tamworth B77 .... 21 D4
Rosewood Cres CV32 ...... 157 B2
Rosewood Ct B77 .... 21 D4
Rosewood Dr
  Barnt Green B45 .... 138 C7
  Birmingham B23 .... 56 D2
  Willenhall WV12 .... 27 B8
Rosewood Gdns WV11 .... 13 B3
Rosewood Pk WS6 .... 4 D2
Rosewood Rd DY1 .... 51 A7
Rosewood Specl Sch
  DY1 .... 50 E1
Roshven Rd B12 .... 87 A4
Roslin Cl B60 .... 137 B1
Roslin Gr B19 .... 66 C6
Roslyn Cl B66 .... 65 A6
Ross B65 .... 63 B2
Ross Cl Coventry CV5 .... 112 A5
  Wolverhampton WV6 .... 24 E2
Ross Dr DY6 .... 60 C7
Ross Hts B65 .... 63 B3
Ross Rd WS3 .... 28 F6
Ross Way CV11 .... 79 B7
Rosse Ct B92 .... 107 F8
Rossendale Cl B63 .... 82 E6
Rossendale Way CV10 ...... 72 C2
Rosslyn Ave CV6 .... 112 E6
Rosslyn Rd B76 .... 57 F6
Roston Dr LE10 .... 71 A1
Rostrevor Rd B10 .... 67 F1
Rosy Cross B79 .... 21 B5
Rotary Ct 2 WV3 .... 25 B2
Rothay B77 .... 35 F8
Rothbury Gn WV10 .... 12 A2
Rotherby Gr B37 .... 90 B7
Rotherfield Cl CV31 ..... 162 B7
Rotherfield Rd B26 .... 89 B8
Rotherham Rd CV6 .... 95 C2
Rotherhams Oak La
  B94 .... 142 F7
Rothesay Ave CV4 .... 112 B2
Rothesay Cl CV10 .... 73 A2
Rothesay Croft B32 ...... 102 B7
Rothesay Dr DY8 .... 60 C3
Rothesay Way WV12 .... 27 B6
Rothwell Dr B91 .... 106 D4
Rothwell Rd CV34 .... 155 C1
Rotten Row WS14 .... 9 C7
Rotten Pk Rd B16 .... 65 D2
Rotton Park St B16 .... 65 F3
Rough Coppice Wlk B35 .... 58 A2
Rough Hay Rd WS10 .... 41 C7
Rough Hay Prim Sch
  WS10 .... 41 C7
Rough Hill Dr
  Blackheath B65 .... 62 F6
  Redditch B98 .... 158 F6
Rough Hills Cl WV2 .... 39 F6
Rough Hills Rd WV2 .... 39 F6
Rough Rd B44 .... 45 A3
Rough The B97 .... 158 D6
Rough Wood Ctry Pk
  WV12 .... 27 E6
Roughknowles Rd CV4 .... 131 D6
Roughlea Ave B36 .... 68 F7
Roughley Dr B75 .... 32 C2

Roughley Farm Rd B75 ..... 32 E3
Rouncil Cl B92 .... 107 D7
Rouncil La CV8 .... 155 C8
Round Cl B90 .... 126 A6
Round Croft WV13 .... 27 A2
Round Hill DY3 .... 39 D2
Round Hill Ave WV9 .... 81 C1
Round House Rd
  Coventry CV3 .... 134 B8
  Dudley DY3 .... 50 E4
Round Moor Wlk B35 .... 58 A3
Round Oak Sch The
  CV32 .... 157 A3
Round Rd B24 .... 57 B2
Round Saw Croft B45 ..... 121 F8
Round St DY2 .... 62 C6
Roundabout The B31 ...... 102 D1
Roundhill Cl B76 .... 46 E4
Roundhill Terr B62 .... 63 E1
Roundhill Way WS8 .... 7 A2
Roundhills Rd B62 .... 83 F8
Roundlea Cl WV12 .... 27 B7
Roundlea Rd B31 .... 102 E2
Rounds Green Prim Sch
  B69 .... 63 E7
Rounds Green Rd B69 ...... 63 E7
Rounds Hill CV8 .... 147 E2
Rounds Hill Rd WV14 ...... 51 D8
Rounds Rd WV14 .... 40 D3
Roundway Down CV3 .... 23 E3
Rousay Cl B45 .... 101 F1
Rousdon Gr B43 .... 54 D8
Rover Dr
  Birmingham, Acock's Green
  B27 .... 88 D4
  Birmingham, Castle Bromwich
  B36 .... 58 F1
Rover Rd CV1 .... 165 B2
Rovex Bsns Pk B11 .... 87 F5
Row The CV7 .... 97 D3
Rowallan Rd B75 .... 32 D2
Rowan Cl
  Binley Woods CV3 .... 135 D7
  Bromsgrove B61 .... 136 E2
  Hollywood B47 .... 125 B5
  Lichfield WS14 .... 9 D8
  Sutton Coldfield B76 .... 58 A6
Rowan Cres Dudley WV14 ... 40 B1
  Redditch B97 .... 153 A4
  Wolverhampton WV3 ...... 38 E7
Rowan Ct
  Birmingham B30 .... 104 A2
  Oldbury B66 .... 64 D8
Rowan Dr
  Birmingham B28 .... 106 A5
  Essington WV11 .... 13 B3
  6 Warwick CV34 .... 160 F8
Rowan Gr Burntwood WV7 ... 6 F7
  Coventry CV2 .... 96 E2
Rowan Rd Cannock WS11 .... 1 C5
  Nuneaton CV10 .... 72 C6
  Redditch B97 .... 153 A4
  Sedgley DY3 .... 39 F3
  Sutton Coldfield B72 .... 46 C3
  Walsall WS5 .... 42 F4
Rowan Rise DY6 .... 60 E6
Rowan Way
  Birmingham, Chelmsley Wood
  B37 .... 70 C1
  Birmingham, Longbridge
  B31 .... 122 F8
  Chapel End CV10 .... 72 A7
Rowans The CV12 .... 77 E2
Rowantrees B45 .... 122 B5
Roway La B69 .... 52 F1
Rowbrook Cl B90 .... 125 E8
Rowcroft Covert B14 .... 104 C2
Rowcroft Rd CV2 .... 115 A6
Rowdale Rd B42 .... 55 C6
Rowden Dr
  Birmingham B23 .... 57 A6
  Solihull B91 .... 106 E2
Rowena Gdns DY3 .... 39 C2
Rowheath Ho B30 .... 103 E5
Rowheath Rd B30 .... 103 F4
Rowington Ave B65 .... 63 D3
Rowington Cl CV6 .... 112 D5
Rowington Grn CV35 .... 144 F1
Rowington Rd B34 .... 69 E6
Rowington Terr B25 .... 88 B7
Rowland Ave B69 .... 159 E3
Rowland Gdns WS2 .... 28 C3
Rowland Hill Ave WS13 ... 7 A1
Rowland Hill Ctr 9
  DY10 .... 116 E6
Rowland Hill Dr DY4 ...... 52 C5
Rowland St WS2 .... 28 C3
Rowland Way (Road 1a)
  DY11 .... 116 E1
Rowlands Ave
  Walsall WS2 .... 27 E3
  Wolverhampton WV1 .... 26 B2
Rowlands Cl WS2 .... 27 E4
Rowlands Cres B91 .... 88 E7
Rowlands Rd B26 .... 88 E7
Rowley Cl WS12 .... 2 B8
Rowley Dr CV3 .... 134 B4
Rowley Gr B33 .... 69 D3
Rowley Hall Ave B65 ...... 63 C4
Rowley Hall Prim Sch
  B65 .... 63 C3
Rowley Hill View B64 ..... 82 F8
Rowley La CV3 .... 134 D3
Rowley Pl WS4 .... 29 B7
Rowley Rd
  Coventry CV3,CV8 .... 134 B3
  Whitnash CV31 .... 162 A2

Rowley Regis Com Hospl
  B65 .... 63 B2
Rowley Regis Ctr (Dudley
  Coll) B65 .... 63 B3
Rowley Regis Sta B65 ..... 63 E2
Rowley St WS1 .... 29 A2
Rowley View
  Bilston WV14 .... 41 A3
  Darlaston WS10 .... 41 C4
  West Bromwich B70 .... 53 B3
Rowley Village B65 .... 63 C3
Rowley's Green La CV6 .... 95 E4
Rowleys Green Lane Ind Est
  CV6 .... 95 E4
Rowney Croft B28 .... 105 E4
Rowney Green La B48 .... 139 F5
Rowood Dr B91,B92 ...... 107 D7
Rowsborough Rd B90 ..... 158 E2
Rowthorn Cl B74 .... 45 A7
Rowthorn Dr B90 .... 127 A6
Rowton Ave WV6 .... 23 E3
Rowton Dr B74 .... 44 F5
Roxall Cl DY10 .... 98 C2
Roxburgh Croft CV32 .... 157 C6
Roxburgh Gr B43 .... 44 C4
Roxburgh Rd
  Nuneaton CV11 .... 73 E1
  Sutton Coldfield B73 .... 46 A3
Roxby Gdns WV6 .... 25 A5
Royal Brierley Glassworks*
  DY5 .... 61 C2
Royal Cl Blackheath B65 .. 63 C5
  Brierley Hill DY5 .... 81 C8
Royal Cres CV3 .... 134 C5
Royal Ct Hinckley LE10 ... 75 D7
  Sutton Coldfield B73 .... 46 B2
Royal Leamington Spa
  Rehabilitation Hospl
  CV34 .... 161 E4
Royal London Bldgs
  WV1 .... 163 C3
Royal Mail St B1 .... 164 B2
Royal Oak La CV7,CV2 ..... 95 C7
Royal Oak Rd
  Blackheath B65 .... 62 F5
  Halesowen B62 .... 83 A5
Royal Oak Yd CV12 .... 78 B4
Royal Orthopaedic Hospl The
  B31 .... 103 B5
Royal Priors 12 CV32 ... 156 F1
Royal Rd B72 .... 46 C4
Royal Scot Gr WS1 .... 42 D5
Royal Sq 5 B97 .... 153 E3
Royal Sta The WV1 ...... 163 D2
Royal Star Cl B33 .... 69 C2
Royal Way DY4 .... 52 A2
Royal Wolverhampton Jun
  Sch The WV3 .... 39 B7
Royal Wolverhampton Sch
  The WV3 .... 39 B7
Royal Worcester Cres
  B60 .... 137 C1
Roydon Rd B27 .... 106 C8
Roylesden Cres B73 .... 45 C2
Royston Cl Coventry CV3 . 115 A3
Royston Croft B12 .... 86 F6
Royston Ct 7 B13 .... 87 B2
Royston Way DY3 .... 50 C5
Rubens Cl Coventry CV5 . 112 C3
  Dudley DY3 .... 50 D5
Rubery Ct WS10 .... 41 C7
Rubery Farm Gr B45 ..... 121 F7
Rubery Field Cl B45 .... 102 B1
Rubery La B45 .... 102 A1
Rubery La S B45 .... 121 F8
Rubery St WS10 .... 41 C8
Ruckleigh Sch B91 ...... 107 C4
Ruckley Ave 1 B19 .... 66 C7
Ruckley Rd B29 .... 103 B8
Rudd Gdns WV10 .... 26 B4
Rudgard Rd CV6 .... 96 A4
Rudge Ave WV1 .... 26 C3
Rudge Cl WV12 .... 27 C4
Rudge Croft B33 .... 69 A4
Rudge Wlk B18 .... 66 B3
Rudgewick Croft 1 B6 .... 66 F6
Rudyard Cl WV10 .... 11 E4
Rudyard Gr B33 .... 69 B3
Rudyngfield Dr B33 .... 68 F4
Rufford B77 .... 22 B3
Rufford Cl
  Birmingham B23 .... 56 D8
  Hinckley LE10 .... 75 D3
Rufford Prim Sch DY9 ..... 81 C5
Rufford Rd DY9 .... 81 D5
Rufford St DY9 .... 81 D5
Rufford Way WS9 .... 29 E7
Rugby Rd
  Binley Woods CV3 .... 135 D8
  Bulkington CV12 .... 79 D2
  Cubbington CV32 .... 157 E6
  Hinckley LE10 .... 75 D8
  Royal Leamington Spa
  CV32 .... 156 D1
  Stourbridge DY8 .... 80 D7
Rugby St WV1 .... 25 B4
Rugeley Ave WV12 .... 27 D8
Rugeley Cl DY4 .... 51 E5
Rugeley Rd
  Burntwood, Chase Terrace
  WS7 .... 6 F8
  Burntwood, Gorstey Ley WS7 7 C7
  Cannock, Hednesford WS12 . 2 D7
  Cannock, Littleworth WS12 . 2 A5
Ruislip Cl B35 .... 58 A4
Ruiton St DY3 .... 50 D4
Rumbow B63 .... 83 B4

Rumbow La B62 .... 100 D3
Rumbush La
  Earlswood B90,B94 ...... 125 F3
  Solihull B90 .... 126 A5
Rumer Hill Bsns Est WS11 . 4 F7
Rumer Hill Rd WS11 .... 4 F8
Runcorn Cl
  Birmingham B37 .... 70 C4
  Redditch B98 .... 158 F8
Runcorn Rd B12 .... 87 A5
Runcorn Wlk 11 CV2 ..... 115 A7
Runnemede Gdns CV10 ...... 72 F3
Runnymede Dr CV7 .... 130 C5
Runnymede Rd B11 .... 87 E3
Rupert Rd CV6 .... 113 B8
Rupert St Birmingham B7 . 67 A4
  Wolverhampton WV3 ...... 25 A2
Rush Gn B32 .... 84 E2
Rush La Redditch B98 .... 146 A6
Rushall Cl Stourbridge DY8 80 E8
  Walsall WS4 .... 29 B4
Rushall Ct B43 .... 54 E7
Rushall JMI Sch WS4 ...... 15 E1
Rushall Manor Cl WS4 ..... 29 B4
Rushall Manor Rd WS4 ..... 29 B4
Rushall Rd WV10 .... 11 E2
Rushbrook Cl
  Clayhanger WS8 .... 15 D6
  Solihull B92 .... 88 E2
Rushbrooke Cl B14 ...... 104 C4
Rushbrooke La B94 ...... 141 D3
Rushbrooke Cl B13 .... 86 F4
Rushbrooke Dr B73 .... 45 C3
Rushbury Cl Bilston WV14 . 40 B5
  Solihull B90 .... 106 D4
Rushden Croft B44 .... 44 F1
Rushes Mill WS3 .... 14 E3
Rushey La B11 .... 88 A5
Rushford Ave WV5 .... 49 A6
Rushford Cl B90 .... 127 A7
Rushlake Gn B34 .... 69 B5
Rushleigh Rd B90 .... 125 E8
Rushmead Gr B45 .... 122 A7
Rushmere Rd DY4 .... 41 B6
Rushmoor Cl B74 .... 46 B6
Rushmoor Dr CV5 .... 112 F3
Rushmore St CV31 .... 162 B7
Rushmore Terr CV31 ..... 162 B7
Rushock Cl B98 .... 159 C7
Rushton Cl CV7 .... 130 C7
Rushwick Croft B34 .... 69 D6
Rushwick Ct B23 .... 56 B3
Rushwood Cl WS4 .... 29 A3
Rushy Piece B32 .... 84 D3
Ruskin Cl CV31 .... 161 F6
Ruskin Ave
  Blackheath B65 .... 63 D2
  Dudley DY3 .... 50 A5
  Kidderminster DY10 ..... 117 C6
  Wolverhampton WV4 .... 39 F2
Ruskin Cl Birmingham B6 .. 66 F7
  Coventry CV6 .... 112 D6
  Nuneaton CV10 .... 72 A5
Ruskin Gr B27 .... 88 B2
Ruskin Rd WV10 .... 12 A1
Ruskin St B71 .... 53 C5
Russel Croft B60 .... 151 A2
Russell Bank Rd B74 ..... 31 E4
Russell Cl
  Tipton, Moxley B64 ...... 41 C1
  Tipton, Tividale B69 .... 52 D2
  Wolverhampton WV11 ...... 12 F1
Russell Ct
  4 Royal Leamington Spa
  CV31 .... 162 A7
  Sutton Coldfield B74 .... 31 D3
  Wolverhampton WV3 ..... 163 A2
Russell St N 8 CV1 ..... 165 C4
Russell St Coventry CV1 . 165 C4
  Dudley DY1 .... 51 B1
  Royal Leamington Spa
  CV32 .... 156 F1
  Wednesbury WS10 .... 41 F2
  Willenhall WV13 .... 27 B2
Russell St N 4 CV1 ..... 165 C4
Russell Terr CV31 ...... 162 A7
Russell's Hall Rd DY1 ... 50 E1
Russells Hall Hospl DY1 . 61 A7
Russells Hall Prim Sch
  DY1 .... 50 E1
Russells The B13 .... 86 D3
Russet Gr CV4 .... 132 D3
Russet Way B31 .... 102 E7
Russett Wlk WV8 .... 10 E1
Russett Cl E Burntwood WS7 6 F6
  Walsall WS5 .... 43 B4
Russett Way DY5 .... 61 B7
Ruston St B16 .... 66 A1
Ruth Chamberlain Ct 5
  DY11 .... 116 D6
Ruth Cl DY4 .... 41 C1
Ruthall Cl B29 .... 103 C7
Rutherford Glen CV11 .... 73 F1
Rutherford Rd
  Birmingham B23 .... 56 E7
  Bromsgrove B60 .... 151 B7
  Walsall WS2 .... 28 A5
Rutherglen Ave CV3 ..... 134 A6
Rutland B77 .... 35 A6
Rutland Ave Hinckley LE10 . 75 C7

Rutland Ave continued
  Nuneaton CV10 .... 72 F4
  Wolverhampton WV4 .... 38 D4
Rutland Cres
  Aldridge WS9 .... 16 B1
  Bilston WV14 .... 40 E7
Rutland Croft 3 CV3 .... 134 F8
Rutland Ct 2 B29 .... 103 C7
Rutland Dr
  Birmingham B26 .... 88 E7
  Bromsgrove B60 .... 151 A8
  Tamworth B78 .... 21 A1
Rutland Pl DY8 .... 80 D8
Rutland Rd Cannock WS12 .. 2 B1
  Smethwick B66 .... 65 A1
  Wednesbury WS10 .... 42 D4
  West Bromwich B71 ...... 53 C7
Rutland St WS3 .... 28 E5
Rutland Terr 5 B18 ...... 66 A5
Rutley Gr B32 .... 84 F4
Rutter St WS1 .... 42 E8
Rutters Mdw B32 .... 84 B4
Ryan Ave WV11 .... 27 A7
Ryan Pl DY2 .... 62 C6
Rycroft Gr B33 .... 69 C2
Rydal B77 .... 36 A7
Rydal Cl Aldridge B74 .... 30 F2
  Allesley CV5 .... 112 B8
  Cannock WS12 .... 2 A8
  Hinckley LE10 .... 74 F7
  Wolverhampton WV11 ..... 26 C7
Rydal Dr WV6 .... 23 F4
Rydal Ho WV1 .... 26 B1
Rydal Ho 4 B69 .... 63 D5
Rydal Way B28 .... 105 F7
Rydding La WS3 .... 28 B3
Rydding Sq B71 .... 53 B8
Ryde Ave CV10 .... 73 D7
Ryde Gr B27 .... 88 A1
Ryder St Birmingham B4 . 164 C3
  Stourbridge DY8 .... 60 D2
  West Bromwich B70 ...... 52 F5
Ryders Green Prim Sch
  B70 .... 52 F4
Ryders Green Rd B70 ..... 52 F4
Ryders Hayes Com Sch
  WS3 .... 15 A5
Ryders Hayes La WS3 ..... 14 B4
Ryders Hill Cres CV10 ... 72 C7
Rye Croft
  7 Birmingham B27 .... 88 C5
  Hollywood B47 .... 125 A5
  Stourbridge DY9 .... 81 E2
Rye Gr B11 .... 87 F4
Rye Grass Wlk B35 .... 58 B3
Rye Hill CV5 .... 112 A6
Rye Piece Ringway CV12 .. 78 C3
Ryebank Cl B30 .... 103 C5
Ryeclose Croft B37 ...... 70 D3
Ryecroft Ave WV4 .... 39 B5
Ryecroft Cl DY3 .... 50 C8
Ryecroft Cotts WV4 ...... 39 B5
Ryecroft Dr 3 WS7 .... 7 A8
Ryecroft Pk 1 WS2 ...... 28 E3
Ryecroft Sh Ctr WS7 ..... 7 A8
Ryecroft St 2 WS2 ...... 28 F6
Ryefield WV8 .... 10 E1
Ryefield La Hagley DY9 ... 99 A4
Ryefields Rd B60 .... 150 C3
Ryegrass La B97 .... 158 C6
Ryemarket DY8 .... 81 A5
Ryhope Cl CV12 .... 77 C1
Ryhope Wlk WV9 .... 11 A3
Ryknild Cl B74 .... 31 F6
Ryknild St WV14 .... 44 F4
Ryle St WS3 .... 14 D1
Rylston Ave CV6 .... 95 A1
Rylstone Way 4 CV34 ... 155 F1
Rymond Rd B34 .... 68 E6
Ryton B77 .... 35 F8
Ryton Cl Coventry CV4 .. 132 A6
  Redditch B98 .... 154 D1
  Sutton Coldfield B73 .... 46 A4
  Wolverhampton WV10 ..... 26 A5
Ryton Gr B34 .... 69 C5
Ryton Organic Gdns*
  CV8 .... 135 E1

S

Sabell Rd B67 .... 64 F6
Sabrina Rd WV6 .... 23 E1
Sackville Ho 1 CV1 ..... 165 D4
Sacred Heart RC Prim Sch
  Coventry CV3 .... 114 A3
  Tipton DY4 .... 52 A4

Sacred Heart Sch B20 .... **55** D1
Saddington Rd CV3 ...... **134** E8
Saddlers Cl
  Halesowen B63 .... **82** B5
  Hinckley LE10 .... **75** F6
  Lichfield WS14 .... **9** E8
Saddlers Court Ind Est
  WS2 .... **28** A7
Saddlers Ctr WS1 .... **28** E2
Saddlers Mews B91 ...... **107** C1
Saddlestones The WV6 ... **23** D4
Saddleworth Rd WS3 ...... **14** A4
Sadler Cres B11 .... **87** D4
Sadler Ctr WS8 .... **16** A8
Sadler Gdns CV12 .... **78** C2
Sadler Ho B19 .... **66** C6
Sadler Rd Brownhills WS8 **16** A8
  Coventry CV6 .... **113** A8
  Sutton Coldfield B75 .... **46** F7
Sadlers Ct WS2 .... **42** B7
Sadlers Mill WS14 .... **16** A7
Sadlers Wlk B16 .... **66** A1
Sadlerswell La B94 ...... **143** B6
Saffron B77 .... **22** B4
Saffron Gdns WV4 .... **39** A4
Saffron Ho ⑪ B38 .... **123** E8
Sage Croft B31 .... **102** F5
Sagebury Dr B60 .... **150** C1
Saint's Peter & Paul RC Prim
  Sch CV2 .... **114** F7
Saintbury Dr B91 .... **127** C8
Sainte Foy Ave WS13 .... **9** A6
Saints Way CV10 .... **73** D5
St Agatha's Rd
  Birmingham B8 .... **68** B5
  Coventry CV2 .... **114** A3
St Agnes Cl
  Birmingham B13 .... **87** B2
  Studley B80 .... **159** C4
St Agnes La CV1 .... **165** B3
St Agnes Rd B13 .... **87** B1
St Agnes Way CV11 .... **73** F4
St Aidan's Ct WV4 .... **39** A5
St Aidans Wlk B10 .... **87** C8
St Alban's Ave CV11 .... **116** A7
St Alban CE Prim Sch
  WV11 .... **27** B8
St Alban's CE Sch B12 .... **86** F7
St Albans RC Prim Sch
  B14 .... **104** F4
St Albans Cl
  Royal Leamington Spa
  CV32 .... **156** C2
  Smethwick B67 .... **64** E6
  Wednesfield WV11 .... **27** A8
  Wolverhampton WV11 ..... **13** A1
St Albans Ct WV13 .... **26** E1
St Albans Ho B32 .... **84** F5
St Albans Rd
  Birmingham B13 .... **87** A4
  Smethwick B67 .... **64** E6
St Alphege CE Inf Sch
  B91 .... **107** C3
St Alphege CE Jun Sch
  B91 .... **107** C2
St Ambrose Barlow RC Prim
  Sch B28 .... **106** A6
St Ambrose Cl B62,B65 ... **83** C8
St Ambrose RC Inf Sch
  DY10 .... **116** F6
St Andrew's CE Inf Sch
  CV5 .... **111** C5
St Andrew's Cl DY3 .... **50** A3
St Andrew's Fst Sch
  B45 .... **138** D8
St Andrew's Gd (Birmingham
  City FC) B9 .... **67** C1
St Andrew's Inf & Jun Sch
  B9 .... **67** B2
St Andrew's Rd B92 ...... **89** A2
St Andrew's Rd
  Birmingham B9 .... **67** B2
  Coventry CV5 .... **132** F8
  Royal Leamington Spa
  CV32 .... **157** B5
St Andrew's St
  Birmingham B9 .... **67** B2
  Dudley DY2 .... **62** C5
St Andrews B77 .... **22** B4
St Andrews Ave WS3 ...... **15** B4
St Andrews CE Prim Sch
  WV6 .... **24** F4
St Andrews Cl
  Birmingham B32 .... **85** A3
  Stourbridge DY8 .... **80** F2
  Wolverhampton WV6 .... **25** A4
St Andrews Ct ⑫ B10 ..... **67** B1
St Andrews Dr
  Nuneaton CV11 .... **74** B1
  Perton WV6 .... **23** D5
  Tipton B69 .... **63** B7
St Andrews Gn DY10 ... **116** E4
St Andrews Ho WV6 ...... **25** B4
St Andrews Ind Est B9 .... **67** C2
St Andrews Rd B75 .... **46** D7
St Andrews Way B61 ... **150** D8
St Ann's Cl CV31 .... **162** C7
St Ann's Rd CV2 .... **114** A3
St Anne's Cl WS7 .... **6** E4

St Anne's Ct
  Birmingham B13 .... **86** E4
  Willenhall WV13 .... **27** B1
St Anne's RC Prim Sch
  B12 .... **87** A8
St Annes RC Prim Sch
  Birmingham, Fordbridge
  B37 .... **70** A2
  Coventry CV3 .... **134** C6
  Nuneaton CV10 .... **72** D7
  Sutton Coldfield B74 ...... **44** E8
St Anne's Rd
  Blackheath B64 .... **62** C1
  Willenhall WV13 .... **27** B3
  Wolverhampton WV10 ...... **11** B1
St Annes Ct B44 .... **54** F4
St Annes Ct B44 .... **56** A7
St Annes Dr B93 .... **128** A6
St Annes Ind Est WV13 ... **27** B3
St Annes Rd WS13 .... **3** B3
St Annes Way B44 .... **56** A7
St Anthony's Dr WS3 ..... **15** B5
St Antony's RC Prim Sch
  B37 .... **70** A5
St Asaphs Ave B80 ..... **159** D4
St Athan Croft B35 .... **58** B3
St Audries Ct B91 .... **106** F2
St Augustine's RC High Sch
  B97 .... **158** D5
St Augustine's RC Prim Sch
  Birmingham B21 .... **54** D2
  Coventry CV6 .... **113** A7
St Augustine's RC Prim Sch
  B91 .... **107** A2
St Augustine's Rd B16 ... **65** D2
St Augustine's Wlk CV6 . **113** A7
St Augustus Cl B70 .... **53** F2
St Austell Cl
  Nuneaton CV11 .... **74** A5
  Tamworth B79 .... **21** A6
St Austell Rd
  Coventry CV2 .... **114** E3
  Walsall WS5 .... **43** E7
St Barnabas CE Prim Sch
  B24 .... **57** A3
St Bartholemews Cl
  CV3 .... **115** A2
St Bartholomew Terr ③
  WS10 .... **41** F3
St Bartholomew's CE Prim
  Sch
  Coventry CV3 .... **134** E7
  Wolverhampton WV4 ...... **38** E3
St Bede's RC Mid Sch
  B98 .... **153** F3
St Benedict Biscop CE Prim
  Sch WV5 .... **49** B7
St Benedict's Cl B70 ..... **53** F2
St Benedict's Inf Sch
  B10 .... **87** F7
St Benedict's RC Prim Sch
  CV1 .... **113** E4
St Benedicts Rd WS7 ...... **7** B6
St Benedicts Rd
  Birmingham B10 .... **87** F8
  Wombourne WV5 .... **49** A6
St Bernadett's RC Prim Sch
  B25 .... **88** B8
St Bernadette's RC Prim Sch
  WS8 .... **15** F8
St Bernard's RC Prim Sch
  B13 .... **87** C1
St Bernard's Rd B92 .... **106** F2
St Bernards Rd B72 ...... **46** C2
St Bernards Wlk CV3 ... **134** D6
St Blaise Ave B46 .... **59** C2
St Blaise Rd B75 .... **32** D3
St Brades Cl B69 .... **63** C7
St Bride's Cl CV31 ...... **162** C6
St Brides Cl DY3 .... **50** C8
St Brigid's RC Prim Sch
  B31 .... **102** F3
St Caroline Cl B70 .... **53** F3
St Catharines Cl WS1 .... **43** A7
St Catherine of Siena RC
  Prim Sch B1 .... **66** D1
St Catherine's LE10 ...... **75** F7
St Catherine's Cl CV3 .. **134** B8
St Catherine's Cres
  Whitnash CV34 .... **161** F3
  Wolverhampton WV4 ...... **38** F4
St Catherine's Lodge ⑦
  CV6 .... **113** A4
St Catherine's Rd B60 . **138** A5
St Catherines Cl
  Blackwell B60 .... **138** A5
  Dudley DY2 .... **52** A1
  Sutton Coldfield B75 ...... **46** F7
St Catherines Rd WS13 .... **3** B3
St Cecilia Cl DY10 ...... **116** E2
St Cecilia's WV11 .... **26** C5
St Chad 'Cath* B4 ...... **164** B4
St Chad's Circus Queensway
  B3 .... **164** B3
St Chad's Cl Cannock WS11 . **2** A4
  Dudley DY3 .... **50** C8
St Chad's RC ⑪ Bilston WV14 . **40** F7
  Birmingham B45 .... **121** F7
  Lichfield WS13 .... **9** B3
  Sutton Coldfield B75 ...... **46** F5

St Chad's Rd continued
  Wolverhampton WV10 ..... **25** F8
St Chad's Stowe CE Prim
  Sch
  WS13 .... **9** C8
St Chads Cl WS13 .... **3** B1
St Chads Cl WS13 .... **9** B8
St Chads Ct B18 .... **66** E5
St Chads Mews B94 .... **144** D3
St Chads Queensway
  B4 .... **164** C4
St Chads RC Sch DY3 .... **50** D7
St Chads Rd B80 .... **159** C4
St Christian's Croft CV3 . **133** E7
St Christian's Rd CV3 ... **133** E8
St Christopher Cl B70 .... **53** E2
St Christopher Prim Sch
  CV5 .... **112** D4
St Christopher's Cl
  CV34 .... **160** D8
St Christopher's Dr B21 . **21** C1
St Christophers B20 ...... **54** F4
St Christophers RC Prim Sch
  WR8 .... **10** A3
St Clare's RC Prim Sch
  B20 .... **55** B1
St Clement's Ave WS3 ... **28** D7
St Clement's CE Prim Sch
  B7 .... **67** C7
St Clement's La B71 ...... **53** D4
St Clements Ct CV2 .... **114** D8
St Clements Ho ⑧ B71 . **53** D4
St Clements Rd B7 .... **67** C6
St Columba's Cl CV1 ... **165** B4
St Columba's RC Prim Sch
  B45 .... **122** D7
St Columbas Dr B45 .... **122** D7
St Cuthbert's Cl B70 ..... **53** F2
St Cuthberts RC Prim Sch
  B8 .... **68** C4
St David's
  Royal Leamington Spa
  CV31 .... **162** C7
  West Bromwich B70 .... **53** F2
St Davids Cl WS3 .... **15** B5
St Davids Dr B32 .... **84** B5
St Davids Gr B20 .... **54** F4
St Davids Orch CV3 .... **134** F7
St Davids Pl WS3 .... **14** D2
St Denis Rd B29 .... **103** B7
St Dominic's Rd B24 ..... **56** E1
St Dunstan's RC Prim Sch
  B14 .... **104** F8
St Edburghs Rd B25 ...... **88** C8
St Edith's Gn ⑤ CV34 .. **161** B8
St Edith's Ho ② CV34 .. **161** B8
St Editha's Cl B79 .... **21** B5
St Editha's Ct B79 .... **21** B7
St Edmund Campion RC Sch
  Birmingham B23 .... **57** B5
  Sutton Coldfield B75 ...... **57** C6
St Edmund's Cl
  West Bromwich B70 .... **53** F2
  Wolverhampton WV6 ..... **24** F3
St Edmund's RC Prim Sch
  B18 .... **66** A4
St Edward's Rd B29 ...... **85** F2
St Edwards RC Prim Sch
  B29 .... **86** B1
St Eleanor Cl B70 .... **53** F3
St Elizabeth's RC Prim Sch
  Coventry CV6 .... **113** E7
  Tamworth B79 .... **20** F8
St Elizabeth's Rd CV6 .. **113** E7
St Francis Ave B91 ..... **106** E6
St Francis CE Prim Sch
  B30 .... **103** D6
St Francis Cl
  Hinckley LE10 .... **71** C3
  Walsall WS3 .... **15** B5
St Francis Factory Est
  B70 .... **53** D2
St Francis of Assisi RC Sch
  Bedworth CV12 .... **78** C3
  Birmingham B19 .... **66** B6
  Walsall WS4 .... **15** C1
St Francis Xavier Sch
  B69 .... **64** A8
St Fremund Way CV31 . **162** C5
St Gabriel's RC Prim Sch
  B71 .... **21** E1
St George Dr B66 .... **65** A7
St George's Ave LE10 .... **71** C1
St George's CE Fst Sch
  DY10 .... **116** F7
St George's CE Prim Sch
  B98 .... **153** F3
  B19 .... **164** B5
St George's Cl
  Darlaston WS10 .... **41** D7
  Sutton Coldfield B75 ...... **46** F6
St George's Ct
  Birmingham B30 .... **103** E7
  Darlaston WS10 .... **41** D7
St George's Gdns ③
  B98 .... **153** F4
St George's Par WV1 ... **163** C2
St George's Pl
  Kidderminster DY10 .... **116** E7
  ④ Walsall WS1 .... **28** F2

St George's Rd
  Coventry CV1 .... **113** F2
  Royal Leamington Spa
  CV31 .... **161** F6
  Solihull B90 .... **126** D8
  Stourbridge DY8 .... **80** D2
St George's St
  Birmingham B19 .... **164** B4
  Darlaston WS10 .... **41** D7
St George's Sta WV1 ... **163** C2
St George's Terr DY10 . **116** F6
St George's Way B77 ..... **21** F4
St Georges Ct B23 .... **57** A5
St Georges Ct B15 .... **86** A7
St Georges Ct
  ⑩ Kidderminster DY10 . **116** E6
  Sutton Coldfield B74 ..... **31** E5
  Walsall WS1 .... **42** E6
St Georges Pl B70 .... **53** C4
St Georges Rd Dudley DY2 . **62** E6
  Redditch B98 .... **153** F4
St Georges Way CV10 .... **78** B8
St Gerards Ct B91 .... **106** E2
St Gerards RC Prim Sch
  B35 .... **58** B4
St Gerards Rd B91 ...... **106** E2
St Gilbert's Cl B65 .... **63** B4
St Giles Cl B65 .... **63** B4
St Giles Cres WV1 .... **26** A2
St Giles Ct B65 .... **63** D3
St Giles Jun Sch CV7 .... **95** F8
St Giles Rd
  Birmingham B33 .... **69** D2
  Burntwood WS7 .... **7** B6
  Coventry CV7 .... **95** D6
  Willenhall WV11 .... **27** B1
  Wolverhampton WV1 ...... **26** A2
St Giles St DY2 .... **62** C5
St Giles' CE Prim Sch
  WV13 .... **27** B2
St Godwald's Cres B60 . **151** B8
St Godwald's Rd B60 ... **151** C7
St Govan's Cl ⑨ CV31 . **162** C6
St Gregory's RC Prim Sch
  Coventry CV1 .... **114** E3
  Smethwick B67 .... **64** F2
St Helen's Rd
  Royal Leamington Spa
  CV31 .... **162** A5
  Solihull B91 .... **107** A6
St Helen's Way CV5 .... **112** B8
St Helens Ave WV4 .... **52** C5
St Helens Pas B1 .... **66** C3
St Helens Rd WS13 .... **3** B3
St Heliers Rd B31 .... **103** C4
St Hubert's RC Prim Sch
  B68 .... **84** C8
St Ives Cl B79 .... **21** B6
St Ives Rd Coventry CV2 **114** E3
  Walsall WS5 .... **43** D7
St Ives Way CV11 .... **73** F5
St James Ave B65 .... **63** B4
St James CE Jun Sch
  Bulkington CV12 .... **79** C2
  Solihull B90 .... **106** B2
St James CE Mid Sch
  CV12 .... **79** C2
St James CE Prim Sch
  Birmingham B21 .... **54** D1
  Stourbridge DY8 .... **80** D7
St James Cl Walsall WS3 . **15** B5
  West Bromwich B70 .... **53** F2
St James Ct
  Bromsgrove B60 .... **137** A3
  Coventry CV3 .... **134** E6
St James Gdns CV12 ..... **79** C2
St James Meadow Rd
  CV32 .... **156** C2
St James Pl
  Birmingham, Edgbaston B15 . **86** B8
  Solihull B90 .... **106** B2
  West Bromwich WS8 ..... **15** F8
St James Rd
  Birmingham, Edgbaston B15 . **86** B8
  Cannock WS11 .... **1** C2
  Norton Canes WS11 .... **6** B5
  Oldbury B69 .... **63** E8
  Sutton Coldfield B75 ...... **32** C2
St James' CE Prim Sch
  Wednesbury WS10 .... **41** E2
  Wolverhampton WV1 ..... **163** D3
St James Wlk WS8 .... **15** F7
St James' La CV3 .... **134** D6
St James' Pl B7 .... **67** A3
St James' RC Jun & Inf Sch
  B45 .... **122** A7
St James' Rd B21 .... **65** D8
St James' Rd B21 .... **54** D1
St James's Cl LE10 .... **75** D5
St James's Rd DY1 .... **51** B2
St James's Terr DY1 ..... **51** A2
St John & St Monica RC Prim
  Sch B13 .... **86** E4
St John Bosco RC Jun & Inf
  Sch B31 .... **53** B7
St John Cl B75 .... **32** D4
St John Fisher RC Fst Sch
  B98 .... **154** D6
St John Fisher RC Prim Sch
  Birmingham B31 .... **123** B7
  Coventry CV7 .... **114** D5
St John St
  Bromsgrove B61 .... **136** F2
  Lichfield WS13 .... **9** B7
St John the Baptist RC Prim
  Sch B36 .... **70** B7

St John the Divine CE Prim
  Sch CV3 .... **134** C5
St John Vianney RC Prim Sch
  CV5 .... **112** B3
St John Wall RC Sch B21 . **54** C2
St John's Arc WV1 ...... **163** B2
St John's Ave
  Kenilworth CV8 .... **148** A3
  Kidderminster DY11 .... **116** B6
St John's CE Foundation
  Mid Sch B61 .... **136** F1
St John's CE Fst Sch
  DY11 ....
St John's CE Mid Sch
  .... **116** B6
St John's CE Prim Sch
  Coventry CV5 .... **112** C4
  Essington WV11 .... **13** A4
  Wednesbury WS10 .... **41** F2
St John's Cl
  Brownhills WS9 .... **15** F3
  Cannock WS11 .... **1** A8
  ⑥ Kidderminster DY11 . **116** C6
  Lichfield WS13 .... **9** B6
  West Bromwich B70 .... **53** F3
  ⑧ Warley CV3 .... **14** B1
St John's Dr WS14 .... **9** F5
St John's Flats CV3 .... **148** A3
St John's Ho WS14 .... **17** F5
St John's Ladywood CE Prim
  Sch B16 .... **66** A2
St John's Mus* CV34 .. **160** F7
St John's Prim Sch CV8 **147** F2
St John's Rd
  Birmingham B17 .... **85** D6
  Cannock WS11 .... **4** D7
  Darlaston WS10 .... **41** C5
  Dudley DY2 .... **51** E1
  Halesowen B63 .... **82** E4
  Royal Leamington Spa
  CV31 .... **162** A6
  Stourbridge DY8 .... **81** A5
  Tipton DY4 .... **51** F8
St John's Sq WV2 .... **163** B2
St John's St
  Coventry CV1 .... **165** C2
  Dudley DY2 .... **62** C5
  Kenilworth CV8 .... **148** A3
  ⑤ Kidderminster DY11 . **116** C6
  Tamworth B79 .... **21** B5
St John's Terr ⑥ CV31 **162** A6
St Johns Hinckley LE10 . **71** E1
  Warwick CV34 .... **160** F7
St Johns Ave B65 .... **63** B4
St Johns CE Prim Sch
  WS9 .... **16** A3
St Johns Cl B93 .... **128** B6
St Johns Ct
  Birmingham B31 .... **103** B1
  ⑳ Brierley Hill DY5 ..... **61** D2
  Warwick CV34 .... **69** F3
St Johns Ho
  Sutton Coldfield B74 ...... **31** E3
  West Bromwich B70 .... **53** C2
St Johns Rd
  Birmingham B11 .... **87** C5
  Brownhills WS8 .... **16** A8
  Essington WV11 .... **13** A3
  Oldbury B68 .... **64** C5
  Walsall, Pelsall WS3 ...... **15** B5
  Walsall, Pleck WS2 .... **42** B8
  St Johns Ret PK WV2 ..... **63** D1
  St Johns Sch WS13 .... **9** B7
St Johns Way B93 ...... **128** C6
St Johns Wood B45 ... **122** B5
St Joseph & St Theresa RC
  Prim Sch WV6 .... **6** E6
St Joseph St ⑰ DY2 ..... **51** D1
St Joseph's Convent Prim
  Sch WV6 .... **24** E6
St Joseph's RC Jun Sch
  CV11 .... **73** C3
St Joseph's RC Prim Sch
  Birmingham B7 .... **67** B6
  Cannock WS10 .... **41** D7
  Dudley DY2 .... **51** E1
  Lichfield WS14 .... **9** C7
  Sutton Coldfield B75 ...... **46** C7
  Whitnash CV31 .... **162** A3
St Joseph's Sch CV8 ... **148** B7
St Josephs Ave B31 ...... **85** D5
St Josephs Ct WV3 .... **15** A4
St Josephs Ct WV4 ...... **38** D6
St Josephs RC Prim Sch
  B30 .... **103** F5
St Josephs Rd B8 .... **68** C5
St Jude's CE Inf Sch WV6 **24** F4
St Jude's CE Jun Sch
  WV3 .... **24** F3
St Jude's Cres CV3 .... **134** D7
St Jude's Ct ⑭ WV6 .... **24** F3
St Jude's Pas B5 .... **164** B1
St Jude's Rd WV6 .... **24** F3
St Jude's Rd W WV6 ..... **24** F3
St Judes Ave B80 ...... **159** D4
St Judes Cl
  Birmingham B14 .... **104** F2
  Sutton Coldfield B75 ...... **46** F6
St Judes Ct B14 .... **104** F7
St Judes RC Prim Sch
  B14 .... **104** F2
St Katherine's Rd B68 ... **64** B2

St Kenelm's CE Sch B62 ...101 A4
St Kenelm's CI B70 ...53 F2
St Kenelm's Pass DY9 ...100 A4
St Kenelm's Rd B62 ...100 E5
St Kenelms Ave B63 ...82 E1
St Kilda's Rd B8 ...67 E5
St Laurence Ave CV34 ...160 D5
St Laurence CE Inf Sch B31 ...103 B4
St Laurence CE Jun Sch B31 ...103 B4
St Laurence CI B48 ...139 B6
St Laurence Rd B31 ...103 B5
St Lawrence CI B93 ...128 B5
St Lawrence Dr WS11 ...2 B2
St Lawrence Mews B31 ...103 A3
St Lawrence Way WS10 ...41 D6
St Lawrence's Rd CV6 ...95 F1
St Leonard's Wlk CV8 ...135 A1
St Leonards CI B37 ...90 A4
St Leonards View B78 ...36 F8
St Loye's CI B62 ...83 D8
St Luke's CE Fst Sch B97 ...153 D1
St Luke's CE Jun & Inf Sch B15 ...86 D8
St Luke's CE Prim Sch WV2 ...39 B7
St Luke's CI WS11 ...4 D8
St Luke's Cotts B97 ...153 D1
St Luke's Rd
Birmingham B5 ...86 E7
Burntwood WS7 ...7 C6
Coventry CV6 ...95 D3
Wednesbury WS10 ...42 A3
St Luke's Terr DY1 ...62 A8
St Lukes CI B65 ...63 A4
St Lukes Inf Sch WV2 ...39 C7
St Lukes St B64 ...62 D1
St Lukes Way CV10 ...72 C4
St Margaret Mary RC Jun & Inf Sch B23 ...56 C6
St Margaret Rd CV1 ...113 F2
St Margaret's B74 ...31 C3
St Margaret's CE Jun Sch CV31 ...162 B3
St Margaret's CE Prim Sch
Birmingham B43 ...43 E4
Solihull B92 ...88 F2
St Margaret's Ho CV31 ...162 B2
St Margaret's Rd
Birmingham B43 ...43 F2
Royal Leamington Spa CV31 ...162 B5
Solihull B92 ...88 E1
Tamworth B79 ...21 B7
St Margarets Ave B8 ...68 B6
St Margarets Dr B63 ...82 F2
St Margarets Rd
Birmingham B8 ...68 B6
Lichfield WS13 ...3 B3
Walsall WS3 ...15 A4
St Mark's Annexe (Coventry & Warwickshire Hospl) CV1 ...165 C4
St Mark's CE Prim Sch DY5 ...61 C7
St Mark's Ct DY5 ...61 D7
St Mark's Mews CV32 ...156 E1
St Mark's RC Prim Sch B42 ...54 F6
St Mark's Rd
Burntwood WS7 ...7 C6
Dudley DY2 ...51 F1
Royal Leamington Spa CV32 ...156 D1
Smethwick B67 ...64 D3
Stourbridge DY9 ...81 D5
Tipton DY4 ...52 A8
Wolverhampton WV3 ...25 B1
St Mark's St WV3 ...163 A2
St Marks CI
Great Wyrley WS6 ...4 F4
Stockingford CV10 ...72 C4
St Marks Cres B1 ...66 B3
St Marks Rd
Brownhills WS8 ...16 A5
Walsall WS3 ...15 A4
St Marks St B1 ...66 B3
St Martin's CE Prim Sch Sch B13 ...87 A3
St Martin's CI
West Bromwich B70 ...53 F2
Wolverhampton WV2 ...39 E6
St Martin's Dr DY4 ...52 A5
St Martin's Mkt B5 ...164 C1
St Martin's Rd CV8 ...133 C2
St Martin's Sch B91 ...107 D3
St Martin's St B15 ...66 B1
St Martin's Terr WV14 ...40 E4
St Martins Ave B80 ...159 D4
St Martins Ind Est B69 ...64 A6
St Martins Rd B75 ...46 F5
St Mary & St John Prim Sch B23 ...56 E3
St Mary & St Margaret's CE Prim Sch B36 ...69 B8
St Mary Magdalene CE Jun & Inf Sch B71 ...53 D6

St Mary of the Angels RC Prim Sch WS9 ...30 B5
St Mary St CV1 ...165 C2
St Mary's & St John's RC Sch WV2 ...163 C1
St Mary's Ave LE10 ...71 F5
St Mary's CE Jun & Inf Sch B20 ...55 B1
St Mary's CE Prim Sch B29 ...85 D1
St Mary's CE Prim Sch
Hinckley LE10 ...75 D8
Kidderminster DY10 ...116 E8
Kingswinford DY6 ...60 D7
St Mary's CI Sedgley DY3 ...50 F8
Sutton Coldfield B24 ...57 D4
Warwick CV34 ...160 D8
St Mary's Coll B73 ...45 D1
St Mary's Cres CV31 ...162 B7
St Mary's Ct
Nuneaton CV11 ...73 B5
Wolverhampton WV11 ...27 A2
St Mary's Hall WV1 ...163 C2
St Mary's Ho 4 B71 ...53 D4
St Mary's Immaculate RC Prim Sch CV34 ...160 E8
St Mary's La DY8 ...81 B3
St Mary's RC Prim Sch B17 ...85 C5
St Mary's RC Prim Sch DY5 ...61 C2
WS11 ...4 E8
St Mary's RC Prim Sch
Coventry CV2 ...113 F3
Studley B80 ...159 E4
Wednesbury WS10 ...41 F4
Wolverhampton WV10 ...26 A7
St Mary's Rd
Hinckley LE10 ...75 D8
Lichfield WS13 ...3 B3
Nuneaton CV11 ...73 B5
St Mary's Row
Birmingham, Moseley B13 ...86 F3
Birmingham, New Town Row B4 ...164 C3
St Mary's St WV1 ...163 C3
St Mary's Terr WV1 ...162 B7
St Mary's The Mount RC Prim Sch WS1 ...42 F8
St Mary's Way
Aldridge WS9 ...30 B5
Tamworth B77 ...21 E4
St Marys CE B72 ...46 B4
St Marys Ct B77 ...61 D2
St Marys Rd B17 ...85 C5
St Marys Ringway DY10 ...116 E6
St Marys View B71 ...56 D8
St Matthew St WV1 ...
St Matthew's Ave WS7 ...7 F7
St Matthew's CE Prim Sch B66 ...65 C5
St Matthew's CI WS1 ...28 F1
St Matthew's Dr WS7 ...7 F7
St Matthews CE Prim Sch B7 ...67 A4
St Matthews Rd
Oldbury B68 ...64 A2
Smethwick B66 ...65 C5
St Mawes Rd WV6 ...24 A3
St Mawgan CI B35 ...58 C4
St Michael Rd WS13 ...9 C8
St Michael St Walsall WS1 ...42 E8
West Bromwich B70 ...53 C3
St Michael's CE High Sch B69 ...63 A4
St Michael's CE Jun & Inf Sch
Birmingham B32 ...102 C8
Wolverhampton WV6 ...24 E5
St Michael's CE Prim Sch CV12 ...78 D3
St Michael's CE Prim Sch WS14 ...9 C8
St Michael's Cres WS13 ...15 A2
St Michael's Ctes B69 ...64 A4
St Michael's Ct B68 ...64 A4
St Michael's Ct
5 Smethwick B66 ...65 A5
Wolverhampton WV6 ...24 E5
St Michael's Gr DY2 ...62 A1
St Michael's Hill B18 ...66 A7
St Michael's Hospl
Lichfield WS13 ...9 D8
Warwick CV34 ...160 D8
St Michael's Mews B69 ...52 A2
St Michael's RC Prim Sch WV3 ...38 D7
St Michael's Rd
Birmingham B18 ...66 A7
Coventry CV2 ...114 A3
Sutton Coldfield B73 ...56 F8
Warwick CV34 ...160 D8
St Michael's Way CV10 ...72 C4
St Michaels CE Inf & Jun Sch
Walsall WS3 ...14 F2
Walsall WS3 ...15 A3
St Michaels CI CV9 ...36 C1
St Michaels Dr WS12 ...2 F5
St Michaels Rd DY3 ...49 F5
St Michaels Way DY4 ...52 A3

St Nicholas Ave CV8 ...147 F3
St Nicholas CE Prim Sch CV8 ...147 F5
St Nicholas Church St CV34 ...160 F6
St Nicholas CI
Coventry CV1 ...113 C5
Walsall WS3 ...15 A4
St Nicholas St
3 Coventry, Edgwick CV6 ...113 F7
Coventry, Radford CV6 ...113 B6
St Nicholas RC Prim Sch B73 ...45 F2
St Nicholas Rd CV31 ...162 F5
St Nicholas St CV1 ...165 B4
St Nicholas Terr CV31 ...162 E4
St Nicholas Wlk B76 ...59 B6
St Nicolas CE Prim Sch CV11 ...73 F6
St Nicolas Gdns B38 ...103 F2
St Nicolas Park Dr CV11 ...73 F7
St Nicolas Rd CV11 ...73 D5
St Osburg's RC Prim Sch CV1 ...165 A3
St Osburg's Rd CV2 ...114 A3
St Oswalds CI CV10 ...116 F8
St Oswalds Rd B10 ...87 E8
St Patrick's CE Prim Sch B94 ...126 C2
St Patrick's Ct DY11 ...116 B1
St Patrick's CE Prim Sch
Birmingham B37 ...70 C2
Coventry CV2 ...96 D1
Walsall WS2 ...28 E3
Wolverhampton WV11 ...26 C5
St Patrick's Rd CV1 ...165 B1
St Patricks Ct B14 ...104 E5
St Patricks RC Prim Sch
Birmingham B18 ...65 F4
Royal Leamington Spa CV31 ...161 F6
St Paul's Ave
Birmingham B12 ...87 A5
Kidderminster DY11 ...116 A6
St Paul's CE Prim Sch
Nuneaton CV10 ...72 C3
Royal Leamington Spa CV32 ...157 B1
St Paul's CI Cannock WS11 ...2 B1
Walsall WS1 ...28 E2
Warwick CV34 ...160 D6
St Paul's Cres
6 Coleshill B46 ...70 F7
West Bromwich B70 ...52 E7
St Paul's Ct B77 ...35 C4
St Paul's Dr DY4 ...52 B4
St Paul's Rd
Birmingham B12 ...87 A5
Burntwood WS7 ...7 C6
Cannock WS12 ...2 F3
Coventry CV6 ...113 E6
Dudley DY2 ...62 D5
Nuneaton CV10 ...72 D3
Smethwick WS10 ...42 C5
St Paul's Sq
4 Royal Leamington Spa CV32 ...157 A1
St Paul's St WS1 ...28 E2
St Paul's Sta B19 ...164 B4
St Paul's Terr CV34 ...160 D6
St Pauls CE Prim Sch B24 ...51 F6
St Pauls CE Sch WV9 ...11 A2
St Pauls Cres WS3 ...15 B5
St Pauls Ct
Blackheath B62 ...63 D1
Water Orton B46 ...59 B3
St Pauls Gdns LE10 ...71 E1
St Pauls Terr B3 ...164 A4
St Peter & Paul RC Prim Sch B24 ...57 C3
St Peter & St Paul RC Prim Sch WS13 ...9 C8
St Peter CI Inf Sch B17 ...85 B4
St Peter's CE Mid Sch B98 ...154 E3
St Peter's CE Prim Sch
Cannock WS12 ...2 D4
Shenstone WS9 ...16 E4
St Peter's CE
Redditch B97 ...158 E5
Stonnall WS9 ...16 E4
Tamworth B77 ...21 D1
Water Orton B46 ...59 D4
West Bromwich DY4 ...52 D4
St Peter's Collegiate CE Sch WV3 ...24 E3
St Peter's Croft B73 ...46 B3
St Peter's Ct CV1 ...165 D4
St Peter's RC Fst Sch B60 ...150 E8
St Peter's RC Prim Sch
Royal Leamington Spa CV32 ...161 F8
St Peter's RC Sch
Hinckley LE10 ...71 E1
Solihull B91 ...107 B2

St Peter's Rd
Birmingham B20 ...66 C8
Burntwood WS7 ...7 C6
Cannock WS12 ...2 D4
Dudley DY2 ...62 D5
Royal Leamington Spa CV32 ...161 F8
Stourbridge DY9 ...81 C1
St Peters CI
Birmingham B28 ...105 D6
Sutton Coldfield B72 ...46 B3
St Peters Ct
2 Hinckley LE10 ...71 E1
Lichfield WS13 ...3 B2
Walsall WS3 ...14 B1
St Peters Dr WS3 ...15 A4
St Peters La B92 ...90 D1
St Peters RC Prim Sch B32 ...84 C1
St Peters Rd B17 ...85 B5
St Peters Terr WS2 ...28 E4
St Philip's Cath* B3 ...164 B3
St Philip's PI B2 ...164 C3
St Philip's RC Jun & Inf Sch B66 ...65 B6
St Philip's Sixth Form Coll B16 ...65 F1
St Phillip's Ave B38 ...38 F7
St Phillip's Gr WV3 ...38 E7
St Phillips Rd WV3 ...38 F8
St Quentin St WV2 ...42 B1
St Saviour's CE Prim Sch B8 ...67 D5
St Saviour's Rd CV2 ...39 F6
St Saviour's Rd B8 ...67 D4
St Silas' Sq B19 ...66 C5
St Simons CI B75 ...46 F6
St Stephan's Ho B97 ...153 E4
St Stephen's Ave WV10 ...25 D4
St Stephen's CE Fst Sch B98 ...153 F5
St Stephen's CE Mid Sch B98 ...153 F5
St Stephen's CI WV10 ...25 F4
St Stephen's Gdns 1 WV13 ...27 A1
St Stephen's Rd WS7 ...7 C6
St Stephens St WS12 ...2 C4
St Stephens Gdns B98 ...153 F5
St Stephens Rd
Birmingham B29 ...104 B8
West Bromwich B71 ...65 B8
St Stephens St B6 ...66 C6
St Teresa's RC Prim Sch B20 ...55 A3
St Teresa's RC Prim Sch WV4 ...39 E5
St Thomas Aquinas RC Sch B38 ...103 D3
St Thomas CE Prim Sch WV11 ...26 D7
St Thomas CI
Stockingford CV10 ...72 C3
Sutton Coldfield B75 ...46 F5
Walsall WS3 ...28 E6
St Thomas More RC Comp Sch WV14 ...41 A7
St Thomas More RC Fst Sch B98 ...159 B7
St Thomas More RC Prim Sch
Coventry CV3 ...133 D5
Great Wyrley WS6 ...5 A4
St Thomas More RC Sch CV10 ...73 A3
St Thomas More's RC Prim Sch B26 ...89 B5
St Thomas of Canterbury RC Prim Sch WS13 ...28 F6
St Thomas' CE Prim Sch DY2 ...62 C5
St Thomas' CE Prim Sch B15 ...86 D8
St Thomas' CI WS9 ...16 B1
St Thomas' Rd
Birmingham B23 ...56 D3
Coventry CV6 ...96 A3
St Thomas's CI CV1 ...113 D2
St Thomas's Ho CV1 ...113 B2
St Valentines CI B70 ...53 F2
St Vincent Cres B70 ...52 F6
St Vincent St B16 ...66 B2
St Vincent St W B16 ...66 A2
St Vincent's CE Prim Sch B7 ...67 B3
St Wilfrid's RC Prim Sch B36 ...68 F8
Saladin Ave B69 ...63 E5
Salcombe Ave B26 ...89 C5
Salcombe CI Cannock WS11 ...4 C7
Nuneaton CV3 ...73 F5
Salcombe Dr DY5 ...81 C7
Salcombe Gr WV14 ...40 D1
Salcombe Rd B8 ...65 B5
Saldavian CI WS2 ...42 B6
Sale St CV1 ...52 D5
Salford CI CV2 ...114 A5
Salford Cir Coventry CV2 ...114 A5
Redditch B98 ...159 B6
Salford St B6 ...67 C8
Salisbury Ave CV3 ...133 C6
Salisbury CI
Birmingham B13 ...86 E3
Dudley DY1 ...50 F3
Lichfield WS13 ...3 C3
Wolston CV8 ...135 F3

Salisbury Dr Cannock WS12 ...2 B1
Kidderminster DY11 ...116 A6
Nuneaton CV10 ...72 B7
Water Orton B46 ...59 C3
Salisbury Gr B72 ...57 C7
Salisbury Ho
3 Birmingham B24 ...56 F4
Hinckley LE10 ...71 C4
Salisbury PI WV3 ...25 B1
Salisbury Prim Sch WS10 ...41 F7
Salisbury Rd
Birmingham, Lozells B19 ...66 D8
Birmingham, Moseley B13 ...86 E3
Birmingham, Saltley B8 ...67 E5
Hinckley LE10 ...76 B7
Smethwick B66 ...65 B4
West Bromwich B70 ...53 E1
Salisbury St
Darlaston WS10 ...41 F2
Wolverhampton WV3 ...25 B1
Salisbury Twr B18 ...66 A3
Sallow Gr WS8 ...7 A1
Sally Ward Dr WS9 ...16 B1
Salop CI B71 ...53 B6
Salop Dr Cannock WS11 ...4 F8
Oldbury B68 ...64 C2
Salop Rd Oldbury B68 ...64 C2
Redditch B97 ...153 D3
Salop St Bilston WV14 ...40 E4
Birmingham B12 ...86 F8
Dudley DY1 ...51 B2
Oldbury B69 ...52 E1
Wolverhampton WV3 ...163 B2
Salstar CI B6 ...66 E6
Salt La CV1 ...165 B2
Saltash Gr B25 ...68 C1
Saltbrook Rd B63 ...82 A7
Saltbrook Trad Est B63 ...82 A7
Salter Rd DY4 ...51 F7
Salter St B94 ...126 C2
Salter's La Redditch B97 ...153 B5
West Bromwich B71 ...53 E4
Salter's Rd WS9 ...16 A3
Salters La B79 ...21 B6
Salters Rd WS9 ...16 B1
Saltisford CV34 ...160 D7
Saltisford Gdns CV34 ...160 C8
Saltley Ind Est B8 ...67 C3
Saltley Rd B8 ...67 B4
Saltley Trad Est B8 ...67 D6
Saltley Viaduct B8 ...67 C5
Saltney CI B24 ...57 D5
Salts La B78 ...34 E5
Saltwells La DY2 ...62 B4
Saltwells Nature Reserve* DY5,DY2 ...62 A3
Saltwells Rd DY2 ...62 C2
Salwarge Gr B29 ...84 F2
Salwarpe Rd B60 ...150 F8
Sam Barber Ct WS12 ...2 E1
Sam Gault CI CV3 ...134 C2
Sam Spencer Ct DY10 ...118 A1
Sambar Rd B78 ...20 F1
Sambourne CI B91 ...107 E6
Sambourne Dr B34 ...69 D7
Sambourne La
Astwood Bank B96 ...158 F1
Sambourne B96 ...159 A1
Sambourne Park La B96 ...159 A1
Sambrook Rd WV10 ...26 A6
Sammons Way CV4 ...111 D1
Sampson CI
Birmingham B21 ...54 C1
Coventry CV2 ...114 C3
Tipton B69 ...63 C7
Sampson Ho B11 ...87 B8
Sampson Rd B11 ...87 B8
Sampson Rd N B11 ...87 B8
Sampson St WS10 ...42 B3
Sams La B70 ...53 C1
Samuel CI WS13 ...3 C2
Samuel Hayward Ho 5 CV2 ...96 B1
Samuel Ho WS3 ...14 B1
Samuel Johnson's Birthplace Mus* WS13 ...9 B8
Samuel St WS3 ...14 B1
Samuel Vale Ho CV1 ...165 B4
Samuels Rd B32 ...84 A5
Sanby CI CV12 ...78 A4
Sand Bank WS3 ...14 A1
Sand Pits B1 ...66 B3
Sand St B70 ...52 F4
Sanda Croft B36 ...70 B6
Sandal Rise B91 ...107 E3
Sandalls CI B31 ...102 D1
Sandals Rise B62 ...83 D3
Sandalwood CI WV12 ...27 B8
Sandbarn CI B90 ...126 F6
Sandbeds Rd WV12 ...27 C4
Sandbourne Rd B8 ...68 A4
Sanderling CI WV10 ...12 B7
Sanderling Ct DY10 ...117 A1
Sanderling Rise
Burntwood WS7 ...7 B8
Kingswinford DY6 ...61 A6
Sanders CI Dudley DY2 ...62 E7
Redditch B97 ...153 B4
Sanders Ct CV34 ...161 C8
Sanders Ind Est B61 ...136 E1
Sanders Rd Bedworth CV6 ...96 B6
Bromsgrove B61 ...136 E1
Sanderson Ct DY11 ...116 C5

Sandfield ❶ B66 .....64 E7
Sandfield Bridge DY5 ....50 B1
Sandfield Cl B90 .....126 B8
Sandfield Gr DY3 .....50 B2
Sandfield Rd
  Stourbridge DY8 .....60 F2
  West Bromwich B71 ....42 E2
Sandfields Ave B10 .....87 B8
Sandfields Rd B68 .....64 C2
Sandford Ave B65 .....63 C3
Sandford Cl Coventry CV2 ..96 D3
  Hinckley LE10 .....71 F1
Sandford Ho WS13 .....9 A7
Sandford Rd
  Birmingham B13 .....87 A3
  Dudley DY1 .....50 E1
Sandford Rise WV6 .....24 E6
Sandford St WS13 .....9 B7
Sandgate Cres CV2 .....114 E2
Sandgate Rd
  Birmingham B28 .....106 A4
  Tipton DY4 .....52 A8
Sandhill Farm Cl ❶ B19 ..66 D7
Sandhill St WS3 .....14 A1
Sandhills Cres B91 .....127 B8
Sandhills Gn B48 .....138 E7
Sandhills La B45 .....138 D7
Sandhills Rd B45 .....138 D8
Sandhurst Ave
  Birmingham B36 .....68 D6
  Stourbridge DY9 .....81 D2
Sandhurst Cl B98 .....154 C6
Sandhurst Dr WV4 .....39 A4
Sandhurst Gr
  Coventry CV6 .....113 B5
  Stourbridge DY8 .....60 E3
Sandhurst Ho B38 .....104 B1
Sandhurst Rd
  Birmingham B13 .....86 F2
  Kingswinford DY6 .....61 A4
  Sutton Coldfield B74 ..31 F5
Sandicliffe Cl DY11 .....116 C8
Sandilands Cl CV2 .....114 E4
Sandland Cl WV14 .....40 F6
Sandland Rd WV12 .....27 D8
Sandmartin Cl DY2 .....62 D2
Sandmartin Way WV10 ..117 A2
Sandmere Gr B14 .....105 D3
Sandmere Rd B14 .....105 D3
Sandon Cl B98 .....154 A3
Sandon Gr B24 .....57 B4
Sandon Ho WV6 .....24 E5
Sandon Rd
  Birmingham B17 .....65 B1
  Nuneaton CV11 .....73 B5
  Stourbridge DY9 .....81 F4
  Wolverhampton WV10 ..11 B2
Sandown B77 .....21 F5
Sandown Ave
  Cheslyn Hay WS6 .....4 E3
  Coventry CV6 .....95 F2
Sandown Cl CV32 .....157 C4
Sandown Ct ⓘ B29 .....103 C7
Sandown Dr Catshill B61 .121 B1
  Perton WV6 .....23 F4
Sandown Rd B36 .....68 D8
Sandown Twr ❸ B31 .....103 A1
Sandpiper B77 .....36 A5
Sandpiper Cl
  Cannock WS12 .....2 C7
  Kidderminster DY10 ...117 B2
  Stourbridge DY9 .....81 F5
Sandpiper Gdns B38 ....123 F7
Sandpiper Rd CV2 .....96 B3
Sandpiper Way B23 .....56 C6
Sandpit Cl WS10 .....42 E2
Sandpits Cl B76 .....59 B6
Sandpits Ind Est ㉓ B1 ...66 B3
Sandpits La CV6 .....94 F2
Sandpits The
  Birmingham B30 .....103 E8
  Bulkington CV12 .....79 C2
Sandra Cl WS9 .....30 B5
Sandringham Ave WV12 .27 B6
Sandringham Cl CV4 ....131 F5
Sandringham Ct CV10 ...72 F6
Sandringham Dr
  Aldridge WS9 .....16 B1
  Blackheath B65 .....63 C4
Sandringham Pl DY8 ....60 D1
Sandringham Rd
  Birmingham B42 .....55 B6
  Halesowen B62 .....83 B7
  Stourbridge DY8 .....60 D1
  Wolverhampton WV4 ...39 A4
Sandstone Ave B45 .....102 A8
Sandstone Cl DY3 .....50 D4
Sandway Gdns B8 .....67 D6
Sandway Gr B13 .....105 C7
Sandwell & Dudley Sta ⓘ B70 .....53 A1
Sandwell Ave WS10 ....41 B5
Sandwell Bsns Development Ctr B66 .....64 C7
Sandwell Bsns Pk B66 ..64 C8
Sandwell Coll B70 .....53 C3
Sandwell Coll (Smethwick Campus) B66 .....65 A5
Sandwell Coll (Wednesbury Campus) WS10 .....42 A1
Sandwell Coll Oldbury Campus B68 .....64 A3
Sandwell Ct B21 .....65 D8

Sandwell Ctr B70 .....53 D3
Sandwell District General Hospl B71 .....53 D5
Sandwell Ho ⓘ WS1 ....42 F8
Sandwell Park Farm* B71 .....53 F3
Sandwell Pl WV12 .....27 D7
Sandwell Rd
  Birmingham B21 .....54 D1
  West Bromwich B70 ...53 C4
  Wolverhampton WV10 ..11 B1
Sandwell Rd N B71 .....53 D4
Sandwell Road Pas B71 .53 C4
Sandwell St WS1 .....42 F8
Sandwell Valley Country Pk* B70,B71 .....53 F3
Sandwell Valley Ctry Pk* B71 .....54 A5
Sandwell Valley Nature Ctr* B43 .....54 C6
Sandwell Wlk ⓼ WS1 ...42 F8
Sandwick Cl CV3 .....134 F8
Sandwood Dr B44 .....55 F8
Sandy Cres Hinckley LE10 .71 C1
  Wednesfield WV11 .....27 A8
  Wolverhampton WV11 ..13 A1
Sandy Croft
  Birmingham B13 .....105 C7
  Sutton Coldfield B72 ..46 C3
Sandy Gr WS8 .....6 F1
Sandy Hill Rd B90 .....106 A4
Sandy Hill Rise B90 ....106 A4
Sandy Hollow WV6 .....24 C2
Sandy La
  Birmingham, Aston B6 ..67 B7
  Birmingham, Great Barr B42 .....55 D8
  Blackdown CV32 .....156 F6
  Blakedown DY10 .....118 C2
  Cannock WS11 .....1 B1
  Codsall WV8 .....10 A4
  Coventry CV1 .....113 C5
  Royal Leamington Spa CV32 .....156 D4
  Wednesbury WS10 .....42 F3
  Wildmoor B61,B62 .....120 E5
  Wolverhampton, Bushbury WV10 .....11 E1
  Wolverhampton, Tettenhall WV6 .....24 E6
Sandy Lane Bsns Pk CV1 .....113 C5
Sandy Mount WV5 .....49 B7
Sandy Mount Rd WS1 ..42 F8
Sandy Rd DY8 .....80 D1
Sandy Way
  Birmingham B15 .....66 B1
  Tamworth B77 .....22 B3
Sandyacre Way DY8 ....81 B5
Sandyfields Rd DY3 ....50 B6
Sandygate Cl B97 .....152 F2
Sandys Gr DY4 .....51 E5
Sandythorpe CV3 .....134 E6
Sangwin Rd WV14 .....51 C2
Sankey Rd WS11 .....1 F3
Sankey's Cnr WS7 .....6 F7
Sansome Rd B90 .....105 F2
Sansome Rise B90 .....105 F2
Sanstone Cl WS3 .....14 C3
Sanstone Rd WS3 .....14 C3
Sant Rd B31 .....123 B7
Santolina Dr WS5 .....43 A3
Santos Cl CV3 .....134 F8
Santridge Ct B61 .....137 A4
Santridge La B61 .....137 A4
Sapcote Bsns Ctr B10 ..87 E6
Sapcote Gr CV6 .....96 B4
Sapcote Ind Est B64 ....62 F3
Sapcote Rd LE10 .....76 B7
Saplings The B76 .....58 A8
Sapphire Cl
  Birmingham B3 .....164 A4
  ❸ Walsall B92 .....88 F1
Sapphire Dr Cannock WS12 .2 C3
  Royal Leamington Spa CV31 .....161 F5
Sapphire Gate CV2 ....114 C2
Sapphire Twr ❷ B6 .....66 F6
Sara Cl B74 .....32 A3
Saracen Dr
  Balsall Common CV7 ...129 E6
  Sutton Coldfield B75 ..47 A6
Sarah Cl WV14 .....40 E1
Sarah Ct B73 .....45 D1
Sarah Gdns WS5 .....42 F4
Sarah Siddons Ho ⓽ WS13 .....9 B7
Sarah St B9 .....67 B2
Saredon Cl B93 .....15 A1
Saredon Rd WS6,WS11, WV10 .....4 B3
Sarehole Mill (Mus)* B13 .....105 D8
Sarehole Rd B28 .....87 E1
Sargeaunt St CV31 .....161 F7
Sargent Ave B44 .....44 D4
Sargent Turner Trad Est DY9 .....81 F6
Sark Dr B36 .....70 B6
Satchwell Cl ⓯ CV32 ...161 F8
Satchwell Wlk ⓴ CV32 .161 F8
Satellite Ind Pk WV11 ..26 D4
Saturday Bridge ⓻ B1 ..66 C1
Saturn Rd WS11 .....2 A5
Saumur Way CV34 .....161 C6
Saunders Ave CV12 ....78 B2
Saunders Ho ⓰ CV32 ..156 F2
Saunderton Rd B31 ....102 E5

Saunton Cl CV5 .....112 B8
Saunton Way B29 .....85 C2
Saveker Dr B76 .....46 E4
Savernake Cl B45 .....102 A2
Saville Cl
  Birmingham B45 .....122 B7
  Hinckley LE10 .....71 E2
Saville Gr CV8 .....148 C5
Savoy Bldgs DY2 .....62 D5
Savoy Cl B32 .....85 A5
Saw Mill Cl WS4 .....28 E3
Saxelby Cl B14 .....104 E2
Saxelby Ho B14 .....104 E2
Saxon Bsns Pk B60 ....150 E2
Saxon Cl
  Binley Woods CV3 .....135 D7
  Great Wyrley WS6 .....5 A2
  Polesworth B78 .....22 F1
  Studley B80 .....159 E5
  Tamworth B77 .....35 F6
Saxon Ct WS13 .....8 E7
Saxon Dr B65 .....63 C4
Saxon Hill Sch WS14 ...9 C6
Saxon Mews CV32 .....156 C2
Saxon Mill La B79 .....21 C4
Saxon Rd CV2 .....114 B4
Saxon Way B37 .....69 F3
Saxon Wlk WS13 .....8 E7
Saxon Wood Cl ⓼ B31 .103 A4
Saxon Wood Rd B90 ...126 D5
Saxoncourt WV6 .....24 C5
Saxondale Ave B26 ....88 F6
Saxonfire B79 .....21 C5
Saxonfields WV6 .....24 C5
Saxons Way B14 .....105 A2
Saxton Dr B74 .....31 F6
Sayer Ho B19 .....66 D6
Scafell Cl CV5 .....112 A4
Scafell Dr Bilston WV14 ..40 F7
  Birmingham B23 .....56 D5
Scafell Rd DY8 .....81 B6
Scaife Rd B60 .....151 B7
Scammerton B77 .....36 B8
Scampton Cl WV6 .....23 C8
Scampton Way B79 .....21 C8
Scar Bank CV34 .....155 E1
Scarborough Cl ❷ WS2 .42 B8
Scarborough Rd WS2 ...42 B8
Scarborough Way CV4 ..131 F7
Scarecrow La B75 .....32 E4
Scarfield Hill B48 .....138 E5
Scarman Rd CV4 .....132 B5
Scarsdale Rd B42 .....55 D8
Schofield Ave B71 .....53 B8
Schofield Rd B37 .....70 A5
Scholars Gate
  Birmingham B33 .....69 B2
  Burntwood WS7 .....7 D7
Scholars Wlk WS4 .....29 B7
Scholefield Twr B19 ....66 D5
Scholfield Rd CV7 .....95 A6
School Ave WS8 .....15 F8
School Bell Mews CV8 ..149 B6
School Cl Birmingham B37 .70 A6
  Burntwood WS7 .....6 D8
  Codsall WV8 .....10 A4
  Coventry CV3 .....113 F2
  Hinckley LE10 .....76 A6
  Norton Canes WS11 .....6 B6
  Stourbridge DY8 .....63 C7
  Wolverhampton WV3 ...38 B7
School Cotts CV35 .....145 F3
School Cres WS11 .....6 A6
School Croft CV35 .....146 C2
School Ct WS12 .....2 C6
School Dr Bilston WV14 ..41 A2
  Bromsgrove B60 .....137 A3
  Dudley DY4 .....40 C1
  Stourbridge DY8 .....80 F8
  Wythall B47 .....125 E3
School Dr The DY2 .....62 D7
School Gn WV14 .....40 C8
School Hill CV10 .....72 A8
School Ho WS7 .....7 D7
School House La CV2 ...115 A6
School La Alvechurch B48 .139 B5
  Bedworth CV7 .....95 F7
  Birmingham, Buckland End B34 .....69 B7
  Birmingham, Kitt's Green B33 .....68 F1
  Brierley Hill DY5 .....61 B4
  Burntwood WS7 .....6 D8
  Hagley DY9 .....99 D6
  Halesowen B63 .....82 F2
  Hopwas B78 .....20 B7
  Kenilworth CV8 .....147 F5
  Lickey End B60 .....137 B6
  Norton Canes WS3 .....5 E2
  Radford Semele CV31 ..162 E5
  Shuttington B79 .....22 F7
  Solihull B91 .....107 D4
  Tamworth B77 .....35 D5
  Walsall WS4 .....14 F4
  Weeford B78 .....19 D2
  Wolverhampton WV10 ..11 E2
  Wroxall CV35 .....145 E4
School of Art, Univ of Wolverhampton WV7 .163 B4
School Rd
  Birmingham, Eachway B45 .121 E6
  Birmingham, Hall Green B28 .....106 A8
  Birmingham, Moseley B13 ..86 F1
  Birmingham, Yardley Wood B14 .....105 C4
  Brierley Hill DY5 .....62 A2
  Bulkington CV12 .....79 C2

School Rd continued
  Himley DY3 .....49 B3
  Hockley Heath B94 ....143 B7
  Norton Canes WS11 .....6 A6
  Solihull B90 .....106 B2
  Trysull WV5 .....37 C1
  Wednesbury WS10 .....42 D2
  Wolverhampton, New Cross WV11 .....26 C6
  Wolverhampton, Tettenhall WV6 .....24 B3
  Wombourne WV5 .....49 B7
School St Blackheath B64 .62 D1
  Brierley Hill DY5 .....61 D5
  Darlaston WS10 .....41 E5
  Dudley, Eve Hill DY1 ...51 B1
  Dudley, Roseville WV14 .51 C8
  Sedgley DY3 .....50 E8
  Stourbridge DY8 .....80 F6
  Tamworth B77 .....21 E4
  Walsall WS4 .....15 D1
  Willenhall WV13 .....26 F1
  Wolverhampton WV3 ...163 B2
School St W WV14 .....51 C8
School Terr ⓘ B29 .....85 F2
School Wlk Bilston WV14 .40 C8
  Burntwood WS7 .....6 D8
  Nuneaton CV11 .....73 E2
Scholacre Rd B34 .....69 B6
Scholacre Rise B74 ....30 E1
Scholfields Rd WS14 ...18 A5
Schoolgate Cl
  Birmingham B8 .....68 A6
  Walsall WS4 .....15 D1
Schoolhouse Cl B38 ...104 B2
Scimitar Cl B79 .....20 E7
Scorers Cl B90 .....106 B6
Scotch Orch WS13 .....3 D1
Scotch Orchard Prim Sch WS13 .....3 D1
Scotchill The CV6 .....95 A1
Scotchings The B36 ....68 E8
Scotia Rd WS11 .....1 D3
Scotland La B32 .....102 C7
Scotland St B1 .....66 C3
Scots Cnr B14 .....104 E8
Scots La CV6 .....112 F6
Scott Arms Sh Ctr B43 ..43 F1
Scott Ave Nuneaton CV10 .73 D8
  Wednesbury WS10 .....42 B2
  Wolverhampton WV4 ...38 E4
Scott Cl Lichfield WS14 ...9 B6
  West Bromwich B71 ....53 D5
Scott Gr B92 .....88 E3
Scott Ho B43 .....54 F7
Scott Rd Birmingham B43 .43 F2
  Kenilworth CV8 .....147 E2
  Redditch B97 .....158 C8
  Royal Leamington Spa CV31 .....162 B6
  Solihull B92 .....88 E2
  Tamworth B77 .....21 E4
  Walsall WS5 .....43 D6
Scott St WS12 .....2 F3
Scott's Green Cl CV1 ...162 A8
Scott's Rd DY8 .....80 F6
Scotts Green Island DY1 .61 F7
  West Bromwich B71 ....42 A4
Scout Cl B33 .....69 C2
Scribban Cl B66 .....65 A8
Scribers La B28 .....105 E4
Scrimshaw Ho ⓘ WS2 ..42 C7
Sculthorpe Rd DY10 ....98 B2
Seacroft Ave B25 .....68 E1
Seafield Cl DY6 .....60 E4
Seafield La Beoley B98 .141 A2
  Portway B48 .....140 E4
Seaford Cl CV6 .....96 B4
Seaforth Dr LE10 .....71 A1
Seaforth Gr WV11 .....13 B1
Seager St B71 .....53 E4
Seager's La DY5 .....61 D2
Seagrave Rd CV1 .....165 D1
Seagull Bay Dr WV14 ...40 D1
Seal Cl B76 .....46 E3
Sealand Dr CV12 .....78 A3
Seals Gn B38 .....123 D7
Sear Hills Cl CV7 .....130 B6
Seaton B77 .....35 F8
Seaton Cl Hinckley LE10 .76 B7
  Nuneaton CV11 .....73 F5
  Wednesfield WV11 .....26 F5
Seaton Gr B13 .....86 D1
Seaton Pl DY8 .....60 C2
Seaton Rd B66 .....65 B5
Seaton St CV31 .....134 B5
Seckham Rd WS13 .....9 A8
Second Ave
  Birmingham, Bordesley Green B9 .....67 F1
  Birmingham, Witton B6 ..55 F3
  Brownhills WS8 .....7 A1
  Coventry CV3 .....114 C1
  Kingswinford, Barrow Hill DY6 .....61 A7
  Kingswinford, Wall Heath DY6 .....60 F8
  Wolverhampton WV10 ..25 E7
Second Exhibition Ave B40 .....90 D4
Securehold Bsns Ctr B98 .....154 B2
Sedge Ave B38 .....103 F3
Sedge Dr B61 .....137 A6
Sedgeberrow Covert ❹ B38 .....123 E8

Sedgeberrow Rd B63 ...83 A2
Sedgebourne Way B31 .102 C1
Sedgefield Cl DY1 .....50 E3
Sedgefield Gr WV6 .....23 D4
Sedgefield Way WS11 ..6 B4
Sedgeford Cl DY5 .....81 D8
Sedgehill Ave B17 .....85 B4
Sedgemere
  Balsall Common CV7 ..130 C5
  Walsall WS4 .....29 C8
Sedgemere Rd B26 .....68 F1
Sedgemoor Ave WS7 ...7 B5
Sedgemoor Rd CV3 ....134 B5
Sedgley Cl B92 .....153 F4
Sedgley Gr B20 .....54 E4
Sedgley Hall Ave DY3 ..50 C8
Sedgley Rd Dudley DY1 .51 B6
  Wombourne WV4 .....38 F2
Sedgley Rd E DY4 .....52 A3
Sedgley Rd W DY4 .....51 D5
Sedgley St WV2 .....39 C7
Seed Field Croft CV3 ...133 E7
Seedhouse Ct B64 .....83 B8
Seeds La WS8 .....15 F8
Seekings The CV31 ....162 B3
Seeleys Rd B11 .....87 E5
Seeswood Cl CV10 .....72 C2
Sefton Dr B65 .....62 F6
Sefton Gr DY4 .....41 C2
Sefton Rd Birmingham B16 .65 F2
  Coventry CV4 .....132 E6
  Tamworth B77 .....35 D4
Segbourne Rd B45 .....121 F8
Segundo Cl WS5 .....42 F4
Segundo Rd WS5 .....42 F4
Seisdon Rd WV5 .....37 A1
Selba Dr DY11 .....116 A6
Selborne Cl WS1 .....29 A1
Selborne Gr B13 .....105 C5
Selborne Rd
  Birmingham B20 .....55 A2
  Dudley DY2 .....62 D7
Selborne St WS1 .....29 A1
Selbourne Cres WV1 ...26 B1
Selby Cl B26 .....68 B1
Selby Gr B13 .....105 C6
Selby Ho B69 .....63 D6
Selby Way Nuneaton CV10 .72 B5
  Walsall WS3 .....13 E2
Selcombe Way B38 ....123 F7
Selcroft Ave B32 .....84 F5
Selecta Ave B44 .....44 D2
Selina Dix Ho CV1 .....165 C4
Selker Dr B77 .....21 F5
Selkirk Cl B71 .....53 C6
Selly Ave B29 .....86 A2
Selly Cl B29 .....86 B2
Selly Hall Croft B30 ....104 A6
Selly Hill Rd B29 .....85 F2
Selly Manor Mus* B30 .103 F7
Selly Oak Colls B29 ....103 D8
Selly Oak Hospl B29 ...85 F1
Selly Oak Ind Est B29 ..85 E1
Selly Oak Rd B30 .....103 E5
Selly Oak Speci Sch B29 .....103 E8
Selly Oak Sta B29 .....85 E2
Selly Park Rd B29 .....86 A2
Selly Park Tech Coll For Girls B29 .....86 B1
Selly Wharf B29 .....86 B1
Selly Wick Dr B29 .....86 B2
Selly Wick Rd B29 .....86 B2
Sellywood Rd B29,B30 .103 E8
Selma Gr B14 .....105 D5
Selman's Par WS3 .....14 C2
Selmans Hill WS3 .....14 C2
Selsdon Cl Kidderminster DY11 .116 B5
  Wythall B47 .....125 C5
Selsdon Rd WS3 .....13 F3
Selsey Ave B66 .....65 B3
Selsey Cl CV3 .....134 C4
Selsey Rd B17 .....65 B3
Selston Rd B6 .....66 E7
Selvey Ave B43 .....44 C3
Selworthy Rd
  Birmingham B36 .....69 F8
  Coventry CV6 .....95 E3
Selwyn Cl WV2 .....39 C7
Selwyn Ho B37 .....70 D3
Selwyn Rd Bilston WV14 .40 F7
  Birmingham B16 .....65 D2
Selwyn Wlk B74 .....31 C4
Semele Cl CV31 .....162 E5
Seneschal Rd CV3 .....133 E7
Senior Cl WV11 .....13 A3
Senneleys Park Rd B31 .84 E1
Sennen Cl Nuneaton CV11 .74 A5
  Willenhall WV13 .....26 F1
Sensall Rd DY9 .....81 F3
Sentry Way B75 .....46 F6
Sephton Dr CV6 .....96 C6
Serin Cl DY10 .....117 A1
Serpentine Rd
  Birmingham, Aston B6 ..56 A1
  Birmingham, Harborne B17 .85 C6
  Birmingham, Selly Oak B29 .86 A2
Serpentine The DY11 ..116 C4
Servite Ct B14 .....105 A2
Servite Ho ❷ Coleshill B46 .70 F7
  Kenilworth CV8 .....147 F3
Seton Ho B74 .....32 C8
Setter Cl B34 .....68 F6
Settle Ave B34 .....69 B6
Settle Croft B37 .....69 F1
Setton Dr DY3 .....50 E7
Seven Acres WS9 .....30 B5
Seven Acres La B98 ....154 C5

Seven Acres Rd
Birmingham B31 103 C1
Halesowen B62 84 A5
Seven Star Rd B91 107 B5
Seven Stars Ind Est
CV3 134 A7
Seven Stars Rd B69 64 A7
Sevendwellings View
DY5 61 C1
Severn Ave LE10 75 A8
Severn Cl Birmingham B36 69 F7
Catshill B61 137 A8
Royal Leamington Spa
CV32 157 C3
Tipton DY4 51 F5
Wednesfield WV12 27 A7
Severn Ct Birmingham B23 56 B3
Sutton Coldfield B73 46 B5
Severn Dr Brierley Hill DY5 61 B7
Burntwood WS7 7 D6
Perton WV6 23 E4
Severn Gr
6 Birmingham B19 66 C7
Kidderminster DY11 116 B3
Severn Ho Dudley DY3 50 D3
4 Oldbury B68 84 B8
Severn Rd Brownhills WS8 6 C2
Bulkington CV12 79 A3
Coventry CV1 113 F1
Halesowen B63 82 B5
Stourbridge DY8 80 F3
Walsall WS3 14 E1
Severn St B1 164 B1
Severn Twr B7 67 B5
Severn Way B47 124 E2
Severne Gr B27 88 C1
Severne Jun & Inf Sch
B27 106 C8
Severne Rd B27 106 C8
Sevington Cl B91 127 C8
Sewall Ct CV6 114 A8
Sewall Highway CV2 114 B6
Seward Cl WS14 9 D6
Seymour Cl
Birmingham B29 86 A2
Cheslyn Hay WS6 4 D1
Coventry CV3 134 C5
Seymour Dr B98 154 A5
Seymour Gdns B74 31 E3
Seymour Gr CV34 161 D6
Seymour Ho CV3 133 C8
Seymour Rd
Kidderminster DY11 116 B8
Nuneaton CV11 73 D3
Oldbury B69 64 C7
Stourbridge DY9 82 A4
Tipton DY4 41 C1
Seymour St B5 164 D3
Shackleton Dr
Hinckley LE10 75 E4
Perton WV6 23 E5
Shackleton Rd WS3 14 D2
Shadow Brook La B92 108 E7
Shadowbrook Rd CV6 113 A5
Shadwell Dr DY3 50 D3
Shadwell St B4 164 C4
Shady La B44 44 E2
Shadymoor Dr DY5 81 C8
Shaft La CV7 93 A4
Shaftesbury Ave
Keresley CV7 95 A7
Stourbridge DY9 81 C2
Shaftesbury Cl B60 137 B2
Shaftesbury Dr WS12 2 C7
Shaftesbury Rd
Coventry CV5 132 F8
Wednesbury WS10 42 B2
Shaftesbury Sq B71 53 C5
Shaftesbury St B70 53 C4
Shaftmoor Ind Est B28 87 F2
Shaftmoor La B27,B28 87 F2
Shaftsbury Ave B63 82 B7
Shaftsbury Cl WV14 40 F7
Shaftsbury Rd B26 89 C5
Shahjalal Rd B8 67 D5
Shakells Cl B97 158 E4
Shakespeare Ave
Bedworth CV12 78 D2
Lichfield WS14 9 B6
Redditch B98 154 A2
Warwick CV34 160 C4
Shakespeare Cl
Dudley WV14 40 D2
Tamworth B79 21 A6
Shakespeare Cres WS3 28 F7
Shakespeare Dr
Hinckley LE10 71 C1
Kidderminster DY10 117 B6
Nuneaton CV11 74 A1
Solihull B90 106 B1
Shakespeare Gr WS11 1 D4
Shakespeare Ho B31 123 A8
Shakespeare Pl WS3 28 F7
Shakespeare Rd
Birmingham B23 56 B3
Burntwood WS7 6 F8
Dudley DY3 50 A4
Smethwick B67 64 E4
Solihull B90 126 D8
Tipton DY4 52 A8
Shakespeare St
Birmingham B11 87 C5
Coventry CV2 114 B4
Wolverhampton WV1 163 D2
Shakleton Rd CV5 113 A2
Shaldon Wlk 4 B66 65 B5
Shale St WV14 40 C5
Shalford Rd B92 88 E4
Shallcross La DY3 50 D3
Shalnecote Gr B14 104 C5
Shambles 2 WS10 41 F2
Shandon Cl B32 84 F3
Shanklin Cl WS6 5 A3
Shanklin Dr CV10 73 D6
Shanklin Rd CV3 134 B4
Shannon B77 35 F8
Shannon Dr WS8 6 C2
Shannon Rd B38 123 E7
Shannon Wlk WS8 6 C2
Shannon's Mill B79 21 A5
Shanti Niketan WV2 39 D7
Shapinsay Dr B45 101 F1
Shard End Cres B34 69 C6
Shardlow Rd WV11 26 E8
Shardway The B34 69 C5
Sharesacre St WV13 27 B3
Sharington Cl 3 DY2 62 E8
Sharman Rd WV10 25 E6
Sharmans Cross Jun Sch
B91 106 E4
Sharmans Cross Rd B91 106 F4
Sharnford Rd LE10 76 F6
Sharon Cl WV4 39 E5
Sharon Ct B27 88 C3
Sharon Way WS12 2 D3
Sharp Cl CV6 95 C2
Sharpe Cl CV34 160 E8
Sharpe St B77 22 A5
Sharpless Rd LE10 75 F7
Sharpley Ct CV2 115 A8
Sharps Cl B45 122 A7
Sharrat Field B75 32 D2
Sharratt Rd CV12 78 A3
Sharrocks St WV1 163 D2
Sharwood Wlk B45 102 B2
Shaw Ave DY10 117 B6
Shaw Dr B33 68 E2
Shaw Hall La WV9 11 C7
Shaw Hill Gr B8 68 A4
Shaw Hill Prim Sch B8 67 F4
Shaw Hill Rd B8 68 A4
Shaw La Lichfield WS13 9 A8
Stoke Prior B60 150 C3
Wolverhampton WV6 24 B3
Shaw Lane Ind Est B60 150 C2
Shaw Park Bsns Village
WV10 25 D6
Shaw Rd
Dudley, Hurst Hill WV14 40 B1
Dudley, Netherton DY2 62 C7
Tipton DY4 52 C4
Wolverhampton, Blakenhall
WV4 39 C6
Wolverhampton, Dunstall Hill
WV10 25 C6
Shaw St B70 52 E7
Shaw's La WS6 5 A2
Shaw's Pas B5 164 D2
Shawbank Rd B98 154 B3
Shawberry Ave B35 58 B4
Shawberry Rd B37 69 F5
Shawbrook Gr 10 B14 105 A3
Shawbury Cl B98 154 E3
Shawbury Gr
Birmingham B12 86 F8
Perton WV6 23 E5
Shawbury Rd WV10 25 F5
Shawe Ave CV10 73 C7
Shawfield B47 125 A5
Shawhellier Ave DY5 61 E2
Shawhurst Croft B47 125 A7
Shawhurst Gdns B47 125 B7
Shawhurst La B47 125 A6
Shawley Croft B27 88 E4
Shaws Cl B97 152 F2
Shawsdale Rd B36 68 F7
Shayler Gr WV2 39 D7
Sheaf La B26 89 B4
Sheapecoate Ho 1 B71 42 F1
Shearwater Cl
Birmingham B45 121 F6
Kidderminster DY10 117 B1
Shearwater Wlk B23 56 B7
Sheaves Cl WV14 40 B3
Shedden St 3 DY2 62 D8
Sheddington Rd B23 56 D7
Sheen Ho CV2 114 D8
Sheen Rd B44 44 E4
Sheepclose Dr B37 70 A3
Sheepcote Cl CV32 157 A1
Sheepcote Grange B61 136 F5
Sheepcote La B77 21 F4
Sheepcote St B16 66 B2
Sheepcroft Cl B97 152 F2
Sheepfold Cl B65 63 A4
Sheepmoor Cl B17 84 F8
Sheepwash La DY4 52 D5
Sheepy Cl LE10 71 F1
Sheerwater Dr DY5 81 D7
Sheffield Rd B73 57 A7
Sheffield St DY5 62 A1
Shefford Rd B6 66 F5
Sheila Ave WV11 26 E7
Shelah Rd B63 83 A6
Shelbourne Cl B69 52 D2
Sheldon Ave WS10 42 A4
Sheldon Cl WV14 40 D4
Sheldon Dr B31 102 D2
Sheldon Gr
Birmingham B26 89 B5
Warwick CV34 155 F2
Sheldon Hall Ave B33 69 D3
Sheldon Heath Com Sch
B33 89 C8
Sheldon Heath Rd B26 89 B8
Sheldon Rd Redditch B98 159 A8
Sheldon Rd continued
West Bromwich B71 53 E8
Wolverhampton WV10 11 A1
Sheldon Wlk B33 69 C1
Sheldonfield Rd B26 89 D5
Sheldrake Cl CV3 115 A1
Shelduck Cl DY10 117 B3
Shelfield Cl
Coventry CV5 112 B3
Hockley Heath B94 143 C6
Shelfield Com Sch WS4 15 C2
Shelfield Rd B14 104 C3
Shell Corner Trad Est
B62 83 D8
Shelley Ave
Kidderminster DY10 116 E7
Tipton DY4 52 B8
Warwick CV34 160 C4
Shelley Cl Bedworth CV12 78 D1
Catshill B61 137 A8
Dudley DY3 50 A5
Redditch B97 158 C8
Stourbridge DY8 81 A8
Shelley Dr
Birmingham B23 56 B3
Sutton Coldfield B74 31 F6
Shelley Gdns LE10 71 E3
Shelley Ho Halesowen B63 82 B5
1 Oldbury B68 64 C4
Shelley Rd
2 Burntwood WS7 7 A8
Cannock WS11 1 E5
Coventry CV2 114 C3
Tamworth B79 21 A7
Willenhall WV12 27 E7
Wolverhampton WV10 11 D2
Shellon Cl CV3 134 F8
Shelly Cl B37 69 F2
Shelly Cres B90 127 B6
Shelly Croft B33 69 A3
Shelly La B90 127 B6
Shelly Twr B31 103 C3
Shelsley Ave B69 63 D5
Shelsley Dr B13 87 B2
Shelsley Way B91 107 B1
Shelton Cl WS10 42 C5
Shelton La B63 82 E5
Shelton Sq CV1 165 B2
Shelton St B77 35 F7
Sheltwood Cl B97 153 A2
Sheltwood La B60,B97 152 A3
Shelwick Gr B93 127 F4
Shenley Ave DY1 51 C6
Shenley Court Sch B29 102 F7
Shenley Fields Dr B31 102 F8
Shenley Fields Rd B29 103 B8
Shenley Gdns B29 103 A7
Shenley Gn B29 102 F6
Shenley Hill B31 102 F6
Shenley La B29 102 F7
Shenstone Ave
Halesowen B62 83 E5
Stourbridge DY8 80 D3
Shenstone Cl
Bromsgrove B60 137 B3
Sutton Coldfield B74 31 E6
Shenstone Ct
Bromsgrove B60 137 B3
Solihull B90 105 D2
Wolverhampton WV3 39 A6
Shenstone Dr
Aldridge WS9 30 A8
Balsall Common CV7 130 A6
Shenstone Flats B62 83 F5
Shenstone Ho WS13 3 E1
Shenstone Lodge Specl Sch
WS14 18 A3
Shenstone Rd
Birmingham, Edgbaston B16 65 C3
Birmingham, Great Barr
B43 54 E8
Birmingham, Highter's Heath
B14 105 A1
Shenstone Sta WS14 17 F6
Shenstone Trad Est B63 83 C4
Shenstone Valley Rd B62 83 F6
Shenton Wlk B37 69 F5
Shepheard Rd B26 89 D5
Shepherd Cl
Coventry CV4 111 F3
Lichfield WS13 3 C3
Shepherd Dr WV12 27 C5
Shepherds Brook Rd
DY9 81 D5
Shepherds Fold B65 63 B2
Shepherds Gdns 8 B15 66 B1
Shepherds Green Rd B24 56 F1
Shepherds Pool Rd B75 32 E2
Shepherds Standing B34 69 B6
Shepherds Way B23 56 C8
Shepherds Wlk
Bromsgrove B60 150 E7
Wolverhampton WV8 10 F2
Shepley Mdw B45 138 B8
Shepley Rd
Barnt Green B45 138 A7
Birmingham B45 122 B6
Shepperton Bsns Pk
CV11 73 C1
Shepperton Ct CV11 73 C1
Shepperton St CV11 73 C2
Sheppey Dr B36 70 B5
Shepwell Gdns WV10 12 C7
Shepwell Gn WV13 27 C1
Sherard Croft B36 70 B6
Sheraton Cl Aldridge WS9 30 B6
Cannock WS12 2 A7
Sheraton Dr DY10 117 B6
Sheraton Grange DY8 80 F2
Sheraton Rd B60 137 C1
Sherborne Cl WS3 28 C7
Sherborne Ct WV10 11 E1
Sherborne Gdns WV8 10 A3
Sherborne Gr B1 66 A3
Sherborne Rd
Hinckley LE10 76 B7
Wolverhampton WV10 11 D1
Sherborne St B16 66 B2
Sherbourne Ave
Cannock WS12 2 E4
Nuneaton CV10 72 B4
Sherbourne Cl B98 154 D2
Sherbourne Cres CV5 112 E4
Sherbourne Ct CV1 165 B1
Sherbourne Dr B27 88 C4
Sherbourne Fields Sch
CV6 112 D5
Sherbourne Rd
Birmingham, Acock's Green
B27 88 C4
Birmingham, Balsall Heath
B12 86 F7
Blackheath B64 83 B8
Stourbridge DY8 81 B4
Sherbourne St CV1 113 A2
Sherbrook Rd WS11 1 C1
Sherbrooke Ave B77 35 E6
Sherdmore Croft B90 126 F6
Sheridan Cl 3 WS2 42 B7
Sheridan Gdns DY3 49 F5
Sheridan St Walsall WS2 42 B7
West Bromwich B71 53 D4
Sheridan Wlk B35 58 A3
Sheriff Ave CV4 132 B7
Sheriff Dr DY5 61 F2
Sheriffs Cl WS14 9 E6
Sheriffs Orch CV1 165 B2
Sherifoot La B75 32 B4
Sheringham B15 85 E8
Sheringham Cl CV11 73 F2
Sheringham Rd B30 104 B3
Sherington Ave CV5 112 C4
Sherington Dr WV4 39 D5
Sherlock Cl WV12 27 D5
Sherlock Rd CV5 112 D3
Sherlock St B5 86 E8
Sherrans Dell WV4 39 D3
Sherratt Cl B76 57 F8
Sherringham Dr WV11 13 C1
Sherron Gdns B12 86 F5
Sherston Covert 11 B30 104 C2
Shervale Cl WV4 39 A6
Sherwin Ave WV14 40 A2
Sherwood Ave DY4 51 F4
Sherwood Cl
Birmingham B28 105 F5
Solihull B92 106 F7
Wood End CV9 36 C1
Sherwood Dr
Brierley Hill DY5 61 F2
Cannock WS11 2 A3
Sherwood Jones Cl CV6 113 B6
Sherwood Mews B28 105 E6
Sherwood Rd
Birmingham B28 105 E7
Bromsgrove B60 151 A6
Smethwick B67 65 A1
Stourbridge DY8 80 E7
Sherwood St WV1 163 B4
Sherwood Wlk
Royal Leamington Spa
CV32 157 C4
Walsall WS9 29 E7
Shetland Ave B77 35 F7
Shetland Cl
Birmingham B16 65 F2
Coventry CV5 112 A4
Wolverhampton WV6 25 B5
Shetland Dr
Nuneaton CV10 73 A2
Smethwick B66 64 D8
Shetland Wlk B36 70 B6
Shevlock Way CV6 114 A6
Shidas La B69 63 E7
Shifnal Wlk B31 122 F8
Shillcock Gr B19 66 E5
Shillingstone Cl CV2 115 A4
Shillingstone Dr
Nuneaton CV10 72 F1
Nuneaton CV10 73 A1
Shilton Cl B90 126 F6
Shilton Gr B29 102 F8
Shilton Ind Est CV7 97 E7
Shilton La
Barnacle CV2,CV7 97 B4
Bulkington CV12 79 D1
Coventry CV2 96 F3
Shilton CV7,CV12 97 D8
Shinwell Cres B69 52 D2
Shipbourne Cl B32 84 F5
Shipley Fields B24 57 A3
Shipley Gr B29 103 A8
Shipston Rd
Birmingham B31 103 B1
Coventry CV2 114 C6
Shipton Cl DY1 50 F3
Shipton Rd B72 46 C3
Shipway Rd B25 88 A7
Shire Brook Cl B6 66 E8
Shire Brook Ct 2 B19 66 D7
Shire Cl Birmingham B16 65 F2
Coventry CV6 96 B1
Oldbury B68 64 B2
Shire Lea WS8 16 B6
Shire Oak Sch WS8 16 A5
Shire Ridge WS9 16 B4
Shirebrook Cl CV2 96 D2
Shirehall Pl WS11 2 B2
Shirehampton Cl B97 152 F2
Shireland Brook Gdns 1
B18 65 D4
Shireland Cl B20 54 F3
Shireland Hall Prim Sch
B66 65 C3
Shireland La B97 153 A4
Shireland Language Coll
B66 65 B3
Shireland Rd B66 65 B3
Shirelea Cl WS7 7 B8
Shires Gate Ret Pk
CV31 161 E6
Shires Gate Trad Est
CV31 161 E6
Shires Ret Pk CV34 161 D6
Shirestone Jun & Inf Sch
B33 69 D2
Shirestone Rd B33 69 E2
Shireview Gdns WS3 15 B4
Shireview Rd WS3 15 B4
Shirewood WS11 1 B2
Shirland Rd B37 70 A1
Shirlett Cl CV2 96 B4
Shirley Dr B72 46 C4
Shirley Heath Jun Sch
B90 106 C1
Shirley La CV7 111 A5
Shirley Park Rd B90 106 B2
Shirley Rd
Birmingham, Hall Green
B27,B28 106 A7
Birmingham, King's Norton
B30 104 A5
Coventry CV2 115 A7
Dudley DY2 62 E8
Oldbury B68 64 C6
Shirley Sta B90 105 F1
Shirley Trad Est B90 106 E1
Shirley Wlk B79 20 F7
Shirleydale 2 B90 126 C8
Shirral Gr B37 69 F5
Shirrall Dr B78 33 E4
Shoal Hill Cl WS11 1 B2
Sholing Cl WV8 10 F1
Shooters Cl B5 86 D6
Shooters Hill B72 46 D2
Shop La WV6 37 B7
Shopping Ctr The CV31 162 B5
Shopping Prec The
CV34 156 A1
Shops The 2 DY6 60 D4
Shopton Rd B34 69 A7
Shoreham Cl WV13 26 D1
Shorncliffe Rd CV6 112 E6
Short Acre St WS2 28 D3
Short Heath Ct B23 56 F5
Short Heath Jun Sch
WV12 27 D5
Short Heath Prim Sch
B23 56 D6
Short Heath Rd B23 56 E6
Short La WS6 4 E3
Short Rd Smethwick B67 64 D3
Wolverhampton WV10 11 E1
Short St Bilston WV14 40 D6
Blackheath B65 63 C2
Brownhills WS8 15 F7
Cannock WS11 1 F3
Coventry CV1 165 C2
Darlaston WS10 41 F7
Dudley DY1 51 A2
Halesowen B63 82 F5
Nuneaton CV10 72 D4
Stourbridge DY8 80 F5
Tipton DY4 51 E8
Walsall WS2 28 D1
Wednesbury WS10 41 E3
Willenhall WV12 27 C5
Wolverhampton WV1 163 C3
Shortbutts La WS14 9 B5
Shorters Ave B14 105 B4
Shortfield Cl CV7 130 B7
Shortland Cl B93 128 A7
Shortlands CV7 95 D6
Shortlands Cl B30 104 A2
Shortlands La WS3 14 F3
Shortley Rd CV3 133 F8
Shorwell Pl DY5 61 B1
Shottery Cl Coventry CV5 112 B3
Sutton Coldfield B76 46 F1
Shottery Gr B76 46 F1
Shottery Rd B90 106 B1
Shotteswell Rd B90 126 B8
Showell Cir WV10 25 E7
Showell Green La B11 87 C3
Showell Ho 10 B69 64 A7
Showell La Meriden CV7 93 A1
Wombourne WV4 38 B3
Showell Rd WV10 25 D6
Showell Road Ind Est
WV10 25 D6
Showells Gdns B7 67 C7
Shrawley Ave DY11 116 B3
Shrawley Cl
Birmingham B45 121 F7
Halesowen B63 83 A2
Shrawley Rd B31 103 C2
Shrewley Cres B33 69 E1
Shrewsbury Cl WS3 13 F1
Shrewsbury Rd DY11 116 A6
Shrewton Ave B14 104 D2
Shrub La B24 57 B4

Shrubberies The CV4 132 E4
Shrubbery Ave DY4 51 D5
Shrubbery Cl B76 57 D6
Shrubbery Ct DY10 116 F7
Shrubbery Rd B61 136 E1
Shrubbery Sch The B76 57 F7
Shrubbery St DY10 116 F7
Shrubbery The
Birmingham B16 65 F3
Dudley DY1 51 B2
Shrubland St CV31 162 A6
Shrubland Street Com Prim Sch CV31 162 A6
Shrublands Ave B68 84 B7
Shuckburgh Gr 4 CV32 157 A2
Shugborough Cl WS3 14 B1
Shugborough Dr DY1 50 E2
Shugborough Way WS11 2 C1
Shulman's Wlk CV2 114 D7
Shultern La CV4 132 D6
Shuna Croft CV2 115 B7
Shustoke La WS5 43 B4
Shustoke Rd
Birmingham B34 69 C6
Solihull B91 107 D5
Shut Mill La B62 100 D2
Shutlock La B13 86 D1
Shutt La B94 126 B1
Shuttington Rd B79 22 B6
Shuttle St CV6 114 B8
Shylock Gr CV34 161 E2
Shyltons Croft B16 66 A2
Sibdon Gr B31 123 A8
Sibree Rd CV3 134 B4
Sibton Cl CV2 96 C1
Sidaway Cl B65 63 C6
Sidaway St B64 62 E1
Sidbury Gr B93 127 E3
Sidbury Rd CV6 113 C6
Sidcup Cl WV14 40 B3
Sidcup Rd B44 45 A1
Siddeley Ave
Coventry CV3 114 B1
Kenilworth CV8 147 E3
Siddons Factory Est B70 52 F8
Siddons Rd WV14 40 D2
Siddons Way B70,B71 53 A7
Sidemoor Fst Sch B61 136 E3
Sidenhill Cl B90 126 B8
Sidford Gdns B24 57 C3
Sidford Gr B23 56 E7
Sidings The
Birmingham B20 66 C8
Cannock WS12 2 C7
Hagley DY9 99 A6
Sidlaw Cl Halesowen B63 82 D2
Wolverhampton WV10 25 C6
Sidmouth Cl
Coventry CV2 114 C7
Nuneaton CV11 73 F5
Sidney St WV2 163 B1
Sidney Stringer Com Tech Coll CV1 165 C3
Sidon Hill Way WS11 2 C2
Sidwick Cres WV2 40 B6
Sigmund Cl WV1 26 B3
Signal Gr WS3 14 A1
Signal Hayes Rd B76 47 A2
Signal Wlk B77 22 A2
Silesbourne Cl B36 69 C8
Silhill Hall Rd B91 107 A5
Silica Rd B77 22 B2
Silken Ct CV11 73 B4
Silksby St CV3 133 D8
Sillins Ave B98 154 A3
Silva Ave DY6 60 F4
Silver Birch Ave CV12 77 E2
Silver Birch Cl B8 67 D6
Silver Birch Coppice B74 31 D5
Silver Birch Dr
Hollywood B47 125 B6
Kidderminster DY10 117 C5
Silver Birch Gr 5 CV31 161 F5
Silver Birch Rd
Aldridge B74 30 F1
Birmingham, Erdington B24 57 B6
Birmingham, Kingshurst B37 69 F6
Huntington WS12 1 D8
Norton Canes WS11 6 B5
Wolverhampton WV2 39 E7
Silver Birches Bsns Pk 3 B60 150 F6
Silver Court Gdns WS8 15 F7
Silver Ct WS8 15 F7
Silver End Ind Est DY5 61 B1
Silver Fir Cl WS12 2 A8
Silver Innage B63 82 C7
Silver Link Rd B77 21 F1
Silver St Birmingham B14 104 E8
Brierley Hill DY5 61 C1
Brownhills WS8 15 F7
Coventry CV1 165 B3
Hollywood B47 124 E5
Kidderminster DY10 116 E7
Redditch B97,B98 153 E4
Tamworth B79 21 B5
Silver Trees Dr CV12 79 B4
Silver Wlk CV10 72 F3
Silver's Cl WS3 14 F4
Silverbirch Cl CV10 72 A7
Silverbirch Ct B24 57 B6
Silverbirch Rd B91 107 E3
Silvercroft Ave B21 54 D3
Silverdale B61 136 F4
Silverdale Cl CV2 96 B4
Silverdale Dr WV10 25 E5
Silverdale Gdns DY8 60 C3
Silverdale Rd B24 57 D5
Silverfield Cl B14 104 E8
Silverlands Ave B68 64 B3
Silverlands Cl B28 87 F1
Silvermead Ct B47 124 F5
Silvermead Rd B73 46 A1
Silvermere Rd B26 89 D6
Silverstone Ave DY11 116 D8
Silverstone Cl WS2 27 D3
Silverstone Dr
Coventry CV6 95 E5
Sutton Coldfield B74 44 F6
Silverthorne Ave DY4 51 D5
Silverthorne La B64 82 B8
Silverton Cres B13 87 D1
Silverton Hts B67 64 F6
Silverton Rd
Coventry CV6 113 F7
Smethwick B67 64 E6
Silverton Way WV11 26 F5
Silvertrees Rd DY4 51 E5
Silvester Ct B70 53 E3
Silvester Rd WV14 40 F7
Silvester Way DY5 81 B8
Silvington Cl B29 103 C7
Simcox Gdns B32 84 D2
Simcox Rd WS10 41 F5
Simcox St WS12 2 D4
Simeon Bissell Cl DY4 52 A5
Simeon's Wlk DY5 81 F7
Simmonds Cl WS3 14 D3
Simmonds Pl WS10 41 F7
Simmonds Rd WS3 14 D3
Simmonds Way WS8 16 A6
Simmons Cl B78 34 B1
Simmons Dr B32 84 D4
Simmons Leasow B32 84 E2
Simmons Rd WV11 13 B1
Simms La Dudley DY2 62 C5
Hollywood B47 125 A5
Simon Cl Nuneaton CV11 73 D2
West Bromwich B71 42 E1
Simon Ct CV7 96 A8
Simon Rd B47 125 A7
Simon Stone St CV6 113 F8
Simpkins Cl WS9 16 A3
Simpson Gr WV10 25 E6
Simpson Rd Lichfield WS13 3 B2
Sutton Coldfield B72 46 C1
Walsall WS2 28 B5
Wolverhampton WV10 25 E6
Simpson St B69 64 A8
Sinclair Ct B13 86 E4
Sinclair Dr CV6 96 C6
Singer Cl CV6 114 B8
Singer Croft B36 58 F1
Singh Cl B21 54 E1
Sion Cl DY5 61 D3
Sir Alfreds Way B76 46 E3
Sir Frank Whittle Prim Sch CV2 114 F8
Sir George's Mall 6 DY10 116 E6
Sir Harrys Rd B5 86 C6
Sir Henry Parkes Prim Sch CV4 132 C8
Sir Henry Parkes Rd CV5 132 D7
Sir Hilton's Rd B31 123 C7
Sir John's Rd B29 86 C3
Sir Richards Dr B17 84 F7
Sir Robert Peel Hospl B78 20 D2
Sir Theodore Pritchett Inf & Jun Sch B14 104 D2
Sir Thomas White's Rd CV5 112 F2
Sir Walter's Mall 8 DY10 116 E6
Sir Wilfrid Martineau Schs B33 69 D3
Sir William Lyons Rd CV4 132 C6
Sir Winston Churchill Pl CV3 135 C7
Sisburn Cl 5 B97 153 B5
Sisefield Rd B38 104 A1
Siskin Cl WS7 7 D5
Siskin Dr Birmingham B12 86 E6
Coventry CV3 134 C4
Siskin Parkway E CV3 134 C1
Siskin Parkway W CV3 134 C2
Siskin Rd DY9 81 C3
Siskin Way DY10 117 B1
Sisley Way LE10 71 A3
Sister Dora Ave WS7 7 F7
Sister Dora Bldgs 2 WS1 28 E1
Sister Dora Gdns 1 WS1 42 E8
Siviter St B63 83 B4
Siviter's Cl B65 63 B3
Siviter's La B65 63 B3
Six Acres B32 84 C4
Six Towers Rd WS2 28 C4
Six Ways B23 56 F4
Six Ways Ho B23 56 F4
Skelcher Rd B90 106 A3
Skelwith Rise CV11 74 A6
Skemp Cl WV14 40 D4
Sketchley Cl B66 65 A6
Sketchley Hall Gdns LE10 75 C5
Sketchley Hill Prim Sch LE10 75 E5
Sketchley La LE10 75 C5
Sketchley La Ind Est LE10 75 B5
Sketchley Manor La LE10 75 D5
Sketchley Mdws LE10 75 C5
Sketchley Meadows Bsns Pk LE10 75 C4
Sketchley Old Village LE10 75 C5
Sketchley Rd LE10 75 E5
Skidmore Ave
Tamworth B77 35 C5
Wolverhampton WV3 38 F8
Skidmore Dr B70 53 A3
Skidmore Rd WV14 40 D2
Skilts Ave B98 153 F1
Skinner La B5 66 E1
Skinner St WV1 163 B3
Skip La WS5 43 E6
Skipness B77 21 E5
Skipton Gdns CV2 114 B6
Skipton Gn WV6 25 A5
Skipton Lodge CV2 114 B6
Skipton Pl WS11 4 B7
Skipton Rd B16 66 A1
Skipworth Rd CV3 115 A1
Skomer Cl B45 101 E1
Sky Blue Way CV1 113 E3
Skydome The CV1 165 A2
Skye Cl Birmingham B36 70 B6
Nuneaton CV10 72 F2
Tamworth B77 35 F7
Skye Wlk 4 B64 62 E1
Skylark Cl Birmingham B23 56 C7
Brierley Hill DY5 50 C1
Huntington WS12 1 C7
Skylark Way DY10 117 A2
Slack La B20 54 E2
Slacky La WS3 14 F1
Slade Ave WS7 7 A8
Slade Cl Nuneaton CV11 79 C8
West Bromwich B71 42 F2
Slade Gdns WV8 10 A4
Slade Gr B93 127 F6
Slade Hill 3 WV6 24 F3
Slade Jun & Inf Sch B23 56 D2
Slade La Birmingham B28 105 E3
Sutton Coldfield B75 33 A3
Tamworth B77 35 C4
Slade Lanker B34 69 A5
Slade Mdw CV31 162 E5
Slade Rd Birmingham B23 56 D3
Halesowen B63 82 C6
Sutton Coldfield B75 32 E3
Wolverhampton WV10 11 C3
Sladefield Inf Sch B8 68 A5
Sladefield Rd B8 68 A5
Sladen CE Mid Sch The DY10 116 F7
Sladepool Farm Rd B14 105 A2
Slaithwaite Rd B71 53 E4
Slaney Rd WS2 42 B6
Slatch House Rd B67 64 E2
Slateley Cres B90 126 F6
Slater Rd B93 127 F4
Slater St Bilston WV14 40 E3
Darlaston WS10 41 D6
Tipton, Dudley Port DY4 52 A4
Tipton, Great Bridge DY4 52 D5
Willenhall WV13 27 C3
Slaters La WS2 42 B7
Slaters Pl WS2 42 B7
Sleaford Gr B28 106 A7
Sleaford Rd B28 106 B7
Sleath's Yd CV12 78 B3
Sledmere Cl CV2 96 B3
Sledmere Prim Sch DY2 62 D6
Sledmore Rd DY2 62 E7
Sleets Yd CV12 78 A2
Slideslow Ave B60 137 B2
Slideslow Dr B60 137 B3
Slieve The B20 55 A3
Slim Ave WV14 40 E3
Slim Rd WS2 27 E2
Slimbridge Cl
Redditch B97 158 E5
2 Solihull B90 127 A6
Slims Gate B63 83 A4
Sling The Dudley DY2 62 C6
Kidderminster DY10 116 E6
Slingfield Mills DY10 116 D6
Slingfield Rd B31 103 C1
Slingsby B77 35 C7
Slingsby Cl CV11 73 F2
Slitting Mill Cl B21 65 C8
Sloane Ho 7 B1 66 C3
Sloane St B1 66 C3
Slough The B97,B80 159 B4
Small Cl B67 64 D5
Small Heath Bridge B10, B11 87 B8
Small Heath Bsns Pk B10 87 F7
Small Heath Highway B10,B11 87 D6
Small Heath Sch
Birmingham B10 87 D7
Birmingham B10 87 D8
Small Heath Sta B10 87 D7
Small Heath Trad Est B11 87 D6
Small La B94 141 E6
Small St Walsall WS1 42 E8
West Bromwich B71 53 B5
Smallbrook La WV5 49 B7
Smallbrook Queensway B5 164 C1
Smalldale Rd B42 55 D7
Smalley Cl WS11 2 A5
Smalley Pl CV8 147 F4
Smallshire Way DY8 80 E8
Smallwood Almshouses B98 153 E3
Smallwood Arch 5 B98 153 E4
Smallwood Cl
Birmingham B24 57 D3
Sutton Coldfield B76 46 E3
Smallwood Rd WV8 10 E2
Smallwood St B98 153 E3
Smarts Ave WS14 32 A7
Smarts Rd CV12 77 F1
Smeaton Cl B18 65 E4
Smedley Crooke Pl B48 123 C2
Smeed Gr B24 57 B3
Smercote Cl CV12 77 D1
Smestow Ho B68 64 B1
Smestow Sch WV3 24 B1
Smestow St WV10 25 D4
Smethwick Galton Bridge Sta B66 64 E7
Smethwick Ho B68 64 C2
Smethwick Rolfe Street Sta B66 65 A6
Smillie Pl WS11 1 F3
Smirrells Rd B28 105 E5
Smith Ave WS10 41 D4
Smith Cl Smethwick B67 64 D3
Wolverhampton WV14 40 A1
Smith Ho WS3 14 C3
Smith Pl DY4 52 B4
Smith Rd Walsall WS2 42 C6
Wednesbury WS10 41 F1
Smith St Bedworth CV12 77 E1
Bilston WV14 40 D5
Birmingham B19 66 C5
Coventry CV6 113 F5
Dudley DY2 62 D7
2 Royal Leamington Spa CV31 161 F7
Warwick CV34 160 F7
Wood End CV9 36 C1
Smith's Cl WS7 6 D6
Smithfield Rd WS3 14 D1
Smithfield Rise WS13 9 C8
Smithfields 3 DY8 81 A5
Smithford Way CV1 165 B3
Smithmoor Cres B71 53 F8
Smiths Cl B32 84 B1
Smiths La B93 127 E7
Smiths Way B46 59 A3
Smiths Wood Sch B36 70 A6
Smithy Dr WS3 15 A4
Smithy La
Aston Flamville LE9 76 C8
Dudley DY5 50 B1
Lichfield WS13 3 A1
Tamworth B77 35 F7
Smithy The B26 89 C6
Smorrall La CV12 77 C2
Smout Cres WV14 39 F2
Smythe Gr CV34 155 E1
Snake La B48 139 A6
Snake Terr B48 139 A6
Snakes Lake La B61 136 D6
Snapdragon Dr WS5 43 A3
Snape Rd Coventry CV2 114 F5
Wolverhampton WV11 13 B1
Sneyd Com Sch WS3 13 E2
Sneyd Hall Cl WS3 28 A8
Sneyd Hall Rd WS3 14 A1
Sneyd Ho WS3 13 F1
Sneyd La Walsall WS3 13 F1
Willenhall WV11 13 C1
Snipe Cl WV10 12 B7
Snow Hill WV2 163 C2
Snow Hill Queensway B4 164 C3
Snow Hill Sta B3 164 B3
Snowberry Dr DY5 50 C1
Snowberry Gdns 6 B27 88 C5
Snowdon Cl CV10 72 B3
Snowdon Gr B63 82 D1
Snowdon Rd Cannock WS11 1 E6
Stourbridge DY8 81 B6
Snowdon Rise DY3 50 D6
Snowdon Way
Willenhall WV12 13 B1
Wolverhampton WV10 25 B6
Snowdrop Cl
Bedworth CV12 77 E1
Clayhanger WS8 15 D6
Snowford Cl B90 105 F1
Snows Drive Hill B90 126 D5
Snowshill Cl
Nuneaton CV11 78 F8
Redditch B98 154 B6
Snowshill Gdns DY1 50 F4
Soar Way LE10 75 A8
Soberton Cl WV11 26 F7
Soden Cl CV3 134 D6
Soden's Ave CV8 135 A1
Soho Ave B18 66 A7
Soho Cl B66 65 C6
Soho Hill B19 66 B7
Soho Ho B66 65 C6
Soho House Mus* B18 66 A7
Soho Rd B21 65 F8
Soho St B66 65 C6
Soho Way B66 65 B6
Soho, Benson Road Sta B18 65 F6
Solari Cl DY4 52 C8
Solent Cl WV9 10 F2
Solent Ct B73 46 B5
Solent Dr CV2 96 F1
Solihull By-Pass B91 107 E4
Solihull Coll B91 107 A3
Solihull Coll (Chelmsley Campus) B37 70 C4
Solihull Hospl B91 107 C4
Solihull La B28 106 A6
Solihull Parkway B37 90 E8
Solihull Parkway Hospl B91 107 E5
Solihull Rd
Birmingham B11 87 D3
Hampton-in-A B92 108 E6
Solihull B90 106 D3
Solihull Ret Pk B90 126 C8
Solihull Sch B91 107 D4
Solihull Sixth Form Coll B91 107 D2
Solihull Sta B91 107 A4
Solly Gr DY4 52 D7
Solva Cl WV1 26 B1
Solway Cl
Royal Leamington Spa CV31 162 C6
Tamworth B79 21 A7
Wednesbury WS10 42 C4
Somerby Dr B91 127 A8
Somercotes Rd B42 55 D8
Somerdale Rd B31 103 C4
Somerfield Cl WS4 15 C1
Somerfield Rd WS3 28 C7
Somerford Cl WS6 4 E1
Somerford Gdns WV10 11 E2
Somerford Pl WV13 26 F1
Somerford Rd B29 102 F8
Somerford Way WV14 51 B8
Somerland Rd B26 69 A1
Somerleyton Ave DY10 117 A5
Somerleyton Ct 3 DY10 117 A5
Somerly Cl CV3 134 F8
Somers Pl 4 CV32 161 E8
Somers Rd Halesowen B62 83 C5
Keresley CV7 95 A6
Meriden CV7 91 F1
Walsall WS2 42 A7
Somerset Cl B78 21 A1
Somerset Cres WS10 42 D4
Somerset Dr
Birmingham B31 122 F7
Nuneaton CV10 72 E4
Stourbridge DY8 80 D7
Somerset Ho B33 69 A2
Somerset Pl WS11 1 F3
Somerset Rd
Birmingham, Edgbaston B15 85 F5
Birmingham, Erdington B23 56 F6
Birmingham, Handsworth B20 54 F2
Coventry CV1 113 C5
Walsall WS4 29 A4
West Bromwich B71 53 D6
Willenhall WV13 27 D2
Somerton Dr
Birmingham, Erdington B23 57 A6
Birmingham, Marston Green B37 90 B7
Somerville Ct
2 Sutton Coldfield B73 46 A2
Tamworth B79 20 D6
Somerville Ho B37 70 D3
Somerville Prim Sch B10 87 D8
Somerville Rd
Birmingham B10 87 E8
Sutton Coldfield B73 46 A3
Somery Rd
Birmingham B29 85 A2
Dudley DY1 51 C3
Sommerfield Rd B32 84 D3
Sommerville Dr B73 46 A4
Sommerville Rd CV2 114 C4
Sonata Rd B60 137 C1
Sonning Dr WV9 10 F2
Sopwith Croft B35 58 A2
Sorbus B77 22 B4
Sorrel B77 22 B5
Sorrel Cl Coventry CV4 131 E8
Featherstone WV10 12 B7
Tipton B69 52 B2
Sorrel Dr Birmingham B27 88 B2
Walsall WS5 43 A3
Sorrel Gr B24 57 D3
Sorrel Ho B24 57 D3
Sorrell Pl CV10 78 D8
Sorrell Rd CV10 78 D8
Sorrell Wlk DY5 81 B6
Soudan B97 153 D2
Souters Ho B32 102 D8
South Ave Coventry CV2 114 A2
Stourbridge DY8 80 F4
Wolverhampton WV11 26 C5
South Bank Rd B64 82 E8
South Birmingham Coll (Digbeth Ctr for Arts &Digital Media) B5 66 F1
South Birmingham Coll (Hall Green Campus) B28 105 E8
South Birmingham Coll (Tech Ctr) B28 87 F1
South Birmingham Coll (The Health & Social Care Ctr) B28 106 B6
South Bromsgrove Com High Sch (Tech Coll) B60 150 F8
South Car Park Rd B40 90 E3
South Cl WS11 4 C8
South Cres
Bromsgrove B60 137 A1
Featherstone WV10 12 C6
South Dene B67 64 F5

South Dr Birmingham B5 . . .86 C4
Coleshill B46 . . . . .70 E6
Sutton Coldfield B75 . . . . . .46 C6
South East Quadrant 8
B98 .153 E4
South Gdns DY9 . . . . .99 A4
South Gn WV4 . . . . .38 D5
South Gr
Birmingham, Aston B6 . . . . .66 D8
Birmingham, Erdington B23 .56 F5
Birmingham, Lozells B19 . . .66 B8
South Holme B9 . . . . .67 C2
South Moons Moat End Est
B98 . . . . .154 D4
South Oval DY3 . . . . .50 E5
South Par B72 . . . . .46 C4
South Park Mews DY5 . . . . .61 C2
South Range 4 B11 . . . . . .87 B6
South Rd
Birmingham, Erdington B23 .56 F4
Birmingham, Hockley B18 . .66 A6
Birmingham, King's Heath
B14 . . . . .104 E8
Birmingham, Northfield
B31 . . . . .102 F2
Birmingham, Sparkbrook
B11 .87 B7
Bromsgrove B60 . . . . .151 B7
Hagley DY9 . . . . .99 A4
Smethwick B67 . . . . .64 E4
Stourbridge DY8 . . . . .80 E4
Tipton DY4 . . . . .52 B8
Wolverhampton WV4 . . . . . .39 F4
South Ridge CV5 . . . . .112 B4
South Road Ave B18 . . . . . .66 A6
South Roundhay B33 . . . . . .69 A3
South St Birmingham B17 . .85 D5
Brierley Hill DY5 . . . . .61 C2
Coventry CV1 . . . . .113 E3
Kidderminster DY10 . . . . . .116 F6
Redditch B98 . . . . .153 E3
Walsall WS1 . . . . .42 D8
Willenhall WV13 . . . . .26 F1
Wolverhampton WV10 . . . . .25 C6
South Staffordshire Bsns Pk
WS11 . . . . .4 E4
South Street Gdns WS1 . . .42 D8
South Terr CV31 . . . . .162 B3
South View
Birmingham B43 . . . . .54 E7
Warwick CV35 . . . . .160 A6
South View Cl
Codsall WV8 . . . . .10 B2
Featherstone WV10 . . . . . . .12 B6
South View Rd
Royal Leamington Spa
CV32 . . . . .157 C5
Sedgley DY3 . . . . .50 C8
South Way B40 . . . . .90 F3
South Wlk B31 . . . . .103 C1
Southacre Ave B5 . . . . .86 E8
Southall Cres WV14 . . . . . . .40 C1
Southall Rd WV11 . . . . .27 A8
Southall's La DY1 . . . . .51 B1
Southam Cl
Birmingham B28 . . . . .105 E8
Coventry CV4 . . . . .131 E7
Southam Dr B73 . . . . .46 B1
Southam Rd
Birmingham B28 . . . . .105 E8
Radford Semele CV31 . . . .162 E6
Southampton St WV1 . . . . .163 C4
Southbank Ct CV8 . . . . .147 F4
Southbank Rd
Blackheath B64 . . . . .82 F8
Coventry CV6 . . . . .112 E5
Kenilworth CV8 . . . . .147 F4
Southbank View DY6 . . . . . .60 E4
Southborough Terr 1
CV31 . . . . .162 A6
Southbourne Ave
Birmingham, Castle Bromwich
B36 .69 B8
Birmingham, Edgbaston
B16 .65 D3
Southfield Cl
Aldridge WS9 . . . . .30 A6
Nuneaton CV10 . . . . .73 D5
Southfield Dr
Birmingham B28 . . . . .106 A5
Kenilworth CV8 . . . . .148 A6
Southfield Gr WV3 . . . . .38 C7
Southfield Rd
Birmingham B16 . . . . .65 D3
Hinckley LE10 . . . . .75 E7
Wednesfield WV11 . . . . .26 F5
Southfield Way WS6 . . . . . . .4 F2
Southfields CV32 . . . . .157 A3

Southfields Prim Sch
CV1 . . . . .113 E3
Southfields Rd WV1 . . . . . .106 F1
Southgate Blackheath B64 .82 D8
Cannock WS11 . . . . .4 B7
Wolverhampton WV1 . . . . .163 A3
Southgate Cl DY11 . . . . . . .116 A4
Southgate End WS1 . . . . . . .4 B7
Southgate Rd B44 . . . . .44 E2
Southlands 8 B31 . . . . . . .162 B7
Southlands Rd B13 . . . . .87 A1
Southlea Ave CV31 . . . . . . .161 E6
Southlea Cl CV31 . . . . .161 E6
Southleigh Ave CV5 . . . . . .132 F7
Southmead Cres B98 . . . . .153 F3
Southmead Dr B60 . . . . . . .137 B6
Southmead Gdns B80 . . . .159 E3
Southminster Dr B14 . . . . .104 C3
Southorn Ct CV31 . . . . .134 B5
Southside Bsns Ctr B12 . . . .87 A5
Southview Ridge DY5 . . . . . .81 D7
Southville Bglws For Old
People B14 . . . . .105 B4
Southwark Cl WS13 . . . . .3 C3
Southway CV31 . . . . .162 A5
Southway Ct DY6 . . . . .60 F4
Southwick Pl WV14 . . . . . . .40 D7
Southwick Rd B62 . . . . .83 D8
Southwold Ave B30 . . . . . . .104 C3
Southwood Ave B34 . . . . . . .69 B7
Southwood Cl DY6 . . . . .60 A7
Southwood Covert B14 . . . .104 C2
Sovereign Cl CV8 . . . . .147 F1
Sovereign Ct 1 B1 . . . . . . .66 C3
Sovereign Dr DY1 . . . . .50 E2
Sovereign Hts B31 . . . . . . .102 C1
Sovereign Rd
Birmingham B30 . . . . .104 A4
Coventry CV5 . . . . .112 A2
Sovereign Row CV5 . . . . . .113 A2
Sovereign Way B13 . . . . . . .86 F4
Sovereign Wlk 7 WS1 . . . .28 F2
Sovereign Works DY1 . . . . . .50 E4
Sowe Valley Prim Sch
CV3 . . . . .134 D7
Sowerby March B24 . . . . . . .57 D4
Sowers Cl WV12 . . . . .27 D5
Sowers Ct B75 . . . . .32 D4
Sowers Gdns WV12 . . . . . . .27 D5
Spa Cl LE10 . . . . .71 E1
Spa Gr B80 . . . . .104 C8
Spa La LE10 . . . . .71 E1
Spa View CV31 . . . . .162 B4
Spadesbourne Rd B60 . . . .137 C6
Spark St B11 . . . . .87 A7
Sparkbrook St CV1 . . . . . . .113 F3
Sparkbrook Workshops
CV1 . . . . .113 F3
Sparrey Dr B30 . . . . .104 A8
Sparrow Cl WS10 . . . . .42 B5
Sparrow Cock La B93 . . . . .129 C1
Spartan Cl CV34 . . . . .161 E4
Spartan Ind Ctr B70 . . . . . . .52 E6
Speakers Cl B69 . . . . .63 B7
Spearhill WS14 . . . . .9 D8
Speed Rd DY4 . . . . .51 E7
Speedway La CV8 . . . . .135 F7
Speedwell Cl
Aldridge WS9 . . . . .30 A5
Birmingham B25 . . . . .88 A6
Wednesfield WV11 . . . . .26 C5
Speedwell Dr CV7 . . . . .130 A6
Speedwell Gdns
Brierley Hill DY5 . . . . .81 B6
Featherstone WV10 . . . . . . .12 B8
Speedwell Rd B38 . . . . .104 A1
Speedwell Rd
Birmingham, Balsall Heath
B5 . . . . .86 D6
Birmingham, Tyseley B25 . .88 A6
Speedwell Trad Est B11 . . . .88 A6
Speedy Cl WS11 . . . . .1 E5
Spencer Ave
Coventry CV5 . . . . .113 A1
Dudley WV14 . . . . .51 C8
Spencer Cl Dudley DY3 . . . .50 A4
Tipton B69 . . . . .63 B8
4 West Bromwich B71 . . . .53 F8
Spencer Dr WS7 . . . . .6 E8
Spencer Rd
Coventry CV5 . . . . .165 A1
Lichfield WS14 . . . . .9 B6
Spencer St
Birmingham B18 . . . . .66 C4
Hinckley LE10 . . . . .71 D1
Kidderminster DY11 . . . . . .116 C4
Spencer Yd CV31 . . . . .161 F7
Spencer's La CV7 . . . . .110 E1
Spennells Fst Sch DY10 . .117 A2
Spennells Valley Rd
DY10 . . . . .117 A3
Spenser Ave B79 . . . . .23 F4
Spenser Cl B79 . . . . .21 A6
Spenser Wlk B61 . . . . .136 E3
Spernal Ash B80 . . . . .159 F1
Spernal La B80 . . . . .159 F1
Spernall Gr B29 . . . . .85 A1
Spetchley Cl B97 . . . . .158 C6
Spey Cl B5 . . . . .86 D6
Spiers Cl Dudley DY3 . . . . . .50 A4
Spiceland Rd B31 . . . . .102 F6
Spiers Cl B93 . . . . .128 A6
Spies Cl B62 . . . . .83 F5
Spies La B62 . . . . .83 F5
Spills Mdw DY3 . . . . .50 E4
Spilsbury Croft B91 . . . . . .156 E2

Spilsbury Croft B91 . . . . . .127 A8
Spindle La B90 . . . . .126 A6
Spindle St CV1 . . . . .113 D6
Spindles The LE10 . . . . .75 F5
Spindlewood Cl 1 WS11 . . .2 D1
Spinners End Dr B64 . . . . . .62 D1
Spinners End Ind Est
B64 .62 D8
Spinney Cl
Binley Woods CV3 . . . . .135 E7
Birchmoor B78 . . . . .36 F8
Birmingham B31 . . . . .103 B3
Kidderminster DY11 . . . . . .116 A2
Norton Canes WS11 . . . . .5 F5
Stourbridge DY8 . . . . .60 C3
Walsall WS3 . . . . .15 A2
Spinney Dr B90 . . . . .126 D4
Spinney Farm Rd WS11 . . . .4 B7
Spinney Hill CV34 . . . . .156 A1
Spinney La CV10 . . . . .72 C4
Spinney Mews B97 . . . . . . .153 C1
Spinney Rd LE10 . . . . .75 C6
Spinney The
Birmingham, Brown's Green
B20 .54 E4
Birmingham, Edgbaston B15 .85 E5
Coventry CV4 . . . . .132 D3
Dudley DY3 . . . . .50 C2
Little Aston B74 . . . . .31 B6
Royal Leamington Spa
CV32 . . . . .156 D1
Solihull B91 . . . . .127 C8
Wolverhampton WV3 . . . . . .24 D1
Wythall B47 . . . . .125 A6
Spinning School La B79 . . .21 B5
Spiral Cl B62 . . . . .83 E8
Spiral Ct Birmingham B24 . .56 E2
Dudley DY1 . . . . .50 D3
Stourbridge DY8 . . . . .81 A4
Sutton Coldfield B76 . . . . . .46 F3
Wednesfield WV11 . . . . .26 E7
Spiral Gn B24 . . . . .57 C4
Spire View B61 . . . . .136 F3
Spirehouse La B60 . . . . . . .137 E5
Spires The Lichfield WS14 . . .9 B6
Nuneaton CV10 . . . . .72 C4
Spitfire Pk B24 . . . . .57 C2
Spitfire Rd B24 . . . . .57 D2
Spitfire Way B35 . . . . .58 A2
Splash La WS12 . . . . .2 C3
Spode Pl WS11 . . . . .2 B2
Spon End CV1,CV5 . . . . . . .113 A3
Spon Gate Ho CV1 . . . . . . .113 A2
Spon Gate Prim Sch
CV1 . . . . .113 A3
Spon La B70 . . . . .53 D1
Spon La S Oldbury B66 . . . .64 D8
Spon Lane Ind Est B66 . . . . .64 D8
Spon Lane Trad Est B70 . . . .64 D8
Spon St CV1 . . . . .165 A3
Spondon Rd WV11 . . . . .26 E8
Spoon Dr B38 . . . . .103 D2
Spooner Croft B5 . . . . .86 E8
Spooners Cl B92 . . . . .107 F7
Spout La Walsall WS1 . . . . . .42 E7
Walsall WS1 . . . . .42 E8
Spouthouse La B43 . . . . .54 F7
Spreadbury Cl B17 . . . . .84 F8
Sprig Croft B36 . . . . .68 C8
Spring Ave B65 . . . . .63 D2
Spring Cl
6 Coventry CV1 . . . . .113 E3
Hagley DY9 . . . . .98 F4
Solihull B91 . . . . .106 F3
Walsall WS4 . . . . .15 C2
Spring Coppice Dr B93 . . . .128 A3
Spring Cres B64 . . . . .82 F7
Spring Ct Walsall WS1 . . . . .43 A8
West Bromwich B70 . . . . . . .53 D2
Spring Gdns
Birmingham B21 . . . . .65 F7
2 Dudley DY2 . . . . .62 D8
Smethwick B66 . . . . .65 A5
Spring Gr B19 . . . . .66 B6
Spring Grove Cres B116 B3 . . . .116 B3
Spring Grove Gdns B18 . . . .65 F6
Spring Grove Rd DY11 . . . .116 B3
Spring Head WS10 . . . . .41 F2
Spring Hill
Birmingham, Erdington B24 .56 F3
Birmingham, Hockley B18 . .66 A4
Spring Hill Ind Est B18 . . . .66 A4
Spring Hill Pas B18 . . . . . . .66 A3
Spring Hill Rd CV10 . . . . . . .72 C3
Spring La Birmingham B24 . .57 A3
Hockley Heath B94 . . . . . . .143 B5
Radford Semele CV31 . . . .162 E5
Romsley B62 . . . . .100 D4
Walsall WS4 . . . . .15 C2
Willenhall WV12 . . . . .27 D5
Spring Mdw
3 Blackheath B64 . . . . .62 F1
Cheslyn Hay WS6 . . . . .4 D1
Halesowen B63 . . . . .82 F2
Tipton DY4 . . . . .52 B5
Spring Meadow Rd DY2 . . .62 C2
Spring Meadows WV8 . . . . .10 B4
Spring Parklands DY1 . . . . . .61 C2
Spring Pool CV34 . . . . .160 E7
Spring Rd Barnacle CV7 . . . .97 B6
Birmingham, Balsall Heath
B15 .86 D7
Birmingham, Tyseley B11 . .87 F3
Coventry CV6 . . . . .95 F1
Dudley DY2 . . . . .62 D6

Spring Rd continued
Lichfield WS13 . . . . .3 D2
Smethwick B66 . . . . .64 D8
Walsall WS1 . . . . .15 D1
Wolverhampton WV4 . . . . . .40 A4
Spring Road Ind Est WV4 . .40 A4
Spring Rd Sta B28 . . . . .88 A2
Spring St Birmingham B15 . .86 D8
Cannock WS11 . . . . .4 E8
Halesowen B63 . . . . .82 D6
Stourbridge DY9 . . . . .81 E4
Tipton DY4 . . . . .52 B8
Spring Terr 1 WS2 . . . . .6 E5
Spring Vale CV14 . . . . .40 A1
Spring Vale Ave WS3 . . . . . .15 A4
Spring Vale Ind Pk WV14 . .40 C5
Spring Vale Island WV14 . .40 C4
Spring Vale Prim Sch
WV4 .39 E4
Spring Vale Rd B65 . . . . .63 A5
Spring Wlk
Halesowen B63 . . . . .82 D1
Oldbury B69 . . . . .64 A4
Walsall WS2 . . . . .28 B3
Springacre Croft B17 . . . . . .85 B6
Springbank B9 . . . . .68 A3
Springbank Rd B15 . . . . .86 D7
Springbrook Cl B36 . . . . . . .58 D1
Springbrook La B94 . . . . . .142 A7
Springcroft Rd B11 . . . . .87 F2
Springdale Ct CV11 . . . . . . .73 D3
Springdale Jun Sch WV4 . .38 D5
Springfield B23 . . . . .56 E3
Springfield Ave
6 Birmingham B12 . . . . . . .87 A6
Bromsgrove B60 . . . . .151 A8
Sedgley DY3 . . . . .39 E1
Stourbridge DY9 . . . . .81 E4
Springfield Cl B65 . . . . .63 A5
Springfield Cres
Bedworth CV12 . . . . .78 B2
Dudley DY2 . . . . .62 F8
Solihull B92 . . . . .89 C3
Sutton Coldfield B76 . . . . . .47 A4
West Bromwich B70 . . . . . . .53 E1
Springfield Ct
Birmingham B28 . . . . .105 F8
Sutton Coldfield B75 . . . . . .47 C5
Wolverhampton WV10 . . . . .11 D4
Springfield Dr B62 . . . . .83 D7
Springfield Gn DY3 . . . . .39 E1
Springfield Gr DY3 . . . . .39 D1
Springfield House Specl Sch
B93 . . . . .129 A5
Springfield Ind Est B69 . . . .64 B7
Springfield Jun Sch B13 . . .87 D2
Springfield La
Kidderminster DY10 . . . . . .116 F8
Wolverhampton WV10 . . . . .11 D4
Springfield Mill Ct WS10 . . .41 E6
Springfield Pk LE10 . . . . . . .71 A3
Springfield Pl CV1 . . . . .165 C4
Springfield Prim Sch
B65 .63 A4
Springfield Rd
Bilston WV14 . . . . .40 E7
Birmingham, Castle Bromwich
B36 .69 D8
Birmingham, King's Heath
B14 . . . . .104 F8
Birmingham, Moseley B13 . .87 D2
Coventry CV1 . . . . .165 C4
Halesowen B62 . . . . .83 D7
Hinckley LE10 . . . . .71 A3
Nuneaton CV11 . . . . .73 E2
Sutton Coldfield B75,B76 . .47 A4
Tamworth B77 . . . . .35 D8
Wolverhampton WV10 . . . . .25 E3
Springfield Rise 8 DY2 . . .62 D8
Springfield St B18 . . . . .66 A3
Springfield Terr B65 . . . . . . .62 F5
Springfields Coleshill B46 . .70 F5
Walsall WS4 . . . . .29 C6
Springfields Rd DY5 . . . . . . .61 B2
Springhill CV10 . . . . .72 A8
Springhill Ave WV4 . . . . . . .38 C4
Springhill Cl Walsall WS4 . .15 D1
Willenhall WV12 . . . . .27 D7
Springhill Gdns B97 . . . . . .152 F2
Springhill Gr WV4 . . . . .38 C4
Springhill La WV4 . . . . .38 B4
Springhill Pk WV4 . . . . .38 B3
Springhill Prim Sch WS7 . . .7 B6
Springhill Rd
Brownhills WS8 . . . . .16 A2
Burntwood WS7 . . . . .7 A6
Walsall WS1 . . . . .28 F1
Wednesfield WV11 . . . . .26 F3
Springmeadow Rd B19 . . . .66 D8
Springs Ave B61 . . . . .121 A1
Springs The B64 . . . . .63 A1
Springside B98 . . . . .159 C8
Springslade B32 . . . . .84 F5
Springslade Dr B24 . . . . . . .57 C4
Springthorpe B24 . . . . .57 D5
Springthorpe Rd
Birmingham, Pype Hayes
B24 .57 D5
Birmingham, Yabarn B24 . . .57 D3
Springvale Ave
Bilston WV14 . . . . .40 B4
Walsall WS5 . . . . .43 C2
Springvale Bsns Pk
WV14 . . . . .40 B4
Springvale Prim Sch
WS11 .4 E8

Springvale Rd B97 . . . . .152 F2
Springvale St WV13 . . . . . . .27 B3
Springvale Way WV14 . . . . .40 C4
Springwell Rd CV31 . . . . . .162 D6
Sproat Ave WS10 . . . . .41 C5
Spruce B77 . . . . .22 B4
Spruce Gr Birmingham B24 .57 B2
4 Royal Leamington Spa
CV31 . . . . .161 F5
Spruce Rd
5 Coventry CV2 . . . . .96 B2
Walsall WS5 . . . . .43 B3
Spruce Way WV3 . . . . .24 D1
Spruces The CV9 . . . . .98 F4
Spur Tree Ave WV3 . . . . .24 A1
Squadron Cl B35 . . . . .58 C4
Square Cl B32 . . . . .84 C3
Square The Aldridge WS9 . .30 B6
Birmingham B31 . . . . .85 B7
Alvechurch B48 . . . . .139 B6
3 Birmingham, Harborne
B17 .85 C5
2 Birmingham, Ladywood
B15 .66 B1
Brierley Hill DY2 . . . . .61 F6
Coventry CV2 . . . . .115 A7
Fazeley B78 . . . . .35 A8
Kenilworth CV8 . . . . .147 F4
Nuneaton CV11 . . . . .73 E2
Solihull B91 . . . . .107 C3
Tipton DY4 . . . . .52 D7
Willenhall WV12 . . . . .27 D8
Wolverhampton WV2 . . . . .163 C1
Squires Croft
Coventry CV2 . . . . .96 F1
Sutton Coldfield B76 . . . . . .47 A2
Squires Ct DY5 . . . . .81 C8
Squires Gate WS7 . . . . .7 C8
Squires Gate Wlk B35 . . . . .58 A3
Squires Gr LE10 . . . . .75 F6
Squires La CV9 . . . . .132 D6
Squirrel Cl B32 . . . . .84 C4
Squirrel Hollow B76 . . . . . . .47 A2
Squirrel Wlk
Little Aston B74 . . . . .31 C5
Wolverhampton WV4 . . . . . .39 A5
Squirrels Hollow B68 . . . . . .84 D7
Squirrels The WV11 . . . . .9 C7
Sring La CV8 . . . . .148 A5
Stable Croft B71 . . . . .53 F7
Stable Ct DY3 . . . . .50 E6
Stable Way B60 . . . . .150 E6
Stable Wlk CV11 . . . . .73 F2
Stableford Cl
Birmingham B32 . . . . .84 F3
Redditch B97 . . . . .158 D7
Stables The
Berkswell CV7 . . . . .110 C4
Birmingham B29 . . . . .86 A2
Hinckley LE10 . . . . .75 D5
Royal Leamington Spa
CV32 . . . . .156 C1
Stacey Cl B64 . . . . .62 E1
Stacey Dr B13 . . . . .105 A5
Stacey Grange Gdns
B45 .122 A6
Stackhouse Cl WS9 . . . . . . .16 A4
Stackhouse Dr WS3 . . . . . . .15 A4
Stadium Cl Coventry CV6 . . .95 D2
Kidderminster DY10 . . . . . .116 F4
Willenhall WV13 . . . . .27 B3
Stafford Cl
Bulkington CV12 . . . . .79 C2
Walsall WS3 . . . . .14 B2
Stafford Ct
Birmingham B43 . . . . .54 E7
Wolverhampton WV10 . . . . .11 C5
Stafford Dr B71 . . . . .53 B6
Stafford Ho B33 . . . . .69 E2
Stafford La WS12 . . . . .2 B5
Stafford Rd
Birmingham B21 . . . . .65 F8
Cannock WS11 . . . . .11 D4
Coven Heath WV10 . . . . . . .11 C6
Darlaston WS10 . . . . .41 C6
Huntington WS11,WS12 . . . .1 C5
Walsall WS3 . . . . .14 B4
Stafford St Bilston WV14 . . .40 D5
Birmingham B5 . . . . .66 F3
Cannock WS12 . . . . .2 E1
Dudley DY1 . . . . .51 B1
Walsall WS2 . . . . .28 E3
Wednesbury WS10 . . . . .41 F2
Willenhall WV13 . . . . .27 A2
Wolverhampton WV1 . . . . .163 C4
Stafford Way B43 . . . . .54 E7
Staffordshire Pool Cl 2
B6 . . . . .55 F1
Staffordshire Univ WS13 . . .9 B7
Stag Cres
Norton Canes WS11 . . . . .6 A6
Walsall WS3 . . . . .28 E6
Stag Dr WS12 . . . . .1 C6
Stag Hill Rd WS3 . . . . .28 E7
Stag Ind Est WV14 . . . . .40 F4
Stag Wlk B76 . . . . .57 D7
Stagborough Way WS12 . . . .2 B4
Staines Ct CV11 . . . . .73 F7
Stainforth Cl CV11 . . . . .73 F7
Stainsby Ave B19 . . . . .66 C5
Stainsby Croft B90 . . . . . . .127 B5
Staircase La CV5 . . . . .112 C7

Stakenbridge La DY10 .....98 D4
Staley Croft WS12 ....1 C4
Stalling's La DY6 ....60 D8
Stallings La Dudley DY6 ...50 A1
  Kingswinford DY6 ....49 F1
Stambermill Cl DY9 ....81 D5
Stambermill Ho DY9 ....81 E5
Stamford Ave CV3 ....133 C6
Stamford Cres WS7 ....7 A8
Stamford Croft B91 ....107 B2
Stamford Gdns CV32 ......156 E1
Stamford Gr B20 ....55 C1

Stamford Rd
  Birmingham B20 ....55 C1
  Brierley Hill DY5 ....81 C6
Stamford St DY8 ....80 F7
Stamford Way WS9 ....16 C1
Stanbrook Rd B90 ....127 A5
Stanbury Ave WS10 ....41 B6
Stanbury Rd B14 ....105 B4
Stancroft Gr B26 ....89 A8
Stand St CV34 ....160 D5
Standard Ave CV4 ....112 B1
Standard Way B24 ....67 F8
Standbridge Way DY4 ......52 A5
Standedge B77 ....36 B7
Standhills Rd DY6 ....60 E6
Standish Cl CV2 ....114 E2
Standlake Ave B36 ....68 D7
Standlake Ho B31 ....102 E5
Standlake Mews 14
  CV31 ....162 C6
Standleys Twr B23 ....57 A6
Stanfield Rd
  Birmingham, Pheasey B43 ...44 D5
  Birmingham, Quinton B32 ...84 E6
Stanford Ave B42 ....55 A7
Stanford Cl B97 ....158 B6
Stanford Gr B63 ....82 C1

Stanford Rd
  Blackheath B65 ....63 B4
  Wolverhampton WV2 ....163 B1
Stanford Way B8 B69 ......81 D8
Stanhoe Cl DY5 ....81 D8
Stanhope Ho B79 ....21 A4
Stanhope Rd B67 ....64 F3
Stanhope St
  Birmingham B12 ....86 F7
  Dudley DY2 ....62 E4
  Wolverhampton WV3 ....163 A2
Stanhope Way B43 ....44 E4
Stanhurst Way B71 ....43 A2
Stanier Ave CV1 ....113 B4
Stanier Cl WS4 ....29 B7
Stanier Gr B20 ....55 B2
Staniforth St B4 ....164 C4
Stanklyn La DY10 ....117 C1

Stanley Ave
  Birmingham B32 ....84 E7
  Solihull B90 ....106 B4
  Sutton Coldfield B75 ....46 F4
Stanley Cl
  Birmingham B28 ....106 A5
  Redditch B98 ....154 A5
  Wednesfield WV11 ....26 F8
Stanley Ct
  Birmingham B13 ....87 B2
  Perton WV6 ....23 E4
  Royal Leamington Spa
  CV31 ....162 C2
Stanley Gr 2 B11 ....87 B6
Stanley Pl Bilston WV14 ....40 A5
  Birmingham B13 ....86 F3
  Walsall WS4 ....29 B6

Stanley Rd
  Birmingham, King's Heath
  B14 ....104 D7
  Birmingham, Nechells B7 ....67 C7
  Cannock WS12 ....2 A6
  Coventry CV5 ....132 F8
  Darlaston WS10 ....41 D5
  Hinckley LE10 ....71 C2
  Nuneaton CV11 ....73 A4
  Oldbury B68 ....84 C7
  Stourbridge DY8 ....80 F3
  Walsall WS4 ....29 B6
  West Bromwich B71 ....53 E7
  Wolverhampton WV10 ....11 D1
Stanley St WS3 ....14 D1
Stanmore Gr B62 ....84 A3
Stanmore Rd B16 ....65 C1
Stansbury Ho 3 WS2 ....42 C8
Stansfield Gr CV8 ....148 D4
Stanton Ave Dudley DY1 ....51 A6
  Sedgley DY1 ....50 F6
Stanton Bridge Prim Sch
  CV6 ....113 F6

Stanton Gr
  Birmingham B26 ....88 F8
  Solihull B90 ....106 A4
  Tipton DY4 ....52 A5
Stanton Ho 2 B71 ....42 F1

Stanton Rd
  Birmingham B43 ....54 D8
  Royal Leamington Spa
  CV31 ....162 C6
  Solihull B90 ....106 A4
  Wolverhampton WV1 ....25 F2
Stanville Rd CV34 ....155 D1
Stanwille Jun & Inf Sch
  B26 ....89 C6
Stanville Rd B26 ....89 C6
Stanway Gdns B71 ....53 D6
Stanway Gr B44 ....44 F3

Stanway Rd
  Coventry CV5 ....133 A8
  Solihull B90 ....106 C4
  West Bromwich B71 ....53 D6
Stanwell Gr B23 ....56 E6
Stanwick Ave B33 ....69 E3
Stapenhall Rd B90 ....127 A5
Staple Flat B60 ....137 C8
Staple Hall Rd B31 ....103 B2
Staple Lodge Rd B31 ......103 C2
Stapleford Croft B14 .....104 C2
Stapleford Gdns WS7 ....7 D6
Stapleford Gr DY8 ....60 E2
Staplehurst Rd B28 ....105 F8
Staples Cl CV12 ....79 C3

Stapleton Cl
  Redditch B98 ....154 D3
  Studley B80 ....159 D3
  Sutton Coldfield B76 ....58 B6
Stapleton Dr B37 ....70 A4
Stapleton La Barwell LE9 ...71 F8
  Hinckley CV13 ....71 A8

Stapleton Rd
  Aldridge WS9 ....29 F5
  Studley B80 ....159 D4
Stapylton Ave B17 ....85 B5
Stapylton Ct B17 ....85 B5
Star Cl Tipton DY4 ....52 C5
  Walsall WS2 ....27 F4
Star Hill B15 ....86 B8
Star Ind Pk CV2 ....114 F5
Star St Stourbridge DY9 ....81 F5
  Wolverhampton WV3 ....38 E8
Starbank Prim Sch B10 .....88 A8
Starbank Prim Sch (Annex)
  B10 ....88 A8
Starbank Rd B10 ....88 A8
Starbold Cres B93 ....128 B5
Starbold Ct B93 ....128 A6
Starcross Cl CV2 ....114 C7
Starcross Rd B27 ....88 C2
Stare Gn CV4 ....132 D5
Stareton Cl CV4 ....132 F6
Starkey Croft B37 ....70 D2
Starkie Dr B68 ....64 C4
Starley Cl CV3 ....133 A4
Starley Pk CV7 ....96 B8
Starley Rd CV1 ....165 A2
Starley Way B37 ....90 C6
Startin Cl CV7 ....95 F7
Starpoint Trad Est B11 ....87 D4
Statham Dr B16 ....65 C2
Station App
  Barnt Green B45 ....138 D8
  Dorridge B93 ....127 F2
  Kidderminster DY10 ....116 F5
  Royal Leamington Spa
  CV31 ....161 F7
  Solihull B91 ....107 A4
  Sutton Coldfield, Hill Hook
  B74 ....31 F6
  Sutton Coldfield, Maney B73,
  B74 ....46 B6

Station Ave
  Birmingham B16 ....65 D1
  Coventry CV4 ....131 D8
  Warwick CV34 ....60 F8
Station Bldgs B46 ....59 B3
Station Cl WS3 ....28 B8
Station Cotts B60 ....138 A4

Station Dr
  Blakedown DY10 ....98 C2
  Brierley Hill, Quarry Bank
  DY5 ....61 E2
  Brierley Hill, Silver End DY5 .61 B1
  Earlswood B94 ....125 D1
  Hagley DY9 ....98 A6
  Sutton Coldfield B74 ....46 B8
  Tipton DY4 ....52 B4
Station La B94 ....144 D3
Station Link Rd B26 ....90 D4
Station Pl WS3 ....28 B8
Station Rd Aldridge WS9 ....30 A5
  Alvechurch B48 ....139 A5
  Balsall Common CV7 ....130 B7
  Bilston WV14 ....40 E5
  Birmingham, Acock's Green
  B27 ....88 C3
  Birmingham, Aston B6 ....55 F1
  Birmingham, Erdington B23 ..56 F5
  Birmingham, Handsworth
  B21 ....65 C8
  Birmingham, Harborne B17 ..85 C6
  Birmingham, King's Heath
  B14 ....104 D7
  Birmingham, King's Norton
  B30 ....103 E4
  Birmingham, Marston Green
  B37 ....90 A8
  Birmingham, Northfield
  B31 ....103 A2
  Birmingham, Stechford B33 ..68 E8
  Blackheath, Haden Cross
  B64 ....83 A8
  Blackheath, Rowley Regis
  B65 ....63 D2
  Blackwell B60 ....138 A5
  Brierley Hill DY5 ....61 C3
  Burntwood WS7 ....8 C1
  Cannock WS12 ....2 C6
  Coleshill B46 ....59 F1
  Great Wyrley WS6 ....4 F4
  Hagley DY9 ....98 A6
  Hampton-in-A B92 ....109 B7
  Hinckley LE10 ....75 D8
  Kenilworth CV8 ....147 F4
  Knowle B93 ....128 B4
  Lapworth B94 ....144 D4

Station Rd continued
  Lichfield WS13 ....9 C7
  Oldbury B69 ....64 A5
  Shenstone WS14 ....77 F8
  Solihull B91 ....107 B4
  Stourbridge DY9 ....81 E6
  Studley B80 ....159 D4
  Sutton Coldfield B73 ....46 A1
  Walsall, Pelsall WS3 ....15 A3
  Walsall, Rushall WV4 ....14 A2
  Warwick CV34 ....160 F7
  Wombourne WV5 ....49 A8
  Wythall B47 ....125 E3
Station Road Ind Est B65 ..63 D2
Station Sq CV1 ....165 A1
Station St Birmingham B5 .164 B2
  Blackheath B64 ....82 C8
  Bromsgrove B60 ....136 F1
  Cheslyn Hay WS6 ....4 E3
  Darlaston WS10 ....41 E7
  Sutton Coldfield B73 ....46 C5
  Tipton DY4 ....52 B5
  Walsall WS2 ....28 E1
  Walsall, Blakenhall Heath
  WS3 ....28 B8
Station St E CV6 ....113 E7
Station St W CV6 ....113 E7
Station Street W Bsns Pk
  CV6 ....113 D7
Station Villas WS10 ....41 E6
Station Way B97 ....153 D3
Staulton Gr 4 B69 ....63 E4
Staunton Rd
  Royal Leamington Spa
  CV31 ....162 A5
  Walsall WS3 ....14 A3
Staveley Rd
  Birmingham B14 ....104 D6
  Wolverhampton WV1 ....25 C4
Staverton Cl CV5 ....112 A3
Stead Cl Tipton DY4 ....41 B1
  Walsall WS2 ....28 C5
Steadman Croft DY4 ....52 D8
Stechford Jun & Inf Sch
  B33 ....68 D2
Stechford La B8 ....68 D5
Stechford Rd B34 ....68 E5
Stechford Sta B33 ....68 D2
Stechford Trad Est B33 ....68 E3
Steel Bright Rd B66 ....65 C6
Steel Dr WV10 ....25 C8
Steel Gr B25 ....88 C7
Steel Rd B31 ....102 F2
Steel Rdbt WS10 ....41 E2
Steelhouse La
  Birmingham B4 ....164 C3
  Wolverhampton WV2 ....39 E8
Steelpark Rd B62 ....83 C7
Steelpark Way WV11 ....26 E4
Steene Gr B31 ....102 D3
Steeplefield Rd CV6 ....113 A5
Steeples The DY8 ....81 B3
Steepwood Croft B30 ......103 D4
Steere Ave B79 ....21 C7
Stella Croft B37 ....70 C2
Stella Rd B4 ....54 C8
Stella Rd DY4 ....51 F6
Stenbury Cl WV10 ....11 F4
Stencills Dr WS4 ....29 B3
Stencills Rd WS4 ....29 B4
Stennels Ave B62 ....83 E4
Stennels Cl CV6 ....112 F8
Stennels Cres B62 ....83 E4
Stephens Cl WV11 ....26 F8
Stephens Ind Est B11 ....87 F4
Stephens Rd B76 ....47 A4
Stephenson Ave
  Royal Leamington Spa
  CV32 ....156 C1
Stephenson Cl 1
  Tamworth B77 ....22 A2
Stephenson Dr
  Birmingham B37 ....70 B2
  Perton WV6 ....23 E5
Stephenson Pl B2 ....164 C2
Stephenson Rd
  Bedworth CV7 ....96 C7
  Hinckley LE10 ....74 E7
Stephenson Sq WS2 ....28 B5
Stephenson St
  Birmingham B2 ....164 B2
  Wolverhampton WV3 ....163 A2
Stephenson Way WS12 ....2 B5
Stepney Rd CV2 ....114 A4
Stepping Stone Ct WS2 ....27 F4
Stepping Stones DY8 ....81 B5
Stepping Stones Rd
  CV5 ....112 F4
Steppingstone St DY1 ......51 B1
Sterling Pk
  Brierley Hill DY5 ....61 F4
  Hinckley LE10 ....74 C8
Sterling Way CV11 ....78 E8
Sterndale Rd B42 ....55 C6
Steven Dr WV14 ....40 E1
Stevenage Wlk 2 CV2 ....115 A7
Stevens Ave B32 ....84 D2
Stevens Dr WS12 ....2 C6
Stevens Gate WV2 ....163 B1
Stevens Ho CV1 ....165 C4
Stevens Rd
  Halesowen B63 ....82 B5
  Stourbridge DY9 ....81 D2
Stevenson Ave B98 ....153 F3
Stevenson Rd
  Coventry CV6 ....113 A8
  Tamworth B79 ....21 A6

Stevenson Wlk WS14 ....9 B6
Steward St B18 ....66 A3
Stewart Cl CV4 ....112 D2
Stewart Ct DY10 ....116 F5
Stewart Rd
  Brownhills WS9 ....16 A3
  Kingswinford DY6 ....60 D4
Stewart St Nuneaton CV11 .73 C3
  Wolverhampton WV2 ....163 B1
Stewarts Rd B62 ....83 D7
Stewkins DY8 ....80 C6
Steyning Rd B26 ....88 E5
Stickley La DY3 ....50 C4
Stidfall Gr CV31 ....162 D6
Stilehouse Cres B65 ....63 C3
Stilthouse Gr B45 ....122 A7
Stirchley Com Sch B30 ....104 A6
Stirchley Trad Est B30 ....104 B6
Stirling Ave Hinckley LE10 .71 A6
  Royal Leamington Spa
  CV32 ....157 B6
Stirling Cl CV3 ....134 F8
Stirling Cres WV12 ....27 B6
Stirling Ct B16 ....65 F1
Stirling Ho B75 ....46 C5
Stirling Pl WS11 ....4 B8
Stirling Rd Bilston WV14 ...40 F2
  Birmingham B16 ....65 F1
  Dudley DY2 ....62 E6
  Solihull B90 ....126 E8
  Sutton Coldfield B73 ....45 E2
Stirrup Cl WS5 ....42 F2
Stivichall Croft CV3 ......133 B6
Stivichall Prim Sch CV3 ..133 A6
Stockbridge Cl WV6 ....23 F2
Stockdale Pl B15 ....85 D8
Stockfield Rd B25,B27 .....88 B5
Stockhay La WS7 ....7 D5
Stockhill Dr B45 ....121 F6
Stocking St DY9 ....81 F5
Stockingford Inf & Jun Sch
  CV10 ....72 D3
Stockland Ct B74 ....44 F8
Stockland Green Sch
  B23 ....56 C4
Stockland Rd B23 ....56 D4
Stockley Cres B90 ....106 D3
Stockley Rd CV6 ....96 C6
Stockmans Cl B38 ....123 E8
Stockton Cl
  Birmingham B76 ....58 C5
  Knowle B93 ....128 B4
  Walsall WS2 ....28 B4
Stockton Ct WV14 ....51 B8
Stockton Gr
  Birmingham B33 ....69 D1
  Royal Leamington Spa
  CV32 ....157 A2
Stockton Rd CV1 ....165 D4
Stockwell Ave DY5 ....81 D8
Stockwell End WV6 ....24 D6
Stockwell Head LE10 ....71 D1
Stockwell Rd
  Birmingham B21 ....54 E2
  Wolverhampton WV6 ....24 D5
Stockwell Rise B92 ....107 D7
Stoke Cross B60 ....151 E7
Stoke Gn CV3 ....114 A2
Stoke Heath Prim Sch
  CV2 ....114 A6
Stoke La B98 ....154 B7
Stoke Park Com Coll
  CV2 ....114 A4
Stoke Park Mews CV2 ......114 A3
Stoke Pound La
  Stoke Pound B60 ....151 A4
  Stoke Prior B60 ....150 F3
Stoke Prim Sch CV2 ....114 A4
Stoke Prior First Sch
  B60 ....150 C3
Stoke Rd
  Bromsgrove, Aston Fields
  B60 ....151 A7
  Bromsgrove,Charford B60 ..150 F7
  Hinckley LE10 ....71 B4
Stoke Row CV2 ....114 A4
Stoke Way B15 ....66 C1
Stoke's La WS11 ....5 F7
Stokes Ave 1 Tipton DY4 ..52 A8
  Willenhall WV13 ....40 F8
Stokes St WS3 ....28 B8
Stokesay Ave WV6 ....23 F3
Stokesay Cl
  Kidderminster DY10 ....116 E2
  Nuneaton CV11 ....73 B3
  Tipton B69 ....63 A8
Stokesay Gr B31 ....122 F8
Stokesay Ho B23 ....56 F6
Stokesay Rise DY1 ....50 E3
Stom Rd WV14 ....40 B5
Stone Ave B75 ....47 A5
Stone CE Fst Sch DY10 ...117 E2
Stone Cl B38 ....103 F2
Stone Cotts B31 ....103 A3
Stone Cross B46 ....59 B3
Stone Hill CV10 ....117 E2
Stone Mdw CV7 ....95 A6
Stone Pine Cl WS12 ....1 F8
Stone Rd B15 ....86 D8
Stone St Dudley DY1 ....51 C1
  Oldbury B69 ....64 A7
Stone Yd Birmingham B12 ..66 F1
  Blackheath B64 ....82 C8
Stonebow Ave B91 ....127 B8
Stonebridge Cres B37 .....69 F4
Stonebridge Highway
  CV3 ....133 C4

Stonebridge Rd
  Coleshill B46 ....70 F5
  Little Packington B46 ....91 A7
Stonebridge Trad Est
  CV3 ....134 B4
Stonebrook Way
  Birmingham B29 ....84 F2
  Coventry CV6 ....95 F3
Stonebury B15 ....85 D8
Stonebury Ave CV5 ....111 E4
Stonechat Cl DY10 ....117 B2
Stonechat Dr B23 ....56 C2
Stonecrop Cl
  Birmingham B38 ....123 F8
  Clayhanger WS8 ....15 D6
Stonedown Cl WV14 ....40 A3
Stonefield Cl CV2 ....115 A8
Stonefield Dr DY5 ....61 A7
Stonefield Rd WV14 ....40 D5
Stoneford Rd B90 ....106 A2
Stonehaven B77 ....21 F5
Stonehaven Dr CV3 ....133 C3
Stonehaven Gr B28 ....106 B8
Stonehenge Croft B14 ....104 D1
Stonehill Croft B90 ....126 F6
Stonehill Wlk B77 ....35 E5
Stonehouse Ave WV13 ......26 F4
Stonehouse Cl
  Redditch B97 ....153 D1
  Royal Leamington Spa
  CV32 ....157 D5
Stonehouse Cres WS10 .....42 B2
Stonehouse Dr B74 ....31 C4
Stonehouse Gr B32 ....84 D2
Stonehouse Hill B29 ....85 A3
Stonehouse La
  Birmingham B32 ....84 E2
  Birmingham B32 ....84 F3
  Coventry CV3 ....134 C4
  Hopwood B48 ....123 E2
Stonehouse Rd
  Bromsgrove B60 ....137 A1
  Sutton Coldfield B73 ....45 F3
Stonehurst Rd B43 ....44 C3
Stonelea WS9 ....30 B5
Stoneleigh Ave B71 ....53 E8
Stoneleigh Ave CV8 ....148 A6
Stoneleigh Cl
  Redditch B98 ....158 F6
  Stoneleigh CV8 ....149 B6
  Sutton Coldfield B74 ....45 B5
Stoneleigh Ct CV11 ....73 C3
Stoneleigh Deer Park Bsns
  Village CV8 ....149 D4
Stoneleigh Gdns CV11 ......73 C3
Stoneleigh Ho B32 ....84 F5
Stoneleigh Rd
  Birmingham B20 ....55 C2
  Blackdown CV32 ....157 A7
  Coventry CV4 ....132 E2
  Kenilworth CV8 ....148 A6
  Solihull B91 ....107 B6
  Stoneleigh CV8 ....149 B3
Stoneleigh Way DY3 ....50 D6
Stonepit B77 ....21 C1
Stonepits La B97 ....158 D4
Stonerwood Ave B28 ....105 E8
Stones Gn B23 ....56 E6
Stoneton Cres CV7 ....130 A6
Stoneton Gr B29 ....103 A8
Stoneway Gr CV31 ....162 D6
Stonewell Cres CV11 ....79 B8
Stoney Cl B92 ....107 E7
Stoney Croft WS11 ....1 F1
Stoney Ct CV3 ....135 A7
Stoney Hill Cl B60 ....137 A1
Stoney La
  Birmingham, Balsall Heath
  B12 ....87 A5
  Birmingham, Quinton B32 ...84 B6
  Birmingham, Stechford B25 .68 E1
  Blackwell B60 ....138 C2
  Churchill DY10 ....98 E3
  Dudley DY2 ....62 C3
  Kidderminster DY10 ....116 E8
  Walsall WS3 ....14 D3
  West Bromwich B71 ....53 D4
  Wolverhampton WV4 ....39 B5
Stoney Lane Ind Est
  DY10 ....116 E8
Stoney Lea Rd WS11 ....1 F1
Stoney Rd
  Coventry CV1,CV3 ....165 B1
  Nuneaton CV10,CV11 ....73 B6
Stoney Stanton Rd CV1,
  CV6 ....113 E5
Stoneycroft Twr 4 B36 .....68 E8
Stoneydelph Prim Sch
  B77 ....22 A1
Stoneyfields Cl 3 WS11 ....2 F2
Stoneyford Gr B14 ....105 B4
Stoneyhurst Rd B24 ....56 F3
Stoneymoor Dr B36 ....58 D1
Stoneythorpe Cl B91 ......107 B1
Stoneywood Rd CV2 ....114 F6
Stonleigh Ave CV5 ....132 F7
Stonnal Gr B23 ....57 A6
Stonnall Gate WS9 ....30 C8
Stonnall Rd WS9 ....30 C8
Stonor Park Rd B91 ....106 F5
Stonor Rd B28 ....106 A5
Stony La B62 ....64 F5
Stony St B67 ....64 F6
Stonydelph La B77 ....36 A7
Stornaway Rd B35 ....58 B4
Storrage La B48 ....139 E3

Storrs Cl B9 . . . . .67 D1
Storrs Pl B10 . . . . .67 D1
Storrs Way The B32 . . . . .102 B7
Stotfold Rd B14 . . . . .104 F2
Stour B7 . . . . .36 A5
Stour Cl Burntwood WS7 . . . . . .7 D6
  Halesowen B63 . . . . .82 E6
Stour Hill DY5 . . . . .62 A6
Stour Ho 2 B68 . . . . .84 B8
Stour St Birmingham B18 . . . . . .66 A3
  West Bromwich B70 . . . . .52 E3
Stour Vale Rd DY9 . . . . .81 F6
Stour Valley Cl DY5 . . . . .81 D7
Stourbridge Coll
  Stourbridge, Old Swinford
  DY8 . . . . .81 A4
  Stourbridge, Wollaston DY8 . . .80 E5
Stourbridge Coll (Church St
  Ctr) DY8 . . . . .81 A5
Stourbridge Coll (Westhill
  Ctr) DY8 . . . . .81 B4
Stourbridge Juntion Sta
  DY8 . . . . .81 B3
Stourbridge Rd
  Belbroughton DY9 . . . . .120 B7
  Blakedown DY9 . . . . .98 F1
  Brierley Hill DY1,DY2,DY5 . . . .61 E6
  Catshill B61 . . . . .136 F7
  Churchill DY10 . . . . .98 A6
  Dudley DY1 . . . . .62 A8
  Fairfield B61 . . . . .120 D2
  Hagley DY9 . . . . .99 C7
  Halesowen B63 . . . . .82 F5
  Harvington DY9,DY10 . . . . . . .118 C4
  Kidderminster DY10 . . . . .116 F8
  Lower Clent DY9 . . . . .99 E3
  Stourbridge DY9 . . . . .81 D5
  Wombourne WV5,DY3 . . . . . . .49 B5
Stourbridge Town Sta
  DY8 . . . . .81 A5
Stourbridge Trad Est
  DY8 . . . . .81 A6
Stourdale Rd B64 . . . . .82 C8
Stourdell Rd B63 . . . . .82 E6
Stourminster Sch DY10 . . . . . .117 B4
Stourmore Cl WV12 . . . . .27 D6
Stourport Rd DY11 . . . . .116 C2
Stourton Cl Knowle B93 . . . . .128 B7
  Sutton Coldfield B76 . . . . .46 F4
Stourton Dr WV4 . . . . .38 C5
Stourton Rd B32 . . . . .84 B5
Stourvale Ind Est DY9 . . . . .81 F6
Stourvale Trad Est B63 . . . . . . .82 D6
Stow Dr DY5 . . . . .81 B6
Stow Gr B36 . . . . .68 E7
Stow Heath La Ind & Inf Sch
  WV13 . . . . .26 D1
Stow Heath La
  Bilston WV1 . . . . .40 B8
  Wolverhampton WV1 . . . . .26 C1
Stow Heath Pl WV1 . . . . .40 B7
Stowe Hill Gdns WS13 . . . . .3 C1
Stowe Pl CV4 . . . . .111 C1
Stowe Rd WS13 . . . . .9 C8
Stowe St Lichfield WS13 . . . . . . .9 C8
  Walsall WS3 . . . . .28 C7
Stowecroft WS13 . . . . .3 C2
Stowell Rd B44 . . . . .55 F8
Stowheath Ind Est & New Ent
  Ctr WV1 . . . . .40 A8
  Stowheath Jun & Inf Sch
  WV1 .40 C8
Stowmans Cl WV14 . . . . .40 B3
Strachey Ave CV32 . . . . .156 E2
Straight Rd WV12 . . . . .27 D6
Straits Dr DY3 . . . . .50 B4
Straits Prim Sch DY3 . . . . .50 B5
Straits Rd DY3 . . . . .50 B3
Straits The DY3 . . . . .50 A4
Strand The B61 . . . . .137 A3
Stratford Cl DY1 . . . . .50 E2
Stratford Ct 1 B46 . . . . .46 B3
Stratford Dr WS9 . . . . .30 C8
Stratford Pl B12 . . . . .87 A8
Stratford Rd
  Birmingham B11 . . . . .87 C5
  Birmingham, Sparkhill B11 . . . .87 B6
  Bromsgrove B60 . . . . .137 A2
  Dorridge B94 . . . . .127 B3
  Solihull B90 . . . . .126 D7
  Tanworth-in-A, Hockley Heath
  B94 .143 C5
  Warwick CV34 . . . . .160 C3
Stratford St
  Birmingham B11 . . . . .87 C5
  Coventry CV1 . . . . .114 A4
  Nuneaton CV11 . . . . .73 C4
Stratford St N B11 . . . . .87 A8
Stratford Way WS11 . . . . .1 F5
Strathdene Gdns B29 . . . . .85 C1
Strathdene Rd B29 . . . . .85 C1
Strathearn Rd CV32 . . . . .156 E1
Strathern Dr WV14 . . . . .40 A4
Strathfield Wlk WV3,WV4 . . . . . .38 C6
Strathmore Ave CV1 . . . . .113 E1
Strathmore Cres WV5 . . . . .49 A7
Strathmore Pl 6 WS11 . . . . .1 F2
Strathmore Rd
  Hinckley LE10 . . . . .75 A7
  Tipton DY4 . . . . .52 A8
Stratton St WV10 . . . . .25 E4
Strawberry Cl B69 . . . . .63 C7
Strawberry Fields CV7 . . . . .92 B1
Strawberry La
  Great Wyrley WS6 . . . . .4 F3
  Willenhall WV13 . . . . .26 D3

Strawberry Lane Ind Est
  WV13 . . . . .26 C2
Strawberry Wlk CV2 . . . . .96 D2
Stray The DY5 . . . . .61 C6
Stream Mdw WS4 . . . . .15 D1
Stream Pk DY6 . . . . .60 E4
Stream Rd DY6,DY8 . . . . .60 D4
Streamside Cl CV5 . . . . .112 A8
Streamside Way
  Solihull B92 . . . . .89 D4
  Walsall WS4 . . . . .29 D8
Streatham Gr B44 . . . . .45 A2
Streather Rd B75 . . . . .32 C2
Streetly Cres B74 . . . . .31 D3
Streetly Dr B74 . . . . .31 D3
Streetly La B74 . . . . .31 D3
Streetly Rd B23 . . . . .56 D5
Streetly Sch The B74 . . . . .45 A6
Streetly Wood B74 . . . . .31 A2
Streets Corner Gdns
  WS9 . . . . .16 A4
Streets La WS6 . . . . .4 F1
Streetsbrook Inf Sch
  B90 .106 C4
Streetsbrook Rd B90,
  B91 .106 D5
Streetway Rd WS14 . . . . .18 B7
Strensham Ct B13 . . . . .86 E4
Strensham Hill B13 . . . . .86 E4
Strensham Rd B12 . . . . .86 E5
Stretton Ave CV3 . . . . .134 C6
Stretton Cl LE10 . . . . .75 D6
Stretton Cres CV31 . . . . .162 B5
Stretton Ct
  Birmingham B24 . . . . .56 E2
  Hinckley LE10 . . . . .75 D3
Stretton Dr B45 . . . . .122 A2
Stretton Gr
  2 Birmingham, Lozells B19 . . .66 C7
  Birmingham, Sparkbrook
  B11 . . . . .87 C6
  Birmingham, Stechford B8 . . . .68 C6
Stretton Ho 7 B97 . . . . .153 A4
Stretton Pl Dudley DY2 . . . . .62 D5
  Wolverhampton WV14 . . . . .40 A1
Stretton Rd
  Kidderminster DY11 . . . . .116 B4
  Nuneaton CV10 . . . . .73 A3
  Solihull B90 . . . . .126 B8
  Willenhall WV12 . . . . .13 D1
Stretton St B77 . . . . .21 E3
Stringer Cl B75 . . . . .32 A4
Stringers Hill WS12 . . . . .2 D4
Stringes Cl WV13 . . . . .27 C3
Stringes La WV13 . . . . .27 B3
Strode Ho B79 . . . . .21 A4
Strode Rd WV2 . . . . .39 C6
Stroma Way CV10 . . . . .72 F2
Stronsay Cl B45 . . . . .101 F1
Stroud Ave WV12 . . . . .27 D5
Stroud Cl WV12 . . . . .27 C4
Stroud Rd B90 . . . . .105 F2
Strutt Cl B15 . . . . .85 D8
Strutt Rd LE10 . . . . .76 A5
Stuart Bathurst RC High Sch
  WS10 . . . . .42 B5
Stuart Cl CV34 . . . . .160 D5
Stuart Cres DY2 . . . . .51 E1
Stuart Ct Coventry CV6 . . . . . .114 A8
  7 Royal Leamington Spa
  CV32 . . . . .157 C2
Stuart Rd Blackheath B65 . . . . . .63 C4
  Halesowen B62 . . . . .83 F5
Stuart St Birmingham B7 . . . . . . .67 B6
  Walsall WS3 . . . . .28 B8
Stuart's Dr B33 . . . . .68 D1
Stuart's Gn B33 . . . . .99 B8
Stuarts Rd B33 . . . . .68 D2
Stuarts Way B32 . . . . .102 B7
Stubbers Green Rd
  Aldridge WS9 . . . . .30 A7
  Walsall WS9 . . . . .29 E8
Stubbington Cl WV13 . . . . .26 D1
Stubbs Cl CV12 . . . . .78 A4
Stubbs Gr CV2 . . . . .114 B5
Stubbs Rd WV3 . . . . .39 A6
Stubby La WV11 . . . . .27 A6
Stubley Dr WV10 . . . . .25 E6
Stud Farm Cotts B78 . . . . .20 E2
Stud La B33 . . . . .68 F4
Studland Gn CV2 . . . . .115 A4
Studland Rd B28 . . . . .106 A8
Studley Cl B98 . . . . .154 D6
Studley Cty Inf Sch B80 . . . . . .159 E4
Studley Dr DY5 . . . . .81 B8
Studley Gate DY8 . . . . .80 D5
Studley High Sch B80 . . . . .159 E3
Studley Rd Redditch B98 . . . . . .154 A2
  Wolverhampton WV3 . . . . .38 C8
Studley St B12 . . . . .87 A5
Studley St Mary's CE Jun Sch
  B80 .159 E3
Studley Twr B12 . . . . .86 F7
Sturgeon's Hill WS14 . . . . .9 C7
Sturley Cl CV8 . . . . .148 B6
Sturman Dr B65 . . . . .63 C1
Sturminster Cl CV2 . . . . .115 A4
Stychbrook Gdns WS13 . . . . .3 B2
Styles Cl CV31 . . . . .162 A7
Styvechale Ave CV5 . . . . .133 A8
Suckling Green La WV8 . . . . .10 A2
Sudbury Cl
  Royal Leamington Spa
  CV32 . . . . .157 C3
  Wednesfield WV11 . . . . .26 E7
Sudbury Gr B44 . . . . .45 B2
Sudeley B77 . . . . .35 C8
Sudeley Cl B36 . . . . .58 B1

Sudeley Gdns DY1 . . . . .50 D2
Sudeley Rd CV10 . . . . .78 C8
Suffield Gr B23 . . . . .56 B5
Suffolk Cl Bedworth CV12 . . . . . .78 A3
  Coventry CV5 . . . . .112 B3
  Nuneaton CV10 . . . . .72 C3
  Oldbury B68 . . . . .64 A4
  Wolverhampton WV11 . . . . .26 C6
Suffolk Dr DY5 . . . . .81 C7
Suffolk Gr WS9 . . . . .30 B8
Suffolk Pl Birmingham B5 . . . . .164 B1
  Walsall WS2 . . . . .28 C5
Suffolk Rd Dudley DY2 . . . . .62 A7
  Wednesbury WS10 . . . . .42 C3
Suffolk St CV32 . . . . .157 A1
Suffolk Street Queensway
  B1 . . . . .164 B2
Suffolk Way B26 . . . . .21 A1
Suffrage St B66 . . . . .65 B4
Sugar Loaf La DY10 . . . . .98 B7
Sugarbrook Ct 1 B60 . . . . .150 F6
Sugarbrook La B60 . . . . .151 A5
Sugarbrook Rd B60 . . . . .151 A7
Sugden Gr B5 . . . . .86 E8
Sulgrave Cl Coventry CV2 . . . . .114 E7
  Dudley DY1 . . . . .51 A3
Sullivan Cl CV6 . . . . .114 B8
Sullivan Ct CV6 . . . . .114 B7
Sullivan Rd WS13 . . . . .3 C2
Sullivan Wlk WS13 . . . . .3 C2
Sumburgh Croft B35 . . . . .58 A3
Summer Croft B19 . . . . .66 D6
Summer Dr DY3 . . . . .50 C3
Summer Gr WS13 . . . . .3 D2
Summer Hill
  6 Halesowen B63 . . . . .83 B3
  Kingswinford DY6 . . . . .60 C6
Summer Hill Ind Pk 2
  B1 . . . . .164 C3
Summer Hill Rd B1 . . . . .66 B3
Summer Hill St B1 . . . . .66 B3
Summer Hill Terr B1 . . . . .66 B3
Summer La
  Birmingham B19 . . . . .66 D5
  Dudley DY3 . . . . .50 C3
  Minworth B76 . . . . .58 D6
  Walsall WS4 . . . . .15 C2
  Summer Pl WV11 . . . . .116 C5
Summer Rd
  Birmingham, Acock's Green
  B27 . . . . .88 A2
  Birmingham, Edgbaston B15 . .86 C7
  Birmingham, Erdington B23 . . .56 F5
  Blackheath B65 . . . . .63 D3
  Dudley DY1 . . . . .51 A4
  Kidderminster DY11 . . . . .116 C3
Summer Row
  Birmingham B3 . . . . .164 A3
  Wolverhampton WV2 . . . . .163 B2
Summer St
  Kingswinford DY6 . . . . .60 D6
  Redditch B98 . . . . .153 E3
  Stourbridge Wollaston DY8 . . .80 F5
  Stourbridge, Lye DY9 . . . . .81 F5
  West Bromwich B71 . . . . .53 D4
  Willenhall WV13 . . . . .26 F2
Summercourt Dr DY6 . . . . .60 C6
Summercourt Sq DY6 . . . . .60 C5
Summerfield Ave
  Kingswinford DY6 . . . . .60 C7
  West Bromwich B70 . . . . .53 C4
Summerfield Cl B77 . . . . .21 D4
Summerfield Cres B16 . . . . .65 E3
Summerfield Ct B15 . . . . .65 C1
Summerfield Gr 8 B29 . . . . . . .103 A7
Summerfield Gr 8 B18 . . . . .65 E4
Summerfield Prim Sch
  B18 . . . . .65 E4
Summerfield Rd
  Birmingham B16 . . . . .65 E3
  Burntwood WS7 . . . . .7 A5
  Clent DY9 . . . . .99 E2
  Dudley DY2 . . . . .62 D7
  Solihull B92 . . . . .89 B1
  Tamworth B77 . . . . .21 D4
  Wolverhampton WV1 . . . . .25 B2
Summerfields Ave B62 . . . . .83 F7
Summergate DY3 . . . . .50 C4
Summerhill WS14 . . . . .16 E8
Summerhill Ave DY11 . . . . .116 A5
Summerhill Rd
  Dudley WV14 . . . . .40 D1
  Tipton DY4 . . . . .51 F7
Summerhill Sch DY6 . . . . .60 B6
Summerhouse CI B97 . . . . .153 A6
Summerhouse Rd WV14 . . . . . . .40 A1
Summerlee Rd B24 . . . . .57 B2
Summerton Rd
  Oldbury B69 . . . . .52 D1
  Whitnash CV31 . . . . .162 A2
Summervale Cl DY9 . . . . .99 A5
Summervale Rd DY9 . . . . .99 A5
Summerville Terr 4 B17 . . . . . . .85 C5
Summit Cres B66 . . . . .64 E8
Summit Gdns B63 . . . . .82 F3
Summit Pl DY3 . . . . .50 B2
Summit The DY9 . . . . .81 D4
Sumner Rd B46 . . . . .70 F6
Sun St Brierley Hill DY5 . . . . . . .61 F1
  Walsall WS1 . . . . .42 E7
  Wolverhampton WV10 . . . . . .163 D3
Sunart Way CV10 . . . . .72 C5
Sunbeam B77 . . . . .21 D1
Sunbeam Cl B36 . . . . .58 F1
Sunbeam Dr WS6 . . . . .4 F3
Sunbeam St WV2 . . . . .163 B2
Sunbeam Way B33 . . . . .69 C2
Sunbury Ave WS14 . . . . .9 E7

Sunbury Cl WV14 . . . . .40 E1
Sunbury Cotts B31 . . . . .103 A4
Sunbury Rd
  Birmingham B31 . . . . .122 E7
  Coventry CV3 . . . . .134 C5
  Halesowen B63 . . . . .82 E6
Suncliffe Dr CV8 . . . . .148 A2
Suncroft B32 . . . . .84 C5
Sunbury Rise B31 . . . . .103 B5
Sunderland Dr DY8 . . . . .81 A8
Sunderton Rd B14 . . . . .104 E4
Sundew Croft B36 . . . . .68 D8
Sundew St CV2 . . . . .96 D2
Sundial La B43 . . . . .43 F1
Sundorne Cl CV5 . . . . .112 A4
Sundour Cres WV11 . . . . .12 E2
Sundridge Prim Sch B44 . . . . . . .44 E4
Sundridge Rd B44 . . . . .44 E4
Sundridge Wlk WV4 . . . . .38 C6
Sunfield Rd WS11 . . . . .1 B1
Sunleigh Gr B27 . . . . .88 E4
Sunley Dr WS12 . . . . .2 D7
Sunningdale
  Bromsgrove B60 . . . . .137 A1
  Halesowen B62 . . . . .83 E4
  Tamworth B77 . . . . .22 C5
Sunningdale Ave
  Coventry CV6 . . . . .95 D2
  Kenilworth CV8 . . . . .148 B4
  Perton WV6 . . . . .23 D5
Sunningdale Cl
  Birmingham B20 . . . . .54 E4
  Nuneaton CV11 . . . . .74 A1
  Redditch B98 . . . . .153 F4
  Stourbridge DY8 . . . . .80 F2
  Sutton Coldfield B73 . . . . .46 A2
Sunningdale Dr B69 . . . . .63 A7
Sunningdale Rd
  Birmingham B11 . . . . .88 A3
  Bromsgrove B61 . . . . .150 D8
  Sedgley DY3 . . . . .39 B3
Sunningdale Way WS3 . . . . .14 A3
Sunny Ave B12 . . . . .87 A5
Sunny Bank Rd B68 . . . . .84 C7
Sunny Hill Cl WV5 . . . . .49 B6
Sunnybank Ave
  Birmingham B44 . . . . .56 B7
  Coventry CV3 . . . . .134 B5
Sunnybank Cl WS9 . . . . .30 E2
Sunnybank Rd Dudley DY3 . . . . .50 F5
  Sutton Coldfield B73 . . . . .57 A8
  Sunnydale Cres LE10 . . . . .74 F7
  Sunnydale Rd LE10 . . . . .74 F7
  Sunnydale Wlk B71 . . . . .53 C4
Sunnydene B8 . . . . .68 A5
Sunnyhill LE10 . . . . .75 F7
  Sunnyhill S LE10 . . . . .75 F6
Sunnymead B60 . . . . .137 A1
Sunnymead Rd
  Birmingham B26 . . . . .88 F6
  Burntwood WS7 . . . . .7 A8
Sunnymead Way B74 . . . . .44 F4
Sunnymede Rd DY6 . . . . .61 A4
Sunnyside Brownhills WS9 . . . . .16 A2
  Hinckley LE10 . . . . .71 D3
  Tipton B69 . . . . .63 B7
Sunnyside Ave B23 . . . . .56 E3
Sunnyside Cl
  Balsall Common CV7 . . . . .130 C7
  Coventry CV5 . . . . .112 F3
Sunnyside Hospl LE10 . . . . .71 D3
Sunnyside Ind Est LE10 . . . . . . .71 D4
Sunnyside La CV7 . . . . .130 C7
Sunridge Ave
  Birmingham B19 . . . . .66 D6
  Wombourne WV5 . . . . .49 A7
Sunrise Hill WS12 . . . . .2 B6
Sunrise Wlk B68 . . . . .64 C3
Sunset Cl Great Wyrley WS6 . . . .4 F3
  Tamworth B79 . . . . .21 A5
Sunset Pl WV4 . . . . .39 F3
Sunshine Cl CV8 . . . . .148 A2
Sunshine Inf Sch The
  WS3 .28 C8
Sunway Gr CV3 . . . . .133 B6
Surfeit Hill Rd B64 . . . . .82 D8
Surrey Cl Cannock WS11 . . . . . . .4 E8
  Hinckley LE10 . . . . .75 E4
  Nuneaton CV10 . . . . .72 E3
Surrey Cres B71 . . . . .53 A8
Surrey Ct CV34 . . . . .160 E8
Surrey Dr
  Kingswinford DY6 . . . . .60 F3
  Tamworth B78 . . . . .21 A1
Surrey Ho 2 DY8 . . . . .80 F8
Surrey Rd Birmingham B44 . . . . .55 F8
  Dudley DY2 . . . . .62 A7
Surrey Wlk WS9 . . . . .30 A8
Sussex Ave Aldridge WS9 . . . . . .30 A8
  Wednesbury WS10 . . . . .42 D4
  West Bromwich B71 . . . . .53 C6
Sussex Cl CV10 . . . . .72 E3
Sussex Ct
  7 Birmingham B29 . . . . .103 C7
  Warwick CV34 . . . . .160 E8
Sussex Dr Cannock WS12 . . . . . . .2 B5
  Wolverhampton WV3 . . . . .24 E1
Sussex Rd CV5 . . . . .112 F4
Sutherland Ave
  Coventry CV5 . . . . .112 A4
  Solihull B90 . . . . .106 C3
  Wolverhampton WV2 . . . . .40 A8
Sutherland Cl
  Birmingham B43 . . . . .44 D4
  Warwick CV34 . . . . .155 E1

Sutherland Dr
  Bedworth CV12 . . . . .78 A4
  Birmingham B13 . . . . .86 F4
  Wombourne WV5 . . . . .38 A1
Sutherland Gr WV6 . . . . .23 F4
Sutherland Ho WV1 . . . . .25 A3
Sutherland Pl WV2 . . . . .163 C2
Sutherland Rd
  Blackheath B64 . . . . .82 E8
  Cheslyn Hay WS6 . . . . .4 E2
  Wolverhampton WV4 . . . . .39 B5
Sutherland St B6 . . . . .67 B8
Sutton App B8 . . . . .68 A4
Sutton Ave Coventry CV5 . . . . .111 D4
  Tamworth B78 . . . . .21 A2
Sutton Cl Hinckley LE10 . . . . . . .71 F3
  Redditch B98 . . . . .154 D2
Sutton Coldfield Coll
  B74 . . . . .46 C6
Sutton Coldfield Coll
  (Erdington Ctr) B24 . . . . .57 A4
Sutton Coldfield Coll Design
  Ctr B72 . . . . .46 B4
Sutton Coldfield Gram Sch
  For Girls B73 . . . . .46 B3
Sutton Coldfield Sta B73 . . . . . .46 B5
Sutton Cottage Hospl
  B72 . . . . .46 B4
Sutton Cres B80 . . . . .53 A3
Sutton Ct
  3 Birmingham, Erdington
  B24 . . . . .57 B6
  Birmingham, Hamstead B43 . . .54 F2
  Sutton Coldfield B74,B75 . . . . .46 F7
  Wolverhampton WV4 . . . . .39 C2
Sutton Lodge B91 . . . . .107 A3
Sutton New Rd B23 . . . . .56 F4
Sutton Oak Cnr B73 . . . . .45 A5
Sutton Oak Rd B73 . . . . .45 A5
Sutton Park Fst Sch
  DY11 . . . . .116 B4
Sutton Park Cl DY11 . . . . .116 C3
Sutton Park Rd DY11 . . . . .116 C3
Sutton Park Rise DY11 . . . . . . .116 B3
Sutton Park Visitor Ctr*
  B74 . . . . .46 A5
Sutton Pk Nuneaton CV10 . . . . .72 B7
Sutton Coldfield B74 . . . . .45 D6
Sutton Rd Aldridge WS9 . . . . . . .30 A1
  Birmingham B23 . . . . .57 B6
  Kidderminster DY11 . . . . .116 C4
  Mile Oak B78 . . . . .34 A7
  Tamworth B78 . . . . .20 C1
  Walsall WS5 . . . . .43 C8
  Wednesbury WS10 . . . . .41 A4
Sutton Specl Sch The
  DY1 . . . . .61 F8
Sutton Sq B76 . . . . .58 E6
Sutton St Birmingham B1 . . . . . .66 D1
  Birmingham, Aston B6 . . . . .66 F6
  Stourbridge DY8 . . . . .60 F1
Sutton Stop CV6 . . . . .96 B5
Sutton's Dr
  Birmingham B43 . . . . .44 A4
  Walsall B43 . . . . .43 F4
Swadling St CV31 . . . . .161 F6
Swaffield Pk WS11 . . . . .2 B2
Swain Crofts CV31 . . . . .162 B6
Swains La LE10 . . . . .75 F6
Swains Gr B44 . . . . .44 F4
Swale Gr Birmingham B38 . . . . .103 F1
  Willenhall WV13 . . . . .27 D2
Swale Rd B76 . . . . .47 A1
Swalecliffe Rd CV11 . . . . .73 A6
Swaledale Cl B60 . . . . .150 E6
Swallow Ave B36 . . . . .70 A8
Swallow Cl
  Birmingham B12 . . . . .87 B5
  Dudley DY2 . . . . .62 D2
  Huntington WS12 . . . . .1 C7
  Wednesbury WS10 . . . . .42 B4
Swallow Croft WS13 . . . . .3 A1
Swallow Ct
  Bedworth CV12 . . . . .95 C8
  Wolverhampton WV10 . . . . .25 D7
Swallow Dr DY10 . . . . .117 A2
Swallow Rd CV6 . . . . .95 C1
Swallow St
  Birmingham B2 . . . . .164 B2
  West Bromwich B70 . . . . .53 A4
Swallowdale
  Brownhills WS9 . . . . .16 A4
  Wolverhampton WV6 . . . . .23 F2
Swallowdean Rd CV6 . . . . .112 E8
Swallowfall Ave DY8 . . . . .80 C4
Swallowfield B79 . . . . .20 C6
Swallowfields Dr WS12 . . . . .2 B3
Swallowfields Rd DY3 . . . . .39 C2
Swallows Cl WS3 . . . . .15 A5
Swallows Ind Est The
  B90 .126 E6
Swallows Rise Bsns Pk
  DY5 . . . . .61 E3
Swallows' Mdw B90 . . . . .126 D8
Swan Bank WV4 . . . . .38 F4
Swan Cl Blakedown DY10 . . . . . .98 B1
  Cheslyn Hay WS6 . . . . .4 D2
Swan Copse B25 . . . . .88 C5
Swan Corner Sh Ctr WV7 . . . . . .24 F5
Swan Cres B69 . . . . .63 F4
Swan Ctr The 7 DY10 . . . . . . .116 E6
Swan Gdns B23 . . . . .56 F4

Swan La Coventry CV2 .....113 F4
Fairfield B61 ....120 E3
Kingswinford DY8 ....60 F2
Stourbridge DY5,DY8 ....61 A2
Upton Warren B61 ....150 A3
West Bromwich B70 ....53 A5
Swan Lane Ind Est B70 ......53 A5
Swan Mews WS13 ....9 A8
Swan Pool Gr WS4 ....15 D1
Swan Rd WS13 ....9 A7
Swan Rdbt B70 ....52 F5
Swan St Alvechurch B48 ....139 B5
Brierley Hill DY5 ....61 C6
Dudley DY2 ....62 C6
Royal Leamington Spa
CV32 ....157 A1
Stourbridge DY8 ....80 E5
Warwick CV34 ....160 E6
Wolverhampton WV1 ....25 F2
Swan Village Ind Pk B70 ....53 A5
Swanage Gn CV2 ....115 A4
Swanage Rd B10 ....87 D8
Swancote Dr WV4 ....38 C6
Swancote Rd
Birmingham B33 ....68 F5
Dudley DY1 ....62 A8
Swancroft Rd
Coventry CV2 ....114 A5
Tipton DY4 ....51 F8
Swanfield Rd
Brierley Hill DY8 ....60 F1
Stourbridge DY8 ....61 A2
Swanfields WS7 ....7 C6
Swanley Cl B62 ....84 A3
Swanmore Cl WV4 ....38 E8
Swanmote B79 ....20 F5
Swann Rd WV14 ....40 A2
Swann Wlk 11 DY4 ....52 A8
Swans Length B48 ....139 A7
Swansbrook Gdns 4
B38 ....104 C2
Swanshurst La B13 ....105 C8
Swanshurst Sch B13 ....105 B7
Swanswell Rd B92 ....106 D7
Swanswell St CV1 ....165 C4
Swanswood Gr 8 B37 ....70 C3
Swarthmore Rd B29 ....103 B7
Sweetbriar La WV12 ....27 D5
Sweetbriar Rd WV2 ....40 A7
Sweetbriar Way WV12 ....2 D2
Sweetbrier 4 DY8 ....60 E1
Sweetman PI WV6 ....25 A3
Sweetman St
Wolverhampton WV6 ....24 F4
Wolverhampton WV6 ....25 A3
Swendover Cl B36 ....69 C8
Sweetpool La DY8 ....98 F5
Swift B77 ....21 E2
Swift Cl Birmingham B36 .....70 A8
Bromsgrove B61 ....150 E8
Kenilworth CV8 ....148 A2
Swift Park Gr DY10 ....117 B2
Swift's Cnr CV3 ....133 E8
Swillington Rd CV6 ....113 B5
Swinbrook Gr B44 ....44 E1
Swinbrook Way B90 ....106 D4
Swinburne Ave CV2 ....114 D2
Swinburne Cl CV10 ....72 A5
Swinburne Rd
Hinckley LE10 ....71 C1
Redditch B97 ....158 C7
Swincross Rd DY8 ....81 B3
Swindale B77 ....36 B7
Swindale Croft CV3 ....134 F8
Swindell Rd DY9 ....81 C1
Swindon Rd
Birmingham B17 ....65 B2
Kingswinford DY6 ....60 A8
Swinfen Broun Rd WS13 .....9 A8
Swinford Gr B93 ....127 E3
Swinford Rd
Birmingham B29 ....85 B3
Stourbridge DY8 ....81 A3
Wolverhampton WV10 ....25 E5
Swiss Dr DY8 ....60 F2
Swiss Lodge Dr B78 ....34 F8
Sword Dr LE10 ....71 B3
Swynnerton Dr WV11 ....12 F4
Sycamore B77 ....35 E7
Sycamore Ave
Birmingham B12 ....87 A5
Redditch B98 ....153 E2
Sycamore Cl
Birmingham B24 ....56 F3
Hinckley LE10 ....75 E5
Kidderminster DY10 ....116 F7
Stourbridge DY8 ....80 D2
Sutton Coldfield B76 ....46 F2
Walsall WS4 ....29 B8
Sycamore Cres
Birmingham, Erdington B24 ..56 F3
Birmingham, Marston Green
B37 ....90 A8
Sycamore Ct
Allesley CV5 ....111 F7
Birmingham, Cotteridge
B30 ....103 C4
Birmingham, Perry Common
B23 ....56 C6
Sycamore Dr
Hollywood B47 ....125 B6
Wolverhampton WV3 ....24 D1
Sycamore Gn
Cannock WS11 ....1 C6
Dudley DY1 ....50 F5

Sycamore Gr CV34 ....156 A1
Sycamore Green Prim Sch
DY1 ....50 F5
Sycamore Ho B13 ....87 A3
Sycamore Ind & Trad Est
B21 ....65 D3
Sycamore Paddock 1
DY8 ....61 A1
Sycamore PI Bilston WV14 ..41 A3
Smethwick B67 ....64 F4
Sycamore Rd
Birmingham, Aston B6 ....67 A8
Birmingham, Bournville
B30 ....103 F7
Birmingham, Erdington B23 ..56 F7
Birmingham, Great Barr
B43 ....43 E3
Birmingham, Handsworth
B21 ....65 D7
Burntwood WS7 ....6 F7
Cannock WS12 ....2 F4
Coventry CV2 ....96 B2
Kingswinford DY6 ....60 E6
Nuneaton CV10 ....72 D6
Oldbury B69 ....64 A4
Smethwick B66 ....65 B3
Tipton DY4 ....51 F7
Walsall, Shelfield WS4 ....29 B8
Walsall, The Delves WS5 .....42 F5
Wednesbury WS10 ....42 A2
Sycamore Terr B14 ....104 C7
Sycamore Way
1 Birmingham B27 ....88 C5
Huntington WS12 ....1 D8
Sycamores The
Bedworth CV12 ....77 E2
Hagley DY9 ....98 F5
Lichfield WS14 ....9 B5
Sutton Coldfield B74 ....31 F2
Wolverhampton, Elston Hall
WV10 ....25 F8
Wolverhampton, New Cross
WV11 ....26 B5
Sydenham Dr CV31 ....162 B6
Sydenham Ind Est CV31 ....162 B6
Sydenham Prim Sch
CV31 ....162 C6
Sydenham Rd
Birmingham B11 ....87 C6
Smethwick B66 ....45 A7
Wolverhampton WV1 ....26 B2
Sydnall Cl B97 ....152 F2
Sydnall Fields CV6 ....95 F4
Sydnall Rd CV6 ....95 F4
Sydney Cl B70 ....53 A7
Sydney Ct 11 CV12 ....77 F2
Sydney Ho B34 ....69 E6
Sydney Rd Birmingham B9 ..67 C2
Blackheath B64 ....82 C8
Bromsgrove B61 ....136 E3
Smethwick B67 ....64 E2
Sykesmoor B77 ....36 B7
Sylvan Ave B31 ....102 F3
Sylvan Dr CV3 ....132 F6
Sylvan Gn B62 ....83 D5
Sylvan Gr B90 ....106 B3
Sylvia Ave B31 ....123 B8
Symphony Ct B16 ....66 B2
Synkere Cl CV7 ....95 A6
Sytch La WV5 ....49 A5

T

Tabbs Gdns DY10 ....117 A6
Table Oak La CV8 ....130 B1
Tachbrook Cl CV2 ....96 C2
Tachbrook Link CV34 ....161 E4
Tachbrook Park Dr
CV34 ....161 E5
Tachbrook Rd CV31 ....161 E5
Tachbrook St CV31 ....162 A6
Tack Farm Rd DY8 ....60 D1
Tackford Cl B36 ....58 D1
Tackford Rd CV6 ....114 A8
Tackley B90 ....126 B8
Tadmore Cl WV14 ....40 D5
Tadworth Cl WV1 ....26 A2
Tainters Hill CV8 ....148 A6
Tait Croft B92 ....107 F8
Talaton Cl WV9 ....11 A2
Talbot B77 ....21 E2
Talbot Ave B74 ....31 B3
Talbot Cl Birmingham B23 ...56 D8
Walsall WS2 ....28 C6
Talbot Ct CV32 ....157 A1
Talbot Ho 6 B24 ....56 F4
Talbot Pass 5 DY8 ....81 A5
Talbot PI WV14 ....40 C6
Talbot Rd
Bromsgrove B60 ....150 E7
Dudley DY2 ....62 A8
Smethwick B66 ....65 A3
Wolverhampton WV2 ....39 C6
Talbot St Birmingham B18 ...66 A6
Brierley Hill DY5 ....61 D3
Halesowen B63 ....82 C6
Kidderminster DY11 ....116 C4
Stourbridge, Lye DY9 ....81 F5
Stourbridge, Stambermill
DY8 ....81 A5
Talbot Way B10 ....87 F7
Talbots La DY5 ....61 F3
Talfourd St B9 ....67 D1
Talgarth Covert B38 ....123 E7
Talisman Cl CV8 ....147 F3
Talisman Sq CV8 ....147 F4
Talke Rd WS5 ....42 F5

Tall Trees Cl Catshill B61 ..136 F8
Sutton Coldfield B74 ....31 D4
Willenhall WV12 ....27 D6
Tall Trees Dr DY9 ....81 D2
Talladale B32 ....102 B7
Talland Ave
Coventry CV6 ....114 A6
Tamworth B77 ....21 E5
Tallants Cl CV6 ....114 A8
Tallants Rd CV6 ....114 A8
Tallington Rd B33 ....89 D7
Talton Cl B90 ....127 A5
Tamar Cl WS8 ....6 C2
Tamar Dr Birmingham B36 ...69 F8
Dudley DY1 ....50 F6
Sutton Coldfield B76 ....58 B7
Tamar Gr Perton WV6 ....23 E4
Willenhall WV13 ....27 C2
Tamar Rd Bulkington CV12 ..79 B2
Tamworth B77 ....36 A5
Tamar Rise DY8 ....81 A8
Tamarisk Cl B29 ....103 B8
Tame Ave Burntwood WS7 ...7 D6
Wednesbury WS10 ....42 C4
Tame Bridge WS5 ....42 F4
Tame Bridge Factory Est
WS5 ....42 F1
Tame Cl WS1 ....42 E6
Tame Cres B71 ....53 C6
Tame Ct Fazeley B78 ....35 B8
Tamworth B79 ....21 A5
Tame Dr WS3 ....15 A1
Tame Gr WS11 ....4 D8
Tame Rd Birmingham B6 ....56 A1
Oldbury B68 ....84 B8
Tipton DY4 ....52 C5
Tame Rise B68 ....84 B8
Tame Road Ind Est B6 ....56 A1
Tame St E WS1 ....42 F6
Tame St Bilston WV14 ....40 F5
Tamworth B77 ....21 C3
Walsall WS1 ....42 E6
West Bromwich B70 ....52 F8
Tame St E WS1 ....42 F6
Tame Valley Bsns Ctr
B77 ....35 E6
Tame Valley Com Sch
B36 ....68 D8
Tame Valley Ind Est B77 ....37 B2
Tame Way LE10 ....75 A8
Tamebridge Ind Est B42 .....55 E4
Tamedrive B78,B79 ....21 A4
Tamerton Rd B32 ....84 D1
Tameside Dr
Birmingham, Castle Bromwich
B35 ....58 A1
Birmingham, Erdington B6 ..56 A3
Tameside Prim Schs
WS10 ....42 C3
Tamworth & Lichfield Coll
B79 ....21 B6
Tamworth Bsns Ctr B77 .....22 B3
Tamworth Bsns Pk B77 ......22 B3
Tamworth Castle* B79 ....21 B4
Tamworth Castle Mus*
B79 ....21 B4
Tamworth Cl WS8 ....6 F2
Tamworth Rd Cliff B78 ......35 C2
Keresley CV6,CV7 ....94 D5
Lichfield WS14 ....9 E5
Polesworth B78 ....22 B5
Sutton Coldfield B75 ....33 A2
Tamworth, Mount Pleasant
B77 ....21 C1
Tamworth, Two Gates B77 ..35 D8
Wood End CV9 ....36 C1
Tamworth Rd (Amington)
B77 ....21 F5
Tamworth Rd (Dosthill)
B77 ....35 C6
Tamworth St WS13 ....8 B8
Tamworth Sta B79 ....21 C5
Tanacetum Dr WS5 ....43 B3
Tancred Cl CV31 ....161 F5
Tandra Cl CV34 ....161 D3
Tandy Dr B14 ....104 F3
Tandy's La DY10 ....118 E4
Tanfield Cl WV6 ....24 B3
Tanfield Rd
Birmingham B33 ....68 F3
Dudley DY2 ....62 B7
Tanford Rd B92 ....89 C3
Tanglewood Cl
Birmingham, Castle Bromwich
B34 ....69 C5
Birmingham, Quinton B32 ...84 B4
Blackwell B60 ....138 A5
Tanglewood Gr DY3 ....39 C2
Tangmere Cl WV6 ....23 E5
Tangmere Dr B35 ....58 A3
Tanhouse Ave B43 ....54 C7
Tanhouse Farm Rd B92 .....89 C2
Tanhouse La
Halesowen B63 ....82 C5
Redditch B98 ....154 C6
Tanners Cl B75 ....47 A6
Tanners Ct WS1 ....42 E8
Tanners Green La B47,
B94 ....125 B2
Tanners' La CV4,CV7 ....111 B1
Tannery Cl WS2 ....28 D3
Tannery Ct CV8 ....147 F4
Tansey Ct DY5 ....61 B7
Tansey Green Rd
Brierley Hill DY5,DY6 ....61 B8

Tansey Green Rd continued
Kingswinford DY6 ....50 A1
Tansley Cl B93 ....127 F4
Tansley Gr B44 ....44 F1
Tansley Hill Ave DY2 ....62 F8
Tansley Hill Rd DY2 ....62 E8
Tansley Rd B44 ....55 F8
Tansley View WV2 ....39 D7
Tansy Sutton Coldfield B74 ..31 F4
Tamworth B77 ....21 C3
Tantallan Dr B32 ....84 D1
Tantany La B71 ....53 C4
Tantarra St Walsall WS1 .....28 F1
Walsall, The Chuckery WS1 ..29 A1
Tanwood Cl
Redditch B97 ....158 A6
Solihull B91 ....127 B8
Tanwood Cross DY10 ....119 B2
Tanwood La DY10 ....119 A2
Tanworth Gr B12 ....86 F6
Tanworth La B90 ....126 C5
Tanworth-in-Arden CE Prim
Sch B94 ....142 A2
Tanyard WS13 ....9 C8
Tanyard Cl
Alvechurch B48 ....139 B6
Coventry CV4 ....111 D1
Tanyard La B48 ....139 B6
Tanyards B27 ....88 D3
Tapcon Way CV2 ....114 F5
Tapestries Ave B70 ....53 A4
Taplow PI WS11 ....1 F4
Tappinger Gr CV8 ....148 C5
Tapster La B94 ....143 F2
Tapton Cl WS3 ....14 C3
Tara Ct CV2 ....114 B4
Tardebigge CE Fst Sch
B60 ....152 B7
Tardebigge Ct B97 ....152 C6
Tardebigge Ho B60 ....137 B3
Tarlington Rd CV6 ....112 E6
Tarmac Rd WV14 ....40 B5
Tarn Cl CV12 ....78 A2
Tarquin Cl CV3 ....134 D7
Tarragon Cl CV2 ....96 D1
Tarragon Gdns B31 ....102 C2
Tarrant B77 ....35 F8
Tarrant Gr B32 ....84 E5
Tarrant Wlk CV2 ....115 A5
Tarrington Covert 6
B38 ....123 E8
Tarry Hollow Rd DY5 ....61 B7
Tarry Rd B8 ....67 E5
Tarvin Mews DY5 ....61 D1
Taryn Dr WS10 ....41 D7
Tasker St Walsall WS1 ....42 D8
West Bromwich B70 ....52 E4
Tasman Gr WV6 ....23 E5
Tat Bank Rd B69 ....64 B6
Tatchbrook Ct 5 CV31 .....161 F6
Tatnall Gr CV34 ....160 E8
Taunton Ave WV10 ....11 D4
Taunton Rd B12 ....87 B4
Taunton Twr B31 ....102 C2
Taunton Way CV6 ....95 A2
Taverner's Gn B20 ....54 F3
Taverners Cl WV12 ....13 C1
Tavistock Cl B79 ....21 C7
Tavistock Rd B27 ....106 C8
Tavistock St CV32 ....156 F1
Tavistock Way CV11 ....73 E5
Tavistock Wlk CV2 ....114 C7
Tavr Cl B36 ....69 F7
Tay Croft B37 ....70 C4
Tay Gr Birmingham B38 ....123 F8
Halesowen B62 ....83 E8
Tay Rd Birmingham B45 ....102 B1
Coventry CV6 ....113 B6
Taylor Ave
Royal Leamington Spa
CV32 ....157 B2
Walsall WS3 ....28 D8
Taylor Cl CV8 ....148 B6
Taylor Ct CV34 ....160 D7
Taylor Ho 4 WS2 ....42 C7
Taylor Rd
Birmingham B13 ....104 F5
Dudley DY2 ....62 E2
Wolverhampton WV4 ....39 F5
Taylor St WV11 ....26 D5
Taylor's La Smethwick B67 ..64 F5
West Bromwich B71 ....53 D4
Taylors La B69 ....63 F2
Taylors Orch B23 ....56 B4
Taynton Covert 4 B30 ......104 C3
Taysfield Rd B31 ....102 E6
Taywood Dr B10 ....87 C7
Tea Gdn The CV12 ....95 E8
Teachers Cl CV6 ....113 A5
Teal Cres DY10 ....117 B3
Teal Dr Birmingham B23 .....56 B3
Hinckley LE10 ....75 A6
Teal Gr WV14 ....41 B3
Teal Rd B80 ....159 F4
Tealby Gr B29 ....86 A1
Teall Ct B27 ....88 C3
Teall Rd B8 ....67 E5
Teal Cl Birmingham B11 .....87 B6
Burntwood WS7 ....7 D6
Teasdale Way DY9 ....81 D4
Teasel Gr WV10 ....12 B7
Teasel Rd WV11 ....26 C5
Teazel Ave B30 ....103 D6
Tebworth Cl WV9 ....10 F2
Ted Pitts La CV5 ....94 B2
Tedbury Cres B23 ....56 E6
Tedder Rd WS2 ....27 F2

Teddesley Ct WS11 ....1 E3
Teddesley Gr B33 ....69 C4
Teddesley St WS4 ....28 F3
Teddesley Way WS12 ....1 C6
Teddington Gr B42 ....55 D3
Tedstone Rd B32 ....84 E5
Tees Gr B38 ....123 F8
Teesdale Ave B34 ....68 F6
Teesdale Cl WV1 ....26 A2
Teeswater Cl B60 ....150 E6
Teign B77 ....36 A5
Teign Bank Cl LE10 ....71 D2
Teign Bank Rd LE10 ....71 D2
Teignmouth Rd B29 ....86 A1
Telephone Rd CV3 ....114 C2
Telfer Rd CV6 ....113 B7
Telford Ave
Great Wyrley WS6 ....4 F3
Royal Leamington Spa
CV32 ....157 B5
Telford Cl Burntwood WS7 ...7 C8
Smethwick B67 ....64 D1
Walsall WS2 ....28 A5
West Bromwich B71 ....53 A8
Telford Dr WS9 ....38 D7
Telford Gdns WV3 ....38 B7
Telford Rd Bedworth CV2 ...96 C8
Tamworth B79 ....20 F8
Walsall WS2 ....28 A5
Telford Way B66 ....64 F8
Telfordinf & Jun Sch
CV32 ....157 C5
Teme Ave DY11 ....116 B3
Teme Ct B23 ....56 B3
Teme Gr WV13 ....27 D2
Teme Rd Halesowen B63 ....82 B5
Stourbridge DY8 ....80 F3
Tempest St Tamworth B79 ..21 A5
Wolverhampton WV2 ....163 C2
Templar Ave CV4 ....112 A1
Templar Ct CV11 ....73 C2
Templars Prim Sch CV4 ...112 A1
Templars The Oldbury B69 ..63 E5
Templars' Fields CV4 ....132 B7
Temple Ave
Balsall Common CV7 ....129 F6
Birmingham B28 ....106 A6
Temple Bar WV13 ....27 A2
Temple Cl B98 ....153 F4
Temple Ct B46 ....59 F1
Temple Gr CV34 ....160 D5
Temple La B93 ....129 A4
Temple Meadow Prim Sch
B64 ....63 A1
Temple Pas B2 ....164 B2
Temple Rd Dorridge B93 ..128 A3
Willenhall WV13 ....27 B3
Temple Row B2 ....164 C3
Temple Row W B2 ....164 B3
Temple Sq WV13 ....27 A3
Temple St Bilston WV14 .....40 E5
Birmingham B2 ....164 B2
Dudley DY3 ....50 D3
West Bromwich B70 ....53 D4
Wolverhampton WV2 ....163 B2
Temple Way Coleshill B46 ...59 F1
Tipton B69 ....52 D2
Templefield Gdns 2 B9 .....67 C1
Templefield Sq B15 ....86 B7
Templefield St B9 ....67 C1
Templemore Dr B43 ....54 E7
Templeton Cl B93 ....128 A3
Templeton Rd B44 ....44 F2
Ten Acres End B30 ....104 B8
Ten Ashes La B45 ....122 C4
Tenacre La DY3 ....50 E6
Tenacres Fst Sch B98 ......154 F3
Tenacres La B98 ....154 F3
Tenbury Cl 11 Aldridge WS9 ..30 C8
Redditch B98 ....154 C6
Willenhall WS2 ....27 D3
Tenbury Ct WV4 ....38 D5
Tenbury Gdns WV4 ....38 D5
Tenbury Ho
Birmingham B33 ....69 A2
2 Halesowen B63 ....83 A3
Tenbury Rd B14 ....104 E6
Tenby Cl CV12 ....77 C1
Tenby Ct CV32 ....161 E8
Tenby Rd B13 ....105 D7
Tenby St N B1 ....66 B4
Tenby St B1 ....66 B4
Tenby Twr B31 ....103 A1
Teneriffe Rd CV6 ....95 F1
Tenlands Rd B63 ....82 F3
Tenlons Rd CV10 ....72 F2
Tennal Dr B32 ....84 F6
Tennal Gr B32 ....84 F6
Tennal La B32 ....84 F6
Tennal Rd B32 ....84 F6
Tennant St
Birmingham B15 ....66 B1
Nuneaton CV11 ....73 E3
Tennis Ct B30 ....103 D4
Tennis Ct The B15 ....86 A5
Tennscore Ave WS6 ....4 E3
Tennyson Ave
Sutton Coldfield B74 ....31 F6
Tamworth B79 ....21 A6
Warwick CV34 ....160 C4
Tennyson Ho
Birmingham B31 ....123 A8
3 Oldbury B68 ....64 C4

Tennyson Rd
Birmingham B10 ....87 E7
Coventry CV2 ....114 C3
Dudley DY1 ....50 A4
Hinckley LE10 ....71 C1
Redditch B97 ....158 C8
Walsall WS3 ....28 E8
Willenhall WV12 ....27 E8
Wolverhampton WV10 ....12 A1
Tennyson St DY5 ....61 D7
Tennyson Way DY10 ....117 C6
Tenter Ct B63 ....83 B4
Tenter Dr B63 ....83 C4
Tenterfields B63 ....83 B4
Tenterfields Prim Sch B63 ....83 C4
Tern Cl WV4 ....39 D3
Tern Gr B38 ....103 E1
Terrace Rd
Birmingham, Edgbaston B15 ....85 F3
Birmingham, Lozells B19 ....66 D7
Terrace St Blackheath B65 ....63 B1
Brierley Hill DY5 ....61 E5
Wednesbury WS10 ....42 A3
Terrace The
Blackheath B64 ....82 E8
Wolverhampton WV3 ....24 C1
Terry Ave CV32 ....156 C1
Terry Dr B76 ....46 F2
Terry Rd CV1 ....113 F1
Terry St DY2 ....51 E1
Terrys La B98 ....153 F5
Terrys La B24 ....57 C3
Tessall La B31 ....102 D2
Tetbury Gr B31 ....102 D3
Tetley Ave WS4 ....29 B4
Tetley Rd B11 ....87 E3
Tetnall St DY2 ....62 D8
Tettenhall Arc WV6 ....24 D5
Tettenhall Coll (The Drive Sch) WV6 ....24 C5
Tettenhall Rd WV1,WV3, WV6 ....24 F4
Tettenhall Wood Sch WV6 ....24 B3
Teviot Gdns DY5 ....61 B6
Teviot Gr B38 ....123 F8
Teviot Twr B19 ....66 C5
Tew Park Rd B21 ....65 F7
Tewe Pl WS13 ....9 A6
Tewkesbury Dr
Bedworth CV12 ....78 C3
Dudley DY2 ....62 D3
Tewkesbury Rd
Birmingham B20 ....55 E2
Walsall WS3 ....13 E2
Thackeray Cl CV10 ....72 A4
Thackeray Dr B79 ....21 A7
Thackeray Rd B30 ....103 D5
Thackhall St CV2 ....113 F4
Thame Ct B47 ....124 E2
Thames Cl
Brierley Hill DY5 ....61 B7
Bulkington CV12 ....79 A3
Thames Ct B23 ....46 B5
Thames Ho DY3 ....50 D3
Thames Rd WS3 ....14 E1
Thames Twr B7 ....67 B5
Thamley Rd CV6 ....113 A4
Thane Cl B80 ....159 F4
Thanet Cl DY6 ....60 C7
Thanet Gr B42 ....55 C4
Thatchers The B62 ....83 E8
Thaxted Rd B33 ....69 E3
Theatre App B5 ....164 C1
Theatre Ct CV34 ....160 D6
Theatre St CV34 ....160 D7
Thebes Cl CV5 ....111 B8
Theddingworth Cl CV3 ....134 E8
Thelbridge Rd B31 ....122 E6
Thelma Rd DY4 ....51 E5
Thelma St ■ WS1 ....42 D7
Thelsford Way WV12 ....107 D8
Theodore Cl
Birmingham B17 ....85 D4
Oldbury B69 ....52 E1
Theresa Rd B11 ....87 B7
Thetford Cl DY4 ....51 D5
Thetford Gdns WV11 ....26 D6
Thetford Rd B42 ....55 B7
Thetford Way WS5 ....43 C3
Thickett Cl WS2 ....42 B8
Thicknall Dr DY9 ....81 C2
Thicknall La DY9 ....99 B3
Thicknall Rise DY9 ....99 B4
Thickthorn Cl CV8 ....148 B2
Thickthorn Mews CV8 ....148 B2
Thickthorn Orchs CV8 ....148 B2
Thimble Dr B76 ....46 F1
Thimble End Rd B76 ....47 A2
Thimble Mill La B6,B7 ....67 B7
Thimblemill Rd B67 ....64 E3
Thimbler Rd CV4 ....132 A6
Thinktank Mus & IMAX Theatre* B4 ....66 F3
Third Ave
Birmingham, Bordesley Green B9 ....67 F2
Birmingham, Selly Oak B29 ....86 C3
Birmingham, Witton B6 ....55 F3
Brownhills WS8 ....7 A1
Kingswinford DY6 ....60 F8
Wolverhampton WV10 ....25 E4
Third Exhibition Ave B40 ....90 D4
Third Rd B61 ....120 F4
Thirlestane Cl CV8 ....148 C6

Thirlmere Ave CV11 ....73 F6
Thirlmere Cl Cannock WS11 ....1 E1
Coventry CV4 ....111 E3
Wolverhampton WV6 ....24 D8
Thirlmere Dr
Birmingham B13 ....105 D8
Essington WV11 ....13 A2
Thirlmere Gr WV6 ....23 F4
Thirlmere Ho B15 ....85 D3
Thirlmere Rd
Bedworth CV12 ....78 A2
Hinckley LE10 ....75 A7
Wolverhampton WV6 ....24 D8
Sutton Coldfield B74 ....45 A7
Thirsk Croft B36 ....68 C8
Thirsk Rd CV3 ....133 C5
Thirsk Way B61 ....121 B1
Thirston Cl WV11 ....27 A5
Thistle Cl DY3 ....50 F6
Thistle Croft WV11 ....26 D5
Thistle Down Cl B74 ....31 A2
Thistle Gn B38 ....123 E7
Thistle Ho B36 ....68 D8
Thistle La B32 ....102 B7
Thistledown Ave WS7 ....7 A6
Thistledown Dr
■ Cannock WS11 ....2 D1
Featherstone WV10 ....12 A7
Thistledown Rd B34 ....69 C7
Thistledown Wlk DY3 ....39 C1
Thistlegreen Cl B65 ....62 F5
Thistlegreen Rd DY2 ....62 E4
Thistlegreen Rd B90 ....145 B6
Thistley Field E CV6 ....113 A7
Thistley Field N CV6 ....113 A7
Thistley Field S CV6 ....112 F6
Thistley Field W CV6 ....112 F7
Thistley Nook WS13 ....3 A1
Thomas Barnes Prim Sch B78 ....20 B7
Thomas Cres ■ B66 ....65 C5
Thomas Greenway WS13 ....3 A2
Thomas Guy Rd B70 ....52 F6
Thomas Hardy Ct B79 ....21 A7
Thomas Ho WS3 ....14 D3
Thomas King Ho ■ CV1 ....113 E4
Thomas Landsdail St CV3 ....133 D8
Thomas Lane St CV6 ....96 A1
Thomas Mason Cl WV11 ....26 D7
Thomas Naul Croft CV4 ....111 F3
Thomas Sharp St CV4 ....132 A7
Thomas St Bedworth CV12 ....78 A2
Birmingham B6 ....66 F6
Royal Leamington Spa CV32 ....157 A1
Smethwick B66 ....65 B5
Tamworth B77 ....21 C4
Walsall WS2 ....28 D2
West Bromwich B70 ....53 D2
Wolverhampton WV2 ....163 B1
Thomas Wlk B35 ....58 B3
Thompson Ave WV2 ....39 E6
Thompson Cl Dudley DY2 ....62 B2
Willenhall WV13 ....27 A3
Thompson Dr B24 ....67 F8
Thompson Gdns B67 ....64 F4
Thompson Ho DY4 ....52 C8
Thompson Rd
Oldbury B68 ....64 B5
Smethwick B67 ....64 F4
Thompson St
Bilston WV14 ....40 D5
Willenhall WV13 ....27 A3
Thompson's Rd CV7 ....94 F6
Thomson Ave B38 ....103 D1
Thor Cl WS11 ....2 A5
Thoresby B79 ....20 E6
Thoresby Croft DY1 ....50 F3
Thornby Ave WS10 ....41 F4
Thorn Rd B30 ....103 E7
Thorn Stile Cl CV32 ....157 E6
Thornberry Dr DY1 ....61 B8
Thornberry Wlk B7 ....67 C6
Thornbridge Ave B42 ....55 D7
Thornbridge Gr WV5 ....15 F3
Thornbrook Cl ■ WS4 ....28 F3
Thornbury Ct WV6 ....24 A3
Thornbury La B98 ....154 C2
Thornbury Rd B20 ....55 D2
Thornby Ave
Kenilworth CV8 ....148 B3
Solihull B91 ....107 B5
Tamworth B77 ....35 E8
Thornby Rd B23 ....56 C8
Thorncliffe Cl B97 ....158 A6
Thorncliffe Rd B44 ....44 E2
Thorncroft Way WS5 ....43 B4
Thorne Ave WV10 ....25 E7
Thorne Pl B65 ....63 C3
Thorne Rd WV13 ....27 A4
Thorne St WV2 ....40 A7
Thornes Croft WS9 ....16 E4
Thorney Rd Aldridge B74 ....30 F1
Coventry CV2 ....114 B4
Thorneycroft La WV10 ....26 A6
Thorneycroft Pl WV11 ....41 B3
Thorneycroft Rd WV14 ....41 B4
Thornfield Cres B14 ....7 A8
Thornfield Croft DY3 ....50 F6
Thornfield Rd B27 ....88 D2
Thornfield Way LE10 ....75 E8
Thorngrove Ave ■ B91 ....127 C8
Thornham Way B14 ....104 D1
Thornhill Dr CV11 ....79 C8
Thornhill Gr B21 ....65 F8
Thornhill Pk B74 ....45 A8

Thornhill Rd
Birmingham, Handsworth B21 ....65 F8
Birmingham, Sparkhill B11 ....87 D3
Brierley Hill DY5 ....81 E8
Cannock WS12 ....1 F7
Coventry CV1 ....113 D5
Dudley DY1 ....51 C4
Halesowen B63 ....82 E3
Little Aston B74 ....31 B1
Redditch B98 ....154 C6
Solihull B91 ....107 C7
Sutton Coldfield B74 ....45 A7
Thornhurst Ave B32 ....84 E7
Thornleigh DY3 ....50 D5
Thornleigh Trad Est DY2 ....62 A7
Thornley Cl
Birmingham B13 ....87 A1
Radford Semele CV31 ....162 F5
Wolverhampton WV11 ....12 F1
Thornley Croft WS6 ....4 D1
Thornley Gr B76 ....58 C6
Thornley Rd WV11 ....12 F1
Thornley St WV1 ....163 C3
Thorns Ave DY5 ....61 E1
Thorns Com Coll DY5 ....81 E8
Thorns Com Inf Sch CV8 ....148 B4
Thorns Prim Sch DY5 ....81 E7
Thorns Rd DY5 ....81 E7
Thornsett Gr B90 ....106 B6
Thornthwaite Cl B45 ....102 B2
Thornton Cl
Coventry CV5 ....111 C4
Tipton B69 ....52 C2
Warwick CV34 ....155 F1
Thornton Dr DY5 ....61 E1
Thornton Ho B19 ....66 C6
Thornton Jun Sch B8 ....68 B5
Thornton Rd
Birmingham B8 ....68 B5
Solihull B90 ....126 E5
Wolverhampton WV1 ....26 B1
Thorntons Way CV10 ....72 A3
Thornwood Cl B68 ....64 C5
Thornycroft Rd LE10 ....75 E8
Thornyfield Cl CV3 ....115 A2
Thornyfield Rd B90 ....106 C3
Thornyhurst La WS14 ....17 A6
Thorp St 164 B1
Thorpe Ave WV7 ....6 D8
Thorpe Cl Burntwood WS7 ....6 D8
Sutton Coldfield B75 ....46 C7
Thorpe Ct B91 ....106 F6
Thorpe Rd WS1 ....42 E7
Thorpe St WS7 ....6 D8
Threadneedle St CV1 ....113 D6
Three Acres La B90 ....125 F6
Three Corner Cl B90 ....125 E8
Three Cornered CV32 ....157 C6
Three Crowns Specl Sch WS5 ....43 F8
Three Oaks Rd B47 ....125 B4
Three Pots Rd LE10 ....75 E4
Three Shires Jct CV6 ....95 A4
Three Shires Oak Rd B67 ....64 F2
Three Spires Ave CV6 ....113 A6
Three Spires Ind Est CV6 ....96 A5
Three Spires Sch CV6 ....112 D6
Three Spires Sh Ctr WS13 ....9 B7
Three Tuns La WV10 ....11 C2
Three Tuns Par WV10 ....11 C2
Threshers Dr WV12 ....27 D6
Threshers Way WV12 ....27 D6
Throckmorton Rd B98 ....159 B8
Throne Cl B65 ....63 D5
Throne Cres B65 ....63 D5
Throne Rd B65 ....63 D5
Throstles Cl B43 ....54 E7
Thrush Rd B68 ....63 F2
Thrushel Wlk WV11 ....26 C5
Thruxton Cl
Birmingham B14 ....104 F3
Redditch B98 ....154 E3
Thurcroft Cl B8 ....67 F4
Thuree Rd B67 ....64 E2
Thurlby Ct WV11 ....25 A3
Thurleigh Cl DY9 ....81 C2
Thurlestone Rd
Birmingham B31 ....122 C7
Coventry CV6 ....112 F8
Thurloe Cres B45 ....101 E1
Thurlston Ave B92 ....88 F4
Thurlstone Dr WV4 ....38 F4
Thurlstone Rd WS3 ....14 B3
Thurne B77 ....35 F8
Thursfield Rd
Royal Leamington Spa CV32 ....157 B3
Tipton DY4 ....52 A6
West Bromwich B71 ....53 E7
Thurso B77 ....21 E5
Thurston Ave B69 ....63 F6
Thynne St B70 ....53 E2
Tibbats Cl B32 ....84 C3
Tibberton Cl
Halesowen B63 ....83 C4
Solihull B91 ....127 A7
Wolverhampton WV3 ....38 D7
Tibberton Ct B60 ....150 E7
Tibbets La B17 ....85 B4
Tibbington Rd DY4 ....51 E6
Tibbington Terr DY4 ....51 F7
Tibbits Ct ■ CV34 ....160 E6
Tibbits Ho ■ WS2 ....28 D3
Tiber Cl CV5 ....111 F4
Tiberius Cl B46 ....59 F1

Tibland Rd B27 ....88 D2
Ticknall Cl B97 ....153 A4
Tidbury Cl B97 ....158 C6
Tidbury Green Sch B90 ....125 E4
Tiddington Cl B36 ....58 B1
Tideswell Cl CV3 ....115 A1
Tideswell Rd B42 ....55 C7
Tidmarsh Cl CV7 ....130 A6
Tidmarsh Rd CV35 ....156 A7
Tidworth Croft ■ B14 ....105 A3
Tierney Dr DY4 ....52 C6
Tiffany La WV9 ....10 F2
Tiffield Rd B25 ....88 C5
Tigley Ave B32 ....84 D1
Tilbury Cl WV3 ....38 A8
Tilbury Gr B13 ....86 D1
Tidasley St B70 ....53 B5
Tildesley Dr WV12 ....27 B5
Tile Cross Rd B33 ....69 E2
Tile Cross Trad Est B33 ....69 E1
Tile Gr B37 ....70 A5
Tile Hill La
Coventry, Allesley CV4, CV5 ....112 D2
Coventry, Tile Hill CV4 ....112 B1
Tile Hill Sta CV4 ....131 D8
Tile Hill Wood Sch & Language Coll CV4 ....111 D2
Tiled House La DY5 ....61 B6
Tilehouse B97 ....153 D2
Tilehouse Green La B93 ....127 F4
Tilehouse La B90 ....125 E6
Tilehurst Dr CV4 ....111 D1
Tilesford Cl B90 ....127 A6
Tilewood Ave CV5 ....111 F4
Tilia Rd B77 ....22 B5
Tiller Gr B75 ....32 D4
Tilshead Cl B14 ....104 E3
Tilsley Gr B23 ....56 B5
Tilston Dr DY5 ....61 D1
Tilton Rd Birmingham B9 ....67 C1
Hinckley LE10 ....75 E6
Timber Mill Ct B17 ....85 B6
Timberdine Cl B63 ....82 D6
Timberhonger La B61 ....136 B2
Timberlake Cl B90 ....127 B6
Timberley La B34 ....69 C6
Timberley Prim Sch B34 ....69 B6
Timbers Way
Birmingham B11 ....87 A6
Sutton Coldfield B72 ....57 F4
Timbertree Cres B64 ....82 E7
Timbertree Prim Sch B64 ....82 E7
Timbertree Rd B64 ....82 F7
Times Square Ave CV31 ....61 F2
Timmins Cl B91 ....107 E6
Timmis Cl WV14 ....40 B3
Timmis Rd DY9 ....81 F6
Timon View CV3 ....134 F7
Timothy Gr CV4 ....112 B1
Timothy Rd B69 ....63 D7
Tinacre Hill WV6 ....23 B4
Tinchbourne St ■ DY1 ....51 C1
Tindal Jun & Inf Sch B12 ....86 F5
Tindal St B12 ....86 F5
Tink-A-Tank CV34 ....160 E6
Tinkers Farm Gr B31 ....102 E3
Tinkers Farm Rd B31 ....102 E3
Tinkers Green Rd B77 ....35 F6
Tinkers La
Earlswood B94 ....142 E2
Lapworth B94 ....143 E1
Tinmeadow Cres B45 ....122 C7
Tinsley St DY4 ....52 B5
Tintagel Cl Coventry CV3 ....134 D5
Perton WV6 ....23 F3
Tintagel Dr DY1 ....50 E2
Tintagel Gr CV8 ....148 B4
Tintagel Way
Nuneaton CV11 ....74 A5
Walsall WS9 ....29 E7
Tintern Cl
Bromsgrove B61 ....136 E1
Sutton Coldfield B74 ....45 A7
Tintern Cres WS3 ....13 F2
Tintern Gr CV6 ....23 E4
Tintern Ho B20 ....84 F5
Tintern Rd B20 ....55 E1
Tintern Villas ■ B12 ....87 B5
Tintern Way
Bedworth CV12 ....78 C3
Walsall WS3 ....13 F2
Tipper Trad Est DY9 ....82 A5
Tipperary Cl B36 ....68 E8
Tippett Cl CV11 ....79 A7
Tipping's Hill B97 ....158 C5
Tippity Gn B65 ....63 B4
Tipps Stone Cl DY4 ....51 E4
Tipton Coll DY4 ....52 B6
Tipton Green Jun Sch DY4 ....51 F4
Tipton Rd
Dudley, Tipton Green DY1 ....51 E3
Dudley, Woodsetton DY3 ....50 F7
Tipton B69 ....52 C2
Tipton St DY3 ....50 E7
Tipton Sta DY4 ....51 F6
Tirley Rd B33 ....69 A4
Tisdale Rise CV8 ....148 B6
Titan Bsns Ctr CV34 ....161 E4
Titan Way LS13 ....9 B8
Titania Cl B45 ....102 A3
Titchfield Cl WV10 ....11 E4
Titford Cl B69 ....63 F5

Titford La B65 ....63 E4
Titford Rd B65 ....63 F4
The Barn La B94 ....142 C6
Tithe Croft WV10 ....25 F3
Tithe Rd WV11 ....26 D6
Titterstone Rd B31 ....123 A8
Tiverton Cl DY6 ....61 A3
Tiverton Dr
Nuneaton CV11 ....73 F5
West Bromwich B71 ....53 C6
Tiverton Gr
Coventry CV2 ....114 D5
Smethwick B67 ....64 F6
Tiverton Jun & Inf Sch B29 ....85 F2
Tiverton Rd
Birmingham B29 ....85 F2
Coventry CV2 ....114 D5
Smethwick B66 ....65 B5
Tiverton Sch CV6 ....112 D5
Tiveycourt Rd CV6 ....96 A3
Tividale Com Prim Sch B69 ....52 B2
Tividale High Sch & Com Coll B69 ....52 C1
Tividale Rd B69 ....52 A2
Tividale St DY4 ....52 A2
Tividale Trad Est B69 ....52 B2
Tixall Rd B28 ....88 D6
Tixall Rd B28 ....105 E5
Tobruk Wlk
Brierley Hill DY5 ....61 D3
Willenhall WV13 ....27 D1
Tocil Croft CV4 ....132 D4
Toler Rd CV11 ....73 B5
Toll End Rd DY4 ....52 C4
Toll House Rd B45 ....122 C7
Tollard Cl CV2 ....114 F5
Tolley Rd DY11 ....116 B1
Tollgate Cl B31 ....122 F8
Tollgate Dr B20 ....66 B7
Tollgate Prec B67 ....64 F6
Tollhouse Rd B60 ....150 E6
Tollhouse Way B66 ....64 F6
Tolman Dr B77 ....21 D3
Tolson Ave B78 ....35 B8
Tolson Cl B77 ....35 D5
Tolworth Gdns WV2 ....39 E7
Tolworth Hall Rd B24 ....57 B3
Tolworth Rd B24 ....57 B3
Tom Ellis Ct CV7 ....96 A8
Tom Henderson Cl CV3 ....134 F7
Tom Hill B94 ....142 B3
Tom Ward Cl CV3 ....134 E7
Tom Williams Way B77 ....25 C8
Tomey Rd B11 ....87 D5
Tomkinson Dr WV11 ....116 B4
Tomkinson Rd CV10 ....72 F4
Tomlan Rd B31 ....123 C2
Tomlinson Rd B36 ....58 D1
Tompstone Rd B71 ....53 F8
Toms Town La B80 ....159 E3
Tomson Ave CV6 ....113 B4
Tonadine Cl WV11 ....13 A1
Tonbridge Rd
Birmingham B24 ....57 A1
Coventry CV3 ....134 A6
Tong Ct ⑨ WV3 ....25 C4
Tong St WS1 ....29 A1
Top Croft Rd B23 ....56 F7
Top Field Wlk B14 ....104 D2
Top Rd Barnacle CV7,CV12 ....97 B7
Wildmoor B61 ....121 A4
Topcliffe Sch B35 ....58 A3
Topfield Ho B14 ....104 E1
Topland Gr B31 ....102 C1
Topp's Dr CV12 ....77 E1
Topp's Heath CV12 ....77 E1
Topsham Croft B14 ....104 D5
Topsham Rd B67 ....64 E6
Tor Way WS3 ....21 E5
Torbay B77 ....21 E5
Torbay Rd CV5 ....112 C4
Torc Ave B77 ....21 E5
Torc High Sch B77 ....21 F1
Torcastle Cl CV6 ....113 F7
Torcross Ave CV2 ....114 C6
Torfield WV8 ....10 E2
Toronto Gdns B32 ....84 E6
Torpoint Cl CV2 ....114 C7
Torre Ave B31 ....102 E2
Torrey Gr B8 ....68 C4
Torridge B77 ....36 A5
Torridge Dr WV11 ....26 C5
Torridon Croft B13 ....86 D3
Torridon Rd WV11 ....13 A1
Torrington Ave CV4 ....131 E8
Torrs Cl B97 ....153 D2
Torside B77 ....36 B7
Torvale Rd WV6 ....24 A2
Torwood Cl CV4 ....131 F6
Totnes Cl CV2 ....114 C7
Totnes Gr ■ B29 ....85 F2
Totnes Rd B67 ....64 F6
Tottenham Cres B44 ....45 B2
Touchstone Rd CV34 ....161 F2
Touchwood Hall Cl B91 ....107 C4
Towbury Cl B98 ....158 F5
Towcester Croft B36 ....68 D8
Tower Croft B37 ....70 B4
Tower Dr B61 ....137 A6
Tower Rd Bedworth CV12 ....78 B2
Birmingham, Aston New Town B6 ....66 F7
Sutton Coldfield B75 ....32 B3

Tower Rd *continued*
Tipton B69 ....63 C7
Tower Rise B69 ....63 C7
Tower St Birmingham B19 ...164 B5
Coventry CV1 ....165 B3
Dudley DY1 ....51 C1
16 Royal Leamington Spa
CV31 ....162 A7
Sedgley DY3 ....39 D1
Walsall WS1 ....28 E2
Wolverhampton WV1 ....25 B2
Tower View Cres CV10 ....72 B3
Tower View Rd WS6 ....13 F8
Towers Cl Kenilworth CV8 ...147 F2
Kidderminster DY10 ....117 B5
Town Fields Cl CV5 ....112 B7
Town Gate Retail Pk DY1 ....51 F2
Town Jun Sch B72 ....46 C4
Town Wharf Bsns Pk
WS2 ....28 D2
Townend St WS2 ....28 E2
Townsend Cl CV34 ....155 F1
Townfields WS3 ....9 A7
Townfold WS3 ....15 A4
Towney Gdns B6 ....55 E1
Townsend Ave
Bromsgrove B61 ....137 B4
Sedgley DY3 ....50 D8
Townsend Croft CV3 ....133 C7
Townsend Dr
Nuneaton CV11 ....73 F3
Sutton Coldfield B76 ....57 F7
Townsend Ho B79 ....21 A4
Townsend Pl DY6 ....60 D6
Townsend Rd CV3 ....133 C8
Townsend Way B1 ....66 B3
Townsends Cl CV11 ....75 A1
Townshend Gr B37 ....69 F4
Townson Rd WV11 ....27 A8
Townwell Fold WV1 ....163 B3
Towpath Cl B9 ....67 B2
Towyn Rd B13 ....87 D2
Toys La B63 ....82 C5
Tozer St DY4 ....51 F7
TP Riley Com Sch WS4 ....14 C2
Traceys Mdw B45 ....122 A7
Tractor Spares Ind Est
WV13 ....26 D2
Trafalgar Cl WS12 ....2 E4
Trafalgar Ct B69 ....52 C1
Trafalgar Gr B25 ....88 A6
Trafalgar Ho
Birmingham B11 ....87 B8
3 Coventry CV1 ....113 B2
Trafalgar Rd
Birmingham, Erdington B24 ...56 F3
Birmingham, Handsworth
B21 ....65 E8
Birmingham, Moseley B13 .....86 F4
Smethwick B66 ....65 C4
Tipton B69 ....52 B1
Trafford Dr CV10 ....72 C6
Trafford Lodge B CV31 ......162 B7
Trafford Pk The B98 ....153 F3
Trafford Rd LE10 ....71 F2
Trajan Hill B46 ....59 F1
Tram St DY10 ....116 E5
Tram Way B66 ....64 C7
Tramway CI Bilston WV14 ....41 A7
Darlaston WS10 ....41 E7
Tranter Ave B48 ....139 A5
Tranter Cres WS11 ....2 B3
Tranter Rd B8 ....68 A5
Tranwell Cl WV9 ....10 F2
Traquain Dr DY1 ....51 A3
Travellers Ct WS7 ....7 A5
Travellers Way B37 ....70 D3
Treaford La B8 ....68 C4
Treasure Ct B77 ....21 E4
Treddles La B70 ....53 D3
Tredington Cl
Birmingham B29 ....103 A7
Redditch B98 ....159 B7
Tredington Rd CV5 ....111 F4
Tree Acre Gr B63 ....82 C4
Treedale Cl CV4 ....131 D8
Treeford Cl WV1 ....106 F1
Trees Rd WS1 ....42 F6
Treeton Croft B33 ....69 A2
Treetops Dr WV12 ....27 E4
Trefoil B77 ....22 B5
Trefoil Cl B29 ....103 A7
Treforest Rd CV3 ....134 C8
Tregarron Rd B63 ....82 C5
Tregea Rise B43 ....54 C7
Tregony Rise WS14 ....9 D6
Tregorrick Rd CV7 ....96 A8
Tregullan Rd CV7 ....96 B8
Trehern Cl B93 ....128 A5
Treherne Rd CV6 ....113 B8
Trehernes Dr DY9 ....81 B1
Trehurst Ave B42 ....55 C7
Trejon Rd B64 ....82 F8
Trelawney Rd CV7 ....96 A7
Tremaine Gdns WV10 ....25 E4
Tremont Ho WV10 ....23 E3
Tremont St WV10 ....25 E3
Trenance Cl WS14 ....9 D7
Trenance Rd CV7 ....96 A8
Trenchard Cl B75 ....46 F5
Treneere Rd CV7 ....96 B8
Trensale Ave CV6 ....112 F4
Trent Cl Burntwood WS7 ......7 D6
Perton WV6 ....23 E4
Stourbridge DY8 ....81 A4

Trent Cres B47 ....124 E2
Trent Ct B73 ....46 B5
Trent Dr B36 ....69 F8
Trent Ho Cannock WS12 ....2 C5
Dudley DY3 ....50 E3
Trent Pl WS3 ....14 D2
Trent Rd Bickenhill B26 ....90 C4
Bulkington CV12 ....79 A2
Cannock WS11 ....1 E5
Hinckley LE10 ....75 A8
Nuneaton CV11 ....73 D5
Walsall WS3 ....15 A1
Trent St B5 ....164 D2
Trent Twr B B7 ....67 A5
Trent Valley Cotts WS13 ....3 F1
Trent Valley Rd WS13,
WS14 ....9 D8
Trentham Ave WV12 ....27 B5
Trentham Ct Cannock WS11 ....2 B1
Nuneaton CV11 ....78 F8
Trentham Gdns CV8 ....148 C5
Trentham Gr B26 ....88 E5
Trentham Rd CV1 ....113 F4
Trentham Rise WV2 ....39 F7
Trenville Ave B11 ....87 B5
Tresco Cl B45 ....101 E1
Trescott Jun & Inf Sch
B31 ....102 D3
Trescott Rd
Birmingham B31 ....102 D4
Redditch B98 ....153 F3
Tresham Rd
Birmingham B44 ....44 F1
8 Kingswinford DY6 ....60 D8
Tresillian Rd CV7 ....96 B8
Tressel Croft CV34 ....161 E2
Trevanie Ave B32 ....84 C6
Trevelyan Ho **1** B37 ......70 C1
Treville Cl B98 ....154 E3
Treviscoe Cl CV7 ....96 A8
Trevithick Cl WS7 ....7 C8
Trevor Ave WS6 ....5 A3
Trevor Cl CV4 ....131 D8
Trevor Rd Hinckley LE10 ......71 F1
Walsall WS3 ....14 F5
Trevor St B7 ....67 C6
Trevor St W B7 ....67 C6
Trevorne Cl B12 ....86 F6
Trevose Ave CV7 ....96 B8
Trevose Cl WS3 ....13 F3
Trevose Retreat B13 ....86 F5
Trewint Cl CV7 ....96 A8
Trewman Cl B76 ....57 F8
Treyamon Rd WS5 ....43 D7
Treynham Cl WV1 ....26 C1
Triangle WS7 ....7 A4
Triangle The
Birmingham B18 ....65 F6
Coventry CV5 ....112 B4
Trianon Rd B60 ....137 C1
Trickley Dr B75 ....46 F6
Trident Bsns Pk CV11 ....73 D3
Trident Cl
Sutton Coldfield, Walmley
B76 ....57 F7
Sutton Coldfield, Wylde Green
B23 ....57 A7
Trident Ct B20 ....55 A3
Trident Ctr The DY1 ....51 C1
Trident Dr Oldbury B68 ....84 B5
Wednesbury WS10 ....41 D3
Trident Ret Pk B9 ....67 A2
Trigo Croft B36 ....68 E8
Trimpley Cl B93 ....127 E3
Trimpley Dr WV11 ....116 A7
Trimpley Gdns WV4 ....38 E3
Trimpley Rd B32 ....84 B1
Trinculo Gr CV34 ....161 F2
Trinder Rd B67 ....64 D2
Trindle Rd DY2 ....51 D1
Tring Ct WV6 ....24 F4
Trinity CE Prim Sch
WV10 ....25 F4
Trinity Churchyard CV1 .....165 B3
Trinity Cl
1 Birmingham B19 ....66 D8
Cannock WS11 ....4 E8
Shenstone WS14 ....17 F6
Solihull B92 ....89 B1
Stourbridge DY8 ....60 D2
Trinity Ct Birmingham B6 ....55 D1
3 Blackheath B64 ....62 E1
Bromsgrove B60 ....151 B7
Hinckley LE10 ....75 C8
4 Kidderminster DY10 ....116 F6
Willenhall WV13 ....26 C2
Wolverhampton WV3 ....25 A2
Trinity Dr B79 ....20 D6
Trinity Fields DY10 ....116 F6
Trinity Gr WS10 ....42 A3
Trinity Grange DY10 ....116 F7
Trinity Hill B77 ....66 C5
Trinity Ho B70 ....53 E1
Trinity La Coventry CV1 .....165 B3
Hinckley LE10 ....71 C1
Trinity RC Sch The
CV32 ....161 C6
Trinity Rd Bilston WV14 ....40 F5
Birmingham B6 ....55 E1
Dudley DY1 ....51 C1
Stourbridge DY8 ....81 A8
Sutton Coldfield B75 ....32 C1
Willenhall WV12 ....27 D7
Wood End B78,CV9 ....36 B3
Trinity Rd N B70 ....53 D2
Trinity Rd S B70 ....53 D1

Trinity St Blackheath B64 ....62 E1
Brierley Hill DY5 ....61 D3
Coventry CV1 ....165 B3
Oldbury B69 ....64 A6
Royal Leamington Spa
CV32 ....156 F1
Smethwick B67 ....65 A6
West Bromwich B70 ....53 D2
Trinity Terr **1** B11 ....87 A8
Trinity Vicarage Rd LE10 ....75 C8
Trinity Way B70 ....53 D2
Trinity Way Sta B70 ....53 D1
Trinity Wlk CV11 ....73 E3
Trippleton Ave B32 ....102 B8
Tristram Ave B31 ....103 B1
Triton Cl WS6 ....4 F1
Trittiford Rd B13 ....105 C6
Triumph Cl B37 ....71 E3
Triumph Cl CV2 ....114 E3
Triumph Wlk B36 ....99 F1
Trojan B77 ....21 E3
Tromans Ind Est DY2 ....62 D3
Troon B77 ....22 C4
Troon Cl
Sutton Coldfield B75 ....46 D8
Walsall WS3 ....14 A3
Troon Ct WV6 ....23 D5
Troon Pl DY8 ....60 C3
Troon Way LE10 ....75 D4
Trossachs Rd CV5 ....111 F3
Trotter's La B71 ....53 A7
Troughton Cres CV6 ....113 A5
Trouse La WS10 ....41 F3
Troutbeck Ave CV32 ....156 C2
Troutbeck Dr DY5 ....81 B8
Troutbeck Rd CV5 ....111 F4
Troy Gr B14 ....104 D4
Troy Ind Est B96 ....159 A3
Troyes Cl CV3 ....133 E7
Truck Stop Bsns Pk B11 ....88 B5
Truda St **1** WS1 ....42 D7
Trueman Cl CV34 ....160 E8
Truemans Heath La
B47,B90 ....125 C7
Truggist La CV7 ....69 D5
Trundalls La B90 ....126 A5
Truro Cl Blackheath B65 ....63 E4
Hinckley LE10 ....71 E4
Lichfield WS13 ....3 B3
Truro Ct Cannock WS11 ....2 F5
Truro Dr DY11 ....116 A5
Truro Pl WS12 ....5 C8
Truro Rd WS5 ....43 D7
Truro Twr **4** B16 ....66 A2
Truro Wlk B37 ....70 C2
Trustin Cres B92 ....107 E8
Tryan Rd CV10 ....72 E4
Tryon Pl WV14 ....40 E6
Tryst The B61 ....137 B5
Trysull Ave B26 ....89 C4
Trysull Gdns WV3 ....38 D7
Trysull Holloway WV5 ....37 C3
Trysull Rd
Wolverhampton WV3 ....38 D7
Wombourne WV5 ....37 E1
Trysull Way DY2 ....62 D8
Tudbury Rd B31 ....102 E4
Tudman Cl B76 ....58 A7
Tudor Ave CV5 ....111 F4
Tudor Bsns Ctr B98 ....153 E3
Tudor Cl
Balsall Common CV7 ....130 A6
Birmingham, Highter's Heath
B14 ....105 A1
Birmingham, King's Heath
B13 ....104 F6
Birmingham, Sparkbrook
B10 ....87 C8
Burntwood WS7 ....7 C6
Cheslyn Hay WS6 ....4 E3
Lichfield WS14 ....9 F6
Sutton Coldfield B73 ....45 D2
Tudor Cres Tamworth B77 .....21 F4
Wolverhampton WV4 ....39 B6
Tudor Croft B37 ....69 F1
Tudor Ct Coventry CV7 ....95 E7
Essington WV11 ....12 F4
Sutton Coldfield B74 ....32 A2
Tipton DY4 ....52 A4
Warwick CV34 ....160 D5
Tudor Gdns
Birmingham B23 ....56 E3
Stourbridge DY8 ....80 E5
Tudor Gr B74 ....44 A8
Tudor Grange Sch B91 ....107 A2
Tudor Hill B73 ....46 A6
Tudor Ho Dudley DY2 ....61 F6
Walsall WS1 ....28 E2
Tudor Park Ct B74 ....31 F3
Tudor Pl DY3 ....50 E6
Tudor Rd Bilston WV14 ....41 B4
Birmingham B13 ....86 F3
Blackheath B65 ....63 C5
Burntwood WS7 ....7 C6
Cannock WS12 ....1 F8
Hinckley LE10 ....71 C3
Nuneaton CV10 ....72 C6
Oldbury B68 ....64 C4
Sutton Coldfield B73 ....46 B5
Tipton DY4 ....52 A4
Wolverhampton WV10 ....26 A4
Tudor Row **8** WS13 ....9 B7
Tudor St Birmingham B18 .....65 E4
Tipton DY4 ....52 A4
Tudor Terr
Birmingham B17 ....85 C6
Dudley DY2 ....51 E1

Tudor Vale DY3 ....50 E6
Tudor Way WS6 ....4 D1
Tufnell Gr B8 ....68 B7
Tugford Rd B29 ....103 C7
Tulsi Ctr B19 ....164 A4
Tulip Tree Ave CV8 ....148 B5
Tulip Tree Ct CV8 ....148 B4
Tulip Wlk B37 ....90 C8
Tulliver Cl CV12 ....78 B3
Tulliver Rd CV10 ....73 C1
Tulliver St CV6 ....113 B5
Tulyar Cl B36 ....68 C8
Tunnel Dr B98 ....153 E3
Tunnel La
Birmingham Brandwood End
B14 ....104 C4
Birmingham, Lifford B30 ....104 B4
Tunnel Rd B70 ....53 A7
Tunnel St WV14 ....51 C8
Tunstall Rd DY6 ....61 A5
Turchill Dr B76 ....58 B8
Turf Cl WS11 ....6 A4
Turf Cotts WV4 ....38 F2
Turf Pitts La B75 ....32 F4
Turfpits La B23 ....56 D6
Turlands Cl CV2 ....115 A7
Turley St DY1 ....51 A6
Turls Hill Rd Sedgley DY3 ....50 E8
Sedgley WV14 ....50 E8
Turls St DY3 ....50 E8
Turnberry B77 ....22 C5
Turnberry Dr CV11 ....79 C8
Turnberry Gr WV6 ....23 D5
Turnberry Rd
Birmingham B42 ....55 B8
Walsall WS3 ....14 A3
Turner Ave WV4,WV14 ....39 F2
Turner Cl Bedworth CV12 ......78 A4
Cannock WS11 ....2 D2
Warwick CV34 ....160 B4
Turner Dr Brierley Hill DY5 ...81 D7
Hinckley LE10 ....71 A3
Turner Gr WV6 ....24 A4
Turner Rd CV5 ....112 D3
Turner St Birmingham B11 .....87 A6
Dudley, Gornalwood DY3 ....50 D3
Dudley, Old Dock DY1 ....62 B8
Tipton DY4 ....51 F7
West Bromwich B70 ....53 A4
Turner's Gr DY3 ....50 C4
Turner's Hill B65 ....63 B6
Turner's Hill Rd DY3 ....50 C4
Turner's La DY5 ....61 D1
Turners Croft B71 ....54 A8
Turney Rd DY8 ....80 F6
Turnham Gn WV6 ....23 E3
Turnhouse Rd B35 ....58 B4
Turnley Rd B34 ....69 C6
Turnpike Cl
Balsall Common CV7 ....130 B7
Birmingham B11 ....87 A6
Turnpike Dr B46 ....59 F1
Turnstone Dr WV10 ....12 B7
Turnstone Rd DY10 ....117 A1
Turpin Ct CV31 ....161 F6
Turquoise Gr WV11 ....2 C3
Turton Cl WS3 ....14 A4
Turton Rd Tipton DY4 ....40 F1
West Bromwich B70 ....53 B2
Turton St DY10 ....117 A8
Turtons Croft WV14 ....40 B3
Turves Gn
Birmingham, Turves Green
B31 ....103 A1
Birmingham, West Heath
B31 ....122 F8
Turves Green Boy's Sch
B31 ....123 A8
Turves Green Girls Sch &
Tech Coll B31 ....103 A1
Turves Green Prim Sch
B31 ....103 A1
Turville Cl LE10 ....75 F5
Turville Rd B20 ....55 C1
Tustin St B27 ....106 C8
Tutbury B77 ....35 C7
Tutbury Ave
Coventry CV4 ....132 E6
Perton WV6 ....24 A3
Tutbury Cl WS11 ....2 C3
Tuthill B77 ....36 B2
Tutnall Cl B60 ....137 F1
Tutnall Dr B60 ....143 B6
Tutnall La Blackwell B60 ....138 A1
Finstall B60 ....137 F1
Tuttle Hill CV10 ....72 F6
Tuttle Hill Ind Est CV10 ....72 E7
Tuxford Cl WV10 ....25 E4
Twatling Rd B45 ....122 A2
Tweed Twr B20 ....55 D2
Tweeds Well B32 ....102 B3
Tweedside Cl LE10 ....71 E3
Twickenham Ct DY8 ....80 D7
Twickenham Prim Sch
B44 ....45 C1
Twickenham Rd B44 ....45 C1
Twickenham Way CV3 ....115 A1
Twiners Rd B98 ....153 F1
Two Gates B63 ....82 C5
Two Gates Com Prim Sch
B77 ....21 C1
Two Gates Ind Est B77 ....35 D7
Two Gates La B63 ....82 C5
Two Locks DY5 ....62 A4
Two Oaks Ave WS7 ....6 D8

Two Woods Ind Est DY5 ....61 E1
Two Woods La DY5 ....61 E1
Two Woods Trad Est DY5 ......61 F1
Twycross Gr B36 ....68 D7
Twycross Rd LE10 ....75 E6
Twycross Wlk CV34 ....155 D1
Twydale Ave B69 ....52 C2
Twyford Cl WS9 ....30 B5
Twyford Gr WV11 ....26 F7
Twyford Rd B8 ....68 C5
Twyning Rd
Birmingham, Edgbaston
B16 ....65 D1
Birmingham, Stirchley B30 ....104 B7
Tybalt Cl Coventry CV3 ......134 C5
Royal Leamington Spa
CV34 ....161 D4
Tyber Dr B20 ....55 B3
Tyberry Cl B90 ....106 A1
Tyburn Gr B24 ....57 D3
Tyburn Rd
Birmingham B24 ....57 C2
Wolverhampton WV1 ....26 C2
Tyburn Sq B24 ....57 D3
Tyburn Trad Est B24 ....57 D2
Tye Gdns DY9 ....81 B1
Tyebeams B34 ....69 C5
Tyler Ct B24 ....56 F3
Tyler Gdns WV13 ....27 B1
Tyler Gr B43 ....44 A1
Tyler Rd WV13 ....27 B1
Tylers Gn B38 ....104 B1
Tylers Gr B90 ....126 F6
Tylney Cl Birmingham B5 .....86 D7
Coventry CV3 ....115 B2
Tyndale Cres B43 ....44 C3
Tyndall Wlk B32 ....84 A2
Tyne Cl Birmingham B37 ......70 C4
Brownhills WS8 ....6 C2
Tyne Ct B73 ....46 B5
Tyne Gr B25 ....88 D8
Tyne Pl DY5 ....61 F2
Tynedale Cres WV4 ....39 E3
Tynedale Rd B11 ....87 F3
Tynemouth Cl CV2 ....96 D5
Tynes The B60 ....150 E7
Tyning Cl WV9 ....11 A2
Tyninghame Ave WV6 ....24 D7
Tynings La WS9 ....30 A5
Tynsall Ave B97 ....152 F2
Tynward Cl CV3 ....133 B5
Tyrley Cl WV6 ....24 B2
Tyrol Cl DY8 ....80 D6
Tyseley Hill Rd B11 ....88 A4
Tyseley Ind Est B11 ....87 E5
Tyseley La B11 ....88 A4
Tyseley Locomotive Wks
Visitor Ctr* B11 ....87 F5
Tyseley Sta B11 ....88 A5
Tysoe Cl
Hockley Heath B94 ....143 C6
Redditch B98 ....158 D5
Tysoe Croft CV3 ....134 F8
Tysoe Dr B76 ....46 F4
Tysoe Rd B44 ....55 F7
Tythe Barn Cl B60 ....150 D6
Tythebarn Dr DY6 ....60 A7
Tythebarn La B90 ....126 A6
Tyzack Cl DY5 ....61 C2

U

Udall Rd WV14 ....40 D3
Uffcumme Rd B30 ....104 D8
Uffcume Specl Sch B13 ....86 E1
Uffmoor Est B63 ....82 E2
Uffmoor La B62 ....100 D7
Ufton Cl B90 ....106 E3
Ufton Cres B90 ....106 D3
Ufton Croft CV5 ....112 A3
Ullapool Cl B97 ....158 D5
Ullenhall Rd Knowle B93 ....128 A6
Sutton Coldfield B76 ....57 F8
Ullenwood B21 ....65 D7
Ulleries Rd B92 ....89 A2
Ullrik Gn B24 ....56 F2
Ullswater B77 ....36 B7
Ullswater Ave
Nuneaton CV11 ....73 F6
Royal Leamington Spa
CV32 ....156 C2
Ullswater Cl B32 ....84 E7
Ullswater Gdns DY6 ....60 D6
Ullswater Ho 4 B69 ....63 D5
Ullswater Pl WS11 ....1 E1
Ullswater Rd
Bedworth CV12 ....78 A2
Coventry CV3 ....114 C1
Willenhall WV11 ....13 B1
Ullswater Rise DY5 ....61 E5
Ulster Cl WS11 ....4 D3
Ulster Dr DY6 ....60 A4
Ulverley Cres B92 ....106 F8
Ulverley Green Rd B92 ....88 F1
Ulverley Sch B92 ....89 B1
Ulverscroft Rd CV3 ....133 D7
Umberslade Rd
Birmingham B29 ....104 A8
Earlswood B94 ....142 C7
Tanworth-In-A-F B94 ....142 E3
Underhill Cl
Coventry CV3 ....133 D3
Redditch B98 ....158 F6
Underhill La WV10 ....12 A2

Underhill Prim Sch
WD10 ....12 B1
Underhill Rd
Birmingham B8 ....67 F3
Tipton DY4 ....52 C6
Underhill St B69 ....64 A5
Underhill Wlk B69 ....64 A5
Underley Cl DY6 ....60 B7
Underpass The B40 ....90 E4
Underwood Cl
Birmingham, Edgbaston
B15 ....85 D4
Birmingham, Stockland B23 ...56 C4
Redditch B97 ....54 E5
Underwood Rd B20 ....58 A5
Unett Ct B B66 ....65 C5
Unett St Birmingham B19 ......66 C5
Smethwick B66 ....65 C4
Unett Wlk B19 ....66 C5
Unicorn Ave CV5 ....111 E4
Unicorn Hill B97 ....153 D4
Unicorn La CV5 ....111 F4
Union Bldgs CV1 ....165 B2
Union Ctr WC10 ....41 F2
Union Dr B73 ....45 F2
Union La WV5 ....37 D2
Union Mill St WV1 ....163 D3
Union Pas B2 ....164 C2
Union Pl Birmingham B29 ......86 B2
Coventry CV6 ....95 F4
Union Rd Birmingham B6 ....67 B5
Oldbury B69 ....52 E2
Royal Leamington Spa
CV32 ....156 E1
Solihull, Lode Heath B91 ......107 C4
Solihull, Shirley B90 ....124 C6
West Bromwich B70 ....52 F2
Union Row B21 ....65 F7
Union St Bilston WV14 ....40 C5
Birmingham B2 ....164 C2
Blackheath B65 ....63 C1
Burntwood WS7 ....6 E5
Cannock WS11 ....4 E6
B Dudley DY1 ....51 C1
Kidderminster DY10 ....116 E7
Redditch B98 ....153 F3
Stourbridge, Lye DY9 ....81 E5
Stourbridge, Stambermill
DY8 ....81 A4
Tipton, Princes End DY1 ....51 F8
Tipton, Tipton Green DY4 .....51 F5
Walsall WS1 ....28 E1
Wednesbury WS10 ....41 F2
West Bromwich B70 ....64 D8
Willenhall WV13 ....27 A2
Wolverhampton WV1 ....163 C3
Unisant Trad Est B64 ....62 F2
United Coll of the Ascension
B29 ....85 C1
Unity Cl WS10 ....41 C4
Unity Ho CV1 ....165 C4
Unity Pl
B Birmingham B29 ....85 F2
Oldbury B69 ....64 A8
Unity Wlk DY4 ....51 F5
Univ of Birmingham B15 ....85 F4
Univ of Birmingham The
(Halls of Residence)
B15 ....66 C1
Univ of Central England
Birmingham B4 ....164 D4
Birmingham, Perry Barr B35 ..86 A8
Univ of Central England
(Perry Barr Campus)
B42 ....55 B2
Univ of Warick (Gibbet Hill)
CV4 ....132 D3
Univ of Warwick CV4 ....132 C4
Univ of Warwick (Westwood)
CV4 ....132 B6
Univ of Warwick Science Pk
CV4 ....132 B6
Univ of Wolverhampton
WV1 ....163 B3
Univ of Wolverhampton
(Annexe) WV1 ....163 C3
Univ of Wolverhampton
(Dudley Campus) DY1 ....51 B2
Univ of Wolverhampton
(Walsall Campus) WS1 ....43 A7
Univ of Wolverhampton
Compton Park Campus
WV6 ....24 E2
University Rd CV4 ....132 C5
University Road W B15 ....85 F4
University Sta B15 ....85 E4
Unketts Rd B67 ....64 E3
Unwin Cres DY8 ....80 E5
Upavon Cl B35 ....58 A4
Upfield Cotts WS7 ....7 E7
Upland Gr B61 ....137 A4
Upland Rd
Birmingham B29 ....86 B3
Bromsgrove B61 ....137 B4
Uplands Coventry CV2 ....114 A5
Halesowen B63 ....82 E2

Uplands Ave
Blackheath B65 ....63 D3
Willenhall WV13 ....26 D1
Wolverhampton WV3 ....38 D8
Uplands Cl DY2 ....62 E7
Uplands Dr Sedgley DY3 ......50 D8
Wolverhampton WV3 ....49 A6
Uplands Gr WV13 ....26 D1
Uplands Jun Sch WV3 ....38 D8
Uplands Manor Prim Sch
B67 ....64 F3
Uplands Rd
Birmingham B21 ....54 D2
Dudley DY2 ....62 F7
Wolverhampton WV13 ....26 C1
Uplands The B67 ....64 F4
Upleadon Cl B97 ....158 A6
Upper Abbey St CV11 ....73 B5
Upper Ashley St B62 ....63 C1
Upper Balsall Heath Rd
B12 ....86 F6
Upper Bond St LE10 ....71 D1
Upper Brook St WS2 ....28 D1
Upper Cape CV34 ....160 D8
Upper Chapel St B69 ....52 B2
Upper Church La DY4 ....52 A6
Upper Clifton Rd B73 ....46 B6
Upper Coneybere St B
B12 ....86 F7
Upper Crossgate Rd
B98 ....159 C8
Upper Eastern Green La
CV5 ....111 E5
Upper Ettingshall Rd
WV14 ....51 B8
Upper Field Cl B98 ....154 C6
Upper Forster St WS4 ....28 F3
Upper Gambolds La
B60 ....151 C5
Upper Gn WV6 ....24 D5
Upper Gough St B1 ....164 B1
Upper Green La WS2 ....28 C4
Upper Grosvenor Rd B20 ......55 B2
Upper Grove St B CV32 ......156 E1
Upper Gungate B79 ....21 B6
Upper Hall Cl B98 ....154 D2
Upper Hall La B B WS1 ....28 E1
Upper Hattons Cotts
WV9 ....10 D5
Upper High St
Blackheath B64 ....62 D1
Wednesbury WS10 ....41 F3
Upper Highgate St B12 ....86 F7
Upper Hill St
Coventry CV1 ....165 A3
Royal Leamington Spa
CV32 ....157 A1
Upper Holland Rd B72 ....46 C4
Upper Holly Wlk CV32 ....157 A1
Upper Ladyes Hills CV8 ....148 A6
Upper Landywood La
Cheslyn Hay WS6 ....4 D1
Great Wyrley WS6 ....13 D8
Upper Lichfield St WV13 ....27 A2
Upper Marshall St B1 ....164 B1
Upper Meadow Rd B32 ....84 C5
Upper Mill La B5 ....164 C1
Upper Navigation St
WS2 ....28 D2
Upper Pk CV3 ....134 D6
Upper Portland St B6 ....67 A7
Upper Ride CV3 ....134 D5
Upper Rosemary Rd
CV8 ....147 F5
Upper Rushall St WS1 ....28 F1
Upper Russell St B
WS10 ....41 F2
Upper Short St WS2 ....28 D1
Upper Sneyd Rd WV11 ....13 B2
Upper Spon St CV1 ....113 A3
Upper Spring La CV8 ....147 E7
Upper St WV6 ....24 D5
Upper St John St WS14 ....9 B6
Upper St Mary's Rd B67 ....64 F5
Upper Stone Cl B76 ....46 E4
Upper Sutton St B6 ....66 F7
Upper Trinity St B9 ....67 A1
Upper Vauxhall WV1 ....25 A2
Upper Villiers St WV2 ....39 C6
Upper Well St CV1 ....165 C1
Upper William St B1 ....66 C1
Upper York St CV1 ....113 B2
Upper Zoar St WV3 ....163 A1
Upperfield Way CV3 ....115 A1
Upton Cl B98 ....154 F3
Upton Ct B23 ....56 B3
Upton Dr CV11 ....78 F8
Upton Gdns WV14 ....40 C5
Upton Gr B33 ....68 C1
Upton Rd B33 ....68 C2
Upton St DY2 ....62 C5
Upwey Ave B91 ....107 A4
Usam Trad Est WV10 ....11 D2
Usk Way B36 ....69 F8
Usmere Rd DY10 ....116 F8
Utrillo Cl CV5 ....112 C6
Uttoxeter Cl WV6 ....25 B5
Uxbridge Ave CV3 ....114 C2
Uxbridge Cl DY3 ....50 D3
Uxbridge Ct Burntwood WS7 ....6 F5
Cannock WS12 ....2 C5
Kidderminster DY11 ....116 D5
Uxbridge St
Birmingham B19 ....66 C5
Cannock WS12 ....2 C4

V

Valbourne Rd B14 ....104 C4
Vale Ave Aldridge WS9 ....30 D3
Vale Cl Birmingham B32 ....84 F3
Lichfield WS13 ....3 B1
Vale Ct B64 ....82 D7
Vale Head Dr WV6 ....24 A2
Vale Ind Est DY11 ....116 C1

Vale Rd DY2 ....62 E4
Vale Row DY3 ....50 D5
Vale St Dudley DY3 ....50 E6
Stourbridge DY8 ....81 A8
West Bromwich B71 ....53 E6
Wolverhampton WV2 ....40 A6
Vale The
Birmingham, Edgbaston B15 ..86 A6
Birmingham, Moseley B11 .....87 B2
Coventry CV3 ....134 C8
Vale View Aldridge WS9 ....30 B4
Nuneaton CV10 ....72 E4
Valencia Croft B35 ....58 B4
Valencia Rd B60 ....137 D1
Valentine Cl B74 ....44 F7
Valentine Ct B14 ....86 E1
Valentine Rd
Birmingham B14 ....86 F1
Oldbury B68 ....64 C2
Valepits Rd B33 ....69 C1
Valerian
Kidderminster DY10 ....116 E2
Sutton Coldfield B74 ....31 F4
Valerie Gr B43 ....44 C1
Vales Cl B76 ....57 E7
Valiant Cl LE10 ....75 E4
Valley Cl B97 ....158 A6
Valley Farm Rd B45 ....122 A6
Valley Gn WS6 ....4 C2
Valley Int Sch B92 ....89 D3
Valley La Lapworth B94 ....144 E7
Lichfield WS13 ....9 D8
Tamworth B77 ....22 A1
Valley Park Nature Reserve*
WV6 ....24 D3
Valley Park Sch WV6 ....24 F5
Valley Rd Birmingham B43 ....54 C7
Blackheath B61 ....82 E7
Bournheath B61 ....136 E7
Cannock WS12 ....2 D6
Coventry CV2 ....114 A6
Dudley DY3 ....50 E6
Earlswood B94 ....126 A1
Halesowen B62 ....83 F8
Nuneaton CV10 ....72 A8
Radford Semele CV31 ....162 E4
Royal Leamington Spa
CV32 ....157 C3
Smethwick B67 ....64 F3
Solihull B92 ....89 D4
Stourbridge DY9 ....81 E6
Sutton Coldfield B74 ....44 F7
Walsall WS3 ....14 D1
Wolverhampton WV10 ....25 F5
Valley Side B WS9 ....14 F2
Valley Stad (Redditch FC)
B97 ....153 C4
Valley The Burntwood WS7 .....6 D8
Radford Semele CV31 ....162 E4
Valley View WS8 ....16 A7
Vallian Croft B36 ....68 F7
Van Dyke Cl CV5 ....112 C3
Van Gogh Cl WS11 ....2 D2
Vanborough Wlk DY1 ....51 A2
Vanbrugh Ct WV6 ....23 E3
Vanguard B77 ....35 D6
Vanguard Ave CV6 ....112 C1
Vanguard B WS1 ....68 E8
Vanguard Rd B26 ....90 C4
Vann Cl B10 ....87 C8
Vantage Point B70 ....53 C2
Varden Croft B5 ....86 D7
Vardon Dr CV3 ....133 D4
Vardon Way B38 ....103 D1
Varley Rd B24 ....57 D4
Varley Vale B24 ....57 D4
Varlins Way B38 ....103 D1
Varney Ave B70 ....53 D2
Vaughan Cl B74 ....31 F6
Vaughan Rd WV13 ....26 C1
Vaughan Trad Est DY4 ....52 C3
Vaughton Dr B75 ....46 C6
Vaughton Ho B15 ....86 C7
Vaughton St B12 ....86 F8
Vaughton St S B12 ....86 E8
Vauxhall Ave B WV1 ....25 A2
Vauxhall Cl B CV1 ....113 E4
Vauxhall Cres B36 ....59 F1
Vauxhall Gdns DY2 ....62 E7
Vauxhall Gr B7 ....67 B3
Vauxhall Ho B WV1 ....25 A2
Vauxhall Pl B7 ....67 A3
Vauxhall Rd
Birmingham B7 ....67 A3
Stourbridge DY8 ....81 A5
Vauxhall St Coventry CV1 ...113 E3
Dudley DY1 ....62 B8
Vauxhall Trad Est B7 ....67 B4
Vaynor Dr B97 ....158 D8
Vaynor Fst Sch The
B97 ....158 C7
Veasey Cl CV11 ....73 F3
Vecqueray St CV1 ....113 E2
Vector Ind Pk B71 ....53 C6
Velsheda Rd B90 ....106 A2
Venetia Rd B9 ....67 D1
Venice Cl B B13 ....87 B2
Venning Gr B43 ....54 D7
Ventnor Ave
Birmingham, Lozells B19 ......66 D7
Birmingham, Ward End B36 ...68 D7
Ventnor Cl Coventry CV3 ....114 E3
Oldbury B68 ....64 A2
Ventnor Rd B92 ....89 C3
Ventnor St CV10 ....73 D6
Ventura Park Rd B78 ....21 A3
Ventura Pk B78 ....21 A3
Ventura Pk Rd B78 ....21 A3
Venture Ct LE10 ....74 E8

Venture Way B7 ....66 F4
Vera Rd B26 ....88 E7
Vera Roberts Way DY11 ......116 B3
Verbena Cl Coventry CV2 .....96 B1
Stoke Prior B60 ....150 C1
Verbena Gdns B7 ....67 A5
Verbena Rd B31 ....102 F6
Vercourt B74 ....31 B3
Verden Ave CV34 ....160 B4
Verdi Ct WS13 ....3 C2
Verdun Cl CV31 ....162 B2
Verdun Cres DY2 ....51 F2
Vere St B5 ....86 D8
Verity Wlk DY8 ....81 A8
Vermont Gn B WS11 ....2 A3
Vermont Gr CV31 ....162 D6
Verney Ave B33 ....89 D7
Vernier Ave DY6 ....61 A5
Vernolds Croft B5 ....86 E8
Vernon Ave
Birmingham B20 ....54 F4
Brownhills WS8 ....16 A8
Tipton DY4 ....51 E4
Vernon Cl
B Coventry CV1 ....113 E3
Essington WV11 ....12 F4
Halesowen B62 ....83 D8
Redditch B98 ....154 A5
Royal Leamington Spa
CV32 ....156 E3
Sutton Coldfield B74 ....31 E5
Willenhall WV13 ....26 E1
Vernon Ct Birmingham B16 ...65 E1
B Coventry CV1 ....113 E3
B Oldbury B68 ....84 B7
Vernon Rd Bilston WV14 ....40 F6
Birmingham B16 ....65 E1
Halesowen B62 ....83 C8
Oldbury B68 ....64 C6
Vernon St B70 ....52 E3
Vernon Trad Est B62 ....83 C8
Vernon Way WS3 ....13 E1
Vernons Cl CV10,CV11 ....72 F4
Vernons La CV11 ....74 A1
Verona Cl CV11 ....74 C4
Verona Ct WV10 ....26 A4
Veronica Ave WV4 ....39 E5
Veronica Cl B29 ....103 A6
Veronica Rd DY6 ....61 A6
Verstone Croft B31 ....103 A3
Verstone Rd B90 ....106 C4
Verwood Cl WV13 ....26 D1
Vesey Cl
Sutton Coldfield B74 ....31 F2
Water Orton B46 ....59 B2
Vesey Rd B73 ....46 B1
Vesey St B4 ....164 C4
Vestry Cl B64 ....62 F1
Vestry Ct DY8 ....80 E6
Viaduct St B7 ....67 A3
Vibart Rd B26 ....88 F8
Vicar St Dudley DY2 ....62 C8
Kidderminster DY10 ....116 E6
Sedgley DY3 ....50 D8
Wednesbury WS10 ....42 A3
Vicar's Cl WS13 ....9 A8
Vicarage Cl
Birmingham, Great Barr
B42 ....55 D7
Birmingham, Stirchley B30 ..104 C7
Brierley Hill DY5 ....81 C8
Bromsgrove B60 ....151 B8
Brownhills WS8 ....16 A7
Dordon B78 ....36 F5
Tipton DY4 ....51 E5
Vicarage Cres
Kidderminster DY10 ....116 F5
Redditch B97 ....153 C3
Vicarage Field CV34 ....161 B8
Vicarage Gdns
Halesowen B62 ....63 D1
Sutton Coldfield B76 ....57 F7
Vicarage Hill
Middleton B78 ....34 B1
Tanworth-In-A B94 ....141 F3
Vicarage La
Brierley Hill DY5 ....61 D7
Coventry CV7 ....95 D7
Warwick CV35 ....160 A1
Water Orton B46 ....59 B2
Vicarage Pl B WS1 ....28 E1
Vicarage Prospect DY1 ....51 B1
Vicarage Rd
Birmingham, Aston B6 ....67 A7
Birmingham, Edgbaston B15 ..85 F8
Birmingham, Handsworth
B18 ....65 D2
Birmingham, Harborne B17 ...85 B5
Birmingham, King's Heath
B14 ....86 F1
Birmingham, Stechford B33 ..68 E1
Brierley Hill DY5 ....61 C7
Brownhills WS8 ....16 A7
Cheswick Green B90,B94 ....126 C3
Dudley, West Coseley
WV14 ....51 C7
Dudley, Woodsetton DY3 ......50 F5
Halesowen B62 ....63 C1
Oldbury B68 ....64 C5
Royal Leamington Spa
CV32 ....157 B3
Sedgley DY3 ....50 E8
Sutton Coldfield B72 ....46 C5
Tamworth B79 ....21 C6
Tipton DY4 ....52 A4
Walsall WS3 ....15 A3
Wolverhampton, New Cross
WV11 ....26 B6
Wolverhampton, Penn WV4 ...38 E3
Wolverhampton, Tettenhall
WV6 ....24 C5
Wolverhampton, Newbolds
WV10 ....25 F5
Wolverhampton, Tettenhall
WV6 ....24 A5

Walsall WS3 ....15 B2
Wednesbury WS10 ....42 A4
West Bromwich B71 ....53 D6
Wolverhampton, Blakenhall
WV2 ....163 C1
Wolverhampton, New Cross
WV11 ....26 B6
Wolverhampton, Penn WV4 ...38 E3
Vicarage St
Nuneaton CV11 ....73 C4
Oldbury B68 ....64 B5
Vicarage Terr B WS2 ....42 C8
Vicarage View B97 ....153 D3
Vicarage Wlk B WS1 ....28 E1
Vicars Wlk DY9 ....81 E2
Viceroy Cl Birmingham B5 ....86 C6
Kingswinford DY6 ....61 A5
Victor Bsns Ctr B98 ....154 B7
Victor Cl WV2 ....40 B6
Victor Rd Birmingham B18 ....65 E6
Solihull B92 ....89 D3
Victor St
Walsall, Caldmore WS1 ....42 E8
Walsall, Pelsall WS3 ....15 A1
Victor Twr B7 ....67 B6
Victoria Arc WV1 ....163 B3
Victoria Ave
Birmingham B21 ....65 F8
Birmingham, Small Heath
B10 ....87 D8
Halesowen B62 ....83 F6
Smethwick B66 ....65 A5
Walsall, Blakenhall Heath
WS3 ....28 D8
Walsall, Wallington Heath
WS3 ....14 C1
Victoria Bldgs B16 ....65 E3
Victoria Bsns Ctr B
CV31 ....162 A7
Victoria Cl
B Birmingham B13 ....86 F4
Brierley Hill DY5 ....61 D3
Coventry CV5 ....112 D4
Halesowen B62 ....83 F6
B Kidderminster DY10 ....116 F6
Norton Canes WS11 ....6 B5
Victoria Dr B78 ....35 A8
Victoria Fold WV1 ....163 B2
Victoria Gdns
Blackheath B64 ....62 F2
Lichfield WS13 ....8 F6
Victoria Gr
B Birmingham B18 ....65 E4
Wombourne WV5 ....49 A8
Victoria Ho
Birmingham B16 ....66 B2
Darlaston WS10 ....41 C6
B Walsall WS3 ....28 D8
Victoria Hospl WS13 ....9 A6
Victoria Infs Sch DY4 ....51 F5
Victoria Lawn Cls DY2 ....164 C3
Victoria Mews
Barnt Green B45 ....138 D8
Coventry CV3 ....114 E2
Oldbury B69 ....63 F3
Walsall WS4 ....29 A3
Warwick CV34 ....160 D7
Victoria Park Rd B66 ....65 B5
Victoria Pas WV1 ....163 B3
Victoria Pass B DY8 ....81 A5
Victoria Pl DY11 ....116 B2
Victoria Rd
Birmingham, Acock's Green
B27 ....88 C2
Birmingham, Aston B6 ....66 F7
Birmingham, Handsworth
B21 ....65 E2
Birmingham, Harborne B17 ...85 B5
Birmingham, Stechford B33 ..68 D3
Birmingham, Stirchley B30 ..104 A7
Birmingham, Stockland Green
B23 ....56 D3
Blackheath B64 ....62 F2
Brierley Hill DY5 ....62 A1
Bromsgrove B61 ....137 D3
Darlaston WS10 ....41 D6
Dodford B61 ....136 A7
Halesowen B62 ....83 D8
Hinckley LE10 ....75 F5
Nuneaton CV10 ....72 B8
Oldbury B68 ....64 D6
Royal Leamington Spa
CV31 ....161 E8
Sedgley DY3 ....50 E8
Sutton Coldfield B72 ....46 C5
Tamworth B79 ....21 C6
Tipton DY4 ....52 A4
Walsall WS3 ....15 A3
Wolverhampton, New Cross
WV11 ....26 B6
Wolverhampton, Penn WV4 ...38 E3
Victoria Specl Sch B31 ....103 A5
Victoria Sq
Birmingham B3 ....164 B2
Wolverhampton WV1 ....163 C3
Victoria St Birmingham B9 ....67 A1
Brierley Hill, Barrow Hill
DY5 ....61 C7
Brierley Hill, Merry Hill DY5 ..61 D3

Victoria St *continued*
Cannock, Bridgtown WS11 . . . . .4 D8
Cannock, Broomhill WS11 . . . . .1 E4
Cannock, Hednesford WS12 . .2 C6
Coventry CV1 . . . . .165 D4
Halesowen B63 . . . . .83 A4
Hinckley LE10 . . . . .71 D1
Kingswinford DY6 . . . . .49 B1
Nuneaton CV11 . . . . .73 C4
7 Redditch B98 . . . . .153 E4
Royal Leamington Spa
CV31 .161 E8
Stourbridge DY8 . . . . .81 A5
Warwick CV34 . . . . .160 D7
Wednesbury WS10 . . . . .41 E2
West Bromwich, Lambert's End
B70 . . . . .53 C3
West Bromwich, Swan Village
B70 . . . . .52 F5
Willenhall WV13 . . . . .27 B3
Wolverhampton WV1 . . . . . . .163 B3
Victoria Terr
Royal Leamington Spa
CV31 .161 F7
4 Walsall WS4 . . . . .28 F3
Victory Ave Burntwood WS7 .6 F7
Darlaston WS10 . . . . .41 C5
Victory Cl WS12 . . . . .2 F4
Victory La WS9 . . . . .28 A4
Victory Rd CV6 . . . . .95 E1
Victory Rise B71 . . . . .53 D5
Victory Terr B78 . . . . .35 B8
Vienna Ho CV5 . . . . .112 E2
View Dr DY2 . . . . .62 E8
View Point B69 . . . . .63 B7
View St WS12 . . . . .1 F6
Viewfield Ave WS12 . . . . .1 F7
Viewfield Cres DY3 . . . . .50 D6
Viewlands Dr WV6 . . . . .24 A2
Vigo Cl WS9 . . . . .15 F2
Vigo Pl WS9 . . . . .30 A8
Vigo Rd WS9 . . . . .15 F2
Vigo Terr WS9 . . . . .15 F2
Viking B77 . . . . .35 D7
Viking Rise B65 . . . . .63 C4
Vilia Cl LE10 . . . . .75 F4
Villa Cl CV12 . . . . .79 C2
Villa Cotts B19 . . . . .66 B7
Villa Cres CV12 . . . . .79 C1
Villa Cross B20 . . . . .66 B7
Villa Park (Aston Villa FC)
B6 . . . . .66 F7
Villa Rd Birmingham B19 . . . .66 B7
Coventry CV6 . . . . .113 B6
Villa St Birmingham B19 . . . . .66 C6
Stourbridge DY8 . . . . .81 A8
Villa Wlk B19 . . . . .66 C6
Village Mews The WV6 . . . .24 C5
Village Rd B6 . . . . .56 A1
Village The DY6 . . . . .60 E7
Village Way WV14 . . . . .40 C5
Village Wlk WS10 . . . . .42 B3
Villebon Way CV31 . . . . .162 A2
Villette Gr B14 . . . . .105 C4
Villiers Ave WV14 . . . . .40 D7
Villiers Ho WV12 . . . . .39 C7
Villiers Ind Est WV12 . . . . . . .39 B7
Villiers Jun & Inf Sch
WV14 .40 D7
Villiers Rd
Bromsgrove B60 . . . . .150 E7
Kenilworth CV8 . . . . .148 B5
Villiers Sq WV14 . . . . .40 D7
Villiers St Birmingham B18 .65 E5
Coventry CV2 . . . . .114 A3
Kidderminster DY10 . . . . .117 A5
Nuneaton CV11 . . . . .73 B3
Royal Leamington Spa
CV32 .157 A1
Walsall WS1 . . . . .42 F7
Vimy Rd Birmingham B13 . . .105 B8
Wednesbury WS10 . . . . .42 A4
Vimy Terr WS10 . . . . .42 A4
Vince St B66 . . . . .65 A3
Vincent Cl B12 . . . . .86 F6
Vincent Dr B15 . . . . .85 E4
Vincent Par B12 . . . . .86 F6
Vincent Rd B75 . . . . .46 E7
Vincent St Birmingham B12 .86 F5
Coventry CV1 . . . . .113 B2
Royal Leamington Spa
CV32 .157 A1
Walsall WS1 . . . . .42 F7
Vincent Wyles Ho CV2 . .114 E3
Vinculum Way WV13 . . . . . . .41 B8
Vine Ave B12 . . . . .87 A5
Vine Cres B71 . . . . .53 D6
Vine Ct Blackheath B64 . . . . . .82 D8
Warwick CV34 . . . . .160 F8
Vine Gdns B64 . . . . .62 C8
Vine La Cannock WS11 . . . . . . .4 D5
Clent DY9 . . . . .99 F3
Halesowen B63 . . . . .83 B3
Warwick CV34 . . . . .160 F8
Vine St Birmingham B6 . . . . . .67 B7
Brierley Hill DY2,DY5 . . . . .61 E5
Coventry CV1 . . . . .165 C3
Kidderminster DY10 . . . . .117 A8
Stourbridge DY8 . . . . .60 E1
Vinecote Rd CV6 . . . . .95 F4
Vineries The B27 . . . . .88 E4
Vineyard Rd B31 . . . . .102 F5
Vinnall Gr B32 . . . . .102 B8

Vintage Cl B34 . . . . .69 A5
Vinyard Cl B18 . . . . .65 F7
Violet Cl CV2 . . . . .96 C3
Violet Croft DY4 . . . . .41 B1
Violet La DY9 . . . . .99 E4
Virginia Dr WV4 . . . . .38 F4
Virginia Pl CV10 . . . . .72 E3
Virginia Rd CV1 . . . . .113 E3
Viscount Cl
Birmingham B35 . . . . .58 A2
Royal Leamington Spa
CV31 .161 F6
Vista Gn B38 . . . . .104 B1
Vista The DY3 . . . . .39 D2
Vittle Dr CV34 . . . . .160 D7
Vittoria St Birmingham B1, B66 .64
Smethwick B66 . . . . .65 D6
Vivian Cl B17 . . . . .85 C5
Vivian Rd B17 . . . . .85 C5
Vixen Cl B76 . . . . .57 D7
Vodena Ct **5** CV32 . . . . . .156 E1
Vogue Cl CV1 . . . . .165 D3
Voyager Dr WS11 . . . . .4 F6
Vulcan Ho
Birmingham B35 . . . . .58 C3
Solihull B91 . . . . .107 C6
Vulcan House Ind Est
B91 . . . . .107 C6
Vulcan Ind Est WS2 . . . . .28 C6
Vulcan Rd Bilston WV14 . . . .40 F5
Lichfield WS13 . . . . .3 E1
Solihull B91 . . . . .107 C7
Vulcan Road Island
WV14 .40 F5
Vyrnwy Gr B38 . . . . .123 E8
Vyse St
Birmingham, Aston B6 . . . . . . .67 B8
Birmingham, Hockley B18 . .66 C4

W

Wackrill Dr CV32 . . . . .157 C3
Wadbarn B90 . . . . .126 A5
Waddam's Pool DY2 . . . . . . .51 D1
Waddell Cl WV14 . . . . .39 F2
Waddens Brook La WV11 .26 E5
Waddington Ave B43 . . . . . .43 E1
Wade Ave CV3 . . . . .133 B5
Wade Gr CV34 . . . . .155 E2
Wade St WS13 . . . . .9 B7
Wadebridge Dr CV11 . . . . . .73 F5
Wadesmill Lawns WV10 . .11 E4
Wadham Cl B65 . . . . .63 C6
Wadham Ho B37 . . . . .70 D3
Wadham's Fold WV1 . . . . . .163 B3
Wadhurst Rd B17 . . . . .85 B2
Wadleys Rd B91 . . . . .106 F6
Waen Cl DY4 . . . . .52 B8
Waggon La DY10 . . . . .98 A3
Waggon St B64 . . . . .62 F2
Waggon Wlk B38 . . . . .123 B8
Waggoner's La B78 . . . . .33 E8
Waggoners Cl **1** B60 . . . .150 E6
Wagon La B26,B92 . . . . .88 F4
Wagoners Cl B8 . . . . .67 F6
Wagstaff Cl WV14 . . . . .51 B8
Wainbody Ave N CV3 . . . .133 A6
Wainbody Ave S CV3 . . . . .132 F5
Wainbody Wood Sch
CV4 . . . . .132 D2
Waine Ho WS8 . . . . .16 A6
Wainrigg B77 . . . . .36 B7
Wainwright Cl DY6 . . . . .60 A7
Wainwright St B6 . . . . .67 A7
Waite Rd WV13 . . . . .40 E8
Wake Gr CV34 . . . . .160 B5
Wake Green Pk B13 . . . . . . .87 B2
Wake Green Rd
Birmingham B13 . . . . .87 A2
Tipton DY4 . . . . .41 A1
Wakefield Cl
Coventry CV3 . . . . .134 F7
Sutton Coldfield B73 . . . . .46 A2
Wakefield Ct B13 . . . . .87 B2
Wakefield Gr B46 . . . . .59 B3
Wakeford Rd B31 . . . . .103 C1
Wakelam Gdns B43 . . . . .43 D1
Wakelams Fold DY3 . . . . .50 C3
Wakeley Hill WV4 . . . . .38 F4
Wakelin Rd B90 . . . . .126 B7
Wakeman Cl WV11 . . . . .12 F5
Wakeman Dr B69 . . . . .63 B8
Wakeman Gr B33 . . . . .89 D7
Wakes Cl WV13 . . . . .27 B1
Wakes Rd WS10 . . . . .42 A2
Walcot Cl B75 . . . . .32 B3
Walcot Dr B43 . . . . .54 F6
Walcot Gdns WV14 . . . . .40 B4
Walcot Gn B93 . . . . .128 A2
Walcote Cl LE10 . . . . .74 F8
Waldale Cl WV11 . . . . .13 C1
Walden Gdns WV4 . . . . .38 C6
Walden Rd B11 . . . . .88 A3
Waldeve Gr B92 . . . . .107 F8
Waldley Gr B24 . . . . .57 D3
Waldon Wlk B36 . . . . .69 F8
Waldron Ave DY5 . . . . .61 A2
Waldron Cl WS10 . . . . .41 F6
Waldrons Moor B14 . . . . . .104 C5
Walford Ave WV3 . . . . .38 F8
Walford Dr B92 . . . . .89 D3
Walford Gr B32 . . . . .102 B7
Walford Gr CV34 . . . . .155 F1
Walford Rd B11 . . . . .87 C6
Walford St CV2 . . . . .96 B2
Walford Wlk **7** B97 . . . . . . .153 E3

Walhouse CE Jun Sch
WS11 . . . . .1 C1
Walhouse Cl **6** WS1 . . . . .28 F2
Walhouse Rd WS1 . . . . .29 A2
Walhouse St WS11 . . . . .4 E8
Walk La WV5 . . . . .49 A6
Walk The DY3 . . . . .39 D1
Walker Ave
Brierley Hill DY5 . . . . .81 D7
Stourbridge DY9 . . . . .81 E3
Tipton B69 . . . . .63 D7
Wolverhampton WV10 . . . . . . .25 E8
Walker Dr B24 . . . . .67 E8
Walker Grange DY4 . . . . .51 F6
Walker Pl WS3 . . . . .28 E8
Walker Rd WS3 . . . . .28 E8
Walker St Dudley DY2 . . . . . . .62 C4
Tipton DY4 . . . . .52 C7
Walkers Croft WS13 . . . . .3 C2
Walkers Fold WV12 . . . . .27 D6
Walkers Heath Rd B38 . . .104 B1
Walkers Orch CV8 . . . . .149 B6
Walkers Rd B98 . . . . .154 E6
Walkers Rise WS12 . . . . .2 D8
Walkers Way
Bedworth CV12 . . . . .77 F1
Kenilworth CV8 . . . . .147 F2
Walkmill Bsns Pk WS11 . . .4 D5
Walkmill La WS11 . . . . .4 D5
Walkmill Way WS11 . . . . .4 D5
Walkwood CE Mid Sch
B97 . . . . .158 C8
Walkwood Cres B97 . . . . . .158 C6
Walkwood Rd B97 . . . . .158 D6
**Wall (Letocetvm) Roman Site
(Town)*** WS14 . . . . .8 E2
Wall Ave B46 . . . . .70 F5
Wall Croft WS9 . . . . .30 B7
Wall Dr B74 . . . . .31 F4
Wall End Cl WS2 . . . . .28 A7
Wall Heath La WS14 . . . . . . .16 F5
Wall Hill Rd CV5,CV7 . . . . . . .94 B3
Wall La WS13,WS14 . . . . .4 D5
**Wall Roman Site (Letocetvm)
Mus*** WS14 . . . . .8 D2
Wall St WV1 . . . . .26 B2
Wall Well B63 . . . . .82 F3
Wall Well La B63 . . . . .82 F3
Wall's Rd B60 . . . . .150 C3
Wallace Cl
Norton Canes WS11 . . . . .5 F5
Oldbury B69 . . . . .63 D6
Wallace Ct WS6 . . . . .4 D1
Wallace Ho
8 Oldbury B69 . . . . .63 D5
Warwick CV34 . . . . .160 D7
Wallace Rd Bilston WV14 . . .41 A2
Birmingham B29 . . . . .86 B2
Brownhills WS8 . . . . .15 E8
Coventry CV6 . . . . .113 A8
Oldbury B69 . . . . .63 D6
Wallace Rise B64 . . . . .82 E7
Wallbank Rd B8 . . . . .68 A6
Wallbrook Prim Sch
WV14 . . . . .51 E8
Wallbrook St WV14 . . . . .51 D8
Waller Cl CV35 . . . . .155 F7
Waller St CV32 . . . . .157 A2
Wallface B71 . . . . .53 B7
Wallheath Cres WS14 . . . . . .16 E5
Walling Croft WV14 . . . . .40 B3
Wallingford Ave CV11 . . . . .73 F7
Wallington Cl WS3 . . . . .14 B2
Wallington Heath WS3 . . . .14 B2
Wallis Ct **1** B13 . . . . .87 B2
Wallows Ind Est The DY5 .61 D5
Wallows La WS1,WS2 . . . . . .42 C6
Wallows Pl DY5 . . . . .61 D5
Wallows Rd DY5 . . . . .61 D5
Wallows Wood DY3 . . . . .50 A4
Wallscourt Cl CV32 . . . . . . .157 B3
Wallwin Ct CV34 . . . . .160 D6
Walmead Croft B17 . . . . .84 F7
Walmer Gr B23 . . . . .56 B5
Walmer Mdw WS9 . . . . .30 B7
Walmer Way B37 . . . . .70 C3
Walmers The WS9 . . . . .30 B7
Walmers Wlk The B31 . . . .102 D1
Walmesley Way B31 . . . . . .102 E2
Walmley Ash Cl B76 . . . . .57 F8
Walmley Ash La B76 . . . . . . .58 C6
Walmley Ash Rd B76 . . . . . . .58 A7
Walmley Cl
Halesowen B63 . . . . .82 B7
Sutton Coldfield B76 . . . . .57 F8
Walmley Jun & Inf Schs
B76 . . . . .58 A7
Walmley Rd B76 . . . . .57 F8
Walney Cl LE10 . . . . .71 B1
Walnut Ave WV8 . . . . .10 B3
Walnut Cl Birmingham B37 .70 B1
Cannock WS11 . . . . .1 C1
Nuneaton, Camp Hill CV10 . . .72 E6
Nuneaton, Hartshill CV10 . . . .72 A8
Stourbridge DY9 . . . . .81 B1
Walnut Dr Cannock WS11 . . . .1 F3
Royal Leamington Spa
CV32 .157 B3
5 Smethwick B66 . . . . .65 B5
Wolverhampton WV3 . . . . .24 D1
Walnut Gn WS14 . . . . .9 F7
Walnut La Finstall B60 . . . . .151 D8
Wednesbury WS10 . . . . .42 A2
Walnut Rd WS5 . . . . .43 A4
Walnut St CV2 . . . . .96 B2
Walnut Tree Cl CV8 . . . . . . .148 A3
Walnut Way B31 . . . . .122 F8

Walpole St WV6 . . . . .25 A3
Walpole Wlk B70 . . . . .53 D1
Walsal End La B92 . . . . .108 F3
Walsall Coll of Arts & Tech
WS1 . . . . .28 E3
**Walsall Coll of Arts & Tech
(Shelley Campus)** WS2 . .28 C1
Walsall New Firms Ctr
WS1 . . . . .42 D8
Walsall Rd Aldridge WS9 . . .30 A5
Birmingham B42 . . . . .55 B6
Cannock WS3 . . . . .4 E7
Darlaston WS10 . . . . .41 E6
Great Wyrley WS6 . . . . .5 A2
Lichfield WS13,WS14 . . . . .8 C5
Norton Canes WS11 . . . . .5 F4
Stonnall WS14 . . . . .16 B8
Sutton Coldfield B74 . . . . .31 D4
Walsall Wood WS9 . . . . .15 E2
Walsall, Pelsall WS3 . . . . .15 A1
Walsall, The Delves WS5 . . . . .42 F4
Wednesbury WS10,B71,
WS5 . . . . .42 F6
West Bromwich B71 . . . . .53 E8
Willenhall WV13 . . . . .27 C2
Walsall St Bilston WV14 . . . .40 D6
Coventry CV4 . . . . .132 B7
Darlaston WS10 . . . . .41 D7
West Bromwich B70 . . . . .53 D3
Willenhall WV13 . . . . .27 B1
Wolverhampton WV1 . . . . . . .163 D2
Walsall Wood Rd WS9 . . . . .30 B7
Walsall Wood Sch WS9 . . . .16 A4
Walsgrave CE Prim Sch
CV2 . . . . .115 A6
Walsgrave Dr B92 . . . . .107 D6
Walsgrave Dr B92 . . . . .107 D6
Walsgrave Gdns **5** CV2 .115 A7
Walsgrave Hospl CV2 . . . . .114 F5
Walsgrave Rd CV2 . . . . .114 B3
Walsgrave Ret Pk CV2 . . . .115 B7
Walsh Dr B76 . . . . .46 F4
Walsh Gr B23 . . . . .56 D8
Walsh La CV7 . . . . .92 E2
Walsham Croft B34 . . . . .69 C5
Walsingham Dr CV10 . . . . . .78 A7
Walsingham St WS1 . . . . .29 A1
Walstead Cl WS5 . . . . .43 C3
Walstead Rd WS5 . . . . .43 B5
Walstead Rd W WS5 . . . . . . .42 E5
Waltdene Cl B43 . . . . .43 D2
Walter Burden Ho B66 . . . . .65 C3
Walter Cobb Dr B73 . . . . . . .46 A1
Walter Nash Rd E DY11 . .116 B2
Walter Nash Rd W
DY11 . . . . .116 A1
Walter Rd Bilston WV14 . . . .40 F3
Smethwick B67 . . . . .64 E6
Walter Scott Rd CV12 . . . . .78 C1
Walter St Birmingham B7 . . .67 B6
Walsall WS3 . . . . .15 A1
West Bromwich B70 . . . . .53 D3
Walters Cl B31 . . . . .122 F6
Walters Rd B68 . . . . .84 B6
Walters Row DY1 . . . . .51 A1
Waltham Cl B61 . . . . .136 E1
Waltham Cres CV10 . . . . .72 B5
Waltham Gr B44 . . . . .45 B2
Waltham Ho
Birmingham B38 . . . . .104 B1
West Bromwich B70 . . . . .53 D3
Walthamstow Ct DY5 . . . . . .61 D1
Walton Ave B65 . . . . .83 B8
Walton Cl Blackheath B65 . . .63 A4
Coventry CV3 . . . . .134 E7
Halesowen B63 . . . . .82 F2
Kidderminster DY11 . . . . .116 B2
Nuneaton CV11 . . . . .73 F7
Redditch B98 . . . . .154 E3
Walton Cres WV4 . . . . .39 E5
Walton Croft B91 . . . . .107 B1
Walton Ct B63 . . . . .82 F3
Walton Dr DY9 . . . . .81 C5
Walton Gr B30 . . . . .104 B2
Walton Heath WS3 . . . . .13 F3
Walton Pool La DY9 . . . . .99 F2
Walton Rd Aldridge WS9 . . . .16 A1
Bromsgrove B61 . . . . .137 B4
Oldbury B68 . . . . .64 A4
Stourbridge DY9 . . . . .81 A6
Wednesbury WS10 . . . . .42 C2
Wolverhampton WV4 . . . . .39 F5
Walton Rise DY9 . . . . .100 A3
Walton St DY4 . . . . .51 F5
Wanderer Wlk B36 . . . . .57 F1
Wanderers Ave WV2 . . . . . . .39 C6
Wandle Gr B11 . . . . .88 A3
Wandsbeck B77 . . . . .35 E8
Wandsworth Rd B44 . . . . . . .44 F3
Wanley Rd CV3 . . . . .133 D6
Wannerton Rd DY10 . . . . . . .98 B1
Wansbeck Gr B38 . . . . .123 E8
Wansbeck Wlk DY3 . . . . .50 F6
Wansfell Cl CV4 . . . . .132 A7
Wanstead Gr B44 . . . . .45 A1
Wantage Rd B46 . . . . .59 E1
Wappenbury Cl CV2 . . . . . . .96 C2
Wappenbury Rd CV2 . . . . . .96 D2
War La B17 . . . . .85 B5
Warbage La
Belbroughton DY9 . . . . .119 F1
Dodford DY9 . . . . .136 A7
Warbank Cl B48 . . . . .139 A6
Warbler Pl DY10 . . . . .117 A2
Warcl Cl B8 . . . . .68 A5
Ward End Cl B8 . . . . .67 F6
Ward End Hall Gr B8 . . . . . . .68 A6

Ward End Park Rd B8 . . . . . .67 F5
Ward End Prim Sch B8 . . . . .68 B6
Ward Gr Warwick CV34 . . . .161 C7
Wolverhampton WV4 . . . . .39 F3
Ward Rd WV4 . . . . .39 D5
Ward St Bilston WV2 . . . . .40 B6
Birmingham B19 . . . . .164 C5
Cannock WS12 . . . . .1 F6
Dudley WV14 . . . . .51 B8
Walsall WS1 . . . . .28 F2
Willenhall WV13 . . . . .27 B3
Wolverhampton WV1 . . . . . . .163 D3
Warden Ave B73 . . . . .56 F8
Warden Rd Coventry CV6 .113 B6
Sutton Coldfield B73 . . . . .56 F8
Wardend Rd B8 . . . . .68 A6
Wardens Ave The CV5 . .112 B6
Wardens The CV8 . . . . .148 C5
Wardle Cl B75 . . . . .32 A4
Wardle Pl WS11 . . . . .1 E5
Wardle St B79 . . . . .21 A5
Wardles La WS6 . . . . .4 F2
Wardlow Cl WV4 . . . . .39 B6
Wardlow Rd B7 . . . . .67 B4
Wardour Dr B37 . . . . .70 C2
Wardour Gr B44 . . . . .56 C8
Wareham Cl WS3 . . . . .28 F5
Wareham Gn CV2 . . . . .115 A5
Wareham Ho B28 . . . . .105 E3
Wareham Rd B45 . . . . .102 B2
Wareing Dr B23 . . . . .56 D8
Warewell Cl **8** WS1 . . . . . . .28 F2
Warewell St WS1 . . . . .28 F2
Waring Cl DY4 . . . . .51 E8
Waring Rd DY4 . . . . .52 A8
Warings Green Rd B94 . .126 D1
Warley Croft B68 . . . . .84 E8
Warley Ct B68 . . . . .64 B2
Warley Hall Rd B68 . . . . .64 D1
Warley High Sch B68 . . . . . . .64 A2
Warley Ho B67 . . . . .64 F2
Warley Inf Both B68 . . . . . .64 C2
Warley Rd B68 . . . . .64 E5
Warmington Cl CV3 . . . . . .134 E8
Warmington Dr B73 . . . . .46 B4
Warmington Gr CV34 . . . . .160 B8
Warmington Rd
Birmingham B26 . . . . .89 C5
Hollywood B47 . . . . .125 A6
Warmley Cl Solihull B91 . .107 D5
Wolverhampton WV6 . . . . .25 B5
Warmwell Cl CV2 . . . . .114 F4
Warneford Mews 9
CV31 .162 A7
Warner Cl CV34 . . . . .155 D1
Warner Dr DY5 . . . . .61 D1
Warner Pl **1** WS3 . . . . .28 F6
Warner Rd Walsall WS3 . . . . .29 A6
Wednesbury WS10 . . . . .42 C2
Warner Row **2** CV6 . . . . . .113 F7
Warner St **1** B12 . . . . .87 A8
Warners Wlk B10 . . . . .87 C8
Warnford Wlk WV4 . . . . .38 C6
Warple Rd B32 . . . . .84 C5
Warren Ave
Birmingham B13 . . . . .86 F2
Wolverhampton WV10 . . . . . . .25 F5
Warren Cl Lichfield WS13 . . . .9 E7
Royal Leamington Spa
CV32 .157 A3
Ryton-on-D CV8 . . . . .135 A1
Tipton DY4 . . . . .52 A7
Warren Dr Blackheath B65 . .62 F5
Dorridge B93 . . . . .128 A3
Sedgley DY3 . . . . .39 C1
Warren Farm Prim Sch
B44 . . . . .56 A8
Warren Farm Rd B44 . . . . . .56 A8
Warren Field CV8 . . . . .135 A1
Warren Gdns DY6 . . . . .60 C6
Warren Gn CV4 . . . . .131 F7
Warren Hill Rd B44 . . . . .56 A7
Warren House Ct B76 . . . . . .46 F1
Warren House Wlk B76 . . . .46 F1
Warren La B45 . . . . .122 B3
Warren Pl WS8 . . . . .16 A7
Warren Rd
Birmingham, Perry B44 . . . . . .56 A7
Birmingham, Stirchley B30 .104 A6
Birmingham, Washwood Heath
B8 . . . . .67 E6
Burntwood WS7 . . . . .7 A5
Warrens Croft WS5 . . . . .43 D5
Warrens End 1 B38 . . . . . .103 F1
Warrens Hall Rd DY2 . . . . . .62 C7
Warrington Cl B76 . . . . .47 A1
Warrington Dr B23 . . . . .56 D7
Warsash Cl WV1 . . . . .40 B8
Warstock La B14 . . . . .105 A4
Warstock Rd B14 . . . . .105 A3
Warston Ave B32 . . . . .84 D3
Warstone Dr B71 . . . . .53 E4
Warstone La B18 . . . . .66 B4
Warstone Mews 2 B18 . . .66 C4
Warstone Par E B18 . . . . . . .66 B4
Warstone Rd WS6 . . . . .13 C7
Warstone Terr B21 . . . . .65 E8
Warstones Cres WV4 . . . . . .38 D5
Warstones Dr WV4 . . . . .38 C6
Warstones Gdns WV4 . . . . .38 C6
Warstones Jun & Inf Sch
WV4 . . . . .38 E6
Warstones Rd WV4 . . . . .38 D5
Wartell Bank DY6 . . . . .60 D7
Wartell Bank Ind Est
DY6 . . . . .60 D7
Warton Cl CV8 . . . . .148 C4

Warwards La B29 .... 104 A8
Warwell La B26 .... 88 D6
Warwick Ave
  Bromsgrove B60 .... 151 A8
  Coventry CV6 .... 133 A8
  Perton WV6 .... 23 F3
  Wednesbury WS10 .... 42 C4
  Willenhall WV13 .... 27 D2
Warwick By-Pass
  Warwick, Hampton Magna
  CV34,CV35 .... 160 A5
  Warwick, Heathcote CV34 .. 161 A1
Warwick Castle* CV34 ...... 160 E6
Warwick Cl Cannock WS11 .... 4 F8
  Dudley B80 .... 64 B2
  Studley B80 .... 159 D3
  West Bromwich B70 .... 52 E7
Warwick Crest B15 .... 86 B7
Warwick Ct
  ■ Birmingham, Acock's Green
  B27 .... 88 C2
  ■ Birmingham, Chelmsley Wood
  B37 .... 70 D2
  Birmingham, Moseley B13 .. 87 A2
  ■ Birmingham, Weoley Castle
  B29 .... 102 B8
  Coventry CV3 .... 165 B1
  Dudley DY3 .... 50 D3
  Solihull B91 .... 107 C3
  Solihull, Lode Heath B91 .. 107 B4
  ■ Wolverhampton WV4 ...... 39 F4
Warwick Gdns
  Hinckley LE10 .... 71 E3
  Nuneaton CV10 .... 72 E4
  Tipton B69 .... 52 C2
Warwick Gn CV12 .... 79 C1
Warwick Gr B92 .... 88 E1
Warwick Grange B91 .... 106 F7
Warwick Hall Gdns B60 .. 151 A8
Warwick Highway W8 .... 154 C2
Warwick Ho
  ■ Birmingham B24 .... 56 F4
  Sutton Coldfield B73 .... 46 A3
Warwick Hospl CV34 ...... 160 E8
Warwick La CV1 .... 165 B2
Warwick New Rd CV32 .. 161 C8
Warwick Park Ct B92 ..... 106 F8
Warwick Pl CV32 .... 156 E1
Warwick Race Course
  CV34 .... 160 C6
Warwick Rd
  Birmingham B42 .... 55 E2
  Birmingham, Sparkhill B11 .. 87 D4
  Chadwick End B93 .... 145 A7
  Coventry CV3 .... 165 B1
  Dudley DY2 .... 62 E3
  Kenilworth CV8 .... 148 A1
  Knowle B93 .... 128 D3
  Leek Wootton CV35 .... 155 F7
  Solihull B27,B91,B92 ..... 106 F7
  Solihull B27,B91,B92 ..... 106 F7
  Stourbridge DY8 .... 60 D1
  Sutton Coldfield B73 .... 45 C2
  Tamworth B77 .... 21 E4
  Wolston CV8 .... 135 F3
Warwick Road Trad Est
  B11 .... 87 D4
Warwick Row CV1 .... 165 B2
Warwick Sch CV34 .... 161 A6
Warwick St Bilston WV14 .. 40 E5
  Birmingham B12 .... 67 A1
  Coventry CV5 .... 112 F1
  Royal Leamington Spa
  CV32 .... 156 F1
  Walsall WS4 .... 28 F3
  Wolverhampton WV1 ...... 163 D2
Warwick Sta CV34 .... 160 F7
Warwick Tech Pk CV34 .. 161 B5
Warwick Terr CV32 .... 156 E1
Warwick Way WS9 .... 16 A1
Warwickshire Coll
  CV32 .... 161 D8
Warwickshire Coll of Ag
  CV11 .... 73 E6
Warwickshire Mus*
  CV34 .... 160 E6
Warwickshire Nuffield Hospl
  The CV32 .... 156 E5
Wasdale Cl CV32 .... 156 C2
Wasdale Dr DY6 .... 60 E6
Wasdale Rd
  Birmingham B31 .... 102 F4
  Clayhanger WS8 .... 15 E5
Waseley Hills Country Pk*
  B45 .... 121 C8
Waseley Hills High Sch
  B45 .... 121 D7
Waseley Rd B45 .... 121 E8
Wash La B25 .... 88 C8
Washbourne Rd CV31 ..... 162 A2
Washbrook La
  Allesley CV5 .... 94 A1
  Norton Canes WS11 .... 5 D5
Washbrook Rd B8 .... 68 A6
Washford Dr B98 .... 159 D7
Washford Gr B25 .... 88 B8
Washford Ind Est B98 .... 159 E8
Washford La B98 .... 159 D8
Washington Ct WV3 .... 24 D1
Washington Ctr DY2 .... 62 D4
Washington Dr B20 .... 55 B3
Washington St
  Birmingham B1 .... 164 A1
  Dudley DY2 .... 62 D3
  Kidderminster DY11 .... 116 C5
Washington Wharf B1 ..... 164 A1

Washwood Heath Rd B8 ... 67 E6
Washwood Heath Tech Coll
  B8 .... 68 C5
Wasperton Cl
  Birmingham B36 .... 69 B8
  ■ Coventry CV3 .... 134 F8
Wassell Ct B63 .... 82 E2
Wassell Grove La B63 .... 82 A2
Wassell Grove Rd DY9 ..... 99 F8
Wassell Rd Bilston WV14 .. 40 D7
  Halesowen B63 .... 82 E2
  Stourbridge DY9 .... 81 E2
Wast Hill Gr B38 .... 123 F7
Waste La
  Balsall Common CV7 .... 130 F5
  Coventry CV6 .... 94 F1
Wasthill La B38,B48 .... 123 D5
Wastwater Ct WS6 .... 23 F4
Watch Cl CV1 .... 165 A3
Watchbury Cl CV36 .... 58 C1
Watchmaker Ct CV1 .... 165 A2
Watchman Ave DY5 .... 81 F7
Watcombe Rd CV2 .... 114 E8
Water Dale WV3 .... 24 E2
Water La B71 .... 53 F7
Water Mill Cl B29 .... 85 D3
Water Mill Cres B76 .... 46 F1
Water Mill Prim Sch B29 .. 85 D3
Water Orton La B76 .... 58 E4
Water Orton Prim Sch
  B46 .... 59 B2
Water Orton Rd B36 .... 58 E1
Water Orton Sta B46 .... 59 A3
Water Rd DY3 .... 50 C2
Water St Birmingham B3 .. 164 B4
  Burntwood WS7 .... 6 E8
  Kingswinford DY6 .... 60 D7
  West Bromwich B70 .... 53 D2
  Wolverhampton WV10 ...... 163 D4
Waterbank Way WS11 .... 4 C6
Watercall Ave CV3 .... 133 C6
Waterdale B90 .... 126 D5
Waterfall Cl Meriden CV7 .. 92 C1
  Smethwick B66 .... 64 E7
Waterfall La B64 .... 63 A1
Waterfall Lane Ind Est
  B64 .... 63 A1
Waterfall Rd DY5 .... 81 D7
Waterfield Cl DY4 .... 51 D5
Waterfield Gdns CV31 .... 162 C7
Waterfield Way
  Birmingham B26 .... 89 C7
  Hinckley LE10 .... 75 C5
Waterford Ct B23 .... 56 B4
Waterford Pl B33 .... 69 D3
Waterford Rd DY6 .... 60 D7
Waterfront Bsns Pk DY5 .. 61 E4
Waterfront E DY5 .... 61 E4
Waterfront W DY5 .... 61 E4
Waterfront Way DY1,DY5 .. 61 E4
Waterglade La WV13 .... 27 A1
Waterhaynes CI B45 .... 122 A6
Waterhead Cl WV10 .... 12 A2
Waterhead Dr WV10 .... 12 B2
Waterlily Cl WS12 .... 2 E2
Waterlinks Blvd B6 .... 67 A7
Waterloo Ave B37 .... 70 B4
Waterloo Bvd WS12 .... 2 E4
Waterloo Cl CV34 .... 161 A8
Waterloo Ind Est B37 .... 70 B5
Waterloo PI ■ CV32 .... 156 F1
Waterloo Rd
  Birmingham, King's Heath
  B14 .... 104 E8
  Birmingham, South Yardley
  B25 .... 88 C6
  Hinckley LE10 .... 75 D8
  Smethwick B66 .... 65 A3
  Wolverhampton WV1 ...... 163 B4
Waterloo St
  Birmingham B2 .... 164 B2
  ■ Coventry CV1 .... 113 E4
  Dudley DY1 .... 62 B8
  Kidderminster DY10 .... 116 E6
  Royal Leamington Spa
  CV31 .... 162 B7
  Tipton DY4 .... 51 F5
Waterloo St E DY4 .... 51 F5
Waterloo Terr WV1 .... 163 A4
Waterman Rd CV6 .... 113 F6
Watermeadow Dr WS4 ...... 15 D1
Watermere WS4 .... 29 D8
Watermill Cl WV10 .... 11 D3
Watermint Cl WS12 .... 2 E4
Waters Dr B74 .... 31 D3
Waters Edge The B1 .... 66 C2
Waters View WS3 .... 15 B5
Watersbridge Gdns CV10 .. 73 C1
Waterside
  Birmingham, Edgbaston B15 .. 86 C8
  Birmingham, Hamstead B43 .. 54 E7
  Coventry CV6 .... 96 C6
  Royal Leamington Spa
  CV31 .... 161 D7
Waterside Cl
  Birmingham, Bordesley B9 .. 67 B2
  Birmingham, Pype Hayes
  B24 .... 58 A5
Waterside Ct
  Birmingham B16 .... 66 B2
  Royal Leamington Spa
  CV31 .... 162 B6
  Tamworth B77 .... 21 F5
Waterside Grange DY10 .. 116 E8
Waterside Ind Est
  Blackheath B65 .... 62 F4

Waterside Ind Est continued
  Wolverhampton WV2 .... 40 A6
Waterside View
  Birmingham B18 .... 66 A5
  Brierley Hill DY5 .... 81 B8
Waterside Way
  Brownhills WS8 .... 6 D2
  Wolverhampton WV9 .... 11 A3
Watermead Cl WS12 .... 2 F4
Watermeet Ho B38 .... 35 B8
Watermeet Rd CV2 .... 114 B6
Waterson Croft B37 .... 70 D3
Waterward Cl B17 .... 85 C5
Waterways Dr B69 .... 63 E8
Waterways Gdns DY8 .... 60 E1
Waterworks Dr B31 .... 102 D4
Waterworks Rd B16 .... 65 F1
Waterworks St B6 .... 67 B8
Watery La
  Alvechurch B48 .... 124 C1
  Belbroughton DY9 .... 118 F7
  Birmingham B46 .... 84 A3
  Cheswick Green B90 ..... 126 A3
  Codsall WV8 .... 10 A5
  Corley CV7 .... 93 D5
  Coventry CV6 .... 95 A4
  Hopwood B48 .... 123 F2
  Keresley CV7 .... 94 F4
  Kingswinford DY6 .... 128 E4
  Lichfield WS13 .... 3 C4
  Portway B48 .... 140 D7
  Redditch B98 .... 154 B2
  Smethwick B67 .... 65 A6
  Stourbridge DY8 .... 60 E2
  Tipton DY4 .... 51 F5
  Walsall WS1 .... 42 E8
  Warwick CV35 .... 160 A1
  Willenhall WV13 .... 26 E3
Watery Lane Ind Est
  WV13 .... 26 E3
Watery Lane Middleway
  B9 .... 67 B2
Watford Gap WS14 .... 32 A7
Watford Gap Rd WS14 ...... 32 A7
Watford Rd B30 .... 103 F5
Wathan Ave WV14 .... 39 F1
Wathen Rd
  Royal Leamington Spa
  CV32 .... 157 A2
  Warwick CV34 .... 160 E8
Watkins Gdns B31 .... 103 C4
Watkins Rd WV12 .... 27 C5
Watland Gn B34 .... 69 B5
Watling Cl CV11 .... 73 F3
Watling Ct CV11 .... 73 F3
Watling Dr LE10 .... 75 C4
Watling Rd CV8 .... 148 B6
Watling St Brownhills WS8 .. 6 D1
  Cannock WS11 .... 4 B6
  Dordon B77,B78 .... 36 D6
  Hinckley CV11,LE10 .... 74 C8
  Hints B78 .... 19 D3
  Norton Canes WS11 .... 5 D3
  Tamworth, Bonehill B78 .... 20 E1
  Tamworth, Two Gates B77 .. 35 D7
Watling Street Jun Mix Inf
  Sch WS8 .... 6 E1
Watney Gr B44 .... 56 C8
Watson Cl
  Sutton Coldfield B72 .... 46 C2
  ■ Warwick CV34 .... 155 E1
Watson Rd Birmingham B7 .. 67 D7
  Birmingham, Nechells B24 .. 67 D8
  Birmingham, Saltley B8 ..... 67 F5
  Coventry CV5 .... 112 D2
  Wednesbury WS10 .... 41 A5
  WV14 .... 39 F2
  Wolverhampton, Pendeford
  WV10 .... 11 B2
Watson Way CV7 .... 130 C8
Watson's Green Fields
  DY2 .... 62 F8
Watson's Green Rd DY2 ... 51 E1
Watsons Cl DY2 .... 62 D8
Watt Ho DY6 .... 60 F7
Watt Rd Birmingham B23 .. 56 E4
  Tipton DY4 .... 52 B8
Watt St Birmingham B21 ... 65 D7
  Smethwick B66 .... 65 B6
Wattis Rd B67 .... 87 D8
Wattis Rd B67 .... 65 A2
Wattisham Sq B35 .... 58 A4
Wattle Rd B70 .... 53 A4
Watton Cl WV14 .... 40 A1
Watton Gr B33 .... 69 D2
Watton La B46 .... 59 D2
Watton St B70 .... 53 D2
Watts Cl DY4 .... 51 D4
Watts Rd B80 .... 159 E2
Wattville Ave B21 .... 65 B8
Wattville Prim Sch B21 .... 65 B8
Wattville Rd B21 .... 65 B8
Watwood Rd B28,B90 ...... 105 F3
Waugh Cl B37 .... 70 B2
Waugh Dr B63 .... 100 D8
Waveley Rd CV1 .... 113 A3
Wavell Rd Birmingham B8 .. 67 E5
  Brierley Hill DY5 .... 81 F7
  Walsall WS2 .... 28 B5
Wavendon Cl CV2 .... 96 F1
Waveney B77 .... 35 E8
Waveney Ave WV6 .... 23 E4
Waveney Cl LE10 .... 75 A8
Waveney Croft B36 .... 69 F8
Waveney Gr WS11 .... 1 B1

Wavenham Cl B74 .... 31 E5
Waverhill Rd B21 .... 65 F7
Waverley Ave
  Birmingham B43 .... 44 B4
  Nuneaton CV11 .... 73 F1
Waverley Cl DY10 .... 117 A8
Waverley Cres
  Romsley B62 .... 100 F4
  Wolverhampton, Lanesfield
  WV4 .... 39 F3
  Wolverhampton, Penn WV4 .. 39 B6
Waverley Gdns WS5 .... 49 B7
Waverley Gr B91 .... 106 F3
Waverley Rd
  Birmingham B10 .... 87 D7
  Darlaston WS10 .... 41 D6
  Kenilworth CV8 .... 148 A4
  Royal Leamington Spa
  CV32 .... 162 B6
  Walsall WS3 .... 13 F2
Waverley Sch B10 .... 88 A8
Waverley Sq CV11 .... 73 F1
Waverley St DY2 .... 62 A8
Waverley Wlk WS14 .... 9 B6
Waverton Mews ■
  CV31 .... 162 C6
Wavytree Cl CV34 .... 160 D7
Waxland Rd B63 .... 83 B2
Wayfield Cl B90 .... 106 C3
Wayfield Rd B90 .... 106 C3
Wayford Dr B72 .... 57 D7
Wayford Glade WV13 .... 40 F8
Wayford Gr B8 .... 68 A5
Waynecroft Rd B43 .... 43 E2
Wayside Birmingham B37 .. 90 A8
  Wolverhampton WV8 .... 10 F2
Wayside Dr B74 .... 31 C3
Wayside Gdns WV12 .... 27 E5
Wayside Wlk WS2 .... 28 A3
Waystone La CV9 .... 119 D4
Wealden Hatch WV10 .... 11 E4
Wealdstone Dr DY3 .... 50 D2
Weale Gr CV34 .... 155 F2
Weaman St B4 .... 164 C3
Weather Oaks B17 .... 85 B6
Weatheroak Cl B97 .... 153 A1
Weatheroak Hill B48 .... 124 B1
Weatheroak Rd B11 .... 87 C5
Weatheroaks
  Brownhills WS9 .... 16 B4
  Halesowen B62 .... 84 A7
Weaver Ave
  Birmingham B26 .... 89 B6
  Sutton Coldfield B76 .... 47 A1
Weaver Cl DY5 .... 61 B6
Weaver Gr WV13 .... 27 D2
Weavers Cl B97 .... 158 D4
Weavers Hill B97 .... 158 D4
Weavers Rise DY2 .... 62 D3
Weavers Wlk CV6 .... 114 B8
Weaving Gdns ■ WS11 ...... 1 E1
Webb Ave WV6 .... 23 E5
Webb La B28 .... 105 E6
Webb Rd DY4 .... 52 C7
Webb St Dudley WV14 .... 40 C1
  Nuneaton CV10 .... 72 D3
  Willenhall WV13 .... 26 F2
Webbcroft Rd B33 .... 68 F4
Webheath Fst Sch B97 .... 153 A2
Webley Rise WV10 .... 11 E4
Webner Ind Est WV2 .... 40 A6
Webster Ave CV8 .... 148 B5
Webster Cl
  Birmingham B11 .... 87 B6
  Sutton Coldfield B72 .... 46 B4
Webster Rd Walsall WS2 ... 28 E5
  Willenhall WV13 .... 27 A3
Webster Steet CV6 .... 113 E7
Webster Way B76 .... 58 B8
Webster Wlk WS11 .... 2 A4
Weddell Wynd WV14 .... 40 F1
Weddington Ctry Wlk*
  CV10 .... 73 B8
Weddington Prim Sch
  CV10 .... 73 D7
Weddington Rd CV10 .... 73 C7
Weddington Terr CV10 ...... 73 D5
Wedgbury Way DY5 .... 61 B1
Wedge St ■ DY5 .... 81 B1
Wedge-Woods CV5 .... 132 F8
Wedgewood Ave B70 .... 52 F7
Wedgewood Cl
  Burntwood WS7 .... 7 C2
  Coventry CV2 .... 114 E8
Wedgewood Ct WS4 .... 15 C1
Wedgewood Ho B37 .... 70 B4
Wedgewood Pl B70 .... 52 F7
Wedgewood Rd B32 .... 84 D5
Wednock Gn CV34 .... 160 D8
Wednock Ind Est CV34 ... 160 C8
Wednock La CV34 .... 155 C1
Wedgwood Cl WV11 .... 26 E5
Wednesbury Oak Prim Sch
  DY4 .... 41 A1
Wednesbury Oak Rd DY4 .. 41 A1
Wednesbury Parkway Sta
  WS10 .... 41 E6
Wednesbury Rd WS1 .... 42 D7
Wednesbury Trad Est
  WS10 .... 41 E4
Wednesbury, Great Western
  Street Sta WS10 .... 41 F1
Wednesfield High Sch
  WV11 .... 26 E5
Wednesfield Rd
  Willenhall WV13 .... 27 A3

Wednesfield Rd continued
  Wolverhampton WV1,
  WV10 .... 163 D4
Wednesfield Village Prim
  Sch WV11 .... 26 D5
Wednesfield Way WV11 .... 26 D4
Wedon Cl CV4 .... 131 E7
Weeford Dell B75 .... 32 E3
Weeford Dr B20 .... 54 F3
Weeford Rd B75 .... 32 F3
Weethley Gr B11 .... 87 C5
Weethley Ho ■ B97 .... 153 A4
Weights La B97 .... 153 C7
Weilerswist Dr CV31 .... 161 F4
Weirbrook Cl B29 .... 103 C7
Welbeck Ave
  Hinckley LE10 .... 75 D4
  Wolverhampton WV10 ...... 25 D7
Welbeck Cl B62 .... 83 E6
Welbeck Dr
  Kidderminster DY11 .... 116 B5
  Walsall WS4 .... 29 D7
Welbeck Gr B23 .... 56 B5
Welby Rd B28 .... 87 F1
Welches Cl B31 .... 103 B5
Welcombe Dr B76 .... 57 F7
Welcombe Gr B91 .... 106 F4
Welcome Dr B61 .... 121 A1
Welford Ave B26 .... 88 F8
Welford Cl B98 .... 158 F5
Welford Gr B74 .... 31 F3
Welford Pl CV6 .... 113 D7
Welford Prim Sch B20 ...... 66 A8
Welford Rd
  Birmingham B20 .... 66 A8
  Solihull B90 .... 106 C4
  Sutton Coldfield B73 .... 45 E1
  Tamworth B77 .... 35 C5
Welgarth Ave CV6 .... 112 F6
Welham Croft B90 .... 127 A6
Welland Gr Birmingham B36 .. 68 E8
  Redditch B97 .... 158 E5
Well La Birmingham B5 .... 164 D2
  Great Wyrley WS6 .... 5 A1
  Hinckley LE10 .... 71 D1
  Tanworth-In-A B94 .... 142 A1
  Walsall WS3 .... 28 E8
  Walsall, Harden WS3 .... 28 D7
  Wolverhampton WV11 ...... 26 C4
Well Mdw B45 .... 122 A6
Well Pl WS3 .... 28 D8
Well St Birmingham B19 ... 66 C5
  Coventry CV1 .... 165 B3
  Darlaston WS10 .... 41 E6
Welland Cl B46 .... 59 B2
Welland Dr DY8 .... 81 A8
Welland Gr
  Birmingham B24 .... 57 D3
  Willenhall WV13 .... 27 C2
Welland Rd Coventry CV1 .. 113 F1
  Halesowen B63 .... 83 A2
Welland Way B76 .... 58 A7
Wellcroft Rd B34 .... 69 A7
Wellcroft St WS10 .... 41 F3
Weller Ct WV3 .... 24 D1
Wellesbourne B79 .... 21 C8
Wellesbourne Cl
  Redditch B98 .... 153 E4
  Wolverhampton WV3 .... 38 B8
Wellesbourne Dr WV14 ..... 51 B7
Wellesbourne Rd
  Birmingham B20 .... 55 B1
  Coventry CV5 .... 112 A3
Wellesbourne Twr ■ B5 .. 86 C8
Wellesley Dr DY4 .... 51 F5
Wellesley Gdns B13 .... 87 D1
Wellesley Rd B68 .... 64 B6
Wellfield Cl
  Balsall Common CV7 ...... 130 D5
  Cannock WS11 .... 4 B7
Wellfield Gdns DY2 .... 62 E6
Wellfield Rd Aldridge WS9 .. 30 B8
  Birmingham B28 .... 106 B6
Wellhead La B42 .... 55 E3
Wellhead Way B42 .... 55 F3
Wellington Ave B13 .... 38 F7
Wellington Cl DY6 .... 60 E4
Wellington Cres B20 .... 55 B2
Wellington Ct
  Birmingham, Beech Lanes
  B32 .... 84 F5
  Birmingham, Handsworth Wood
  B20 .... 55 A3
  Blackheath B64 .... 62 F2
  Kidderminster DY11 .... 116 C5
Wellington Dr WS11 .... 4 B8
Wellington Gdns ■
  CV1 .... 113 B2
Wellington Gr B91 .... 106 F6
Wellington Ho B32 .... 84 F4
Wellington Ind Est WV14 .. 51 C7
Wellington Pl WV13 .... 26 F3
Wellington Rd
  Bilston WV14 .... 40 D6
  Birmingham B20 .... 55 C2
  Birmingham, Edgbaston B15 .. 86 C7
  Bromsgrove B60 .... 151 A8
  Dudley DY1 .... 51 B1
  CV32 .... 157 C2
  Smethwick B67 .... 65 A3
  Tipton DY4 .... 52 A4
  Walsall WS5 .... 43 C6
Wellington St
  Birmingham B18 .... 65 D5

Wellington St continued
Blackheath B64 .....62 F2
Coventry CV1 .....165 D4
Oldbury B69 .....64 B6
6 Redditch B98 .....153 E4
Walsall WS1 .....42 B7
West Bromwich B71 .....53 C4
Wellington St S B70 .....53 C4
Wellington Terr 3 B19 .....66 B7
Wellington Twr 4 B31 .....103 A1
Wellington Way B35 .....58 B2
Wellman Croft B29 .....85 D1
Wellman's Rd WV13 .....27 C1
Wellmead Wlk B45 .....121 F8
Wellmeadow Gr B92 .....109 A7
Wells Ave WS10 .....41 B6
Wells Cl Cannock WS11 .....1 E6
  Kidderminster DY11 .....116 A6
  Perton WV6 .....23 D4
  Tipton DY4 .....41 A1
  West Bromwich B71 .....53 D8
Wells Ct Coventry CV3 .....133 F7
  Dudley DY2 .....62 C5
Wells Green Rd B92 .....89 A4
Wells Rd Bilston WV14 .....40 E3
  Blackheath B65 .....63 E4
  Brierley Hill DY5 .....61 B3
  Solihull B92 .....89 C4
  Wolverhampton WV4 .....38 F5
Wells Twr B16 .....66 A2
Wellsford Ave B92 .....89 B4
Welney Gdns WV9 .....11 A3
Welsby Ave B43 .....54 E7
Welsh Cl CV34 .....155 E2
Welsh House Farm Com Sch
  B32 .....84 F4
Welsh House Farm Rd
  B32 .....84 F4
Welsh Rd Coventry CV2 .....114 B4
  Cubbington CV32,CV33 .....157 F2
Welshmans Hill B73 .....45 C3
Welton Cl B76 .....47 A2
Welton Rd CV34 .....155 D1
Welwyn Rd LE10 .....71 F1
Welwyndale Rd B72 .....57 C6
Wem Gdns WV11 .....26 D6
Wembley Gr B25 .....88 C8
Wembley La WS7 .....6 D8
Wembrook Cl CV11 .....73 D2
Wembrook Ho CV11 .....73 E2
Wembrook Prim Sch
  CV11 .....73 C2
Wembury B77 .....21 E5
Wendell Crest WV10 .....11 F4
Wendiburgh St CV4 .....132 B7
Wendover Dr LE10 .....71 E4
Wendover Rd
  Birmingham B23 .....56 C7
  Blackheath B65 .....63 A5
  Wolverhampton WV4 .....39 F2
Wendover Rise CV5 .....112 C4
Wenlock Cl B60 .....137 B2
Wenlock Dr B14 .....104 D4
Wenlock B77 .....21 D3
Wenlock Ave WV3 .....38 E8
Wenlock Cl
  Halesowen B63 .....82 D2
  Sedgley DY3 .....50 C7
Wenlock Dr B61 .....137 A5
Wenlock Gdns WS3 .....28 E5
Wenlock Rd
  Birmingham B20 .....55 F1
  Stourbridge DY8 .....81 B6
Wenlock Way CV10 .....72 B3
Wenman St B12 .....86 F6
Wensley Croft B90 .....106 B6
Wensley Rd B26 .....88 F6
Wensleydale Rd B43 .....55 B6
Wensum Cl LE10 .....75 B8
Wentbridge Rd WV1 .....26 C1
Wentworth Ave B36 .....69 B8
Wentworth Cl
  Burntwood WS7 .....7 C7
  Hinckley LE10 .....71 E3
Wentworth Ct
  Birmingham B24 .....56 F2
  Sutton Coldfield B75 .....32 B1
Wentworth Dr
  Blackwell B60 .....138 A5
  Coventry CV6 .....95 B4
  Lichfield WS14 .....9 D5
  Nuneaton CV11 .....74 A1
  Tipton B69 .....63 A7
Wentworth Gate B17 .....85 B6
Wentworth Gr WV6 .....23 D5
Wentworth Park Ave B17 .....85 B6
Wentworth Rd
  Birmingham B17 .....85 B6
  Royal Leamington Spa
  CV31 .....162 D6
  Solihull B92 .....88 F3
  Stourbridge DY8 .....80 E7
  Sutton Coldfield B74 .....46 A8
  Walsall WS3 .....13 F3
  Wolverhampton WV11 .....11 F3
Wentworth Rise B62 .....83 D3
Wentworth Way B32 .....84 F3
Wenyon Cl DY4 .....52 B4
Weoley Ave B29 .....85 F2
Weoley Castle Rd B29 .....84 F1
Weoley Hill B29 .....103 C8
Weoley Park Rd B29 .....85 C1
Wergs Dr WV6 .....24 A7

Wergs Hall Rd
  Codsall WV8 .....23 F8
  Wolverhampton WV6,WV8 .....24 A7
Wergs Rd Codsall WV8 .....23 F7
  Wolverhampton WV6 .....24 B6
Werneth Gr WS3 .....14 A4
Wesley Ave
  Cheslyn Hay WS6 .....4 D3
  Codsall WV8 .....10 B2
  Halesowen B63 .....82 B8
Wesley Cl B64 .....62 E3
Wesley Ct Blackheath B64 .....82 F8
  Cannock WS11 .....1 E1
  Willenhall WV13 .....26 E1
  8 Wolverhampton WV4 .....39 F4
Wesley Gr WS10 .....41 E3
Wesley Ho 3 WS2 .....42 C7
Wesley Pl Cannock WS12 .....2 C7
  Tipton DY4 .....52 C7
Wesley Rd
  Birmingham B23 .....56 F5
  Brierley Hill DY5 .....61 B5
  Codsall WV8 .....10 B2
  Willenhall WV12 .....27 C6
Wesley St Bilston WV14 .....40 E2
  Oldbury B69 .....64 A8
  West Bromwich B70 .....53 B3
  Wolverhampton WV2 .....40 A6
Wesley Way B77 .....21 F4
Wesley Wlk B60 .....150 E7
Wesley's Fold WS10 .....41 D6
Wessenden B77 .....36 B7
Wessex Cl Bedworth CV12 .....78 A4
  Brownhills WS8 .....15 F7
Wessex Ct B79 .....22 F7
Wessex Dr WS11 .....1 F2
Wessex Rd WV2 .....39 F6
Wesson Gdns B63 .....83 A3
Wesson Rd WS10 .....41 C8
West Acre WV13 .....26 F1
West Ave Bedworth CV12 .....78 D2
  Birmingham, Castle Bromwich
  B36 .....69 D8
  Birmingham, Handsworth
  B20 .....55 A4
  Coventry CV7 .....95 A5
  Coventry, Middle Stoke
  CV2 .....114 A2
  Redditch B98 .....153 E3
  Tipton B69 .....63 B7
  Wolverhampton WV11 .....26 C6
West Bromwich Rd WS5 .....42 F5
West Bromwich Ringway
  B70 .....53 D2
West Bromwich St
  Oldbury B69 .....52 F1
  Walsall WS1 .....42 E7
West Bvd B32 .....84 F4
West Cl LE10 .....75 D7
West Coppice Rd WS8 .....15 C8
West Cross Sh Ctr B66 .....64 D7
West Ct B60 .....150 F6
West Dr
  Birmingham, Edgbaston B5 .....86 C5
  Birmingham, Handsworth
  B20 .....66 B8
  Fazeley B78 .....20 E2
West End Ave B66 .....64 D7
West End Villas B18 .....103 F2
West Gate B16 .....65 C3
West Gn WV4 .....38 C5
West Green Cl B15 .....85 F8
West Heath Hospl B38 .....123 C8
West Heath Jun & Inf Sch
  B38 .....123 C8

West Heath Rd
  2 Birmingham, Edgbaston
  B18 .....65 D4
  Birmingham, Northfield
  B31 .....103 B1
West Hill Ave WS10 .....2 B6
West Hill Cl B14 .....104 C4
West Hill Prim Sch WS12 .....2 B6
West Holme B7 .....67 C2
West House Sch B15 .....86 B8
West Lodge WV1 .....25 A3
West Mead Dr B14 .....104 E6
West Mews B44 .....44 D2
West Midlands (Private)
  Hospl B63 .....82 D5
West Mill Croft B38 .....123 E7
West Orchards Sh Ctr
  CV1 .....165 B3
West Park Ave B31 .....102 E2
West Park Ct WV1 .....25 A2
West Park Hospl WV1 .....25 A2
West Park Inf Sch WV1 .....163 A4
West Park Jun Sch
  WV1 .....163 A4
West Park Rd B67 .....64 D6
West Pathway B17 .....85 C6
West Point B17 .....85 C8
West Rd
  Birmingham, Hamstead B43 .....54 F7
  Birmingham, Handsworth
  B6 .....55 C2
  Bromsgrove B60 .....137 A2
  Halesowen B63 .....82 B6
  Tipton DY4 .....52 B8
  Wolverhampton WV4 .....39 F5
West Rd S B63 .....82 B6
West Ridge CV5 .....112 A5
West Rise B45 .....46 C6
West Rock CV34 .....160 D7
West Side Bsns Ctr CV4 .....131 F8

West St Birmingham B7 .....66 F4
  Blackheath B65 .....63 C1
  Brierley Hill DY5 .....81 F8
  Cannock WS11 .....4 E6
  Coventry CV1 .....113 E3
  Dudley DY1 .....51 B2
  Redditch B98 .....153 E3
  17 Royal Leamington Spa
  CV31 .....162 A7
  Stourbridge DY8 .....80 F5
  Tamworth B79 .....21 C5
  Tamworth, Kettlebrook B77 .....21 C3
  Walsall WS3 .....28 C7
  Warwick CV34 .....160 D5
  West View B8 .....68 C4
  West View Dr DY6 .....60 D5
West View Rd
  Royal Leamington Spa
  CV32 .....157 C5
  Sutton Coldfield B75 .....46 E6
West Way WS4 .....15 B2
West Winds WV10 .....12 C7
Westacre Cres B14 .....24 C1
Westacre Dr DY5 .....81 F8
Westacre Gdns B33 .....68 F3
Westacre Inf Sch WV3 .....24 C1
Westbourne Ave
  Birmingham B34 .....68 E6
  Cannock WS11 .....1 D3
  Cheslyn Hay WS6 .....4 E3
Westbourne Cl B61 .....136 E1
Westbourne Cres
  Birmingham B15 .....86 A8
  Burntwood WS7 .....7 B7
Westbourne Ct
  Darlaston WS10 .....41 F7
  Walsall WS4 .....29 A3
Westbourne Gdns B15 .....86 A7
Westbourne Gr B21 .....65 F7
Westbourne Rd
  Birmingham, Edgbaston B15 .....86 A8
  Birmingham, Handsworth
  B21 .....54 D1
  Darlaston WS10 .....41 F7
  Halesowen B62 .....83 E7
  Solihull B92 .....106 E8
  Walsall WS4 .....29 A4
  West Bromwich B70 .....53 B2
  Wolverhampton WV4 .....39 A5
  Westbourne St 5 WS4 .....28 F3
Westbourne Terr B61 .....136 E1
Westbrook Ave WS9 .....29 F5
Westbrook Ct CV5 .....112 A4
Westbury Ave WS10 .....41 F6
Westbury Ct
  22 Brierley Hill DY5 .....61 D2
  Coventry CV2 .....114 A3
  Warwick CV34 .....161 A7
Westbury Ho B97 .....153 B2
Westbury Rd
  Coventry CV5 .....112 D5
  Nuneaton CV10 .....72 D3
  Smethwick B17 .....65 B3
  Wednesbury WS10 .....41 F6
Westcliff Dr CV2 .....114 C8
Westcliff Dr CV34 .....160 D6
Westcliffe Dr CV3 .....133 B5
Westcombe Gr B32 .....84 A1
Westcote Ave B31 .....102 C2
Westcote Cl B92 .....89 A2
Westcotes CV4 .....112 B1
Westcott Cl DY6 .....60 F3
Westcott Rd B26 .....89 A8
Westcroft Ave WV10 .....12 A1
Westcroft Gr B38 .....103 D3
Westcroft Rd Sedgley DY3 .....39 B2
  Wolverhampton WV6 .....23 F6
Westcroft Sch WV10 .....12 B2
Westcroft Way B14 .....105 B1
Westerdale Cl DY3 .....51 A7
Westerham Cl B93 .....127 F6
Westerhope Gr B19 .....66 C5
Westeria Cl B36 .....69 C8
Westeria Ho B36 .....69 C8
Westering Parkway
  WV10 .....11 F4
Westerings B20 .....55 C2
Western Ave
  Brierley Hill DY5 .....61 B2
  Halesowen B62 .....83 E4
  Sedgley DY3 .....50 B8
  Willenhall WS7 .....27 D3
Western Bsns Pk
  Birmingham B18 .....65 E6
  Halesowen B62 .....83 B7
Western By-Pass WS13 .....8 F8
Western Cl WS2 .....27 D3
Western Hill Cl B96 .....158 E1
Western Rd
  Birmingham, Edgbaston B18 .....65 F4
  Birmingham, Erdington B24 .....57 A3
  Blackheath B64 .....82 E8
  Cannock WS12 .....2 B6
  Hagley DY9 .....99 B4
  Stourbridge DY8 .....64 B5
  Sutton Coldfield B73 .....46 A1
Western Way
  Kidderminster DY11 .....116 A5
  Wednesbury WS10 .....41 C3
Westfield Ave B14 .....105 B1
Westfield Cl
  Dorridge B93 .....127 F2
  Nuneaton CV10 .....73 D5

Westfield Cl LE10 .....75 C7
Westfield City Prim Sch
  WV5 .....49 A7
Westfield Dr WS9 .....30 A6
Westfield Gr WV3 .....38 C8
Westfield Hall 6 B16 .....65 D1
Westfield Ho B36 .....70 A7
Westfield Jun & Inf Schs
  LE10 .....75 B7
Westfield Manor B75 .....32 A4
Westfield Rd
  Bilston WV14 .....40 B7
  Birmingham, Acock's Green
  B27 .....88 B3
  Birmingham, Edgbaston
  B15 .....85 D7
  Birmingham, Moseley B14 .....86 E1
  Brierley Hill DY5 .....81 F8
  Dudley DY2 .....62 D7
  Halesowen B62 .....63 E1
  Hinckley LE10 .....75 B7
  Sedgley DY3 .....39 E1
  Smethwick B67 .....64 F5
  Willenhall WV13 .....40 E8
Westfields B61 .....136 F8
Westford Gr B28 .....105 E3
Westgate Aldridge WS9 .....29 E6
  Birmingham B15 .....85 E4
  Cannock WS12 .....2 F6
  Oldbury B65 .....63 E4
Westgate Cl Sedgley DY3 .....50 E7
  Warwick CV34 .....160 D6
Westgate Ho 3 CV34 .....160 E6
Westgate Prim Sch
  CV34 .....160 D6
Westgate Trad Est WS9 .....29 E6
Westgrove Ave 6 B90 .....127 A6
Westgrove Terr 1
  CV32 .....161 D8
Westhall Gate WS3 .....14 B2
Westham Ho B37 .....70 B4
Westhaven Dr B31 .....102 E7
Westhaven Rd B72 .....46 C5
Westhay Rd B28 .....106 B7
Westhill WV3 .....24 C2
Westhill Cl B92 .....106 E8
Westhill Coll (Univ
  Birmingham) B29 .....103 D8
Westhill Rd
  Birmingham B38 .....103 F3
  Blackdown CV32 .....157 A6
  Coventry CV6 .....112 F6
Westholme Croft B30 .....103 E8
Westhouse Gr B14 .....104 D4
Westland Ave WV3 .....24 F2
Westland Cl B23 .....56 F5
Westland Gdns
  Stourbridge DY8 .....80 F7
  6 Wolverhampton WV3 .....25 A2
Westland Rd WV6 .....24 F2
Westland Wlk B35 .....57 F2
Westlands Rd
  Birmingham B13 .....87 A1
  Sutton Coldfield B76 .....57 F6
Westlea Rd CV31 .....161 E6
Westleigh Ave CV5 .....132 F7
Westley Brook Cl B26 .....89 B5
Westley Cl B28 .....106 B6
Westley Rd B27 .....88 B3
Westley St 2 Birmingham B9 .....67 A2
  7 Dudley DY1 .....62 B8
Westmead Ave B80 .....159 E4
Westmead Cres B24 .....57 C4
Westmead Dr B60 .....150 E6
Westmede Ctr CV5 .....112 C4
Westminster B37 .....69 F5
Westminster Ave WV4 .....39 B5
Westminster Cl
  Bromsgrove B61 .....136 D1
  Dudley DY1 .....51 A2
Westminster Ct
  Birmingham B20 .....55 C2
  2 Bromsgrove B60 .....137 A2
Westminster Dr
  Birmingham B14 .....104 E6
  Hinckley LE10 .....75 F4
  Nuneaton CV10 .....72 D7
Westminster Ind Est DY2 .....62 D2
Westminster Prim Sch
  B67 .....65 A5
Westminster Rd
  Birmingham, Handsworth
  B20 .....55 C1
  Birmingham, Stirchley B29 .....104 A8
  Cannock WS11 .....1 C6
  Coventry CV1 .....165 A1
  Kidderminster DY11 .....116 A6
  Stourbridge DY9 .....60 D2
  Walsall WS4 .....29 B7
  West Bromwich B71 .....53 D8
Westminster Sch The
  B67 .....65 A5
Westmore Way WS10 .....42 D5
Westmorland Ave CV10 .....72 E4
Westmorland Ct B71 .....53 D7
Westmorland Ct B71 .....21 A1
Westmorland Rd
  Coventry CV2 .....114 F4
  West Bromwich B71 .....53 D7
Weston Ave
  Birmingham B11 .....87 C6
  7 Birmingham B19 .....66 C7
  Tipton B69 .....52 B1
Weston Cl Cannock WS11 .....2 C1
  Dorridge B93 .....128 A2
  Hinckley LE10 .....71 A1
  5 Royal Leamington Spa
  CV31 .....162 C6

Weston Ct continued
  Walsall WS1 .....42 E6
  Warwick CV34 .....160 F7
Weston Cres WS9 .....30 B4
Weston Ct 10 WS1 .....25 C4
Weston Dr Bilston WV14 .....40 B5
  Great Wyrley WS6 .....4 F1
  Tipton DY4 .....41 C2
Weston Hall Stables
  CV12 .....79 A3
Weston Ho
  Birmingham B19 .....66 C6
  Wolverhampton WV6 .....24 E7
Weston Ind Est B11 .....87 E4
Weston La
  Birmingham B11 .....87 E4
  Bulkington CV12 .....79 B3
Weston Rd
  Birmingham B19 .....66 B8
  Lichfield WS13 .....3 A2
  Smethwick B67 .....64 F2
Weston St Coventry CV1 .....165 C4
  Walsall WS1 .....42 E7
Weston Terr 3 B19 .....66 D8
Westonbirt Cl CV8 .....148 C6
Westonhall Rd B60 .....150 D1
Westover Rd B20 .....54 E4
Westport Cres WV11 .....26 F5
Westray Cl B45 .....101 F1
Westray Dr LE10 .....71 C1
Westridge B32 .....84 D1
Westridge DY3 .....50 C8
Westridge Rd B13 .....105 C6
Westside Dr B32 .....84 D1
Westville Ave B16 .....116 A5
Westville Rd WS2 .....28 A3
Westward Cl B44 .....55 F8
Westway WS4 .....15 B1
Westwick Cl WS9 .....16 C4
Westwood Ave
  Birmingham B11 .....87 D4
  Stourbridge DY8 .....80 D3
Westwood Bsns Pk
  Birmingham B6 .....56 B1
  Coventry CV4 .....131 F6
Westwood Cl CV10 .....72 E3
Westwood Ct B73 .....45 B4
Westwood Dr B45 .....102 B1
Westwood Gr B91 .....106 F2
Westwood Heath Rd
  CV4 .....131 E6
Westwood Holdings WS12 .....1 B6
Westwood Rd
  Birmingham, Aston B6 .....56 A2
  Birmingham, Kingstanding
  B73 .....45 A4
  Coventry CV5 .....113 A1
Westwood St DY5 .....61 A1
Westwood View B24 .....57 C3
Westwood Way CV4 .....132 A6
Westwoods Hollow WS7 .....7 B8
Wetherby Cl
  Birmingham B36 .....68 D8
  Wolverhampton WV10 .....11 D5
Wetherby Rd
  Birmingham B27 .....88 C2
  Walsall WS3 .....14 A4
Wetherfield Rd B11 .....88 A3
Wexford Cl DY1 .....50 F2
Wexford Rd CV2 .....96 D1
Weybourne Rd B44 .....44 E2
Weycroft Rd B23 .....56 B7
Weyhill Cl WV9 .....10 F2
Weymoor Rd B17 .....85 B3
Weymouth Cl CV3 .....134 D5
Weymouth Dr B74 .....31 F4
Weymouth Ho B79 .....21 B5
Whaley's Croft CV6 .....113 B8
Whar Hall Rd B92 .....107 E8
Wharf App WS9 .....29 C7
Wharf Cl WS14 .....9 F7
Wharf La Birmingham B18 .....66 A6
  Burntwood WS8 .....6 F3
  Lapworth B94 .....143 D4
  Solihull B91 .....107 D6
  Stourbridge B60 .....138 B1
Wharf Lodge CV31 .....161 D7
Wharf Rd
  Birmingham, King's Norton
  B30 .....104 A2
  Birmingham, Tyseley B11 .....88 B5
  Coventry CV6 .....113 F5
Wharf St
  Birmingham, Aston B6 .....67 A7
  Birmingham, Hockley B18 .....66 A6
  Walsall WS2 .....28 C1
  Warwick CV34 .....161 A8
  Wolverhampton WV1 .....163 D2
Wharf The B1 .....164 A2
Wharfdale Rd B11 .....88 A5
Wharfedale St DY6 .....60 F4
Wharfside St WS10 .....42 A2
Wharfside St B1 .....164 B2
Wharnside B70 .....63 F7
Wharrington Cl B98 .....159 A8
Wharrington Hill B98 .....159 A8
Wharton Ave B92 .....107 C7
Wharton Rd B66 .....65 C4
Wharton St B7 .....67 A8
Wharton St Ind Est B7 .....67 D8
Wharwell La WS6 .....5 A1
Whatcote Gn B92 .....107 E8
Whatcroft The B17 .....85 B6
Whateley Ave WS3 .....28 F6
Whateley Cres B36 .....69 D8
Whateley Gn B36 .....69 C8
  Sutton Coldfield B74 .....44 A8
Whateley Hall Cl B93 .....128 C7
Whateley Hall Rd B93 .....128 B7
Whateley La B77,B78 .....35 F4
Whateley Lodge Dr B36 .....69 C8

Whateley Pl WS3 28 F6
Whateley Rd
Birmingham B21 65 E8
Walsall WS3 28 F6
Whateley Villas CV9 36 A2
Whateley's Dr CV8 148 A5
Wheat Hill WS5 43 E8
Wheat St CV11 73 D4
Wheatcroft Cl
Burntwood WS7 7 A5
Halesowen B62 83 F8
Sutton Coldfield B75 32 E3
Wheatcroft Dr B37 70 C1
Wheatcroft Gr DY2 51 F1
Wheatcroft Rd B33 68 F2
Wheate Croft CV4 111 F2
Wheaten Cl B37 70 D3
Wheatfield Cl B36 70 A7
Wheatfield View B31 102 D6
Wheatfield Way LE10 71 C4
Wheathill Cl
Royal Leamington Spa CV32 156 E2
Wolverhampton WV4 38 E3
Wheatlands Cl [1] WS11 2 C1
Wheatlands Croft B33 69 E3
Wheatlands The WV6 23 D3
Wheatley Cl Oldbury B68 84 C8
Solihull B92 107 E8
Sutton Coldfield B75 32 C3
Wheatley Grange B46 70 F6
Wheatley Rd B68 84 D8
Wheatley St
West Bromwich B70 53 A3
Wolverhampton WV2 39 F6
Wheatmill Cl DY10 98 B2
Wheatmoor Rd B75 47 A6
Wheatmoor Rise B75 46 E6
Wheaton Cl WV10 25 C7
Wheaton Vale B20 54 E3
Wheatridge Cl DY6 60 A8
Wheatridge Rd B60 150 E6
Wheats Ave B17 85 B3
Wheatsheaf Rd
Birmingham B16 65 D2
Tipton B69 63 A8
Wolverhampton WV8 10 E1
Wheatstone Cl DY3 50 E6
Wheatstone Gr B33 68 F5
Wheeldon Ho B26 88 E4
Wheeler Cl B93 145 B7
Wheeler Ho [12] B69 64 A7
Wheeler Rd WV11 26 C8
Wheeler St
Birmingham B19 66 D7
Stourbridge DY8 80 F5
Wheeler Street Sh Ctr B19 66 D6
Wheeler's Fold WV1 163 C3
Wheeler's La B13 105 A7
Wheelers La B13 104 F7
Wheelers Lane Boys Sch B13 104 F7
Wheelers Lane Inf Sch B13 104 F7
Wheelers Lane Jun Sch B13 104 F7
Wheelers Lane Jun Sch (Annexe) B13 105 A6
Wheeley Moor Rd B37 70 A5
Wheeley Rd
Alvechurch B48 138 D5
Solihull B92 107 D7
Wheeley's La B15 66 C1
Wheeleys Rd B15 86 B8
Wheelock Cl B74 44 F7
Wheelwright Cl B60 150 E6
Wheelwright Ct [5] B24 56 E2
Wheelwright La CV6,CV7 95 C4
Wheelwright Lane Prim Sch CV7 95 D5
Wheelwright Rd B24 56 F1
Wheldrake Ave B34 69 C6
Wheler Rd CV3 134 A7
Whernside Dr WV6 25 A5
Wherretts Well La B91 107 E6
Whetstone Cl B15 85 F5
Whetstone Field Prim Sch WS9 30 B4
Whetstone Gn WV10 11 D1
Whetstone Gr WV10 25 D8
Whetstone La WS9 30 B4
Whetstone Rd WV10 25 D8
Whetty La B45 121 F7
Whettybridge Rd B45 121 E6
Whichcote Ave CV7 92 C1
Whichford Cl B76 57 D6
Whichford Gr B9 68 C2
While Rd B72 46 B4
Whilmot Cl WV10 12 B6
Whimbrel Gr DY10 117 A1
Whinberry Rise DY5 50 C1
Whinchat Gr DY10 117 A2
Whinfield Rd B61 136 B6
Whinyates Rise WS11 4 F8
Whisley Brook La B28 87 F2
Whiston Ave WV11 27 A7
Whiston Gr B29 103 B8
Whiston Ho [9] WS1 28 F1
Whitacre La WS14 16 E7
Whitacre Rd
Birmingham B9 67 F3
Knowle B93 128 B7
Nuneaton CV11 73 E4
[3] Royal Leamington Spa CV32 157 A2
Whitacre Rd Ind Est CV11 73 E4
Whitaker Rd CV5 112 C3
Whitbourne Cl B12 87 B5
Whitburn Ave B42 55 A5
Whitburn Cl
Kidderminster DY11 116 B5
Wolverhampton WV9 11 A2
Whitburn Rd CV12 77 C1
Whitby Cl WS3 13 F3
Whitby Rd B12 87 A4
Whitby Way WS11 4 C8
Whitchurch Cl B98 158 F6
Whitchurch Way CV4 131 F8
Whitcot Gr B31 122 F8
White Bark Cl WS12 2 A8
White Beam Rd B37 90 D8
White City Rd DY5 62 A1
White Cl DY9 81 C2
White Falcon Ct B91 106 F2
White Farm Rd B74 31 E4
White Field Ave B17 85 A6
White Friars La CV1 165 C2
White Friars St CV1 165 C2
White Hart The [8] WS1 42 E8
White Hill B31 103 B6
White Ho B19 66 D6
White Hollies WS3 14 F4
White Horse Rd WS8 6 E2
White House Ave WV11 26 F7
White House Cl B91 106 F3
White House Dr B45 122 A2
White House Gn B91 106 F3
White House Way B91 107 A3
White Houses La WV10 12 B5
White Oak Dr
Kingswinford DY6 60 C6
Wolverhampton WV3 24 C1
White Rd
Birmingham, Quinton B32 84 D6
Birmingham, Sparkbrook B11 87 C7
Smethwick B67 64 F6
White Rose Ho [4] CV32 156 F2
White Row WV5 37 C1
White St Birmingham B12 87 A5
Coventry CV1 165 C3
Walsall WS1 42 E8
White's Dr DY3 50 E8
White's Rd B71 53 C6
Whitebeam Cl
Clayhanger WS8 15 E6
Coventry CV4 111 D1
Dudley DY3 50 C4
Whitebeam Croft [3] B38 103 E1
Whitecrest B43 44 A2
Whitecrest Prim Sch B43 44 A2
Whitecroft Rd B26 89 D5
Whitefield Cl Codsall WV8 10 B2
Coventry CV4 131 D6
Whitefields Cres B91 107 B2
Whitefields Gate B91 107 A1
Whitefields Rd B91 107 A2
Whitefriars Dr B63 83 A4
Whitegate Dr DY11 116 A3
Whitegates Rd WV14 40 D2
Whitehall Com Jun Sch WS1 42 F6
Whitehall Ct WV3 38 F6
Whitehall Dr Dudley DY1 51 A2
Halesowen B63 83 B4
Whitehall Ind Pk DY4 52 E5
Whitehall Inf Sch WS1 42 E7
Whitehall Rd
Birmingham, Bordesley Green B9 67 E1
Birmingham, Handsworth B21 66 A8
Blackheath B64 82 C8
Halesowen B63 83 B4
Kingswinford DY6 60 C6
Stourbridge DY8 81 B2
Tipton DY4,B70 52 E4
[2] Walsall WS1 42 E7
Wolverhampton WV4 39 B4
Whitehead Dr
Kenilworth CV8 148 C7
Minworth B76 58 D6
Whitehead Gr CV7 130 B7
Whitehead Rd B6 66 E8
Whiteheath CE Jun Sch B69 63 D5
Whiteheath Ct [5] B65 63 E4
Whiteheath PRU B65 63 D4
Whitehill La B29,B31 103 A5
Whitehill Rd DY11 116 A4
Whitehorn Dr CV32 157 B2
Whitehorse Cl CV6 96 B6
Whitehouse Ave
Darlaston WS10 41 B7
Wednesbury WS10 41 F3
Wolverhampton WV3 38 D8
Whitehouse Common Prim Sch B75 46 D7
Whitehouse Common Rd B75 46 E7
Whitehouse Cres
Burntwood WS7 7 B7
Nuneaton CV10 72 D3
Sutton Coldfield B75 46 E7
Wolverhampton WV11 12 F1
Whitehouse Ct B75 46 F6
Whitehouse Dr B66 65 A7
Whitehouse La
Codsall WV8 10 A6
Redditch B98 154 E4
Whitehouse Pl B45 121 F6
Whitehouse Rd
Dordon B78 36 F7
Kidderminster DY10 116 D4
Whitehouse St
Birmingham B6 66 F6
Dudley WV14 51 C8
Tipton DY4 52 A2
Walsall WS2 28 D3
Whitehouse Way WS9 29 F4
Whitelaw Cres CV5 112 C6
Whitemoor Dr B90 127 A7
Whitemoor Rd CV8 148 B5
Whitepits La B48 140 F4
Whitepoplars Cl DY5 61 C4
Whites Row CV8 148 A3
Whites Wood WV5 49 A5
Whitesands Cl B77 21 E5
Whiteside Cl CV3 134 F8
Whiteslade Cl B93 128 A7
Whitesmith Cl DY3 50 D8
Whitesmith Croft B14 104 E8
Whitesmore Sec Sch B37 69 F1
Whitestitch La CV7 92 C3
Whitestone Inf Sch CV11 79 A8
Whitestone Rd
Halesowen B63 83 A6
Nuneaton CV11 79 B7
Whitethorn Cl WS12 2 A8
Whitethorn Cres B74 30 D1
Whitethorn Rd
[2] Brierley Hill DY8 60 F1
Stourbridge DY8 61 A1
Whitewood Glade WV12 27 E4
Whitfield Gr B15 86 D8
Whitfield Rd WS12 2 C7
Whitford Bridge Rd B60 151 A2
Whitford Cl B61 150 D8
Whitford Dr B90 127 C7
Whitford Gdns B61 136 D2
Whitford Rd B61 136 D2
Whitgreave Ave
Featherstone WV10 12 B7
Wolverhampton WV10 25 F8
Whitgreave Ct WV10 12 B6
Whitgreave Inf Sch WV10 25 E8
Whitgreave Jun Sch WV10 25 E8
Whitgreave Prim Sch WV10 12 B7
Whitgreave St B70 52 E3
Whiting B77 35 D7
Whitland Cl B45 122 B6
Whitland Dr B14 104 F3
Whitley Abbey Com Sch CV3 133 F5
Whitley Abbey Prim Sch CV3 134 A6
Whitley Ave B77 21 E5
Whitley Cl WV6 24 B2
Whitley Court Rd B32 84 C6
Whitley Ct
Birmingham B20 54 E3
Coventry CV3 133 F7
Whitley Dr B74 45 A8
Whitley St WS10 41 E3
Whitley Village CV3 133 F7
Whitlock Gr B14 105 A3
Whitlocks End Halt B90 125 E7
Whitminster Ave B24 57 B3
Whitminster Cl WV12 27 C4
Whitmore Hill WV1 163 B3
Whitmore Ho WV6 25 A4
Whitmore Park Prim Sch CV6 95 A1
Whitmore Park Rd CV6 95 D3
Whitmore Rd
Birmingham B10 87 C8
Stourbridge DY8 80 D5
Whitnash CV31 162 A3
Whitmore St
Birmingham B18 66 B6
Walsall WS1 42 D7
Wolverhampton WV1 163 C3
Whitnash Cl CV7 130 A6
Whitnash Gr CV2 114 D5
Whitnash Prim Sch CV31 162 A4
Whitnash Rd CV31 162 B4
Whitney Ave DY8 80 D6
Whittaker St WV2 39 E6
Whittall Dr E DY11 116 B1
Whittall Dr W DY11 116 A1
Whittall St B4 164 C3
Whittimere St WS1 28 F2
Whittingham Gr WV11 26 F6
Whittingham Rd B63 83 A5
Whittington Cl
Birmingham B14 104 E5
[4] Warwick CV34 161 B8
West Bromwich B71 53 F8
Whittington Gr B33 68 F2
Whittington Hall La DY7 80 B3
Whittington Ho WS13 3 E1
Whittington Oval B33 69 A2
Whittington Rd DY8 80 E3
Whittle Cl CV3 134 F8
Whittle Croft B35 57 F3
Whittle Ct [9] CV32 157 A1
Whittle Rd LE10 74 E7
Whittleford Gr B36 58 C1
Whittleford Rd CV10 72 C4
Whitton St WS10 41 E6
Whitville Cl DY11 116 C7
Whitwell Dr B90 127 A6
Whitworth Ave
Coventry CV3 114 B1
Whitworth Ave *continued*
Hinckley LE10 74 F7
Whitworth Cl WS10 41 E7
Whitworth Dr B71 42 E1
Whitworth Ind Pk B9 67 C2
Whoberley Ave CV5 112 D2
Whoberley Hall Prim Sch CV5 112 C3
Whyley St B70 53 A4
Whyley Wlk B69 64 A5
Whynot Cl B60 150 C2
Whynot St B63 82 B5
Wibert Cl B29 86 A1
Wichnor Rd B92 88 F5
Wickam Sq B70 53 B2
Wickets Twr B5 86 C5
Wickham Cl CV6 94 F2
Wickham Ct CV32 157 B3
Wickham Gdns WV11 26 A6
Wickham Rd B80 159 F4
Wicklow Cl B63 82 D1
Wickmans Dr CV4 111 C2
Wiclif Way CV10 72 B3
Widdecombe Cl CV2 114 D7
Widdrington Rd CV1 113 C5
Wide Acres B45 101 F1
Wideacre Dr B44 55 E7
Widney Ave Aldridge WS9 16 B1
Birmingham B29 85 C1
Widney Cl B93 127 F5
Widney Jun Sch B91 106 F1
Widney La B91 127 B8
Widney Manor Rd B91 127 D7
Widney Manor Sta B91 127 C8
Widney Rd B93 127 F5
Wigeon Gr WV10 12 B7
Wigford Rd B77 35 C5
Wiggin Cotts [5] B17 85 C5
Wiggin Ho WS3 14 C3
Wiggin St B16 65 F3
Wiggin Twr [5] B19 66 D7
Wiggins Croft B76 46 F3
Wiggins Hill Rd B76 58 F7
Wigginsmill Rd WS10 41 D1
Wigginton Rd B79 21 B7
Wight Croft B36 70 B6
Wightman Cl WS14 9 E6
Wightwick Bank WV6 24 A2
Wightwick Cl WS3 14 B1
Wightwick Ct WV6 24 A2
Wightwick Gr WV6 24 A2
Wightwick Hall Rd WV6 23 E1
Wightwick Hall Sch WV6 23 E2
Wightwick Manor* WV6 23 F1
Wigland Way B38 104 A1
Wigmore Gr B44 56 B8
Wigmore La B71 54 A8
Wigorn Ho B67 84 F8
Wigorn La DY9 99 B8
Wigorn Rd B67 64 F1
Wigston Rd CV2 96 F1
Wilberforce Way B92 107 F7
Wilbraham Rd WS2 28 C1
Wilcote Gr B27 106 C8
Wilcox Ave WS12 2 B7
Wild Goose La B98 159 D8
Wildacres DY8 80 C6
Wilday Cl DY4 52 A5
Wildcroft Rd CV5 112 C3
Wilde Cl B14 104 D4
Wilden Cl B31 102 C3
Wilden La DY10 116 E1
Wilderness La B43 43 D3
Wildey Rd CV12 77 D2
Wildfell Rd B27 88 D2
Wildmoor Cl CV2 96 B4
Wildmoor La B61 121 A3
Wildmoor Rd B90 106 B5
Wildtree Ave WV10 12 A2
Wiley Ave WS10 41 C5
Wiley Ave S WS10 41 C5
Wilford Gr Solihull B91 107 B2
Sutton Coldfield B76 58 B6
Wilford Rd B71 53 D6
Wilkes Ave WS2 27 F2
Wilkes Cl WS3 14 E3
Wilkes Croft DY3 50 D7
Wilkes Green Jun & Inf Sch B21 54 E1
Wilkes St
West Bromwich B71 53 E7
Willenhall WV13 27 A1
Wilkin Rd WS8 6 C2
Wilkins Ho WS3 14 A1
Wilkins Rd WV14 40 D7
Wilkinson Ave WV14 40 E3
Wilkinson Cl
Burntwood WS7 7 B8
Sutton Coldfield B73 46 A2
Wilkinson Croft B8 68 C6
Wilkinson Jun & Inf Sch WV14 40 F3
Wilkinson Rd WS10 41 A4
Wilks Gn B21 54 D3
Willard Rd B25 88 C6
Willaston Rd B33 89 D7
Willclare Rd B26 89 A6
Willcock Rd WV2 39 E6
Willenhall Ind Est WV13 27 C3
Willenhall La
Coventry CV3 134 F7
Walsall WS3 28 A8
Willenhall Lane Ind Est WS3 28 A8
Willenhall Rd
Bilston WV14 40 F7
Darlaston WS10 41 D8
Wolverhampton WV1,WV13 26 C1
Willenhall Sch Sports Coll WV12 27 E5
Willenhall St WS10 41 C7
Willenhall Trad Est WV13 27 A1
Willenhall Wood Prim Sch CV3 134 D6
Willerby Fold WV10 11 F4
Willersey Rd B13 105 D8
Willes Ct [2] CV31 162 B7
Willes Rd Birmingham B18 65 E6
Royal Leamington Spa CV31,CV32 162 A8
Willes Terr CV31 162 B8
Willett Ave WS7 6 E5
Willett Rd B71 53 E8
Willetts Dr B63 82 B4
Willetts Rd B31 103 A1
Willetts Way B64 62 F2
Willey Gr B24 57 B2
William Arnold Cl CV2 114 A4
William Batchelor Ho CV1 165 B4
William Baxter Com Sch WS12 2 A6
William Beesley Cres CV11 79 E6
William Bentley Ct WV11 26 C5
William Booth La B4 164 B4
William Bree Rd CV5 111 C5
William Bristow Rd CV3 133 E7
William Cook Rd B8 68 B5
William Cowper Prim Sch B19 66 E6
William Cree Cl CV8 135 F3
William Ct B16 65 E1
William Edward St [1] B12 86 F7
William Green Rd WS10 42 C3
William Groubb Cl CV3 134 D7
William Harper Rd WV13 27 B1
William Hawke Ind Est DY5 61 E1
William Henry St B7 67 A6
William Iliffe St LE10 75 B7
William Ker Rd DY4 52 C5
William Lunn's Homes [2] WS14 9 C8
William MacGregor Prim Sch B77 21 D4
William Malcolm Ho CV2 114 E3
William McCool Cl CV3 134 F7
William McKee Cl CV3 134 E7
William Morris Gr WS11 1 E4
William Rd B67 64 D3
William Sheriden Ho CV2 114 E3
William St Bedworth CV12 78 D2
Birmingham B15 66 C1
Brierley Hill DY5 61 C3
Nuneaton CV11 73 E3
Redditch B97 153 E4
Royal Leamington Spa CV32 162 A8
Walsall WS4 28 F3
West Bromwich B70 52 E5
William St N B19 164 B4
William St W B66 65 B7
William Tarver Cl CV34 161 A7
William Thomson Ho [2] CV1 165 D4
Williams Cl WV12 27 C5
Williams Rd CV31 162 E4
Williamson St WV3 163 A2
Willingsworth High Sch DY4 41 B2
Willingsworth Rd WS10 41 D1
Willington Rd B79 21 B7
Willington St CV11 73 B5
Willingworth Cl WV14 40 A3
Willis Gr CV12 78 C3
Willis Pearson Ave WV14 41 A3
Willis St DY11 116 C5
Willmore Gr [4] B38 123 F8
Willmore Rd B20 55 D2
Willmott Cl B75 32 D3
Willmott Rd B75 32 D3
Willoughby Ave CV8 147 E3
Willoughby Cl CV3 134 E8
Willoughby Ct B76 46 F2
Willoughby Dr B91 107 B1
Willoughby Gr B29 85 A1
Willoughby Rd B79 20 E7
Willow Ave
Birmingham B17 65 A2
Burntwood WS7 7 C6
Wednesbury WS10 41 F4
Wolverhampton WV11 26 B8
Willow Bank WV3 24 C1
Willow Bank Rd B93 127 F6
Willow Brook Rd B48 139 A7
Willow Cl Bedworth CV12 78 B5
Blackheath B64 62 E1
Bromsgrove B61 136 E2
Hagley DY9 98 F5
Hinckley LE10 75 E5
Nuneaton CV10 72 A7
Whitnash CV31 162 B2
Willow Coppice B32 84 C1
Willow Ct Birmingham B13 87 A3
Bromsgrove B61 136 E3
Lichfield WS14 9 C5
Oldbury B66 64 D8
Smethwick B17 65 A2

Willow Ctyd CV2 ....114 D7
Willow Dr Birmingham B21 ..54 C1
  Cheswick Green B90 ....126 D4
  Codsall WV8 ....10 B3
  Tipton B69 ....63 C7
Willow End DY9 ....81 D3
Willow Gdns
  Birmingham B16 ....65 F4
  Bromsgrove B61 ....136 E3
Willow Gr Coventry CV4 ...112 B2
  Essington WV11 ....13 B3
Willow Ho Birmingham B7 ..67 B4
  Walsall WS2 ....15 D1
Willow Hts B64 ....83 A8
Willow Meer CV8 ....148 B5
Willow Mews B29 ....85 B1
Willow Park Dr B18 ....81 B2
Willow Way
  Birmingham, Bournville
  B29,B30 ....103 F8
  Birmingham, Great Barr
  B43 ....44 A2
  Bromsgrove B61 ....136 E3
  Dudley DY1 ....51 A4
  Nuneaton CV10 ....72 F5
  Solihull B91 ....106 E2
  Wolverhampton WV3 ....38 D8
Willow Rise DY5 ....61 C1
Willow Sheets Mdw
  CV32 ....157 E6
Willow Tree Dr B45 ......138 D8
Willow Way
  Birmingham B37 ....70 B1
  Redditch B97 ....153 B4
  Studley B80 ....159 E2
Willow Wlk WS12 ....1 D8
Willowbank B78 ....23 B1
Willowbank Rd LE10 ......75 C7
Willowdale LE10 ....75 A7
Willowdale Grange WV6 ..24 E5
Willowfield Dr DY11 ......116 C8
Willowfields Rd CV11 ....74 A1
Willowherb Cl
  Cannock WS11 ....2 C2
  ⑤ Coventry CV3 ....134 F8
  ⑤ Walsall WS5 ....43 A3
Willowherb Way WV10 ...126 A5
Willows Cres B12 ....86 E5
Willows Prim Sch WS13 ....3 B2
Willows The
  Bedworth CV12 ....77 E2
  Birmingham B27 ....88 B2
  Cannock WS11 ....1 C1
  Hollywood B47 ....125 A6
  Sutton Coldfield, Streetly
  B74 ....31 F2
  Sutton Coldfield, Walmley
  B76 ....46 F2
  Wolverhampton WV3 ....26 B5
Willowsbrook Rd B62 .....83 F8
Willowside WS4 ....29 C8
Willowsmere Dr WS14 ......9 F7
Willows Ave CV13 ....3 B2
Wills Ho B70 ....53 C2
Wills St B19 ....66 C7
Wills Way B66 ....65 C4
Willsbridge Covert ⑧
  B14 ....104 C2
William Croft B28 ....105 D3
Wilmcote Cl B32 ....86 E6
Wilmcote Ct B61 ....150 D8
Wilmcote Dr B75 ....32 B3
Wilmcote Gn CV5 ....112 A3
Wilmcote Ho B97 ....153 B4
Wilmcote Rd B91 ....106 F6
Wilmcote Twr ⑤ B12 .....86 F7
Wilmhurst Rd CV34 ......160 C8
Wilmington Rd B32 ....84 B6
Wilmore Ho B20 ....55 D1
Wilmore La B47 ....124 F4
Wilmot Ave B46 ....70 F6
Wilmot Cl CV7 ....130 B8
Wilmot Dr
  Birmingham B23 ....57 A6
  Tipton DY4 ....51 E6
Wilmot Gdns DY1 ....51 A2
Wilmott Cl WS13 ....9 A7
Wilncote Gr
  Birmingham B42 ....55 D4
  Royal Leamington Spa
  CV31 ....162 B5
Wilncote High Sch B77 ...35 F6
Wilncote Jun Sch B77 ....35 F7
Wilncote La B77 ....21 D2
Wilncote St B77 ....35 D7
Wilner's View WS3 ....14 F5
Wilsford Cl
  Birmingham B14 ....104 D1
  Walsall WS4 ....29 C8
Wilson Dr B75 ....47 A5
Wilson Gn CV3 ....114 F1
Wilson Gr Cannock WS11 ....2 C2
  Kenilworth CV8 ....148 C4
Wilson Rd
  Birmingham B19 ....66 D8
  Brierley Hill DY5 ....61 C4
  Dudley WV14 ....51 C7
  Oldbury B68 ....64 D1
  Smethwick B66 ....65 B3
Wilson St Tipton DY4 .....52 A5

Wilson St continued
  Wolverhampton WV1 ....163 C4
Wilson Stuart Sch B23 ...56 C6
Wilson's La CV6 ....95 F6
Wilsons La CV7 ....96 A6
Wilsons Rd B93 ....128 C6
Wiltell Rd WS14 ....9 B6
Wilton Ave DY11 ....116 B8
Wilton Cl DY3 ....50 E7
Wilton Rd
  Balsall Common CV7 ....130 C8
  Birmingham, Balsall Heath
  B11 ....87 B5
  Birmingham, Erdington B23 .57 A5
  Birmingham, Handsworth
  B20 ....55 B1
Wilton St B19 ....66 D8
Wiltshire Cl
  Bedworth CV12 ....78 A3
  Coventry CV5 ....112 B3
  Walsall WS2 ....28 D4
Wiltshire Ct ⑩ B29 .....103 C7
Wiltshire Dr B63 ....82 B7
Wiltshire Ho ⑤ DY8 ......80 F8
Wiltshire Way B71 ....53 C7
Wimberger Ho ⑧ B71 ....53 D4
Wimbledury Rd
  Cannock, Heath Hayes WS12 .2 F2
  Cannock, Wimblebury WS12 .2 F4
Wimbledon Dr DY9 ....81 E7
Wimborne Dr CV2 ....115 A4
Wimborne Rd WV10 ....26 A6
Wimbourne Cl CV10 ....72 B5
Wimbourne Rd
  Birmingham B16 ....65 D3
  Sutton Coldfield B76 ....47 A4
Wimperis Way B43 ....44 C4
Wimpole Gr B44 ....56 B7
Wimshurst Mdw WV10 ...11 F4
Wincanton Croft B36 .....68 C8
Winceby Pl CV4 ....111 D1
Winceby Rd WV6 ....23 F3
Winchat Cl CV3 ....114 F1
Winchcombe Cl
  Dudley DY1 ....50 E3
  Solihull B92 ....89 B2
Winchcombe Rd B92 ....89 B2
Winchester Ave
  Kidderminster DY11 ....116 A6
  Nuneaton CV10 ....73 C7
Winchester Cl
  ⑦ Blackheath B65 ....63 E4
  Hagley DY9 ....99 A6
  Lichfield WS13 ....3 C3
Winchester Ct B74 ....31 F7
Winchester Dr
  Birmingham B37 ....70 A2
  Hinckley LE10 ....76 B7
  Stourbridge DY8 ....81 A3
Winchester Gdns B31 ....103 A3
Winchester Gr B21 ....65 C8
Winchester Mews WS9 ...30 B4
Winchester Rd
  Birmingham B20 ....55 D1
  Cannock WS11 ....2 A4
  Tamworth B78 ....20 F3
  West Bromwich B71 ....53 B8
  Wolverhampton WV10 ......11 C3
Winchester Rise DY1 ......51 A2
Winchester St CV1 ....113 E3
Winchfield Dr B17 ....84 F7
Wincote Dr WV6 ....24 C4
Wincrest Way B34 ....69 C5
Windermere Dr B74 ....36 A7
Windermere Ave
  Coventry, Binley CV3 ....114 E1
  Coventry, Upper Eastern Green
  CV5 ....111 E4
  Nuneaton CV11 ....73 F6
Windermere Dr
  Aldridge B74 ....30 F3
  Royal Leamington Spa 60 D6
  Royal Leamington Spa
  CV32 ....156 D2
Windermere Ho
  Kidderminster DY10 ....116 C7
  ⑩ Oldbury B69 ....63 D5
Windermere Pl WS11 ......1 E1
Windermere Rd
  Birmingham, Handsworth
  B21 ....54 E2
  Birmingham, Moseley B13 ..87 B1
  Wolverhampton WV6 ....24 D8
Windermere Ho B15 ....35 D3
Winding House La CV6,
  CV7 ....95 C4
Winding Mill N DY5 ....81 E7
Winding Mill S DY5 ....81 E7
Windings The WS13 ....3 A1
Windleaves Rd B36 ....69 E8
Windley Ho B73 ....45 C2
Windmill Ave
  Birmingham B45 ....121 E8
  ④ Coleshill B46 ....70 F7
Windmill Bank WV5 ....49 A7
Windmill Cl
  Birmingham B31 ....103 C5
  Kenilworth CV8 ....148 A6
  Lichfield WS13 ....3 A2
  Tamworth B79 ....21 A8
Windmill Cres
  Smethwick B66 ....65 C5
  Wolverhampton WV3 ....38 B6
Windmill Croft CV32 .....157 D5
Windmill Ct CV6 ....96 A3
Windmill Dr B97 ....158 C6
Windmill End DY2 ....62 E5
Windmill Gdns B97 ....158 B6

Windmill Gr DY6 ....60 B8
Windmill Hill
  Birmingham B31 ....103 B5
  Halesowen B63 ....82 D5
  Royal Leamington Spa
  CV32 ....157 D5
Windmill Hill The CV5 ...112 A7
Windmill Ind Est CV5 ....111 F7
Windmill La
  Balsall Common CV7 ....130 D4
  Corley CV7 ....93 D6
  Dorridge B93 ....127 F1
  Lichfield WS13 ....3 A2
  Smethwick B66 ....65 B5
  Tanworth-in-A B94 ....144 A8
  Wolverhampton WV3 ....24 A1
Windmill Prec B66 ....65 C5
Windmill Rd
  Bedworth CV7 ....96 A8
  Coventry CV6 ....96 A3
  Nuneaton CV10 ....72 D7
  Royal Leamington Spa
  CV31 ....161 F5
  Solihull B90 ....105 E2
Windmill St
  Birmingham B1 ....164 B1
  Dudley, Eve Hill DY1 ....51 A2
  Dudley, Gornalwood DY3 ...50 D5
  Walsall WS1 ....42 F8
  Wednesbury WS10 ....42 A3
Windmill Terr WS10 ....42 A3
Windmill View DY1 ....51 B7
Windmill Works Ind Pk
  DY2 ....62 B6
Windridge Cl CV3 ....134 C6
Windridge Cres B92 .....107 F8
Windrow The WV6 ....23 D4
Windrush Cl
  Redditch B97 ....158 D6
  Sedgley DY3 ....50 D3
  Solihull B92 ....89 A2
Windrush Dr LE10 ....75 A8
Windrush Gr B29 ....104 A8
Windrush Ho B31 ....102 E5
Windrush Rd
  Cannock WS11 ....1 E6
  Hollywood B47 ....125 B7
Winds Point DY9 ....99 A6
Windsor Arc B2 ....164 C3
Windsor Ave Cannock WS12 ..2 B6
  Oldbury B68 ....64 A3
  Wolverhampton WV4 ....38 E6
Windsor Cl
  Birmingham, Coft Common
  B31 ....123 A6
  Birmingham, Frankley B45 102 A2
  Blackheath B65 ....63 C4
  Dudley DY3 ....50 B2
  Halesowen B63 ....82 F3
  Tamworth B79 ....21 C7
Windsor Cres DY2 ....62 D6
Windsor Ct
  Birmingham B38 ....103 F1
  Cannock WS12 ....2 B6
  Coventry CV4 ....112 B2
  Hinckley LE10 ....76 A5
  Lichfield WS14 ....9 B6
  Nuneaton CV10 ....72 E6
Windsor Dr
  Birmingham B24 ....57 C5
  Kidderminster DY10 ....116 E7
  Solihull B92 ....89 B2
Windsor Gate WV12 ......27 C4
Windsor Gdns
  Bromsgrove B60 ....137 A2
  Nuneaton CV10 ....72 E4
  Wolverhampton WV3 ....38 A8
Windsor Gr
  Stourbridge DY8 ....60 E1
  Walsall WS4 ....15 C2
  Windsor High Sch B63 .....82 F4
Windsor Ho
  Birmingham B23 ....56 F6
  Dudley DY2 ....61 F7
  Windsor Ind Est B7 ....67 A5
Windsor Lodge B92 ......106 D8
Windsor Pl Birmingham B7 .67 A3
  Birmingham, Erdington B23 .56 E3
  ⑧ Royal Leamington Spa
  CV32 ....156 F1
Windsor Rd
  Birmingham, Castle Bromwich
  B36 ....69 F7
  Birmingham, New Oscott
  B73 ....45 D1
  Birmingham, Stirchley B30 .104 B5
  Blackheath B65 ....63 C5
  Cheslyn Hay WS6 ....4 E4
  Halesowen B63 ....82 F4
  Oldbury B68 ....64 A3
  Redditch B97 ....153 D5
  Stourbridge DY8 ....80 E3
  Tipton DY4 ....52 A8
  West Bromwich B71 ....42 B1
  Wolverhampton WV4 ....39 F5
Windsor St Bilston WV14 ..40 C6
  Birmingham B7 ....67 A4
  Bromsgrove B60 ....137 A2
  Coventry CV1 ....113 B2
  Hinckley LE10 ....76 A5
  Nuneaton CV11 ....73 B4
  Royal Leamington Spa
  CV32 ....161 F8
  Walsall WS1 ....42 E7
Windsor St S B7 ....67 A4
Windsor Terr ⑤ B16 ......65 F1

Windsor View B32 ....102 B7
Windsor Way WS4 ....29 D7
Windsor Wlk WS10 ....41 D8
Windward Way B36 ....70 B6
Windyridge Ind Est
  B36 ....69 F8
Windy Arbor Prim Sch
  B37 ....70 D2
Windy Arbour CV8 ....148 B4
Windyridge Rd B76 ....58 A6
Winfield Rd CV11 ....73 B5
Winford Ave DY6 ....60 E4
Winforton Cl B98 ....154 E3
Wing Cl WS2 ....27 E4
Wingate Cl B30 ....103 F4
Wingate Ct B74 ....31 E4
Wingate Rd WS2 ....27 E2
Wingfield Cl B37 ....69 F3
Wingfield Ho B37 ....69 F5
Wingfield Rd
  Birmingham B42 ....55 C7
  Coleshill B46 ....70 F5
Wingfield Way CV6 ....95 A2
Wingfoot Ave WV10 ....25 E8
Wingrave Cl CV5 ....112 A6
Winifred Ave CV5 ....113 A1
Winifride Ct B17 ....85 B5
Winkle St B70 ....53 B4
Winleigh Rd B20 ....54 F2
Winn Ho ⑧ WS2 ....28 D3
Winnall Cl WV14 ....40 D2
Winnallthorpe CV3 ......134 E6
Winnie Rd B29 ....85 E1
Winnington Rd B8 ....68 A7
Winnipeg Rd B38 ....124 A8
Winscar Croft DY3 ....50 D3
Winsford Ave CV5 ....112 B4
Winsford Cl
  Balsall Common CV7 ....130 A6
  Halesowen B63 ....82 A6
  Sutton Coldfield B76 ....46 E3
Winsford Ct CV5 ....112 C4
Winsham Gr B21 ....65 E8
Winsham Wlk CV3 ....133 D3
Winslow Ave B8 ....68 F4
Winslow Cl Coventry CV5 .112 B3
  Redditch B98 ....154 F3
  Royal Leamington Spa
  CV32 ....156 C1
Winslow Dr WV6 ....24 E4
Winslow Ho ⑪ CV1 ....113 B2
Winson Green Rd B18 .....65 E5
Winson Green, Outer Circle
  Sta B21 ....65 E7
Winson St B18 ....65 D4
Winspear Cl CV7 ....92 B1
Winstanley Rd B33 ....68 D2
Winster Ave B93 ....127 E4
Winster Cl CV7 ....95 A7
Winster Gr B44 ....44 D2
Winster Grove Ind Ctr
  B44 ....44 D2
Winster Rd
  Birmingham B43 ....54 D8
  Wolverhampton WV1 ....26 B1
Winston Ave CV2 ....114 D8
Winston Churchill Ct
  WV14 ....40 C8
Winston Cl CV2 ....114 D8
Winston Dr
  Birmingham B20 ....55 B1
  Romsley B62 ....101 A4
Winstone Cl B98 ....154 A4
Winter Cl WS13 ....3 D2
Winterbourne Croft
  B14 ....104 C1
Winterbourne Rd B91 ....106 F4
Winterdene CV7 ....130 B7
Winterfold Cl DY10 ......117 B6
Winterley Gdns DY3 ....50 E6
Winterley La WS4 ....29 C6
Winterton Rd
  Birmingham B44 ....45 A3
  Bulkington CV12 ....79 C2
Winthorpe Dr B91 ....127 C8
Winton Cl B17 ....85 A7
Winton Ho B16 ....65 E1
Wintour Wlk B60 ....150 E7
Winward Rd B98 ....154 F1
Winwood Ct DY8 ....80 F4
Winwood Heath Rd B62 .100 E2
Winwood Rd B65 ....63 D3
Winwoods Gr B32 ....102 A8
Winyate Hill B98 ....154 A2
Winyates Crafts Ctr
  B98 ....154 E3
Winyates Ctr B98 ....154 E3
Winyates Way B98 ....154 E4
Wirehill Dr B98 ....153 F1
Wiremill Cl B44 ....55 E6
Wirral Rd B31 ....102 F6
Wise Gr CV34 ....155 D3
Wise St CV31 ....161 F7
Wise Terr CV31 ....161 F7
Wiseacre Croft B90 ......105 E2
Wiseman Gr B23 ....45 D1
Wisemore WS2 ....28 E2
Wishaw Cl Redditch B98 ..159 A8
  Solihull B90 ....105 E2
Wishaw Gr B37 ....69 F5
Wishaw La Curdworth B76 .59 A7
  Middleton B78 ....48 C6
  Minworth B76 ....58 E7
Wisley Gr CV8 ....148 C5
Wisley Way B32 ....84 F5
Wissage Cft WS13 ....9 D8
Wissage La WS13 ....3 D1
Wissage Rd WS13 ....9 D8

Wistaria Cl
  Birmingham B31 ....103 A6
  ② Coventry CV2 ....96 B2
Wisteria Gr B44 ....44 E2
Wistmans Cl DY1 ....50 E2
Wistwood Hayes WV10 ...11 F4
Witham Croft B91 ....107 C1
Withdean Cl B11 ....87 D6
Witherford Cl B29 ....103 E8
Witherford Croft B91 ...106 E2
Witherford Way B29 .....103 C8
Withern Way DY3 ....50 D3
Withers Rd WV8 ....10 B3
Withers Way B71 ....53 D4
Withington Covert B14 .104 D2
Withington Gr B93 ....127 E4
Witham Cl B76 ....47 A1
Withy Gr B37 ....69 F5
Withy Hill Rd B75 ....47 B8
Withy Rd WV14 ....40 C3
Withy Road Ind Est
  WV14 ....40 C3
Withybed Cl B48 ....139 A6
Withybed La B48 ....139 A6
Withybrook Cl CV2 ....96 D2
Withybrook La CV7 ....97 F5
Withybrook Rd
  Bulkington CV12 ....79 D2
  Solihull B90 ....126 B8
Withymere La WV5 ....49 C8
Withymoor Prim Sch
  DY5 ....61 D1
Withymoor Rd Dudley DY2 .62 E4
  Stourbridge DY8 ....81 A7
Withy Cl DY11 ....116 B2
Witley Cres B69 ....63 E5
Witley Farm Cl B91 ......107 C2
Witley Rd B31 ....103 D2
Witnell Rd CV6 ....113 C6
Witney Cl B79 ....20 F7
Witney Dr B37 ....69 F2
Witney Gr WV10 ....11 B3
Wittersham Ct WV13 ......27 B2
Witton Bank B62 ....83 F7
Witton La Birmingham B6 .55 F1
  West Bromwich B71 ....53 B8
Witton Lodge Rd B23 ......56 D7
Witton Rd Birmingham B6 .66 C8
  Wolverhampton WV4 ....39 A6
Witton St Birmingham B9 .67 B2
  Stourbridge DY8 ....80 F4
Witton Sta B6 ....55 F2
Wixford Gr B90 ....106 D2
Wobaston Rd Codsall WV9 .10 E4
  Wolverhampton WV9,WV10 .11 B4
Woburn B77 ....21 D3
Woburn Ave WV12 ....27 B6
Woburn Cl
  Bromsgrove B61 ....136 D1
  Hinckley LE10 ....71 E3
  Royal Leamington Spa
  CV32 ....162 C6
Woburn Cres B43 ....43 D1
Woburn Dr
  Brierley Hill DY5 ....81 B8
  Halesowen B62 ....83 B7
Woburn Gr B27 ....88 C1
Woburn Ho B15 ....86 C7
Wodehouse La WV5,DY3 ...49 E8
Woden Ave WV11 ....26 C6
Woden Cres WV11 ....26 C6
Woden Prim Sch WV10 ....25 E4
Woden Rd WV10 ....25 E4
Woden Rd E WS10 ....42 B4
Woden Rd N WS10 ....41 F5
Woden Rd S WS10 ....42 A1
Woden Rd W WS10 ....41 D4
Woden Way WV11 ....26 C6
Wodensborough Com Tech
  Coll WS10 ....42 B2
Wodensfield Inf & Jun Sch
  WV11 ....26 B6
Wodensfield Twr WV11 ....26 C5
Wold Wlk B13 ....105 C6
Wolfe Rd CV4 ....131 F8
Wolfsbane Dr WS5 ....43 A3
Wolfson Dr B15 ....85 E4
Wollaston Cres WV11 ......26 D6
Wollaston Ct
  Stourbridge DY8 ....80 C6
  ① Walsall WS1 ....28 F2
Wollaston Rd
  Stourbridge, Amblecote DY8 .80 F8
  Stourbridge, Wollaston DY7 .80 C7
Wollerton Gr B75 ....46 F6
Wollescote Bsns Pk ⑧
  DY9 ....81 F5
Wollescote Dr B91 ....107 B2
Wollescote Prim Sch
  DY9 ....81 F4
Wollescote Rd DY9 ....81 D3
Wolmer Rd WV11 ....13 A2
Wolseley B77 ....22 A3
Wolseley Ave B27 ....88 D4
Wolseley Bank WV10 ....25 F7
Wolseley Cl
  Birmingham B36 ....59 A1
  Wolverhampton WV10 ......25 F7
Wolseley Dr B8 ....68 A7
Wolseley Gate WV10 ....25 F7
Wolseley Rd Bilston WV14 .40 C7
  West Bromwich B70 ....52 F6
Wolseley St B9 ....67 B2

Wolston Cl B90 ....106 B5
Wolston La CV8 ....135 E2
Wolverhampton & Midland
Ctics Eye Infmy WV3 ....25 A2
Wolverhampton Coll Wulfrun
Campus WV6 ....24 E3
Wolverhampton Girls High
Sch WV6 ....24 F3
Wolverhampton Gram Sch
WV3 ....24 F2
Wolverhampton Rd
Cannock WS11 ....4 D8
Cheslyn Hay WV10,WS6 ...4 E2
Codsall WV8 ....10 A3
Essington WV11 ....13 A3
Kingswinford DY6 ....49 C1
Norton WV6 ....23 A3
Oldbury B69 ....63 F4
Sedgley DY3 ....39 D2
Walsall, Birchills WS2 ...28 B2
Walsall, Pelsall WS3 ...14 F3
Walsall, Wallington Heath
WS3 ....14 B1
Wedges Mills WS11 ......4 B6
Wolverhampton WV10,
WV11 ....26 B4
Wolverhampton Rd E
WV4 ....39 D5
Wolverhampton Rd S
B32 ....84 E7
Wolverhampton Rd W
WV13,WS2 ....27 D2
Wolverhampton St
Bilston WV14 ....40 C6
Darlaston WS10 ....41 C6
Dudley DY1 ....51 B1
Walsall WS2 ....28 D2
Willenhall WV13 ....27 A1
Wolverhampton Sta
WV1 ....163 C3
Wolverley Ave
Stourbridge DY8 ....80 C6
Wolverhampton WV4 ....38 D5
Wolverley Cres B69 ....63 E5
Wolverley Rd
Birmingham B32 ....102 B8
Halesowen B63 ....82 F2
Solihull B92 ....89 D2
Wolverson Cl WV12 ....27 C4
Wolverson Rd WS9 .....16 A4
Wolverton Cl B98 .....154 E2
Wolverton Rd
Birmingham, Marston Green
B37 ....90 B7
Birmingham, Rednall B45 .122 C6
Coventry CV5 ....112 A3
Dudley DY2 ....51 E1
Wolvey CE Prim Sch (annex)
CV7 ....97 E5
Wolvey Rd
Bulkington CV12 ....79 E2
Hinckley LE10 ....75 E4
Wombourne Cl DY3 .....50 C8
Wombourne Pk WV5 ....49 A4
Wood Ave Dudley DY3 ...50 C4
Wednesfield WV11 .....26 D6
Wood Bank Rd WV3 ....38 A8
Wood Cl B46 ....70 F7
Wood Common Grange
WS3 ....14 F4
Wood Croft B47 ....125 B6
Wood Ct Birmingham B20 .55 A2
Coventry CV2 ....114 D7
Wood End Dr B45 .....138 A8
Wood End Jun & Inf Sch
WV11 ....26 C7
Wood End La
Birmingham B24 ....56 F3
Lichfield WS13 ....3 B7
Tamworth-In-A B94 ....141 F5
Wood End Prim Sch
Coventry CV2 ....96 D1
Coventry CV2 ....36 C1
Wood End Rd
Birmingham B24 ....56 F3
Walsall WS5 ....43 D8
Wednesfield WV11 .....26 D7
Wood End Way WV5 ....16 B1
Wood Green High Sch
WS10 ....42 B5
Wood Green Jun Sch
WS10 ....42 A4
Wood Green Rd
Birmingham B18 ....65 D4
Wednesbury WS10 .....42 B4
Wood Hayes Rd WV11 ...12 C1
Wood Hill Rise CV6 .....95 D2
Wood La 1 WS1 ....42 E7
Wood La Aldridge B74 ...30 E2
Birmingham, Erdington B24 .57 C1
Birmingham, Handsworth
B20 ....55 C8
Birmingham, Harborne B17 .85 A6
Birmingham, Marston Green
B37 ....90 A8
Birmingham, Woodgate B32 .84 A1
Cannock WS12 ....2 D4
Earlswood B94 ....125 E1
Fairfield B61 ....120 C3
Hampton-in-A B92 .....108 F2
Nuneaton CV10 ....72 A8
Shenstone WS14 ....17 B2
Shilton CV7 ....97 D5
Walsall WS3 ....14 F4
Wedges Mills WS11 ......4 A6
West Bromwich B70 .....53 A3
Willenhall WV12 ....27 E7

Wood La continued
Wolverhampton WV10 ....11 D2
Wood Lane Cl WV12 .....27 E7
Wood Leasow B32 ....84 D2
Wood Leigh Cl B63 .....83 A6
Wood Piece La B98 ....154 D7
Wood Rd Dudley DY3 ....50 C4
Wolverhampton WV6 ....24 C3
Wombourne WV5 ....49 B7
Wood Ridings WS3 ......3 A1
Wood Side WV11 ....27 A8
Wood St Bedworth CV12 .78 B5
Bilston WV14 ....40 D5
Birmingham B16 ....66 A2
Darlaston WS10 ....41 F6
Dudley DY2 ....61 F6
Hinckley LE10 ....71 D1
Kidderminster DY11 ...116 D5
Nuneaton CV10 ....72 F4
Royal Leamington Spa
CV32 ....162 A8
Stourbridge, Lye DY9 ...81 F5
Stourbridge, Wollaston DY8 .80 D6
Tipton DY4 ....51 E5
Willenhall WV13 ....27 B2
Wolverhampton, Lanesfield
WV4 ....40 A3
Wolverhampton, Park Village
WV10 ....25 F5
Wood End CV9 ....36 C1
Wood Street Cl LE10 ...71 E1
Wood Terr B96 ....159 B1
Woodacre Rd B24 ......57 C4
Woodall Ho WS3 ....28 C8
Woodall Rd B6 ....55 F1
Woodall St
Blackheath B64 ....62 C1
Walsall WS3 ....28 C8
Woodard Rd DY4 ....52 C7
Woodbank LE10 ....76 A7
Woodbank Dr B61 .....136 F8
Woodbank Rd DY3 .....50 C7
Woodberrow La B97 ...158 D6
Woodberry Dr B76 .....47 A2
Woodberry Wlk B27 ....88 D3
Woodbine Ave B10 .....87 D8
Woodbine Cotts 2
CV32 ....161 E8
Woodbine Croft B26 ....89 A6
Woodbine St 1 CV32 ..161 E8
Woodbine Wlk B37 .....70 D2
Woodbourne WS5 ....85 D8
Woodbourne Rd
Birmingham B15,B16 ....85 C8
Smethwick B67 ....64 E2
Woodbridge Cl
Walsall, Heath Heath WS4 ..15 D1
Walsall, Wallington Heath
WS3 ....14 A3
Woodbridge Rd B13 ....86 F3
Woodbrook Ho 8 B37 ...70 B2
Woodbrooke Rd B30 ...103 E7
Woodburn Cl CV5 .....112 B4
Woodburn Rd B66 .....65 D7
Woodbury Cl
Brierley Hill DY5 ......61 E2
Halesowen B62 ....83 F8
Redditch B97 ....158 A6
Woodbury Gr B91 .....107 B1
Woodbury Rd
Halesowen B62 ....84 A8
Kidderminster DY11 ...116 B2
Rowchester DY9 ....99 B4
Woodchester Rd B93 ..127 E2
Woodclose Ave CV6 ...112 F6
Woodclose Rd B37 .....69 F3
Woodcock Cl
Birmingham B31 ......102 C1
Tamworth-In-A B94 ....141 E3
Woodcock Gdns WV10 ...12 B7
Woodcock Hill Jun & Inf Sch
B31 ....102 C2
Woodcock La
Birmingham, Acock's Green
B27 ....88 D3
Birmingham, Northfield
B31 ....102 E8
Woodcock La N B27 ....88 D4
Woodcock St B7 ....66 F4
Woodcombe Cl DY5 ....81 B7
Woodcote Ave
Kenilworth CV8 ....147 D6
Nuneaton CV11 ....73 F8
Woodcote Cl B98 .....154 E3
Woodcote Dr
Birmingham B8 ....67 F5
Dorridge B93 ....128 B2
Leek Wootton CV35 ...155 F7
Woodcote La
Balsenhope DY9 ....119 E1
Leek Wootton CV8,CV35 .155 F7
Woodcote Rd
Birmingham B24 ....57 D5
Royal Leamington Spa
CV32 ....156 F3
Warwick CV34 ....160 F8
Wolverhampton WV6 ....24 C4
Woodcote Way
Birmingham B18 ....66 A4
Sutton Coldfield B74 ...44 F6
Woodcraft Cl CV4 ....112 A2
Woodcroft Ave
Birmingham B20 ....54 E3
Dudley DY4 ....51 C4
Tamworth B79 ....21 B6
Woodcroft Cl
Blackheath B64 ....82 F8
Blackwell B60 ....137 F5

Woodcross La WV14 ....40 A2
Woodcross St WV14 ....39 F2
Woodend B20 ....54 E6
Woodend Cl B97 ......153 B2
Woodend Croft CV4 ...131 E8
Woodend Pl WV6 ....24 B4
Woodfall Ave B30 ....104 A5
Woodfield DY9 ....119 E7
Woodfield Ave
Blackheath B64 ....82 D8
Brierley Hill DY5 ......61 B7
Oldbury B69 ....64 A4
Stourbridge DY9 ....81 F2
Wolverhampton WV4 ....38 F6
Woodfield Cl
Norton Canes WS11 ......5 F7
Redditch B98 ....154 A5
Sutton Coldfield B74 ...46 B8
Walsall WS5 ....43 E5
Woodfield Cres
Birmingham B12 ....87 A6
Kidderminster DY11 ...116 D5
Woodfield Dr WS11 ......5 F7
Woodfield Hts WV6 ....24 D4
Woodfield Jun Sch WV4 .38 F6
Woodfield La B62 ....120 D8
Woodfield Rd
Birmingham, Balsall Heath
B12 ....87 A6
Birmingham, King's Heath
B13 ....104 F8
Coventry CV5 ....132 E8
Dudley DY3 ....50 C4
Hinckley LE10 ....75 C6
Solihull B91 ....107 B6
Woodfield St 4 DY11 ..116 C6
Woodfields Dr WS14 ....9 C8
Woodfold Croft WS9 ...30 B7
Woodford Ave B36 .....69 B8
Woodford Cl
Ash Green CV7 ....95 D5
Nuneaton CV10 ....72 D4
Wolverhampton WV9 ....10 F2
Woodford Cres WS7 ....7 B7
Woodford End WS11 ....1 F4
Woodford Green Rd
B28 ....106 B8
Woodford Way WS12 ....2 D1
Woodfort Rd B43 ......54 E7
Woodgate Bsns Pk B32 .84 B2
Woodgate Dr B32 .....84 A1
Woodgate Gdns B32 ...84 A4
Woodgate Ho B97 ....153 B4
Woodgate Jun & Inf Sch
B32 ....84 B1
Woodgate La B32 ......84 A2
Woodgate Rd
Hinckley LE10 ....76 A8
Stoke Prior B60 ......151 B1
Woodgate Valley Ctry Pk★
B32 ....84 D3
Woodgate Way DY9 ...119 E7
Woodglade Croft B38 ..103 E2
Woodgreen WS6 ....4 E5
Woodgreen Cl B97 ....158 B7
Woodgreen Croft B68 ..84 C7
Woodgreen Rd B68 ....84 C7
Woodhall Cl
Nuneaton CV11 ....74 A2
Tipton DY4 ....52 A8
Woodhall Croft B92 ....88 F3
Woodhall Rd WV4 ......38 E5
Woodham Cl B45 .....101 C1
Woodhaven Walsall WS4 .15 D1
Wedges Mills WS11 .....4 B5
Woodhouse Cl CV3 ...134 E8
Woodhouse Fold WV11 ..26 D5
Woodhouse Hill Jun Sch
B77 ....21 F4
Woodhouse La B77 .....22 A5
Woodhouse Orch DY9 ..119 E7
Woodhouse Prim Sch
B32 ....84 E6
Woodhouse Rd
Birmingham B32 ....84 E5
Wolverhampton WV6 ....24 B4
Woodhouse Rd N WV6 ..24 B4
Woodhouse St CV34 ...160 D6
Woodhouse Way B64 ...62 C1
Woodhouses La WS7 ....7 F6
Woodhouses Rd WS7 ....8 A7
Woodhurst Cl B7 ......21 F5
Woodhurst Rd B13 .....87 A4
Wooding Cres DY4 .....41 B1
Woodington Rd B75 ....47 B5
Woodland Ave
Brierley Hill DY5 ......62 A1
Coventry CV5 ....132 F7
Dudley DY1 ....51 C3
Hagley DY8 ....98 F5
Hinckley LE10 ....76 A7
Kidderminster DY11 ...116 C7
Wolverhampton WV6 ....24 B3
Woodland Cl WS12 Canck .2 B8
Stourbridge DY9 ....81 D2
Willenhall WV12 ....27 D6
Woodland Cres WV3 ....38 D7
Woodland Ct
Cannock WS12 ....1 C4
Shenstone WS14 ....32 A7
Woodland Dr
Birmingham B45 ......122 A2
Cheslyn Hay WS6 ....4 E4
Smethwick B66 ....64 E7
Woodland Gr
Birmingham B43 ....43 E3

Woodland Gr continued
Dudley DY3 ....50 B3
Woodland Rd
Birmingham, Handsworth
B21 ....65 C8
Birmingham, Northfield
B31 ....103 B3
Dodford B61 ....136 A7
Halesowen B62 ....83 D8
Hinckley LE10 ....71 F1
Kenilworth CV8 ....148 B7
Redditch B97 ....153 B3
Tamworth B77 ....22 A4
Wolverhampton WV3 ....38 D7
Woodland Rise
Blackheath B64 ....82 F8
Sutton Coldfield B73 ...46 B4
Woodland Way
Birchmoor B78 ....36 F8
Burntwood WS7 ....7 A6
Woodlands Ave
Walsall WS5 ....43 E5
Water Orton B46 ....59 B2
Woodlands Cotts WV4 ..38 F3
Woodlands Cres WS3 ...14 F5
Woodlands Ct
Binley Woods CV3 .....135 D7
Coventry CV5 ....133 A8
Woodlands Farm Rd B24 .57 F4
Woodlands Inf Sch B90 .126 B8
Woodlands Jun & Inf Sch
B36 ....70 B6
Woodlands La
Bedworth CV12 ....77 E4
Solihull B90 ....126 B8
Woodlands Paddock
WV4 ....38 E4
Woodlands Park Rd
B30 ....103 C5
Woodlands Prim Sch
Tamworth B77 ....21 E4
Willenhall WV12 ....27 D6
Woodlands Rd
Bedworth CV12 ....77 F3
Binley Woods CV3 .....135 D7
Birmingham, Moseley B11 .87 C2
Birmingham, Rubery B45 .121 D7
Birmingham, Saltley B8 ..67 F3
Wombourne WV5 ....49 A5
Woodlands Sch The
CV5 ....111 D3
Woodlands St B66 .....65 C5
Woodlands The
Blackheath B64 ....83 A7
Lichfield WS13 ....9 D8
Nuneaton CV10 ....72 A8
Stourbridge DY8 ....81 A2
Sutton Coldfield B75 ...47 A6
Wood End CV9 ....36 C1
Woodlands Way B37 ....70 D3
Woodlawn Gr DY6 ......60 D5
Woodlea Dr
Birmingham B24 ....56 F2
Solihull B91 ....106 E4
Woodleaves B47 ......124 F8
Woodleigh Ave B17 ....85 D4
Woodleigh Cl B38 ....103 F1
Woodleigh Rd
Coventry CV4 ....131 F5
Sutton Coldfield B72 ...46 C1
Woodleys The B14 ....105 B4
Woodloes Ave N CV34 .155 F2
Woodloes Ave S CV34 .155 F1
Woodloes Inf Sch CV34 .155 E1
Woodloes Jun Sch
CV34 ....155 F1
Woodloes La CV34,CV35 .155 F2
Woodloes Rd B90 ....126 B7
Woodman Cl
Halesowen B63 ....83 C3
Wednesbury WS10 .....42 B4
Woodman La
Cheslyn Hay WS6 ....4 E4
Clent DY9 ....99 E4
Woodman Rd
Birmingham B14 ......105 A1
Halesowen B63 ....83 C3
Woodman Wlk B23 .....56 A5
Woodmeadow Rd B30 ..104 B3
Woodmill Mdw CV4 ...148 B6
Woodnorton Dr B13 ....86 E2
Woodnorton Rd B65 ...63 F2
Woodpecker Gr
Birmingham B36 ....70 A7
Kidderminster DY10 ...117 A7
Woodpecker Way WS11 ..2 C3
Woodpeery Ave B91 ...107 C1
Woodridge B20 ....55 E1
Woodridge Ave
Birmingham B32 ....84 B4
Coventry CV5 ....112 A6
Woodridge Rd B63 ....83 A5
Woodroffe Wlk CV6 ....96 A4
Woodrough Dr B13 ....86 F2
Woodrow Cl B61 .....120 F1
Woodrow Cres B93 ...128 A5
Woodrow Ctr B98 ....159 B8
Woodrow Dr B98 .....159 B6
Woodrow Fst Sch B98 .159 B7
Woodrow La
Bluntington DY10 ....118 E3
Catshill B61 ....121 B2
Woodrow N B98 ......159 A7
Woodrow S B98 ......159 A7
Woodrow W B98 .....159 A7
Woodruff Way WS5 ....43 A3
Woodrush Dr B47 ....125 A5

Woodrush High Sch The
B47 ....125 A6
Woods Bank Terr WS10 ..41 C5
Woods Cres DY5 ....62 A1
Woods Croft WS13 ......3 A1
Woods La Blackheath B64 .82 C8
Brierley Hill DY5 ......81 D7
Woods Piece CV7 ......94 F6
Woods The B14 ....86 F1
Woodsbank Ind Est The
WS10 ....41 C5
Woodsetton Cl DY1 ....51 B6
Woodsetton Specl Sch The
DY3 ....50 F7
Woodshill Ave B45 ...122 A2
Woodshires Rd
Coventry CV6 ....95 F5
Solihull B92 ....106 D7
Woodside Birmingham B37 .69 E4
Sutton Coldfield B74 ...31 E2
Woodside Ave B97 ....153 B2
Woodside Ave N CV3 ..132 E5
Woodside Ave S CV3 ..132 F5
Woodside Cl Walsall WS5 .43 D6
Wood End CV9 ....36 C1
Woodside Cres B93 ...128 B4
Woodside Dr
Barnt Green B45 .....138 B8
Little Aston B74 ....31 C5
Woodside Gr WV8 .....10 B2
Woodside Ind Est DY2 ..61 F5
Woodside Pl WS11 ......1 A3
Woodside Rd
Birmingham B29 ....86 A1
Dudley DY2 ....61 F7
Walsall WS5 ....43 E6
Woodside Way
Aldridge WS9 ....30 B5
Birmingham B32 ......102 A8
Solihull B91 ....106 E5
Willenhall WV12 ....27 E2
Woodsome Gr B23 .....56 C7
Woodsorrel Rd DY1 ....51 A4
Woodstile B34 ....69 B6
Woodstile Cl B75 .....32 D3
Woodstock Cl Dudley DY1 .62 A8
Hinckley LE10 ....76 A5
Stourbridge DY8 ....60 C1
Woodstock Cres B93 ..127 F3
Woodstock Dr B74 .....31 B3
Woodstock Rd B13 ....87 B4
Woodstock Dr
Huntington WS12 ....1 C7
Stourbridge DY8 ....60 C2
Sutton Coldfield B74 ...31 D4
Woodstock Rd
Birmingham, Handsworth
B21 ....65 E8
Birmingham, Moseley B13 .87 B3
Coventry CV3 ....133 D7
Nuneaton CV11 ....73 E1
Wolverhampton WV1 ...26 B1
Woodston Gr B91 ....127 C8
Woodthorne Cl DY1 ....50 D2
Woodthorne Prim Sch
WV6 ....24 B4
Woodthorne Rd WV6 ...24 A5
Woodthorne Rd S WV6 .24 A5
Woodthorne Wlk DY6 ...60 E8
Woodthorpe Dr DY9 ....81 D3
Woodthorpe Gdns B14 .104 E5
Woodthorpe Inf & Jun Sch
B14 ....104 E5
Woodthorpe Rd B14 ..104 E5
Woodvale Dr B28 .....105 E4
Woodview Dr
Birmingham, Woodgate B32 .84 A1
Birmingham, Yardley Wood
B28 ....105 E4
Woodville Ct B13 .....86 C7
Woodville Gdns DY3 ...39 F1
Woodville Rd
Birmingham, Harborne B17 .85 A6
Birmingham, King's Heath
B14 ....104 E8
Warwick CV34 ....160 E8
Woodward Cl CV31 ...162 A2
Woodward Pl DY9 ......81 C4
Woodward Rd DY11 ...116 C4
Woodward St B71 .....53 E4
Woodwards Cl WS2 ....42 B8
Woodwards Pl WS2 ....42 B8
Woodwards Rd WS2 ...42 B8
Woodway B24 ....57 B5
Woodway Cl CV2 .....114 F8
Woodway La CV2 ....96 F1
Woodway Park Sch & Com
Coll CV2 ....96 F1
Woodway Wlk CV2 ...114 E8
Woodwells Rd B8 ......68 B5
Woody Bank WS6 ......4 E2
Woolacombe Lodge Rd
B29 ....85 C2
Woolaston Rd B98 ....159 C8
Woolgrove St CV6 .....96 A3
Woolhope Cl B98 ....154 F3
Woolmore Rd B23 .....56 C5
Woolpack Cl B65 ......63 A4
Woolpack St WV1 ....163 B3
Woolpack The 9 CV34 .160 E6
Woolwich Rd CV11 .....79 F6
Wooton Ct CV32 .....153 A4
Wooton Gr B44 ....56 C8

Wootton Ave WV11 ....26 D7
Wootton Cl WS11 ....2 B2
Wootton Ct
Coventry CV2 ....114 D7
6 Royal Leamington Spa
CV32 ....156 F2
Wootton Green La CV7 .130 A8
Wootton Rd CV9 ....109 E1
Wootton Rd
Birmingham B31 ....103 A6
Wolverhampton WV3 ....38 D8
Wootton St CV12 ....78 D3
Woottons Ct WS11 ....1 F1
Worcester Cl
Allesley CV5 ....112 B7
Cannock WS11 ....4 F8
Hagley DY9 ....99 A5
Lichfield WS13 ....3 C3
Sutton Coldfield B75 ....32 D3
Worcester Cross ⬛
DY10 ....116 E5
Worcester Ct
Coventry CV6 ....96 B4
Wolverhampton WV3 ....39 A6
Worcester Gn B71 ....53 C7
Worcester Gr WV6 ....23 D4
Worcester Ho
Birmingham B36 ....70 A8
4 Halesowen B63 ....83 A3
Worcester La
Stourbridge DY9 ....99 B7
Sutton Coldfield B75 ....32 D4
Worcester Rd
Birmingham B6 ....55 F2
Bromsgrove B61 ....136 F1
Dudley DY2 ....62 E3
Hagley DY9 ....99 A5
Hagley DY9 ....99 F3
Kenilworth CV8 ....148 B3
Kidderminster DY10 ....116 E2
Mustow Green DY10 ....117 F1
Oldbury B68 ....84 A8
Stoke Heath B61 ....150 B4
Willenhall WV13 ....27 D2
Worcester Rise B29 ....86 B1
Worcester St ⬛ B97 ....153 E4
Worcester St
Kidderminster DY10 ....116 E5
Kidderminster DY10 ....116 E6
Stourbridge DY8 ....81 A4
Wolverhampton WV2 ....163 B2
Worcester Wlk B37 ....70 A1
Word Hill B17 ....84 F7
Wordsley Cl B98 ....154 B7
Wordsley Ct DY8 ....60 E3
Wordsley Green Sh Ctr
DY8 ....60 D2
Wordsley Hospl DY8 ....60 E3
Wordsworth Ave
Redditch B97 ....158 C8
Tamworth B79 ....21 A6
Warwick CV34 ....160 D5
Wolverhampton WV4 ....39 F4
Wordsworth Cl
Cannock WS11 ....1 D4
Lichfield WS14 ....9 B5
Tipton DY4 ....52 A8
Wordsworth Cres CV10 .117 B6
Wordsworth Ct WV6 ....23 E4
Wordsworth Dr CV8 ....148 C4
Wordsworth Ho
Birmingham B31 ....123 A8
Halesowen B63 ....82 B5
6 Oldbury B68 ....64 C4
Wordsworth Rd
Bedworth CV12 ....78 D1
Birmingham B10 ....87 D7
Burntwood WS7 ....7 A8
Coventry CV2 ....114 C4
Dudley DY3 ....50 B5
Walsall WS3 ....28 E8
Willenhall WV12 ....27 E7
Wolverhampton WV10 ....26 A8
Wordsworth St B71 ....53 C5
Worfield Cl WS4 ....29 A4
Worfield Gdns WV3 ....38 F6
Workhouse La LE10 ....76 A4
Works Rd B26 ....90 A3
World's End Ave B32 ....84 D6
World's End La
B32 ....84 D5
World's End La B32 ....84 D5
Worlds End Rd B20 ....55 A3
Worleys Wharf Ave
WS10 ....42 E2
Worsdell Cl CV1 ....113 B4
Worsey Dr DY4 ....52 D6
Worsfold Cl CV5 ....112 A7
Worthen Gr B31 ....123 A8
Worthings The B30 ....104 B6
Worthy Down WV10 ....26 F5
Worthy Down Wlk B35 ....58 B3
Wortley Ave WV10 ....25 E6

Worton Rd DY9 ....81 F2
Wr Twr La CV8 ....147 F6
Wragby Cl WV9 ....11 B3
Wrekin Cl Halesowen B63 ......82 C1
Kidderminster DY11 ....116 B2
Wrekin Ct B74 ....31 F2
Wrekin Dr
Bromsgrove B61 ....137 A5
Stourbridge DY9 ....81 D4
Wolverhampton Penn WV3 ..38 E8
Wolverhampton, Tettenhall
WV6 ....24 A5
Wrekin Gr WV11 ....13 B1
Wrekin La WV6 ....24 A5
Wrekin Rd
Birmingham B44 ....56 A6
Sutton Coldfield B73 ....46 A1
Wrekin View
Brownhills WS8 ....16 A5
Wednesbury WS12 ....1 C7
Wolverhampton WV1 ....163 B3
Wrekin View Rd DY3 ....50 C8
Wren Ave WV6 ....23 D3
Wren St Coventry CV2 ....113 F3
Dudley, Netherton DY2 ....62 B5
Dudley, Swan Village DY1 ....51 C6
Wren's Nest Cl B90 ....126 A5
Wren's Nest Nature
Reserve * DY1 ....51 B4
Wren's Nest Prim Sch
DY1 ....51 A4
Wren's Nest Rd DY1 ....51 A5
Wrenbury Dr CV6 ....96 A4
Wrens Ave Dudley DY4 ....51 D4
Kingswinford DY6 ....61 A4
Wrens Hill Rd DY1 ....51 B5
Wrens Nest Pl DY1 ....51 A5
Wrens Nest Rd DY1 ....51 A4
Wrens Park Ave B76 ....57 E2
Wrentham St B5 ....86 E8
Wretham Ct B19 ....66 B7
Wretham Rd B19 ....66 B6
Wrexham Ave WS2 ....27 F1
Wright Ave WV11 ....26 E7
Wright Rd B8 ....68 A5
Wright St Bilston WV14 ....40 E4
Birmingham B10 ....87 D8
Coventry CV1 ....113 E4
Halesowen B63 ....83 B4
Wolverhampton WV10 ....25 D8
Wrighton Dr WV11 ....11 F5
Wright's La B64 ....63 A1
Wrighton Cl WV12 ....27 C8
Wrighton Dr DY5 ....50 C1
Wrigsham St CV3 ....133 D8
Wrottesley Park Rd WV6,
WS 25 D5
Wrottesley Rd
Birmingham B43 ....43 D1
Wolverhampton WV6 ....24 B5
Wrottesley Rd W
Perton WV6 ....23 F6
Wolverhampton WV6 ....24 A6
Wrottesley St B5 ....164 C1
Wroxall Cl DY5 ....81 C8
Wroxall Gr B13 ....105 A6
Wroxall Rd B91 ....106 E6
Wroxham Glen WV13 ....40 F8
Wroxton Rd B26 ....88 E8
Wulfrun Coll Annexe,
Newhampton Ctr WV1 ....163 A4
Wulfrun Ctr WV1 ....163 C2
Wulfrun Sq WV1 ....163 C2
Wulfrun Trad Est WV6 ....25 C5
Wulfruna Gdns WV3 ....24 F1
Wulfruna St WV1 ....163 B3
Wyatt Cl B5 ....86 C5
Wyatt Ct CV12 ....78 B3
Wyatt Ho CV2 ....114 D7
Wyatt Rd B75 ....47 B5
Wych Elm ⬛ CV31 ....161 F5
Wych Elm Rd WS8 ....15 E5
Wychall Dr WV10 ....11 E4
Wychall La B38 ....103 E2
Wychall Park Gr B38 ....103 D2
Wychall Prim Sch B31 ....103 C2
Wychall Rd B31 ....103 C3
Wychbold Cl
Redditch B97 ....158 A6
Willenhall WV12 ....13 D1
Wychbold Cres B33 ....69 C3
Wychbold Ct DY9 ....99 C8
Wychbold Way WV12 ....13 D1
Wychbury B76 ....47 A1
Wychbury Ct B63 ....82 E5
Wychbury Dr DY9 ....99 C7
Wychbury Grange DY9 .81 C1
Wychbury Rd
Birmingham B32 ....102 B7
Brierley Hill DY5 ....81 E8
Stourbridge DY9 ....81 E8
Wolverhampton WV3 ....38 C7
Wyche Ave B14 ....104 D4
Wyche Cotts B60 ....150 C1

Wychelm Farm Rd B14 ..105 A1
Wychnor Gr B71 ....42 E2
Wychwood Ave
Coventry CV3 ....133 C3
Knowle B93 ....128 B8
Wychwood Cres B26 ....89 A6
Wychwood Dr B97 ....158 D6
Wyckham Cl B17 ....85 A5
Wyckham Rd B36 ....69 F8
Wycliffe Gr CV2 ....114 B5
Wycliffe Rd W CV2 ....114 C5
Wycome Rd B28 ....106 A7
Wye Cl Bulkington CV12 ....79 B2
Hinckley LE10 ....75 A8
Perton WV6 ....23 F4
Royal Leamington Spa
CV32 ....157 C3
Sutton Coldfield B76 ....58 B7
Wye Cliff Rd B20 ....66 B8
Wye Ho DY3 ....50 D3
Wye Rd WS3 ....14 E1
Wyemanton Cl B43 ....43 C1
Wyke Rd CV2 ....114 C4
Wykeham Gr WV6 ....23 D3
Wykeley Rd CV2 ....114 C4
Wyken Ave CV2 ....114 D5
Wyken Cl B93 ....127 E2
Wyken Croft CV2 ....114 D6
Wyken Croft Nature Pk*
CV2 ....114 D6
Wyken Croft Prim Sch
CV2 ....114 D5
Wyken Grange Rd CV2 .114 C5
Wyken Way CV2 ....114 B5
Wykin Rd LE10 ....71 A3
Wyld Cl B71 ....53 A8
Wyld Ct CV5 ....112 B5
Wylde Cres B65 ....63 C4
Wylde Green Prim Sch
B73 ....57 B7
Wylde Green Rd B72,B76 .46 D1
Wylde Green Sta B73 ....46 B1
Wyley Rd CV6 ....113 B5
Wymering Ave WV11 ....26 F7
Wyn-Griffith Dr DY4 ....52 A3
Wynall La DY9 ....81 F3
Wynall La S DY9 ....82 A3
Wynbrook Gr B90 ....127 A6
Wynchcombe Ave WV4 ....38 D4
Wyncote Cl CV8 ....148 A4
Wynd The DY3 ....39 D1
Wyndcliff Rd B9 ....67 D1
Wyndcliffe Jun Com Sch
B9 ....67 C1
Wyndham Gdns B30 ..103 D4
Wyndham Rd B16 ....65 F1
Wyndhurst Rd B33 ....68 E5
Wyndley Dr B73 ....46 B4
Wyndley L Ctr B73 ....46 A5
Wyndley La B73 ....46 A4
Windmill Cres B71 ....42 F1
Wynds Covert B14 ....104 D2
Wynds Point B31 ....103 B5
Wynfield Gdns B14 ....104 F5
Wynford Road Ind Est
B27 ....88 C5
Wynn Rd WV4 ....38 F5
Wynn St B15 ....86 D8
Wynne Cres WV4 ....38 C3
Wynstead Covert ⬛
B14 ....104 C2
Wyntor La B71 ....53 B8
Wynyates B79 ....20 E6
Wyre Cl Birmingham B45 .102 B1
Brownhills WS9 ....15 F4
Wyre Rd DY8 ....80 E7
Wyrley Brook Pk WS11 ..4 D5
Wyrley Brook Ret Pk
4 ....4 C5
Wyrley Cl Burntwood WS8 ..6 F3
Lichfield WS14 ....9 A5
Willenhall WV12 ....27 D7
Wyrley Ho
Birmingham B23 ....56 C6
Tipton DY4 ....52 B3
Wyrley La WS3 ....14 E8
Wyrley Rd Birmingham B6 .56 A2
Sutton Coldfield B75 ....32 D1
Wednesfield WV11 ....27 A6
Wyrley St WV10 ....26 A6
Wyrley Way B23 ....56 A1
Wythall Green Way B47 .124 E3
Wythall Rd B63 ....83 A2
Wythall Sta B47 ....125 C4
Wythwood CI DY9 ....81 D1
Wythwood Gr
Hollywood B47 ....125 C6
Tipton DY4 ....52 A8
Wythwood Rd B47 ....125 C6
Wyton Ave B68 ....84 C5
Wyvern CI CV5 ....112 C3
Wyvern Gr ⬛ B31 ....103 A2
Wyvern Rd B74 ....46 B7
Wyvis Cl WV6 ....24 E2

Y

Yale Dr WV11 ....26 E5
Yardley Cl Oldbury B68 ....64 B1
Redditch B98 ....154 E3
Warwick CV34 ....155 F2
Yardley Fields Rd B33 ..68 E2
Yardley Green Hospl
B10 ....68 A1
Yardley Green Rd B9,B25,
B33 ....65 A2
Yardley Jun Sch B26 ....88 D7
Yardley Jun Sch B26 ....88 D7
Yardley Rd Barford CV35 ....156 A3
Darlaston WS10 ....41 C7
Stourbridge DY9 ....81 C6
Yardley Wood Com Prim Sch
B14 ....105 D4
Yardley Wood Rd B13,
B14 ....105 B5
Yardley Wood Sta B28 .105 D5
Yardley Works DY9 ....81 C5
Yardleys Sch B11 ....87 F4
Yare Gr WV13 ....27 D1
Yarmouth Gn CV4 ....131 E8
Yarn Cl B47 ....125 A5
Yarnborough Hill DY8 ..81 A2
Yarnbury Cl B14 ....104 E1
Yarner Cl DY1 ....50 E2
Yarnfield Prim Sch B11 .88 A3
Yarnfield Rd B11 ....88 A3
Yarningale Cl B98 ....158 F6
Yarningale Rd
Birmingham B14 ....104 D5
Coventry CV3 ....134 D5
Yarningdale 7 B90 ..126 C8
Yarnold La
Bournheath B61 ....136 C8
Fairfield B61 ....120 C1
Yarrow Cl Walsall WS3 ....15 A5
Wednesfield WV11 ....26 F5
Yarrow Dr B38 ....123 F8
Yarwell Cl WV10 ....163 C4
Yateley Ave B42 ....55 A7
Yateley Cres B42 ....55 A7
Yateley Rd B15 ....85 F2
Yates Croft B74 ....31 F6
Yates La B65 ....63 F2
Yatesbury Ave B35 ....58 A3
Yeadon Cl B97 ....153 A1
Yeadon Gdns WV3 ....38 D8
Yeames Cl B43 ....44 C4
Yellowhammer Ct
DY10 ....117 A1
Yelverton Cl WS3 ....14 B4
Yelverton Dr B15 ....85 E8
Yelverton Rd CV6 ....113 D8
Yeman Rd B68 ....64 D3
Yems Croft WS4 ....29 A6
Yemscroft WS6 ....14 A8
Yenton Cl B78 ....21 A1
Yenton Gr B24 ....57 C6
Yenton Jun & Inf Schs
B24 ....57 C6
Yeoman Cl CV10 ....116 E3
Yeomanry Cl 10 CV34 ..160 F7
Yeomans Way B75 ....46 E5
Yeomans Wlk B60 ....150 E8
Yeovil Ct 2 DY5 ....61 D2
Yeovilton B79 ....21 C8
Yerbury Gr B23 ....56 B4
Yew Cl CV3 ....114 C1
Yew Croft Ave B17 ....85 B6
Yew St WV3 ....25 A1
Yew Tree Ave
Bellbroughton DY9 ....119 E8
Birmingham B26 ....88 E7
Lichfield WS14 ....9 E8
Yew Tree Cl
Lapworth B94 ....144 D3
Norton Canes WS11 ....6 A5
Redditch B97 ....153 A4
Yew Tree Com Jun & Inf Sch
B6 ....56 A1
Yew Tree Ct 1 CV31 ..161 F5
Yew Tree Gdns B26 ....88 E7
Yew Tree Hills DY2 ....62 C4
Yew Tree Inf & Jun Sch
B91 ....107 E6
Yew Tree La
Birmingham, Frankley B32 .101 E3
Birmingham, Yardley B26 ......88 E7
Dudley WV14 ....40 D1
Fairfield B61 ....120 B1
Lapworth B94 ....144 B1
Solihull B91 ....107 E5
Wednesbury WS10 ....42 A2
Wolverhampton WV6 ....24 A5

Yew Tree Pl
Romsley B62 ....101 A5
Walsall WS3 ....14 D3
Yew Tree Prim Sch WS5 .43 C4
Yew Tree Rd
Birmingham, Castle Bromwich
B36 ....69 E8
Birmingham, Edgbaston B15 .86 C8
Birmingham, Handsworth
B6 ....56 A1
Birmingham, Moseley B13 .86 D2
Dudley DY2 ....62 C4
Halesowen B63 ....82 F3
Kidderminster DY10 ....116 F5
Smethwick B67 ....64 E4
Walsall, High Heath WS4 .15 B1
Walsall, The Delves WS5 .43 A5
Yew Tree Rise B26 ....88 E7
Yew Tree Villas B73 ....57 A7
Yew Wlk B37 ....70 B2
Yewdale B17 ....84 F5
Yewdale Cres CV2 ....96 E1
Yewdale Cl CV2 ....96 E1
Yewhurst Rd B91 ....106 E4
Yews The CV12 ....77 E2
Yewtree Dr B60 ....137 B2
Yewtree La B65 ....63 B2
Yewtree Rd

Yockleton Rd B33 ....69 E2
Yoemanry Ct B75 ....47 A6
York Ave Bedworth CV12 .78 D2
Bromsgrove B61 ....136 E4
Walsall WS2 ....28 B2
Wolverhampton WV2 ....27 D2
York Cl DY10 ....116 E7
York Dr B36 ....68 B8
York Gdns WV3 ....24 E1
York Rd Birmingham B23 .56 F4
Birmingham, Edgbaston B16 .65 E1
Birmingham, Handsworth
B21 ....65 F8
Birmingham, King's Heath
B14 ....104 E8
Birmingham, Tyseley B28 .87 D2
Blackheath B65 ....63 E3
Bromsgrove B61 ....136 F4
Cannock WS11 ....4 F7
Dudley DY2 ....62 E3
Hinckley LE10 ....71 D3
Royal Leamington Spa
CV31 ....161 F8
Walsall WS4 ....29 D7
Wolverhampton WV3 ....38 B8
York St Birmingham B17 .85 D6
Coventry CV1 ....113 B2
Kidderminster DY10 ....116 E7
Nuneaton CV11 ....73 A4
Wolverhampton WV1 ....163 D2
York Terr B18 ....66 C5
Yorkbrooke Dr B26 ....89 B5
Yorkdale Cl DY3 ....50 D3
Yorke Ave DY5 ....61 A1
Yorklea Croft B37 ....69 F2
Yorkmead Jun & Inf Sch
B28 ....87 F2
Yorkminster Dr B37 ....70 D3
Yorks Wood Dr B37 ....69 E5
Yorksand Rd B78 ....34 F8
Yorkswood Prim Sch
B37 ....69 F5
Young Cl CV34 ....160 B5
Young St B70 ....53 A3
Yoxall Gr B33 ....69 A3
Yoxall Rd B90 ....106 D2
Yule Rd CV2 ....114 D5
Yvonne Rd B97 ....158 D7

Z

Zealand Cl LE10 ....71 F3
Zion Cl WS6 ....4 D3
Zion St DY4 ....51 F8
Zions Cl B64 ....62 F1
Zoar St Dudley DY3 ....50 C3
Wolverhampton WV3 ....25 B1
Zorrina Cl CV10 ....72 B5
Zouche Cl DY8 ....80 E8

Using the Ordnance Survey National Grid

Any feature in this atlas can be given a unique reference to help you find the same feature on other Ordnance Survey maps of the area, or to help someone else locate you if they do not have a Street Atlas.

The grid squares in this atlas match the Ordnance Survey National Grid and are at 500 metre intervals. The small figures at the bottom and sides of every other grid line are the National Grid kilometre values (**00** to **99** km) and are repeated across the country every 100 km (see left).

To give a unique National Grid reference you need to locate where in the country you are. The country is divided into 100 km squares with each square given a unique two-letter reference. The atlas in this example falls across the junction of four such squares. Start by working out on which two-letter square the page falls. The Key map and Administrative map are useful for this.

The bold letters and numbers between each grid line (**A** to **F**, **1** to **8**) are for use within a specific Street Atlas only, and when used with the page number, are a convenient way of referencing these grid squares.

Example The railway bridge over DARLEY GREEN RD in grid square B1 on page 128

Step 1: Identify the two-letter reference, in this case page 128 is in **SP**

Step 2: Identify the 1 km square in which the railway bridge falls. Use the figures in the southwest corner of this square: Eastings **17**, Northings **74**. This gives a unique reference: **SP 17 74**, accurate to 1 km.

Step 3: To give a more precise reference accurate to 100 m you need to estimate how many tenths along and how many tenths up this 1 km square the feature is (to help with this the 1 km square is divided into four 500 m squares). This makes the bridge about **8** tenths along and about **1** tenth up from the southwest corner.

This gives a unique reference: **SP 178 741**, accurate to 100 m.

Eastings (read from left to right along the bottom) come before Northings (read from bottom to top). If you have trouble remembering say to yourself "Along the hall, THEN up the stairs"!

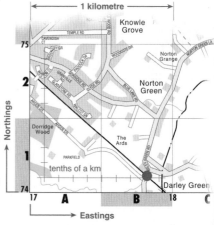